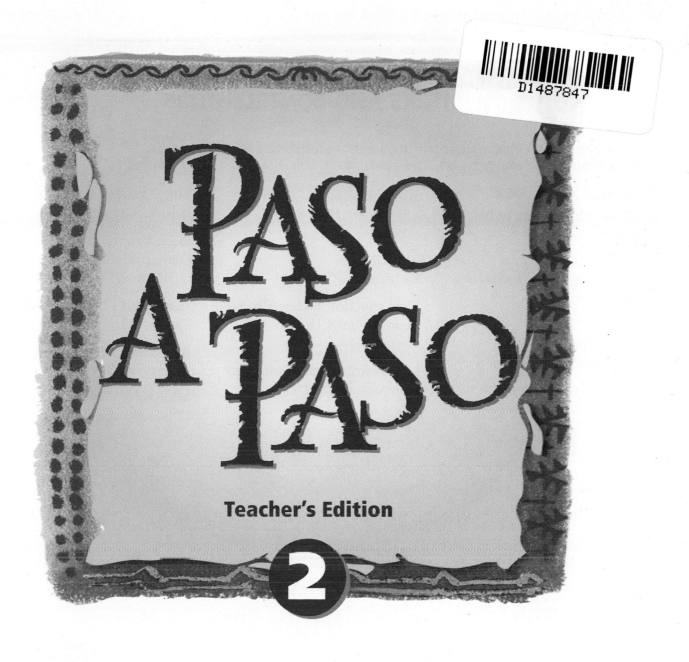

PASO A PASO

Teacher's Edition

2

Myriam Met
Coordinator of Foreign Languages
Montgomery County Public Schools
Rockville, MD

Richard S. Sayers
Longmont, CO

Carol Eubanks Wargin
Glen Crest Junior High School
Glen Ellyn, IL

Prentice Hall

Glenview, Illinois
Needham, Massachusetts
Upper Saddle River, New Jersey

Visit our Web site at http://www.pasoapaso.com

ADDITIONAL WRITERS AND CONTRIBUTORS

The following individuals contributed their expertise and creativity in developing the many notes and features in this Teacher's Edition.

Lynn Andersen
Chattahoochee High School
Alpharetta, GA

Peggy Boyles
Foreign Language Coordinator
Putnam City Schools
Oklahoma City, OK

Mary Louise Carey
Natick (MA) High School

JoAnn DiGiandomenico
Natick (MA) High School

Susan Dobinsky
Niles North High School
Skokie, IL

Gail Glover
San Antonio, TX

Marjorie Hall Haley, Ph. D.
George Mason University
Fairfax, VA

Thomasina Pagán Hannum
Albuquerque, NM

Mary Maggi
Bristow, OK

Lucía Nuñez
Stanford University
Stanford, CA

Bernadette M. Reynolds
Parker, CO

Luz Nuncio Schick
Naperville, IL

Michael S. Werner
University of Chicago (IL)

ISBN: 0-673-58926-9

3 4 5 6 7 8 9 10 DOW 03 02 01 00

Prentice Hall
Upper Saddle River, New Jersey 07458

TABLE OF CONTENTS

PHILOSOPHY OF THE PROGRAM

Welcome to *PASO A PASO!*

This program is based on the belief that the purpose of learning Spanish is to communicate with the people who speak it and to understand their cultures. *PASO A PASO* is designed to help your students achieve that goal by getting them to communicate right from the start.

PASO A PASO reflects the most current thinking in the foreign language field. It reflects state-of-the-art research on how students learn languages and what teachers and materials need to do to help them become proficient language users, whether they are using their new language for oral or written communication.

Let's take a look at some basic premises about language and language learning, the components of *PASO A PASO,* and how each of these components contributes to developing language proficiency.

What is communication?

Communication is an authentic exchange of information for a real purpose between two or more people. By this we mean that people tell each other (through speech or writing) something the other person doesn't already know.

Communicating meaning has several aspects. Students need to learn to listen to and read Spanish in order to interpret intended meanings, to express meaning by conveying their own messages for a purpose and to a real audience, and to negotiate meaning through the natural give-and-take involved in understanding and in making oneself understood (Savignon, 1991). Research tells us that classroom activities must provide students practice in interpreting, expressing, and negotiating meaning through extensive and frequent peer interactions, preferably in pairs or small groups.

Communication is driven not only by meaning, but also by purpose. In real life, people communicate to get things done. They may communicate to transact business, to get to know someone

else, or to find out something they really need to know. In authentic communication, people give and get new ideas or information. The information that one partner has and the other doesn't is often called an *information gap* or an *opinion gap.* How unlike the classrooms of old, where we typically asked students questions to which we (and everyone else) already knew the answer, questions such as, "Tom, what's your name?" and "Sally, are you a boy or a girl?" These questions are not heard in real life because they lack a communicative purpose: There is no information or opinion gap.

PASO A PASO is organized around the principle that just as meaning and purpose drive all language use, so too should they drive all language learning. Students are engaged in understanding messages, in sending their own messages, and thus in communicating on every page of every chapter. Because *PASO A PASO* structures almost all activities for pair or group interaction, students find themselves active participants in every lesson, every day. They communicate real ideas and real meanings for real purposes. Every component of *PASO A PASO* is designed with the goal of communication in mind.

Interpreting meaning

In the last decade we have learned more than ever before about how language is acquired. We know that students learn best when they have ample opportunities to internalize meanings before they have to produce them. That is, we know that comprehension precedes production. Many teachers will be familiar with the term "comprehensible input," first used by Stephen Krashen, who suggests that learners acquire language by understanding what they hear. Students need many opportunities to match what they hear with visual cues (pictures, video, or teacher pantomime) or experiences (physical actions) so that they can associate meanings with forms. This is as true for comprehending language structure and syntax as it is for vocabulary development.

In keeping with research on the importance of matching language with meaning, *PASO A PASO* gives students many opportunities to comprehend new language before producing it. The video allows students to hear native speakers using the language in a new and exciting soap-opera format. Students learn by matching what they hear with what they see. Numerous activities for providing comprehensible input are suggested in this Teacher's Edition, activities that involve visuals (transparencies and pictures) and that physically engage students as they acquire new language. Whenever possible, in the pupil's text, vocabulary is visualized, providing examples of language in context.

What kind of practice promotes communication skills?

The first and most critical step in the language development process is getting meaning—learning to understand by matching what is heard with what is seen or experienced. But by itself, understanding is not enough. Students also need to use their new knowledge.

Research tells us that students need extensive practice in using their new language to create and convey their own messages. While there may be a legitimate role for simply drilling new structures or vocabulary, the most valuable practice comes from using them to send messages that have meaning for the learner and serve a legitimate communicative purpose. When teachers (or texts) structure activities so there is only one right answer, clearly students are sending messages that convey someone else's thoughts, not their own, and are serving someone else's communicative purpose. In these kinds of activities students are *practicing* language, but they are not really *using* language to communicate.

In contrast, when the answers are determined by the students themselves—and are therefore unpredictable, with no single correct response—students are involved in authentic communica-tion. In these information- or opinion-gap activities, answers will vary. Research suggests that these types of activities are extremely important. After all, if the purpose of learning Spanish is to communicate, then students will need practice in doing just that! In contrast, if practice consists only (or mainly) of producing right answers determined by others, students will have difficulty spontaneously creating their own messages when needed. Thus language activities and tasks should not proceed from rote or de-contextualized to meaningful practice. All practice should be meaningful, with a predominance of activities that are truly communicative, activities in which students' answers will vary.

Research also tells us that pair and group language practice is far more effective than student-teacher practice alone. Cooperative learning and pair and group work both provide increased time for communicative language practice and promote the give-and-take necessary for negotiating meaning.

Working with a partner to make and share meaning lies at the heart of *PASO A PASO*. Everything students learn in each chapter is tied together in a meaningful way. The parts of language are taught and practiced (with a partner) within the context of the whole, with vocabulary and related grammar closely intertwined. Students use language in context to convey meaning and for a real purpose. All activities involve meaning, and most allow students to choose the meanings they want to convey. These are the kinds of information- and opinion-gap events that are characteristic of real-life communication. Even in structured activities designed to provide specific practice of forms and to elicit certain responses, teachers will find that students may still respond in ways that are personal and true for them. The activities are, however, focused, and you will often find "answers will vary, but look for correct use of . . ." in the answer keys.

To promote the development of communicative ability, *PASO A PASO* integrates vocabulary and grammar. They are then re-integrated continually, with gradually increasing complexity. In addition to the personalized and open-ended responses found in the vocabulary and grammar sections of the chapter, the *Todo junto* feature specifically focuses on weaving together newly learned material with material from previous chapters. It promotes the use of all the language students have learned to that point, in oral tasks and through reading and writing.

Teaching for understanding: The whole is greater than the parts

In many academic disciplines today, instructional practices are based on constructivist theory, which suggests that learners are more likely to be successful when instruction focuses on making meaning, on students' pursuing their natural inclination to try to make sense of what they are experiencing, and on ensuring that the parts are carefully integrated. In foreign languages, we traditionally taught the parts (grammar rules, vocabulary, pronunciation) hoping that eventually students would have the opportunity and ability to integrate them into the "whole" of communicating their own ideas. Today, integration of the parts of language takes place right from the start. It has been suggested that the relationship between learning the parts vs. integration with the whole is like learning to play a musical instrument. The focus is always on making music, and from the outset, learners need to have many experiences producing it. But they can't learn to play an instrument without knowing something about how to produce sounds (e.g., use the violin bow or play scales) or without practice.

Just as students learn the specific skills they need to produce a piece of music in learning to play an instrument, in language-learning we proceed today by identifying the learner's communicative needs (that is, the "music" they want to be able to produce) and then identifying the vocabulary, structures, and cultural skills needed to accomplish their purpose. Vocabulary and grammar are thus taught in the context of the situations in which students will be communicating or the topics they will be communicating about. Everything ties together naturally.

All effective learning is rooted in a meaningful context. We know from research that information is most likely to be retained when it is connected to other information in a meaningful way. Thus, language learning is more successful and retention more likely when we present new language organized into topics or by situations. This also means that some things we have taught in the past may not get taught at the same point or in the same way. For example, students may need to learn the stem-changing verbs *jugar, perder,* and *querer* to describe leisure or sports activities. However, since *dormir, morir,* and *pedir* do not naturally fit with the theme of sports or leisure, they may not be introduced until another theme or situation arises that will logically involve the use of one or more of them.

PASO A PASO is organized into thematic chapters. All material—vocabulary, grammar, culture—is rooted in a context and used meaningfully. All the elements of a chapter tie together. Students learn the vocabulary related to the theme, the grammar they need to communicate about the theme, and the information that helps anchor language in its cultural context. The themes have been chosen to reflect what students want or need to talk about. And the end-of-chapter vocabulary list is organized to reflect how the new words are used to create and convey meaning.

Critical thinking: Understanding and making meaning

We know from research that language learners are active makers of meaning. They learn by creating their own understandings, not by memorizing ours. This means that students are more likely to remember vocabulary when they have acquired it by figuring out its meaning in a logical context (video situation, visual, teacher pantomime). Grammar is most likely to be understood and rules applied when students have been guided to discover underlying patterns or have formulated the rules for themselves. In contrast, retention and applicability are greatly reduced when students simply memorize lists or rules without real understanding.

In order for students to construct their own understandings and generate rules of language usage, they need to be guided through interaction with teacher and text. Strategic questioning (in the text or by the teacher) plays an important role in this process, a process that is not at all the same as groping blindly to make a random discovery. Rather, through well-chosen examples and appropriate, inductive questioning, students can be led to make significant discoveries on their own, leading to a deep understanding that is much more likely to stay with them and be reflected in their own language use.

Understanding grammar

Understanding and critical thinking are reflected throughout *PASO A PASO*. This text is unique in its approach to the development of grammar skills, emphasizing as it does the critical roles that comprehensible input and student construction of knowledge play in language learning. New structures are foreshadowed through lexical presentation in the vocabulary section, and by the use of the *yo / tú* verb forms in vocabulary practice prior to the grammar presentation. Vocabulary activities familiarize students with new grammar before it is formally presented, allowing them to construct their own understanding.

To further facilitate grammar learning, students observe patterns of use in the comprehensible input that introduces the grammar section. This is done through a visualized context and strategic inductive questions. Through interaction with the teacher and the text, observation and analysis lead students to understand grammar, not merely to memorize formulas to be applied in rote fashion.

Understanding culture

Guided discovery is also an effective means of helping students construct an understanding of culture. Not only do we want our students to know about the cultures of the people who speak Spanish, we also want them to understand the cultural framework that determines what people say or do. In other words, we want students to understand the *why* of culture that determines the *what*. Whenever and wherever students may encounter speakers of Spanish, they will likely confront cultural practices and behaviors that are new to them. Cultural understanding begins with developing sensitivity to the possibility that people vary in how they think, live, and behave. Students must learn to observe other cultures without judging and to use what they see to help them discover the meanings that underlie cultural practices or behaviors. Specific information provides knowledge that aids in understanding the system of attitudes, values, and beliefs that frames cultural practices or behaviors. Students also need to understand other cultures in relation to their own, so that they may gain a deeper understanding of why they think, live, and behave as they do.

Background knowledge can serve as an important tool for the construction of meaning. It may be contextual (What normally happens in a restaurant?), topical (What are some typical leisure activities?), linguistic (What words do I already know that look like this new word?), or cultural (I know that interpersonal relationships are very important in Hispanic cultures, so that may be why people put so much value on greeting one another). This can serve to help students interpret new cultural information or contrast that information with values and practices common to their own culture. Students should be encouraged to understand the close relationship between language and culture. The social / cultural meanings of words (What does "friendship" mean in Hispanic cultures?) should be taught along with their dictionary meanings.

PASO A PASO develops important cultural understandings through a unique guided-discovery approach. It provides students with a progression of activities that lead them from thoughtful observation to knowledge and understanding of Hispanic cultures and then to reflection on their own culture. A photo essay with strategic inductive questions leads them to reflect on what they are observing. An informative reading then provides cultural information or insights that expand upon the visual information and allows students to validate or reject the ideas they formulated at the beginning. They are then asked thought-provoking questions to lead to reflection upon their own culture and their own cultural perspectives.

Strategies for success

Effective learners not only construct their own understanding of new concepts, they also know how to help themselves be successful learners. One way they do this is by using specific problem-solving strategies. When confronted with unknown words in a reading passage, successful learners don't run for a dictionary or just give up. They know how to get around that obstacle.

PASO A PASO teaches students to use strategies to be effective listeners, readers, and writers. Each reading selection takes students through a multi-step process (Phillips, 1984). Before reading, they are encouraged to use their background knowledge to help them predict or anticipate information they are likely to encounter in the text. A first reading helps them focus on general ideas (gist) without getting mired in details or difficult expressions. Reading closely for specific information, with specific strategies for dealing with difficult aspects of a text, is a strategy frequently emphasized in the reading sections. Students are then encouraged to use what they have learned in the reading by applying it in a new way. Thus, from the start, students are empowered to deal with authentic print materials.

Effective writing is promoted through a process

approach in *PASO A PASO*. In the pre-writing stage, students think about the topic, generate needed language, and organize their ideas. They then write a first draft. Reviewing this draft with a peer yields insights into needed revisions or clarification and results in a revision that may be published or placed in a portfolio. This approach is consistent with the ways in which many students are learning to write in their English classes. It also provides them with a strategy or model for independent writing.

Authenticity in language learning

Language teaching today places great value on authenticity. The content that students are expected to learn and how they practice it (objectives and tasks) should be authentic to the learner's interests and to real-life uses. Tasks should require an authentic exchange of meaning (an information or opinion gap) and should have an authentic purpose. Students should be taught authentic, not "textbook," language. Most important, information and, to the extent possible, materials should be culturally authentic.

PASO A PASO opens authentic avenues to communication and culture. Students continually engage in authentic communicative tasks. Pair and group activities in which students fill information or opinion gaps constitute the great majority of exercises. These activities allow students to express their own views on topics and questions of interest to them. The language presented is culturally accurate. Videos, photos, realia, and readings provide authentic contacts with the cultures of Spanish speakers.

PASO A PASO and the student

PASO A PASO is a learner-friendly series. It is friendly to the interests of students and provides extensive opportunities for them to talk about themselves, to explore with peers, and to be engaged, thoughtful learners. Each chapter opens with clearly stated communicative objectives that help focus on what students are expected to learn. Knowing what's expected of them makes students more comfortable.

Because we know that it is impossible for students to learn all the vocabulary related to a given theme at one time, and because we know that it is unusual for students to "master" the grammar the first time they are exposed to it, *PASO A PASO* reviews each Book 1 theme in Book 2. However, the review is not simply repetition, re-entry, or recycling. Rather, our approach is recursive: Each review allows students to expand to new levels of achievement, so that their language becomes more refined, more elaborate, and more complex. Students will find comfort in knowing that there is more than one chance to learn the material and that they don't need to know everything perfectly all at once. *PASO A PASO* is a program in which students are continually getting better at communicating in Spanish and are regularly made aware of their progress at specific points in every chapter.

The student book and tests convey a powerful message. Both emphasize knowledge in action. Students are asked to use what they know to communicate real messages to a real audience for a real purpose. Practice activities make it clear to students that they are expected to learn to communicate in the language. End-of-chapter tests reinforce the message, assessing students' ability to use what they have learned for receptive and productive purposes and allowing them to demonstrate their understanding of related aspects of Hispanic cultures.

We know more today than ever about how foreign languages are learned. Using that knowledge to help students become proficient communicators, and to acquire an understanding and appreciation of other cultures, can be facilitated by appropriate instructional materials. *PASO A PASO* is based on solid research on second-language acquisition, on accepted theories about the teaching of culture, and on sound pedagogical practices that are common to all disciplines. We

are sure that you and your students will find this an exciting, engaging, and enormously successful approach to learning Spanish.

Bibliography

Adair-Hauck, Bonnie, Richard Donato and Philomena Cumo. 1994. "Using a Whole Language Approach to Teach Grammar," in Eileen Glisan and Judith Shrum, Eds. *Contextualized Language Instruction,* Boston: Heinle and Heinle Publishers. pp. 90–111.

Brooks, Jacqueline and Martin G. Brooks. 1993. *In Search of Understanding: The Case for Constructivist Classrooms.* Alexandria, VA: Association for Supervision and Curriculum Development.

Doughty, Catherine and Teresa Pica. 1986. "Information Gap Tasks: Do They Facilitate Second Language Acquisition?" *TESOL Quarterly.* 20:3, 305–325.

Ellis, Rod. 1993. "The Structural Syllabus and Second Language Acquisition." *TESOL Quarterly.* 27:1, 91–112.

Kagan, Spencer. 1992. *Cooperative Learning.* San Juan Capistrano, CA: Resource for Teachers Inc.

Krashen, Stephen. 1982. *Principles and Practice in Second Language Acquisition.* Oxford: Pergamon Press.

Nunan, D. 1991. "Communicative Tasks and the Language Curriculum." *TESOL Quarterly.* 25:2, 279–295.

Phillips, June K. "Practical Implication of Recent Research in Reading." *Foreign Language Annals* 17:4 (September 1984), 285–299.

Resnick, Lauren B. 1989. *Knowing, Learning, and Instruction: Essays in Honor of Robert Glaser.* Hillsdale, New Jersey: Lawrence Erlbaum Associates, Publishers.

Savignon, S. J. 1991. "Communicative Language Teaching: State of the Art." *TESOL Quarterly.* 25:2, 261–277.

Swain, Merrill. 1985. "Communicative Competence: Some Roles of Comprehensible Input and Comprehensible Output in Its Development." In Susan Gass and Madden, C. (Eds.) *Input in Second Language Acquisition.* Rowley, MA: Newbury House.

ASO A PASO AND THE NATIONAL STANDARDS

National standards provide an important and useful framework to guide the teaching and learning of foreign languages. This framework should result in a new generation of language learners prepared to meet the demand for competence in other languages that our nation will face as we move toward an increasingly interdependent world. The work of teachers and students will be facilitated by instructional resources aligned with the National Standards. *PASO A PASO* provides these resources. The program at all levels, with its rich array of ancillary materials (including print and technological resources), is designed to help students develop the competencies delineated in the Standards for *Foreign Language Learning.*

Goal 1. Communication

Communicate in Languages Other than English

Standard 1.1:	Students engage in conversations, provide and obtain information, express feelings and emotions, and exchange opinions.
Standard 1.2:	Students understand and interpret written and spoken language on a variety of topics.
Standard 1.3:	Students present information, concepts, and ideas to an audience of listeners or readers on a variety of topics.

From the very first oral activity in *PASO A PASO,* students work with a partner. They use language to convey meaning and for a real purpose that allows them to choose the meanings they want to convey, which is the basic characteristic of real-life communication. Even in structured activities designed to provide practice of specific forms, students may still interact with partners to exchange real information.

PASO A PASO gives students many opportunities to comprehend new language before producing it. The video allows students to hear native speakers using new vocabulary and grammar in a context that makes the meanings clear. Numerous activities for providing comprehensible input are

suggested in this Teacher's Edition, including hands-on activities that physically engage students as they acquire new language. In the student book, vocabulary is visualized, rather than translated or buried in cartoons or *fotonovelas,* so that print and video materials provide different but complementary examples of language in context.

An important characteristic of both the audio and video materials is that they do not repeat material from the text, but rather extend it. Simply hearing what they read does not develop students' ability to understand Spanish when it is spoken, because spoken language and written language are not alike. Even more important, students need to develop the ability to understand the spoken message without being able to predict every word they will hear.

Reading activities can also be found in every chapter and at every level of *PASO A PASO.* As students begin to gain control of new chapter material, they are presented with short reading passages. Later in the chapter, more extensive reading selections are presented, along with strategies that empower students to be successful independent readers. In Book 2, cultural essays are presented in Spanish. As students progress through the program, reading selections increase in challenge level, culminating in a 68-page *Fondo literario* in Book 3. The various Web-based activities at www.pasoapaso.com provide still more opportunities for reading authentic materials.

The presentational mode (Standard 1.3) differs from the interpersonal mode (Standard 1.1) in that the opportunity for direct interaction (conversational give-and-take) between speaker and listener (or reader and writer) is absent. Examples of the former include leaving messages and giving speeches. At the earliest stages of language development, students are more likely to engage in the presentational mode in writing than in speaking. Nonetheless, students have many opportunities for making oral presentations in the *Todo junto* sections at the end of each chapter. As they move through the program, the presentational speaking activities become more frequent and more challenging.

Various challenge levels of writing occur throughout each chapter of *PASO A PASO*. Initial writing tasks are limited in scope and audience, but at the end of every chapter at every level a more extended and comprehensive writing task requires student communication on the chapter topic. Because writing always has an intended audience and purpose, these are made clear in each writing task, with suggestions for ways in which students can publish their writing.

The interactive CD-ROMs *(Pasos vivos 1* and *Pasos vivos 2: La Catrina)* provide outstanding opportunities for both spoken and written presentations. The Word Processor, Slide Presentation Maker, and Video Presentation Maker are the three magic multimedia features aimed at achieving Standard 1.3.

Goal 2. Cultures

Gain Knowledge and Understanding of Other Cultures

Standard 2.1:	Students demonstrate an understanding of the relationship between the practices and perspectives of the culture studied.
Standard 2.2:	Students demonstrate an understanding of the relationship between the products and perspectives of the culture studied.

Cultural understanding is at the heart of Goal 2. Cultural information (knowing about the practices and products of other cultures) is important. However, it is equally important for students to understand that the perspectives of a culture (its attitudes, values, beliefs) both determine that culture's practices and products and may in turn be influenced by them. Resources for teaching toward Goal 2 of the Standards are found throughout the student books in cultural photo essays *(¡Piensa en la cultura!)*, cultural readings *(Perspectiva cultural)*, and in cultural notes

(Pasos culturales). There are also culture notes throughout this Teacher's Edition. Significant cultural information abounds in the video program.

Too often in teaching foreign languages, it is easier to focus on the informational aspects of culture and to ignore the perspectives that underlie them. *PASO A PASO* helps students know about the cultures of the people who speak Spanish, but it also highlights the cultural framework that determines what people say or do. In other words, we want students to understand the *why* of culture that determines the *what*.

These important cultural understandings are developed through guided discovery, an approach unique to *PASO A PASO*. The program provides students with a progression of activities that lead them from thoughtful observation, to knowledge and understanding of Hispanic cultures, as well as to reflection on their own culture. A photo essay in the opening section of the textbook chapter with strategic inductive questions leads students to reflect on what they are observing. An informative cultural reading provides information and insights that expand upon the visual information in the photo essay and allows students to validate or reject the ideas they formulated earlier. Most important, students are asked thought-provoking questions for reflection upon the cultural perspectives they have encountered.

Goal 3. Connections

Connect with Other Disciplines and Acquire Information

Standard 3.1:	Students reinforce and further their knowledge of other disciplines through the foreign language.
Standard 3.2:	Students acquire information and recognize the distinctive viewpoints that are only available through the foreign language and its cultures.

In *PASO A PASO A-B, 1,* and *2* a section of each chapter, entitled *Conexiones,* gives students an opportunity to use their language skills to acquire information in other disciplines, such as mathematics, science, social studies, and so on. Certain chapter themes (the environment, health, art) directly relate to the content of the school curriculum. The Internet-based activities found at www.pasoapaso.com provide activities that connect to other curriculum areas as well as access to information that is available only through the Spanish language. In the Teacher's Editions of Books 1–3, cross-curricular connections are noted at the beginning of each chapter, including suggestions for student activities.

Another important way in which *PASO A PASO* connects with other disciplines is through the development of learning strategies, learning processes, and higher order thinking skills. We teach students to use strategies to be effective readers, listeners, and writers. For example, the *¡Vamos a leer!* takes students through a multistep process similar to the strategic approach they may be using in their language arts courses. Similarly, effective writing is promoted through a process approach. In the pre-writing stage, students think about the topic, generate needed language, and organize their ideas. They then write a first draft. Reviewing this draft with a peer results in a revision, which may be published or placed in a portfolio. This approach is not only consistent with the ways in which many students are learning to write effectively in their English classes, but it also provides them with a strategy or model for independent writing.

Higher order thinking skills are emphasized throughout, with suggestions for developing critical thinking and for enrichment activities included in the Teacher's Edition. In addition, deep understanding, rather than rote memorization, is a key feature of grammar and culture instruction. *PASO A PASO* is unique in its approach to the development of grammar understanding. It emphasizes the critical roles that comprehensible input and the construction of knowledge play in language learning. To provide comprehensible input, new structures are foreshadowed through lexical presentation in the vocabulary section, for example, by the use of first- and second-person singular verb forms in vocabulary practice prior to the grammar presentation. Both the video and vocabulary activities familiarize students with new grammar before it is formally presented, allowing students to construct their own understanding. Students then discuss with a partner the grammatical patterns under observation. This is done through actual or simulated realia highlighted by inductive questions in the text. This approach of observation and analysis leads students to understand the grammar, eventually leading to a more consistently correct use of the structures being studied.

Goal 4. Comparisons

Gain Insight into the Nature of Language and Culture

Standard 4.1:	Students demonstrate understanding of the nature of language through comparisons of the language studied and their own.
Standard 4.2:	Students demonstrate understanding of the concept of culture through comparisons of the cultures studied and their own.

Myriad opportunities exist in *PASO A PASO* for students to compare their own language and culture to Spanish and to Hispanic cultures. Take, for example, the very first chapter of Books A and 1. Students are introduced to the concept that most adjectives change if they are describing a boy or a girl. They note how this can help them as a reading strategy (was the self-descriptive poem "Yo" written by a male or a female?). They learn the very different cultural connotations of the supposedly equivalent words *amigo(a)* and "friend."

Such comparisons between the student's own language and culture and the target language and culture(s) are found in every chapter. Guided discovery is a prime feature of *PASO A PASO* as a means to help students gain insight into language and culture. For example, at the end of every culture section, students are asked to reflect upon what they have read from their own cultural perspective. This heightened consciousness of their own language and cultural beliefs and practices can only evoke a deeper understanding of those being studied.

Goal 5. Communities

Participate in Multilingual Communities at Home and Around the World

Standard 5.1:	Students use the language both within and beyond the school setting.
Standard 5.2:	Students show evidence of becoming life-long learners by using the language for personal enjoyment and enrichment.

Of the five goals in the National Standards, Goal 5 involves application of Goals 1–4, and is most closely aligned with experiences that take place outside the classroom. These experiences may be within the school itself, but are also likely to be in the community and even beyond the student's enrollment in a given course.

For students with direct access to Spanish speakers in their school or community, there are many suggestions in *PASO A PASO* that address Standard 5.1. Many of these are found in the Teacher's Edition (labeled "Spanish in Your Community"). Other opportunities to use Spanish in or beyond the school setting are included in suggestions for publishing student writing, in activities that involve collecting information from the local community, and in chapters related to the environment (Books A-B, 1, and 2) and community service (Book 3). In fact, two chapters in Book 3 directly address Standard 5.1: a chapter on community service and another on the importance of knowing another language. Indeed, the latter chapter also addresses Standard 5.2, for the personal enrichment derived from knowing

Spanish is highlighted. Each chapter provides at least two Internet links that take students into the Spanish-speaking world.

As for Standard 5.2, it is hard to do much more than promote this Standard, for it is neither text- nor schoolroom-based. However, users of the first edition of *PASO A PASO* share with us their students' enthusiasm for the study of Spanish, of going beyond the textbook, of wanting to interact with Spanish speakers both in school and in the community. And we also know that the award-winning *telenovela, La Catrina,* that accompanies *PASO A PASO 2* moves students toward achieving Standard 5.2, for we have seen the essays, reports, and taped sequels that it has prompted individuals and small groups of students to create.

Page-by-Page Correlations to the Standards

In this Teacher's Edition, you will find page-by-page correlations to the Standards. These are located in the bottom left- or right-hand corner of each page. All material in the Teacher's Edition pages and in the reduced Student Edition are correlated. So when the audio program is listed in the margin of the Teacher's Edition, Standard 1.2 will be noted; if an activity in *Un paso más* requires writing, Standard 1.3 will be noted; if a video activity asks students to compare cultures, Standard 4.2 is noted, and so on.

Each chapter supports the Standards, but not all Standards are supported on every page. Some pages contain no correlations, because the material on those pages is not Standard-specific. It is important to recognize that not every activity in a textbook or ancillary component supports a Standard, and we have been very strict in our interpretation. For example, a fill-in-the-blank exercise designed for skill-building writing practice is a valid activity, but it is *not* aimed at fulfilling a Standard.

COMPONENTS OF THE PROGRAM

PASO A PASO is a complete, three-level series with a full range of ancillary components that allow you to tailor the materials to the needs of your students and to your teaching style.

Student's Edition

Presentation material begins with maps of Spanish-speaking countries and *Pasodoble,* a unique magazine-format contextual review of basic Book 1 material (regular verbs, *ir, querer, gustar,* and the like). This is followed by fourteen thematic chapters and an appendix offering verb charts, Spanish-English / English-Spanish vocabularies, and a grammar index.

Ancillaries

Multisensory / Technology

Overheads: A package of 90 full-color overhead visuals that reproduce the vocabulary-teaching illustrations without labels or captions. Also included are maps, a pronoun chart, the realia from the *Gramática en contexto,* and additional teaching transparencies. Suggestions for use are provided in a separate booklet.

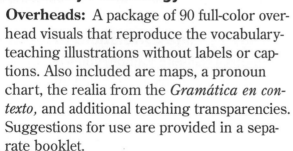

Audio Cassettes / CDs: A set of ten 60-minute audio tapes on cassette or CD containing listening activities for each chapter and separate tapes for assessment, pronunciation and vocabulary, and songs. The primary focus is on developing listening comprehension, with secondary emphasis on supporting the intermediate stages of speaking, including practice with pronunciation of new words and some focused speaking opportunities.

Vocabulary Art Blackline Masters for Hands-On Learning / CD-ROM: All teaching vocabulary art reproduced on blackline masters and available on the Resource Pro® CD-ROM, ideal for making manipulatives or flashcards.

Classroom Crossword: A wall-size crossword puzzle to be completed over the course of the school year.

La Catrina: A storyline video series taped on location in Mexico. Available on both tape and disc, *La Catrina* incorporates the chapter themes, vocabulary, and grammar into an engaging tale of romance, intrigue, and adventure. A Teacher's Guide is included with complete transcriptions, cultural information, teaching suggestions, and reduced reproductions of the Video Activities pages *(see next page)* with overprinted answers.

La Catrina: **Interactive CD-ROM:** Real-world activities based on *La Catrina* offer creative, interactive practice opportunities for listening, speaking, reading, and writing, while extending students' knowledge of Hispanic cultures.

Multisensory / Technology *(continued)*

 Internet-based activities at www.pasoapaso.com: Chapter-by-chapter support for the culture and content of each chapter through engaging internet-based activities. Students can explore sites from around the Spanish-speaking world via selected web sites and can interact with the information provided at each while expanding language skills and cultural understanding. Additional chapter-by-chapter activities provide games and drill-and-skill practice with vocabulary and grammar.

Print

 Practice Workbook: (with separate Teacher's Answer Key): Worksheets for basic, one-step writing practice for all vocabulary and grammar sections of the student text. Exercises include the support of learning strategies. Each chapter also has an Organizer that allows students to record and keep track of new vocabulary and structures.

 Writing, Audio & Video Activities: Writing Activities provide chapter-by-chapter practice that is at the same level as (or slightly higher level than) that in the student text. Audio Activities offer exercises necessary to focus attention on listening comprehension as students work with the audio tapes. Video Activities focus attention as students view the video. Follow-up activities verify and extend their understanding of what they have seen.

Teacher's Edition: Writing, Audio & Video Activities: Student material with overprinted answers and a complete tapescript of the audio tapes and CDs.

 Communicative Activities Blackline Masters (Pair and Small-Group Activities with Situation Cards): Oral activities for pair and group practice.

 Un paso más: Actividades para ampliar tu español: A worktext for Spanish-speaking students designed to supplement the textbook activities.

Assessment

 Assessment Program: Blackline master quizzes *(Pruebas)* for each vocabulary section and each grammar topic in the student text; fourteen chapter quizzes *(Pruebas cumulativas);* fourteen chapter proficiency tests *(Exámenes de habilidades);* a chapter test for *Pasodoble (Prueba Pasodoble);* and *Bancos de ideas,* several sets of cumulative proficiency sections for use in creating mid-term and special end-of-year tests to highlight teachers' own objectives or areas of concern. Suggestions for administering and scoring proficiency tests are included.

 ¿Lo sabes bien? **Video Quiz:** This end-of-chapter video quiz provides ten multiple-choice questions that review key concepts. The questions appear on the monitor and are read aloud.

 Test Generator: A multiple-choice test generator. Teachers can add their own questions to the question bank.

Teacher's Resource File: This convenient, desk-top organizer contains the Teacher's Edition of the Writing, Audio & Video Activities, the Assessment Program, and the Communicative Activities Blackline Masters.

RESOURCE◉PRO®

Resource Pro®: Teachers have complete support for developing lesson plans through this multipurpose CD-ROM. The Teaching Resources Library allows teachers to view and print out all print ancillaries. Planning Express builds complete lesson plans for regular and block scheduling with objectives and correlations to local and national standards. The Vocabulary Clip Art Library contains clip art for all visualized vocabulary in all levels of the program. Teacher and students can copy and use images for manipulatives and flashcards.

CHAPTER ORGANIZATION

Organization of the Text

PASO A PASO 2 contains a review section (*Pasodoble*) and 14 thematically organized chapters in which students learn to communicate about their own lives and how to interact with Hispanic cultures. The 14 themes are:

CAPÍTULO 1   School

CAPÍTULO 2   Daily routine

CAPÍTULO 3   Clothing

CAPÍTULO 4   Leisure activities

CAPÍTULO 5   Childhood

CAPÍTULO 6   Special occasions

CAPÍTULO 7   Luxuries and necessities

CAPÍTULO 8   Shopping

CAPÍTULO 9   Health

CAPÍTULO 10   Movies and TV

CAPÍTULO 11   The future

CAPÍTULO 12   Travel

CAPÍTULO 13   Food

CAPÍTULO 14   Nature

Using *Pasodoble*

The magazine-format review, *Pasodoble,* is designed to help students recall certain major vocabulary sets and structure taught in Chapters 1–12 of *PASO A PASO 1.* Previously taught concepts are uniquely integrated to provide meaningful communication combined with purposeful review.

Chapter organization

The 14 chapters follow a consistent organization that increases student confidence while allowing for easy classroom management. Chapters are organized according to the latest research on how students learn a second language and follow a clear pedagogical model:

1 Introduce/Preview   **4** Apply

2 Present   **5** Summarize/Assess

3 Practice

Each chapter follows this model:

Chapter Sections	**Pedagogical Support**
Objectives	Introduce
¡Piensa en la cultura!	Preview
Vocabulario para conversar	
• *Visualized vocabulary*	Present
• También necesitas ...	Present
• Empecemos a conversar	Practice
• Empecemos a escribir (y a leer)	Apply
• ¡Comuniquemos!	Practice
• ¿Qué sabes ahora?	Practice / Assess
Perspectiva cultural	Preview / Present
• La cultura desde tu perspectiva	Apply
Gramática en contexto	Preview / Present / Practice
• Ahora lo sabes	Practice / Assess
Todo junto	
• Actividades	Apply
• Conexiones	Apply
• ¡Vamos a leer!	Apply
• ¡Vamos a escribir!	Apply
Repaso: ¿Lo sabes bien?	Apply / Assess
Resumen del vocabulario	Summarize

USING A CHAPTER

Chapter Opener (Introduce)

The chapter theme is introduced through a photograph and related communicative and cultural objectives.

Teaching ideas for the Chapter Opener

Wrap-around notes give many suggestions. Here are a few basic ideas for these two pages:

1 Prior to discussing the objectives, have students look at the photos and skim the chapter. Ask them to suggest objectives based upon what they have seen. Write these on the chalkboard and see if they compare with those listed.

2 Show additional pictures, posters, or slides that preview the chapter theme.

Objectives:
Relate to real-life, purposeful communication and relevant cultural information. These will be referred to throughout the chapter so that students can monitor their own progress. Chapter assessment is based on the objectives.

VISIT www.pasoapaso.com

CAPÍTULO 5
¿Qué te gustaba hacer de pequeño?

Objectives
At the end of this chapter, you will be able to:
► tell what you were like as a child
► tell what you used to like to do
► talk about what you learned to do
► understand how experiences in José Martí's early life affected his later life

PASO CULTURAL
El primero de noviembre en San Juan Sacatepéquez, Guatemala, se ven grandes cometas de muchos colores subir al cielo. Es el Día de Todos los Santos, cuando la gente de este pueblo construye cometas para llevar cartas a sus familiares que han muerto (who have died). Hay varias palabras en español para *kite*: "cometa," "barrilete" y "papalote." Una de estas palabras viene del náhuatl, el idioma de los aztecas antiguos. ¿Qué palabra es? ¿Cómo sabes que es esa palabra?

Festival de cometas en Guatemala   159

158 Capítulo 5

Paso cultural:
Culture notes lead students to an understanding of cultural practices, products, and perspectives, and to comparisons with their own culture.

¡Piensa en la cultura! *(Preview)*

This section continues to preview the chapter theme. Students use their own experiences and background information to interact with the photographs.

Teaching ideas for *¡Piensa en la cultura!*

1 Ask students to study the photographs and to suggest as many words, phrases, or short sentences as they can about them. Focus on previously taught vocabulary.

2 Use the inductive questions to elicit the similarities and differences. Focus on the similarities.

3 At the end of the chapter, return to these photos. See how extensively students can describe the pictures. Choose a photo and have students bring it to life by acting out the situation.

Questions:
Students use critical thinking to answer inductive questions.

Captions:
Easy-to-guess cognates and recycled vocabulary help build students' confidence. New vocabulary and structures are previewed.

¡Piensa en la CULTURA!

Juegos de niños en Honduras, Venezuela y en la España antigua

Mira las fotos. Los niños que vemos están haciendo sus actividades favoritas. ¿Qué te gustaba hacer cuando eras niño(a)?

"¡Dos y dos son cuatro; cuatro y dos son seis; seis y dos son ocho y ocho dieciséis!"

¿Qué te gustaba jugar de niño(a)? Si saltabas a la cuerda, ¿cantabas canciones como ésta?

"Aquí está mi nueva tarjeta de Juan González."

Cuando eras niño(a), ¿coleccionabas algo? ¿Tenías una colección grande? ¿Todavía la tienes?

Caracas, Venezuela

Un niño de Caracas les muestra su colección de tarjetas de béisbol a unos amigos.

Niños hondureños saltando a la cuerda

160   Capítulo 5

Guanaja, Honduras

¿Tenías gatos, perros o pájaros cuando eras niño(a)?

PASO CULTURAL   Francisco José de Goya y Lucientes (1746–1828) es uno de los pintores más importantes de España. En este cuadro, podemos ver que esta familia es importante por la manera en que está vestido el hijo. Describe otras cosas que ves en este cuadro. ¿Puedes leer lo que dice el papel que el pájaro tiene en su pico?

Don Manuel Osorio Manrique de Zúñiga (1788); Francisco de Goya

¡Piensa en la cultura!   161

Locator globes:
Expand students' knowledge of geography.

Painting:
Photos of a wide variety of art and handicrafts reinforce the chapter theme and broaden knowledge of Hispanic cultures.

Vocabulario para conversar (Present, Practice & Apply)

New vocabulary is presented in a visualized context in two short, manageable sections.

Teaching ideas

1 Use the Overheads, the Vocabulary Audio Tape, and /or the Vocabulary Art Blackline Masters/ CD-ROM to introduce the new vocabulary.

2 Combine auditory, visual, and kinesthetic activities. Present the vocabulary using comprehensible input. Here are several suggestions:

A. Getting meaning from comprehensible input

The purpose of these activities is to allow students to match new language with its meaning.

■ Using the Overhead, point to pictures as you simply and clearly name and talk about them in Spanish. Students should be able to understand new vocabulary from your body language and gestures. For example: *Aquí hay unos animales de peluche. Hay un oso de peluche, un gato de peluche y una tortuga de peluche.*

■ You might also pantomime new vocabulary.

■ As you progress through *PASO A PASO,* your descriptions will expand to include previously learned language.

Visualized vocabulary:
Research indicates that we learn best in logical sets or categories and through immediately associating words with objects.

¡No olvides!:
This recycling feature reminds students at appropriate moments of previously taught concepts and vocabulary.

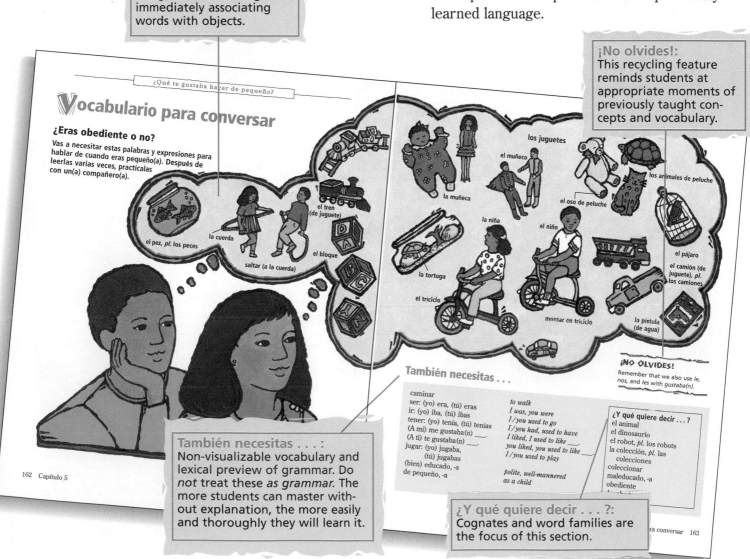

También necesitas . . . :
Non-visualizable vocabulary and lexical preview of grammar. Do *not* treat these *as grammar.* The more students can master without explanation, the more easily and thoroughly they will learn it.

¿Y qué quiere decir . . . ?:
Cognates and word families are the focus of this section.

B. Demonstrating comprehension through physical response

The purpose of these activities is to allow students to demonstrate their comprehension non-verbally.

■ After presenting two or three pictures of new vocabulary, review by asking yes / no questions: *¿Es un pájaro? ¿Es una cuerda? ¿Tenías un triciclo?* Students may respond as a group with thumbs up / down *(sí / no)*. Individuals may also be asked to respond in this way.

■ As students become more proficient, vocabulary from previous chapters can be used in these questions: *¿Dónde viven las tortugas? ¿Y los peces?*

■ Continue alternating the steps in the first two paragraphs until all new vocabulary has been presented.

■ Distribute Vocabulary Art BLMs or make photocopies from the CD-ROM printout. As you name each new item, point to it on the transparency. Have students point to the corresponding picture. Tell students: *Señalen el tren. Señalen la muñeca.* This time, do not point to the picture on the transparency until students have pointed to it on their worksheet. Confirm student responses on the transparency.

■ Have students point to pictures on the Overhead as you describe the picture: *Al niño le encanta montar en triciclo* (student points to picture of tricycle).

■ Have students open their books and point to pictures you name or describe: *Señalen su juguete favorito. ¿Qué animal de peluche es mejor para una niña de tres años?*

■ Have students pantomime vocabulary.

■ Have students respond to commands: *Dale el bloque a Matilde. Muestra el tren a la clase.*

■ Provide each student with a worksheet from the Vocabulary Art BLMs/CD-ROM. Direct them to cut out each picture. Have students move the pictures as you direct: *Pongan el bloque a la derecha de los peces. Pongan el tren entre el bloque y los peces. Pongan los juguetes en tres columnas: Juguetes para niños, niñas o los dos.* Or students may use them to make your sentence true by arranging pictures to match your oral description: *El tren y el camión están en la mesa.*

Each chapter provides suggestions for Learning Spanish Through Action (TPR).

C. Limited verbal response

Once students have had an opportunity to internalize meaning and to demonstrate comprehension of new language physically, they may respond verbally.

■ Ask yes / no or true / false questions: *¿Saltabas a la cuerda? Un pez sabe saltar a la cuerda.*

■ Ask questions that require comprehension of new vocabulary but do not require using it in the answer. Responses will use language from previous chapters: *¿De qué color era tu triciclo?*

■ Ask questions in which the correct answer is embedded: *¿Es un pez o un pájaro? ¿Preferías jugar con muñecas o con animales de peluche?*

■ Have students repeat after you for pronunciation practice.

3 On subsequent days, add details by recycling previously learned vocabulary. Retell an earlier narration without visual support. Ask students to draw their own visual representation of what has been said.

Empecemos a conversar (Practice)

Students practice the new vocabulary in paired activities that provide models for real-life language.

Teaching ideas for *Empecemos a conversar*

1 Place students in pairs. (There are many ways of doing this.) You may want to pair students of different abilities. Assign "study buddies" for each week or chapter. They are not only pair-practice partners, but they also keep track of each other's papers and assignments. (Be sure they exchange phone numbers.) You might award extra credit for partners who work well together and show improvement.

2 Always model the pair practice. Quickly review the vocabulary so that students can be more successful.

3 Set a time limit. Finish an activity when approximately three fourths of the class have finished. Walk around the class, listening for areas of difficulty such as pronunciation or grammar. Focus on these at a later time.

4 Ask pairs of students to do selected items for the whole class.

5 Have students work in pairs to answer the questions, then with another group to compare responses. Ask individuals to write this section as homework. Use the more open-ended questions as one-on-one questions with students or as topics for class discussion.

6 See the list of ancillaries for additional resources to help students work with the new vocabulary.

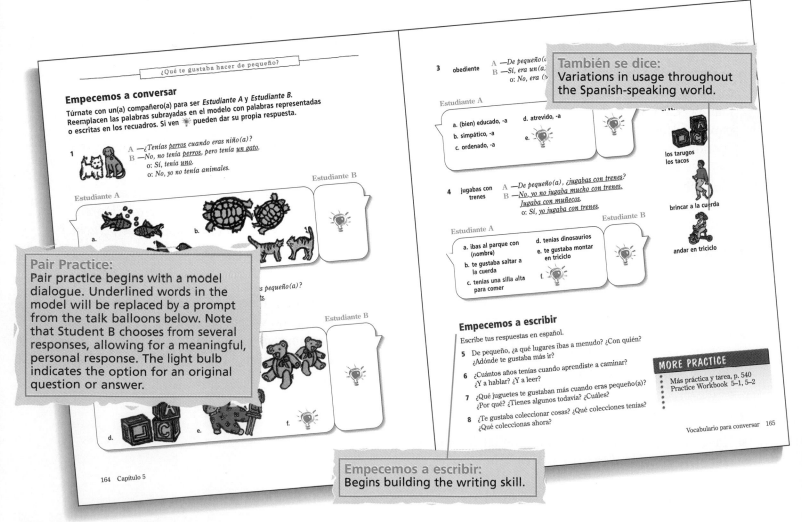

Empecemos a conversar

Túrnate con un(a) compañero(a) para ser *Estudiante A* y *Estudiante B*.
Reemplacen las palabras subrayadas en el modelo con palabras representadas o escritas en los recuadros. Si ven 💡 pueden dar su propia respuesta.

1 A —¿Tenías *perros* cuando eras niño(a)?
   B —*No, no tenía perros, pero tenía un gato.*
   o: *Sí, tenía uno.*
   o: *No, yo no tenía animales.*

Pair Practice:
Pair practice begins with a model dialogue. Underlined words in the model will be replaced by a prompt from the talk balloons below. Note that Student B chooses from several responses, allowing for a meaningful, personal response. The light bulb indicates the option for an original question or answer.

3 obediente A —*De pequeño(...)
             B —Sí, era un(a)...*
             o: *No, era (...*

También se dice:
Variations in usage throughout the Spanish-speaking world.

Estudiante A

a. (bien) educado, -a   d. atrevido, -a
b. simpático, -a   e. 💡
c. ordenado, -a

los tarugos
los tacos

4 jugabas con   A —*De pequeño(a), ¿jugabas con trenes?*
   trenes   B —*No, yo no jugaba mucho con trenes.*
                  Jugaba con muñecos.
                  o: *Sí, yo jugaba con trenes.*

Estudiante A

a. ibas al parque con   d. tenías dinosaurios
   (nombre)   e. te gustaba montar
b. te gustaba saltar a   en triciclo
   la cuerda   f. 💡
c. tenías una silla alta
   para comer

brincar a la cuerda

andar en triciclo

Empecemos a escribir

Escribe tus respuestas en español.

5 De pequeño, ¿a qué lugares ibas a menudo? ¿Con quién? ¿Adónde te gustaba más ir?

6 ¿Cuántos años tenías cuando aprendiste a caminar? ¿Y a hablar? ¿Y a leer?

7 ¿Qué juguetes te gustaban más cuando eras pequeño(a)? ¿Por qué? ¿Tienes algunos todavía? ¿Cuáles?

8 ¿Te gustaba coleccionar cosas? ¿Qué colecciones tenías? ¿Qué coleccionas ahora?

MORE PRACTICE

Más práctica y tarea, p. 540
Practice Workbook 5–1, 5–2

Vocabulario para conversar 165

164 Capítulo 5

Empecemos a escribir:
Begins building the writing skill.

¡**C**omuniquemos! *(Practice)*

This section offers additional practice with the new vocabulary. The varied activities guide students to personalized communication.

Teaching ideas

Follow the guidelines for paired practice. At this point, students are familiar with the new vocabulary and the activities should go quickly, but choose from among them. Do not attempt to do them all.

¡Comuniquemos!

¿Qué te gustaba hacer de pequeño?

Aquí tienes otra oportunidad para usar el vocabulario de este capítulo.

1 Habla con un(a) compañero(a) de cómo eras antes y cómo eres ahora. Usa las características de la lista.
A —Cuando eras niño(a), ¿eras (muy) perezoso(a)?
B —Sí, pero ahora soy (muy) trabajador(a).
o: No. Era (muy) trabajador(a).

a. simpático(a)
b. obediente
c. ordenado(a)
d. serio(a)
e. tacaño(a)
f. paciente
g. educado(a)
h. atrevido(a)
i.

maleducado(a)
impaciente
desobediente
prudente
generoso(a)
antipático(a)
divertido(a)
desordenado(a)

2 Con un(a) compañero(a), habla de los juguetes para niños. ¿Cuáles son los mejores y por qué? Después, trabajen con otros dos estudiantes para hablar sobre lo que escogieron.

170 Capítulo 5

3 La profesora de una guardería infantil no sabe qué hacer. Con un(a) compañero(a), describe los problemas que hay en la guardería.

Fernanda
Rubén
Patricia
Gabriel
Ignacio
Anita

Ahora decidan lo que debe hacer la profesora en cada situación. Pueden usar estos u otros verbos.

ayudar
dar   lavar   poner
           limpiar   preguntar

¿Qué sabes ahora?

Can you:

■ tell what you were like when you were a child?
—De pequeño(a), yo era ___, y ___ mucho.
■ tell what you liked to play with?
—Me ___ jugar con ___.
■ talk about how old you were when you learned to do something?
—Aprendí a ___ cuando ___ años.

Vocabulario para conversar 171

¿Qué sabes ahora?:
Students begin to check their own progress toward achieving the chapter objectives.

Perspectiva cultural (Preview, Present & Apply)

This section offers a unique perspective into understanding the richness of Hispanic cultures. Using a combination of a photographic and narrative essay, it asks students to think about culture in such a way as to develop real cross-cultural understanding and sensitivity.

Teaching ideas for the *Perspectiva cultural*

1 Have students answer the inductive questions as a whole-class or small-group activity. Write their responses on the board. This will activate background information, prompt and recycle related vocabulary, and show that, even in their own class, they will find a variety of customs and traditions.

2 Use the photographs to encourage students to make observations about cultural perspective. Describe the photo(s) in Spanish, adding more information.

3 Add personal information or anecdotes. If any students have personal knowledge about the cultural topic, let them share their experiences. Ask Spanish speakers to share family traditions.

4 In small groups or as a whole class, have students answer the questions in *La cultura desde tu perspectiva*. This is your best opportunity for helping students understand their own culture and the beliefs and attitudes they have formed.

5 Ask students to use the cultural insight gained to reflect on their own culture. For example, whom would students cite as a United States figure similar to José Martí if a Spanish-speaking student should ask?

Critical questioning:
A series of inductive questions focusing on students' background knowledge and on the photos.

Cultural reading:
Cultural information and insights that expand upon the information in the photos. Students validate or reject the ideas they formulated earlier.

La cultura desde tu perspectiva:
Students reflect upon and interact with new cultural information from the perspective of their own culture.

ramática en contexto (*Preview, Present & Practice*)

A realia-based reading provides comprehensible input for the new grammar. This gives students meaningful understanding of the structures by letting them intuit the rules. This inductive approach allows students to internalize and gain a deeper understanding of the grammar. Students were shown these structures in the vocabulary presentation and have practiced using them. They should not be uncomfortable with the structures themselves.

Realia-based reading:
The reading combines cognates and previously learned vocabulary with the chapter's key grammar concepts.

Teaching ideas for *Gramática en contexto*

1 Show the Overhead. Activate students' own experience by asking questions such as: How many students have studied about colonial life in America? How was life different then? Have they ever visited a site of colonial life that has been preserved or reconstructed?

2 Have students read the captions and study the pictures. Have them answer the questions individually or in pairs. Let them verify their answers with another pair or as a whole-class activity.

3 As students generate explanations, write them on the chalkboard along with examples from the reading.

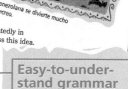

Inductive questions:
Students scan for information that leads them to produce their own explanation for the structures used.

Easy-to-understand grammar explanations:
Rules developed by the student are reinforced in easily understood explanations. Grammar terminology is kept to a minimum.

In a truly thematic approach, grammar is tied to the communicative objectives. What is not relevant is not presented. Here, for example, students work with understanding and using the imperfect in the context of what they were like as children and what they used to do. Students focus on content relevant to the theme. Students will, in later chapters, continue to work with the imperfect as related to other themes. This thematic approach builds in regular review and recycling as students are reminded of structures and vocabulary sets through the *¡No olvides!* feature. There are three to four grammar topics per chapter, each followed by a variety of activities.

¿Qué te gustaba hacer de pe

3 Túrnate con un(a) compañero(a) para hablar de lo que te
personas cuando Uds. eran pequeños(as).

tus abuelos   A —¿Qué tenían tus abuelos
              B —Tenían un proyector de

a. tus tíos   d. tus hermanos
b. tus primos   e. tu vecino(a)
c. tú   f. 💡

4 Pregúntale a dos compañeros(as) qué
en la escuela primaria.

obedecer siempre   A —¿Uds. obedecían
a sus padres   B —Sí, obedecíamos
                   o: No, desobede

a. comer en la cafetería todos los
b. hacer fila antes de las clases
c. ver videos en las clases
d. leer libros en la biblioteca a
e. tener tarea
f. soler visitar museos
g. escribir cartas a estudiant
   de otras escuelas
h. mentir mucho o siempre
   decir la verdad
i. 💡

178 Capítulo 5

El imperfecto de l
terminan en -er e

Here are all the forms of
have the same pattern of

comer / vivir

(yo)	comía
	vivía
(tú)	comías
	vivías
Ud.	comía
(él)	vivía
(ella)	

• The verb *ver* is
are added to th

(yo)	veía
(tú)	ve'
Ud.	
(él)	
(ella)	

• *Haber* is
know th
form is
En l
En

Unas niñas españolas saltan a la cuerda
delante de su casa en Andalucía.

Ahora lo sabes

Can you:

■ talk about your life as a child?

—De pequeño(a) ___ en
un apartamento muy pequeño.
Me ___ jugar con trenes.

■ tell what people used to do regularly?

—Los vecinos ___ de lunes a viernes.
Y los fines de semana ___ de pesca.

■ compare what people used to do with
what they do now?

—Cuando ___ pequeño(a), yo ___ los
platos. Ahora ___ la comida.

Este mes

CRECER *feliz*

• TU PELO, TU SONRISA...
¿Qué heredará
tu hijo de ti?

• JUGUETES
INTELIGENTES
Informática
para bebés

92 PAPILLAS
PARA ELEGIR
LA MEJOR

• SUS DIBUJOS
HABLAN
Aprende a
descifrarlos

• ALERGIAS
Cómo afectan
al embarazo

REGALO
Una cuchara
para comidas muy divertidas

Gramática en contexto 181

Ahora lo sabes (Assess):
Students continue assessing their
progress toward achieving the
chapter objectives.

Todo junto (Apply)

Todo junto is composed of four integrative sections: *Actividades, Conexiones, ¡Vamos a leer!,* and *¡Vamos a escribir!*

Teaching ideas for *Actividades*

1 To complement what students have learned up to this point, use the video segments for *La Catrina.* (See pp. T50–T52 for details.) See the Teacher's Guide that accompanies the video program for teaching suggestions.

2 You may want to use different activities for different ability groupings.

3 Use activities for performance-based assessment. Refer to the section in the Assessment Program book on the development and use of rubrics to evaluate student performance.

Teaching ideas for *Conexiones*

1 Use these activities to extend the chapter language skills.

2 Include additional activities if students express interest in the connection. Work with other subject area teachers for ideas or let students develop their own ideas.

Actividades (Apply):
Pick and choose from among these activities.

Conexiones:
Activities connect to other disciplines through the chapter theme and content.

¡Vamos a leer! (Apply)

Students learn how to become efficient readers through a four-step process. Real comprehension is achieved through strategies, questions, and activities in the *Infórmate* and *Aplicación*. Students encounter unknown vocabulary, but gain confidence by realizing they don't need to know every word to read successfully.

Teaching ideas

1 *Antes de leer:* Use the globe on p. 185 or the maps on the Overheads to point out where Nicaragua is located. Ask students if anyone has heard of Roberto Clemente. Does anyone have one of his baseball cards? Encourage answers to the questions to activate prior knowledge. Write responses on the chalkboard.

2 *Mira la lectura:* Have students work individually or in groups and report back to the class. Compare their answers to what they brainstormed in *Antes de leer.*

3 *Infórmate:* This can be done individually or in pairs.

4 *Aplicación:* Students will complete this activity successfully because of the careful structuring of the early steps in the reading process. You might have students work in pairs or small groups.

• **Step 1**
Antes de leer: Activates students' background knowledge to help them predict or anticipate.

• **Step 2**
Mira la lectura: Pre-reading section focusing on a specific reading strategy.

Todo junto

¡Vamos a leer!

Antes de leer

STRATEGY ➤ Using prior knowledge

Have you ever known a really amazing athlete? What was he or she like? What information would you expect to find in the life story of an outstanding athlete? How is a biography usually organized?

El campeón

—¡Roberto! ¡Roberto, ven! ¡Ya es hora de comer!

El pequeño Roberto no prestaba atención. Era un muchacho obediente, pero en ese momento, sólo pensaba en lo que hacía—jugar béisbol.

Roberto Clemente nació en 1934 en la pequeña comunidad de Carolina, Puerto Rico. Jugaba béisbol todos los días, pero también tenía que ir a la escuela y trabajar. Trabajaba porque quería comprarse una bicicleta. Después de trabajar tres años, tuvo bastante dinero para comprarse una. En la escuela secundaria, Roberto era un muchacho tímido, pero en el campo de béisbol su timidez desaparecía.

En 1953 representantes de los Brooklyn Dodgers fueron a

Puerto Rico para observar y contratar a nuevos jugadores. —¡Tenía que contratarlo! Era el mejor atleta innato que había visto,— dijo el scout de los Dodgers cuando vio al joven Roberto jugar. Los Dodgers lo mandaron a su equipo de Montreal, Canadá. De allí pasó a los Piratas de Pittsburgh en 1955. Cinco años más tarde los Piratas ganaron el campeonato de la Liga Nacional y la Serie Mundial. Clemente fue nombrado el Jugador Más Valioso de la liga en 1966. El 24 de julio de 1970 se celebró la Noche de Roberto Clemente en el estadio Three [Rivers] Pittsburgh para ho[nrar al] pelotero más famo[so y] querido del equipo.

En diciembre de 19[72] un terrible terrem[oto]

Mira la lectura

Read the story through quickly. Did you find the information you expected?

Esta estatua de Roberto Clemente queda enfrente del estadio en Pittsburgh.

Nicaragua. En seguida Clemente organizó un vuelo de ayuda. Llevaba alimentos, ropa y medicina para las víctimas del desastre. El avión era viejo y pequeño y pesaba mucho, pero Clemente insistió en ir.

Infórmate

STRATEGY ➤ Recognizing time expressions

Time expressions will help you understand writing that is organized chronologically, as a biography usually is. Some of the time expressions in this biography are:

• …en 1934…
• Cinco años más tarde…
• En diciembre de 1972…

Other expressions can help you to keep track of time by referring to activities associated with a certain stage of life. For example:

• …tenía que ir a la escuela…
• En la escuela secundaria, …

1. Now reread the biography. When you come [to] an expression that helps you fix the time, st[op] and quickly calculate how old Roberto was [...]

2. Why is Roberto Clemente one of baseball's most honored players? Why is he considered a great humanitarian?

Managua, Nicaragua

La ciu[dad...]

BOB CLEMENTE — PIRATES

• **Step 3**
Infórmate: Students read for specific information or details, using strategies for dealing with difficult aspects of the text. Questions help focus on key information.

18

Aplicación

Write three to five sentences with time expressions about a famous athlete or other famous person. Then read one sentence to a partner and ask him or her to guess who it is about. If your partner can't guess, read the next sentence, and so on. For example, these statements are about Nancy López.

1. Ganó el Torneo de Golf Femenino de Nuevo México cuando tenía 12 años.
2. En 1978 ganó nueve torneos de golf, entre ellos el de la Asociación de Mujeres Golfistas Profesionales (LPGA en inglés).
3. Siete años después, ganó cinco torneos, entre ellos el LPGA una vez más.

¡Vamos a leer! 185

• **Step 4**
Aplicación: Students use what they have learned by applying it in a different way.

¡Vamos a escribir! *(Apply)*

As with reading, students develop effective writing through a process approach consistent with the way they are learning to write in their English classes. It also provides a strategy or model for writing independently. Each writing task provides a creative, personalized opportunity to expand the chapter theme.

• Step 1
Pre-writing questions have students think about the topic, generate needed language, and organize their ideas. They then write the first draft.

• Steps 2 & 3
Through peer review students gain insights into needed revisions or clarifications for preparing the final draft.

Teaching ideas

1 This may be done in class or as homework. Students can work individually, in pairs, or in small groups to brainstorm the topic and needed vocabulary. Be sure to review the model interviews that accompany the photographs. They can jot down answers to the questions and share them with other students. They then use the questions and responses as a starting point for writing their first draft. Have students skip lines on the first draft so that there is room for comments during the peer review.

2 Have students share their first draft with one or more partners. Peer reviewers should check for thoroughness and comprehensibility, as well as for errors in spelling, grammar, and punctuation. (Each reviewer should say at least one good thing about the writing sample.)

3 Students may might want to include final drafts in their writing portfolios.

Todo junto

¡Vamos a escribir!

Todos tenemos una persona especial en la vida. Puede ser un(a) pariente(a), un(a) amigo(a) o un(a) profesor(a). Vamos a escribir una biografía breve de una persona especial.

1 Primero entrevista a la persona o a alguien que la conoce. Contesta éstas preguntas:

- ¿Cuándo y dónde nació?
- ¿Dónde vivía la familia cuando nació?
- ¿Cómo era de pequeño(a)?
- ¿Qué hacía de pequeño(a)? ¿De joven?
- ¿Cómo es ahora?
- ¿Qué hace ahora?

2 Organiza tus ideas en orden cronológico. Escribe el primer borrador. Sigue los pasos del proceso de escribir.

Ahora escribe una anécdota de la vida de la persona que escogiste. Debe ser una anécdota que revele algo de su carácter. Por ejemplo, ¿hizo alguna vez algo muy difícil? ¿Algo increíble?

3 Para distribuir las biografías y anécdotas, pueden:

- enviarlas a las personas de quienes escribieron
- enviarlas al periódico o a la revista literaria escolar
- incluirlas en un libro titulado *Personas especiales*
- ponerlas en sus portafolios

Un gaucho de San Antonio de Areco, Argentina

Entrevista con un gaucho

ESTUDIANTE	¿Qué es un gaucho?
GAUCHO	Somos vaqueros.
ESTUDIANTE	¿La ropa que usa es típica?
GAUCHO	Sí. El poncho, el sombrero negro, los pantalones flojos, el cinturón de plata y las botas son muy típicos.

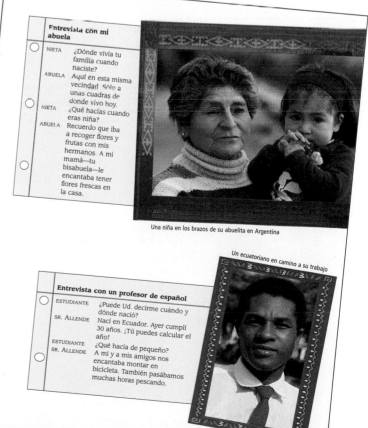

Entrevista con mi abuela

	NIETA	¿Dónde vivía tu familia cuando naciste?
	ABUELA	Aquí en esta misma vecindad. Sólo a unas cuadras de donde vivo hoy.
	NIETA	¿Qué hacías cuando eras niña?
	ABUELA	Recuerdo que iba a recoger flores y frutas con mis hermanos. A mi mamá—tu bisabuela—le encantaba tener flores frescas en la casa.

Una niña en los brazos de su abuelita en Argentina

Un ecuatoriano en camino a su trabajo

Entrevista con un profesor de español

	ESTUDIANTE	¿Puede Ud. decirme cuándo y dónde nació?
	SR. ALLENDE	Nací en Ecuador. Ayer cumplí 30 años. ¡Tú puedes calcular el año!
	ESTUDIANTE	¿Qué hacía de pequeño?
	SR. ALLENDE	A mí y a mis amigos nos encantaba montar en bicicleta. También pasábamos muchas horas pescando.

epaso: ¿Lo sabes bien? *(Apply, Assess & Summarize)*

In this section students practice tasks similar to those they will encounter on the *Examen de habilidades.* They focus on the chapter objectives and show what they can do with the language.

Teaching ideas

1 Point out how this pre-test and the vocabulary on the following page prepare for the *Examen de habilidades.*

2 Do this as a whole-class activity or have pairs complete the sections at home and then compare their responses with those of a partner. Or, with a partner, they can work through each section in class and then compare their answers with those of another pair.

3 Students who do well should feel confident about performing well on the test. Those having difficulty will know where they need to focus attention as they study for the test.

Resumen del vocabulario *(Summarize)*

This section organizes the chapter vocabulary to reflect how it can be used to meet the communicative objectives. The objectives were stated in the chapter overview, and students have been given regular opportunities to assess their progress in the *¿Qué sabes ahora?, Ahora lo sabes,* and *Repaso: ¿Lo sabes bien?*

CAPÍTULO 5

Repaso ¿Lo sabes bien?

Esta sección te ayudará a prepararte para el examen de habilidades.

Listening
Can you understand when people talk about what they were like as children? Listen as your teacher reads a sample similar to what you will hear on the test. How were Tina and her sister different? Why were they different?

Reading
Read the following fragment of an autobiography. Then complete the sentences with the right time expressions. (One choice will not be used.)

Cuando yo era niño, mi mamá me hacía animales de peluche. Mi papá me hacía juguetes de madera. ___ me hizo una casa de madera en un árbol. Yo no entendía por qué mis padres no me compraban juguetes de plástico, como los de mis compañeros. ___ por fin entendí. Estudiamos el medio ambiente y la importancia de reciclar los materiales. Mis padres estaban reciclando las cosas. ___ yo también hago juguetes de madera para mi hija.

Writing
Clara is going to spend a year in Guatemala as an exchange student. A Guatemala City newspaper has asked for a brief description of her as a child. This is what a long-time friend wrote. Write a similar description of *your* best friend.

Recuerdo que Clara era una niña muy simpática y trabajadora. Cuando no conocía a la gente, era un poco tímida, pero después era sociable. Éramos vecinos. Íbamos a la misma escuela. Los fines de semana jugábamos en el parque. Yo sé que Clara va a tener muchos amigos en Guatemala.

Culture
If you had been a friend of José Martí, would you have helped him fight for Cuban independence? Why?

Speaking
With a partner, talk about your childhood. Ask one another some questions to find out what you were like as young children. Here is a sample dialogue.

A —*Cuando tenías cinco años, ¿cómo eras?*
B —*Obediente pero a veces un poco travieso. ¿Y tú?*
A —*Casi siempre me portaba bien, pero también era traviesa. ¿Con qué te gustaba jugar?*
B —*Me gustaban los bloques, los trenes eléctricos y las pistolas de agua. ¿Qué preferías tú?*
A —*A mí me encantaba montar en triciclo y saltar a la cuerda.*

a. cuando estaba en la escuela secundaria
b. el año pasado
c. ahora
d. cuando cumplí ocho años

Self Test   www.pasoapaso.com

188 Capítulo 5

Teaching ideas

1 Have pairs review the vocabulary. They might make up a sentence or dialogue in each category. For example, *Tenía un pez cuando era niño* or:
—*¿Tenías un pájaro cuando eras niño?*
—*No, pero tenía una tortuga.*

2 If students have created flashcards, have them organize these according to the communicative categories.

3 Have students quiz each other using the list in the book or their flashcards. Ask them to indicate any words their partner had trouble with by writing them on a sheet of paper or placing a check on the flashcard. This will focus their test preparation on problem areas.

Assessment options

1 The *Prueba cumulativa* is a prochievement instrument that focuses on students' knowledge of the chapter vocabulary and grammar in a communicative context.

2 The *Examen de habilidades* is a proficiency-oriented instrument that focuses on what students can do with the language in a real-world context.

3 The Test Generator provides a test bank of multiple-choice questions to which you can add your own questions.

Resumen del vocabulario

Usa el vocabulario de este capítulo para:
· tell what you were like as a child
· tell what you used to like to do
· talk about what you learned to do

to talk about animals
el animal, *pl.* los animales
el pájaro
el pez, *pl.* los peces
la tortuga

to talk about people
de pequeño, -a
el niño, la niña
el vecino, la vecina
obediente
desobediente
(bien) educado, -a
maleducado, -a
consentido, -a
tímido, -a
travieso, -a

to name toys
el juguete
la muñeca
el muñeco
el robot, *pl.* los robots
el animal de peluche, *pl.* los
    animales de peluche
el oso de peluche
el dinosaurio
el camión, *pl.* los camiones
el tren (de juguete)
el bloque
la pistola (de agua)

to discuss things you used to do
ser: (yo) era, (tú) eras
caminar
montar en triciclo
el triciclo
saltar (a la cuerda)
la cuerda
ir: (yo) iba, (tú) ibas
recordar *(o → ue)*
coleccionar
la colección, *pl.* las colecciones
la verdad
mentir *(e → ie)*
obedecer *(c → zc)*
desobedecer *(c → zc)*
portarse (bien / mal)
molestar
pelearse (con)
llorar

to talk about places children go
la guardería infantil
el kindergarten
la escuela primaria

to talk about playground equipment
el patio de recreo
el cajón de arena, *pl.* los
    cajones de arena
el carrusel
el columpio
el sube y baja
el tobogán, *pl.* los toboganes

Resumen **189**

USING THE TEACHER'S EDITION

This Teacher's Edition provides all the support needed to work with the wide range of students in today's Spanish classes.

Each teacher chapter begins with a spread that provides organizational and cultural information for instructional planning.

> Additional information and insight into the chapter's cultural theme

> List of the chapter communication, culture, and grammar objectives

> List of ancillaries available, each represented by an icon that will be shown at suggested point of use

This Teacher's Edition is organized to provide for maximum ease of use. The student page is slightly reduced. Teacher notes appear regularly in the same place on the page.

Sidenotes are organized around the five-step pedagogical model used throughout *PASO A PASO*:

- **Introduce / Preview**
- **Present**
- **Practice**
- **Apply**
- **Summarize / Assess**

Notes provide answers, teaching suggestions, ancillary cross-references, recycling references, and other useful information.

Previously taught vocabulary sets that are re-entered in the chapter

Activities that expand the chapter theme into other curricular areas

Activities in which students can look beyond the classroom to find the influence of Hispanic cultures

Ideas for planning, strategies for reaching all students, and expansions on cultural themes

References to help with planning and instruction

Chapter theme

Communicative objectives

Ideas for recycling previously taught material

Additional perspectives from throughout the Spanish-speaking world

Icons for ancillary references

Lexical preview of grammar

Suggestions for multiple intelligence-based activities and extensions

Additional written practice for in-class assignments or homework

Ideas to help reach the wide range of learners in your classroom

Page-by-page correlations to the Standards addressed in the student text, ancillaries, and Teacher's Edition suggestions

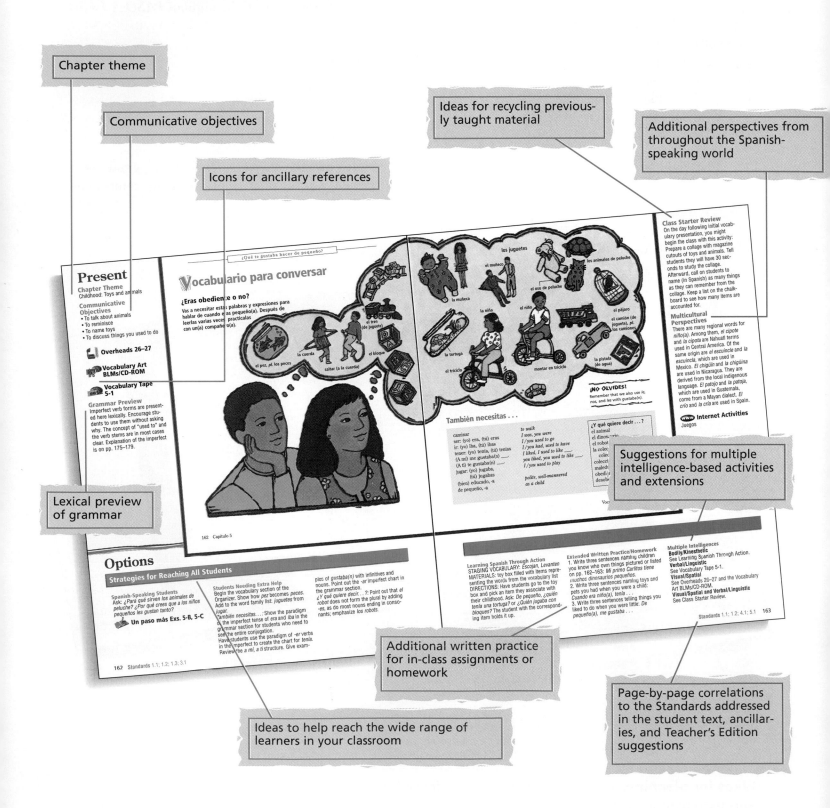

CLASSROOM MANAGEMENT AND LESSON PLANS

PASO A PASO 2 has been carefully developed to provide the instructional materials for one school year. The authors had as a goal the development of a realistically paced and easy-to-manage program that would relieve teacher and student frustration. There is flexibility and choice among the textbook activities and ancillaries. To help work with the wide variety of learners in your classroom, *PASO A PASO 2* offers unprecedented support on every page. We developed the Scope and Sequence to give students the tools needed to communicate about their interests. Thematic chapter organization allows for real integration of vocabulary, grammar, and culture, while avoiding unneeded grammatical content.

We present vocabulary in logical sets and, when possible, with visuals. Research shows that both of these approaches lead to more efficient and more permanent learning. Above all, lexical and contextual introduction of grammar allows students to learn structures in a truly natural way. *Fui* is not "the first-person singular preterite of the verb *ir*," but, quite simply, "I went"—a concept that presents no difficulty. (This is particularly true for students who neither know nor care that "I went" is a past-tense form of the verb "to go.")

We would urge you to allow this process to unfold. Avoid explanations in the vocabulary section. Allow students to use the words naturally. By the time they reach the explanations they will feel confident in their ability to use the language.

Management and Lesson Plans for the Traditional Class Schedule

Teachers working in a traditional class schedule (meeting daily for approximately 40–50 minutes) should comfortably reach Chapter 12 in one school year.

Pacing for *Pasodoble*

The *Pasodoble* contains 14 theme-based review sections that recycle the vocabulary and grammar of Chapters 1–12 of *PASO A PASO 1*. Study the overview of *Pasodoble* on pages 1A–B to see the thematic review, recycling, and ancillary support. We suggest that you incorporate the review gradually into the first few weeks of instruction. Spend the first three days of school on it, and then move into Chapter 1. Return to *Pasodoble* sections throughout the first chapter (or the first few chapters) as a warm-up activity. You will find that students remember the key concepts and that the *Pasodoble*'s integrated review will help them move easily into *PASO A PASO 2*.

Pacing for Chapters 1–14

We suggest that approximately 11–13 instructional days be spent on each chapter, including assessment. This time will vary based upon the amount of instructional time and the range of students in the class.

As you begin teaching with *PASO A PASO 2*, you will sense a rhythm, a flow within each chapter that helps students move smoothly and successfully. The thematic integration and spiraling within a chapter, the extensive use of context and comprehensible input for vocabulary and grammar, the inductive questioning that leads to real understanding, and the recycling of previously taught material are part of the carefully thought out chapter design. You should be able to move quickly through the chapters in the suggested time period.

The following Lesson Plans show how Chapter 1 might be organized for instruction. Feel free to adapt these sample lessons to your teaching style, students, and schedule. As you become more familiar with the program, you will find many more ways to use all of the *PASO A PASO* components.

Pasodoble
Capítulo 1   ¿Cómo es tu escuela?

	Instructional Process	Tasks/Activities	Components
Day #1	Preview	Explanation of *Pasodoble* review	Text, p. 1
	Presentation/Practice	*Pasodoble*	Text, pp. 2–3
	Practice	Vocabulary review and practice	Level 1 Overheads 38–39 Level 1 Communicative Activity BLMs 7-1
	Closing/Assignments	Review day's objectives and tasks to be done Preview Day #2	Practice Wkbk. PD-1
Day #2	Introduction/Review	Review homework *Pasodoble*	Practice Wkbk. PD-1 Text, pp. XII–XV, 4
	Presentation/Practice	*Pasodoble* Vocabulary review	Text, p. 5 Level 1 Overheads 8–10
	Application	Writing Activity	WAVA: Writing Activity A
	Closing/Assignments	Review day's objectives and tasks to be done Preview Day #3	Practice Wkbk. PD-2, PD-3
Day #3	Introduction/Review	Review homework	Practice Wkbk. PD-2, PD-3
	Presentation/Practice	*Pasodoble* Vocabulary review	Text, pp. 6–7 Level 1 Vocabulary Art BLMs, pp. 8–9, 18, 20–21
	Presentation/Practice	*Pasodoble* Writing Activity	Text, pp. 10–11 WAVA: Writing Activity B (p. 1)
	Closing/Assignments	Review day's objectives and tasks to be done Preview Day #4	Practice Wkbk. PD-4, PD-5

Day #4	Introduction/Review	Review homework	Practice Wkbk. PD-4, PD-5
	Application	Interview/Writing Activity	WAVA: Writing Activity B (p. 2)
	Presentation	*Capítulo 1* Cultural Overview, Objectives	Text, pp. 25B–27
	Presentation/Practice	*¡Piensa en la cultura!*	Text, pp. 28–29
	Closing/Assignments	Review day's objectives and tasks to be done Preview Day #5	Practice Wkbk. PD-6, PD-7
Day #5	Introduction/Review	Review homework Audio Activities	Practice Wkbk. PD-6, PD-7 WAVA: Audio Activities P.1–P.2
	Presentation/Practice	*Pasodoble* Vocabulary review Video Activity	Text, pp. 12–13 Level 1 Overheads 21–24 *En vivo:* Episode 4, *Todo junto*
	Presentation	Vocabulary presentation /Input	Text, pp. 30–31 Overheads 6–7 Vocabulary Art DLMs
	Closing/Assignments	Review day's objectives and tasks to be done Preview Day #6	Vocabulary Art BLMs
Day #6	Introduction/Review	Audio Activities Vocabulary Review	WAVA: Audio Activities P.3–P.4 Vocabulary Art BLMs
	Presentation/Practice	Vocabulary presentation/Input *También necesitas . . .*	Text, pp. 30–31 Text, p. 31
	Practice	Paired practice	Text, pp. 32–33
	Application	Video Activity	*En vivo:* Episode 2, *Todo junto*
	Closing/Assignments	Review day's objectives and tasks to be done Preview Day #7	Practice Wkbk. 1-1, 1-2

Day #7	Introduction/Review	Review homework	Practice Wkbk. 1-1, 1-2
		Review vocabulary	Text, pp. 30–31
		Pronunciation Review	Vocabulary Tape 1-1
	Practice	Communicative Activity	Communicative Activity BLMs 1-1
		Choose from:	
		Enrichment	Text, pp. 32–33
		Cooperative Learning	
	Application	Audio Activity	WAVA: Audio Activity 1.1
	Assessment	Quiz	*Prueba* 1-1
	Closing/Assignments	Review day's objectives and tasks to be done	Text, p. 33, *Empecemos a escribir*
		Preview Day #8	
Day #8	Introduction/Review	Review homework	Text, p. 33, *Empecemos a escribir*
	Assessment	Quiz	*Prueba* 1-2
	Presentation/Practice	*Pasodoble*	Text, pp. 14–15
		Vocabulary review	Level 1 Overheads 56–60 and/or Level 1
			Vocabulary Art BLMs, pp. 58–62
	Closing/Assignments	Review day's objectives and tasks to be done	Practice Wkbk. PD-8, PD-9
		Preview Day #9	
Day #9	Introduction/Review	Review homework	Practice Wkbk. PD-8, PD-9
	Application	Choose from:	
		Video Activity	*En vivo:* Episode 11, *Todo junto*
		Writing Activity	WAVA: Writing Activity D
		Communicative Activity	Level 1 Communicative Activity
			BLMs 11-1
		CD-ROM Activities	*Pasos vivos 1* CD-ROM
	Presentation	Vocabulary presentation/Input	Text, pp. 34–35
			Overheads 8–9
			Vocabulary Art BLMs
	Practice	Paired practice	Text, p. 36
	Closing/Assignments	Review day's objectives and tasks to be done	Vocabulary Art BLMs
		Preview Day #10	

Day #10	Introduction/Review	Class Starter Review Review vocabulary	Text, p. 35 Vocabulary Art BLMs
	Presentation/Practice	*También necesitas . . .* Pronunciation review	Text, p. 35 Vocabulary Tape 1-2
	Practice	Paired practice	Text, p. 37
	Application	Audio Activities	WAVA: Audio Activities 1.2, 1.3
	Closing/Assignments	Review day's objectives and tasks to be done Preview Day #11	Practice Wkbk. 1-3, 1-4
Day #11	Introduction/Review	Review homework Review vocabulary	Practice Wkbk. 1-3, 1-4 Vocabulary Art BLMs
	Practice	Communicative Activity	Communicative Activity BLMs 1-3
	Application	Writing Activities	WAVA: Writing Activities 1-A, 1-B
	Assessment	Quiz Self-assessment	*Prueba* 1-3 Text, p. 39, *¿Qué sabes ahora?*
	Closing/Assignments	Review day's objectives and tasks to be done Preview Day #12	Text, p. 37, *Empecemos a escribir y a leer*
Day #12	Introduction/Review	Review homework	Text, p. 37, *Empecemos a escribir y a leer*
	Assessment	Quiz	*Prueba* 1-4
	Application	*¡Comuniquemos!*	Text, pp. 38–39
	Presentation	*Perspectiva cultural*	Text, pp. 40–41
	Closing/Assignments	Review day's objectives and tasks to be done Preview Day #13	Text, pp. 40–41 WAVA: Writing Activity C
Day #13	Introduction/Review	Review homework	Text, pp. 40–41 WAVA: Writing Activity C
	Presentation/Practice	*Gramática en contexto*	Text, pp. 42–45 Overhead 10
	Closing/Assignments	Review day's objectives and tasks to be done Preview Day #14	Practice Wkbk. 1-5, 1-6

Day #14	Introduction/Review	Review homework	Practice Wkbk. 1-5, 1-6
	Presentation/Practice	*Gramática en contexto*	Text, pp. 45–49
	Application	Video Activity	*La Catrina:* Episode 1 WAVA: Video Activities, pp. 151–152, A–C
	Closing/Assignments	Review day's objectives and tasks to be done Preview Day #15	Practice Wkbk. 1-7, 1-8
Day #15	Introduction/Review	Review homework	Practice Wkbk. 1-7, 1-8
	Practice	Communicative Activity	Communicative Activity BLMs 1-2
	Application	Choose from: *Todo junto* CD-ROM Activities *Actividades en grupo* Audio Activities Video Activity	 Text, pp. 50–51 *Pasos vivos 2* CD-ROM Communicative Activity BLMs 1-4 WAVA: Audio Activities 1.4, 1.5 *La Catrina:* Episode 1
	Assessment	Quizzes	*Pruebas* 1-5, 1-6, 1-7
	Closing/Assignments	Review day's objectives and tasks to be done Preview Day #16	Practice Wkbk. 1-9, 1-10
Day #16	Introduction/Review	Review homework	Practice Wkbk. 1-9, 1-10
	Assessment	Quizzes	Pruebas 1-8, 1-9
	Application	*¡Vamos a leer!*	Text, pp. 52–53
	Closing/Assignments	Review day's objectives and tasks to be done Preview Day #17	Choose from: Practice Wkbk. Organizer, p. 11 WAVA: Writing Activities 1-D to 1-H

Day #17	Introduction/Review	Review homework	Practice Wkbk. Organizer, p. 11
			WAVA: Writing Activities 1-D to 1-H
	Application	Choose from:	
		Todo junto	Text, pp. 50–51
		¡Vamos a escribir!	Text, pp. 54–55
		Actividades en grupo	Communicative Activity BLMs 1-4
		CD-ROM Activities	*Pasos vivos 2* CD-ROM
		Video Activity	*La Catrina:* Episode 1
	Application	Self-assessment	Text, p. 56, *Repaso: ¿Lo sabes bien?*
	Closing/Assignments	Review for Chapter Test	
Day #18	Assessment	Chapter Test	Assessment Program: Choose from
			Prueba cumulativa or
			Examen de habilidades
			(or)
			Use components such as: Situation Cards,
			Communicative Activity BLMs, p. 7;
			Pasos vivos 2 CD-ROM; Test Generator
	Preview	Preview Day #1 of *Capítulo 2*	Text, pp. 58–59

Management and Lesson Plans for the Block Schedule

PASO A PASO is ideal for the block schedule. The theme-based approach in each chapter allows for a more holistic presentation of content. Since the vocabulary, grammar, and culture are based upon the theme and recycle naturally throughout the chapter, there is flexibility in the way the material can be presented. The wide range of activities in the student book and the many ancillary components allow for individual, paired, and small group activities, as well as for the incorporation of different learning modalities. A variety of formal and informal assessment options are provided.

For teachers using the block schedule (85–90 minutes of instructional time), you should com-

fortably reach between Chapters 10–12 in one block.

Do not spend more than two days on the *Pasodoble* review. While students will need to recognize the vocabulary through listening and reading, they will not need spelling mastery at this point. Use this chapter to let students learn the beginning communication tools, cultural insights, and learning strategies. All of the concepts presented will be recycled throughout the text.

We suggest approximately 6–8 instructional days for each chapter. Start planning by looking at the year as a whole. Determine how many class periods you will have for instruction and how these are grouped around grading periods, testing, and vacation. Determine what your goals will be and then develop a general plan for the entire year using the following sample lesson plans as a guide. To develop a daily lesson plan, you might want to divide each day into a five- or six-step instructional sequence: Introduction/Review; Preview/Presentation; Practice; Application; Assessment; and Closing/Assignments. The amount of time devoted to each and how it is sequenced each day will vary based upon daily goals. You will notice variations in these sample plans. Feel free to adapt them to your teaching style, students, and class schedule. As you become more familiar with the program, you will find many more ways to use all of the *PASO A PASO* components.

Pasodoble
Capítulo 1   ¿Cómo es tu escuela?

Note: We suggest combining the *Pasodoble* review section with *Capítulo 1.* (See p. T36.)

	Instructional Process	Tasks/Activities	Components
Day #1	Preview	Explanation of *Pasodoble* review	Text, p. 1
	Presentation/Practice	*Pasodoble* Vocabulary review and practice	Text, pp. 2–3 Level 1 Overheads 38–39 Level 1 Communicative Activity BLMs 7-1
	Presentation/Practice	*Pasodoble* Vocabulary review	Text, p. 5 Level 1 Overheads 8–10
	Application	Writing Activity	WAVA: Writing Activity A
	Closing/Assignments	Review day's objectives and tasks to be done Preview Day #2	Practice Wkbk. PD-1 to PD-3
Day #2	Introduction/Review	Review homework *Pasodoble*	Practice Wkbk. PD-1 to PD-3 Text, pp. XII–XV, 4
	Presentation/Practice	*Pasodoble* Vocabulary review	Text, pp. 6–7 Level 1 Vocabulary Art BLMs, pp. 8–9, 18, 20–21
	Presentation/Practice	*Pasodoble*	Text, pp. 10–11
	Application	Writing Activity	WAVA: Writing Activity B
	Presentation	*Capítulo 1* Cultural Overview, Objectives *¡Piensa en la cultura!*	Text, pp. 25B–27 Text, pp. 28–29
	Closing/Assignments	Review day's objectives and tasks to be done Preview Day #3	Practice Wkbk. PD-4 to PD-6

Day #3	Introduction/Review	Review homework Audio Activities	Practice Wkbk. PD-4 to PD-6 WAVA: Audio Activities P.1–P.2
	Presentation/Practice	*Pasodoble* Vocabulary review Video Activity	Text, pp. 12–13 Level 1 Overheads 21–24 *En vivo:* Episode 4, *Todo junto*
	Presentation	Vocabulary presentation/Input	Text, pp. 30–31 Overheads 6–7 Vocabulary Art BLMs
	Closing/Assignments	Review day's objectives and tasks to be done Preview Day #4	Practice Wkbk. PD-7 Vocabulary Art BLMs
Day #4	Introduction/Review	Review homework Audio Activities Vocabulary Review Pronunciation Review	Practice Wkbk. PD-7 WAVA: Audio Activities P.3–P.4 Vocabulary Art BLMs Vocabulary Tape 1-1
	Presentation	Vocabulary presentation/Input *También necesitas . . .*	Text, pp. 30–31 Text, p. 31
	Practice	Paired practice	Text, pp. 32–33
	Practice	Communicative Activities	Communicative Activity BLMs 1-1
	Application	Video Activity	*En vivo:* Episode 2, *Todo junto*
	Closing/Assignments	Review day's objectives and tasks to be done Preview activities for Day #5	Practice Wkbk. 1-1, 1-2
Day #5	Introduction/Review	Review homework Review vocabulary	Practice Wkbk. 1-1, 1-2 Text, pp. 30–31
	Practice	Writing Practice	Text, p. 33, *Empecemos a escribir*
	Application	Audio Activity	WAVA: Audio Activity 1.1
	Assessment	Quiz	*Prueba* 1-1
	Presentation/Practice	*Pasodoble* Vocabulary review	Text, pp. 14–15 Level 1 Overheads 56–60 and/or Level 1 Vocabulary Art BLMs, pp. 58–62
	Closing/Assignments	Review day's objectives Preview activities for Day #6	Practice Wkbk. PD-8

Day #6	Assessment	Quiz	*Prueba* 1-2
	Introduction/Review	Review homework Choose from: Video Activity Writing Activity Communicative Activity	Practice Wkbk. PD-8 *En vivo*: Episode 11 WAVA: Writing Activity D Level 1 Communicative Activity BLMs 11-1
	Presentation	Vocabulary presentation/Input	Text, pp. 34–35 Overheads 8–9 Vocabulary Art BLMs
	Practice	Paired practice	Text, p. 36
	Closing	Review day's objectives and tasks to be done Preview activities for Day #7	Practice Wkbk. 1-3 Vocabulary Art BLMs
Day #7	Introduction/Review	Class Starter Review Review homework Pronunciation Review Writing Activity	Text, p. 35 Practice Wkbk 1-3 Vocabulary Art BLMs Vocabulary Tape 1-2 WAVA: Writing Activity 1-A
	Presentation	*También necesitas . . .*	Text, p. 35
	Practice	Paired practice	Text, p. 37
	Application	Audio Activities Communicative Activity	WAVA: Audio Activities 1.2, 1.3 Communicative Activity BLMs 1-3
	Closing/Assignments	Review day's objectives and tasks to be done Preview Day #8	Practice Wkbk. 1-4 Text, p. 37, *Empecemos a escribir y a leer*

Day #8	Introduction/Review	Review homework	Practice Wkbk. 1-4
			Text, p. 37, *Empecemos a escribir y a leer*
		Writing Activities	WAVA: Writing Activities 1-B, 1-C
	Application	Choose from *¡Comuniquemos!* activities	Text, pp. 38–39
	Assessment	Self-Assessment	Text, p. 39, *¿Qué sabes ahora?*
		Quizzes	*Pruebas* 1-3, 1-4
	Presentation/Practice	*Perspectiva cultural*	Text, pp. 40–41
	Presentation	*Gramática en contexto*	Text, pp. 42–44
			Overhead 10
	Closing/Assignments	Review day's objectives and tasks to be done	Text, p. 40, *La cultura desde tu perspectiva*
		Preview Day #9	Practice Wkbk. 1-5
Day #9	Introduction/Review	Review homework	Text, p. 40, *La cultura desde tu perspectiva*
			Practice Wkbk 1-5
	Presentation/Practice	*Gramática en contexto*	Text, pp. 44–45
			Overhead 10
	Presentation/Application	Choose from:	
		Todo junto	Text, pp. 50–51
		CD-ROM Activities	*Pasos vivos 2* CD-ROM
	Presentation/Practice	*Gramática en contexto*	Text, pp. 46–49
	Application	Video Activity	*La Catrina:* Episode 1
			WAVA: Video Activities, pp. 151–152, A–C
		CD-ROM Activities	*Pasos vivos 2* CD-ROM
	Closing/Assignments	Review day's objectives and tasks to be done	Practice Wkbk. 1-6 to 1-10
		Preview Day #10	

Day #10	Introduction/Review	Review homework	Practice Wkbk. 1-6 to 1-10
		Writing Activities	WAVA: Writing Activities 1-D to 1-F
	Practice	Communicative Activity	Communicative Activity BLMs 1-2
	Application	*¡Vamos a leer!*	Text, pp. 52–53
		Choose from:	
		Actividades en grupo	Communicative Activity BLMs 1-4
		Audio Activities	WAVA: Audio Activities 1.4, 1.5
		Video Activity	*La Catrina:* Episode 1
		CD-ROM Activities	*Pasos vivos 2* CD-ROM
	Assessment	Quizzes	*Pruebas* 1-5, 1-6, 1-7
	Closing/Assignments	Review day's objectives and tasks to be done	Text, pp. 54–55
		Preview Day #11	
Day #11	Introduction/Review	Partner work based on homework	Text, pp. 54–55
	Assessment	Quizzes	*Pruebas* 1-8, 1-9
	Application	Writing Activities	WAVA: Writing Activities 1-H, 1-I
		Self-assessment	Text, p. 56, *Repaso: ¿Lo sabes bien?*
		CD-ROM activities	*Pasos vivos 2* CD-ROM
	Presentation/Practice	*Pasodoble*	Text, pp. 20–21
			Practice Wkbk. PD-9
	Closing/Assignments	Review for Chapter Test	Practice Wkbk. Organizer, p. 11
Day #12	Introduction/Review	Review homework	Practice Wkbk. Organizer, p. 11
	Assessment	Chapter Test	Assessment Program: Choose from *Prueba cumulativa* or *Examen de habilidades*
			(or)
			Use other components such as: Situation Cards, Communicative Activities BLMs, p. 7; *Pasos vivos 2* CD-ROM; Test Generator
	Presentation	*Capítulo 2* Cultural Overview,	Text, pp. 57B–61
		Objectives	
		¡Piensa en la cultura!	
	Closing/Assignments	Review day's objectives and tasks to be done	
		Preview Day #1 of *Capítulo 2*	

Bridging *to PASO A PASO 3*

As students move into *PASO A PASO 3,* it is expected that they will have completed the content in Chapters 1–12 of Book 2. The grammar and vocabulary in Chapters 13–14 will be retaught as if new in *PASO A PASO 3.*

Review and reteaching

As students move into *PASO A PASO 3,* they will continually be exposed to material they will have learned in this book.

PASO A PASO 3 begins with a lively, communicative magazine-like section entitled *Pasodoble* that reactivates the major vocabulary sets and structures of the early chapters of *PASO A PASO 2.*

The charts on the following pages show the reteaching and expansion of specific grammar points from book to book.

rammar

Grammar	PASO A PASO 1	PASO A PASO 2
ser	1, **5***	*Pasodoble*, **4, 5, 7**
adjectives	**1**, 3, **4, 5, 6, 7, 8, 9**	*Pasodoble*, **1**, 3
negatives	**1**, 2, **14**	**8**
regular *-ar* verbs	**2**	*Pasodoble*
tener	2, 4, **5**	*Pasodoble*, **1**
ir	**3**	*Pasodoble*, **5**
estar	**3**	*Pasodoble*, **8**
stem-changing verbs: *o→ue*	3, **7, 9**	**2**
stem-changing verbs: *e→ie*	3, 4, **7, 8**	**2**
regular *-er* verbs	**4**	*Pasodoble*
possessive adjectives	**5, 8**	*Pasodoble*, **7**
demonstrative adjectives	**6**	1, **3**
direct object pronouns	**6**, 10, **11**, 12, 13	**1**, 9
preterite	6, 7, 9, **10, 11, 12**, 13	**3, 4, 6, 9, 10**
salir	**7**	**1**
personal *a*	**7**	*Pasodoble*
regular *-ir* verbs	**8**	*Pasodoble*
hacer	**8**	*Pasodoble*
poner	**8**	**9**
indirect object pronouns	**9, 11, 12**	2, 3, 5, 9
dar	11, **14**	**6**
comparatives / superlatives	**11**	*Pasodoble*, **1**, 3
stem-changing verbs: *e→i*	**12**	**2, 6**
traer	**12**	**1**, 9
saber	**13**	**4**, 8
decir	**13**	*Pasodoble*, **7**
tú affirmative commands	**13**	**12, 13**
conocer	**14**	**1**, 5
present progressive	**14**	**8**, 9

*Lightface numbers represent lexical introduction or quick review;
 boldface numbers represent presentation of the grammar point.

rammar

Grammar	PASO A PASO 2	PASO A PASO 3
ir	*Pasodoble*	*Pasodoble*
hacer	*Pasodoble*	*Pasodoble*
tener	*Pasodoble,* **1***	*Pasodoble*
comparatives / superlatives	*Pasodoble,* **1, 3**	*Pasodoble*
demonstratives	1, **3**	*Pasodoble*
ser	*Pasodoble,* **4, 5, 7**	*Pasodoble*
possession	*Pasodoble,* **7**	*Pasodoble*
estar	*Pasodoble,* **8**	*Pasodoble*
direct object pronouns	**1,** 9	*Pasodoble,* **1, 6**
indirect object pronouns	2, 3, 5, 9	*Pasodoble,* **1, 6**
reflexive verbs	**2, 4,** 6	*Pasodoble*
stem-changing verbs: $e \rightarrow i$	**2, 6**	*Pasodoble,* 8
preterite	**3, 4, 6, 9, 10**	*Pasodoble,* **3, 4,** 11, 12
imperfect	**5, 6, 10**	*Pasodoble,* 2
negatives	**8**	*Pasodoble*
present progressive	**8,** 9	**5**
imperfect progressive	**9**	**3**
future	**11**	**6**
tú commands	**12, 13,** 14	*Pasodoble,* **1, 9**
subjunctive	**13, 14**	**7, 8, 9, 10, 11, 12**

*Lightface numbers represent lexical introduction or quick review;
boldface numbers represent presentation of the grammar point.

INTEGRATING TECHNOLOGY IN THE *PASO A PASO* CLASSROOM

PASO A PASO provides a complete, state-of-the-art technology package for each chapter at all levels, including Internet-based activities, award-winning video programs, lively audio activities, interactive CD-ROMs that combine practice and performance-based tasks, easy-to-use test generators, and vocabulary art on CD-ROM. *PASO A PASO* also provides extensive overheads that build upon the time-tested approach of presenting vocabulary visually.

Throughout this Teacher's Edition, there are clear cross-references to the various technology components. The following chart shows how to integrate these in a chapter.

Chapter section	Technology component
Vocabulario para conversar	*Pasos vivos 2* CD-ROM
	Audio program
	www.pasoapaso.com
	Vocabulary Art CD-ROM
	Overheads
Perspectiva cultural	www.pasoapaso.com
	Pasos vivos 2 CD-ROM
Gramática en contexto	Overheads
	Pasos vivos 2 CD-ROM
	Audio program
Todo junto: Actividades	*La Catrina* video
	Pasos vivos 2 CD-ROM
Todo junto: ¡Vamos a leer!	www.pasoapaso.com
Todo junto: ¡Vamos a escribir!	*Pasos vivos 2* CD-ROM
Resumen: Exámenes	Audio program
	Test generator
	Pasos vivos 2 CD-ROM

Internet-based Activities: www.pasoapaso.com

Standards: 1.2; 1.3; 2.1; 2.2; 3.1; 3.2; 4.1; 4.2; 5.1; 5.2

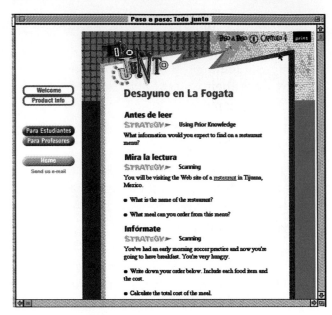

A quick trip via cyberspace to www.pasoapaso.com provides access to a wide range of activities, from authentic sources and cultural resources found on web sites to vocabulary and grammar games and extra drill-and-skill opportunities. All chapters in *PASO A PASO* have specific activities that integrate vocabulary, grammar, and culture. You will also find additional resources, articles, updates, teaching ideas, and ways to network with other *PASO A PASO* users.

La Catrina Video Program

Standards: 1.2; 2.1; 2.2; 3.1; 3.2; 4.1; 4.2; 5.1; 5.2

La Catrina is the storyline video program that accompanies *PASO A PASO 2*. Why a storyline video? For many students, the second year of language learning is especially difficult and they lose motivation. We have thus developed an energizing, motivating, teen-centered *telenovela* that will help students feel a sense of accomplishment as they work their way through the 14 episodes (and the 14 chapters). It is performed by professional actors, most of them well known to Mexican television viewers.

Students can benefit in many ways from viewing *La Catrina*. They expand their ability to understand native speakers of Spanish as they move beyond the textbook. They experience the integration and recycling of previously learned vocabulary and grammar. They grow in confidence as they encounter and understand new content embedded in a meaningful context. They gain in cultural understanding as they observe contemporary Mexican culture, with special emphasis on the day-to-day lives of young adults. Students improve in proficiency as they work with the video's content and the activities that accompany *La Catrina*. In addition, students' motivation to learn Spanish grows as they become involved in the engaging plot and characters that bring *La Catrina* to life.

The plot of *La Catrina*

Jamie González, a bilingual high-school student from Los Angeles, spends the summer in Querétaro, Mexico. A scholarship from the Comité de Intercambio Cultural has made this trip possible. Accompanying her on the trip is a classmate, Philip Armstrong. While there, Jamie hopes to learn about her great-grandmother, La Catrina, who lived in Querétaro during the time of the Mexican Revolution. To help in this search, Jamie brings the family's only connection to this mysterious relative: an old, faded photograph. Awaiting Jamie is a summer of mystery, adventure, and romance . . . and the discoveries involving La Catrina, which will change her life forever.

The organization of *La Catrina*

Each of the 14 episodes is organized around three segments. In the first chapter, segment 1 is an introduction to the story. In subsequent chapters, it is entitled *¿Recuerdas?*, and is a brief summary of the plot up to that point to help students prepare for the upcoming episode. The second segment, approximately eight minutes long, contains the episode itself. The third segment, *Para entender mejor,* is a one-minute review focusing on a key plot concept. It includes additional narration and on-screen text to support students' understanding. The Teacher's Guide accompanying the video contains plot synopses as well as a complete video transcript.

Using *La Catrina* with *PASO A PASO 2*

La Catrina incorporates the themes and vocabulary of *PASO A PASO 2*. But the video moves the students well beyond the book as they experience Spanish in real-world contexts. Each of the 14 episodes corresponds to the similarly numbered chapter in the text. The chapter theme and some of its vocabulary are integrated into the plot. For example, the theme in Chapter 2 of *PASO A PASO 2* is school. In episode 2 of *La Catrina,* Jamie is getting to know María Linares, with whose family she will live while in Mexico. The two girls talk about their school experiences and how schools differ in the United States and Mexico.

You might find it most successful to show *La Catrina* as students begin working with the chapter section entitled *Todo junto,* where chapter vocabulary and grammar are integrated with previously learned content. This philosophy is reflected in *La Catrina,* where students continually build upon language they already know.

As you work with *La Catrina,* we suggest you use the material in the video section of the student Writing, Audio & Video Activities workbook, which contains both pre- and post-viewing activities. Before viewing, have students recall the previous episode by brainstorming what happened.

Then show segment 1 to verify their recall. Let students see segment 2 several times. You might want to break the episode up by scenes and show them over several days, first showing portions with the sound off. Encourage students to brainstorm what the episode might be about. What are the locales? Who are the characters? What are they doing? Use segment 3 after students have viewed the episode in its entirety. After they view this video explanation of a key concept, they might want to see the entire episode again, as they will have still more insight into the plot. After completing the entire episode, you might focus on the scenes that integrate the chapter theme. See the Video Teacher's Guide for additional teaching ideas.

There is an additional workbook of activities based on *La Catrina*. It contains different and more extensive activities than those in the Writing, Audio & Video Activities workbook. A novelization of *La Catrina* is also available.

While it is certainly possible to teach *PASO A PASO 2* without using the video, you will find it a powerful tool in promoting the development of the listening skills students need to function outside the sheltered environment of the classroom, and in bringing the culture of Mexico into the classroom in a vivid and motivating way.

Vocabulary Art CD-ROM

Standards: 1.1; 1.2

This clip art (part of the Resource Pro® CD-ROM) includes all visualized vocabulary from Books 1–3 of *PASO A PASO*. Teachers can modify the clip art to create a variety of hands-on learning tools, such as flashcards, posters, and games.

Audio Program

Standards: 1.2; 3.1

Each chapter contains a variety of audio activities, including vocabulary/pronunciation practice, contextualized listening activities, songs, and listening comprehension tests. The audio activities help students learn the vocabulary and grammar of each chapter. Student activity sheets appear in the Writing, Audio & Video Activities workbook.

Pasos vivos 2 CD-ROM

Standards: 1.2; 1.3; 2.1; 2.2; 3.1; 3.2; 4.2; 5.1; 5.2

Students enter the world of broadcast station KPSO, where they encounter a wide range of interactive games and activities that allow them to practice and apply the chapter vocabulary and grammar, to view short video clips from *La Catrina,* to record their own voices, and to produce a slide presentation, a video presentation, or a writing project using the built-in word processor. Students can develop oral and written portfolios and explore the many open-ended resources. Cultural notes, music, and beautiful, theme-based photographs expand the cultural support for each chapter.

Test Generator

Standards: 1.2; 1.3; 2.1; 2.2; 4.2

Teachers can access ready-made tests for each chapter that contain multiple choice, true/false, matching, fill-in-the-blank, short answer, and essay questions. You can integrate these as intra-chapter quizzes, prepare end-of-chapter tests, or combine questions from various chapters to create semester or year-end tests. The templates can also be used to create your own questions.

Overheads

Standards: 1.1; 1.2

Each chapter provides complete overheads for vocabulary and grammar presentation and practice.

STRATEGIES FOR REACHING ALL STUDENTS

PASO A PASO 2 provides teachers the support and strategies needed to reach all students in the Spanish classroom. We offer an unprecedented commitment to providing materials that help meet the realities of today's classroom. This article focuses on strategies from *PASO A PASO 2* that will help you and all of your students enjoy a successful year learning Spanish . . . step by step!

 Material that builds upon students' experiences

Language students learn best by using what they know, by building new knowledge on old, and by experiencing and doing. As you use the text, you will see that *PASO A PASO 2* provides for an authentic, meaningful experience for the learner. The fourteen chapter themes were developed by asking, "What do students want to talk about?" The vocabulary taught is high-frequency language that students want to learn. The grammar supports communication and is practiced communicatively. The cultural content provides a means toward understanding and a global perspective that will be meaningful to all students. The activities ask students to interact, to become active participants in the learning process, and to express real ideas and real meanings for real purposes.

A multisensory approach to learning

Each student enters the Spanish classroom with different learning styles and abilities. Some work best with an aural / oral approach; others need a strong visual approach. Many need to touch and be physically involved in learning. An approach that addresses the needs and strengths of each student lays the groundwork for reaching all.

PASO A PASO 2 provides a strong multisensory approach to language learning. Students have varied opportunities for success by working with activities that recognize different learning styles and employ more than one modality. Each chapter provides suggestions for incorporating TPR,

which we call Learning Spanish Through Action. The *Todo junto* offers activities that involve different learning skills and interests (creating a collage, preparing a skit, drawing a house).

The cornerstone of success in Scott Foresman's foreign language programs has always been our strong visual approach. We have expanded this in *PASO A PASO 2*. Each chapter opens with culturally authentic photographs (*¡Piensa en la cultura!*) that call upon students' background knowledge in discussing the chapter theme. Vocabulary presentation is facilitated by contextual visualization that is then recycled in the practice activities to reinforce learning. This approach is supported by the Overheads and the Vocabulary Art Blackline Masters/CD-ROM. We have enhanced the visual approach through a photo essay in the *Perspectiva cultural*. A new, realia-based approach offers students an opportunity to study grammar in a real-life context. And reading and writing practice are made more accessible through the strong use of visual cues.

The multisensory approach is further expanded through use of the chapter-by-chapter audio tapes, video, and the interactive multimedia CD-ROM. The video program brings the culture to students through a story that represents language in a truly authentic context. The *La Catrina:* Interactive CD-ROM provides opportunities for students to work at their own pace while engaging all learning styles.

 Learning strategies

PASO A PASO 2 reinforces the strategies and skill-building techniques that students are using in their other classes. Some of these may be new to you but are easily implemented in the Spanish classroom. Strategies include building on background knowledge and experience, making lists or webs to organize their learning, inductive questioning, and consistent application of reading strategies and process writing.

4 **Higher-order and inductive thinking**

It sometimes seems that every day researchers are discovering new facts about the workings of the brain. We now know that information is stored in many areas of the brain and connected by a rich network of neurons. The goal of instruction should be to maximize the use of this network by helping students make connections and to learn information from a variety of perspectives and in a variety of ways. Activities aimed toward this goal are inherently interesting and motivating.

Students learn more successfully when they create their own understanding. Throughout *PASO A PASO 2* you will find activities that ask students to do just this. Inductive questions, for example, are the starting point of the following chapter features: *¡Piensa en la cultura!*, *Perspectiva cultural*, *Gramática en contexto*, and *¡Vamos a leer!* Activities that engage students in higher-level thinking skills are the initial focus in each of these sections, as well as in the *Actividades/Conexiones* and *¡Vamos a escribir!* We sequence these activities so that all students can be successful.

Another important learning strategy, informed guessing, is embedded in the vocabulary section entitled *¿Y qué quiere decir . . . ?* and is focused on in the inductive questions about photographs, as well as in the process reading and writing sections of each chapter.

5 **Multiple learning opportunities**

We know that students will improve at different rates and will be stronger in some areas than in others. In addition, developing proficiency takes time for everyone, no matter how gifted. Therefore, instruction must provide multiple opportunities for learning and improvement.

PASO A PASO 2 offers these opportunities. New vocabulary is presented, practiced, and recycled throughout a chapter and in subsequent chapters. Students are first exposed to grammar lexi-

cally, use it as they practice, and have some degree of understanding and control of it before it is presented and practiced as grammar. It is presented in easy-to-deal-with increments. The imperfect, for example, is first explained in Chapter 5, with additional information being presented in Chapters 6 and 10. Similarly, reflexive constructions are explained in Chapter 2, with reminders or additional information in Chapters 4, 6, and 8. In addition, recursive themes from one level to the next allow for regular review, expansion, and elaboration.

Throughout the text you will find reminder notes to students entitled *¡No olvides!* These focus on previously learned concepts that students will need in order to do a particular exercise or to understand better an extension of a given structure. These reminders are not crutches, but rather important tools for mastery.

6 **Additional opportunities for students who need them**

A regular on-page feature of this Teacher's Edition entitled "Strategies for Reaching All Students" provides you support for working with:

- Spanish-speaking students
- those having difficulty learning
- the gifted
- cooperative learning groups
- students needing extra practice
- multiple intelligences

For working with Spanish speakers, there are suggestions throughout the text, as well as a specially written supplemental worktext, *Un paso más: Actividades para ampliar tu español.* Notes under the heading "Students Needing Extra Help" suggest adaptations of the textbook activities or grammar explanations for those with real learning difficulties. Enrichment suggestions allow students who are capable of doing so to move beyond the textbook.

Varied assessment options

Students will do better in assessment situations if they have a clear understanding of the objectives and of how they will be assessed, and if they are assessed in such a way as to focus on their strengths.

PASO A PASO 2 offers a variety of options. Besides the *Pruebas* and *Exámenes de habilidades* in the Assessment Program, the *Actividades/Conexiones* in the integrative *Todo junto* offer you different types of opportunities for assessment, asking students to draw upon auditory, visual, and kinesthetic strengths. The Communicative Activities Blackline Masters include Situation Cards that are ideal for use in assessing speaking proficiency. (For additional ideas, see the article on assessment, pp. T59–T63, and the Introduction to the Assessment Program itself.)

Through the clearly stated objectives at the beginning of each chapter and the mini-assessments within the chapter *(¿Qué sabes ahora?* and *Ahora lo sabes),* students are able to monitor their own progress. In addition, the end-of-chapter pre-test *(Repaso: ¿Lo sabes bien?)* gives them a clear picture of how they will be assessed on the *Examen de habilidades.*

PASO A PASO 2 is committed to helping every teacher reach every student in the Spanish class. By providing materials that are strategy-based and that have built-in teacher support, we believe that we are enabling both you and your students to experience real enjoyment and unparalleled success.

MULTIPLE INTELLIGENCES

Education, like most institutions, has weathered storms of quick fix-it methodologies or theories that look promising on paper but have little or no practical application or realistic hope of success in an actual classroom. The Multiple Intelligences Theory is in no way intended to be a quick fix-it approach for teaching second languages, yet it is easily applicable in any classroom with careful planning and reflection on the teacher's part. Additionally, the Multiple Intelligences Theory does not demand that you teach in a certain way or falsely promise an easy ten-step process which, if followed precisely, will transform the entire class into straight A students! However, what the theory does do is remind us of what we already know: Everyone learns in different ways, and if you present new material in a variety of formats, then more students will likely learn and be able to demonstrate proficiency with the new material.

The notion that a person's intellectual worth can be based on a narrowly focused standardized test was challenged in 1983 by Howard Gardner in his book, *Frames of Mind,* which proposed the theory of Multiple Intelligences. Gardner believes that a person has many different ways of both acquiring and demonstrating intelligence (Armstrong, 1994). For instance, some students can remember just about anything as long as it is learned to the tune of a jingle, while someone else may be able to grasp an idea, concept, or grammatical form provided it is presented visually in the form of a graph, chart, or picture. Gardner has identified and labeled eight main styles of acquiring and demonstrating knowledge; those eight intelligences are Verbal/Linguistic, Visual/Spatial, Bodily/Kinesthetic, Logical/Mathematical, Interpersonal/Social, Intrapersonal/Introspective, Musical/Rhythmic, and Naturalist. Allowing students the opportunity to learn and acquire knowledge in the manner in which they are most receptive maximizes their potential to become successful students (Armstrong, 1994; Beckman, 1998).

When Gardner introduced his theory of Multiple Intelligences in 1983, he marked a new trend in cognitive psychology, broadening perspectives on human brain functions and views on human potential in terms of learning, and facilitating attempts to explain human differences. Gardner presents the notion that there is no "general intelligence," but rather that the mind is organized around distinct functional capacities, which he defines as "intelligences." Though each of the intelligences is developed independently of the others over the course of a lifetime, they usually work together and do not often appear in isolation.

In this Teacher's Edition you will find frequent specific suggestions for accommodating and teaching to the Multiple Intelligences. This is not meant to be construed as a paradigm for labeling every student in your class. On the contrary, we must continue to recognize each student as unique, complex, and highly individualistic. Therefore, we must regard students holistically and as individuals, recognizing that they are intelligent in many ways and that their overall "intelligence" is based on the sum of all of their intelligences.

Given the nature of the subject, foreign language teachers traditionally work most often with the **Verbal/Linguistic Intelligence.** Individuals who demonstrate strength in this area think and express themselves through words and have a strong ability to understand and use language to communicate effectively (Chapman, 1993). They enjoy reading, writing, telling stories, playing word games, and often excel in memorizing.

Musical/Rhythmic Intelligence is reflected in an individual's ability to analyze or create musical compositions. This intelligence can be used in a foreign language classroom in a variety of ways, such as teaching about culture through music or having students create their own raps or jingles to enhance vocabulary/grammar learning. It is important to note that Gardner does not believe that music played in the background during an activity or test is necessarily engaging the Musical Intelligence. If it is merely background music, its function is "unlikely to be different from that of a dripping faucet or a humming fan" (Gardner, 1995). The following are opportunities for accommodating this intelligence: Students research Spanish dances and are prepared to discuss them and teach them to the class; students compose a song about traveling and favorite places to visit; students make up rhymes to practice vocabulary; students create and demonstrate an aerobic exercise routine.

Interpersonal/Social Intelligence operates primarily through person-to-person relationships and communication. A common misconception is that it applies only to extroverted individuals (Gardner, 1995). One of the most effective ways to utilize this intelligence is through pair, group, and cooperative learning activities.

Intrapersonal/Introspective Intelligence is the ability to understand oneself and to think introspectively. Such students often enjoy working alone, being allowed to pursue their own interests, being provided with individualized projects and self-paced instruction. The following activities will provide opportunities to accommodate this intelligence: Students write poems describing themselves; students write a report on their views about recycling; students write a personal agenda for improving the environment.

Bodily/Kinesthetic Intelligence is related to physical movement and the ability to manipulate objects. These students enjoy most physical activities, e.g., moving, touching, body language, jumping, and running. Learning Spanish Through Action provides a wide variety of activities that accommodate this intelligence. Other production activities include role-playing, drama, creative movements, and gross motor and whole body activities.

Visual/Spatial Intelligence relies on the sense of sight and being able to visualize an object through mental images or pictures. These students enjoy opportunities to work with art and construction materials and to create projects. The use of video, movies, slides, imagination games, mazes, and puzzles will accommodate this intelligence.

Logical/Mathematical Intelligence deals with inductive and deductive reasoning, numbers, and the recognition of abstract patterns. Individuals who enjoy analyzing similarities and differences and manipulating numbers and graphs are strong in this intelligence. These students will perform well by working with numbers, exploring patterns and relationships, and using manipulatives. The following activities will provide opportunities to accommodate this intelligence: Students use a Venn diagram to compare Spanish and U.S. homes; students create a survey to determine what one should do to prevent catching a cold and display the results in a graph or chart; students use a logic puzzle to figure out which primary colors combine to produce the secondary colors on their TV screen.

Naturalist Intelligence is the latest intelligence added by Gardner. It includes the capacity to recognize flora and fauna, to make distinctions in the natural world, and to use this ability productively in activities such as gardening, farming, and biological science. This intelligence involves the ability to see the natural world from a larger perspective—an understanding of how nature interacts with civilization, the symbiotic relationships inherent in nature, and the life cycles of nature. Students exhibiting this intelligence will learn best through working in nature, exploring living things, learning about plants and natural events.

It should be stressed that the eight intelligences were not designed to be used as a new set of labels for teachers to assign to students (Edwards, 1998). Instead, by identifying a student's preferred intelligence, you can encourage the learning process while also fostering the other intelligences through appropriate activities.

As a rule, the eight intelligences should not be thought of as independent and isolated approaches, but rather should be intertwined and used in conjunction with each other to create the best possible learning experience for all students (Armstrong, 1994).

Integrating the use of Multiple Intelligences into the classroom does not require a major overhaul of lesson plans or a reworking of the curriculum. Generally, all that is required is supplementing and enhancing already existing lesson plans with a few creative and imaginative activities (Campbell, 1997). Some first-hand accounts are reassuring because many teachers find that in a very short time thinking and planning within the framework of the eight intelligences becomes second nature and quite painless (Campbell, 1989). Another suggestion from veteran Multiple Intelligences teachers is to team teach or team plan with teachers who have strengths in the intelligences that complement your own (Campbell, 1997).

The idea of Multiple Intelligences is a wonderful concept because it recognizes and validates the fact that every person is an individual who acquires and demonstrates knowledge through different means. However inclined, students should all be given the same opportunity to function in the manner in which they are most receptive and proficient. Some of those students may even discover that they actually enjoy learning—and that is the goal of every teacher: to instill the love of learning for learning itself.

References

Armstrong, Thomas. *Multiple Intelligences in the Classroom.* State of Virginia: Association for Supervision and Curriculum Development (1994).

Beckman, Marian S. *Multiple Ways of Knowing: Howard Gardner's Theory of Multiple Intelligences Extend and Enhance Student Learning.* http://www.earlychildhood.com/articles/artmi.html (1998).

Campbell, Bruce. "Multiplying Intelligences in the Classroom." New Horizons for Learning: *On the Beam,* IX, No. 2, (Winter 1989).

Campbell, Linda. "Variations on a Theme: How Teachers Interpret MI Theory." *Educational Leadership,* Vol. 55, No. 1 (September 1997).

Campbell, L., B. Campbell, and D. Dickinson. *Teaching and Learning Through Multiple Intelligences.* Tucson, AZ: Zephyr Press (1996).

Chapman, C. *If the Shoe Fits . . . How to Develop Multiple Intelligences in the Classroom.* Palatine, IL: IRI/Skylight (1993).

Edwards, Jack. *Multiple Intelligences and Technology.* http://www.firn.edu/~face/about/dec95/multi_int.html (1995).

Gardner, Howard. *Frames of Mind: The Theory of Multiple Intelligences.* New York: Basic Books (1983).

————. *Multiple Intelligences: The Theory in Practice: A Reader.* New York: Basic Books (1993).

SSESSMENT

Various methods of assessment are appropriate in a standards-driven classroom. Chapter tests, student conferences, teacher notes, checklists, portfolios, and performance demonstrations are all part of a well-rounded assessment program. All have advantages and disadvantages, and to use any one method exclusively would block your view of the total student picture. *PASO A PASO 2* offers a multi-faceted assessment program based on the premise that the main purpose of learning a language is to communicate in a meaningful and culturally appropriate way. As you begin to use the assessment program, you might want to start by asking yourself a few key questions: What do I expect my students to learn? What do I want them to be able to do? and How can I assess what I am looking for in student performance? Your answers to these questions can help define your philosophy in regard to assessment.

Self-Assessment of Chapter Objectives

Essential to any assessment program is the inclusion of self-assessment opportunities, which allow students to become independent evaluators of their own progress and to take more responsibility for their own learning. They engage students in the process of learning and promote greater involvement and reflection. The chapter objectives offer the basis for a self-assessment checklist of what each student should be able to do at the end of the chapter. The stated objectives can be rewritten by you and distributed as "I can . . ." statements to be used as a checklist as students move through the chapter. For example, a checklist for *Capítulo 1* might look like this:

Student Checklist		*Capítulo 1*
Using the Spanish I have learned . . .	**Yes**	**No**
1. I can name the school subjects that I am taking this year.	☐	☐
2. I can describe my teachers.	☐	☐
3. I can describe the type of homework I have to do in each of my classes and can ask others about their homework.	☐	☐

4. I can talk about the classes that I like best and those that I like least.	☐	☐
5. I can ask others about their classes and which ones they like best and least.	☐	☐
6. I can describe the school day (e.g., times school day starts and ends, number of minutes per class).	☐	☐
7. I can explain at least one thing that is prohibited and one thing that is allowed in my school.	☐	☐
8. I can talk about extracurricular activities associated with school.	☐	☐
9. I can name places in a school and the equipment used in them.	☐	☐
10. I can describe, in English, at least two differences between Mexican and American schools.	☐	☐

Two Types of Assessment

Both traditional and authentic assessment are part of the *PASO A PASO 2* program. *Traditional assessments* test knowledge of limited materials presented in a given chapter, and therefore are achievement based. *Authentic assessments* evaluate what learners can *do* with the language being learned, and are therefore competency-based. Both have a valid place in today's classroom. While the former assess for "coverage," the latter assess for "uncoverage." In other words, it is important to know that students can prove mastery of the material covered, but it is also important to "uncover" how they can use this language to express their own meanings.

PASO A PASO 2 offers you opportunities to assess the students' knowledge of specific vocabulary and grammar points through the use of several *pruebas* provided for each chapter. These prompt the student to progress from simple vocabulary recognition to limited production of a specific grammatical structure. The *prueba cumulativa* can be used as a final quiz to assess students' ability to apply learned material in a new context. The *Test Generator,* a bank of multiple-choice questions, offers yet another option for end of chapter assessment. It serves especially well as a make-up assessment for those who were unable to attend class on final quiz day.

A unique assessment tool in *PASO A PASO 2,* the *Examen de habilidades,* provides a vehicle for evaluating students' ability to apply what they have learned in a realistic, yet controlled context. For example, students may be asked to role-play a situation in which they are buying clothes. These more revealing, performance-based assessments provide engaging tasks from which to evaluate students' ability to use acquired language more creatively. Both the *Test Generator* and the *Banco de ideas* section offer additional test questions and assessment tasks, providing students opportunities to demonstrate real-life applications of the language they are learning.

Many of the activities in the *Todo junto* and *¡Vamos a escribir!* sections of the textbook provide the basis for *performance demonstrations,* such as individual writing projects, small group presentations, and paired conversations. Tasks in the very engaging CD-ROM package, *Pasos vivos 2,* include making videos and replying to faxes in the imaginary setting of radio station KPSO. Such performance assessments allow you to see the students' actual use of language in several types of tasks. Another source of mini-performance asssessments can be found in the *Communicative Activity Blackline Masters,* which offer small group tasks, paired activities, and situation cards.

Grading Performance Assessments

PASO A PASO 2 provides you with several templates for *scoring rubrics.* These include numerical values associated with performance levels, such as Below Average (1 point), Average (3 points), and Good (5 points). The criteria are precisely defined in terms of what students actually do to demonstrate performance at that level and they reflect what are considered to be appropriate communication skills and strategies. These criteria can be changed at any time to reflect a different emphasis. A rubric should be explained in advance to the students so that they have a clear understanding of what is expected of them and the level of performance needed to receive the highest score.

Grading a Paired Conversation

Throughout *PASO A PASO 2,* there are many activities that can serve as a basis for a performance assessment. For example, in the *Todo junto* section of Chapter 6, students ask each other questions about a family celebration that is shown in a photograph. What would your expectations be for your students in this activity? How can you be consistent in the way you grade performances? The following rubric can serve as a template for this paired activity, as well as for many similar tasks in any chapter:

Paired Conversation Rubric

	1 point	3 points	5 points
Language Use	Heavy reliance on English words, word order, and pronunciation.	Frequently uses English words, word order, and pronunciation.	Can "talk around" an exact word in order to maintain conversation in Spanish.
Ability to Sustain Conversation	Can only answer partner's direct questions.	Can both ask and answer questions.	Can state opinions and give reasons for them.
Conversational Interaction	Interaction is nonexistent. No conversational reaction to what is said by partner.	Limited conversational reaction to what is said by partner. Responds, but quickly moves to next question.	Natural interaction between partners. Each responds by following up on what the other person says.

15 pts. = A; 11–13 pts. = B; 7–9 pts. = C; 3–5 pts. = D

This particular rubric makes clear to students that getting their message across to their partners and maintaining a conversational flow are your top priorities at this point.

Although performance levels will vary greatly, your expectations are firmly anchored in the rubric's descriptors and in the models you give as examples of the different levels. For example, *My familia celebrando Thanksgiving* is an example of *language use* at the 1-point level, whereas *Mi familia estaba celebrando Thanksgiving* is at the 3 point level. *Mi familia estaba celebrando ... hmmm. No sé, el día de comer mucho y de ver fútbol americano* is at the 5-point level because even while forgetting the Spanish word for Thanksgiving, the student was able to substitute a description of what is done on that day. A student able both to answer and ask questions would receive 3 points for *ability to sustain conversation.* To perform at the 5-point level in this category, the student would respond with a reason for his or her statement by saying something such as, *Me gustaba mucho porque era una comida muy deliciosa. Comíamos todo el día.*

Conversational interaction focuses on whether the partners are listening and responding appro-priately. For example, after hearing that one's partner really likes Thanksgiving with the family, the student responds at the 1-point level by ignoring the information and saying *Es una foto de mi cumpleaños.* At the 3-point level, the student might respond with *A mí también.* A performance in conversational interaction at the 5-point level would elicit a response such as *A mí me gusta comer todo el día también.*

Grading a Writing Sample

Throughout *PASO A PASO 2,* students are led through the writing process to enable them to organize both their thinking and writing. There are several writing tasks strategically placed in each chapter's *¡Vamos a escribir!* sections. These can serve as stand-alone writing assessments, or as writing assignments for homework. In either case, you want to be able to grade the sample objectively and fairly. For example, students are asked in Chapter 4 to write a review of a concert, movie, TV show, or play, based on process writing strategies, possibly to be published in a class newspaper. The following rubric could be used for this activity and many similar writing tasks in the program:

Writing Rubric

CRITERIA	1 point	3 points	5 points
Use of prewriting strategies	Only turns in final product.	Turns in lists or planning notes along with final product.	Turns in planning notes, first draft, and final product.
Accuracy	Many spelling errors and repeated patterns of subject/verb agreement errors.	Several spelling errors and repeated patterns of subject/verb agreement errors.	Few spelling or subject/verb agreement errors.
Content	Gives no examples or details about the topic.	Gives a few examples or details about the topic	Consistently adds examples and/or details about topic.

15 pts. = A; 11–13 pts. = B; 7–9 pts. = C; 3–5 pts. = D

Assessment of Cultural Awareness

Both the *Foreign Language Standards* and *PASO A PASO 2* emphasize the importance of students' using their language and cultural understanding outside of the classroom in order to connect to and reflect on their own and the target culture. At several points in each chapter, students are called upon to reflect about the products, practices, and perspectives of people in the Spanish-speaking world, and as they progress through the program, they gain increasing awareness of Hispanic influences around them.

In the *Examen de habilidades,* students are consistently asked to compare their own culture to that of the Spanish-speaking world and to reflect about the differences and similarities. For example, merely stating that in many Mexican schools girls are not allowed to wear makeup or high heels would earn the student points. However, reflecting about why that difference between Mexico and the United States exists would earn the student additional points. Rather than awarding points for a "correct" reflection, you are awarding points for the students who go through the process and show evidence of reflective thinking.

Personal Culture Logs

In order to encourage cultural awareness, you might want to ask students to keep a log of at least ten instances in which they have encountered the target language or target culture in their own communities. Their entries might include chance meetings with Spanish speakers, snippets of conversation in movies or TV programs, street or store signs, product information, references noted from other classes where Spanish culture or language was mentioned, or any other experience in which students realized that "something Spanish" was going on.

Each of the ten entries would be graded as 2-point, 4-point, or 6-point entries. The following rubric could be distributed to students and used for giving an objective grade to their log entries. The rubric guides students to go beyond the recognition level to a more reflective level of thinking about culture and language. The following is an example of a student entry in a culture log that would earn six points because of the evidence of reflection:

Personal Language and Culture Log

Date	Recognition—2 points "Hey, that's Spanish!"	Comprehension—4 points "Hey, that's Spanish and I know what it means!"	Reflection—6 points "Hey, that's Spanish and I think I know why they did that!"
1.			We went to the arts festival in the city's Paseo District. *Paseo* means "walk" in Spanish. I bet they named it that because it is one of the few places where there are sidewalks for people who like to walk!

Portfolios

A portfolio is a purposeful collection that exhibits a student's performance efforts, progress, and achievement over a period of time. Some teachers, especially those working on a block schedule, have found that portfolios have given their students an avenue to pursue some things outside of class that they don't have time to develop in the class period. For example, students could compare the reporting of a major international news story in newspapers from around the Spanish-speaking world to that in the United States by accessing foreign newspapers on the Internet outside of class. Portfolios can allow students to document aspects of their learning that do not show up well in traditional assessments, yet are part of the overall assessment program.

One of the most common uses of portfolios is to showcase the students' favorite examples of their work. This type of portfolio can include both assigned and student-selected projects. Since the student chooses some of the work to be showcased, the portfolio can link the student personally to his or her own assessment in a way that traditional assessment can never create. The final portfolio can then be shared with parents, friends, and other teachers.

Another type of portfolio might have the focus of documenting student progress over time. You could collect baseline samples of work, such as the first piece of writing for the year and the first oral interview, and then regularly update and add to the portfolio. It can be a unique opportunity for your students to monitor and evaluate their own progress.

NDEX OF CULTURAL REFERENCES

PASO A PASO

2

Myriam Met
Coordinator of Foreign Languages
Montgomery County Public Schools
Rockville, MD

Richard S. Sayers
Longmont, CO

Carol Eubanks Wargin
Glen Crest Junior High School
Glen Ellyn, IL

Prentice Hall

Glenview, Illinois
Needham, Massachusetts
Upper Saddle River, New Jersey

Visit our Web site at http://www.pasoapaso.com

I

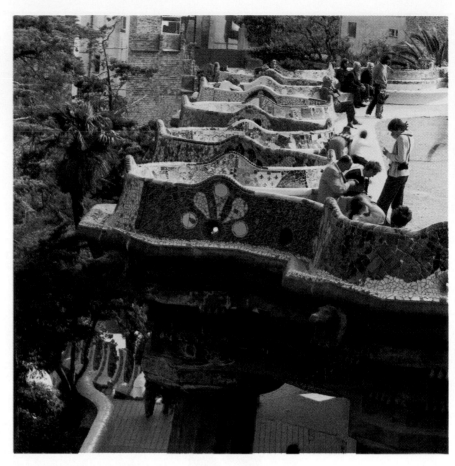

En el Parc Güell, Barcelona

Acknowledgments

Chapter 4, p. 144: Biographies of Gloria Estefan and Jon Secada. Reprinted by permission of Foreign Imported Productions & Publishing, Inc.

Chapter 8, pp. 286–287: *¿De qué país es esta bandera?*, map and flags. Adapted from MATERIALES QUINTO CENTENARIO, NOVIEMBRE-DICIEMBRE 1992, page 22. Text, p. 287, adapted from "Tarjetas de Información" from MATERIALES QUINTO CENTENARIO, NOVIEMBRE-DICIEMBRE 1992. Copyright © 1992 Consejería de Educación - Embajada de España. Reprinted by permission.

Chapter 9, p. 320: "Chana y su rana" from CHANA Y SU RANA by Cecilia Ávalos. Text copyright © 1992 Scholastic Inc. Reprinted by permission of Scholastic Inc.

Chapter 13, p. 450: From "El aceite de oliva" from DA QUE HABLAR, Número 14, Octubre-Noviembre 1993, page 13. Reprinted by permission of Consejería de Educación - Embajada de España.

The modernist style of Spanish architect Antonio Gaudí (1852–1926) is reflected in these benches found in Parc Güell, an unfinished hillside park that Gaudí designed for his most important patron, Eusebio Güell. Gaudí favored using the richest, most colorful textures possible, and he often created mosaics made of broken tile scraps. Gaudí's work inspired a twentieth-century revival in the use of tile in architecture.

Contributing Writers

Eduardo Aparicio
Miami, FL

Margaret Juanita Azevedo
Stanford University
Palo Alto, CA

Louis Carrillo
Miami, FL

Madela Ezcurra
New York, NY

Thomasina Pagán Hannum
Albuquerque, NM

Mary de López
Río Rancho Public Schools
Río Rancho, NM

Reader Consultants

The authors and editors would like to express our heartfelt thanks to the following team of reader consultants. Each of them read the manuscript, chapter by chapter, offering suggestions and providing encouragement. Their contribution has been invaluable.

Rosario Martínez-Cantú
Northside Health Careers High School
San Antonio, TX

Kelley Domínguez
Ledford Senior High School
Thomasville, NC

Greg Duncan
InterPrep
Marietta, GA

Walter Kleinmann
Sewanhaka Central High School District
New Hyde Park, NY

Joanna Lowe
Apopka High School
Apopka, FL

Bernadette M. Reynolds
Parker, CO

Rudolf L. Schonfeld, Ph.D.
Parsippany-Troy Hills School District
Parsippany, NJ

Connie Johnson Vargas
Apple Valley High School
Apple Valley, CA

Marcia Payne Wooten
Starmount High School
Boonville, NC

Tabla de materias

PASODOBLE
Una revista escolar para los jóvenes

CAPÍTULO 3 ¿Qué ropa está de moda?

Theme

► Clothing

Objectives

► Describe clothing in detail
► Indicate clothing preferences and make comparisons
► Say how you paid for purchases
► Talk about the currency in Spain and in various Latin American countries

CAPÍTULO 4 ¿Cómo te diviertes?

Theme

► Leisure-Time Activities

Objectives

► Talk about past and present activities
► Extend, accept, or reject an invitation
► Discuss and evaluate a leisure-time activity
► Talk about the paintings of two Mexican artists and what their work tells us about them and their culture

CAPÍTULO 5 ¿Qúe te gustaba hacer de pequeño?

Theme

► Childhood

Objectives

► Tell what you were like as a child

► Tell what you used to like to do

► Talk about what you learned to do

► Understand how experiences in José Martí's early life affected his later life

CAPÍTULO 6 ¡Celebremos!

Theme

► Special Occasions

Objectives

► Name and describe members of an extended family

► Describe special family occasions, holidays, and other celebrations

► Greet people in several different ways

► Discuss how one culture can influence another

CAPÍTULO 11　¿Cómo será el futuro?

Theme

▶ The Future

Objectives

▶ Discuss various professions

▶ Say what you think the world will be like in the future

▶ Discuss how to protect the environment

▶ Compare attitudes toward the future in Latin America and the United States

CAPÍTULO 12　¡El pasaporte, por favor!

Theme

▶ Travel

Objectives

▶ Give advice

▶ Discuss travel arrangements

▶ Make recommendations about what to do and see in your community

▶ Discuss the variety of travel accommodations in Spain

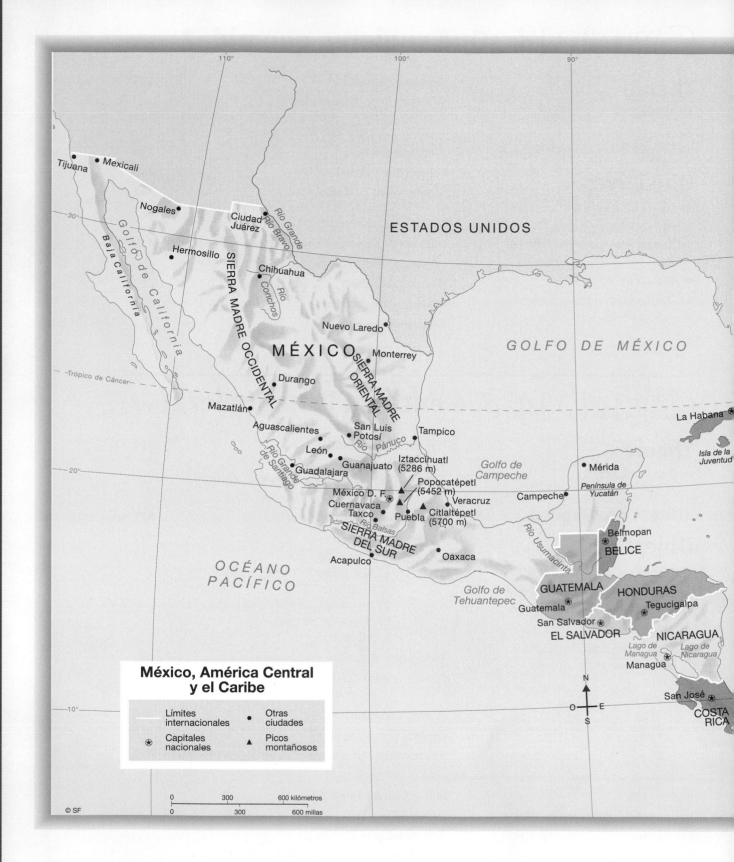

110° 100° 90°

ESTADOS UNIDOS

Tijuana • Mexicali

Nogales •
Ciudad Juárez
Río Grande / Río Bravo

Hermosillo •
Chihuahua •
Río Conchos

SIERRA MADRE OCCIDENTAL

Golfo de California
Baja California

30°

GOLFO DE MÉXICO

Nuevo Laredo •
Monterrey •
MÉXICO SIERRA MADRE ORIENTAL

Trópico de Cáncer

Durango •

Mazatlán •

Aguascalientes •
San Luis Potosí •
Río Pánuco
Tampico •

León •
Río Grande de Santiago
Guanajuato •
Guadalajara •

20°

Iztaccíhuatl (5286 m)
Popocatépetl (5452 m)
México D. F. ⊛
Cuernavaca •
Taxco •
Río Balsas
Puebla •
Citlaltépetl (5700 m)
Veracruz •

Golfo de Campeche

Mérida •
Península de Yucatán
Campeche •

La Habana ⊛
Isla de la Juventud

SIERRA MADRE DEL SUR

Acapulco •

OCÉANO PACÍFICO

Oaxaca •

Río Usumacinta

Belmopan ⊛
BELICE

Golfo de Tehuantepec

GUATEMALA

Guatemala ⊛
San Salvador ⊛
EL SALVADOR

HONDURAS
Tegucigalpa •

NICARAGUA

Lago de Managua
Lago de Nicaragua
Managua ⊛

N
O E
S

San José ⊛
COSTA RICA

México, América Central y el Caribe

— Límites internacionales
• Otras ciudades
⊛ Capitales nacionales
▲ Picos montañosos

0   300   600 kilómetros
0   300   600 millas

© SF

10°

XII

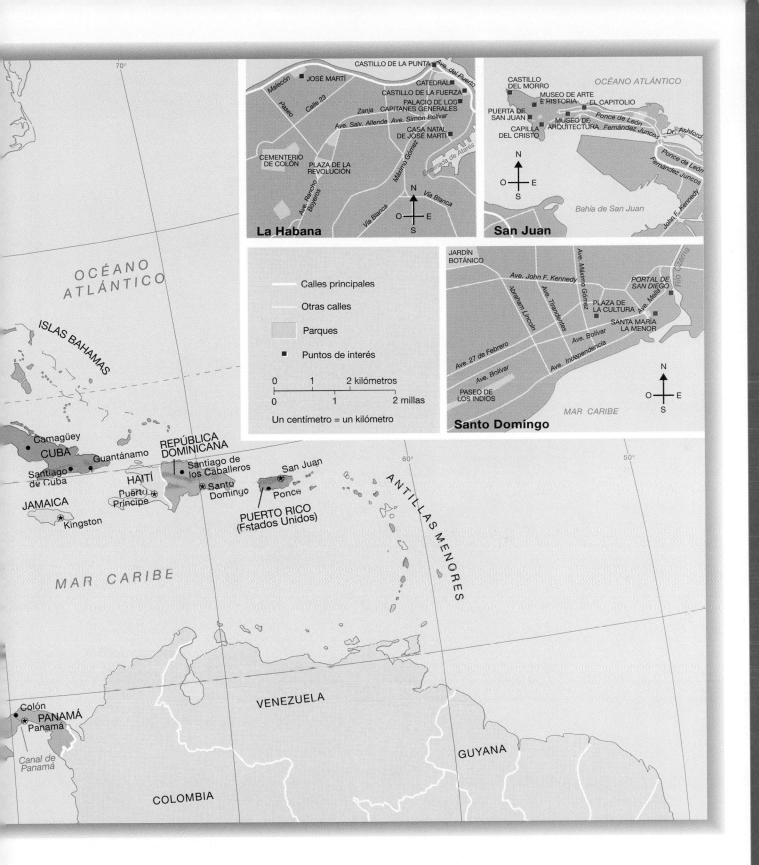

La Habana

CASTILLO DE LA PUNTA · Ave. del Puerto
Malecón · JOSÉ MARTÍ
CATEDRAL
CASTILLO DE LA FUERZA
PALACIO DE LOS
CAPITANES GENERALES
Calle 23
Paseo
Zanja
Ave. Salv. Allende · Ave. Simón Bolívar
CASA NATAL
DE JOSÉ MARTÍ
CEMENTERIO
DE COLÓN
PLAZA DE LA
REVOLUCIÓN
Ave. Rancho Boyeros
Máximo Gómez
Ensenada de Atarés
Vía Blanca
Vía Blanca
N
O · E
S

San Juan

OCÉANO ATLÁNTICO
CASTILLO
DEL MORRO
MUSEO DE ARTE
E HISTORIA · EL CAPITOLIO
PUERTA DE
SAN JUAN
Ponce de León
CAPILLA
DEL CRISTO
MUSEO DE
ARQUITECTURA · Fernández Juncos
Dr. Ashford
Ponce de León
Fernández Juncos
John F. Kennedy
Bahía de San Juan
N
O · E
S

OCÉANO
ATLÁNTICO

ISLAS BAHAMAS

Calles principales
Otras calles
Parques
■ Puntos de interés

| 0 | 1 | 2 kilómetros |
| 0 | 1 | 2 millas |

Un centímetro = un kilómetro

Santo Domingo

JARDÍN
BOTÁNICO
Ave. John F. Kennedy
Ave. Máximo Gómez
PORTAL DE
SAN DIEGO
Río Ozama
Ave. Trinientes
Abraham Lincoln
Ave. Máximo Gómez
PLAZA DE
LA CULTURA
Ave. Melia
SANTA MARÍA
LA MENOR
Ave. 27 de Febrero
Ave. Bolívar
Ave. Bolívar
Ave. Independencia
PASEO DE
LOS INDIOS
MAR CARIBE
N
O · E
S

Camagüey
CUBA
Guantánamo
Santiago
de Cuba
JAMAICA
Kingston

REPÚBLICA
DOMINICANA
Santiago de
los Caballeros
Puerto
Príncipe
HAITÍ
✹ Santo
Domingo
San Juan
Ponce
PUERTO RICO
(Estados Unidos)

ANTILLAS MENORES

MAR CARIBE

Colón
PANAMÁ
✹ Panamá
Canal de
Panamá

VENEZUELA

GUYANA

COLOMBIA

Mapas XIII

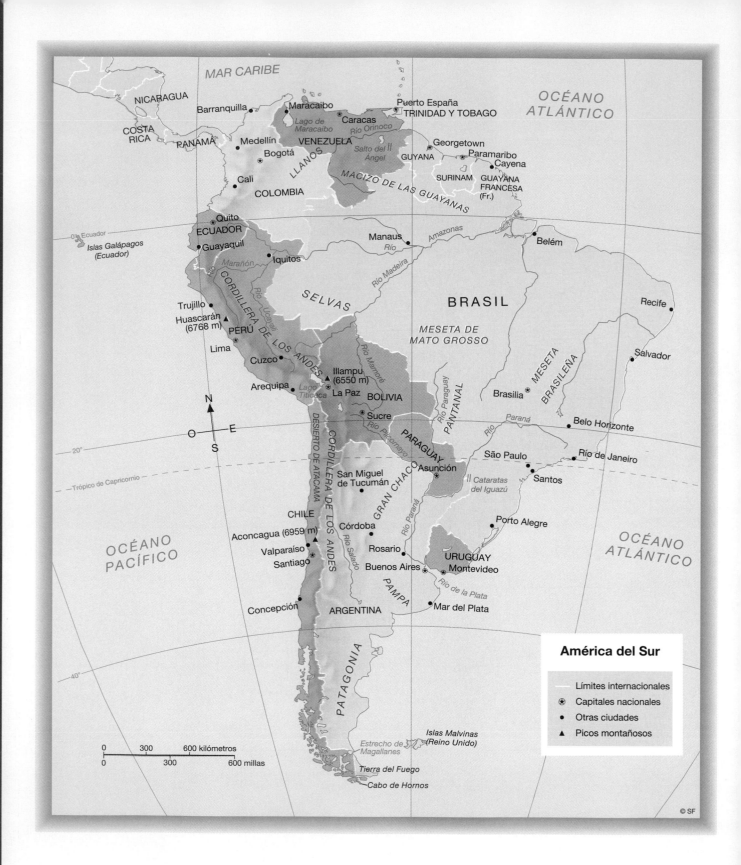

América del Sur

	Límites internacionales
⊛	Capitales nacionales
●	Otras ciudades
▲	Picos montañosos

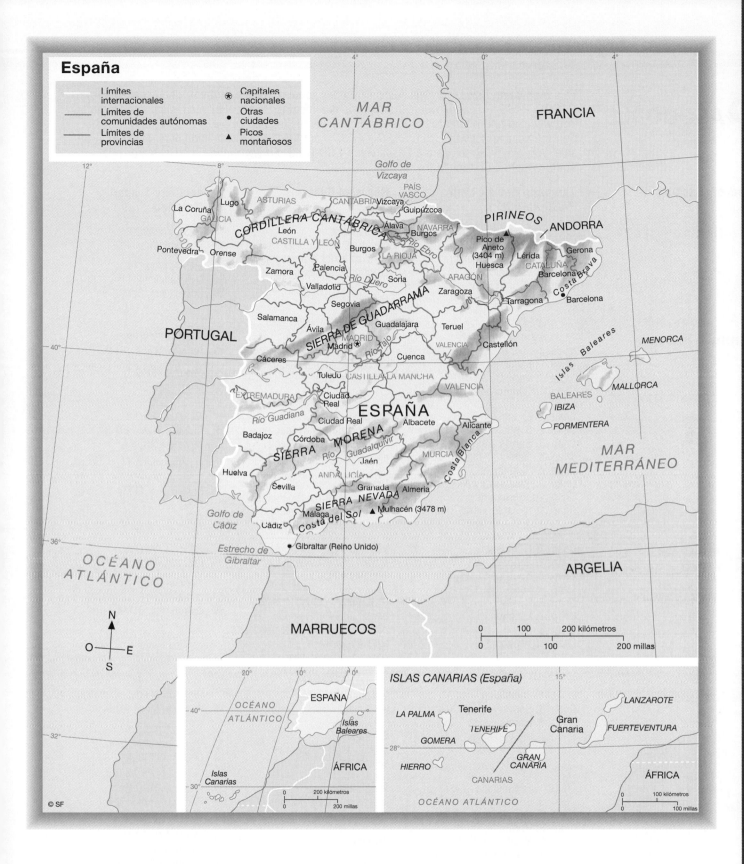

España

- ─── Límites internacionales
- ─── Límites de comunidades autónomas
- ─── Límites de provincias
- ✳ Capitales nacionales
- • Otras ciudades
- ▲ Picos montañosos

FRANCIA

MAR CANTÁBRICO

Golfo de Vizcaya

La Coruña
Lugo
ASTURIAS
GALICIA
CANTABRIA
Vizcaya
PAÍS VASCO
Guipúzcoa
CORDILLERA CANTÁBRICA
León
Álava
NAVARRA
Burgos
PIRINEOS
ANDORRA
Pontevedra
Orense
CASTILLA Y LEÓN
Río Ebro
Pico de Aneto (3404 m)
Huesca
Lérida
Gerona
Zamora
Palencia
LA RIOJA
Soria
ARAGÓN
CATALUÑA
Costa Brava
Valladolid
Burgos
Río Duero
Zaragoza
Barcelona
Segovia
SIERRA DE GUADARRAMA
Tarragona
Barcelona
Salamanca
Ávila
Guadalajara
Teruel

PORTUGAL

MADRID
Madrid ✳
Río Tajo
VALENCIA
Castellón

Cáceres
Toledo
Cuenca
CASTILLA-LA MANCHA
VALENCIA

Islas Baleares
MENORCA

EXTREMADURA
Ciudad Real
BALEARES
MALLORCA

Río Guadiana
ESPAÑA
IBIZA

Badajoz
Ciudad Real
Albacete
Alicante
FORMENTERA

Córdoba
SIERRA MORENA
Río Guadalquivir
MURCIA
Costa Blanca

MAR MEDITERRÁNEO

Huelva
Jaén
ANDALUCÍA

Sevilla
Granada
Almería

SIERRA NEVADA
Mulhacén (3478 m)

Golfo de Cádiz
Málaga
Costa del Sol
Cádiz

Estrecho de Gibraltar
Gibraltar (Reino Unido)

OCÉANO ATLÁNTICO

ARGELIA

MARRUECOS

N
O   E
S

| 0 | 100 | 200 kilómetros |
| 0 | 100 | 200 millas |

OCÉANO ATLÁNTICO
ESPAÑA
Islas Baleares
Islas Canarias
ÁFRICA

| 0 | 200 kilómetros |
| 0 | 200 millas |

ISLAS CANARIAS (España)

LA PALMA
Tenerife
TENERIFE
GOMERA
HIERRO
Gran Canaria
GRAN CANARIA
CANARIAS
LANZAROTE
FUERTEVENTURA
ÁFRICA

OCÉANO ATLÁNTICO

| 0 | 100 kilómetros |
| 0 | 100 millas |

© SF

Mapas   XV

PASODOBLE

This motivating magazine-style section recycles some of the major themes and concepts from *PASO A PASO 1*. The following chart shows the integrative review of vocabulary and grammar. You will also find references to the ancillary materials for *Pasodoble*. Some of the Communicative Activities from *PASO A PASO 1* are listed to provide additional review. If available, you may wish to use the *Pasos vivos 1* CD-ROM, *En vivo* video, Test Generator, and Audiocassettes/CDs for further review.

Pasodoble Sections	Thematic Review from *PASO A PASO 1*	Recycled Concepts	Ancillary Support Materials
¿Qué tiempo hace?	*El primer paso:* Spanish-speaking world Chap. 3: Sports and leisure Chap. 7: Vacation Chap. 10: Community	**Vocabulary:** countries and capitals, numbers, calendar expressions, seasons, weather, directions **Grammar:** *estar*	*PASO A PASO 2:* Practice Wkbk. PD-1 *PASO A PASO 1:* Overheads 14, 17, 27, 38–40 Comm. Act. BLM 7-1
El mundo hispano	*El primer paso:* Spanish-speaking world Chap. 5: Family Chap. 7: Vacation Chap. 10: Community	**Vocabulary:** countries and capitals, physical characteristics, nature, directions, *estar*	*PASO A PASO 2:* Practice Wkbk. PD-2 *PASO A PASO 1:* Overheads 78–81
Tenis y más	Chap. 1: Friendship Chap. 2: School Chap. 3: Sports and leisure Chap. 5: Family Chap. 6: Clothing Chap. 7: Vacation Chap. 10: Community Chap. 12: Restaurants	**Vocabulary:** personal questions, personality traits, school subjects, leisure activities, colors **Grammar:** *gustar, -ar* verbs, *jugar,* age, *ser,* adjective agreement, personal *a,* preterite tense	*PASO A PASO 2:* Practice Wkbk. PD-3 Writing Activity A *PASO A PASO 1:* Overheads 8–10 Comm. Act. BLMs 1-1, 1-2, 1-3
Dos amigas de Puerto Rico	Chap. 1: Friendship Chap. 2: School Chap. 3: Sports and leisure Chap. 4: Food Chap. 5: Family Chap. 7: Vacation Chap. 8: Home Chap. 9: Health	**Vocabulary:** school subjects, leisure activities, household chores **Grammar:** *gustar, ir a* + inf., *poder, querer, -er* verbs, *encantar,* age, *ser, quisiera, pensar, tener que, hacer, vivir,* indirect object pronouns	*PASO A PASO 2:* Practice Wkbk. PD-4 *PASO A PASO 1:* Overheads 16, 18, 42, 45 Comm. Act. BLMs 3-1, 3-3
¿Qué les gusta hacer?	Chap. 1: Friendship Chap. 3: Sports and leisure Chap. 8: Home	**Vocabulary:** leisure activities **Grammar:** *gustar, estar,* possessive adjectives	*PASO A PASO 2:* Practice Wkbk. PD-5 *PASO A PASO 1:* Overheads 18–19, 42 Comm. Act. BLM 2-3
A ti, ¿qué te gusta hacer?	Chap. 1: Friendship Chap. 3: Sports and leisure Chap. 7: Vacation Chap. 8: Home Chap. 9: Health Chap. 10: Community Chap. 12: Restaurants	**Vocabulary:** leisure activities, household chores **Grammar:** *ni . . . ni, poder, pensar,* negative constructions, preterite tense	*PASO A PASO 2:* Practice Wkbk. PD-6 Writing Activity B *PASO A PASO 1:* Overheads 18–19, 42 Comm. Act. BLMs 3-2, 8-1
¿Bueno o malo para la salud?	Chap. 2: School Chap. 3: Sports and leisure Chap. 4: Food Chap. 6: Clothing Chap. 8: Home Chap. 9: Health Chap. 11: Movies and TV	**Vocabulary:** leisure activities, food, health **Grammar:** *-ar* verbs, *comer, deber, -er* verbs, demonstrative adjectives, *hacer, tener que,* comparatives, superlatives	*PASO A PASO 2:* Practice Wkbk. PD-7 Writing Activity C *PASO A PASO 1:* Overheads 21–24 Comm. Act. BLM 4-1

Pasodoble Sections	Thematic Review from PASO A PASO 1	Recycled Concepts	Ancillary Support Materials
¿Qué hay en la tele esta noche?	El primer paso: Spanish-speaking world Chap. 1: Friendship Chap. 2: School Chap. 3: Sports and leisure Chap. 4: Food Chap. 5: Family Chap. 7: Vacation Chap. 13: Environment	**Vocabulary:** calendar expressions **Grammar:** hay, se dice, leer, time-telling, poder, creer, llamarse, pensar, hay que + inf.	PASO A PASO 2: Practice Wkbk. PD-8 Writing Activity D PASO A PASO 1: Overheads 13, 16, 56–60 Comm. Act. BLM 11-1
¡Hola, Andy!	Chap. 5: Family Chap. 10: Community Chap. 11: Movies and TV Chap. 12: Restaurants	**Vocabulary:** family members **Grammar:** preterite tense, comparatives	PASO A PASO 1: Overheads 29–30 Comm. Act. BLMs 10-2, 10-3
¡Sí, puedo! ¡Soy joven!	Chap. 1: Friendship Chap. 3: Sports and leisure Chap. 5: Family Chap. 9: Health	**Vocabulary:** personality traits, physical characteristics **Grammar:** ir a + inf., querer, poder, negative expressions	PASO A PASO 1: Overheads 8, 10, 28–29 Comm. Act. BLM 7-2
Caricaturas	Chap. 3: Sports and leisure Chap. 4: Food Chap. 9: Health Chap. 11: Movies and TV	**Grammar:** estar, deber, negative expressions, indefinite pronouns	PASO A PASO 2: Writing Activity E
¿Qué quiere decir "casa"?	Chap. 5: Family Chap. 6: Clothing Chap. 8: Home Chap. 13: Environment	**Vocabulary:** rooms in a house, furniture **Grammar:** tener, direct object pronouns, decir	PASO A PASO 2: Practice Wkbk. PD-9 PASO A PASO 1: Overheads 41–43 Comm. Act. BLM 8-3
Vacaciones mágicas	Chap. 3: Sports and leisure Chap. 4: Food Chap. 5: Family Chap. 7: Vacation Chap. 10: Community Chap. 11: Movies and TV Chap. 12: Restaurants Chap. 13: Environment	**Vocabulary:** leisure activities, travel, environmental terms **Grammar:** gustar expressions, poder, preferir, tener, pensar, preterite tense, superlatives	PASO A PASO 2: Practice Wkbk. PD-10 Writing Activity F PASO A PASO 1: Overheads 36–37, 40 Comm. Act. BLM 7-3
Ana Laura	Chap. 1: Friendship Chap. 4: Food Chap. 5: Family Chap. 6: Clothing Chap. 7: Vacation	**Vocabulary:** personality traits, physical characteristics **Grammar:** -er and -ir verbs, adjective agreement, quisiera	PASO A PASO 2: Writing Activity G Audio Activities P.1, P.2, P.3, P.4 PASO A PASO 1: Overheads 8–10, 28–29

Present

Pasodoble is a motivating, maga-zine-style recycling of major themes and concepts from *PASO A PASO 1*. Its purpose is to help students bridge the time gap between Levels 1 and 2 and to give teachers interesting and pur-poseful materials to use during the first days of a course when class rosters may continue to change. There are different ways in which *Pasodoble* can be used, depending on student needs. Here are some options to consider:

1 Complete all sections of *Pasodoble* before beginning Chapter 1. In order to ensure appropriate pacing, this use of *Pasodoble* should last no longer than two weeks on a schedule of daily 45- to 50-minute classes.

2 Choose five to six sections of *Pasodoble* to use during the first days of class. The chart on pp. 1A–1B, which lists the recy-cling of *PASO A PASO 1* themes, vocabulary, and grammar, is use-ful in helping you make those choices. After approximately one week, on a schedule of 45- to 50-minute classes, begin Chapter 1. Keep track of the *Pasodoble* sec-tions that were not used and intro-duce them at appropriate times during the year. For example, *¡Hola, Andy!* can be used with Chapter 3 to introduce or practice the preterite. Use *¿Qué quiere decir "casa"?* to review house-

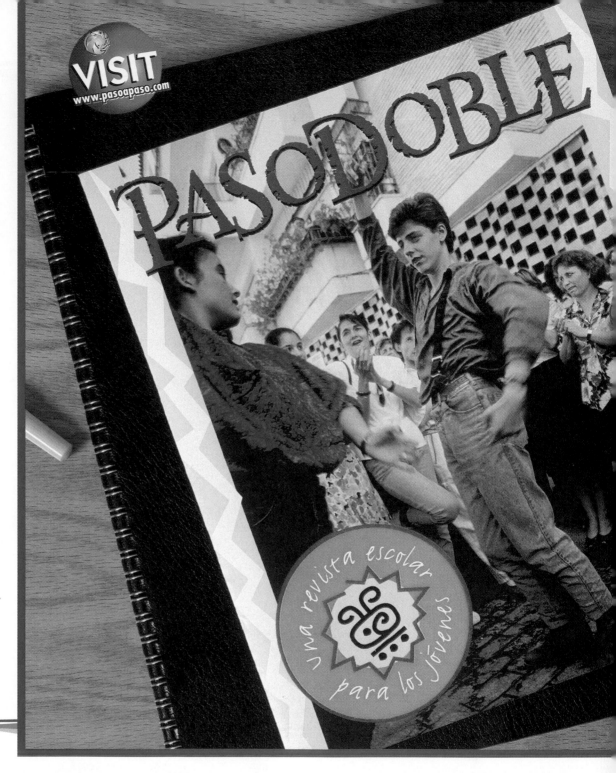

Options

Strategies for Reaching All Students

Students Needing Extra Help
Point out the magazine format to those who do not recognize it. Emphasize that just as magazines reprint popular articles, the authors have re-entered important concepts studied the previous year.

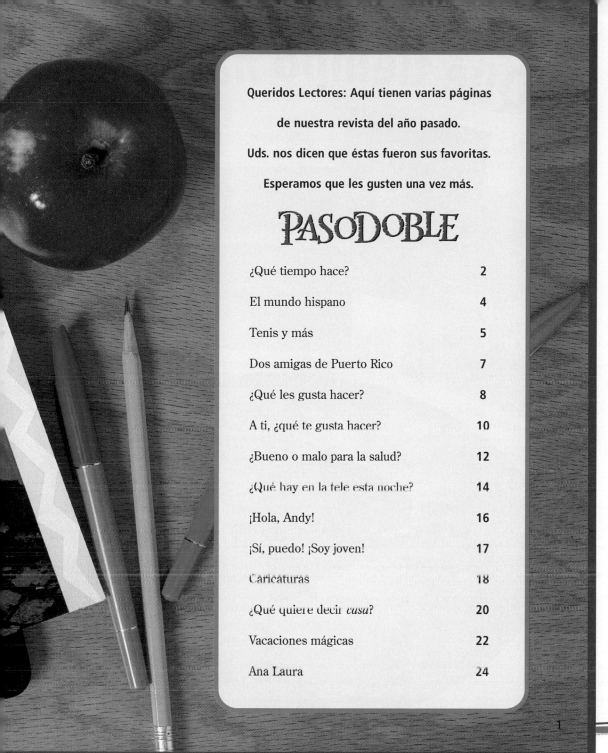

Queridos Lectores: Aquí tienen varias páginas
de nuestra revista del año pasado.
Uds. nos dicen que éstas fueron sus favoritas.
Esperamos que les gusten una vez más.

PASODOBLE

related vocabulary before starting Chapter 7. You might reserve some *Pasodoble* sections for days when a substitute teacher is in class.

3 Begin Chapter 1 within the first week of class. During the first two weeks, develop lessons in which you combine *Pasodoble* sections with elements of Chapter 1 on a daily basis. Sections that are not used now can be introduced later (see option #2).

The *Pasodoble* articles can be complemented by ancillary support materials from *PASO A PASO 1* and *2*. These provide additional practice of vocabulary and grammar, as well as development of language skills, for classroom use or as homework. Refer to pp. 1A–B for a listing of these support materials.

Cultural Notes

(p. xvi, photo)
El pasodoble, a familiar ballroom dance, actually refers to the dramatic march music played at bullfights and other public events in Spain. Each measure of its music consists of eight beats in 2/4 time, creating an even rhythm. Although the term literally means "two-step," the dance is a march step accentuated by movements reminiscent of the *torero.* The popular meaning came into use as professional dancers of the 1920s and '30s used the music to improvise encores after classical dance performances.

Review

Recycled Concepts

Countries and capitals, calendar expressions *(El primer paso)*; numbers *(El primer paso* and Chaps. 2, 5, 6, and 10); *estar* and seasons (Chap. 3); weather (Chap. 7); directions (Chaps. 8 and 10)

Ancillaries available for use with *Pasodoble*

 Practice Wkbk. PD-1

Ancillaries suggested from *PASO A PASO 1*

 Overheads 14, 17, 27, 38–40

 Comm. Act. BLM 7-1

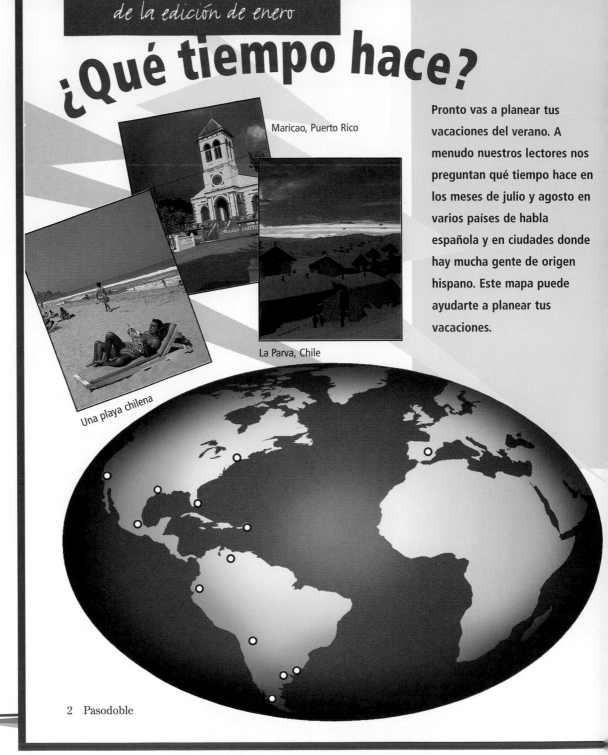

de la edición de enero

¿Qué tiempo hace?

Maricao, Puerto Rico

Una playa chilena

La Parva, Chile

Pronto vas a planear tus vacaciones del verano. A menudo nuestros lectores nos preguntan qué tiempo hace en los meses de julio y agosto en varios países de habla española y en ciudades donde hay mucha gente de origen hispano. Este mapa puede ayudarte a planear tus vacaciones.

2   Pasodoble

Options

Strategies for Reaching All Students

Spanish-Speaking Students
¿Has vivido en otro país o estado? ¿Cuál era el promedio de temperatura en ese lugar en julio?

Students Needing Extra Help
Remind students that they already know this material. Emphasize that they don't need to understand every word to comprehend the material.

Ex. 1: Have a map available for students having difficulty identifying the states and countries. You may also want to make this a homework assignment after students have tried it in class.
Ex. 3: Make sure students realize that *meses* is the plural of *mes.*
Ex. 4: Brainstorm words that describe your community in the chosen season. Give students a definite number of sentences to create.

Multiple Intelligences
Naturalist
Have students choose two cities on p. 3 to research and do a comparison of their climate and environmental conditions.
Visual/Spatial
See Practice Wkbk. PD-1; Overheads 14, 17, 27, and 38–40 (from Book 1); Comm. Act. BLM 7-1 (from Book 1); Students Needing Extra Help; and Activate Prior Knowledge.

*e*n el mes de julio, la temperatura promedio de estas ciudades es diferente. ¿Puedes decir por qué? ¿Por qué hay dos temperaturas para cada ciudad? (El símbolo ° se dice "grado.")

Bariloche: 3° (38°)

Buenos Aires: 11° (51°)

Caracas: 22° (72°)

Ciudad de México: 18° (64°)

Houston: 34° (93°)

La Paz: 9° (48°)

Los Ángeles: 21° (70°)

Madrid: 24° (75°)

Miami: 32° (89°)

Montevideo: 10° (50°)

Nueva York: 25° (77°)

Quito: 14° (67°)

San Juan: 27° (80°)

Aguadilla, Puerto Rico

1. ¿Puedes decir en qué país o estado está cada una de las ciudades mencionadas?

2. ¿Cuántos países de habla española pueden nombrar tú y un(a) compañero(a)? ¿Cuántos pueden indicar en el mapa?

3. ¿Qué tiempo hace en tu ciudad en el verano? ¿Y en el invierno? ¿Nieva mucho? ¿Hay meses en que llueve mucho? ¿Cuáles?

4. Si pensamos ir de vacaciones a tu ciudad, ¿en qué estación debemos ir: en la primavera, en el verano, en el otoño o en el invierno? Trabaja con un(a) compañero(a) para escribir una tarjeta postal en que describes la estación más bonita del lugar donde vives.

3

Cultural Notes

(p. 2, center photo)
Maricao, located in the Cordillera Central of Puerto Rico, is known for its coffee plantations. Every February the *plaza* is transformed into a coffee plantation of the past, in the colorful three-day celebration of the coffee harvest. Townspeople dress in indigenous costumes, and folkloric *trovadores* entertain the crowds with their musical improvisations.

(p. 2, photos)
Chile is a land of extreme climatic variation, due in great part to its 5,000-mile length. During the summer months of January and February, many Chileans spend time at beach resorts. From June to September, skiing is a popular activity.

(p. 3, photo)
These fishing boats are on Crashboat Beach, one of Aguadilla's most beautiful beaches, with sparkling white sand, calm waters, and sunny weather. Its beauty is clouded, however, by the mystery of the Bermuda Triangle, which supposedly touches the area around the beach. Divers frequently discover sunken boats about a mile offshore.

Review

Recycled Concepts

Countries and capitals, *(El primer paso)*; physical characteristics (Chap. 5); nature (Chap. 7); directions (Chaps. 8 and 10)

Ancillaries available for use with *Pasodoble*

 Practice Wkbk. PD-2

Ancillaries suggested from *PASO A PASO 1*

 Overheads 78–81

Activate Prior Knowledge

To prepare students for this reading, have a wall map available or use the overhead. Ask students to identify various Spanish-speaking countries and capitals. For example: *¿Dónde está Paraguay? ¿Es Lima la capital de Paraguay? ¿Qué países hispanos son islas?*

Answers

1. d; 2. c; 3. c; 4. a; 5. b; 6. b; 7. a; 8. b; 9. a; 10. c

Writing Extensions

As homework or an in-class writing assignment, have students create five additional multiple-choice questions for this survey. Have pairs exchange surveys and try to answer them.

---

de la edición de febrero

El mundo hispano

1 ¿Cuál de estos países no está en América Central?

a. Costa Rica
b. El Salvador
c. Honduras
d. México

2 Tres capitales tienen el nombre de un santo: San José, San Juan y Santiago. Son las capitales de:

a. Honduras, El Salvador y Uruguay
b. Colombia, Bolivia y Ecuador
c. Costa Rica, Puerto Rico y Chile
d. Nicaragua, Paraguay y Perú

3 Montevideo es:

a. la montaña más alta de América del Sur
b. un videojuego muy popular
c. la capital y la ciudad más grande de un país
d. el país más pequeño de las Américas

4 Hay más de veinte países donde el español es la lengua oficial. En área, ¿cuál es el más grande?

a. Argentina
b. Brasil
c. España
d. México

5 Managua es:

a. el nombre de la selva en Ecuador
b. una ciudad y capital centroamericana
c. una isla en el Caribe
d. una pirámide azteca en México

6 La República Dominicana queda en una isla. ¿Qué otro país está en esa isla?

a. Cuba
b. Haití
c. Panamá
d. Puerto Rico

7 ¿Cuál de estos países no está al lado de Perú?

a. Argentina
b. Bolivia
c. Chile
d. Colombia

8 La capital de Colombia es:

a. Asunción
b. Bogotá
c. La Paz
d. Lima

9 ¿Cuál de estos países es una isla?

a. Cuba
b. Guatemala
c. Paraguay
d. Uruguay

10 El país de habla española que está más cerca de los Estados Unidos es:

a. Colombia
b. Cuba
c. México
d. Puerto Rico

MORE PRACTICE

Más práctica y tarea, p. 525
Practice Workbook PD–1, PD–2

4 Pasodoble

Options

Strategies for Reaching All Students

Spanish-Speaking Students
El mundo hispano: Escribe tres a cinco preguntas más acerca de los países hispanohablantes. Hazles las preguntas a tus compañeros. ¿Eran tus preguntas demasiado fáciles o difíciles? ¿Las contestaron bien?
Tenis y más: Have students write and discuss with other Spanish-speaking students, if possible: *Usa esta información para escribir sobre tu compañero(a). No des el nombre. Léeles la descripción a otros com-pañeros para ver si pueden adivinar de quién escribes.*

Students Needing Extra Help
El mundo hispano: Have maps and other research materials available. Have pairs of students answer the questions.
Tenis y más: Read the information about Conchita Martínez aloud as students follow along in their texts.

Enrichment
El mundo hispano: As a homework assignment, ask students to research Hispanic countries and then make up three more multiple-choice questions regarding them. Have them write one of their questions on the chalkboard for the entire class to try to answer.

4 Standards 1.1; 1.2; 3.1

TENIS y más

Conchita Martínez juega tenis profesional desde los dieciséis años. En 1994 ganó el torneo internacional de Wimbledon.

de la edición de marzo

Nació en: *España, el 18 de abril de 1972*

Vive en: *Barcelona*

Colores favoritos: *el negro y el blanco*

Actor favorito: *Patrick Swayze*

Pasatiempo favorito: *ir al cine*

Le gusta: *jugar golf y fútbol, montar a caballo, escuchar toda clase de música, estar con sus amigos y su familia y trabajar como voluntaria*

No le gusta: *la guerra*

Admira a: *la gente que ayuda a otros*

Característica principal: *es perfeccionista*

Le interesa: *la psicología y la literatura*

Mejor momento en la cancha de tenis: *cuando venció a Gabriela Sabatini 7-5, 6-1 en Roma en mayo de 1994.*

Entrevista a un(a) compañero(a). Puedes usar estas preguntas u otras:

1 ¿Cuándo es tu cumpleaños?

2 ¿Cuál es tu dirección?

3 ¿Cuál es tu color favorito?

4 ¿Quiénes son tu actor y actriz favoritos?

5 ¿Cuáles son tus pasatiempos favoritos?

6 ¿Qué no te gusta hacer?

7 ¿A quién o a quiénes admiras?

8 ¿Cómo eres? ¿paciente o impaciente? ¿atrevido(a) o prudente? ¿ordenado(a) o desordenado(a)? ¿perezoso(a) o trabajador(a)? ¿gracioso(a) o serio(a)? ¿Eres artístico(a)? ¿deportista? ¿callado(a)? ¿amable?

5

Review

Recycled Concepts
Question words (*El primer paso* and Chaps. 1–2); personality traits (Chap. 1); leisure activities (Chaps. 1 and 3); *gustar* (Chaps. 1 and 5); school subjects and *-ar* verbs (Chap. 2); *jugar* (Chap. 3); age and *ser* (Chap. 5); colors and adj. agreement (Chap. 6); personal *a* (Chap. 7); preterite tense (Chaps. 10 and 12)

Ancillaries available for use with *Pasodoble*

Practice Wkbk. PD-3

Ancillaries suggested from *PASO A PASO 1*

Overheads 8–10

Comm. Act. BLMs 1-1, 1-2, 1-3

Activate Prior Knowledge
Brainstorm what information would likely be in an interview. Have students determine which information is most important, and when in the interview it should be requested.

Answers
1–8 Answers will vary.

Writing Extensions

Writing Activity A

Cultural Notes

(p. 5, photo)
Spain's Conchita Martínez is one of the world's most successful women tennis players. Together with her countrywoman, Arantxa Sánchez-Vicario, she consistently ranks in the top five players in terms of earnings. In 1994, Martínez became the first Spanish woman to win at Wimbledon.

Review

Recycled Concepts

Leisure activities (Chaps. 1 and 3); school subjects (Chap. 2); *ir a +* inf. (Chap. 3); *poder* and *querer* (Chaps. 3 and 7); *-er* verbs (Chap. 4); *gustar, encantar, ser,* and age (Chap. 5); *quisiera* (Chap. 7); *pensar* (Chaps. 7 and 11); *tener que, hacer, vivir,* and household chores (Chap. 8); indirect object pronouns (Chap. 9)

Ancillaries available for use with *Pasodoble*

 Practice Wkbk. PD-4

Ancillaries suggested from *PASO A PASO 1*

 Overheads 16, 18, 42, 45

 Comm. Act. BLMs 3-1, 3-3

Querido Pasodoble.

¡Hola! Somos seis amigos de la clase de español de segundo año de El Toro High School, en El Toro, California. Nos encanta Pasodoble. Todos los artículos de su revista son interesantes y originales.

Queremos leer más sobre los jóvenes de diferentes países de América Latina: qué ropa llevan, qué música les gusta, qué hacen para divertirse y si tienen algunos intereses especiales, como la ecología.

Saludos a todos los lectores de Pasodoble. ¡Y muchas gracias por una revista fantástica!

Options

Strategies for Reaching All Students

Spanish-Speaking Students

Have students work in pairs, if possible, to respond either orally or in writing: *Imaginen que contestan estas preguntas. ¿Qué dirían Uds.? Para las últimas preguntas, sustituyan Puerto Rico con los Estados Unidos u otro país donde hayan vivido.*

Students Needing Extra Help

Remind students that they don't need to know every word to understand the material. If necessary, explain *lo que.* Divide students into groups of three to conduct interviews similar to this one. When the class has completed *Pasodoble,* have students write a letter similar to this one, commenting on the magazine.

Enrichment

As an in-class written assignment, students can answer the questions in this section as if they were being interviewed. For the last question, they can say what they like best about living where they do.

DOS AMIGAS

de Puerto Rico

Gretel Cathiard es una joven de quince años. Su amiga Magda Ramos tiene dieciséis años. Las dos viven en San Juan, la capital de Puerto Rico. A Gretel le encantan las ciencias, y a Magda el inglés y las ciencias sociales. Lo que más les gusta es ir a la playa, tomar el sol, nadar y jugar vólcibol. **Pasodoble** habla con las dos amigas.

PD: ¿Qué les gusta hacer los fines de semana?

Gretel: Nos gusta estar con nuestros amigos. Vamos al cine o a la playa donde jugamos vóleibol, nadamos y paseamos en bote.
Magda: Y cuando no podemos estar juntos, hablamos por teléfono.

PD: ¿Adónde van Uds. con sus familias?

Magda: A veces vamos a pasear al parque. Y por supuesto vamos juntos a la iglesia los domingos. También vamos al centro comercial, pero sólo cuando necesito ir de compras. Cuando no tengo que comprar cosas, voy allí con amigos.

PD: ¿Qué piensan hacer después de terminar la escuela secundaria?

Gretel: Todavía no sé, pero me interesa mucho la medicina.
Magda: Quiero ser psicóloga. Quisiera ayudar a otros, y creo que tengo el potencial para hacerlo.

PD: ¿Qué no les gusta hacer?

Gretel: No me gustan nada los quehaceres de la casa: pasar la aspiradora, sacudir los muebles, lavar platos . . . ¡Bah!
Magda: A mí no me gusta hacer mi tarea de matemáticas. Afortunadamente, Gretel me ayuda a hacerla.

PD: ¿Qué diferencias ven Uds. entre los jóvenes de los Estados Unidos y los de Puerto Rico?

Gretel: Creo que los puertorriqueños somos menos nerviosos.
Magda: En los Estados Unidos un muchacho y una muchacha pueden ser novios a los doce años. Aquí no es común tener novio antes de los catorce.

PD: ¿Qué es lo que más les gusta de la vida en Puerto Rico?

Gretel: ¡El tiempo y el campo! Es un lugar muy bonito, ¿no?
Magda: A mí lo que más me gusta es la gente de mi país. Los puertorriqueños son generosos y simpáticos. De veras comprenden lo que es importante en la vida.

7

Answers
Answers to inductive questions will vary.

Writing Extensions
As an in-class written assignment, have students interview a classmate. Each interview should contain five questions about what the person likes to do, and why. Have students write out the questions beforehand, leaving space between them for answers.

 Writing Activity B

Review

Recycled Concepts
Leisure activities (Chaps. 1 and 3); *gustar* (Chaps. 1 and 5); *estar* (Chap. 3); possessive adjectives (Chap. 8)

Ancillaries available for use with *Pasodoble*

 Practice Wkbk. PD-5

Ancillaries suggested from *PASO A PASO 1*

 Overheads 18–19, 42

 Comm. Act. BLM 2-3

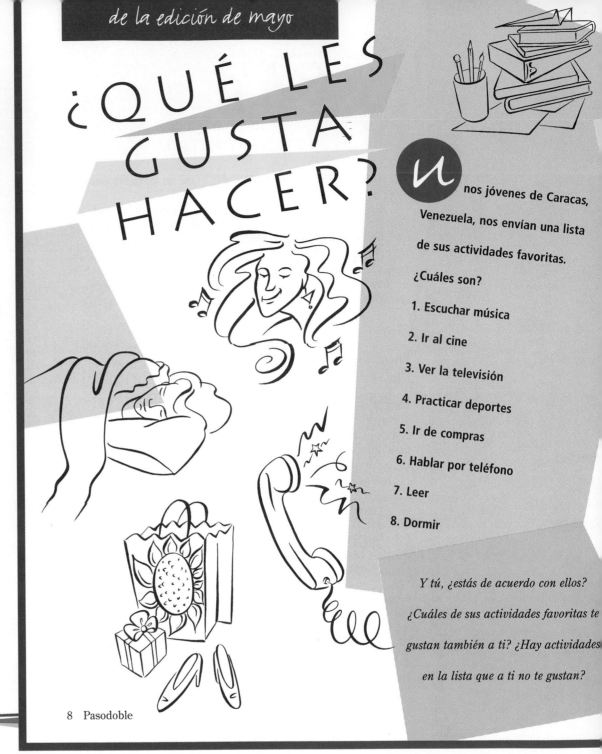

de la edición de mayo

¿QUÉ LES GUSTA HACER?

U nos jóvenes de Caracas, Venezuela, nos envían una lista de sus actividades favoritas. ¿Cuáles son?

1. Escuchar música
2. Ir al cine
3. Ver la televisión
4. Practicar deportes
5. Ir de compras
6. Hablar por teléfono
7. Leer
8. Dormir

Y tú, ¿estás de acuerdo con ellos? ¿Cuáles de sus actividades favoritas te gustan también a ti? ¿Hay actividades en la lista que a ti no te gustan?

8   Pasodoble

Options

Strategies for Reaching All Students

Spanish-Speaking Students
Responde a las preguntas por escrito.

Students Needing Extra Help
Review *estar de acuerdo*.

Multiple Intelligences
Logical/Mathematical
See Activate Prior Knowledge.
Visual/Spatial
See Practice Wkbk. PD-5; Overheads 18–19 and 42 (from Book 1); Comm. Act. BLM 2-3 (from Book 1); and Writing Extensions.
Visual/Spatial and Bodily/Kinesthetic
Have students create a collage with Spanish labels called *Mis pasatiempos favoritos* and share it with the class.

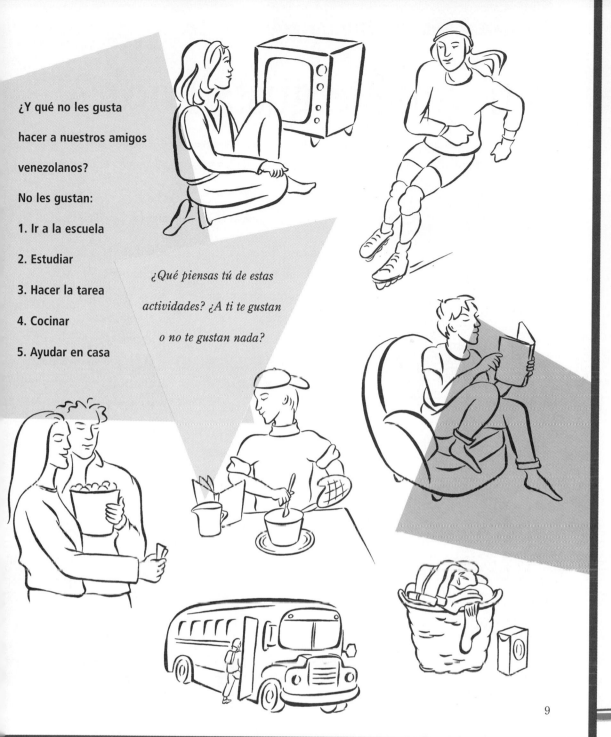

¿Y qué no les gusta hacer a nuestros amigos venezolanos?

No les gustan:

1. Ir a la escuela

2. Estudiar

3. Hacer la tarea

4. Cocinar

5. Ayudar en casa

¿Qué piensas tú de estas actividades? ¿A ti te gustan o no te gustan nada?

Activate Prior Knowledge

Have students generate a list of five favorite and five least favorite activities among young people across the U.S. Compare this list with the ones given in the reading.

Answers

Answers to inductive questions will vary.

Writing Extensions

As a homework assignment, have students generate a reason why young people may not like the activities listed as least favorite. Students should give a different reason for people not liking each activity. For example, *No les gusta ir a la escuela porque quieren dormir, y las clases empiezan a las ocho de la mañana.*

Review

Recycled Concepts

Ni . . . ni (Chap. 1); leisure activities (Chaps. 1 and 3); *poder* (Chaps. 3 and 7); household chores (Chap. 8); negative constructions (Chap. 9); preterite tense (Chaps. 10 and 12); *pensar* (Chap. 11)

Ancillaries available for use with *Pasodoble*

 Practice Wkbk. PD-6

Ancillaries suggested from *PASO A PASO 1*

 Overheads 18–19, 42

 Comm. Act. BLMs 3-2, 8-1

de la edición de junio

A ti, ¿qué te gusta hacer?

El mes pasado un grupo de jóvenes venezolanos nos enviaron una lista de sus actividades favoritas. Este mes tú puedes hacer una lista similar.

Aquí tienes varias actividades. ¿Qué piensas de ellas?

ayudar en casa (sacar la basura, lavar platos, hacer la cama, sacudir los muebles, pasar la aspiradora, etc.)

cocinar

comer

comprar cosas (ropa, libros, etc.)

cortar el césped

dibujar

dormir

escuchar música

estudiar/hacer la tarea

hablar por teléfono

hacer ejercicio

ir al centro comercial

ir al cine

ir al parque de diversiones

ir al museo

ir de pesca

jugar videojuegos

practicar deportes

sacar fotos

ver la televisión

Options

Strategies for Reaching All Students

Spanish-Speaking Students
Responde a las preguntas por escrito. Después de decidir cuáles de las actividades son quehaceres, di con cuáles deben ayudar todos y por qué.

Students Needing Extra Help
Review the present tense.
Ex. 2: Make sure students understand how the parentheses are used. Review *ni . . . ni.*

Multiple Intelligences
Visual/Spatial
See Practice Wkbk. PD-6, Overheads 18–19 and 42 (from Book 1), Comm. Act. BLMs 3-2 and 8-1 (from Book 1), and Writing Extensions.
Visual/Spatial and Bodily/Kinesthetic
Have students create a comic strip with characters portraying several activities they enjoy doing.

1. ¿Cuáles de estas actividades te gustan más? ¿Cuáles no te gustan nada? ¿Cuáles son pasatiempos y cuáles son quehaceres? Haz dos listas: *Me gusta mucho* y *No me gusta nada.* Escribe por lo menos cinco actividades en cada lista.

2. Con un(a) compañero(a), hablen de las actividades que sí les gustan y de las que no les gustan. ¿Cuáles no les gustan ni a él (ella) ni a ti?

3. Haz una encuesta (*poll*) para decidir cuáles son las actividades favoritas y las menos favoritas de la clase.

Activate Prior Knowledge
Brainstorm additional activities that can be included in the list on p. 10 *(bailar, pasear en bote, dibujar, lavar ropa, nadar, poner la mesa, jugar béisbol).*

Answers
1 Answers will vary but may include:
pasatiempos: comer, comprar cosas, dibujar, dormir, escuchar música, hablar por teléfono, ir al centro comercial, ir al cine, ir al museo, ir al parque de diversiones, ir de pesca, jugar videojuegos, practicar deportes, sacar fotos, ver la televisión
quehaceres: ayudar en casa, cocinar, cortar el césped, estudiar, hacer la tarea, hacer ejercicio

2–3 Answers will vary.

Writing Extensions

 Writing Activity B

11

Review

Recycled Concepts
Leisure activities (Chaps. 1 and 3); -ar verbs (Chap. 2); *comer, deber, -er* verbs, and food (Chap. 4); demonstrative adjectives (Chap. 6); *hacer,* and *tener que* (Chap. 8); health (Chap. 9); comparatives and superlatives (Chap. 11)

Ancillaries available for use with *Pasodoble*

 Practice Wkbk. PD-7

Ancillaries suggested from *PASO A PASO 1*

 Overheads 21–24

 Comm. Act. BLM 4-1

---

de la edición de julio

¿Bueno o malo para la salud?

¿Qué debes comer y qué debes hacer para tener buena salud? Y, lo que es más importante, ¿comes esa comida y haces esas actividades?

¿Haces ejercicio cada día? ¿Nadas o patinas? ¿Juegas básquetbol, vóleibol, fútbol o béisbol? ¿Esquías en el invierno?

¿Cuántas frutas (manzanas, naranjas, plátanos, uvas, etc.) comes al día?

¿Cuántas clases de verduras comes (guisantes, judías verdes, lechuga, tomates, zanahorias)? ¿Te gustan las ensaladas?

¿Comes pan, arroz o papas más o menos tres veces al día?

Cuando tienes sed, ¿tomas agua, leche o jugo de naranja o de manzana? ¿O bebes siempre un refresco, café o té?

Compara lo que comes en el desayuno con lo que come un(a) compañero(a).

1. Haz una encuesta para decidir quién come el mejor desayuno. ¿Por qué creen Uds. que ese desayuno es el mejor?

2. Mira el menú. En tu opinión, ¿cuál de estas pizzas es mejor para la salud?

3. Para comprar la pizza más saludable, ¿qué tienes que hacer?

12 Pasodoble

Options

Strategies for Reaching All Students

Spanish-Speaking Students
Have students respond orally or in writing: *De las meriendas que comes todos los días, ¿cuál crees que es la más nutritiva y cuál es la menos nutritiva? ¿Por qué?*

Students Needing Extra Help
After answering the questions, have students discuss how healthy or unhealthy their habits are as a class. Also discuss the health aspects of skipping breakfast.
Ex. 1: Review the vocabulary necessary to talk about breakfast. If available, use the vocabulary section of the Book 1, Chap. 4 Organizer. Categorize the words according to food groups. Have a food pyramid available.

Ex. 3: Remind students to read the fine print on the menu. Refer them to the questions discussing exercise earlier in the selection for clues.

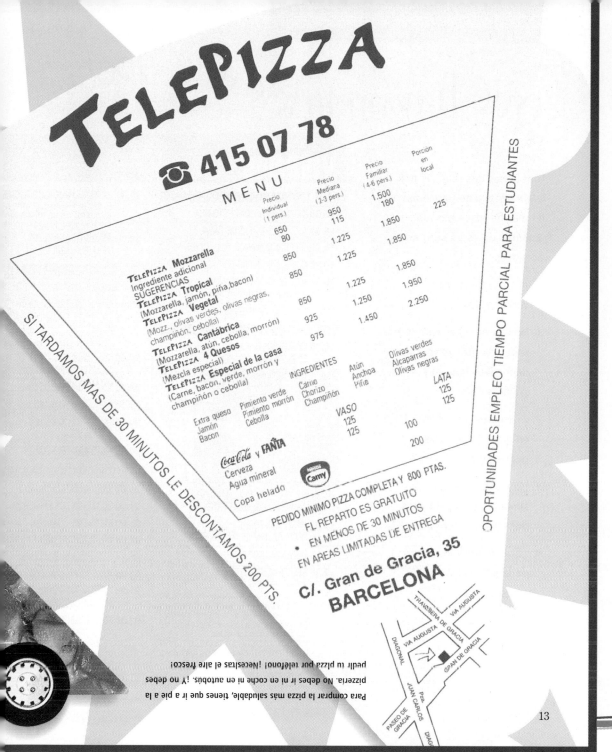

TELEPIZZA

☎ 415 07 78

Activate Prior Knowledge

To prepare students for this reading, brainstorm healthy foods from each food group. Have a food pyramid available so that students can categorize foods correctly.

Answers

Answers to inductive questions will vary, but look for correct use of the present tense.

1–2 Answers will vary.

3 (printed upside down on the bottom of p. 13) To buy the healthiest pizza, walk to the pizza parlor. You need the fresh air!

Writing Extensions

As an in-class written assignment, have pairs of students create a list of their ten favorite foods, indicate to which food groups they belong, and how frequently students eat them in a week. Pairs should share this information with the class, to see which pair has the healthiest eating habits.

 Writing Activity C

Enrichment

Conduct a class discussion on the Telepizza ad, asking students to comment on similarities and differences between this ad and pizza ads they see in the local newspaper. Encourage students to comment on the different kinds of pizza listed, saying which they would order. You may want to have pairs of students act out a call to the pizza place in front of the class, with one student ordering and the other taking the order, writing it down, and reading it back for verification.

Multiple Intelligences

Interpersonal/Social and Visual/Spatial
See Writing Extensions.
Verbal/Linguistic
See Enrichment.

Visual/Spatial
See Practice Wkbk. PD-7, Overheads 21–24 (from Book 1), and Comm. Act. BLM 4-1 (from Book 1).
Visual/Spatial and Logical/Mathematical
Have students bring in a pizza ad from a local newspaper and make comparisons with the ad in the book.

Review

Recycled Concepts
Hay, se dice, and calendar expressions *(El primer paso); leer* (Chap. 1); time-telling (Chap. 2); *poder* (Chaps. 3 and 7); *creer* (Chap. 4); *llamarse* (Chap. 5); *pensar* (Chap. 11); *hay que* + inf. (Chap. 13)

Ancillaries available for use with *Pasodoble*

 Practice Wkbk. PD-8

Ancillaries suggested from *PASO A PASO 1*

 Overheads 13, 16, 56–60

 Comm. Act. BLM 11-1

de la edición de agosto

¿Qué hay en la tele esta noche?

Aquí tienes dos páginas del *Teleprograma* de Barcelona del mes de mayo pasado. ¿Cuántos de estos programas reconoces?

¿Eres buen lector? Vamos a ver . . .

1. No hay que leer nada para saber cuántos programas deportivos hay esta noche. ¿Cuántos hay?

2. ¿Y cuántos programas hay en que las personas pueden ganar dinero?

3. ¿Por qué crees que hay símbolos sólo para esas dos clases de programas?

4. ¿Qué piensan los editores de la película *Agárralo como puedas 2 1/2?*

14 Pasodoble

VIERNES 14 MAYO

18.00
18.00 2-TVE BALONCESTO NBA
18.00 ANTENA-3 COSAS DE CASA
18.20 CANAL+ AVANCE. REDACCIÓN
18.25 CANAL+ PREVIO TOROS
18.30 ANTENA-3 LA MERIENDA
Espacio infantil en el que se ofrecen varios concursos y la serie CHICHO TERREMOTO.

19.00
19.00 TELE-5 HABLANDO SE ENTIENDE LA BASCA

Jesús Vázquez entabla cada tarde una interesante conversación con sus jóvenes invitados.

19.00 CANAL+ TOROS. FERIA DE SAN ISIDRO (Codificado)
19.25 TVE-1 NOTICIAS
19.30 TVE-1 MacGYVER: "COSECHA AMARGA"
El coche de MacGyver se para en la localidad de Kasabian, donde un grupo de trabajadores del campo se enfrentan a los propietarios de las tierras que trabajan. INTÉRPRETES: RICHARD DEAN ANDERSON, DANA ELCAR, ABE VIGODA, DICK BUTKUS.
19.30 2-TVE JARA Y SEDAL

19.30 ANTENA-3 NUEVOS POLICÍAS
El oficial Penhall y Hoffs in la muerte de un atleta olím consumo de anabolizantes
19.30 TELE-5 LA RULETA DE LA FORTUNA

20.00
20.00 2-TVE EL INFORME DEL
20.00 TELE-5 PRIMER AMOR (C
Armando da su aprobac adopción de la niña de Rossana visita al médico dice que está embarazada
20.30 TVE-1 VUELTA CICLISTA A ESPAÑA (Resumer
20.30 2-TVE DÍAS DE CINE
20.30 ANTENA-3 NOTICIAS
20.30 2-TVE (Canarias) A TODA VELA
20.45 TELE-5 TELECUPÓN

21.00
21.00 TVE-1 TELEDIARIO-2
21.00 2-TVE LOS PRIMEROS
21.00 2-TVE (Canarias) CAMP
21.05 TELE-5 SU MEDIA NARAN
21.15 ANTENA-3 BUSCAVIDAS
21.25 TVE-1 EL TIEMPO
21.25 CANAL+ INFORMACIÓN METEOROLÓGICA
21.30 TVE-1 UN, DOS, TRES...: "EL LEJANO OESTE"
En esta ocasión se cuenta c sencia de Cher, La Frontera pa los pollos y Abuelo Jone
21.30 2-TVE TAL CUAL

86   ○○○○ EXCELENTE ○○○ MUY BUENA ○○ BUENA ○

Options

Strategies for Reaching All Students

Spanish-Speaking Students
¿Has visto algunos de estos mismos programas? ¿Cuáles recomiendas? ¿Por qué?

Students Needing Extra Help
Emphasize that this listing is for people watching TV in Barcelona. Point out context clues for students having difficulty with *baloncesto.* If necessary, help students find the icons representing sports and game shows, as well as the film rating guide at the bottom left-hand page.

Multiple Intelligences
Interpersonal/Social and Visual/Spatial
See Writing Extensions.
Visual/Spatial
See Practice Wkbk. PD-8; Overheads 13, 16, and 56–60 (from Book 1); Comm. Act. BLM 11-1 (from Book 1); and Writing Extensions.

The following is the TV guide realia (left portion):

14 MAYO VIERNES

.30 **CANAL+** REDACCIÓN. NOTICIAS

.30 **2-TVE** (Canarias) CANARIOS EN SU RINCÓN

.45 **ANTENA-3** CINE
LOS JACKSON (Cap. 2 y último)

.55 **CANAL+** INFORMACIÓN DEPORTIVA

.00

.00 **TELE-5** SENSACIÓN DE VIVIR:
"PERFECTAMENTE PERFECTO"
Serie estadounidense. Mientras Kelly sigue obsesionada con su exceso de peso, sus amigos están preparando para ella una gran fiesta de cumpleaños.
(Reportaje en páginas 8 a 11)

.00 **CANAL+** AGÁRRALO COMO PUEDAS 2 1/2 ◦◦
ESTRENO (Codificado)
Producción estadounidense de 1990. Título original: "Nacked gun 2/2: the smell of fear". Duración: 82 minutos. Color. Comedia.
INTÉRPRETES: LESLIE NIELSEN, PRISCILLA PRESLEY, GEORGE KENNEDY. Director: D. ZUCKER.

.55 **TELE-5** MELROSE PLACE (Cap.30)
Serie estadounidense. Billy y Allison quieren que su relación se mantenga en secreto.

Los chicos de Melrose Place tienen multitud de problemas sentimentales.

23.00

23.00 **2-TVE** PAVAROTTI Y SUS AMIGOS
Gran gala concierto, celebrada en Modena (Italia), en la que intervienen intérpretes de los más diversos estilos musicales: Pavarotti, Sting, Zucchero, Lucio Dalla, Neville Brothers, Aaron Neville, Suzanne Vega, Mike Oldfield, Brian May, Bob Geldof y Patricia Kaas.

23.20 **CANAL+** SOLO EN CASA
CINE (Codificado) (Repetición)

23.30 **ANTENA-3** CON USTEDES ...
PEDRO RUIZ

23.50 **TELE-5** CONTACTO, CON TACTO

24.00

24.00 **TVE-1** PARA ELISA (Capítulo 14)
Vicente consigue que Laura acceda a encontrarse con él fuera de Madrid. Por otro lado, Óscar y Natalia siguen con su romance sin que Claudio sepa nada. Se va a celebrar en Madrid el premio "la señorita España" y Jana está segura de que será nominada.
INTÉRPRETES: ASSUMPTA SERNA, XABIER ELORRIAGA, FERNANDO VALVERDE.

24.00 **2-TVE** DOCTOR EN ALASKA (3)
Serie estadounidense que comenzó a emitirse el pasado 30 de Abril sin previo aviso. Shelly se queda embarazada y Holling se ve obligado a casarse con ella. En el pueblo todos preparan la ceremonia y en el último momento Holly no se presenta. Pese a todo, Shelley vuelve a aceptar la propuesta de matrimonio.
INTÉRPRETES: ROB MORROW, BARRY CORBIN, JOHN CORBETT, JANINE TURNER.

00.35 **TVE-1** ENTRE HOY Y MAÑANA

00.45 **ANTENA-3** NOTICIAS

87

---

5. ¿Cómo se llama el programa "Wheel of Fortune" en España?

6. ¿Cómo se llama "Doctor en Alaska" en los Estados Unidos?

7. ¿Cómo se dice "básquetbol" en España?

8. Jesús Vázquez entrevista a jóvenes invitados a su programa. ¿Cómo se llama su programa? ¿A qué hora pueden verlo los barceloneses?

9. ¿A qué hora hay que ver la televisión para saber qué tiempo va a hacer mañana? ¿En qué canales puedes ver esos programas?

10. Imagina que la fecha de hoy es el 14 de mayo. Con un(a) compañero(a), hablen de los programas que quieren ver. Después, hablen con otro grupo y decidan qué van a ver esta noche.

15

Activate Prior Knowledge

Brainstorm with students the different types of programs available on television during prime-time. Ask students which types they prefer, and which types appeal to other age brackets, such as older people or small children.

Answers
1. 4
2. 4
3. porque estas dos clases son las más populares
4. Piensan que es buena. (See rating scale, bottom of left-hand page of the guide.)
5. "La ruleta de la fortuna"
6. "Northern Exposure"
7. En España, se dice "baloncesto."
8. Su programa se llama "Hablando se entiende la basca." Pueden verlo a las siete de la noche.
9. Pueden ver Canal + o TVE-1 a las nueve y veinticinco.
10. Answers will vary.

Writing Extensions

In pairs or small groups, have students create a TV Guide page of the programs they watch in a given week. It should include a grid listing day of the week, time, channel, title, and type of show. Students should write a two-sentence summary of three of the programs they saw.

 Writing Activity D

Cultural Notes

(pp. 14–15, realia)
Many popular U.S. television programs shown in Barcelona retain their original names: "MacGyver" and "Melrose Place," for example. Others are given new titles: *Sensación de vivir* is "Beverly Hills 90210." *Su media naranja* means, colloquially, "your better half."

La ruleta de la fortuna, the Spanish equivalent of "Wheel of Fortune," is as popular as the show is in the U.S. The variety game show *Un, dos, tres* is thematic: *El lejano oeste* is the theme listed for this day, so contestants are required to wear western wear. For more information about this game show, see p. 329.

Review

Recycled Concepts
Family members (Chap. 5); preterite tense (Chaps. 10 and 12); comparatives (Chap. 11)

Ancillaries suggested from *PASO A PASO 1*

 Overheads 29–30

 Comm. Act. BLMs 10-2, 10-3

Activate Prior Knowledge
Brainstorm vocabulary that would be used in a performer's biography *(estudió, trabajó, vivió, película, jugó, televisión, cantó)*.

Writing Extensions
Have students write a short biography about their favorite performer, using the format shown here and the vocabulary they came up with in the **Activate Prior Knowledge** section.

de la edición de septiembre

¡HOLA, Andy!

¿Quién es Andy García? Es un actor del cine norteamericano, famoso por su talento y por su amabilidad natural. Pero, ¿quién es en la vida real?

Nació en La Habana, Cuba, el 12 de abril de 1956. Cinco años más tarde, llegó a los Estados Unidos con sus padres. Vivieron en Miami, donde reside la comunidad cubana más grande de este país. Cuando decidió ser actor, fue a Los Ángeles.

Cuando no trabaja, Andy se dedica a su familia—su esposa, que también es cubana, y sus tres hijas. Para Andy, la familia es lo más importante. En su casa se habla español y él quiere educar a sus hijas en la tradición en que le enseñaron sus padres a él—con mucha dedicación y disciplina.

MORE PRACTICE

- Más práctica y tarea, p. 525–527
- Practice Workbook PD–3, PD–8

16 Pasodoble

Options

Strategies for Reaching All Students

Spanish-Speaking Students
¡Hola, Andy!: ¿Conoces a otro(a) artista hispano(a)? ¿Quién es?
¡Sí, puedo! ¡Soy joven!: ¿Tienes la misma confianza que este(a) poeta? ¿Qué quieres ser y hacer tú?

Students Needing Extra Help
¡Hola, Andy!: Review preterite-tense verb forms. Discuss any other well-known Spanish-speaking people students may know (Jimmy Smits, Paul Rodríguez, Rosie Pérez, José Canseco).
¡Sí, puedo! ¡Soy joven!: Review *nada* and *nadie*. Students do not yet know the future tense, but context should make it clear here. Emphasize the theme rather than poetic language and style.

Enrichment
¡Sí, puedo! ¡Soy joven!: For a homework assignment, ask students to write a paragraph or poem in which they tell what they want to do to improve the world.

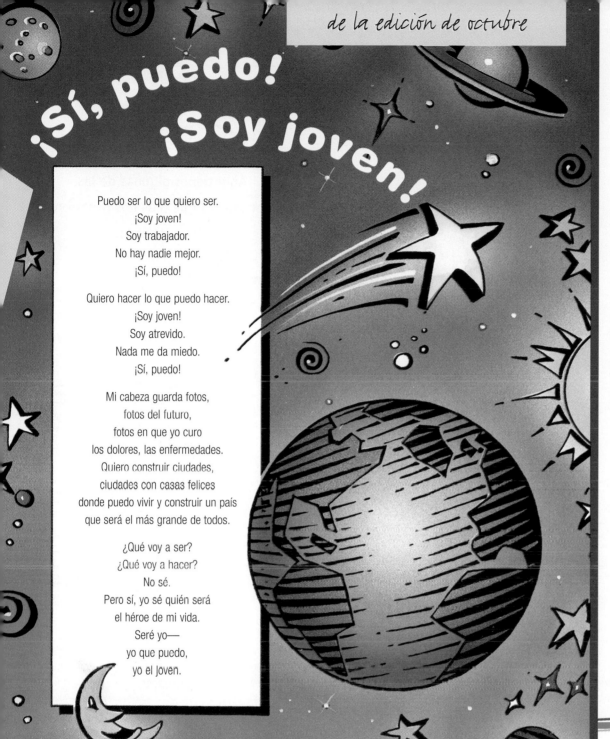

¡Sí, puedo! ¡Soy joven!

Puedo ser lo que quiero ser.
¡Soy joven!
Soy trabajador.
No hay nadie mejor.
¡Sí, puedo!

Quiero hacer lo que puedo hacer.
¡Soy joven!
Soy atrevido.
Nada me da miedo.
¡Sí, puedo!

Mi cabeza guarda fotos,
fotos del futuro,
fotos en que yo curo
los dolores, las enfermedades.
Quiero construir ciudades,
ciudades con casas felices
donde puedo vivir y construir un país
que será el más grande de todos.

¿Qué voy a ser?
¿Qué voy a hacer?
No sé.
Pero sí, yo sé quién será
el héroe de mi vida.
Seré yo—
yo que puedo,
yo el joven.

Review

Recycled Concepts
Ir a + inf. Chap. 3; *querer* and *poder* (Chaps. 3 and 7); negative expressions (Chaps. 5 and 9)

Ancillaries suggested from *PASO A PASO 1*

 Overheads 8, 10, 28–29

 Comm. Act. BLM 7-2

Activate Prior Knowledge
To prepare students for this reading, have each write a short description of his or her future goals, and what qualities they possess that will help them achieve those goals. Ask for volunteers to share their descriptions with the class.

Cultural Notes

Multiple Intelligences
Intrapersonal/Introspective
See Activate Prior Knowledge.
Intrapersonal/Introspective and Visual/Spatial
See Enrichment.
Visual/Spatial
See Overheads 8, 10, and 28–30 (from Book 1); Comm. Act. BLMs 7-2, 10-2, and 10-3 (from Book 1); and Writing Extensions.

(p. 16, photos)
Andy García's popularity skyrocketed in 1990 with the release of *Godfather Part III, A Show of Force,* and *Internal Affairs.* He co-wrote the latter. The plot of *A Show of Force* revolves around the true story of the fatal political shooting of two young pro-

independence Puerto Ricans, one of whom was the son of novelist Pedro Juan Soto. García is one of the first Hispanics, along with Edward James Olmos and Paul Rodríguez, to enter the U.S. film production business.

Review

Recycled Concepts
Estar (Chap. 3); *deber* (Chap. 4);
negative expressions (Chaps. 5
and 9); *alguien* (Chap. 14)

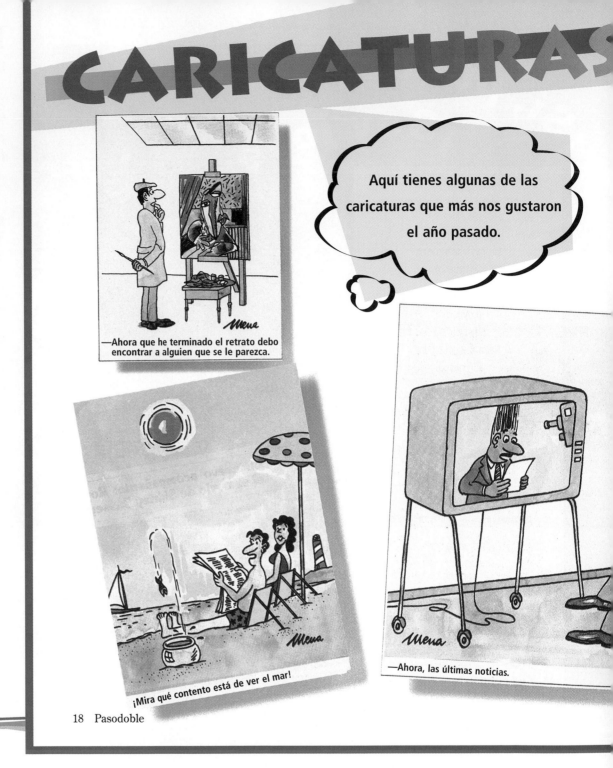

CARICATURAS

Aquí tienes algunas de las caricaturas que más nos gustaron el año pasado.

—Ahora que he terminado el retrato debo encontrar a alguien que se le parezca.

¡Mira qué contento está de ver el mar!

—Ahora, las últimas noticias.

18   Pasodoble

Options

Strategies for Reaching All Students

Spanish-Speaking Students
¿Cuál de las caricaturas crees que es más cómica? ¿Por qué?

Students Needing Extra Help
Review the concept of cartoons making points rather than just being humorous. Before discussing the cartoon of the painter, emphasize that the subject of a portrait is always a person.

Multiple Intelligences
Visual/Spatial
1) If accessible, have students use a computer draw-and-paint program to create cartoons with Spanish captions.
2) See Students Needing Extra Help, Activate Prior Knowledge, and Writing Extensions.

—¡Me aburro! ¡No hay nada interesante en la tele!

19

Have some local political or satirical cartoons available to share with students. Discuss how to read these types of cartoons to understand the point the artist was making. Point out that the artwork is often used to complement the text, not only to illustrate it. Students do not know the verb forms in the cartoon showing the painter. Help them as they work to figure out its meaning.

Writing Extensions
Students might enjoy drawing their own cartoons and generating captions for them.

Writing Activity E

Review

Recycled Concepts
Tener (Chap. 5); rooms in a house and furniture (Chap. 8); *decir* (Chap. 13)

Ancillaries available for use with *Pasodoble*

 Practice Wkbk. PD-9

Ancillaries suggested from *PASO A PASO 1*

 Overheads 41–43

 Comm. Act. BLM 8-3

---

de la edición de noviembre

¿Qué quiere decir "casa"?

Una casa no es *a house*. La imagen que tiene una persona española cuando dice "mi casa" normalmente no incluye ni césped grande ni garaje ni sótano con lavadero y sala de estar. Pero sí puede incluir un patio bonito (muchas veces en el centro de la casa) con flores y sillas. El patio es un "cuarto" muy importante en una casa española o latinoamericana.

¿Qué ves tú cuando dices *house*?

20   Pasodoble

Maracaibo, Venezuela

San Cristóbal de las Casas, México

Córdoba, España

Options

Strategies for Reaching All Students

Spanish-Speaking Students
Ask students to write a paragraph answering the following questions: *El primer párrafo dice que el patio es un "cuarto" importante. ¿Por qué será? ¿Cómo se usa el patio de una casa en España o en América Latina? ¿Qué se usa en los Estados Unidos para las mismas actividades?*

Students Needing Extra Help
Use the vocabulary section of the Book 1, Chap. 8 Organizer, if available. Have students use extra-large paper so they can spread out their work. Have magazines available for them to cut out pictures of furniture or rooms of a house. Give students guidelines as to what you expect the description to include.

Multiple Intelligences
Visual/Spatial
See Practice Wkbk. PD-9, Overheads 41–43 (from Book 1), Comm. Act. BLM 8-3 (from Book 1), and Activate Prior Knowledge.

el segundo piso

el primer piso

el sótano

Mira las fotos de las casas y patios. Mira también el plano de una casa típica de los Estados Unidos. Trabaja con dos o tres compañeros(as) para diseñar la casa ideal. Pueden combinar aspectos de los dos tipos de casas.

Uno de ustedes debe dibujar la casa. Después, descríbanla. ¿Dónde están las puertas y ventanas? Una persona puede describir los muebles de la sala o de la sala de estar (sofás, sillones, sillas, mesas, lámparas). Otra persona debe describir los dormitorios (camas, cómodas, guardarropas, etc.). ¿Hay escritorio? ¿Equipos de sonido? ¿Videocaseteras? ¿Dónde hay espejos o carteles o fotos?

Con otro grupo hablen de los dos diseños.

Cuando una persona hispanohablante dice, "Mi casa es su casa," ¿qué quiere decir? ¿Hay una expresión de hospitalidad similar en inglés?

21

Review

Recycled Concepts
Leisure activities (Chaps. 1 and 3); *gustar* expressions (Chap. 3); *poder* (Chaps. 3 and 7); *preferir* (Chaps. 4 and 8); *tener* (Chap. 5); travel (Chap. 7); *pensar* (Chaps. 7 and 11); preterite tense (Chaps. 10 and 12); superlatives (Chap. 11); environmental terms (Chap. 13)

Ancillaries available for use with *Pasodoble*

 Practice Wkbk. PD-10

Ancillaries suggested from *PASO A PASO 1*

 Overheads 36–37, 40

 Comm. Act. BLM 7-3

de la edición de diciembre

Vacaciones mágicas
¿Adónde piensas ir de vacaciones? ¿Qué tipos de lugares y qué actividades prefieres? En América Latina hay una gran variedad de lugares interesantes y divertidos.

Para el deportista

¿Te gustaría esquiar en verano? Puedes ir a Chile o a Argentina, donde es invierno cuando es verano en los Estados Unidos. El mes de agosto es cuando hay mejor nieve para esquiar. El lugar más popular para esquiar está en Bariloche, un centro turístico en el sur de Argentina. Es similar a Suiza por su arquitectura y su belleza natural. Sólo necesitas llevar la ropa apropiada. Los esquís, las botas . . . puedes alquilar allí todo lo que necesitas.

Para el ecólogo

Si prefieres el clima tropical y la ecología, puedes pasar unas vacaciones ideales en Costa Rica. Muchos turistas van para tomar el sol en sus playas del Caribe y del Pacífico, para pasear en bote por sus ríos o para explorar la selva. Si te interesa la ecología, puedes ir a la provincia de Guanacaste para ver la gran variedad de animales y plantas en los parques nacionales.

Y para los más aventureros, hay programas donde pueden trabajar como voluntarios ayudando a proteger el medio ambiente.

Para el antropólogo

Imagina una ciudad muy moderna, donde también hay arquitectura colonial y ruinas de ciudades de hace quinientos años. Si te interesan las civilizaciones precolombinas, el lugar ideal para ti es la Ciudad de México. Tienes que visitar el Museo Nacional de Antropología para ver los antiguos artefactos de esas civilizaciones indígenas. Cerca de la plaza del Zócalo, puedes ver las ruinas del Templo Mayor de Tenochtitlán, la ciudad más importante de los aztecas, que descubrieron unos trabajadores en 1978. ¿Hay más ruinas debajo de esta ciudad moderna? ¡Claro que sí! Pero qué son y cuándo las vamos a descubrir es todavía un misterio.

22 Pasodoble

Options

Strategies for Reaching All Students

Spanish-Speaking Students
Describe otro lugar que atraería a los turistas. Menciona los lugares de interés y la mejor estación para visitar.

Students Needing Extra Help
Refer to pp. 2–3 where Bariloche is mentioned. Have visuals available to help students understand the concepts of anthropology, pre-Columbian civilizations, etc.

Multiple Intelligences
Visual/Spatial
See Practice Wkbk. PD-10, Overheads 36–37 and 40 (from Book 1), Comm. Act. BLM 7-3 (from Book 1), Activate Prior Knowledge, and Writing Extensions.

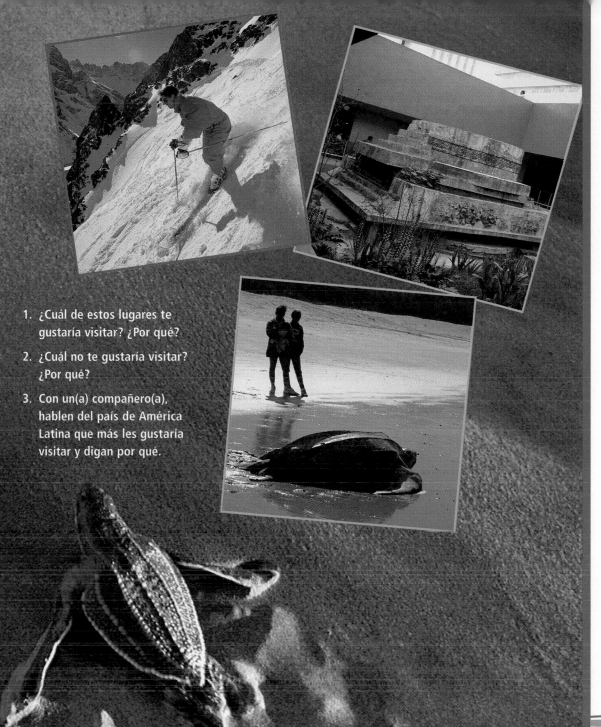

1. ¿Cuál de estos lugares te gustaría visitar? ¿Por qué?

2. ¿Cuál no te gustaría visitar? ¿Por qué?

3. Con un(a) compañero(a), hablen del país de América Latina que más les gustaría visitar y digan por qué.

Cultural Notes

(p. 23, top left photo)
Chile offers many impressive ski resorts. Valle Nevado, near Santiago, is the largest in South America, with almost 50 ski lifts and 22,000 acres of Andean ski slopes. Some runs are 10 miles long and 17,908 feet high. Other popular ski resorts are Chillán, Farellones, Lagunillas, and Portillo.

(p. 23, top right photo)
Mexico City's *metro* system is quiet, smooth, and efficient. During the construction of the Pino Suárez station in the city's center, engineers unearthed an Aztec pyramid, which has been left in the station. Modern Mexico is juxtaposed with the ancient past as commuters stream past the little pyramid.

(p. 23, bottom photo)
Leatherback turtles, the largest existing sea turtles, have a flexible shell made of small bones embedded in soft, leathery skin. Weighing over 1,600 pounds and reaching lengths of over 7 feet, they maintain a constant body temperature in or out of the water. Leatherbacks go ashore to lay their eggs, and tourists often visit Costa Rican beaches to watch the hatchlings work their way into the water.

Review

Recycled Concepts

Personality traits (Chap. 1); -er and -ir verbs (Chap. 4); physical characteristics (Chap. 5); adjective agreement (Chap. 6); quisiera (Chap. 7)

Ancillaries suggested from PASO A PASO 1

 Overheads 8–10, 28–29

Éste es un bio-poema. El poeta (la poetisa) describe su personalidad y sus emociones. Aquí tienes la estructura de un bio-poema. Síguela y ¡tú también puedes ser poeta!

Escribe tu nombre: ___ .

Escribe 4 adjetivos que te describen: ___ .

Escribe el nombre de uno de tus padres: ___ .

Escribe: A quien le encantan: ___ , ___ y ___ .

Escribe: Quien se siente: ___ , y ___ .

Escribe: Quien necesita: ___ , ___ y ___ .

Escribe: Quien ofrece (offers): ___ y ___ .

Escribe: Quien teme a (fears): ___ , ___ y ___

Escribe: Quien quisiera tener: ___ , ___ y ___ .

Escribe: Quien quisiera ver: ___ y ___ .

Escribe: Quien vive en: ___
(tu ciudad), ___ (tu dirección).

Escribe tu apellido: ___ .

MORE PRACTICE

- Más práctica y tarea, p. 527
- Practice Workbook PD–9, PD–10

24 Pasodoble

Ana Laura

Alta, impaciente, cariñosa y callada.
Hija de Adriana.

A quien le encantan:
los elefantes, la lluvia y los ojos de Daniel.

Quien se siente:
emocionada por la generosidad, y triste por los
que tienen hambre.

Quien necesita:
la música, el océano y a su amiga Raquel.

Quien ofrece:
puerta abierta a los amigos
y hamburguesas sabrosas.

Quien teme a:
la ignorancia, la tacañería
y la contaminación de la Tierra.

Quien quisiera tener:
la visión del poeta, la vida de un rockero
y un perro labrador de color chocolate.

Quien quisiera ver:
cómo se hace una película
y a Paula lavar los platos.

Quien vive en:
Gilboa, calle Blossom.
Cáceres, León.

Options

Strategies for Reaching All Students

Students Needing Extra Help
Brainstorm other vocabulary in each category for students to use in the poem.

Multiple Intelligences
Musical/Rhythmic and Naturalist
Ask students to select (or create) a piece of music that might reflect the mood of the scene in the photo on p. 25.
Visual/Spatial
See Overheads 8–10 and 28–29 (from Book 1) and Writing Extensions.

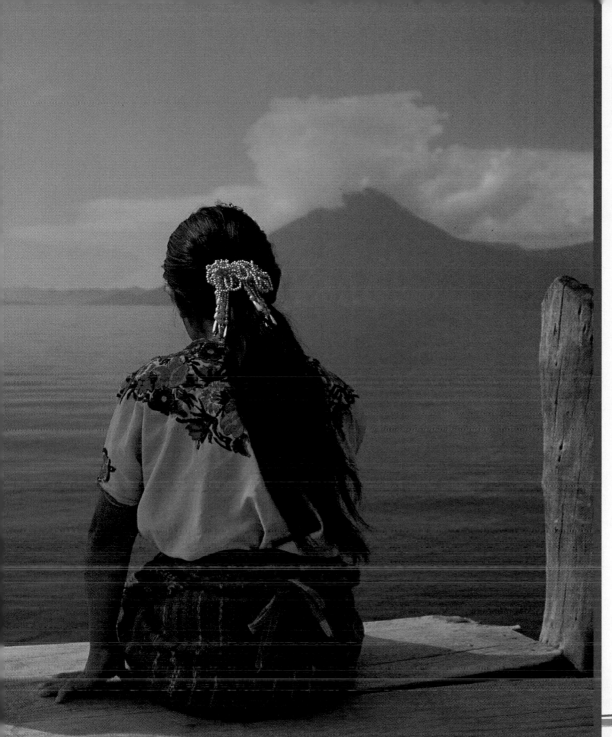

Activate Prior Knowledge
To prepare students for this activity, brainstorm vocabulary describing personality traits and physical characteristics.

Answers
Answers will vary, but look for a wide variety of appropriate vocabulary.

Writing Extensions

 Writing Activity G

 Audio Activities P. 1, P. 2, P. 3, P. 4

 Internet Activities
Have students go to www.pasoapaso.com for additional activities and practice.

Assessment

 Prueba Pasodoble

 Internet Activities
Self-Test

Cultural Notes

(p. 25, photo)
This Guatemalan woman looks out over Lake Atitlán, known for its beaches, mountains, and volcanoes. Volcán San Pedro, in the background, rises 9,920 feet above sea level. The other two volcanoes overlooking the lake are Tolimán (10,340 feet) and Atitlán (11,560 feet). Temperatures around this tropical shoreline range narrowly from 50° to 70° F.

CAPÍTULO 1

THEME: SCHOOL

COMMUNICATION

Topics

School subjects

School equipment

School activities

Homework

Objectives

To compare schooling in Spanish-speaking countries and in the U.S.

To name school subjects

To name people who work at a school

To name places in a school

To describe school equipment

To talk about activities associated with school

To talk about homework

To make comparisons

CULTURE

Schooling

GRAMMAR

El verbo salir

La forma comparativa: tan ... como

Repaso: La forma comparativa

Repaso: El complemento directo

Ancillaries available for use with Chapter 1

Multisensory/Technology

 Overheads, 6–10

 Audio Tapes and CDs

 Vocabulary Art Blackline Masters for Hands-On Learning, pp. 8–12/CD-ROM

 Classroom Crossword

 La Catrina

 Pasos vivos 2 CD-ROM

 Internet Activities www.pasoapaso.com

Print

 Practice Workbook, pp. 1–11

 Writing, Audio & Video Activities, pp. 5–10, 93–95, 151–152

 Communicative Activity Blackline Masters

Pair and Small Group Activities, pp. 1–6

Situation Cards, p. 7

 Un paso más: Actividades para ampliar tu español, pp. 1–6

RESOURCE PRO®

Planning Express, Teaching Resources Library, and Clip Art Library

Assessment

 Assessment Program

Pruebas, pp. 9–20

Examen de habilidades, pp. 21–24

 Test Generator

 ¿Lo sabes bien? Video Quiz

Video still from Chap. 1

High School in Latin America

Although there are similarities between the high-school experience in the U.S. and in Spanish-speaking countries, there are also some striking differences.

In the U.S., high-school students take between five and seven subjects per year, but in Latin America, students usually take between ten and twelve. These classes do not meet each day, however. A geography class may meet only three days a week, a music class, twice a week. As a result, student schedules vary from day to day. Furthermore, although physical education is taught, team athletics do not form part of the curriculum. On the other hand, the study of English is mandatory in many schools.

Schools in Latin America rarely have the amenities that students take for granted in the U.S. For example, most schools are not equipped with lockers. As a result, many students use *mochilas* (backpacks) or *bolsos* (book bags) to carry their books and personal items. As a rule, Latin American students have much more homework than American students, thus providing another reason for owning a good, sturdy backpack or book bag.

The grading scale varies from country to country, but letter grades are rarely used. For example, in Mexico grades range from 0–10; in Ecuador, the scale is 1–20; and in Chile, it is 1–7. Although in this chapter we use the terms *nota* (grade, as in evaluation of work) and *año* (grade, as in year in school), the word *grado,* to mean both, is current in some Spanish-speaking regions of the U.S.

Private schools are common in Latin America. Many are Roman Catholic and run by specific orders of nuns and priests. Parochial schools in Latin America are usually not coeducational. But there are many coed private schools that are not church-affiliated. Many of these are associated with ethnic or cultural traditions and require the study of the appropriate foreign language. In this category are many American, German, British, Italian, and French schools.

The most obvious difference between our school system and that of Spanish-speaking countries is the use of uniforms. In some cases the uniform is the same throughout the country, but usually a school—especially a private school—can be identified by the uniform. For girls, this may consist of a jumper, a blouse, and tie, or a pleated skirt, a blouse, and a vest or blazer. Boys must wear slacks, a shirt with a tie, and sometimes a sweater or blazer as well. Some schools have variations of the girls' uniforms for special occasions, such as honor roll assemblies or celebrations honoring the patron saint of their institution.

Introduce

The following list represents words, expressions, and grammar topics re-entered from Book 1: numbers 0–31, physical characteristics, school subjects, school supplies, *gustar* expressions, time-telling, food, family, pets, clothing, personal hygiene items, places and buildings, health-care items

26   Capítulo 1

Planning

Cross-Curricular Connections

Art Connection *(pp. 31–32)*
Have students design textbook covers. Let them choose one of the subjects listed in the *Vocabulario para conversar.* Encourage them to be as creative as possible. Display the completed covers or have students use them to cover their books.

Journalism Connection *(pp. 40–41)*
Have pairs of students write an article about an imagined conversation between a Mexican student and an American student who is visiting Mexico. With each student assuming one of the roles, have them compare experiences and tell about the advantages and disadvantages of attending their particular schools.

Career Connection *(pp. 50–51)*
Have individuals pretend that they are interviewing for the position of high-school principal. The screening committee has asked them to provide the following: a) a description of the types of teachers they will hire; b) five main rules for students and staff; and c) a list of extracurricular activities to be offered.

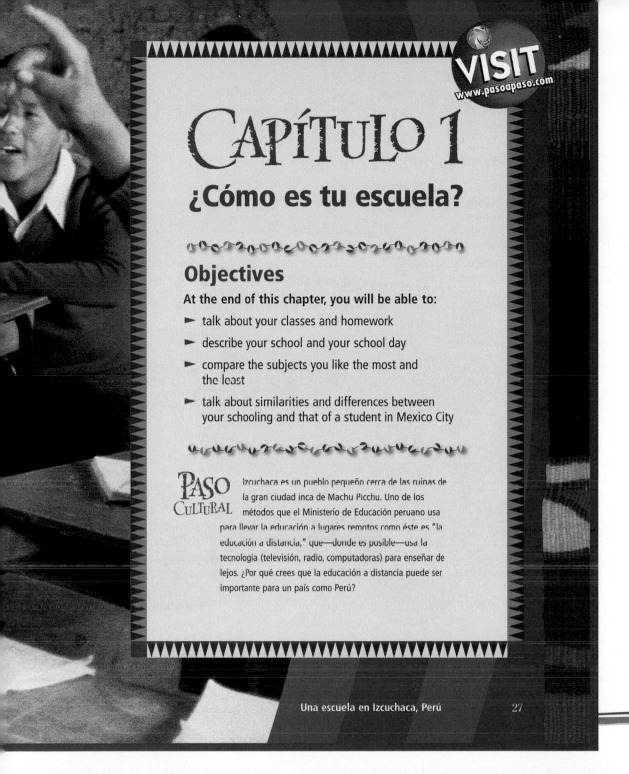

CAPÍTULO 1
¿Cómo es tu escuela?

Objectives

At the end of this chapter, you will be able to:

► talk about your classes and homework

► describe your school and your school day

► compare the subjects you like the most and the least

► talk about similarities and differences between your schooling and that of a student in Mexico City

PASO CULTURAL

Izcuchaca es un pueblo pequeño cerca de las ruinas de la gran ciudad inca de Machu Picchu. Uno de los métodos que el Ministerio de Educación peruano usa para llevar la educación a lugares remotos como éste es "la educación a distancia," que—donde es posible—usa la tecnología (televisión, radio, computadoras) para enseñar de lejos. ¿Por qué crees que la educación a distancia puede ser importante para un país como Perú?

Una escuela en Izcuchaca, Perú   27

Spanish in Your Community
Have students interview exchange students, students from a Spanish-speaking country, or adults in the community who studied in a Spanish-speaking country. During the interview, students should find out what their school was like compared to a U.S. school (school hours, courses, and school activities). Have students share their findings with the class.

Paso cultural
Los Andes de Perú son altos y difíciles de pasar. También es difícil la geografía de la selva amazónica *(Amazon)*. Por eso el Ministerio de Educación busca maneras nuevas de llevar información a los estudiantes.

(pp. 26–27, photo)
Peru is the third-largest country in South America and has an 87 percent literacy rate. Izcuchaca is a small town with a population of only about 1,700. Located in a valley in the Andean Sierra Central, it is 2,800 (9,100 feet) meters above sea level.

Preview

Cultural Objective
- To compare school subjects in a Spanish-speaking country with those in the U.S.

¡Piensa en la CULTURA!

Escuelas en California y Argentina

Mira las fotos. Los estudiantes que vemos están hablando de su escuela, de sus clases y de sus tareas.

"¿Cuál es el número de tu armario?"

¿Tienes un armario en tu escuela? ¿Qué contiene? ¿Cómo te gustaría decorarlo?

Don Quixote (1955), Pablo Picasso

"Esta semana vamos a empezar a leer Don Quijote."

¿Qué sabes de la literatura española o latinoamericana?

28   Capítulo 1

Options

Strategies for Reaching All Students

Spanish-Speaking Students
Ask: *¿Has estudiado en otra secundaria? ¿Cómo era igual y cómo era diferente? ¿Te gustaría seguir estudiando después de graduarte de la escuela secundaria? ¿Por qué?*

 Un paso más Ex. 1-A

Students Needing Extra Help
(p. 28, right photo): Tell students briefly about *Don Quijote* or have them research the subject. Bring in some Spanish literature.
(p. 29, top photo): Students may not have the vocabulary to answer questions about biology, chemistry, or physics. Let them move ahead to find the necessary words.
(p. 29, bottom photo): Review Book 1, Chap. 2, for school-related words.

Cultural Notes

(p. 28, left photo)
In U.S. high schools, students may often chat with friends between classes at their lockers. Students in Latin America don't usually have lockers; they carry their class materials with them. Most students remain in their classroom and the teachers travel from class to class. Study groups are commonly formed within a classroom, and individuals may meet outside of school for cooperative study sessions and test preparation.

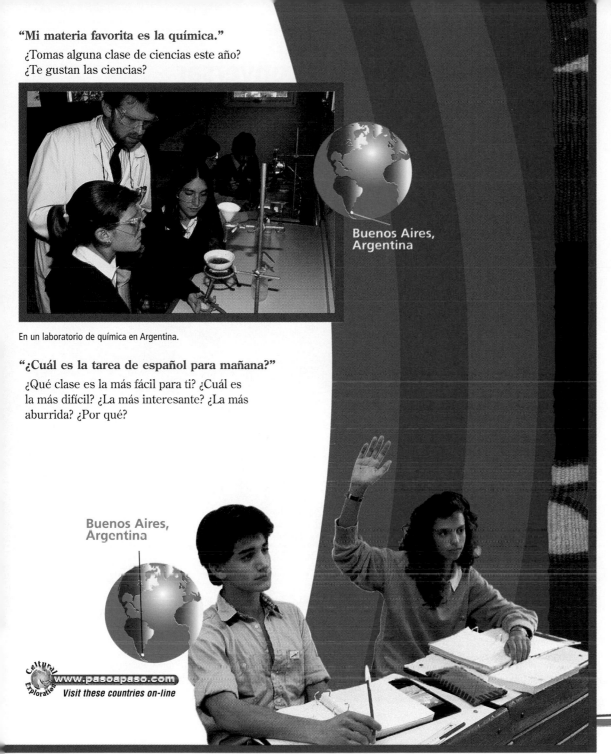

"Mi materia favorita es la química."

¿Tomas alguna clase de ciencias este año?
¿Te gustan las ciencias?

Answers: ¡Piensa en la cultura!
Answers to inductive questions will vary.

En un laboratorio de química en Argentina.

"¿Cuál es la tarea de español para mañana?"

¿Qué clase es la más fácil para ti? ¿Cuál es
la más difícil? ¿La más interesante? ¿La más
aburrida? ¿Por qué?

Buenos Aires,
Argentina

Buenos Aires,
Argentina

www.pasoapaso.com
Visit these countries on-line

Paso cultural
Picasso pintó a Don Quijote y Sancho como
siluetas *(silhouettes)* negras./Como indica el
texto, *El ingenioso hidalgo, Don Quijote de
la Mancha* es una novela muy importante en
la historia de la literatura. Sus personajes
(characters) son héroes folklóricos en
España y puede ser por eso que Picasso los
escogió para pintar.

(p. 28, right photo)
Don Quijote de la Mancha has long been a
favorite folk hero in Spanish literature. He
and his squire, Sancho Panza, are rendered
in this lithograph by Pablo Picasso, who
examined literary themes during the 1950s.
*El ingenioso hidalgo, Don Quijote de la
Mancha* was originally published in two
parts, the first in 1605 and the second in
1615. Cervantes's story is often considered
to be the first true novel in Western literature.

(p. 29, photos)
Argentina has one of the highest literacy
rates in Latin America and one of the highest rates of secondary school enrollment,
exceeded only by Cuba. As in the U.S., there
has been a renewed emphasis in Argentine
high schools on mathematics and science
courses to prepare students for jobs in technology and science. Ask students: What are
some other subjects or skills that you feel
schools should emphasize?

Present

Chapter Theme
School: Subjects and equipment

Communicative Objectives
- To name school subjects
- To describe school equipment
- To make comparisons

 Overheads 6–7

 Vocabulary Art BLMs/CD-ROM

 Vocabulary Tape 1-1

Grammar Preview
El / la más and *el / la menos* + adj. are reviewed here lexically. A review of superlatives appears on pp. 44–45.

Teaching Suggestions
Preparing students to speak: Use one or two options from each of the categories of Comprehensible Input, Physical Response, or Limited Verbal Response. For a complete explanation of these categories and some sample activities, see pp. T20–T21.

Vocabulario para conversar

¿Cuándo tienes geografía?

Vas a necesitar estas palabras y expresiones para hablar sobre tus clases. Después de leerlas varias veces, practícalas con un(a) compañero(a).

el reloj*

sacar una buena / mala nota

la bandera

el armario

la computadora

el bolso

* We also use the word *el reloj* or *el reloj pulsera* for "wristwatch."

30   Capítulo 1

Options

Strategies for Reaching All Students

Spanish-Speaking Students

 Un paso más Exs. 1-B, 1-C

Students Needing Extra Help
Have students begin to fill in their Organizers. Review reading directions in the target language. Remind students that names of languages are not capitalized. Give some examples of *sacar: ¿Por qué sacas buena nota en la clase de español?* Get a sample report card to encourage discussion.
Give some examples using *álgebra* so that students can manipulate the adjective: *El álgebra es aburrida.*

If necessary, refer to Book 1, Chap. 11, to review superlatives.
Give some examples with *el problema* so that students can use the proper form of the adjective.

el laboratorio

la literatura

la geografía

el álgebra (f.)*

el alemán

la geometría

el francés

la biología

la química

la historia

la página

¡NO OLVIDES!

Hacer ejercicio means "to exercise." *Hacer unos ejercicios* means "to do exercises," as for a homework assignment.

También necesitas . . .

el idioma[†]	*language*		
la materia	*school subject*		
el informe	*report*		
próximo, -a	*next*		
alguno (algún), -a	*some*		
repasar	*to review*		
por suerte	*luckily*		
tan + *adj.* + como	*as* + adj. + *as*		

¿Y qué quiere decir . . . ?

escribir	el examen
el capítulo	la lección
la composición	el problema[†]
el ejercicio	la prueba

* Note that *álgebra* is a feminine noun. However, we use the article *el* with feminine nouns beginning with stressed *a* or *ha*.
† Note that *el idioma* and *el problema* are masculine nouns although they end in *a*.

Class Starter Review

On the day following the initial vocabulary presentation, you might begin the class with this activity:
Have students ask three classmates for their favorite and least favorite classes. Record responses to see which received the most votes.

Multicultural Perspectives

In ancient Mexico, education was important to the Aztecs. Students attended a temple-school called a *telpochcalli,* where they received instruction on temple services and also learned to prepare for war. The children of the nobles attended *calmecac.* Students of other classes were allowed to attend these schools if they exhibited certain special abilities. The *cuicacalli* were special schools for music and dance for those students who showed talents in these areas. Ask students to share any information they may have about the educational systems of other past or present cultures.

Internet Activities
Juegos
Have students go to www.pasoapaso.com for additional activities and practice.

Learning Spanish Through Action
STAGING VOCABULARY: *Levanten, Pongan*
MATERIALS: students' books
DIRECTIONS: Direct students to put all the books they have with them on their desks. Ask them to hold up a book for the class you mention. You might choose to review locations by giving directions to put books in certain places.

Multiple Intelligences
Bodily/Kinesthetic
See Learning Spanish Through Action.
Logical/Mathematical
See Class Starter Review.
Verbal/Linguistic
See Vocabulary Tape 1-1.
Verbal/Linguistic and Visual/Spatial
Place ten school items on a table. Give students one minute to look at the objects. Then cover the table with a cloth. Ask students to write down the Spanish names of as many of the objects as they can remember. Students who have all ten items should turn their papers over, and those who don't have all ten should share what they remembered with each other until everyone's list is complete.
Visual/Spatial
See Overheads 6–7 and the Vocabulary Art BLMs/CD-ROM.

Practice & Apply

Reteach / Review: Vocabulary

Ex. 1: To extend this dialogue, *Estudiante A* can respond to *Estudiante B*'s news with expressions of disappointment, disbelief, or relief (*¡Vaya! ¡Qué bueno! ¡Qué lástima!*).

Ex. 2: To extend this dialogue *Estudiante A* can react to *Estudiante B*'s reply and then name the subject that is most interesting in his or her opinion. Encourage students to begin their extended responses with an expression of surprise or interest (*¡No me digas! ¿De veras?*).

Answers: Empecemos a conversar

1 ESTUDIANTE A

a. ¿Cuál es la tarea de historia?

b. ...de química?

c. ...de biología?

d. ...de literatura?

e. ...de geografía?

f. ...de álgebra?

g. ...de español?

h. Questions will vary, but look for *de* + school subject.

ESTUDIANTE B

a.–h. Answers will vary, but look for *tenemos que* + inf.

Empecemos a conversar

Túrnate con un(a) compañero(a) para ser *Estudiante A* y *Estudiante B*. Reemplacen las palabras subrayadas en el modelo con las palabras representadas o escritas en los recuadros. Si ven pueden dar su propia respuesta.

1

A —¿Cuál es la tarea de <u>geometría</u>?
B —Tenemos que <u>hacer los problemas 20 y 21 de la página 10</u>.
   o: *Por suerte no tenemos tarea.*

Estudiante A

a.
b.
c.
d.
e.
f.
g.
h.

Estudiante B

hacer los problemas 20 y 21 de la página 10

escribir una composición

hacer un informe

repasar la lección

leer un capítulo

estudiar dos páginas

hacer algunos ejercicios

2   interesante

A —*Para ti, ¿qué materia es la más <u>interesante</u>?*
B —*Para mí, <u>la química</u>.*

Estudiante A

a. fácil
b. difícil
c. aburrida
d. divertida
e. importante
f.

Estudiante B

32   Capítulo 1

Options

Strategies for Reaching All Students

Students Needing Extra Help

Ex. 3: Brainstorm the location of these objects before beginning the exercise.

Exs. 4–5: Brainstorm possible responses to *¿Por qué?*

Ex. 5: Remind students that they can use the preterite (*Saqué buena nota porque estudié mucho*) or the present (*Saco buena nota porque estudio mucho*).

Ex. 6: Brainstorm why learning another language is important. Review *para* + inf. Give some examples.

Ex. 7: Review adjectives describing color, size, and material (Book 1, Chap. 9).

Enrichment

Ex. 2: Once students have finished this exercise, have the class vote on which subject they consider most interesting, important, etc., by raising their hands as you call out subjects. Keep a tally on the chalkboard. Discuss the results, asking individuals whether they agree or disagree with what the majority of the class said. Ask them to justify their opinions.

Cooperative Learning

Divide the class into groups of three or four. Tell the groups to rank each of the subjects listed in the vocabulary section from favorite to least favorite. (You might like to add other subjects to the list.) Have students use 1 for favorite, 2 for second favorite, and so on. Appoint one student in each group to compile the results. Write each group's listings on the chalkboard and tabulate.

3

A —¿Hay _bandera_ en la sala de historia?
B —_Claro que sí. En (casi) todas las salas hay
una bandera._
    o: _No, en esa sala no hay bandera._

¡NO OLVIDES!

Este, esta; estos, estos = this; these
Ese, esa; esos, esas = that; those

Estudiante A   **Estudiante B**

a.

b.   c.   d.

e.   f.   g.

Empecemos a escribir

Escribe tus respuestas en español.

4 ¿Qué materia te gusta más? ¿Y cuál te gusta menos? ¿Por qué?

5 ¿En qué materias sacas buena nota? ¿Y en cuáles sacas mala nota? ¿Por qué?

6 ¿Hay clases de alemán y francés en tu escuela? ¿Crees que es importante aprender otro idioma? ¿Por qué?

7 ¿Usas una mochila o un bolso para llevar tus cosas? ¿Cómo es? ¿Cuántos compartimientos tiene? Generalmente, ¿qué llevas allí?

MORE PRACTICE

- Más práctica y tarea, p. 528
- Practice Workbook 1-1, 1-2

También se dice

Con frecuencia, en los países donde se habla español, se usan palabras diferentes para decir lo mismo. En esta sección puedes ver algunas de esas palabras.

el computador
el ordenador

el guardarropa
el guardalibros
el casillero
el ropero

la bolsa
la cartera

For _la materia,_ we can also say _la asignatura._

For _el informe,_ we can also say _la presentación_ or _el reporte._

Vocabulario para conversar   33

Present

Chapter Theme
School: Locations

Communicative Objectives
- To name places in a school
- To talk about activities associated with school
- To name people who work at a school

 Overheads 8–9

 Vocabulary Art BLMs/CD-ROM

 Vocabulary Tape 1-2

Grammar Preview
Conozco / conoces are presented here lexically. The paradigm of present-tense *conocer* is presented on p. 48.

Vocabulario para conversar

¿Conoces a todos los profesores?

Aquí tienes el resto del vocabulario que necesitas en este capítulo para hablar sobre tus clases.

el auditorio

el mapa

el escenario

el asiento

el sacapuntas, *pl.* los sacapuntas

la grapadora

el sujetapapeles, *pl.* los sujetapapeles

el proyector

la diapositiva

34   Capítulo 1

Options

Strategies for Reaching All Students

Spanish-Speaking Students

 Un paso más Ex. 1-D

Students Needing Extra Help
También necesitas . . . : Show how *escolar* is used as an adjective: *el año escolar, el periódico escolar.*
Because *entregar* follows *escolar,* emphasize that this is a verb. Give an example of how it is used.
Show the entire *conocer* paradigm to those who need to see the whole conjugation.

Learning Spanish Through Action
STAGING VOCABULARY: *Apunten, Señalen, Toquen*
MATERIALS: transparency of vocabulary and / or drawings of items listed that are not in the room
DIRECTIONS: Direct students to point to or touch items in the room. As each item is shown, make a true or false statement about it. *(El sacapuntas está a la derecha del escritorio.)* The class signals with thumbs up for true or thumbs down for false.

la oficina

hacer fila

el bufet de ensaladas

la pared

la cafetería

También necesitas . . .

escolar	*school* (adj.)	se prohíbe	*it's prohibited*
entregar	here: *to hand in*	la respuesta	*answer*
hacer una pregunta	*to ask a question*	el consejero,	*counselor*
contestar	*to answer*	la consejera	
explicar	*to explain*	el director,	*principal*
conocer *(c → zc):*	*to know, to be*	la directora	
	acquainted with:		
(yo) conozco	*I know*	**¿Y qué quiere decir . . . ?**	
(tú) conoces	*you know*	usar	preguntar
se permite	*it's allowed*	la pregunta	el edificio

Vocabulario para conversar 35

Teaching Suggestions
Preparing students to speak: Use one or two options from each of the categories of Comprehensible Input, Physical Response, or Limited Verbal Response. For a complete explanation of these categories and some sample activities, see pp. T20–T21.

Point out the similarity between *el mapa* and previous vocabulary in this chapter *(el idioma, el problema).*

Class Starter Review
On the day following initial vocabulary presentation, you might begin the class with this activity: Have pairs of students take turns naming objects in the classroom.

Internet Activities
Juegos
Have students go to www.pasoapaso.com for additional activities and practice.

Extended Written Practice/Homework
1. Choose four objects from pp. 34–35 and write sentences telling where they are found or who has them in your school: *El profesor de geografía tiene muchas diapositivas.*
2. Write two sentences telling the name of a counselor and a principal at your school. Include a brief description of each person.

3. Write two sentences telling when the school year begins and ends. Tell how many months it lasts.

Multiple Intelligences
Bodily/Kinesthetic and Visual/Spatial
See Learning Spanish Through Action.
Verbal/Linguistic
See Vocabulary Tape 1-2 and Class Starter Review.
Visual/Spatial
See Overheads 8–9, the Vocabulary Art BLMs/CD-ROM, and Students Needing Extra Help.

Practice & Apply

Ex. 8: Students can extend this dialogue and review their vocabulary for directions by having *Estudiante A* ask *Estudiante B* where the room in question is located.

Answers: Empecemos a conversar

8 ESTUDIANTE A

a. ¿Qué hay en la cafetería?

b. ... en la oficina?

c. ... en la sala de clase?

d. ... en la biblioteca?

e. ... en la escuela?

f. Questions will vary.

ESTUDIANTE B

a.–f. Answers will vary.

9 ESTUDIANTE A

a. Necesito un proyector. ¿Dónde hay uno?

b. ... un mapa. ... uno?

c. ... una bandera. ... una?

d. ... un diccionario. ... uno?

e. ... una grapadora. ... una?

f. ... unos sujetapapeles. ... unos?

g. Questions will vary, but look for correct use of the indefinite article.

ESTUDIANTE B

a.–g. Answers will vary.

Empecemos a conversar

8

A —¿Qué hay en *el auditorio*?

B —*Muchos asientos y un escenario grande.*

Estudiante A   **Estudiante B**

a.   b.   c.

d.   e.   f.

9

A —*Necesito un sacapuntas. ¿Dónde hay uno?*

B —*Hay uno en la sala de arte.*

o: *No sé. Lo siento.*

Estudiante A   **Estudiante B**

a.   b.   c.

en la sala de ___

en la oficina de ___

en el escritorio de ___

d.   e.   f.   g.

36   Capítulo 1

Options

Strategies for Reaching All Students

Spanish-Speaking Students

Ex. 8: After this exercise, ask: *¿En qué clase dan más tarea? ¿En qué clase tienes poca tarea? ¿Por qué es importante hacer la tarea? ¿Siempre la haces?*

Ex. 15: After this exercise, have Spanish-speaking students respond in writing: *Describe tu escuela. ¿Es nueva o vieja? ¿Es de un piso o de varios? ¿Tiene gimnasio, auditorio o teatro u otros salones especiales?*

 Un paso más Ex. 1-E

Students Needing Extra Help

Ex. 8: Brainstorm what things could be found in these rooms.

Ex. 9: Brainstorm in what area of the building you could find these. If you find them all in the room you are in, review location words so that students can say *Hay uno cerca del libro,* etc.

Ex. 10: Brainstorm possible answers. These responses require a lot of vocabulary and some sophisticated structures. There could be many responses for students to formulate, depending on your school's environment and individual teacher rules.

Ex. 11: Start with responses from Ex. 10 and brainstorm others: eating in class, etc.

Ex. 12: If students can't think of any situations in which they stand in line, remind them of middle and elementary school, sporting events, movies, etc.

Ex. 14: Review location words.

10 entregar la tarea tarde

A —¿*Se permite entregar la tarea tarde?*
B —*No. Debemos entregar la tarea a tiempo.*
   o: *Sí, se permite.*

Estudiante A

a. usar las computadoras después de las clases

b. llevar pantalones cortos

c. hacer preguntas en un examen

d. escuchar música en clase

e. contestar en inglés en la clase de español

f.

Estudiante B

Empecemos a escribir y a leer

Escribe tus respuestas en español.

11 ¿Qué se prohibe en la escuela? ¿Y en la clase de español?

12 En tu escuela, ¿tienes que hacer fila en la cafetería? ¿Para qué más debes hacer fila?

13 ¿A qué hora empieza el día escolar? ¿A qué hora termina? ¿Cuántas horas estás en la escuela?

14 ¿Dónde queda la oficina del director (de la directora)? ¿Y la oficina de los consejeros? ¿Cómo se llama el director (la directora)? ¿Conoces a los consejeros? ¿Cómo son?

15 ¿Qué clase es? Lee las frases y escribe la respuesta.

a. Hay diccionarios en dos idiomas sobre el escritorio del profesor y un mapa de América Central en la pared. Las preguntas del profesor y las respuestas de los estudiantes son en otro idioma.

b. Hay una regla en el escritorio de la profesora. La profesora explica un problema. Algunos estudiantes usan sus calculadoras. Estudian círculos y triángulos.

c. Hay mapas de todos los países en las paredes. El profesor tiene diapositivas de océanos y montañas. Los estudiantes van a la biblioteca a menudo. Deben hacer muchos informes.

www.pasoapaso.com

También se dice

el tajador
el sacaminas

formar fila
hacer cola

el salón de actos

la butaca

el comedor

el foro

MORE PRACTICE

• Más práctica y tarea, p. 529
• Practice Workbook 1–3, 1–4

Vocabulario para conversar   37

10 ESTUDIANTE A

a. ¿Se permite usar las computadoras después de las clases?
b. ... llevar pantalones cortos?
c. ... hacer preguntas en un examen?
d. ... escuchar música en clase?
e. ... contestar en inglés en la clase de español?
f. Questions will vary, but should include *Se permite* + inf.

ESTUDIANTE B

a.–f. Answers will vary; look for *Debemos* + inf.

Answers: Empecemos a escribir y a leer

11 Answers will vary; look for the expression *Se prohibe* + inf.

12 Answers will vary, but look for use of *tengo*.

13 Answers will vary, but look for correct use of time expressions.

14 Answers will vary.

15 a. español; b. geometría; c. geografía

 Practice Wkbk. 1-3, 1-4

 Audio Activity 1.2

 Writing Activities 1-A, 1-B, 1-C

Pruebas 1-3, 1-4

Enrichment
Ex. 10: As a homework assignment, have students go to their public library and report on the rules of a specific department (children's, young adult, adult, audiovisual). Students can list the rules under either of two columns: *Se prohibe* and *Se permite*. If they wish, students can also write what they think of these rules and suggest changes. As a class, discuss what students wrote, comparing the rules of the various departments of the library.

Extended Written Practice/Homework
1. Using the vocabulary from *También necesitas...* on p. 35 and other words you know, write three sentences saying what teachers should do and what students should do: *Los estudiantes deben entregar las tareas a tiempo.*
2. Write three sentences saying what is allowed or is *not* prohibited in the ideal class: *En la clase ideal ...*

Multiple Intelligences
Verbal/Linguistic
See Exs. 8–10 and Audio Activity 1.2.
Visual/Spatial
See Exs. 11–15, Practice Wkbk. 1-3 and 1-4, and Writing Activities 1-A, 1-B, and 1-C.

Practice

Answers:
¡Comuniquemos!

1 Answers will vary. Look for correct use of *el señor / la señora / la señorita* and a variety of appropriate adjectives.

2 Answers will vary. Look for correct use of time expressions and *nos gustaría.*

3 Answers will vary. Look for a variety of appropriate adjectives and nouns and logical verbs for the rooms being discussed. For example: *el auditorio (ver / escuchar / hablar), la biblioteca (buscar / leer / estudiar / hacer tarea), la cafetería (cocinar / comer / hablar con), la oficina de los consejeros (hablar / aprender)*

¡Comuniquemos!

Aquí tienes otra oportunidad para usar el vocabulario de este capítulo.

1 Haz una lista de las tres materias que te gustan más. Compárala con la lista de un(a) compañero(a). Hablen de:

- por qué les gustan más esas tres clases
- quiénes son los profesores y cómo son
- cuánta tarea tienen que hacer

2 Compara tu horario con el de un(a) compañero(a). Hablen de:

- a qué hora empieza y a qué hora termina el día escolar
- qué clases toman juntos *(together)* y cuáles no
- qué les gustaría cambiar *(change)* en sus horarios para tener un horario ideal

Pueden escribir su horario ideal y compararlo con los horarios de otros compañeros.

3 Con un(a) compañero(a) discutan sobre algunas salas de la escuela, por ejemplo: el auditorio, la biblioteca, la cafetería, la oficina de los consejeros. Hablen de:

- cómo es la sala
- qué hay en esa sala
- qué hacen las personas allí

Dos muchachas mexicanas se preparan para un examen de inglés.

Horario de un estudiante en Madrid

38   Capítulo 1

Options

Strategies for Reaching All Students

Spanish-Speaking Students
Ex. 1: Have Spanish-speaking students survey the class and report the results orally or in writing. *Haz una encuesta. Ve de grupo en grupo para aprender cuáles son las clases más populares y qué características tienen en común los profesores de estas clases. Después de hablar con cada grupo, presenta tus resultados a la clase entera oralmente o en forma escrita.*

Students Needing Extra Help
Rather than have students do all exercises, divide them into groups, assign an activity to them, and have them report back to the class. Ex. 1 is the easiest; Ex. 2 is the most challenging.
Use the vocabulary sections from Book 1 Organizers.
¿Qué sabes ahora?: Have students write out this section so they can check off what they have mastered.

Enrichment
Ex. 2: To extend this dialogue, *Estudiante A* can ask *Estudiante B* which school he or she prefers and why.

ENGLISH SUMMER S.A. SCHOOLS

UN VERANO "EXCLUSIVO" PARA SUS HIJOS

COLEGIOS RESIDENCIALES DE INGLES EN VERANO (ESPAÑA)

- Empresa familiar, dirigida por Mrs. Margaret Wright.
- 14 años de Experiencia.
- 6,000 familias de toda España nos avalan.
- INGLES, deporte, diversión, formación humana y convivencia.
- Centros de propiedad en la provincia de Tarragona.
- Antiguo Hotel-Balneario "La Capella" (a 200 m. Monasterio de Poblet).
- Casa Señorial de Vallclara.
- Estancias de 4 o 3 semanas.
- Edades: De 6 a 13 y de 14 a 18 años.

PARA MAS INFORMACION: Solicite nuestro folleto

Oficinas centrales:
ENGLISH SUMMER, S.A.
Rambla vella 2. Edif. Hotel Imperial Tárraco - 43003 TARRAGONA.

Tfno. 977/ 23.45.08. Fax: 977/ 23.45.19

ACADEMIAS DE LENGUA INGLESA - CURSOS DE IDIOMAS EN EL EXTRANJERO - COLEGIOS DE INGLES EN VERANO

¿Qué sabes ahora?

Can you:

- talk about your classes and homework?
  —Para la clase de _____ tengo que _____ .
- express your opinion about your subjects?
  —Para ti, ¿qué materia es la más _____?
  —Para mí, _____ .
- talk about rules and regulations in your Spanish class?
  —En mi clase de español se permite _____ y se prohibe _____ .

Multiple Intelligences
Interpersonal/Social, Logical/Mathematical, and Verbal/Linguistic
See Ex. 1.
Interpersonal/Social and Verbal/Linguistic
See Exs. 2–3.
Verbal/Linguistic
See Audio Activity 1.3.

Cultural Notes

(p. 39, realia)
This advertisement from a Spanish publication asks parents to consider enrolling their children in a summer English-language program. Students live on campus, experiencing immersion in the foreign language. The ability to speak English has acquired added value in Europe in recent years, as countries continue to integrate their economies in the European Union.

Present & Apply

Cultural Objective

• To compare schooling in Spanish-speaking countries and the U.S.

Critical Thinking: Identifying Stereotypes

After students have read the *Perspectiva cultural,* review the term "stereotype." Make sure they understand that not all high schools in Mexico are like the one attended by Gilda and her friends. In rural Mexico, schools are less formal and have fewer amenities. Have students offer suggestions as to how a rural school in Mexico and in the U.S. might be different from one in a large city.

Multicultural Perspectives

One of the major reforms of the Mexican Revolution of 1910 was to change the educational system so that all children could receive a free public education. Today, the educational system is divided into levels: elementary, secondary, and higher education. At the elementary level, children first attend a kindergarten, or *jardín de niños.* They then go on to *la primaria,* which takes six years, and then to *la enseñanza media básica (secundaria),* which takes three years. After finishing this basic

Perspectiva cultural

¿A qué hora llegas a la escuela? Imagina un día escolar en que los estudiantes llegan a las dos de la tarde. ¿Cómo es su día? ¿A qué hora regresan a la casa?

Gilda va a la escuela por la tarde. Sus clases empiezan a las dos de la tarde y terminan a las ocho de la noche. Hay tantos estudiantes en la Ciudad de México que la mayoría de las escuelas tienen que ofrecer dos sesiones. La sesión de la mañana, el turno matutino, es para estudiantes menores de once años. La sesión de la tarde, el turno vespertino, es para estudiantes mayores de once años.

"Me encanta ir a la escuela por la tarde," dice Gilda. "Puedo levantarme tarde."

Gilda toma doce clases y pasa 30 horas por semana en la escuela. Sus clases incluyen español, historia, geografía de México, educación cívica, biología, química, física, inglés, arte y educación física. Las clases de computadoras y de matemáticas son sus clases favoritas. Gilda estudia las mismas materias durante todo el año.

La escuela de Gilda tiene reglas muy estrictas. Por ejemplo, las muchachas pueden llevar pantalones sólo cuando hace frío. Y nunca pueden llevar maquillaje ni tacones altos. Los muchachos no pueden llevar ni gorras ni aretes.

Gilda siempre sale de la escuela con Sonia y Enrique, que son hermanos y viven cerca de su casa. Inmediatamente después de salir de la escuela, Gilda y Sonia se maquillan y Enrique se pone su gorra de béisbol.

La cultura desde tu perspectiva

1 Para ti, ¿quiénes tienen un horario más difícil, los estudiantes mexicanos o tú y tus compañeros? ¿Por qué?

2 ¿Te gustaría tomar clases por la tarde y por la noche? ¿Por qué? ¿Cuáles crees que son las ventajas *(advantages)* y las desventajas de un sistema de dos sesiones al día?

www.pasoapaso.com

Jóvenes colombianos escuchando cintas en un laboratorio de idiomas en Cali

40 Capítulo 1

Options

Strategies for Reaching All Students

Spanish-Speaking Students

Have Spanish-speaking students respond in writing: *¿Tienes las mismas clases que Gilda? ¿Cuáles tienen en común? ¿Cómo sería tu día si tuvieras clases en turno vespertino?*

 Un paso más Ex. 1-F

Students Needing Extra Help

Have students take notes to use as they study for the chapter test.
Discuss cultural differences with regard to strictness and discipline.
Exs. 1–3: Review comparatives (Book 1, Chap. 11).
The last question may pose a challenge for some students. Guide them through it.

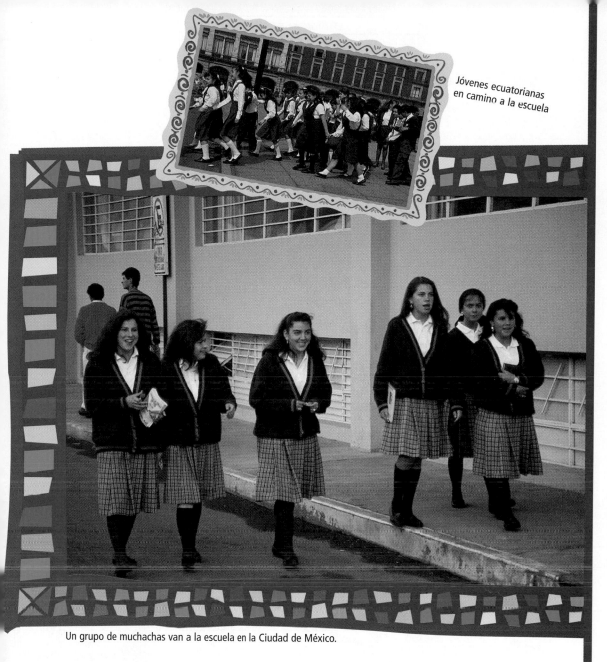

Jóvenes ecuatorianas en camino a la escuela

Un grupo de muchachas van a la escuela en la Ciudad de México.

cycle, students can elect to continue to receive their *bachillerato* or *preparatoria*. This will prepare students for such careers as nursing, social work, or vocational jobs. Students who have finished their *preparatoria* can select from among universities, teachers' colleges, or technical educational institutions. Encourage students to share any knowledge they may have of the educational systems of other countries.

Answers
Answers to inductive questions will vary, but may include some time between 7:30 and 9:00 A.M. / Students in the *turno vespertino* return home some time late in the evening.

Answers: La cultura desde tu perspectiva
1–2 Answers will vary.

 Pasos vivos 2 CD-ROM
Maps, Notas culturales

 Internet Activities
Perspectiva cultural
Have students go to www.pasoapaso.com for additional activities and practice.

Cultural Notes

(p. 40, photo)
Almost all Colombian high-school students study a foreign language. The most commonly studied are English, French, and German. Many young people attend private high schools, approximately 40 percent of which are bilingual. In addition, various institutes in Colombia offer private instruction in a second language.

(p. 41, photos)
Students in Latin America often wear uniforms, such as those worn by the girls in these photos. Both public and private school students wear uniforms, which tend to be conservative in appearance. Girls usually wear skirts and boys wear dark slacks and a tie. School uniforms are often viewed as a way to contribute a sense of community and equality within a student body.

Preview

 Overhead 10

Answers

A There are four forms of *salir: salgo, sales, salimos, salir. Salgo* is the *yo* form. Verbs with a similar *yo* form include *hacer (hago), traer (traigo),* and *tener (tengo).*

B The word that comes before *bonita* is *tan.* The word that comes after is *como.* / The new employee is not as pretty as Marianela.

Gramática en contexto

42   Capítulo 1

Options

Strategies for Reaching All Students

Students Needing Extra Help
Have students begin to fill in the grammar section of the Organizer.

Extended Written Practice/Homework
1. Write three sentences telling when different people leave school: *Los estudiantes que practican deportes salen a las seis de la tarde.*
2. Write three sentences telling to what places different people go out: *A veces mis padres salen a un restaurante con sus amigos.*

Multiple Intelligences
Logical/Mathematical
Have students work in groups to create a word search made of a grid of small squares with a letter in each one. These letters form hidden words of consecutive letters in any direction. The hidden words should be chapter vocabulary for school subjects. When the word searches are complete, have groups trade papers and see how many words they can circle.

¿Qué va a hacer Pablo? ¿Va a salir con Marianela o con la empleada nueva? ¡Vea el próximo capítulo de *Marianela* mañana, a la misma hora y en el mismo canal!

Present

Teaching Suggestions
Refer to Book 1, Chap. 9, to review regular *-ir* endings.

A As you know, *salir* means "to leave, to go out." How many forms of *salir* can you find in the scenes of this *telenovela?* Which is the *yo* form? What other verbs do you know that have a similar *yo* form?

B One way to make comparisons is by using *más / menos* + adjective + *que*. We can also make other kinds of comparisons. Find the sentence in Frame 4 in which Pablo compares Marianela to the new employee. What word comes before *bonita?* And after? What do you think Pablo is saying?

El verbo *salir*

Salir follows the pattern of regular *-ir* verbs except in the *yo* form, *salgo*. Here are all its present-tense forms:

(yo)	sal**go**	(nosotros) (nosotras)	sal**imos**
(tú)	sal**es**	(vosotros) (vosotras)	sal**ís**
Ud. (él) (ella)	sal**e**	Uds. (ellos) (ellas)	sal**en**

Gramática en contexto   43

Visual/Spatial
See Overhead 10.

Present & Practice

Class Starter Review

On the day following the presentation of comparatives, you might begin the class with this activity: Post pairs of pictures with obvious similarities on the chalkboard (two famous actresses, two ugly dogs, two tall basketball stars, etc.). Have students develop comparative statements. *(Sally Field es tan famosa como Whoopi Goldberg.)*

Answers

1 ESTUDIANTE A

a. ¿A qué hora sale de la casa tu padre (madre)?

b. ... salen tus abuelos?

c. ... sale tu hermano(a) mayor (menor)?

d. ... sales tú?

e. ... salen tú y tu hermano(a)?

ESTUDIANTE B

Answers will vary, but look for correct use of time expressions.

a. Sale ...

b. Salen ...

c. Sale ...

d. Salgo ...

e. Salimos ...

2 ESTUDIANTE A

Questions may vary, but may include: *¿A qué hora sales de tu (la) casa por la mañana en un día escolar? ¿Cuánto tiempo necesitas para llegar a la escuela?*

1 Habla de un sábado típico con un(a) compañero(a). Imagina que todas estas personas viven contigo. ¿A qué hora sale de la casa cada *(each)* persona y qué hace cuando sale?

tu hermano

A —*¿A qué hora sale de la casa tu hermano?*
B —*Sale a las nueve de la mañana para practicar deportes.*

a. tu padre / tu madre

b. tus abuelos

c. tu hermano(a) mayor / menor

d. tú

e. tú y tu hermano(a)

2 Ahora pregunta a tres personas a qué hora salen de su casa por la mañana en un día escolar. ¿Cuánto tiempo necesitan para llegar a la escuela?

La forma comparativa: *tan ... como*

To compare things that are the same, we use *tan* + adjective + *como*. In English we use "as ... as."

Elena es **tan** alta **como** su madre, pero no es **tan** deportista **como** ella.

3 Con un(a) compañero(a), comparen a los estudiantes de su clase. Usen los dibujos.

A —*(Patricia) es tan trabajadora como (Daniel), ¿no?*
B —*Sí, tienes razón.*
   o: *No, no tienes razón. (Patricia) es más / menos trabajadora que (Daniel).*

a.

b.

c.

¡NO OLVIDES!

• To make unequal comparisons, we use *más / menos* + adj. + *que*. *El álgebra es **más** fácil **que** la química.*

• We do not use *más / menos* with the words *mayor / menor* and *mejor / peor*. *Juan es **menor que** su hermano Luis.*

Options

Strategies for Reaching All Students

Students Needing Extra Help

Ex. 1: Use the vocabulary sections of the Book 1 Organizers to help determine which activities the people can do when they leave. Remind students that the exercise specifies activities done on Saturday.

Review how verb forms change when going from a question to an answer.

Ex. 2: Model. Remind students to use the *tú* form.

La forma comparativa: Students may find this concept and structure difficult.

Elaborate on *tan ... como.* Give some examples in English.

¡No olvides!: If available, review the grammar section of the Organizer from Book 1, Chap. 11.

Give a model using *menos.*

Review meanings of *mayor / menor* and *mejor / peor.* Give examples.

Emphasize by example that the noun can be dropped.

Give a sample using the English "good, better, best."

La forma superlativa: Write this formula on the chalkboard or overhead for each kind of noun: masculine singular, feminine singular, etc. Write it out in one straight line. Have students come to the chalkboard and fill in the formula with the information you have given them. Then add *de* to the formula. Emphasize this because students want to use *en.* Review *del.*

d.

e.

f.

g.

h.

i.

Repaso: La forma superlativa

Remember that to say something is the "most" or the "least," we use:

el / la / los / las + noun + *más / menos* + adjective

la prueba **más** difícil
el informe **menos** interesante

- To say something is the "most" or the "least" in a group or category, we use *de* after the adjective. For example:

Esta prueba es **la más** difícil **de** todas.
Estos informes son **los menos** interesantes **del** día.

4 Túrnate con un(a) compañero(a) para combinar palabras de las tres listas y expresar tu opinión. Por ejemplo:

Central Park es el parque más grande de la ciudad de Nueva York.

a. el profesor / la profesora
b. el edificio
c. la persona
d. la escuela
e. el almacén
f. el actor / la actriz
g.

alto, -a
bonito, -a
viejo, -a
grande
simpático, -a
guapo, -a
pequeño, -a

los Estados Unidos
la escuela
(nombre de un país)
(nombre de una comunidad)
(nombre de una ciudad)

¡NO OLVIDES!

We also use the irregular forms *mejor* and *peor, mayor* and *menor* in the superlative.
*Pepe es **el mejor** estudiante **de** la clase.*
*Pepe es **el menor de** la familia.*

Gramática en contexto 45

Present & Practice

Reteach / Review: Vocabulary

Ex. 5: To extend this dialogue, have *Estudiante A* ask *Estudiante B* for directions to the store.

Answers

5 ESTUDIANTE A

Adjectives may vary.

a. ¡Qué (bonitos) son tus jeans! / ¿Dónde los compraste?

b. ¡Qué (bonito) es tu suéter! / ¿Dónde lo compraste?

c. ¡Qué (bonitos) son tus calcetines! / ¿Dónde los compraste?

d. ¡Qué (bonita) es tu camiseta! / ¿Dónde la compraste?

e. ¡Qué (bonitos) son tu camisa y tus pantalones! / ¿Dónde los compraste?

f. ¡Qué (bonitas) son tus botas! / ¿Dónde las compraste?

g. ¡Qué (bonito) es tu bolso! / ¿Dónde lo compraste?

h. ¡Qué (bonita) es tu chaqueta! / ¿Dónde la compraste?

i. Questions will vary, but should follow the model. Look for correct adjective agreement and verb form with proper placement of correct direct object pronoun.

Repaso: El complemento directo: los pronombres *lo, la, los, las*

Remember that a direct object tells who or what receives the action of the verb. Here are the direct object pronouns in Spanish:

lo	*him, it, you* (formal)	**los**	*them, you* (m. pl.)
la	*her, it, you* (formal)	**las**	*them, you* (f. pl.)

* Direct object pronouns agree in number and gender with the nouns they replace. They usually come right before the verb.

—¿Tomaste **la prueba** la semana pasada?
—Sí, **la** tomé el viernes.

* When a pronoun replaces both a masculine and a feminine noun, we use *los*.

—¿Tomaste **la prueba** y **el examen**?
—Sí, **los** tomé.

5 Admira algo que tiene uno(a) de tus compañeros(as). Luego pregúntale dónde lo compró. Usa los dibujos.

A —*¡Qué (bonitos) son tus zapatos!*
B —*Gracias.*
A —*¿Dónde los compraste?*
B —*Los compré en el almacén Rogers.*

a.　　b.　　c.　　d.

e.　　f.　　g.　　h.　　i.

Options

Strategies for Reaching All Students

Students Needing Extra Help

Ex. 5: Avoid replacing *bonitos* with another adjective. Simply remind students of the four forms of direct object pronouns so that they won't be concerned about which adjective to use. The emphasis should be on direct object pronouns.

Review *tener, traer,* and *conocer.* If students have them available, they can use the Organizers from Book 1, Chaps. 5, 8, 9, 12, and 14.
El complemento directo: Refer to Book 1, Chap. 6, for a review.

Extended Written Practice/Homework

1. Write three pairs of sentences naming different foods that you do or do not like. Tell how often you eat them: *Me encantan las enchiladas. Las como a menudo.*
2. Write three pairs of sentences telling what classroom objects students have and if they bring them to class every day: *Sara tiene un bolso para libros. Lo trae a clase todos los días.*

Repaso: Los verbos *tener* y *traer*
El verbo *conocer*

Review the present-tense forms of *tener*.

(yo)	**tengo**	(nosotros) (nosotras)	**tenemos**
(tú)	**tienes**	(vosotros) (vosotras)	**tenéis**
Ud. (él) (ella)	**tiene**	Uds. (ellos) (ellas)	**tienen**

• Remember that we use *tener* in many different expressions:

—¿Cuántos años **tienes**?
—Dieciséis.

—**Tengo** hambre / sed.
—Pues **tienes que** comer / beber algo.

Review the present-tense forms of *traer*.

(yo)	**traigo**	(nosotros) (nosotras)	**traemos**
(tú)	**traes**	(vosotros) (vosotras)	**traéis**
Ud. (él) (ella)	**trae**	Uds. (ellos) (ellas)	**traen**

—¿Qué **traes** en la mochila?
—**Traigo** libros, lápices, bolígrafos y un sacapuntas.

En un restaurante mexicano,
Novato, California

ESTUDIANTE B
a. Los compré en . . .
b. Lo compré en . . .
c. Los compré en . . .
d. La compré en . . .
e. Los compré en . . .
f. Las compré en . . .
g. Lo compré en . . .
h. La compré en . . .
i. Answers will vary, but look for correct verb form with proper placement of correct direct object pronoun.

 Practice Wkbk. 1-8

 Writing Activity 1-G

 Prueba 1-8

Multiple Intelligences
Bodily/Kinesthetic and Verbal/Linguistic
Use the cube made of plastic foam from Book 1 for further practice in reviewing *tener, traer,* and *conocer.* If not available, you may take a plastic foam cube and write six subject pronouns *(yo, tú, Ud., nosotros, vosotros, Uds.)* in bold letters on each of the six sides. Toss the cube to the class and when a student catches it, name a verb in the infinitive and ask for the appropriate form of the verb using the pronoun that is facing upwards. Have more capable students form a complete sentence.
Visual/Spatial
See Practice Wkbk. 1-8 and Writing Activity 1-G.

Present & Practice

Answers

6 ESTUDIANTE A

a. Tengo que comprar un libro. ¿Adónde puedo ir?

b. ...comestibles...

c. ...zapatos...

d. ...pasta dentífrica...

e. ...un sello...

f. ...una falda...

g. Statements will vary.

ESTUDIANTE B

a. Yo conozco una librería por aquí.

b. ...un supermercado...

c. ...una zapatería...

d. ...una farmacia...

e. ...un correo...

f. ...una tienda (de ropa) / un almacén...

g. Answers will vary.

7 ESTUDIANTE A

a. ¿Quién trae el queso?

b. ...los refrescos?

c. ...la ensalada?

d. ...las frutas?

e. ...el pollo?

f. ...la leche?

g. ...la limonada?

h. ...el pan?

i. ...las naranjas?

Here are the present-tense forms of *conocer* ("to know, to be acquainted with").

(yo)	**conozco**	(nosotros) (nosotras)	**conocemos**
(tú)	**conoces**	(vosotros) (vosotras)	**conocéis**
Ud. (él) (ella)	**conoce**	Uds. (ellos) (ellas)	**conocen**

- Remember that we use *a* before the direct object if it refers to a person or an animal (especially a pet).

  Conozco a María Teresa. *but:* **Conozco** Madrid.

6 Pregúntale a un(a) compañero(a) si conoce algún lugar que quede cerca. Usa los dibujos.

A —*Tengo que comprar un regalo. ¿Adónde puedo ir?*
B —*Yo conozco una tienda (de regalos) por aquí.*

a.   b.   c.

d.   e.   f.   g.

Options

Strategies for Reaching All Students

Students Needing Extra Help
Ex. 7: Remind students that there may be two changes: one to the direct object and one to the verb.
Use the subject pronoun icon overhead transparency.
Ahora lo sabes: Have students write out this section so they can check off what they have mastered.

Extended Written Practice/Homework
1. Write three sentences saying that different students have classes during different hours: *Marta y yo tenemos la clase de química en la cuarta hora.*
2. Write three sentences telling whether your classmates or teachers know members of your family: *Mi profesor de biología conoce a mi hermano mayor.*

3. Write two pairs of sentences naming a teacher, counselor, or principal. Tell if you know them well: *La Sra. Blanco es consejera. No la conozco bien.*

7 La clase planea un picnic. Túrnate con tu compañero(a) para decir qué va a traer cada persona.

A —¿Quién trae el jamón?
B —Pedro y Sara lo traen.

(dos nombres)

a.
b.
c.
d.
e.
f.
g.
h.
i.

(nombre)
(dos nombres)

Ahora lo sabes

Can you:

- talk about the time you leave a place?
  —Nosotros _____ de la escuela a las tres de la tarde.
- make equal comparisons of people or things?
  —Margarita está _____ cansada _____ Pablo.
- talk about the most or the least in a certain category?
  —Este libro es _____ interesante _____ la biblioteca.

> **MORE PRACTICE**
>
> Más práctica y tarea, pp. 529–530
> Practice Workbook 1–5, 1–10

Gramática en contexto 49

ESTUDIANTE B
Answers will vary, but look for the correct direct object pronoun and conjugated verb form of *traer*.
a. lo + *conjugated form of* traer
b. los
c. la
d. las
e. lo
f. la
g. la
h. lo
i. las

Answers: Ahora lo sabes
- salimos
- tan / como
- el más (menos) / de

Practice Wkbk. 1-9, 1-10

Audio Activities 1.4, 1.5

Writing Activity 1-H

Prueba 1-9

Comm. Act. BLM 1-2

Pasos vivos 2 CD-ROM
Fax Task, Slide Presentation Maker, Spindle, Treadmill

Multiple Intelligences
Verbal/Linguistic
See Audio Activities 1.4 and 1.5.
Visual/Spatial
See Practice Wkbk. 1-9 and 1-10, Writing Activity 1-H, and Comm. Act. BLM 1-2.

Using the Video

In this initial presentation of *La Catrina*, we meet Jamie González, a high school student from Los Angeles. Jamie has a grant to spend the summer in Querétaro, Mexico. She wants to find out about her paternal great-grandmother, "La Catrina," who disappeared during the Mexican Revolution.

In Spanish class at Jamie's school, the teacher wishes Jamie and fellow classmate Philip Armstrong (also a grant recipient) a good trip. After the plane flight to Mexico City, Jamie and Philip (Felipe) travel by train to Querétaro, where they meet their host families. The Navarro family is surprised to learn that the boy they were expecting, "Jaime," is a girl named "Jamie."

Meanwhile, at the local library, Demetrio Alcocer receives a phone call from Santana, who has been spying on Jamie and Felipe.

In subsequent episodes, each chapter's video is divided into three segments: a) a summary of the previous episode, b) the main

Actividades

1 ¡Tu mascota—perro, gato, etc.—va a participar en un concurso *(contest)!* Trae una foto de tu mascota para exhibir en clase. Luego, la clase va a votar y a preparar medallas. Por ejemplo:

el /la más feo(a)
el /la más grande
el /la más pequeño(a)
el /la más perezoso(a)
el /la más inteligente
el /la más …

En Santiago, Chile, unos jóvenes deportistas celebran una victoria.

2 La clase va a preparar un "Guinness Book of Class Records." El libro debe tener un nombre en español. Puedes usar estas categorías. Piensa también en otras.

¿Quién es el (la) estudiante más /menos atrevido(a)?
¿Quién tiene el pelo más largo /más corto?
¿Quién escribe más rápido en la computadora?
¿Quién dibuja mejor?
¿Quién saca las mejores notas?

Cada estudiante debe traer una foto. Todos deben comparar las fotos y decidir qué información van a escribir debajo de cada una. Pueden exhibir el libro en la sala de clases o en la biblioteca escolar.

50   Capítulo 1

Options

Strategies for Reaching All Students

Spanish-Speaking Students
Ex. 1: Give this assignment to Spanish-speaking students: *Prepara un artículo de periódico que describe este concurso. Debes incluir dónde y cuándo tuvo lugar, los premios que se dieron y las mascotas que los recibieron.*

 Un paso más Exs. 1-G, 1-H

Students Needing Extra Help
Actividades: Assign one of these to a group of students if time is limited.
Ex. 1: Put the formula on the chalkboard so students can fill it in.
Ex. 2: Brainstorm other categories: use the Organizer from Book 1, Chap. 1, if available.

Cooperative Learning
Tan + adj. + *como* can also be used to construct similes such as "She is as quiet as a mouse." Explain what a simile is and how to construct one, then divide the class into groups of three or four. Have them use *tan* + adj. + *como* to create five or six similes. For example: *"La geometría es tan divertida como leer una guía telefónica"* or *"La química es tan interesante como arreglar mi cuarto."* Collect the similes and read the most humorous ones to the class.

Conexiones

Un día escolar

Esta gráfica indica cuántos estudiantes hay en una escuela durante un día escolar. Mírala con un(a) compañero(a). Decidan:

- cuánto tiempo indica cada cuadrado
- las horas del almuerzo
- más o menos cuántos estudiantes almuerzan en la escuela
- qué indican los puntos A, B, C, D y E

Después, trabajen en grupo. En una hoja de papel cuadriculado, hagan una gráfica para la escuela de ustedes. Tienen que considerar:

- el número total de estudiantes de la escuela
- las horas de clase
- las horas en que los estudiantes entran y salen de la escuela

Marquen los puntos críticos e indíquenlos con letras.

Todo junto 51

story, and c) a review of a difficult concept from the second segment.

La Catrina: Capítulo 1

Play

Video Activity B

Para entender mejor

Play

Video Activity C

Answers: Actividades
1–2 Responses will vary.

Answers: Conexiones
- media hora
- 12:45–2:00
- 500
- los cambios del número total de estudiantes durante el día
Graphs will vary.

Comm. Act. BLMs 1-3, 1-4, 1-5

Pasos vivos 2 CD-ROM

A Jugar, Boom Box, Laboratorio de grabar, Maps, Video Monitor, Video Presentation Maker

---

Cultural Notes ☼

Multiple Intelligences
Interpersonal/Social and Visual/Spatial
See Cooperative Learning and Exs. 1–2.
Logical/Mathmatical
See *Conexiones*.
Visual/Spatial
See Using the Video and Comm. Act. BLMs 1-3, 1-4, and 1-5.

(p. 50, photo)
It is likely that these young Chileans are celebrating a soccer victory. As in most of South America, soccer is by far the most popular sport in Chile, and women's soccer is also increasing in popularity. Soccer is not the only popular sport for Chilean youths, however, as evidenced by the rise of young Marcelo Ríos to the ranks of the world's elite men's tennis players.

Apply

Process Reading

Make sure students understand the four headings in this section and the tasks they represent:
- *Antes de leer:* prereading activity for activating prior knowledge; emphasis on one or more strategies for overcoming the tendency to read slowly, word by word, and instead to focus on receiving the message being communicated in the text
- *Mira la lectura:* scanning / skimming for general ideas or information, looking for cognates, proper nouns, headings, numbered or bulleted items, familiar words, etc.
- *Infórmate:* reading for more detailed information
- *Aplicación:* post-reading activity

Answers
Antes de leer
Answers will vary.

Mira la lectura
Answers will vary, but students may say that the play will be a comedy.

¡Vamos a leer!

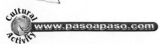 www.pasoapaso.com

Antes de leer

STRATEGY Using prior knowledge

This is a play about an unusual mosquito. How do you feel about insects? How do you react when you see one?

Mira la lectura

STRATEGY Using the title and illustrations as context clues

Read the title and look at the illustrations. What do you think the play will be like?

Infórmate

STRATEGY Using context clues

Now read the play. When you come to something you don't know, use the words you do know and your knowledge of the situation to help you figure it out. For example, toward the end of the play, the word *grita* occurs twice in stage directions. Both times it comes before something Eduardo says. And what Eduardo says begins and ends with exclamation marks, which tells you that he is speaking louder than normal. Read the stage directions to see what word makes sense. Is your answer confirmed when Alfonso asks, "*¿Por qué gritas?*" That is a natural question if you can't understand why someone is excited.

El EXTRAÑO
caso del mosquito

EDUARDO ROBLES BOZA (TÍO PATOTA)

Acto I

(Eduardo está en su dormitorio escuchando música. Lleva un libro en la mano mientras da vueltas por el cuarto. Abre, repasa y cierra el libro continuamente. Está nervioso. Es de noche.)

EDUARDO: Mañana tengo examen y no sé nada.

(Eduardo da vueltas otra vez; trata de leer y memorizar. Ve un mosquito. Pone el libro en la cama, recoge un periódico y va a la pared a matar el mosquito. Pero el mosquito empieza a hablar.)

MOSQUITO: ¡No me mates, por favor!

EDUARDO: ¿Tú hablas?

52   Capítulo 1

Options

Strategies for Reaching All Students

Spanish-Speaking Students
Add: *Después de leer "El extraño caso del mosquito," piensa en los refranes que siguen: "Nunca dejes para mañana lo que puedas hacer hoy" y "Lo mal ganado se lo lleva el diablo." ¿Cuál es un buen refrán para Eduardo? ¿Por qué?*

Students Needing Extra Help
Infórmate: Explain the concept of stage directions.
As an example of using prior knowledge, show students where *grita* is. See if they pick up on the exclamation points *before* you read the *Infórmate* to them. Discuss what they mean. Emphasize that they have taken something they already know (that exclamation points are used to show excitement, a raised voice, etc.) and transferred it to *this* situation. Show them how you have to guess sometimes and try again.
Aplicación 2: When students make suggestions, help them with the vocabulary they need and add it to the story.

MOSQUITO: Sí, y en dos idiomas. Soy bilingüe.

EDUARDO: ¡Caramba! No lo puedo creer . . . Pues, tengo que matarte. *(Levanta el periódico.)*

MOSQUITO: ¡No! ¡No! Puedo ayudarte.

EDUARDO: ¿Ayudarme? ¿Tú? ¿A qué?

MOSQUITO: A estudiar. Tengo memoria y sé leer también.

(Eduardo coloca el mosquito, con cuidado, en la palma de su mano. Lo lleva y lo pone sobre el libro abierto que está en la cama.)

EDUARDO: Bueno, lee lo que hay en esa página.

MOSQUITO: Aquí dice que Cristóbal Colón fue un navegante español que . . .

EDUARDO: ¡Está bien, está bien! Eres un mosquito muy preparado.

MOSQUITO: ¿No me vas a matar?

EDUARDO: No sé. ¿Cómo vas a ayudarme?

MOSQUITO: Muy fácil. Yo estudio esta noche. Tú duermes y mañana me escondo en tu oreja, . . . y te explico todo. *(Eduardo no contesta.)* Bueno, ¿cuándo empiezo?

EDUARDO: *(Recoge el libro, lo pone sobre el escritorio y lo abre en una página.)* Puedes empezar ahora. Tienes que estudiar desde esta página y hasta terminar el libro . . . y yo me voy a dormir. ¡Hasta mañana, compañero!

Aplicación

Make a list of three to five new words you figured out from the context. Discuss them with a classmate to see if he or she agrees. Then look them up in a dictionary to see if you were right.

Acto II

(Es de día. Eduardo duerme. La luz del escritorio todavía está encendida. Entra un muchacho.)

ALFONSO: ¡Eduardo! ¡Hoy tenemos examen! ¿Estudiaste?

EDUARDO: ¿Cómo dices? ¡Sí, sí, claro que estudié!

(Eduardo se levanta, recoge su ropa y entra en el baño. Alfonso da vueltas por el cuarto.)

ALFONSO: Veo que estudiaste mucho porque la luz todavía está encendida y el libro abierto.

EDUARDO: *(Grita desde el baño.)* ¡Sí, hoy sé todo!

(Alfonso recoge el libro y lo cierra. Eduardo sale del baño y ve lo que está haciendo Alfonso. Se pone las manos en la cara y le grita.)

EDUARDO: ¡Qué horror! ¿Qué haces, Alfonso?

ALFONSO: ¿Por qué gritas? Sólo cerré tu libro.

EDUARDO: *(Corre rápido adonde está Alfonso y toma el libro, busca nerviosamente en las páginas y ve que el mosquito está aplastado.)* Creo que no voy a poder tomar el examen . . . ¡Ya olvidé todo!

If you were Eduardo at the end of the play, what would you do? In a small group, decide on some suggestions for him.

Infórmate
Answers will vary.

Aplicación
Answers will vary.

www Internet Activities
Have students go to www.pasoapaso.com for additional activities and practice.

Multiple Intelligences
Visual/Spatial and Verbal/Linguistic
See *Aplicación.*

Apply

Process Writing

Inform students in advance that their work will be kept in a portfolio of their writing. Explain that their portfolio will help them keep a record of their progress throughout the year.

Portfolios represent a systematic process involving both learner and teacher. They document progress toward specific standards by applying clearly stated criteria in selecting, monitoring, and evaluating significant products and performance. (For a more detailed explanation of portfolio writing and assessment, see pp. T57–T61.)

In preparation for the writing assignment, you may wish to briefly review adjective agreement. For step 4, remind students about correct accent placement, question marks, and exclamation points. For spelling checks, tell students that they may always refer back to the vocabulary sections or the *Resumen del capítulo* at the end of the chapter.

Before beginning this exercise, you may want to review the five steps of process writing with your students.

NOTE: *¡Vamos a escribir!* offers two related activities. The first is more basic; the second is an

¡Vamos a escribir!

Con un(a) compañero(a), prepara un folleto *(pamphlet)* en español sobre tu escuela. El folleto va a servirles a los estudiantes que sólo hablan español.

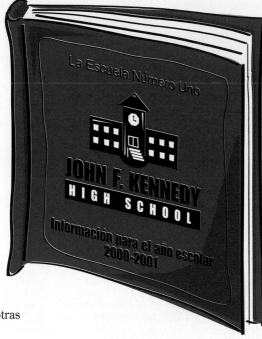

1 Primero, contesta estas preguntas con un(a) compañero(a).

- El horario
  ¿A qué hora empieza el día escolar? ¿A qué hora termina? ¿Cuánto dura cada clase?

- Las salas
  ¿Hay cafetería, auditorio, gimnasio, piscina? ¿Cómo son? ¿Dónde quedan?

- Las materias
  ¿Qué materias toman los estudiantes de tu año?

- Las actividades
  ¿Qué deportes pueden practicar? ¿En qué otras actividades pueden participar?

- El personal
  ¿Cómo se llaman el (la) director(a) y los consejeros? ¿Dónde están sus oficinas? ¿Cuáles son sus números de teléfono? ¿Cómo se llama el (la) enfermero(a)? ¿Dónde está la enfermería?

- Las reglas
  ¿Qué se prohibe hacer? ¿Hay ropa que se prohibe llevar? ¿Qué debes hacer si te sientes mal y no puedes ir a la escuela? ¿Y si te sientes mal en la escuela?

Usa tus respuestas para preparar el folleto. Si quieres, puedes hacer un dibujo de la mascota u otra insignia de tu escuela.

¡NO OLVIDES!

Hay cinco pasos.
1. Primero, piensa en el tema *(topic)* y escribe tus ideas.
2. Luego, escribe el primer borrador *(draft)*.
3. Comparte *(share)* tu borrador con un(a) compañero(a) y pídele recomendaciones o ideas. Escribe el segundo borrador.
4. Revisa tu trabajo para corregir los errores de ortografía y puntuación.
5. Ahora, distribuye tu trabajo entre las personas a quienes pueda interesar, y guarda otra copia en tu portafolio.

54   Capítulo 1

Options

Strategies for Reaching All Students

Students Needing Extra Help
Because students are used to having the directions given in English, turn to a *Vamos a escribir* section from the end of Book 1. Show students how similar and consistent the formats are.
Have students keep a list in their notebooks of words such as *el tema, el borrador,* etc., that will keep reappearing in this section throughout the book.

If students have them available, they can use the vocabulary sections of the Organizers from Book 1, Chap. 2, and this chapter.
Review sports vocabulary (Book 1, Chap. 3). Have students use *guitarra, música, periódico,* etc.
El personal: Have a student handbook available.
Las reglas: Use the Organizer from this chapter.

Step 2: If you do this activity, supply some vocabulary. Do this as a large group and brainstorm.
This is a sophisticated format. Students can supply the vocabulary while you provide the structure of the sentences and the grammar.

Multiple Intelligences
Visual/Spatial and Interpersonal/Social
See step 2.

2 Ahora, tú y tu compañero(a) deben preparar una carta para enviarles con el folleto a las familias que hablan español. En la carta pueden incluir:

- una bienvenida a la escuela
- quién escribió el folleto
- para quién es el folleto
- una invitación a visitar la escuela

La carta debe empezar con la fecha y un saludo formal. Al final, escriban una despedida (Cordialmente o Atentamente).

_____ de septiembre de 200__

Estimada familia,

¡Bienvenidos a la escuela _____ !
xxxxxxxxxxxxxxxxxxxxxxxxxxx
xxxxxxxxxxxxxxxxxxxxxxxxxxx
xxxxxxxxxxxxxxxxxxxxxxxxxxx
xxxxxxxxxxxxxxxxxxxxxxxxxxx

Atentamente,

_____
(firma)

Estudiantes en Ambato, Ecuador, se preparan para los Juegos Nacionales.

PASO CULTURAL

Cada cuatro años, deportistas en todo Ecuador participan en los Juegos Nacionales, que son administrados por los gobiernos provinciales y el gobierno nacional. Los estudiantes de secundaria, como éstos, participan cada año en campeonatos provinciales y nacionales en varios juegos, entre ellos básquetbol, fútbol, ajedrez y tae kwon do. ¿Qué sabes de estos juegos? ¿En qué continentes tuvieron su origen?

3 Ahora pueden:

- darles folletos a los estudiantes nuevos de la escuela que hablan español
- enviarles folletos a los estudiantes de la escuela media *(middle)* que hablan español
- exhibir los folletos en la sala de clases
- incluirlos en su portafolio

inglés en QUICK LEARNING

¡hablas o hablas!
como aprendiste a hablar el español,
sin reglas gramaticales, sin tareas en casa,
¡así de fácil !, ¡así de natural !

346-87-18
GARANTIZAMOS RESULTADOS
O TE DEVOLVEMOS
TU DINERO

INICIAMOS
CURSOS
LUNES 17
DE ENERO

CENTROS DE INFORMACION: • Mty: 346-87-18 y 346-87-19
B. F.: 538-71-80 • Gdl: 625-75-55 • Tij: 84-24-23

¡Vamos a escribir! 55

extension and should be reserved for more able students. The second is also appropriate for any native speakers of Spanish who may be in your class. (If your school doesn't have any Spanish-speaking students, ask students to share their pamphlet with someone they know who speaks Spanish.)

Using Realia
Using context clues, ask students if they can figure out what the phrase *¡hablas o hablas!* means ("You will speak, no matter what!" or "We guarantee you will speak English!").

 Pasos vivos 2 CD-ROM
Word Processor

Assess & Summarize

Test Preparation

You may want to assign parts of this section as written homework or as an in-class writing activity prior to administering the *Examen de habilidades*.

Answers

Listening: *Tomo muchas materias este año. Y todos los días tengo que entregar tareas. En geometría tenemos que hacer problemas y todos los viernes hay prueba. Tomo química también, pero no es tan interesante. Para mí, la historia es la materia más interesante y más fácil de todas.* / History is the easiest subject. / The student expects a weekly test in geometry.

Reading: The picture of the dejected soccer player does not agree with the student's note, which says the soccer team is in first place.

Writing: Letters will vary.

Culture: Answers will vary, but students may say that in a Mexican school, the school day is divided into a morning session and an afternoon session, that students take more classes, have more homework, etc.

Speaking: Dialogues will vary.

Repaso ¿Lo sabes bien?

Esta sección te ayudará a prepararte para el examen de habilidades, donde tendrás que hacer tareas semejantes. Recuerda, sin embargo, que en el examen no habrá *(there won't be)* modelos.

Listening

Can you understand when people talk about their classes and assignments? Listen as your teacher reads a sample similar to what you will hear on the test. According to this student, which subject is the easiest? In which subject does the student expect a weekly test?

Reading

Can you understand a written description in which a student compares one school with others? Which picture does not agree with this student's note to a friend?

Me gusta mucho mi escuela. No es tan grande como otras, pero es muy moderna. Tenemos computadoras en todas las salas de clase. Tomamos las mismas materias que en otras escuelas. Pero también podemos estudiar varios idiomas y ciencias avanzadas. ¡Y el equipo de fútbol está en el primer lugar de la liga!

56   Capítulo 1

Writing

Can you write a letter in which you describe your school to someone else? Here is a sample.

Culture

Can you explain how the school day of a Mexican student might differ from yours?

Speaking

Can you talk about your school and your classes? With a partner, create a dialogue between an old student and a new one. What are some questions a new student might ask about your school? Here is a sample dialogue:

Querida Toña,

Hay muchas cosas que me gustan de esta escuela nueva. Primero, no está tan lejos de mi casa y salgo casi media hora más tarde por la mañana. Hay armarios también, y no tengo que llevar todo en mi bolso. ¡Y se permite salir a comer al mediodía! Ya conozco a muchos de los profesores. Creo que son mejores que los del año pasado, pero ninguno de ellos es tan divertido como el Sr. Gómez.

Tu amiga,

María

A —¿Cómo es la clase de matemáticas?
B —No es mi clase favorita, pero la profesora explica bien y se permite hacerle preguntas.
A —Y los exámenes, ¿son muy difíciles?
B —No mucho. Por suerte, a la profesora le encanta repasar.
A —¿Y hay mucha tarea?
B —Ah, eso sí. Todos los días tenemos que hacer tres páginas de ejercicios.

Self Test   www.pasoapaso.com

Options

Strategies for Reaching All Students

Students Needing Extra Help
Have students write out this section so they can check off what they have mastered. Present this as a sample test or a pretest. Be sure that students understand that this is not the actual test. Some students will study *only* what they see here.
Listening: Read slowly, pausing after each sentence so that students can absorb the material. Remember that many of your students are visual, and that listening, without visual input, is difficult.

Remind students that they are only listening for two pieces of information. See if they can suggest some of the words they might hear.
Reading: Have the students look at the three pictures first so they can get an idea of what they are looking for. Again, emphasize that they don't have to know each word in order to understand.
Writing: Have students use the Organizer and write a sample letter as practice.

Culture: Have students review any notes they may have taken during their first reading of the *Perspectiva cultural.*
Speaking: Use the Organizer to create some dialogues.
Review the *¡Comuniquemos!* section, where students created a similar dialogue.

Resumen del vocabulario

Usa el vocabulario de este capítulo para:
- talk about your classes and homework
- describe your school and your school day
- compare the subjects you like the most and the least

to name school subjects
el alemán
el álgebra (f.)
la biología
el francés
la geografía
la geometría
la historia
el idioma
la literatura
la materia
la química

to name people who work at a school
el consejero, la consejera
el director, la directora

to name places in a school
el auditorio
el bufet de ensaladas
la cafetería
el escenario
el laboratorio
la oficina

to describe school equipment
el armario
el asiento
la bandera
el bolso
la computadora

la diapositiva
la grapadora
el mapa
la pared
el proyector
el reloj
el sacapuntas,
   pl. los sacapuntas
el sujetapapeles,
   pl. los sujetapapeles
el edificio

to talk about activities associated with school
conocer (*c → zc*):
   (yo) conozco
   (tú) conoces
contestar
escribir
explicar
hacer fila
hacer una pregunta
preguntar
repasar
sacar una buena / mala nota
la pregunta
la respuesta
se permite
se prohibe
usar
escolar

to talk about homework
entregar
el capítulo
la composición
el ejercicio
el examen
el informe
la lección
la página
el problema
la prueba

to make comparisons
tan + *adj.* + como

other useful words and expressions
alguno (algún), -a
por suerte
próximo, -a

Resumen 57

Assessment

 Prueba cumulativa

 Examen de habilidades

 Test Generator

Additional Assessment Options

 Comm. Act. BLMs
Small Group Activities
Situation Cards

 Pasos vivos 2 CD-ROM
Slide Presentation Maker, Video Presentation Maker, Word Processor, Spindle

¿Lo sabes bien? Video Quiz

Internet Activities
Self-Test

CAPÍTULO 2
THEME: DAILY ROUTINE

SCOPE AND SEQUENCE Pages 58–89

COMMUNICATION

Topics

Personal hygiene items

Before-school activities

After-school activities

Musical instruments

Objectives

To compare students' extracurricular activities in Guatemala and in the U.S.

To describe daily routine

To indicate time

To discuss extracurricular activities

To discuss music

CULTURE

Extracurricular activities in Guatemala

GRAMMAR

Los verbos reflexivos

Repaso: Verbos con los cambios o → ue, e → ie, *y* e → i

Antes de / después de + inf.

Ancillaries available for use with Chapter 2

Multisensory/Technology

 Overheads, 11–15

 Audio Tapes and CDs

 Vocabulary Art Blackline Masters for Hands-On Learning, pp. 13–17/CD-ROM

 Classroom Crossword

 La Catrina

Pasos vivos 2
CD-ROM

 Internet Activities
www.pasoapaso.com

Print

 Practice Workbook, pp. 12–22

 Writing, Audio & Video Activities, pp. 11–16, 96–98, 153–154

 Communicative Activity Blackline Masters

Pair and Small Group Activities, pp. 8–13

Situation Cards, p. 14

 Un paso más: Actividades para ampliar tu español, pp. 7–12

 RESOURCE PRO®

Planning Express, Teaching Resources Library, and Clip Art Library

Assessment

 Assessment Program

Pruebas, pp. 25–34

Examen de habilidades, pp. 35–38

Test Generator

¿Lo sabes bien? Video Quiz

Video still from Chap. 2

57A

¿Qué haces todos los días?

Although daily routines and activities of young people in Spanish-speaking countries vary from place to place and from one socioeconomic group to another, many of these activities are shared among them.

As in the U.S., school plays an important role. Much of young people's social life stems from the relationships they establish there. Many students, particularly those in private schools, have been classmates since grade school. Because of this, the few extracurricular activities that are offered take on added significance. Among these activities are school performances, field trips, and dances.

Unlike young people in the U.S., teens in most Spanish-speaking countries rarely hold outside jobs. Families sometimes employ maids and gardeners—even middle-class families. Teenagers are expected to dedicate time at home to their studies. As in the U.S., they are sometimes provided special tutors to ensure that they do well.

In large Spanish-speaking cities, many young people study English, French, German, or other languages at language academies. This instruction is in addition to the foreign language education offered in the schools. There are also educational opportunities away from school. Many students study dance, voice, guitar, art, or gymnastics.

Young Hispanics enjoy socializing in groups—giving or attending parties is one important aspect of this. They can often be seen at *cafés,* public parks, town *plazas,* as well as at the local shopping mall. Weekend activities might include camping, going to the beach, or going on a skiing trip (depending on the country or season).

Eating habits and schedules for teens in Spanish-speaking countries differ considerably from those of young people in the U.S. Most eat a light breakfast of bread and jam with juice and coffee. Lunch, however, includes several courses: soup, a meat dish with vegetables and / or salad, dessert, fruit, and coffee. Lunch may take place as late as 1:30 or 2:00 in the afternoon. It is a time considered important for the family to come together and relax. For most families, the evening meal is light because of the heavy and late lunch, but some families have a complete dinner around 9:00 P.M. or later.

Introduce

Re-entry of Concepts
The following list represents words, expressions, and grammar topics re-entered from Book 1 and Book 2 (Chap. 1):

Book 1
numbers 0–31, calendar terms, *gustar* expressions, time-telling, seasons, leisure-time activities, places in a community, vacation activities, chores, recycling activities

Chapter 1
school subjects

58   Capítulo 2

Planning

Cross-Curricular Connections

Career / Home Economics Connection (pp. 66–67)
Have pairs or small groups of students role play being instructors for a parenting class. Using dolls or stuffed animals, they will instruct the class or another group on how to care for a new baby and also how to treat older siblings. They may want to make posters as a follow-up. Brainstorm with students additional necessary vocabulary before beginning.

Art / Business Connection (pp. 74–75)
Have students create an ad poster for a new personal hygiene item. Have them use reflexive verbs and vocabulary from the first *Vocabulario para conversar* to create ads such as these: *Debe bañarse con jabón Fiesta. ¡Es el mejor!* or *Yo me lavo el pelo con el champú Color Bonito. ¡Me encanta!* Display the posters around the classroom.

Spanish in Your Community
Have students find out what type of Spanish music is available in their community. If possible, have them listen to a Spanish-language radio station for at least 15 minutes and take notes on what they hear. What do they recognize (advertisements, newscasts, DJ "talk")? What could they understand (store names, addresses)? Have students visit a local store that sells CDs and cassettes to find out the names of popular Hispanic bands or singers.

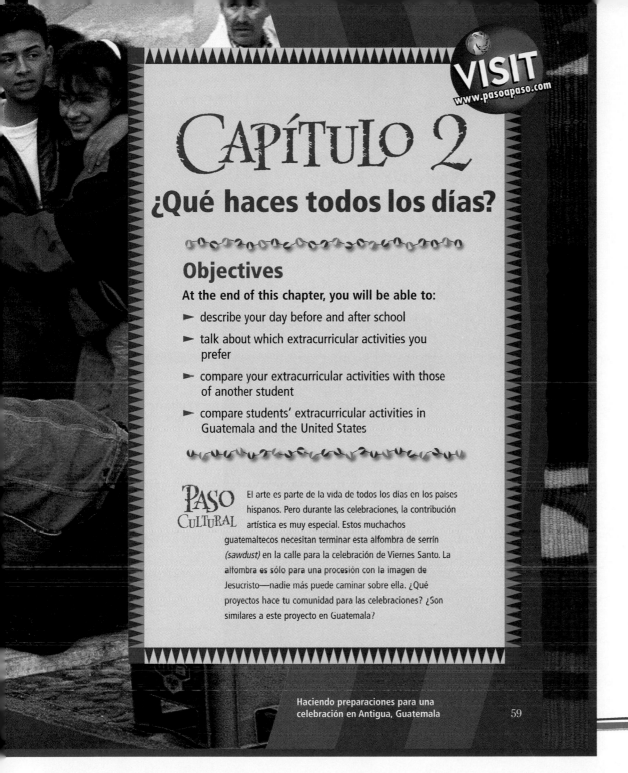

CAPÍTULO 2

¿Qué haces todos los días?

Objectives

At the end of this chapter, you will be able to:

► describe your day before and after school

► talk about which extracurricular activities you prefer

► compare your extracurricular activities with those of another student

► compare students' extracurricular activities in Guatemala and the United States

PASO CULTURAL El arte es parte de la vida de todos los días en los países hispanos. Pero durante las celebraciones, la contribución artística es muy especial. Estos muchachos guatemaltecos necesitan terminar esta alfombra de serrín *(sawdust)* en la calle para la celebración de Viernes Santo. La alfombra es sólo para una procesión con la imagen de Jesucristo—nadie más puede caminar sobre ella. ¿Qué proyectos hace tu comunidad para las celebraciones? ¿Son similares a este proyecto en Guatemala?

Haciendo preparaciones para una celebración en Antigua, Guatemala

59

Cultural Notes

(pp. 58–59, photo)
On Maundy Thursday (Holy Thursday) in Guatemala, teens from different churches work into the night making decorative carpets out of sawdust for the next day's procession—rather like rolling out the red carpet. They lay wood cutouts on the pavement and fill in the holes with colored sawdust, until they have completed the carpet.

Paso cultural
Answers will vary.

Preview

Cultural Objective

- To compare the daily routines and activities of students in Spanish-speaking countries and those in the U.S.

¡Piensa en la CULTURA!

"Cada semana mi tutora, Anita, me ayuda. Ella es muy simpática."

¿Te gustaría ser tutor(a)? ¿En qué materias?

Actividades fuera de la escuela en México, California y España

Mira las fotos. Los estudiantes que vemos aquí están hablando de lo que hacen antes y después de las clases. ¿Qué haces tú?

Torreón, México

Fullerton, California

"Siempre tengo que hacer mi cama antes de salir para la escuela."

¿Hay quehaceres de la casa que tú tienes que hacer por la mañana? ¿Cuáles?

60   Capítulo 2

Options

Strategies for Reaching All Students

Spanish-Speaking Students

Ask: *¿Por qué crees que a los estudiantes les falta tiempo para hacer lo que tienen que hacer? Además de ir a clases, ¿qué otras cosas tienes que hacer todos los días? ¿Qué haces después de las clases?*

 Un paso más Ex. 2-A

Cultural Notes

(p. 60, top photo)
The Boys' and Girls' Clubs is a national network that offers a variety of recreation and support services in neighborhood-based settings. The clubs include approximately 2.8 million members in all fifty states. In addition to other professional support staff, the clubs have more than eight thousand trained youth workers who provide tutoring, mentoring, and other support to younger children and peers.

PASO CULTURAL

Picasso pintó muchos cuadros en el estilo del cubismo, que ves aquí y que él ayudó a inventar. El cubismo manipula el espacio y las formas para demolir las ideas tradicionales realistas de cómo representar los objetos. En este cuadro, Picasso usa formas geométricas para representar a los músicos y sus instrumentos. ¿Qué otros estilos de arte presentan los objetos de una perspectiva no realista?

Tres músicos (Three Musicians) (1921), Pablo Picasso

"¡Nos encanta tocar en la banda!"

A estos jóvenes en San Sebastián, España, les gusta mucho esta actividad extracurricular. ¿Hay banda en tu escuela? ¿Tocas tú algún instrumento musical?

San Sebastián, España

www.pasoapaso.com
Visit these countries on-line

Cultural Exploration

Paso cultural
Possible answers: impresionismo, fauvismo, expresionismo, surrealismo, expresionismo abstracto y otros estilos abstractos.

(p. 61, top photo)
"Three Musicians" is an example of Picasso's cubist style. In this painting, for example, the center musician's legs and torso are represented by triangles. The guitar is a composite of geometric shapes, yet remains recognizable as a guitar.

(p. 61, bottom photo)
In Spain, extra-curricular activities traditionally perform a much smaller role in school life than in the U.S. For young people, activities such as music and athletics usually take place at clubs outside of school. The band pictured here may represent one of these clubs. Churches also have similar bands that take part in the religious processions that form an important part of Spanish cultural life.

Present

Chapter Theme
Before-school activities

Communicative Objectives
• To describe daily routine
• To indicate time

 Overheads 11–12

 Vocabulary Art BLMs/CD-ROM

 Vocabulary Tape 2-1

Grammar Preview
Reflexive verbs; verbs with the stem change *o → ue, e → ie,* and *e → i;* and *antes de / después de* + inf. are presented lexically. Their explanation appears in the grammar section. Avoid explaining or treating these as grammar at this point. Allow students to use them naturally, and the grammar will be much more readily comprehended later.

Vocabulario para conversar

¿Te despiertas temprano?

Vas a necesitar estas palabras y expresiones para hablar sobre lo que haces antes y después de la escuela. Después de leerlas varias veces, practícalas con un(a) compañero(a).

despertarse *(e → ie)* — levantarse — lavarse la cara

cepillarse los dientes — ducharse — lavarse el pelo

62   Capítulo 2

Options

Strategies for Reaching All Students

Spanish-Speaking Students

 Un paso más Exs. 2-B, 2-C

Students Needing Extra Help
Begin to fill in the vocabulary section of the Organizer.
Reflexive verbs may be difficult for some students. Point out that these are *-ar* and *-ir* verbs with *-se* attached at the end.
Remind them that *e → ie* and *e → i* are boot verbs. Review this concept. Show them

the sample in *También necesitas . . . .*
También necesitas . . . : Provide some expressions using *hay que, antes de, después de,* and *soler* with regular verbs and reflexives. Remind students that they have seen *me* and *te* used before with *gusta(n), encanta(n),* etc.
This vocabulary may seem complicated to some. Keep in mind that some students may need to understand concepts before they can manipulate the words.
Give examples of *de buen / mal humor.*

Enrichment
Present this vocabulary in conjunction with a game of charades. You can play the game with the entire class, having individuals or groups of students perform a given action in front of the class as you call out a word or expression and then having a vote for who did the clearest pantomime, the funniest, etc.

62   Standards 1.1; 1.2; 3.1; 4.1

secarse el pelo

cepillarse el pelo

peinarse

vestirse *(e → i)*

bañarse

acostarse *(o → ue)*

Teaching Suggestions
Preparing students to speak: Use one or two options from each of the categories of Comprehensible Input, Physical Response, or Limited Verbal Response. For a complete explanation of these categories and some sample activities, see pp. T20–T21.

Class Starter Review
On the day following initial vocabulary presentation, you might begin the class with this activity: Prepare a transparency with five or six morning activities in the infinitive form. Have students put them in logical order.

www Internet Activities
Juegos
Have students go to www.pasoapaso.com for additional activities and practice.

También necesitas . . .

hay que + *inf.*	*It's necessary to ___.*	antes de + *inf.*	*before + verb + -ing*
(yo) me despierto	*I wake up*	después de + *inf.*	*after + verb + -ing*
(tú) te despiertas	*you wake up*	de buen / mal humor	*in a good / bad mood*
(yo) me levanto	*I get up*	mismo, -a	*same*
(tú) te levantas	*you get up*	soler *(o → ue)* + *inf.*	*to be in the habit of*
uno	here: *one, a person*		
sin	*without*		
según	*according to*		
por lo menos	*at least*		

¿Y qué quiere decir . . . ?

depender	es necesario
desayunar	fácilmente

Vocabulario para conversar 63

Learning Spanish Through Action
STAGING VOCABULARY: *Hagan pantomimas*
MATERIALS: copies from the Vocabulary Art BLMs/CD-ROM or actual items to represent vocabulary: toothbrush, shampoo, comb, brush, alarm clock, etc.
DIRECTIONS: Direct students to use the props, if available, to act out the activities that you mention: *Hay que lavarse el pelo. Hay que cepillarse los dientes,* etc.

Extended Written Practice/Homework
1. Refer to the actions on pp. 62–63 and write three sentences telling how often one should do them: *Uno siempre debe lavarse las manos antes de comer.*
2. Write three sentences saying what people often do at night before going to bed: *Antes de acostarse, muchos jóvenes escuchan música.*
3. Write three sentences telling things you usually do on the weekends: *Suelo ir al cine con mis amigos los fines de semana.*

Multiple Intelligences
Bodily/Kinesthetic
See Enrichment and Learning Spanish Through Action.
Verbal/Linguistic
See Vocabulary Tape 2-1.
Visual/Spatial
See Overheads 11–12 and Class Starter Review.

Practice & Apply

Reteach / Review: Vocabulary

Ex. 1: As an extension exercise, have students redo this exercise with *Estudiante A* and *Estudiante B* talking about whether various people or pets have breakfast early or late, or whether they have breakfast at all. Encourage students to extend their dialogues as best they can by asking each other what they eat and why they eat breakfast when they do *(porque me despierto temprano, porque tengo que ir a la escuela temprano)*, and any other appropriate questions.

Answers: Empecemos a conversar

1 ESTUDIANTE A
a. ¿A qué hora te levantas los días de semana?
b. . . . en el verano?
c. . . . en las vacaciones?
d. . . . el sábado?
e. . . . el domingo?

ESTUDIANTE B
a.–e. Answers will vary, but look for *me levanto* and a correct time expression.

Empecemos a conversar

Túrnate con un(a) compañero(a) para ser *Estudiante A* y *Estudiante B*. Reemplacen las palabras subrayadas en el modelo con palabras representadas o escritas en los recuadros. Si ven 💡 pueden dar su propia respuesta.

1   los fines de semana   A —¿A qué hora te levantas *los fines de semana*?
              B — *Depende. Algunas veces me levanto a las 8:00, otras a las 9:00.*

Estudiante A   **Estudiante B**

a. los días de semana
b. en el verano
c. en las vacaciones
d. el sábado
e. el domingo

2   temprano   A —¿Te despiertas *temprano*?
            B —*Sí, me despierto temprano.*
               o: *No, no me despierto temprano.*
               o: *No, me despierto tarde.*

Estudiante A   **Estudiante B**

a. de buen humor
b. fácilmente
c. sin despertador
d. siempre a la misma hora
e.

64   Capítulo 2

Options

Strategies for Reaching All Students

Spanish-Speaking Students
Ex. 7: After this exercise, ask Spanish-speaking students: *¿Cuándo preparas la ropa que vas a llevar a la escuela? ¿Cuándo te bañas? ¿Cuándo preparas tus libros y cuadernos? ¿Quién te prepara el desayuno?*

 Un paso más Exs. 2-D, 2-E

Students Needing Extra Help
Ex. 1: Give *Estudiante B* time to develop appropriate responses. Review time-telling. Remind students that not only will the verb form change in the answer, but also the reflexive pronoun. Give them extra practice, both oral and written.
Ex. 2: Do this exercise three times. Do each example answering *sí* to everything, then with the first negative response, and finally answer all examples with the last response. In this way, students can focus on the *me /*

te changes and the verb endings.
Ex. 3: Show students that they only have to change the verb and number.
Exs. 4 and 6: Students may need some help with the vocabulary in order to answer the *¿por qué?* portions of these exercises.
Ex. 5: Allow students time to do a quick survey to answer these questions.
Ex. 7: Many students probably don't eat breakfast or may eat at a free breakfast program provided by the school. Emphasize the importance of breakfast.

3

A —¿Cuánto tiempo necesita uno para _vestirse_?
B —Pues, por lo menos _veinte_ minutos.

Estudiante A

Estudiante B

a.

b.

c.

d.

e.

f.

g.

Empecemos a escribir

Escribe tus respuestas en español.

4 ¿Te despiertas de buen humor? ¿Es fácil o difícil despertarse temprano? ¿Crees que es importante levantarse temprano? ¿Y acostarse temprano? ¿Por qué?

5 ¿Cuántas personas de tu clase suelen bañarse por la mañana? ¿Y antes de acostarse?

6 ¿Es necesario cepillarse los dientes por lo menos tres veces al día? Según los dentistas, ¿cuándo hay que cepillarse los dientes? ¿Y hay que lavarse las manos antes de comer? ¿Por qué?

7 ¿Desayunas siempre a la misma hora? ¿Sueles desayunar antes de salir de casa? ¿Con quién? Si no, ¿cuándo y dónde desayunas?

MORE PRACTICE

- Más práctica y tarea, p. 531
- Practice Workbook 2–1, 2–2

También se dice

lavarse los dientes

**tomar un baño / una ducha
darse un baño / una ducha**

Vocabulario para conversar **65**

Present

Chapter Theme
After-school activities

Communicative Objectives
- To discuss extracurricular activities
- To discuss music

 Overheads 13–14

 Vocabulary Art BLMs/CD-ROM

 Vocabulary Tape 2-2

Teaching Suggestions
Preparing students to speak: Use one or two options from each of the categories of Comprehensible Input, Physical Response, or Limited Verbal Response. For a complete explanation of these categories and some sample activities, see pp. T20–T21.

Vocabulario para conversar

¿Qué haces después de las clases?

Aquí tienes el resto del vocabulario que necesitas en este capítulo para hablar sobre lo que haces antes y después de las clases.

Las actividades extracurriculares

el coro

el anuario

las artes marciales (pl.)

el periódico (de la escuela)

Viajes

la revista (literaria)

Options

Strategies for Reaching All Students

Students Needing Extra Help
También necesitas . . . : Remind students that *ganar* also means "to win."

Learning Spanish Through Action
STAGING VOCABULARY: *Señalen*
MATERIALS: large calendar with various activities from the vocabulary list and *También necesitas . . .* pictured under various dates

DIRECTIONS: Make several true / false statements about routines and activities, using days of the week: *El jueves toco en la banda. El coro practica sólo los lunes. Los viernes los estudiantes trabajan en el anuario.* Students will signal thumbs up for true statements and thumbs down for false ones.

Cooperative Learning
Divide students into groups of four. Ask them to rank the extracurricular activities on p. 66 from most to least popular. Have them add other activities if they know them in Spanish. Call on each group to report results, and tally them on the chalkboard.

La banda
Los instrumentos musicales

la trompeta

la flauta

el violín,
pl. los violines

el clarinete

el saxofón, *pl.* los saxofones

el contrabajo

el piano

el tambor

la canción, *pl.* las canciones

cantar

Ojos negros

Class Starter Review
On the day following initial vocabulary presentation, you might begin the class with this activity: Ask students to list five extracurricular activities offered at your school. Keep a list of their responses on the chalkboard for reporting purposes.

www **Internet Activities**
Juegos
Have students go to www.pasoapaso.com for additional activities and practice.

También necesitas . . .

ganar	here: *to earn (money)*	
cuidar niños	*to baby-sit*	
repartir	here: *to deliver*	
el equipo	*team*	
el miembro	*member*	

¿Y qué quiere decir . . . ?

el club, *pl.* los clubes	literario, -a
el consejo estudiantil	participar (en)
la orquesta	ser miembro de
el tutor, la tutora	trabajar como voluntario (a)

Vocabulario para conversar   67

Extended Written Practice/Homework
1. Refer to the musical instruments on p. 67 and write three sentences naming famous people or people you know who play them: *Billy Joel toca el piano muy bien.*
2. Choose four of the activities on pp. 66–67 and name people you know who participate in these activities: *Mi hermano es miembro del consejo estudiantil.*
3. Refer to the activities on pp. 66–67 and write three sentences telling things you would like to do.

Multiple Intelligences
Bodily/Kinesthetic
See Learning Spanish Through Action.
Interpersonal/Social and Logical/Mathematical
See Cooperative Learning.

Intrapersonal/Introspective
Have students write a brief paragraph about the extracurricular activities they participate in or enjoy the most.
Verbal/Linguistic
See Vocabulary Tape 2-2.
Visual/Spatial
See Overheads 13–14, the Vocabulary Art BLMs/CD-ROM, and Class Starter Review.

Practice & Apply

Re-enter / Recycle
Ex. 9: school subjects from Chap. 1

Answers: Empecemos a conversar

8 ESTUDIANTE A
a. ¿Qué haces de pasatiempo?
b ...como voluntario(a)?
c. ...después de las clases?

ESTUDIANTE B
a.–c. Answers will vary, but may include any of the following:
Practico artes marciales. Toco los tambores. Participo en el anuario. Trabajo en el hospital. Canto en el coro.

9 ESTUDIANTE A
a. ¿Qué clases son las más populares de la escuela?
b. ...deportes son los más populares...?
c ...profesores son los más populares...?
d. ...pasatiempos son los más populares...?
e. ...clubes son los más populares...?
f. Questions will vary, but should include the construction *de la escuela.*

ESTUDIANTE B
a.–f. Answers will vary.

Empecemos a conversar

8 después de las clases

A —¿Qué haces <u>después de las clases</u>?
B —<u>Practico artes marciales todos los miércoles</u>.

Estudiante A

a. de pasatiempo
b. como voluntario(a)
c. después de las clases

Estudiante B

practicar

tocar

participar en

trabajar en

cantar en

9 actividades extracurriculares

A —¿Qué <u>actividades extracurriculares</u> son <u>las más populares de la escuela</u>?
B —Creo que <u>son la revista literaria y la banda</u>.

Estudiante A

a. clases
b. deportes
c. profesores
d. pasatiempos

e. clubes
f.

Estudiante B

EL CLUB DE ESPAÑOL

Options

Strategies for Reaching All Students

Spanish-Speaking Students
Ex. 15: After this exercise, have students respond to the following in writing: *¿Cuáles son los beneficios de participar en actividades extracurriculares? ¿En actividades para voluntarios? ¿Participan todos Uds. en estas actividades? ¿Por qué?*

Students Needing Extra Help
Ex. 8: Remind students that *haces* is rarely answered with *hago.* Tell them to look for a logical answer.

Ex. 9: Ask students what will happen to *las* when you do a sentence with a masculine subject.
Ex. 10: Brainstorm possible work places for response *b.*
Ex. 11: Brainstorm possible responses to *¿por qué?*
Ex. 14: Students will need help with the structures needed to express these ideas.

Enrichment
Ex. 9: Have students redo this exercise with *Estudiante A* asking *Estudiante B* which activities or classes are least popular.
Ex. 10: You may want to keep a class tally of how many students do various things to earn money.
Exs. 12–14: Additional questions: *¿En qué actividades extracurriculares te gustaría participar? ¿Por qué? ¿Hay estas actividades extracurriculares en tu escuela? ¿Por qué sí o no?*

10 cuidar niños   A —*¿Cuidas niños para ganar dinero?*
B —*No. Trabajo en un supermercado.*
o: *No. No hago nada para ganar dinero.*

Estudiante A

Estudiante B

a. ayudar en casa

b. trabajar en ____

c. repartir periódicos

d. trabajar de tutor(a)

e. tocar un instrumento

f. cortar céspedes

Empecemos a escribir y a leer

Escribe tus respuestas en español.

11 ¿Qué actividades extracurriculares te gustan más? ¿En cuál(es) no participas? ¿Por qué? ¿Haces algo para ganar dinero? ¿Qué?

12 En tu comunidad, ¿dónde puede uno trabajar como voluntario?

13 ¿Hay banda u orquesta en tu escuela? ¿Tocas algún instrumento musical o te gustaría tocar alguno? ¿Cuál? ¿Te gusta cantar? ¿Qué canciones sabes cantar o tocar?

14 ¿Qué día de la semana estás más ocupado(a)? ¿Por qué? ¿Estás de buen o de mal humor cuando estás ocupado(a)? ¿Por qué?

15 Lee las frases siguientes con un(a) compañero(a). ¿Con cuáles están de acuerdo? ¿Con cuáles no?

- A los estudiantes de hoy no les gusta trabajar.
- Las actividades extracurriculares ayudan a formar líderes *(leaders)*.
- El consejo estudiantil es la actividad más importante de la escuela.
- Los estudiantes de hoy deben jugar menos y estudiar más.
- Una persona ocupada es una persona contenta.
- Los deportes son buenos para la salud.

Si no están de acuerdo con estas frases, cámbienlas *(change them)* y escriban otras.

También se dice

la memoria

PASO CULTURAL La calidad de las figuras de porcelana de Lladró es el resultado de un proceso especial inventado en los años 1950 por tres hermanos, Juan, José y Vicente Lladró, en Almacera, un pueblo pequeño en el noreste de España. ¿Qué otros objetos de artesanía española conoces? ¿Te gustaría coleccionarlos o no? ¿Por qué?

MORE PRACTICE

Más práctica y tarea, p. 532
Practice Workbook 2–3, 2–4

Vocabulario para conversar 69

---

10 **ESTUDIANTE A**
a. ¿Ayudas en casa para ganar dinero?
b. ¿Trabajas en ___ . . .
c. ¿Repartes periódicos . . .
d. ¿Trabajas de tutor(a) . . .
e. ¿Tocas un instrumento . . .
f. ¿Cortas el césped . . .
ESTUDIANTE B
a.–f. Answers will vary

Answers: Empecemos a escribir y a leer
11–15 Answers will vary.

 Practice Wkbk. 2-3, 2-4

 Audio Activity 2.2

 Writing Activities 2-A, 2-B, 2-C

 Pruebas 2-3, 2-4

 Comm. Act. BLM 2-2

Cultural Notes
(p. 69, realia)
Manufactured in Valencia, Spain, Lladró ceramics are known for their pastel colors and fine detailing. The Lladró factory, "Porcelain Town," employs more than two thousand people. Each figurine is made of several pieces, which are shaped separately and then glued together. The figurine is then hand-painted and fired once. Lladró distributes its porcelains to more than ninety-seven hundred stores worldwide.

Cultural Notes

Extended Written Practice/Homework
1. Write three sentences describing a musical group that you are familiar with.
Include: what instruments they play, how many people sing, if you like their songs.
2. Write four sentences telling how different people you know earn money: *Mi hermana trabaja en un banco para ganar dinero.*
3. Write three sentences describing extracurricular activities in your school: *En nuestra escuela el club de español es muy activo.*

Multiple Intelligences
Interpersonal/Social and Visual/Spatial
See Ex. 15.
Verbal/Linguistic and Interpersonal/Social
See Exs. 9–10.
Visual/Spatial
See Exs. 11–14.

Paso cultural
Answers will vary: Otros objetos de artesanía española son cerámicas, objetos de cuero y damasquinado *(gold inlaid Damascene jewelry).*

Practice

Answers:
¡Comuniquemos!

1 Answers will vary, but look for *puede* + inf. and logical time expressions.

2 Answers will vary.

¡Comuniquemos!

Aquí tienes otra oportunidad para usar el vocabulario de este capítulo.

1 El día escolar empieza a las 8 de la mañana y Luz suele llegar tarde todos los días. Con un(a) compañero(a), digan qué puede hacer Luz para llegar a tiempo a la escuela. Usen las palabras y expresiones de las dos columnas para formar frases.

acostarse	por la noche
despertarse	a las (6:45)
levantarse	en (5) minutos
ducharse	antes de ...
lavarse el pelo	temprano
secarse el pelo	en seguida
cepillarse los dientes	después de ...
peinarse	a la misma hora
vestirse	puntualmente
desayunar	
salir de su casa	
llegar a la escuela	

Luz puede despertarse a las seis y cuarenta y cinco y levantarse en seguida.
Puede ducharse por la noche ...
Puede ...

2 Con un(a) compañero(a), hablen de sus tareas escolares y de sus actividades extracurriculares.

A —*¿Cuándo haces tus tareas?*
B —*Creo que es mejor ...*
A —*¿Por qué?*
B —*Porque ...*
A —*Y después de las clases, ¿qué haces?*

70 Capítulo 2

Options

Strategies for Reaching All Students

Spanish-Speaking Students
Ex. 3: As an alternative to this exercise, give this assignment: *Haz una descripción corta de cada actividad ilustrada aquí. Luego, di qué características debe tener una persona para participar en cada una.*

 Un paso más Ex. 2-F

Students Needing Extra Help
Ex. 1: Finish the model, giving students more of a framework. Assign a minimum number of sentences to be produced.
Ex. 2: If students respond that they don't do homework, have them respond when they *should* do homework. Complete this model. Help students organize their thoughts and develop correct responses to *¿por qué?*
Ex. 3: If available, use the vocabulary section from the Book 1, Chap. 1 Organizer.

Because some students may not participate in these activities, they may not see the connections between some of these traits and the corresponding activity. Explain the connections.
¿Qué sabes ahora?: Have students write out this section so they can check off what they have mastered.

3 Recomiéndales a las siguientes personas alguna actividad extracurricular según sus características. Puedes usar las ideas del dibujo u otras.

serio(a) / escribir

A —*Soy serio y me gusta escribir. ¿Qué actividad crees que me gustaría?*
B —*La revista literaria.*

a. ordenado(a) / dibujar

b. deportista / hacer ejercicio

c. atrevido(a) / sacar fotos

d. paciente / tocar la flauta

e. trabajador(a) / leer

f.

¿Qué sabes ahora?

Can you:

- describe typical morning routines?
  —Antes de ir a la escuela, es necesario ___, ___ y ___.

- talk about which extracurricular activities you prefer?
  —A mí me gusta(n) ___ y ___.

- tell what you do after school?
  —Después de las clases, hago la tarea, ___ y ___.

---

3 ESTUDIANTE A

a. Soy ordenado(a) y me gusta dibujar. ¿Qué actividad crees tú que me gustaría?

b. ... deportista ... hacer ejercicio ...

c. ... atrevido(a) ... sacar fotos ...

d. ... paciente ... tocar la flauta ...

e. ... trabajador(a) ... leer ...

f. Answers will vary.

ESTUDIANTE B

Answers will vary, but may include:

a. El anuario.

b. El equipo de fútbol.

c. El periódico (de la escuela).

d. La banda. / La orquesta.

e. El periódico (de la escuela).

f. Answers will vary, but look for logical answers.

Answers: ¿Qué sabes ahora?

- Answers will vary, but should include a variety of reflexive verbs.
- Answers will vary, but should include chapter vocabulary.
- Answers will vary, but look for logical verbs in the first person singular.

 Audio Activity 2.3

Pasos vivos 2 CD-ROM
Boom Box, Clip Art Album, Slide Projector, Laboratorio de grabar

---

Enrichment
Ex. 3: Have students choose three friends and write two sentences about each, describing his or her personality and the activities he or she enjoys most.

Multiple Intelligences
Verbal/Linguistic
See Audio Activity 2.3.
Verbal/Linguistic and Interpersonal/Social
See Exs. 1–3.
Visual/Spatial
See Enrichment.

Cultural Notes

(p. 70, realia)
This advertisement for a teeth-whitening system offers the potential user a dazzling smile. The ad's headlines, *Si tus dientes no están blancos es porque no quieres,* uses the *tú* form of address to imply intimacy with the reader, while promising a "natural" method of whitening teeth.

Present & Apply

Cultural Objective
• To compare students' extra-curricular activities in Guatemala and in the U.S.

Multicultural Perspectives
What young people do after school in Guatemala depends on whether they live in a small *aldea* in the highlands or if they live in Guatemala City. In rural towns, young boys may help their fathers in the *milpa,* planting, tending, and harvesting corn for their families' use. Rural girls might work at home weaving *huipiles* (dresses), *servilletas* (cloths used to wrap tortillas and bread), and other items that their families will then sell. On religious holidays and other special days, everyone in town helps prepare for a *fiesta.* Men's associations called *cofradías* organize and conduct many of the ceremonies during a *fiesta.* Have students familiar with other cultures share information about how holidays are celebrated.

Answers
Answers to inductive questions will vary, but students may say a student council provides students a voice in decision-making and gives students a sense of power and self-esteem.

Perspectiva cultural

¿Hay muchos estudiantes que quieren estar en el consejo estudiantil de tu escuela? ¿Por qué? ¿Cómo puede un consejo estudiantil mejorar una escuela?

"Vamos a mejorar la escuela," dice Maya. "Por ejemplo," dice Javier, "el próximo año queremos tener un club de inglés." Éstas son las palabras de dos candidatos al consejo estudiantil del Colegio Interamericano, una escuela privada en la Ciudad de Guatemala. Es una escuela bilingüe donde todos los estudiantes toman unas clases en inglés y otras en español. Por eso, la idea de un club de inglés es muy popular.

Hay dos grupos rivales que esperan ganar el consejo estudiantil. El grupo de Maya y Javier es el más organizado. Su equipo tiene cuatro estudiantes: Maya es candidata a presidenta, Javier a vicepresidente, Luis Enrique a secretario y Margarita a tesorera.

En el Colegio Interamericano hay muchas actividades extracurriculares. La mayoría de los estudiantes participan en algún deporte. Muchos trabajan en el periódico escolar o en la nueva revista literaria. También hay un club de teatro. A veces los grupos hacen fiestas o venden dulces, pasteles o frutas para ganar dinero para algún proyecto.

"El próximo año voy a estar muy ocupada," dice Maya, "y no voy a poder participar en el club de teatro. Para mí el club es muy importante, pero ser presidenta del consejo estudiantil es todavía más importante."

72 Capítulo 2

En una biblioteca escolar, tres jóvenes mexicanos hablan de lo que debe hacer el consejo estudiantil.

La cultura desde tu perspectiva

1 ¿Qué actividades extracurriculares tiene tu escuela? ¿Hay actividades en el colegio de Maya que no hay en tu escuela? ¿Y viceversa? ¿Cuáles?

2 ¿Hay un programa bilingüe en tu escuela? ¿Quiénes participan en ese programa? ¿Cómo es el programa bilingüe en el Colegio Interamericano? ¿Qué piensas de él?

www.pasoapaso.com

Options

Strategies for Reaching All Students

Spanish-Speaking Students
After reading the *Perspectiva cultural,* have Spanish-speaking students make campaign posters based on the following questions: *Si fueras candidato(a) a presidente(a) del consejo estudiantil de tu escuela, ¿qué prometerías? ¿Por qué?* Display the posters around the classroom and encourage the other students to read them.

 Un paso más Ex. 2-G

Students Needing Extra Help
Explain what a student council tries to accomplish and how. Students will need some additional vocabulary.
Ex. 1: Some students may not participate in extracurricular activities. In order to get a response, ask if they work after school, or baby-sit a younger brother or sister. If not, elicit negative responses. Help them with the vocabulary.

Ex. 2: Some students may not be aware of the bilingual program. This would be a good opportunity to have bilingual students or the director come in and talk about the program. If your school doesn't have a bilingual (or ESL) program, brainstorm with students what they would need to do to start one.

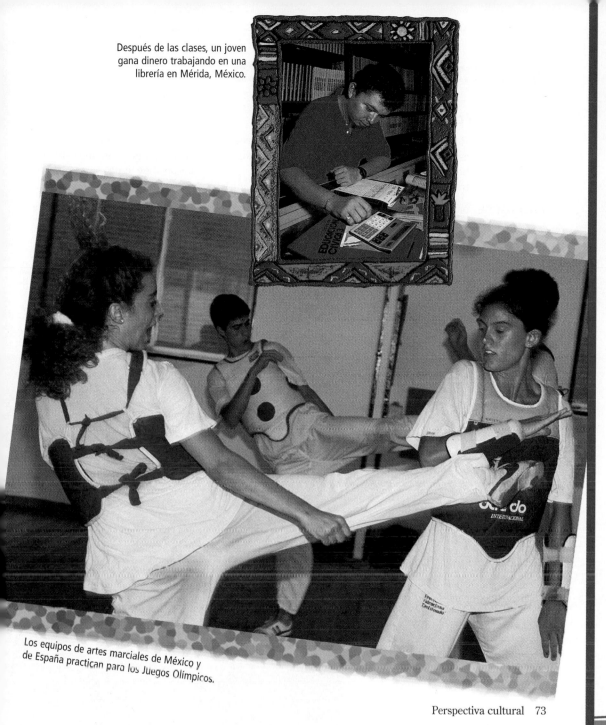

Después de las clases, un joven gana dinero trabajando en una librería en Mérida, México.

Los equipos de artes marciales de México y de España practican para los Juegos Olímpicos.

Perspectiva cultural   73

Answers: La cultura desde tu perspectiva

1–2 Answers will vary, but students may say that in the bilingual program in the *Colegio Interamericano* all students take some classes in Spanish and some in English.

 Pasos vivos 2 CD-ROM

Maps, Notas culturales

 Internet Activities

Perspectiva cultural
Have students go to
www.pasoapaso.com for
additional activities and practice.

Cultural Notes

(p. 72, photo)
These students are meeting to discuss student council matters. Education is free of cost and compulsory for students between the ages of 6 and 14 in Mexico. While the quality of public education in rural Mexico has improved in recent years, urban areas continue to offer greater educational opportunities, especially for study above the *primaria* level. About 80 percent of university students study in Mexico City.

(p. 73, top photo)
It is more common than it once was for high-school students in Latin America to work part-time after school. Among other school expenses, Mexican students must purchase all of their own textbooks which are not provided by the schools. Specialized *librerías* in Latin America sell primarily school texts and supplies.

Standards 2.1; 5.1   **73**

Preview

Overhead 15

Answers

A Other forms of *despertarse: se despiertan, nos despertamos; cepillarse: se cepillan, nos cepillamos; bañarse: se bañan, nos bañamos.* The words that precede the forms of these verbs are pronouns, *se* and *nos.* The *nosotros* form of *levantarse: nos levantamos;* the *Uds. / ellos / ellas* form: *se levantan.*

B *Despertarse* is an *e → ie* stem-changing verb. *Dormir* is an *o → ue* verb. The stem doesn't change in the *nosotros* form.

Gramática en contexto

Entrevista con un astronauta

REPORTERO   Hoy está con nosotros un astronauta, el señor Montero. Señor Montero, ¿es muy difícil trabajar en el espacio?

ASTRONAUTA   No tanto. Uno se acostumbra rápido.

REPORTERO   ¿Duermen en camas?
ASTRONAUTA   Bueno, dormimos en sacos de dormir atados a la pared.

REPORTERO   ¿Cómo se despiertan?
ASTRONAUTA   Nos despertamos con música.

REPORTERO   ¿Y cómo se cepillan los dientes?
ASTRONAUTA   Nos cepillamos los dientes con pasta dentífrica, como todo el mundo.

REPORTERO   ¿Y cómo se bañan?
ASTRONAUTA   Nos bañamos con una esponja y un poco de agua.

REPORTERO   ¿Dónde se lavan las manos?
ASTRONAUTA   En una fuente de agua que está debajo de una cúpula de plástico.

REPORTERO   Bueno. Gracias por su visita, Sr. Montero. Y gracias a ustedes por ver este programa. Hasta la próxima semana.

A Can you find in the interview two other forms of each of these verbs: *despertarse, cepillarse,* and *bañarse?* What words precede those forms? What would be the *nosotros* form of *levantarse?* And the *Uds. / ellos / ellas* form?

B You know that *querer* is an *e → ie* stem-changing verb and *poder* is an *o → ue* stem-changing verb. Which verb in the interview is an *e → ie* verb? Which one is an *o → ue* verb? In which form do you <u>not</u> see the stem change?

74   Capítulo 2

Options

Strategies for Reaching All Students

Students Needing Extra Help
Begin to fill in the grammar section of the Organizer.
A: When students find the forms, put them on the chalkboard. Have them note what is unusual.
B: Have students write out the paradigms for *querer* and *poder* (Book 1, Chap. 7). If they have difficulty, refer them to letter A. Have them start with those three verbs to look for a stem change.

Los verbos reflexivos: 1) Write *levantarse,* drawing a line through the *-se.* 2) Now write out the subject pronoun chart underneath the infinitive. 3) Draw a blank space after each subject pronoun. 4) After each blank space, place the correct conjugated form of *levantar,* pointing out that it is a regular *-ar* verb. 5) Fill in the reflexive pronouns in the blanks next to the corresponding subject pronoun. Point out that students have seen a similar construction in Book 1, Chaps. 7

and 11 (Chap. 12 with infinitives), and in Book 2, Chap. 1.
Provide more examples of placing the reflexive in both positions. Emphasize the use of the definite article. This may be confusing for students because the translation from English suggests using *mi, tu,* etc., instead of *el, la,* etc. Show them that the possession is in the reflexive pronoun because you are doing the action to yourself.

Saturno

Present

Class Starter Review

On the day following presentation of reflexive verbs, you might begin class with this activity:
Have students list three morning activities *(levantarse, ducharse, cepillarse los dientes)*. They then ask three classmates at what time they do each activity (nine questions total). Record the responses.

Los verbos reflexivos

Reflexive verbs are generally used to tell that a person does something to or for him- or herself. A reflexive verb has two parts: a reflexive pronoun *(me, te, se, nos, os)* and a verb form. Here are all the present-tense forms of *levantarse:*

(yo)	**me** levanto	(nosotros) (nosotras)	**nos** levantamos
(tú)	**te** levantas	(vosotros) (vosotras)	**os** levantáis
Ud. (él) (ella)	**se** levanta	Uds. (ellos) (ellas)	**se** levantan

- Except for *se,* the reflexive pronouns are the same as the indirect object pronouns. They usually come before the verb, but they may also be attached to an infinitive.

  Me voy a lavar el pelo.
  Voy a lavar**me** el pelo.

- When using reflexive verbs to talk about parts of the body, we usually use the definite article.

  Nos lavamos **el** pelo.　　*We're washing our hair.*
  ¿Te cepillas **los** dientes?　*Are you brushing your teeth?*

¡NO OLVIDES!

Do you remember the expression *debes quedarte en la cama?* It uses the reflexive verb *quedarse,* "to remain, to stay."

¡NO OLVIDES!

You know the indirect object pronouns.

me	*(to / for) me*
te	*(to / for) you*
le	*(to / for) him, her, it, you (formal)*
nos	*(to / for) us*
os	*(to / for) you (pl.)*
les	*(to / for) them, you (pl.)*

Gramática en contexto　75

Cooperative Learning

Divide the class into groups of three or four. Have them make charts with the following headings: *bañarse (ducharse), vestirse, peinarse, cepillarse los dientes, secarse el pelo.* Under each heading, have the groups list the amount of time it takes to perform each activity. Have groups tabulate their results and report to the class.

Extended Written Practice/Homework

1. Using vocabulary from pp. 62–63, write four sentences telling what you do to get ready in the morning. Include the times at which you do these things.
2. Refer to the actions on pp. 62–63 and write three sentences telling what young people typically do: *Generalmente los jóvenes no se despiertan muy temprano.*
3. Using verbs from pp. 62–63, write three questions that you can ask a classmate about his or her daily schedule.

Multiple Intelligences

Interpersonal/Social, Visual/Spatial, and Logical/Mathematical
See Cooperative Learning.
Visual/Spatial
See *Gramática en contexto* and Overhead 15.
Visual/Spatial and Verbal/Linguistic
See Class Starter Review.

Practice

Answers

1 Answers will vary, but look for a logical progression of actions and the correct reflexive construction. Answers may include: *Primero me levanto. Segundo me cepillo los dientes. Luego me ducho. Después me seco el pelo. Luego me peino.*

Using Realia

Ask: *¿Qué quiere decir "se limpian solas"?*

1 Dile a tu compañero(a) qué haces por la mañana.
Puedes usar *a las (6:00), primero, segundo, después, luego.*

Me despierto a las 6:00.

a.   b.

c.   d.   e.

SE LIMPIAN SOLAS

CON **OXYSEPT** COMFORT TUS **LENTES** DE **CONTACTO**
TAMBIÉN SE **LIMPIAN SOLAS**
Y EN... **1** PASO   ⊛ **ALLERGAN S.A.**

DUERMA DE NOCHE. DESCANSE DE DIA.

76   Capítulo 2

Options

Strategies for Reaching All Students

Students Needing Extra Help
Ex. 2: Have students match the verbs to the pictures and then go back and conjugate the verbs according to the people (or animals) shown. As a reference for students, project the transparency of the reflexive vocabulary pictures.

Ex. 3: Remind students of compound subjects and that the verb form as well as the reflexive pronoun will change in the answer. Model a few of these sentences. If students seem uncertain, do this as a whole-class exercise on the chalkboard or with pairs of students formulating answers.

Extended Written Practice/Homework
1. Write two sentences telling how your schedule and that of another person are different: *Mi papá se levanta a las cinco pero yo me levanto a las seis y cuarto.*
2. Write three sentences telling when you are going to do the actions on pp. 62–63: *Voy a ducharme después de jugar tenis.*

76

2 ¿Qué ocurre en estos dibujos? Usa los verbos de la lista para decirle a tu compañero(a) lo que pasa en cada uno.

Rosario y Mónica se secan el pelo.

Rosario y Mónica

acostarse	lavarse	quedarse
cepillarse	peinarse	secarse
despertarse		

a. ellos   b. Carlos y Ricardo   c. Pilar

d. yo   e. nosotros   f. tú

3 Túrnate con un(a) compañero(a) para hacer preguntas y respuestas.

a qué hora
levantarse / tú y
tus hermanos

A —¿A qué hora se levantan tú y tus hermanos?
B —Nos levantamos temprano.
    o: No tengo hermanos, pero yo me levanto temprano.

a. con qué lavarse las manos / María

b. con qué lavarse el pelo / Manuel y Óscar

c. cuántas veces al día cepillarse los dientes / Uds.

d. cuándo ducharse / tú

e. en cuánto tiempo secarse el pelo / Silvia

a las 7:00

con champú

con jabón

media hora

temprano

tres veces al día

2 Answers
a. Ellos se lavan.
b. Carlos y Ricardo se peinan.
c. Pilar se lava el pelo.
d. Yo me despierto.
e. Nosotros nos cepillamos el pelo.
f. Tú te quedas en la cama.

3 ESTUDIANTE A
a. ¿Con qué se lava María las manos?
b. ¿Con qué se lavan Manuel y Óscar el pelo?
c. ¿Cúantas veces al día se cepillan Uds. los dientes?
d. ¿Cúando te duchas?
e. ¿En cúanto tiempo se seca Silvia el pelo?

ESTUDIANTE B
a. Se lava las manos con jabón.
b. Se lavan el pelo con champú.
c. Nos cepillamos los dientes tres veces al día.
d. Me ducho temprano (a las 7:00).
e. Se seca el pelo en media hora.

 Practice Wkbk. 2-5, 2-6

 Writing Activity 2-D

 Prueba 2-5

Cultural Notes

Multiple Intelligences
Verbal/Linguistic
See Exs. 1–3.
Visual/Spatial
1) Have students create a chart showing their daily schedule.
2) See Practice Wkbk 2-5 and 2-6 and Writing Activity 2-D.

(p. 76, realia)
Note that this advertisement employs both informal and formal forms of address. The *S.A.* following the manufacturer's name stands for *sociedad anónima:* a publicly held corporation with stock holders. The abbreviation is the equivalent of "Inc." in the U.S.

Present & Practice

Class Starter Review

On the day following the presentation of stem-changing verbs, you might begin the class with this activity:

Have students make two columns: 1) *durante las vacaciones* and 2) *durante el año escolar.* Using *acostarse, despertarse,* and *vestirse,* have them write sentences describing at what time they do these activities during vacation and during the school year.

Answers

4 ESTUDIANTE A

a. ¿A qué hora crees que se despierta un actor (una actriz)?

b. . . . se despierta una persona muy trabajadora?

c. . . . se despierta una persona perezosa?

d. . . . se despierta un(a) profesor(a)?

e. . . . se despierta un(a) médico(a)?

f. . . . nos despertamos mi familia y yo los fines de semana?

ESTUDIANTE B

a.–f. Answers will vary, but look for logical times and proper use of the reflexive construction. In *f.,* the answer will be in the *Uds.* form *(Creo que Uds. se despiertan . . .).*

Repaso: Verbos con los cambios *o → ue,* *e → ie* y *e → i*

You know three kinds of stem-changing verbs:

o → ue   *(poder)*   e → ie   *(pensar)*   e → i   *(pedir)*

Here are all the present-tense forms of *acostarse (o → ue), despertarse (e → ie),* and *vestirse (e → i).*

(yo)	me ac**ue**sto	(nosotros) (nosotras)	nos acostamos
(tú)	te ac**ue**stas	(vosotros) (vosotras)	os acostáis
Ud. (él) (ella)	se ac**ue**sta	Uds. (ellos) (ellas)	se ac**ue**stan

(yo)	me desp**ie**rto	(nosotros) (nosotras)	nos despertamos
(tú)	te desp**ie**rtas	(vosotros) (vosotras)	os despertáis
Ud. (él) (ella)	se desp**ie**rta	Uds. (ellos) (ellas)	se desp**ie**rtan

(yo)	me v**i**sto	(nosotros) (nosotras)	nos vestimos
(tú)	te v**i**stes	(vosotros) (vosotras)	os vestís
Ud. (él) (ella)	se v**i**ste	Uds. (ellos) (ellas)	se v**i**sten

78   Capítulo 2

Options

Strategies for Reaching All Students

Students Needing Extra Help

Verbos con los cambios . . . : Have students review the *poder* paradigm from Book 1, Chap. 7. Then have them write out the *acostar* paradigm based on their review of *poder.* Follow this with a review of *pensar* (Book 1, Chap. 7). Then write out *despertar.* Finally, review *pedir* (Book 1, Chap. 12), writing out *vestir.* Let them discover similar patterns. Show them the pattern of "boot" verbs.

Exs. 4–5: Show students what stays the same and what changes.

Brainstorm the times for each kind of personality or job.

Remind students to be careful with *f.* because of the verb change to *nosotros / Uds.* Have students answer, using the second choice, so they can practice attaching the pronoun to the infinitive.

Ex. 6: Brainstorm what activities would need particular clothing. Then conjugate the verb. Add pictures of clothing if it helps students to focus.

Extended Written Practice/Homework

1. Write three sentences describing some of your habits and those of your family related to daily care: *Suelo cepillarme los dientes por lo menos dos veces al día.*

2. Write three sentences telling who wants to participate in different extracurricular activities: *Mi amiga Graciela quiere cantar en el coro.*

Después de jugar jai alai, hay que descansar.

4 ¿A qué hora crees que se despiertan estas personas? Trabaja con un(a) compañero(a).

un(a) camarero(a)

A —¿A qué hora crees que se despierta un(a) camarero(a)?
B —Creo que se despierta a las cinco de la mañana.
  o: Depende. Puede despertarse a las seis o las siete de la mañana.

a. un actor, una actriz
b. una persona muy trabajadora
c. una persona perezosa
d. un(a) profesor(a)
e. un(a) médico(a)
f. mi familia y yo los fines de semana

5 Ahora, trabaja con un(a) compañero(a) para decir a qué hora se acuestan las personas del Ejercicio 4.

un(a) camarero(a)

A —¿A qué hora crees que se acuesta un(a) camarero(a)?
B —Creo que se acuesta a las diez y media de la noche.
  o: Depende. Puede acostarse a medianoche.

6 Túrnate con un(a) compañero(a). Digan para qué se visten estas personas. Usen expresiones de las dos columnas.

a. yo   para practicar ___
b. mis compañeros y yo   para cantar en ___
c. (nombre)   para ir a ___
d. los miembros del (de la) ___   para jugar ___
e. tu profesor(a) de español   para

Gramática en contexto   79

---

5 ESTUDIANTE A
a. ¿A qué hora crees que se acuesta un actor (una actriz)?
b. ...se acuesta una persona muy trabajadora?
c. ...se acuesta una persona perezosa?
d. ...se acuesta un(a) profesor(a)?
e. ...se acuesta un(a) médico(a)?
f. ...nos acostamos mi familia y yo los fines de semana?

ESTUDIANTE B
a.–f. Answers will vary, but look for the proper use of the reflexive or *puede* + reflexive *inf.*

6 Answers will vary, but should begin in the following manner:
a. Yo me visto para ...
b. Mis compañeros y yo nos vestimos para ...
c. (Nombre) se viste para ...
d. Los miembros del coro se visten para ...
e. Mi profesor(a) de español se viste para ...

 Practice Wkbk. 2-7, 2-8

 Writing Activity 2-E

 Prueba 2-6

Cultural Notes

3. Write three sentences telling what people wear when they get dressed for different events: *Cuando se viste para un baile, mi mamá prefiere llevar un vestido.*

Multiple Intelligences
Bodily/Kinesthetic
Have volunteers research jai alai and come to class prepared to explain and demonstrate the sport.

Paso cultural
Possible answers: karate, tae kwon do, judo, yoga/Sí, también son antiguos.

(p. 79, photo)
The game of jai alai was first played by the Basques who named this sport *pelota vasca*. Around 1900 the game was introduced to Cuba and from there has become popular in Spain, France, Italy, Mexico, the Philippines, Indonesia, and in parts of the U.S. There is an international jai alai federation that holds championship games every four years.

Present & Practice

Class Starter Review

On the day following presentation of *antes de / después de,* you might begin the class with this activity:

Have students form groups of three and then take turns playing three roles: *Estudiante A* gives a reflexive verb, *Estudiante B* says what he or she does before the verb mentioned *(Antes de lavarme el pelo, yo me levanto),* and *Estudiante C* says what he or she does afterward.

Answers

7 ESTUDIANTE A

a. ¿Qué haces antes de pasar la aspiradora?

b. . . . nadar en la piscina?

c. . . . ir al centro comercial?

d. . . . salir para la escuela?

e. . . . acostarte?

f. Questions will vary, but look for the construction *antes de* + inf.

ESTUDIANTE B

Answers will vary, but may include the following:

a. Sacudo los muebles.

b. Me ducho (me baño).

c. Saco dinero.

d. Me visto. / Me cepillo los dientes.

e. Me cepillo los dientes.

f. Answers will vary, but may include a reflexive verb in the first person singular.

Antes de /después de + infinitivo

When *antes de* or *después de* is followed by a verb, the verb is in the infinitive form.

Me gusta leer **antes de acostarme.**

Después de preparar la mochila, salgo de la casa.

7 Pregúntale a un(a) compañero(a) qué hace antes de hacer estas actividades.

ir al dentista   A —¿Qué haces antes de ir al dentista?
                 B —Me cepillo los dientes.

Estudiante A   **Estudiante B**

a. pasar la aspiradora

b. nadar en la piscina

c. ir al centro comercial

d. salir para la escuela

e. acostarse

f.

A esta joven española le encanta cuidar niños.

80   Capítulo 2

Options

Strategies for Reaching All Students

Students Needing Extra Help

Ex. 7: Remind students that *hace* is usually answered with another verb.

Use the vocabulary sections from the Book 1 Organizers, if available.

Ex. 8: Give additional models, showing students the combination of regular and reflexive verbs in a dialogue.

Ex. 9: Remind students that the verb form won't change if the answer involves com-

pound subjects. However, if only one student answers a question, the verb form will change. Everyone should keep a list in order to answer the questions in Ex. 10.

Ex. 10: Remind students to answer in the *nosotros* form.

Ahora lo sabes: Have students write out this list so they can record what they have mastered.

Extended Written Practice/Homework

1. Think of three things you do before leaving the house in the morning. Write sentences describing these actions:
Generalmente me ducho antes de salir de casa por la mañana.

2. Write three sentences naming a pair of actions that you always do in sequence:
Siempre bebo agua después de practicar deportes.

8 Ahora pregúntale a tu compañero(a) qué hace después de hacer estas actividades.

levantarse   A —¿*Qué haces después de levantarte?*
                  B —*Hago la cama.*

Estudiante A

a. ducharse   d. lavarse el pelo

b. practicar artes marciales   e. desayunar

c. poner la mesa

f.

Estudiante B

hacer la cama   ducharse

comer algo   vestirse

secarse el pelo

9 Trabajen en grupo. Un miembro del grupo va a hacer estas preguntas. Escriban el nombre de los estudiantes que contestan cada pregunta.

a. ¿Quiénes se levantan antes de las 6:30?
b. ¿Quiénes se acuestan después de las 10:30 los días de semana?
c. ¿Quiénes hacen la tarea antes de la cena?
d. ¿Y quiénes la hacen después de la cena?
e. ¿Quiénes se visten antes de desayunar el sábado?
f. ¿Quiénes se cepillan los dientes después del desayuno?

10 Luego, compara las respuestas del Ejercicio 9 y dile a un(a) compañero(a) el nombre de un(a) estudiante que dio la misma respuesta que tú.

Pablo y yo nos levantamos antes de las 6:30.

Ahora lo sabes

Can you:

■ talk about your daily routine?
   —Todas las mañanas ___ levanto temprano, me ___ y me ___ para ir a la escuela.

■ talk about people's habits?
   —Mi hermanito nunca ___ los dientes ni ___ la cara.

■ talk about a sequence of events?
   —Es necesario cepillarse los dientes ___ de comer.

> **MORE PRACTICE**
>
> Más práctica y tarea, pp. 532–533
> Practice Workbook 2–5, 2–10

Cultural Notes

(p. 80, photo)
This Spanish girl is helping care for her younger brother. While child care has traditionally been considered to be a woman's responsibility, gender roles in Spanish society are gradually changing. Today many men also perform such domestic tasks as child care, cleaning, and cooking.

Apply

 ¿Recuerdas?

Play

 Video Activity A

Using the Video

Episode 2 begins as Jamie arrives at the Navarro family's house in Querétaro. The Navarros had previously agreed to Jamie's sharing a bedroom with their son Carlos because they thought she was a boy named *Jaime*. On discovering the truth, the Navarros send Jamie to stay with the family of Carlos' former girlfriend, María Linares. Meanwhile, in the Querétaro Central library, the mysterious figure who appeared on the train in Episode 1, Santana, is meeting privately with the library's director, Demetrio. Santana has been spying on Jamie, secretly following her everywhere. Demetrio tells Santana to continue keeping an eye on Jamie.

In the final scene, don Silvestre Aguilar, a powerful local politician, makes a secret visit to María's house, where Jamie is now staying.

El básquetbol es muy popular en los países hispanos.

Actividades

1 En grupo, hagan una lista de las actividades extracurriculares que ofrece la escuela.

• Hablen de las actividades más populares.
• Digan por qué son tan populares.
• Digan qué es necesario hacer para participar en estas actividades.
• Díganles a otros estudiantes por qué deben participar.

2 En grupos pequeños, inventen una entrevista con una persona famosa. Pregúntenle sobre:

• cuándo se levanta y se acuesta
• sus actividades por la mañana
• su familia
• sus pasatiempos
• sus planes para el futuro

Escojan *(choose)* a dos personas del grupo para practicar la entrevista. Grábenla *(record it)* si es posible. Luego, preséntenla a la clase.

En Cali, Colombia, dos muchachos practican el tiro al arco.

82   Capítulo 2

Options

Strategies for Reaching All Students

Spanish-Speaking Students
Ex. 2: After this activity, have Spanish-speaking students answer in writing: *¿Qué personas famosas te interesan más? ¿Por qué? ¿Por qué crees que nos interesan tanto las vidas de personas famosas?*

 Un paso más Ex. 2-H

Students Needing Extra Help
If pressed for time, divide the class into groups. Assign an activity to each group.
Ex. 1: This could be a whole-class activity. Use the vocabulary section of the Organizer. Offer a model for the list of activities.
Ex. 2: If available, use the vocabulary sections of the Book 1 Organizers for help with words relating to families, activities, pastimes, etc.
Brainstorm how to form the questions the interviewer will ask.

Multiple Intelligences
Interpersonal/Social and Visual/Spatial
See Exs. 1–2.
Visual/Spatial
See Using the Video, Writing Activities 2-G and 2-H, and Comm. Act. BLMs 2-4 and 2-5.
Visual/Spatial and Logical/Mathematical
See *Conexiones*.

Conexiones

Prepararse por la mañana

Vas a hacer un diagrama de flujo *(flow chart)* para organizarte por la mañana. Observa el diagrama que hizo un estudiante de Perú.

LEVANTARSE: 7h.* → PREPARARSE → SALIR: 7h.45m.*

levantarme

lavarme la cara 1m. → cepillarme los dientes 2m. → ducharme 7m.

peinarme 2m. → vestirme 5m.

arreglar el cuarto y desayunar 18m. → pasear al perro 10m.

salir

*h. = hora(s); m. = minuto(s)

Haz tu propio diagrama de flujo como el modelo. Debes considerar:

- el tiempo que necesitas para prepararte
- todo lo que debes hacer antes de salir
- la duración de cada actividad (la suma del tiempo de cada actividad debe ser igual al tiempo total que necesitas para prepararte)

Compara tu diagrama con el de un(a) compañero(a). Hablen de las actividades que Uds. hacen por la mañana y de la diferencia en el orden en que las hacen.

Todo junto 83

Answers: Conexiones
Flow charts will vary. Look for logical time sequence and use of chapter vocabulary.

 La Catrina: Capítulo 2

Play

 Video Activity B

 Para entender mejor

Play

 Video Activity C

 Writing Activities 2-G, 2-H

 Comm. Act. BLMs 2-4, 2-5

 Pasos vivos 2 CD-ROM
A Jugar, Laboratorio de grabar, Maps, Video Monitor, Video Presentation Maker

Cultural Notes

(p. 82, top photo)
Basketball is beginning to rival soccer as a sport without national boundaries. The only sport whose origins are wholly within the U.S., basketball was invented in 1891 by James A. Naismith in Springfield, Massachusetts. In recent years, it has gained greatly in popularity throughout the world.

(p. 82, bottom photo)
With about two million people, Cali is the third-largest city in Colombia. Located just three degrees north of the equator, it has a year-round warm climate, which is tempered by its altitude of almost 3,500 feet. In equatorial regions such as southern Colombia, altitude is the biggest factor in the climate. Lowlands are hot and humid, and much cooler conditions prevail higher in the Andes.

Apply

Process Reading
For a description of process reading, see p. 52.

Multicultural Perspectives
Fútbol is not the same game played by the San Francisco 49ers or Green Bay Packers. It is, however, one of the most popular games in Latin America and the most popular worldwide. Soccer, as it is called in the U.S., is only beginning to become popular here. The World Cup *(la Copa Mundial),* soccer's international championship tournament, was held for the first time in the U.S. in the summer of 1994. This event takes place only every four years, and millions follow their favorite team from even the most remote areas. The Hispanic American countries of Argentina, Bolivia, Colombia, and Mexico all had qualifying teams for the 1994 World Cup. (Brazil defeated Italy for the championship.) Since the tournament began in 1930, two Spanish-speaking countries have won the World Cup: Uruguay (1930, 1950) and Argentina (1978, 1986). Ask students who are familiar with other cultures to share their knowledge of popular sports in those cultures.

¡Vamos a leer!

Antes de leer

STRATEGY ➤ Using prior knowledge

Which sports are the most popular at your school? Are you on a sports team? How long do you practice each day?

Mira la lectura

STRATEGY ➤ Identifying the main idea

Skim this article to see if you can identify the main idea. Which of these would make the best title for the selection?

- Mi deporte favorito
- Me encanta nadar
- Menos práctica, por favor
- ¡Abajo los deportes!

¿De Acuerdo?

¿Cómo son los deportes en las escuelas secundarias de los Estados Unidos? Creo que tomamos los deportes demasiado en serio.

Soy nadadora. Me paso todo el día en mis clases y en la piscina, y el resto durmiendo. Tengo que levantarme a las seis de la mañana y acostarme a las nueve de la noche o antes. Mi equipo practica dos horas antes de entrar a clase y dos horas y media después de salir de la escuela. Las prácticas son muy duras. En una tarde,

nadamos más de 9.000 yardas y tenemos sólo seis minutos para descansar. ¡Pero no estamos entrenando para las olimpiadas!

No comprendo por qué los deportes son tan importantes. Es posible que las escuelas quieran tener una buena reputación, pero el resultado es la tensión innecesaria y a veces los accidentes. Creo que se debe fijar un máximo de tiempo para el entrenamiento de los atletas. Si hay deportistas

que quieren practicar más, pueden hacerlo en clubes fuera de la escuela.

Options

Strategies for Reaching All Students

Spanish-Speaking Students
Aplicación: After this activity, have Spanish-speaking students answer in writing: *¿Crees que es mejor tener equipos para varios deportes en la escuela o sólo en clubes fuera de la escuela? ¿Por qué?*

Students Needing Extra Help
Antes de leer: Remind students to follow the four-step procedure (predict, skim, reread, summarize) recommended in Chap. 1. A cooperative learning method appropriate for this reading selection is to form teams of three students. Each team member is responsible for reading and answering the questions in one of the three *¡Vamos a leer!* sections. After each student has completed his or her individual section, the team meets together, and the three members report on

the content of their sections to the rest of the team. However, each member is responsible for reading all parts.
Mira la lectura: Be sure students understand the meaning of the four possible title selections. Bring students back to the four titles. They may lose track of the assignment as they skim through.
Infórmate: Be sure students understand the four attitudes.
Aplicación: Ask for volunteers to approach the athletes, or use the athletes in your own

Infórmate

STRATEGY ➤ Identifying the writer's attitude

A reading selection can not only tell us what the writer *thinks* about a subject, but also what he or she *feels* about it. However, the writer's attitude is often not stated directly. We have to figure it out from clues that might include choice of words, choice of details, and what is left out.

Read the article carefully. Which of these statements best expresses the writer's attitude toward sports?

1. Le gustan los deportes, pero no todos.
2. No le gustan los deportes escolares.
3. Le gustan los deportes. Sobre todo le gusta nadar.
4. Le gustan los deportes, pero quiere darles menos énfasis.

SONDEO DE OPINIÓN

	Equipo de fútbol americano	Equipo de fútbol	Equipo de básquetbol	La banda	El coro
Practicamos demasiado					
No practicamos demasiado					
Practicamos muy poco tiempo					

Aplicación

Take a poll of ten members of your school's athletic teams. Ask them if the amount of practice required is too much, too little, or just enough. Then report the results to the class.

For example:

Hay (número) personas que están de acuerdo con la autora.

Hay (número) personas que creen que no practican demasiado.

Hay (número) personas que creen que practican muy poco tiempo.

Answers
Antes de leer
Answers will vary.

Mira la lectura
Menos práctica, por favor

Infórmate
Statement 4 best expresses the writer's attitude toward sports.

Aplicación
Answers will vary.

WWW Internet Activities
Have students go to www.pasoapaso.com for additional activities and practice.

class to answer this. Also, this might spark a great discussion with members of non-athletic clubs who put in as much practice time, but are not recognized for doing so.

Multiple Intelligences
Logical/Mathematical
See *Aplicación*.

Apply

Process Writing

For more information regarding developing a writing portfolio, see p. 54.

¡Vamos a escribir!

1 ¿Quieres ser jugador(a) de béisbol? ¿Conoces a algunos médicos? Piensa en el horario de una persona con una profesión interesante (policía, actor, actriz, etc.). Si puedes, entrevista a la persona. Contesta estas preguntas.

- ¿Cuándo se levanta?
- ¿Trabaja por la noche?
- ¿A qué hora sale para el trabajo?
- ¿Qué hace en el trabajo?
- ¿A qué hora regresa a casa?
- ¿Cómo se siente al final del día?

Luego escribe un informe con el título "Un día en la vida de ..." Sigue los cinco pasos del proceso de escribir. (Si es necesario, mira la página 54.)

2 Lee el informe de otro estudiante y escribe tu reacción. Lo puedes titular "(No) me gustaría ser ...". Explica por qué te gustaría o no te gustaría ser piloto, por ejemplo. Sigue los cinco pasos del proceso de escribir. Puedes usar expresiones como éstas:

- porque soy (muy) ...
- fácil / difícil
- prefiero ...

3 Para distribuir tu trabajo, puedes:

- incluirlo en un libro titulado *Un día en la vida de ...*
- enviarlo a la revista literaria de la escuela
- incluirlo en un boletín para los padres
- exhibirlo en la sala de clases
- incluirlo en tu portafolio

Un soldador ecuatoriano construyendo un edificio

Options

Strategies for Reaching All Students

Students Needing Extra Help
Step 1: Give students time to think about how to respond to these questions. Model using the student's own life. Interview school personnel in your building: custodians, nurse, administrator, etc. Send students in pairs.

Assign this in advance and give enough time. Remind students that the essay will be written using the reflexive *se*.
Step 2: If students wrote an essay as suggested in Step 1, the class could respond to it here. They may need more vocabulary to write the essay.

Cultural Notes

(p. 86, photo)
This man in Quito, Ecuador, is practicing *soldadura* (welding). The frequent use of sheet metal in the construction of Latin American housing calls for the skills of trained welders at construction sites. Door and window frames in homes are often constructed of steel, and the internal support structure typically is constructed in part with iron rods.

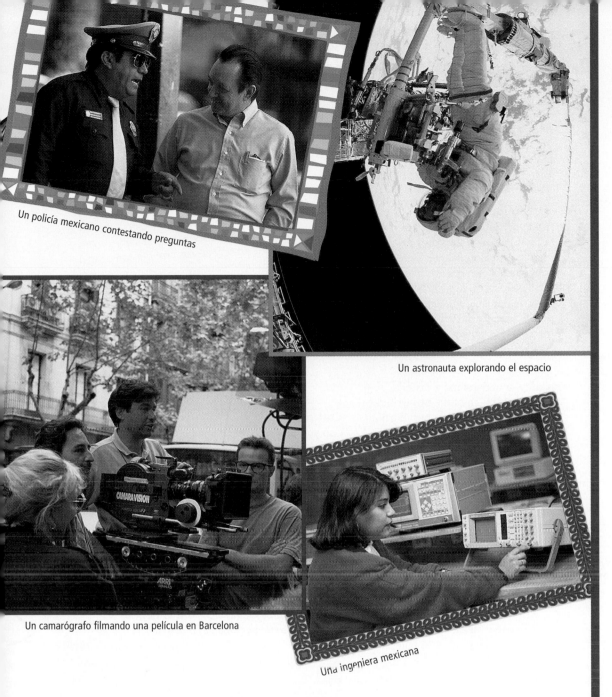

Un policía mexicano contestando preguntas

Un astronauta explorando el espacio

Un camarógrafo filmando una película en Barcelona

Una ingeniera mexicana

¡Vamos a escribir! 87

(p. 87, top left photo)
Mexico has both national and local police forces. In Mexico City, local police often work out of small *cabinas* situated at traffic intersections. The *cabinas* are staffed 24 hours a day.

(p. 87, bottom left photo)
These filmmakers are shooting on location in Barcelona, which is one of the filmmaking centers of Spain. Barcelona vies with Madrid as the cultural capital. Barcelona is a bilingual city, with most residents speaking both Castillian and Catalan.

(p. 87, bottom right photo)
This young Mexican woman is using her engineering skills on a project. In Mexico, as in many other countries, women are participating in formerly male-dominated occupations in ever-increasing numbers. The enrollment of women in technical university courses is on the upswing. More women work outside the home, and more than ever, families have both parents working.

Assess & Summarize

Test Preparation

You may want to assign parts of this section as homework or as an in-class writing activity prior to administering the *Examen de habilidades.*

Answers

Listening: *Yo siempre me levanto temprano. Me levanto a las cinco porque tengo que repartir el periódico antes de las seis. Casi todos los días cuido niños después de la escuela. No puedo practicar deportes ni tocar en la banda como tú. Pero estoy de buen humor. Sé que en dos o tres meses voy a poder comprarme una computadora nueva.* The student is talking about after-school activities. The student is unable to participate in sports or play in the band because he or she is earning money for a new computer through a paper route and a baby-sitting job.

Reading: The writer of the second passage probably enjoys his or her morning routine; he or she seems less rushed.

Writing: Letters will vary.

Esta sección te ayudará a prepararte para el examen de habilidades, donde tendrás que hacer tareas semejantes. Recuerda, sin embargo, que en el examen no habrá *(there won't be)* modelos.

Listening

Can you understand when people talk about the things they do before and after school? Listen as your teacher reads a sample similar to what you will hear on the test. Is this student talking about extracurricular activities or outside-of-school activities? What is this student not able to do and why?

Reading

Can you understand a writer's attitude? Which of the two writers probably enjoys his or her morning routine?

1. Todos los días el despertador me despierta a la misma hora. Tengo que levantarme inmediatamente. Me ducho, me cepillo los dientes y me visto rápido porque mi hermana tiene que usar el baño después.

2. Todos los días el despertador me despierta a la misma hora. Me baño, me cepillo los dientes y me visto. Luego preparo el desayuno. Desayuno y repaso mis lecciones antes de salir para la escuela.

88 Capítulo 2

Writing

Can you write a letter to a friend describing what you do during the week? Here is a sample.

> Querido Alonso,
>
> Mi semana es bastante típica. Antes de regresar a casa practico con la banda los lunes, miércoles y viernes. Los martes y jueves trabajo como tutor voluntario. Enseño flauta y clarinete en una escuela que está cerca. Me gusta despertarme tan tarde como posible porque siempre me acuesto tarde.
>
> Tu amigo,
>
> Sebastián

Culture

Can you describe what teenagers in Guatemala might do as extracurricular activities? Which of these are similar to what you and your friends do?

Speaking

Can you talk with someone about your day before or after school? Create a dialogue with your partner. Here is a sample:

A —*¿A qué hora te despiertas de lunes a viernes?*
B —*Me despierto a las seis y media. Por suerte, los fines de semana puedo levantarme más tarde.*
A —*¿Qué haces por la mañana?*
B —*Antes de ir a la escuela me ducho y me visto. Después de desayunar salgo para la escuela.*
A —*¿Participas en alguna actividad extracurricular?*
B —*Sí, en la banda y también escribo para la revista literaria. ¿Y tú?*

Self Test www.pasoapaso.com

Options

Strategies for Reaching All Students

Students Needing Extra Help

Have students write out this section so they can keep track of what they have mastered. Remind them that this is just a sample of what the test will be like.
Listening: Ask students for which information they should be listening. What words do they think will be used? Emphasize that they don't have to understand everything in order to be successful in this exercise.
Allow students to jot down words as they hear them. Many with poor auditory processing might hear the word but have difficulty recalling it. Read the sample more than once.
Another method is to let students write down the words they think might be contained in the paragraph and then check them off as they hear them.
Reading: If this is too subtle for some students to pick up, add words to the second paragraph that mean the opposite of *inmediatamente* and *rápido.*

Writing: Use the vocabulary section of the Organizer.
Culture: Have students review the *Perspectiva cultural.* Follow up with a discussion of important points.
Speaking: Review both sections of *Empecemos a conversar* in order to find expressions that would be useful here. Set a specific time for this assignment.

Resumen del vocabulario

Usa el vocabulario de este capítulo para:
- describe your day before and after school
- talk about which extracurricular activities you prefer
- compare your extracurricular activities with those of another student

to indicate daily routine
acostarse *(o → ue)*
bañarse
la cara
cepillarse (los dientes / el pelo)
desayunar
el despertador
despertarse *(e → ie)*
ducharse
lavarse (la cara / el pelo)
levantarse
peinarse
secarse (el pelo)
soler *(o → ue)* + *inf.*
vestirse *(e → i)*

to indicate time
antes de + *inf.*
después de + *inf.*

to discuss extracurricular activities
la actividad extracurricular
el anuario
las artes marciales
el club, *pl.* los clubes
el consejo estudiantil
cuidar niños
el equipo
ganar
literario, -a
el miembro
participar (en)
el periódico (de la escuela)
repartir
la revista (literaria)
ser miembro de
trabajar como voluntario(a)
el tutor, la tutora

to discuss music
la banda
la canción, *pl.* las canciones
cantar
el coro
la orquesta
el instrumento musical
  el clarinete
  el contrabajo
  la flauta
  el piano
  el saxofón, *pl.* los saxofones
  el tambor
  la trompeta
  el violín, *pl.* los violines

other useful words and expressions
depender
de buen / mal humor
fácilmente
es necesario
hay que + *inf.*
mismo, -a
por lo menos
según
sin
uno

Resumen 89

Assessment

Prueba cumulativa

Examen de habilidades

Test Generator

Additional Assessment Options

Comm. Act. BLMs
Small Group Activities
Situation Cards

Pasos vivos 2 CD-ROM
Slide Presentation Maker, Video Presentation Maker, Word Processor, Spindle

¿Lo sabes bien? Video Quiz

Internet Activities
Self-Test

CAPÍTULO 3

THEME: CLOTHING

COMMUNICATION

Topics
Clothing
Currency

Objectives
To understand relative values of currencies

To indicate articles of clothing

To describe clothing in detail

To describe fabrics and patterns

To indicate sizes

To indicate clothing preferences and make comparisons

To discuss ways of paying for purchases

CULTURE

Currency in Spain and Latin America

GRAMMAR

Repaso: El pretérito de los verbos regulares

Adjetivos y pronombres demostrativos

Los comparativos: tanto(a) . . . como

Ancillaries available for use with Chapter 3

Multisensory/Technology

 Overheads, 16–20

 Audio Tapes and CDs

 Vocabulary Art Blackline Masters for Hands-On Learning, pp. 18–22/CD-ROM

 Classroom Crossword

 La Catrina

 Pasos vivos 2 CD-ROM

 Internet Activities www.pasoapaso.com

Print

 Practice Workbook, pp. 23–33

 Writing, Audio & Video Activities, pp. 17–22, 99–101, 155–156

 Communicative Activity Blackline Masters
  Pair and Small Group Activities, pp. 15–20
  Situation Cards, p. 21

 Un paso más: Actividades para ampliar tu español, pp. 13–18

 RESOURCE PRO®

Planning Express, Teaching Resources Library, and Clip Art Library

Assessment

 Assessment Program
  Pruebas, pp. 39–50
  Examen de habilidades, pp. 51–54

 Test Generator

 ¿Lo sabes bien? Video Quiz

Video still from Chap. 3

89A

¿Qué ropa está de moda?

School uniforms show school affiliation and are very practical. Many Latin American and Spanish teens wear them. Away from school, however, these teens are often fashionable and enjoy wearing trendy clothing.

Many of the same clothes that are "in" in the U.S. are also popular in Spanish-speaking countries. For example, teens love T-shirts and sweatshirts. Those sporting the names of American universities or that have some writing in English are always in vogue. Athletic shoes are also considered fashionable for informal occasions, and blue jeans are as popular there as here. However, even though the casual look is acceptable, sloppiness is frowned upon. Generally, shorts, other than for children, are considered improper anywhere except the beach or a resort town.

Teens in Spanish-speaking countries often express their individuality through clothing styles. Leather boots and jackets are common in cold climates, and accessories might include scarves, thick leather belts and, for girls, more jewelry than a typical U.S. teen might wear. Colors are generally subdued. In tropical countries, embroidered, bright-colored cotton clothing is popular. Each Spanish-speaking country is different. You are likely to see more teens dressed in up-to-date fashions in countries with a heavy European influence and a large middle class, such as Argentina and Chile, than in countries whose populations are heavily Indian or part Indian such as Bolivia or Peru.

It would be amiss to speak of clothing in Latin America and fail to mention the beautiful native clothing worn by many indigenous people. For example, the colorful and intricate patterns worn by the Mayas of Guatemala are hand-woven on looms designed centuries ago. Throughout Latin America, Indian villages have their own unique style of dress, and on market days, when villagers from a specific region converge on the market town, one can identify their origins by the clothing they wear. Today, this is more true of the women than the men, but in areas where there is less contact with urban areas, the men, too, wear the clothing of their village. Traditional costumes may be worn on *días de fiesta*.

Introduce

Re-entry of Concepts

The following list represents words, expressions, and grammar topics re-entered from Book 1 and Book 2 (Chaps. 1–2):

Book 1
numbers 0–61, *gustar* expressions, school supplies, colors, clothing, vacation places, household chores, formal attire

Chapter 1
school activities
school supplies

Chapter 2
daily routine

90   Capítulo 3

Planning

Cross-Curricular Connections

Consumer Education Connection
(pp. 98–99)
Ask students to put together a wardrobe for school with a budget of $150. Have them consider these factors: Can the item be worn with more than one thing? Is the fabric durable? Is the item multifunctional (for example, a scarf that doubles as a waist wrap)? Have students present their wardrobe choices to the class.

Career Connection *(pp. 108–109)*
In small groups, have students create a line of clothing on a large piece of construction paper. Have them include a designer name, a logo, and a category of clothing for the current season. Students can draw or use magazine pictures to illustrate their line, and they should write a brief description of each item or ensemble and give it a price in dollars and *pesos* (or another currency used in the Spanish-speaking world).

Math Connection *(pp. 116–117)*
Provide students with a chart comparing the cost of common items (for example, a ballpoint pen, a soft drink, etc.) in U.S. currency and currency from Spanish-speaking countries. Using a currency conversion chart from a newspaper, compare the actual cost of the items in U.S. currency and calculate the percentage difference.

CAPÍTULO 3

¿Qué ropa está de moda?

Objectives

At the end of this chapter, you will be able to:

► describe clothing in detail

► indicate clothing preferences and make comparisons

► say how you paid for purchases

► talk about the currency in Spain and in various Latin American countries

PASO CULTURAL

La ropa tradicional de la gente indígena de Latinoamérica es mucho más que algo para llevar. Es una forma de comunicar información como, por ejemplo, de qué pueblo es la persona que la lleva. Las molas de los indios cuna de Panamá, como éstas, se usan generalmente para decorar blusas. ¿Por qué crees que la ropa tradicional es tan importante para esta gente? Compara la actitud de la gente en los Estados Unidos hacia *(toward)* la ropa con la de la gente indígena de Latinoamérica. ¿En qué son iguales y diferentes las dos actitudes?

Comprando molas en un mercado de Panamá

91

Cultural Objective
• To discuss students' clothes-pur-chasing habits and preferences

Critical Thinking: Classifying Information
Ask students what factors they consider when making a clothing purchase. After writing each response on the chalkboard, poll students to find out the three most important factors.

¡Piensa en la CULTURA!

De compras en México, Chile y España

Mira las fotos. Los estudiantes que vemos aquí están hablando de la ropa que usan.

"¿Quieres entrar en esta tienda o en ésa?"
¿Te gusta ir al centro comercial los fines de semana? ¿Qué tiendas de ropa prefieres?

PASO CULTURAL
Cancún es uno de los lugares de vacaciones más populares de México. Tiene un clima tropical y playas hermosas. En algunas de estas playas y en otros lugares cerca están todavía las ruinas de las pirámides de los mayas. Cerca de los centros comerciales en el norte de la ciudad hay un museo arqueológico con tesoros descubiertos en la región. Y cerca de Cancún está también Chichén Itzá, donde los turistas pueden comprar *huipiles* y otra ropa típica de los mayas. ¿Qué diferencias puede haber entre comprar ropa en un centro comercial como éste y comprar ropa en Chichén Itzá?

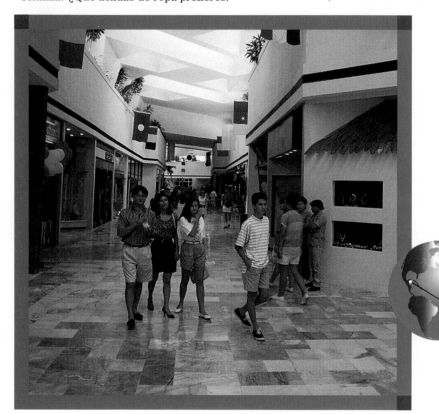

Plaza Flami
Cancún, Mé

92   Capítulo 3

Options

Strategies for Reaching All Students

Spanish-Speaking Students
Ask: *¿Quién te compra ropa o te da dinero para comprarla? ¿Qué tipo de ropa te gusta llevar? ¿Por qué crees que a muchos jóvenes les gusta la ropa un poco exagera-da? ¿Cuál es el estilo más popular ahora?*

 Un paso más Ex. 3-A

Multiple Intelligences
Visual/Spatial and Verbal/Linguistic
Have students research clothing styles of various Spanish-speaking countries and write a report comparing their fashion to ours in the U.S. Have volunteers read their reports to the class.

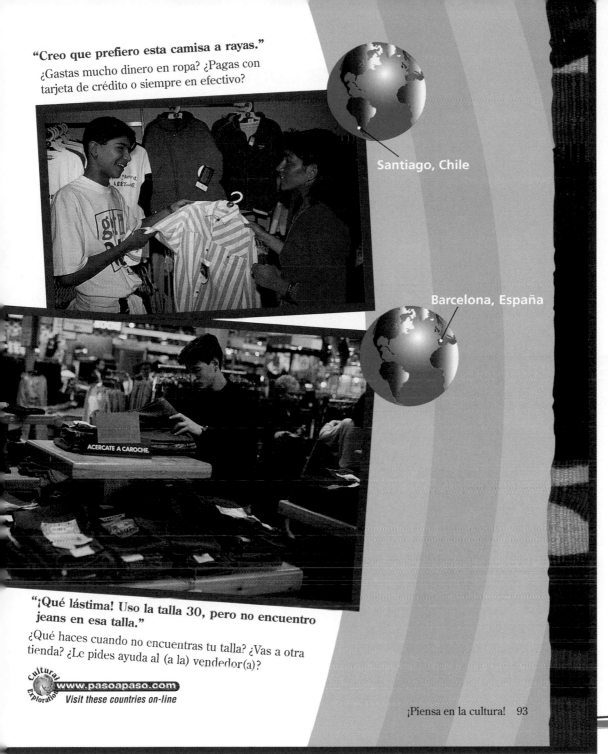

"Creo que prefiero esta camisa a rayas."
¿Gastas mucho dinero en ropa? ¿Pagas con tarjeta de crédito o siempre en efectivo?

Santiago, Chile

Barcelona, España

"¡Qué lástima! Uso la talla 30, pero no encuentro jeans en esa talla."
¿Qué haces cuando no encuentras tu talla? ¿Vas a otra tienda? ¿Le pides ayuda al (a la) vendedor(a)?

Cultural Exploration
www.pasoapaso.com
Visit these countries on-line

¡Piensa en la cultura! 93

Multicultural Perspectives

Tell students to look at the labels on their clothing at home. Where are these articles of clothing made? Many may have been partially manufactured at one of the many U.S.-owned *maquiladoras* (assembly plants) in Mexico, Honduras, and other Latin American countries. In 1992 there were more than 2,000 *maquiladoras* in Mexico alone. About one-fifth of these plants produced clothing and textiles. Generally, unfinished pieces of clothing are sent to the *maquiladoras* to be sewn or otherwise assembled. The finished items are then shipped back to the U.S. Ask students to research other industries that use *maquiladoras* to assemble their products.

Answers: ¡Piensa en la cultura!
Answers will vary.

Cultural Notes

(p. 92, photo)
As international trade agreements, such as NAFTA, between the U.S., Mexico, and Canada are put into effect, more consumer products are exchanged between countries. Approximately two thirds of Mexico's exports go to the U.S. and the same percentage of Mexico's imports are from the U.S. Thus, shopping malls in different countries may carry many of the same products and have a similar appearance.

Paso cultural
En el centro comercial se encuentran muchos tipos de ropa moderna en un ambiente moderno. En Chichén Itzá se encuentra sólo ropa tradicional que se compra de vendedores(as) indígenas.

(p. 93, bottom photo)
El Corte Inglés is a well-known department store chain in Spain. Here a young man examines blue jeans in the Barcelona store. Jeans are the quintessential U.S. export product. Although they were first produced as heavy-duty work pants, jeans are popular casual attire throughout the world. In Spain, jeans are called *tejanos* or *vaqueros,* while in other places they may be referred to as simply *jeans.*

Present

Chapter Theme
Clothing

**Communicative
Objectives**
• To indicate articles of clothing
• To describe fabrics and patterns

 Overheads 16–17

 **Vocabulary Art
BLMs/CD-ROM**

 **Vocabulary Tape
3-1**

Teaching Suggestions
Preparing students to speak: Use one or two options from each of the categories of Comprehensible Input, Physical Response, or Limited Verbal Response. For a complete explanation of these categories and some sample activities, see pp. T20–T21.

Multicultural Perspectives
Dyed fabrics from Guatemala, alpaca sweaters from Peru, woven fabrics from Nigeria—what do these items have in common? Chances are you'll see these items and others incorporated into the fashions of some of the most renowned designers. From the friendship bracelets made by Guatemalan Indians to the woven hats worn by the Rastafari in

Vocabulario para conversar

¿Qué va bien con este chaleco?

Vas a necesitar estas palabras y expresiones para hablar sobre la ropa que usas. Después de leerlas varias veces, practícalas con un(a) compañero(a).

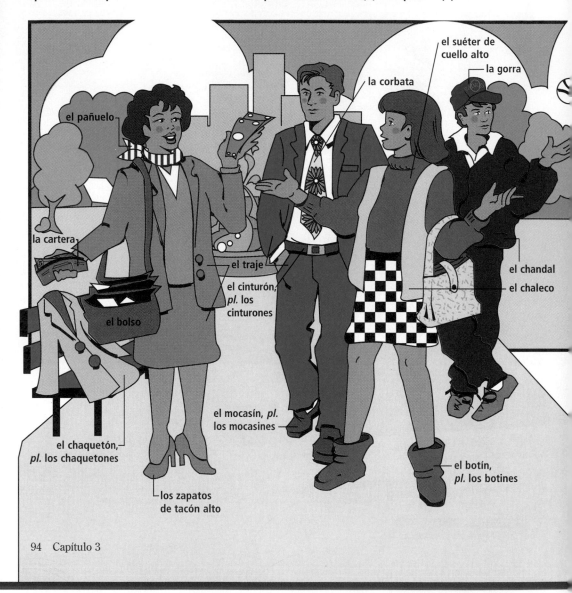

el suéter de cuello alto
la gorra
la corbata
el pañuelo
la cartera
el traje
el cinturón, pl. los cinturones
el bolso
el chandal
el chaleco
el mocasín, pl. los mocasines
el chaquetón, pl. los chaquetones
el botín, pl. los botines
los zapatos de tacón alto

94   Capítulo 3

Options

Strategies for Reaching All Students

Spanish-Speaking Students
Ask: ¿Puedes añadir otras palabras a las que están aquí? ¿Cuál(es) de las variaciones usas o prefieres tú?

 Un paso más Exs. 3-B, 3-C

Students Needing Extra Help
Make a clear distinction between words with similar spellings such as chaquetón, chaleco, and chandal; and lona and lana.
Remind students that un gorro is a ski cap and una gorra is a baseball cap.
También necesitas . . . : Give some examples of ¿De qué es . . . ? and Es de . . . .
Write out the probar (verb) forms.
¿Y qué quiere decir . . . ?: Give examples and write out all the forms for estar de moda.

Learning Spanish Through Action
STAGING VOCABULARY: Apunten, Levántense, Siéntense
MATERIALS: none
DIRECTIONS: Direct students to stand if they are wearing the items you mention. Tell them to sit if the item is a certain color or is made of a certain material, such as cotton or wool. Tell them to point to a classmate who's wearing a certain item of clothing.

las telas

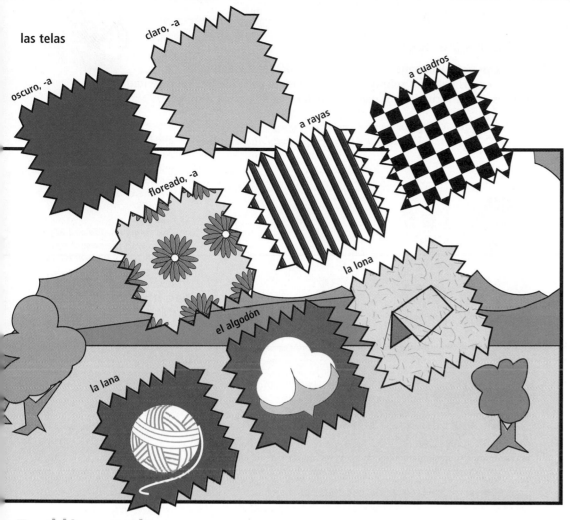

oscuro, -a

claro, -a

a cuadros

a rayas

floreado, -a

la lona

el algodón

la lana

También necesitas . . .

la moda	*fashion*	
liso, -a	*plain*	
sencillo, -a	*simple*	
probarse *(o → ue)*	*to try on*	
usar	*here: to wear*	
¿De qué es ___?	*What's (it) made of?*	
Es de ___.	*It's made of . . .*	

¿Y qué quiere decir . . . ?
estar de moda
el nilón
el plástico
elegante
sintético, -a

Jamaica, these accessories are part of a "global" look popular with many young people. Ask students to think about what is fashionable today and to trace the origin of those fashions.

Class Starter Review
On the day following initial presentation, begin the class with either of these activities:
1) Have a volunteer write the three categories *Hombres, Mujeres,* and *Los dos* on the chalkboard. As you call out each clothing item, have the class respond with the correct category. The volunteer then writes each in the appropriate column.
2) Have students form pairs and have one face toward the class and the other away from the class. *Estudiante A,* who is facing the class, describes someone's clothing to *Estudiante B,* who draws the outfit and then turns around to guess whose clothing he or she has drawn.

www Internet Activities
Juegos
Have students go to www.pasoapaso.com for additional activities and practice.

Extended Written Practice/Homework
1. Choose four items of clothing on p. 94. Write sentences saying how often or where you wear them: *Uso una corbata cuando voy a la iglesia.*
2. Write four sentences describing the clothing worn by the people on p. 94. Include vocabulary from p. 95 in your sentences: *La joven a la izquierda usa una falda a cuadros.*

3. Refer to the types of material on p. 95 and write three sentences telling what kinds of clothing you buy: *Siempre compro camisas de algodón.*

Multiple Intelligences
Bodily/Kinesthetic
See Learning Spanish Through Action.
Interpersonal/Social and Verbal/Linguistic
See Class Starter Review activity 2.

Logical/Mathematical and Verbal/Linguistic
See Class Starter Review activity 1.
Musical/Rhythmic
Have students create a jingle to advertise a particular clothing item.
Verbal/Linguistic
See Vocabulary Tape 3-1.
Visual/Spatial
See Overheads 16–17 and the Vocabulary Art BLMs/CD-ROM.

Practice & Apply

Teaching Suggestions

Review clothing (Book 1, Chap. 6), before presenting new vocabulary.

Answers: Empecemos a conversar

1 ESTUDIANTE A

a. ¿Qué va bien con este pañuelo floreado?

b. ... este traje (de color) oscuro?

c. ... esta corbata a rayas?

d. ... esta cartera?

e. ... estos botines rosados?

f. Questions will vary.

ESTUDIANTE B

a.–f. Answers will vary, but should begin *Yo creo que* ....

2 ESTUDIANTE A

a. ¿De qué son estos mocasines?

b. ... es este chaquetón?

c. ... es esta cartera?

d. ... es esta gorra?

e. ... es este chandal?

f. Questions will vary.

ESTUDIANTE B

Answers will vary, but may include the following:

a. Son de plástico. Yo prefiero los de cuero.

b. Es de tela sintética. ... los de lana.

c. Es de plástico. ... los de cuero.

d. Es de lona. ... las de algodón.

e. Es de nilón. ... los de algodón.

f. Answers will vary.

Empecemos a conversar

Túrnate con un(a) compañero(a) para ser *Estudiante A* y *Estudiante B.*
Reemplacen las palabras subrayadas en el modelo con palabras representadas
o escritas en los recuadros. Si ven 💡 pueden dar su propia respuesta.

1
A —¿Qué va bien con *este chaleco a cuadros*?
B —*Yo creo que un suéter de cuello alto liso, ¿no?*

Estudiante A   Estudiante B

a.

b.   c.

d.   e.   f.

¡NO OLVIDES!

When comparing two similar things, we can avoid repeating the noun:
—*Prefieres la corbata roja o la amarilla?*
—*La roja.*
The definite article and adjective agree with the noun they refer to. Similarly with expressions that include *de*:
No me gusta ni el bolso de Juana ni el de María.

2
A —*¿De qué es este cinturón?*
B —*Es de plástico. Yo prefiero los de cuero.*

Estudiante A   Estudiante B

a.   b.   c.

d.   e.   f.

plástico	nilón
cuero	algodón
lona	
lana	
tela sintética	

96   Capítulo 3

Options

Strategies for Reaching All Students

Spanish-Speaking Students

Ex. 6: After this exercise, ask: *Algunas personas creen que la ropa refleja la personalidad del que la lleva. ¿Crees que es verdad? ¿Por qué? ¿Qué ropa llevas tú que refleja o indica cómo eres?*

 Un paso más Ex. 3-D

Students Needing Extra Help

Empecemos a conversar: Begin to fill in the vocabulary section of the Organizer.
Give students time to describe the articles of clothing with the patterns.
¡No olvides!: Give additional examples of agreement, using masculine and feminine and singular and plural.
Ex. 2: Remind students that names of materials are always in the singular form: *los de cuero.*

Ex. 3: To practice the use of indefinite pronouns, have students repeat this exercise, using the third choice in the model: *No, pero me gustaría comprar uno.*
Ex. 5: Review colors from Book 1, Chap. 6.
Ex. 6: Be aware that this discussion may be uncomfortable for students of limited economic means. Provide additional vocabulary for students to answer ¿*Por qué?*

3

A —¿Tienes <u>chaquetón</u>?
B —<u>Sí, tengo un chaquetón de lona.</u>
   o: *No. No uso <u>chaquetón</u>.*
   o: *No. Pero me gustaría comprar <u>uno</u>.*

¡NO OLVIDES!

You can also use *uno/una* to avoid repeating a noun.
—*¿Tienes mochila?*
—*No, necesito* **una.**

Estudiante A   **Estudiante B**

Empecemos a escribir

Escribe tus respuestas en español.

4 Generalmente, ¿qué ropa usas cuando vas a la escuela? ¿Usas la misma ropa los fines de semana?

5 ¿Qué colores de ropa sueles usar más? ¿Prefieres los colores claros o los oscuros? ¿Prefieres la ropa floreada, a cuadros o a rayas? ¿O prefieres ropa muy sencilla de sólo un color?

6 ¿Qué ropa está de moda ahora? ¿Crees que es necesario o importante estar de moda? ¿Por qué?

7 ¿Sueles probarte la ropa antes de comprarla? ¿Por qué?

MORE PRACTICE

- Más práctica y tarea, p. 534
- Practice Workbook 3-1, 3-2

También se dice

el cincho
la faja
el cinto

el monedero
la billetera
el portamonedas

el suéter de cuello de tortuga

el tailleur
el saco
el paltó

Vocabulario para conversar 97

Present

Chapter Theme
Clothing sizes

Communicative Objectives
- To describe clothing in detail
- To indicate sizes
- To discuss ways of paying for purchases

 Overheads 18–19

 Vocabulary Art BLMs/CD-ROM

 Vocabulary Tape 3-2

Teaching Suggestions
Preparing students to speak: Use one or two options from each of the categories of Comprehensible Input, Physical Response, or Limited Verbal Response. For a complete explanation of these categories and some sample activities, see pp. T20–T21.

Vocabulario para conversar

¿Qué talla usas?

Aquí tienes el resto del vocabulario que necesitas en este capítulo para hablar sobre la ropa que usas.

*Note that we use *la talla* for clothing sizes and *el número* for shoe size.

98   Capítulo 3

Options

Strategies for Reaching All Students

Spanish-Speaking Students
 Un paso más Ex. 3-E

Students Needing Extra Help
Explain that *tamaño, pequeño, mediano,* and *grande* can refer to many things besides clothes. However, the word *talla* refers only to clothes and accessories.
También necesitas . . . : Give examples of half sizes *(Mi número de zapato es siete y medio).*
Show the connection between *guardarropa* (closet) and *guardar* (to put away).
Give examples in which *(me) da igual* would be an appropriate answer. Refer to Ex. 11.

Learning Spanish Through Action
STAGING VOCABULARY: *Cuelguen, Encuentren, Guarden, Pongan*
MATERIALS: items of clothing labeled either *sucio(a)* or *limpio(a)* scattered on the floor; hangers; boxes; laundry hamper (or a box with label: *ropa sucia*)
DIRECTIONS: Direct students to find the items you call out. If the item is clean, direct them to hang it up or put it away. If the item is dirty, direct them to put it in the laundry hamper.

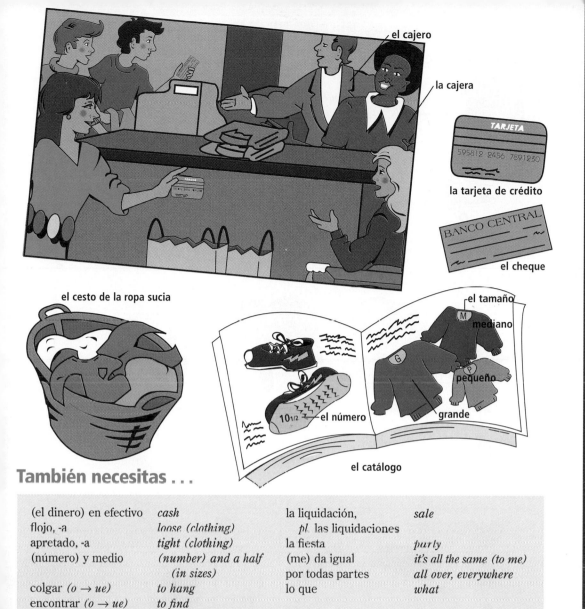

el cajero

la cajera

TARJETA
595818 2456 7891230

la tarjeta de crédito

BANCO CENTRAL

el cheque

el cesto de la ropa sucia

el tamaño

M mediano

G

P pequeño

grande

10 1/2 — el número

el catálogo

También necesitas . . .

(el dinero) en efectivo	*cash*	la liquidación,	*sale*
flojo, -a	*loose (clothing)*	*pl.* las liquidaciones	
apretado, -a	*tight (clothing)*	la fiesta	*party*
(número) y medio	*(number) and a half*	(me) da igual	*it's all the same (to me)*
	(in sizes)	por todas partes	*all over, everywhere*
colgar *(o → ue)*	*to hang*	lo que	*what*
encontrar *(o → ue)*	*to find*		
escoger*	*to choose*		
guardar	*to put away, to keep*		
alguien	*someone*		

> **¿Y qué quiere decir . . . ?**
> estar en liquidación

* *Escoger* is a regular *-er* verb. However, the *g* changes to *j* in the *yo* form: *(yo) escojo.*

Practice

Grammar Preview

Encontraste is used lexically in Ex. 9. A review of the preterite of *-ar* verbs is on p. 109.

Answers: Empecemos a conversar

8 ESTUDIANTE A
a. ¿Qué número de zapato (tenis) usas?
b. ...tamaño (talla) de chandal ...
c. ...tamaño (talla) de cinturón ...
d. ...tamaño (talla) de chaquetón ...
e. ...tamaño (talla) de traje ...
f. ...tamaño (talla) de vestido ...
g. Questions will vary.

ESTUDIANTE B
a.–g. Answers will vary.

9 ESTUDIANTE A
a. ¿Encontraste el chaleco?
b. ...la cartera?
c. ...el pañuelo?
d. ...la corbata?
e. ...el suéter de cuello alto?
f. Questions will vary.

ESTUDIANTE B
Answers will vary, but look for logical fabrics or materials and adjectives that agree with them rather than with the article of clothing.
a. Sí. Esogí uno de lana blanca.
b. ...una de ...
c. ...uno de ...
d. ...una de ...
e. ...uno de ...
f. Answers will vary.

Empecemos a conversar

8
A —¿Qué talla de *pantalones* usas?
B —Uso *la talla treinta y cuatro.*

Estudiante A

Estudiante B

talla 30, 32, 34, ...

tamaño pequeño / mediano / grande

talla 4, 6, 8, ...

número 6, 6½, 7, ...

a.   b.   c.   d.   e.   f.   g.

9
A —¿Encontraste *los mocasines?*
B —Sí. Escogí *unos de cuero rojo.*

Estudiante A   **Estudiante B**

a.   b.   c.   d.   e.   f.

Zapatos hechos a mano en un mercado mexicano

100   Capítulo 3

Options

Strategies for Reaching All Students

Students Needing Extra Help
Ex. 8: Review when to use *talla* versus *número,* and *talla* versus *tamaño.*
Ex. 9: Give students time to come up with combinations of patterns and materials. Since the model uses the plural, model a question in the singular.
Ex. 10: Point out that item *e.* is plural.

Enrichment
Ex. 8: Point out that this exercise uses American sizes. However, many Spanish-speaking countries use a different sizing system. In Spain, for example, a size 38 dress, blouse, or coat is equivalent to a U.S. size 6; a 40 is equal to size 8; 42 to size 10, and so on. For both men's and women's shoes, the sizes are 36, 37, 38, and so on. Use the chart on p. 101 so students can figure out what sizes they wear in Spanish-speaking countries.

Multiple Intelligences
Verbal/Linguistic, Visual/Spatial, and Interpersonal/Social
Have one student describe a classmate's outfit while another one draws it, writing in the colors. If available, use markers or pens of different colors. The first student will then check the drawing for accuracy.

10
A —¿Cómo me queda *este chandal*?
B —*Te queda muy apretado.*

¡NO OLVIDES!

Remember that the verb *quedar* is like *gustar*, and that we use it with the indirect object pronouns *me, te, nos,* and *le(s)*.

Estudiante A

a.

b.

c.

d.

e.

f.

Estudiante B

10 ESTUDIANTE A
a. ¿Cómo me queda este chaquetón?
b. . . . queda esta chaqueta?
c. . . . queda este suéter de cuello alto?
d. . . . queda esta gorra?
e. . . . quedan estos pantalones cortos?
f. Questions will vary, but look for the correct use of *me queda(n)*.

ESTUDIANTE B
a. Te queda muy flojo.
b. . . . queda muy floja.
c. . . . queda apretado (pequeño).
d. . . . queda apretada (pequeña).
e. . . . quedan muy bien.
f. Answers will vary, but look for the correct use of *te queda(n)* and adjective agreement.

TALLAS	blusas y vestidos						
españolas	36	38	40	42	44	46	
norteamericanas	4	6	8	10	12	14	
	pantalones para hombre y mujer						
españolas	36	38	40	42	44	46	
norteamericanas	35	36	37	38	39	40	
	camisas para hombre						
españolas	36	37	38	40	41	42	43
norteamericanas	14	14½	15	15½	16	16	17
NÚMEROS	zapatos para hombre y mujer						
españoles	36	37	38	39	40	41	42
norteamericanos	5	6	7	8	9	9½	10

Cultural Notes ☀

(p. 101, photo)
Mexico has a tradition of skilled leather work both in folk arts and in manufacturing. Shoes are a major product from the states of Jalisco and Guanajuato. In Guadalajara, Jalisco, a major commercial center and Mexico's second-largest city, an entire district is devoted to shoe stores. Cow hide is not a commodity native to the Americas: cattle were first introduced to Mexico in 1519 by the Spanish explorer Cortés.

Practice & Apply

11 ESTUDIANTE A

a. ¿Te gusta usar ropa de algodón?

b. . . .pantalones con cremallera?

c. . . .suéteres sin bolsillos?

d. . . .zapatos de tacón alto?

e. . . .vestidos de tela sintética?

f. Questions will vary.

ESTUDIANTE B

a.–f. Answers will vary.

Answers: Empecemos a escribir y a leer

12–15 Answers will vary.

11 camisas de manga larga

A —¿Te gusta usar *camisas de manga larga*?

B —*Depende, pero prefiero las de manga corta en el verano.*
o: *Me da igual.*
o: *No, nunca uso camisas de manga larga.*

Estudiante A

a. ropa de algodón

b. pantalones con cremallera

c. suéteres sin bolsillos

d. zapatos de tacón alto

e. vestidos de tela sintética

f.

Estudiante B

Empecemos a escribir y a leer

Escribe tus respuestas en español.

12 En tu cuarto, ¿está la ropa en el suelo por todas partes? ¿Dónde pones la ropa sucia? ¿Dónde guardas la ropa limpia? ¿Qué ropa cuelgas en el guardarropa?

13 ¿Qué ropa te gusta usar cuando vas a fiestas? ¿Te ayuda alguien a escoger lo que vas a llevar?

14 ¿Sueles comprar cosas que están en liquidación? ¿Por qué? ¿Qué te gusta comprar en liquidación?

15 ¿Compras a veces por catálogo? ¿Qué compras? ¿Pagas con tarjeta de crédito? ¿O paga alguno de tus padres con cheque? Generalmente, ¿qué cosas pagas en efectivo?

www.pasoapaso.com

MORE PRACTICE

Más práctica y tarea, p. 534–535
Practice Workbook 3–3, 3–4

COMPLEMENTOS DE ITALIA
Protagonistas de la moda

Options

Strategies for Reaching All Students

Spanish-Speaking Students
Ex. 13: Ask: *¿Tienes ropa diferente para cada estación del año? ¿Cuál te gusta más usar: la de la primavera, del verano, etc.? ¿Por qué?*

 Un paso más Ex. 3-F

Students Needing Extra Help
Ex. 11: Discourage students from always answering with *Me da igual.* Encourage them to give reasons for the kind of clothing they prefer: *Prefiero la ropa de lana porque me gusta la ropa cómoda. Prefiero los suéteres con bolsillos para poner mi dinero,* etc.
Ex. 12: Make a distinction between *el suelo* and *yo suelo* if it presents a problem for students. Explain that they are homonyms, like the word "rose" in the sentence "He rose to hand her a pink rose." If available, use the vocabulary section of the Book 1, Chap. 6 Organizer.
Ex. 15: Be sensitive to socioeconomic issues.
Ex. 16: Discuss the dialogue that usually occurs between a customer and a salesperson or cashier. Be sure everyone is starting with the correct sentence.

El Corte Inglés en Madrid, España

Las gangas son increíbles cuando los almacenes ponen las cosas en liquidación.

16 Lee las frases de este diálogo y ponlas en un orden lógico. Después, decide quién dice cada frase. Puede ser el cajero (la cajera), el vendedor (la vendedora) o la clienta.

—Tenemos unos en liquidación, señorita. Son muy baratos. Mire, dos por $30.

—Entonces sólo puede pagar en efectivo o con tarjeta de crédito.

—No, no tengo.

—Depende. ¿Tiene Ud. alguna identificación con foto?

—Quiero dos, uno rojo mediano y otro azul pequeño. ¿Puedo pagar con cheque?

—Perdón, señor, busco un suéter de cuello alto.

También se dice

el cierre
el cierre relámpago
el síper

la bolsa

el canasto de la ropa sucia
el ropasuciero

Vocabulario para conversar   103

16 [CL = clienta;
V = vendedor(a); CA = cajero(a).]
Order of dialogue is as follows:
CL —Perdón, señor, busco un suéter de cuello alto.
V —Tenemos unos en liquidación, señorita . . . .
CL —Quiero dos, . . .
CA —Depende. ¿Tiene Ud. . . .
CL —No, no tengo.
CA —Entonces sólo puede pagar . . .

Practice Wkbk. 3-3, 3-4

Audio Activity 3.2

Writing Activities 3-A, 3-B, 3-C

Pruebas 3-3, 3-4

Cultural Notes
(p. 103, photo)
Originally a tailors shop in Madrid, El Corte Inglés was bought in 1928 by Ramón Areces Rodríguez, who expanded and transformed it into a luxury department store with branches throughout Spain. El Corte Inglés now also has travel, insurance, and publishing businesses. Ask students to discuss U.S. stores that started out small and local, like El Corte Inglés, and have grown in a similar way.

Extended Written Practice/Homework
1. Write three sentences telling the sizes of clothing and shoes that you wear: *Uso tenis de número 12.*
2. Write three sentences telling if you do the following when you go shopping: *buscar liquidaciones, encontrar muchas gangas, escoger ropa que está de moda.*
3. Write three sentences saying whether or not you prefer to wear tight or loose items of clothing: *Prefiero usar sudaderas flojas.*

Multiple Intelligences
Bodily/Kinesthetic and Verbal/Linguistic
Have students present a fashion show describing what their classmates are wearing.
Intrapersonal/Introspective
See Exs. 12–15.
Verbal/Linguistic
See Ex. 11 and Audio activity 3.2.
Visual/Spatial
See Practice Wkbk. 3-3 and 3-4 and Writing Activities 3-A, 3-B, and 3-C.

Cultural Notes

(p. 102, realia)
This advertisement from El Corte Inglés, a trend-setting Spanish department store, promotes Italian clothing and personal accessories. Spain and Italy maintain strong commercial ties. Italy continues to be a leader in European fashion, and Italian styles frequently set the pace in Spain.

Practice

¡Comuniquemos!

Aquí tienes otra oportunidad para usar el vocabulario de este capítulo.

1 Dile a un(a) compañero(a) qué ropa usas cuando vas a estos lugares.

A —¿Qué ropa usas cuando vas al cine?
B —*Generalmente uso algo sencillo: jeans, camiseta y una chaqueta.*

a.

b.

c.

d.

e.

f.

2 Con un(a) compañero(a) hablen de la última prenda de ropa *(article of clothing)* que compraron. Hablen de:
- qué es
- cómo es (el color, etc.)
- dónde la compraron
- cómo pagaron
- si la compraron en liquidación o no
- cuándo la usan

104   Capítulo 3

Options

Strategies for Reaching All Students

Spanish-Speaking Students
Ex. 3: Have students write out this exercise. *Lee las instrucciones. En vez de decirle a tu compañero(a) cómo organizar su guardarropa, escríbele tus recomendaciones.*

 Un paso más Ex. 3-G

Students Needing Extra Help
Ex. 1: If available, use the vocabulary sections from the Book 1, Chaps. 6, 7, and 14 Organizers.
Ex. 2: Students may need help constructing their narrative. Provide them with an opening sentence and give them time to prepare. Use the vocabulary section of the Organizer.
Ex. 3: Brainstorm other expressions of emotion. Use the vocabulary section of the

Organizer. Review commands for some words that students might want to use: *separar, lavar,* etc.
Review furniture from Book 1, Chap. 9.
¿Qué sabes ahora?: Have students write out this list so that they can record what they have mastered.

3 ¡Qué desastre! Dile a un(a) compañero(a) cómo organizar su dormitorio. Puedes usar las siguientes expresiones u otras.

Guarda ___ en ___   Pon ___ en ___   Hay que colgar ___

¿Qué sabes ahora?

Can you:

■ describe clothing in detail?

—La blusa es de manga ___ y de color verde ___.

■ indicate clothing preferences?

—Prefiero los suéteres de ___ y los zapatos ___.

■ say how you paid for your purchases?

—Compré estas dos camisetas en ___, pero pagué por el chaquetón con ___.

Vocabulario para conversar   105

3 Answers will vary, but should be logical.

Answers: ¿Qué sabes ahora?

• corta (larga) / claro (oscuro)
• Answers will vary.
• efectivo / cheque (tarjeta de crédito)

 Audio Activity 3.3

 Pasos vivos 2 CD-ROM

Boom Box, Clip Art Album, Slide Projector, Laboratorio de grabar

Enrichment
Ex. 1: Have students redo this exercise with *Estudiante B* saying that he or she plans to wear clothes that are obviously unsuitable for the situation mentioned. *Estudiante A* can then react in a shocked manner and suggest more appropriate clothes.

Cooperative Learning
In groups of three or four, tell students they have each been given $500. Have them create a list of clothing that they would buy for themselves or for a family member or a friend. Tell them to include details such as style, material, and cost. Have them explain their choices. Groups should then tabulate the results to find the most popular item. Call on groups to report results.

Multiple Intelligences
Interpersonal/Social and Logical/Mathematical
See Cooperative Learning.
Verbal/Linguistic
See Audio Activity 3.3.
Verbal/Linguistic and Interpersonal/Social
See Exs. 1–3.

Present & Apply

Cultural Objective
• To understand relative values of currencies

Teaching Suggestions
If possible, go to a major bank and exchange a few dollars' worth of U.S. money for currency from Spanish-speaking countries. Bring in coins from your trips to Spanish-speaking countries.

Answers
Answers to inductive questions will vary.

Answers: La cultura desde tu perspectiva

1 *El colón es la moneda oficial de Costa Rica y de El Salvador. Se llama así por Cristóbal Colón. El quetzal es la moneda oficial de Guatemala y el guaraní es la de Paraguay.*

2 Answers will vary.

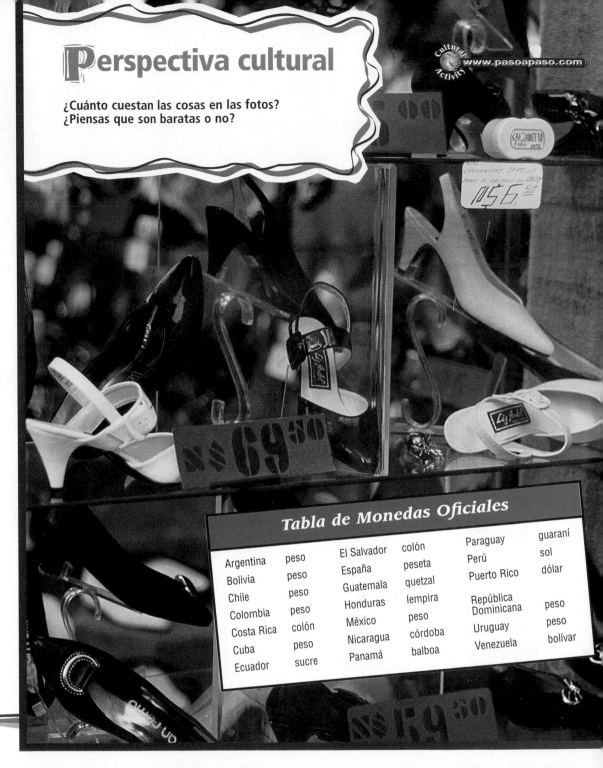

Perspectiva cultural

¿Cuánto cuestan las cosas en las fotos?
¿Piensas que son baratas o no?

www.pasoapaso.com

Tabla de Monedas Oficiales

Argentina	peso	El Salvador	colón	Paraguay	guaraní
Bolivia	peso	España	peseta	Perú	sol
Chile	peso	Guatemala	quetzal	Puerto Rico	dólar
Colombia	peso	Honduras	lempira	República Dominicana	peso
Costa Rica	colón	México	peso	Uruguay	peso
Cuba	peso	Nicaragua	córdoba	Venezuela	bolívar
Ecuador	sucre	Panamá	balboa		

Options

Strategies for Reaching All Students

Spanish-Speaking Students
Ask: *¿Has visto el dinero de otro(s) país(es)? ¿Cuál es el más interesante? ¿Por qué?*

 Un paso más Ex. 3-H

Students Needing Extra Help
Have students take notes to help them when reviewing for the chapter test.
Bring in a currency-conversion table from a newspaper. Explain the concept of the difference in the value of money from country to country. Explain the "weight" concept of currency. You might give the example of weighing a gold chain to determine its price.

Enrichment
Explain the origin of the currency from other Spanish-speaking countries: the *guaraní* was named for the indigenous people and language of Paraguay. *Lempira* was a fallen hero in Honduras' battle against the Spaniards. The *sol* was originally called *inti*, after the sun god of the people inhabiting what is now Peru.

La respuesta a las preguntas de la izquierda depende del país en que se sacaron las fotos. Por ejemplo, un paraguas que cuesta 1.500 pesetas en España no es caro. Una peseta vale más o menos tres cuartos de un centavo americano. Por eso, el paraguas sólo cuesta diez dólares estadounidenses.

Si estás en un país extranjero, siempre tienes que saber el valor de la moneda para saber si lo que compras es una ganga. ¡Y no olvides que el valor puede cambiar de un día a otro!

La moneda oficial no es la misma en cada país. En España se usa *la peseta.* En México y en algunos otros países se usa *el peso.* ¿Sabías que esas dos palabras están relacionadas con el verbo *pesar,* que quiere decir *"to weigh"*? Hace muchos años una moneda de oro o de plata valía lo que pesaba. Piensa, por ejemplo, en la moneda inglesa—¡*pound*!

La moneda puede decirte mucho sobre un país. La moneda oficial panameña, por ejemplo, se llama *el balboa* y la de Nicaragua se llama *el córdoba.* ¿Por qué? Vasco Nuñez de Balboa era el conquistador que llevó a los primeros soldados españoles por Panamá hasta el Océano Pacífico. Francisco Hernández de Córdoba fundó las ciudades nicaragüenses de Léon y Granada.

En el dinero de muchos países puedes ver a personajes literarios, líderes políticos y animales y paisajes locales. Mirando con cuidado su dinero, puedes aprender mucho sobre un país.

A este joven chileno le interesan las liquidaciones.

La cultura desde tu perspectiva

1   Mira la tabla de monedas. ¿Cómo se llaman las monedas costarricense y salvadoreña? ¿Por qué se llaman así? ¿De qué país es el quetzal la moneda oficial? ¿Y el guaraní? Si no las conoces, busca esas palabras en un diccionario de inglés.

2   Imagina que el dinero de nuestro país va a cambiar y que tú puedes sugerir un nuevo nombre y un nuevo diseño. ¿Qué nombre va a tener la moneda oficial? ¿Qué símbolos vas a poner en el dinero para reflejar nuestros valores más importantes?

Estos zapatos en México se venden muy baratos ahora.

Perspectiva cultural   107

Cultural Notes ✦

(p. 106, photo)
A Cancún shop window at a women's shoe store. The *peso* is the Mexican unit of currency and it is expressed by a sign similar to the U.S. dollar sign. A *peso* is made up of 100 *centavos.* During the 1980s, Mexico experienced high inflation and the value of the revaluated *peso* fell dramatically in relation to the U.S. dollar. In 1993, *nuevos pesos* (N$) came into circulation.

(p. 107, realia)
The Guatemalan monetary note depicts the *quetzal,* an endangered bird that is also the country's national symbol. *Quetzales* have brilliant green and red plumage and a strikingly long tail. Populations of *quetzales* are still found in northeastern Guatemala, in the forests of the area known as El Petén.

The Venezuelan *bolívar* is named after Simón Bolívar (known as *el Libertador*) (1783–1830). He led several South American countries, including Venezuela, in their fight for independence from Spain. The Republic of Bolivia was named in his honor.

Preview

 Overhead 20

Reteach / Review: Direct Object Pronouns

A: Point out the direct object pronoun *los* in these phrases: *los busqué, los llevaste, los lavé.* Remind students that direct object pronouns usually come before the verb.

Answers:

A The forms are *lavé* and *lavo:* "I washed" (preterite), "I wash" (present). The endings change the meanings.

B Two *ellos / ellas* forms (panel 5): *entraron, salieron. Entraron* is an *-ar* verb *(entrar); salieron* is an *-ir* verb *(salir).*

C *Busqué* (panel 2) is a verb whose infinitive ends in *-car (buscar).* The preterite *yo* form differs from that of other *-ar* verbs because the consonant *(c)* changes (to *qu*). The preterite *yo* form of *tocar* is *toqué.*

Gramática en contexto

¡Los busqué por toda la casa!

108   Capítulo 3

A The boy uses two forms of *lavar* to talk about washing clothes. What are they? How do they differ in meaning? What is it about these two verb forms that changes the meaning?

B Find the two *ellos / ellas* forms of the preterite. Which one is an *-ar* verb and which is an *-ir* verb?

C Find a verb whose infinitive ends in *-car.* How is its *yo* form in the preterite different from that of other *-ar* verbs? What do you think the preterite *yo* form of *tocar* would be?

Options

Strategies for Reaching All Students

Students Needing Extra Help
Begin to fill in the grammar section of the Organizer. Review Book 1, Chaps. 10 and 12. Students will more likely remember the preterite of irregular verbs, which they saw in the latter part of their previous academic year; they will therefore need to review the preterite of regular verbs.

C: If students are having trouble identifying the *-car* verbs, have them give the present tense of *buscar* and *lavar.* Now have them compare these verb forms to the corresponding ones in the reading.

Extended Written Practice/Homework
1. Write three pairs of sentences telling what items of clothing your friends or family members bought and how they paid for them.
2. Write three sentences telling what items of clothing your friends chose when they went shopping: *Cuando mi amigo Juan fue de compras, escogió un suéter de lana.*

Repaso: El pretérito de los verbos regulares

You have learned to use the preterite tense to talk about things that happened in the past. Remember that, in general, verb endings tell who did an action and when it was done. Here are all the preterite forms of regular -ar, -er, and -ir verbs:

comprar

(yo)	compr**é**	(nosotros) (nosotras)	compr**amos**
(tú)	compr**aste**	(vosotros) (vosotras)	compr**asteis**
Ud. (él) (ella)	compr**ó**	Uds. (ellos) (ellas)	compr**aron**

comer

(yo)	com**í**	(nosotros) (nosotras)	com**imos**
(tú)	com**iste**	(vosotros) (vosotras)	com**isteis**
Ud. (él) (ella)	com**ió**	Uds. (ellos) (ellas)	com**ieron**

vivir

(yo)	viv**í**	(nosotros) (nosotras)	viv**imos**
(tú)	viv**iste**	(vosotros) (vosotras)	viv**isteis**
Ud. (él) (ella)	viv**ió**	Uds. (ellos) (ellas)	viv**ieron**

Gramática en contexto 109

Present

Using Realia
Remind students that they saw *alegre* in Chap. 4 as meaning "happy, festive." Have them brainstorm to figure out what *alegre* means in this advertisement ("bright, sunny").

Multiple Intelligences
Visual/Spatial
See Overhead 20.

Practice

Re-enter / Recycle
Ex. 1: school activities from Chap. 1
Ex. 2: daily routine from Chap. 2

Answers
1 Answers will vary, but look for the correct preterite forms.

2 ESTUDIANTE A
a. Pepe encontró los chandales, ¿verdad?
b. Julia lavó la ropa sucia . . .
c. Tú guardaste la ropa limpia . . .
d. Mi padre buscó su corbata . . .
e. Tú y tu hermano compraron los mocasines . . .
f. Tía Carmen escogió el pañuelo . . .
g. José colgó los chaquetones . . .

ESTUDIANTE B
a.–g. Answers may vary, but look for the correct preterite forms and direct object pronouns.

3 Answers will vary, but may include the following:
a. Generalmente reparto periódicos por la mañana. Pero ayer repartí periódicos por la tarde.
b. . . . llevo ropa elegante. . . . llevé ropa sencilla.
c. . . . saco una buena nota. . . . saqué una mala nota.
d. . . . desayuno temprano. . . . desayuné tarde.
e. . . . llego a casa a las 8:00. . . . llegué a las 9:00.
f. . . . uso vestidos de colores claros. . . . usé uno (un vestido) de color oscuro.

• Remember that *-ar* and *-er* verbs that have a stem change in the present tense do *not* have a stem change in the preterite.

cerrar (e → ie):
C**ie**rro las ventanas de mi cuarto todas las noches.
Pero ayer no c**e**rré las ventanas.

devolver (o → ue):
Siempre dev**ue**lvo los libros los miércoles.
Ayer dev**o**lví tres libros.

• Remember that in the preterite, verbs whose infinitive ends in *-gar* or *-car* have a spelling change in the *yo* form. All of their other preterite forms are regular.

pa**gar**	yo pa**gué**
lle**gar**	yo lle**gué**
ju**gar**	yo ju**gué**
sa**car**	yo sa**qué**
bus**car**	yo bus**qué**
to**car**	yo to**qué**

1 Formen grupos para describir lo que hicieron Uds. y otras personas en el pasado. Usen una expresión de cada columna. Den *(Give)* más información si pueden.

Mario *Mario tocó el violín anoche.*

a. mis amigos	tocar el violín	anoche
b. mi hermano(a)	ver la televisión	ayer
c. tú y tu tío	practicar deportes	hace una hora
d. yo	comer tacos	el año pasado
e. tú	entregar el informe	el mes pasado
f. nosotros	cerrar la puerta	la semana pasada
g. 💡	encontrar la cartera 💡	el (día de la semana) 💡

En un mercado de San Blas, Panamá, se vende ropa típica de los indios cuna además de ropa hecha para los turistas.

PASO CULTURAL
Los indios cuna de las islas de San Blas hacen y venden molas, un tipo de artesanía en forma de paneles de tela. Las molas se hacen con varias capas *(layers)* de tela de colores diferentes. Estas capas se cosen juntas a mano para crear diseños de pájaros, animales, plantas o flores. Piensa en *quilting,* una artesanía tradicional en los Estados Unidos. ¿Cómo es similar a coser molas? ¿Cómo son los diseños tradicionales de *quilting?*

Options

Strategies for Reaching All Students

Students Needing Extra Help
El pretérito de los verbos regulares: Give additional examples of stem changes that occurred in the present but won't in the preterite. Write them on the chalkboard. Point out that the *yo* form is irregular.
Ex. 1: Remind students to form logical answers; this is not a linear match. Review the preterite of the verbs in column 2 and words that indicate past in column 3.

Ex. 2: Review object pronouns. Model the exercise, choosing the correct pronoun. Then go through it again, changing the verbs to the preterite.
Ex. 3: Explain that the parenthetical phrase in the model is optional. Brainstorm words that mean the opposite of the words given: *mañana (tarde); elegante (sencillo).*

Extended Written Practice/Homework
1. Write three sentences telling what different people did to earn money: *El verano pasado repartí periódicos.*
2. Write three questions that you could ask classmates about the last time they went shopping for clothes: *¿Encontraste muchas gangas?*
3. Write three sentences telling what happened in one of your classes recently: *Ayer la profesora de historia usó diapositivas en su clase.*

2 Trabaja con un(a) compañero(a) para corregir estos malentendidos (*misunderstandings*).

tú / pagar la cuenta	A —*Pagaste la cuenta, ¿verdad?* B —*No, yo no la pagué. Anita la pagó.*

a. Pepe / encontrar los chandales	mi padre
b. Julia / lavar la ropa sucia	Miguel y Roberto
c. tú / guardar la ropa limpia	mi madre
d. mi padre / buscar su corbata	Tomás
e. tú y tu hermano / comprar los mocasines	la abuela Anita
f. tía Carmen / escoger el pañuelo	yo
g. José / colgar los chaquetones	nosotros

3 Túrnate con un(a) compañero(a) para hablar sobre algo que no suelen hacer pero que hicieron ayer.

salir de casa a las 7:00	*Generalmente salgo de casa a las 7:00. Pero ayer salí a las cinco de la mañana (para ir de pesca con mi padre).*

a. repartir periódicos por la mañana
b. llevar ropa elegante
c. sacar una buena nota
d. desayunar temprano
e. llegar a casa a las 8:00
f. usar vestidos de colores claros
g. ver la televisión durante el día
h. pagar en efectivo
i. 💡

PASO CULTURAL

Este anuncio sobre etiquetas bordadas *(sew-on labels)* usa nombres de figuras importantes de la cultura española. ¿Qué nombres de este anuncio conoces? ¿Qué sabes de estas personas? Imagina que vas a hacer etiquetas bordadas con los nombres de figuras de la cultura americana. ¿Qué nombres vas a escoger?

PERSONALICE SU ROPA CON

ETIQUETAS BORDADAS

Una forma práctica y sencilla de identificar su ropa. Con las etiquetas bordadas puede marcar, con su nombre, las prendas del colegio, del trabajo, militares, batas de hospitales... y todas aquellas prendas que quiera personalizar. Así no habrá confusiones.
Sólo tiene que rellenar el cupón respuesta con sus datos y recibirá en su domicilio, en breve plazo, las etiquetas bordadas, en el color que elija.

36 unidades por solo **990 PTAS.**	72 unidades por solo **1.490 PTAS.**

más gastos de envío

UN TOQUE DE DISTINCION
C/. Cuatro Amigos, 1 - 28029 MADRID
Tel.: **733 33 66**

• JUEGOS DE 36 ó 72 UNIDADES POR NOMBRE.
• 36 UNIDADES HASTA 20 LETRAS: 990 PTAS; 21-40: 2.000 PTAS.
• 72 UNIDADES HASTA 20 LETRAS: 1.490 PTAS; 21-40: 2.500 PTAS.
• COLORES ROJO O AZUL SOBRE CINTA BLANCA, COLORES SOLIDOS.
• PAGO CONTRA REEMBOLSO.

LETRAS PARA BORDAR

DESTINATARIO: _____
DIRECCION _____ C.P. _____
CIUDAD _____ D.N.I. _____
TELEFONO _____
INDIQUE: COLOR: ☐ ROJO ☐ AZUL   CANTIDAD: ☐ 36 ☐ 72
Recorte y envíe este cupón a:
UN TOQUE DE DISTINCION: C/. Cuatro Amigos, 1 - 28029 MADRID

Gramática en contexto 111

---

g. . . . veo la televisión durante el día. . . . vi la televisión durante la noche.
h. . . . pago en efectivo. . . . pagué con un cheque.
i. Statements will vary.

 Practice Wkbk. 3-5, 3-6, 3-7

 Writing Activity 3-D

 Pruebas 3-5, 3-6

 Comm. Act. BLM 3-2

Cultural Notes
(p. 111, realia)
A sense of humor increases the consumer's interest in these personalized sew-on labels. The choice of "Francisco de Goya," "Don Juan Tenorio," etc., reflect the prominence of these figures in Spanish culture. The purchaser can call the manufacturer or fill out a mail-in order form to take advantage of this offer.

Cultural Notes

Paso cultural
Possible answers: *Quilting* es similar a coser molas donde también se usan paneles de tela de varias capas que se cosen juntas a mano para crear diseños./Los *quilts* generalmente tienen diseños geométricos, pero a veces tienen diseños de animales o plantas como las molas.

(p. 110, photo)
Panama's Cuna Indians are known for their *molas,* colorful reverse-appliquéd fabrics. Panama's population is highly diverse. Nearly half of the country's inhabitants are of African descent, about a third are *mestizos* (of mixed Indian and black or white heritage), and about seven percent are indigenous peoples.

Paso cultural
Answers: En las etiquetas bordadas se ven estos nombres: Don Quijote de la Mancha, héroe de la literatura; María Eugenia de Montijo, aristócrata española y emperatriz *(empress)* de Francia; Antonio Gaudí, arquitecto; Don Juan Tenorio, personaje de la literatura *(literary character)*; Cristóbal Colón *(Columbus),* explorador de las Américas; Francisco de Goya y Diego Velázquez, pintores./Figures from U.S. culture will vary.

Present & Practice

Re-enter / Recycle

Ex. 4: school supplies from Chap. 1

Adjetivos y pronombres demostrativos

Remember that we use demonstrative adjectives to point out people or things that are nearby. A demonstrative adjective always comes before the noun and agrees with it in gender and number.

este bolso	*this bag*	**estos** bolsos	*these bags*
esta cartera	*this wallet*	**estas** carteras	*these wallets*
ese bolso	*that bag*	**esos** bolsos	*those bags*
esa cartera	*that wallet*	**esas** carteras	*those wallets*

- To point out things that are farther away, we use these demonstrative adjectives.

aquel chaleco	*that vest*	**aquellos** chalecos	*those vests*
aquella chaqueta	*that jacket*	**aquellas** chaquetas	*those jackets*

- Demonstrative adjectives can also be used as pronouns to replace nouns. In that case they have a written accent.

> **Este** chaleco no me gusta; me gusta **ése.**
> No voy a comprar **ésta.** Prefiero **aquélla.**

Options

Strategies for Reaching All Students

Students Needing Extra Help
Adjetivos y pronombres demostrativos: For a quick review, refer to Book 1, Chap. 6. Emphasize gender agreement; students tend to use only the masculine form. Demonstrate *aquel* as "over there" (the farthest one from you). Provide additional examples. Sress the importance of the accents on the pronouns (i.e., when the noun is not used).

Ex. 4: Provide an assortment of school supplies that represent the masculine, feminine, singular, and plural forms.
Start with a simple model: *este libro.* Then present the pronouns: *éste, ése.* Repeat until all supplies have been mentioned.

Extended Written Practice/Homework
1. Write three sentences that you might say as you point at items in a store window: *No me gustan nada aquellos zapatos de tacón alto.*

2. Write three questions that you might ask classmates to find out where they bought certain items of clothing: *¿Dónde compraste ese chaleco de cuero?*
3. Identify items of clothing in the photos in Chapter 3 that you would or would not like to buy. Write three sentences: *No me gustaría comprar estos zapatos blancos.*

Here are all of the demonstrative adjectives and pronouns.

	Close to you		Closer to the person you are talking to		Far from both of you	
Adjectives	este	estos	ese	esos	aquel	aquellos
	esta	estas	esa	esas	aquella	aquellas
Pronouns	éste	éstos	ése	ésos	aquél	aquéllos
	ésta	éstas	ésa	ésas	aquélla	aquéllas

4 Pon varios útiles escolares *(school supplies)* sobre la mesa. Describe los de tu mesa, los de la mesa de tu compañero(a) y los de una mesa que está un poco más lejos.

Este libro es negro y grande.
Ése es gris y pequeño.
Aquél es un diccionario.

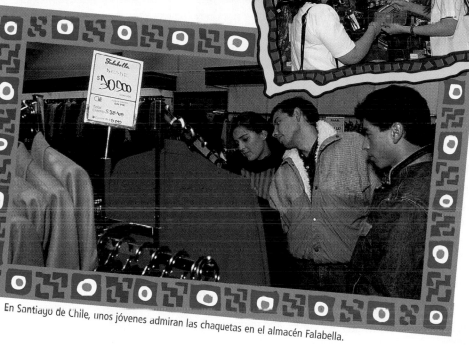

Esta joven chilena trabaja de cajera en una tienda.

En Santiago de Chile, unos jóvenes admiran las chaquetas en el almacén Falabella.

Gramática en contexto   113

Class Starter Review
On the day after reviewing demonstrative adjectives and pronouns, you might begin the class with this activity:
Cut out pictures of various fashion models from magazines. Have students form groups of three, and hand out three pictures to each group. Each group takes turns describing the differences in clothing among the three photos. *(Esta mujer lleva . . . Ésa lleva . . . Aquélla lleva . . .)*

4 Answers will vary, but look for correct agreement of subject and verb, correct adjective agreement, and correct use of demonstrative adjectives and pronouns.

Practice Wkbk. 3-8, 3-9

Writing Activity 3-E

Pruebas 3-7, 3-8

Cultural Notes ☼

Multiple Intelligences
Interpersonal/Social and Verbal/Linguistic
See Class Starter Review.
Visual/Spatial
See Practice Wkbk. 3-8 and 3-9 and Writing Activity 3-E.

(p. 113, top photo)
Store clerks in Latin America often play a different role than their U.S. counterparts. In the U.S., customers typically search through merchandise and select their own purchases. In Latin America, the clerk often locates and shows goods to the customer in a one-on-one interchange with more personalized service.

(p. 113, bottom photo)
Santiago is the cultural, political, and financial capital of Chile. Over 90 percent of the population lives in and around the capital in the central part of the country. The Chilean economy has rebounded in recent years, and many Chileans have acquired a greater amount of disposable income.

Present & Practice

Answers

5 Order of questions and answers will vary, but may include the following:

MAMÁ

¿De quién son estos pantalones azules oscuros?

…son estos jeans blancos?

…son estos jeans negros?

…es esta sudadera verde clara?

…es esta sudadera roja?

…es este suéter rosado?

…es este suéter verde oscuro?

VÍCTOR

Ésos son de Pedro.

Ésos son de Julia.

Ésos son de Pedro.

Ésa es de Julia.

Ésa es de Pedro.

Ése es de Julia.

Ése es de Pedro.

MAMÁ

¿De quién es aquella sudadera anaranjada clara?

…es aquel suéter rojo?

…son aquellos tenis blancos?

…son aquellos tenis negros?

VÍCTOR

¿Aquélla? Es de Julia.

¿Aquél? Es de Pedro.

¿Aquéllos? Son de Julia.

¿Aquéllos? Son de Pedro.

---

5 Víctor ayuda a su madre a guardar la ropa después de lavarla. La ropa de su hermano Pedro es de colores oscuros. La de su hermana Julia es de colores claros. Con un(a) compañero(a) digan de quién es la ropa de los dibujos.

Mamá —*¿De quién son estos pantalones marrones claros?*
Víctor —*Ésos son de Julia.*

Mamá —*¿De quién son aquellos pantalones verdes oscuros?*
Víctor —*¿Aquéllos? Son de Pedro.*

Los comparativos: *tanto(a) . . . como*

You know that we use *tan* + adjective + *como* ("as . . . as") to make equal comparisons of people or things. To make the same kind of comparison with nouns, we use *tanto(a)* + noun + *como.*

Rosa es **tan** elegante **como** su prima.	*Rosa is **as** elegant **as** her cousin.*
Tiene **tanto** dinero **como** su prima.	*She has **as much** money **as** her cousin.*
Compró **tantas** blusas **como** faldas.	*She bought **as many** blouses **as** skirts.*

Since *tanto* is an adjective, it agrees in number and gender with the noun.

114   Capítulo 3

Options

Strategies for Reaching All Students

Spanish-Speaking Students

 Un paso más Ex. 3-I

Students Needing Extra Help

Los comparativos: Provide a few more examples with *tan,* stressing its use with an adjective. Then give some masculine, feminine, singular, and plural examples of *tanto,* stressing its use with a noun.

To emphasize that *tanto* refers to objects, provide examples with objects in the room: *Marcos tiene tantos libros como Rosa.* If there is confusion with *tan,* review examples from Chap. 1.

Ex. 5: Point out that in the first sentence of the sample dialogue, the adjective is used; in the second, the pronoun is used. Review the concept of distance (over there). Instruct students to pay close attention to the illustration.

Ex. 6: Go through the exercise, using only *tanto* + noun + *como: tantos cinturones como.* Then form the verb in the preterite: *escogió.* Finally, put the two together: *escogió tantos cinturones como.*

Ahora lo sabes: Have students write out this section so they can record what they have mastered.

6 Túrnate con un(a) compañero(a) para decir qué hicieron estas personas.

Julia sacó tanto dinero como Juan.
o: *Juan sacó tanto dinero como Julia.*

Julia / Juan / sacar

a. **Susana / Rosita / escoger**   b. **Felipe / Anita / tocar**   c. **Rosario / Pablo / comprar**

d. **María / Roberto / repartir**   e. **Lucía / Tomás / escribir**   f. **Diego / Luis / comer**

Ahora lo sabes

Can you:

■ tell what happened in the past?
—Ayer compré un(a) ___ y lo (la) ___ con tarjeta de crédito.

■ refer to people and things at various distances from you?
—Ese chaleco es bonito, pero ___ es más elegante.

■ compare quantities that are the same?
—Julio tiene ___ gorras ___ su hermano.

MORE PRACTICE

• Más práctica y tarea, pp. 535–536
• Practice Workbook 3–5, 3–10

Gramática en contexto   115

---

6 a. Susana (Rosita) escogió tantos cinturones como Rosita (Susana).
b. Felipe (Anita) tocó tanta música como Anita (Felipe).
c. Rosario (Pablo) compró tantas corbatas como Pablo (Rosario).
d. María (Roberto) repartió tantos periódicos como Roberto (María).
e. Lucía (Tomás) escribió tantas tarjetas postales como Tomás (Lucía).
f. Diego (Luis) comió tantos sandwiches como Luis (Diego).

Answers: Ahora lo sabes
• *Answers will vary.* / pagué
• éste (aquél)
• tantas / como

Practice Wkbk. 3-10

Audio Activities 3.4, 3.5

Writing Activity 3-F

Pruebas 3-9

Comm. Act. BLM 3-3

Pasos vivos 2 CD-ROM
Bulletin Board, Slide Presentation Maker, Spindle, Treadmill

Extended Written Practice/Homework
1. Write three sentences comparing items of clothing using any of these adjectives: *cómodo(a), elegante, flojo(a), apretado(a), sencillo(a): Mis zapatos de tacón alto no son tan cómodos como mis mocasines.*
2. Write three sentences comparing the quantities of clothing that people have: *Mi prima no tiene tantos vestidos como yo, pero tiene más pantalones que yo.*

Multiple Intelligences
Verbal/Linguistic
See Exs. 5–6 and Audio Activities 3.4 and 3.5.
Visual/Spatial
1) With a permanent marker, draw stick figures on an overhead transparency. Copy chapter vocabulary words that refer to

clothing items onto index cards and distribute them to students. Call on individuals to draw the clothing item on their index cards on one of the figures on the transparency.
2) See Practice Wkbk. 3-10, Writing Activity 3-F, and Comm. Act. BLM 3-3.

Apply

 ¿Recuerdas?

Play

 Video Activity A

Using the Video
In Episode 3, Carlos, María and Jamie are having breakfast in Carlos's father's restaurant when an ominous fax arrives with the message *¡Cuidado!*

Later that morning Carlos and Jamie visit the state building of Querétaro. The building is named after La Corregidora, a heroine of the Mexican Independence movement.

In an antique store, Jamie discovers a photo of her great-grandmother, La Catrina. She learns that "catrina" is a term for a rich woman.

Later María, Carlos and Jamie shop for clothes. Afterward they go to a hotel restaurant, where they are spied on again by don Silvestre Aguilar. He tells his companions that Jamie poses a threat to his political campaign, since she is the heir to all of La Catrina's property, and Demetrio Alcocer, the librarian, has the will.

¿Se visten como tú y tus amigos estos muchachos en Bariloche, Argentina?

Artículos de cuero en venta en la Plaza Flamingo, Cancún

116   Capítulo 3

Actividades

1 Piensa en un día muy especial. Túrnate con un(a) compañero(a) para hablar de lo que hiciste ese día. Puedes hablar de:

- las actividades del día
- la hora, el lugar
- las personas que participaron
- lo que ocurrió

2 Hagan una "tienda de ropa" en la clase. Pueden traer ropa de su casa o fotos de revistas. Usen toda la sala. Pongan algunas cosas cerca de ustedes y otras más lejos. Inventen diálogos entre vendedores, cajeros y clientes. Usen estas u otras ideas en sus diálogos:

- saludar *(to greet)* y preguntar al cliente (a la clienta) qué busca
- hablar de la tela, de la talla (del número) y del color
- si puede probarse la ropa
- decir el precio y preguntar cómo quiere pagar
- dar las gracias y despedirse *(say good-by)*

Options

Strategies for Reaching All Students

Spanish-Speaking Students
Exs. 1–2: Pair bilingual with non-bilingual students if possible.

 Un paso más Ex. 3-J

Students Needing Extra Help
If pressed for time, divide the class into groups and assign an activity to each group.
Ex. 1: Brainstorm examples of important days. Remind students to use the preterite.

Help them with vocabulary referring to holidays, sports victories, special ceremonies, etc. Provide a model.
Ex. 2: Allow time to prepare this exercise. Suggest a question-and-answer format for students' dialogues. If necessary, refer to the dialogues in the Book 1, Chap. 6 *Vocabulario para conversar* exercises.

Enrichment
Ex. 1: Before doing this exercise, brainstorm activities that someone may do on a special day: a party, a trip, a visit to the museum or to visit relatives, for example. Follow up this exercise by having students take notes on the narrative and write about their classmate's day.
Ex. 2: For extra credit, have groups of students prepare a videotape of their dialogue at home.

Conexiones

Las ciencias sociales

Los zapatos en la historia

El estilo del zapato refleja las tendencias sociales y culturales de la época. Lee el texto y mira las ilustraciones de diferentes estilos de zapatos a lo largo de los siglos *(across the centuries)*.

Zapato con plataforma: De moda en diversas épocas. La plataforma representa el deseo de "estar en lo alto."

Zapato del siglo XIV: Usado por los nobles, de hasta 46 cm de largo. Era un símbolo de prestigio social aunque la iglesia lo consideraba producto del diablo.

Choclo japonés: Para usar en el exterior. Suelas gruesas *(thick soles)* de madera de hasta 10 cm. La persona parecía más alta y caminaba con más elegancia.

Zapato chino: La costumbre de vendar *(to bind)* los pies de las mujeres duró en China hasta el comienzo del siglo XX. Los pies pequeños daban una imagen delicada de la mujer y hacían difícil su escape.

Zapatilla de deporte: Un símbolo de la sociedad actual. Las usan tanto las mujeres como los hombres y crean la imagen de un estilo de vida sano.

Túrnate con un(a) compañero(a) para decir si estas afirmaciones son verdaderas o falsas según el texto. Cambia las falsas para transformarlas en verdaderas.

1. A lo largo de los siglos, la comodidad del zapato ha sido *(has been)* una cuestión muy importante.
2. La costumbre de vendar los pies de las mujeres todavía se practica en China.
3. El antiguo zapato japonés es una clase de zapato con plataforma.

Ahora escribe tres preguntas sobre estos estilos de zapatos u otros y hazlas a un(a) compañero(a).

Todo junto   117

La Catrina: Capítulo 3

Play

Video Activity B

Para entender mejor

Play

Video Activity C

Writing Activities 3-G, 3-H

Comm. Act. BLMs 3-4, 3-5

Pasos vivos 2 CD-ROM
A Jugar, Laboratorio de grabar, Maps, Video Monitor, Video Presentation Maker

---

Cooperative Learning
Divide the class into groups of three or four. Photocopy pictures from magazines and distribute a different one to each group. On one sheet of paper, each group member should write one descriptive sentence about the picture and then pass the paper to the right. After each student has written three sentences, have the groups organize the sentences to create a story or logical description. Call on groups to share their stories with the class.

Multiple Intelligences
Bodily/Kinesthetic and Verbal/Linguistic
See Ex. 2.
Interpersonal/Social and Visual/Spatial
See Cooperative Learning.
Verbal/Linguistic
See Ex. 1.
Visual/Spatial
See Using the Video, Writing Activities 3-G and 3-H, and Comm. Act. BLMs 3-4 and 3-5.

Cultural Notes

(p. 116, bottom photo)
In 1970, the Mexican government chose Cancún as the site of a planned tourist development. In a short period of time it became home to a wide range of hotels, an active night life, and exclusive shops, such as this leather goods store. The main attractions, however, are Cancún's Caribbean beaches. Tourists can go snorkeling to see spectacular and colorful tropical fish, or travel to the nearby Mayan ruins of Tulum and Chichén Itzá.

Apply

Process Reading
For a description of process reading, see p. 52.

Answers
Antes de leer
Answers will vary. Students may say that advice columns deal with relationship problems, finances, health and beauty, or consumer issues.

Mira la lectura
Answers will vary.

¡**V**amos a leer!

www.pasoapaso.com

Antes de leer

STRATEGY ➤ Using prior knowledge

What kinds of problems are discussed in advice columns? What advice might you give someone who was unhappy about his or her wardrobe?

Mira la lectura

STRATEGY ➤ Skimming

Skim the column to get an overall idea of what it is about. Were some parts of it not clear? Make a list of three to five words that seemed to prevent you from understanding something important.

Querida Aurora...

Aurora:

Por favor, ¡dime qué debo hacer! Mis hermanitos y yo vivimos con mi papá. Él trabaja desde temprano por la mañana hasta tarde por la noche para mantenernos. El problema es que mi ropa está vieja, descolorida y me queda muy apretada. Pero no tengo dinero para comprar ropa nueva. Me da envidia cuando veo a mis amigas tan bien vestidas. Yo solamente tengo 17 años y ya me siento infeliz.

Alma Rosa Calderón

Alma Rosa:

Hay varias cosas que puedes hacer para no sentirte infeliz y para mejorar tu situación. Primero, ¡cambia de actitud! Claro que sí es normal querer ropa nueva, pero no olvides que hay otras cosas más importantes. Segundo, ¿por qué no encuentras una manera de ganar dinero? Puedes cuidar niños o trabajar en un restaurante o en una tienda. Además de comprar la ropa que necesitas, también vas a sentirte mejor porque podrás ayudar a tu padre. Sobre todo, ¡no descuides tus estudios! Recuerda que son más importantes que nada.

Aurora

118 Capítulo 3

Options

Strategies for Reaching All Students

Spanish-Speaking Students
Aplicación: Have students respond in writing: *Imagina que Alma Rosa te escribió a ti con su problema. ¿Qué le dirías? Escribe una carta dándole consejos.*

Students Needing Extra Help
Mira la lectura: If students come up with too many words that they don't know, show them which ones aren't important to getting the gist of the reading.
Infórmate: Provide examples of prefixes in English. This is a concept with which they are probably familiar. Have students work in pairs to figure out the meaning of the words listed.

Aplicación: Be alert to the mention of illegal means of earning money. It is easier to change Alma Rosa's letter first; then change Aurora's response. Brainstorm ways that Alma Rosa's letter can change: complaints against a disorganized sibling, an impatient parent, unmanageable school work, etc.

Infórmate

STRATEGY ➤ Understanding prefixes

Your list may have included the words *infeliz, descolorida,* and *descuides.* These words begin with a prefix that changes the meaning of the base word to its opposite. For example, you already know these pairs of opposites.

cómodo   incómodo
ordenado   desordenado
paciente   impaciente

Here are some other words with the negative prefixes *des-* and *in-/im-*.

necesario   innecesario
ocupado   desocupado
posible   imposible
prudente   imprudente

Use the meanings of these words to figure out the words with the prefixes in the reading.

feliz   *happy*
colorida   *colorful*
cuidar   *to take care of*

¿NECESITA AYUDA CON LOS NIÑOS?

Mi nombre es Alma Rosa Calderón. Tengo 17 años de edad y busco trabajo cuidando niños los fines de semana. Como soy la hermana mayor en mi familia, tengo mucha experiencia con los niños pequeños y con los quehaceres de la casa.

Soy honesta, responsable y muy buena estudiante. Por favor llame al teléfono (745) 555-2841

¡NO BUSQUE MÁS!

Aplicación

What do you think of Aurora's advice? How do teenagers earn money in your community? Change Aurora's letter to reflect the way things are where you live. Use the pairs of opposites in *Infórmate* and this section if you can.

Use the meanings of these words to figure out their opposites:

cansar   descansar *(to rest)*
contento *(happy)* descontento
justo   injusto *(unfair)*
maduro *(mature)*   inmaduro

¡Vamos a leer!   119

Infórmate

infeliz: unhappy; *descolorida:* discolored, washed out; *descuidar:* to neglect

Aplicación

cansar: to tire; *descontento:* unhappy; *justo:* fair; *inmaduro:* immature

🌐 Internet Activities

Have students go to www.pasoapaso.com for additional activities and practice.

Enrichment
Aplicación: Additional activities: 1) Imagine you are the brother or sister of the young woman who wrote the letter. Write to Aurora to explain your sister's problem from your perspective. 2) Write to Aurora to explain the problem from the point of view of a friend or parent. 3) Write to Aurora about a problem of your own.

Apply

Process Writing

For information regarding developing a writing portfolio, see p. 54.

¡Vamos a escribir!

Imagina que tu escuela necesita uniformes nuevos: uno para usar en clase, uno para un equipo deportivo y uno para la banda.

 Primero, escoge un uniforme para diseñar. Piensa en estas cosas:

- las telas
- los colores
- el costo

Luego escribe una descripción del uniforme. Haz un dibujo para acompañar la descripción. No olvides ponerle el nombre o el símbolo de la escuela. Sigue los cinco pasos del proceso de escribir. (Si es necesario, mira la página 54.)

A estos jóvenes mexicanos les quedan bien los uniformes escolares.

Estudiantes de camino a la escuela en Quito, Ecuador

Estudiantes en Santiago, República Dominicana

120   Capítulo 3

Options

Strategies for Reaching All Students

Students Needing Extra Help
Ex. 1: Students need design only one uniform.
Ex. 2: Help students with the words *afectar* and *mejorar*. Remind them of the *tanto . . . como* formula and demonstrative adjectives.

Multiple Intelligences
Interpersonal/Social
See step 2.
Naturalist
Have students create a chart/diagram that shows clothing made from natural fibers such as *algodón* or *lana* and those made from synthetic materials.
Visual/Spatial and Bodily/Kinesthetic
See step 3.

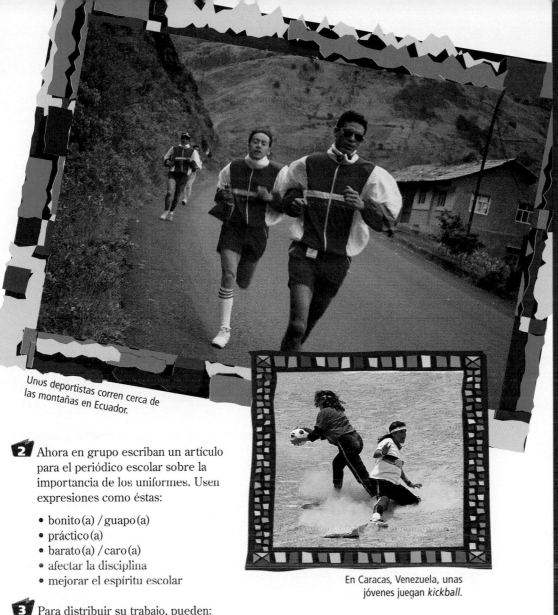

Unos deportistas corren cerca de las montañas en Ecuador.

2 Ahora en grupo escriban un artículo para el periódico escolar sobre la importancia de los uniformes. Usen expresiones como éstas:

- bonito (a) / guapo (a)
- práctico (a)
- barato (a) / caro (a)
- afectar la disciplina
- mejorar el espíritu escolar

En Caracas, Venezuela, unas jóvenes juegan *kickball*.

3 Para distribuir su trabajo, pueden:

- exhibir las descripciones y los dibujos en la sala de clases
- exhibirlos en el vestíbulo o la biblioteca escolar
- enviar el artículo al periódico escolar
- enviarlo al director o a la directora de la escuela
- poner todo en el portafolio

¡Vamos a escribir!   121

Cultural Notes ☼

(pp. 120–121, photos)
Uniforms contribute to a sense of equality and common purpose within a group. For this reason, athletic teams employ uniforms that identify their members. School uniforms contribute to this same goal. In Latin America, many schools enforce a dress code in which girls wear dark skirts or dresses, while boys wear ties and conservative style slacks.

(p. 121, photo)
Kickball is popular in many parts of Latin America. The game is similar to baseball, except that the "pitcher" bowls the ball to the "batter," who kicks it into play.

Test Preparation

You may want to assign parts of this section as written homework or as an in-class writing activity prior to administering the *Examen de habilidades*.

Answers:

Listening: *¡Mamá! Luz María me invitó a pasar una semana en el campo con ella y su familia. Me gustaría llevar esta chaqueta de cuero, pero ya no está de moda. Creo que debo llevar aquel suéter de cuello alto y los pantalones de lana. ¿Están limpios? También necesito un chandal. Ese de tela sintética ya no me queda bien. ¡Mamá! ¡Tenemos que ir de compras!*
Answers may vary, but students should mention cold or cool weather.

Reading: The bottom right picture

Writing: Answers will vary.

Culture: Answers will vary, but students may say they'd need to know the exchange rate before buying something. / By looking carefully at a country's currency one can see literary figures, political leaders, and national flora and fauna: the *quetzal,* the currency of Guatemala, is also the name of that country's national bird.

Esta sección te ayudará a prepararte para el examen de habilidades, donde tendrás que hacer tareas semejantes. Recuerda, sin embargo, que en el examen no habrá modelos.

Listening

Can you understand when someone talks about clothes in detail? Listen as your teacher reads a sample similar to what you will hear on the test. Based on the clothing mentioned, what do you think the weather will be like in the country?

Reading

Can you understand written descriptions of clothes? Which picture matches one of the articles described?

Pagué veinte dólares por esta blusa a cuadros y me queda floja. Estos pantalones de algodón no tienen bolsillos, y no me gusta la chaqueta porque los botones son demasiado pequeños. Los zapatos que llegaron para papá son de color marrón, y no negro, y el cinturón para mi hijo no es de la talla que él usa.

Querida Mónica,

Debes traer ropa sencilla y cómoda. Por aquí está muy de moda usar jeans con un chaleco, también los suéteres de cuello alto y las camisas lisas de algodón. ¿Compraste aquel chaquetón que vimos en el almacén González? Por la noche hace frío. No tienes que traer traje de baño. Aquí hay tres de tamaño mediano. Me regalaron dos y compré uno. Pero papá dice que necesitas una tarjeta de crédito si quieres comprar algo muy caro. Hasta pronto.

Tu amiga,
Gloria

Writing

Can you write a letter to a friend about an upcoming visit? See the sample above.

Culture

If you were planning to visit several Latin American countries, what would you need to know before buying something? What can you tell about a country by looking carefully at its currency? Give an example from a Spanish-speaking country.

Speaking

Can you ask and answer questions about clothes? Create a dialogue with your partner between a salesperson and a customer. Here is a sample dialogue:

A —¿De qué son estos cinturones?
B —Éstos son de cuero y aquéllos de lona.
A —Este cinturón me queda apretado. ¿Lo tiene en la talla mediana?
B —Sí. Aquí hay uno. ¿Necesita algo más?
A —Me gustarían unos pantalones flojos y oscuros.
B —Éstos a rayas están muy de moda.

www.pasoapaso.com

Options

Strategies for Reaching All Students

Students Needing Extra Help
Have students write out this section so they can check off what they have mastered.
Listening: Review weather expressions. Ask students what they would wear in different types of weather: *¿Qué llevas cuando hace frío?* Review the vocabulary section of the Organizer.
Reading: Have students first look at the pictures so that they know what to look for. Read slowly so students pick up subtleties.

Writing: Brainstorm other activities that require special clothing because of the weather. Limit the number of sentences.
Culture: Have students review the *Perspectiva cultural.*
Speaking: Use the vocabulary section of the Organizer. Review dialogues in the *Vocabulario para conversar* and *Todo junto* sections.

Resumen del vocabulario

Usa el vocabulario de este capítulo para:

- describe clothing in detail
- indicate clothing preferences and make comparisons
- say how you paid for purchases

to indicate articles of clothing
el bolso
el botín, *pl.* los botines
la cartera
el chaleco
el chandal
el chaquetón, *pl.* los chaquetones
el cinturón, *pl.* los cinturones
la corbata
la gorra
el mocasín, *pl.* los mocasines
el pañuelo
el suéter de cuello alto
el traje
los zapatos de tacón alto

to indicate parts of clothing
el bolsillo
el botón, *pl.* los botones
la cremallera
la manga

to discuss making purchases
el cajero, la cajera
el catálogo
el cheque
(el dinero) en efectivo
la liquidación, *pl.* las liquidaciones
estar en liquidación
la tarjeta de crédito
el vendedor, la vendedora
encontrar *(o → ue)*
escoger

to discuss clothing
apretado, -a
flojo, -a
elegante
sencillo, -a
la moda
estar de moda
probarse *(o → ue)*
usar

to discuss fabrics and patterns
¿De qué es ___?
Es de ___.
la tela
el algodón
la lana

la lona
el nilón
el plástico
sintético, -a
a cuadros
a rayas
floreado, -a
liso, -a
claro, -a
oscuro, -a

to indicate sizes
el número (de zapatos)
(número) y medio
la talla
el tamaño
  grande
  mediano, -a
  pequeño, -a

other useful words and expressions
alguien
el cesto de la ropa sucia
el suelo
la fiesta
colgar *(o → ue)*
guardar
lo que
(me) da igual
por todas partes

Resumen 123

Assessment

Prueba cumulativa

Examen de habilidades

Test Generator

Additional Assessment Options

Comm. Act. BLMs
Small Group Activities
Situation Cards

Pasos vivos 2 CD-ROM
Slide Presentation Maker, Video Presentation Maker, Word Processor, Spindle

¿Lo sabes bien? Video Quiz

www Internet Activities
Self-Test

CAPÍTULO 4

THEME: LEISURE-TIME ACTIVITIES

SCOPE AND SEQUENCE Pages 124–157

COMMUNICATION

Topics

Sports and sports equipment

Music

Games

Objectives

To discuss the paintings of Frida Kahlo and Diego Rivera

To discuss sports

To discuss leisure activities

To describe people or things

To discuss activities in the past

CULTURE

The paintings of Frida Kahlo and Diego Rivera

GRAMMAR

El pretérito del verbo ser

El pretérito de los verbos hacer, poder *y* tener

Repaso: El verbo saber

El pretérito de verbos reflexivos

Ancillaries available for use with Chapter 4

Multisensory/Technology

 Overheads, 21–25

 Audio Tapes and CDs

 Vocabulary Art Blackline Masters for Hands-On Learning, pp. 23–27/CD-ROM

 Classroom Crossword

 La Catrina

 Pasos vivos 2 CD-ROM

 Internet Activities www.pasoapaso.com

Print

 Practice Workbook, pp. 34–44

 Writing, Audio & Video Activities, pp. 23–28, 102–104, 157–158

 Communicative Activity Blackline Masters
  Pair and Small Group Activities, pp. 22–27
  Situation Cards, p. 28

 Un paso más: Actividades para ampliar tu español, pp. 19–24

 RESOURCE PRO®

Planning Express, Teaching Resources Library, and Clip Art Library

Assessment

 Assessment Program
  Pruebas, pp. 55–66
  Examen de habilidades, pp. 67–70

 Test Generator

 ¿Lo sabes bien? Video Quiz

Video still from Chap. 4

Outdoor Fun

Most leisure-time activities in Spanish-speaking countries take place in the streets, parks, and cafés in the commercial areas of the cities—often in the downtown areas. Because towns and cities are designed with the pedestrian in mind, street life is full of things to see and do.

People of all ages commonly enjoy each other's company in local outdoor cafés, or in the many parks, often replete with monuments, fountains, and gazebos. Vendors selling ice cream, fresh fruit, cold beverages, and brightly colored balloons add to the liveliness of the parks and *plazas*. Occasionally entertainment may be provided by a group of musicians playing songs of the region, or by a clown juggling, or by a city-organized concert. Local artists and artisans display paintings, jewelry, and other handicrafts in outdoor areas. Some locales with temperate climates offer year-round art fairs.

One of Latin America's most renowned parks lies in the heart of Mexico City. It is called Chapultepec, which is the Aztec, or Nahuatl, word for "grasshopper hill." Chapultepec Park contains spacious areas for walking and playing, a small lake for boating, outdoor restaurants, and the city zoo. It is also the site of several museums, including the historical museum known as *El Castillo*—former home of the French-imposed emperor and empress Maximiliano and Carlota, who ruled Mexico between 1864 and 1867. Other museums include the *Museo Nacional de Antropología,* which houses the most complete collection of pre-Columbian art and artifacts in the world, and *El Museo de Arte Moderno,* which features twentieth century paintings by Mexico's most accomplished artists. In all Spanish-speaking countries, the citizens are very proud of their rich cultural heritage, and museums are considered to be important and enjoyable places to relax and learn.

Undoubtedly, the most popular team sport throughout Spain and most of Latin America is soccer *(fútbol)*. Youngsters of all ages can be seen playing it in parks, on sports fields, or neighborhood streets. As a spectator sport, soccer is also extremely important. People fill the stadiums for games, and many of the events are televised. In countries that have not adopted soccer as a national sport, such as the Dominican Republic and Nicaragua, baseball is the preferred game. Skiing is popular during the winter months in Argentina, Chile, and Spain. Each of these nations boasts several internationally known ski resorts. In addition, of course, beaches are popular in all Spanish-speaking countries except the two landlocked South American nations of Bolivia and Paraguay.

Introduce

Re-entry of Concepts

The following list represents words, expressions, and grammar topics re-entered from Book 1 and Book 2 (Chaps. 1–3):

Book 1
calendar expressions, *gustar* expressions, time-telling, family members, places and buildings, television shows

Chapter 1
school activities

Chapter 2
daily routine

124   Capítulo 4

Planning

Cross-Curricular Connections

Physical Education Connection
(pp. 128–129)
Have pairs of students choose a favorite sport or invent a new one. Have them make a poster and / or prepare an oral report in Spanish stating the rules, the equipment needed, and the reasons that this sport is so much fun.

Communications Connection
(pp. 146–147)
In small groups, have students prepare a TV sportscast. Each student should report on a different game from that day or evening. They should include key plays, errors, and other crucial information. If time permits, you might want to videotape some of the best reports to share with other classes.

Literature / History Connection
(pp. 154–155)
Have each student choose a famous person, past or present, and write a short biography using the past tense. Focus should be on the person's most significant moment or success and the factors that led to it.

CAPÍTULO 4

¿Cómo te diviertes?

Objectives

At the end of this chapter, you will be able to:

► talk about past and present activities

► extend, accept, or reject an invitation

► discuss and evaluate a leisure-time activity

► talk about the paintings of two Mexican artists and what their work tells us about them and their culture

PASO CULTURAL

El grupo de *rock* Santana y su líder, el guitarrista mexicano Carlos Santana, tienen más de 18 álbumes de oro y 12 de platino. Su estilo combina influencias de *rock*, *blues* y música latina. Santana es miembro del Rock and Roll Hall of Fame desde 1998. En este mural en San Francisco, *Inspire to Aspire*, pintado por Michael Ríos en 1987, vemos a Carlos con imágenes de todas sus influencias musicales. ¿Cuáles son los elementos mexicanos en este mural? ¿Cuáles representan el *rock*, los *blues* y la música latina?

Mural dedicado a Carlos Santana, San Francisco, California

125

Cultural Notes

Spanish in Your Community
Have students select three activities from the chapter vocabulary and name at least one Hispanic person famous for each. For example, they might name Seve Ballesteros, a Spaniard, for golf. Afterwards, have each student ask five people outside of the classroom to provide additional names for the categories. Have students share the results of their surveys with the class and discuss the contributions of Hispanics to sports and other activities.

Paso cultural
Possible answers: Elementos mexicanos son los mariachis, los bailarines *(dancers)* y las caras indígenas detrás de Santana. *Rock* y *blues* se representan por su guitarra eléctrica. La música latina se representa por el señor que toca el bongó.

(pp. 124–125, photo)
This mural depicts Carlos Santana, the son of a *mariachi* violinist. Santana is considered to be the father of fusion Latin rock and was one of the first Latino musicians to become popular with mainstream audiences in the U.S. Michael Ríos was a member of *Galería de la raza,* and an active muralist at the start of the contemporary mural movement. Ríos and his peers are influenced by Rivera's and other Mexican muralists' works.

• To discuss leisure-time activities in Spanish-speaking countries

Critical Thinking: Synthesizing

Have students write one or two descriptive sentences about the photographs. Refer to Book 1, Chap. 3, to review leisure-time activities.

Cultural Notes

(p. 126, bottom photo)
Most CD stores in Argentina would probably feature a wide range of music, including Mexican *mariachi,* Caribbean *salsa,* Colombian *cumbia,* Venezuelan and Andean folk music, and Argentinean *tangos.* Perhaps because of its mostly European roots, Argentina also has a highly developed classical music tradition. In addition, a flourishing music industry produces U.S.-style popular music.

¡Piensa en la CULTURA!

Diversiones en Argentina, Venezuela y Cuba

Mira las fotos. Las personas están hablando de varias diversiones. ¿Qué pasatiempos te gustan a ti?

PASO CULTURAL

El ajedrez empezó en India en el siglo VI, pasó a Persia, y fue llevado a España por los moros *(Moors)* de África en el siglo VIII. La palabra *ajedrez* viene del árabe. Muchas palabras del español que empiezan con *al-* son de origen árabe, como *almacén* y *algodón.* Una es el nombre de un tipo de matemáticas. ¿Qué palabra es?

"Ayer fuimos al parque para jugar ajedrez."

El ajedrez es un pasatiempo muy popular por todas partes. ¿Sabes jugar?

Jugando ajedrez en Caracas, Venezuela

Caracas, Venezuela

Una tienda de discos compactos en Buenos Aires

Buenos Aires, Argentina

"Dicen que el último disco compacto de Los Lobos tiene muchas canciones muy buenas."

¿Qué clase de música te gusta más? ¿Conoces algunos artistas que cantan en inglés y en español? ¿Te gusta su música?

126   Capítulo 4

Options

Strategies for Reaching All Students

Spanish-Speaking Students

Ask students to respond orally or in writing: *Describe tus actividades favoritas cuando estabas en la escuela primaria. ¿En qué participabas fuera de la escuela? ¿Te gustaban los deportes, los videos, los videojuegos y el baile? ¿En qué quisieras participar después de terminar tus estudios?*

 Un paso más Ex. 4-A

Cultural Notes

Paso cultural
(p. 126)
Answer: álgebra

(p. 127)
Possible answers: Rusia, otros países del este de Europa, los Estados Unidos, Francia, Holanda e Inglaterra tienen compañías prestigiosas de ballet clásico. México, Irlanda y muchos otros países tienen compañías prestigiosas de ballet folklórico.

"No sé por qué a tantos jóvenes no les gusta el ballet. ¡Los bailarines son atletas fantásticos!"

¿Crees que es más difícil meter un gol en fútbol o bailar por una hora?

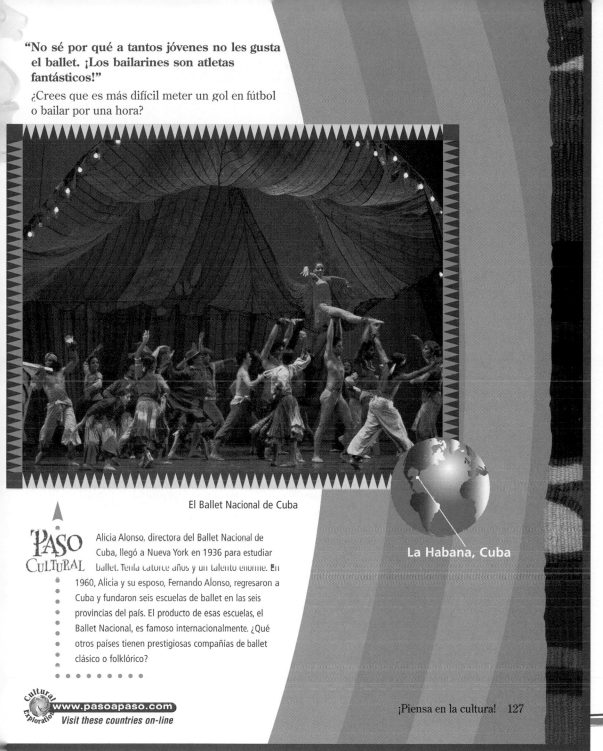

El Ballet Nacional de Cuba

PASO CULTURAL

Alicia Alonso, directora del Ballet Nacional de Cuba, llegó a Nueva York en 1936 para estudiar ballet. Tenía catorce años y un talento enorme. En 1960, Alicia y su esposo, Fernando Alonso, regresaron a Cuba y fundaron seis escuelas de ballet en las seis provincias del país. El producto de esas escuelas, el Ballet Nacional, es famoso internacionalmente. ¿Qué otros países tienen prestigiosas compañías de ballet clásico o folklórico?

Cultural Exploration
www.pasoapaso.com
Visit these countries on-line

La Habana, Cuba

Multicultural Perspectives

Sports were just as important to the people of ancient Meso-america as they are today. Some of these sports, however, were more than simple *diversiones.* For example, the ancient ball game of *ulama,* a version of which is still played today in rural Mexico, may have had a religious significance. Players had to hit the ball, which may have represented the sun, through a stone ring in order to score. The sport was much more physical than modern football or rugby. In fact, players sometimes died from injuries suffered during what was aptly called *el juego de vida y muerte.* Ask students to analyze current sports and describe what significance they have to a given culture.

Answers: ¡Piensa en la cultura!

Answers to inductive questions will vary. *(p. 126, bottom photo)* Some names of artists who sing in English and in Spanish may include: Santana, Plácido Domingo, The Barrio Boyzz, Lisette Meléndez, and Selena.

(p. 127, photo)
El Ballet Nacional de Cuba, based in Havana, was founded in 1960 by ballerina Alicia Alonso (1921–). Although she was allowed to study ballet, her parents did not intend for her to dance professionally. However, she defied them by eloping with a fellow classmate, Fernando Alonso, to New York City, where they both wished to pursue a career in ballet. She joined the American Ballet Theater and was with the theater from 1941–1960. In 1960, the couple returned to Cuba with the dream of creating their own company. By 1966, Cuban dancers were winning recognition in competitions all over Europe. El Ballet Nacional de Cuba, headed by its star and founder, performed all over the world, except in the U.S, where she was not allowed to perform because of her political affiliation. Then, in 1975, in a gesture of international goodwill, Alonso was allowed to perform once again in the city that had made her a star: she danced *Swan Lake* with the American Ballet Theater at Lincoln Center. At the end of her performance, she received an 18-minute standing ovation. Before returning to Havana, she said: *El arte no tiene fronteras. Le pertenece al mundo, y el mundo somos tú y yo.*

Present

Chapter Theme
Sports and sports equipment

Communicative Objectives
- To discuss sports
- To discuss activities in the past

 Overheads 21–22

 Vocabulary Art BLMs/CD-ROM

 Vocabulary Tape 4-1

Teaching Suggestions
Preparing students to speak: Use one or two options from each of the categories of Comprehensible Input, Physical Response, or Limited Verbal Response. For a complete explanation of these categories and some sample activities, see pp. T20–T21.

Vocabulario para conversar

¿Me prestas tu raqueta?

Vas a necesitar estas palabras y expresiones para hablar sobre las diversiones. Después de leerlas varias veces, practícalas con un(a) compañero(a).

el palo (de golf, de hockey)

el casco

el disco (de hockey)

los bolos

el golf

el hockey

el entrenador

las pesas

la bicicleta

montar en bicicleta

el patín, *pl.* los patines

patinar sobre hielo

levantar pesas

la entrenadora

correr

el campeón, *pl.* los campeones; la campeona

128   Capítulo 4

Options

Strategies for Reaching All Students

Spanish-Speaking Students
Ask: *¿Usas otras palabras para estos deportes o este equipo? ¿Cuáles son? Haz una lista.*

 Un paso más Exs. 4-B, 4-C

Students Needing Extra Help
Vocabulario para conversar: Have students begin filling in the vocabulary section of the Organizer.
Distinguish between *pelota* and *balón: pelota* is a small ball, such as a baseball or tennis ball; *balón* is a large, inflated ball such as a basketball or volleyball. Remind students to use *jugar* with sports words. Point out word families such as *patinar / patín*, etc.

También necesitas . . . : Distinguish between *prestar* (to lend) and *pedir prestado* (to borrow).

Learning Spanish Through Action
STAGING VOCABULARY: *Busquen, Levanten*
MATERIALS: envelopes containing pictures of vocabulary items
DIRECTIONS: Pass out envelopes to groups. Direct them to look for and then hold up pictures of sports equipment related to the sport that you mention.

empatar

perder (e → ie)   ganar

JAGUARES TIGRES
5   5

JAGUARES TIGRES
5   6

¡NO OLVIDES!

Ganar can also mean "to earn."

el esquí, *pl.* los esquíes

la jugadora
(de golf)

la raqueta
(de tenis)

el bate

el jugador
(de béisbol)

el balón, *pl.*
los balones

la pelota (de golf, de béisbol)

el guante (de béisbol)

También necesitas . . .

prestar	*to lend*	el partido	*match, game*
pedir prestado, -a (a)	*to borrow*	meter un gol	*to score a goal*
tener que:			
(yo) tuve que	*I had to*		
(tú) tuviste que	*you had to*		
la liga	*league*		

> **¿Y qué quiere decir . . . ?**
> el campeonato

Vocabulario para conversar   129

Explain to students that this chapter is about leisure-time activities. They should be prepared to state what they are in the habit of doing (using *soler*) on weekends.

Grammar Preview
(Yo) tuve que / (tú) tuviste que are presented here lexically. The complete paradigm of *tener* in the preterite is found on p. 146. Avoid grammar discussion at this point.

Class Starter Review
On the day following initial vocabulary presentation, you might begin the class with either of these activities:
1) In pairs, have students take turns naming a sport and listing the equipment necessary for it.
2) Prepare a transparency listing outcomes of sports matches, real or imaginary (*Los Leones 21, Los Tigres 20*). In pairs, students take turns reading the scores and then saying who won (*ganó, ganaron*), who lost (*perdió, perdieron*), or if it was a tie (*empataron*).

ᴡᴡᴡ Internet Activities
Juegos
Have students go to www.pasoapaso.com for additional activities and practice.

Extended Written Practice/Homework
1. Choose three activities from pp. 128–129 and write sentences telling when you did them last.
2. Choose three items from pp. 128–129 and write sentences telling how long different people have had them: *Hace seis meses que tengo mi nuevo casco de hockey.*

3. Write three pairs of sentences telling activities you would like to do and whether or not you need to borrow certain equipment for these activities: *Quisiera patinar sobre hielo. No necesito pedir prestado los patines.*

Multiple Intelligences
Bodily/Kinesthetic
See Learning Spanish Through Action.
Interpersonal/Social and Verbal/Linguistic
See Class Starter Review, Ex. 1.
Verbal/Linguistic
See Vocabulary Tape 4-1.
Visual/Spatial
See Overheads 21–22.
Visual/Spatial and Verbal/Linguistic
See Class Starter Review, Ex. 2.

Practice

Reteach / Review: Time-telling

Ex. 1: Pairs of students can extend this dialogue by having *Estudiante A* ask *Estudiante B* at what time he or she would like to do the activity named.

Answers: Empecemos a conversar

1 ESTUDIANTE A

a. Tengo un palo de golf nuevo. ¿Jugamos golf mañana?

b. Tengo esquíes nuevos. ¿Esquiamos mañana?

c. Tengo un (balón de) básquetbol nuevo. ¿Jugamos básquetbol mañana?

d. Tengo patines nuevos. ¿Patinamos sobre hielo mañana?

e. Tengo una raqueta de tenis nueva. ¿Jugamos tenis mañana?

f. Tengo un (balón de) fútbol nuevo. ¿Jugamos fútbol mañana?

ESTUDIANTE B

a.–f. Answers will vary, but encourage students to use a variety of answers.

You might want students to note the use of the present tense implying future. It is the same as the English "are we playing tomorrow?"

Empecemos a conversar

Túrnate con un(a) compañero(a) para ser *Estudiante A* y *Estudiante B*. Reemplacen las palabras subrayadas en el modelo con palabras representadas o escritas en los recuadros. Si ven 💡 pueden dar su propia respuesta.

1

A —Tengo <u>un palo de hockey</u> nuevo. ¿<u>Jugamos hockey</u> mañana?

B —¡<u>Por supuesto</u>!

Estudiante A

a.   b.   c.

d.   e.   f.

Estudiante B

Sí, me gustaría mucho.

No, yo nunca ___.

No, mañana no puedo. Tengo que ___.

No, mañana no. ¿Por qué no jugamos ___?

Pero yo no sé ___.

¡Por supuesto!

💡

Levantando pesas, Palos Verdes, California

130   Capítulo 4

Options

Strategies for Reaching All Students

Students Needing Extra Help

Ex. 1: Discuss what kinds of words will go in the blank for *Estudiante B*.

Ex. 2: Remind students that this is not a linear match for answers.

Extended Written Practice/Homework

1. Refer to the activities on pp. 128–129 and write three questions that you can ask classmates to see if they would like to do different activities with you.

2. Write three sentences telling which persons or teams won, lost, or tied in a game or competition: *En 1998 y 1999 los Broncos ganaron el campeonato de fútbol americano.*

3. Write three sentences naming activities you didn't do because of other things you had to do: *No jugué golf con mis amigos porque tuve que trabajar en el almacén.*

2   A —¿Me prestas tu *pelota de béisbol*?
  B —*Claro que sí. ¿Necesitas el bate también?*

Estudiante A

Estudiante B

Patinando afuera de
un centro comercial,
Santiago, Chile

2 ESTUDIANTE A

a. ¿Me prestas tu bicicleta?
b. ...guante de béisbol?
c. ...raqueta de tenis?
d. ...casco de fútbol americano?
e. ...disco de hockey?
f. Questions will vary.

ESTUDIANTE B

a. Claro que sí. ¿Necesitas el casco de bicicleta también?
b. ...el bate (de béisbol) también?
c. ...las pelotas de tenis también?
d. ...el balón de fútbol americano también?
e. ...el palo de hockey también?
f. Answers will vary.

Multiple Intelligences
Bodily/Kinesthetic
Have students play "Name that Sport."
Students mime a particular sport and have others guess the name of it.
Bodily/Kinesthetic and Visual/Spatial
Have students make a collage depicting their favorite sports or leisure activities, creating colorful labels for the pictures.
Verbal/Linguistic
See Exs. 1–2.

Cultural Notes ☀

(p. 131, photo)
Santiago, Chile, has many shopping malls: two of the largest are Parque Arauco and Alto de los Condes. Malls have become a popular place for socializing or to enjoy such unconventional activities as roller skating.

Practice & Apply

Answers:
Empecemos a conversar

3 ESTUDIANTE A
a. ¿Quién ganó el partido de fútbol?
b. ...hockey?
c. ...tenis?
d. ...básquetbol?
e. ...bolos?
f. Questions will vary.

ESTUDIANTE B
a.–f. Answers will vary, but encourage students to use a variety of answers. Be alert for appropriate use of preterite forms.

4 ESTUDIANTE A
a. ¿Fuiste a patinar sobre el hielo el sábado pasado?
b. ...a montar en bicicleta...
c. ...a jugar bolos...
d. ...a levantar pesas...
e. ...a esquiar...
f. Questions will vary, but should include *a* + inf.

ESTUDIANTE B
a.–f. Answers will vary, but encourage students to use a variety of excuses. Look for the construction *tuve que* + inf.

3

A —¿Quién ganó el partido de <u>béisbol</u>?
B —<u>Nosotros ganamos (cuatro a dos)</u>.

Estudiante A

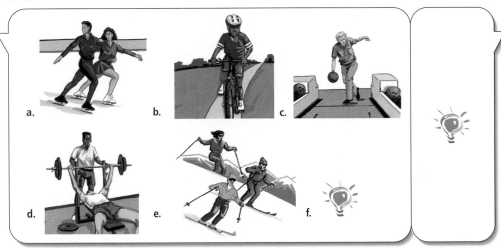

a. b. c.

d. e. f.

Estudiante B

(nombre) ___.

El otro equipo ___.

Nosotros perdimos.

Nadie ___. Empatamos.

Nosotros. Metimos ___ goles.

4

A —¿Fuiste a <u>correr</u> el sábado pasado?
B —<u>No, tuve que llevar a mi hermano menor al parque</u>.

Estudiante A

a. b. c.

d. e. f.

Estudiante B

132 Capítulo 4

Options

Strategies for Reaching All Students

Spanish-Speaking Students
Ex. 8: After this exercise, ask: *¿Juegan fútbol en tu escuela? ¿Participas tú? ¿Cómo es el equipo? ¿Cuándo practican? ¿Cuándo son los partidos? ¿Tienen que viajar mucho para los partidos?*

Students Needing Extra Help
Ex. 3: In the list of possible responses for *Estudiante B,* explain what will go in the blanks and how the *nombre* response fits in.

Ex. 4: Brainstorm possible responses for *Estudiante B.* Have students alternate *Estudiante A* and *Estudiante B* parts in order to practice both constructions.
Ex. 5: Explain the general nature of the first question and how the second question is really asking if there was a variance in routine during the past weekend. Students may see this as redundant. Remind them that the first question is answered in the present tense, while the second is answered in the preterite.

Ex. 7: You may need to get some information from the athletic director in order to answer these questions.

Enrichment
Ex. 4: Encourage *Estudiante B* to use a variety of excuses: *estudiar, ir a la biblioteca, ayudar en casa, cocinar, ir a una fiesta,* etc., or you may want to brainstorm excuses.

132   Standards 1.1

Empecemos a escribir

Escribe tus respuestas en español.

5 Generalmente, ¿qué tienes que hacer los fines de semana? ¿Y qué tuviste que hacer el fin de semana pasado?

6 Cuando no tienes algo, ¿sueles pedirlo prestado? ¿A quién? Generalmente, ¿qué cosas pides prestado?

7 ¿Qué equipos hay en tu escuela? ¿Cuántos jugadores hay en cada equipo? ¿Quiénes son los entrenadores?

8 ¿Quiénes son los campeones de la liga escolar de fútbol americano? ¿Y de béisbol? ¿Cuándo ganaron el campeonato?

También se dice

el boliche
el bowling

hacer pesas
hacer halterofilia

la manopla

la bola

MORE PRACTICE

- Más práctica y tarea, p. 537
- Practice Workbook 4–1, 4–2

Un participante de los Juegos Paraolímpicos en Barcelona

Vocabulario para conversar 133

Answers: Empecemos a escribir

5 Answers will vary, but look for *tengo que / tuve que* + inf.

6–8 Answers will vary, but encourage use of chapter vocabulary.

 Practice Wkbk. 4-1, 4-2

 Audio Activity 4.1

 Pruebas 4-1, 4-2

 Comm. Act. BLM 4-1

Cooperative Learning

Divide the class into groups of three. One student will be a world-class athlete in one of the sports mentioned in this chapter. Another student will be a clothing designer, and the third will be a graphic designer. As a group, they should develop a new line of clothing for the sport, to be promoted by the athlete. The ad should include such things as a logo, name, and description of the line. Have them present their ad on a poster to be displayed in the classroom.

Multiple Intelligences

Interpersonal/Social and Visual/Spatial
See Cooperative Learning.
Verbal/Linguistic
See Audio Activity 4.1 and Exs. 3–8.
Visual/Spatial
See Practice Wkbk. 4-1 and 4-2 and Comm. Act. BLM 4-1.

Cultural Notes

(p. 133, photo)
The ninth *paralímpicos* (Paralympics), or Olympic Games for the Disabled, were held in Barcelona following the 1992 Olympics. Sixteen events, including fencing, cycling, judo and wheelchair basketball, were included in the '92 games. Volunteers from all parts of Spain contributed translation, technical, and information services to the event. Queen Sofía of Spain hosted the games as Honorary President.

Present

Chapter Theme
Games and music

Communicative Objectives
• To discuss leisure-time activities
• To discuss activities in the past

 Overheads 23–24

 Vocabulary Art BLMs/CD-ROM

 Vocabulary Tape 4-2

Teaching Suggestions
Preparing students to speak: Use one or two options from each of the categories of Comprehensible Input, Physical Response, or Limited Verbal Response. For a complete explanation of these categories and some sample activities, see pp. T20–T21.

Vocabulario para conversar

¿Cómo estuvo el concierto?

Aquí tienes el resto del vocabulario que necesitas en este capítulo para hablar sobre las diversiones.

la fiesta de disfraces

la obra de teatro

la exposición, *pl.* las exposiciones (de arte)

la música clásica

la música rock

el desfile

(hacer) un picnic

las damas

134   Capítulo 4

Options

Strategies for Reaching All Students

Students Needing Extra Help
Vocabulario para conversar: Review the forms of *hacer.*
También necesitas . . . : Write out the two reflexive paradigms. Give examples of *soportar, pasarlo bien / mal* and *bastante.* Write out the entire *saber* paradigm for students who need to see all six forms.
¿Y qué quiere decir . . . ?: Give some examples of *tener tiempo de* + inf.

Learning Spanish Through Action
STAGING VOCABULARY: *Señalen, Levántense*
MATERIALS: transparency of the vocabulary page
DIRECTIONS: Direct students to decide which is their favorite activity. Ask them to stand if the activity you mention is their favorite. Write the number of standing students on the transparency. Make comments about the favorite activities of the class. If you have other classes of the same level, you might use different-colored markers for each class so that you can make comparisons between classes.

(hacer) un crucigrama

(hacer) un rompecabezas

el ajedrez

el disco compacto

el casete

el video musical

También necesitas . . .

saber: (yo) sé	*to know: I know,*	alegre	*happy, festive*
(tú) sabes	*you know*	último, -a	*last*
divertirse *(e → ie)*	*to have fun*	bastante	here: *quite*
aburrirse	*to be bored*		
soportar	*to tolerate, to stand*		
pasarlo bien / mal	*to have a good /*		
	bad time		
estuvo *(from: estar)*	*he / she / it was*		
fue *(from: ser)*	*he / she / it was*		

¿Y qué quiere decir . . . ?
tener tiempo de + *inf.*
la diversión, *pl.* las diversiones
el desastre
el horror

Vocabulario para conversar 135

Grammar Preview
(Yo) sé / (tú) sabes are presented here lexically. The paradigm of present-tense *saber* is reviewed on p. 148.
Fue is presented here lexically. The paradigm of *ser* in the preterite is on p. 145. Alert students may realize that it is the same as the preterite form of *ir.*

Class Starter Review
On the day following initial vocabulary presentation, you might begin the class with this activity: Have students rank the activities from this and the previous vocabulary section in order of preference. Have a volunteer keep a class tally on the chalkboard.

www Internet Activities
Juegos
Have students go to www.pasoapaso.com for additional activities and practice.

Extended Written Practice/Homework
1. Write two pairs of sentences telling when you did two of the activities pictured on pp. 134–135 and whether you had a good or bad time.
2. Write three questions you can ask classmates to find out when they did the activities on pp. 134–135 the last time: *¿Cuándo viste un desfile la última vez?*
3. Write three sentences telling when you have fun or when you get bored: *Me divierto cuando hago un picnic en el verano.*

Multiple Intelligences
Bodily/Kinesthetic
See Learning Spanish Through Action.
Logical/Mathematical
See Class Starter Review.
Musical/Rhythmic
Bring in a number of audio selections from these or other categories: *música clásica, música rock, música mexicana,* and *jazz.* Have students close their eyes while you play the first selection. Then tell them to answer the following questions (keeping

their eyes closed) by a show of hands. Ask: *¿Cuántos piensan que esta selección es música clásica? ¿Música rock? ¿Música mexicana? ¿Jazz?* Keep track of students' responses and then tell them the results and the correct answer.
Verbal/Linguistic
See Vocabulary Tape 4-2.
Visual/Spatial
See Overheads 23–24 and the Vocabulary Art BLMs/CD-ROM.

Practice

Reteach / Review: Vocabulary
Ex. 9: You may want to review vocabulary from Book 1, Chap. 11 before doing this exercise.

Teaching Suggestions
Ex. 10: To review direct object pronouns, ask students questions such as these: *¿Viste la película Jurassic Park? (Sí la vi.) ¿Hiciste la tarea de matemáticas? (No, no la hice.) ¿Quién corta el césped en tu casa? (Mi hermano lo corta* or *Yo lo corto.)*

Answers: Empecemos a conversar
9 ESTUDIANTE A
a. ¿Cómo estuvo el último programa de entrevistas que viste?
b. . . . la última película . . .
c. . . . la última obra de teatro . . .
d. . . . la última exposición de arte . . .
e. . . . la última telenovela . . .
f. Questions will vary, but look for adjective agreement.
ESTUDIANTE B
a.–f. Answers will vary, but look for logical answers and adjective agreement.

Empecemos a conversar

9 A —¿Cómo estuvo *el último video musical* que viste?
B —*Bastante divertido.*

Estudiante A   **Estudiante B**

a.   b.   c.

d.   e.   f.

genial
bastante divertido(a)
(muy) aburrido(a)
horrible
Me encantó.
No me gustó nada.
(muy) bueno(a) / malo(a)

10 A —¿Te gustan *los picnics?*
B —*Sí, son muy divertidos.*
o: *No, son demasiado aburridos.*
o: *No, no los soporto.*

Estudiante A   **Estudiante B**

a.   b.   c.

d.   e.   f.

aburrido(a)
alegre
divertido(a)
interesante
largo(a)

136   Capítulo 4

Options

Strategies for Reaching All Students

Students Needing Extra Help
Ex. 9: Show how *último, divertido,* and *aburrido* will change with a feminine noun.
Ex. 11: Brainstorm what kinds of words will go in the blank for the second response.

Enrichment
Ex. 10: Have students justify their answers about what they like or don't like by explaining their own tastes or personalities.

Extended Written Practice/Homework
1. Write three sentences telling when or with whom you usually do the activities pictured on pp. 134–135: *Suelo ir al museo de arte cuando tienen una nueva exposición.*

2. Choose three activities and write sentences telling who likes to do them: *A mi abuelo le encanta hacer rompecabezas.*
3. Write three sentences telling things or situations that you can't stand and why: *No puedo soportar la clase de química porque el profesor es muy aburrido.*

11 A —¿Fuiste *a la exposición de arte de tus amigos*?

B —Sí. Y *lo pasé muy bien*.

   o: *No, no fui. Fui a ___.*

de tus amigos

Estudiante A

a. del 4 de julio   b. de la escuela   c. de (nombre)

d. de (nombre)   e. con tu familia   f.

Estudiante B

me encantó

(no) me gustó

me aburrí

(no) me divertí

fue un desastre / horror

Estos carteles anuncian presentaciones de grupos de baile peruanos, dominicanos, mexicanos y colombianos.

Una orquesta sinfónica en el Teatro Real de Madrid

Vocabulario para conversar   137

Practice & Apply

Answers:
Empecemos a conversar

12 ESTUDIANTE A

a. ¿Prefieres las películas o las obras de teatro?

b. ...los discos compactos o los casetes?

c. ...los desfiles o los picnics?

d. ...los rompecabezas o los crucigramas?

e. ...la música rock o la música clásica?

f. Questions will vary, but should include logical pairs.

ESTUDIANTE B

a.–f. Answers will vary.

Answers: Empecemos a escribir y a leer

13–17 Answers will vary.

 Practice Wkbk. 4-3, 4-4

 Audio Activity 4.2

 Writing Activities 4-A, 4-B, 4-C

 Pruebas 4-3, 4-4

12

A —¿Prefieres _jugar damas_ o _ajedrez_?

B —Prefiero _jugar ajedrez_. Pero a veces _juego damas_.

o: _No me gustan ni las damas ni el ajedrez._

Estudiante A   Estudiante B

a.   b.

c.   d.

e.   f.

Empecemos a escribir y a leer

Escribe tus respuestas en español.

13 ¿Qué diversiones prefieres tú? ¿Tienes tiempo para todas las diversiones que te gustan?

14 ¿Qué tipo de música sueles escuchar? ¿Vas a conciertos? ¿Con quién? La última vez que fuiste a un concierto, ¿cómo lo pasaste?

15 ¿Piensas que es difícil hacer crucigramas? ¿Por qué? ¿Sabes jugar ajedrez? ¿Quién te enseñó a jugar? ¿Con quién juegas? En tu opinión, ¿es fácil aprender?

www.pasoapaso.com

MORE PRACTICE

- Más práctica y tarea, p. 538
- Practice Workbook 4–3, 4–4

138   Capítulo 4

Options

Strategies for Reaching All Students

Spanish-Speaking Students

Ex. 14: _¿Qué tipo de música es más popular en tu comunidad?_

Ex. 16: _Describe la última película que viste. Debes dar el nombre de la película y de los artistas, un resumen de la acción, y decir si te gustó o no y por qué._

 Un paso más Ex. 4-D

Students Needing Extra Help

Ex. 12: Have students go through the exercise once using the infinitives and then using the second response. Brainstorm which infinitives will go with movies, CDs, etc.

Ex. 14: Review possible kinds of music.

Ex. 15: Students will need help with the vocabulary to answer _¿Por qué?_ If no one plays chess, ask _¿Por qué?_

Ex. 17: Brainstorm other possibilities of things to do with little or no money. Bring in the section of the weekend newspaper relating to this theme.

16 ¿Sueles ver películas en el cine o en video? ¿Cuál prefieres? ¿Por qué?

17 Lee este párrafo sobre diversiones que cuestan muy poco o nada. Luego describe una diversión similar.

Quieres salir con tus amigos y no tienes dinero. ¿Qué haces? Pues, la diversión no tiene que costar mucho. En muchos museos la entrada es gratis por lo menos un día a la semana. Además, siempre hay exposiciones en bancos, bibliotecas y agencias del gobierno que son gratis. Y si hace buen tiempo, ¿por qué no vas a un parque o al zoológico? Sólo necesitas buscar en el periódico local para ver qué hay y pasar un día muy divertido.

Linda Ronstadt a menudo se viste de charra en sus conciertos.

Miles de Discos
Compactos Diferentes
Usted puede escoger su música latina favorita y **nosotros se la enviamos** a cualquier lugar del país o del extranjero el mismo día que recibimos su orden.

MÚSICA LATINA DE TODOS LOS PAÍSES Y TODAS LAS ÉPOCAS

CASA DE DISCOS
7249 Point Loma Blvd. N.
San Diego, CA 92165
TEL: (800) 555-7979

Aceptamos las principales tarjetas de crédito.

Cultural Notes

Enrichment
Ex. 14: Students can also answer a negative version of this question: *¿Qué tipo de música no te gusta nada? ¿Por qué no?*

Multiple Intelligences
Interpersonal/Social and Verbal/Linguistic
See Ex. 12.
Verbal/Linguistic
See Audio Activity 4.2 and Exs. 13–17.
Visual/Spatial
See Practice Wkbk. 4-3 and 4-4 and Writing Activities 4-A, 4-B, and 4-C.

(p. 139, photo)
Linda Ronstadt was born in 1946 in Tucson, Arizona. At nineteen, Ronstadt joined *The Stone Poneys* and had one hit song, "Different Drum," in 1967. Her career has taken many turns, moving from rock to country and even to opera. She drew upon her Mexican American heritage in *Canciones de mi padre* (1987), an album of traditional Mexican songs accompanied by *mariachi*.

Practice

Reteach / Review: Accepting and declining invitations

Ex. 1: Have students name creative ways to accept and decline invitations. Write the expressions on the chalkboard as they are said. Some suggestions: *¡Sí! ¡Cómo no! / ¡Por supuesto! / ¡Me gustaría mucho! / ¡Genial!* or *No puedo. Tengo que... / ¿No podemos otro día? / ¡Qué lástima! Debo... / Me gustaría mucho, pero... / Lo siento mucho, pero...*

Answers: ¡Comuniquemos!

1 ESTUDIANTE A

a. ¿Quieres ir al concierto el domingo? ... (a las siete)

b. ...a la fiesta de disfraces el viernes? ... (a las ocho)

c. ...al parque de diversiones el sábado? ... (al mediodía)

d. ...al restaurante el miércoles? ... (a las siete y media)

e. Questions will vary.

ESTUDIANTE B

a.–e. Answers will vary, but look for a variety of acceptances and refusals. If students use *¿A qué hora?* in their responses, look for correct use of time-telling by *Estudiante A*.

2 Answers will vary.

¡Comuniquemos!

Aquí tienes otra oportunidad para usar el vocabulario de este capítulo.

1 Túrnate con un(a) compañero(a) para aceptar o rechazar *(refuse)* las siguientes invitaciones.

A —¿Quieres ir a jugar fútbol el sábado?

B —¡Claro que sí! (¿A qué hora? ¿Dónde?)
   o: *Lo siento. No juego fútbol.*
   o: *El sábado no puedo. ¿Podemos ir... ?*

a.

b.

c.

d.

e.

2 La nueva revista para jóvenes *¡Ya!* pregunta a sus lectores qué les gustaría leer. Con un(a) compañero(a), escojan dos de las secciones siguientes:

- televisión
- deportes
- cine y video
- moda
- música

¿Qué les gustaría ver en las secciones que escogieron?

—*Me gustaría leer algo sobre ___ porque ___.*
—*A mí me gustaría saber más sobre ___. Creo que ___.*

Después, hablen con otros grupos que escogieron las mismas secciones.

En la sección de deportes nos gustaría encontrar / leer / aprender / saber más sobre...

140   Capítulo 4

Options

Strategies for Reaching All Students

Spanish-Speaking Students

 Un paso más Ex. 4-E

Students Needing Extra Help
Ex. 1: Use the vocabulary section of the Organizer. Brainstorm *dónde* responses. Review days of the week. Discourage students from responding with only *lo siento*.
Ex. 3: Model. Show students that *encontrar, leer, aprender,* and *saber* are interchangeable. Brainstorm the possibilities for the

blanks. If available, use the vocabulary sections of Level 1, Chaps. 1 and 11, to help students express why they like to read these sections. Have each group do only two sections.
¿Qué sabes ahora?: Have students write this out so they can record what they have mastered.

3 Ayuda al recepcionista del hotel con las maletas de estos jugadores. Túrnate con un(a) compañero(a) para ser el recepcionista y el ayudante. Por ejemplo:

A —*¿De quién es esta maleta?*
B —*Es de un jugador de . . .*
A —*¿Cómo lo sabes?*
B —*Porque aquí hay un(a) . . .*
A —*¿Y aquel(la) . . . ?*

¿Qué sabes ahora?

Can you:

■ compare what you usually do with what you did?

—Generalmente ___ los sábados, pero el sábado pasado ___.

■ extend, accept, or reject an invitation?

—¿Quieres ir a ___?

—___.

■ discuss and evaluate a leisure-time activity?

—¿Cómo ___ la fiesta de ___?

—(No) Me ___. Estuvo muy ___.

Vocabulario para conversar   141

Es de un jugador de béisbol. / Porque aquí hay una pelota de béisbol, un bate y un guante de béisbol.

. . . de tenis. / . . . una raqueta, una pelota y zapatos de tenis.

. . . de golf. / . . . palos de golf.

. . . de hockey. / . . . patines, un palo y un disco de hockey.

. . . de básquetbol. / . . . un balón y una camiseta de básquetbol.

. . . de fútbol americano. / . . . un balón y un casco de fútbol americano.

. . . de fútbol. / . . . un balón y una camiseta de fútbol.

Answers: ¿Qué sabes ahora?

• Answers will vary, but look for the *yo* form of the present tense in the first blank and of the preterite in the second.

• Answers will vary, but should be logical.

• *estuvo* / Answers will vary. / *aburrí* or *divertí* / Answers will vary.

 Audio Activity 4.3

 Pasos vivos 2 CD-ROM

Boom Box, Clip Art Album, Notas culturales, Slide Projector, Laboratorio de grabar

---

Enrichment
Ex. 2: After pairs of students have completed this activity, have them share their ideas with other groups or with the class: *En la sección de deportes a nosotros nos gustaría . . . Nos gustaría saber más sobre . . . .*

Multiple Intelligences
Interpersonal/Social and Verbal/Linguistic
See Exs. 1–3.
Verbal/Linguistic
See Audio Activity 4.3.

Cultural Objective

• To discuss the paintings of Diego Rivera and Frida Kahlo, and what their work tells us about them and their culture

Critical Thinking: Identifying Stereotypes

Diego Rivera is a world-renowned artist, most famous for his enormous murals depicting facets of Mexican life. Discuss the different ways of looking at Rivera's work. Stress that these are his viewpoints and that they don't necessarily reflect a national consciousness.

Multicultural Perspectives

Muralismo in Mexico dates back to ancient times when artists portrayed important events on the walls of temples and palaces. Twentieth-century muralists such as Diego Rivera and José Clemente Orozco, recording Mexico's past, present, and future, took this indigenous art form to truly remarkable levels. Rivera's murals depict clear messages of the poverty of the Indians, of the failure of land redistribution, and of corrupt politicians. Orozco's powerful fresco of Cortés and Malinche shows Mexico's roots. Have students find examples of

Perspectiva cultural

¿Qué quieren expresar los artistas en estas pinturas? ¿Cómo comunican las pinturas esas ideas? Míralas con cuidado. ¿Te dicen algo sobre las personas que las pintaron?

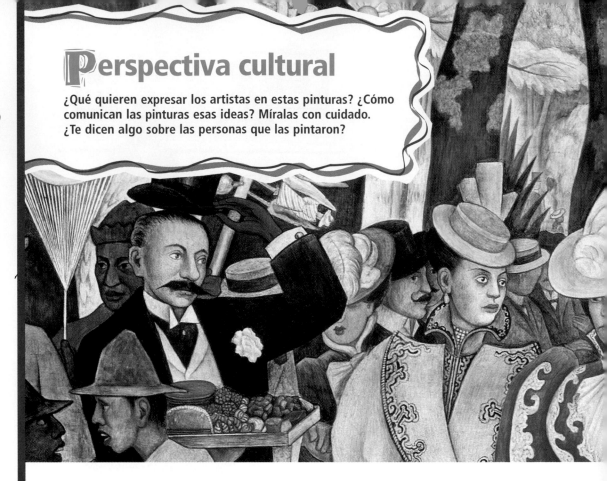

Roberto es un estudiante mexicano que está pasando un año en Detroit. Tiene un nuevo amigo, Mauricio, que espera visitar a Roberto en México en la primavera.

—Primero vamos a visitar el Palacio Nacional— dice Roberto—. Tienes que ver los murales de Diego Rivera. Te ayudarán a comprender la historia y la gente de México. Y después vas a ver varios de los autorretratos maravillosos de Frida Kahlo, su esposa.

—Los conozco a los dos—dice Mauricio—. Hay murales increíbles de Rivera aquí, en el museo de arte.

—Sí, es un pintor muy importante. ¡Y la obra de Kahlo es única! No hay nadie como ella. Diego Rivera es conocido sobre todo por los grandes murales que pintó. Quería ayudar a la gente a apreciar la historia de su país.

Kahlo es igualmente conocida. Vivió una vida muy triste. De niña, tuvo polio y, de mujer joven, casi murió en un accidente de tranvía *(trolley)*. Después, siempre sufrió de un dolor extremo. En su obra vemos la tristeza y los dolores que tan bien conocía.

Mira con cuidado las obras de arte. Pueden decirte mucho.

142 Capítulo 4

Options

Strategies for Reaching All Students

Spanish-Speaking Students
Ask: *¿Conoces a otros pintores? Haz una investigación sobre un pintor hispano. Luego escribe uno o dos párrafos sobre su vida y su obra.*

 Un paso más Ex. 4-F

Students Needing Extra Help
Perspectiva cultural: Students may not have much information about artists. Ask the art teacher to help them gain an appreciation. Ex. 1: If your community doesn't have outdoor art, talk about places students have visited that do, and / or cities near you that do have this type of art. Contact the Visitors' Bureau or the Chamber of Commerce. They may be able to give you pictures.

Multiple Intelligences
Logical/Mathematical
Have students plan an imaginary surprise trip to Mexico City for you. The school has given $2,000 to fund the trip. Using the Internet or other sources, students must find out the cost of airfare and hotels and determine how many days in Mexico City they can give you. (Your other expenses will not be covered.) They may present you with your itinerary in a special ceremony.

Detalle del *Sueño de una tarde dominical en la Alameda Central* (1947-1948), Diego Rivera

Las Dos Fridas (1939), Frida Kahlo

La cultura desde tu perspectiva

1 Mirando *La Alameda* de Diego Rivera, ¿qué puedes decir sobre la historia de México? ¿Hay murales en tu comunidad? ¿Son similares a o diferentes de los de Rivera?

2 ¿Qué atracciones culturales hay en tu ciudad o estado? ¿Qué comunican sobre la historia de la comunidad y sus habitantes?

Perspectiva cultural   143

---

murals in their communities or in books and try to determine their messages.

Answers: La cultura desde tu perspectiva

1 Answers will vary, but students may make references to *La Catrina*—subject of the video they are watching—the skeleton with the feather boa around her neck. Through this character, Rivera pokes fun at the upper class of society. Students may mention the images of wealth and poverty, issues that still confront Mexico today.

2 Answers will vary.

 Pasos vivos 2 CD-ROM

Maps

Internet Activities

Perspectiva cultural
Have students go to www.pasoapaso.com for additional activities and practice.

Cultural Notes ☀

(pp. 142–143, photo)
The Alameda Central is the oldest public park in Mexico City and the setting for this Diego Rivera mural, in which he visually summarizes Mexican history from the pre-Colombian era until the early twentieth century. From left to right: *(man with top hat)* **Manuel Gutiérrez Nájera,** poet and precursor of modernist poetry; **Lucecita Díaz,** daughter of Porfirio Díaz, who was president of Mexico (1876–1880 and 1884–1911); **Carmen Romero Rubio de**

Díaz, Porfirio Díaz's second wife; *(man tipping hat)* **José Martí,** poet who led the fight for Cuba's independence; **Diego Rivera** as a boy and, behind him, **Frida Kahlo,** his wife; *(skeleton)* **La Calavera Catrina,** character created by artist **José Guadalupe Posada** (represented at the far right of the mural) to poke fun at the aristocracy of the Díaz era. Rivera embellished the character with a feather boa, symbol of Quetzal-cóatl ("plumed serpent" in Nahuatl), a pre-Columbian god.

(p. 143, bottom photo)
This double self portrait by Frida Kahlo was created during her divorce from Diego Rivera in 1940. (They were later remarried in 1941.) The Frida whom Diego no longer loves wears a white dress that is ripped. Her heart is broken and bleeding. The other Frida is still loved by Rivera. Her heart is connected to his small portrait. Kahlo represents her dual European and indigenous heritage through the dress and features of the two figures.

Preview

 Overhead 25

Multicultural Perspectives

In Latin America, tastes in music are diverse and vary from region to region. In the Caribbean, *salsa, soca, calypso,* and *merengue* are popular. The Mighty Sparrow, a well-known entertainer in the Caribbean, is best known for *calypso,* a type of music that dates back to the days of slavery. The slaves passed information from person to person through these simple rhythmic tunes. Juan Luis Guerra, a popular performer in the Dominican Republic, combines the rhythms of *merengue* and *salsa* with social commentary about the country's economic woes. Ask students if they are familiar with other kinds of music from Latin America.

Answers

A Elicit *nació, trabajó, ganó, sacó,* and *llegó.* The accented final *o* is a clue.

B *Fue a vivir: ir; Fue estudiante: ser; Fue después: ir; Fue representante: ser*

C *Tuvo un accidente*: He had an accident, *tener; Tuvo su primer gran hit:* She had her first great hit, *tener; Tuvo un accidente:* She had an accident, *tener; Hizo una donación:* She made a donation, *hacer*

Gramática en contexto

¿Quiénes son?

¿Sabes quiénes son estas personas famosas? (Sus nombres están al pie de la página.)

- Nació en La Habana, Cuba, en 1957.
- Llegó con sus padres a los Estados Unidos dos años después.
- Tuvo su primer gran hit, "Conga," en 1985.
- Fue después a Inglaterra, Holanda, Japón, México, Canadá y Bélgica, donde ganó discos de oro y plata en 1989.
- Tuvo un accidente de autobús muy grave en 1990.
- Hizo una donación de $2.000.000 para las víctimas del huracán Andrew en 1992.
- Fue representante de los Estados Unidos ante las Naciones Unidas también en 1992.

★ Nació en La Habana, Cuba, en 1962.

★ Fue a vivir con sus padres a Miami, Florida, en 1970.

★ Fue estudiante en la Universidad de Miami.

★ Trabajó en el restaurante de sus padres antes de ser famoso.

★ Ganó un "Grammy" en 1992 por su álbum, *Otro día más sin verte.*

★ Tuvo un accidente en el escenario cantando para la Copa Mundial en 1994.

★ Sacó su segundo álbum llamado *Si te vas* en 1994.

A Look at the verbs at the beginning of every sentence in the biographies. Which ones have regular preterite endings? What helps you recognize them?

B Look at the four sentences that begin with *fue.* In these sentences the verb *fue* has two different meanings. In each case, what is the infinitive form of the verb?

C Find the preterite verb forms *tuvo* and *hizo.* Can you figure out what they mean? What are their infinitive forms?

Respuestas: Gloria Estefan; Jon Secada

Options

Strategies for Reaching All Students

Students Needing Extra Help
Gramática en contexto: Begin the grammar section of the Organizer.
A: Find the verbs. If students have difficulty, review preterite endings.
B: Use context clues. If available, have students look at the Organizer from Level 1, Chap. 10. Write the four examples on the chalkboard. Point out that two examples have *fue + a.*

C: Point out specific clues.
El pretérito del verbo ser: Have students call out the present tense of *ser* and *ir* as you write the words on the chalkboard. Then write the preterite next to it. Write *hoy* and *ayer* next to the appropriate tenses.
Ex. 1: Again, emphasize that *fue + a = went.*

Multiple Intelligences
Interpersonal/Social and Verbal/Linguistic
See Ex. 1.
Visual/Spatial
See Overhead 25 and Exs. A–C.

El pretérito del verbo *ser*

Here are all the preterite forms of *ser.* They are identical to the preterite forms of *ir.* The context makes the meaning clear.

(yo)	**fui**	(nosotros) (nosotras)	**fuimos**
(tú)	**fuiste**	(vosotros) (vosotras)	**fuisteis**
Ud. (él) (ella)	**fue**	Uds. (ellos) (ellas)	**fueron**

Compare the following sentences:

Jon Secada **fue** estudiante en la Universidad de Miami.
*Jon Secada **was** a student at the University of Miami.*

Gloria Estefan **fue** a Inglaterra y Holanda en 1989.
*Gloria Estefan **went** to England and Holland in 1989.*

1 Túrnate con un(a) compañero(a) para decir cuándo fue la última vez que fuiste a los siguientes lugares. Por ejemplo:

A —*¿Cuándo fue la última vez que fuiste a un restaurante?*
B —*La última vez fue hace dos días.*
   o: *Nunca voy a restaurantes.*

a.　　　　　b.　　　　　c.　　　　　d.

e.　　　　　f.　　　　　g.　　　　　h.

Gramática en contexto　145

Present

Answers

1 ESTUDIANTE A
a. ¿Cuándo fue la última vez que fuiste a un concierto?
b. ...a un desfile?
c. ...al cine?
d. ...a una exposición de arte?
e. ...a una fiesta de disfraces?
f. ...a una biblioteca?
g. ...a un picnic?
h. Questions will vary.
ESTUDIANTE B
a.–h. Answers will vary, but look for *fue* + time expression or the correct use of *hace* + time expression.

Cultural Notes

(p. 144, bottom left photo)
Gloria Estefan was born in Cuba and moved with her family to Miami after Fidel Castro came to power. In 1976 she began her career with the Miami Sound Machine, led by her then future husband Emilio Estefan, performing songs in English and Spanish.

Their song "Conga" was the first to place on pop, dance, black, and Latin music charts. She is shown here performing at the 1994 *Premio Lo Nuestro a la Música Latina,* an awards show honoring international performers of Latin music. It is produced in Miami by Univisión.

(p. 144, right photo)
Jon Secada received a Master of Arts degree in jazz vocal performance from the University of Miami. He sang backup vocals for Miami Sound Machine before making his first solo album in 1991. His first two hits, "Just Another Day" *(Otro día más)* and "Angel" *(Ángel),* reached the top 40 in both the Spanish- and English-language pop charts simultaneously.

¿Cómo te diviertes?

Present & Practice

Re-enter / Recycle
Ex. 3: daily routine from Chap. 2
Ex. 4: school activities from
Chap. 1

Answers
2 Questions and answers will vary, but look for correct preterite forms of *ir*.

 Practice Wkbk. 4-5, 4-6

 Writing Activity 4-D

 Prueba 4-5

3 ESTUDIANTE A
a. ¿Melba no tuvo tiempo de lavarse el pelo?
b. ¿(Tú) no tuviste tiempo de secarte el pelo?
c. ¿Sara y María no tuvieron tiempo de correr?
d. ¿Tomás no tuvo tiempo de hacer el crucigrama?
e. ¿Ud. no tuvo tiempo de cepillarse los dientes?
f. ¿Enrique y tú no tuvieron tiempo de desayunar?

ESTUDIANTE B
a. No, no pudo lavarse el pelo.
b. No, no pude secarme el pelo.
c. No, no pudieron correr.
d. No, no pudo hacer el cruci-grama.

---

2 Túrnate con un(a) compañero(a) para hablar de un viaje que hiciste con tu familia. Dile adónde fuiste. Después tu compañero(a) debe preguntarte:

• cuándo fueron
• quiénes fueron
• cómo fueron

A —*Fui a Los Ángeles.*
B —¿ . . . ?

El pretérito de los verbos *hacer, poder* y *tener*

You already know *hizo* and *hiciste.* Here are all the preterite forms of *hacer.*

(yo)	hice	(nosotros) (nosotras)	hicimos
(tú)	hiciste	(vosotros) (vosotras)	hicisteis
Ud. (él) (ella)	hizo	Uds. (ellos) (ellas)	hicieron

The preterite forms of *poder* and *tener* follow a similar pattern.

(yo)	pude tuve	(nosotros) (nosotras)	pudimos tuvimos
(tú)	pudiste tuviste	(vosotros) (vosotras)	pudisteis tuvisteis
Ud. (él) (ella)	pudo tuvo	Uds. (ellos) (ellas)	pudieron tuvieron

146   Capítulo 4

Options

Strategies for Reaching All Students

Students Needing Extra Help
Ex. 2: Some students don't take family trips. Suggest a place. Review months and means of transportation. Write the questions on the chalkboard. Model.
El pretérito de los verbos hacer, poder *y* tener: Review the present tense of each of these verbs. Point out that these preterite forms have no written accent marks.
Ex. 3: Review compound subjects. Provide a non-reflexive model.

Ex. 4: Have students do more than four subjects. Remind them that this is not a linear match for answers.

Enrichment
Ex. 4: Have students redo this exercise, giving far-fetched or obviously untrue excuses: *Tuve que lavar las ventanas del Empire State Building* or *Tuve que cuidar a la prima del Presidente de los Estados Unidos.*

Extended Written Practice/Homework
1. Write three pairs of sentences describing a movie, concert, or other event that was really bad, telling whether you were able to stand it: *La fiesta de disfraces de la escuela fue un horror. No pude soportarla.*
2. Write three sentences telling when you did not have time to do something: *Anoche no tuve tiempo de terminar mi composición.*

3 El autobús que va al partido de tenis va a salir. Y nadie quiere llegar tarde. Con un(a) compañero(a) di qué no pudieron hacer estas personas antes de salir de sus casas.

A —¿Luz no tuvo tiempo de peinarse?
B —No, no pudo peinarse.

Luz

a. Melba   b. (tú)   c. Sara y María

d. Tomás   e. Ud.   f. Enrique y tú

4 ¿Por qué no pudieron hacerlo? Con un(a) compañero(a), contesta usando expresiones de cada lista.

A —¿No pudiste ir al desfile?
B —No, tuve que estudiar para un examen.

a. tú	ver el partido de hockey	hacer la tarea
b. (nombre)	ir a la exposición de arte	ayudar en casa
c. (nombre) y tú	ir a patinar sobre hielo	escribir un informe
d. (dos nombres)	ir al concierto	cuidar a mi hermana menor
	jugar bolos	salir con mi / su familia
	ir a la fiesta de disfraces	hacer la cena
	escuchar el disco compacto	estudiar para un examen

Gramática en contexto   147

e. No, no pude cepillarme los dientes.
f. No, no pudimos desayunar.

4 ESTUDIANTE A
Questions will vary, but look for the correct preterite form of *poder* + an infinitive phrase from the second column.
a. ¿No pudiste . . .
b. ¿No pudo . . .
c. ¿No pudieron . . .
d. ¿No pudieron . . .

ESTUDIANTE B
Answers will vary, but look for the correct preterite form of *tener que* + an infinitive phrase from the third column.
a. No, tuve que . . .
b. No, tuvo que . . .
c. No, tuvimos que . . .
d. No, tuvieron que . . .

 Practice Wkbk. 4-7, 4-8

 Writing Activities 4-E, 4-F

 Prueba 4-6

 Comm. Act. BLM 4-2

3. Use *hacer* and three of the following activities to write sentences telling who did them and when: *un crucigrama, un rompecabezas, ejercicio, un picnic.*

Multiple Intelligences
Naturalist and Logical/Mathematical
Have students make three columns: *Adentro, Al aire libre,* and *Adentro o al aire libre.* Ask them to list as many sports or activities as they can think of under each of the appropriate categories.
Verbal/Linguistic
See Exs. 2–4.
Visual/Spatial
See Practice Wkbk. 4-5, 4-6, 4-7, and 4-8; Writing Activities 4-D, 4-E, and 4-F; and Comm. Act. BLM 4-2.

(p. 146, photo)
The circus comes to town! Exotic animals, performance artists, and references to far-away places promise excitement. The *feria* is an annual event in Sevilla, a week of flamenco dancing, bullfights, and parades. Note that this poster makes reference to Columbus, whose voyage to the New World brought great wealth to the city.

Present & Practice

Answers

5 Answers will vary, but look for the correct forms of *saber* and a logical reason in the second sentence.

a. Mi madre sabe mucho sobre el arte.

b. Mis amigos *(dos nombres)* saben mucho sobre las bicicletas.

c. Tú y *(nombre)* saben mucho sobre los rompecabezas.

d. Mis hermanos y yo sabemos mucho sobre las pesas.

e. Tú sabes mucho sobre libros.

f. Yo sé mucho sobre películas.

g. Answers will vary.

 Prueba 4-7

Repaso: El verbo *saber*

We use *saber* to talk about knowing facts or information. Here are all of its present-tense forms.

(yo)	sé	(nosotros) (nosotras)	sabemos
(tú)	sabes	(vosotros) (vosotras)	sabéis
Ud. (él) (ella)	sabe	Uds. (ellos) (ellas)	saben

¿**Sabes** dónde juega hockey Javier?
¿**Saben** Uds. quién ganó el partido ayer?
Sabemos que ellos empataron.

- *Saber* followed by an infinitive means "to know how."

  Yo **sé** jugar ajedrez.
  ¿**Sabe** Eduardo patinar sobre hielo?

- Both *saber* and *conocer* mean "to know." *Conocer* means "to know" in the sense of being acquainted or familiar with a person, place, or thing.

¡NO OLVIDES!

Remember that we can often omit the word "that" in English, but in Spanish we must always use *que*.

Jugando fútbol en Matapalo, Costa Rica

5 Túrnate con un(a) compañero(a) para decir sobre qué cosas saben mucho estas personas y por qué. Por ejemplo:

Mateo y Carmen / la moda *Mateo y Carmen saben mucho sobre la moda. Trabajan en una tienda de ropa. (o: Leen mucho sobre ella / Les gusta mucho la ropa, etc.)*

a. Mi madre / el arte

b. Mis amigos *(dos nombres)* / las bicicletas

c. Tú y *(nombre)* / los rompecabezas

d. Mis hermanos y yo / las pesas

e. Tú / libros

f. Yo / películas

g. 💡 / 💡

148   Capítulo 4

Options

Strategies for Reaching All Students

Spanish-Speaking Students

 Un paso más Exs. 4-G, 4-H

Students Needing Extra Help

El verbo saber: Emphasize *sé*. Some students will insist on saying *sabo*. Remind them that this is the present tense. They have been doing preterite with the other verbs. They may interpret the note about *que* as meaning *que* always has to be used with *saber*. Give many examples to dispel that idea. In trying to show the distinction between *conocer* and *saber*, show students how *saber* is followed by question words or an infinitive. Students want to use *cómo* with *saber* in order to say *know how*. Tell them that "how" is included in the verb. Give examples of *conocer* and *saber*. See Level 2, Chap. 1 for examples of *conocer*. Ex. 5: Brainstorm possible places of employment and activities associated with the *gustar* statement. Be careful not to let *saber* get lost in this exercise.

Ex. 6: Put both paradigms on the board or overhead. Have students decide first which verb to use. Point out the clues. Then conjugate and decide who the person is who does know the information. Be sure students vary the "knower," using singular and plural. *El pretérito de los verbos reflexivos:* Review the present tense of reflexives, especially the pronouns. Then review the preterite endings of *-ar* and *-ir* verbs. Remind students that there are no stem changes in the

6 Túrnate con un(a) compañero(a). Escojan el verbo *saber* o *conocer* para hacerse preguntas. Pueden usar estas u otras frases.

A —*¿Sabes dónde es el concierto de rock este sábado?*
B —*Yo no sé, pero creo que Mateo sabe.*
   o: *Sí sé. Es en el . . .*

a. ¿. . . dónde puedo comprar un casco de hockey?
b. ¿. . . a esa entrenadora?
c. ¿. . . quiénes juegan en el partido de tenis mañana?
d. ¿. . . a quién puedo pedirle prestado un bate de béisbol?
e. ¿. . . a los campeones de la liga escolar de béisbol?
f. ¿. . . cuántos goles metieron los jugadores de la escuela en el último partido?
g. ¿. . . quién ganó el campeonato de la Liga Nacional de Fútbol?
h. ¿. . . a algún entrenador de tenis?
i. ¿. . . dónde es el partido de bolos mañana por la noche?
j.

El pretérito de los verbos reflexivos

Reflexive verbs have the same endings in the preterite as non-reflexive verbs.

7 Escoge verbos de la lista de la derecha para escribir lo que hiciste esta mañana antes de ir a la escuela.

Me desperté a las . . .

Luego, túrnate con tu compañero(a) para hacerse preguntas y contestar sobre lo que hicieron. Después, escriban un informe. Por ejemplo:

Nos despertamos a las . . . Ana se duchó en seguida, pero yo . . .

Ahora lo sabes

Can you:

- talk about a person or an event in the past?
  Ayer Luis ___ el que metió todos los goles.
- talk about what you did and why?
  —Yo no ___ la tarea porque no ___ tiempo.
- talk about things that happened to you?
  —Me ___ la pierna jugando fútbol y me ___ en cama todo el día.
- talk about someone you're acquainted with who knows a lot about a certain subject?
  —(Yo) ___ a la madre de Luis. Ella ___ mucho sobre el arte.

¡NO OLVIDES!

Here are some of the reflexive verbs that you know:

aburrirse
acostarse (o → ue)
bañarse
cepillarse
despertarse (e → ie)
ducharse
lastimarse
lavarse
peinarse
probarse (o → ue)
quedarse
secarse

MORE PRACTICE

Más práctica y tarea, pp. 538–539
Practice Workbook 4–5, 4–10

Gramática en contexto   149

preterite of -ar verbs but there are in -ir verbs.
Ex. 7: The list is alphabetical. Separating it into -ar and -ir verbs can help students keep the endings straight. Give students a finite number of things to write about. Remind them that if two of them did the same thing, the response becomes *nosotros.* Brainstorm possible questions.
Ahora lo sabes: Have students write out this section so they can record what they have mastered.

Multiple Intelligences
Verbal/Linguistic
See Ex. 5 and Audio Activities 4.4 and 4.5.
Visual/Spatial
See Practice Wkbk. 4-9 and 4-10 and Writing Activities 4-G and 4-H.

Cultural Notes

(p. 148, photo)
Matapalo is part of the Osa Peninsula in the southeastern region of Costa Rica. Surfing and soccer are popular sports there, and after church on Sundays, many soccer clubs get together to play and socialize.

Apply

 ¿Recuerdas?

Play

 Video Activity A

Using the Video

Episode 4 opens in the library, where Demetrio Alcocer is receiving a threatening phone call from don Silvestre Aguilar. Don Silvestre tells Demetrio never to reveal that Jamie is the real heir to La Catrina's fortune, which don Silvestre has acquired illegally. Moments later, Jamie arrives at the library looking for information about her great-grandmother. Demetrio offers to do what he can and instructs Jamie to return in a few days.

In the final scene, Jamie and María meet Felipe (Jamie's classmate from Los Angeles) in the recreational area of the university and decide to go swimming at the pool. María and Felipe have an especially good time together and she invites him to an upcoming party for international students. Meanwhile, Santana is spying on them from his end of the pool.

BICICLETA DE MONTAÑA DE MIGUEL INDURÁIN

DESCÚBRELA EN BANESTO

PASO CULTURAL

El gran ciclista español Miguel Induráin nació en 1964. Estuvo en el ciclismo profesional por doce años, participando en competiciones importantes. Es el único ciclista que ha ganado cinco veces consecutivas el Tour de Francia. En 1997, Induráin dijo adiós al ciclismo profesional. Mira este anuncio. ¿Por qué crees que la gente compra productos recomendados por alguien famoso?

150   Capítulo 4

Actividades

1 Cuéntale a un(a) compañero(a) cómo aprendiste a nadar, a cocinar, a montar en bicicleta o a hacer otra cosa. Usa estas u otras frases:

hace + *time expression*
aprender a / con
enseñarme a
ser difícil / fácil
cuando
una vez / dos (tres / muchas) veces
tener que
después de / antes de

2 Entrevista a tu compañero(a) o a un(a) amigo(a) sobre el último partido que vio o en el cual *(in which)* participó. Pregúntale, por ejemplo:

• qué tipo de partido fue
• quiénes jugaron
• cómo estuvo el partido
• quién ganó
• quién perdió
• si se lastimó alguien
• si alguien recibió un premio
• ¿ . . . ?

Prepara un informe para la clase. Si quieres, puedes incluir fotos o dibujos en tu informe.

Options

Strategies for Reaching All Students

150   **Standards** 1.1; 1.3; 3.1

Conexiones

 El razonamiento lógico

¿Qué hicieron el fin de semana pasado?

Este triple diagrama de Venn muestra las actividades que hicieron el fin de semana pasado 15 estudiantes de una clase. Los números indican cuántos estudiantes participaron en cada actividad.

1 Túrnate con un(a) compañero(a) para contestar estas preguntas.
a. ¿Cuántos estudiantes jugaron bolos pero no montaron en bicicleta?
b. ¿Cuántos jugaron bolos y montaron en bicicleta?
c. ¿Cuántos montaron en bicicleta y corrieron?
d. ¿Cuál fue la actividad más popular? ¿La menos popular?

2 ¿A qué sector (de *a* a *g*) del diagrama se refiere?
Sólo corrieron.   Jugaron bolos y corrieron.
Sólo jugaron bolos.   Montaron en bicicleta y corrieron.
Hicieron las tres actividades.   Sólo montó en bicicleta.

3 ¿A qué sector del diagrama corresponden los nombres de estos estudiantes? ¿Qué hicieron ellos?
a. Rebeca y Susana no montaron en bicicleta.
b. Andrés, Laura y Pablo participaron en todas las actividades.
c. Juan Carlos ni jugó bolos ni corrió.
d. Patricia no corrió.
e. Adán, Felipe, Pilar y Elisa hicieron una sola actividad de las tres.
f. A Sara y a Manuel no les gusta jugar bolos.
g. A Rosa y a Jorge no les gusta ni jugar bolos ni montar en bicicleta.

Trabajen en grupos grandes para hacer un diagrama que indique las actividades favoritas del grupo el fin de semana pasado. Comparen su diagrama con el de otros grupos de la clase.

montar en bicicleta

jugar bolos

a   1   c   4   f
    d
  2   3   2
  b   2   e
      g

Todo junto   151

 La Catrina: Capítulo 4

Play

 Video Activity B

Para entender mejor

Play

 Video Activity C

Writing Activities 4-I, 4-J

 Comm. Act. BLMs 4-3, 4-4, 4-5

 Pasos vivos 2 CD-ROM
A Jugar, Laboratorio de grabar, Maps, Video Monitor, Video Presentation Maker

---

Cooperative Learning
In groups of four, have students create a "Who Is It?" game in which each group writes out the clues to describe a famous person or celebrity on an index card. Allow about ten minutes for each group to write at least five sentences. Then have each group read its clues to another group and ask: *¿Quién soy yo?*

Multiple Intelligences
Logical/Mathematical
See *Conexiones.*
Verbal/Linguistic
See Exs. 1–2.
Visual/Spatial
See Using the Video, Writing Activities 4-I and 4-J, and Comm. Act. BLMs 4-3, 4-4, and 4-5.
Visual/Spatial and Verbal/Linguistic
See Cooperative Learning.

Cultural Notes

Paso cultural
Answers will vary.

(p. 150, realia)
Bicycling has increased in popularity during the last decade and bicycle technology has kept pace. This new mountain bike model advertised in a Spanish magazine is named for that country's retired cycling champion: Miguel Induráin. Cycling is popular across Europe, and Induráin is famous throughout the continent.

Apply

Process Reading

For a description of process reading, see p. 52.

Answers
Antes de leer

Answers will vary, but students may say that masks or whole-body costumes best conceal the wearer's identity.

Mira la lectura

Answers will vary.

¡Vamos a leer!

www.pasoapaso.com

Antes de leer

STRATEGY ➤ Using prior knowledge

Have you ever been to a costume party? What did people wear? What kinds of costumes best conceal the wearer's identity?

Mira la lectura

STRATEGY ➤ Predicting the outcome

Read the first part of this story. Then ask yourself what comes next. See if you can predict what will happen.

Una fiesta curiosa

Había una fiesta de disfraces en la casa de los Márquez. Los invitados fueron al baile vestidos con muchos tipos de disfraces: de levantadora de pesas, de bailarina, de princesa, de astronauta, de médico, de Frankenstein y de torero. Pero, ¿por qué había tantas personas vestidas de fantasma? Una vez la señora Márquez vio a cuatro fantasmas cerca de la mesa de postres y tres cerca de la de ensaladas y sandwiches. ¿Y por qué entraban y salían tan frecuentemente del dormitorio de su hija Natalia?

La señora Márquez ya no pudo soportarlo. Se decidió a averiguar esta situación tan curiosa. Con mucho cuidado, sin hacer ningún ruido, fue al dormitorio de su hija. Se acercó a la puerta, escuchó por un momento el sonido alegre de mucha gente divirtiéndose, abrió la puerta y encontró . . .

152 Capítulo 4

Options

Strategies for Reaching All Students

Spanish-Speaking Students
Aplicación: ¿Te gustan las fiestas de disfraces? Si te invitaran a una fiesta de disfraces, ¿qué disfraz te gustaría llevar? Descríbelo y di por qué te gustaría llevarlo.

Students Needing Extra Help
Mira la lectura: Talk about context and picture clues. Call attention to the pictures.
Infórmate: Write word families on the chalkboard, drawing arrows to indicate the connection: *vestidas → el vestido.* Return to the text to see how the words are used in context. Give additional examples of word families.
Aplicación: You can prepare students for this activity by asking them to find the noun forms of *beber* and *comer* in the story and

to come up with the verb form of *disfraz.* Students know many more words. Have them keep a running list in their notebooks to be added to periodically. To avoid mention of inappropriate types of parties, suggest that the funny story be about a party students attended as a young child. Or have them model a "Once upon a time" story. Brainstorm as a class. Use the vocabulary section of the Organizer.

Infórmate

STRATEGY ➤ Recognizing word families

In the reading there are probably several unknown words that resemble words you already know. Use what you know about the meaning of the root (for example, *invit-*) and how the word is used in the sentence to help you figure it out. For example, *invitados* should remind you of *invitar*, "to invite." In the phrase *Los invitados fueron . . .* you see that the definite article *los* is used, that *invitados* is plural, and that it comes before a verb. So you probably figured out that *invitados* is a noun meaning "invited ones," or "guests."

1. Now try to figure out the meaning of these italicized words in the same way.

   - *vestidos* con muchos tipos de disfraces
   - de *levantadora* de pesas
   - de *bailarina*
   - con mucho *cuidado*
   - *se acercó* a la puerta

   What helped you figure out the new words?

2. Now turn the book upside down and read the ending to see if you predicted it correctly. If you did, or came close, what clues helped you? What happened in the first part of the story that led you to your prediction?

Aplicación

Use your knowledge of word families to complete this chart. Use a separate piece of paper.

dibujar	dibujo
	regalo
	entrevista
	lavadero

Find out if any of your classmates has a funny story about a party. Write a brief account of the story in Spanish.

. . . a Natalia y a una docena de sus amigos y amigas. Los más pequeños estaban sobre los hombros de los más grandes y se quitaban sus disfraces fantasmales. Y en sus manos ¡llevaban platos de la comida deliciosa que servían los Márquez en su fiesta!

Infórmate

1. *vestidos,* from *vestir* (dressed), *lavantadora,* from *levantar* (lifter), *bailarina,* from *bailar* (dancer), *cuidado,* from *cuidar* (care), *se acercó,* from *cerca* (she approached)

Aplicación

regalar, entrevistar, lavar

🌐 Internet Activities

Have students go to www.pasoapaso.com for additional activities and practice.

Enrichment
Aplicación: Additional activities: 1) Create a celebration that highlights something special about your school or your region's history, local culture, or a special natural feature. Decide on a name for the festival, the theme, and one or two events. Share your ideas with a classmate. 2) Describe seasonal festivals or celebrations in your area or in another area that you've visited or heard about. 3) Go to the library and research the kinds of festivals that used to be held in your area or state but that are no longer held. Try to find answers to these questions: What was celebrated at these festivals? What did people do? Why did the festivals die out? Would you like to have gone to one of these festivals? What has replaced them? Are there festivals in your area with a period or nostalgia theme? Have you gone or would you like to go to one of them?

Multiple Intelligences
Visual/Spatial
See *¡Vamos a leer!*

Apply

Process Writing
For information regarding developing a writing portfolio, see p. 54.

¡Vamos a escribir!

Las reseñas (*reviews*) se publican en los periódicos y las revistas para informar al público sobre las películas, los programas de televisión y las obras de teatro. ¡Vamos a escribir una reseña!

1 Primero, escoge una obra para ver y describir en la reseña. Puede ser un programa de televisión, una película, una obra de teatro o un concierto. Después de ver la obra, escribe la reseña.

Para empezar, organiza tus ideas. Piensa en estas cosas:

- el nombre de la obra o del *show*
- cuándo y dónde lo (la) viste
- los artistas / actores / actrices
- lo que te gustó y por qué
- lo que no te gustó y por qué

Luego escribe el primer borrador. Sigue los pasos del proceso de escribir.

Los Lobos en concierto

Una exposición de arte en una plaza en México

154 Capítulo 4

Options

Strategies for Reaching All Students

Students Needing Extra Help
¡Vamos a escribir!: You may want to do these activities in groups or pairs.
Use the vocabulary section of the Organizer and, if available, the vocabulary section of the Organizer from Level 1, Chap. 11.
Ex. 1: Assign in advance. Students will need help with the descriptive vocabulary. Do a model based on a show or movie they saw.

Ex. 2: Brainstorm and model on the chalkboard or a transparency. Students may find it redundant to review a review. Have them start by critiquing the teacher's model.

Extended Written Practice/Homework
1. Write three sentences naming people who know how to do a sport or activity well.

2. Write three questions you can ask classmates to see if they know something about different activities: *¿Sabes quién ganó el campeonato de tenis?*
3. Write three pairs of sentences telling what different people had to do at night and what time they went to bed: *Juan tuvo que trabajar en el restaurante el sábado pasado. No se acostó hasta las dos de la mañana.*

2 Ahora escoge una reseña de un(a) compañero(a) y escribe tu
opinión sobre ella. Escribe por qué estás o no estás de acuerdo.
Puedes usar estas expresiones entre otras:

- creo que ...
- para mí
- porque
- por eso
- por ejemplo
- además (*in addition*)

3 Para distribuir su trabajo, pueden:

- enviar las reseñas y las reacciones al periódico escolar
- incluirlas en un periódico publicado en su clase
- exhibirlas en la sala de clases
- ponerlas en su portafolio

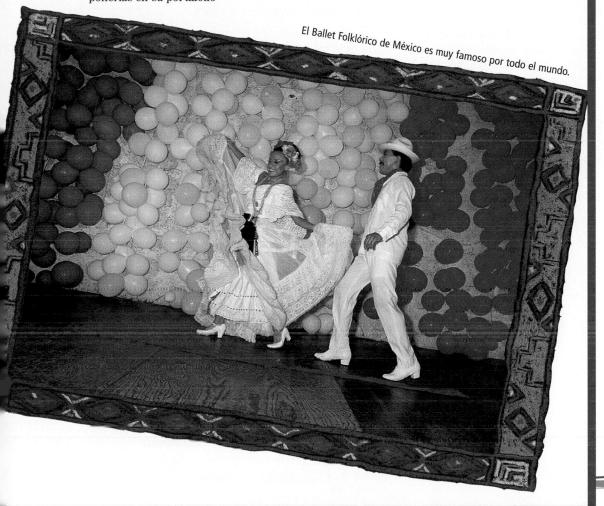

El Ballet Folklórico de México es muy famoso por todo el mundo.

Cultural Notes

(p. 154, photo)
Los Lobos are a popular Mexican American rock group who count among their influences traditional *norteña,* or Tex-Mex *conjunto,* music. It is characterized by the accordion and the *bajo sexto,* a twelve-string guitar. *Norteña* music is basically a joining of the polka and mazurka rhythms of the German immigrants in Texas and the Latin rhythms brought by the Mexicans.

(p. 155, photo)
Supported in part by the Mexican Department of Tourism, the Ballet Folklórico de México is one of Mexico's premier cultural institutions. It was founded by choreographer Amalia Hernández in 1952 and had eight dancers. Now the company has two troupes: one which performs in Mexico and another which tours abroad.

Assess & Summarize

Test Preparation

You may want to assign parts of this section as homework or as an in-class writing activity prior to administering the *Examen de habilidades.*

Answers

Listening: *¿Francisco? Soy yo, Andrés. Francisco, ¿me prestas el casco, los patines de hielo y el palo? Me desperté tarde esta mañana y tuve que correr de casa. No tengo nada conmigo. Te puedo devolver todo esta noche. ¿Vas a estar en casa?*

Andrés has telephoned his friend Francisco in order to borrow his helmet, ice skates, and hockey stick. He is planning to play ice hockey.

Reading: 1. b; 2. a; 3. c

Writing: Notes will vary.

Culture: Answers will vary, but students may cite references to the *Perspectiva cultural:* Rivera's paintings reveal Mexico's struggles with poverty and the people's day-to-day survival, selling candy, balloons, newspapers, and so on, in the streets. Frida Kahlo's paintings, especially her self-portraits, tell of her sad, painful life: of having polio as a child, of nearly dying in a bus accident, and the subsequent pain she lived with.

Speaking: Dialogues will vary.

Esta sección te ayudará a prepararte para el examen de habilidades, donde tendrás que hacer tareas semejantes.

Listening

Can you understand when people talk about their leisure-time activities? Listen as your teacher reads a sample similar to what you will hear on the test. Why has Andrés telephoned his friend Francisco? What is Andrés planning to do?

Reading

Read the following excerpts from a teen magazine. Then match each excerpt with the right ending.

1. ¡Un desastre total! Nadie va a creer en estas aventuras de un niño que busca un jaguar grande que está amenazando a una comunidad pequeña del Amazonas. . . .
2. Por fin ganó el equipo de la secundaria Muñoz Marín. Y los ganadores defenderán el campeonato en un partido la semana que viene en el Estadio Bolívar. . . .

3. Las canciones incluyen la que cantó Ricky Gómez, "No me olvides." El grupo de jóvenes tiene mucho talento, pero todavía no encuentran su sonido especial. . . .

   a. . . . dijo el entrenador en un momento muy emocionante.
   b. . . . Seguramente va a salir en video pronto.
   c. . . . Quiero decir que todavía cantan como muchos otros.

Writing

Write a note to a friend to persuade him or her to accompany you to a special event. Here is a sample.

> Querido Felipe,
>
> ¿Sabes que Patricia va a jugar en el campeonato de tenis de la liga escolar? El último partido va a ser el jueves. ¿Puedes ir conmigo? Va a ser muy emocionante porque las jugadoras de la Escuela Nacional también son muy buenas. Después podemos salir todos a celebrar—si gana Patricia. (No pude ir al partido el jueves pasado porque tuve que ir al dentista. Dicen que fue una ocasión muy alegre.)
>
>   Tu amigo,
>   Enrique

Culture

What do the paintings of Diego Rivera tell us about Mexican life? What do the paintings of Frida Kahlo tell us about her life?

Speaking

Work with a partner inviting him or her to join you in an activity. Here is a sample dialogue:

A —*¿Te gustaría ir a la exposición de obras de estudiantes en el Museo Universitario?*
B —*Ya la vi. Fui con mi hermana menor y me aburrí.*
A —*Pues, ¿sabes que hay un concierto en el parque el miércoles a la una?*
B —*¿Es de música clásica?*
A —*No. Es de jazz. Va a tocar Carlos Baker.*

www.pasoapaso.com

Options

Strategies for Reaching All Students

Students Needing Extra Help

¿Lo sabes bien?: Remind students that this is just a sample, not the actual text.
Listening: Read the sample more than once. Remind students that they only need to listen for two pieces of information. Brainstorm what words they should listen for.
Reading: Tell students to watch for context clues. Because many tests have had narrations as opposed to excerpts, this format may cause confusion for some students.

Writing: Have students use the Organizer and write a sample note as pre-test practice. Brainstorm other special events and the corresponding vocabulary.
Culture: Have students review any notes they took during their first reading of the *Perspectiva cultural.*
Speaking: Brainstorm other places. Limit the number of lines of dialogue. You may want to have students accept or reject the invitation, not both, within one dialogue.

Resumen del vocabulario

Usa el vocabulario de este capítulo para:

- talk about past and present activities
- extend, accept, or reject an invitation
- discuss and evaluate a leisure-time activity

to talk about sports
el bate
el guante (de béisbol)
la pelota (de béisbol, de tenis)
la raqueta (de tenis)
los bolos
el golf
el hockey
el palo (de golf, de hockey)
el disco de hockey
meter un gol
correr
levantar pesas
las pesas
montar en bicicleta
la bicicleta
el casco
el balón, *pl.* los balones
el patín, *pl.* los patines
patinar sobre hielo
el esquí, *pl.* los esquíes
el partido
la liga
el jugador, la jugadora
el campeón, *pl.* los campeones,
 la campeona
el campeonato
el entrenador, la entrenadora
empatar
ganar
perder *(e → ie)*

to discuss leisure activities
la diversión, *pl.* las diversiones
el desastre
el horror
el ajedrez
las damas
el desfile
la exposición, *pl.* las
 exposiciones (de arte)
(hacer) un crucigrama
(hacer) un picnic
(hacer) un rompecabezas
la música clásica
la música rock
la obra de teatro
la fiesta de disfraces
el casete
el disco compacto
el video musical
aburrirse
divertirse *(e → ie)*
pasarlo bien / mal
soportar

to describe people or things
alegre
último, -a

to discuss activities in the past
estuvo *(from:* estar)
fue *(from:* ser)
(yo) tuve que / (tú) tuviste que
 (from: tener que)

other useful words and expressions
bastante
prestar
pedir prestado, -a (a)
saber
tener tiempo de + *inf.*

Resumen 157

Assessment

¿? **Prueba cumulativa**

¿? **Examen de habilidades**

 Test Generator

Additional Assessment Options

 Comm. Act. BLMs

Small Group Activities
Situation Cards

 Pasos vivos 2 CD-ROM

Slide Presentation Maker, Video
Presentation Maker, Word
Processor, Spindle

¿Lo sabes bien? Video Quiz

www **Internet Activities**
Self-Test

CAPÍTULO 5

THEME: CHILDHOOD

COMMUNICATION

Topics

Toys

Animals

Playground equipment

Childhood activities

Objectives

To discuss the life and importance of José Martí

To talk about animals

To reminisce

To name toys

To discuss things you used to do

To talk about places children go

To talk about playground equipment

CULTURE

José Martí

GRAMMAR

El imperfecto de los verbos que terminan en -ar

El imperfecto de los verbos que terminan en -er *e* -ir

El imperfecto de los verbos ir *y* ser

Ancillaries available for use with Chapter 5

Multisensory/Technology

 Overheads, 26–29

 Audio Tapes and CDs

 Vocabulary Art Blackline Masters for Hands-On Learning, pp. 28–32/CD-ROM

 Classroom Crossword

 La Catrina

 Pasos vivos 2 CD-ROM

 Internet Activities www.pasoapaso.com

Print

 Practice Workbook, pp. 45–54

 Writing, Audio & Video Activities, pp. 29–34, 105–107, 159–160

 Communicative Activity Blackline Masters

   Pair and Small Group Activities, pp. 29–34

   Situation Cards, p. 35

 Un paso más: Actividades para ampliar tu español, pp. 25–30

 RESOURCE◉PRO®

Planning Express, Teaching Resources Library, and Clip Art Library

Assessment

 Assessment Program

   Pruebas, pp. 71–80

   Examen de habilidades, pp. 81–84

 Test Generator

 ¿Lo sabes bien? Video Quiz

Video still from Chap. 5

157A

Childhood in Spain and Latin America

As a general rule, children in Spain and Latin America are shown great verbal and physical affection. Adults are very tolerant of their behavior. However, children must show respect to adults, and are taught to treat their parents' friends courteously. They must address them as *usted*, and in some countries, such as Mexico, Nicaragua, and Colombia, are expected to address their parents formally as well. In these cases, the young child is addressed as *usted* as he or she is learning to speak. The difference between *usted* and *tú* is learned with the advent of increasing peer interaction.

When not in school, most children are cared for by parents, other family members, or maids, who either live with them or come to their homes on an almost daily basis. *Jardines de niños* (or *guarderías infantiles)* are common. They are similar to nursery schools where pre-kindergarteners learn social skills and have fun. Because many children attend private schools, and those who don't most likely spend their childhood in the same home, children who begin kindergarten together often remain classmates through high school. As a result, lifelong friendships begin at an early age, and there is much camaraderie.

In cities, small yards are the norm, even in upper-class neighborhoods. Children are often seen playing in the street, local parks, or *plazas.* They enjoy soccer, riding bicycles, flying kites, playing with marbles and tops, and jumping rope. Social interaction during play is much more important than possession of toys. Children in Spanish-speaking countries have dogs and cats for pets, but it is unusual for animals to be allowed in the house. They are generally not made members of the family, contrary to common practice in the U.S.

Birthdays and first communions are two important events in the lives of children throughout Spain and Latin America. First communion usually occurs around the age of ten. Although it is primarily a religious event, the child is often honored by his or her parents with a formal party that includes relatives, godparents, and family friends. A child celebrates a birthday with his or her peers, at parties that tend to be elaborate. Guests are expected to wear party clothes. In Mexico and Central America, one of the highlights of the birthday celebration is the breaking of the *piñata,* filled with candies the children scramble to pick up. Birthday party entertainment may also include a clown, magician, or puppet show. Each guest is presented with a party favor, which may be a beautifully sculpted piece of candy or another small but carefully chosen gift. The guests give the honoree presents, but unlike birthday parties in the U.S., they are usually not opened until all the guests have left.

Introduce

Re-entry of Concepts

The following list represents words, expressions, and grammar topics re-entered from Book 1 and Book 2 (Chaps. 1–4):

Book 1

numbers 0–31, *gustar* expressions, family members, places and buildings, household chores

Chapter 1

school subjects

Chapter 2

daily routine

Chapter 4

sports

158   Capítulo 5

Planning

Cross-Curricular Connections

Language Arts Connection *(pp. 162–163)*
Have students pretend that they are part of a large family from a Spanish-speaking country. Have them write a letter to Santa telling him what to give each member of the family and why they deserve their gift.

Sociology Connection *(pp. 166–167)*
As a homework assignment, have students interview their parents or an older relative about their childhood. Then have them write a brief composition about what their parents or other relatives did for fun, what they themselves did, and what they think their children will do in the future. Have students include any insights that they might have about the differences and similarities among the three groups.

Spanish in Your Community
Have students create bilingual posters for a daycare center or kindergarten in your community. Assign each one a color or a number (1–10). Provide a design format to ensure consistency. For the numbers, have them use simple shapes, such as circles, squares, and triangles for counting. For the colors, have them use easily identifiable objects, such as fruit or animals. Have a volunteer deliver the posters after you have made arrangements ahead of time.

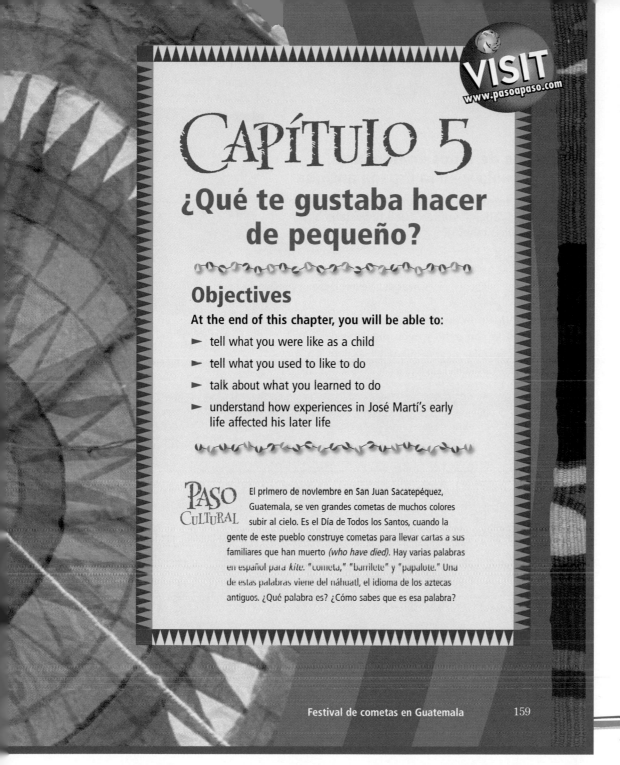

CAPÍTULO 5

¿Qué te gustaba hacer de pequeño?

Objectives

At the end of this chapter, you will be able to:

► tell what you were like as a child

► tell what you used to like to do

► talk about what you learned to do

► understand how experiences in José Martí's early life affected his later life

PASO CULTURAL

El primero de noviembre en San Juan Sacatepéquez, Guatemala, se ven grandes cometas de muchos colores subir al cielo. Es el Día de Todos los Santos, cuando la gente de este pueblo construye cometas para llevar cartas a sus familiares que han muerto *(who have died)*. Hay varias palabras en español para *kite*: "cometa," "barrilete" y "papalote." Una de estas palabras viene del náhuatl, el idioma de los aztecas antiguos. ¿Qué palabra es? ¿Cómo sabes que es esa palabra?

Cultural Notes

(pp. 158–159, photo)
The skies over San Juan Sacatepequez just outside of Guatemala City are invaded once a year by giant flying animals, objects, people, and weird abstract forms swirling overhead! It is the *festival de barriletes* (Giant Kite Festival) held every November 1 to commemorate *el día de todos los santos* (All Saints' Day). People of all ages build kites and take part in the competition.

Paso cultural
La palabra "papalote" viene del náhuatl. Palabras del náhuatl con frecuencia terminan en *-ote* o *-ate* (antes *-otl* y *-atl*), como "aguacate," "cacahuate" *(peanut)* y "guajolote" *(turkey)*.

Preview

Cultural Objective
- To discuss childhood activities in Spanish-speaking countries

¡Piensa en la CULTURA!

Juegos de niños en Honduras, Venezuela y en la España antigua

Mira las fotos. Los niños que vemos están haciendo sus actividades favoritas. ¿Qué te gustaba hacer cuando eras niño(a)?

"¡Dos y dos son cuatro; cuatro y dos son seis; seis y dos son ocho y ocho dieciséis!"

¿Qué te gustaba jugar de niño(a)? Si saltabas a la cuerda, ¿cantabas canciones como ésta?

"Aquí está mi nueva tarjeta de Juan González."

Cuando eras niño(a), ¿coleccionabas algo? ¿Ten una colección grande? ¿Todavía la tienes?

Caracas, Venezuela

Un niño de Caracas les muestra su colección de tarjetas de béisbol a unos amigos.

Niños hondureños saltando a la cuerda

Guanaja, Honduras

160   Capítulo 5

Options

Strategies for Reaching All Students

Spanish-Speaking Students
Ask: *¿Sabes algunos trabalenguas o juegos infantiles? ¿Cómo son? Enséñale uno a un(a) compañero(a) de clase.*

 Un paso más Ex. 5-A

Multiple Intelligences
Intrapersonal/Introspective and Visual/Spatial
Have students research the artist Francisco de Goya to find more of his works. Ask students to compare the painting on p. 161 to others they find.

Cultural Notes

(p. 160, top photo)
Baseball has long been played in Venezuela, and it is popular throughout the Spanish-speaking countries of the Caribbean region. Over the years, professional baseball in the U.S. has benefited from a steady flow of players from such countries as Venezuela, Mexico, Cuba, Nicaragua, and the Dominican Republic.

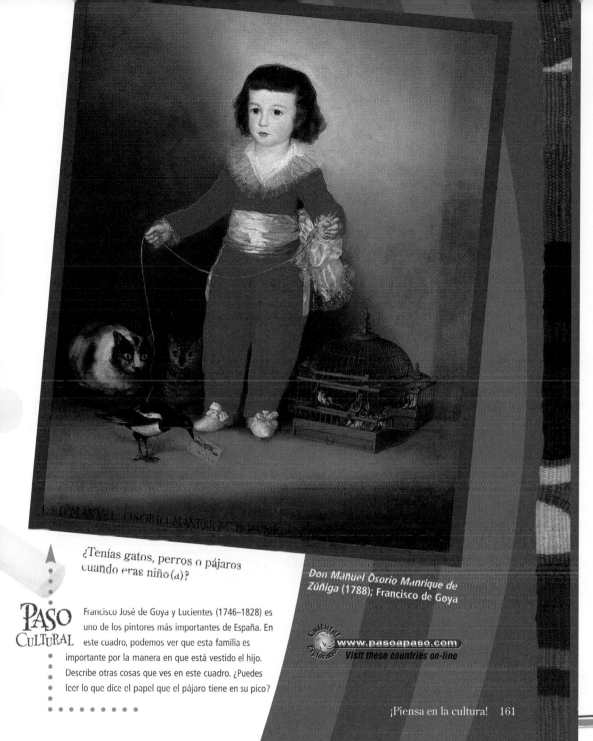

¿Tenías gatos, perros o pájaros cuando eras niño(a)?

Don Manuel Osorio Manrique de Zúñiga (1788); Francisco de Goya

PASO CULTURAL

Francisco José de Goya y Lucientes (1746–1828) es uno de los pintores más importantes de España. En este cuadro, podemos ver que esta familia es importante por la manera en que está vestido el hijo. Describe otras cosas que ves en este cuadro. ¿Puedes leer lo que dice el papel que el pájaro tiene en su pico?

www.pasoapaso.com
Visit these countries on-line

¡Piensa en la cultura! 161

Multicultural Perspectives

Before television and video games, children in many countries throughout Spain and Latin America were entertained by *canciones, adivinanzas,* and *trabalenguas* (tongue twisters). An *adivinanza* is a riddle in the form of a short poem that describes some object. Ask students if they can guess these *adivinanzas:*

Para uno es poco.
Para dos es suficiente.
Para tres no es nada.
(un secreto)

¿Qué animal salta más alto que una casa?
(Todos, porque las casas no saltan.)

Ask students if they can say this *trabalengua:*

Cuando cuentes cuentos,
cuenta cuántos cuentos cuentas
cuando cuentas cuentos.

Ask students to create *adivinanzas* or *trabalenguas* for each other to guess.

Answers: ¡Piensa en la cultura!
Answers will vary.

(p. 160, bottom photo)
These girls are skipping rope in Guanaja, Departamento de Islas de la Bahía, Honduras. The three islands that compose this department—Utila, Roatán, and Guanaja—are noted for their diverse population. Many residents are Black Caribs. Other residents are of German and Middle Eastern ancestry; still others are English-speakers descended from inhabitants of the Cayman Islands. Fishing and tourism are important industries.

Paso cultural
Descriptions will vary./El papel en el pico del pájaro tiene el nombre del artista.

(p. 161, photo)
Francisco Goya (1746–1828) completed this painting of Don Manuel Osorio de Zúñiga around 1788. Don Manuel was the son of the Count of Altamira, a Spanish aristocrat and patron of Goya. Although Goya had wealthy patrons among the Spanish nobility, his disillusionment with the Spanish court led to a self-imposed exile in France.

Standards 1.2; 2.1; 2.2; 3.1 **161**

Present

Chapter Theme
Childhood: Toys and animals

Communicative Objectives
- To talk about animals
- To reminisce
- To name toys
- To discuss things you used to do

 Overheads 26–27

 Vocabulary Art BLMs/CD-ROM

 Vocabulary Tape 5-1

Grammar Preview
Imperfect verb forms are presented here lexically. Encourage students to use them without asking why. The concept of "used to" and the verb stems are in most cases clear. Explanation of the imperfect is on pp. 175–179.

Vocabulario para conversar

¿Eras obediente o no?

Vas a necesitar estas palabras y expresiones para hablar de cuando eras pequeño(a). Después de leerlas varias veces, practícalas con un(a) compañero(a).

el pez, *pl.* los peces

la cuerda

saltar (a la cuerda)

el tren (de juguete)

el bloque

162   Capítulo 5

Options

Strategies for Reaching All Students

Spanish-Speaking Students
Ask: *¿Para qué sirven los animales de peluche? ¿Por qué crees que a los niños pequeños les gustan tanto?*

 Un paso más Exs. 5-B, 5-C

Students Needing Extra Help
Begin the vocabulary section of the Organizer. Show how *pez* becomes *peces.* Add to the word family list: *juguetes* from *jugar.*
También necesitas. . . : Show the paradigm of the imperfect tense of *era* and *iba* in the grammar section for students who need to see the entire conjugation.
Have students use the paradigm of *-er* verbs in the imperfect to create the chart for *tenía.* Review the *a mí, a ti* structure. Give exam-

ples of *gustaba(n)* with infinitives and nouns. Point out the *-ar* imperfect chart in the grammar section.
¿Y qué quiere decir. . . ?: Point out that *el robot* does not form the plural by adding *-es,* as do most nouns ending in consonants; emphasize *los robots.*

los juguetes

el muñeco

los animales de peluche

el oso de peluche

la muñeca

la niña

el niño

la tortuga

el pájaro

el camión (de juguete), pl. los camiones

el triciclo

montar en triciclo

la pistola (de agua)

¡NO OLVIDES!

Remember that we also use *le, nos,* and *les* with *gustaba(n).*

También necesitas . . .

caminar	*to walk*
ser: (yo) era, (tú) eras	*I was, you were*
ir: (yo) iba, (tú) ibas	*I / you used to go*
tener: (yo) tenía, (tú) tenías	*I / you had, used to have*
(A mí) me gustaba(n) ___.	*I liked, I used to like ___.*
(A ti) te gustaba(n) ___.	*you liked, you used to like ___.*
jugar: (yo) jugaba, (tú) jugabas	*I / you used to play*
(bien) educado, -a	*polite, well-mannered*
de pequeño, -a	*as a child*

¿Y qué quiere decir . . . ?
el animal
el dinosaurio
el robot, *pl.* los robots
la colección, *pl.* las colecciones
coleccionar
maleducado, -a
obediente
desobediente

Practice & Apply

Answers: Empecemos a conversar

1 ESTUDIANTE A

a. ¿Tenías peces cuando eras niño(a)?

b. ...tortugas...

c. ...pájaros...

d. ...gatos...

ESTUDIANTE B

a–d. Answers will vary.

2 ESTUDIANTE A

a. ¿Te gustaban los animales de peluche cuando eras pequeño(a)?

b. ...los camiones de juguete...

c. ...los osos de peluche...

d. ...los bloques...

e. ...las muñecas...

f. Questions will vary.

ESTUDIANTE B

a.–f. Answers will vary.

3 ESTUDIANTE A

a. De pequeño(a), ¿eras (bien) educado(a) o no?

b. ...simpático(a)...

c. ...ordenado(a)...

d. ...atrevido(a)...

e. Questions will vary.

ESTUDIANTE B

Answers will vary.

a. No, era (muy) maleducado(a).

b. ...antipático(a).

c. ...desordenado(a).

d. ...prudente.

e. Answers will vary.

Empecemos a conversar

Túrnate con un(a) compañero(a) para ser *Estudiante A* y *Estudiante B*. Reemplacen las palabras subrayadas en el modelo con palabras representadas o escritas en los recuadros. Si ven 💡 pueden dar su propia respuesta.

1
A —¿Tenías *perros* cuando eras niño(a)?
B —No, no tenía *perros*, pero tenía *un gato*.
　o: Sí, tenía *uno*.
　o: No, yo no tenía animales.

Estudiante A　　　　　　　　　　　　　　　　Estudiante B

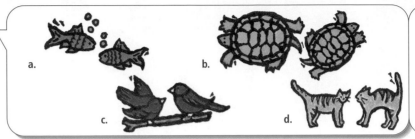

a.　　b.　　c.　　d.

2
A —¿Te gustaban *los coches* cuando eras pequeño(a)?
B —Sí, y también me gustaban *los robots*.
　o: No, pero me gustaban *los robots*.

Estudiante A　　　　　　　　　　　　　　　　Estudiante B

a.　　b.　　c.　　d.　　e.　　f.

Options

Strategies for Reaching All Students

Spanish-Speaking Students

 Un paso más Ex. 5-D

Students Needing Extra Help

Ex. 1: Demonstrate how you got *uno* from *perros*.

Discourage students from giving the final response too often.

Brainstorm responses involving other animals. If available, use the Organizer from Book 1, Chap. 13.

Ex. 3: Brainstorm antonyms for responding in the negative: (bien) *educado, -a (maleducado, -a); simpático, -a (antipático, -a),* etc.

Ex. 4: Explain to students that they need to supply a name in answer *a*.

Brainstorm other possibilities for responding in the negative.

Ex. 5: Brainstorm names of places frequented by children.

Ex. 6: Discuss the typical ages for these childhood milestones to occur. Give broad ranges; some students may have been on the outer limits.

Ex. 7: Provide necessary vocabulary for answering the *¿Por qué?* question. Ask why they still have the toys.

Ex. 8: Brainstorm types of collections. Review vocabulary for coins, stamps, photos, postcards, etc.

3 obediente   A —*De pequeño(a), ¿eras* <u>*obediente*</u> *o no?*
               B —*Sí, era un(a) niño(a) (muy)* <u>*obediente*</u>.
                  o: *No, era (muy)* <u>*desobediente*</u>.

Estudiante A   **Estudiante B**

a. (bien) educado, -a   d. atrevido, -a

b. simpático, -a

c. ordenado, -a   e.

4 jugabas con trenes   A —*De pequeño(a), ¿jugabas con trenes?*
               B —*No, yo no jugaba mucho con trenes.*
                  Jugaba con muñecos.
                  o: *Sí, yo jugaba con trenes.*

Estudiante A   **Estudiante B**

a. ibas al parque con (nombre)   d. tenías dinosaurios

b. te gustaba saltar a la cuerda   e. te gustaba montar en triciclo

c. tenías una silla alta para comer   f.

Empecemos a escribir

Escribe tus respuestas en español.

5 De pequeño, ¿a qué lugares ibas a menudo? ¿Con quién? ¿Adónde te gustaba más ir?

6 ¿Cuántos años tenías cuando aprendiste a caminar? ¿Y a hablar? ¿Y a leer?

7 ¿Qué juguetes te gustaban más cuando eras pequeño(a)? ¿Por qué? ¿Tienes algunos todavía? ¿Cuáles?

8 ¿Te gustaba coleccionar cosas? ¿Qué colecciones tenías? ¿Qué coleccionas ahora?

También se dice

el velocípedo

los tarugos
los tacos

brincar a la cuerda

andar en triciclo

> ### MORE PRACTICE
>
> Más práctica y tarea, p. 540
> Practice Workbook 5–1, 5–2

Vocabulario para conversar   165

---

4 ESTUDIANTE A
a. De pequeño(a), ¿ibas al parque con (nombre)?
b. ...te gustaba saltar a la cuerda?
c. ...tenías una silla alta para comer?
d. ...tenías dinosaurios?
e. ...te gustaba montar en triciclo?
f. Answers will vary, but look for the correct use of imperfect tense.
ESTUDIANTE B
a.–f. Questions will vary, but look for correct agreement of subject and verb.

Answers: Empecemos a escribir

5–8 Answers will vary, but look for correct tense of verbs.

 Practice Wkbk. 5-1, 5-2

Audio Activity 5.1

Pruebas 5-1, 5-2

Comm. Act. BLM 5-1

Present

Chapter Theme
Playground and behavior

Communicative Objectives
- To reminisce
- To talk about playground equipment
- To discuss things you used to do
- To talk about places children go

 Overhead 28

 Vocabulary Art BLMs/CD-ROM

 Vocabulary Tape 5-2

Grammar Preview
Again, imperfect forms are presented here lexically. Encourage students to use them without explanation. If necessary, however, see pp. 175–177.

Teaching Suggestions
Preparing students to speak: Use one or two options from each of the categories of Comprehensible Input, Physical Response, or Limited Verbal Response. For a complete explanation of these categories and some sample activities, see pp. T20–T21.

Vocabulario para conversar

¿Cómo te portabas cuando eras pequeño(a)?

Aquí tienes el resto del vocabulario que necesitas en este capítulo para hablar de cuando eras pequeño(a).

el patio de recreo
el columpio
el tobogán, *pl.* los toboganes
el sube y baja
el carrusel
el cajón de arena, *pl.* los cajones de arena

166 Capítulo 5

Options

Strategies for Reaching All Students

Spanish-Speaking Students
 Un paso más Ex. 5-E

Students Needing Extra Help
También necesitas . . . : Present *portarse bien* and *portarse mal* separately. Avoid giving grammatical explanations until later on in the chapter. Review stem-changing verbs and their rules with *mentir.*

Because of the amount of vocabulary, you may want to organize the list into nouns, adjectives, and verbs. Divide the verbs by endings and / or reflexive vs. non-reflexive, etc.

Ex. 9: Review numbers. Discuss the ages at which these events usually occur.

Enrichment
Ex. 9: To extend the dialogue, students can ask each other: *¿Te gustaba más jugar con otros niños o solo(a)? ¿Por qué?*

Learning Spanish Through Action
STAGING VOCABULARY: *Pongan*
MATERIALS: pictures of playground equipment from the Vocabulary Art BLMs/ CD-ROM
DIRECTIONS: Direct students to place items in the "play area" of a nursery school as you describe them.

También necesitas . . .

la guardería infantil	*day-care center*	llorar: (yo) lloraba	*to cry: I used to cry*
el vecino, la vecina	*neighbor*	pelearse: (yo) me	*to fight: I used to fight*
decir: (yo) decía	*I used to say / tell*	peleaba	
mentir *(e → ie):*	*to lie: I used to lie*	tímido, -a	*shy*
(yo) mentía		travieso, -a	*mischievous, naughty*
obedecer *(c → zc):**	*to obey: I used to obey*	consentido, -a	*spoiled*
(yo) obedecía			
molestar:	*to bother, to annoy: I*		
(yo) molestaba	*used to bother, annoy*		
portarse (bien / mal):	*to behave (well / badly)*		
(yo) me portaba	*I / you used to behave*		
(tú) te portabas			
recordar *(o → ue)*	*to remember*		
preferir: (yo) prefería	*I preferred*		

> **¿Y qué quiere decir . . . ?**
> el kindergarten
> la escuela primaria
> la verdad
> desobedecer *(c → zc)*

Empecemos a conversar

9

jugar con
otros niños

A —*¿Cuántos años tenías cuando empezaste
a <u>jugar con otros niños</u>?*

B —*Tenía <u>tres años</u>.*
  o: *No recuerdo. Era
  muy pequeño(a).*

Estudiante A

a. vestirte solo(a)
b. prestar tus
   juguetes a
   otros niños
c. ir a fiestas
d. estudiar
   español
e. ir a la escuela
f.

Estudiante B

* *Obedecer* and *desobedecer* follow the pattern of *conocer:*
(yo) obedezco, (tú) obedeces, etc.

Los columpios y el tobogán ocupan un lugar central en el patio de esta casa en Santiago, República Dominicana.

Vocabulario para conversar   167

Practice & Apply

Una familia hondureña

10 la guardería infantil

A —¿*Cómo te portabas en* <u>*la guardería infantil*</u>?
B —<u>*Me portaba bien*</u>.
    o: *No recuerdo (pero creo que* <u>*me portaba mal*</u>).

Estudiante A

a. el kindergarten
b. la escuela primaria
c. tu casa
d. la casa de (los vecinos)
e. el patio de recreo
f. el cine

Estudiante B

portarse bien / mal
molestar mucho a ___
llorar a menudo
ser muy (travieso, -a)

(nunca) obedecer a nadie
pelearse con los otros niños

168   Capítulo 5

Options

Strategies for Reaching All Students

Spanish-Speaking Students
Additional questions to expand responses:
Cuando eras pequeño(a), ¿tenías un(a) profesor(a) favorito(a)? ¿Cómo era? (Describe su apariencia física y su personalidad.)

 Un paso más Ex. 5-F

Students Needing Extra Help
Ex. 10: Remind students that the verbs in the responses for *Estudiante B* need to be conjugated: *ser* becomes *era*. Direct students to the *También necesitas...* list. Remind them to put a name in the blank for the *molestar mucho a ___* response. Brainstorm other possibilities for *ser muy (____)*.
Ex. 11: Brainstorm possibilities for *e*. If available, use the Organizer for Book 1, Chap. 1.

Ex. 13: Students may need help with the structure of the responses to *¿Cuándo mentías?*.
Ex. 14: Point out that the last question is in the present tense; provide necessary vocabulary.
Ex. 15: Students may need help with the vocabulary for the *¿Por qué?* response.
Ex. 16: Show some possibilities for rewriting the sentences.

11 hermanos menores / educados

A —¿Tus *hermanos menores* son *educados*?
B —Sí, son *muy educados*.
o: *No. Son muy maleducados y traviesos.*
o: *No tengo hermanos menores.*

Estudiante A

a. primos(as) / obedientes
b. vecinos(as) / simpáticos(as)
c. sobrinos(as) / consentidos(as)
d. amigos(as) / tímidos(as)
e.

Estudiante B

Empecemos a escribir y a leer

Escribe tus respuestas en español.

12 Cuando eras pequeño(a), ¿ibas a una guardería infantil? ¿Te gustaba o no?

13 De pequeño(a), ¿decías siempre la verdad o mentías a menudo? ¿Cuándo mentías? Y ahora, ¿mientes a veces?

14 Cuando ibas al parque, ¿te gustaba jugar en el columpio, en el tobogán o en el sube y baja? ¿Te gustaba el carrusel? ¿O preferías el cajón de arena? ¿Por qué crees que a los niños les gusta tanto el cajón de arena?

15 De pequeño(a), ¿eras consentido(a)? ¿Y ahora? ¿Te gusta estar con los (las) niños(as) consentidos(as)? ¿Por qué?

16 Discute estas frases con un(a) compañero(a). Decidan si están de acuerdo o no. Si no están de acuerdo, cambien las frases y escríbanlas otra vez.

a. Los niños antipáticos suelen ser muy consentidos.
b. Es necesario portarse bien en la casa y en la escuela.
c. Los niños no deben jugar con pistolas de agua.
d. Los niños deben obedecer a todos los adultos.
e. Hay que decir la verdad siempre.

También se dice

el resbaladero
el deslizadero

el trapecio
la hamaca

el tiovivo
la calesita
los caballitos

www.pasoapaso.com

MORE PRACTICE

Más práctica y tarea, p. 540–541
Practice Workbook 5–3, 5–4

ENSEÑA A PENSAR CON LAS MANOS.

Vocabulario para conversar   169

Practice

Answers
¡Comuniquemos!

1 Answers will vary for *Estudiante B*, but look for use of antonyms and correct adjective agreement.
a. antipático(a)
b. desobediente
c. desordenado(a)
d. divertido(a)
e. generoso(a)
f. impaciente
g. maleducado(a)
h. prudente
i. Answers will vary.

2–3 Answers will vary, but may include the following:
Rubén se pelea con los niños porque quiere el camión (de juguete). (La profesora debe poner el camión en el estante.) Anita tiene ropa sucia. (La profesora debe limpiarla.) Gabriel llora. (La profesora debe preguntarle por qué llora.) Patricia dibuja en las paredes. (La profesora debe ayudarle a limpiar las paredes.) Fernanda quiere un libro que está en el estante. (La profesora debe darle el libro.) Ignacio no puede ponerse la chaqueta. (La profesora debe ayudarle.)

¡Comuniquemos!

Aquí tienes otra oportunidad para usar el vocabulario de este capítulo.

1 Habla con un(a) compañero(a) de cómo eras antes y cómo eres ahora. Usa las características de la lista.

A —*Cuando eras niño(a), ¿eras (muy) perezoso(a)?*
B —*Sí, pero ahora soy (muy) trabajador(a).*
    o: *No. Era (muy) trabajador(a).*

a. simpático(a)	maleducado(a)
b. obediente	impaciente
c. ordenado(a)	desobediente
d. serio(a)	prudente
e. tacaño(a)	generoso(a)
f. paciente	antipático(a)
g. educado(a)	divertido(a)
h. atrevido(a)	desordenado(a)
i.	

2 Con un(a) compañero(a), habla de los juguetes para niños. ¿Cuáles son los mejores y por qué? Después, trabajen con otros dos estudiantes para hablar sobre lo que escogieron.

170   Capítulo 5

Options

Strategies for Reaching All Students

Spanish-Speaking Students
 Un paso más Exs. 5-G, 5-H

Students Needing Extra Help
Ex. 2: Model. Students may need help with the vocabulary needed to answer *¿Por qué?* Develop some questions for students to ask each other. The idea of choosing the "best" toys may be confusing.
Ex. 3: Remind students that there are two parts to this activity: identifying the problem and giving a solution.
¿Qué sabes ahora?: Have students write out this section so they can keep track of their progress.

Enrichment
Ex. 2: As an additional assignment, have students describe and draw a toy they would like to invent. Have them tell why they think this toy would be appealing to children.
Ex. 3: The whole class may enjoy acting out the scene in the picture. Have students decide who will be the children and who will be the teacher (there may be more than one teacher). Suggest this plot line for the class

3 La profesora de una guardería infantil no sabe qué hacer. Con un(a) compañero(a), describe los problemas que hay en la guardería.

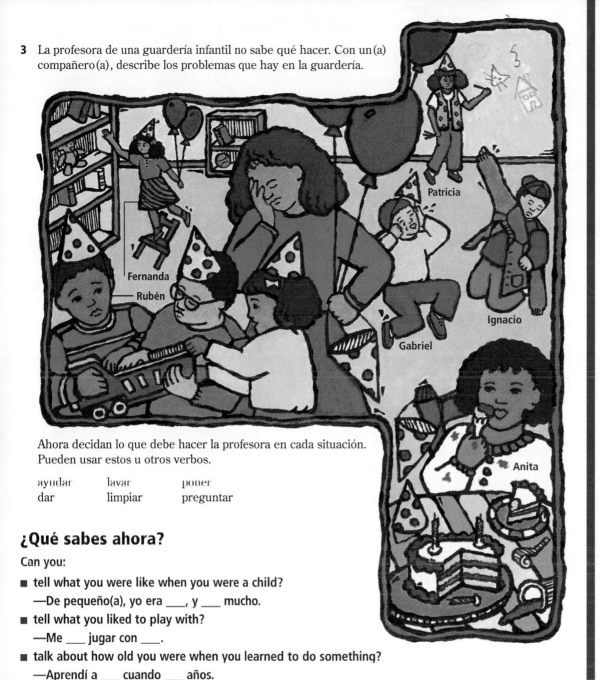

Fernanda

Rubén

Patricia

Ignacio

Gabriel

Anita

Ahora decidan lo que debe hacer la profesora en cada situación. Pueden usar estos u otros verbos.

ayudar	lavar	poner
dar	limpiar	preguntar

¿Qué sabes ahora?

Can you:

■ tell what you were like when you were a child?

—De pequeño(a), yo era ___, y ___ mucho.

■ tell what you liked to play with?

—Me ___ jugar con ___.

■ talk about how old you were when you learned to do something?

—Aprendí a ___ cuando ___ años.

Vocabulario para conversar   171

Present & Apply

Cultural Objective

• To understand how childhood experiences affected José Martí's later life

Multicultural Perspectives

Gabriela Mistral was the first Latin American writer to be awarded the Nobel Prize for Literature. A native of Chile, Mistral loved children and wrote *Canciones de cuna,* a collection of lullabies. When the United Nations International Children's Emergency Fund (UNICEF) was created, Mistral said, *"Las Naciones Unidas son más que una Asamblea y una hechura política; ellas son la yema de una conciencia universal."* Make available a book of Mistral's poetry (or an equivalent in translation), and ask students to select a poem to present to the class.

Critical Thinking: Making Comparisons

Ask students if they know of anyone in U.S. history whose life or deeds paralleled those of Martí. Encourage discussions.

Answers

Answers to inductive questions will vary, but students may say that Martí participated in organizing Cuba's revolution while he lived in New York.

Perspectiva cultural

¿Por qué crees que hay una estatua de este héroe cubano en Nueva York? ¿Hay estatuas de héroes de otros países en tu ciudad? ¿Quiénes son?

EL CRIMEN: Incitar a la gente a rebelarse
EL VEREDICTO: Culpable
LA SENTENCIA: Seis años de trabajo forza
EL ARMA CON QUE SE COMETIÓ EL CRIMEN: La pluma del poeta
LA EDAD DEL CRIMINAL: 16 años

Imagina que es el año 1870. Cuba es una colonia de España. Hay mucha intriga y mucha actividad política entre los españoles y los que están a favor de la independencia.

Tú tienes dieciséis años. Eres estudiante de secundaria. Escribes artículos políticos que se distribuyen no sólo en la escuela sino también en la ciudad. Y escribes poesía. Todo lo que escribes tiene el mismo tema: la independencia de Cuba.

Ahora estás en la corte en La Habana. Te dan una sentencia de seis años de trabajo forzado. ¿Por qué? Porque en una carta acusaste a un amigo de no ayudar a la revolución.

Ésta era la situación de un joven cubano, José Julián Martí y Pérez.

Martí pasó menos de un año en la prisión. Lo exiliaron a España en 1871 por sus actividades revolucionarias. En España, estudió y continuó su trabajo a favor de la independencia de Cuba. Escribió artículos, folletos, discursos y poesía.

En los años siguientes, Martí vivió y trabajó en México, Guatemala, los Estados Unidos y Venezuela. Escribía poemas y artículos, entre ellos, una columna en el periódico *La nación* de Buenos Aires. Era famoso en toda América Latina.

Cuando vivió en Nueva York, participó en la organización de la revolución cubana. Regresó a Cuba y murió en una batalla contra los españoles cerca de Dos Ríos en 1895. Siete años después, Cuba por fin obtuvo su independencia.

172 Capítulo 5

La cultura desde tu perspectiva

1 ¿Conoces a artistas de hoy que se dedican a una causa importante como hizo Martí? ¿Quiénes? ¿Qué hacen para la causa?

2 Imagina que José Martí vive hoy. ¿A qué causa se dedica? ¿Qué escribe?

www.pasoapaso.com

Options

Strategies for Reaching All Students

Spanish-Speaking Students

Ask: *En la biblioteca de tu escuela o comunidad (o entre los estantes de libros en el salón de clase), busca información sobre la obra de un(a) poeta hispano(a). Puede ser Martí u otro(a) que te interese. Lee algunos de sus poemas, escoge uno que te guste y escribe tu interpretación del poema o tu reacción al leerlo.*

 Un paso más Ex. 5-I

Students Needing Extra Help

Have students take notes that can be reviewed in the *¿Lo sabes bien?* section. Read the questions from *La cultura desde tu perspectiva* first so that students can be looking for the information.
Ex. 1: Discuss the necessary qualities and then tie them in to people in the news. Students will tend to mention celebrities in sports and music.

Enrichment

Students can work in groups of three or four to research the name of a park, building, or street, and present their findings to the rest of the class.

Multiple Intelligences

Interpersonal/Social
See Enrichment.

Estatua de José Martí en el Central Park de Nueva York

Cultural Notes ☼

(p. 172, photo)
Rubén Darío, the Nicaraguan poet, once said that José Martí did not "belong to Cuba alone, but to all of humanity." Martí, both through his writings and his actions, spoke out against the oppression and suffering of all people. When he was nine, Martí accompanied his father to work in a Matanzas sugar cane field. There he saw slaves for the first time and began to learn about the Caribbean plantation system. He was horrified, and the outrage he experienced at that moment guided his actions throughout his life. As an adult he wrote a poem describing himself in Matanzas and his determination to help end the cruelty and suffering of slavery and exploitation. These are the last two stanzas of that poem, *Versos sencillos:*

*Rojo, como en el desierto,
Salió el sol al horizonte:
Y alumbró a un esclavo muerto,
Colgado a un ceibo del monte.*

*Un niño lo vió: tembló
De pasión por los que gimen:
¡Y, al pie del muerto, juró
Lavar con su vida el crimen!*

(from *José Martí: Revolutionary Democrat,* 1986)

Standards 1.1; 1.3; 3.1; 5.1   **173**

Preview

Overhead 29

Teaching Suggestions

A: You may want to add another question: Which ending do you think goes with *Uds. / ellos / ellas?* Which one with *Ud. / él / ella?*

Answers:

A The ending *-aban* is found on the verbs *caminar, usar, jugar,* and *cantar.* The ending *-aba* is found on the verb *tocar.*

B The verb is *iban* from the infinitive *ir.*

C The verbs are *vivir, hacer, comer,* and *divertirse.*

Gramática en contexto

¿Cómo era la época colonial?

Mucha gente vivía en fincas. La gente hacía su propia ropa y comía lo que la finca producía.

Los niños iban a la escuela a pie. Generalmente caminaban largas distancias para llegar allí.

Los niños usaban juguetes hechos a mano y jugaban con otros niños de la familia. Todos se divertían.

A menudo el padre o la madre le leía algo a la familia por la noche. Muchas veces alguien tocaba un instrumento y los otros cantaban o bailaban.

A When reading about what colonial families used to do, what endings do you find on the verbs *caminar, usar, jugar, tocar,* and *cantar?*

B Find the sentence that tells how children used to go to school. What is the verb? What is its infinitive form?

C The writer uses the words *vivía, hacía, comía,* and *se divertían.* What verbs do you think they come from?

174   Capítulo 5

Options

Strategies for Reaching All Students

Students Needing Extra Help
B: Begin the grammar section of the Organizer.
Students may have difficulty going from *iba* to *ir.*
El imperfecto de los verbos que terminan en -ar: The concept of two past tenses may be difficult. Give many examples: "When I was your age, I used to..."

Because the concept may be difficult but the forms relatively easy, emphasize the ease with which they will learn the endings. Emphasize keeping the subject pronoun.

Extended Written Practice/Homework
1. Choose four of these expressions and tell whether or not you and your friends or you and your family used to do them: *tocar un instrumento musical, cantar en un coro, jugar damas, jugar ajedrez, patinar sobre hielo.*
2. Write four sentences describing the behavior of your friends and/or your brothers and sisters when they were little. Use these verbs: *pelearse, molestar, portarse, llorar.*

174   **Standards** 1.2; 1.3; 3.1; 4.1

El imperfecto de los verbos que terminan en -ar

You have already learned to talk about the past using the preterite tense for actions that began and ended at a definite time.

> Ana **cantó** en la fiesta anoche.
> *Ana **sang** at the party last night.*

The imperfect tense is another way to talk about the past. We use it to describe past actions without any indication of their beginning or end.

> Ana **cantaba**.
> *Ana **was singing**.*

Esta niña venezolana se divierte mucho durante el recreo.

• We use the imperfect to talk about actions that happened repeatedly in the past. In English we often say "used to" or "would" to express this idea.

> Generalmente **caminaban** mucho.
> *Generally **they would walk** a lot.*

> **Jugaban** con otros niños de la familia.
> ***They used to play*** *with other children in the family.*

• Expressions such as *generalmente, a menudo, muchas veces, todos los días, siempre,* and *nunca* can cue us to use the imperfect.

Here are all the forms of *-ar* verbs in the imperfect. Notice the accent mark on the *nosotros* form.

caminar

(yo)	camin**aba**	(nosotros) (nosotras)	camin**ábamos**
(tú)	camin**abas**	(vosotros) (vosotras)	camin**abais**
Ud. (él) (ella)	camin**aba**	Uds. (ellos) (ellas)	camin**aban**

• Since the *yo* and the *Ud. / él / ella* forms are the same, we often use the subject pronouns to avoid confusion.

Gramática en contexto 175

Present

Teaching Suggestions

Make two columns, one titled "preterite" and the other "imperfect." Fill them in with the clue words for each tense.

3. Using *usar* or *llevar,* write three sentences telling what kinds of clothes different people used to wear.

Multiple Intelligences
Musical/Rhythmic
Have students create a rhythmic chant or rap to help remember the imperfect endings.
Verbal/Linguistic and Bodily/Kinesthetic
Have students make personalized verb form charts and use them to practice the imperfect tense.
Visual/Spatial
See Teaching Suggestions, Overhead 29, and Exs. A–C.

Present & Practice

Re-enter / Recycle
Ex. 1: sports from Chap. 4

Answers

1 ESTUDIANTE A

a ¿Qué deportes practicabas (tú) en la escuela primaria?

b. . . . practicaba tu madre. . .

c. . . . practicaban tú y tu hermano(a). . .

d. . . . practicaban tus hermanos(as) menores / mayores. . .

e. . . . practicaba tu abuelo(a). . .

f. . . . practicaban tus amigos(as). . .

g. Questions will vary, but look for the correct use of *practicar* in the imperfect.

ESTUDIANTE B

Answers will vary, but look for correct endings of *practicar* and a variety of appropriate sports.

a. Practicaba. . . .

b. Practicaba. . . .

c. Practicábamos. . . .

d. Practicaban. . . .

e. Practicaba. . . .

f. Practicaban. . . .

g. Answers will vary, but look for correct endings of *practicar.*

1 Con un(a) compañero(a), habla de los deportes que practicaban tú y otras personas en la escuela primaria.

tu padre

A —*¿Qué deportes practicaba tu padre en la escuela primaria?*

B —*Practicaba fútbol americano.*
   o: *No practicaba deportes.*

a. tú

b. tu madre

c. tú y tu hermano(a)

d. tus hermanos(as) menores / mayores

e. tu abuelo(a)

f. tus amigos(as)

g. 💡

2 Pregúntale a un(a) compañero(a) si hacía estas cosas a menudo cuando era pequeño(a).

patinar

A —*¿Patinabas a menudo cuando eras pequeño(a)?*

B —*Sí, patinaba todas las semanas.*
   o: *No, nunca patinaba.*

a. cantar

b. saltar a la cuerda

c. llorar

d. montar en triciclo

e. molestar a tus compañeros(as)

f. jugar con muñecos

g. 💡

Ahora, dile a otro estudiante una o dos cosas que tu compañero(a) hacía a menudo.

—*Miguel patinaba todas las semanas y jugaba con muñecos todos los días.*

176   Capítulo 5

Options

Strategies for Reaching All Students

Students Needing Extra Help

Ex. 1: Ask students to determine the meaning of the question in order to cement in the idea of "used to." Review sports vocabulary. Let students guess what parents or other adults used to do.

Ex. 2: Ask students to identify the clue words in the directions. Point out that this exercise consists of two parts.

El imperfecto de los verbos que terminan en -er e -ir: Stress the simplicity of these endings.

Give more examples of *haber.* Give an example with *hay* and *había: Hay un gato en el sofá. Había un gato en el sofá.*

Extended Written Practice/Homework

1. Write three sentences using *hacer* to tell who used to do the following: *ejercicios, rompecabezas, un picnic, crucigramas.*

2. Write three sentences describing the home of friends or relatives that you remember from your childhood. Use: *tener, vivir, había.*

El imperfecto de los verbos que terminan en -er e -ir

Here are all the forms of -er and -ir verbs in the imperfect. Note that they have the same pattern of endings. Notice the accent mark on each ending.

comer / vivir

(yo)	comía vivía	(nosotros) (nosotras)	comíamos vivíamos
(tú)	comías vivías	(vosotros) (vosotras)	comíais vivíais
Ud. (él) (ella)	comía vivía	Uds. (ellos) (ellas)	comían vivían

• The verb *ver* is irregular in the imperfect only because the endings are added to the stem *ve-*:

(yo)	veía	(nosotros) (nosotras)	veíamos
(tú)	veías	(vosotros) (vosotras)	veíais
Ud. (él) (ella)	veía	Uds. (ellos) (ellas)	veían

• *Haber* is a special verb because it has only one form. You already know the present-tense form, *hay* ("there is / are"). The imperfect form is *había* ("there was / were, there used to be").

En la escuela **había** un patio de recreo muy grande.
En mi casa **había** dos baños.

Present & Practice

Re-enter / Recycle
Ex. 4: daily routine from Chap. 2

Answers

3 ESTUDIANTE A
a. ¿Qué tenían tus tíos cuando tú eras pequeño(a)?
b. ¿Qué tenían tus primos...
c. ¿Qué tenías tú...
d. ¿Qué tenían tus hermanos y tú...
e. ¿Qué tenía tu vecino(a)...
f. Questions will vary.

ESTUDIANTE B
Answers will vary, but should include the following forms of *tener:*
a. Tenían...; b. Tenían...;
c. Tenía...; d. Teníamos...;
e. Tenía...; f. *Answers will vary.*

4 ESTUDIANTE A
a. ¿Uds. comían en la cafetería todos los días?
b. ...hacían fila antes de las clases?
c. ...veían videos en las clases?
d. ...leían libros en la biblioteca a menudo?
e. ...tenían tarea?
f. ...solían visitar museos?
g. ...escribían cartas a estudiantes de otras escuelas?
h. ...mentían mucho o siempre decían la verdad?
i. Answers will vary.

3 Túrnate con un(a) compañero(a) para hablar de lo que tenían estas personas cuando Uds. eran pequeños(as).

tus abuelos A —*¿Qué tenían tus abuelos cuando eras pequeño(a)?*
B —*Tenían un proyector de diapositivas.*

a. tus tíos   d. tus hermanos y tú
b. tus primos   e. tu vecino(a)
c. tú   f. 💡

4 Pregúntale a dos compañeros(as) qué hacían ellos (ellas) en la escuela primaria.

obedecer siempre A —*¿Uds. obedecían siempre a sus padres?*
a sus padres   B —*Sí, obedecíamos siempre a nuestros padres.*
                      o: No, desobedecíamos a menudo.

a. comer en la cafetería todos los días
b. hacer fila antes de las clases
c. ver videos en las clases
d. leer libros en la biblioteca a menudo
e. tener tarea
f. soler visitar museos
g. escribir cartas a estudiantes de otras escuelas
h. mentir mucho o siempre decir la verdad
i. 💡

Aquí hay un avión reactor, un Fórmula 1, un tren, una lancha motora, un camión, un robot y una nave espacial.

Aquí también.

MECCANO
El juguete de hacer juguetes

178   Capítulo 5

Options

Strategies for Reaching All Students

Students Needing Extra Help
Ex. 3: Review the model. Frame the exercise for students by saying: "When you were little, and you used to visit your grandparents, what things did they have that you used to play with or used to like to see?"
El imperfecto de los verbos ir *y* ser: Emphasize that the written accent mark is only on the *nosotros* form.
Have charts of all the different tenses of these two verbs posted around the room, with an example of usage.

178 Standards 1.1; 1.3

Enrichment
Ex. 5: As an additional assignment to review location vocabulary, students can choose three of the places named in this exercise and describe where they were located and how they or the people named used to go there. Encourage use of expressions such as *quedaba cerca / lejos de, enfrente / detrás de, a la izquierda / derecha de,* etc.

Extended Written Practice/Homework
1. Write three sentences telling how often or where you and your friends (or you and your family) used to do the following: *ir de compras, ir a fiestas, ir a la playa.*
2. Write three sentences describing characters from TV or comic strips that you remember from your childhood: *Godzilla y King Kong eran muy feos y antipáticos.*
3. Write three sentences describing relatives, friends, or famous people from the past: *Helen Keller era una mujer muy atrevida.*

l imperfecto de los verbos *ir* y *ser*

he verbs *ir* and *ser* are irregular in the imperfect. Here are all
eir imperfect forms:

(yo)	iba	(nosotros) (nosotras)	íbamos
(tú)	ibas	(vosotros) (vosotras)	ibais
Ud. (él) (ella)	iba	Uds. (ellos) (ellas)	iban

er

(yo)	era	(nosotros) (nosotras)	éramos
(tú)	eras	(vosotros) (vosotras)	erais
Ud. (él) (ella)	era	Uds. (ellos) (ellas)	eran

Usa las dos listas para decir adónde iban a menudo tú
y otras personas cuando eran pequenos(as).

Cuando yo era pequeño(a), iba a menudo a la biblioteca.

a. yo — la biblioteca
b. mi hermano(a) — la escuela
c. mi hermano(a) y yo — la tienda cerca de mi casa
d. mi primo(a) — el centro comercial
e. mis primos(as) — el parque
f. mi vecino(a) — el cine
g. mis vecinos(as) — el supermercado
h.

PASO CULTURAL
La ciudad de San Sebastián es la capital de Güipúzcoa, una de las provincias vascas en el norte de España. San Sebastián tiene algo para todos: bonitas playas, restaurantes, museos, acuarios, palacios y, para los niños, un bonito parque de diversiones en lo alto del Monte Igueldo. También es famosa por dos festivales internacionales que se celebran allí todos los años, uno de cine y otro de jazz. ¿Qué lugares en los Estados Unidos ofrecen algo para todos, como San Sebastián? ¿Qué hay en esos lugares?

Algunas plazas tienen área de recreo, como ésta en San Sebastián, España.

Gramática en contexto   179

Cultural Notes

(p. 178, realia)
Toy model construction kits were patented by Frank Hornby of Liverpool, England in 1901. His original company, *Meccano,* has been producing kits since that time. Over the years they have been produced and marketed in various parts of the world, including the U.S., Spain, and Argentina. This Spanish ad suggests that, with this single toy, a child really has many different toys at the same time.

Paso cultural
Answers will vary.

(p. 179, photo)
These children in San Sebastián, España, are enjoying the swings in a park playlot. San Sebastián, whose inhabitants are known as *donostiarras,* has substantial manufacturing, chemical and metallurgical industries. The city is famous for its beautiful bay and was one of Ernest Hemingway's favorite locations in Europe.

Practice

Re-enter / Recycle
Ex. 7: daily routine from Chap. 2

Answers

6 Answers will vary, but should follow the format and include:
a. Mi . . . era muy maleducada, pero ahora es bastante educada.
b. . . . tímido(a) / sociable.
c. . . . antipático(a) / simpático(a).
d. . . . desobediente / obediente.
e. . . . gracioso(a) / serio(a).
f. Answers will vary, but look for agreement of adjectives.

7 Answers will vary, but may include the following verbs:
a. Cuando era pequeño(a) hacía la cama. Y ahora todavía hago la cama.
b. . . . sacaba / saco. . .
c. . . . lavaba / lavo. . .
d. . . . limpiaba / limpio. . .
e. . . . pasaba / paso. . .
f. . . . sacudía / sacudo. . .
g. Answers will vary.

8 Answers will vary, but should follow the format:
Ahora hay. . .
Cuando era pequeño(a) había. . .

---

6 Describe cómo han cambiado *(have changed)* tú, otras personas de tu familia, tus amigos(as) y tus vecinos(as). Por ejemplo:

travieso(a)
> *Mi vecino Jorge era muy travieso, pero ahora es bastante obediente.*
> o: *Mi vecino Jorge era muy travieso y todavía es bastante travieso.*

a. maleducado(a)   d. desobediente
b. tímido(a)   e. gracioso(a)
c. antipático(a)   f. 💡

7 Con un(a) compañero(a), compara lo que haces en casa ahora con lo que hacías en casa cuando eras pequeño(a). Puedes usar estas expresiones u otras:

poner la mesa
> *Cuando era pequeño(a) ponía la mesa. Y ahora todavía la pongo.*
> o: *Pero ahora debo pasar la aspiradora una vez por semana.*

a. hacer la cama
b. sacar la basura
c. lavar el suelo de la cocina
d. limpiar mi dormitorio
e. pasar la aspiradora
f. sacudir los muebles
g. 💡

8 Di qué hay en tu casa ahora que es diferente de lo que había antes. Por ejemplo:

Ahora hay un sofá blanco de cuero en mi casa. Cuando era pequeño(a) había un sofá negro de lona.

Un muchacho hondureño muestra a su hermanito cómo montar en bicicleta.

180   Capítulo 5

Options

Strategies for Reaching All Students

Students Needing Extra Help
Ex. 6: Brainstorm more possibilities. Have students make a list of who they will use as the subject of their sentences. Point out that in this exercise and in Ex. 7, each sentence contains a verb in the imperfect and one in the present tense.
Ex. 8: Brainstorm things that might have been different in their homes when they were little: furniture, color of walls, etc. If available, use the Organizers from Book 1, Chap. 8.

Ahora lo sabes: Have students write out this list so that they can record what they have mastered.

Enrichment
Ex. 7: Students can also tell each other which chores they liked doing as children and why they enjoyed them.

Cooperative Learning
Divide the class into groups of three of four. Have each group construct a composite diary that recalls the students' experiences as young children. Each group member should supply at least two entries for the diary. Entries shouldn't exceed one or two sentences and need not be real remembrances. Have a volunteer in each group record the entries. Afterward, the remaining group members can take turns reading their group's diary to the class.

Unas niñas españolas saltan a la cuerda delante de su casa en Andalucía.

Ahora lo sabes

Can you:

■ talk about your life as a child?

—De pequeño(a) ____ en
un apartamento muy pequeño.
Me ____ jugar con trenes.

■ tell what people used to do regularly?

—Los vecinos ____ de lunes a viernes.
Y los fines de semana ____ de pesca.

■ compare what people used to do with what they do now?

—Cuando ____ pequeño(a), yo ____
los platos. Ahora ____ la comida.

Este mes
CRECER feliz
LA REVISTA DE LOS NUEVOS PADRES · Nº 45 · MARZO 1992 · 300 PTAS.

• TU PELO, TU SONRISA...
¿Qué heredará
tu hijo de ti?

• JUGUETES
INTELIGENTES
Informática
para bebés

92 PAPILLAS
PARA ELEGIR
LA MEJOR

• SUS DIBUJOS
HABLAN
Aprende a
descifrarlos

• ALERGIAS
Cómo afectan
al embarazo

REGALO
Cuchara-tren

REGALO
Una cuchara
para comidas muy divertidas

MORE PRACTICE

- Más práctica y tarea, pp. 541–542
- Practice Workbook 5–5, 5–9

Gramática en contexto   181

Answers: Ahora lo sabes
• vivía / gustaba
• trabajaban / iban
• era / lavaba / hago or preparo

 **Practice Wkbk. 5-8,
5-9**

 **Audio Activities 5.4,
5.5**

 **Writing Activities
5-G, 5-H**

 Prueba 5-7

 Comm. Act. BLM 5-2

 **Pasos vivos 2
CD-ROM**
Phone Task, Slide Presentation
Maker, Spindle, Treadmill

Using Realia
Having students use reading
strategies they've learned thus far,
ask: *¿De qué se trata esta revista?
¿Cuáles son las palabras que te
ayudaron a saberlo?*

Multiple Intelligences
Interpersonal/Social and Visual/Spatial
See Cooperative Learning.
Verbal/Linguistic
See Audio Activities 5.4 and 5.5 and
Enrichment.
Visual/Spatial
See Practice Wkbk. 5-8 and 5-9, Writing
Activities 5-G and 5-H, and Comm. Act.
BLM 5-2.

Cultural Notes ☀

(p. 181, photo)
These two girls are skipping rope on a cobblestone street in Casares, near Estepona,
Andalucía, about 75 kilometers south of
Málaga on the Costa del Sol. Brilliant white
walls are a common sight in southern
Spain, reflecting the intense Mediterranean
sunlight. Residents whitewash *(blanquear)*
the exterior walls of their homes using a
solution of *cal* (lime) and water.

(p. 181, realia)
This monthly magazine published in Spain
reflects contemporary interest in child care
and child development. Directed toward new
and prospective parents, this issue carries
articles on such topics as inherited characteristics and how to interpret a child's artwork.

Apply

Actividades

1 Cada estudiante debe traer una foto de cuando era pequeño(a) o una foto de alguna revista. Pongan todas las fotos en una bolsa y escojan una. Según la foto van a inventar cómo era y qué hacía ese (esa) niño(a). Escriban un informe y léanlo en clase.

Este niño era muy... Lloraba...

2 ¿Cómo era tu comunidad hace 50 o 100 años? En grupo, investiguen sobre:

- las casas
- los trabajos
- la comida
- la ropa
- los pasatiempos
- los deportes
- el transporte

Preparen un informe para la clase. Pueden usar la selección de la página 174 como modelo e incluir dibujos o fotos de revistas. Por ejemplo:

En nuestra comunidad, había muy pocas casas...

182   Capítulo 5

Options

Strategies for Reaching All Students

Spanish-Speaking Students
Ex. 2: After this exercise, have students do this assignment: *Prepara una cápsula que se va a abrir en el futuro. ¿Qué te gustaría incluir en ella para indicar cómo era tu familia, cómo eras tú y cómo vivías? Explica por qué escogiste cada artículo.*

Students Needing Extra Help
Ex. 1: Using magazine pictures is a good alternative to having students bring in their own pictures: some may not have any or won't want to bring them in. Have extra magazine photos available.
Brainstorm possible characteristics and verbs that would apply to children.
Ex. 2: Divide the class into three groups and assign them specific areas. Have resources available or give them a few days to investigate.

Enrichment
Ex. 2: Additional topics to investigate: *¿Cómo eran las escuelas en tu comunidad? ¿Las tiendas? ¿Qué cosas no había en la biblioteca que sí hay ahora?*

Conexiones

Las ciencias sociales

Ayer y hoy

Vas a hacer una comparación entre la época colonial y la de hoy.

1 Mira con un(a) compañero(a) las escenas de la época colonial de la página 174. Copia esta red *(web)* de categorías en una hoja de papel.

Escoge con tu compañero(a) dos categorías de la red. Cada uno debe escribir una frase para cada categoría escogida. Lean las frases. Por ejemplo:

Categoría: Los muebles
Los muebles eran . . . (No) había . . . La gente . . .

2 Con tu compañero(a) vas a hacer una red para hablar de lo que pasa ahora. Deben escribir "Ahora" en el centro, escoger dos de las categorías y seguir los mismos pasos que en la red anterior. Por ejemplo:

Los muebles son . . . (No) hay . . . Nosotros . . .

3 Completen todas las categorías de las dos redes. Después, escojan las dos comparaciones mejores y léanlas a la clase.

Todo junto   183

Answers: Conexiones
1–3 Answers will vary, but look for use of chapter vocabulary and logical information regarding the historical eras.

 La Catrina: Capítulo 5

Play

 Video Activity B

 Para entender mejor

Play

 Video Activity C

 Writing Activities 5-I, 5-J

 Comm. Act. BLMs 5-3, 5-4, 5-5

 Pasos vivos 2 CD-ROM
A Jugar, Laboratorio de grabar, Maps, Video Monitor, Video Presentation Maker

Multiple Intelligences
Logical/Mathematical
See *Conexiones.*
Naturalist
Have students research and write a brief paragraph (using the imperfect) that describes their town or area in the past. How has the land or area changed?
Visual/Spatial
See Using the Video, Writing Activities 5-I and 5-J, and Comm. Act. BLMs 5-3, 5-4, and 5-5.

Standards 1.1; 1.2; 2.1; 3.1; 3.2; 4.2; 5.2   **183**

Apply

Process Reading
For a description of process reading, see p. 52.

Teaching Suggestions
You may want to set parameters and time limits for this activity. Each group could choose one or two topics and write two to three sentences about each. You could also assign a topic to each group to answer on a given day.

Multicultural Perspectives
Baseball is especially popular in the Caribbean countries of Cuba, the Dominican Republic, and Puerto Rico. Many players from these countries have become major leaguers in the U.S. The Dominican Republic has produced more professional major leaguers than any other Latin American country. Quisqueya Stadium in the capital of Santo Domingo is the national center of baseball. Young players aspire to be seen there by a scout from the U.S. Ask students if they can name any U.S. baseball players from the Dominican Republic.

¡Vamos a leer!

Antes de leer

STRATEGY ▸ Using prior knowledge

Have you ever known a really amazing athlete? What was he or she like? What information would you expect to find in the life story of an outstanding athlete? How is a biography usually organized?

El campeón

—¡Roberto! ¡Roberto, ven! ¡Ya es hora de comer!

El pequeño Roberto no prestaba atención. Era un muchacho obediente, pero en ese momento, sólo pensaba en lo que hacía—jugar béisbol.

Roberto Clemente nació en 1934 en la pequeña comunidad de Carolina, Puerto Rico. Jugaba béisbol todos los días, pero también tenía que ir a la escuela y trabajar. Trabajaba porque quería comprarse una bicicleta. Después de trabajar tres años, tuvo bastante dinero para comprarse una. En la escuela secundaria, Roberto era un muchacho tímido, pero en el campo de béisbol su timidez desaparecía.

En 1953 representantes de los Brooklyn Dodgers fueron a

Puerto Rico para observar y contratar a nuevos jugadores. —¡Tenía que contratarlo! Era el mejor atleta innato que había visto,— dijo el scout de los Dodgers cuando vio al joven Roberto jugar. Los Dodgers lo mandaron a su equipo de Montreal, Canadá. De allí pasó a los Piratas de Pittsburgh en 1955. Cinco años más tarde los Piratas ganaron el campeonato de la Liga Nacional y la Serie Mundial. Clemente fue nombrado el Jugador Más Valioso de la liga en 1966. El 24 de julio de 1970 se celebró la Noche de Roberto Clemente en el estadio Three Rivers de Pittsburgh para honrar al pelotero más famoso y más querido del equipo.

En diciembre de 1972, ocurrió un terrible terremoto en

184   Capítulo 5

Mira la lectura
Read the story through quickly. Did you find the information you expected?

Esta estatua de Roberto Clemente queda enfrente del estadio en Pittsburgh.

Nicaragua. En seguida Clemente organizó un vuelo de ayuda. Llevaba alimentos, ropa y medicina para las víctimas del desastre. El avión era viejo y pequeño y pesaba mucho, pero Clemente insistió en ir.

Cuando desapareció el avión en el mar poco antes de la medianoche del 31 de diciembre, murió no sólo un gran atleta sino un gran hombre.

Options

Strategies for Reaching All Students

Students Needing Extra Help
Antes de leer: As a class, generate a list of what students might expect to find in the life story of an outstanding athlete. Have them check off the items as they find them.
Infórmate: Students may have some difficulty recognizing the verb tense and making the connection with age and high school. After each entry on the list generated for *Antes de leer,* have students fill in Clemente's age.

Aplicación: Emphasize that the preterite is used for events in the past that have a definite beginning and end and that the imperfect is used to describe.
Have students form small groups to figure out the name of the person being described. Then have them list the person's accomplishments. They may need help putting the words into sentences.

Infórmate

STRATEGY > Recognizing time expressions

Time expressions will help you understand writing that is organized chronologically, as a biography usually is. Some of the time expressions in this biography are:

- ...en 1934...
- Cinco años más tarde...
- En diciembre de 1972...

Other expressions can help you to keep track of time by referring to activities associated with a certain stage of life. For example:

- ...tenía que ir a la escuela...
- En la escuela secundaria,...

1. Now reread the biography. When you come to an expression that helps you fix the time, stop and quickly calculate how old Roberto was then.

2. Why is Roberto Clemente one of baseball's most honored players? Why is he considered a great humanitarian?

Managua, Nicaragua

La ciudad de Managua después del terremoto de 1972

BOB CLEMENTE — OUTFIELD PIRATES

18

Aplicación

Write three to five sentences with time expressions about a famous athlete or other famous person. Then read one sentence to a partner and ask him or her to guess who it is about. If your partner can't guess, read the next sentence, and so on. For example, these statements are about Nancy López.

1. Ganó el Torneo de Golf Femenino de Nuevo México cuando tenía 12 años.
2. En 1978 ganó nueve torneos de golf, entre ellos el de la Asociación de Mujeres Golfistas Profesionales (LPGA en Inglés).
3. Siete años después, ganó cinco torneos, entre ellos el LPGA una vez más.

¡Vamos a leer!   185

Answers
Antes de leer
Answers will vary, but students may say they'd expect to find details of the athlete's childhood, how he became an outstanding athlete, and his current statistics. Students may say a biography is usually organized chronologically.

Mira la lectura
Answers will vary.

Infórmate
2. Answers will vary, but students may say that Clemente was one of baseball's most honored players because of his role in helping the Pirates win the World Series in 1960. He was considered a great humanitarian because he organized relief efforts for the victims of the earthquake in Nicaragua in 1972.

Aplicación
Answers will vary.

www Internet Activities

Cultural Notes

(p. 184, photo)
Artist Susan Wagner's 12-foot-high bronze sculpture of Roberto Clemente, located at Three Rivers Stadium in Pittsburgh, was dedicated at the start of the 1994 All Star Games hosted by the Pirates. 1994 would have marked Clemente's 60th birthday and is the 22nd year since his death. Clemente wears a sleeveless 1960s uniform and is rendered in an action pose, dropping his special knobless bat after a hit. The black granite base of the statue reads "The Great One" and a baseball field design below his feet incorporates soil from Puerto Rico (first base), the old Forbes Field ball park (second base), and Three Rivers Stadium (third base). A timeline encircles the base with highlights from Clemente's career. However, the section between third base and home is left blank to symbolize the incompleteness of Clemente's life.

(p. 185, realia)
Roberto Clemente's early baseball cards remain a favorite among collectors. A 1955 Roberto Clemente "rookie" card in mint condition sells for about $2,000 on the market today. Clemente's second year (1956) card earns as much as $400. Clemente's cards are popular in part because of the star's reputation for generosity and kindness.

Apply

Process Writing
For information regarding developing a writing portfolio, see p. 54.

see p. 54.

Todo junto

¡Vamos a escribir!

Todos tenemos una persona especial en la vida. Puede ser un(a) pariente(a), un(a) amigo(a) o un(a) profesor(a). Vamos a escribir una biografía breve de una persona especial.

1 Primero entrevista a la persona o a alguien que la conoce. Contesta estas preguntas:

- ¿Cuándo y dónde nació?
- ¿Dónde vivía la familia cuando nació?
- ¿Cómo era de pequeño(a)?
- ¿Qué hacía de pequeño(a)? ¿De joven?
- ¿Cómo es ahora?
- ¿Qué hace ahora?

2 Organiza tus ideas en orden cronológico. Escribe el primer borrador. Sigue los pasos del proceso de escribir.

Ahora escribe una anécdota de la vida de la persona que escogiste. Debe ser una anécdota que revele algo de su carácter. Por ejemplo, ¿hizo alguna vez algo muy difícil? ¿Algo increíble?

3 Para distribuir las biografías y anécdotas, pueden:

- enviarlas a las personas de quienes escribieron
- enviarlas al periódico o a la revista literaria escolar
- incluirlas en un libro titulado *Personas especiales*
- ponerlas en sus portafolios

Un gaucho de San Antonio de Areco, Argentina

Entrevista con un gaucho

ESTUDIANTE	¿Qué es un gaucho?
GAUCHO	Somos vaqueros.
ESTUDIANTE	¿La ropa que usa es típica?
GAUCHO	Sí. El poncho, el sombrero negro, los pantalones flojos, el cinturón de plata y las botas son muy típicos.

186   Capítulo 5

Options

Strategies for Reaching All Students

Students Needing Extra Help
Ex. 1: Point out that three tenses are being used. Use the verb charts in the room, or if available, from Organizers from Book 1. Students will need help formulating sentences. Model, using yourself.
Ex. 2: Explain that an anecdote is a short account of an interesting or funny incident in someone's life. Some suggestions for topics: a friend who helped someone, a student who won an award, an athlete who scored the winning basket.

Enrichment
Point out that when speaking to their grandparents, many Spanish speakers use the *Ud.* form as a sign of respect.

Entrevista con mi abuela

○	NIETA	¿Dónde vivía tu familia cuando naciste?
	ABUELA	Aquí en esta misma vecindad. Sólo a unas cuadras de donde vivo hoy.
○	NIETA	¿Qué hacías cuando eras niña?
	ABUELA	Recuerdo que iba a recoger flores y frutas con mis hermanos. A mi mamá—tu bisabuela—le encantaba tener flores frescas en la casa.
○		

Una niña en los brazos de su abuelita en Argentina

Un ecuatoriano en camino a su trabajo

Entrevista con un profesor de español

○	ESTUDIANTE	¿Puede Ud. decirme cuándo y dónde nació?
	SR. ALLENDE	Nací en Ecuador. Ayer cumplí 30 años. ¡Tú puedes calcular el año!
	ESTUDIANTE	¿Qué hacía de pequeño?
○	SR. ALLENDE	A mí y a mis amigos nos encantaba montar en bicicleta. También pasábamos muchas horas pescando.

Cultural Notes

(p. 186, photo)
Gauchos are part of the national identity of Argentina. They represent freedom, independence, and strength. *Gauchos* are the cowboys who work on the *pampas,* herding cattle and doing other agricultural work. Some *gauchos* claim to have both Spanish and indigenous parentage and thus are among Argentina's small *mestizo* population. The modern *gaucho* in this photo leans on a pick-up truck instead of a horse.

(p. 187, top photo)
This girl and her grandmother are residents of Tucumán, a province in northern Argentina. The capital of the province, also called Tucumán, played a significant role in the history of Argentina. In 1816, members of the Congreso General Constituyente met there to proclaim their independence from Spain.

Assess & Summarize

Test Preparation

You may want to assign parts of this section as homework or as an in-class writing activity prior to administering the *Examen de habilidades*.

Answers

Listening: *De pequeña yo lloraba mucho y me peleaba con los otros niños. Era una niña muy traviesa y desobediente. Mi hermana, al contrario, se portaba bien y nunca se peleaba con nadie. Creo que es porque ella fue a una guardería infantil y yo no.*

Tina cried a lot and fought with other children; she was mischievous and disobedient. Her sister was polite and never fought with anyone. They were probably different because her sister went to a daycare center and Tina didn't.

Reading: d, a, c

Writing: Descriptions will vary.

Culture: Answers will vary.

Speaking: Dialogues will vary.

Esta sección te ayudará a prepararte para el examen de habilidades.

Listening

Can you understand when people talk about what they were like as children? Listen as your teacher reads a sample similar to what you will hear on the test. How were Tina and her sister different? Why were they different?

Reading

Read the following fragment of an autobiography. Then complete the sentences with the right time expressions. (One choice will not be used.)

Cuando yo era niño, mi mamá me hacía animales de peluche. Mi papá me hacía juguetes de madera. ___ me hizo una casa de madera en un árbol. Yo no entendía por qué mis padres no me compraban juguetes de plástico, como los de mis compañeros. ___ por fin entendí. Estudiamos el medio ambiente y la importancia de reciclar los materiales. Mis padres estaban reciclando las cosas. ___ yo también hago juguetes de madera para mi hija.

188   Capítulo 5

Writing

Clara is going to spend a year in Guatemala as an exchange student. A Guatemala City newspaper has asked for a brief description of her as a child. This is what a long-time friend wrote. Write a similar description of *your* best friend.

> Recuerdo que Clara era una niña muy simpática y trabajadora. Cuando no conocía a la gente, era un poco tímida, pero después era sociable. Éramos vecinos. Íbamos a la misma escuela. Los fines de semana jugábamos en el parque. Yo sé que Clara va a tener muchos amigos en Guatemala.

Culture

If you had been a friend of José Martí, would you have helped him fight for Cuban independence? Why?

Speaking

With a partner, talk about your childhood. Ask one another some questions to find out what you were like as young children. Here is a sample dialogue.

A —*Cuando tenías cinco años, ¿cómo eras?*
B —*Obediente pero a veces un poco travieso. ¿Y tú?*
A —*Casi siempre me portaba bien, pero también era traviesa. ¿Con qué te gustaba jugar?*
B —*Me gustaban los bloques, los trenes eléctricos y las pistolas de agua. ¿Qué preferías tú?*
A —*A mí me encantaba montar en triciclo y saltar a la cuerda.*

a. cuando estaba en la escuela secundaria
b. el año pasado
c. ahora
d. cuando cumplí ocho años

Self Test www.pasoapaso.com

Options

Strategies for Reaching All Students

Students Needing Extra Help

Have students write out this section so that they can check off what they have mastered. Remind students that this is just a sample of what will be on the test.
Listening: Read the listening sample more than once. Remind students that they only have to listen for two pieces of information. Brainstorm the words for which students should be listening.

Reading: Emphasize that one choice won't be used. Review the meanings of the choices. Put the choices in chronological order: eight years old, high school, last year, and now. This should help them as they try to connect the reading material to the time that it happened. See if students can recognize that one choice is a preterite.
Writing: Have students use the Organizer and write a sample description before the

test as practice. Brainstorm other description words. If available, use the Organizers from Book 1.
Culture: Have students review any notes they took during their reading of the *Perspectiva cultural*. Discuss the pros and cons of joining forces with Martí.
Speaking: Limit the number of lines of dialogue. Use the vocabulary section of the Organizer.

Resumen del vocabulario

Usa el vocabulario de este capítulo para:

- tell what you were like as a child
- tell what you used to like to do
- talk about what you learned to do

to talk about animals
el animal, *pl.* los animales
el pájaro
el pez, *pl.* los peces
la tortuga

to talk about people
de pequeño, -a
el niño, la niña
el vecino, la vecina
obediente
desobediente
(bien) educado, -a
maleducado, -a
consentido, -a
tímido, -a
travieso, -a

to name toys
el juguete
la muñeca
el muñeco
el robot, *pl.* los robots
el animal de peluche, *pl.* los
  animales de peluche
el oso de peluche
el dinosaurio
el camión, *pl.* los camiones
el tren (de juguete)
el bloque
la pistola (de agua)

to discuss things you used to do
ser: (yo) era, (tú) eras
caminar
montar en triciclo
el triciclo
saltar (a la cuerda)
la cuerda
ir: (yo) iba, (tú) ibas
recordar *(o → ue)*
coleccionar
la colección, *pl.* las colecciones
la verdad
mentir *(e → ie)*
obedecer *(c → zc)*
desobedecer *(c → zc)*
portarse (bien / mal)
molestar
pelearse (con)
llorar

to talk about places children go
la guardería infantil
el kindergarten
la escuela primaria

to talk about playground equipment
el patio de recreo
el cajón de arena, *pl.* los
  cajones de arena
el carrusel
el columpio
el sube y baja
el tobogán, *pl.* los toboganes

Resumen 189

Assessment

 Prueba cumulativa

 Examen de habilidades

 Test Generator

Additional Assessment Options

 Comm. Act. BLMs

Small Group Activities
Situation Cards

 Pasos vivos 2 CD-ROM

Slide Presentation Maker, Video
Presentation Maker, Word
Processor, Spindle

 ¿Lo sabes bien? Video Quiz

www **Internet Activities**
Self-Test

CAPÍTULO 6

THEME: SPECIAL OCCASIONS

SCOPE AND SEQUENCE Pages 190–221

COMMUNICATION

Topics

Family celebrations

Extended family members

Holidays

Objectives

To discuss how one culture can influence another

To discuss celebrations

To identify family members

To talk about holidays

To greet people and say good-by

CULTURE

How cultures adopt, often in altered forms, aspects and traditions of other cultures

GRAMMAR

El pretérito de los verbos e → i

El pretérito del verbo dar

Otros usos del imperfecto

Los verbos reflexivos recíprocos

Ancillaries available for use with Chapter 6

Multisensory/Technology

 Overheads, 30–34

 Audio Tapes and CDs

 Vocabulary Art Blackline Masters for Hands-On Learning, pp. 33–37/CD-ROM

 Classroom Crossword

 La Catrina

 Pasos vivos 2 CD-ROM

 Internet Activities www.pasoapaso.com

Print

 Practice Workbook, pp. 55–65

 Writing, Audio & Video Activities, pp. 35–40, 108–110, 161–162

 Communicative Activity Blackline Masters

Pair and Small Group Activities, pp. 36–41

Situation Cards, p. 42

 Un paso más: Actividades para ampliar tu español, pp. 31–36

RESOURCE⊙PRO®

Planning Express, Teaching Resources Library, and Clip Art Library

Assessment

 Assessment Program

Pruebas, pp. 85–95

Examen de habilidades, pp. 96–99

 Test Generator

 ¿Lo sabes bien? Video Quiz

Video still from Chap. 6

Los días de fiesta

Some holidays are celebrated differently in Latin America and Spain than in the U.S. *La Nochebuena,* or Christmas Eve, is when most of the Spanish-speaking world celebrates Christmas. January 6, *el Día de los Reyes,* marks the formal end of the Christmas holidays because it is believed that on this date the three Wise Men arrived in Bethlehem. In Puerto Rico, it marks the last in a series of parties and is often held outdoors. *El Año Nuevo,* which falls in the summer in the southern hemisphere, is celebrated with fireworks in many parts of Latin America.

Unlike in the U.S., Mother's Day is always celebrated on May 10 in Spain and Latin America, regardless of the day of the week it falls on. Spanish-speaking countries also tend to celebrate *el Día de los Abuelos* and *el Día del Niño,* and the dates can vary from country to country.

Columbus Day is generally known as *el Día de la Raza.* The holiday honors the blending of the Spanish and indigenous cultures. In some Spanish-speaking countries it is also referred to as *el Día de la Hispanidad,* recognizing the impact of the Spanish culture on the American continent. In recent years, it has lost standing as a holiday in favor of holidays of greater national meaning: September 15 is *el Día de la Independencia* for Guatemala, Honduras, El Salvador, Nicaragua, and Costa Rica. Paraguay celebrates its independence from Spain on May 14; Venezuela, July 5; Argentina, July 9; Colombia, July 20; Peru, July 28; Bolivia, August 6; Ecuador, August 10; and Uruguay, August 25.

Extended families and close friends often get together during these *fiestas patrias.* In Chile, for example, Independence Day (September 18) may be celebrated with a *parrillada,* where a variety of grilled meats and *empanadas de pino* (turnovers of ground beef) are served.

In contrast, *Carnaval,* which corresponds somewhat to Mardi Gras, is a celebration that draws large crowds. Perhaps one of the most famous *Carnavales* is held in Oruro, Bolivia. Both indigenous and Spanish elements are present as throngs of spectators watch costumed dancers wind their way through the streets as a form of pilgrimage in honor of *la Virgen Morena.*

Introduce

Re-entry of Concepts

The following list represents words, expressions, and grammar topics re-entered from Book 1 and Book 2 (Chaps. 2–5):

Book 1
numbers 0–31, calendar terms, *gustar* expressions, foods, family members, clothing, formal clothing

Chapter 2
daily routine

Chapter 3
clothing

Chapter 4
leisure activities

Chapter 5
toys

190   Capítulo 6

Planning

Cross-Curricular Connections

Sociology Connection *(pp. 194–195)*
As homework, have students interview their own families to find out where their grandparents and great-grandparents came from, and where their aunts, uncles, cousins, nieces, or nephews live today. Have them share this information with the class.

Language Arts Connection *(pp. 198–199)*
Have students write a letter to a Spanish-speaking pen pal, describing how they celebrate Thanksgiving. Have them include which family members are present, which foods are served, and any traditional activities they participate in. When completed, have them seal the letter in an envelope and give it to you. The next day, pass out the envelopes at random. Have students read the letters and try to guess who wrote them.

Spanish in Your Community
Many shops offer greeting cards in Spanish. Have students visit stores in their community to see if they can find cards celebrating *cumpleaños, quinceañera, bautismo,* or other occasions. Encourage them to purchase a card to share with the class or place on a bulletin board.

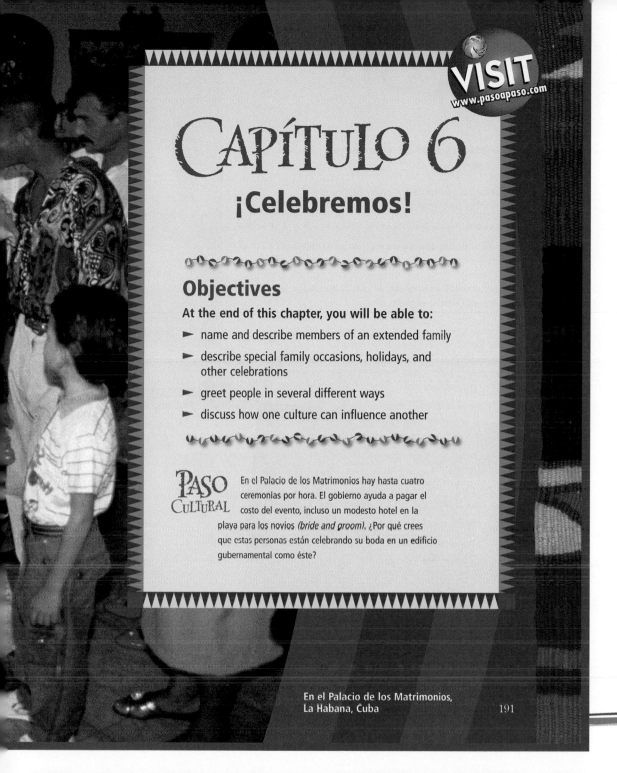

CAPÍTULO 6
¡Celebremos!

Objectives
At the end of this chapter, you will be able to:

► name and describe members of an extended family

► describe special family occasions, holidays, and other celebrations

► greet people in several different ways

► discuss how one culture can influence another

PASO CULTURAL
En el Palacio de los Matrimonios hay hasta cuatro ceremonias por hora. El gobierno ayuda a pagar el costo del evento, incluso un modesto hotel en la playa para los novios *(bride and groom)*. ¿Por qué crees que estas personas están celebrando su boda en un edificio gubernamental como éste?

En el Palacio de los Matrimonios,
La Habana, Cuba

191

VISIT
www.pasoapaso.com

Cultural Notes

Paso cultural
Los matrimonios en Cuba generalmente son civiles porque las iglesias perdieron muchas de sus funciones después de la revolución de Castro. Los palacios de matrimonios (hay catorce en la Habana) son edificios elegantes y el costo de la boda es bajo.

(pp. 190–191, photo)
Although every municipality in Cuba has its own *Palacio de matrimonios*, the most famous and beloved is the one on Calle Paseo in La Habana Vieja. Approximately every two hours a wedding takes place in this ornate colonial building, which was originally a theater. Family and friends gather to watch the ceremony and take pictures, and then the group moves elsewhere for the reception.

Preview

Cultural Objective
• To discuss how holidays are celebrated in Spanish-speaking countries

**Critical Thinking:
Summarizing Information**
Discuss with students similarities and / or differences they see between typical families in the U.S. and those depicted in the photos.

¡Piensa en la CULTURA!

Una familia (1989), Fernando Botero

Familias en las obras de Goya, Picasso y Botero

**Mira las pinturas. ¿Cómo son estas familias?
¿Qué diferencias ves en estas pinturas?**

PASO CULTURAL

En los cuadros, dibujos y esculturas del artista colombiano Fernando Botero (1932–), casi todas las figuras son redondas, enormes y sin emoción. Botero dice que con este estilo quiere comunicar la igualdad *(sameness)* de las cosas. Para ti, ¿qué está comunicando el artista en este cuadro?

Muchos de los cuadros del artista español Francisco de Goya (1746–1828) presentan escenas de la aristocracia y la familia real *(royal)* española. Sus cuadros son famosos por su variedad y su realismo. En tu opinión, ¿cuál de estos tres cuadros es el más realista? ¿Por qué crees eso?

Cultural Exploration
www.pasoapaso.com
Visit these countries on-line

Carlos IV y su familia (1800), Francisco de Goya

192   Capítulo 6

Options

Strategies for Reaching All Students

Spanish-Speaking Students
Ask *¿Cuáles son los días de fiesta que celebra tu familia? ¿Y tu comunidad? ¿Se reúne mucha gente? ¿Por qué son tan importantes (y tan divertidas) estas celebraciones?*

 Un paso más 6-A

Cultural Notes ☀

(p. 192, top photo)
Colombian painter and sculptor Fernando Botero (b. 1932) is a native of Medellín. Botero's early career was spent abroad, studying and traveling in Europe, Latin America, and the U.S. As his work matured, he turned to the daily life, religious myths, and folk art of Colombia. Here he depicts a middle-class family in a surrealistic setting with his typically humorous disregard of normal proportion.

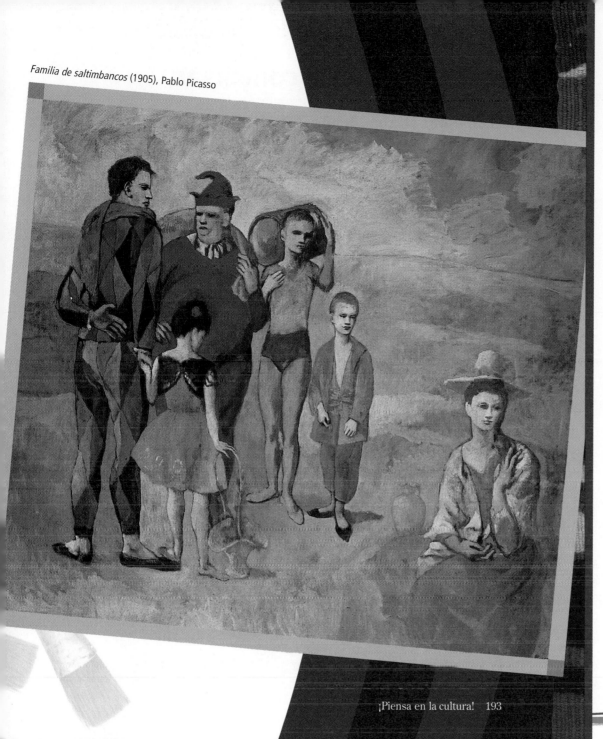

Familia de saltimbancos (1905), Pablo Picasso

¡Piensa en la cultura!   193

(p. 192, bottom photo)
Goya rendered this painting of Carlos IV (1748–1819), King of Spain (1788–1808) and his wife, Queen María Luisa, shown here surrounded by family members. The King's eldest son Ferdinand, in blue, stands to the left. The woman next to Ferdinand, with her face averted, represents his yet-to-be-chosen bride. María Luisa is flanked by her youngest children. Goya has included himself in the background, to the left of the painting, behind an easel.

(p. 193, photo)
Pablo Picasso (1881–1973) was born in Málaga. By the age of 20, he had developed a mature, personal style marked by melancholy subject matter and a blue palette. The years 1901–1904 are referred to as his "blue period." In 1905 he began to paint portraits of circus performers, dancers, and acrobats in warmer, pink tones in what is referred to as his "rose period."
Picasso's inspiration for *Familia de saltimbancos* (acrobatic performers) was

the *Cirque Médrano* in Paris's Montmarte district. He attended the circus and made studies of acrobats and other performers. He combined these into a family portrait. Included in the painting are likenesses of the French poet Guillaume Apollinaire (the jester) and of the artist himself (the harlequin at the far left).

Present

Chapter Theme
Family celebrations

Communicative Objectives
- To discuss celebrations
- To identify family members
- To greet people and say good-by

 Overheads 30–31

 Vocabulary Art BLMs/CD-ROM

 Vocabulary Tape 6-1

Grammar Preview
Reciprocal reflexive verbs are presented here lexically. Their explanation appears on p. 213. Allow students to practice these without explaining them at this point unless they express a need to understand the concept.

Teaching Suggestions
Preparing students to speak: Use one or two options from each of the categories of Comprehensible Input, Physical Response, or Limited Verbal Response. For a complete explanation of these categories and some sample activities, see pp. T20–T21.

Vocabulario para conversar

¿Cómo celebras tu cumpleaños?

Vas a necesitar estas palabras y expresiones para hablar sobre reuniones familiares y otras celebraciones. Después de leerlas varias veces, practícalas con un(a) compañero(a).

encender *(e → ie)*

apagar

La fiesta de cumpleaños

la vela
el pastel

La graduación, *pl.* las graduaciones

graduarse
abrazarse

Options

Strategies for Reaching All Students

Spanish-Speaking Students

 Un paso más Ex. 6-B

Students Needing Extra Help
Begin the vocabulary section of the Organizer. Show word families with *abrazarse (brazo)* and *besarse (beso)*. Have a reflexive verb chart and a stem-change chart available. Help them see that these verbs are used only in the *nosotros(as)* and *Uds. / ellos / ellas* forms.

También necesitas . . . : Point out that *nacer* is rarely used in the present tense. Stress how *nieto* looks like the English *niece* and shouldn't be confused with its true meaning. Stress the pronunciation and meaning of *familiar.*

¿Y qué quiere decir . . . ?: Review the paradigm of *estar.* Explain the difference between *el cumpleaños* and *cumplir años.* Again, emphasize word families.

Learning Spanish Through Action
STAGING VOCABULARY: *Nombren, Señalen*
MATERIALS: transparency of a family tree, including four generations, some unmarried people, and birth and death dates
DIRECTIONS: Direct students to point to an appropriate person as you give definitions of the relationships.

194 Standards 1.1; 1.2; 3.1; 4.1

La boda

casarse (con)

el esposo

la esposa

despedirse *(e → i)* (de)

darse la mano

besarse

decirse "¡Hola!"

Class Starter Review
On the day following the initial presentation of vocabulary, you may want to begin the class with this activity:
Prepare an overhead transparency of a family tree that includes vocabulary from this chapter, and from Book 1, Chap. 5. Label one person *yo* and ask students who other people are in relation to *yo*. On subsequent days, label different people *yo* and have them write out their answers.

www Internet Activities
Juegos

También necesitas . . .

la reunión, *pl.* las reuniones	*gathering, get-together*
saludar	*to greet*
nacer	*to be born*
(estar) casado, -a (con)	*(to be) married (to)*
(estar) soltero, -a	*(to be) single*
(estar) muerto, -a	*(to be) dead*
el bisabuelo, la bisabuela	*great-grandfather / great-grandmother*
el nieto, la nieta	*grandchild*
el cuñado, la cuñada	*brother-in-law / sister-in-law*
el sobrino, la sobrina	*nephew, niece*
familiar	*family* (adj.)
de nuevo	*again*

¿Y qué quiere decir . . . ?
el cumpleaños
cumplir años
el aniversario (de boda)
la celebración, *pl.* las celebraciones
celebrar
regalar
invitar
especial
(estar) divorciado, -a (de)
(estar) separado, -a (de)

Vocabulario para conversar   195

Extended Written Practice/Homework
1. Write three sentences telling how your family or friends celebrate birthdays: *Siempre cantamos "Feliz cumpleaños" a la persona que cumple años.*
2. Using expressions from p. 195, write three sentences telling whether or not different people are married: *Mi hermano no está casado.*
3. Write three sentences telling when you and other people were born.

Multiple Intelligences
Bodily/Kinesthetic and Visual/Spatial
See Learning Spanish Through Action.
Logical/Mathematical and Visual/Spatial
Have students work together to create a chart which shows the birthdays of all the students in the class.

Verbal/Linguistic
1) See Vocabulary Tape 6-1.
2) Read True/False statements about the pictures on pp. 194–195 and have students answer *Verdad* or *Falso*. For example: *Quince personas llegaron a la fiesta de cumpleaños. (Falso)*
Visual/Spatial
See Overheads 30–31, the Vocabulary Art BLMs/CD-ROM, and Class Starter Review.

Practice & Apply

Reteach / Review: Vocabulary

Encourage students to use known vocabulary to vary their answers.
Ex. 1: *Sí, me encantan las fiestas de disfraces. / No, no me gusta nada ir a fiestas de disfraces.*

Re-enter/ Recycle

Ex. 1: leisure-time activities from Chap. 4

Answers: Empecemos a conversar

1 ESTUDIANTE A

a. ¿Sueles ir a fiestas de cumpleaños?

b. . . . a graduaciones?

c. . . . a conciertos?

d. . . . a obras de teatro?

e. . . . a bodas?

f. Questions will vary.

ESTUDIANTE B

a.–f. Answers will vary, but look for the correct forms: *me divierto, me aburro, lo paso bien / mal.*

2 ESTUDIANTE A

a. Generalmente, ¿cómo saludas a tus cuñados(as)?

b. . . . a tu madre / padre?

c. . . . a tu abuelo(a)?

d. . . . a tus amigos(as)?

e. . . . a tus bisabuelos(as)?

f. . . . al director (a la directora) de la escuela?

g. Questions will vary.

Empecemos a conversar

Túrnate con un(a) compañero(a) para ser *Estudiante A* y *Estudiante B*. Reemplacen las palabras subrayadas en el modelo con palabras representadas o escritas en los recuadros. Si ven pueden dar su propia respuesta.

1

A —¿Sueles ir a *fiestas de disfraces*?

B —*Sí, y me divierto bastante*.

　o: *No. Nunca voy a fiestas de disfraces.*

　o: *Sí, pero no las soporto.*

Estudiante A　　　　　　　　　　　　　　　　**Estudiante B**

a.　　b.　　c.

d.　　e.　　f.

divertirse

aburrirse

pasarlo bien / mal

2　tu tío(a)

A —*Generalmente, ¿cómo saludas a tu tío(a)*?

B —*Nos abrazamos*.

　　o: *No tengo tíos*.

Estudiante A　　　　**Estudiante B**

a. tus cuñados(as)

b. tu madre / padre

c. tu abuelo(a)

d. tus amigos(as)

e. tus bisabuelos(as)

f. el director / la directora de la escuela

g.

196　Capítulo 6

Options

Strategies for Reaching All Students

Spanish-Speaking Students

Exs. 1–4: Pair bilingual with non-bilingual students if possible.
After Ex. 5: *Piensa en cuando eras más joven y en tu fiesta de cumpleaños favorita. Descríbela. Di por qué te gustó. ¿Qué hicieron? ¿Qué regalos recibiste? ¿Quién fue a tu fiesta? ¿Qué comieron?*

 Un paso más Exs. 6-C, 6-D

Students Needing Extra Help

Ex. 1: Review reflexive verbs if necessary. With *pasarlo bien,* remind students to put the *lo* before the conjugated verb form. Discourage them from using *aburrirse* for every answer.
Ex. 3: Discourage students from always answering with *no recuerdo.* However, some students will not want to share the information requested in the question. Let them respond accordingly. Review the imperfect.

Previous activities have focused on the present tense.
Ex. 4: Some students will hesitate to discuss family celebrations. Don't obligate them to share their writing. Point out that this exercise uses three verb tenses. Review the preterite if necessary.
Ex. 5: Not all students have had joyous celebrations. Encourage them to come up with something imaginary if this seems more comfortable.

3
cumplir años

A —*Cuando eras pequeño(a), ¿qué hacía tu familia cuando alguien cumplía años?*
B —*Comprábamos un pastel.*
   o: *No recuerdo.*

Estudiante A

a. celebrar su aniversario de boda
b. graduarse
c. casarse
d. nacer

Estudiante B

comprar un pastel
invitar a ___
hacer una fiesta / cena / almuerzo
hacer una reunión familiar
no hacer nada

Empecemos a escribir

Escribe tus respuestas en español.

4 ¿Te diviertes cuando cumples años? ¿Cómo celebraste tu último cumpleaños? ¿A quiénes invitaste? ¿Qué te regalaron? ¿Había pastel? ¿Quién encendió las velas? ¿En qué pensaste cuando las apagaste?

5 ¿Qué ocasiones especiales celebra tu familia? ¿Cuándo fue la última vez que celebraron algo? ¿Cómo lo pasaste? Generalmente, ¿quiénes van a las reuniones familiares? ¿Qué haces tú en esas reuniones? ¿Qué hacías cuando eras pequeño(a)?

6 De tus actores o cantantes *(singers)* favoritos, ¿sabes quiénes están casados? ¿Quiénes están separados o divorciados? ¿Y solteros? ¿Quiénes están divorciados y casados de nuevo?

MORE PRACTICE

- Más práctica y tarea, p. 543
- Practice Workbook 6–1, 6–2

También se dice

el casamiento
el matrimonio

la colación

la torta   el ponqué
la tarta   el bizcocho
el queque

la candela

Vocabulario para conversar   197

Present

Chapter Theme
Holidays

Communicative Objectives
• To discuss celebrations
• To talk about holidays

 Overheads 32–33

 Vocabulary Art BLMs/CD-ROM

 Vocabulary Tape 6-2

Grammar Preview
Reflexive reciprocal verbs are presented here lexically. Their explanation appears on p. 213.

¡Celebremos!

Vocabulario para conversar

¿Cómo celebras los días de fiesta?

Aquí tienes el resto del vocabulario que necesitas en este capítulo para hablar sobre reuniones familiares y otras celebraciones.

¡Una fiesta de sorpresa!
FECHA:
HORA:
LUGAR:

la invitación, *pl.* las invitaciones

la flor

el Día de la Madre (el segundo domingo de mayo)

Enero

el Año Nuevo

Febrero

el Día de los Enamorados

Mayo

los fuegos artificiales (*m.pl.*)

Junio

bailar

el baile

el Día del Padre (el tercer domingo de junio)

Julio

el Día de la Independencia

Options

Strategies for Reaching All Students

Spanish-Speaking Students

 Un paso más Ex. 6-E

Students Needing Extra Help

También necesitas . . . : Go over *encontrarse* for students who need to see all the verb forms. Help them see that this is used only in the *nosotros(as)* and *Uds. / ellos / ellas* forms. Give complete sentences for *desde* and *desde que.* Remind students that *pariente* is a false cognate, and that it means "relative."

Enrichment

Ask students to share information they know about two Mexican holidays that are widely celebrated in the U.S.: *Cinco de mayo* and Mexican Independence Day. You may also ask them if they know of other foreign holidays that are celebrated in the U.S. (Bastille Day, Chinese New Year). Have information ready about these holidays so that you can present it to the class.

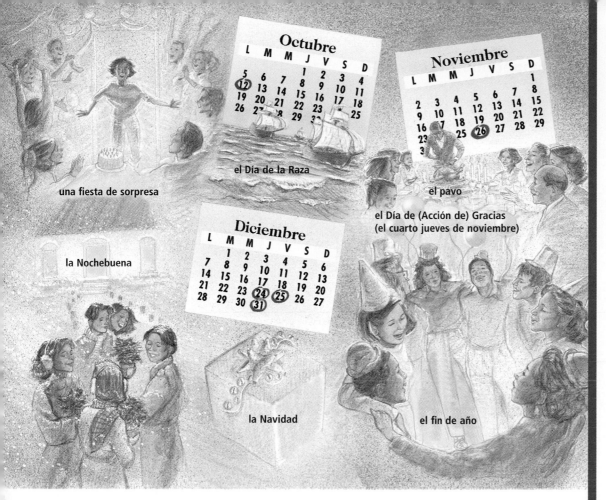

una fiesta de sorpresa

Octubre
L	M	M	J	V	S	D
			1	2	3	4
⑫	6	7	8	9	10	11
19	13	14	15	16	17	18
26	20	21	22	23	24	25
	27	28	29	30	31	

el Día de la Raza

Noviembre
L	M	M	J	V	S	D
						1
2	3	4	5	6	7	8
9	10	11	12	13	14	15
16	17	18	19	20	21	22
23	24	25	㉖	27	28	29
3						

el pavo

el Día de (Acción de) Gracias
(el cuarto jueves de noviembre)

la Nochebuena

Diciembre
L	M	M	J	V	S	D
	1	2	3	4	5	6
7	8	9	10	11	12	13
14	15	16	17	18	19	20
21	22	23	㉔	25	26	27
28	29	30	㉛			

la Navidad

el fin de año

También necesitas . . .

charlar	*to chat*
encontrarse (*o → ue*)	*to meet (each other)*
felicitar	*to congratulate*
lanzar fuegos artificiales	*to shoot / set off fireworks*
¿a qué edad . . . ?	*at what age . . . ?*
a los ___ años	*at the age of ___*
desde (que + *verb*)	*since, from*
el pariente, la parienta	*relative*

¿Y qué quiere decir . . . ?
escribirse
hablarse
verse
el día de fiesta
la fiesta de fin de año
¡felicidades!

Vocabulario para conversar   199

Teaching Suggestions
Preparing students to speak: Use one or two options from each of the categories of Comprehensible Input, Physical Response, or Limited Verbal Response. For a complete explanation of these categories and some sample activities, see pp. T20–T21.

Class Starter Review
On the day following the presentation of vocabulary, you might begin the class by asking students questions about their childhood: *¿A qué edad empezaste a ir a la escuela? ¿A qué edad empezaste a hablar?*

www Internet Activities
Juegos

Learning Spanish Through Action
STAGING VOCABULARY: *Levanten*
MATERIALS: index cards with copies from the Vocabulary Art BLMs/CD-ROM mounted on them
DIRECTIONS: Hand out the cards to the class. Direct students to raise the card corresponding to the holiday you describe: *Este día lanzamos fuegos artificiales. En este día en mayo le regalo flores a mi mamá.*

Extended Written Practice/Homework
1. Choose three special occasions from pp. 198–199 and tell why you do or do not like to celebrate them: *Me gusta celebrar la Nochebuena porque vamos a la iglesia y comemos una cena especial.*
2. Choose one special occasion that you remember from your childhood and write three sentences telling what you used to do then: *Cuando era niño(a), siempre íbamos a la casa de mis abuelos para celebrar el Día de Gracias.*

Multiple Intelligences
Bodily/Kinesthetic
See Learning Spanish Through Action.
Verbal/Linguistic
See Vocabulary Tape 6-2.
Visual/Spatial
See Overheads 32–33 and the Vocabulary Art BLMs/CD-ROM.

Practice

Re-enter / Recycle
Ex. 9: clothing from Chap. 3

Answers: Empecemos a conversar

7 ESTUDIANTE A

a. ¿Cuándo es la Navidad?

b. ...el Año Nuevo?

c. ...el Día del Padre?

d. ...el Día de (Acción de) Gracias?

e. ...el Día de los Enamorados?

f. ...la Nochebuena?

g. Questions will vary.

ESTUDIANTE B

a. Es el veinticinco de diciembre.

b. ...primero de enero.

c. ...tercer domingo de junio.

d. ...cuarto jueves de noviembre.

e. ...catorce de febrero.

f. ...veinticuatro de diciembre.

g. Answers will vary.

Empecemos a conversar

7

A —¿Cuándo es *el Día de la Madre*?

B —Es *el segundo domingo de mayo*.

Estudiante A

a.

b.

c.

d.

e.

f.

g.

Estudiante B

SIEMPRE QUE QUIERAS.

Cuando las palabras no bastan, las flores lo dicen todo. No importa la distancia. Todo es tan sencillo como entrar en una floristería donde veas el distintivo de Interflora, elegir las flores o plantas que desees y... ¡Ya está! En pocas horas llegarán allí donde quieras tú.

interflora
Digaselo con flores

200 Capítulo 6

Options

Strategies for Reaching All Students

Students Needing Extra Help
Ex. 7: Be sure that calendars are available. Provide a model using a date. *(Es el veinticinco de diciembre.)*
Ex. 8: Brainstorm the possibilities for celebrating these holidays.
Ex. 9: Review *desde que*.

Extended Written Practice/Homework
1. Choose a special occasion from pp. 194–195 or 198–199 when you meet with friends or relatives. Write three sentences describing the occasion and telling what you usually do.
2. Write three questions that you can ask classmates to find out at what age they did different things: *¿A qué edad aprendiste a montar en bicicleta?*

Multiple Intelligences
Verbal/Linguistic
See Exs. 7–9.
Visual/Spatial and Verbal/Linguistic
Use the vocabulary Overheads from this chapter and number each item. Say the Spanish word for the pictures at random. Students should call out the numbers of the corresponding pictures in Spanish. Then call out the numbers of the pictures and have students say the Spanish words.

8

tus amigos(as)

A —¿*Cómo celebran tus amigos(as) el Día de los Enamorados?*

B —*Envían tarjetas, regalan flores,* . . .
o: *No hacen nada.*

Estudiante A

a. tu ciudad

b. tu familia

c. Uds.

d. tú

e. tú y tus amigos

f. tu familia   g.

Estudiante B

9

trabajar

A —¿*A qué edad vas a trabajar?*

B —*A los (18) años.*
o: *Trabajo desde que tengo 12 años.*

Estudiante A

a. graduarte*

b. usar corbata / zapatos de
tacón alto

c. comprar un coche

d. vivir sólo(a)

e. casarte

f. tener hijos

g.

Estudiante B

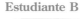

* When a reflexive verb is used in the infinitive (*graduarte, casarte*),
the reflexive pronoun (*te*) agrees with the subject (*tú*).

Vocabulario para conversar   201

8 ESTUDIANTE A

a. ¿Cómo celebra tu ciudad el Día de la Raza?

b. . . . celebra tu familia el Día de (Acción de) Gracias?

c. . . . celebran Uds. el Día de la Madre?

d. . . . celebras tú el Día de la Independencia?

e. . . . celebran tú y tus amigos el fin de año?

f. . . . celebra tu familia la Nochebuena?

g. Questions will vary.

ESTUDIANTE B

a.–g. Answers will vary.

9 ESTUDIANTE A

a. ¿A qué edad vas a graduarte?

b. . . . vas a usar corbata / zapatos de tacón alto?

c. . . . comprar un coche?

d. . . . vivir sólo(a)?

e. . . . casarte?

f. . . . tener hijos?

g. Questions will vary.

ESTUDIANTE B

a.–g. Answers will vary.

Practice & Apply

Re-enter / Recycle
Ex. 13: leisure-time activities from Chap. 4

Teaching Suggestions
Ex. 10: Explain to students that they can choose any family members they want in the question. Review reflexive verbs.

Answers: Empecemos a conversar

10 **ESTUDIANTE A**

a. ¿Se hablan por teléfono a menudo tú y ___?

b. ¿Se escriben a menudo tú y ___?

c. ¿Se encuentran a menudo tú y ___?

d. Questions will vary.

ESTUDIANTE B

a.–d. Answers will vary, but look for correct use of reflexive verbs *(nos hablamos / escribimos / encontramos)* and logical time expressions.

¡Celebremos!

10
verse

A —*¿Se ven a menudo tú y <u>tu bisabuelo(a)</u>?*
B —*<u>Nos vemos todos los días.</u>*
　　o: *Casi nunca nos vemos.*
　　o: *Mis bisabuelos están muertos.*

Estudiante A

a. **hablarse por teléfono**　　b. **escribirse**

c. **encontrarse**　　d.

Estudiante B

una vez (dos veces) al mes / año

a veces

hace (3 meses) que no nos ___

El padre de la quinceañera baila el primer vals con su hija.

Una familia se reúne delante de una iglesia en la Ciudad de México después de un bautizo.

Options

Strategies for Reaching All Students

Spanish-Speaking Students
Exs. 10: Pair bilingual with non-bilingual students if possible.
After Ex. 14: *Escribe una nota de sociedad sobre una fiesta fabulosa. Puede ser una fiesta verdadera o una imaginaria ¿Qué tipo de fiesta fue? Cuándo y dónde fue? ¿Quiénes fueron a la fiesta? ¿Cómo se vistieron?*

 Un paso más Ex. 6-F

Students Needing Extra Help
Ex. 11: Encourage students to stay focused, as there are many questions that may seem redundant.
Ex. 12: Show students the difference between the third and fourth questions. One is indicating a specific day, while the other indicates when something occurs.
Ex. 13: Students will need help with the vocabulary to answer the first *¿por qué?*

Enrichment
As homework, have students write a newspaper article covering events mentioned in this letter. Have them invent details: How many people attended? What was the most interesting costume? What foods were served? What music was played? Or they can write tabloid-type articles: *¿De veras "perdió" su abrigo de piel la Srta. de la Luna en la fiesta de disfraces?* or *La Srta. de la Luna se lastima la pierna. ¡Algunos dicen que no fue accidente!*

Empecemos a escribir y a leer

11 ¿Cómo te gustaría celebrar tu próximo cumpleaños? ¿Piensas enviarles invitaciones a tus parientes y amigos? Generalmente, ¿qué haces de especial el día de tu cumpleaños? ¿Qué hacen tus parientes y amigos? ¿Cómo te saludan ese día? ¿Qué te dicen?

12 ¿Cuál es tu día de fiesta favorito? ¿Por qué? ¿En qué días de fiesta les dices "felicidades" a otras personas? ¿Cuándo felicitas a tus amigos(as) y a los miembros de tu familia? ¿En qué días de fiesta le envías tarjetas a la gente? ¿En qué días lanza la gente fuegos artificiales?

13 ¿Qué tipo de fiestas prefieres, las de sorpresa o las de disfraces? ¿Por qué? Cuando vas a un baile, ¿prefieres charlar o bailar? ¿Por qué?

14 ¿Cómo celebra tu familia el Día de Acción de Gracias?

15 Lee esta carta de agradecimiento *(thank you)*. En grupo, hablen de la visita de la señorita de la Luna. ¿Lo pasó bien o mal? ¿Cómo lo saben? Después, hagan una lista de las cosas positivas de su visita y otra lista de las cosas negativas.

Estimado Sr. Gastelotodo:

Gracias por su generosa invitación a La Vega durante el Primer Festival Internacional de Cine. Ya no recuerdo que llovió todos los días y que Ud. y yo sólo nos encontramos una vez. Recuerdo la fantástica fiesta de disfraces cuando bailé toda la noche con un hombre vestido de leopardo. Todavía pienso en el abrigo de piel que perdí. Lloré mucho, pero ahora ya no estoy tan triste. ¡Estaba un poco aburrida de llevar el mismo abrigo desde 1994! Y me compré uno más bonito y más caro.

¡Qué feliz me hizo ganar el plátano de oro para la mejor actriz del año! Pero la pierna que me lastimé cuando salía del escenario todavía me duele mucho.

Muchos besos y un abrazo fuerte,

Lucía de la Luna

También se dice

el Día de San Valentín

la Nochevieja

**el guajolote
el chompipe**

www.pasoapaso.com

MORE PRACTICE

- Más práctica y tarea, p. 544
- Practice Workbook 6–3, 6–4

Vocabulario para conversar   203

Cultural Notes

(p. 202, left photo)
The *fiesta de quince años*, a lavish fifteenth birthday party, is an important event in the life of a young woman in many Spanish-speaking countries and among families of Hispanic heritage in the U.S., such as this one in Novato, California. The celebration marks a young girl's passage into adulthood. The young woman dances first with her father and then with her *chambelán*, or escort.

(p. 202, right photo)
A baptism brings family and friends together to celebrate a baby's acceptance into the Church. Following a mass and the baptismal ceremony, the celebrants often meet at the parents' home for a reception. The child's parents and godparents are *compadres* in a relationship known as *compadrazgo*. *Compadres* (literally, "co-parents") help raise the child in the Church and provide legal guardianship if necessary.

Practice

Answers:
¡Comuniquemos!
1–3 Answers will vary, but look for correct use of present, preterite, and imperfect tenses.

¡Comuniquemos!

Aquí tienes otra oportunidad para usar el vocabulario de este capítulo.

1 Túrnate con un(a) compañero(a) para hablar de alguna fiesta a la que fue cada uno de ustedes. Pregunten:

- qué tipo de fiesta era y dónde fue
- qué celebraban
- quiénes fueron (¿parientes? ¿amigos?)
- qué hicieron
- 💡

Pueden usar las expresiones de la lista u otras para contestar las preguntas.

abrir los regalos
cantar "Feliz cumpleaños"
charlar
cortar / comer pastel
despedirse
encender / apagar las velas
felicitar
regalar
sacar fotos
saludar

Después, dile a otro(a) estudiante cómo fue la fiesta de tu compañero(a). Por ejemplo:

Miguel fue a una fiesta el sábado. Era el aniversario de boda de sus . . . Fue en . . . Había . . .

2 Hazle una entrevista a un(a) pariente(a) o a un(a) amigo(a). Luego, prepara su biografía. Puedes usar estas u otras preguntas:

- cuándo nació
- a qué edad empezó a ir a la escuela y cuándo se graduó
- a qué edad empezó a trabajar
- cuándo le pasó algo importante y qué le pasó

Luego, dile a tu compañero(a) lo que averiguaste *(found out):*

Mi prima María Rosa nació el 7 de octubre de 1978 . . .

Estas dos amigas en Montevideo, Uruguay, se saludan con un beso en la mejilla.

PASO CULTURAL Cuando los amigos hispanohablantes se encuentran en la calle, muchas veces se dan la mano o se saludan con un besito o un abrazo. Generalmente se acercan más físicamente que los anglohablantes para saludarse y conversar. ¿Te gustaría incorporar esta costumbre a nuestra cultura? ¿Por qué sí o no?

Options

Strategies for Reaching All Students

Spanish-Speaking Students
Ex. 1: Pair Spanish-speaking students. Have them act out the conversation for the class. Use as a listening comprehension activity. To check comprehension, have other students write answers to the questions.
Ex. 2: Have Spanish-speaking students write out the biography of a relative: *Escribe una biografía de un(a) pariente(a) o de un(a) buen amigo(a). Usa las preguntas en el ejercicio 2 como guía.*

Students Needing Extra Help
¡Comuniquemos!: Have models ready for these activities.
Ex. 1: Tell students that they need not discuss the same party. Remind the person responding to the question to use the preterite. Explain that *fiesta* doesn't always have the same meaning we give it in English; it may imply a celebration such as an anniversary. Have pairs take notes so that they can give the information to someone else. Remind them to use a different

form of the verb when reporting the celebration to a third student.
Ex. 2: Have students take notes before reporting the information.
Ex. 3: Help students choose the correct form of the verb when asking the second group of questions.
¿Qué sabes ahora?: Have students write out this section so they can record their progress.

3 Con un(a) compañero(a) inventa una conversación por teléfono. Él (Ella) te invita a una fiesta y te dice:

- la fecha
- la hora
- la dirección
- el tipo de fiesta que va a ser
-

Tú le preguntas sobre:

- el regalo
- la ropa que debes llevar
- las personas que van a ir
- qué van a hacer
- si debes llevar algo de comida
-

Pueden comenzar así:

A —¡Hola, Olga! Soy Luis. ¿Cómo estás?
B —Bien, gracias, Luis. ¿Y tú?
A —Muy bien. Yo quisiera invitarte a . . .

¿Qué sabes ahora?

Can you:

■ **talk about how your family celebrates certain occasions?**

—Mi familia celebra _____ todos los años. Hacemos un(a) _____ .

■ **talk about holiday celebrations?**

—El 4 de julio, día de _____ , la gente lanza _____ en la calle

■ **talk about how you greet people?**

—Mi bisabuela y yo siempre nos _____ cuando nos _____ .

Día del Padre

Vía Digital
+
6 Partidos Gratis*
+
5 Películas Gratis*

(Tu padre siempre dice que quiere lo mejor para vosotros, ¿no?)

Abónate, antes del 19 de Marzo, llamando al 902 200 035 o en cualquiera de nuestros distribuidores autorizados.

Vocabulario para conversar 205

Present & Apply

Cultural Objective
- To discuss how cultures adopt, often in altered form, aspects and traditions of other cultures

Critical Thinking: Identifying Stereotypes
Celebrations represent only one aspect of the many diverse cultures in Latin America. Dispel any stereotypical ideas students might have that life in Latin America is one long string of parties.

Multicultural Perspectives
In Uruguay, groups perform for prize money in the month-long celebration for *Carnaval. Los parodistas*, wearing brightly colored clothes and painted faces, perform musical skits and parodies accompanied by electric guitar and keyboard. *Una revista* performs dances from the U.S. and Latin America, such as samba, salsa, and Charleston. A combo accompanies them, playing the music to special lyrics written by the group. *Los lubolos* paint their faces black and perform musical numbers of African origin, such as *milonga* and *candombe*. Ask students if they are familiar with Mardi Gras traditions in other parts of the world. (Those in New Orleans, Rio, and Nice, France, are proba-

Perspectiva cultural

¿Qué te dicen estas fotos sobre la religión en América Latina? ¿Qué influencias de diferentes culturas puedes observar en ellas?

La gente se disfraza con colores brillantes en un desfile de carnaval en Ponce, Puerto Rico.

Probablemente sabes que el catolicismo es la religión principal en los países hispanos. Es verdad, pero también se practican el protestantismo, el islamismo, el judaísmo, el budismo, la religión ortodoxa griega y las religiones indígenas. En el Caribe, mucha gente practica la santería, una combinación entre la religión yoruba africana y el catolicismo.

Hay celebraciones de origen religioso muy populares entre gente de todas las religiones. *Los carnavales*, por ejemplo, son desfiles con danza, música y disfraces que se celebran por toda América Latina. Empiezan en febrero, el fin de semana antes del Miércoles de Ceniza, que es el comienzo de los 40 días de la Cuaresma *(Lent)*.

Los carnavales se celebran de diferentes maneras. En Perú, Bolivia y el norte de Argentina, se ven las tradiciones incas. En la región del Caribe vemos símbolos cristianos mezclados con tradiciones africanas que llegaron a este hemisferio con los esclavos.

En los Estados Unidos también se ven tradiciones hispanas de origen religioso. Una de ellas es la tradición de las *luminarias.* Éstas son bolsas de papel con arena y una vela encendida adentro. Originalmente se usaban para iluminar la casa en la Nochebuena. Ahora se usan para iluminar la acera, una piscina o un patio cuando hay una fiesta.

www.pasoapaso.com

206 Capítulo 6

Options

Strategies for Reaching All Students

Spanish-Speaking Students
Ask: *¿Cuáles son los días religiosos que celebra tu familia o tu comunidad? ¿Cómo los celebran? ¿Vas a continuar esas tradiciones? ¿Por qué?*

 Un paso más Ex. 6-G

Students Needing Extra Help
Explain Ash Wednesday and Lent.
Ex. 1: Direct students to paragraphs 3–4 if they are having difficulty.
Ex. 2. Explain the concept of the origin of holidays. Students probably haven't given much thought to how holidays began. Give an example as a model to help with a concept that may be difficult.

Cultural Notes

(pp. 206–207, photo)
In Ponce, Puerto Rico, *Carnaval* celebrants often wear brightly painted horned masks. Floats and parades are features of the festival, along with dancing to *plena* music, folk music with African roots. Slavery brought an African presence to Puerto Rico during the eighteenth and nineteenth centuries. In

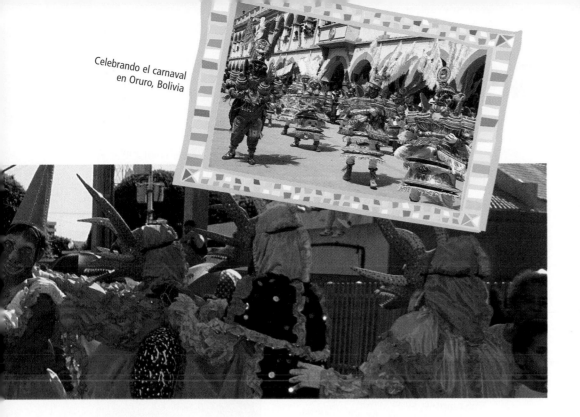

Celebrando el carnaval en Oruro, Bolivia

bly the best known.) Discuss the historical and present-day importance of *carnaval*. The etymology of the word is tied to the idea of abstaining from meat. *Carnaval* is the three-day period preceding Ash Wednesday and the 40 meatless days of Lent.

Answers

Students may say that religion plays an important part in public celebrations in Latin America. African and Indian traditions and costumes are a part of these celebrations in regions where those groups represent a large percentage of the population. In the U.S. one can see the Hispanic influence in the use of traditional *luminarias* at Christmas time.

Answers: La cultura desde tu perspectiva

1 Answers will vary; students may say the celebration takes on aspects of the other culture: *Carnaval* in Bolivia, Peru, and Argentina shows Incan traditions, and in the Caribbean, African traditions.

2 Answers will vary, but may include Christmas and Chanukah, centering on gift-giving and decorations, and Easter, with its child-centered bunny and colored eggs.

La cultura desde tu perspectiva

1 ¿De qué manera puede modificarse una costumbre religiosa cuando se encuentra con otra cultura? Da un ejemplo.

2 ¿Qué días de fiesta de origen religioso que tú celebras o conoces se celebran hoy de otra manera?

 Pasos vivos 2 CD-ROM
Maps, Notas culturales

 Internet Activities
Perspectiva cultural

Casa de Nuevo México decorada con luminarias para la Navidad

207

---

addition, European influences came through immigration, mostly from Cataluña, Asturias, Galicia, and Mallorca. Although Puerto Rico had originally been populated by the Arawak people, only a very few traces of indigenous culture remain.

(p. 207, top photo)
Oruro, a small town on the high plateau of Bolivia, is famous for its *Carnaval*. Young Bolivians, members of *fraternidades,* travel from all parts of the country to dance during the celebration.

(p. 207, bottom photo)
Originally, *luminarias* were small fires of burning sticks, but today they are paper bags, weighted with sand, into which a lit candle is placed. *Luminarias* still have a religious significance in Mexico and parts of the U.S. Southwest. Placed along the sidewalks leading to a home, they provide a pathway for the Christchild.

Preview

 Overhead 34

Reteach / Review:
Indirect object pronouns
You may want to review indirect object pronouns by asking who or what *le* refers to in the lower left-hand caption: *le di su comida favorita . . . .* (The dog Rex)

Answers
A Clues are described in the preterite: endings *-ió* and *-ieron,* and the words *pasado* and *ayer.*

B These are *e → i* stem-changing verbs in the preterite.

C Preterite forms of *dar: dieron* and *di.* The preterite endings are irregular.

Gramática en contexto

NOTAS DE SOCIEDAD

El perro de Pilar Ramírez, Rex, ganó una medalla en el concurso que tuvo lugar ayer en el Estadio Central. Hablando de Rex, Pilar dijo, "Como siempre, no me pidió nada. Pero yo le di su comida favorita: un hueso muy grande."

El domingo pasado el señor Pablo Rosas y la señora Matilde López de Rosas dieron una fiesta para celebrar el cuarenta aniversario de su boda. Sirvieron una espléndida cena.

A Find the forms of *servir* and *pedir.* How can you tell that these events are described in the preterite tense?

B Compare the infinitives of these verbs to the forms used in the captions. What do you notice about the stem?

C In the captions, preterite forms of the verb *dar* are used. What are they? Are the endings of this *-ar* verb regular or irregular?

208   Capítulo 6

Options

Strategies for Reaching All Students

Students Needing Extra Help
Gramática en contexto: Begin the grammar section of the Organizer.
A: Use the grammar section from Chaps. 3 and 4 to review.
El pretérito de los verbos e → i: Give more examples using *vestirse* and *servir.* On the Organizer, have students highlight the irregular forms or write them in a different color.

Extended Written Practice/Homework
1. Write three sentences telling what foods different people ordered on different occasions: *Cuando celebramos el cumpleaños de mi abuela en el restaurante mexicano, ella pidió chiles rellenos con arroz.*

2. Write two pairs of sentences using *pedir, vestirse, servir,* or *despedirse* to tell what different people usually do vs. what they did recently: *Generalmente me despido de mis padres cuando salgo de casa. Ayer no me despedí de ellos porque salí muy temprano.*

El pretérito de los verbos con el cambio e → i

First, review the present-tense forms of e → i stem-changing verbs. Note that the change occurs in all except the *nosotros* and *vosotros* forms:

pedir

(yo)	**pido**	(nosotros) (nosotras)	pedimos
(tú)	**pides**	(vosotros) (vosotras)	pedís
Ud. (él) (ella)	**pide**	Uds. (ellos) (ellas)	**piden**

In the preterite, these verbs also have a stem change, but **only** in the *Ud./él/ella* and *Uds./ellos/ellas* forms:

(yo)	pedí	(nosotros) (nosotras)	pedimos
(tú)	pediste	(vosotros) (vosotras)	pedisteis
Ud. (él) (ella)	**pidió**	Uds. (ellos) (ellas)	**pidieron**

1 Imagina que Rosario, Luis, tu compañero(a) y tú son camareros en un restaurante donde van a celebrar una boda. Hay nueve mesas. Dile a tu compañero(a) qué mesas sirve cada uno.

Rosario /#8   *Rosario sirve la mesa número 8.*

a. yo / #2
b. Luis y yo / #9
c. Rosario y Luis / #6
d. tú / #3
e. nosotros(as) dos / #7
f. Luis / #5
g. 🔦 / 🔦

Esta pareja argentina celebra su aniversario con una fiesta familiar en el campo.

209

Class Starter Review
On the day following the presentation of the preterite of *-ir* verbs, you may want to begin the class with this activity:
Have students tell their classmates what they ordered the last time they went to a restaurant and what they served at their last family celebration. To practice the *-ieron* form, have students take notes on what three classmates ordered and served.

Answers
1 a. Yo sirvo la mesa número 2.
b. Luis y yo servimos la mesa número 9.
c. Rosario y Luis sirven la mesa número 6.
d. Tú sirves la mesa número 3.
e. Nosotros(as) dos servimos la mesa número 7.
f. Luis sirve la mesa número 5.
g. Statements will vary.

Multiple Intelligences
Musical/Rhythmic
There are several different Spanish lyrics to the tune of the English-language "Happy Birthday" song. Try singing the following version with your students. Write the words on the board or on an overhead transparency.
Feliz cumpleaños a ti.
Feliz cumpleaños a ti.
Feliz cumpleaños, [person's name].
¡Feliz cumpleaños a ti!

Verbal/Linguistic
See Class Starter Review.
Verbal/Linguistic and Visual/Spatial
1) Using Overhead 34, have students describe the pictures.
2) Have students bring in a photo of a celebration with family or friends and describe it to the class.
Visual/Spatial
See Overhead 34 and Exs. A–C.

Present & Practice

Re-enter / Recycle
Ex. 4: Daily routine from Chap. 2

Answers

2 ESTUDIANTE A
¿Qué pidió la Sra. González?
¿Qué pidió la hermana del Sr. González?
¿Qué pidió el cuñado del Sr. González?
¿Qué pidieron los niños?
¿Qué pediste tú?

ESTUDIANTE B
El Sr. González pidió pavo y papas al horno.
La Sra. González pidió sopa de tomate y pollo.
La hermana del Sr. González pidió pavo y ensalada.
El cuñado del Sr. González pidió sopa de verduras y pescado.
Los niños pidieron hamburguesas y leche.
Yo pedí . . . *(Answers will vary.)*

3 El camarero le sirvió al Sr. González hamburguesas y papas fritas.
. . . le sirvió a la Sra. González café y sopa de verduras.
. . . le sirvió a la hermana del Sr. González pastel y un refresco.
. . . le sirvió al cuñado del Sr. González sopa de tomate y pollo.
. . . les sirvió a los niños pescado y papas al horno.
. . . me sirvió . . . *(Answers will vary.)*

2 Túrnate con un(a) compañero(a) para decir qué pidieron estas personas en la cena de fin de año.

el cuñado del Sr. González

la hermana del Sr. González

Sr. González

Sra. González

los niños de los González

tú

A —¿Qué pidió el señor González?
B —Pidió . . .

3 Ahora, imagina que el camarero confundió lo que pidieron. Dile a tu compañero(a) lo que les sirvió el camarero.

¡NO OLVIDES!

Remember that we use indirect object pronouns to tell to whom or for whom an action is done.

me	nos
te	os
le	les

To make the meaning of *le* and *les* clear, we can add *a* + noun or pronoun. For example:
*El camarero **le** sirvió ensalada **al señor Rosas**.*
*Después **me** sirvió **a mí**.*

El camarero le sirvió . . . al señor González.

Options

Strategies for Reaching All Students

Students Needing Extra Help
Ex. 2: Remind students to use the definite article with *Sr. / Sra.* If available, use the vocabulary section of the Organizer from Book 1, Chap. 4.
¡No olvides!: Give additional examples of the use of *le* and *les* and ask students to help you do so.
Ex. 3: Remind students that *le* will change to *les* in some examples.
El pretérito del verbo dar: Stress that there are no written accents on these verb forms.

Ex. 5: Decide with students what the objects will be. They could use anything they might have with them, such as jewelry. Make sure they have three objects. Have extras on hand so that everyone doesn't use the same objects. Remind students that they have just reviewed indirect object pronouns. Model with three students so they can see the verbal exchange. Review *a mí, a ti,* etc. for this exercise and for Ex. 6.

Extended Written Practice/Homework
1. Write three sentences telling what people served on different celebrations or special occasions in the last year: *Mis tíos sirvieron hamburguesas y perros calientes en el Día de la Independencia.*
2. Write three sentences telling who gave different things to people at school: *La profesora de álgebra nos dio mucha tarea ayer.*

4 Imagina que fuiste a la fiesta de disfraces de los Abreu. Cuéntale a tu compañero(a) de qué se vistieron tú y otras personas.

Pilar y Carlos se vistieron de astronautas.

a. yo
b. (nombre)
c. tú y (nombre)
d. (dos nombres)

e. las sobrinas del señor Abreu
f. la nieta de Ricardo Calderón
g.

> **¡NO OLVIDES!**
>
> Remember that we use *vestirse de* to mean "to be dressed as": *Me vestí de pirata.*

El pretérito del verbo *dar*

Dar is an *-ar* verb, but its preterite endings are the same as those of *-er* and *-ir* verbs.

(yo)	**di**	(nosotros) (nosotras)	**dimos**
(tú)	**diste**	(vosotros) (vosotras)	**disteis**
Ud. (él) (ella)	**dio**	Uds. (ellos) (ellas)	**dieron**

> **¡NO OLVIDES!**
>
> Do you remember the present-tense forms of *dar*?
>
> doy   damos
> das   dais
> da   dan

5 Formen grupos de tres. Cada miembro del grupo debe tener tres objetos. Intercambien *(exchange)* esos objetos. Túrnense para decir lo que hicieron. Por ejemplo:

Yo te di un sujetapapeles a ti.
Tú le diste un sacapuntas a Francisco.
Y Francisco me dio una grapadora a mí.

Gramática en contexto   211

Present & Practice

Re-enter / Recycle

Ex. 6: clothing from Chap. 3, toys from Chap. 5

Answers

6 Answers will vary, but look for correct use of indirect object pronouns and preterite forms of *dar.*

 Practice Wkbk. 6-5, 6-6, 6-7, 6-8

 Writing Activities 6-D, 6-E

 Pruebas 6-5, 6-6

 Comm. Act. BLM 6-2

7 imperfect: *vivían*
imperfect: *eran*
imperfect: *Iban*
imperfect: *se hablaban*
imperfect: *tenían*
imperfect: *Jugaban*
imperfect: *tenían*
preterite: *se lastimó*
preterite: *corrió*
preterite: *pudo*
preterite: *fue*
preterite: *metió*
preterite: *ganó*

Students' paragraphs will vary, but look for correct imperfect and preterite forms.

6 Piensa en los regalos que tú y tu familia intercambiaron el año pasado para Navidad, Chanuka o alguna otra ocasión. Habla con un(a) compañero(a).

A —*Yo le di un bolso a mi mamá para su aniversario de boda.*
B —*¿Y qué le dio tu papá a ella?*
A —*Él le dio flores y un chaquetón de cuero.*
B — . . .

Otros usos del imperfecto

You know how to use the imperfect tense to talk about what someone **used to do** or **would do** in the past. We also use the imperfect tense:

* to describe people, places, or situations in the past.

    Era una casa muy grande.
    *It **was** a very big house.*

* to talk about a past action that was continuous or that kept on happening.

    Todavía **había** gente a las tres de la mañana.
    *People **were** still there at 3 A.M.*

7 Con un(a) compañero(a) termina de escribir la historia de Lola y Alba. Decidan si los verbos en paréntesis deben estar en el pretérito o en el imperfecto.

Lola y Alba *(vivir)* en la misma calle cuando *(ser)* pequeñas. *(Ir)* a la misma escuela y *(hablarse)* por teléfono casi todos los días. Las dos *(tener)* una gran pasión por el fútbol. *(Jugar)* desde que *(tener)* siete años. Un día, en un partido muy importante, Lola *(lastimarse)* una pierna. Alba *(correr)* a ayudarla y no *(poder)* jugar más. Pero no *(ser)* un día triste. El equipo *(meter)* tres goles y *(ganar)* el partido.

Ahora, escriban un párrafo similar.

LA NAVIDAD ES EL MEJOR REGALO

GUÍA DE SUGERENCIAS Y SERVICIOS DE El Corte Inglés

212   Capítulo 6

Options

Strategies for Reaching All Students

Students Needing Extra Help

Ex. 6: Brainstorm occasions and gifts.
Otros usos del imperfecto: Give additional examples.
Ex. 7: Brainstorm a storyline. Because of the number of tasks to be completed (creating a storyline, choosing the tense, conjugating the verb), do this as a class. Give help with the storyline and let students conjugate the verbs.

Los verbos reflexivos recíprocos: Compare this to regular reflexive verbs in which the action is done to oneself. Give examples.
Ex. 8: Remind students that this is the present tense. You may want to tell students to pretend rather than to use the *no tengo* response: it takes the focus away from the reflexive verbs.
Ahora lo sabes: Have students write out this section so they can keep track of their progress.

Cooperative Learning

Divide the class into groups of three. Pass out magazine cutouts of animals and / or people. On one sheet of paper, using Ex. 8 as a model, the first student provides a descriptive noun about the cutout: *El pescado azul y la tortuga.* The second student continues with a reciprocal reflexive verb: *. . . se visitan.* The third student finishes the sentence: *El pescado azul y la tortuga se visitan en la piscina.* Poll students to see which sentences are logical.

Los verbos reflexivos recíprocos

Sometimes we use the reflexive pronouns *se* and *nos* to express the idea of "(to) each other."

Los vecinos siempre **se saludan.**
The neighbors always greet each other.

Mis amigos y yo **nos abrazamos** cuando **nos encontramos.**
My friends and I hug each other when we meet.

8 Túrnate con un(a) compañero(a) para decir qué cosas hacen estas personas a menudo. Usa elementos de las tres listas. Por ejemplo:

A —¿Tus padres y tíos se escriben a menudo?
B —No se escriben nunca, pero se hablan por teléfono a menudo.
    o: No tengo tíos.

a. tus parientes   escribirse   algunas veces
b. tus amigos   ayudarse   a menudo
c. tus abuelos y tú   visitarse   todos los días
d. tus hermanas   verse   mucho
c. tu cuñado y tú   hablarse por teléfono siempre
f. (nombre) y tú   saludarse   casi nunca
g. 💡   pelearse

Ahora lo sabes

Can you:

- talk about food that was ordered and served?
  —Yo ____ pescado pero el camarero me ____ pollo.

- talk about gifts that someone gave?
  —Mi mamá me ____ un violín para mi cumpleaños.

- describe something in the past?
  —A las dos de la mañana José todavía no ____ sueño.

- talk about actions that refer to "each other"?
  —Mi cuñada y yo ____ vemos todas las semanas.

Muchas familias mexicanas tienen un árbol de la vida.

MORE PRACTICE

Más práctica y tarea, pp. 544–545
Practice Workbook 6–5, 6–10

PASO CULTURAL

El árbol de la vida es una figura muy antigua en muchas culturas. En la cerámica mexicana, el árbol a veces presenta escenas bíblicas como la Natividad o, en este caso, el jardín del Edén. Imagina que vas a hacer un árbol de la vida. ¿Cuál va a ser el tema de tu árbol, y qué vas a incluir?

213

Using Realia
Ask students: *¿Qué se vende en este catálogo?*

8 a.–g. Answers will vary, but should include three plural verb forms in all questions and in the answers to *a*, *b*, and *d*. Answers should be in the *nosotros* form for questions *c*, *e*, and *f*.

Answers: Ahora lo sabes
- pedí / sirvió
- dio
- tenía
- nos

 Practice Wkbk. 6-9, 6-10

 Audio Activities 6.4, 6.5

 Writing Activities 6-F, 6-G

 Pruebas 6-7, 6-8

 Pasos vivos 2 CD-ROM
Bulletin Board, Slide Presentation Maker, Spindle, Treadmill

Extended Written Practice/Homework
1. Write four sentences describing a social occasion from your childhood: *Siempre íbamos a la casa de mis tíos para la Navidad.*
2. Refer to pp. 194–195 and write four sentences saying what people are doing with respect to each other: *Un padre y su hija se abrazan en la graduación.*
3. Write three sentences telling what you and others used to do with respect to each other: *Cuando éramos niños, mis primos y yo nos veíamos frecuentemente.*

Multiple Intelligences
Bodily/Kinesthetic, Interpersonal/Social, and Visual/Spatial
See Cooperative Learning.
Interpersonal/Social and Verbal/Linguistic
See Exs. 6–8.
Verbal/Linguistic
See Audio Activities 6.4 and 6.5.
Visual/Spatial
See Practice Wkbk. 6-5, 6-6, 6-7, 6-8, 6-9, and 6-10; Writing Activities 6-D, 6-E, 6-F, and 6-G; and Comm. Act. BLM 6-2.

Cultural Notes

Paso cultural
Answers will vary.

(p. 213, photo)
The town of Metepec, located in the State of Mexico, is famous for its ceramic *artesanía.* The pieces produced by local craftspeople often reflect Biblical motifs. Metepec's "tree of life" *(árbol de la vida)* sculptures are especially famous and are found in many Mexican homes.

Apply

 ¿Recuerdas?

Play

 Video Activity A

Using the Video
María and Susana, a girl from Spain, meet Felipe.
The next day, María and Jamie meet Carlos and Felipe in the university recreation area.
Afterwards, as the four of them are talking, they notice that Paco Aguilar (the son of Silvestre Aguilar) is staring at Jamie. Paco takes off in his new sports car, and the conversation turns to relationships. Carlos and María ask themselves what will happen after Jamie and Felipe go back to the U.S.
The next scene is set in the office of Operación Aztlán, the environmental organization where Carlos works. A girl arrives with a letter from her mother, whose husband works at the hacienda La Jacaranda. The letter informs Carlos that the pesticides used on the produce grown there are affecting the health of the workers

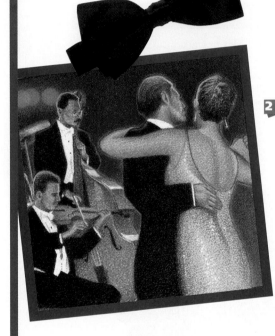

Actividades

1 Trae fotos de eventos sociales de alguna revista. Formen un grupo y escriban comentarios sobre esos eventos. Al final, expliquen por qué les gustaría o no ir a cada evento. Sus comentarios pueden ser divertidos. Por ejemplo:

Era una cena muy aburrida en . . . La señora (nombre) llevaba . . . y el esposo de la señora (nombre) llevaba . . . Había . . .

A mí (no) me gustaría ir a esa fiesta porque . . .

Pueden poner sus fotos y comentarios en un cartel en la pared.

2 Trae una foto de una celebración familiar cuando tú eras pequeño(a) o trae una foto de revista. Intercámbiala *(exchange it)* con tu compañero(a). Túrnense para hablar sobre las circunstancias de la foto. Pregunten, por ejemplo:

• quiénes son las personas
• qué estaban celebrando
• cuándo y dónde fue la celebración
• qué sirvieron de comida

Luego, cada uno debe hablar con otro(a) estudiante sobre la foto de su compañero(a).

En esta foto Patricia tenía . . .

214   Capítulo 6

Options

Strategies for Reaching All Students

Spanish-Speaking Students
 Un paso más Ex. 6-H

Students Needing Extra Help
Ex. 1: Use the vocabulary section of the Organizer. Brainstorm vocabulary used to describe the party, food, clothing, etc. Have pictures available, because the magazines students know won't have this type of photo. Continue the model.
Ex. 2: Have extra photos on hand. Show students that three verb tenses are involved. Model a conversation. Have students take notes in order to report.

Enrichment
Ex. 2: As preparation for this exercise, bring in a poster or large book of photographs showing a celebration. Conduct a class discussion covering any of the questions listed that are applicable.

Conexiones

La estadística

La mejor edad para casarse

¿Qué edad les parece buena para casarse a ti y a tus compañeros? ¿Antes de los 20 años? ¿Entre los 20 y los 25? ¿Entre los 25 y los 30? ¿Después de los 30? ¿Ninguna?

Esta gráfica de sectores presenta las opiniones de 25 estudiantes sobre la mejor edad para casarse.

- Trabajen en grupos grandes o con toda la clase. Hagan su propia gráfica de sectores para indicar la opinión de su clase sobre esta cuestión.

Con un(a) compañero(a), estudia las estadísticas de la tabla.

Antes de los 20 años — 12%
20-25 años — 8%
Ninguna — 4%
Después de los 30 años — 40%
Entre los 25 y los 30 años — 36%

Edad promedio de casarse en los Estados Unidos

AÑO	HOMBRES	MUJERES
1990	26.1	23.9
1993	26.5	24.5
1994	26.7	24.5
1995	26.9	24.5

Source: *1998 Information Please Almanac* (Boston: Houghton Mifflin Company, 1997)

- ¿Qué tendencias se observan respecto a la edad promedio de casarse de los hombres? ¿De las mujeres? Hablen en grupos sobre las razones por estas tendencias.

- ¿Con qué porcentaje de la opinión de tu clase están de acuerdo las estadísticas? ¿Se está casando la gente a la edad que la mayoría de ustedes considera la mejor? Si no, ¿por qué no están de acuerdo ustedes con la edad en que se está casando la gente?

Todo junto   215

and putting consumers at risk. When Carlos discusses the matter with Silvia, another member of the organization, he remembers that La Jacaranda belongs to don Silvestre Aguilar.

Answers: Conexiones
La edad promedio de casarse de los hombres y de las mujeres sube un poco./Answers and opinions will vary.

 La Catrina: Capítulo 6

Play

 Video Activity B

 Para entender mejor

Play

 Video Activity C

 Writing Activities 6-H, 6-I

 Comm. Act. BLMs 6-3, 6-4, 6-5

 Pasos vivos 2 CD-ROM
A Jugar, Laboratorio de grabar, Maps, Video Monitor, Video Presentation Maker

---

Multiple Intelligences
Logical/Mathematical
See *Conexiones*.
Musical/Rhythmic
Have students form small groups to create new Spanish-language lyrics to the "Happy Birthday" song. Or, if the Book 1 Writing, Audio & Video Activities workbook and recordings are available, have small groups sing "Las mañanitas" (p. 140) for the rest of the class.

Verbal/Linguistic and Visual/Spatial
See Exs. 1–2.
Visual/Spatial
See Using the Video, Writing Activities 6-H and 6-I, and Comm. Act. BLMs 6-3, 6-4, and 6-5.

Apply

Process Reading
For a description of process reading, see p. 52.

Answers
Antes de leer
Answers will vary, but students may say *piñatas* are for children's birthday parties.

Mira la lectura
2. Un símbolo de alegría

¡Vamos a leer!

www.pasoapaso.com

Antes de leer

STRATEGY➤ Using prior knowledge

A *piñata* is often part of a Latin American family celebration. Have you ever seen a *piñata* for sale or been to a party where there was one? What are *piñatas* for?

¡Crac! La piñata se rompe y cae una lluvia de dulces, monedas y juguetitos. Los niños corren para recoger todo lo que pueden. Saltan, gritan, se pelean y lloran, pero están contentos. Así terminan muchas fiestas en América Latina, sobre todo en México y el Caribe.

Una piñata es muchas cosas. Es una obra de arte. En una fiesta puede haber un concurso para ver quién hace la piñata más original. La piñata también es un juego. Los niños (¡o adultos!) tienen los ojos vendados y tratan de romper la piñata con un palo. También es un regalo, o mejor dicho, muchos regalitos que caen de la piñata cuando se rompe.

216   Capítulo 6

Mira la lectura

STRATEGY➤ Identifying the main idea

Read the following selection about *piñatas*. Then choose the best title from these choices:

a. La piñata en China
b. La piñata ayer y hoy
c. Cómo hacer una piñata

Options

Strategies for Reaching All Students

Spanish-Speaking Students
Aplicación: ¿Es verdad que la piñata es un símbolo de alegría? ¿Has recibido una piñata alguna vez? ¿Cuál fue la ocasión? ¿Qué hiciste con ella?

Students Needing Extra Help
Mira la lectura: Discuss the information that would be included in an article with each title.
Infórmate: Have students write down the supporting details.
Aplicación: Brainstorm the vocabulary needed to describe the shape, color, size, and contents of *piñatas.*

Multiple Intelligences
Visual/Spatial
See *¡Vamos a leer!*

Algunos creen que la costumbre de la piñata es de origen chino. No sabemos si es verdad. Pero sí sabemos que la costumbre es muy antigua. En Italia, en el siglo dieciséis, ponían regalitos en una olla de barro que después rompían con un palo. De allí la costumbre llegó a España, y los españoles la llevaron al Nuevo Mundo. Ahora la piñata en forma de estrella, burro, tambor o tortuga ninja es un símbolo de fiesta y de alegría.

Vendedora de piñatas,
Ciudad de Guatemala

Infórmate

STRATEGY➤ Identifying supporting details

One way of organizing information is to give a general statement followed by supporting details. For example, after the general statement *Un perro puede ser más que una mascota* you would expect to find examples of the ways dogs can help us (as guard dogs, as seeing-eye dogs, etc.). These details explain or support the general statement. Reread the second paragraph and identify the details that support the general statement *Una piñata es muchas cosas.*

Aplicación

Which of the following supports the general statement *La costumbre de la piñata es muy antigua?*

a. A los adultos también les gustan las piñatas.
b. Una piñata no se puede usar más de una vez.
c. Nadie sabe el origen de la piñata.

Design a *piñata* for a holiday that you celebrate, and describe it in two or three sentences.

¡Vamos a leer! 217

Infórmate
Answers will vary, but may include *Es obra de arte, juego, regalo.*

Aplicación
c. Nadie sabe el origen de la piñata.

www **Internet Activities**

Cultural Notes ☀

(p. 217, photo)
Piñatas are a form of folk art and some, such as these displayed in a Guatemala City shop, can be very elaborate. Originally made out of clay pots, they are now usually made by covering a blown-up balloon with papier-mâché, letting it dry for a few days, then popping the balloon. This makes for a safer *piñata* than the one made out of clay, which can shatter into dangerous shards when broken.

Apply

Process Writing
For information regarding developing a writing portfolio, see p. 54.

¡Vamos a escribir!

Piensa en las ocasiones especiales que celebras. ¿Hay otro día que te gustaría celebrar? Puedes honrar a alguien (como el Día del Niño que se celebra en Japón) o celebrar una fecha importante (el día que ganó el campeonato tu equipo de fútbol americano).

 Escoge una ocasión y piensa en estas cosas:

- ¿Qué nombre le vas a dar al día de fiesta?
- ¿Cuándo se va a celebrar?
- ¿Cómo se va a celebrar? (¿Con ropa, comida o música especial? ¿Con eventos especiales?)

Organiza tus ideas y escribe el primer borrador. Sigue los pasos del proceso de escribir.

 Ahora escribe una carta al editor de un periódico (nacional, local o escolar) y explícale por qué se debe celebrar ese día de fiesta. Puedes usar estas frases entre otras:

- celebrar / honrar
- el aniversario
- es necesario / importante

 Al terminar la descripción y la carta, puedes:

- enviarlas a un periódico
- enviarlas a una organización relacionada con la ocasión
- exhibirlas en la sala de clases
- incluirlas en tu portafolio

 PASO CULTURAL

Más de dos millones de personas indígenas viven en los Andes y muchos de éstos hablan quechua, el idioma de los antiguos incas. Cada 24 de junio en Cuzco, la capital del imperio inca, celebran el solsticio de invierno con un festival que se llama Inti Raymi, o Fiesta del dios-sol. La gente lleva ropa tradicional, canta, baila y hace hogueras *(bonfires)* en las montañas para celebrar el regreso del sol. ¿Por qué crees que el sol es tan importante en la cultura andina?

Celebrando el festival del solsticio de invierno, Inti Raymi, en Cuzco, Perú

218   Capítulo 6

Options

Strategies for Reaching All Students

Students Needing Extra Help
¡Vamos a escribir!: Do these activities in small groups or as a whole class. Students may have difficulty expressing why the day should be a holiday.
Give possibilities for the special day: the day Louis won the tennis match, the day Brian wasn't late, the day Tony received an A on his test, etc. Use the vocabulary section of the Chap. 4 Organizer.

Multiple Intelligences
Musical/Rhythmic and Bodily/Kinesthetic
Write the words to the song "La fiesta campesina" (see Writing, Audio & Video Activities, p. 142) on the board or an overhead transparency. Ask students to identify words they learned in this chapter. Circle those words and assign two or three volunteers to each circled word. Tell students that you will play the song and they should carefully follow the lyrics.

Before playing it again, tell the volunteers that this time, whenever their word comes up as the song is being sung, they must stand.
Naturalist
Have students use the Internet or other sources to find out if there is an equivalent to Earth Day in Latin America. Ask those who find relevant information to share it with the class.
Visual/Spatial
See steps 1–3.

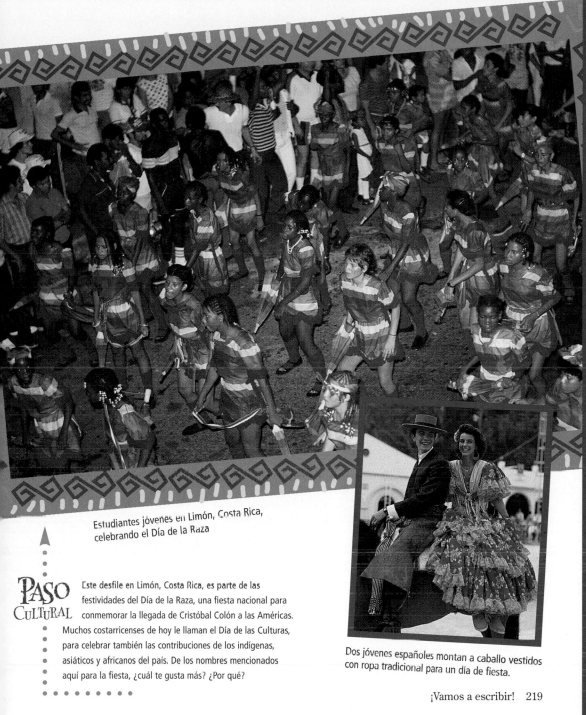

Estudiantes jóvenes en Limón, Costa Rica, celebrando el Día de la Raza

PASO CULTURAL

Este desfile en Limón, Costa Rica, es parte de las festividades del Día de la Raza, una fiesta nacional para conmemorar la llegada de Cristóbal Colón a las Américas. Muchos costarricenses de hoy le llaman el Día de las Culturas, para celebrar también las contribuciones de los indígenas, asiáticos y africanos del país. De los nombres mencionados aquí para la fiesta, ¿cuál te gusta más? ¿Por qué?

Dos jóvenes españoles montan a caballo vestidos con ropa tradicional para un día de fiesta.

¡Vamos a escribir!   219

Cultural Notes

Paso cultural
(p. 218)
La gente indígena tiene una relación muy fuerte con la naturaleza *(nature)*. El clima de los Andes altos es frío. El sol de los Andes es muy fuerte y da mucho calor porque las montañas son muy altas y están cerca de la línea ecuatorial *(equator)*.

(p. 219)
Answers will vary.

(p. 219, top photo)
Columbus Day in Limón is a time for dancing and street festivities. Groups of musicians and dancers called *comparsas* perform, each group distinguished by unique costumes and special dance steps. Many *limonenses* are descended from Jamaican immigrants who came to Costa Rica during the nineteenth century.

(p. 219, bottom photo)
This young woman wears the *traje de flamenca* and the man the *traje de corto*, recalling the traditions of Andalucía, where horsemanship has long been valued. Jerez de la Frontera is home to one of the most important riding schools in Spain: the *Real Escuela Andaluza del Arte Ecuestre*.

Assess & Summarize

Test Preparation

You may want to assign parts of this section as written homework or as an in-class writing activity prior to administering the *Examen de habilidades.*

Answers

Listening: *Nosotros celebramos dos Días de Independencia, el de los Estados Unidos, que es el 4 de julio, y el de México, que es el 16 de septiembre. El 4 de julio toda la familia va al parque. Comemos hamburguesas y jugamos béisbol. Por la noche lanzamos fuegos artificiales. El 16 de septiembre vamos a la casa de mis abuelos. Comemos enchiladas y jugamos fútbol. Por la noche escuchamos música mexicana.*

Cristina is contrasting the celebration of Independence Day in the U.S. and in Mexico. On July 4 the whole family goes to the park, they eat hamburgers and play baseball, and at night they shoot fireworks. On September 16 they go to their grandparents' house, where they eat enchiladas and play soccer and listen to Mexican music.

Reading: 2. Algunas fiestas son para la familia.

Writing: Letters will vary.

Esta sección te ayudará a prepararte para el examen de habilidades, donde tendrás que hacer tareas semejantes.

Listening

Can you understand when people talk about a special occasion? What is Cristina contrasting? Name two differences between the two celebrations.

Reading

Read the following selection. Then choose the sentence that goes at the beginning.

… Parientes llegan de todas partes para estar con su familia en el Día de Acción de Gracias. Y mucha gente suele reunirse con su familia en la Navidad. ¿Y una boda? ¡Es muy importante ir a la boda de un hijo o un hermano!

1. Uno debe estar con los amigos en una fiesta de fin de año.
2. Algunas fiestas son para la familia.
3. Es fácil pasar tiempo con la familia.

Writing

Can you write a letter to a good friend describing a graduation party you gave or attended? Here is an example:

> Hola Ramón,
>
> Nuestro vecino Rodrigo se graduó el fin de semana pasado. (Le di una cartera de regalo.) Celebraron la graduación con una fiesta genial en que sirvieron comida fabulosa. Charlábamos y comíamos mucho cuando ocurrió algo muy divertido. Cuando llegó el cuñado de Rodrigo, ellos se abrazaron, pero Rodrigo olvidó que tenía el pastel en la mano. ¡Qué desastre! Su cuñado tuvo que pedir prestada una chaqueta al Sr. Ramírez. ¡Nunca vamos a olvidar esa fiesta!
>
> Un abrazo,
>
> Lorenzo

Culture

Can you explain why the celebration of the same holiday or festival can vary greatly from country to country in the Spanish-speaking world?

Speaking

Talk to a partner about a birthday party you attended recently. Discuss when and where the celebration took place and who attended. Here is a sample dialogue:

A —*¿Cuándo fue la fiesta de cumpleaños de Laura?*
B —*La semana pasada en casa de mis tíos.*
A —*¿Quiénes fueron?*
B —*Todas las amigas de Laura, ¡y ella tiene muchas amigas! También estuvieron sus hermanos y varios otros invitados que yo no conocía.*
A —*¿Cómo la celebraron?*
B —*Bailamos, encendimos las velas del pastel, le cantamos y todos comimos mucho.*

220   Capítulo 6

Self Test · www.pasoapaso.com

Options

Strategies for Reaching All Students

Students Needing Extra Help
Have students write out this section so that they can check off what they have mastered. *¿Lo sabes bien?:* Remind students that this is just a sample, not the actual test.
Listening: Read the sample more than once. Remind students that they only need to listen for two pieces of information. Brainstorm for which words they should be listening.

Reading: Familiarize students with the three choices, then read the article. If students still are having difficulty, have them read the paragraph, discuss the contents, and then choose the sentence.
Writing: Have students use the Organizer and write a sample letter before the test. Brainstorm other things that might happen at a party. Discuss some ordinary happenings (opened presents, went swimming,

etc.) so that students don't feel that they have to generate something unusual. But encourage creativity to the extent possible.
Culture: Have students review any notes they took during their reading of the *Perspectiva cultural.*
Speaking: Limit the number of lines of dialogue. Use the vocabulary section of the Organizer.

Resumen del vocabulario

Usa el vocabulario de este capítulo para:
- name and describe members of an extended family
- describe special family occasions, holidays, and other celebrations
- greet people in several different ways

to discuss celebrations
invitar
la invitación, *pl.* las invitaciones
la reunión, *pl.* las reuniones
la celebración,
   pl. las celebraciones
celebrar
felicitar
¡felicidades!
la boda
casarse (con)
el aniversario (de boda)
la fiesta de sorpresa
la fiesta de cumpleaños
el cumpleaños
cumplir años
el pastel
la vela
encender
apagar
regalar
charlar
bailar
el baile
la graduación,
   pl. las graduaciones
graduarse

to describe family members
familiar
el bisabuelo, la bisabuela
el cuñado, la cuñada
el esposo, la esposa
el nieto, la nieta
el pariente, la parienta
el sobrino, la sobrina
(estar) casado, -a (con)
(estar) divorciado, -a (de)
(estar) separado, -a (de)
(estar) soltero, -a
nacer
(estar) muerto, -a

to talk about holidays
el día de fiesta
el Año Nuevo
el Día de los Enamorados
el Día de la Madre
la flor
el Día del Padre
el Día de la Independencia
los fuegos artificiales *(m.pl.)*
lanzar fuegos artificiales
el Día de la Raza
el Día de (Acción de) Gracias
el pavo
la Nochebuena
la Navidad
el fin de año
la fiesta de fin de ano

**to greet people
and say good-by**
abrazarse
besarse
darse la mano
decirse "¡Hola!"
despedirse *(e → i)*
encontrarse *(o → ue)*
hablarse
saludar

**other useful words
and expressions**
¿a qué edad ...?
a los ___ años
de nuevo
desde (que + *verb*)
especial
escribirse
verse

Resumen 221

Culture: Answers will vary, but students may say that many factors influence how a holiday is celebrated. For example, *los carnavales* in Bolivia feature Incan traditions. In the Caribbean, however, they are celebrated with African traditions.

Speaking: Dialogues will vary.

Assessment

 Prueba cumulativa

 Examen de habilidades

 Test Generator

Additional Assessment Options

 Comm. Act. BLMs
Small Group Activities
Situation Cards

 Pasos vivos 2 CD-ROM
Slide Presentation Maker, Video Presentation Maker, Word Processor, Spindle

 ¿Lo sabes bien? Video Quiz

www Internet Activities
Self-Test

Enrichment
To help students organize their letter, encourage them to think of something outstanding or memorable about the graduation party, as in the model. You may also want to go over the model in class and ask students to help you list the information each sentence carries. Remind students that they do not have to follow the model exactly, but that they should try to convey equally pertinent information to make their letters substantial.

CAPÍTULO 7

THEME: LUXURIES AND NECESSITIES

SCOPE AND SEQUENCE Pages 222–255

COMMUNICATION

Topics

Personal possessions

Necessities and luxuries

Early American civilizations

Objectives

To discuss early American civilizations

To name and discuss personal possessions

To name home appliances and furnishings

To talk about emergencies

To talk about conservation

To express an opinion

CULTURE

Early American civilizations

GRAMMAR

Los adjetivos posesivos

Los pronombres posesivos

Repaso: Los usos del verbo ser

Ancillaries available for use with Chapter 7

Multisensory/Technology

 Overheads, 35–38

 Audio Tapes and CDs

 Vocabulary Art Blackline Masters for Hands-On Learning, pp. 38–42/CD-ROM

 Classroom Crossword

 La Catrina

 Pasos vivos 2 CD-ROM

 Internet Activities www.pasoapaso.com

Print

 Practice Workbook, pp. 66–74

 Writing, Audio & Video Activities, pp. 42–46, 111–113, 163–166

 Communicative Activity Blackline Masters

    Pair and Small Group Activities, pp. 43–48

    Situation Cards, p. 49

 Un paso más: Actividades para ampliar tu español, pp. 37–42

 RESOURCE⊙PRO®

Planning Express, Teaching Resources Library, and Clip Art Library

Assessment

 Assessment Program

    Pruebas, pp. 100–109

    Examen de habilidades, pp. 110–113

 Test Generator

 ¿Lo sabes bien? Video Quiz

Video still from Chap. 7

Possessions in Spanish-Speaking Countries

In many Spanish-speaking countries, wealthy families do not have as many items in their homes as middle class families in the U.S. do. Kitchen appliances, for example, are much less common; middle- and upper-class Hispanic families usually employ full-time maids and cooks. Because these people are paid to do domestic work, time-saving devices like electric can openers, food processors, or dishwashers are not necessary. In warm or dry climates, clothes are generally washed by hand and hung out to dry, so washing machines and dryers are rare. Most *electrodomésticos* are manufactured in other countries and imported, therefore making them too expensive for the general population.

Furniture is frequently more sparse in homes in Spanish-speaking countries than in the U.S., and it is rare to find a home with wall-to-wall carpeting, even among wealthy families. What is found, especially in countries with warmer climates, are courtyards filled with plants, and, in some cases, colorful caged birds. Hammocks and rocking chairs are plentiful, as people enjoy resting in them from the heat of the more tropical climates.

In Spain and Latin America, possessions which bring enjoyment or enrichment are prized. Music is highly valued in many Latin American countries; almost every home has a source of music, whether it is an inexpensive radio or a sophisticated stereo system. Dressing up is more common in Spanish-speaking countries than in the U.S. Stylish clothes are important: from hand-embroidered shirts and blouses in Central America to leather jackets and fur coats in South America. Hispanic women tend to wear more jewelry than American women. Most girls like to wear bracelets and earrings, and most have their ears pierced as infants.

Automobiles are considered a luxury in Spanish-speaking countries because of high import tariffs and high gasoline costs. They are not the necessity that they are in the U.S. because public transportation, taxis, and collective taxis (taxis that run the same routes repeatedly and carry four or five passengers) are so common.

Possessions can tell us about the way in which ancient peoples lived, including the Aztecs, Incas, and Mayas. The placement and types of objects found in undisturbed sites throughout Latin America have helped anthropologists deduce much of what is known about these indigenous cultures.

Introduce

Re-entry of Concepts

The following list represents words, expressions, and grammar topics re-entered from Book 1 and Book 2 (Chaps. 1–6):

Book 1
calendar expressions, numbers 32–59, school supplies, time-telling, expressions of frequency, family, adjectives describing things, clothing, colors, household items, numbers 500–1,000, places in the community, *hay que* + inf., conservation, parties

Chapter 1
school subjects

Chapter 3
clothing

Chapter 4
sports
leisure-time activities

Chapter 6
special occasions

Planning

Cross-Curricular Connections

Art Connection (pp. 230–231)
Have students design an advertisement for a company that produces electrical appliances. Have them choose the items in the second *Vocabulario para conversar*. Encourage them to be as creative as possible. They should include a logo, the name of the item, its features, and the price. Display completed billboards around the classroom.

History Connection (pp. 238–239)
Have students choose an item from either *Vocabulario para conversar*. Have them think about the item's purpose and use today. What would the early American civilizations from the *Perspectiva cultural* have used instead? For example, instead of using a washing machine, they probably washed their clothes in a stream or a river.

Spanish in Your Community
Have students look for information in Spanish in the print material (instructions, warnings, etc.) that accompanies small appliances, make-up, and other personal products. Have them share this information with the class. Are students able to read and understand the information? Are the instructions in any other language besides Spanish and English? Do students think it is important to have these materials in many languages? Why?

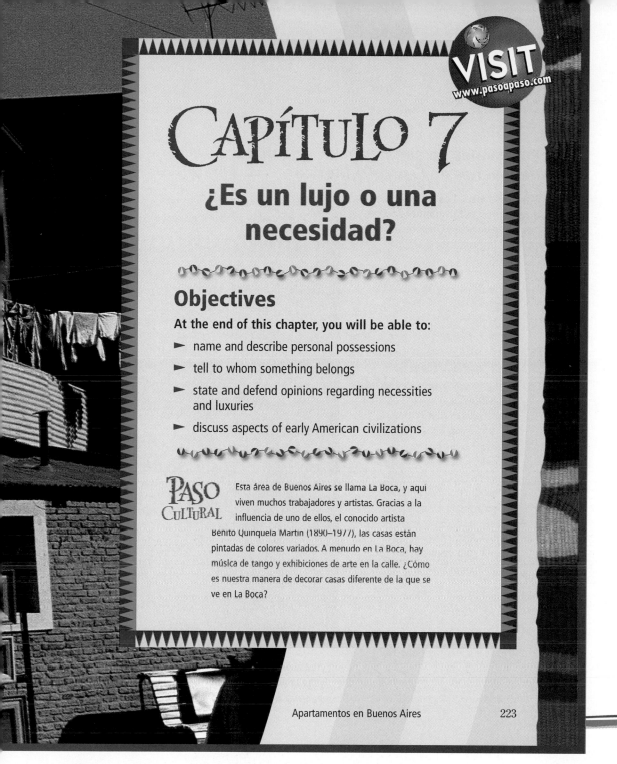

CAPÍTULO 7

¿Es un lujo o una necesidad?

Objectives

At the end of this chapter, you will be able to:

► name and describe personal possessions

► tell to whom something belongs

► state and defend opinions regarding necessities and luxuries

► discuss aspects of early American civilizations

PASO CULTURAL Esta área de Buenos Aires se llama La Boca, y aquí viven muchos trabajadores y artistas. Gracias a la influencia de uno de ellos, el conocido artista Benito Quinquela Martín (1890–1977), las casas están pintadas de colores variados. A menudo en La Boca, hay música de tango y exhibiciones de arte en la calle. ¿Cómo es nuestra manera de decorar casas diferente de la que se ve en La Boca?

Apartamentos en Buenos Aires

Cultural Notes

Paso cultural
Possible answers: Los colores de estas casas son muy fuertes y variados.

(pp. 222–223, photo)
Apartment or condominium-style buildings are common in Buenos Aires, a city of 10 million. Not all such buildings include washers and dryers, so a trip to the *lavandería* is a weekly chore for many *porteños.* Air-drying of clothes is a frequently seen alternative to a machine dryer.

Cultural Objective
• To discuss what personal belongings are important to Hispanic teens

Critical Thinking: Summarizing Information
Have students summarize the activities that are depicted in the photos on these pages. Discuss similarities and differences between the possessions shown here and what they have at home.

¡Piensa en la CULTURA!

Sevilla, España

Posesiones personales en la vida diaria de jóvenes en España y México

Mira las fotos. Los estudiantes que vemos están hablando de sus posesiones. ¿Qué tienes que es muy importante para ti?

Dos jóvenes españoles tocando la guitarra en Sevilla

PASO CULTURAL
Estos guitarristas están en la Plaza de España, una gran plaza semicircular en Sevilla donde todas las provincias de España están representadas con decoraciones cerámicas. Los mosaicos muestran los escudos, mapas y eventos históricos más importantes de cada provincia. Imagina que vas a hacer un mosaico como éste para representar el estado donde vives. ¿Qué aspectos de tu estado quieres mostrar?

"Sabemos tocar casi todas las canciones de los Beatles."
¿Tienes una guitarra o algún otro instrumento musical? ¿Es importante para ti? ¿Por qué?

224   Capítulo 7

Options

Spanish-Speaking Students
Ask: ¿Cuáles de estas posesiones son necesarias en tu vida? ¿Por qué?

 Un paso más Exs. 7-A, 7-B

Cultural Notes ☀

Paso cultural
Answers will vary.

"Me gusta esta raqueta de tenis. ¿Cuánto cuesta?"

¿Cuál es tu deporte favorito? ¿Necesitas muchas cosas para jugarlo? ¿Cuesta mucho jugarlo?

Málaga, España

San Miguel de Allende, México

"Para mí, la computadora es una necesidad. La uso todos los días."

Cultural Exploration
www.pasoapaso.com
Visit these countries on-line

¡Piensa en la cultura! 225

(p. 224, photo)
The classical guitar, of Arabic and Greco-Roman ancestry, is central to Spanish and Latin American music. As Spanish explorers followed Columbus, they brought guitars and other stringed instruments with them. During the Conquest, their guitar music blended with the ancient flutes and panpipes of the indigenous American peoples and the drums of the African peoples brought to the continent as slaves.

(p. 225, top photo)
This sporting goods store in Spain prominently displays gear for tennis, soccer, and basketball, all of which took their modern forms in nineteenth-century England or the U.S. Ask students: Why do you think these sports are popular in Spain?

(p. 225, bottom photo)
Mexico has the highest rate of computer ownership in Latin America. Most computer users are in cities, where there is better access to reliable power supplies, customer support, and parts and supplies. They also tend to be better educated and to know English, which is necessary since much software and documentation are not available in Spanish. Ask students: How does this compare with computer use in the U.S.?

Present

Chapter Theme
Personal possessions

Communicative Objectives
- To name personal possessions
- To discuss personal possessions
- To express an opinion

 Overhead 35

 Vocabulary Art BLMs/CD-ROM

 Vocabulary Tape 7-1

Grammar Preview
Possessive pronouns are presented here lexically. Their explanation appears on p. 243.

Teaching Suggestions
Preparing students to speak: Use one or two options from each of the categories of Comprehensible Input, Physical Response, or Limited Verbal Response. For a complete explanation of these categories and some sample activities, see pp. T20–T21.

Vocabulario para conversar

¿Siempre llevas carnet de identidad?

Vas a necesitar estas palabras y expresiones para hablar sobre tus posesiones. Después de leerlas varias veces, practícalas con un(a) compañero(a).

la plata

el oro

el carnet de identidad

el televisor

el secador de pelo

el arete

el anillo (de plata)

el collar

la pulsera

el control remoto

el reloj (pulsera)

el radio

la moneda

el llavero

el peine

los lentes de contacto (m.pl.)

la llave

el tocacintas, pl. los tocacintas

los anteojos (m.pl.)

la cadena (de oro)

Options

Strategies for Reaching All Students

Spanish-Speaking Students
Vocabulario para conversar: ¿Usas otras palabras para los artículos que se ven aquí? ¿Cuáles? Haz una lista.
Ex. 1: Pair bilingual with non-bilingual students, if possible.

 Un paso más Ex. 7-C

Students Needing Extra Help
Begin to fill in the vocabulary section of the Organizer. Reorganize the list according to categories: jewelry and accessories; entertainment gadgets.
También necesitas . . . : Write out the *mostrar* paradigm for those students who need to see the whole chart. Give examples of *te parece* and *me parece*.

Learning Spanish Through Action
STAGING VOCABULARY: *Levanten*
MATERIALS: actual items from the vocabulary list (or Vocabulary Art BLMs/CD-ROM)
DIRECTIONS: Hand out the props or BLMs. As you call out an item from the vocabulary list, have students hold up the item.

También necesitas . . .

mostrar (o → ue)	to show	(A mí) Me parece	I think . . .; it seems
el lujo	luxury	que . . .	to me (that) . . .
propio, -a	(one's) own		
(yo) mismo, -a	here: I myself		
el mío, la mía	mine		
el tuyo, la tuya	yours		
de vez en cuando	sometimes		
¿(A ti) Te parece	Do you think		
que . . . ?	(that) . . . ?		

> **¿Y qué quiere decir . . . ?**
> la identificación
> la necesidad

Empecemos a conversar

Túrnate con un(a) compañero(a) para ser *Estudiante A* y *Estudiante B*.
Reemplacen las palabras subrayadas en el modelo con palabras
representadas o escritas en los recuadros. Si ven 💡 pueden dar su
propia respuesta.

1

A — *¿Siempre llevas <u>carnet de identidad</u>?*
B — *Sí, siempre.*
   o: *No, nunca.*
   o: *Sólo de vez en cuando.*

Estudiante A   Estudiante B

Practice & Apply

Reteach / Review: Vocabulary

Ex. 2: Students can extend this dialogue by asking each other *¿Dónde compraste el tuyo (la tuya)? ¿Cuánto costó el tuyo (la tuya)?*

2 ESTUDIANTE A
a. Mi collar es de plata, ¿y el tuyo?
b. Mi pulsera es de oro, ¿y la tuya?
c. Mi reloj (pulsera) es de plástico, ¿y el tuyo?
d. Mi cartera es de cuero, ¿y la tuya?
e. Mi cadena es de plata, ¿y la tuya?
f. Questions will vary.

ESTUDIANTE B
a.–f. Answers will vary, but look for proper use of *el mío, la mía.*

2
A — Mi *anillo* es de *oro*, ¿y *el tuyo*?
B — *El mío* es de *plata*.
   o: *El mío* es de *oro* también.
   o: *Yo no tengo anillo*.

Estudiante A   Estudiante B

a.   b.   c.

d.   e.   f.

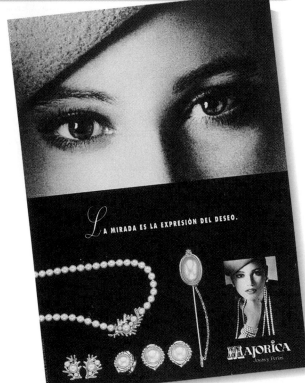

*L*A MIRADA ES LA EXPRESIÓN DEL DESEO.

MAJORICA
Joyas y Perlas

228   Capítulo 7

Options

Strategies for Reaching All Students

Spanish-Speaking Students
Exs. 2–3: Pair Spanish-speaking students, if possible.
Ex. 6: *¿Qué te gustaría tener en tu casa ideal? ¿Dónde puedes obtenerlo o comprarlo? ¿Por qué te gustaría tenerlo(la)?*

 Un paso más Ex. 7-D

Students Needing Extra Help
Ex. 2: Remind students that they have practiced *es de* with materials in Chap. 3.
Show students how *tuyo* in the question becomes *mío* in the answer.
For the first run-through, don't allow the *no tengo* response, as it doesn't provide practice of the possessive pronouns.
Encourage students to use responses involving more vocabulary and to use all the responses at least once.

Ex. 4: Model possible ways to answer question 2. Brainstorm possible responses to the *¿Por qué?* question. Remind students that *te parece* becomes *me parece*.
Ex. 5: Brainstorm possible responses to the *¿Por qué?* question.
Direct students to include household items.
Ex. 7: Brainstorm possible responses.
Students may need help with the vocabulary for all the questions.

3

A — *En tu casa, ¿tienes tu propio televisor?*
B — *Sí. Fue un regalo de (mi madre).*
  o: *No, sólo hay uno para toda la familia.*

Estudiante A

a.
b.
c.
d.
e.
f.

Estudiante B

No, sólo hay uno(a) para toda la familia.

Sí, lo (la) compré con mi propio dinero.

No, no tengo.

Sí, lo (la) compré yo mismo(a).

No, uso el (la) de ___.

Empecemos a escribir

Escribe tus respuestas en español.

4 ¿Quién usa anteojos o lentes de contacto en tu casa? ¿Desde cuándo los usan? Y tú, ¿necesitas anteojos? ¿A ti te parece necesario usar anteojos de sol? ¿Por qué?

5 ¿Qué haces para ganar dinero? ¿Te parece importante ganar tu propio dinero? Generalmente, ¿qué compras con tu propio dinero? ¿Y con el dinero de tus padres? ¿Por qué?

6 ¿Crees que un tocacintas es un lujo? ¿Y un control remoto? Haz una lista de cinco cosas que son necesidades y de cinco que son lujos. Compara tu lista con la de un(a) compañero(a).

7 ¿Por qué es importante llevar identificación? ¿Qué tipo de identificación tienes tú? ¿Dónde, a quiénes y para qué debes mostrarla?

MORE PRACTICE

- Más práctica y tarea, p. 546
- Practice Workbook 7-1, 7-2

También se dice

los lentes
las gafas
los espejuelos

los chapas
las pantallas
los zarcillos

Vocabulario para conversar 229

---

3 ESTUDIANTE A
a. En tu casa, ¿tienes tu propio secador de pelo?
b. . . . propio radio?
c. . . . propia computadora?
d. . . . propia cámara?
e. . . . propio tocacintas?
f. Questions will vary.
ESTUDIANTE B
a.–f. Answers will vary.

Answers: Empecemos a escribir

4–6 Answers will vary.

7 Answers will vary, but students may say that it is important to carry identification to provide vital information in case of an emergency. Some form of identification must be presented when making a purchase by check, when proof of age is required, and when requested by a police officer.

 Practice Wkbk. 7-1, 7-2

 Audio Activity 7.1

 Writing Activity 7-A

 Pruebas 7-1, 7-2

Cultural Notes

For the last question, write out the three questions that are included in one: *¿Dónde debes mostrarla? ¿A quiénes debes mostrarla? ¿Para qué debes mostrarla?*

Extended Written Practice/Homework
1. Write three sentences describing a possession that belongs to another person and contrasting it to one of your own: *La calculadora de Tomás es grande, pero la mía es bastante pequeña.*

2. Write three sentences expressing your opinions about items of luxury vs. items of necessity: *Me parece que el coche es una necesidad para los jóvenes.*

Multiple Intelligences
Verbal/Linguistic
See Exs. 2–3 and Audio Activity 7.1.
Visual/Spatial
See Exs. 4–7, Practice Wkbk. 7-1 and 7-2, and Writing Activity 7-A.

(p. 228, realia)
In Spain and Latin America, women are exposed to jewelry at a very early age. Tiny gold earrings are made for baby girls, many of whom have their ears pierced at birth. Several years later, gem-studded earrings replace those worn since birth. Rings and ID bracelets are also popular gifts for girls. *Medallas,* pendants depicting a religious figure, are usually given to a girl by her godparents at important religious ceremonies.

Standards 1.1; 1.2; 2.2 **229**

Present

Chapter Theme
Home appliances and furnishings

Communicative Objectives
- To name home appliances and furnishings
- To talk about emergencies
- To talk about conservation

 Overheads 36–37

 Vocabulary Art BLMs/CD-ROM

 Vocabulary Tape 7-2

Teaching Suggestions
Preparing students to speak: Use one or two options from each of the categories of Comprehensible Input, Physical Response, or Limited Verbal Response. For a complete explanation of these categories and some sample activities, see pp. T20–T21.

Vocabulario para conversar

¿Es necesario tener un detector de humo?

Aquí tienes el resto del vocabulario que necesitas en este capítulo para hablar sobre tus posesiones.

el bombillo
el detector de humo
el microondas
el incendio
el extinguidor de incendios
el ventilador
el fregadero
el tostador
el horno
el lavaplatos
el aire acondicionado

Options

Strategies for Reaching All Students

Spanish-Speaking Students

 Un paso más Ex. 7-E

Learning Spanish Through Action
STAGING VOCABULARY: *Apaguen, Enciendan, Pongan*
MATERIALS: flashlight, smoke detector, batteries, and items included in vocabulary that may be found in the classroom
DIRECTIONS: Direct students to turn off the heat, put dictionaries on the shelf, turn on the flashlight, etc.

Extended Written Practice/Homework
1. Write four pairs of sentences naming items from pp. 230–231 that your family has and telling how often you use them: *Tenemos un lavaplatos. Lo usamos todos los días.*
2. Write three sentences telling what people used to do when they didn't have certain appliances: *Antes mi abuela no tenía secadora. Secaba la ropa en el patio.*

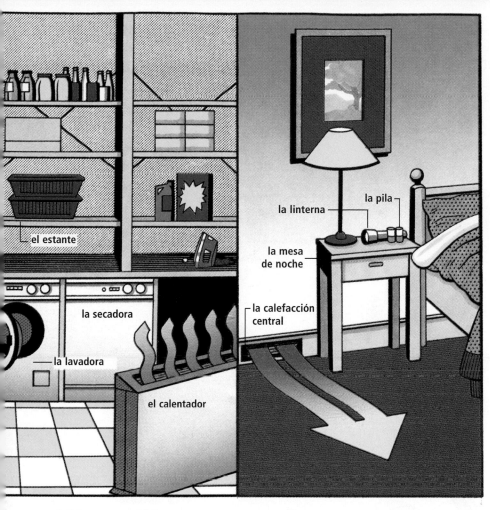

el estante

la linterna

la pila

la mesa
de noche

la calefacción
central

la secadora

la lavadora

el calentador

También necesitas . . .

encender *(e → ie)* here: *to turn on*
apagar here: *to turn off*
funcionar *to work, to function*
el aparato *appliance, device*
ahorrar *to save*

¿Y qué quiere decir . . . ?
la electricidad conservar
eléctrico, -a reparar
la emergencia en caso de
la energía suficiente
la posesión, *pl.* las
  posesiones

Critical Thinking: Categorizing Information
Call on individuals to write in the name of an item under one of the following categories: *Aparatos grandes, Aparatos pequeños, Joyas, Objetos para emergencias.* Keep the chart on a bulletin board. Encourage students to add to the lists from time to time.

Reteach / Review: Vocabulary
También necesitas . . . : To review vocabulary appropriate to environmental conservation, refer to Book 1, Chap. 13.

Class Starter Review
On the day following initial vocabulary presentation, you might begin the class with one or both of these activities:
1) In pairs, have students say which of the vocabulary items is most essential in a house and explain why. Keep a class tally on the chalkboard.
2) Prepare a list of words from previous chapters associated with each vocabulary item. For example, *el pan (tostado)* for *el tostador.* Read the list aloud and have students respond with possible associated words.

www Internet Activities
Juegos

Multiple Intelligences
Bodily/Kinesthetic
See Learning Spanish Through Action.
Logical/Mathematical
See Class Starter Review, Activity 1.
Verbal/Linguistic
See Vocabulary Tape 7-2 and Class Starter Review, Activity 2.

Visual/Spatial
1) Have students write a list of things that they do in their home to maintain a safe environment.
2) See Overheads 36–37 and the Vocabulary Art BLMs/CD-ROM.

Practice

Teaching Suggestions

Ex. 8: Encourage students to give a reason when answering positively: *Es necesario tener un microondas para cocinar más rápidamente cuando uno no tiene mucho tiempo.*

Answers: Empecemos a conversar

8 ESTUDIANTE A

a ¿Te parece que hay que tener aire acondicionado?

b. . . . un lavaplatos?

c. . . . calefacción central?

d. . . . un tostador?

e. Questions will vary.

ESTUDIANTE B

Answers will vary, but negative responses may include the following:

a. A mí me parece que un ventilador es suficiente.

b. . . . un fregadero . . .

c. . . . un calentador . . .

d. . . . un horno . . .

9 ESTUDIANTE A

a. ¿Crees que es necesario tener una linterna?

b. . . . un extinguidor de incendios?

c. . . . un radio?

d. . . . un despertador?

e. . . . pilas?

f. Questions will vary.

Empecemos a conversar

8

A —¿Te parece que hay que tener <u>un microondas</u>?

B —<u>Claro que sí.</u> Ahorra mucha energía y mucho tiempo.

o: A mí me parece que <u>un horno</u> es suficiente.

o: ¡No! ¡No soporto tantos aparatos!

Estudiante A   Estudiante B

9

A —¿Crees que es necesario tener <u>un detector de humo</u>?

B —¡Cómo no! Puedes <u>necesitarlo en caso de incendio</u>.

Estudiante A   Estudiante B

para despertarse por la mañana

en caso de incendio / emergencia

si no hay electricidad

para escuchar las noticias

para ver en la noche

No, no es necesario.

232   Capítulo 7

Options

Strategies for Reaching All Students

Spanish-Speaking Students

Exs. 8–11: Pair bilingual with non-bilingual students if possible.

Students Needing Extra Help

Ex. 8: For the first run-through, eliminate the *Claro que sí* and the *¡No! ¡No soporto . . . !* responses.

Help students with the association between air conditioner and fan, dishwasher and sink, etc.

Ex. 10: Brainstorm the possibilities for what may be found in their rooms. If available, use the vocabulary section of the Level 1, Chap. 9 Organizer.

Cooperative Learning

Have students form groups of three. Instruct groups to select one option from Ex. 10 for the question *¿Qué tienes en el / la ___ de tu dormitorio?* One student interviews the other members of the group, while the second one writes down the answers. The third student reports the results to the class: *Ana María tiene un espejo, perfume, y joyas en la cómoda de su dormitorio.*

10

A —¿Qué tienes en *la mesa de noche* de tu dormitorio?

B —Tengo *una lámpara, un radio y un despertador.*

o: *No tengo mesa de noche.*

¡NO OLVIDES!

Do you remember these words?
el cartel
la cómoda
el escritorio
el guardarropa

Estudiante A

a.
b.
c.
d.
e.

Estudiante B

f.

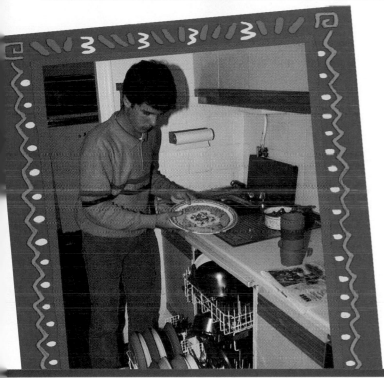

¿Lujo o necesidad? Este joven de Madrid usa el lavaplatos.

Vocabulario para conversar   233

ESTUDIANTE B

Answers will vary, but may include the following:

a. ¡Como no! Puedes necesitarla para ver en la noche.

b. . . . necesitarlo en caso de incendio.

c. . . . necesitarlo para escuchar las noticias.

d. . . . necesitarlo para despertarte por la mañana.

e. . . . necesitarlas si no hay electricidad.

f. Answers will vary.

10 ESTUDIANTE A

a. ¿Qué tienes en los estantes de tu dormitorio?

b. . . . la pared . . .

c. . . . la cómoda . . .

d. . . . el escritorio . . .

e. . . . el guardarropa . . .

f. Questions will vary.

ESTUDIANTE B

a.–f. Answers will vary.

Extended Written Practice/Homework

1. Write three sentences telling in what parts of your house different items from pp. 230–231 are located: *Hay un extinguidor de incendios en la cocina debajo del fregadero.*

2. Write three sentences saying what you wouldn't like to live without and why: *No me gustaría vivir sin calefacción central porque hace demasiado frío en el invierno.*

3. Write three sentences telling what you and others do to conserve energy: *Para ahorrar la electricidad, apago las luces que no uso.*

Multiple Intelligences

Interpersonal/Social
See Cooperative Learning.

Verbal/Linguistic
See Exs. 8–10.

Cultural Notes

(p. 233, photo)
Spanish women have joined the workforce in large numbers in recent years, which means that other family members are increasingly called upon to do domestic work. Double incomes in a family and increased work hours outside the home make dishwashers not only affordable, but often necessary to keep up with chores.

Standards 1.1; 2.1   **233**

Practice & Apply

11 ESTUDIANTE A

a. ¿Para qué sirve un lavaplatos?

b. . . . una cámara?

c. . . . una cartera?

d. . . . una secadora?

e. . . . un bombillo?

f. . . . una mesa de noche?

g. Questions will vary.

ESTUDIANTE B

Answers will vary, but may include the following:

a. Sirve para lavar platos.

b. . . . sacar fotos.

c. . . . llevar dinero.

d. . . . secar ropa.

e. . . . dar luz.

f. . . . poner el despertador.

g. Answers will vary.

11

A — ¿*Para qué sirve una lavadora*?

B — *Sirve para lavar ropa*.

Estudiante A

Estudiante B

a. b. c.

d. e. f. g.

Empecemos a escribir y a leer

Escribe tus respuestas en español.

12 ¿Qué podemos hacer todos los días para conservar energía? En tu casa, ¿encienden todas las luces por la noche? ¿Cómo podemos conservar agua? Tú mismo, ¿qué puedes hacer hoy para conservar energía y agua?

13 ¿Qué aparato eléctrico es el más necesario para ti? ¿Y para tus padres? Cuando no funciona un aparato, ¿te parece mejor repararlo o comprar uno nuevo? ¿Ahorras dinero si lo reparas? ¿Qué aparatos necesitan pilas?

14 Entre todas tus posesiones, ¿cuáles son las más importantes para ti? ¿Por qué? De esas posesiones, ¿hay cosas que ya no necesitas? ¿Cuáles?

15 En caso de incendio, ¿sabes qué hacer? ¿A qué número debes llamar? ¿Y en caso de alguna otra emergencia? ¿A quién le puedes pedir ayuda?

www.pasoapaso.com

MORE PRACTICE

Más práctica y tarea, p. 547
Practice Workbook 7–3, 7–4

Options

Strategies for Reaching All Students

Spanish-Speaking Students
Ex. 12: *¿Qué puedes hacer con las cosas que no necesitas? ¿A quién o a qué organización puedes ofrecérselas?*

 Un paso más Exs. 7-F, 7-G

Students Needing Extra Help
Ex. 11: Brainstorm possible *Estudiante B* responses.
Exs. 12–14: Choose a few from each group in order to help students stay focused. Many students haven't given these issues much thought. They will need help with the vocabulary.
Ex. 15: Students will need help with vocabulary. Review telephone numbers.
Ex. 16: Brainstorm possibilities for the other three rules. Supply vocabulary as needed.

Enrichment
Ex. 11: As a homework assignment, have students choose an electrical or battery-powered appliance and describe it (how it works, what it looks like) to someone who has never seen one before. Encourage students to be imaginative and thorough in their descriptions. You might have them present their descriptions orally and have the class guess what the appliance is.

16 Aquí tienes una serie de reglas *(rules)* para conservar energía y agua. Con un(a) compañero(a), cámbienlas si no están de acuerdo con ellas. Después, escriban otras tres reglas.

Para conservar energía y agua es necesario:

- apagar los aparatos eléctricos por la mañana
- encender solamente las luces necesarias por la noche
- ducharse rápidamente
- usar la lavadora sólo cuando hay mucha ropa sucia
- usar el aire acondicionado sólo de vez en cuando
- reparar los aparatos que no funcionan bien

Pinnnn...

NOVEDAD MUNDIAL

...zassss

Toast Taurus, con pinzas. Para no quemarse.

La tostadora automática Toast Taurus tiene exterior frío. Cuenta, además, en exclusiva, con unas pinzas integradas que permiten coger las tostadas sin quemarse.
Por otra parte, está especialmente preparada para descongelar. La intensidad del tostado del pan se gradúa automáticamente. Su amplia abertura admite todo tipo de rebanadas, desde las de pan de molde hasta las de pan de hogaza.

taurus crea

También se dice

la tostadora

la batería

la bombilla
la bujía

el abanico

el lavatrastos
el lavatrastes

el foco

la repisa

la mesa de luz
la mesilla

Vocabulario para conversar   235

Answers: Empecemos a escribir y a leer

12 Answers will vary, but students may say that they can save energy by turning off the lights when not in use, and riding a bike or walking instead of using a car. They can save water by not leaving the water running while brushing their teeth, by not using as much water when washing dishes, or by saving up clothes for a large laundry load.

13–14 Answers will vary.

15 Answers will vary, but students may say they should dial 911 *(nueve once)* in case of a fire or other emergency.

16 Answers will vary.

 Practice Wkbk. 7-3, 7-4

Audio Activity 7.2

Writing Activities 7-B, 7-C, 7-D

Pruebas 7-3, 7-4

Comm. Act. BLM 7-1

Multiple Intelligences
Naturalist
Have students write a short paragraph discussing the effects that appliances have on their lives. They can discuss positive or negative effects on daily life as well as on the environment.

Verbal/Linguistic
See Enrichment, Exs. 12–16, and Audio Activity 7.2.
Visual/Spatial
See Practice Wkbk. 7-3 and 7-4; Writing Activities 7-B, 7-C, and 7-D; and Comm. Act. BLM 7-1.

Cultural Notes

(p. 235, realia)
Pinzas, the selling point of this toaster, are used to create this onomatopeic ad:
Pinnnn . . . the toaster hums as it toasts the bread. Suddenly, *¡ . . . zassss!* The toast pops up and in one fell swoop, it is snatched up and placed on the plate. To facilitate this maneuver without burning oneself, this toaster comes equipped with *pinzas* (tongs).

Apply

Answers:
¡Comuniquemos!
1–3 Answers will vary.

Using Photos

Having students use what they've learned about word families *(dominical / domingo)*, ask: *¿Cuándo van de compras estos jóvenes?*

¡Comuniquemos!

Aquí tienes otra oportunidad para usar el vocabulario de este capítulo.

1 Imagina que eres un(a) millonario(a). ¿Qué aparatos eléctricos te gustaría comprar? ¿Para quién? ¿Por qué? Trabaja con un(a) compañero(a).

para tu familia / $1.500

A —*¿Qué aparato eléctrico te gustaría comprar para tu familia con $1.500?*
B —*Un televisor muy grande con control remoto.*
A —*¿Por qué?*
B — . . .

a. para ti / $250
b. para la escuela / $500
c. para tu mejor amigo(a) / $100
d. para tu familia / $1.000
e. para la guardería infantil a la cual ibas cuando eras niño(a) / $500
f. para tus vecinos / $50
g. para algún (alguna) niño(a) que conoces / $50
h. 💡

2 Hay un incendio en el horno eléctrico cuando tú y tu compañero(a) están cocinando. ¿Qué hacen? Escribe un diálogo con tu compañero(a).

A —*¡Aaaaay! ¡Mira, Luis, un incendio!*
B —*Hay que . . .*
A —*¡No! Trae . . .*
B — . . .

Unos jóvenes madrileños en un mercado dominical

Options

Strategies for Reaching All Students

Students Needing Extra Help
Ex. 1: Students will need help with the response to *¿Por qué?* Use the vocabulary section of the Organizer.
Ex. 2: Discuss what to do during a kitchen fire (throw salt, not water). Model a complete dialogue. Students will most likely give the correct response first, not noticing that the third line of dialogue begins with *¡No! Trae . . .*

Ex. 3: If available, use the vocabulary section of Level 1, Chaps. 6 and 7 Organizers. *¿Qué sabes ahora?:* Have students write out this list so that they can keep track of their progress.

Enrichment
Have pairs of students embellish their dialogues and present them as skits to the rest of the class the next day. Encourage students to use real newspaper ads or mailings for props. Remind them that the shopping vocabulary from Chap. 3 would be helpful.

3 Túrnate con un(a) compañero(a). Van a ser el padre o la madre y su hijo(a). Quieres algo, pero tu padre o madre no quiere comprarlo. ¿Cómo puedes convencerlo(la)? Explícale:

- qué quieres
- por qué lo quieres
- dónde lo viste
- cómo es
- cuánto cuesta

¿Qué sabes ahora?

Can you:

- name some personal possessions?

    —Tengo ___, ___ y ___ en mi dormitorio.

- describe personal possessions and ask about those of other people?

    —Mi anillo es de ___, ¿y el ___?

- state and defend opinions regarding necessities and luxuries?

    —Me parece que tener ___ es una necesidad, pero tener ___ es un lujo.

Answers: ¿Qué sabes ahora?

- Answers will vary, but each blank should contain a noun.
- Answers will vary, but the first blank should contain a material and the second a possessive pronoun.
- Answers will vary, but both blanks should contain nouns.

 Audio Activity 7.3

 Pasos vivos 2 CD-ROM

Boom Box, Clip Art Album, Notas culturales, Slide Projector, Laboratorio de grabar

Cooperative Learning

Have students form groups of three. Two will act as though they are looking for an apartment; the third will be a landlord. Two apartments are available. One has a sink, an electric fan, and a refrigerator; it costs $450. The other has a microwave, a dishwasher, and central air conditioning; it costs $700. The renters have a combined monthly income of $1,000. The landlord must describe both apartments and try to convince the students to lease the more expensive one. The renters need to decide between themselves which one they will rent, and be prepared to explain their reasons to the class.

Multiple Intelligences

Bodily/Kinesthetic and Interpersonal/Social
See Cooperative Learning.
Verbal/Linguistic
See Audio Activity 7.3, Exs. 1–3, and Enrichment.

Cultural Notes

(p. 236, photo)
A Sunday morning excursion to *el Rastro,* Spain's famous flea market, is a Madrid tradition. Filled with surprises and discoveries, this market is not a destination for someone with a specific shopping list. Browsing is what brings real success. True flea markets such as this are disappearing from modern cities as malls, shopping centers, and discount malls grow more common.

Standards 1.1; 2.1; 3.1   **237**

Present & Apply

Cultural Objective
- To discuss early American civilizations

Critical Thinking: Synthesizing
Have small groups of students use encyclopedias or social studies texts to prepare maps showing the areas of the Aztec, Mayan, and Incan civilizations. Have them label each civilization's capital and important geographical features. In addition, they might illustrate their maps with drawings or descriptions of key accomplishments of each civilization.

Multicultural Perspectives
The Aztec description of the Spanish conquest of Tenochtitlán in the Codex Florentine reveals a difference in perceptions of what was considered valuable by the two cultures. The Spanish wanted gold and gold alone. The Aztecs were surprised when the Spanish tore off the *quetzal* feathers decorating the gold ornaments and burned them. For the Aztecs and the Maya, the *quetzal* was a spiritual protector, and its feathers were extremely valuable. Ask students if they know of any objects that are valued in one culture that are not necessarily valued in another.

Perspectiva cultural

¿Según las fotos, cómo se sabe que estas civilizaciones eran muy avanzadas en la agricultura? ¿En las ciencias? ¿En el arte?

En el año 1500, los aztecas dominaban lo que hoy es México. La ciudad de Tenochtitlán, la capital azteca, tenía más o menos 200.000 habitantes, más que cualquier ciudad europea de ese tiempo. Esta ciudad tenía grandes templos y avenidas y un estadio para un deporte similar al básquetbol. Cultivaban maíz, verduras y flores en grandes jardines acuáticos. Hacían joyas de cobre, oro y plata. ¡Y hacían todo sin instrumentos de metal ni sistema alfabético de escribir!

Esta cabeza hecha de estuco está en una pared de la antigua ciudad maya de Comalcalco, México.

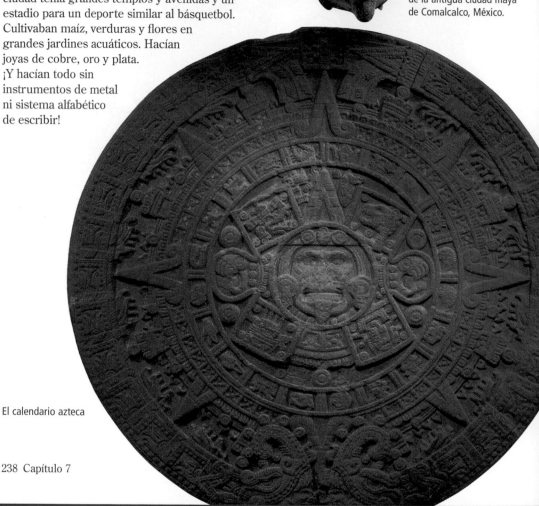

El calendario azteca

238 Capítulo 7

Options

Strategies for Reaching All Students

Spanish-Speaking Students
After Ex. 2: *Haz una investigación sobre un aspecto de la vida diaria de una de estas civilizaciones indígenas. Luego, descríbelo en una composición breve. Puedes ilustrar tu informe y exhibirlo en la sala de clase.*

 Un paso más Ex. 7-H

Students Needing Extra Help
Have students take notes, as an aid in reviewing for the exam.
Have some background material on hand.
Ex. 1: Students will have very little knowledge of the Greeks and Romans. Be prepared to give them this information. You may want to invite the Latin teacher or someone from the history department to come to your class.
Ex. 2: Brainstorm possible solutions. Supply the vocabulary.

Cultural Notes

(p. 238, bottom photo)
The Calendar Stone was completed about 1479 A.D. From the center, the six circles contain 1) Tonatiuh, the Aztec sun god; 2) four ovals individually representing the previous stages of the world, and together representing our present world; 3) symbols for 20 days in the Aztec calendar; 4) symbols for jade or turquoise meaning "precious," referring to the sky's color; 5) glyphs for "star" penetrated by the sun's rays; 6) fire snakes symbolizing time.

Cuando el imperio romano estaba perdiendo su influencia en el año 200 d. C., en América Central crecía el imperio maya. Los mayas también tenían grandes ciudades. En el centro de Tikal, por ejemplo, había más de 300 edificios. Los mayas tenían observatorios astronómicos. Su calendario de 365 días era más preciso que el calendario europeo de esa época. Y todavía podemos admirar sus joyas, su cerámica y sus monumentos de piedra.

La civilización que dominaba la región de los Andes en el año 1500 era la de los incas. Construyeron caminos y puentes en las montañas. Hicieron edificios grandes y elegantes. Construyeron estos edificios tan bien que aun hoy no se puede poner un cuchillo entre las piedras de sus paredes.

"El Caracol," observatorio astronómico maya de Chichén Itzá, Yucatán, México

Vista de Machu Picchu, una ciudad incaica en los Andes peruanos

La cultura desde tu perspectiva

1   ¿Cuál de estas civilizaciones antiguas te parece más similar a la civilización romana o griega? ¿Por qué?

2   Imagina que tienes que hacer una pirámide como las de los aztecas o los mayas sin usar instrumentos de metal. ¿Qué problemas vas a tener? ¿Cómo los vas a solucionar?

(p. 238, top photo)
This stucco head is part of a wall relief in Comalcalco, a site in the Mexican state of Tabasco, at what was the western limit of the Mayan Civilization. Comalcalco flourished during the middle classic period (approximately 450–600 A.D.) The architecture and brick and stucco construction methods here are similar to those of Palenque.

(p. 239, left photo)
El Caracol (800–1000 A.D.) is believed to have had a purpose similar to that of an astronomical observatory. Through astronomy, the Mayas devised a calendar system more accurate than any except our Gregorian calendar. El Templo de los Guerreros *(right)* was built during the post-classic Maya period (1000–1200). The building features images of Quetzalcóatl, one of the legendary rulers of the Toltecs.

(p. 239, right photo)
Located in the Andes Mountains, at more than 8,000 feet above sea level, Machu Picchu is one of the best preserved archeological sites in South America. The ruins were rediscovered in 1911 by Hiram Bingham. These remains tell us many things about pre-Columbian Incan culture. The great stone temples and large above-ground cemeteries tell of the Incan belief in the afterlife and of the importance of religion to their civilization.

Preview

Overhead 38

Answers

A He uses the word(s) *(los) míos.* If he were talking about *un disco compacto,* the word(s) would be *(el) mío.*

B The words used to describe characteristics of the robot are *(una) necesidad, (una) maravilla, fantástico, mágico,* and *resistente.* The verb used with the descriptions is *ser.*

Gramática en contexto

¡El último triunfo de la tecnología!

HACELOTODO funciona con electricidad o con pilas.

HACELOTODO da lecciones por computadora.

HACELOTODO juega video-juegos, damas y ajedrez.

HACELOTODO muestra video y toca discos compactos.

HACELOTODO envía mensajes por fax.

HACELOTODO es mucho mejor que una linterna. Tiene bombillos en las manos.

HACELOTODO tiene detector de humo y puede apagar incendios. ¡Y al final del día, cuando Ud. lo apaga, **HACELOTODO** no está cansado!

¿Qué dicen nuestros clientes?

❝**HACELOTODO** *no es un lujo, es una necesidad. ¡Es una maravilla! El mío ayuda a los niños en sus tareas.*❞
JUAN SOTO, MONTEREY PARK

❝**HACELOTODO** *es fantástico. Yo misma no puedo vivir sin él.*❞
CARLOTA SANTOS, LOMA LINDA

❝*Yo uso a* **HACELOTODO** *para escuchar música. Saco fácilmente los discos compactos de mis hijos y pongo los míos.*❞
FRANK ÁVALOS, MONTEBELLO

El mágico **HACELOTODO** *es de metal fuerte, no de plástico. Es resistente al calor y al frío.* **HACELOTODO** *puede ser suyo por sólo $899. Reserve su propio* **HACELOTODO** *ahora mismo.*

A Frank Ávalos talks about "my children's CDs and mine." What word does he use for "mine"? If he were talking about *un disco compacto,* what form do you think that word would take?

B In this ad, users describe characteristics of the robot. What are they? At the bottom of the ad, other expressions tell what the robot is made of. What verb is used with both types of descriptions?

240   Capítulo 7

Options

Strategies for Reaching All Students

Students Needing Extra Help
Begin the grammar section of the Organizer. Ex. A: On the chalkboard or overhead, write out *los discos compactos → los míos un disco compacto → _____.*
Show the pattern that connects *los discos* and *los míos.*
Ex. B: Direct students to the words that describe characteristics.

Give examples of how these adjectives agree in number and, when applicable, in gender. You may now want to do Ex. 1 on p. 242. Give more examples using *su* and *sus* with *de.* Show how *my key* becomes *mine* (two words becoming one). Construct a chart in which you show students that you have really said the same thing in two different ways.

Enrichment
As an in-class written assignment, have students create more comments praising HACELOTODO, citing other things the robot has done for them. When students have finished, call on them to share their comments with the class.

Los adjetivos posesivos

You know that possessive adjectives agree in gender and number with the nouns they describe. They are always used before a noun.

mi, tu, su nuestro	televisor	mis, tus, sus nuestros	televisores
mi, tu, su nuestra	linterna	mis, tus, sus nuestras	linternas

• Since *su* and *sus* have many meanings, for clarity or emphasis we can use a prepositional phrase instead.

de	Ud. él ella	de	Uds. ellos ellas

—¡**Sus** zapatos son   *(His / Her / Your / Their)*
muy elegantes!   *shoes are very elegant!*
—¿Los zapatos **de ella**?   *Her shoes?*
—No, los **de Ud**.   *No, yours.*

• Like English, Spanish has another set of possessive adjectives that come *after* the noun. Compare these sentences.

Ésa es **mi** llave.   *That's my key.*
Esa llave es **mía**.   *That key is mine.*

Here are the possessive adjectives that follow a noun:

mío(s), mía(s)	*my, mine*	nuestro(s), nuestra(s)	*our, ours*
tuyo(s), tuya(s)	*your, yours*	vuestro(s), vuestra(s)	*your, yours*
suyo(s), suya(s)	*your, yours his her, hers*	suyo(s), suya(s)	*your, yours their, theirs*

Gramática en contexto   241

Present
Class Starter Review
On the day following the presentation of possessive adjectives, you might begin the class with this activity:
Ask individual students about objects in the classroom: *¿De quién es ese suéter? (Es mío, es suyo.) ¿De quién es ese escritorio? (Es suyo, profesora.)*

Cooperative Learning
Tell students they will create a time capsule. In groups of three, using the Vocabulary Art BLMs/CD-ROM or magazine cutouts representing similar items, have each student mount a cutout on a sheet of paper, writing a description of the item underneath. When they are finished, students pass their papers to the left, and the receiving students write the use for the cutout item on their new paper. After passing their papers to the left again, students will write whether the item is a luxury or a necessity. Have each group collect the three papers and roll them into a "time capsule" tube, securing it with a rubber band or piece of yarn. Then each group passes its time capsule to another group. The receiving group represents Aztecs from the year 1500. Each student will examine a paper from the previous group and answer in writing: What item do you use for the same purpose? How is it similar or different from this item? Is your item a luxury or a necessity for you? Call on students to report results.

Multiple Intelligences
Bodily/Kinesthetic and Interpersonal/Social
See Cooperative Learning.
Verbal/Linguistic
See Class Starter Review.
Visual/Spatial
See Overhead 38 and Enrichment.

Present & Practice

Multicultural Perspectives

Appliances such as refrigerators may be considered necessities in some places and luxuries in others. In some small towns in Latin America, for example, people who don't have refrigerators use other methods to preserve food. Raw meat is sometimes salted or smoked. In cold regions such as the Andes Mountains in South America, food may be frozen outside. Many people also buy the exact amount of food needed for that particular day, keeping perishable items cold in an ice-filled cooler. Ask students what appliances they use every day and how they would survive without these items.

Answers

1 ESTUDIANTE A

a. ¿Son tus llaveros?
b. ¿Es tu carnet de identidad?
c. ¿Son tus collares?
d. ¿Son tus lentes de contacto?
e. ¿Son tus pulseras?
f. Questions will vary.

ESTUDIANTE B

a. No, son los de ellos.
b. No, es el de Mauricio.
c. No, son los de Luz y Estela.
d. No, son los de nosotros.
e. No, son las de Uds.
f. Answers will vary.

• To clarify or emphasize, we can use *de* + pronoun instead of a form of *suyo*.

¿Es el ventilador **suyo**?   *Is it (**his/her/your/their**) fan?*
Sí, es el ventilador **de ella**.   *Yes, it's **her** fan.*

Note that the pronoun agrees in number and gender with the noun it refers to.

1 Pregúntale a un(a) compañero(a) si estas cosas son de él (ella).

A — *¿Es tu anillo?*
B — *No, es el de Mercedes.*

Mercedes

| a. ellos | b. Mauricio | c. Luz y Estela | d. nosotros | e. Uds. | f. |

2 ¿De quién son estos aparatos? Pregúntale a un(a) compañero(a).

A — *Éste es el calentador de Myriam, ¿verdad?*
B — *Sí, es el calentador suyo.*
   o: *No, no es el calentador suyo.*

Myriam

| a. ella | b. Carmina y Manuel | c. él |

| d. Uds. | e. ellas | f. Mateo | g. |

242   Capítulo 7

Options

Strategies for Reaching All Students

Students Needing Extra Help
Ex. 1: You may want to do this exercise right after reviewing the possessive adjectives that come before a noun *(mi, tu,* etc.) and the prepositional phrase using *de (de Ud., de él).*
Ex. 2: Review demonstrative pronouns. Point out that the possessive adjective agrees with the object, not the person.

Show on the board or overhead that students only need to eliminate the *de* phrase and replace it with the possessive adjective.

Extended Written Practice/Homework
1. If you and a brother or sister had to identify to whom different items belonged, what would you say is or is not yours? Write four sentences: *Los aretes de oro no son míos.*
2. Write three questions you can ask classmates to find out if different items belong to them: *¿Las llaves son tuyas?*

Los pronombres posesivos

A possessive pronoun takes the place of a noun and a possessive adjective.

	el mío	la mía	los míos	las mías
	el tuyo	la tuya	los tuyos	las tuyas
	el suyo	la suya	los suyos	las suyas
	el nuestro	la nuestra	los nuestros	las nuestras
	el suyo	la suya	los suyos	las suyas

- The possessive pronouns agree in number and gender with the nouns they replace. They are generally used with the appropriate definite article.

  Mi linterna está en el armario. ¿Dónde está **la tuya**?

- When possessive pronouns are used after the verb *ser*, we usually omit the definite article.

  —¿De quién es esta cartera?
  —Es **mía**.

Gramática en contexto   243

a. Éste es el microondas de nosotros, ¿verdad?
b. ...el secador de pelo de Carmina y Manuel ...
c. ...el tocacintas de él ...
d. ...el tostador de Uds. ...
e. Éste es el radio de ellas ...
f Éste es el extinguidor de incendios de Mateo ...
g. Questions will vary.

ESTUDIANTE B
a. Sí, es (No, no es) el microondas nuestro (*or:* suyo).
b. ...el secador de pelo suyo.
c. ...el tocacintas suyo.
d. ...el tostador nuestro.
e. Sí, es (No, no es) el radio suyo.
f. Sí, es (No, no es) el extinguidor de incendios suyo.
g. Answers will vary.

 Practice Wkbk. 7-5

 Writing Activity 7-E

 Prueba 7-5

3. Write three sentences saying that a person has an item that does not belong to him or her: *Juan tiene unas monedas que no son suyas.*

Multiple Intelligences
Visual/Spatial
See Practice Wkbk. 7-5 and Writing Activity 7-E.

Practice

Re-enter / Recycle
Exs. 3, 4, 6: clothing from Chap. 3
Ex. 4: school from Chap. 2
Ex. 6: sports from Chap. 4

Answers

3 ESTUDIANTE A
a. El anillo de plata, ¿es tuyo o de Rosa?
b. El reloj de plástico, ¿es tuyo o de Mario?
c. La mesa de noche de metal, ¿es tuya o de él?
d. La cartera negra, ¿es tuya o del profesor / de la profesora?
e. La camisa (blusa) a cuadros, ¿es tuya o de ella?
f. Questions will vary.

ESTUDIANTE B
Answers will vary.
a. Es suyo. El mío es de oro.
b. Es suyo. El mío es de cuero.
c. Es suya. La mía es de madera.
d. Es suya. La mía es marrón.
e. Es suya. La mía es a rayas.
f. Answers will vary.

4 Answers will vary.

5 ESTUDIANTE A
a. No encuentro mi champú. ¿Me prestas el tuyo?
b. . . . mi pasta dentífrica. . . . la tuya?
c. . . . mis pesas. . . . las tuyas?
d. . . . mi tocacintas. . . . el tuyo?
e. . . . mi raqueta de tenis. . . . la tuya?
f. . . . mi radio. . . . el tuyo?
g. . . . mi secador de pelo. . . . el tuyo?

3 Túrnate con un(a) compañero(a) para preguntar de quién es cada uno de estos objetos.

A —El peine azul, ¿es tuyo o de Eva?
B —Es suyo. El mío es rojo.

Eva

a. Rosa   b. Mario   c. él

d. el (la) profesor(a)   e. ella   f.

4 Con un(a) compañero(a), hablen de sus posesiones. Por ejemplo:

A —Mi cartera es negra. ¿Y la tuya?
B —La mía es verde. Es de plástico.
    o: La mía es negra también.
    o: No tengo cartera.

244   Capítulo 7

Options

Strategies for Reaching All Students

Students Needing Extra Help
Ex. 3: Use vocabulary sections of Chap. 3. Do as a whole class, as this exercise involves multiple steps. Show students that a form of *tuyo, suyo,* and *mío* is used in each dialogue, just as in the model. One picture will be paired with a form of *tuyo.* Show how the *de* phrase becomes a form of *suyo.* Finally, show how the *tuyo* in statement A becomes the *el mío* in statement B. Provide more examples.

Ex. 4: Show students how *mi cartera* becomes *la tuya.* Demonstrate how a form of *tuyo* in the question becomes a form of *mío* in the answer. Do more examples using masculine, plurals, etc.
Ex. 5: You may want to have students answer only with the second response because it does not involve object pronouns. Remind students of the vocabulary they can use to excuse themselves if they do not have the item in question: *Lo siento (perdón), yo no tengo peine.*

Ex. 6: Use the vocabulary section of Chap. 3 Organizer. Remind students that the adjective in each sentence will be a form of *horrible.* Students may be confused to see *tu* and *tus* instead of *tuyo.* Explain.
Ex. 7: Practice the entire exercise, answering with only the first B response. This will help students stay focused on dropping the article before a form of *ser.* Then repeat, using the second response, reminding students of why *los* is present.

5 Estás con tu compañero(a) en el club deportivo y no encuentras tus cosas. Pídele las suyas.

peine   A —*No encuentro mi peine. ¿Me prestas el tuyo?*
        B —*¿El mío? Aquí lo tienes.*
           o: *¿El mío? Yo no tengo peine.*

a. champú
b. pasta dentífrica
c. pesas
d. tocacintas

e. raqueta de tenis
f. radio
g. secador de pelo
h. reloj

6 Rosita siempre prefiere las cosas de sus hermanas mayores. Con un(a) compañero(a), sigue el modelo.

A —*¿Por qué no usas tus propios anteojos de sol?*
B —*Porque los míos son horribles. Prefiero los suyos.*

7 Después de un incendio en un edificio de apartamentos, los bomberos preguntan de quién son estas cosas en la calle.

aparatos   A —*¿Son suyos estos aparatos?*
         B —*Sí, señor, son nuestros.*
           o: *No, señor, no sabemos dónde están los nuestros.*

a. estantes
b. mesas de noche
c. juguetes
d. lámparas

e. sillas
f. televisores
g. trajes
h. lavadora y secadora

Gramática en contexto   245

h. ...mi reloj. ...el tuyo?
ESTUDIANTE B
a. ¿El mío? Aquí lo tienes.
b. ¿La mía? ...la ...
c. ¿Las mías? ...las ...
d. ¿El mío? ...lo ...
e. ¿La mía? ...la ...
f. ¿El mío? ...lo ...
g. ¿El mío? ...lo ...
h. ¿El mío? ...lo ...

6 Answers will vary.

7 ESTUDIANTE A
a. ¿Son suyos estos estantes?
b. ...suyas estas mesas de noche?
c. ...suyos estos juguetes?
d. ...suyas estas lámparas?
e. ...suyas estas sillas?
f. ...suyos estos televisores?
g. ...suyos estos trajes?
h. ...suyas esta lavadora y secadora?
ESTUDIANTE B
a. Sí, señor, son nuestros. / No, señor, no sabemos dónde están los nuestros.
b. ...nuestras. / ...las nuestras.
c. ...nuestros. / ...los nuestros.
d. ...nuestras. / ...las nuestras.
e. ...nuestras. / ...las nuestras.
f. ...nuestros. / ...los nuestros.
g. ...nuestros. / ...los nuestros.
h. ...nuestras. / ...las nuestras.

 Practice Wkbk. 7-6, 7-7

 Prueba 7-6

 Comm. Act. BLM 7-2

Extended Written Practice/Homework
1. Write four sentences contrasting possessions of your neighbors and other people with those of your family: *Los muebles de mis vecinos son nuevos, pero los nuestros son antiguos y cómodos.*
2. Write three pairs of sentences contrasting your possessions with those of other students: *Antonio y yo llevamos suéteres de vez en cuando. Los míos son de algodón; los suyos son de lana.*

Multiple Intelligences
Verbal/Linguistic and Bodily/Kinesthetic
Have students write an original dialogue based on the picture in Ex. 6. Have them bring in props and present the dialogue to the class.
Visual/Spatial
See Practice Wkbk. 7-6 and 7-7 and Comm. Act. BLM 7-2.

Present & Practice

Re-enter / Recycle

Ex. 9: school supplies from Chap. 2

Ex. 10: school subjects from Chap. 2, sports and leisure activities from Chap. 4, special occasions from Chap. 6

Class Starter Review

On the day following the review of *ser*, you might begin the class with this activity:

Using *nuestro* and *mi,* a vocabulary item from the chapter, and *ser* and *estar,* have students write a statement describing the item and where it is in their house. *(Nuestro tostador es bastante viejo; está en la cocina.)*

Answers

8–9 Answers will vary.

10 ESTUDIANTE A

a. ¿Sabes cuándo (dónde) va a ser el partido de hockey?

b. . . . la fiesta de cumpleaños de Teresa?

c. . . . el desfile?

d. . . . la graduación?

e. . . . la boda de Luis y Pilar?

f. . . . la reunión del coro?

g. . . . la próxima prueba de química?

h. . . . la exposición de arte?

i. Questions will vary.

Repaso: Los usos del verbo *ser*

Review the present-tense forms of *ser*.

soy	somos
eres	sois
es	son

Remember that we use *ser* to describe a characteristic that usually does not change from one minute to the next or over time.

> Carlos **es** alto y tiene pelo castaño.
> El helado **es** frío.

• We also use *ser* to indicate origin, material, or possession.

> Mi profesora **es** de Honduras.
> La linterna **es** de plástico.
> El llavero **es** del señor Durán.

• *Ser* is also used to tell where and when an event takes place.

> La reunión del consejo estudiantil **es** a las ocho.
> **Es** en el gimnasio.

8 Descríbele a tu compañero(a) tu posesión más importante. Debes decirle cómo es, pero no le digas qué es. Tu compañero(a) debe adivinarlo. Puedes decirle:

- el color, el tamaño
- de dónde es (si lo sabes)
- para qué sirve
- si lo (la) compraste tú o fue un regalo

Si tu compañero(a) no adivina, él o ella debe decirle la descripción a otro(a) estudiante. Por ejemplo:

Clara dice que su posesión más importante es bastante grande, verde, de cuero. La compró . . .

9 Ahora túrnate con tu compañero(a) para describir dos salas diferentes de la escuela y lo que hay en ellas.

La sala de computadoras es grande, pero no hay ventanas. Las computadoras son . . . Hay . . .

¡NO OLVIDES!

Do you remember the present-tense forms of *decir?*

digo	decimos
dices	decís
dice	dicen

246   Capítulo 7

Options

Strategies for Reaching All Students

Students Needing Extra Help

Ex. 8: Model a whole description (or more). Say it, but have copies of it ready to give to students so they can repeat it. Otherwise, they will have difficulty remembering the details and will lose the emphasis of the exercise, which is a review of *ser.* Show how when repeating it to another classmate, the student must change the form of the verb. Review object pronouns. Do in small groups.

Brainstorm vocabulary to use in this section.

Ex. 10: Model an example using a place. *Ahora lo sabes:* Have students write out this list so students can record their progress.

Extended Written Practice/Homework

1. Choose four items from pp. 226–227 and write sentences naming two or more basic characteristics of each one: *La mesa de noche en mi dormitorio es de madera y es bastante pequeña.*

2. Refer to the vocabulary on p. 123 and write four sentences describing your clothing and that of other people: *La falda de Maribel es de lana y es muy elegante.*

10 Túrnate con tu compañero(a) para decir dónde o cuándo van a ser estas actividades.

picnic / sábado /   A —¿Sabes cuándo va a ser el picnic?
10 A.M.   B —Sí, el sábado a las 10 de la mañana.

a. el partido de hockey / jueves / gimnasio
b. la fiesta de cumpleaños de Teresa / viernes / 7 P.M.
c. el desfile / domingo / el parque
d. la graduación / martes / 4 P.M.
e. la boda de Luis y Pilar / sábado / 3 P.M.
f. la reunión del coro / miércoles / el auditorio
g. la próxima prueba de química / mañana / el laboratorio
h. la exposición de arte / la próxima semana / la biblioteca
i. 💡

PASO CULTURAL

La corrida de toros *(bullfighting)* es una combinación de arte, deporte, espectáculo y ceremonia, con elementos de las antiguas culturas y de la sociedad moderna. En España, hay corridas de toros desde la primavera hasta el otoño. Mucha gente pregunta si las corridas son un abuso de los animales. Otras personas consideran que la interacción entre el matador y el toro es un arte y debe continuar. ¿Qué piensas tú?

Trajes de luces: Sólo los matadores pueden llevar trajes de oro. Los banderilleros—asistentes del matador—llevan los de plata.

Ahora lo sabes

Can you:

■ say what is yours and what belongs to someone else?
—Esa ___ es ___; la otra es de ___.

■ describe things?
—Mi reloj es de ___; no ___ de plata.

■ tell the time and place of an event?
—La graduación ___ el 23 de mayo.
Es ___ 5 de la tarde.

Gramática en contexto   247

a. Sí, el jueves en el gimnasio.
b. Sí, el viernes a las siete de la noche.
c. Sí, el domingo en el parque.
d. Sí, el martes a las cuatro de la tarde.
e. Sí, el sábado a las tres de la tarde.
f. Sí, el miércoles en el auditorio.
g. Sí, mañana en el laboratorio.
h. Sí, la próxima semana en la biblioteca.
i. Answers will vary.

Answers: Ahora lo sabes
• Answers will vary, but the first should be a feminine noun, the second *mía,* and the third a name or personal pronoun.
• Answers will vary, but the first blank should be a material, and the second *es.*
• es / a las

 Practice Wkbk. 7-8

 Audio Activities 7.4, 7.5

 Writing Activity 7-F

 Prueba 7-7

 Comm. Act. BLM 7-3

 Pasos vivos 2 CD-ROM
Phone Task, Slide Presentation Maker, Spindle, Treadmill

Cultural Notes ☀

Multiple Intelligences
Verbal/Linguistic
See Audio Activities 7.4 and 7.5.
Visual/Spatial
See Practice Wkbk. 7-8, Writing Activity 7-F, and Comm. Act. BLM 7-3.

Paso cultural
Answers will vary.

(p. 247, photo)
In Spain and Latin America, the *matador's* outfit is a symbol of grace and courage. To earn the privilege of wearing the traditional gold-sequinned *traje de luces* (suit of lights), one must be given the title *matador de toros.* This is accomplished in a special ceremony known as *la alternativa.* Only the most skilled, experienced *matadores* are invited to participate. The *matador's* assistants, *los banderilleros,* wear silver to signify their desire to become a *matador.*

Apply

 ¿Recuerdas?

Play

 Video Activity A

Using the Video

In Episode 7, Carlos calls up Jamie to go to the market to look for contaminated produce from the Hacienda la Jacaranda. Jamie finds corn which a local woman tells her is contaminated and is from La Jacaranda.

Carlos and Jamie take the corn to the university science laboratory. Carlos's former biology teacher offers to conduct pesticide tests. Next, Carlos and Jamie go to the city's health department. Roberto, an old friend of Carlos's who works there, locates a folder in which there are complaints of chemical abuse made against La Jacaranda. However, no action has been taken because the owner of the hacienda has not been located. Jamie finds that the owner's name is Josefa de González, La Catrina . . . Jamie's great-grandmother.

Actividades

 En una hoja de papel haz dos listas de tus posesiones más importantes según el modelo.

Mis posesiones

Una necesidad   Un lujo

Escribe el nombre de tres objetos en cada columna. Compara tus listas con las de un(a) compañero(a). Luego, comparen sus listas con las de otros(as) compañeros(as). ¿Cuáles son los tres objetos que aparecen más en las listas de toda la clase? Discutan por qué cada objeto es un lujo o una necesidad.

2 Entrevista a una persona mayor. Puede ser un(a) pariente(a), amigo(a) de la familia o un(a) profesor(a) de la escuela. Pregúntale sobre las cosas que tenía cuando era joven y lo que tiene ahora. Toma notas. Pregúntale, por ejemplo:

* si tenía (aparatos eléctricos)
* si había (computadora, tocacintas, televisión, radio) cuando era niño(a)
* cuándo compró su primer (televisor, radio, coche)
* cuál era su posesión más importante, cómo era y si todavía la tiene
* si tenía animales y cómo se llamaban

Ahora, con tus notas, prepara un informe para la clase. Compara la vida de antes con la de hoy. Puedes empezar así:

Mi bisabuelo se llama . . . Nació en 19 . . . Cuando era pequeño no había . . . Compró su . . . en 19 . . .

Las figuras de madera hechas en Oaxaca son famosas por sus colores brillantes.

248   Capítulo 7

Options

Strategies for Reaching All Students

Spanish-Speaking Students
Ex. 2 *¿Qué cosas tenía que ya no tiene? ¿Qué cosas había que ya no hay? ¿Cuál es la cosa más importante que uno puede tener?*

 Un paso más Ex. 7-I

Students Needing Extra Help
Ex. 1: Students will need help with the vocabulary in order to answer the *¿Por qué?* of the last statement.
Ex. 2: Model. Review preterite and imperfect tenses. Use vocabulary section of the Organizer. Remind students that they can interview in English.

Multiple Intelligences
Intrapersonal/Introspective
See Ex. 1.
Logical/Mathematical
See *Conexiones*.
Visual/Spatial
See Using the Video, Writing Activities 7-G and 7-H, and Comm. Act. BLMs 7-4 and 7-5.

Conexiones

La ecología

El uso mundial de energía

Las fuentes *(sources)* de energía tradicionales contaminan el medio ambiente y algún día pueden terminarse. Es mejor usar fuentes renovables, que son menos peligrosas para el medio ambiente y de mayor duración.

Fuentes tradicionales	Fuentes renovables
petróleo	marina
carbón	eólica o del viento
gas natural	solar

Con un(a) compañero(a), observa esta gráfica de barras.

- ¿Cuál es la clase de energía más usada en el mundo? ¿Es renovable o no?
- ¿Cuáles son las menos usadas? ¿Son renovables o no?

Trabajen en grupos para determinar la clase de energía que se usa más en las casas o apartamentos de tus compañeros(as). Averigüen qué clase de energía se usa en cada casa o apartamento para la calefacción, para calentar el agua y para cocinar. En la pizarra, hagan una tabla como ésta para anotar todas las respuestas.

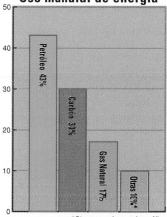

Uso mundial de energía

Petróleo 43%
Carbón 30%
Gas Natural 17%
Otras 10%*

*Otras = nuclear, solar, eólica

Nombre	Gas natural	Petróleo o derivados	Carbón	Electricidad	Solar	Otra
Pablo	✓			✓		
Anita		✓	✓			

Con un(a) compañero(a), haz una gráfica de barras en una hoja de papel cuadriculado para indicar las fuentes de energía más usadas por los miembros de tu clase.

Todo junto   249

La Catrina: Capítulo 7

Play

Video Activity B

Para entender mejor

Play

Answers: Conexiones

La clase de energía más usada en el mundo es el petróleo. No es renovable./Las menos usadas son las energías eólica *(wind),* solar y nuclear. Sí, son renovables.

Video Activity C

Writing Activities 7-G, 7-H

Comm. Act. BLMs 7-4, 7-5

Pasos vivos 2 CD-ROM
A Jugar, Laboratorio de grabar, Maps, Video Monitor, Video Presentation Maker

Cultural Notes

(p. 248, realia)
Folk art *(el arte popular)* is born of human creativity and learned through experience and experimentation with little formal training. Skills are passed from generation to generation by family or community tradition. Having worked anonymously for many years, *artesanos(as)* in Mexico have begun to be recognized for their work in recent years.

Apply

Process Reading
For information regarding process reading, see p. 52.

Answers
Antes de leer
Answers will vary, but students may say they would expect to find information such as brand names, product features, and prices.

Mira la lectura
Answers will vary.

¡Vamos a leer!

Antes de leer

STRATEGY➤ Using prior knowledge

This is an ad for electrical appliances from El Corte Inglés, a Spanish department store. What information would you expect to find?

Mira la lectura

STRATEGY➤ Skimming

In advertisements, sentences are often short. Punctuation and capitalization may be unusual. Look over the selection to get the gist of it.

OCEAN

La magi del diser

El Corte Inglés presenta en exclusiva algo que le a encantar, un número u en diseño italiano y toda novedad en España: Electrodomésticos Ocean Una gama de electrodomésticos tecnológicamente avanzad con los sistemas más revolucionarios y el diseño más innovador. Además co garantía y servicios qu proporciona El Corte Inglés:
— Transporte y entrega a domicilio.
— Instalación por especialistas.
— Garantía por un año.
— Servicio post-venta.
— Financiación hasta 24 meses, sin entrada, a partir de 5.000 pts. mensuales.

OCEAN
diseño

una exclusiva de

El Corte Inglés

Options

Strategies for Reaching All Students

Students Needing Extra Help
Mira la lectura: Bring in an ad from an English language magazine to show how they also sometimes contain unusual punctuation, capitalization, or spelling.

Multiple Intelligences
Musical/Rhythmic
Have students create a jingle to go with the ad on p. 250.
Visual/Spatial
See *¡Vamos a leer!*

Infórmate

STRATEGIES➤   Using cognates
                  Recognizing false cognates

You already know how to use cognates—for example, *sistemas, revolucionarios,* and *transporte*—to help you understand a selection. However, sometimes a Spanish word has a different meaning from that of the English word that it resembles.

When you come across a word that is important for understanding the selection, and the English meaning doesn't make sense, use the context to help you figure it out.

1 In the phrase *Además con la garantía y servicios que proporciona El Corte Inglés,* the word *proporciona* is similar to the English word "proportion." But the position of the word tells you that it probably is a verb. The ending tells you that it is an *él / ella* form. So *proporciona* is something that El Corte Inglés does. Ask yourself what verb best tells what a store does with regard to delivery, installation, etc.

2 The word *entrada* means "entrance," but it has another meaning here. Use the context to help you figure it out.

3 If you were going to buy an electrical appliance, would you go to El Corte Inglés? Why?

Aplicación

List as many words as you can that you learned from this selection. Underline the cognates. Then compare your list with a classmate's.

Aplicación

Answers will vary, but the list of cognates may include: *presenta, exclusiva, tecnológicamente, garantía, instalación, especialistas*

www **Internet Activities**

Cultural Notes ☀

(p. 250, realia)
As in the U.S., washing machines are common appliances in most households in Spain. In much of Latin America, however, clothing is frequently washed by hand. Foreign-produced machines are expensive and labor is relatively inexpensive. Many people therefore wash their own clothing by hand or hire someone else to do it. Ask students: Is a washing machine a luxury or a necessity? Give reasons to support your point of view.

Apply

Process Writing
For information regarding developing a writing portfolio, see p. 54.

Using Realia
Remind students of *¡No olvides!* What do they think that means? Then ask: *¿Qué quiere decir "inolvidable regalo"?*

¡Vamos a escribir!

Imagina que tu familia necesita hacer una lista de sus posesiones para la compañía de seguros *(insurance company)*. ¿Qué cosas tuyas quieres poner en la lista?

1 Primero, haz una lista de tres a cinco cosas que son importantes para ti; por ejemplo, una colección de monedas. Escribe una breve descripción para cada una. Piensa en estas cosas:

- ¿Qué es el artículo?
- ¿Cómo es?
- ¿Cuánto tiempo hace que lo tienes?
- ¿Lo compraste o fue un regalo?
- ¿Cuánto costó?
- ¿Puedes comprar otro como éste?

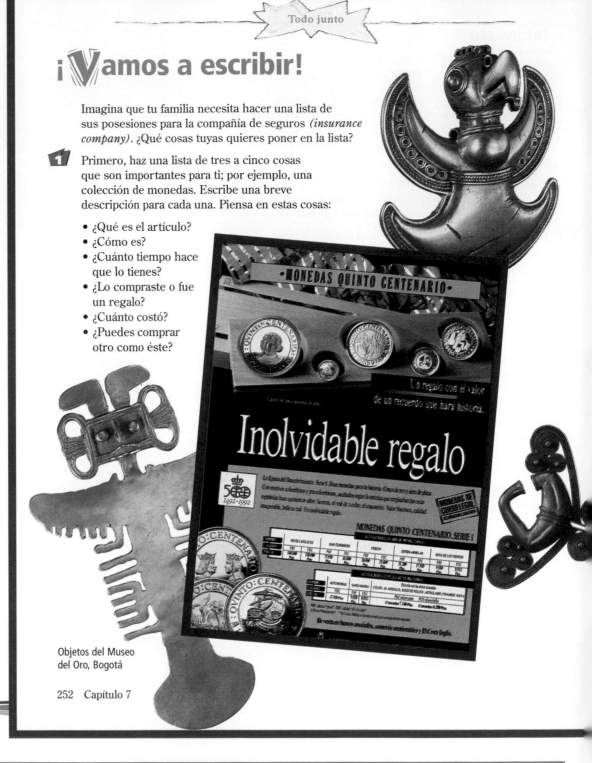

Objetos del Museo del Oro, Bogotá

252 Capítulo 7

Options

Strategies for Reaching All Students

Students Needing Extra Help
Ex. 1: Discuss the reasons why this list would be made in reality. Most students will not be familiar with this insurance concept. Review *hace que* construction and the preterite. Teacher should have one ready as a model.
Ex. 2: Model. Brainstorm why their things are important to them. Students will need help with the vocabulary, particularly as to why things are important to them.

Multiple Intelligences
Visual/Spatial
1) Have students design a poster similar to the one on p. 252.
2) See steps 1–3.

"Para mí, mis tarjetas de béisbol son
muy preciosas."

"Paso mucho tiempo con mi colección de sellos."

2 Ahora imagina que tu familia va a mudarse
(to move) y no puede llevar todo. Tienes
que dejar una de las cosas que describiste.
Escoge una cosa y la persona más
apropiada para recibirla. Escribe una carta
breve a la persona y explícale:

• qué le vas a dar
• por qué vas a hacerlo
• qué importancia tiene la cosa para ti

3 Para distribuir tu trabajo, puedes:

• incluirlo en un libro titulado *Cosas
  preciosas*
• ofrecerlo a la revista literaria escolar
• exhibirlo en la sala de clases
• incluirlo en tu portafolio

¡Vamos a escribir!   253

Cultural Notes ☀

(p. 252, realia)
These specially minted gold and silver
Spanish coins honor the 500th anniversary
of Columbus' landing in the Americas. Each
coin is named for some aspect of Spanish
or Latin American history or culture and
struck in authentic denominations. *El real de
a ocho,* one type of coin produced for this
edition, was a common coin in seventeenth-
century Spain, and was minted in the New
World. The *pinzón,* also offered in this set,
is valued at about $400 U.S.

Assess & Summarize

Test Preparation
You may want to assign parts of this section as written homework or as an in-class writing activity prior to administering the *Examen de habilidades*.

Answers

Listening: —*¿Tenías dinero en la cartera?*
—*No tenía mucho dinero en efectivo, pero tenía mis tarjetas de crédito y el carnet de identidad. Menos mal que tenía mi llavero, anillo y cadena en el bolsillo de mi chaqueta.*
—*Ya viene el policía. Explícale lo que pasó.*
Horacio has lost his wallet, or it has been stolen.

Reading: Answers should be the modern counterparts to the items listed, for example, *el bombillo* for *la vela* and *el tocacintas* (or *el televisor*) for *el radio eléctrico*.

Writing: Thank you notes will vary.

Repaso ¿Lo sabes bien?

Esta sección te ayudará a prepararte para el examen de habilidades, donde tendrás que hacer tareas semejantes.

Listening
Can you understand when people talk about their personal possessions? Listen as your teacher reads a sample similar to what you will hear on the test. What do you think Horacio's problem is?

Reading
Part of an advertisement for new appliances included comparisons between old and new. Add two modern items to complete the comparisons.

Antes	Ahora
el ventilador	el aire acondicionado
el fregadero	el lavaplatos
la vela	
el radio eléctrico	

Writing
Write a thank you note in which you explain to a relative how you used a gift of clothing. On the right is a sample.

Culture
How were the early American civilizations more advanced than those of Europe? How were they less advanced?

Speaking
In a discussion with your partner can you state and opinion about some recent purchases you made?

A —*¿Te gusta el nuevo televisor que compré? Me encanta el control remoto.*

B —*¡Pero Uds. tienen muchos televisores! Me parece que es un lujo tener tantos aparatos.*

A —*Pues, a mí no me parece así. Somos una familia grande y todos tenemos nuestros programas favoritos. ¡Y lo compré con mi propio dinero!*

Querida abuela,

Muchas gracias por el abrigo de lana. Ya tenía un suéter y unos pantalones de lana, pero necesitaba un abrigo para el viaje a las montañas. (La familia de Maribel me invitó a su casa en Portillo.) ¡Olvidé llevar la bufanda y los guantes! Pero Maribel me prestó los suyos. Sí llevé una linterna y pilas en caso de emergencia, pero no las necesité. La casa tiene electricidad. También tiene calefacción central, una lavadora, una secadora ¡y un microondas!

Un beso,
Chelita

 www.pasoapaso.com

Options

Strategies for Reaching All Students

Students Needing Extra Help
Have students write out this section so they can check off what they have mastered. Remind students that this is just a sample of what the actual test will be like.
Listening: Read the sample more than once. Remind students that they only need to listen for one piece of information. Brainstorm for what words students should be listening.

Writing: Have students use the Organizer and write a sample note before the test as practice. Brainstorm other possibilities that are more low key for how a gift might be used. For example, the student could be simple and direct: the gift was worn to a party, was taken when he / she went skiing, has become his / her favorite sweater, etc. Give a required number of sentences to write.

Culture: Have students review the notes they took during their first reading of *Perspectiva cultural*.
Speaking: The statement "state and defend your opinion" may be confusing for students. Explain. Limit the number of lines of dialogue. Use the vocabulary section of the Organizer.

Resumen del vocabulario

Usa el vocabulario de este capítulo para:

- name and describe personal possessions
- tell to whom something belongs
- state and defend opinions regarding necessities and luxuries

to name personal possessions

la posesión, *pl.* las posesiones
la necesidad
el lujo
el oro
la plata
el anillo
el arete
la cadena
el collar
la pulsera
el reloj (pulsera)
los anteojos *(m.pl.)*
los lentes de contacto *(m.pl.)*
la llave
el llavero
la moneda
el peine
el secador de pelo
la identificación
el carnet de identidad

to discuss personal possessions

propio, -a
mío, -a
tuyo, -a
suyo, -a
nuestro, -a
el mío, la mía; los míos, las mías

el tuyo, la tuya; los tuyos, las tuyas
el suyo, la suya; los suyos, las suyas
el nuestro, la nuestra; los nuestros, las nuestras

to name home appliances and furnishings

el aparato
la electricidad
eléctrico, -a
el bombillo
apagar
encender (e → ie)
funcionar
el horno
el lavaplatos
la lavadora
la secadora
el microondas
el tostador
el ventilador
el aire acondicionado
la calefacción central
el calentador
el fregadero
el estante
la mesa de noche
el radio
el televisor

el control remoto
el tocacintas, *pl.* los tocacintas

to talk about emergencies

el detector de humo
la emergencia
el incendio
el extinguidor de incendios
la linterna
la pila
en caso de

to talk about conservation

la energía
ahorrar
conservar
reparar

to express an opinion

¿(A ti) Te parece que...?
(A mí) Me parece que...

other useful words and expressions

mostrar (o → ue)
suficiente
de vez en cuando
(yo) mismo, -a

Culture: Answers will vary, but students may say that very early American civilizations were more advanced than ours because they were able to accomplish so much with limited resources. For example, the Aztecs built great temples and avenues without the use of metal instruments or a written means of communication.

Speaking: Dialogues will vary.

Assessment

¿? **Prueba cumulativa**

¿? **Examen de habilidades**

Test Generator

Additional Assessment Options

Comm. Act. BLMs

Small Group Activities
Situation Cards

Pasos vivos 2 CD-ROM

Slide Presentation Maker, Video Presentation Maker, Word Processor, Spindle

¿Lo sabes bien? Video Quiz

www **Internet Activities**
Self-Test

CAPÍTULO 8

THEME: SHOPPING

SCOPE AND SEQUENCE   Pages 256–291

COMMUNICATION

Topics

Specialty shops

Asking for and giving directions

Places in a community

Pharmacy items

Departments in a store

Objectives

To compare bargaining in Guatemala and in the U.S.

To name things and places in a community

To name specialty shops

To ask for or give directions

To describe places

To identify personal hygiene items

To name and indicate departments in a store

To talk about shopping

CULTURE

Bargaining procedures in Guatemala

GRAMMAR

Repaso: Los usos de estar

Repaso: El presente progresivo

Construcciones negativas

El se impersonal

Ancillaries available for use with Chapter 8

Multisensory/Technology	Print	Assessment

 Overheads, 39–43

 Audio Tapes and CDs

 Vocabulary Art Blackline Masters for Hands-On Learning, pp. 43–47/CD-ROM

 Classroom Crossword

 La Catrina

Pasos vivos 2 CD-ROM

 Internet Activities
www.pasoapaso.com

 Practice Workbook, pp. 75–84

 Writing, Audio & Video Activities, pp. 47–52, 114–116, 165–166

 Communicative Activity Blackline Masters

Pair and Small Group Activities, pp. 50–55

Situation Cards, p. 56

 Un paso más: Actividades para ampliar tu español, pp. 43–48

 RESOURCE PRO®

Planning Express, Teaching Resources Library, and Clip Art Library

 Assessment Program

Pruebas, pp. 114–124

Examen de habilidades, pp. 125–128

 Test Generator

 ¿Lo sabes bien? Video Quiz

Video still from Chap. 8

Running Errands

In Spain and Latin America, the downtown area is considered the hub of commercial activity. It usually features a main *plaza,* filled with shoeshine stands, newspaper kiosks, small candy stands, flower stands, and vendors selling everything from handcrafted jewelry to popcorn. Money exchange houses downtown provide foreign travelers a convenient way to exchange their currency. Another feature of the commercial area is the telephone company office, where local, long-distance, and international calls can be placed by those who do not have a telephone.

Larger cities may have several major commercial areas, with a large superstore as the anchor. *Supermercados* such as Comercial mexicana or Gigante are stocked with a variety of products. These stores offer the ultimate one-stop shopping experience: deli, bakery, dairy, hardware, electronics, books, clothing, CDs and cassettes—even carry-out buffets with such typical dishes as *mole poblano* and *nopalitos,* served hot and weighed at the checkout counter. Picnic tables outside the store offer a convenient place to enjoy lunch.

Some people, however, may go to specialty shops and open-air markets for their grocery shopping. A grocery run for the day's meal may include a stop at the *carnicería,* then to the *frutería* or *verdulería* and finally to the *tortillería.* Most towns have an open-air market, and if the market is especially large, it is divided into specialty sections. A characteristic of the marketplace is the custom of bargaining for the final price of an item. Vendors usually state their prices higher than they expect to receive, and shoppers often succeed in paying a lower price than the one originally offered. Bargaining is as much a part of the shopping experience in the marketplace as using cents-off coupons is in the U.S.

Introduce

Re-entry of Concepts

The following list represents words, expressions, and grammar topics re-entered from Book 1 and Book 2 (Chaps. 2–4):

Book 1
numbers 0–31, physical sensations, leisure-time activities, family members, household chores, places in a community, personal hygiene items, directions

Chapter 2
daily routine

Chapter 3
greetings and leavetakings

Chapter 4
sports

Planning

Cross-Curricular Connections

Business Education Connection
(pp. 260–261)
In groups of three, have students choose a type of shop from the given vocabulary, and create a poster to advertise it. They should include a name, logo, and slogan for the store, as well as a few special items for sale there. Display the posters, and have students tell why they would or would not shop there.

Geography Connection *(pp. 278–279)*
At a given hour in New York on Eastern Standard Time, it is two hours ahead in Buenos Aires, Argentina; eight hours ahead in Moscow, Russia; 12 hours ahead in Tokyo, Japan; and 15 hours ahead in Sydney, Australia. Create a transparency chart, adjusting the time differences for your local time zone. Ask students to write two responses for each city to the question: *¿Qué están haciendo ellos ahora?* Have them share their responses.

Spanish in Your Community
Have students name places in their community where they may have spotted the following items: a *piñata;* restrooms labeled for *damas* and *caballeros, bacalao* (salted, dried cod); chocolate disks for making Mexican hot chocolate; *piloncillo* (raw cone-shaped sugar); Spanish *chorizo* (sausage); yucca; a *panadería;* an exit sign labeled *salida.*

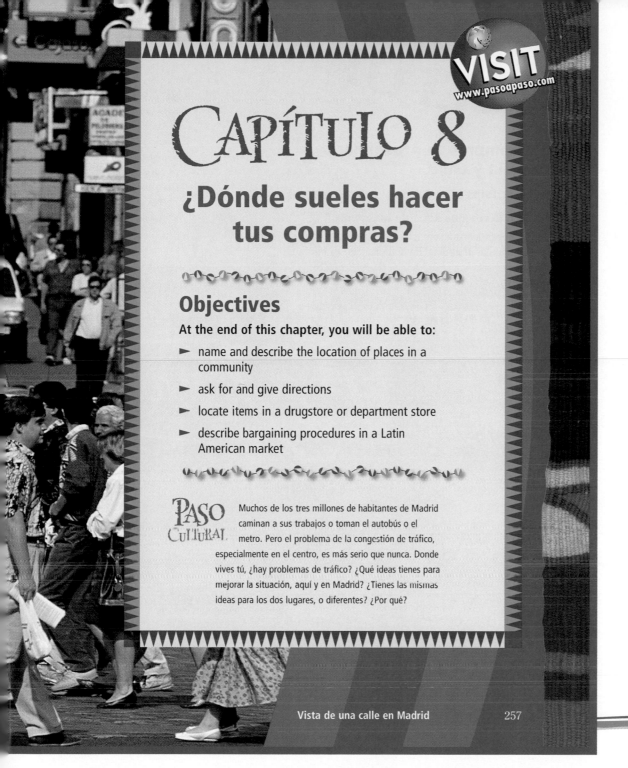

VISIT
www.pasoapaso.com

CAPÍTULO 8

¿Dónde sueles hacer tus compras?

Objectives

At the end of this chapter, you will be able to:

► name and describe the location of places in a community

► ask for and give directions

► locate items in a drugstore or department store

► describe bargaining procedures in a Latin American market

PASO CULTURAL
Muchos de los tres millones de habitantes de Madrid caminan a sus trabajos o toman el autobús o el metro. Pero el problema de la congestión de tráfico, especialmente en el centro, es más serio que nunca. Donde vives tú, ¿hay problemas de tráfico? ¿Qué ideas tienes para mejorar la situación, aquí y en Madrid? ¿Tienes las mismas ideas para los dos lugares, o diferentes? ¿Por qué?

Vista de una calle en Madrid   257

Preview

Cultural Objective
• To compare specialty shops in Spain and Latin America with those in the U.S.

Critical Thinking: Summarizing Information
Have students summarize the activities depicted in the chapter opener photographs. Discuss any similarities and differences they may see between where they shop and the places shown here.

¡Piensa en la CULTURA!

De compras en Argentina, España y Chile

Mira las fotos. ¿Dónde compras tú estas cosas?

"Voy a llevar dos kilos de manzanas."

¿Prefieres las manzanas rojas o las amarillas? ¿Dónde compras las frutas? ¿Hay fruterías en tu ciudad?

PASO CULTURAL Las tiendas de especialidades como éstas son muy importantes en la vida diaria de los habitantes de los países hispanos. Mucha gente va a estas tiendas por la mañana para comprar lo que necesita para el día y, a la vez, para conversar con sus amigos y vecinos. ¿Hay tiendas de especialidades cerca de tu casa? ¿Prefieres ir a tiendas como éstas o a los supermercados? ¿Por qué?

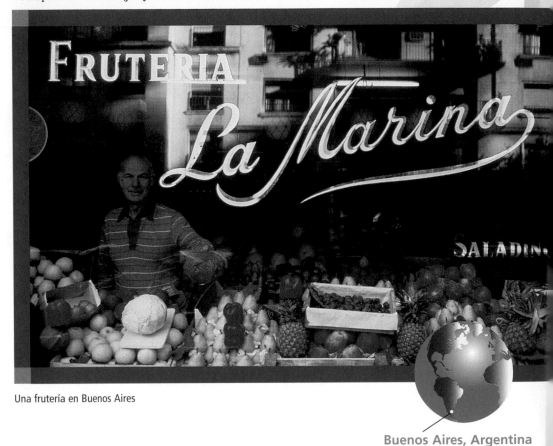

FRUTERIA La Marina

SALADIN

Una frutería en Buenos Aires

Buenos Aires, Argentina

258   Capítulo 8

Options

Strategies for Reaching All Students

Spanish-Speaking Students
Ask: *¿Cuáles de estos lugares hay en tu comunidad? ¿Prefiere tu familia comprar en tiendas grandes como almacenes y super-mercados, o en tiendas más pequeñas como fruterías, pescaderías, etc.? ¿Por qué?*

 Un paso más Ex. 8-A

Multiple Intelligences
Verbal/Linguistic
See Critical Thinking.

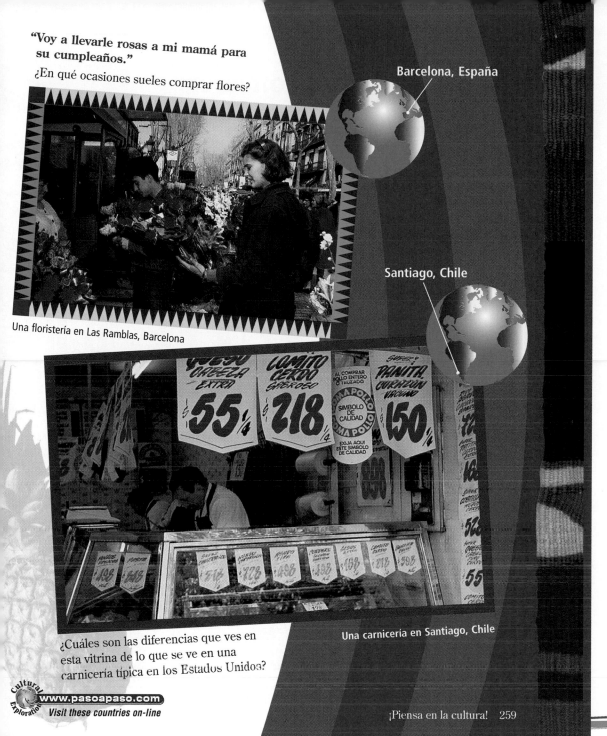

"Voy a llevarle rosas a mi mamá para su cumpleaños."

¿En qué ocasiones sueles comprar flores?

Una floristería en Las Ramblas, Barcelona

Barcelona, España

Santiago, Chile

¿Cuáles son las diferencias que ves en esta vitrina de lo que se ve en una carnicería típica en los Estados Unidos?

Una carnicería en Santiago, Chile

www.pasoapaso.com
Cultural Exploration
Visit these countries on-line

Cultural Notes ☀

Paso cultural
Answers will vary.

(p. 259, top photo)
Newspaper kiosks, flower stalls, bird sellers, and *cafés* fill Las Ramblas, a boulevard linking Barcelona's port with Plaza Cataluña, the city's commercial and banking center. Las Ramblas is the nexus of community life for many *barceloneses*.

(p. 259, bottom photo)
Sale banners entice passersby to buy some *queso cabeza* (head cheese), *lomito* (pork loin), or *panita* (beef liver). Specialty shops such as this *carnicería* are common in Latin America and Spain. They lend a personable atmosphere to even the largest cities, and serve as congenial meeting places where neighbors exchange greetings and keep abreast of local happenings.

Present

Chapter Theme
Downtown

Communicative Objectives
- To name things and places in a community
- To name specialty shops
- To ask or give directions
- To talk about shopping

 Overheads 39–40

 Vocabulary Art BLMs/CD-ROM

 Vocabulary Tape 8-1

Teaching Suggestions
Preparing students to speak: Use one or two options from each of the categories of Comprehensible Input, Physical Response, or Limited Verbal Response. For a complete explanation of these categories and some sample activities, see pp. T20–T21.

Vocabulario para conversar

¿Podría indicarme dónde queda una floristería?

Vas a necesitar estas palabras y expresiones para hablar sobre dónde puedes encontrar ciertas cosas y lugares.

El centro

la carretera

el quiosco (de periódicos)

el semáforo

el teléfono público

la panadería

CALLE SAN JUAN

ESTÁS AQUÍ

la señal de alto

la carnicería

AVENIDA SAN JOSÉ

260 Capítulo 8

Options

Strategies for Reaching All Students

Spanish-Speaking Students
Have students list other words they might use for these places in the community.
¿Usas otras palabras para estos lugares en una comunidad? Haz una lista.

 Un paso más Exs. 8-B, 8-C

Students Needing Extra Help
Begin the vocabulary section of the Organizer.
Students may think *señal* sounds like signal, and make the assumption that it is a traffic light. Emphasize that it is a stop sign. Present the shops (all of which end in *-ía*) as a group. Show the root words in this group: *carne → carnicería; fruta → frutería*, etc.
También necesitas . . . : Give examples of *por* + place.

Learning Spanish Through Action
STAGING VOCABULARY: *Pongan*
MATERIALS: transparency of a downtown area with squares and rectangles to indicate locations; cutouts of symbols for buildings, shops, etc.
DIRECTIONS: Direct students to place the symbols in the correct squares or rectangles as you give the location of each.

También necesitas . . .

seguir (e → i): siga (Ud.)	*to follow, to continue:*
	follow! continue!
doblar: doble (Ud.)	*to turn: turn!*
cruzar	*to cross*
¿Podría (Ud.) / Podrías (tú) + *inf.?*	*Could you . . . ?*
el centro	*downtown*
el metro	here: *meter* (measurement)
la milla	*mile*
por + (*place*)	*by, through, at*

¿Y qué quiere decir . . . ?
indicar
hacer las compras
el transporte público
perdonar: perdone (Ud.)
el kilómetro
histórico, -a

¡NO OLVIDES!
Remember: *comprar* = to buy and
ir de compras = to go shopping.

- la pescadería
- AVENIDA SAN ANTONIO
- la estación de bomberos
- la verdulería
- el cruce
- el bombero
- la bombera
- la frutería
- AVENIDA SAN FELIPE
- la floristería
- CALLE SANTIAGO
- la heladería
- la dirección, *pl.* las direcciones
- el buzón, *pl.* los buzones

Class Starter Review

On the day following the presentation of vocabulary, you might
begin the class with either of
these activities:
1) Call out the name of a store
and have students respond with
what can be bought there. On a
subsequent day, name an item and
have students respond with the
name of the store.
2) Play a game of *Ojo atento:*
Show students pictures of places
in a community with items that
clearly do not belong; for example,
a fish in a *floristería;* a loaf of
bread in a *quiosco,* etc. Have students identify what doesn't belong
in the picture and say where it
does belong:
*El pescado debe estar en la pesca-
dería.*

www **Internet Activities**
Juegos

Extended Written Practice/Homework
1. Write four sentences telling where
different places are located in the drawing
on pp. 260–261: *La estación de bomberos
queda en la esquina de la avenida San
Antonio y la calle Santiago.*
2. Write four sentences telling where
different places are located in your
community: *Hay una frutería a media milla
de mi casa, enfrente de la panadería.*

3. Write three sentences telling where
different people went in your community
and what they did there.

Multiple Intelligences
Bodily/Kinesthetic
See Learning Spanish Through Action.
Verbal/Linguistic
See Vocabulary Tape 8-1 and Class Starter
Review, Activity 1.
Visual/Spatial
1) Have students make and label a map of a
nearby shopping area.
2) See Overheads 39–40, the Vocabulary Art
BLMs/CD-ROM, and Class Starter Review,
Activity 2.

Practice

Reteach / Review: Singular and Plural

Ex. 1: Remind students that, just as in English, when we talk about *flores* and *verduras,* we use the plural, and for *pan, pescado, carne,* and *helado,* we use the singular. Fruit takes either the singular or the plural.

Refer to vocabulary from Book 1, Chaps. 4 and 10 for a review of foods.

Answers: Empecemos a conversar

1 ESTUDIANTE A
a. Necesito comprar flores.
b. . . . verduras.
c. . . . pan.
d. . . . pescado.
e. . . . frutas.
f. . . . helado.
g. Statements will vary.

ESTUDIANTE B
a. Pues vamos, hay una floristería muy cerca.
b. . . . una verdulería . . .
c. . . . una panadería . . .
d. . . . una pescadería . . .
e. . . . una frutería . . .
f. . . . una heladería . . .
g. Answers will vary.

Empecemos a conversar

Túrnate con un(a) compañero(a) para ser *Estudiante A* y *Estudiante B.* Reemplacen las palabras subrayadas en el modelo con palabras representadas o escritas en los recuadros. Si ven 💡 pueden dar su propia respuesta.

1
  A — *Necesito comprar <u>carne</u>.*
  B — *Pues vamos, hay una <u>carnicería</u> muy cerca.*

Estudiante A   Estudiante B

2
  A — *Perdone, señor(ita), ¿sabe si hay una farmacia por aquí?*
  B — *Sí. Hay una a media cuadra.*

¡NO OLVIDES!

Sabe is the *Ud.* form of *saber.* It is a regular *-er* verb except for its *yo* form: *sé.*

Estudiante A   Estudiante B

a (dos) cuadras

a media cuadra

enfrente de ____

en la esquina

262   Capítulo 8

Options

Strategies for Reaching All Students

Spanish-Speaking Students
Exs. 1–4: If possible, pair bilingual with non-biligual students.

Students Needing Extra Help
Ex. 2: Help students use the map.
Ex. 3: Review location words. If available, use the Organizer from Book 1, Chap. 10. Give several examples on the overhead so students don't start each one the same way.

Extended Written Practice/Homework
1. Tell how close to your home the following are located: *un semáforo, un buzón, un quiosco de periódicos.*
2. Give two sets of directions telling someone how to go from your school to other places in your community: *Para ir de la escuela al correo, ...*
3. Write three sets of sentences recalling from your childhood different places in your community: *Cuando era niño(a), había una panadería cerca de mi casa. A veces iba allí con mi padre.*

AV. SAN FELIPE

AV. SAN ANTONIO

CALLE SAN JUAN

CALLE SANTIAGO

AV. SAN JOSÉ

ÁS AQUÍ

3

A —¿*Podría indicarme dónde queda una pescadería?*

B —*Sí, señor(ita). Siga por esta calle. En la segunda esquina, doble a la derecha.*

Estudiante A

Estudiante B

a.

b.

c.

d.

e.

f.

2 ESTUDIANTE A

a. Perdone, señor(ita), ¿sabe si hay un buzón por aquí?

b. ...un quiosco ...

c. ...un teléfono público ...

d. ...una parada del autobús ...

e. ...una estación de bombe-ros ...

f. Questions will vary.

ESTUDIANTE B

a. Sí. Hay uno a una cuadra.

b. ...uno a dos cuadras.

c. ...uno a una cuadra.

d. ...una a dos cuadras.

e. ...una a tres cuadras.

f. Answers will vary.

3 ESTUDIANTE A

a. ¿Podría indicarme dónde queda una heladería?

b. ...una frutería?

c. ...una verdulería?

d. ...una floristería?

e. ...una panadería?

f. Questions will vary.

ESTUDIANTE B

Directions will vary, but may include the following:

a. Sí, señor(ita). Siga por la avenida San José. En la primera esquina, doble a la izquierda.

b. ...En el semáforo, doble a la derecha.

c. ...En el semáforo, doble a la derecha. Está al lado de la frutería.

d. ...En el semáforo, doble a la derecha. Está enfrente de la frutería.

e. ...En el semáforo, doble a la izquierda.

f. Directions will vary.

Practice & Apply

Reteach / Review: Vocabulary

Review this additional location vocabulary from Book 1, Chap. 10 to help students vary their answers to the exercises that follow: *a la izquierda (de), al lado (de), detrás (de), entre.* Ask two volunteers to help you act out the different locations for the rest of the class.

Ex. 4: Encourage students to say more. For example, *cerca de ___, enfrente de___, por ___.* You can extend the exercise by asking students to ask for a specific shop: *la panadería La Esperanza, la pescadería De Martino's,* etc.

Answers: Empecemos a conversar

4 ESTUDIANTE A

a. ¿Sabes si está lejos de aquí la estación de policía?
b. . . . la iglesia de ___?
c. . . . el templo de ___?
d. . . . el correo?
e. . . . el centro?
f. . . . (nombre de una comunidad)?
g. Questions will vary.

ESTUDIANTE B

a.–g. Answers will vary, but should reflect locations in your community.

---

4 Aquí hablamos de tu propia ciudad.

la estación de bomberos

A — ¿Sabes si está lejos de aquí *la estación de bomberos*?
B — *Un poco; está a dos millas de aquí, en la Calle Lincoln.*
    o: *Lo siento, pero no lo sé.*

Estudiante A

a. la estación de policía
b. la iglesia de ___
c. el templo de ___
d. el correo
e. el centro
f. (nombre de una comunidad)
g.

Estudiante B

(número) kilómetros
(número) metros
(número) cuadras
(número) millas
medio kilómetro
media milla

Vista de una calle antigua al pie de las montañas en Quito, Ecuador

San Antonio de Oriente (1957), José Antonio Velásquez

264   Capítulo 8

Options

Strategies for Reaching All Students

Spanish-Speaking Students
Ex. 8: *¿Cuál es tu lugar favorito en tu comunidad? ¿Se lo recomendarías a otras personas? ¿Por qué?*

 Un paso más Ex. 8-D

Students Needing Extra Help
Ex. 4: Discourage overuse of the second response. Using the classroom as a starting point gives everyone the same perspective. Give more than one example, so students

don't always repeat the model dialogue.
Ex. 5: Refer students to the envelope in the visualized vocabulary section. Remind them that in Spanish the street name is written first, then the number.
Ex. 6: Students may need to sketch maps. Help them focus.
Ex. 7: Discuss the layout of the local market to help students think in terms of sections.
Ex. 8: Have students imagine they are in a new town. Discuss which places are important to know in case of emergency.

Enrichment
Ex. 4: As a homework assignment, ask students to choose an item or place from the vocabulary list that they would like to have on the corner of their block and to give reasons for their choice. Example: *Me gustaría mucho tener un semáforo en la esquina. Siempre hay accidentes.*
Ex. 6: Additional questions: *¿Cuánto tiempo necesitas para ir al centro en coche? ¿Y en transporte público?*

Empecemos a escribir

Escribe tus respuestas en español.

5 ¿Cuál es tu dirección? ¿Y la de la escuela? Escríbele una nota a un(a) amigo(a) explicándole cómo ir de la escuela a tu casa.

6 ¿Cuáles son las calles y carreteras más importantes de tu comunidad o ciudad? Para ir de tu casa al centro comercial, ¿qué calles o carreteras hay que tomar? ¿Más o menos cuántos cruces y señales de alto debes pasar? Y para ir al centro de la ciudad, ¿usas el transporte público o vas en coche?

7 ¿Dónde hace las compras tu familia? ¿Quién las hace? ¿Qué tiendas de comestibles hay cerca de tu casa? ¿Dónde quedan? ¿Qué tiene el supermercado (carnicería, panadería, etc.) donde hace las compras tu familia?

8 ¿Qué edificios históricos hay en tu comunidad o ciudad? ¿Los visitas de vez en cuando? En tu opinión, ¿qué lugares hay que conocer en una ciudad? ¿Por qué?

Niños montando en bicicleta en Puerto Plata, República Dominicana

También se dice

la florería

el puesto de periódicos

la sorbetería
la nevería

el pare
el stop

MORE PRACTICE

- Más práctica y tarea, p. 549
- Practice Workbook 8–1, 8–2

Vocabulario para conversar 265

Cooperative Learning
In pairs, one student is given a blank map of a *plaza* with four surrounding streets. Without letting his or her partner see the map, *Estudiante A* fills in eight symbols for the shop vocabulary. *Estudiante B* asks if a given shop is nearby. If the symbol is on the map, *Estudiante A* says where it is *(Está en la esquina)*. If not, he or she responds accordingly. *Estudiante B* records *Estudiante A*'s responses to read to the class, who checks responses against the map.

Multiple Intelligences
Interpersonal/Social and Visual/Spatial
See Cooperative Learning.
Intrapersonal/Introspective
See Exs. 5–8.
Verbal/Linguistic
See Audio Activity 8.1.
Visual/Spatial
See Practice Wkbk. 8-1 and 8-2 and Writing Activity 8-A.

Cultural Notes

(p. 264, bottom left photo)
Honduran artist José Antonio Velásquez (1906–1983) created this painting of his native village. A self-taught artist who never learned to read or write, Velásquez achieved recognition as one of Latin America's leading artists. San Antonio de Oriente still retains much of the character captured in this painting.

Present

Chapter Theme
Store sections

Communicative Objectives
- To ask or give directions
- To identify personal hygiene items
- To name and indicate departments in a store
- To talk about shopping

 Overheads 41–42

 Vocabulary Art BLMs/CD-ROM

 Vocabulary Tape 8-2

Grammar Preview
Se vende is presented here lexically. The explanation of impersonal *se* is on p. 282. Encourage its use without explanation.

Teaching Suggestions
Preparing students to speak: Use one or two options from each of the categories of Comprehensible Input, Physical Response, or Limited Verbal Response. For a complete explanation of these categories and some sample activities, see pp. T20–T21.

Vocabulario para conversar

¿Los ascensores están al fondo?

Aquí tienes el resto del vocabulario que necesitas en este capítulo para hablar sobre dónde puedes encontrar ciertas cosas y lugares.

La farmacia

Options

Strategies for Reaching All Students

Spanish-Speaking Students

 Un paso más Ex. 8-E

Students Needing Extra Help
Show root words and word families.

Learning Spanish Through Action
STAGING VOCABULARY: *Levanten*
MATERIALS: Vocabulary Art BLMs/CD-ROM of vocabulary
DIRECTIONS: Distribute cutouts to students. Direct them to hold up the cutouts when they hear them named.

El almacén

los servicios (m.pl.)

la salida

el ascensor

la ropa para niños

la caja

la escalera

el mostrador

la escalera mecánica

la ropa para caballeros

la ropa para damas

la entrada

También necesitas . . .

al fondo	*in the back*	
gastar	*to spend*	
ponerse	*to put on (clothing, make-up, etc.)*	
quitarse	*to take off (clothing, make-up, etc.)*	
vender; se vende(n)	*to sell; is (are) sold*	
mientras	*while*	

¿Y qué quiere decir . . . ?
afeitarse
maquillarse
la distancia
la sección, *pl.* las secciones

Class Starter Review
On the day following the presentation of vocabulary, you might begin the class with this activity: Give pairs of students one minute to list everything they can think of that can be bought in a pharmacy.

www Internet Activities
Juegos

Extended Written Practice/Homework
1. Write three sentences telling where different items are located in the pharmacy on p. 266: *El jabón está entre los desodorantes y los perfumes.*
2. Choose four items on p. 266 that you or another person bought. Write sentences telling when and where they were purchased.

3. Write three questions that you might ask a person in order to find out where different things are located in a store: *¿Podría Ud. decirme dónde queda la sección de perfumes?*

Multiple Intelligences
Bodily/Kinesthetic
1) See Learning Spanish Through Action.

2) Divide the class into pairs. Without revealing the destination, have one of them use the imperative to direct the other to a destination in the room.
Verbal/Linguistic
See Vocabulary Tape 8-2.
Visual/Spatial
See Overheads 41–42, the Vocabulary Art BLMs/CD-ROM, and Class Starter Review.

Practice

Reteach / Review: Vocabulary

Ex. 9: Note that there is more than one way to express location. Accept all appropriate answers. Tell students that in this context the plural forms *lápices de labios* and *perfumes* would be used. You may want to review vocabulary from Book 1, Chaps. 4 and 10.

Answers: Empecemos a conversar

9 ESTUDIANTE A

a. Por favor, ¿dónde puedo encontrar el desodorante?

b. ...los cepillos de dientes?

c. ...los perfumes?

d. ...los lápices de labios?

e. ...la crema de afeitar?

f. ...el esmalte de uñas?

g. ...las vendas?

h. Questions will vary.

ESTUDIANTE B

Answers will vary, but may include the following:

a. En la sección tres, enfrente de las pastillas para la garganta.

b. En la sección dos, al lado de la pasta dentífrica.

c. En la sección tres, al lado del jabón.

d. En la sección dos, al lado de los cepillos de dientes.

e. En la sección dos, enfrente de la pasta dentífrica.

f. En la sección tres, detrás de los lápices de labios.

Empecemos a conversar

9

A — *Por favor, ¿dónde puedo encontrar la seda dental?*

B — *En la sección dos, enfrente de los champús.*

Estudiante A · Estudiante B

268 Capítulo 8

Options

Strategies for Reaching All Students

Spanish-Speaking Students
If possible, pair Spanish-speaking students for Ex. 9 and bilingual with non-bilingual students for Exs. 10–11.

Students Needing Extra Help
Ex. 9: Review location words.
Help students refer to the pharmacy layout. Use the Vocabulary section of the Organizer.
Ex. 10: If the answer is negative, have students complete the response by telling where these places are. Provide a model.

Enrichment
As an in-class written assignment, pairs of students can create a dialogue to present to the rest of the class. This dialogue will vary from the one in Ex. 9 in that *Estudiante B* tells *Estudiante A* that he or she has none of the items named. Encourage students to come up with a range of reactions on the part of *Estudiante A:* from ordinary questions regarding where else the item is sold

10 ESTUDIANTE A

a. ¿El mostrador está al fondo?

b. ¿La caja está . . .

c. ¿Los servicios están . . .

d. ¿La escalera mecánica está . . .

e. ¿La salida está . . .

f. ¿La escalera está . . .

ESTUDIANTE B

Answers will vary, but may include the following information:

a. No. Está al lado de la caja.

b. No. Está al lado del mostrador.

c. Sí, señor(ita).

d. No. Está cerca de la entrada.

e. Sí, señor(ita).

f. Sí, señor(ita).

10

A — *¿Los ascensores están al fondo?*

B — *Sí, señor(ita), a la derecha de la salida.*
   o: *No, están . . .*

Estudiante A

a.

b.

c.

d.

e.

f.

Estudiante B

or when they are going to have it, to extraordinary, dramatic statements about how tired or sick he or she is, how badly he or she needs the item, etc.

Extended Written Practice/Homework

1. Write four sentences describing a department store.

2. Write three sentences using verbs from pp. 89 and 267 to tell what you do to get ready for school or to go out with friends.

3. Write three sentences telling how someone would go up to a higher floor in different places: *Para subir al segundo piso de la escuela, debes usar las escaleras.*

Multiple Intelligences

Interpersonal/Social and Verbal/Linguistic

See Enrichment.

Visual/Spatial

1) Have students make a comic strip about holiday shopping.

2) Have students write a recommendation for a friend applying for after-school work.

Practice & Apply

Re-enter / Recycle
Ex. 16: daily routine from Chap. 2

Answers: Empecemos a conversar

11 ESTUDIANTE A

a. ¿Se venden sellos en una farmacia?

b. ¿Se venden revistas . . .

c. ¿Se vende ropa para damas . . .

d. ¿Se venden lápices de labios . . .

e. ¿Se venden verduras . . .

f. ¿Se vende crema de afeitar . . .

g. ¿Se vende perfume . . .

h. ¿Se venden flores . . .

i. ¿Se venden vendas . . .

j. Questions will vary.

ESTUDIANTE B

a.–j. Answers will vary, but should reflect your community.

---

11 periódicos   A —¿Se vende(n) _periódicos_ en una farmacia?
B — _En algunas sí._
o: _No sé, pero hay un quiosco en la esquina._

Estudiante A

a. sellos

b. revistas

c. ropa para damas

d. lápices de labios

e. verduras

f. crema de afeitar

g. perfume

h. flores

i. vendas

j.

Estudiante B

Claro que sí / no.

En algunas sí.

No sé.

Empecemos a escribir y a leer
Escribe tus respuestas en español.

12 ¿A qué distancia de tu casa está la farmacia que queda más cerca? ¿Qué compras en la farmacia generalmente? ¿En qué tipo de tienda gastas más dinero?

13 ¿A qué edad empiezan a maquillarse las muchachas de tu comunidad? ¿Qué color de lápiz de labios está de moda ahora? ¿Y de esmalte de uñas? ¿Con qué se afeitan los hombres de tu familia?

www.pasoapaso.com

MORE PRACTICE
- Más práctica y tarea, p. 550
- Practice Workbook 8–3, 8–4

270   Capítulo 8

El perfume que inspiró Carmen sólo se encuentra en Sevilla.

CARMEN
VICTORIO & LUCCHINO
SEVILLA

Comprando lápices de labios en El Corte Inglés, Madrid

Options

Strategies for Reaching All Students

Spanish-Speaking Students
Ex. 15: _¿Te gusta ir a los centros comerciales con tus amigos(as)? ¿Cuándo van? ¿Van sólo a comprar? ¿Qué otras cosas hacen?_

 Un paso más Ex. 8-F

Students Needing Extra Help
Ex. 12: Refer students to the _Empecemos a conversar,_ Exs. 2 and 4 on pp. 262 and 264. Review types of stores. If available, use the Organizer from Book 1, Chap. 6.
Ex. 14: Students may need help with the _¿por qué?_ response.
Ex. 15: Students may need help formulating the answer to the last question.
Ex. 16: Model the changes for a statement that students disagree with. Show which part of the statement changes.

Multiple Intelligences
Intrapersonal/Introspective
See Exs. 12–16.
Verbal/Linguistic
See Audio Activity 8.2.
Visual/Spatial
See Practice Wkbk. 8-3 and 8-4, Writing Activity 8-B, and Comm. Act. BLM 8-1.

14 Para ir al piso cinco de un almacén, ¿usas la escalera, el ascensor o la escalera mecánica? ¿Por qué?

15 Cuando vas de compras, ¿usas el transporte público? ¿Con quiénes sueles ir de compras? Cuando vas con un adulto, ¿qué haces tú mientras él o ella hace sus propias compras?

16 En grupo decidan si están de acuerdo con las siguientes frases. Si no están de acuerdo, escríbanlas de nuevo según su opinión y digan por qué.

a. La ropa para caballeros es más cara que la de damas.
b. La ropa para caballeros es más cómoda que la de damas.
c. Una mujer debe quitarse todo el maquillaje antes de acostarse.
d. Uno debe ponerse la camisa antes de peinarse.
e. Uno debe cepillarse los dientes antes de usar la seda dental.
f. Un hombre debe lavarse la cara antes de afeitarse.

También se dice

el hilo dental

la escalera eléctrica

la pintura de uñas
el barniz de uñas

la pintura de labios
el crayón de labios
el lápiz labial

la máquina de rasurar
la rastrilla
la rasuradora

el elevador

Vocabulario para conversar   271

Cultural Notes ☀

(p. 270, realia)
The opera *Carmen,* by Georges Bizet, is presumably the inspiration for this perfume. The ad implies that only a city like Sevilla would inspire such an opera or such a perfume.

(p. 271, realia)
The time of the year *(el tiempo)* when we are plagued with bad weather *(mal tiempo)* is time for Vitamin C. Using a play on words, this ad emphasizes the role of Vitamin C in preventing illnesses brought on by cold, wet weather. The product claims to replenish one's supply of Vitamin C with an effervescent tablet dissolved in water.

Practice

Teaching Suggestions

Ex. 2: Draw a simple map of your neighborhood or community on the chalkboard to help students do this activity. Include important landmarks such as *el correo, la estación de policía, la biblioteca pública, el parque,* etc. Students should give authentic answers. You may want to focus on school instead. Use *la cafetería, la oficina del director / de la directora, la enfermería, la biblioteca, el gimnasio,* and *el auditorio.* Be sure students know *el pasillo, el (segundo) piso, el patio de recreo,* if appropriate.

Ex. 3: You may want to have students use a guide from a store in your community.

Answers:
¡Comuniquemos!

1 Answers will vary, but may include the following:

ESTUDIANTE A

¿Cómo se llama el lugar donde se venden periódicos? / . . . el lugar donde se vende bronceador? / . . . la tienda donde se venden verduras? / . . . el lugar donde se venden vendas? / . . . el lugar donde hay un semáforo? / . . . el lugar donde se pagan las compras?

ESTUDIANTE B

Se llama un quiosco. / . . . una farmacia. / . . . una verdulería. / . . . una farmacia. / . . . un cruce. / . . . una caja.

¡Comuniquemos!

Aquí tienes otra oportunidad para usar el vocabulario de este capítulo.

1 A veces uno no sabe la palabra correcta y necesita preguntar cómo se llama algo. Usa palabras como *lugar, cosa, tienda.* Túrnate con un(a) compañero(a). Puedes usar éstas u otras ideas. Por ejemplo:

A — *¿Cómo se llama el lugar donde se ponen las cartas?*
B — *Se llama un buzón.*

MARIBEL VERDÚ PRESENTA
LOS NUEVOS COLORES DE GIOVANNA

Giovanna se llena de color con la nueva línea de maquillaje Gio de Giovanna. Atrevida. Osada. Moderna. Para ponerte guapísima. Irresistible. Con los lápices de labios más audaces que nunca hayas visto. Unas sombras de ojos arrebatadoras, para asombrarte... y asombrar. Y con unos rabiosos coloretes de auténtica locura. ¡Échale imaginación y ponte a la moda! ¿Te atreves? Gio, I nuovi colori di Giovanna.

Gio
de Giovanna

Maribel Verdú

Options

Strategies for Reaching All Students

Spanish-Speaking Students

Exs. 1–3: If possible, pair bilingual with non-bilingual students.

 Un paso más Ex. 8-G

Students Needing Extra Help

Students may need help formulating the questions and retrieving the appropriate vocabulary. Do as a class or assign one example to each group.

Ex. 2: Give students time to make the map, or have a map ready. Do a complete model. Use the vocabulary section of the Organizer. *¿Qué sabes ahora?:* Have students write out this exercise so that they can record their progress.

Cooperative Learning

In groups of four, students will design a layout for a new department store having the following departments: *juguetes, aparatos eléctricos, cosméticos, muebles, ropa para niños,* and *zapatos.* Have two students decide where each department should go, and where the cash registers, elevators,

2 Túrnate con un(a) compañero(a) para ser el (la) policía y el (la) turista. Hagan un mapa de su comunidad y úsenlo para pedir y dar direcciones.

A —*Señor(ita), ¿me podría indicar dónde queda la biblioteca pública?*
B —*Claro que sí,...*

3 Túrnense para pedir y dar información. Uno de ustedes trabaja en el mostrador de información en el primer piso de un almacén. Usen la información en la tabla de la derecha.

A —*Perdone, señor(ita), ¿dónde están los perfumes?*
B —*Al fondo, señor(ita), cerca de la escalera mecánica.*

a. b. c.

d. e. f. g.

DIRECTORIO

administración	2
aparatos eléctricos	5
juguetes	6
maquillaje	1
muebles	4
perfumes	1
restaurante	sótano
ropa para caballeros	sótano
ropa para damas	2
ropa para niños	3
servicios	6
zapatos	3

¿Qué sabes ahora?

Can you:

- name and describe the location of places in a community?
  —Pon las cartas en ___. Está ___ el correo.
- ask for and give directions?
  —Perdone, señorita, ¿___ indicarme dónde ___ la estación de bomberos?
  —Cruce ___, siga por ___ y ___ a la izquierda.
- locate items in a drugstore or department store?
  —¿La ropa de niños está en   ?
  —No, señor, está en ___.

Vocabulario para conversar   273

2 Answers will vary.

3 ESTUDIANTE A
a. Perdone, señor(ita), ¿dónde están los microondas?
b. ...los trajes de hombre?
c. ...los lápices de labios?
d. ...los zapatos?
e. ...las muñecas?
f. ...las faldas?
g. Questions will vary.

ESTUDIANTE B
a. En el quinto piso, señor(a).
b. ...sótano...
c. ...primer piso...
d. ...tercer piso...
e. ...sexto piso...
f. ...segundo piso...
g. Answers will vary.

Answers: ¿Qué sabes ahora?

- el buzón / *Answers will vary, but should be a preposition.*
- Podría / queda, está / la calle (por aquí) (la carretera) / la calle / doble
- el primer (segundo, etc.) piso / el sótano

 Audio Activity 8.3

 Writing Activity 8-C

Pasos vivos 2 CD-ROM
Boom Box, Clip Art Album, Slide Projector, Laboratorio de grabar

escalators, and restrooms should be located. They should then tell a third student, so he or she can sketch out the layout of the store. As the group work proceeds, the fourth student should make a chart with the headings *Departamento, Lugar,* and *¿Por que?* and be prepared to present the data to the class.

Multiple Intelligences
Interpersonal/Social and Bodily/Kinesthetic
See Cooperative Learning.
Verbal/Linguistic
See Exs. 1–3 and Audio Activity 8.3.
Visual/Spatial
See Writing Activity 8-C.

Present & Apply

Cultural Objective
• To discuss bargaining procedures in Guatemala

Critical Thinking: Hypothesizing
Based on information in the *Perspectiva cultural* and students' general knowledge of U.S. history, what do they think might happen to the present-day Guatemalan system of buying goods in the next decade or so? Will bargaining become a thing of the past or will it remain a strong part of the Guatemalan economic system? Why? What is the likelihood of its becoming a part of our daily life?

Perspectiva cultural

¿Cómo sabe la gente los precios de las cosas en el mercado? ¿Crees que todos pagan el mismo precio? ¿Por qué crees eso? ¿Y en el almacén? ¿Por qué crees que sí o que no?

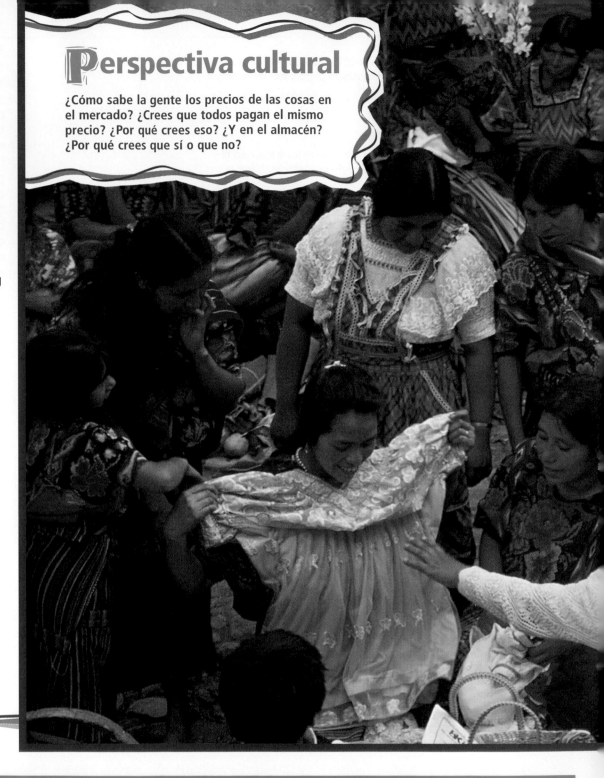

Options

Strategies for Reaching All Students

Spanish-Speaking Students
Ask: *¿Te gusta regatear, o prefieres comprar en un lugar con precios fijos? ¿Por qué? ¿Crees que los vendedores que tienen que regatear ganan mucho dinero? ¿Tienen un sueldo seguro? ¿Has regateado con un vendedor alguna vez? ¿Cómo te fue? ¿Qué compraste?*

 Un paso más Ex. 8-H

Students Needing Extra Help
Have students take notes to use when reviewing for the test. Discuss the idea of bargaining. Point out the differences in the photos, such as no price tags in the market, etc.
La cultura desde tu perspectiva: Students may need help defining yard sales, car purchases, etc.

Enrichment
Ex. 2: It might be helpful for students to make lists with the following headings to help them answer this question: *Aquí siempre se regatea, Aquí nunca se regatea, Aquí se regatea de vez en cuando.*
Additional questions: *¿Cómo debe ser una persona para poder regatear bien? ¿Qué tipo de personalidad debe tener? ¿Te gusta (gustaría) regatear? ¿Por qué sí o no?*

Roberto es un estudiante estadounidense que está viviendo con una familia guatemalteca en una comunidad pequeña. Hoy acompañó a doña* Francia, la madre de la familia, al mercado.

DOÑA FRANCIA	Buenos días, don Pancho.
VENDEDOR	Buenos días, doña Francia. ¿Cómo está?
DOÑA FRANCIA	Muy bien, gracias. ¿Y usted?
VENDEDOR	Bien, gracias a Dios.
DOÑA FRANCIA	Su hijo mayor es de la misma edad que Roberto, ¿verdad? ¿Ya se graduó?
VENDEDOR	No, todavía no. Se gradúa el año que viene, si Dios quiere. Está sacando buenas notas.
DOÑA FRANCIA	Me alegro.
VENDEDOR	Las manzanas están muy buenas hoy. Están a 75 centavos el kilo.
DOÑA FRANCIA	(inspeccionando las manzanas) Mmmm.
VENDEDOR	(en voz baja) Sesenta centavos.
DOÑA FRANCIA	Me da dos kilos, don Pancho. (Don Pancho le entrega las manzanas, y doña Francia le paga.) Gracias, don Pancho. Hasta la próxima vez. Salúdeme a su señora.
VENDEDOR	¡Cómo no, doña Francia! Que estén bien por su casa.

*Don and doña are titles of respect used with a person's first name.

De compras en el mercado de Momostenango, Guatemala

Unas mujeres admiran una blusa en el mercado de Chichicastenango, Guatemala.

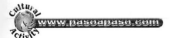
www.pasoapaso.com

Doña Francia y don Pancho charlan un poco antes de hablar de lo que ella va a comprar porque las relaciones personales son muy importantes en su cultura. Es necesario confirmarlas antes de negociar.

Más tarde Roberto va a un mercado turístico para comprar unos recuerdos.

ROBERTO	Buenas tardes, señor.
VENDEDOR	Buenas tardes, joven.
ROBERTO	¿A cuánto están estas bolsas?
VENDEDOR	A cien quetzales cada una. Son de pura lana y de colores firmes.
ROBERTO	¿No me puede dar una por ochenta quetzales?
VENDEDOR	No, lo siento. Pero sí por noventa.

La cultura desde tu perspectiva

1 Compara los dos diálogos según estas preguntas: ¿Se conocen el cliente y el vendedor? ¿Cómo lo sabes? ¿De qué hablan? ¿Quién menciona el precio primero? ¿Cambia mucho el precio?

2 ¿Cuándo y dónde se regatea (bargain) en los Estados Unidos? Compara la manera de regatear en los Estados Unidos y en Guatemala.

Perspectiva cultural 275

Cultural Notes

(p. 274, photo)
Chichicastenango, in the Department of Quiché, Guatemala, is known for its market, held every Sunday and Thursday. The colorful huipil (embroidered blouse made of handwoven fabric) worn by the woman in this photo identifies her as a member of a particular community. Each village designs a signature pattern into its huipil. Also situat-

ed on the plaza is Santo Tomás, the church where the Popol Vuh, a book written in Maya-Quiché about the indigenous peoples of Guatemala, was first translated into Spanish.

(p. 275, photo)
Momostenango is a small town in the Department of Huehuetenango, one of the most mountainous regions of Guatemala. Temperatures range from 40–70° F. Momostenango is known for its production of heavy wool blankets, called ponchos, which typically feature the design of two quetzales facing each other.

Preview

 Overhead 43

Teaching Suggestions

A: Have students predict what the present participle of *servir* would be. Then ask them to find that form in the text to see if their prediction is correct. *75 años sirviendo a nuestros clientes.*

B: Ask students to guess what *Se prohíbe fumar* means. ("Smoking is prohibited" or "No smoking.")

Answers

A The line is *¡Aprenda español mientras está durmiendo!* The form of *dormir* is *durmiendo.* The stem of the present participle contains the stem change *(o → u).* The present participle of *pedir* is *está pidiendo;* the present participle of *servir* is *está sirviendo.*

B People in general (also expressed as "we") perform the action. The word that follows the verb (in this case, the subject of the sentence) determines whether the verb is singular or plural.

C The expression is *Ud. no paga nada.* Two negative words *(no* and *nada)* are used. *No* comes before the verb, and *nada* comes after. "I don't see anything" is said *(Yo) no veo nada.*

Gramática en contexto

¡Aprenda español mientras está durmiendo!

¿Imposible? ¡Sí es posible con el fabuloso y nuevo **método Dormex!**

Llame hoy al 555-7777 y ¡ábrale las puertas a un nuevo futuro!

Librería El Quijote
Paseo de la Reforma 327

Se venden libros, revistas, periódicos, mapas y guías turísticas

75 años sirviendo a nuestros clientes

— Se habla inglés. —

Taller Hermanos Gómez

Se vende gasolina.

Se reparan coches y camiones.

Si su vehículo no queda en perfectas condiciones, ¡Ud. no paga nada!

A You know that we use *estar* + present participle to talk about something that is happening right now. Find the sentence that talks about sleeping in the first ad. How is the stem different from *dormir?* What do you think the present participle of *pedir* and *servir* might be?

B In these ads, *se habla, se reparan,* and *se vende(n)* are used. In these sentences, who do you think performs the action? In some cases the verb is singular; in others, plural. What do you think determines this?

C Find the expression that means "you pay nothing." How many negative words are used? Where do they appear in relation to the verb? How would you say "I don't see anything"?

276 Capítulo 8

Options

Strategies for Reaching All Students

Students Needing Extra Help
Begin the grammar section of the Organizer.
B: Students may have difficulty explaining the impersonal *se* in these sentences. Give more examples (in columns) to help them determine when the verb is singular and when it is plural.
Repaso: Los usos de estar: Give additional examples. If available, use the Organizer from Book 1, Chap. 3.
Ex. 1: Create additional examples to include the points made in the *estar* explanation.

Extended Written Practice/Homework
1. Choose four items on p. 266 and tell where they are now in your home: *Mi perfume está sobre mi cómoda.*
2. Choose three of the following words and write sentences describing people you know: *casado(a), divorciado(a), separado(a), soltero(a), muerto(a). Mis vecinos están separados.*

Multiple Intelligences
Visual/Spatial
See Overhead 43, Exs. A–C, and Practice Wkbk. 8-5.

276 **Standards** 1.2; 3.1; 4.1

Repaso: Los usos de *estar*

Review the present-tense forms of *estar*.

(yo)	**estoy**	(nosotros) (nosotras)	**estamos**
(tú)	**estás**	(vosotros) (vosotras)	**estáis**
Ud. (él) (ella)	**está**	Uds. (ellos) (ellas)	**están**

- Remember that we use *estar* to indicate location.

  Los servicios **están** al fondo.

- We also use *estar* to talk about conditions and characteristics that are not always associated with that person or thing.

  La venda **está** limpia.
  La máquina de afeitar **está** sucia.

Compare this use of *estar* with the use of *ser* for conditions and characteristics that usually *are* associated with a person or thing.

Juan **es** guapo.	*Juan is good-looking.*
¡Qué guapo **estás** hoy!	*How nice you look today!*

- *Estar* is also used to form the present progressive tense.

  Patricia **está cruzando** la calle.

1 Tu equipo ganó el partido de fútbol. Túrnate con un(a) compañero(a) para decir cómo están estas personas.

> **yo**　　　*Estoy (muy) cansado.*

a. el entrenador de tu equipo　　　alegre
b. el entrenador del otro equipo　　　triste
c. los jugadores de tu equipo　　　de buen / mal humor
d. los jugadores del otro equipo　　　cansado(a)
e. algunos amigos tuyos　　　callado(a)
f. Uds.
g. la esposa de tu entrenador

Present & Practice

Reteach / Review: Uses of *estar*
After reviewing the examples, call on students to give other sentences illustrating uses of *estar*.

Re-enter / Recycle
Ex. 1: sports from Chap. 4

Answers
1 Answers will vary, but may include:
a. Está (muy) alegre.
b. Está de mal humor.
c. Están (muy) cansados.
d. Están (muy) callados.
e. Están de buen humor.
f. Están (muy) alegres.
g. Está alegre.

 Practice Wkbk. 8-5

 Writing Activity 8-D

 Prueba 8-5

Present & Practice

Re-enter / Recycle

Ex. 3: greetings and leavetakings from Chap. 6
Ex. 5: daily routine from Chap. 2

Answers

2 a. Está bebiendo (un vaso de) agua.
b. Están escribiendo en la pizarra.
c. Están sacando la basura.
d. Están encendiendo las velas.
e. Está tocando la trompeta.
f. Está patinando (en la acera).

3 a. Carla está durmiendo.
b. Yo estoy vistiendo al niño.
c. Él está pidiendo una venda.
d. Ellas se están diciendo "¡Hola!"
/ Ellas están diciéndose "¡Hola!"
e. Uds. se están divirtiendo. /
Uds. están divirtiéndose.
f. (Nosotros) nos estamos despidiendo. / (Nosotros) estamos despidiéndonos.

4 ESTUDIANTE A
a. ¿Quién está haciendo las compras?
b. ... está reparando la escalera mecánica?
c. ... (es) está(n) buscando la verdulería?
d. ... está comprando la crema de afeitar?
e. ... (es) está(n) apagando el incendio?
f. ... está colgando la ropa?
g. ... está enviando las cartas?

Repaso: El presente progresivo

You know that when we want to express that an action is happening right now, we use the present progressive tense. We form it using the present tense of *estar* + the present participle of another verb. To form the present participle, we add *-ando* to the stem of *-ar* verbs and *-iendo* to the stem of *-er* and *-ir* verbs.

habl**ar**	**estoy** habl**ando**
com**er**	**estamos** com**iendo**
escrib**ir**	**están** escrib**iendo**

- Verbs that have the stem change $o \to u$ or $e \to i$ in the preterite have the same change in the present participle. For example:

INFINITIVE	PRETERITE	PRESENT PARTICIPLE
dormir $(o \to u)$	**durm**ieron	**durm**iendo
servir $(e \to i)$	**sirv**ieron	**sirv**iendo

Juan todavía **está durmiendo**.
El camarero **está sirviendo** la comida.

- Reflexive or object pronouns can be placed before the form of *estar,* or they can be attached to the end of the present participle. If they are attached to the present participle, a written accent is needed.

Ahora **me** estoy **divirtiendo**.	Ahora estoy **divirtiéndome**.
Lo está **haciendo** ahora.	Está **haciéndolo** ahora.

2 Mira los dibujos y di qué están haciendo estas personas.

Está hablando por teléfono.

a.   b.   c.
d.   e.   f.

278   Capítulo 8

Options

Strategies for Reaching All Students

Students Needing Extra Help
Repaso: El presente progresivo: If available, use the Organizer from Book 1, Chap. 14. Review all the verbs having the stem change: *vestirse, conseguir, despedirse, pedir.* Write them on the chalkboard and have students copy the list. Give more examples of the reflexive and object pronoun construction. If students are having

difficulty, review indirect object pronouns with infinitives. Encourage students to use the construction that is most comfortable for them.
Ex. 2: Remind students that this exercise contains *-ar, -er,* and *-ir* verbs.
Ex. 3: Point out that this exercise uses stem-changing verbs.

Ex. 4: Point out where the *lo* came from. Model with a feminine object pronoun. Go through the exercise, using the first response, then again using the second response.
Ex. 5: If available, use the vocabulary section of the Organizer from Chap. 2.

3 ¿Y qué están haciendo estas otras personas?

Ramón / servir   *Ramón está sirviendo los refrescos.*
los refrescos

a. Carla / dormir
b. yo / vestir al niño
c. él / pedir una venda

d. ellas / decirse "¡Hola!"
e. Uds. / divertirse
f. nosotros / despedirse

4 ¿Quién está haciendo estas cosas? Túrnate con otro(a) compañero(a).

lavar el   **A** —*¿Quién está lavando el coche?*
coche / Jorge   **B** —*Jorge está lavándolo.*
           o: *Jorge lo está lavando.*

a. hacer las compras / Rafael
b. reparar la escalera mecánica / Patricia
c. buscar la verdulería / ellos
d. comprar la crema de afeitar / Mario
e. apagar el incendio / los bomberos
f. colgar la ropa / Juana
g. enviar las cartas / Marco

5 Son las siete de la mañana. ¿Qué está haciendo la familia de Javier?
Túrnate con otro(a) compañero(a).

Su padre está afeitándose.

su padre

a. su madre   b. sus hermanos menores   c. su hermana mayor

d. Javier   e. su bisabuela   f. su hermana menor

Gramática en contexto   279

ESTUDIANTE B
a. Rafael está haciéndolas (las está haciendo).
b. Patricia está reparándola (la está reparando).
c. Ellos están buscándola (la están buscando).
d. Mario está comprándola (la está comprando).
e. Los bomberos están apagándolo (lo están apagando).
f. Juana está colgándola (la está colgando).
g. Marco está enviándolas (las está enviando).

5 a. Su madre está maquillándose.
b. Sus hermanos menores están vistiéndose.
c. Su hermana mayor está poniéndose esmalte de uñas.
d. Javier está cepillándose los dientes.
e. Su bisabuela está levantándose.
f. Su hermana menor está peinándose.

 Writing Activity 8-E

 Comm. Act. BLM 8-2

Enrichment
Use the examples showing the placement of reflexive or object pronouns for a quick review. Write these sentences on the chalkboard and call on students to change them according to your cue for a different reflexive verb or pronoun: *Ahora Javier se está divirtiendo. Ahora está divirtiéndose. (nosotros / aburrirnos; yo / quedarme en cama; tú / sentirte mal)*

Extended Written Practice/Homework
1. Imagine you are in a department store right now. Write four sentences saying what different people are doing: *Mi amiga está probándose zapatos nuevos.*
2. Write three sentences telling things that are happening in your school or community: *El equipo de básquetbol está preparándose para el campeonato.*

Multiple Intelligences
Visual/Spatial
See Enrichment, Writing Activity 8-E, and Comm. Act. BLM 8-2.
Visual/Spatial and Verbal/Linguistic
See Ex. 2.

Present & Practice

Reteach / Review: Negative constructions
To reinforce affirmative and negative words, call out a word and have students call out the antonym.

Re-enter / Recycle
Ex. 9: daily routine from Chap. 2

Answers

6 Answers will vary, but look for the correct forms of *estar* + present participle.

7 **ESTUDIANTE A**
a. ¿Celebraste algo especial esta semana?
b. ¿Compraste . . .
c. ¿Encontraste . . .
d. ¿Escribiste . . .
e. ¿Viste . . .
f. ¿Hiciste . . .
ESTUDIANTE B
Answers will vary; look for correct first-person preterite forms.
a. (No) Celebré . . .
b. (No) Compré . . .
c. (No) Encontré . . .
d. (No) Escribí . . .
e. (No) Vi . . .
f. (No) Hice . . .

8 **ESTUDIANTE A**
a. ¿Ves alguna máquina de afeitar por aquí?
b. . . . algún perfume . . .
c. . . . algún desodorante . . .

---

6 Imagina qué están haciendo varias personas (el presidente de los Estados Unidos, el (la) director(a) de la escuela, etc.) en este momento. Túrnate con un(a) compañero(a).

A — ¿Qué está haciendo ___?
B — Creo que está ___.

Construcciones negativas

Here are some affirmative and negative words that you already know. Remember that they are antonyms.

AFFIRMATIVE	NEGATIVE
alguien	nadie
algo	nada
alguno, alguna *(pronoun)*	ninguno, ninguna *(pronoun)*
algún, alguna *(adj.)*	ningún, ninguna *(adj.)*
siempre	nunca
también	tampoco

Algún and *ningún* are always written with an accent.

• Affirmative words usually come before the main verb of the sentence. In a question they may come after the verb.

Ella **también** lo recuerda.   ¿Se repartió **algo**?
¿**Alguien** cumplió años?   ¿**Siempre** vas a la panadería?

• Negative words may come before or after the verb. But if they come after, we must use *no* before the verb.

Nadie fue a la reunión.   **No** fue **nadie** a la reunión.
Nunca llora.   **No** llora **nunca**.
Ninguno de ellos se quitó el abrigo.   **No** se quitó el abrigo **ninguno** de ellos.

7 Túrnate con un(a) compañero(a) para contestar las preguntas.

comer

A — ¿Comiste algo especial esta semana?
B — Sí, comí ___.
o: No, no comí nada especial.

a. celebrar   c. encontrar   e. ver
b. comprar   d. escribir   f. hacer

280   Capítulo 8

Options

Strategies for Reaching All Students

Students Needing Extra Help
Ex. 6: Brainstorm people and their activities as a whole class.
Construcciones negativas: continuación:
Help pairs of students read the chart. Give additional examples of the placement of affirmative words. If available, refer to the grammar section of the Organizer for Book 1, Chap. 14.
Give additional examples of negative constructions using *no,* emphasizing that this is just another way of saying the same thing.

Ex. 7: Model more of these responses, especially a positive response. Brainstorm possible responses.
Ex. 8: Remind students that *alguno(a)* and *ninguno(a)* must agree with the nouns they replace. Point out the artwork, and remind students that their response depends on it. Give an example using the second response.
Ex. 9: Do the exercise twice, as an oral and as a written exercise, using the two negative responses separately. Remind students that

this practices two ways of saying the same thing.

Enrichment
Construcciones negativas: As a homework assignment, have students write on the following topic, using as many appropriate affirmative and negative words as possible: *Rodrigo perdió su carnet de identidad. ¿Qué le dice un optimista? ¿Qué le dice un pesimista?*

8 Con un(a) compañero(a) contesta las preguntas.
Por ejemplo:

pasta dentífrica

A —¿*Ves alguna pasta dentífrica*
por aquí?
B —*No, no veo ninguna.*
o: *Sí, aquí está.*

a. máquina de afeitar
b. perfume
c. desodorante
d. cepillo de dientes

e. lápiz de labios
f. jabón
g. 💡

9 ¿Qué haces todas las mañanas? Con un(a)
compañero(a) contesta las preguntas.

A —¿*Siempre te bañas por la mañana?*
B —*No, nunca me baño por la mañana.*
o: *No, no me baño nunca por la mañana.*
o: *Sí, siempre. / Sólo de vez en cuando.*

a.

b.

c.

d.

e.

f.

Gramática en contexto 281

d. ...algún cepillo de dientes ...
e. ...algún lápiz de labios ...
f. ...algún jabón ...
g. Questions will vary.

ESTUDIANTE B
a. No, no veo ninguna.
b. Sí, aquí está.
c. No, no veo ninguno.
d. Sí, aquí está.
e. Sí, aquí está.
f. No, no veo ninguno.
g. Answers will vary.

9 **ESTUDIANTE A**
a. ¿Siempre te maquillas por la
mañana?
b. ...te cepillas los dientes ...?
c. ...te duchas ...?
d. ...te peinas ...?
e. ...te lavas la cara ...?
f. ...te secas el pelo ...?

ESTUDIANTE B
Answers will vary, but should
include the following:
a. ...me maquillo ...
b. ...me cepillo ...
c. ...me ducho ...
d. ...me peino ...
e. ...me lavo ...
f. ...me seco ...

 **Practice Wkbk. 8-6,
8-7, 8-8**

Writing Activity 8-F

¿? Pruebas 8-6, 8-7

Comm. Act. BLM 8-3

Ex. 9: You may want to do this exercise with
the entire class, with you posing the same
question four times and eliciting from students the four different responses provided
in the example. Remind students that they
can use other time expressions such as *a
veces, muchas veces, a menudo, casi siempre,* and *casi nunca.*

Extended Written Practice/Homework
1. Refer to pp. 260–261 and write three
sentences saying what places are not found
near your home: *No hay ninguna pescadería
en mi comunidad.*
2. Using words from pp. 221 and 280, write
three sentences describing social events
that were disasters: *En mi fiesta de
cumpleaños, nadie me regaló nada.*

3. Refer to p. 189 and write three sentences
saying what did not used to happen when
you were a child: *Cuando era niño(a), no
me peleaba con nadie.*

Multiple Intelligences
Interpersonal/Social and Verbal/Linguistic
See Exs. 6–9.
Visual/Spatial
See Enrichment; Practice Wkbk 8-6, 8-7,
and 8-8; Writing Activity 8-F; and Comm.
Act. BLM 8-3.

Present & Practice

El *se* impersonal

In English we often use *they, you, one,* or *people* in an impersonal or indefinite sense meaning "people in general." In Spanish we use *se* + the *Ud. / él / ella* or the *Uds. / ellos / ellas* form of the verb.

Se habla español.   *Spanish is spoken (here).*

Se venden perfumes en   *They sell perfume in that store.*
        esa tienda.

¿**Se permite** sacar fotos?   *Can you take pictures?*

10 Con un(a) compañero(a), habla de un club nuevo. Por ejemplo:

tocar música   A — *¿Aquí se toca música rock o clásica?*
rock o clásica   B — *Aquí se toca música rock.*

a. bailar bailes latinos o americanos
b. servir comida o sandwiches
c. permitir sacar fotos o no
d. ver gente famosa o no
e. llevar ropa elegante o deportiva

Options

Strategies for Reaching All Students

11 Pregúntale a un(a) compañero(a) qué se hace en estos lugares.

A —¿Qué se repara aquí?
B —Se reparan zapatos.

reparar

a. vender

b. servir

c. hacer

d. comprar

e. pedir prestado

f. practicar

Ahora lo sabes

Can you:

■ talk about actions that are happening right now?

—¡Silencio! Pablo está ___ .

■ use negative words?

—___ compré ___ revista porque no encontré el quiosco.

■ talk about actions without specifying who does them?

—En una estación de servicio, se ___ gasolina y algunas
veces ___ reparan coches.

11 ESTUDIANTE A
a. ¿Qué se vende aquí?
b. ...se sirve...
c. ...se hace...
d. ...se compra...
e. ...se pide prestado...
f. ...se practica...
ESTUDIANTE B
a. Se vende maquillaje.
b. Se sirve(n) helado (refrescos).
c. Se hacen llaves.
d. Se compran pasta dentífrica y cepillos de dientes.
e. Se pide prestado dinero.
f. Se practica básquetbol.

Answers: Ahora lo sabes
• Answers will vary, but should be a present participle.
• No / ninguna
• vende / se

 Practice Wkbk. 8-9

 Audio Activities 8.4, 8.5

 Writing Activity 8-G

 Prueba 8-8

 Pasos vivos 2 CD-ROM
Phone Task, Slide Presentation Maker, Spindle, Treadmill

Multiple Intelligences
Logical/Mathematical
Have students check the prices for the exact same item in at least three stores. Have them show the results in a graph and share them with the class.
Verbal/Linguistic
See Exs. 10–11 and Audio Activities 8.4 and 8.5.
Visual/Spatial
See Practice Wkbk. 8-9 and Writing Activity 8-G.

Apply

Teaching Suggestions

Ex. 1: You may want to use different settings, such as a classroom, a department store, a drugstore, etc.

Answers: Actividades

1–2 Answers will vary.

 ¿Recuerdas?

Play

 Video Activity A

Using the Video

In Episode 8, Jamie and Carlos drop off the vegetables they bought for Sr. Navarro, who tells them that the produce from La Jacaranda is overpriced and of inferior quality.

The next day, Jamie, Carlos, María and Felipe go shopping together. There is tension between Felipe and Carlos over María; Felipe thinks Carlos is still interested in María until he finds Carlos singing a serenade to Jamie that night. Later, Jamie and Carlos visit Operación Aztlán for the results of the tests: the pesticides used at La Jacaranda are illegal. In the final scene, Jamie and Carlos talk about the future.

Estas señales indican lugares de interés en una sección histórica de Colonia del Sacramento, Uruguay.

Actividades

1. En grupo, van a jugar Veinte Preguntas. Una persona piensa en un objeto. Las otras le hacen preguntas. Ella sólo puede contestar sí o no. Por ejemplo:

   A —*Estoy pensando en algo que está en la esquina de una calle.*
   B —*¿Se ponen cartas allí?*
   A —*No.*
   B —*¿Se venden . . . ?*

2. Túrnate con un(a) compañero(a) para darle direcciones. Tu compañero(a) tiene que adivinar adónde lo llevas. Puedes usar lugares del mapa de las páginas 260–261, de la escuela o de tu comunidad. Por ejemplo:

   Estás en la pescadería. Camina media cuadra hasta llegar al banco. Allí, dobla a la izquierda y camina una cuadra. Ahora, dobla a la izquierda de nuevo. El lugar queda al lado de la verdulería. ¿Dónde estás?

PASO CULTURAL Cuzco fue la antigua capital de los incas. Tiene ahora menos de 300.000 habitantes, pero en su época fue el centro de un imperio que incluía parte de lo que hoy es Colombia, Ecuador, Perú, Bolivia, Chile y Argentina. Cuando el conquistador Francisco Pizarro llegó a Cuzco en 1533, empezó la destrucción del imperio. ¿Por qué piensas tú que Pizarro no respetaba la civilización inca?

Mapa de la ciudad de Cuzco, Perú

284 Capítulo 8

Options

Strategies for Reaching All Students

Students Needing Extra Help

Ex. 1: Limit the possibilities to things that students can clearly see: for example, objects in the classroom or playground. Review the present progressive, the uses of *estar,* and the impersonal *se.* Brainstorm possible questions. If, for example, the objects are all in the classroom, necessary vocabulary would deal with size, shape, color, material, usage, etc.

Ex. 2: Use the vocabulary section of the Organizer. Review location words and words such as *caminar, doblar, quedar,* etc. Give students a place on the map from which to begin.

Multiple Intelligences
Visual/Spatial
See *Conexiones,* Writing Activities 8-H and 8-I, and Comm. Act. BLMs 8-4 and 8-5.

Enrichment

Ex. 1: Pairs of students can play a guessing game in which one student can give hints about a famous person or date in history and the other can try to name it. Example: *Estoy pensando en el jugador de básquetbol que después jugó béisbol. / Estoy pensando en algo que pasó en la luna el 20 de julio de 1969. / Estoy pensando en la persona que dijo, "Un paso pequeño para un hombre, un salto gigante para la humanidad."*

Conexiones

Las ciencias sociales

La evolución de las compras

Vas a hacer una comparación entre cómo se compraba antes y cómo se compra ahora.

Con un(a) compañero(a), mira este diagrama para hacer una comparación entre la Edad Media y el siglo XVIII.

EN LA EDAD MEDIA   EN EL SIGLO XVIII

a. Se vendía(n)... en...
b. Se pagaba(n) con/en...
c. (No) Se podía(n) comprar...

- Haz una lista de palabras que se pueden usar para completar las tres categorías indicadas. Después, escribe frases usando las palabras de tu lista. Por ejemplo:

  En la Edad Media se vendía ropa en una plaza o en la calle.

  En el siglo XVIII se vendía ropa en tiendas pequeñas.

- Con tu compañero(a), túrnate para leer las frases que Uds. escribieron y combínenlas.

  En la Edad Media . . . , pero en el siglo XVIII . . .

- En grupo, hagan una tabla similar mostrando lo que pasa hoy: *Se vende(n) . . . en . . . ,* etc. Formen frases en el presente para cada categoría y escríbanlas.

  Ahora se vende ropa en centros comerciales.

- Entre todos, combinen frases del pasado y del presente para hacer comparaciones.

  Antes se vendía . . . , pero ahora se vende . . .

Todo junto 285

 La Catrina: Capítulo 8

Play

 Video Activity B

 Para entender mejor

Play

 Video Activity C

Answers: Conexiones
Possible answers:
a. See example.
b. En la Edad Media se pagaba con materiales o bienes (goods). En el Siglo XVIII se pagaba con oro y plata.
c. En la Edad Media se podía comprar cerámica en la calle. En el Siglo XVIII no se podía pagar con materiales./Answers and charts will vary.

 Writing Activities 8-H, 8-I

 Comm. Act. BLMs 8-4, 8-5

 Pasos vivos 2 CD-ROM
A Jugar, Laboratorio de grabar, Maps, Video Monitor, Video Presentation Maker

---

Cultural Notes

Cooperative Learning
Divide students into groups of four. Tell each group that they are going on a picnic. Assign each student a responsibility: planning the menu, organizing sports and activities, listing paper goods, and planning musical entertainment. Ask: *¿Qué llevaste al picnic? ¿Dónde lo (la) compraste? ¿Cuánto costó? ¿Qué hiciste en el picnic?* Have one student from each group compile the data and another present it to the class.

Paso cultural
Answers will vary.

(p. 284, top photo)
Colonia del Sacramento, Uruguay, originally a seventeenth-century Portuguese settlement, still retains a colonial atmosphere. Narrow cobblestone streets and ornate wrought-iron work decorate residential buildings in the vicinity. (Note that the word *pulpería* is a regionalism for "general store.") A hydrofoil crosses the Río de la Plata three times daily, connecting Colonia del Sacramento and nearby Buenos Aires.

Apply

Process Reading

For a description of process reading, see p. 52.

Teaching Suggestions

Aplicación: The flags of Puerto Rico (No. 3), Argentina (No. 5), and Panamá (No. 6) are not described in the text. You may want to have groups of three work together, with one student giving the description and the other two guessing.

Answers
Antes de leer

Answers will vary, but students may say that they will find information about Central and South American countries and their flags.

¡Vamos a leer!

www.pasoapaso.com

Antes de leer

STRATEGY ➤ Using prior knowledge

These are excerpts from a geography textbook. Look at the map and flags. What kind of information do you think will be in the text?

Mira la lectura

STRATEGY ➤ Skimming

Now skim the text to get a general idea of what it says. Was your guess correct?

¿DE QUÉ PAÍS ES ESTA BANDERA?

286   Capítulo 8

Options

Strategies for Reaching All Students

Spanish-Speaking Students
Aplicación: Have students research the history of one of the flags shown on p. 287: *Haz una investigación sobre la historia de una bandera en la página 287.*

 Un paso más Ex. 8-I

Students Needing Extra Help
Mira la lectura: Go over each description carefully after the answer has been given to ensure that students understand it. You may want to use a large wall map and have one student point as you read aloud.
Aplicación: Have students describe the location and flag of the U.S. Let them use this and other models to write their own descriptions.

Cultural Notes

Flags of Spain and Latin America

Argentina: (1818) Sun represents independence. Blue and white worn by patriots who fought off British invaders in 1806 and 1807.
Bolivia: (1888) Coat of arms has a breadfruit tree, a bundle of wheat, and a mountain. Also pictures a condor and an alpaca.
Chile: White star, progress and honor; red, blood of heroes; white, snow of Andes; blue, sky.
Colombia: (1861) Yellow represents New World; red, the blood of heroes; blue, the ocean.
Costa Rica: (1848) Coat of arms shows three volcanoes, the Caribbean, and seven stars, each representing a province.

Este país está situado en el norte de América del Sur y al este de Colombia. La bandera tiene una franja central azul con siete estrellas blancas. La primera franja es amarilla y la última roja.

Este país está situado en América Central y está al norte de Nicaragua. La bandera tiene una franja central blanca con cinco estrellas azules. Las otras dos franjas también son azules.

Este país está situado al sur de Brasil y es un país pequeño bañado por el Océano Atlántico. La bandera tiene cinco franjas blancas, cuatro azules y un sol amarillo.

Este país está situado en el sur de América del Sur, está bañado por el Océano Pacífico y limita con Perú, Bolivia y Argentina. La bandera tiene una franja superior blanca y otra roja. También tiene una estrella blanca en un cuadrado azul.

Infórmate

STRATEGY ➤ Coping with unknown words

You already know that some words are essential to understanding and some aren't. In this selection, the word *franja* occurs often, and it is important for understanding the text. What do you think it means?

Here are some clues. Look at the flags and name some features they have in common. Then look at the text and the color adjectives used with the word *franja*. Can you guess the meaning? Now do the same with the word *estrella*. Verify your guesses by consulting a dictionary.

Which flag goes with each of the four countries and descriptions?

Infórmate
Franja means "stripe." *Estrella* means "star."
Venezuela (No. 2)
Honduras (No. 4)
Uruguay (No. 7)
Chile (No. 1)

Aplicación
Answers will vary.

www **Internet Activities**

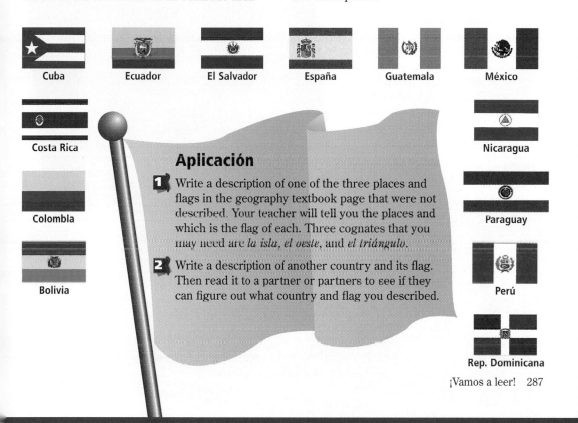

Cuba Ecuador El Salvador España Guatemala México

Costa Rica

Colombia

Bolivia

Nicaragua

Paraguay

Perú

Rep. Dominicana

Aplicación

1 Write a description of one of the three places and flags in the geography textbook page that were not described. Your teacher will tell you the places and which is the flag of each. Three cognates that you may need are *la isla*, *el oeste*, and *el triángulo*.

2 Write a description of another country and its flag. Then read it to a partner or partners to see if they can figure out what country and flag you described.

¡Vamos a leer!   287

Flags of Spain and Latin America cont'd.

Cuba: (1902) Star represents independence.
Dominican Republic: Blue, liberty; white, salvation; red, blood of heroes.
Ecuador: Coat of arms has a condor, Chimborazo mountain, and the first steamboat built in Ecuador.
El Salvador: (1912) Blue stripes represent unity; white, peace.
Guatemala: (1971) Blue stripes represent the Atlantic and Pacific; coat of arms has quetzal with scroll bearing date of independence.
Honduras: (1866) Stars represent the five Central American republics that formed a union in early 1880s.

Mexico: (1821) Coat of arms in the center. Green, independence; white, religion; red, union.
Nicaragua: (1908) Coat of arms features volcanoes representing Central American union; triangle, equality; rainbow, peace; cap, liberty.
Panama: (1903) Blue star, honesty and purity; red star, authority and law.
Paraguay: Red, white, and blue stripes honor French ideals. Coat of arms on front; treasury seal with a lion and liberty cap on back.
Peru: (1825) Symbols represent abundant animal, plant, and mineral resources.

Puerto Rico: (1952) Resembles Cuban flag recalling 1890s when both countries opposed Spanish rule.
Spain: (1981) Shield represents Aragón, Castilla, and other historic kingdoms of Spain.
Uruguay: Stripes represent political division at time of independence. The sun represents independence.
Venezuela: (1954) Red, blood of heroes; blue, Atlantic; yellow, prosperity. Stars represent original states that united to proclaim independence.

Apply

Process Writing
For information regarding developing a writing portfolio, see page 54.

Teaching Suggestions
Students may need help identifying local landmarks. Use this as an opportunity to instill pride in their hometown. Have students contact The Chamber of Commerce, the Visitors' Bureau if there is one, or the public library to learn more about local history and any places of interest that they may be unaware of.

¡Vamos a escribir!

¿Qué lugares de interés hay en tu comunidad, ciudad o estado? Vamos a preparar una guía turística con descripciones de los lugares de más interés.

1 Primero, identifiquen los lugares históricos, famosos o importantes de su comunidad. Piensen en estas cosas:

- cómo se llama el lugar
- dónde queda
- cuál es su historia o qué importancia tiene
- cómo se llega a él
- el horario y el precio de la entrada

Cada estudiante o grupo pequeño debe escoger un lugar y escribir el primer borrador. Consulten con un(a) compañero(a), y sigan los otros pasos del proceso de escribir. Escriban la versión final en un procesador de texto si es posible. Usen dibujos o fotos para ilustrar la guía.

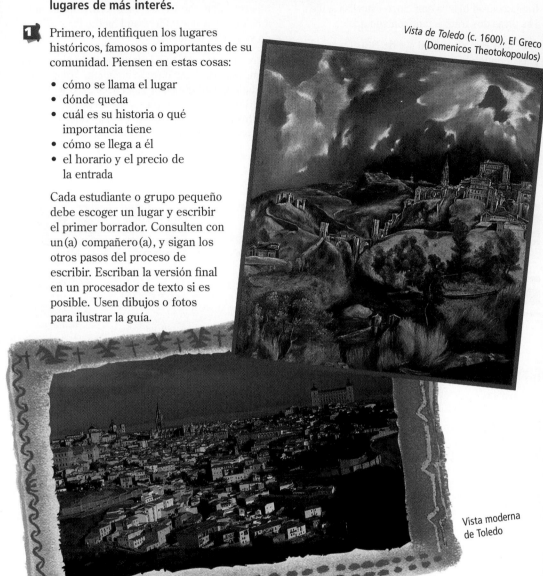

Vista de Toledo (c. 1600), El Greco (Domenicos Theotokopoulos)

Vista moderna de Toledo

Options

Strategies for Reaching All Students

Students Needing Extra Help
After discussing your community, divide the class into two groups: one to work on places of interest, one for the community as a whole. Have tourist guides and community information available. Show how tourist guides keep descriptions short.
As a class, brainstorm places to include in the guide. Model one description, using the vocabulary section of the Organizer. If available, use the Organizer from Book 1, Chap. 10. Remind students that they may have to contact these places for more information. Limit paragraph length. Review the preterite and imperfect tenses and their uses. Give students time to research. They may also need help with the vocabulary and the structure of the sentences. Assign four or five areas to cover: population, number of schools, etc.

Multiple Intelligences
Interpersonal/Social
See Exs. 2–3.
Naturalist
Looking at the painting and photograph of Toledo on p. 288, have students discuss the differences that they observe between the city in 1600 and today. Discuss the changes that have occurred in your own area.

2 Ahora, en grupo escriban uno o dos párrafos sobre su comunidad, ciudad o estado para incluir en la guía. Piensen en estas cosas:

- de dónde viene el nombre de la comunidad
- quiénes eran los primeros habitantes del área
- cuándo llegaron los europeos
- qué se cultivaba o qué industria había
- cómo es la comunidad hoy

3 Para distribuir su trabajo, pueden:

- enviarlo a los hoteles o moteles de la comunidad
- enviarlo a la cámara de comercio (*chamber of commerce*) de la comunidad
- exhibirlo en la biblioteca escolar
- ofrecerlo a una revista o un periódico hispano
- exhibirlo en la sala de clases
- incluirlo en su portafolio

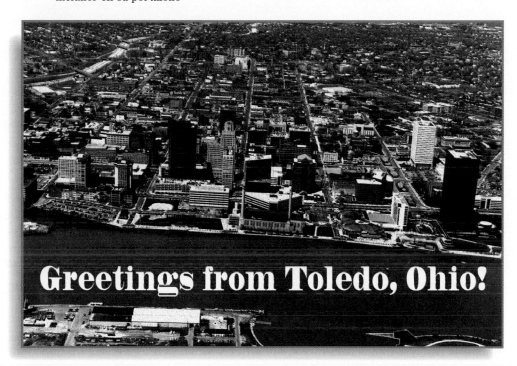

Greetings from Toledo, Ohio!

¡Vamos a escribir!   289

Cultural Notes ☀

(p. 288, top photo)
Domenikos Theotokopoulos, El Greco (1541–1614), was born in Crete. Around 1560, he left to study in Venice, where he began to experiment with the style of painting called "mannerism," characterized by graceful lines, elongated figures, and unusual perspectives. Seeking patronage, he went to Toledo in 1577, where he settled permanently and completed many paintings of its landscape.

(p. 288, bottom photo)
Toledo has long been a crossroads of culture and religion. The Romans entered the already existing city in 193 B.C. The Visigoths and the Moors occupied Toledo in later centuries. In 1085 King Alfonso I took the city from the Moors during the Reconquest and established the political center of Castilla there. During the middle ages, Toledo was an intellectual and artistic center, home to a multicultural citizenry of large numbers of Jews, Muslims, and Christians. The Alcázar, a fortress built in the Moorish style in 1531, dominates this view on the right.

Assess & Summarize

Test Preparation

You may want to assign parts of this section as homework or as an in-class writing activity prior to administering the *Examen de habilidades*.

Answers

Listening: —*Sí, señor. Hay uno muy cerca, a tres cuadras de aquí. Siga por esta calle dos cuadras. En el semáforo, doble a la derecha. Siga por esa calle y el quiosco de periódicos está al final de la cuadra, enfrente de una estación de metro.*
Answers will vary, but may include *¿Hay un quiosco (de periódicos) cerca de aquí?*

Reading: *Rebaja* means "reduction" or "discount."
Answers will vary, but students may say the use of "50 percent" or that they could not be combined with any other discount clued them in to its meaning.

Writing: Directions should be accurate for your community.

Culture: Answers will vary, but students may mention that if the buyer and seller know each other, the bargaining process is subtle. The seller is the first to mention the price of an item, and the buyer then offers a lower amount.

Repaso ¿Lo sabes bien?

Esta sección te ayudará a prepararte para el examen de habilidades, donde tendrás que hacer tareas semejantes.

Listening
Can you understand when someone gives directions? Listen as your teacher reads a sample similar to what you will hear on the test. What question is this the response to?

Reading
Can you understand a written advertisement describing a department store sale? What do you think *rebaja* means? How do you know?

¡Gran Liquidación— Sólo Hoy!

En los Almacenes Flores, donde las rebajas son fantásticas

♦ ropa para damas, caballeros y niños ♦
♦ maquillaje y productos personales ♦
♦ muebles ♦

Rebajas especiales de hasta 50% en todas las secciones.*

*Estas rebajas especiales no se pueden combinar con ningún otro descuento.

Writing
Can you write a note giving directions to a friend who is going to the public library? This is an example.

Carlos,
Es muy fácil ir a la biblioteca desde la parada del autobús en la Calle Franklin. Primero, dobla a la izquierda en la Calle Monroe. Camina dos cuadras. (Hay una señal de alto en la esquina y una heladería cerca.) Dobla a la derecha. Camina por seis cuadras. La biblioteca está en esa esquina. No hay ningún otro edificio grande allí. (En la biblioteca se están vendiendo bolsos muy bonitos esta semana.)
Anabel

Culture
Can you explain how a price is usually negotiated while bargaining in Guatemala?

Speaking
Create a dialogue with your partner about a customer trying to find some things in a department store.

A —*Por favor, ¿dónde puedo encontrar la ropa para damas?*
B —*Está en el tercer piso.*
A —*¿Y dónde están los ascensores? ¿Están al fondo?*
B —*No. Están cerca de la entrada. Siga por aquí. Doble a la derecha en la sección de perfumes. Están enfrente de la caja.*
A —*Muchas gracias. Usted es muy amable.*

Self Test www.pasoapaso.com

Options

Strategies for Reaching All Students

Students Needing Extra Help
Have students write out this exercise so that they can check off what they have mastered. Remind students that this is just a sample of what the test will be like.
Listening: Read more than once. Remind students they only need to listen for one piece of information. Brainstorm for what words they should be listening.
Reading: Remind students of context clues.

Writing: Have students use the Organizer and write a sample note as practice. Give students a common starting point. Remind them to give clues, such as buildings, street names, etc. Allow them to use a map as they write their directions, and give a required number of sentences to write.
Culture: Have students review the notes they took during their first reading of the *Perspectiva cultural*. Role play a bargaining scene with a student, or videotape one with a colleague before-

hand. Review the *Perspectiva cultural*.
Speaking: Choose a store that everyone in the class is familiar with. Discuss the layout of the store, and get students to think in terms of sections. Draw a layout on the chalkboard that students can refer to while speaking. Remind them to give clues such as floor numbers, front, entrance, etc. Use the vocabulary section of the Organizer. Limit the number of lines of the dialogue.

Resumen del vocabulario

Usa el vocabulario de este capítulo para:

- name and describe the location of places in a community
- ask for and give directions
- locate items in a drugstore or department store

to name things and places in a community
el centro
el semáforo
la señal de alto
el cruce
la carretera
el buzón, *pl.* los buzones
el teléfono público
el transporte público
la estación de bomberos
el bombero, la bombera

to name places where you shop
la carnicería
la floristería
la frutería
la heladería
la panadería
la pescadería
el quiosco (de periódicos)
la verdulería

to ask or give directions
la dirección, *pl.* las direcciones
indicar
perdonar: perdone (Ud.)
¿Podría (Ud.) /
    Podrías (tú) + *inf.?*
seguir *(e → i)*: siga (Ud.)
por + *(place.)*
doblar: doble (Ud.)

cruzar
la distancia
la milla
el kilómetro
el metro

to describe places
histórico, -a

to talk about personal care
el cepillo de dientes
la seda dental
el desodorante
la crema de afeitar
la máquina de afeitar
afeitarse
la venda
ponerse
quitarse
maquillarse
el maquillaje
el lápiz de labios,
    pl. los lápices de labios
los labios
el esmalte de uñas
la uña
el perfume

to name and indicate places in a store
el ascensor
la escalera
la escalera mecánica
la caja
el mostrador
la entrada
la salida
al fondo
los servicios
la ropa para caballeros
la ropa para damas
la ropa para niños
la sección, *pl.* las secciones

to talk about shopping
vender: se vende(n)
hacer las compras
gastar

other useful words
mientras

Resumen 291

Assessment

 Prueba cumulativa

 Examen de habilidades

 Test Generator

Additional Assessment Options

 Comm. Act. BLMs
Small Group Activities
Situation Cards

 Pasos vivos 2 CD-ROM
Slide Presentation Maker, Video Presentation Maker, Word Processor, Spindle

 ¿Lo sabes bien? Video Quiz

www Internet Activities
Self-Test

CAPÍTULO 9
THEME: ACCIDENTS AND ILLNESS

COMMUNICATION

Topics

Parts of the body

Medical procedures

Medicines

Allergies

Objectives

To compare pharmacies in Spanish-speaking countries with those in the U.S.

To identify parts of the body

To discuss an illness

To talk about allergies

To talk about treatment for medical conditions

To describe how an accident occurred

To indicate time

CULTURE

Medical care

GRAMMAR

El imperfecto progresivo

El uso del pretérito y del imperfecto progresivo

El pretérito de caerse

El pretérito de poner

Ancillaries available for use with Chapter 9

Multisensory/Technology

Overheads, 44–47

Audio Tapes and CDs

Vocabulary Art Blackline Masters for Hands-On Learning, pp. 48–52/CD-ROM

Classroom Crossword

La Catrina

Pasos vivos 2 CD-ROM

Internet Activities www.pasoapaso.com

Print

Practice Workbook, pp. 85–94

Writing, Audio & Video Activities, pp. 53–58, 117–119, 167–168

Communicative Activity Blackline Masters
  Pair and Small Group Activities, pp. 57–62
  Situation Cards, p. 63

Un paso más: Actividades para ampliar tu español, pp. 49–54

RESOURCE PRO®

Planning Express, Teaching Resources Library, and Clip Art Library

Assessment

Assessment Program
  Pruebas, pp. 129–139
  Examen de habilidades, pp. 140–143

Test Generator

¿Lo sabes bien? Video Quiz

Video still from Chap. 9

Medical Care in Latin America

Latin Americans rely on many different forms of health care, depending on the resources available to them. Doctors and nurses trained in Latin America and abroad work in private practice, clinics, and hospitals in every country. In rural areas where hospitals are not accessible, women often rely on the wisdom and experience of midwives *(parteras).* Some people go to holistic healers known as *curanderos,* who use traditional spiritual, herbal, and other remedies.

A visit to a Latin American doctor's office can be both similar to and different from a typical visit in the U.S. The office is frequently in the doctor's home, and he or she will often take the time to discuss the patient's problems at length. Although advanced medical training and technology may not be readily available to them, many doctors have a reading knowledge of one or more foreign languages and stay aware of the latest developments in their fields through medical journals from all over the world. In the specialized fields of rural medicine and parasitic diseases, Latin American doctors often have more expertise than their counterparts in other countries. Cuba, in fact, is a world leader in rural medicine.

Conventional pharmacies abound in Latin America. They often do not require a prescription for dispensing medication. In this case, if a person is fairly certain of his or her ailment, a simple description of the symptoms will enable the patient to obtain the necessary medicine. In some Spanish-speaking countries, homeopathic pharmacies specializing in remedies based on natural foods and plants are commonplace. They carry products similar to those found in U.S. health food stores. In addition, roots and herbs are popular for healing many illnesses, from liver ailments to insomnia. An impressive variety of these natural medicines is displayed in small packages on sidewalks and in marketplaces. Herbal teas *(agüitas)* are also popular, especially chamomile *(té de manzanilla)* for soothing stomach upsets. (See the reading selection, p. 320.)

In many small villages, doctors, nurses, and modern medicines are scarce. In these areas, *curanderos* and *parteras* have long been able to help and heal with their detailed knowledge of natural remedies. Health projects that provide additional resources are frequently organized by national governments in conjunction with local volunteers and international health organizations.

Introduce

Re-entry of Concepts

The following list represents words, expressions, and grammar topics re-entered from Book 1 and Book 2 (Chaps. 2–7):

Book 1
numbers 0–31, calendar expressions, leisure-time activities, family members, vacation items and activities, household chores, parts of the body, physical symptoms

Chapter 2
daily routine

Chapter 4
sports

Chapter 7
pharmacy items

Planning

Cross-Curricular Connections

Health Connection *(pp. 296–297)*
Divide the class into three groups, giving each group one of the following situations: *Se rompieron el codo; Se quemaron la mano; Se cortaron el dedo.* Within each group, students should divide into three groups, each group creating three sentences. One group should discuss how the injury occurred, another what type of treatment they need, and the third should tell how long they will be injured, and what they won't be able to do because of the injury. Have groups present their scenarios to the class.

History/Science Connection
(pp. 308–309)
The use of medicinal herbs was common in early American civilizations. These herbs were complemented with other natural elements, such as mud for healing open wounds and rocks used as surgical instruments. Have students investigate other natural healing methods used by any of the early American civilizations they have studied.

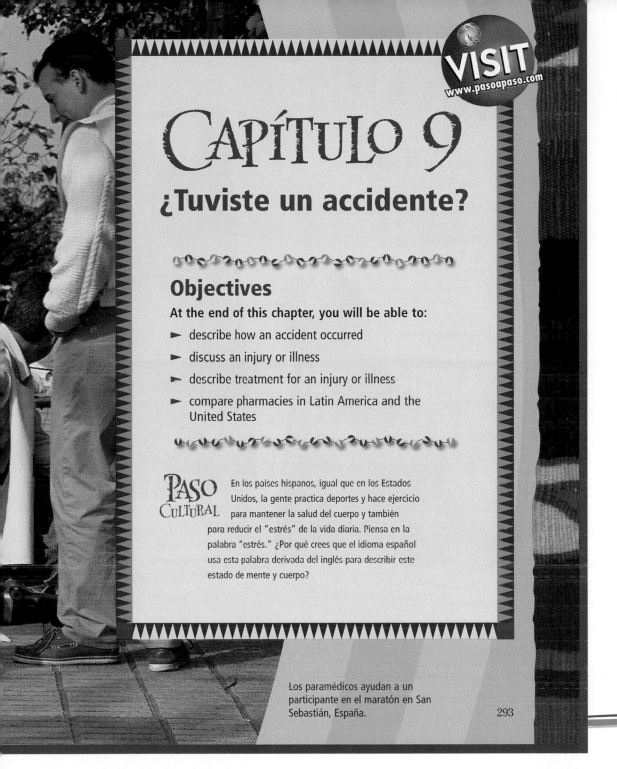

CAPÍTULO 9
¿Tuviste un accidente?

Objectives
At the end of this chapter, you will be able to:

► describe how an accident occurred

► discuss an injury or illness

► describe treatment for an injury or illness

► compare pharmacies in Latin America and the United States

PASO CULTURAL En los países hispanos, igual que en los Estados Unidos, la gente practica deportes y hace ejercicio para mantener la salud del cuerpo y también para reducir el "estrés" de la vida diaria. Piensa en la palabra "estrés." ¿Por qué crees que el idioma español usa esta palabra derivada del inglés para describir este estado de mente y cuerpo?

Los paramédicos ayudan a un participante en el maratón en San Sebastián, España.

293

VISIT
www.pasoapaso.com

Cultural Notes

Spanish in Your Community
Have students go to their local pharmacy to look for over-the-counter medical supplies (aspirin, bandages, etc.) that are either imported from Spanish-speaking countries or have an extra set of instructions in Spanish. Tell them to make a list of the products they find, including: pharmacy name, product name, product type, price, and whether or not it was imported.

Paso cultural
Possible answer: Esta palabra no existe en español. A veces se puede usar una palabra o frase de otro idioma, como el "estrés," con una pronunciación española.

(pp. 292–293, photo)
Located in the heart of the Basque country, San Sebastián-Donostia is home to two of Spain's most famous races. The flat course of the *Maratón Popular San Sebastián* attracts runners from all over the world. The 20K Behobia-San Sebastián race is frequented more by locals. Starting in the village of Behobia on the French border, the race winds through the Pyrenees Mountains before ending in San Sebastián.

Cultural Objective

• To discuss health care in Spanish-speaking countries and in the U.S.

Critical Thinking: Summarizing Information

Have students summarize what they see in the photographs. Discuss student summaries as a whole class. Ask students what clues in the photos led them to their conclusions.

Answers: ¡Piensa en la cultura!

Answers will vary.

¡Piensa en la CULTURA!

Santiago, Chile

Unas jóvenes charlando en Santiago, Chile

La medicina en El Salvador, Chile y España

Mira las fotos. Las personas que vemos están hablando de sus enfermedades y de lo que les pasó. ¿Te rompiste alguna vez la pierna o el brazo? ¿Qué ocurrió?

San Salvador, El Salvador

En el Hospital Benjamín Bloom, San Salvador, El Salvador

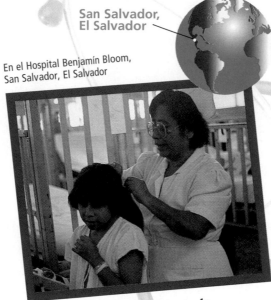

"Me lastimé el brazo. Por eso la enfermera tuvo que cepillarme el pelo."

¿Sabes cómo son los hospitales de tu ciudad? ¿Son los enfermeros y las enfermeras tan amables como ésta?

"¿Cómo te rompiste la pierna?" "Aprendiendo a esquiar."

¿Alguien en tu clase lleva un yeso? ¿Por cuánto tiempo tiene que llevarlo? ¿Qué hueso se rompió? ¿Cómo se lo rompió?

294   Capítulo 9

Options

Strategies for Reaching All Students

Spanish-Speaking Students

Ask: *¿Has estado en una sala de emergencia? ¿Estabas herido o enfermo? ¿Quién te ayudó y cómo? ¿Qué más viste allí? ¿Quiénes deben ir a salas de emergencia? ¿Cuándo debes ir al médico? ¿Cuándo usas remedios caseros en vez de ir al médico? ¿Cuáles son algunos de esos remedios?*

 Un paso más Ex. 9-A

Multiple Intelligences

Intrapersonal/Introspective and Logical/Mathematical

Have students list five things they do to prevent illness: *Duermo mucho. Como buenas comidas.* Have them survey the class and make a graph with the results.

Verbal/Linguistic

See Critical Thinking.

Madrid, España

Letreros en un hospital en Madrid

Consultorios ala Sur Y Norte

Puerta A principal

Gerencia

Dirección Médica

Administración General

Recepción Enfermos →

Urgencias →

Entradas ala Norte y Sur →

Donantes de Sangre →

"Perdone. ¿Podría indicarme dónde puedo ir
para donar sangre?"

www.pasoapaso.com
Visit these countries on-line

¡Piensa en la cultura! 295

Cultural Notes

(p. 294, left photo)
Hospital Benjamín Bloom, named for its benefactor, is a large, modern facility located in the center of San Salvador. A private hospital serving the city's health care needs, it has a well-known pediatric department with notable diagnostic capabilities.

(p. 294, right photo)
Due to the Andes mountains rising sharply out of the Pacific coast, the people of Santiago can reach ski slopes and beaches in just a couple of hours. With its location in the foothills, however, the city suffers from severe air pollution. Smog becomes trapped against the rising mountains, contributing to a high incidence of respiratory diseases. The government is studying methods to cut down on vehicle emissions as well as other ways to reduce pollution.

(p. 295, photo)
City hospitals in Spain are often large, multipurpose facilities engaged in medical research and teaching as well as healing. These medical centers may offer less personalized service, but they provide state-of-the-art medical technology for precise diagnosis and specialized treatment. As in most countries, rural areas in Spain often have limited access to the advanced facilities located in the more populated areas.

Present

Chapter Theme
In the emergency room

Communicative Objectives
- To identify parts of the body
- To talk about treatment for medical conditions
- To describe how an accident occurred
- To indicate time

 Overhead 44

 Vocabulary Art BLMs/CD-ROM

 Vocabulary Tape 9-1

Grammar Preview
(*Yo*) *me caí* and *(usted / él / ella) puso* are presented here lexically. The preterite forms of *caerse* and *poner* are on pp. 314 and 316, respectively.

Teaching Suggestions
Preparing students to speak: Use one or two options from each of the categories of Comprehensible Input, Physical Response, or Limited Verbal Response. For a complete explanation of these categories and some sample activities, see pp. T20–T21.

Vocabulario para conversar

¿Te rompiste el tobillo?

Vas a necesitar estas palabras y expresiones para hablar sobre ciertos accidentes y enfermedades. Después de leerlas varias veces, practícalas con un(a) compañero(a).

la sala de emergencia

la sangre
el hueso
el enfermero, la enfermera
la inyección, *pl.* las inyecciones
el codo
la muñeca
la rodilla
el tobillo
los frenillos *(m.pl.)*
poner una inyección
la medicina
la radiografía
sacar una radiografía
la ambulancia
el yeso
las puntadas *(f.pl.)*
la silla de ruedas
las muletas *(f.pl.)*
hacer puntadas

296   Capítulo 9

Options

Strategies for Reaching All Students

Spanish-Speaking Students
Ask: *¿Sabes otras palabras que se pueden incluir aquí? Haz una lista.*

 Un paso más Ex. 9-B

Students Needing Extra Help
Begin the vocabulary section of the Organizer.
Show students that *la muñeca* has two meanings (they saw it in Chap. 5 as "doll"). Point out the cognates.
También necesitas . . . : Show examples of the reflexives.

Give examples of *por* + time expression.
Ex. 1: If available, refer to the Organizer from Book 1, Chap. 9.
Review reflexive verbs in the preterite. Encourage students to use both positive and negative responses.
Remind students that in Spanish "the leg" is used as opposed to "my leg."

También necesitas . . .

el análisis, *pl.* los análisis	*medical test*	¿Qué te pasó?	*What happened to you?*
caerse: (yo) me caí	*to fall down: I fell down*	por + *time expression*	*for*
		además	*in addition, besides*
poner: (Ud. / él / ella) puso	*you / he / she put*		
cortarse	*to cut oneself*		
quemarse	*to burn oneself*		
romperse (un hueso)	*to break (a bone)*		
roto, -a	*broken*		

> **¿Y qué quiere decir . . . ?**
> el accidente
> el antibiótico
> el músculo
> la operación, *pl.* las operaciones

Empecemos a conversar

Túrnate con un(a) compañero(a) para ser *Estudiante A* y *Estudiante B*. Reemplacen las palabras subrayadas en el modelo con palabras representadas o escritas en los recuadros. Si ven 💡 pueden dar su propia respuesta.

1

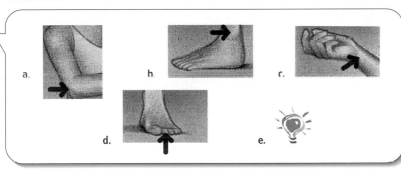

A —¿Te rompiste *el brazo*?
B —Sí, me rompí *el brazo*.
   o: *No. Me rompí el codo.*

Estudiante A

a.
h.
c.
d.
e. 💡

Estudiante B

💡
💡

¡NO OLVIDES!

Do you remember these body parts?
   el brazo
   la mano
   el dedo
   la espalda
   la pierna
   el pie
   el dedo del pie

Vocabulario para conversar   297

Practice & Apply

Reteach / Review: Vocabulary

Ex. 2: *Estudiante A* can ask *Estudiante B*: *¿Y qué te parece?* regarding the treatment he or she is being told to follow. Encourage *Estudiante B* to express a range of emotions, including agreement, disagreement, fear, impatience, boredom, or anger.

Answers: Empecemos a conversar

2 ESTUDIANTE A

a. ¿Te van a poner un yeso?
b. ... sacar una radiografía?
c. ... dar una medicina?
d. ... poner sangre?
e. ... poner una inyección?

ESTUDIANTE B

Answers will vary, but may include:
a. Sí, y además dicen que necesito usar muletas.
b. ... más análisis.
c. ... quedarme en cama.
d. ... una operación.
e. ... antibióticos.

3 ESTUDIANTE A

a. ¿Qué te pasó en el brazo? ¿Te quemaste?
b. ... el codo? ¿Te caíste?
c. ... la espalda? ¿Te lastimaste?
d. ... la rodilla? ¿Te lastimaste?
e. ... el dedo? ¿Te cortaste?
f. ... la mano? ¿Te cortaste?

2
poner

A — *¿Te van a poner una venda?*
B — *Sí, y además dicen que necesito antibióticos.*

Estudiante A

a. poner   b. sacar   c. dar

d. poner   e. poner

Estudiante B

antibióticos

más análisis

una operación

quedarme en cama

usar muletas

3
caerse

A — *¿Qué te pasó en la pierna? ¿Te caíste?*
B — *Sí, me caí cuando estaba subiendo una escalera.*

Estudiante A

a. quemarse   b. caerse   c. lastimarse

d. lastimarse   e. cortarse   f. cortarse

Estudiante B

preparar la ensalada

reparar la bicicleta

patinar

levantar pesas

encender el horno

jugar___

298   Capítulo 9

Options

Strategies for Reaching All Students

Spanish-Speaking Students
Exs. 1–3: Pair bilingual with non-bilingual students if possible.
Ex. 8: Ask: *¿Por qué son necesarios los frenillos?*

 Un paso más Ex. 9-C

Students Needing Extra Help
Ex. 2: Help students make the correct association between the two parts of the answers. Show them what changes and what does not.
Ex. 3: Remind them that these are all -*ar* reflexive verbs except for *caerse*.
Remind students there are two tenses here: the preterite and the imperfect progressive. Remind them to fill in the blank after *jugar*. Provide students with the following steps:

a.) identify the body part, b.) form the question in the preterite, c.) answer using the preterite, d.) make the association, and e.) form the imperfect progressive.
Ex. 4: Brainstorm the time frames. Review calendar expressions.
Ex. 6: Use the vocabulary section of the Organizer.
Ex. 7: Help students stay focused.
Ex. 9: Summarize treatment of burn victims.

4

A —*Doctor(a), ¿por cuánto tiempo tengo que llevar el yeso?*
B —*Por seis semanas.*

llevar

Estudiante A

a. llevar   b. usar   c. tomar

d. quedarme en   e. usar

Estudiante B

Empecemos a escribir

Escribe tus respuestas en español.

5 Piensa en alguien que conoces que se rompió un hueso. ¿Le sacaron radiografías? ¿Tuvo que llevar un yeso? ¿Tuvo que usar una silla de ruedas o muletas? ¿Por cuánto tiempo?

6 ¿Cuándo te lastimaste la última vez? ¿Qué te pasó? ¿Fuiste al (a la) médico(a)? ¿Qué te dio? ¿Qué te puso?

7 Piensa en alguien que conoces que estuvo en un hospital. ¿Tuvo un accidente o le hicieron una operación? ¿Lo (la) tuvieron que llevar en ambulancia o fue en coche? ¿Le tuvieron que poner sangre? ¿Le hicieron muchos análisis? ¿Le hicieron puntadas? ¿Por cuánto tiempo se quedó en el hospital?

8 Generalmente, ¿por cuánto tiempo tiene uno que llevar los frenillos?

9 ¿Dónde está la sala de emergencia más cerca de la escuela? ¿Y de tu casa? Generalmente, ¿qué le hacen a una persona que tiene un hueso roto? ¿Qué le hacen a una persona que se corta? ¿Y a una persona que se quema?

MORE PRACTICE

* Más práctica y tarea, p. 552
* Practice Workbook 9–1, 9–2

También se dice

la sala de urgencia
el servicio de emergencia

los frenos
los aparatos (para los dientes)

la escayola

el medicamento

Vocabulario para conversar   299

Present

Chapter Theme
Allergies

Communicative Objectives
- To discuss an illness
- To talk about allergies
- To talk about treatment for medical conditions
- To describe how an accident occurred

 Overheads 45–46

 Vocabulary Art BLMs/CD-ROM

 Vocabulary Tape 9-2

Teaching Suggestions
Preparing students to speak: Use one or two options from each of the categories of Comprehensible Input, Physical Response, or Limited Verbal Response. For a complete explanation of these categories and some sample activities, see pp. T20–T21.

Vocabulario para conversar

¿Eres alérgico a los antibióticos?

Aquí tienes el resto del vocabulario que necesitas en este capítulo para hablar sobre ciertos accidentes y enfermedades.

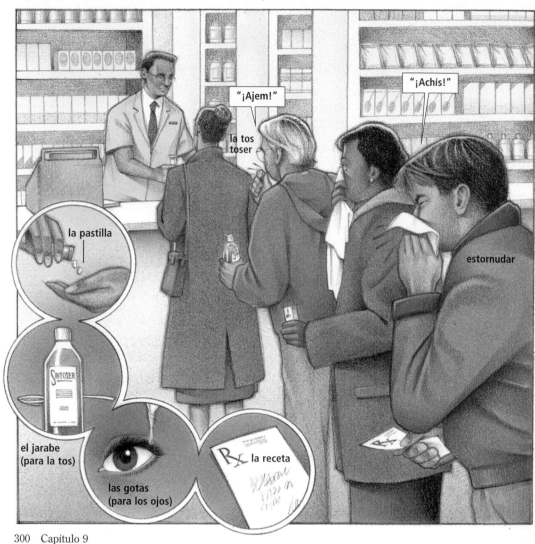

300   Capítulo 9

Options

Strategies for Reaching All Students

Spanish-Speaking Students

 Un paso más Ex. 9-D

Students Needing Extra Help
Show the connection of *tos* to *toser*.
Point out that *tos* is singular, even though it ends in *s*.
Show word families: *picar, picadura; insecto, insecticida;* etc.
Tambien necesitas . . . : Write out the whole verb chart in the present tense for *sentirse* and *protegerse.*

Learning Spanish Through Action
STAGING VOCABULARY: *Dibujen*
MATERIALS: paper and pencil
DIRECTIONS: Describe a walk that you took in the woods. Tell students to draw what you saw. Include insects and known vocabulary for nature and animals.

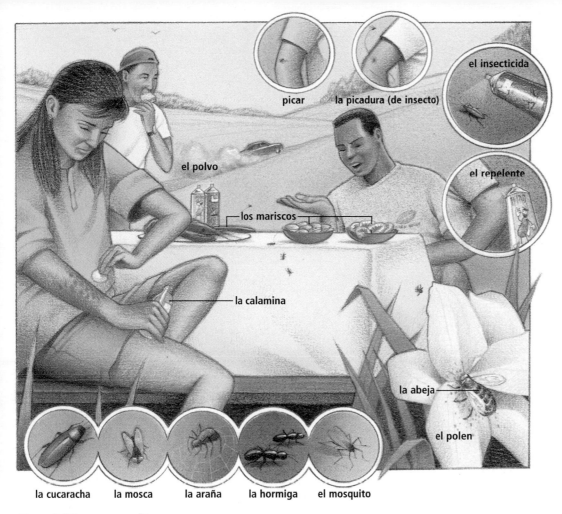

picar

la picadura (de insecto)

el insecticida

el polvo

el repelente

los mariscos

la calamina

la abeja

el polen

la cucaracha la mosca la araña la hormiga el mosquito

También necesitas . . .

proteger(se) (g › j)*	to protect (oneself)
sentirse (e → ie)	to feel
la enfermedad	illness
antialérgico, -a	nonallergenic
fuerte	strong
leve	light, minor

¿Y qué quiere decir . . . ?

la alergia	el síntoma
la infección,	el virus
pl. las infecciones	(ser) alérgico, -a (a)
la reacción,	recetar
pl. las reacciones	vomitar

*Infinitives that end in *-ger* change the g to a j in the yo form of the present tense: *proteger: (yo) protejo.*

Vocabulario para conversar   301

Class Starter Review
On the day following the presentation of vocabulary, you might begin the class with this activity: Have students form groups of three. Give a specific time limit in which they use vocabulary from this and previous chapters to prepare two lists: one of things that make you sneeze *(el perfume, el polen, el polvo),* the other of things that make you cough *(el humo, el polvo, el repelente).* Keep a list on the chalkboard.

www Internet Activities
Juegos

Extended Written Practice/Homework
1. Write four sentences naming people you know who have allergies and how they react: *Mi tía es alérgica a los mariscos. Le dan una reacción muy fuerte.*
2. Write three sentences describing situations when you feel bad: *Me siento mal cuando hay mucho polvo y me duelen los ojos.*
3. Use the following verbs and write three sentences about the different pests pictured on p. 301: *dar miedo, molestar, picar.*

Multiple Intelligences
Bodily/Kinesthetic and Naturalist
See Learning Spanish Through Action.
Verbal/Linguistic
See Vocabulary Tape 9-2.
Visual/Spatial
See Overheads 45–46 and the Vocabulary Art BLMs/CD-ROM.

Standards 1.1; 1.2; 3.1; 4.1; 5.1   301

Practice

Answers: Empecemos a conversar

10 ESTUDIANTE A

a. ¿Te dan miedo los mosquitos?
b. ... las arañas?
c. ... las hormigas?
d. ... las cucarachas?
e. ... las moscas?
f. Questions will vary.

ESTUDIANTE B

Answers will vary, but may include the following:

a. Sí, porque pican.
b. Sí, porque son feas.
c. No. No me dan miedo.
d. Sí, porque son sucias.
e. Sí, porque traen enfermedades.
f. Answers will vary.

11 ESTUDIANTE A

a. ¿Eres alérgico(a) al polen?
b. ... a los mariscos?
c. ... a las picaduras de insecto?
d. ... al bronceador?
e. ... al polvo?
f. Questions will vary.

ESTUDIANTE B

a.–f. Answers will vary.

Empecemos a conversar

10 A —¿Te dan miedo *las abejas*?
    B —Sí, porque *pican*.
        o: *No. No me dan miedo.*

Estudiante A   **Estudiante B**

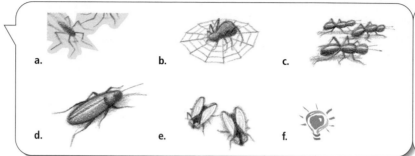

picar
ser feo
ser sucio
traer
enfermedades

11 A —*¿Eres alérgico(a) a los gatos?*
    B —*Sí, y me dan una reacción (muy) fuerte.*
        o: *Sí, pero sólo me dan una reacción leve.*
        o: *No, no tengo ninguna reacción.*

Estudiante A   **Estudiante B**

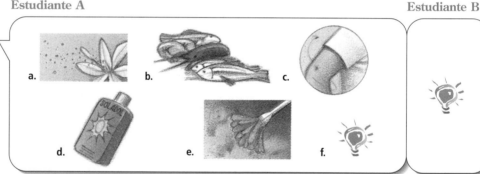

302   Capítulo 9

Options

Strategies for Reaching All Students

Spanish-Speaking Students
Exs. 10–12: Pair bilingual with non-bilingual students if possible.

Students Needing Extra Help
Ex. 10: Encourage students not to use the negative response.
Ex. 11: Brainstorm possible responses.
Ex. 12: Brainstorm possibilities for the blanks in the *Estudiante A* choices and for additions to the *Estudiante B* responses: *Me siento mejor, pero necesito antibióticos.*

Enrichment
Ex. 12: To extend this dialogue, *Estudiante A* can ask *Estudiante B* what he or she took or did to feel better.

12 el resfriado   A —¿*Cómo estás del resfriado?*
                 B —*Me siento (mucho) mejor, gracias.*

Estudiante A

a. la infección en ___

b. la alergia

c. el virus

d. el dolor de ___

e. el tobillo

f. la gripe

g. 💡

Estudiante B

(mucho) mejor

(mucho) peor

💡

¡NO OLVIDES!

Do you remember these words related to health?
dolor de cabeza
        estómago
        garganta
        oído
        muelas
tengo fiebre
        gripe
        resfriado
las pastillas para la garganta

Vocabulario para conversar   303

12 ESTUDIANTE A
a. ¿Cómo estás de la infección en (el oído / el ojo / la garganta)?
b. . . . de la alergia?
c. . . . del virus?
d. . . . del dolor de (cabeza / estómago / muelas)?
e. . . . del tobillo?
f. . . . de la gripe?
g. Questions will vary.
ESTUDIANTE B
a.–g. Answers will vary.

Using Realia
Refer students to the heading on the ad. Ask: *¿A qué se refiere el verbo "piquen"? (a los mosquitos) ¿Y "pica"? (a la medicina)*

Cooperative Learning
Brainstorm with students three things they might be afraid of in addition to those listed in Ex. 10 *(los perros, los pájaros, los exámenes,* etc.). In groups of four, have each student list the insects from Ex. 10, plus any brainstormed items, in order of how they fear them: from the most to the least. Have two students from each group combine the lists and determine which three things the group fears most. Another student can report the findings to the class. Write each group's findings on the chalkboard, and tabulate which three things the class fears most.

Extended Written Practice/Homework
1. Refer to the items on pp. 300–301 that you might use or take. Choose three and write sentences telling how often you take or use them: *Me pongo mucho repelente en el verano cuando juego béisbol por la noche.*
2. Write three sentences telling how people should protect themselves from different sicknesses: *Para protegerse de los resfriados, uno debe lavarse las manos frecuentemente.*

Practice & Apply

Re-enter / Recycle
Ex. 13: pharmacy items from Chap. 7

Answers: Empecemos a conversar

13 ESTUDIANTE A

a. ¿Estás tomando las pastillas?
b. . . . poniéndote las gotas para los ojos?
c. . . . tomando el jarabe?
d. . . . poniéndote una venda?
e. . . . poniéndote la calamina?
f. . . . tomando la receta?
g. Questions will vary.

ESTUDIANTE B

Answers will vary, but may include the following:

a. Sí, porque todavía tengo fiebre.
b. . . . una leve infección.
c. . . . tos.
d. . . . puntadas.
e. . . . muchas picaduras.
f. . . . un dolor fuerte en el músculo.
g. Answers will vary.

Answers: Empecemos a escribir y a leer

14–17 Answers will vary, but look for correct use of present, preterite, and imperfect tenses.

13   A —¿Estás *tomando las pastillas para la garganta*?
       B —*Sí, porque tengo dolor de garganta*.

tomar

Estudiante A

a. tomar   b. ponerse   c. tomar

d. ponerse   e. ponerse   f. tomar   g.

Estudiante B

tos

una leve infección

muchas picaduras

fiebre

un dolor fuerte en el músculo

puntadas

Empecemos a escribir y a leer

Escribe tus respuestas en español.

14 ¿Qué haces cuando no te sientes bien? Y después, ¿generalmente te sientes mejor?

15 ¿Qué síntomas tienes cuando tienes gripe? ¿Estornudas? ¿Vomitas? ¿Qué te duele? Generalmente, ¿qué te receta el (la) médico(a) cuando tienes tos o gripe? ¿Y cuando tienes una infección fuerte?

16 ¿Cuándo fue la última vez que te pusiste gotas en los ojos? ¿Qué tenías?

MORE PRACTICE

- Más práctica y tarea, p. 552
- Practice Workbook 9–3, 9–4

www.pasoapaso.com

Una joven busca un libro en un quiosco en la Ciudad de México.

304   Capítulo 9

Options

Strategies for Reaching All Students

Spanish-Speaking Students
Ex. 13: Pair bilingual with non-bilingual students if possible.
After Ex. 18, Have Spanish-speaking students take a class survey.
Pregúntales a tus compañeros(as) sobre las alergias: ¿Tienen alergias? ¿A qué son alérgicos(as)? ¿Cuáles son los síntomas? ¿Qué remedios o medicinas usan o prefieren?

📖 **Un paso más Ex. 9-E**

¿Cuáles son los alergias más comunes entre tus compañeros(as)? Escoge cuatro o cinco y prepara una hoja en tres columnas con esta información: Alergia, Síntomas, Remedio preferido. Exhíbela en el salón de clase o en la oficina de la enfermera o del enfermero de la escuela.

Students Needing Extra Help
Ex. 13: Students may need help associating the ailment with the cure.
Review the present progessive tense.
Ex. 14: Use the vocabulary section of the Organizer.
Ex. 17: Students will need help with the vocabulary for answering the fourth question about how to protect oneself from allergies.
Ex. 18: Students may need help with the vocabulary.

18 Answers will vary, but might include the following:
- *sacando la basura cada día*
- *siempre lavando los platos después de comer*
- *usando camisas con mangas largas*
- *quedándose en casa cuando hay muchos mosquitos*

 Practice Wkbk. 9-3, 9-4

 Audio Activity 9.2

 Writing Activities 9-B, 9-C

 Pruebas 9-3, 9-4

 Comm. Act. BLM 9-1

También se dice

la píldora

el piquete

el zancudo

la avispa

Vocabulario para conversar   305

Cooperative Learning
Divide the class into groups of three. Within each group, students will decide on an allergy they have, and write a list of three symptoms. They then exchange lists with another group, who will act as doctors. The doctors must diagnose the allergy and prescribe a treatment in writing. After papers are returned to the original groups, call on students to tell the class their allergy and the prescription, letting the class decide if the treatment was appropriate.

Multiple Intelligences
Interpersonal/Social and Visual/Spatial
See Cooperative Learning.
Intrapersonal/Introspective
See Exs. 14–18.
Verbal/Linguistic
See Audio Activity 9.2.
Visual/Spatial
See Practice Wkbk. 9-3 and 9-4, Writing Activities 9-B and 9-C, and Comm. Act. BLM 9-1.

Cultural Notes

(p. 305, photo)
Browsing for books is easy in many of Mexico City's *colonias* (neighborhoods). Open-air *librerías* display numerous popular titles, magazines, and other printed materials. Some sell school books, for most students in Mexico must purchase their own texts. This stall displays packets of study sheets illustrating the human anatomy.

Practice

Re-enter / Recycle:
Ex. 2: sports from Chap. 4

Answers:
¡Comuniquemos!

1 Answers will vary.

2 ESTUDIANTE A
¿Cómo puedes protegerte de los accidentes cuando cambias un bombillo?
. . . cuando corres?
. . . cuando cocinas?
. . . cuando paseas en bote?
. . . cuando montas en bicicleta?
. . . cuando levantas pesas?
. . . cuando cruzas la calle?

ESTUDIANTE B
Answers will vary, but may include:
Puedo protegerme apagando la lámpara.
Puedo protegerme corriendo con un amigo.
Puedo tener un extinguidor de incendios cerca de la estufa.
Puedo protegerme no paseando cuando hace mal tiempo.
Puedo protegerme usando casco.
Puedo protegerme usando un cinturón.
Puedo protegerme mirando el semáforo.

3 Answers will vary, but look for correct use of the preterite and imperfect tenses.

¡Comuniquemos!

Aquí tienes otra oportunidad para usar el vocabulario de este capítulo.

1 Túrnate con un(a) compañero(a). Pregúntale sobre la última vez que estuvo enfermo(a).

A —¿Qué tenías la última vez que estuviste enfermo(a)?
B —Tenía una infección en . . .
A —¿Y qué síntomas tenías?
B —Me dolía mucho . . .

2 Túrnate con otro(a) compañero(a). Habla de cómo protegerse de los accidentes al hacer estas actividades.

A —¿Cómo puedes protegerte de los accidentes cuando montas en bicicleta?
B —Puedo protegerme usando . . .

Options

Strategies for Reaching All Students

Spanish-Speaking Students
Exs. 1–3: Pair Spanish-speaking students to prepare these dialogues and present them orally or on tape. Use as listening comprehension exercises with true / false statements.

Students Needing Extra Help
Ex. 1: Review *doler* and point out that *dolía* is the imperfect tense.
Use the vocabulary section of the Organizer.
Ex. 2: Brainstorm the possibilities for protecting yourself. Help students with the vocabulary.
Ex. 3: Refer to Ex. 3 in the *Vocabulario para conversar*.
Present a complete model.

Help students with the *Pues* response: Brainstorm situations that would lead to each outcome listed.
¿Qué sabes ahora?: Have students write out this list so that they can record their progress.

3 Escoge dos de las siguientes ideas. Pregúntale a tu compañero(a) si alguna vez tuvo que:

llevar un yeso   tomar medicina antialérgica
llevar una venda grande   usar muletas
ponerse gotas para los ojos   usar una silla de ruedas

A —*¿Tuviste que usar muletas alguna vez?*
B —*Sí, cuando . . .*
A —*¿Y qué te pasó después?*
B —*Pues, . . .*

Para tus ojos irritados: **Visadron.**

La tensión, el cansancio, el cloro de las piscinas, el humo, la permanencia ante la pantalla de T.V. y ordenador, la polución, los cosméticos, todo ello puede provocar irritación, enrojecimiento, molestias en tus ojos.
Unas gotas de Visadrón, aliviarán la irritación y el enrojecimiento de tus ojos devolviéndoles el blanco natural.

Visadrón descongestivo ocular con clorhidrato de fenilefrina y ácido bórico. Lea las instrucciones. No usar más de tres días seguidos sin consultar a su médico o farmacéutico ni en niños menores de 3 años.

Visadron. Fher   Laboratorios

¿Qué sabes ahora?

Can you:

■ describe how an accident occurred?
—Anita se ___ el brazo cuando estaba ___ básquetbol.

■ tell the cause of an accident?
—Estaba ___ una escalera cuando me ___.

■ talk about someone's health?
—Él se ___ mejor pero todavía tiene ___.

Vocabulario para conversar   307

Answers: ¿Qué sabes ahora?
• rompió / jugando
• subiendo / caí
• siente / *Answers will vary, but may include:* infección, virus, tos

  Audio Activity 9.3

Pasos vivos 2 CD-ROM
Boom Box, Clip Art Album, Slide Projector, Laboratorio de grabar

---

Enrichment
Ex. 2: Students can also talk about hazards for children and how they can be protected in the following situations: at a picnic, at a pool, on the playground, in the kitchen, in the bathroom.

Cooperative Learning
Brainstorm with students other situations in which one might want to protect oneself (at the beach, preparing food, etc.). Instruct groups of three to select one topic and develop two protection strategies. Exchange strategies with another group, who will edit the work for clarity and gramatical correctness and prepare a poster with slogans and pictures describing the methods of protection. Display the posters so the original group can see how their ideas evolved.

Multiple Intelligences
Interpersonal/Social
See Cooperative Learning.
Interpersonal/Social and Verbal/Linguistic
See Exs. 1–3.
Verbal/Linguistic
See Enrichment and Audio Activity 9.3.

Apply

Cultural Objective
• To discuss pharmacies in Spanish-speaking countries

Critical Thinking: Formulating Questions

After reading the *Perspectiva cultural,* have small groups formulate questions that they might have. Collect the questions and read them to the class. Encourage students familiar with Latin American pharmacies to provide answers and additional information.

Answers

Answers to inductive questions will vary, but students may say that they knew they were pharmacies by the merchandise displayed. *Una inyectología* is a place where injections or shots are given. *Una farmacia de turno* is a pharmacy whose turn it is to stay open overnight.

Perspectiva cultural

¿Qué tiendas son éstas? ¿Cómo lo sabes? ¿Qué lugar crees que es una *inyectología*? ¿Qué crees que significa *farmacia de turno*?

En América Latina, para ciertas enfermedades uno puede decidir ir a un médico o a un curandero. Mucha gente cree que los dos sistemas, uno basado en la ciencia y la medicina moderna y el otro en las hierbas y la tradición, son igualmente válidos.

Imagina que estás viajando en un país latinoamericano. Ya no tienes el antibiótico que te recetó tu médico. Decides ir a una farmacia.

Encuentras una muy pequeña. Las medicinas están detrás del mostrador y hay que pedir lo que quieres comprar. Le explicas al farmacéutico el problema, y él te vende la medicina en seguida.

En algunas farmacias, también ponen inyecciones. Si te enfermas y sabes lo que necesitas, puedes ir a una farmacia donde se ve el letrero *inyectología* y allí te ponen la inyección.

Ahora imagina que despiertas con un ataque fuerte de asma y no tienes medicina. ¿Qué haces? Puedes ir a la sala de emergencia de un hospital. Pero si sólo necesitas medicina, puedes ir a una farmacia. Las farmacias de una comunidad se turnan para quedar abiertas por la noche. El horario se publica en el periódico, y en la vitrina se ve el letrero *farmacia de turno*. Así se pueden obtener medicinas en caso de emergencia.

"Dicen que estas hierbas pueden curar muchas enfermedades."

308 Capítulo 9

La cultura desde tu perspectiva

1 Compara lo que puede hacer un farmacéutico en América Latina con lo que puede hacer uno en los Estados Unidos.

2 ¿Cuáles son las ventajas y las desventajas de vender medicinas sin receta, como, por ejemplo, los antibióticos? En caso de urgencia médica, ¿qué hay que hacer en los Estados Unidos?

www.pasoapaso.com

Options

Strategies for Reaching All Students

Spanish-Speaking Students

Ask: *¿Conoces a una persona que sepa utilizar hierbas y plantas para curar o aliviar a alguien? ¿Quién es? ¿Dónde aprendió estos remedios? ¿Se pueden encontrar hierbas medicinales en tu comunidad? ¿Dónde?*

 Un paso más Ex. 9-F

Students Needing Extra Help

Have students take notes for use in reviewing for the test.
Discuss the idea of alternative medicine versus standard medical practices.
Ex. 2: Encourage discussion, emphasizing the dangers of misusing medicine.

Enrichment

Additional question: *Pregunta a tus padres u otras personas mayores cómo eran las farmacias cuando eran pequeños.*

Multiple Intelligences
Verbal/Linguistic
See Critical Thinking.

308 Standards 1.1; 1.2; 1.3; 2.1; 3.1

Una farmacia en Buenos Aires

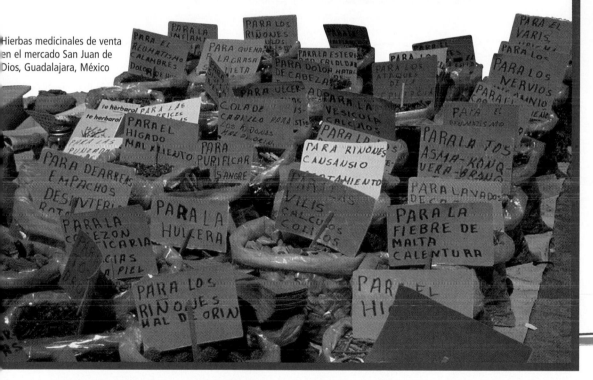

Hierbas medicinales de venta en el mercado San Juan de Dios, Guadalajara, México

Cultural Notes

(p. 308, photo)
Very common in Mexican markets is a section of *botánicas* selling medicinal herbs used to treat ailments ranging from a stomachache to a "broken heart." El Mercado San Juan de Dios, el Mercado Corona and el Mercado Libertad are three well-known Guadalajaran markets having large *botánicas.*

(p. 309, top photo)
Although large chain stores are becoming more common in Latin America, smaller *farmacias* are still prevalent. These privately owned businesses typically sell only medical supplies, vitamins, and personal hygiene and beauty products.

(p. 309, bottom photo)
Many people learn from their elders how to use traditional healing methods. Chamomile *(manzanilla)*, for example, reduces fever. *Té de canela* treats a stomachache. *Té de orégano* soothes a colicky baby. *Flor de tilo* (lime blossom), *flor de valeriana* (valerian blossom), and *flor de azahar* (orange blossom) relax the nerves. *Gordolobo* (mullein) is used to treat a cough and *té de linaza* (linseed) works as a laxative.

Preview

 Overhead 47

Answers

A The similar form is *estaba limpiando*. The action takes place in the past. The meaning is "was cleaning."

B *Sonó* and *corrí* tell what happened at a specific moment. *Estaba limpiando* and *estaba jugando* tell what was going on when the phone rang.

The other verbs that tell what happened are *regresé, fui, vi,* and *(no le) pasó (nada)*.

C The verb is *se cae*. The stem of *caer* is *ca-*. The ending is *-e*. The preterite form is *se cayó*. The stem is *ca-*. The ending is *-yó*. It is different in that the *i* of the *ió* ending changes to *y*.

Gramática en contexto

¡Niña se cae de tercer piso y vive!

Ayer, en un accidente casi mortal, una niña de tres años y medio se cayó del tercer piso de su casa y ¡salió con vida! El accidente ocurrió cuando la madre, la Sra. Luz María López de Chávez, estaba limpiando las ventanas. La señora Chávez dice que la niña estaba jugando en el suelo.

"Sonó el teléfono y corrí al otro cuarto a contestarlo. Cuando regresé, ¡mi hija ya no estaba! Fui a la ventana y la vi tres pisos más abajo en la nieve. ¡Mi pobre niña! Había tanta nieve que, milagrosamente, no le pasó nada."

A You know the present progressive form *está limpiando*. What similar form is used in this article? Does the action take place in the present or in the past? What do you think this verb form means?

B When Sra. Chávez describes the accident, she uses the verbs *sonó (el teléfono)* and *corrí*. The reporter uses the verbs *estaba limpiando* and *estaba jugando*. Which pair of verbs tells what happened at a specific moment, and which pair tells what was going on when that happened?

What other verbs tell what happened at a specific moment?

C In the headline, what verb is used to say "child falls"? What is the stem, and what is the ending?

Now look for the corresponding preterite form ("fell") at the beginning of the article. What is the stem, and what is the ending? How is this preterite form different from the preterite form of other *-er* verbs?

310 Capítulo 9

Options

Strategies for Reaching All Students

Spanish-Speaking Students

📖 **Un paso más Ex. 9-G**

Students Needing Extra Help
Begin the grammar section of the Organizer.
A: Review the meaning of *está limpiando* before contrasting it with *estaba limpiando*.
B: In a two-column chart headed *¿Qué ocurrió?* and *¿Qué estaba pasando?,* have students write the correct words in the appropriate columns.
C: Write the answers *(se cae* and *se cayó)* on the chalkboard.

El imperfecto progresivo: Model the present progressive to help students remember. Have students add additional examples. If available, use the Organizer from Book 1, Chap. 14.
Review *estar* in the imperfect, and how to form present participles.
Ex. 1: Have students list the infinitive expressions, then conjugate the verbs according to the pictures. If available, use the Organizers from Book 1.

El imperfecto progresivo

You have learned to use the present progressive tense to describe an action or event that is taking place right now. To describe something that was taking place at a certain time in the past, we use the imperfect progressive. We form this tense by using the imperfect forms of *estar* + the present participle.

Cuando el niño se cayó, la señora Chávez **estaba hablando** por teléfono.
Sus otros hijos **estaban haciendo** la tarea.
Su esposo **estaba preparando** la cena.

1 ¿Qué estaban haciendo estas personas cuando ocurrió el accidente?

Cuando ocurrió el accidente, una mujer estaba cortando el césped. Una muchacha ...

Reteach / Review: Vocabulary
Ex. 1: As an extension of this exercise, have students play the role of reporters writing an article describing an accident at one of the following places: *un restaurante, una estación de servicio, un centro comercial, un parque de atracciones, una parada de autobús.* Tell students to include the time of the accident, what happened, people who were witnesses, and the outcome (people who went to the hospital, etc.).

Answers
1 Order of answers will vary, but should include:
Una muchacha estaba montando en bicicleta.
Un cartero estaba repartiendo cartas.
Unos niños estaban jugando béisbol.
Un hombre estaba poniéndose bronceador.
Una señora estaba cruzando la calle.
Una mujer estaba hablando por teléfono.
Un muchacho estaba estornudando.
Dos hombres estaban comprando flores.
Una mujer estaba cortando el césped.

Extended Written Practice/Homework
1. Write what you and other students were doing when the class bell rang: *Miguel y yo estábamos terminando la tarea.*
2. Imagine that the people on p. 296 are people you know. Write four sentences telling what was happening when you saw them: *Cuando vi a Juana, estaba sacando una radiografía.*

3. Recall a time when you arrived at a social gathering. Write three sentences telling what different people were doing: *Cuando llegué a la fiesta, todos estaban comiendo.*

Multiple Intelligences
Visual/Spatial
See Overhead 47.
Visual/Spatial and Bodily/Kinesthetic
Have students cut out or draw pictures similar to the photo on p. 310. Ask them to write descriptions of what is happening in their pictures.

Present & Practice

Reteach / Review: Indirect object pronouns

Ex. 2: Remind students that some of these verbs, like *sacar una radiografía, poner una inyección,* and *dar medicina* take the indirect object pronoun *le(s)* and the preposition *a.*

Have students also tell what each person was doing by using the construction that attaches the object pronoun to the participle. *Cuando llegó la ambulancia, el médico estaba poniéndole un yeso a Luisa. La enfermera estaba . . .*

Re-enter / Recycle

Exs. 3–4: daily routine from Chap. 2

Answers

2 La enfermera le estaba dando el jarabe a Angélica.
Gloria estaba poniéndose una venda en el tobillo.
El enfermero le estaba poniendo una inyección a Mateo.
La médica le estaba haciendo puntadas a Fernando en el codo.
La médica estaba mirando una radiografía.

2 Di qué estaban haciendo estas personas cuando llegó la ambulancia. Usa los dibujos.

Cuando llegó la ambulancia, el médico le estaba poniendo un yeso a Luisa. La enfermera le . . .

Angélica

Gloria

Fernando

Luisa

Carmen

Mateo

312   Capítulo 9

¡NO OLVIDES!

Remember that object pronouns can be placed before the form of *estar* or attached to the end of the present participle. If they are attached to the present participle, a written accent is needed:

El enfermero le estaba poniendo (estaba poniéndole) una inyección a Martín.

Options

Strategies for Reaching All Students

Students Needing Extra Help

Ex. 2: Write the sentence included in *¡No olvides!* and the model sentence for Ex. 2 on the chalkboard. With as much help as students can give, write the second clause of the model sentence again, attaching the *le* to the present participle as in the *¡No olvides!* Help them see the need for the added accent mark. Remind students that both structures mean the same thing. Show students they are doing the same

thing as they did in Ex. 1, except that the scene has changed.
Use the vocabulary section of the Organizers.
El uso del pretérito y del imperfecto: In the two examples, have students show which actions have a beginning and an end, and which are ongoing. Using the same examples, reverse the order of the verbs to show students that the *cuando* clause does not always come first. Give additional examples.

Ex. 3: Present another model that does not use a reflexive verb. Remind students that the imperfect phrase stays in the *yo* form. Review *estar* in the imperfect tense. Review the preterite endings using the grammar section of the Chap. 3 Organizer. Create further examples to accustom students to the structure.
Ex. 4: Organize the list into morning, afternoon, and evening activities where appropriate. Remind students that the people

312

El uso del pretérito y del imperfecto progresivo

The preterite tense is used to tell that something began and ended in the past, and the imperfect progressive describes something that was taking place. They are often used together.

Cuando **llegó** la ambulancia, el niño **estaba llorando**.
*When the ambulance **arrived**, the child **was crying**.*

Cuando **sacamos** esta foto, la señora Chávez **estaba hablando** con la periodista.
*When we **took** this photograph, Mrs. Chávez **was talking** to the reporter.*

3 Di lo que estabas haciendo cuando pasaron estas cosas. Por ejemplo:

ponerse las gotas / *Yo estaba poniéndome*
alguien / llamarme *las gotas cuando alguien*
por teléfono *me llamó por teléfono.*

a. tomar el jarabe / tú / estornudar
b. dormir / mi mamá / caerse de la escalera
c. comer / (nombre) / quemarse la mano
d. peinarse / mi hermano menor / vomitar
e. ponerse la venda / mi padre / despertarse
f.

4 Di qué estaban haciendo algunas personas que conoces ayer cuando ocurrió otro evento.

afeitarse	encontrar(se)	pelearse
buscar	escoger	ponerse
comprar	escuchar	probarse
cortar(se)	estornudar	quemar(se)
desayunar	hacer	reparar
despertarse	levantarse	romperse
empezar	maquillarse	toser

Freddy y Paula estaban comprando pastillas cuando empezaron a estornudar.

PASO CULTURAL La salud no es sólo algo personal—es nacional también. En muchos países de Latinoamérica, voluntarios de la comunidad trabajan con el gobierno para mejorar la salud de todos. La Organización Panamericana de la Salud (OPS) de las Naciones Unidas ayuda a financiar muchos de estos proyectos, como el de esta foto. ¿Crees que el gobierno debe interesarse en la salud de sus habitantes? ¿Por qué? ¿Qué puede hacer el gobierno?

Un cartel en La Paz motiva a los padres a mantener la salud de sus hijos.

Gramática en contexto 313

Class Starter Review
On the day following the presentation of the uses of the preterite and imperfect, you might begin the class with this activity: Choose a recent news event (local or national) to begin a sentence using the preterite tense, which students will finish using the imperfect progressive *(Cuando + preterite . . . yo + imperfect progressive).*

Answers
3 a. Yo estaba tomando el jarabe cuando tú estornudaste.
b. Yo estaba durmiendo cuando mi mamá se cayó de la escalera.
c. Yo estaba comiendo cuando *(nombre)* se quemó la mano.
d. Yo estaba peinándome cuando mi hermano menor vomitó.
e. Yo estaba poniéndome la venda cuando mi padre se despertó.
f. Answers will vary.

4 Answers will vary, but look for the correct forms of *estar* in the imperfect + present participle followed by a clause in the preterite.

Practice Wkbk. 9-5, 9-6

Writing Activities 9-D, 9-E

Pruebas 9-5, 9-6

Cultural Notes

named should be people they know. Review time expressions. Remind students that some of the verbs are reflexive.
Point out that *buscar, comprar, escuchar, empezar, escoger, hacer, ponerse, probarse,* and *reparar* will need other vocabulary. Brainstorm the possibilities.
Have students make a four-column grid to organize themselves: time, people, activity, other words.

Paso cultural
Answers will vary.

(p. 313, photo)
Children's health is a critical part of a national medical program. In this banner for a national health campaign, a Bolivian soldier helps a mother to vaccinate her child. Children are given vaccines against diseases including *difteria* (diptheria), *tos ferina* (pertussis, or whooping cough), *tétanos, poliomielitis, sarampión* (measles), *parótidas* (mumps), and *hepatitis B.*

Present & Practice

Re-enter / Recycle
Ex. 5: sports from Chap. 4

El pretérito de *caerse, creer* y *leer*

Here are the preterite forms of *caerse*.

(yo)	me **caí**	(nosotros) (nosotras)	nos **caímos**
(tú)	te **caíste**	(vosotros) (vosotras)	os **caísteis**
Ud. (él) (ella)	se **cayó**	Uds. (ellos) (ellas)	se **cayeron**

We add *y* to the stem in the *Ud. / él / ella* and *Uds. / ellos / ellas* forms.
We use an accent over the *i* in all the other forms.

• *Creer* and *leer* follow the same pattern in the preterite.

creí	creímos	leí	leímos
creíste	creísteis	leíste	leísteis
creyó	creyeron	leyó	leyeron

¡NO OLVIDES!

Remember that in the present tense *caerse* follows the same pattern as *traer*. It is a regular *-er* verb except in the *yo* form.

me caigo	nos caemos
te caes	os caéis
se cae	se caen

Esta gente de Santander, España, mantiene su salud montando en bicicleta.

314   Capítulo 9

Options

Strategies for Reaching All Students

Students Needing Extra Help
El préterito de caerse, creer y leer: Use the grammar section of the Chap. 1 Organizer to review *traer*.
Emphasize that all the forms have written accent marks, except the *Uds. / ellos / ellas* form.
Remind students of the spelling change in both singular and plural third person forms.

Ex. 5: Present a model with a non-reflexive verb.
Have students go through the exercise in two steps, the first time giving the imperfect progressive of the verb represented by the art, the second time putting both verb phrases together.

Extended Written Practice/Homework
1. Write four sentences telling what was happening when someone had an accident: *Mi vecino estaba trabajando en el garaje cuando se cortó la mano.*
2. Write three sentences telling when someone fell and what happened to the person: *Mi mejor amigo se cayó el año pasado y se lastimó la espalda.*

5 Di qué estaban haciendo estas personas cuando se cayeron.

Mateo estaba duchándose cuando se cayó.

Mateo

a. (yo)

b. el señor Soto

c. (tú)

d. Teresa y Lourdes

e. mi amigo y yo

f. Uds.

Estudiantes españolas
haciendo un examen de
educación física en Mallorca

Gramática en contexto   315

Answers

5 a. (Yo) estaba esquiando cuando me caí.
b. El señor Soto estaba jugando tenis cuando se cayó.
c. (Tú) estabas corriendo cuando te caíste.
d. Teresa y Lourdes estaban patinando cuando se cayeron.
e. Mi amigo y yo estábamos montando en bicicleta cuando nos caímos.
f. Uds. estaban subiendo la escalera cuando se cayeron.

Cultural Notes

3. Write two pairs of sentences telling what someone did because of something that was happening: *Estaba estornudando mucho. Por eso, tomé unas pastillas para el resfriado.*

Multiple Intelligences
Intrapersonal/Introspective
Have students write a paragraph describing a recent illness or accident and what they did to get better.

(p. 314, bottom photo)
Europeans love bicycle racing, and some of the most competitive races are held in Spain. The *Semana catalana* race takes place in March. *La Vuelta del país vasco* is held in April and is considered a preliminary for the April–May Tour of Spain, or, simply, *la Vuelta*. Each cycle of *la Vuelta* is held in a different location in Spain. Spain's racing season concludes with the *Clásica de San Sebastián* in August.

(p. 315, photo)
These young people are taking their high-school physical fitness test. A program of exercise begun in childhood has lifelong benefits. Schools around the world try to generate positive attitudes toward exercise by teaching fitness to young students.

Practice

Re-enter / Recycle
Ex. 6: pharmacy items from
Chap. 7

Answers

6 a. (Tú) te pusiste gotas para
los ojos.
b. Tomás se puso calamina.
c. Ellos se pusieron crema de
afeitar.
d. Nosotros nos pusimos bronceador.
e. (Yo) me puse repelente.
f. La señora Bonilla se puso
perfume.
g. Juan y Víctor se pusieron
desodorante.

7 ESTUDIANTE A
a. ¿Dónde pusieron Miguel y
Carlota los platos sucios?
b. . . . pusieron Uds. la ropa
sucia?
c. . . . pusiste el libro?
d. . . . puso Carolina el video?
e. . . . puso tu padre la carta?
f. . . . puse la leche?
g. Questions will vary.
ESTUDIANTE B
a. Los pusieron en el lavaplatos,
¡por supuesto!
b. La pusimos en el cesto de la
ropa sucia . . .
c. Lo puse en el estante . . .
d. Lo puso en la videocasetera . . .
e. La puso en el escritorio . . .
f. La pusiste en el refrigerador . . .
g. Answers will vary, but should
be in the preterite.

El pretérito del verbo *poner*

Here are the preterite forms of *poner*.

(yo)	**puse**	(nosotros) (nosotras)	**pusimos**
(tú)	**pusiste**	(vosotros) (vosotras)	**pusisteis**
Ud. (él) (ella)	**puso**	Uds. (ellos) (ellas)	**pusieron**

6 Di qué se pusieron estas personas.

Eva se puso maquillaje.

Eva

a. (tú) b. Tomás c. ellos

d. nosotros e. (yo) f. la señora Bonilla g. Juan y Víctor

316   Capítulo 9

Options

Strategies for Reaching All Students

Students Needing Extra Help
El pretérito de poner: Emphasize that *poner*
is irregular in the preterite.
Write the *ponerse* chart on the chalkboard.
Ex. 6: Use the vocabulary section of the
Organizer.
Ex. 7: Review direct object pronouns.
Remind students to fill in the blank after *el
cesto de (la ropa sucia).*
Remind students that the verb changes from
the question to the answer.

Ahora lo sabes: Have students write these
out so they can keep track of their progress.

Extended Written Practice/Homework
1. Write four sentences telling where you
and your classmates put different items
today: *Javier puso su cuaderno en mi
mochila.*
2. Write three sentences using *ponerse* to
tell who used the following and in what
situation: *gotas para los ojos, insecticida,
calamina. Mi mamá se puso gotas para los
ojos porque tenía una infección de los ojos.*

7 No puedes encontrar nada, pero todos te dicen que pusieron las cosas en un lugar lógico. Con un(a) compañero(a), pregunta y contesta.

(tú) / el pastel   A — ¿Dónde pusiste el pastel?
                        B — Lo puse en el horno, ¡por supuesto!

a. Miguel y Carlota / los platos sucios

b. Uds. / la ropa sucia

c. (tú) / el libro

d. Carolina / el video

e. tu padre / la carta

f. (yo) / la leche

g.

el escritorio

el lavaplatos

la videocasetera

el cesto de ___

el refrigerador

el estante

MORE PRACTICE

Más práctica y tarea, pp. 553–554
Practice Workbook 9–5, 9–9

Un letrero bonito de una farmacia en Pamplona, España

Ahora lo sabes

Can you:

■ talk about conditions or situations in the past?

—Antes de la clase, los estudiantes estaban charlando y ___.

■ talk about what was going on when something happened?

—Yo estaba ___ cuando alguien me ___.

■ talk about an accident?

—María se ___ y se ___ un músculo.

Gramática en contexto   317

Answers: Ahora lo sabes
• Answers will vary, but look for the correct form of the present participle.
• Answers will vary, but look for the correct *yo* form of the preterite / *estaba*
• Answers will vary.

 Practice Wkbk. 9-7, 9-8, 9-9

 Audio Activities 9.4, 9.5

 Writing Activities 9-F, 9-G, 9-H, 9-I

 Pruebas 9-7, 9-8

 Comm. Act. BLMs 9-2, 9-3

 Pasos vivos 2 CD-ROM
Fax Task, Slide Presentation Maker, Spindle, Treadmill

Multiple Intelligences
Bodily/Kinesthetic and Verbal/Linguistic
Bring in samples of the items pictured on p. 316. Place them in a bag and have students select one. Then ask them to make a sentence using the vocabulary word with the preterite of *poner*.

Verbal/Linguistic
See Audio Activities 9.4 and 9.5.
Visual/Spatial
See Practice Wkbk. 9-7, 9-8, and 9-9; Writing Activities 9-F, 9-G, 9-H, and 9-I; and Comm. Act. BLMs 9-2 and 9-3.

Apply

 ¿Recuerdas?

Play

Using the Video

Episode 9 begins as Jamie and María are waiting in the doctor's office. They listen as an agricultural worker tells his wife that his illness was caused by pesticides (from working at La Jacaranda). María then sees the doctor and returns to report that she has a cold.

As Jamie and María are walking home, Felipe shows up and excitedly tells María that he wants to see her soon.

At María's house, Jamie listens to a phone message from Rogelio Salazar, the library assistant, who wants to talk to Jamie.

The next evening, Jamie, Carlos, María and Felipe attend a conference on environmental pollution. After the conference, Rogelio explains to Jamie that Demetrio Alcocer wants to help her but is afraid of don Silvestre. At the same moment, another scene shows an ambulance arriving at the library.

Actividades

Un hombre recibe tratamiento para el cáncer en San Juan, Puerto Rico.

1 ¡Tantos pacientes y cada uno con su historia! En grupo, inventen diálogos entre un(a) enfermero(a) y los pacientes en la sala de espera *(waiting room)*. El (la) enfermero(a) va a preguntar:

- tu nombre
- tu edad y fecha de nacimiento
- tu dirección y número de teléfono
- por qué quieres ver al (a la) médico(a)
- cuáles son tus síntomas
- hace cuánto tiempo que los tienes

Después, el (la) médico(a) va a decirte lo que debes hacer.

Vas a quedarte en . . .

2 Entrevista a uno de tus abuelos o a una persona de 60 ó 70 años. Pregúntale cómo eran los servicios médicos cuando él (ella) er joven. Luego, haz un informe. Habla sobre:

- cómo eran los médicos y los dentistas
- las medicinas y los remedios
- los hospitales
- las farmacias
- cuánto costaba ir al médico

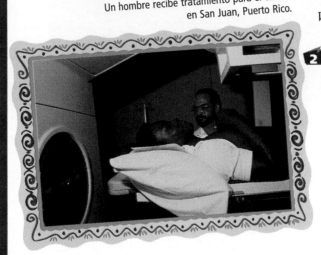

318   Capítulo 9

Options

Strategies for Reaching All Students

Spanish-Speaking Students
Ex. 2: Have students write out what they learned from the person they interviewed. Since others will most likely conduct their interviews in English, Spanish speakers might be enlisted to help them put their interviews into the target language.

Students Needing Extra Help
Ex. 1: Use the vocabulary section of the Organizer.
Help students brainstorm and formulate the structure of the questions as a class. Brainstorm possible remedies.
Model possible dialogues.

Ex. 2: Remind students to conduct the interviews in English.
Students should already have the questions written before the interview with space between them so they can take complete notes.
Help them translate their notes into Spanish, and decide what information should be included in the report.

Conexiones

La biología

Las enfermedades infecciosas

Imagina que trabajas como voluntario(a) en una clínica. Antes de poner este cartel en la pared, quieres incluir un ejemplo para cada caso.

Lee estos ejemplos y, con un(a) compañero(a), decide qué ejemplo corresponde a cada caso del cartel.

a. como el virus de la hepatitis B

b. como la bacteria *Salmonella*

c. como pasa con los hongos *(fungi)* del pie de atleta

d. como el protozoo *Plasmodium* que causa la malaria

e. como el virus de la gripe

Escoge dos de estas enfermedades y escribe consejos para protegerse o curarse de ellas (sin mencionar qué enfermedades son). Lee tus consejos a la clase, que debe adivinar de qué enfermedades hablas.

¿Cómo se transmiten las enfermedades infecciosas?

¡Achís!
Por el aire

Por agua o comida contaminada

Por contacto directo

Por fluidos corporales

¡Ojo!

Por animales vectores

Todo junto 319

 Video Activity A

 La Catrina: Capítulo 9

Play

 Video Activity B

 Para entender mejor

Play

 Video Activity C

Answers: Conexiones

a. Por fluidos corporales
b. Por agua o comida contaminada
c. Por contacto directo
d. Por animales vectores
e. Por el aire

Responses will vary, but look for use of chapter vocabulary.

 Comm. Act. BLMs 9-4, 9-5

 Pasos vivos 2 CD-ROM

A Jugar, Laboratorio de grabar, Maps, Video Monitor, Video Presentation Maker

---

Cooperative Learning
Tell pairs of students they are preparing a scene for an upcoming live episode of a popular TV hospital drama, but they should not discuss the scene beforehand. Each student will be reponsible for four lines of dialogue. On one sheet of paper, have *Estudiante A* write the first line of the dialogue. *Estudiante B* should read the line and write the next one. When they have completed the eight-line dialogue, they should practice it before presenting it to the class.

Multiple Intelligences
Interpersonal/Social
See Exs. 1–2.
Interpersonal/Social and Verbal/Linguistic
See Cooperative Learning.
Visual/Spatial
See Using the Video, *Conexiones,* and Comm. Act. BLMs 9-4 and 9-5.

Cultural Notes

(p. 318, photo)
Puerto Rico is a commonwealth of the U.S. and, to this point, the people have voted against becoming a U.S. state. The life expectancy in Puerto Rico is nearly 75 years, almost as high as in the U.S. and much higher than many Latin American countries. While health care is relatively successful, high unemployment is a severe problem, and many Puerto Ricans migrate to the U.S. in search of jobs.

Apply

Process Reading
For a description of process reading, see p. 52.

Answers
Antes de leer
Students may say that the child would become ill and have to go to the hospital. The child would receive medicine there, and would probably not eat that much again.

Mira la lectura
Ask at random what students think the poem is about. Avoid correcting misunderstandings.

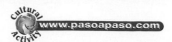

¡Vamos a leer!

Antes de leer

STRATEGY ➤ Using prior knowledge

What would happen if a child ate too much of something? Where might a parent take the child, and what might happen there? Do you think he or she would ever do it again?

Mira la lectura

STRATEGY ➤ Skimming

Skim this poem to get a general idea of what happens.

Chana y su rana

—Cecilia Ávalos

Doña Chana tenía una rana
que le gustaba comer manzana.
Cien manzanas se comió.
Y la rana se empachó.

Doña Chana llevó a su rana
con la curandera Doña Sana.
Una sobada Doña Sana le dio,
y té de manzanilla le recetó.

Doña Chana, con su rana,
a su casita regresó.
Tomando té de manzanilla cada día
del empacho la rana sanó.

Doña Chana le dijo a su rana:
—¡Ya NO vuelvas a comer manzana!
Y triste su rana suspiró:
—¡Ay, mamita, yo creo que NO!

320   Capítulo 9

Options

Strategies for Reaching All Students

Spanish-Speaking Students
Ask: *¿Crees que cuentitos de este tipo impresionan a los niños más que las advertencias de sus padres? ¿Por qué?*

Students Needing Extra Help
Mira la lectura: Read the poem aloud so students can hear the rhyme and rhythm. Remind them to look at the pictures carefully for clues.
Students may think *manzanilla* means some type of apple. Explain that it is chamomile tea.

Infórmate: For point 3 write the last two lines of the third stanza on the chalkboard. Then, insert *se* before *sanó*. Give students choices of meaning: became sane, was clean, was cured.
Review the meaning of "idiom" in point 4.
Aplicación: Encourage students to use words directly from the poem in the new title.

Infórmate

 STRATEGY Using context to get meaning

1 Sometimes *se* is used to make the meaning of a verb stronger; for example, *caer* = "to fall," *caerse* = "to fall down" and *beber* = "to drink," *beberse* = "to drink (something) up." Given this information, what do you think *comerse* means?

2 In this poem, what is another way to say *se empachó*?

  a. comió mucho
  b. le dolió el estómago porque comió demasiado
  c. tenía hambre

3 Sometimes *se* is left out so that a line will "flow" better. For example, line 4 of stanza 3 could read, *del empacho la rana se sanó.* Does that help you understand the meaning of *sanó*? What do you think it means?

4 *Volver a* + infinitive is an idiom. Which phrase comes closest to expressing the meaning of *no vuelvas a comer manzana*?

  a. no vas a comer tantas manzanas otra vez
  b. no tienes que comer manzanas
  c. no te gustan las manzanas

Aplicación

1 Choose another title for this story that gives a clue to what happens in it.

2 Do you know other stories in which animals behave like people? How is this story similar or different?

Infórmate
1. to eat (something) up
2. b
3. was cured
4. a

Aplicación
Titles will vary. Some possibilities: *La rana que comió demasiado, La rana que nunca va a comer demasiado.*

Names of stories will vary, but students may mention *Charlotte's Web,* or *The Wind in the Willows,* or Aesop's fables. *Chana y su rana* is the same as these stories in that the animals are personified, and there is a moral.

 Internet Activities

Apply

Process Writing
For information regarding developing a writing portfolio, see p. 54.

¡Vamos a escribir!

Vamos a escribir una entrevista divertida sobre el tema de la salud.

1 Primero, piensa en un insecto u otro animalito que causa enfermedades. Piensa en lo que hace y por qué. ¿Qué va a decir el insecto en una entrevista? Por ejemplo, una entrevista con un mosquito puede empezar así:

> **REPORTERO** Buenos días, señor Mosquito. En su opinión, ¿cuál es el problema entre los mosquitos y las personas?

> **SR. MOSQUITO** Pues, yo no sé por qué no le gustamos a la gente. No somos malos. Somos muy simpáticos y trabajadores.

Escribe el primer borrador y consulta con un(a) compañero(a). Sigue los otros pasos del proceso de escribir. Puedes usar estas palabras u otras:

- picar /picadura
- sangre
- piel (*skin*)
- brazo /mano
- protegerse
- repelente /insecticida
- calamina
- enfermedad
- dolerle a uno
- tener razón

2 Ahora, imagina que lees en una revista una de las entrevistas que escribieron tus compañeros. Escribe tu opinión en una carta al redactor (*editor*). Debes atacar o defender el punto de vista del insecto. Puedes hacer sugerencias (*suggestions*) para resolver el problema. Usa estas frases u otras:

- a mí me parece que
- creo que
- para mí
- es verdad que
- (no) estoy de acuerdo
- además
- por ejemplo

322   Capítulo 9

Options

Strategies for Reaching All Students

Students Needing Extra Help
Ex. 1: Brainstorm insects or small animals that might provide possibilities for this exercise.
Assign a specific number of lines, perhaps three for each character. Have students work in pairs.
Help students with sentence structure.

Ex. 2: Use your local paper to review the idea behind letters to the editor. Why might they write a letter to the editor? Emphasize the idea of freedom of thought, opinion, and speech.
Have students use as much vocabulary from the interview as they can when writing the letter.
Help students incorporate their opinions using the phrases listed in section 2.

Multiple Intelligences
Visual/Spatial
Have students create an ad for a product similar to the one on p. 323 or p. 324.
Visual/Spatial and Intrapersonal/Introspective
See steps 1–2.

3 Para compartir tu trabajo, puedes:

- presentar las entrevistas como obras de teatro
- grabarlas en audio o video
- enviar las entrevistas y las cartas
  al periódico o revista escolar
- enviarlas a un periódico local
- incluirlas en tu portafolio

¡Vamos a escribir!   323

Assess & Summarize

Test Preparation

You may want to assign parts of this section as written homework or as an in-class writing activity prior to administering the *Examen de habilidades.*

Answers

Listening: —*Nuestro gato estaba en un árbol y yo subí para sacarlo. Yo me caí y me lastimé el tobillo. El gato está bien, pero yo tengo que llevar una venda y usar muletas por tres semanas. ¡Caramba!* Students may say the cause of the accident was either the cat or loss of footing. The person speaking has to wear a bandage and use crutches for three weeks.

Reading: Answers will vary, but may include the following:
mal
cabeza
Usted puede ser
Debe comprar
Salud

Writing: Questions will vary, but should include a variety of chapter vocabulary.

Repaso ¿Lo sabes bien?

Esta sección te ayudará a prepararte para el examen de habilidades, donde tendrás que hacer tareas semejantes.

Listening

Can you understand when someone describes an accident? Listen as your teacher reads a sample similar to what you will hear on the test. What caused the accident? What treatment did the person speaking receive?

Reading

Alicia read the following advertisement on the side of a bus. But she couldn't remember all of it. Supply the missing text in the blanks so that the ad makes sense.

Writing

Can you write questions for a health-services survey in a Spanish-speaking community? Add three more to these.

1. ¿Va a un(a) médico(a) por lo menos una vez al año?
2. ¿Dónde queda la sala de emergencia más cerca?

Culture

Can you explain how to find a pharmacy late at night in Latin America? What kind of medicine can you buy there that you would not be able to buy without a prescription in the United States?

Speaking

Create a dialogue with your partner in which you discuss an injury with a doctor.

A —*¿Qué te pasó? ¿Tuviste un accidente?*
B —*Sí, doctor(a). Estaba corriendo por el parque con mis amigos cuando me caí.*
A —*¿Te duele mucho la rodilla?*
B —*Sí.*
A —*Mmmm. Necesito sacarte una radiografía y hacer algunos análisis.*

¿Ud. estornuda de la mañana a la noche?
¿Se siente _____?
¿Tiene dolor de _____?
¿No puede dormir?

_____ alérgico a:
• el polen de la primavera
• el pelo de las mascotas
• el polvo de los muebles

_____ pastillas
QUITALERGIA
¡_____!

Self Test   www.pasoapaso.com

Options

Strategies for Reaching All Students

Students Needing Extra Help
Have students write out this section so that they can check off what they have mastered. Remind students that this is just a sample of what the actual test will be like.
Listening: Read more than once. Remind students that they need only listen for two pieces of information. Brainstorm for what words they should listen.
Reading: Review commands. Point out that some blanks can be filled in with verbs.

Bring in magazine ads for allergy medications to use as a model.
Writing: Have students use the Organizer and write a sample survey as practice. Discuss health surveys, pointing out that they are taken to improve local services. Brainstorm what other questions might be important.
Culture: Have students review any notes they may have taken during their reading of the *Perspectiva cultural.*

Speaking: Use the vocabulary section of the Organizer.
Limit the number of lines of dialogue.
Remind students to use the preterite and the imperfect progressive.

Resumen del vocabulario

Usa el vocabulario de este capítulo para:

- describe how an accident occurred
- discuss an injury or illness
- describe treatment for an injury or illness

to identify parts of the body
el codo
el hueso
la muñeca
el músculo
la rodilla
el tobillo

to discuss an illness
la enfermedad
la infección, *pl.* las infecciones
el síntoma
la tos
el virus
estornudar
sentirse *(e →ie)*
toser
vomitar

to talk about allergies
la alergia
(ser) alérgico, -a (a)
antialérgico, -a
la abeja
la araña
la cucaracha
la hormiga
el insecticida
los mariscos
la mosca

el mosquito
la picadura (de insecto)
picar
el polen
el polvo
la reacción,
   pl. las reacciones
el repelente

to talk about treatment for medical conditions
la ambulancia
el análisis, *pl.* los análisis
el antibiótico
la calamina
el enfermero, la enfermera
los frenillos *(m.pl.)*
las gotas (para los ojos)
la inyección, *pl.* las inyecciones
poner una inyección
el jarabe (para la tos)
la medicina
las muletas *(f.pl.)*
la operación, *pl.* las
   operaciones
la pastilla
las puntadas *(f.pl.)*
hacer puntadas
la radiografía
sacar una radiografía

la receta
recetar
la sala de emergencia
la sangre
la silla de ruedas
el yeso

to describe how an accident occurred
el accidente
caerse: (yo) me caí
cortarse
proteger(se) *(g →j)*
quemarse
romperse (un hueso)
roto, -a

to indicate time
por + *time expression*

other useful words and expressions
poner: (Ud. / él / ella) puso
además
fuerte
leve
¿Qué te pasó?

Resumen 325

Culture: Students may say they can go to a *farmacia de turno.* The schedule can be found in the newspaper, and there is a sign in the window. You can receive antibiotics at a pharmacy in Latin America, but in the U.S. you must go to a doctor to get a prescription.

Speaking: Dialogues will vary.

Assessment

 Prueba cumulativa

 Examen de habilidades

 Test Generator

Additional Assessment Options

 Comm. Act. BLMs
Small Group Activities
Situation Cards

 Pasos vivos 2 CD-ROM
Slide Presentation Maker, Video Presentation Maker, Word Processor, Spindle

 ¿Lo sabes bien? Video Quiz

www **Internet Activities**
Self-Test

Enrichment
Pairs of students can also create a dialogue in which one person is trying to persuade the other to seek medical care for an ailment that clearly needs professional attention. The reluctant person can be a child, friend, relative, or older person.

CAPÍTULO 10

THEME: MOVIES AND TELEVISION

SCOPE AND SEQUENCE   Pages 326–359

COMMUNICATION

Topics

Movie character types

Television shows

Natural disasters

Objectives

To compare soap operas in Spanish-speaking countries with those in the U.S.

To talk about movie-making

To talk about various kinds of films

To talk about natural disasters

To summarize movies and TV programs

To talk about TV programs

CULTURE

Soap operas in Latin America

GRAMMAR

El pretérito y el imperfecto

El pretérito del verbo decir

Ancillaries available for use with Chapter 10

Multisensory/Technology

 Overheads, 48–51

 Audio Tapes and CDs

Vocabulary Art Blackline Masters for Hands-On Learning, pp. 53–57/CD-ROM

Classroom Crossword

La Catrina

 Pasos vivos 2 CD-ROM

 Internet Activities www.pasoapaso.com

Print

 Practice Workbook, pp. 95–104

 Writing, Audio & Video Activities, pp. 59–64, 120–122, 169–170

 Communicative Activity Blackline Masters

Pair and Small Group Activities, pp. 64–69

Situation Cards, p. 70

Un paso más: Actividades para ampliar tu español, pp. 55–60

 RESOURCE PRO®

Planning Express, Teaching Resources Library, and Clip Art Library

Assessment

 Assessment Program

Pruebas, pp. 144–154

Examen de habilidades, pp. 155–158

 Test Generator

 ¿Lo sabes bien? Video Quiz

Video still from Chap. 10

¿Qué prefieres, el cine o la televisión?

Movies, television, and VCRs are all part of the growing entertainment industry in Spain and Latin America. In theaters, movies are shown from one month to a year, depending on the success of the film. Then, they go to video rental stores and to cable systems. Movies made in the U.S. are the most popular. *Jurassic Park (Parque jurásico)* or *Schindler's List (La lista de Schindler)* were as successful in Latin America as they were in the U.S. Movies such as *La belle époque,* from Spain, and *Como agua para chocolate (Like Water for Chocolate),* from Mexico, have also won recognition in film festivals around the world. The former won the Academy Award for the best foreign film in 1993; the latter broke the record for box office sales in New York. These films are becoming more and more popular in Spain and Latin America.

There is a long tradition of movies and filmmaking in Spanish-speaking countries. *Un perro andaluz (An Andalusian Dog),* 1928, and *Los olvidados (The Forgotten Ones),* 1950, both by the great Spanish director Luis Buñuel, are still shown in universities and video clubs. Also, any new film by Pedro Almodóvar, creator of *Matador* and *Mujeres al borde de un ataque de nervios (Women on the Verge of a Nervous Breakdown),* is received with as much excitement in Spain and Latin America as in the U.S.

Just as in the U.S., TV talk shows, sports programs, news broadcasts, educational TV, and music videos are offered in Spanish-speaking countries. One of the most popular variety shows is also broadcast in the U.S.: *Sábado gigante* from Miami and Chile. Soap operas are normally broadcast in the evening in Latin America, running a few months at a time. News programs always cover other Spanish-speaking countries as well as major news stories from the U.S. and other countries. Television programs from the U.S. are frequently shown in Latin America, almost invariably dubbed into Spanish.

The Spanish and Latin American TV industry is also expanding. For example, the Mexican news channel ECO (Echo) broadcasts 24 hours a day in more than 20 countries. Soap operas from Latin America are not only shown in Venezuela and Peru, but also in the Soviet Union and Poland.

Introduce

Re-entry of Concepts
The following list represents words, expressions, and grammar topics re-entered from Book 1 and Book 2 (Chaps. 2 and 4):

Book 1
numbers 0–31, time-telling, expressing likes or preferences, indicating hunger, weather expressions, rooms in a house, household chores, making comparisons, expressing opinions

Chapter 2
daily routine

Chapter 4
leisure-time activities

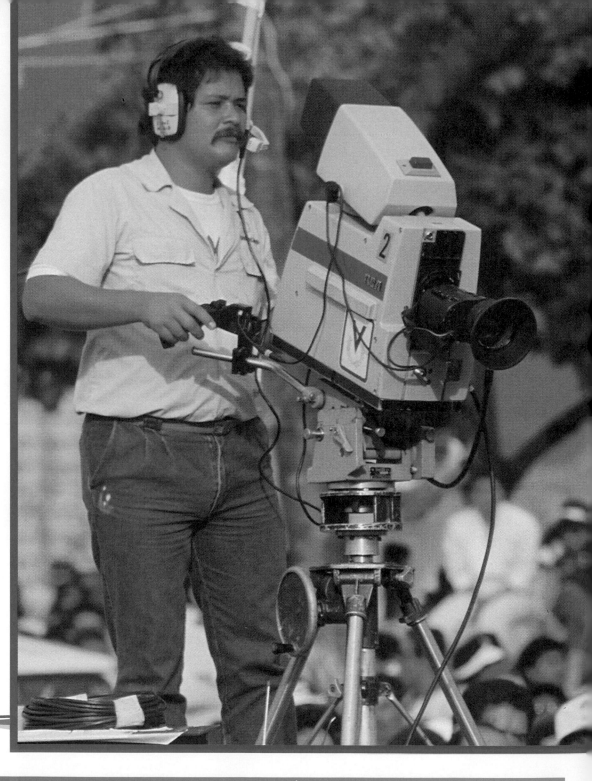

Planning

Cross-Curricular Connections

Language Arts Connection *(pp. 346–347)*
In pairs, have students choose a famous fairy tale and retell it from the point of view of the villain or anti-hero, using the preterite and imperfect tenses. Students may follow up with a book cover or an oral presentation to the class.

Drama Connection *(pp. 352–353)*
In groups of four, have students choose a current event or controversial situation in the news. They then create a soap opera title and a short (three-minute) scene depicting the events or issues involved. Encourage satire, comedy, and exaggeration. Have students present their skits in class or videotape them.

Spanish in Your Community
Assign pairs of students to watch one game show on Spanish-language TV and one on English-language TV. Have them take notes during the broadcasts in order to create a two-column table headed "English-language" and "Spanish-language." Have them write about what they see (similarities and differences) in the types of games played and prizes awarded.

CAPÍTULO 10

¿De qué se trataba la película?

Objectives

At the end of this chapter, you will be able to:

► summarize the plot of a movie or television program

► describe the characters and settings of a movie or television program

► describe conditions when something happened

► compare soap operas in Latin America and the United States

PASO CULTURAL

Los programas de televisión son un importante producto de exportación en Venezuela. Las compañías de televisión, privadas y del gobierno, venden sus programas a muchos países, con doblaje *(dubbing)* si es necesario. Las telenovelas venezolanas son especialmente populares en Latinoamérica. ¿Tienes oportunidades de ver programas de televisión en español? ¿En qué aspectos son diferentes de los programas en los Estados Unidos? ¿En qué aspectos son similares?

Filmando en Caracas, Venezuela   327

Paso cultural
Answers will vary.

(pp. 326–327, photo)
Venezuela is a center of television production in Latin America. Both government-owned and private Venezuelan television broadcasting companies produce programs to be seen all over the world. Venezuelan productions are exported and dubbed into many languages. Venezuela is especially well known for its production of *telenovelas*.

Preview

Cultural Objective

• To discuss movies and television in Spanish-speaking countries

Multicultural Perspectives

Como agua para chocolate, one of the greatest international successes in Mexican cinematic history, is based on the popular novel of the same name by Laura Esquivel, who also wrote the screenplay. Her husband, Alfonso Arau, directed the film which was nominated for the Best Foreign Film Oscar in 1992, and in the same year won 10 *Arieles,* the Mexican equivalent of the Oscar. The story is set in the early 1900s in Texas and Coahuila, Mexico. Tita, the protagonist, is forced to give up the man she loves (Pedro) in order to care for her domineering mother. Pedro then marries her older sister so as to be near his true love. This situation proves to be very difficult, but all Tita can do is take out her frustrations through cooking. Ask students if they are familiar with it, or with other Spanish-language films. Have students research what Spanish-language films are available in their local video store.

¡Piensa en la CULTURA!

San Juan Chamula, México

La televisión en México, Colombia y España

Mira las fotos. ¿Qué hay en las fotos que se parece y que no se parece a lo que tú sueles ver y hacer?

"A toda la familia le gusta este programa. No se aburre nadie."

Una familia maya viendo la televisión en San Juan Chamula, México

PASO CULTURAL

La televisión llega a los lugares más remotos de México. En esta foto, del estado de Chiapas, la cultura moderna electrónica coexiste con la vieja cultura española / católica y la antigua cultura maya. ¿Cuáles son los elementos indígenas que ves en esta casa, y cuáles son los españoles / católicos?

Options

Strategies for Reaching All Students

Spanish-Speaking Students

Ask: *¿Has visto películas en español? ¿Cuál te gustó más? ¿Qué clases de programas en la televisión te gustan más? ¿Por qué?*

 Un paso más Ex. 10-A

Multiple Intelligences
Visual/Spatial
See Critical Thinking.

Cultural Notes ☼

Paso cultural
Possible answers: La decoración del pelo de la señora es un elemento indígena. El altar al lado de la televisión es un elemento católico (la religión del lugar también mantiene elementos indígenas). La televisión es un elemento español o de la cultura occidental.

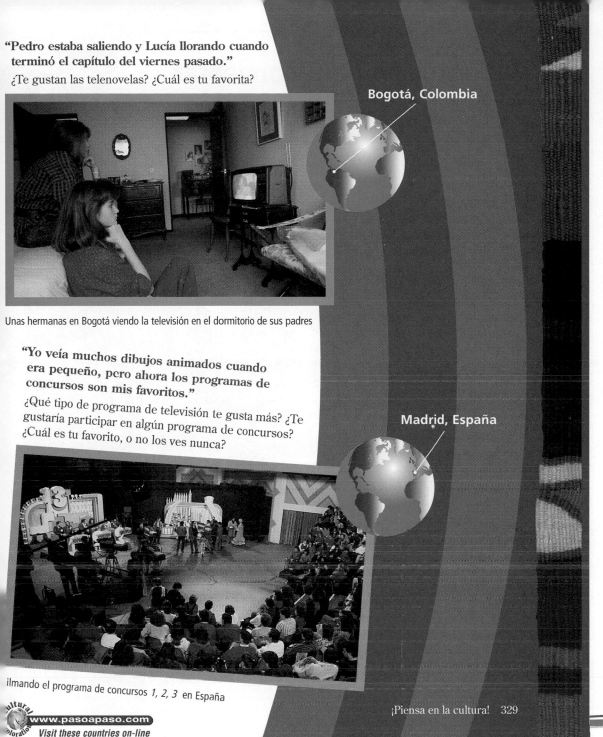

"Pedro estaba saliendo y Lucía llorando cuando terminó el capítulo del viernes pasado."

¿Te gustan las telenovelas? ¿Cuál es tu favorita?

Bogotá, Colombia

Unas hermanas en Bogotá viendo la televisión en el dormitorio de sus padres

"Yo veía muchos dibujos animados cuando era pequeño, pero ahora los programas de concursos son mis favoritos."

¿Qué tipo de programa de televisión te gusta más? ¿Te gustaría participar en algún programa de concursos? ¿Cuál es tu favorito, o no los ves nunca?

Madrid, España

Filmando el programa de concursos 1, 2, 3 en España

¡Piensa en la cultura! 329

www.pasoapaso.com
Visit these countries on-line

Critical Thinking: Formulating Appropriate Questions
After reviewing the photos and captions, have students write three questions they might ask their classmates about what they like to watch on TV.

Answers: ¡Piensa en la cultura!
Answers will vary.

(p. 328, photo)
Traditional life and modern technology are juxtaposed in this Mayan home in San Juan Chamula, a village in the Chiapas highlands, near the colonial city of San Cristóbal de las Casas. The Chamula church, famous for its fusion of Mayan and Catholic rituals, is a major cultural and ceremonial center for the people of this area.

(p. 329, top photo)
The *telenovela* is a genre that is unique to Latin American television (including Brazil), but its popularity is beginning to spread to other parts of the world. Spanish-language *telenovelas* have long been popular with Latino audiences in the U.S., but in the 1990s they have had great success in countries as diverse as Denmark, Russia, and Indonesia.

(p. 329, bottom photo)
The game show 1, 2, 3 is very popular in Spain. To play, three contestants are asked trivia questions and awarded points for answering correctly. The winner goes on to the next phase in which he or she must choose between prizes concealed behind doors, in boxes, or behind curtains, in the hope of finding the grand prize—a car, a condo, or cash. However, they may be asked to perform a stunt, or they may go home with a pumpkin or a lump of coal.

Standards 1.1; 2.1; 2.2; 3.1   **329**

Present

Chapter Theme
Movies and movie characters

Communicative Objectives
- To talk about movie-making
- To talk about various kinds of films
- To summarize movies and TV programs

 Overheads 48–49

 Vocabulary Art BLMs/CD-ROM

 Vocabulary Tape 10-1

Teaching Suggestions
Preparing students to speak: Use one or two options from each of the categories of Comprehensible Input, Physical Response, or Limited Verbal Response. For a complete explanation of these categories and some sample activities, see pp. T20–T21.

Inform students that the word for "victim" (*la víctima*) is always feminine.

Vocabulario para conversar

¿De qué se trata tu película favorita?

Vas a necesitar estas palabras y expresiones para hablar sobre películas y programas de televisión. Después de leerlas varias veces, practícalas con un(a) compañero(a).

Options

Strategies for Reaching All Students

Spanish-Speaking Students
Haz una lista de otras palabras que tú sabes que se relacionan a este tema.

 Un paso más Exs. 10-B, 10-C

Students Needing Extra Help
Vocabulario para conversar: Begin the vocabulary section of the Organizer.
Write out the *dirigir* paradigm for those students who need to see it completed.
Point out how similar these words are to the English.
También necesitas . . . : Give some examples with *enamorarse de*, *tratarse de,* and *¿Qué tal es . . . ?*
¿Y qué quiere decir . . . ?: Give examples of *esconder* and *esconderse.*

Enrichment
Ask students to name recent or older television programs in which various types of characters appear. For example: *¿Cuáles son algunas películas en que vemos extraterrestres?* As a homework assignment, students can make up the names of television programs or movies in which these characters would appear, and write a brief description of what the program or movie would be about.

la víctima

la ladrona

esconder

robar

el criminal

matar

el ladrón,
pl. los ladrones

la policía

la criminal

el /la detective

la directora

el policía

arrestar

También necesitas . . .

actuar*	to act
la actuación	acting
enamorarse (de)	to fall in love (with)
hacer el papel (de)	to play the part / role (of)
el papel	here: part, role
tratarse de	to be about
el argumento	plot
el crimen	crime
la escena	scene
el guión, pl. los guiones	script
el personaje	character
¿Qué tal es . . . ?	How is . . . ?

¿Y qué quiere decir . . . ?
la ayuda
la dirección
los efectos especiales
la fotografía
la película de acción
esconderse
investigar
excelente
principal
típico, -a

* *Actuar* has an accent on the *u* in all present-tense forms except the *nosotros* and *vosotros* forms: *actúo, actúas, actúa, . . . actúan.*

Vocabulario para conversar   331

Class Starter Review
On the day following initial pre-sentation of vocabulary, you might begin the class with this activity: On a transparency, have a list of Spanish movie titles and their English counterparts. Have students match the titles.

Reteach / Review: Vocabulary
También necesitas . . . : Review Book 1, Chap. 11 vocabulary.

www Internet Activities

Juegos

Learning Spanish Through Action
STAGING VOCABULARY: *Actúen, Levanten*
MATERIALS: flashcards for the types of movies listed in Book 1, Chap. 11; cards of current vocabulary, including items from *También necesitas . . .*
DIRECTIONS: Direct students to form groups of three and pantomime the kind of program they see on the card.

Extended Written Practice/Homework
1. Write four sentences naming actors who play different roles in movies: *Will Smith hace el papel de un detective en la película* Men in Black.
2. Choose a movie you saw recently and write three sentences telling things that happened: *Los policías arrestaron a un ladrón.*
3. Using the same movie as in number 2 or a different movie, write sentences describing three aspects listed in *También*

necesitas...: Los efectos especiales son fantásticos y realistas.

Multiple Intelligences
Bodily/Kinesthetic
See Learning Spanish Through Action.
Verbal/Linguistic
See Vocabulary Tape 10-1.
Visual/Spatial
See Overheads 48–49 and the Vocabulary Art BLMs/CD-ROM.

Practice

Answers: Empecemos a conversar

1 **ESTUDIANTE A**
a. ¿Qué personaje es típico en una película romántica?
b. ...de acción?
c. ...de aventuras?
d. ...del oeste?
e. ...de ciencia ficción?

ESTUDIANTE B
a. Un galán.
b. Una detective.
c. Un ladrón.
d. Un vaquero.
e. Un extraterrestre.

Empecemos a conversar

Túrnate con un(a) compañero(a) para ser *Estudiante A* y *Estudiante B.*
Reemplacen las palabras subrayadas en el modelo con palabras
representadas o escritas en los recuadros. Si ven 💡 pueden dar
su propia respuesta.

1   de terror   A — *¿Qué personaje es típico en una película de terror?*
B — *Un monstruo.*

Estudiante A
a. romántica
b. de acción
c. de aventuras
d. del oeste
e. de ciencia ficción

Estudiante B

Options

Strategies for Reaching All Students

Spanish-Speaking Students
Exs. 1–3: Pair bilingual with non-bilingual students, if possible.

Students Needing Extra Help
Ex. 2: Show how the relationship in the question is incorrect, and that it is corrected in the response.
Ex. 3: Help students understand how to judge a film's script and direction. Brainstorm the titles of films. Encourage them to vary their responses.

Enrichment
Ex. 2: To extend this exercise, you may want to elicit the titles of some current movies. Have students apply the questions in this exercise to those movies.

2

A —*Generalmente, ¿investiga el crimen el galán?*
B —*No. El detective investiga el crimen.*

investigar el crimen

Estudiante A

Estudiante B

a. enamorarse   b. montar a caballo   c. matar a la gente

d. arrestar al criminal   e. pedir ayuda   f. robar el banco   g. esconderse de la policía

3 el argumento

A —*¿Qué tal es el argumento en (nombre de película)?*
B —*(Es) excelente.*

Estudiante A

a. la dirección
b. la actuación
c. los efectos especiales
d. el guión
e. la fotografía
f. la música

Estudiante B

excelente   terrible
un desastre
así, así

Vocabulario para conversar   333

---

2 ESTUDIANTE A
a. Generalmente, ¿se enamora la criminal?
b. . . . monta a caballo la extraterrestre?
c. . . . mata a la gente la policía?
d. . . . arresta al criminal el científico?
e. . . . pide ayuda el monstruo?
f. . . . roba el banco el detective?
g. . . . se esconde de la policía la víctima?

ESTUDIANTE B
Answers will vary, but may include the following:
a. No. El galán y la heroína se enamoran.
b. . . . El vaquero monta a caballo.
c. . . . El criminal mata a la gente.
d. . . . El detective o la policía arrestan al criminal.
e. . . . La víctima pide ayuda.
f. . . . El ladrón (la ladrona) roba el banco.
g. . . . El criminal o el ladrón (la ladrona) se esconde de la policía.

3 ESTUDIANTE A
If possible, provide Spanish titles of recent films students will know.
a. ¿Qué tal es la dirección en (nombre de película)?
b. . . . es la actuación . . .
c. . . . son los efectos especiales . . .
d. . . . es el guión . . .
e. . . . es la fotografía . . .
f. . . . es la música . . .

ESTUDIANTE B
a.–f. Answers will vary.

Extended Written Practice/Homework
1. Write four sentences telling what different movies are about: The Wedding Singer *se trata de un cantante que se enamora de una camarera.*
2. Write four sentences telling why you like or dislike different types of movies: *No me gustan las películas violentas porque los criminales matan a muchas personas.*
3. Refer to *También necesitas . . .* on p. 331 and write three sentences saying what

aspects of a movie are most important to you: *El argumento de una película es muy importante para mí.*

Multiple Intelligences
Verbal/Linguistic
See Exs. 1–3.
Verbal/Linguistic and Interpersonal/Social
Have students in groups make lists of the ways that television influences their lives and then share them with the class.

Visual/Spatial
Make lists of movies made in the U.S. and of the titles that are used in the Spanish translations of the same movies. *(My Best Friend's Wedding/La boda de mi mejor amigo; Home Alone/Solo en casa; As Good as it Gets/Mejor, imposible).* Have students match movies with their Spanish counterparts. Explain that titles are not always translated literally.

Practice & Apply

Answers: Empecemos a conversar

4 ESTUDIANTE A

a. ¿De qué se trata *Frankenstein?*
b. ... *Parque Jurásico?*
c. ... *La bella y la bestia?*
d. ... *Ricitos de oro?*
e. ... *La bella durmiente?*
f. ... *E.T.?*
g. Questions will vary.

ESTUDIANTE B

a. Se trata de un científico que hace un monstruo.
b. ... unos dinosaurios que viven en una isla.
c. ... un monstruo que se enamora de la heroína.
d. ... una niña que encuentra la casa de unos osos.
e. ... una muchacha que duerme por muchos años y un galán que la despierta.
f. ... un extraterrestre que llega a los Estados Unidos y un niño que lo protege.
g. Answers will vary.

Answers: Empecemos a escribir

5–7 Answers will vary, but should include a variety of chapter vocabulary.

¿De qué se trataba la película?

Una escena de la película
El Norte

4 *Romeo y Julieta*

A — ¿De qué se trata <u>Romeo y Julieta</u>?
B — Se trata de <u>una muchacha y un muchacho que se enamoran</u>.

Estudiante A

a. *Frankenstein*
b. *Parque Jurásico*
c. *La bella y la bestia*
d. *Ricitos de oro* (Goldilocks)
e. *La bella durmiente*
f. *E.T.*
g.

Estudiante B

una muchacha que duerme por muchos años y un galán que la despierta

un científico que hace un monstruo

un extraterrestre que llega a los Estados Unidos y un niño que lo protege

un monstruo que se enamora de la heroína

unos dinosaurios que viven en una isla

una niña que encuentra la casa de unos osos

Options

Strategies for Reaching All Students

Spanish-Speaking Students
Ask: *¿Quién es tu actor favorito o tu actriz favorita? ¿En qué película o programa de televisión ha actuado? ¿Por qué te gusta?*

 Un paso más Ex. 10-D

Students Needing Extra Help
Ex. 4: Have students create more examples.
Ex. 5: If available, use the vocabulary section of the Organizer from Book 1, Chap. 11. Point out that the first question is similar to those in Ex. 4. Review *¿Qué tal es?* so that students do not confuse it with *¿Qué tal?* Model the answers for questions regarding photography, script, and favorite scene.
Ex. 6: Students may have difficulty articulating their thoughts regarding their choices. Brainstorm possible answers.

Cooperative Learning
In groups of four, have students decide who will interview and who will play three famous actors from three different types of films. In front of the class, the interviewer will ask each person three questions designed to reveal his or her identity without revealing the name. The actors must answer truthfully according to their characters, and when all three have finished, the class must try to guess the identity of each.

Empecemos a escribir

Escribe tus respuestas en español.

5 ¿De qué se trata tu película favorita? ¿Qué tipo de película es? ¿Qué actor y actriz hacen los papeles principales? ¿Qué tal es la actuación? ¿La fotografía? ¿El guión? Describe tu escena favorita.

6 ¿Qué es más importante en una película, un buen director o buenos actores? ¿Un buen argumento o efectos especiales? Explica por qué. ¿Hay tipos de películas en que la fotografía es mejor en blanco y negro que en colores? ¿Cuáles? ¿Por qué piensas eso?

7 ¿Qué tipo de película te gustaría dirigir? ¿O en qué tipo te gustaría actuar? ¿Qué tipo de papel te gustaría hacer? ¿Por qué? ¿Qué te gustaría más, escribir un guión o hacer los efectos especiales? ¿Por qué?

¿En Qué Se Parece Cristina A La Mona Lisa?

La Mona Lisa es morena, Cristina es rubia.
La Mona Lisa es Europea, Cristina es Latina.
La Mona Lisa es antigua, Cristina es moderna.
¿En qué se parece La Mona Lisa a Cristina?
En que las dos son únicas.

Cristina: Lunes a viernes 4pm-3pm Centro.
Cristina Edición Especial: Lunes 10pm-9pm Centro.

Univisión

MORE PRACTICE

- Más práctica y tarea, p. 555
- Practice Workbook 10–1, 10–2

También se dice

el marciano / la marciana

el héroe

el bandido
el villano
el malo
el maleante

Una escena de la película
argentina La historia oficial

Vocabulario para conversar   335

Multicultural Perspectives

El Show de Cristina is becoming the most popular television talk show for Spanish-speaking audiences in the U.S., as well as in Puerto Rico and Latin America. The show follows the same format with the same controversial topics as many of the popular daytime talk shows for English-speaking audiences. Cristina is also heard on radio. Ask students to compile a list of topics for a talk show. Have them write questions in Spanish for their panel of guests.

Practice Wkbk. 10-1, 10-2

Audio Activity 10.1

Writing Activity 10-A

Pruebas 10-1, 10-2

Strategies for Reaching All Students
MULTIPLE INTELLIGENCES
Interpersonal/Social and Verbal/Linguistic
See Cooperative Learning.
Verbal/Linguistic
See Ex. 4 and Audio Activity 10.1.
Visual/Spatial
See Practice Wkbk. 10-1 and 10-2 and Writing Activity 10-A.

Cultural Notes

(p. 334, photo)
The events in *El Norte* take place in three locations: the Guatemalan highlands, Mexico, and California. Characters may speak Maya Quiché, Spanish, or English. The Guatemalan Spanish used includes the *voseo* (for example: *vos sos, vos sabés, vos salís*) of Central America. The plot revolves around the journey of a brother and sister, Rosa and Enrique, to the U.S., upon the death of their father and disappearance of their mother.

(p. 335, realia)
Cristina Saralegui is well known for her forthright interview style. In 1989 she became executive producer and host of Univisión's *El show de Cristina,* now ranked among the top ten Spanish-language programs in the U.S. In 1992 Saralegui became executive producer and host of "Cristina," an English-language version of her talk show, making her the first person to host daily programs in two languages.

(p. 335, photo)
The 1985 Academy Award winner for Best Foreign Film was *The Official Story.* Produced in Argentina and based on a true story, the film tells of a young couple's search for the natural father of their adopted daughter. They discover that he has been imprisoned for political reasons, and become involved in trying to secure his release.

Present

Chapter Theme
Television

Communicative Objectives
- To talk about natural disasters
- To summarize movies and TV programs
- To talk about TV programs

 Overhead 50

 Vocabulary Art BLMs/CD-ROM

 Vocabulary Tape 10-2

Teaching Suggestions
Preparing students to speak: Use one or two options from each of the categories of Comprehensible Input, Physical Response, or Limited Verbal Response. For a complete explanation of these categories and some sample activities, see pp. T20–T21.

¿De qué se trataba la película?

Vocabulario para conversar

¿No te parecen exageradas las telenovelas?

Aquí tienes el resto del vocabulario que necesitas en este capítulo para hablar sobre películas y programas de televisión.

el terremoto

el huracán, pl. los huracanes

la tormenta

la erupción, pl. las erupciones

el derrumbe

la inundación, pl. las inundaciones

el locutor

la locutora

Anillo de oro
$499 $449
1-800-555-2345
el programa de compras

$1.500 $900
el programa de concursos

336   Capítulo 10

Options

Strategies for Reaching All Students

Spanish-Speaking Students
Tell students: *Agrega otras palabras relacionadas con el tiempo a tu lista de vocabulario.*

 Un paso más Ex. 10-E

Students Needing Extra Help
Tambien necesitas . . . : Give examples of *el comentario (sobre).*
Review *hay* and *había.* Call students' attention to the footnote.
¿Y qué quiere decir . . . ?: Create some examples for *(estar) basado, -a (en).*
Ex. 8: Review time expressions.

Enrichment
Ex. 8: To extend this exercise, you may want to ask: *¿Qué hubo en la televisión ayer a las . . . ?*

Learning Spanish Through Action
STAGING VOCABULARY: *Señalen*
MATERIALS: transparency of a page from a Spanish-language television guide
DIRECTIONS: Direct students to point to the listing for programs as you describe them.

También necesitas . . .

el comentario (sobre)	*review (of)*	sensacionalista*	*sensational*
el fracaso	*failure*		
el hecho	*fact*		
dañar	*to damage*		
destruir:	*to destroy:*		
Ud. / él / ella	*you / he / she*		
destruyó	*destroyed*		
hubo *(preterite of* haber)	*there was / were*		
tener éxito	*to be successful*		

¿Y qué quiere decir . . . ?

la entrevista	ocurrir
la información	(estar) basado, -a (en)
la violencia	exagerado, -a
violento, -a	internacional
cambiar	local

Empecemos a conversar

8

A — *Generalmente, ¿qué hay en la televisión a las seis de la tarde?*
B — *Las noticias.*

Estudiante A

a.
b.
c.
d.
e.
f.

Estudiante B

las noticias

telenovelas

programas de concursos

programas de acción
y comedias

programas de entrevistas

programas de compras

dibujos animados

documentales

*Sensacionalista is used with both masculine and feminine singular nouns: un programa de televisión sensacionalista; una noticia sensacionalista.

Vocabulario para conversar   337

Practice

Class Starter Review
On the day following initial presentation of vocabulary, you might begin the class with this activity: In pairs, have students create a chart, categorizing as many television shows as they can think of in 60 seconds according to the types of shows taught on p. 336 and from Book 1, Chap. 11. Call on students to share their list for certain categories with the class.

Answers: Empecemos a conversar
8 ESTUDIANTE A
a. Generalmente, ¿qué hay en la televisión a las siete de la tarde?
b. . . . a las cinco y media . . .
c. . . . a las dos . . .
d. . . . a las ocho . . .
e. . . . a las once y media . . .
f. Questions will vary.
ESTUDIANTE B
a.–f. Answers will vary. You may want to ask students to give examples mentioning title, time, and channel *(en el canal . . .)*.

 Internet Activities

Juegos

Extended Written Practice/Homework
1. Write four sentences telling your reactions to different types of television programs: *No me interesan nada los programas de concursos.*
2. Write sentences describing three disasters that have taken place: *Hubo un huracán en Honduras que mató a más de 10.000 personas.*

3. Refer to *También necesitas...* and write three sentences describing news and talk shows that are on TV: *Me gusta escuchar los comentarios del locutor en el canal 12.*

Multiple Intelligences
Bodily/Kinesthetic
See Learning Spanish Through Action.
Logical/Mathematical and Interpersonal/Social
See Class Starter Review.

Musical/Rhythmic
Have students in pairs select a well-known television program and, without having to change the melody, write a theme song for the show.
Verbal/Linguistic
See Vocabulary Tape 10-2 and Ex. 8.
Visual/Spatial
See Overhead 50 and the Vocabulary Art BLMs/CD-ROM.

Practice & Apply

Answers: Empecemos a conversar

9 ESTUDIANTE A
a. ¿Viste las noticias locales?
b. ...la información deportiva?
c. ...el anuncio de perfume?
d. ...el comentario sobre (nombre de película)?
e. ...la entrevista con (nombre)?
f. ...las noticias internacionales?

ESTUDIANTE B
a. Sí. Robaron un banco en el centro.
b. ...Nuestro equipo perdió.
c. ...Lo venden en muchas farmacias.
d. ...Dicen que la actuación es excelente.
e. ...La locutora dijo que estaba haciendo otro video.
f. ...Dicen que hubo un derrumbe en Guatemala.

10 ESTUDIANTE A
a. ¿Viste que hubo un terremoto en Costa Rica?
b. ...una erupción en Perú?
c. ...una tormenta en Cuba?
d. ...una inundación en Argentina?
e. ...un derrumbe en Chile?
f. Questions will vary.

ESTUDIANTE B
a.–f. Answers will vary, but should include correct use of the preterite tense.

¿De qué se trataba la película?

9 el pronóstico del tiempo
A — ¿Viste *el pronóstico del tiempo*?
B — Sí. *Va a llover este fin de semana*.

Estudiante A

a. las noticias locales
b. la información deportiva
c. el anuncio de perfume
d. el comentario sobre (nombre de película)
e. la entrevista con (nombre)
f. las noticias internacionales

Estudiante B

Dicen que la actuación es excelente.
La locutora dijo que estaba haciendo otro video.
Nuestro equipo perdió.
Dicen que hubo un derrumbe en Guatemala.
Lo venden en muchas farmacias.
Robaron un banco en el centro.

10

Puerto Rico

A — ¿Viste que hubo *un huracán* en *Puerto Rico*?
B — Sí. *Destruyó muchos edificios*.

Estudiante A

a. Costa Rica   b. Perú

c. Cuba   d. Argentina   e. Chile   f.

Estudiante B

destruir ___
dañar ___
matar a ___

338   Capítulo 10

Options

Strategies for Reaching All Students

Spanish-Speaking Students
Exs. 9–11: Pair Spanish-speaking students, if possible.
Ex. 16: *Trata de convencer a un compañero que el programa que quieres ver es el mejor. Haz una lista de las razones que le vas a dar.*

 Un paso más Ex. 10-F

Students Needing Extra Help
Ex. 9: Show students that they need to provide additional information for *d* and *e*.
Ex. 10: Brainstorm the information that will go in the blanks for *Estudiante B*. Remind students to use the preterite. Review the *a personal*.
Ex. 11: Review the *Estudiante A* list with the class, choosing the correct endings for the adjectives before students begin the exercise.

Ex. 12: Students may need help with the *¿Por qué?* questions.
Ex. 13: Students may need help with the vocabulary for the first question.
Ex. 14: Brainstorm book titles that were made into movies. Have background information available in order to discuss the last question.
Ex. 15: Students may need help with the vocabulary for the last question.

338   Standards 1.1; 3.2

11 exagerado(a) / A —¿*No te parecen exageradas las telenovelas?*
las telenovelas B —*Sí, no las soporto.*

Estudiante A   **Estudiante B**

a. **tonto(a) / los dibujos animados**

b. **sensacionalista / los programas de entrevistas**

c. **exagerado(a) / las comedias**

d. **aburrido(a) / los programas de compras**

e. **violento(a) / los programas de detectives**

Sí, no los (las) soporto.

Sí, pero me fascinan.

No. Me encantan.

También se dice

el presentador /
la presentadora

 www.pasoapaso.com

Empecemos a escribir y a leer

Escribe tus respuestas en español.

12 En tu opinión, ¿qué programa de televisión tiene más éxito? ¿Por qué tiene éxito? ¿Qué personajes son populares hoy? ¿Quiénes hacen esos papeles? ¿Qué programa es un fracaso? ¿Por qué?

13 ¿Cómo se debe preparar alguien para participar en un programa de concursos?

14 ¿Conoces alguna película que está basada en un libro? ¿Leíste el libro? ¿Viste la película? ¿Cuál te gustó más? ¿Por qué? ¿Conoces alguna película basada en un hecho de la vida real? ¿Cuál? ¿Ocurre en la película lo mismo que en la realidad?

15 ¿Qué piensas de la violencia en la tele? ¿Crees que se debe hacer algo?

MORE PRACTICE

- Más práctica y tarea, pp. 555–556
- Practice Workbook 10–3, 10–4

16 Lee esta lista de programas de televisión. Sólo puedes ver la tele por dos horas. Escoge lo que quieres ver. Compara tus programas con los de un(a) compañero(a). Imaginen que hay un sólo televisor y que necesitan ponerse de acuerdo.

	Canal 2	Canal 4	Canal 6
6:00	Moda: La chica de hoy	Noticias locales	Busca tu fortuna
7:00	Información deportiva	Telenovela: Marianela	Música de hoy
8:00	Película: Batman	Telenovela: Corazones tristes	Palabra de Dios
9:00	El chef francés: pasteles	Telenovela: Vidas exageradas	¡Bailemos!
10:00	Cine 2: El otoño de un vaquero	Noticias locales	Película: Derrumbe de noche
11:00		Noticias latinoamericanas	Noticias internacionales

Vocabulario para conversar 339

Practice

Teaching Suggestions

Ex. 1: Encourage students to watch the news the day before doing this exercise.

Answers:
¡Comuniquemos!
1–3 Answers will vary, but should include a variety of chapter vocabulary.

¡Comuniquemos!

Aquí tienes otra oportunidad para usar el vocabulario de este capítulo.

1 Con un(a) compañero(a), habla de las noticias en la televisión.

A — *¿Viste las noticias ayer?*
B — *Sí. Me interesaron mucho.*
A — *¿Y qué piensas de lo que dijo el locutor sobre . . . ?*
B — *. . .*

2 Con un(a) compañero(a), compara dos programas de televisión.

A — *¿Qué programa de televisión te gusta más, (nombre) o (nombre)?*
B — *A mí . . .*
A — *¿Por qué?*
B — *Porque los personajes son . . .*
A — *. . .*

3 Habla con un(a) compañero(a) sobre la película que tiene más éxito en estos días. Discutan por qué tiene éxito. Hablen de estas cosas:

• el nombre de la película
• el tipo de película
• el argumento
• los personajes
• la actuación y los actores
• la fotografía
• el guión
• la dirección

340 Capítulo 10

Options

Strategies for Reaching All Students

Spanish-Speaking Students
Ex. 3: Have students write out this exercise.

 Un paso más Ex. 10-G

Students Needing Extra Help
Ex. 1: Encourage students to create a news story using the vocabulary section of the Organizer. Do a complete model. Assign this a day in advance so that students will watch the news and take notes.

Ex. 3: Model. Students may have difficulty with the concept of judging the script, photography, and acting.
¿Qué sabes ahora?: Have students write out this section so that they are able to record their progress.

Cooperative Learning
Instruct students in groups of four to create a newscast. Each person will be responsible for three sentences on one of the following topics: national news, international news,

weather, or sports. Students should read aloud within the group to check for clarity and correctness. Each group should then present its newscast to the class. You may want to videotape these presentations.

Multiple Intelligences
Interpersonal/Social and Verbal/Linguistic
See Exs. 1–3 and Cooperative Learning.
Verbal/Linguistic
See Audio Activity 10.3.

340 **Standards** 1.1; 1.3; 5.1

Esta joven puertorriqueña aprende sobre la televisión en la Universidad de San Juan.

Una locutora de un canal hispanohablante en Chicago

Answers: ¿Qué sabes ahora?
• Answers will vary.
• Answers will vary, but will proba-bly be in present tense.
• name of a country / *hubo*

 Audio Activity 10.3

 Pasos vivos 2
CD-ROM
Boom Box, Clip Art Album, Slide Projector, Laboratorio de grabar

¿Qué sabes ahora?

Can you:

■ discuss a film?

—Lo que más me gustó de la película fue el ___ y la ___.

■ summarize the plot of a movie or television program?

—(Nombre) se trata de un(a) ___ que ___.

■ discuss a major news story?

—El terremoto en ___ fue horrible, pero no ___ muchas víctimas.

Vocabulario para conversar   341

Cultural Notes ☀

(p. 340, realia)
The pop art style of Roy Lichtenstein plays a prominent role in this *telenovela* ad. His distinctive work often uses arrangements of large, colored dots to create cartoonlike images. This exaggeration adds to the "larger-than-life" appeal of the *novela*.

(p. 341, top photo)
Students learn to direct their own television productions as they pursue degrees in telecommunications at the University of Puerto Rico. Courses leading to this degree include film and video production techniques and processes, writing for film and television, and the role of media in contemporary culture and society. The University of Puerto Rico in San Juan is well known for its classes in radio production.

(p. 341, bottom photo)
Carla Sánchez, reporter and anchorperson for TV Channel 44 in Chicago, was born in Blue Island, Illinois, but moved to Guadalajara, when she was in fourth grade. She finished *primaria* and *secundaria* there, and returned to Chicago to attend Columbia College where she majored in radio. She began working as a part-time DJ on Chicago's WIND radio, and later became the first Hispanic airborne traffic reporter in the city.

Present & Apply

Cultural Objective
- To compare soap operas in Spanish-speaking countries with those in the U.S.

Multicultural Perspectives

Telenovelas were originally adaptations of great literary works, broadcast over the radio as *radionovelas*. A few *telenovelas* have remained true to the meaning of the word *novela*, with complex characters and quality production. *Escalona* is one such *novela de época* (thus called because it takes place in the 1940s) that stars the popular singer Carlos Vives as Rafael Escalona, a young student dedicated to composing songs, romancing women, and enjoying life. This *novela* makes several literary allusions: in one episode Escalona refers to a woman as a *. . . diosa coronada de mi compadre Leandro Díaz* (Leandro Díaz is a popular Colombian composer; "La Diosa Coronada" is one of his songs. Gabriel García Márquez, in the epigraph of his novel, *Amor en los tiempos de cólera,* also mentions this *diosa coronada.*). This *novela* has been compared to the MGM musicals of the '40s, with Carlos Vives bursting into song at any moment. You may

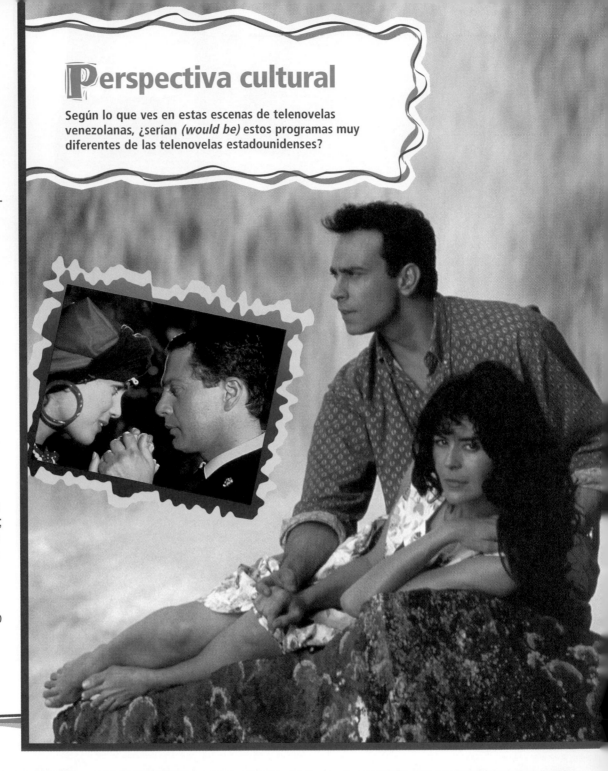

Perspectiva cultural

Según lo que ves en estas escenas de telenovelas venezolanas, ¿serían *(would be)* estos programas muy diferentes de las telenovelas estadounidenses?

Options

Strategies for Reaching All Students

Spanish-Speaking Students
Have students answer either orally or in writing: *¿Ves telenovelas o las ve alguien en tu familia? Di por qué te gustan a ti o por qué le gustan a los miembros de tu familia.*

 Un paso más Ex. 10-H

Students Needing Extra Help
Perspectiva cultural: Have students take notes to use later in the *¿Lo sabes bien?* section.
La cultura desde tu perspectiva, Ex. 1: Make a two-column chart in which students list a feature of the *telenovela* in one column and, in the second column, write how it would be different in the English version.
Ex. 2: Videotape a *telenovela* presented on your local channel.

Enrichment
If possible, videotape an episode of a U.S. soap opera. Show parts of it to generate class discussion in Spanish about how American cultural values are represented in the episode. Ask students to compare these with what they know about Hispanic cultural values.

Multiple Intelligences
Visual/Spatial and Verbal/Linguistic
See Enrichment.

Las telenovelas en español son muy populares. Generalmente se dan episodios todos los días por dos o tres meses. El episodio final tiene una audiencia muy grande y mucha gente se reúne con su familia y amigos para verlo. Éstas son dos escenas de la telenovela *Ladrón de corazones*.

La hermana mayor de la familia se divorció y regresó a vivir con sus padres. La hermana menor, Claudia, quiere tener su propio apartamento.

CLAUDIA: Pero, papá, ahora no hay espacio para mí en el dormitorio.

PAPÁ: Hija, tú eres el sol de esta casa. No lo olvides. Mientras este viejo cuerpo tenga vida, ¡no te voy a permitir vivir sola!

El presidente de Aerolíneas del Caribe, el señor Bastos, está hablando con su hijo David.

DAVID: Pero, papá, yo quiero ser músico. No me gusta el negocio, y me da miedo volar.

SR. BASTOS: ¡Eso no importa! Toma. *(Le da su carnet de identidad de las aerolíneas y lo besa.)* No te olvides de quién eres y de tus responsabilidades como el nuevo presidente de la línea aérea más grande del Caribe.

En todas las telenovelas, tanto en inglés como en español, la manera de hablar es exagerada porque se trata de situaciones exageradas. Pero en las culturas latinoamericanas, palabras y expresiones poéticas como "tú eres el sol de esta casa" y "mientras este viejo cuerpo tenga vida" se usan en la vida diaria y no son exageraciones.

María Conchita Alonso y Jorge Schubert hacen el papel de médicos en la telenovela venezolana *Alejandra*.

Inset: Flavio Caballero y Ruddy Rodríguez, el galán y la heroína de la telenovela venezolana *Volver a ti*

En las telenovelas en español también se expresa muy abiertamente el cariño *(affection)* entre parientes y amigos. En las telenovelas, como en la vida real, la gente se abraza y se besa con frecuencia. También los hombres expresan sus emociones más abiertamente. Por ejemplo, el papá besa a su hijo para felicitarlo en *Ladrón de corazones*.

Las telenovelas tienen argumentos, personajes y guiones muy exagerados, pero también pueden indicar cosas importantes sobre la cultura.

La cultura desde tu perspectiva

1 Imagina que hay una telenovela en inglés con el mismo argumento que *Ladrón de corazones*. ¿En qué sería diferente? ¿Qué nos dicen las diferencias sobre las dos culturas?

2 Si puedes ver telenovelas en español, ve un episodio. Haz una lista de por lo menos tres cosas que te parecen diferentes de las telenovelas en inglés.

www.pasoapaso.com

Claudia Venturini actúa en la telenovela venezolana *Inocente en línea*.

Perspectiva cultural   343

want to obtain a videotape to show students.

Answers
Answers to inductive questions will vary.

Answers: La cultura desde tu perspectiva

1 Answers will vary, but may include: The English-language soap opera would be longer. Less affection would be shown among family members. Males would usually not express emotion openly. The language would be neither poetic nor flowery. This tells us that in Hispanic cultures, family members show affection frequently as part of normal life. Latin cultures also encourage the expression of emotion by males, as well as what others might consider exaggerated or flowery language.

2 Answers will vary, but may include the following: exaggerated actions, language, sets, and make-up. The expression of affection is more frequent. The expression of emotion by males is shown. Children are included in the plot. The plot moves faster.

 Pasos vivos 2 CD-ROM
Maps, Notas culturales

 Internet Activities
Perspectiva cultural

Cultural Notes

(p. 342, photo)
María Conchita Alonso plays the title role in *Alejandra*, a *telenovela* about a young doctor struggling for respect in a male-dominated hospital. Jorge Schubert plays the *galán* who ridicules Alejandra, saying she should be at home cooking and cleaning instead of playing doctor. He of course winds up falling in love with her.

(p. 342, inset photo)
Volver a ti portrays the story of a young woman, played by Ruddy Rodríguez, who travels back in time to the era of Venezuela's military dictatorship. Rodríguez, a popular television personality and Miss Venezuela 1985, has acted in French, Latin American, and U.S. films. Her work is known throughout the Spanish-speaking world and in France.

(p. 343, photo)
Inocente en línea revolves around the murder of a beautiful young woman. When all the evidence points to Aguirre, the woman's husband, he is arrested and jailed for a crime he didn't commit. Only Gamboa, a special agent, believes Aguirre is innocent and sets out to free him. In the end, Aguirre's innocence is proven and the real murderer is put behind bars.

Preview

Overhead 51

Answers

A The expression is *Había una vez*. The verb *había* is in the imperfect tense. The other verb is *vivían*.

B The verb *estaba caminando* tells what was going on. It is in the imperfect progressive. The verb *encontró* tells what happened. It is in the preterite.

C *Dijo* is used to tell what Ricitos de oro said. The verb ending has no *i* and ends in an unaccented *o*, unlike the verb *vivió*, for example.

D The expression *tenía mucha hambre* tells what Ricitos de oro was feeling. The verb *(tenía)* is in the imperfect. The verbs that tell what she did are *entró, vio,* and *decidió*. They are in the preterite.

Gramática en contexto

Ricitos de oro y los tres osos

Había una vez una familia de tres osos: El papá oso, la mamá osa y el bebé oso. Vivían en el bosque.

Un día la mamá osa preparó tres platos de avena. La familia decidió dar un paseo porque la avena estaba muy caliente.

Una niña estaba caminando en el bosque cuando encontró la casa de los osos. "¡Qué casita tan bonita!" dijo ella. La niña se llamaba Ricitos de oro.

Entró en la casa y vio los tres platos de avena. Ricitos de oro tenía mucha hambre y decidió probar la avena.

A In caption 1, what expression corresponds to "Once upon a time there was"? What is the verb? What tense is it in? What is the other verb in caption 1?

B In caption 3, which verb tells what action was going on when something happened? Which verb tells what happened? What tense is each verb in?

C In caption 3, which verb is used to tell what Ricitos de oro said? How is this form different from the equivalent preterite form of other -*ir* verbs?

D In caption 4, what expression tells what Ricitos de oro was feeling? What tense is the verb in? Find the verbs that tell what she did. What tense are they in?

344   Capítulo 10

Options

Strategies for Reaching All Students

Students Needing Extra Help
B: Caption 2 offers another example of a contrast between a condition *(estaba muy caliente)* and an action *(decidió dar un paseo)*.
C: Point out that the unaccented *o* ending in *dijo* is like the *Ud. / él / ella* form of *hacer, poder,* and *tener* in the preterite.

Students may have to refer to the *decir* chart to see that there are no written accents in the preterite paradigm.
El pretérito y el imperfecto 1: Give additional examples.

Extended Written Practice/Homework
1. Write three sentences describing the weather conditions when different accidents occurred: *Hacía mucho viento cuando la niña se cayó y se lastimó la rodilla.*
2. Write three sentences telling what time it was when different people left or arrived at your home: *Eran las seis cuando mi mamá llegó a casa.*

El pretérito y el imperfecto 1

We often use the preterite and the imperfect together. The imperfect may be used to put an action in the context of what time it was or what the weather was like.

Eran las seis de la mañana cuando Ricitos de oro **se despertó.**

El día **estaba** muy bonito. **Hacía** sol. No **hacía** frío.

1 ¿Qué tiempo hacía en España la semana pasada? Usa este pronóstico del tiempo y haz una frase por cada ciudad. Por ejemplo:

En Sevilla hacía mucho sol y viento. Hacía fresco.

Gramática en contexto   345

¡NO OLVIDES!

Remember these words and expressions to talk about the weather:

llover
nevar
hacer buen/mal tiempo
    sol
    calor
    frío
    fresco
    viento

Present & Practice

Answers

1 En Madrid llovía y también hacía (un poco de) sol.
En Barcelona llovía y hacía viento.
En Bilbao llovía (mucho) y hacía (mucho) frío.
En Cádiz hacía sol y viento.
En Málaga hacía sol y (mucho) calor.
En los Pirineos nevaba.

 Writing Activities 10-D, 10-E

Multiple Intelligences
Visual/Spatial
See Overhead 51 and Writing Activities 10-D and 10-E.

Present & Practice

Teaching Suggestions

El pretérito y el imperfecto 2:
Have students identify the verbs in the examples that describe Goldilocks' feelings. Ask: What tense is each of the verbs in? Then have students locate the sentences and verbs that express action. Ask: What tense is each of those verbs in?

Re-enter / Recycle

Ex. 3: daily routine from Chap. 2

Answers

2 Answers will vary, but look for the correct form of *ser* in the imperfect with the expressions of time and the correct form of the preterite in the second part of the sentence.

2 Aquí tienes posibles situaciones en las noticias del día. Con un(a) compañero(a), túrnense haciendo preguntas y contestando.

A —¿Cuándo empezó la tormenta?
B —Eran las 9:45 de la noche cuando empezó.

la tormenta / empezar

a. la víctima / subir a la ambulancia   b. el incendio / empezar   c. el ladrón / robar el banco

d. el niño / caerse del segundo piso   e. el ascensor / romperse   f. el científico / quemarse las manos

g. el derrumbe / ocurrir   h. la policía / arrestar a los criminales

El pretérito y el imperfecto 2

Sometimes we use the preterite and imperfect tenses to contrast a physical, mental, or emotional state with an action.

Ricitos de oro **vio** la avena. **Tenía** mucha hambre.
Ricitos de oro **quería** comerla. No **sabía** qué hacer.
Tomó la cuchara y **empezó** a comer.

346   Capítulo 10

Options

Strategies for Reaching All Students

Students Needing Extra Help

Ex. 2: Review preterite endings and time-telling.
Point out that *d.–f.* include reflexive verbs.
El pretérito y el imperfecto 2: Have students decide which verb in each example indicates the physical state. Then repeat separately for the mental and emotional states. Give further examples.

Ex. 3: Have students identify which answers contain examples of the physical, mental, and emotional states.
Ex. 4: Brainstorm possible excuses.

Extended Written Practice/Homework

1. Use *tener* and three of these expressions to write sentences explaining why someone did or did not do something: *sueño, fiebre, gripe, un hueso roto, una alergia, la tos, una infección. Paco no jugó en el partido porque tenía fiebre.*

2. Write four sentences telling what different characters in movies did. Include a description of their physical, mental, or emotional state: *En* The Lost World *la mamá dinosaurio mató a muchas personas porque quería encontrar a su bebé.*

3 Dí por qué están pasando estas cosas en un estudio de cine.

la heroína /
ir al baño /
sentirse mal
La heroína fue al baño porque se sentía mal.

a. el niño / esconderse / darle miedo el monstruo
b. el director y el galán / pelearse / estar de mal humor
c. el vaquero / acostarse / estar muy cansado
d. el caballo / comer las flores / tener hambre
e. el extraterrestre / quitarse el disfraz / tener calor
f. los músicos / salir de la escena / aburrirse

Delante de un cine en Madrid

4 Con un(a) compañero(a), termina estas excusas diciendo por qué. Puedes usar estos u otros verbos: *tener (que), querer, estar, poder* y *hacer.*

no ir a
la escuela
A —*¿Por qué no fuiste a la escuela?*
B —*No fui a la escuela porque tenía fiebre.*

a. no hacer la tarea
b. no ir al partido de fútbol
c. levantarse tarde
d. no ayudar a limpiar la casa
e. no tomar la medicina
f. no llamar a nadie

En Madrid

Gramática en contexto 347

a. El niño se escondió porque le daba miedo el monstruo.
b. El director y el galán se pelearon porque estaban de mal humor.
c. El vaquero se acostó porque estaba muy cansado.
d. El caballo comió las flores porque tenía hambre.
e. El extraterrestre se quitó el disfraz porque tenía calor.
f. Los músicos salieron de la escena porque se aburrían.

4 ESTUDIANTE A
a. ¿Por qué no hiciste la tarea?
b. . . . no fuiste al partido de fútbol?
c. . . . te levantaste tarde?
d. . . . no ayudaste a limpiar la casa?
e. . . . no tomaste la medicina?
f. . . . no llamaste a nadie?
ESTUDIANTE B
a.–f. Answers will vary, but look for the correct forms of the preterite and imperfect and logical responses.

 **Practice Wkbk.
10-5, 10-6, 10-7**

 **Writing Activity
10-F**

 Pruebas 10-5, 10-6

Cultural Notes ☼

Multiple Intelligences
Verbal/Linguistic
See Ex. 2.
Visual/Spatial
See Practice Wkbk. 10-5, 10-6, and 10-7 and Writing Activity 10-F.

(p. 347, photos)
Hollywood movie stars such as Leonardo DiCaprio, Kate Winslet, and Jack Nicholson have become household names in Spain, gracing the covers of popular magazines and winning the hearts of the moviegoing public. Although Spanish films regularly take top honors in international film festivals, Spain is also the eighth-largest market for Hollywood movies.

Present & Practice

Class Starter Review

On the day following the presentation of the preterite and imperfect 3, you might begin the class with the following activity:
Compile a list of 20 basic action verbs *(bailar, comer, nadar,* etc.) and write them on the chalkboard. Have students stand and pantomime a verb from the list, while watching a classmate at the same time. When you say *alto,* all students write what the student they were watching was doing *(Cuando el profesor / la profesora dijo "alto," Andrés estaba llorando).*

Re-enter / Recycle

Ex. 5: daily routine from Chap. 2

Answers

5 Answers will vary, but may include:
En el 1-A un señor estaba viendo la televisión y unos jóvenes estaban lavando los platos.
En el 1-B una niña y su mamá estaban saludándose en el comedor.
En el 2-A unos muchachos estaban tocando música y otro estaba cantando. Un niño estaba cepillándose los dientes.

El pretérito y el imperfecto 3

Sometimes the preterite and the imperfect (or the imperfect progressive) contrast a continuing action with an action that has a definite beginning and end.

Una niña **estaba caminando** por el bosque cuando **vio** la casa de los osos.

5 Con un(a) compañero(a), di qué estaba pasando en los apartamentos del dibujo cuando ocurrió el terremoto. Escoge por lo menos seis situaciones.

A —*¿Qué estaba pasando en el apartamento 3-A cuando ocurrió el terremoto?*
B —*En el 3-A un señor estaba afeitándose en el baño.*

6 Inventa tres escenas divertidas para una película. Usa una sola frase para cada descripción.

Una señora estaba desayunando cuando el gato saltó y se cayó en el plato de cereal.

Después, formen un grupo para escoger las tres escenas más divertidas.

348   Capítulo 10

Options

Strategies for Reaching All Students

Students Needing Extra Help
El pretérito y el imperfecto 3: Give additional examples.
Ex. 5: Have students decide on the vocabulary before conjugating the verbs. Point out that in some apartments, more than one action is taking place.
Ex. 6: Do as a whole class. Help students by giving them the beginning phrase (the setting). Encourage them to create the *cuando* phrase.

Extended Written Practice/Homework
1. Choose three situations from p. 331 and write sentences telling what different people were doing when something happened: *El detective estaba investigando el crimen cuando vio a la víctima.*
2. Choose three photographs from this book and tell what different people were doing when the photographer took their picture: (p. 256) *Las personas estaban cruzando la calle cuando el fotógrafo sacó la foto.*

Multiple Intelligences
Bodily/Kinesthetic
See Class Starter Review.
Naturalist
Have students watch a nature program on TV and write a brief paragraph describing it.
Verbal/Linguistic and Interpersonal/Social
See Exs. 5–6.
Visual/Spatial
See Practice Wkbk 10-8 and Writing Activity 10-G.

En el 2-B un hombre estaba poniéndose la corbata y una mujer estaba usando un extinguidor de incendios en la cocina.

En el 3-A una mujer estaba maquillándose en el baño.

En el 3-B un hombre estaba haciendo un crucigrama, una muchacha estaba haciendo un rompecabezas y un muchacho estaba levantando pesas.

En el 4-A un muchacho estaba bañándose mientras alguien estaba pasando la aspiradora y otra persona estaba hablando por teléfono.

En el 4-B un ladrón estaba robando unas joyas.

En el 5-A un perro y un gato estaban peleándose.

En el 5-B un hombre estaba encendiendo la luz.

6 Answers will vary, but look for the correct use and forms of the imperfect progressive and the preterite.

 Practice Wkbk. 10-8

 Writing Activity 10-G

 Prueba 10-7

Present & Practice

Answers

7 ESTUDIANTE A

a. ¿Qué dijeron tú y *(nombre)* de la película de aventuras?

b. ... dijeron Felipe y Susana de la película romántica?

c. ... dijo Ramón de la película de ciencia ficción?

d. ... dijeron Roberto y Marina de la película del oeste?

e. ... dijiste (tú) de la película de acción?

f. Questions will vary.

ESTUDIANTE B

Answers will vary, but should begin as follows:

a. (Nosotros) dijimos ...

b. (Ellos) dijeron ...

c. (Él) dijo ...

d. (Ellos) dijeron ...

e. (Yo) dije ...

f. Answers will vary.

El pretérito del verbo *decir*

In the preterite tense, the stem of *decir* is *dij-*, and the endings follow the pattern of *hacer, poder,* and *tener*. Notice that the *Uds. /ellos /ellas* form does not have an *i* in the ending.

(yo)	**dije**	(nosotros) (nosotras)	**dijimos**
(tú)	**dijiste**	(vosotros) (vosotras)	**dijisteis**
Ud. (él) (ella)	**dijo**	Uds. (ellos) (ellas)	**dijeron**

7 ¿Qué tal fueron los comentarios de estas personas sobre la última película que vieron? Con un(a) compañero(a), usa los dibujos para preguntar y contestar. Por ejemplo:

A —*¿Qué dijo Marta de la película de terror?*
B —*Dijo que era un fracaso.*

Marta

Estudiante A

Estudiante B

a. (nombre) y tú

b. Felipe y Susana

c. Ramón

d. Roberto y Marina

e. (tú)

f.

350   Capítulo 10

Options

Strategies for Reaching All Students

Students Needing Extra Help
El pretérito del verbo decir: Review the preterite forms of *hacer, poder,* and *tener* by writing them on the chalkboard. Stress that there is no *i* in the third person plural ending. Ex. 7: Brainstorm the possible reactions. Remind students that they need to adjust the verb endings. If available, use the vocabulary section of the Book 1, Chap. 11 Organizer.

Ahora lo sabes: Have students write this so that they can record their progress.

Enrichment
To extend this exercise, name a movie or television show that students can question each other about. In groups of three, have students ask questions and take notes about what their group members answer. Students will report the comments to the rest of the class when called on to answer the following question: *En tu grupo, ¿qué dijeron las personas de* (name of movie or TV program)? *Explica por qué dijeron eso.*

Ahora lo sabes

Can you.

- describe the conditions when something happened?
  —Cuando el incendio empezó, ___ mucho viento.

- tell what happened and why?
  —La película ___ éxito porque los actores principales ___ excelentes.

- report what someone said?
  —Felipe ___ que quería ver una película de acción, pero yo ___ que no.

MORE PRACTICE

- Más práctica y tarea, pp. 556–557
- Practice Workbook 10–5, 10–9

Gramática en contexto 351

Answers: Ahora lo sabes
- hacía
- tuvo / eran
- dijo / dije

 Practice Wkbk. 10-9

 Audio Activities 10.4, 10.5

 Writing Activity 10-H

 Prueba 10-8

 Comm. Act. BLM 10-2

 Pasos vivos 2 CD-ROM
Fax Task, Slide Presentation Maker, Spindle, Treadmill

Extended Written Practice/Homework
1. Write three sentences telling what the announcer of different TV shows or news programs said: *La locutora de las noticias del canal 11 dijo que hubo una inundación en el norte de México.*
2. Write three sentences telling what different people said about movies they saw: *Mis amigos dijeron que* The Nutty Professor *era una película muy cómica.*

Multiple Intelligences
Verbal/Linguistic -
See Ex. 7, Audio Activities 10.4 and 10.5, and Enrichment.
Visual/Spatial
See Practice Wkbk. 10-9, Writing Activity 10-H, and Comm. Act. BLM 10-2.

Cultural Notes

(p. 351, realia)
This ad lists the full range of thematic, regional, and international channels offered by Vía Digital, one of the two digital TV services in Spain. Have students note the ad's use of puns. S. T. Hilo, for example, is a play on the word *estilo*. The name of the science fiction channel AluCine plays on the noun *cine* and the verb *alucinar*. Ask students: What other examples of wordplay are there in this ad?

Apply

¿Recuerdas?

Play

Video Activity A

Using the Video

In Episode 10, Jamie learns that Demetrio Alcocer has injured himself trying to catch a thief attempting to steal La Catrina's will. Demetrio tells Jamie that Silvestre Aguilar's grandfather was the lawyer in charge of La Catrina's will. Instead of finding an heir to her estate, he kept the estate for himself. Demetrio then gives Jamie the will.

At the Hacienda la Jacaranda, Jamie and Carlos talk to a worker about the pesticides used on the corn.

At home with María, Jamie watches a TV program about *El día de los muertos*. That night, she dreams that don Silvestre threatens to harm her if she claims the estate. Then La Catrina appears and confirms that Jamie is her true heir.

La Catrina: Capítulo 10

Play

Actividades

 Describe una ocasión cuando tuviste que:

- hacer un informe oral
- asistir a una boda (o a algún otro evento importante)
- recibir un premio (o un diploma)
- actuar, cantar, bailar o tocar un instrumento

En dos o tres frases dile a un(a) compañero(a) qué día era, qué tiempo hacía, cómo te sentías y por qué. Luego, formen grupos. Tu compañero(a) debe contarle al grupo lo que le dijiste.

Un día tuve que ... Era ...

 Piensa en algún crimen o desastre natural reciente. Habla con un(a) compañero(a) sobre:

- qué pasó
- cuándo
- dónde

Usen palabras y expresiones como las siguientes:

(No) había ...	la emergencia
ayudar	estar muerto(a)
pedir ayuda	matar a
la ambulancia	quedarse sin casa / ropa / comida
los bomberos	las víctimas
la policía	la vida

352   Capítulo 10

Options

Strategies for Reaching All Students

Spanish-Speaking Students
Ex. 1: Have students write out this activity, choosing two of the options and giving more details.

Students Needing Extra Help
Ex. 1: Do a complete model. Remind students to change the verb form to third person when reporting. Review uses of preterite and imperfect.
Ex. 2: Do a complete model. Remind students not to use the entire list.

Cooperative Learning
Divide the class into groups of five. One student from each group writes a sentence about his or her favorite movie or TV program as a child, using the imperfect tense. He or she then gives that paper to you. Each group forms a circle. *Estudiante A* whispers that sentence to *Estudiante B,* who then whispers *Él / ella me dijo que ...* and the rest of the message as he / she heard it. This repeats to the right until *Estudiante E* receives the message. He / she must report the message to the class. You will report the original message.

Conexiones

La estadística

¿Qué programas de tele prefieren?

Vas a hacer un pictograma para ilustrar los tipos de programas de televisión que prefiere tu clase. El pictograma de abajo refleja los gustos de los jóvenes españoles.

Preferencias televisivas de los jóvenes españoles

Categoría	
Películas, series	
Noticias, documentales	
Deportes	
Musicales	
Telenovelas	
De la naturaleza y animales	
Concursos	
Debates y mesas redondas	
Programación infantil	
Anuncios	
Otros	CLAVE: =10% =1%

Source: *Jóvenes: Lo que hacen y lo que piensan,* Materiales N° 17 (nov.–dic. 1994), Consejería de Educación, Embajada de España, p. 20

¿Qué dibujo indica el 10 por ciento? ¿Y el 1 por ciento? ¿Qué porcentaje de los jóvenes españoles prefieren los programas deportivos? ¿Y las telenovelas?

- Trabaja con toda la clase para hacer un pictograma que refleje la clase de programas que Uds. prefieren. Pueden usar la misma clave u otra.

- Comparen su pictograma con el de los jóvenes españoles. ¿Les gusta a Uds. la misma clase de programas que a los jóvenes españoles? ¿En qué se parecen sus gustos a los de ellos y en qué se diferencian?

Todo junto   353

Cultural Notes

(p. 352, realia)
The collection of *Believe It or Not* stories by American cartoonist Robert Ripley continues to have new books published in ten languages around the world. Originally published in 1918 as single-panel newspaper cartoons, they once had a peak daily readership of 80 million.

(p. 353, realia)
The Spanish subsidiary of the French digital TV giant Canal Plus has signed exclusive deals with U.S.-based entertainment conglomerates Universal, Fox, and Time-Warner, as well as CNN. These deals have been expensive, however, and both Canal Plus and its main rival, Vía Digital, posted losses in 1997. Ask students: Which of the films in this ad might appeal most to a Spanish audience? Which might appeal least?

Apply

Process Reading
For a description of process reading, see p. 52.

Answers
Antes de leer
Answers will vary, but will most likely include: 1, 2, 3, 5, 8, 10.

Mira la lectura
Students should skim the story to get a general idea of what happens.

¡Vamos a leer!

www.pasoapaso.com

Antes de leer

STRATEGY ➤ Using prior knowledge

Decide which of the following events is likely to occur in a soap opera. Write down the numbers of those that are likely to occur, then compare your choices with those of a partner.

1. Alguien tiene un accidente grave.
2. Dos jóvenes se enamoran a primera vista.
3. Unos criminales roban una joyería.
4. Un joven va a clases todos los días y estudia mucho.
5. Alguien pierde la memoria.
6. Una joven monta a caballo.
7. Un hombre y una mujer se casan y no tienen ningún problema.
8. Madre e hijo se separan.
9. Un consejero de campamento se cae de un árbol.
10. La gente cree que la heroína mató a alguien.

Mira la lectura

STRATEGY ➤ Skimming

Read the selection once through to get the gist of it.

Cómo escribir una telenovela

Las telenovelas latinas no son tan complicadas como parecen. Todas están hechas con la misma fórmula.

La heroína es, por lo general, joven, linda e inocente. Es pobre y sufre mucho para pagar sus estudios.

354   Capítulo 10

Se cree todo lo que le dicen y por eso tiene tantos problemas. No es raro que, en un momento u otro, termine en la cárcel, acusada de un crimen que no cometió. Si tiene un hijo, no le permiten verlo y pasa mucho tiempo buscándolo. Últimamente, las pobres heroínas están perdiendo la memoria con frecuencia. Al final siempre recibe una gran fortuna y entonces puede vengarse.

Y, por supuesto, hay un galán. Es muy guapo, rico y se enamora de la heroína a primera vista. Pero es un muñeco en las manos de su mamá, que es un monstruo. Él también se cree todo lo que le dicen, sobre todo si es algo malo sobre la heroína. Es terrible ver cómo el galán trata a la heroína en el período en que la cree mala: la humilla y la maltrata delante de la gente. Al final, por supuesto, comprende que ella es buena y que la quiere de veras.

Si usted quiere escribir una telenovela, tiene que incluir estos personajes, y nunca olvide que todo es fórmula y repetición.

Options

Strategies for Reaching All Students

Spanish-Speaking Students
Have students write out a short scene from one of the types of TV programs or movies listed. *Escribe una escena de uno de los tipos de obra mencionados. Luego, con unos compañeros, puedes presentarla en clase.*

Students Needing Extra Help
Mira la lectura: Remind students that they don't have to understand every word, that they are just looking for the main idea of each paragraph.
Infórmate: Explain the reason for reading the selection more than once. Read aloud as students follow along. Read aloud again, one sentence at a time, giving students an opportunity to write down the unfamiliar words.

Have students work in pairs or small groups in order to share their knowledge of the vocabulary. Collect their lists and combine them into one for the next day's class. Put this list on the chalkboard (or have it copied for each student). As a class, decide which words are not important for an understanding of the reading.

Infórmate

STRATEGIES Distinguishing essential from nonessential words
Identifying supporting details

1 Now read the selection more carefully, and make a list of those words you don't know. Read the selection a third time, and cross out on your list the words that are not important for understanding the selection.

2 Were any of the events that you identified in *Antes de leer* mentioned in the selection? Read aloud to your partner the places in the selection where they are mentioned.

3 List at least four events that are part of the formula for soap operas in Spanish.

DE LUNES A SABADO
A LAS 9 DE LA NOCHE

Manuela
Un Apasionante Romance Para Tus Noches De Amor

Ahora, Grecia Colmenares te invita a vivir nuevas y fuertes emociones. Con "Manuela", la dramática historia de dos hermanas, Isabel y Manuela, enfrentadas por el amor de un mismo hombre: Fernando. Intrigas, celos, pasiones y odios. "Manuela". La nueva telenovela de TELECINCO que mantendrá tu corazón en vilo desde el primer al último capítulo. ¡Vívela todas las noches en tu pantalla amiga!

Engánchate a
TELE5

Aplicación

Many kinds of books, movies, and television shows have their own formulas. List at least four events that are likely to occur in one of these: a teen romance, a western, a situation comedy, a detective story.

¡Vamos a leer!   355

Infórmate

1.–2. Answers will vary.

3. Answers will vary, but may include the following:
La heroína busca a su hijo.
La heroína termina en la cárcel.
La heroína pierde la memoria.
La heroína consigue una gran fortuna y puede vengarse.
El galán maltrata a la heroína.
El galán comprende que quiere a la heroína de veras.

Aplicación

Answers will vary, but may include the following:
Teen romance: Dos jóvenes se enamoran, pero los padres de la muchacha no están de acuerdo con el romance. El jóven tiene que mostrarles que él es un buen muchacho.
Western: Hay un nuevo sheriff. El hombre que mató al antiguo sheriff regresa; se pelean; el asesino muere y el sheriff es un héroe.
Sit-com: Un niño saca mala nota, y la cambia con un marcador. La profesora, los padres y el niño se encuentran en el supermercado, y hablan sobre las notas del niño.
Detective story: El detective habla con la persona que vio el robo de una joyería. El detective encuentra al ladrón, y devuelve las joyas a la joyería.

 Internet Activities

Apply

Process Writing

For information regarding developing a writing portfolio, see p. 54.

¡Vamos a escribir!

Todo junto

A veces tenemos una buena idea para una película. Vamos a inventar una película y a hacer un cartel para anunciarla al público.

 Piensa en estas cosas:

- qué tipo de película es
- quiénes son los personajes principales
- de qué se trata
- los comentarios que van a escribir los críticos

Escribe el primer borrador y consulta con un(a) compañero(a). Sigue los otros pasos del proceso de escribir.

¿Eran seres humanos o . . .?

LA TIERRA EN RUINAS

¿Por qué llegaron los extraterrestres a la Tierra? ¿Sólo buscaban agua, o querían algo más?

Rosalía Rodríguez (la heroína de *Marianela*) y Jorge Cantú (el galán de *Vidas exageradas*) en los papeles más emocionantes de su vida

Con la música de Tito Gómez y Los Muchachos

"¡Los efectos especiales son fantásticos, sobre todo la inundación de Caracas!"
—Francisco Rivera, *Telenoticias nacionales*

356   Capítulo 10

Options

Strategies for Reaching All Students

Students Needing Extra Help

Bring in the movie section of the weekend paper so that students can see how a movie they are familiar with is publicized. Compare one of the full-page ads to the model in the book, pointing out that students don't have to create something as sophisticated as the one in the paper. Remind students that they are creating a new movie, not translating a current ad into Spanish. Use the vocabulary section of the Organizer.

Enrichment

Have students create posters for real movies. Discuss how English movie titles translated into Spanish can sometimes be quite different from the original.

Multiple Intelligences

Bodily/Kinesthetic and Visual/Spatial
See Enrichment.

2 Ahora escoge el cartel que más te guste. Quieres que una compañía de cine filme esta película. Escribe una descripción de la película según este modelo.

nombre:	La Tierra en ruinas
personajes:	una científica y un policía
lugar:	Caracas en el año 2050
argumento:	Los extraterrestres necesitan agua. Llegan a la Tierra y empiezan a destruir las grandes ciudades.
audiencia:	jóvenes de 12 a 18 años

3 Para distribuir su trabajo, pueden:

- exhibir los carteles en la sala de clases
- exhibirlos en el vestíbulo o en la biblioteca escolar
- enviar las descripciones al periódico o a la revista escolar
- enviarlas a un periódico local
- escoger la mejor descripción, escribir el guión para una escena y presentarla a otras clases de español
- incluir todo en sus portafolios

¡Vamos a escribir! 357

Assess & Summarize

Test Preparation
You may want to assign parts of this section as written homework or as an in-class writing activity prior to administering the *Examen de habilidades*.

Answers
Listening: —*Era muy interesante. Se trataba de un vaquero que llega a una comunidad pequeña y se pelea con algunos criminales. La heroína tiene un rancho. El vaquero se enamora de ella. Hay una pelea terrible, y el vaquero mata a los criminales. Luego se monta a caballo y se va. La heroína se queda llorando. La película estuvo muy buena.*
A western movie is being discussed. The speaker likes the film.

Reading: 1. No vale la pena verla. 2. La recomiendo.
Words that one would *not* need to know will vary, but may include: *varios, anciano, sucesos.*

Writing: Summaries will vary.

Culture: Answers will vary, but may include the following: The expression of affection is frequent. Men express emotion openly. Language and actions are often exaggerated.

Speaking: Dialogues will vary.

Repaso ¿Lo sabes bien?

Esta sección te ayudará a prepararte para el examen de habilidades, donde tendrás que hacer tareas semejantes.

Listening
Can you understand when people talk about a movie or TV program? Listen as your teacher reads a sample similar to what you will hear on the test. What kind of movie is being discussed? Did the speaker like it or not?

Reading
Read what two critics have written about a film. List at least three words that you *would not* need to know in order to understand these reviews. Then assign the correct last sentence to each review.

1 En Tijuana, un detective investiga un crimen que se cometió hace varios años. El argumento es muy complicado, y nunca se explica el crimen. Después de muchas aventuras exageradas, escenas sensacionalistas y un derrumbe que casi no daña nada, termina la película. . . .

2 Un detective descubre un crimen horrible en Tijuana. Conoce a un anciano que puede ser el criminal y a su hija, de quien se enamora. Tienen muchas aventuras. Casi los mata un derrumbe. No comprendemos muy bien los sucesos, pero la película es divertida. . . .

a. No vale la pena verla.
b. La recomiendo.

Writing
Can you write a summary of a television drama or comedy? Here is an example for a teen drama.

Culture
Can you give three characteristics of a Spanish-language soap opera?

Speaking
Talk to your partner about your favorite actor. Discuss the actor's movies and / or television shows.

A —¿Qué actor o actriz te gusta más?
B —Arnold Schwarzenegger.
A —¿Por qué?
B —Porque hace películas de acción y comedias muy buenas.
A —¿Te gustó su actuación en (nombre de película)?
B —...

www.pasoapaso.com

Se trata de unos jóvenes que van a la misma escuela secundaria. Los muchachos son muy guapos y las muchachas muy bonitas. La semana pasada, uno de los muchachos se enamoró de una chica pobre. Los jóvenes se querían mucho y querían casarse, pero sus padres no lo permitieron y el joven se peleó con ellos.

Options

Strategies for Reaching All Students

Students Needing Extra Help
Have students write out this exercise so that they can check off what they have mastered. *¿Lo sabes bien?:* Remind students that this is just a sample of what the test will be like.
Listening: Read more than once. Remind students that they only need to listen for two pieces of information. Brainstorm for which words they should be listening.

Reading: Show students where the choices are located on the page. They may have difficulty distinguishing which words are unimportant. They will probably choose smaller words, such as *en, un, a,* etc.
Writing: Have students use the Organizer and write a sample summary before the test as practice. Limit the number of required sentences. Brainstorm possible plot lines. Create with students the first sentence or two.

Culture: Have students review the notes they took during their first reading of the *Perspectiva cultural.* Also, review the reading in *¡Vamos a leer!*
Speaking: Use the vocabulary section of the Organizer. Limit the number of lines of dialogue. Do a complete model. Remind students to think about which tenses they need to use.

Resumen del vocabulario

Usa el vocabulario de este capítulo para:

■ summarize the plot of a movie or television program
■ describe the characters and settings of a movie or television program
■ describe conditions when something happened

to talk about moviemaking
actuar
la actuación
dirigir (g → j)
el director, la directora
la dirección
los efectos especiales
la escena
la fotografía
el guión, pl. los guiones

to talk about various kinds of films
la película de acción
montar a caballo
el caballo
el vaquero, la vaquera
enamorarse (de)
el galán, pl. los galanes
la heroína
arrestar
investigar
matar
robar

el /la criminal
el crimen
el /la detective
el ladrón, pl. los ladrones; la ladrona
el /la policía
la víctima
el científico, la científica
el /la extraterrestre
el monstruo

to talk about natural disasters
dañar
destruyó *(from:* destruir)
el derrumbe
la erupción, pl. las erupciones
el huracán, pl. los huracanes
la inundación, pl. las inundaciones
el terremoto
la tormenta

to summarize movies and TV programs
(estar) basado, -a (en)
tratarse de
el argumento
hacer el papel (de)
el papel

el personaje
principal
tener éxito
el fracaso
ocurrir
el hecho
la información
la violencia
violento, -a
exagerado, -a
excelente
sensacionalista
típico, -a

to talk about TV programs
el comentario (sobre)
la entrevista
el locutor, la locutora
el programa de compras
el programa de concursos
internacional
local

other useful words and expressions
la ayuda
cambiar
esconder(se)
hubo *(from:* haber)
¿Qué tal es...?

 Prueba cumulativa

 Examen de habilidades

 Test Generator

Additional Assessment Options

 Comm. Act. BLMs
Small Group Activities
Situation Cards

 Pasos vivos 2 CD-ROM
Slide Presentation Maker, Video Presentation Maker, Word Processor, Spindle

¿Lo sabes bien? Video Quiz

Internet Activities
Self-Test

CAPÍTULO 11

THEME: THE FUTURE

COMMUNICATION

Topics
Professions

Space

Environment

Recyclables

Objectives
To compare Latin American and U. S. attitudes toward the future

To discuss professions

To discuss career education

To describe homes of the future

To describe the world of the future

To discuss the environment

CULTURE

Latin American attitudes toward the future

GRAMMAR

El futuro

Ancillaries available for use with Chapter 11

Multisensory/Technology

 Overheads, 52–56

 Audio Tapes and CDs

 Vocabulary Art Blackline Masters for Hands-On Learning, pp. 58–62/CD-ROM

 Classroom Crossword

 La Catrina

 Pasos vivos 2 CD-ROM

 Internet Activities www.pasoapaso.com

Print

 Practice Workbook, pp. 105–114

 Writing, Audio & Video Activities, pp. 65–70, 123–125, 171–172

 Communicative Activity Blackline Masters

   Pair and Small Group Activities, pp. 71–76

   Situation Cards, p. 77

 Un paso más: Actividades para ampliar tu español, pp. 61–66

 RESOURCE PRO®

Planning Express, Teaching Resources Library, and Clip Art Library

Assessment

 Assessment Program

   Pruebas, pp. 159–169

   Examen de habilidades, pp. 170–173

 Test Generator

 ¿Lo sabes bien? Video Quiz

Video still from Chap. 11

El año 2000 comienza en febrero

Education is an investment for the future, and many Latin American countries, such as Mexico, have made changes in their educational systems.

The government of Mexico emphasized the connection between education and the future by encouraging parents to register their children in February for the upcoming elementary school year. The 1982 slogan for this campaign was *El año 2000 comienza en febrero.* Prior to this time, students were registered just before the school year, in September. From their first year on, these students will study a comprehensive variety of subjects, including English, which are important to Mexico's success in the areas of technology, health care, tourism, and trade.

During the Salinas de Gortari administration (1988–1994), the country experienced a sweeping educational reform. Course curriculum was updated and the role of the teacher was re-evaluated, along with the relationship of families and school authorities. Another change during this time was the decentralization of the educational system, which gave the individual states more control of the schools.

Science and technology are key to building a competitive economy, and the budget allocated to these areas has increased each year since 1989. More resources have been allocated to the development of public universities and technological institutes. In 1994, 114 technological high schools and 16 higher education institutes were created. CONALEP (Colegio Nacional de Educación Profesional), ITESM (Instituto Tecnológico de Estudios Superiores de Monterrey), and CBTIS (Centro de Bachillerato Técnico Industrial y de Servicios) are a few examples of technological schools. A new alternative, the technological university, is being offered in seven Mexican states.

Although Mexico faces a challenge in providing enough schools to keep up with its population growth, the reform of Mexico's educational system offers hope for the future.

Introduce

Re-entry of Concepts
The following list represents words, expressions, and grammar topics re-entered from Book 1 and Book 2 (Chaps. 2 and 10):

Book 1
school subjects, conservation, recyclable items, environment

Chapter 2
school subjects

Chapter 10
TV and movie character types

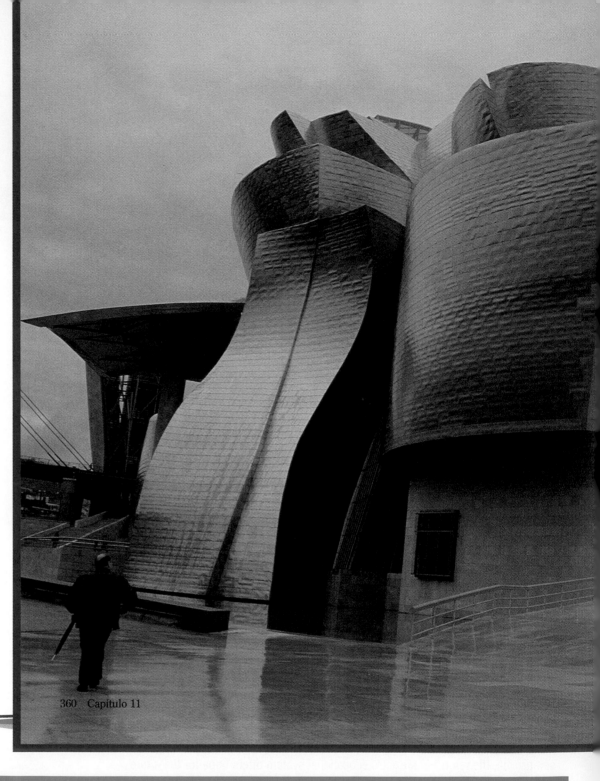

360   Capítulo 11

Planning

Cross-Curricular Connections

Vocational Education Connection *(pp. 364–365)*
In pairs, have students develop a job interview for one of the careers shown. They should include a cover sheet with the preferred educational, professional, and personal qualifications. These can be passed to another pair, who can conduct a mock interview or write a letter of introduction for the job. As follow-up, have each pair write a classified ad for the Classified section. Compile these for use in class review and questioning.

Industrial Arts Connection *(pp. 370–371)*
Have students individually design a poster of a house of the future and label it using vocabulary from Chaps. 8 and 11. They should then write a paragraph describing one room of the house in detail. Both posters and paragraphs could be displayed.

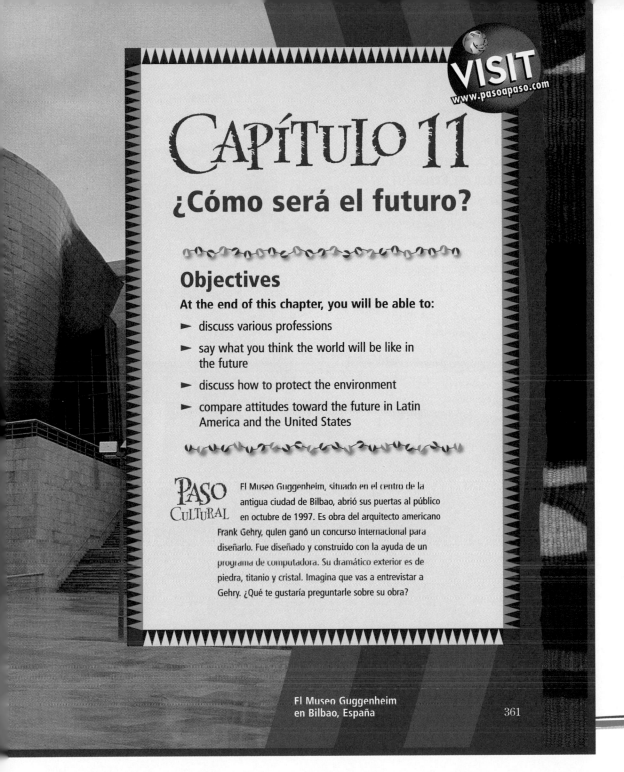

CAPÍTULO 11

¿Cómo será el futuro?

Objectives

At the end of this chapter, you will be able to:

► discuss various professions

► say what you think the world will be like in the future

► discuss how to protect the environment

► compare attitudes toward the future in Latin America and the United States

PASO CULTURAL El Museo Guggenheim, situado en el centro de la antigua ciudad de Bilbao, abrió sus puertas al público en octubre de 1997. Es obra del arquitecto americano Frank Gehry, quien ganó un concurso internacional para diseñarlo. Fue diseñado y construido con la ayuda de un programa de computadora. Su dramático exterior es de piedra, titanio y cristal. Imagina que vas a entrevistar a Gehry. ¿Qué te gustaría preguntarle sobre su obra?

El Museo Guggenheim en Bilbao, España

361

Cultural Notes

Spanish in Your Community
In pairs, have students choose a profession and create a strategy to attract Spanish-speaking customers or clients. They should list five things that they think will influence the local Hispanic communities. Ask local Spanish-speaking merchants or business-people to comment on students' lists.

Paso cultural
Answers will vary.

(pp. 360–361, photo)
The Bilbao Guggenheim Museum houses part of the Solomon R. Guggenheim Foundation's collection of modern and contemporary art. The building's titanium-paneled curves and concrete blocks recall the wharves, slag heaps, and bridges of Bilbao, a former shipbuilding center in the heart of the Basque Country. Ask students: How would you design a museum to blend into your neighborhood or city?

Cultural Objective
• To discuss possible future professions in Spanish-speaking countries

Critical Thinking: Paraphrasing
Have students write a description of the activities in the photographs. As a class, brainstorm ways to describe things for which students have not yet learned the vocabulary. For example, students have not learned the Spanish word for "test tube," but they could paraphrase using *botella larga de vidrio.*

¡Piensa en la CULTURA!

El futuro se enfrenta con el presente en Ecuador, España y México

Mira las fotos. ¿A qué piensas dedicarte en el futuro, o piensas raramente en eso? ¿Te interesa lo que hacen estas personas?

Madrid, España

"¡Está muy bien! Pesa nueve kilos y doscientos gramos."

¿Por qué crees que los médicos pesan casi siempre a sus pacientes? ¿Puedes nombrar una o dos cosas más que hacen los médicos en un chequeo?

"Todavía no sabemos todos los usos que este aceite pueda tener."

¿Te interesan las ciencias? ¿Te gustaría ser médico(a), enfermero(a) o científico(a)? ¿Por qué?

Científicos españoles investigando los usos del aceite de oliva

En una clínica ecuatoriana

Riobamba, Ecuador

362   Capítulo 11

Options

Strategies for Reaching All Students

Spanish-Speaking Students
Ask: *¿Cuál(es) de estas profesiones te interesa(n)? ¿Por qué?*

 Un paso más 11-A

Multiple Intelligences
Verbal/Linguistic
Have students discuss the major health concerns that will remain with us going into the twenty-first century.
Visual/Spatial
See Critical Thinking.

Cultural Notes

(p. 362, top photo)
Olives *(las aceitunas),* so important to Mediterranean culture, have been cultivated since approximately 3500 B.C. Olive oil *(el aceite de oliva)* has multiple uses and is classified by grade, from cooking to industrial quality. Diamond cutters use an abrasive paste of diamond dust and olive oil to polish the facets of newly cut stones. Coin collectors clean rare copper coins by rubbing them with olive oil. Olive trees *(los olivos)* may live as long as 1,500 years.

"¿En qué puedo servirle?"

¿Te interesa algún trabajo de servicio público, como por ejemplo, el de policía, bombero(a) o paramédico(a)? ¿Por qué?

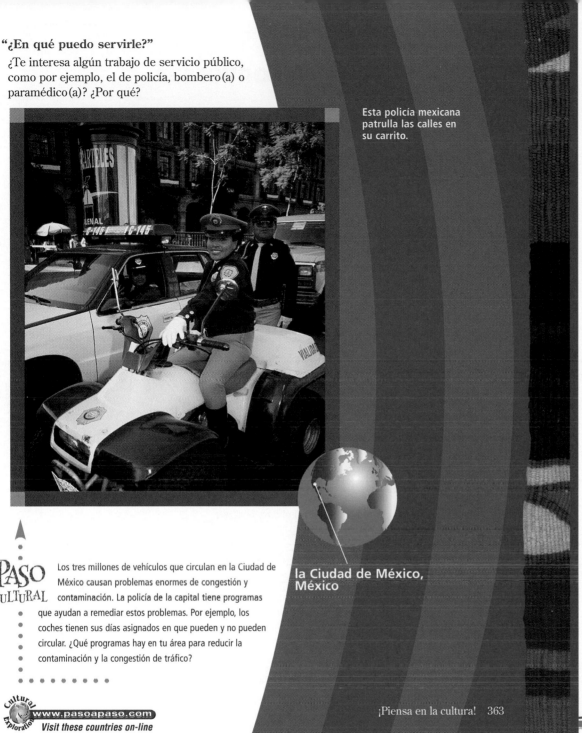

Esta policía mexicana patrulla las calles en su carrito.

la Ciudad de México, México

¡Piensa en la cultura! 363

Present

Chapter Theme
Professions

Communicative Objectives
• To discuss professions
• To discuss career education

 Overheads 52–53

 Vocabulary Art BLMs/CD-ROM

 Vocabulary Tape 11-1

Teaching Suggestions
Preparing students to speak: Use one or two options from each of the categories of Comprehensible Input, Physical Response, or Limited Verbal Response. For a complete explanation of these categories and some sample activities, see pp. T20–T21.

Vocabulario para conversar

¿A qué vas a dedicarte?

Vas a necesitar estas palabras y expresiones para hablar sobre el futuro. Después de leerlas varias veces, practícalas con un(a) compañero(a).

el /la astronauta

el /la deportista

el mecánico, la mecánica

el técnico, la técnica (de computadoras)

el obrero, la obrera

el político, la política

el veterinario, la veterinaria

el escritor, la escritora

la novela

364   Capítulo 11

Options

Strategies for Reaching All Students

Spanish-Speaking Students
Haz una lista de otras profesiones que puedes nombrar.

 Un paso más Ex. 11-B

Students Needing Extra Help
Have students begin to fill in the Vocabulary section of the Organizer. Group the vocabulary by spelling. Put the words that remain the same for both masculine and feminine in one group, those that follow the regular pattern in another group, those that end in a consonant for masculine and -a for feminine in another, etc.

Keep *novela* separate from the occupations. Point out the change in the plural form of *juez.*
También necesitas . . . : Give examples of *dedicarse a.*

Enrichment
As a homework assignment, have students write about three persons they most admire in each of the given professions. Have them explain why they admire each person.

la abogada

el abogado

el juez, *pl.* los jueces

la juez, *pl.* las jueces

el músico, la música

el /la cantante

el bailarín la bailarina

el pintor, la pintora

el hombre de negocios el secretario

la mujer de negocios la secretaria

También necesitas . . .

la ventaja	*advantage*
querer: (yo) quisiera / (tú) quisieras	*I'd like; you'd like*
dedicarse (a)	*to be involved in*

¿Y qué quiere decir . . . ?

la desventaja	la profesión, *pl.*
la educación	las profesiones
el futuro	la tecnología
los negocios	la universidad
la política	ganarse la vida

Vocabulario para conversar 365

Practice

Re-enter / Recycle
Ex. 2: TV and movie character types from Chap. 10

Answers: Empecemos a conversar

1 ESTUDIANTE A

a. ¿Conoces a algún cantante?
b. ...algún bailarín?
c. ...algún veterinario?
d. ...algún obrero?
e. ...algún técnico?
f. ...algún hombre de negocios?
g. Questions will vary.

ESTUDIANTE B

a.–g. Answers will vary, but should include *(No) conozco a....*

Empecemos a conversar

Túrnate con un(a) compañero(a) para ser *Estudiante A* y *Estudiante B*. Reemplacen las palabras subrayadas en el modelo con palabras representadas o escritas en los recuadros. Si ven 💡 pueden dar su propia respuesta.

1

A — *¿Conoces a algún dentista?**
B — *Sí, conozco a uno(a) / muchos(as).*
   o: *No, no conozco a ninguno.*

¡NO OLVIDES!

Do you remember these words for professions?
el actor, la actriz
el bombero, la bombera
el / la dentista
el / la detective
el director, la directora (de cine, de orquesta, de una escuela)
el locutor, la locutora (de radio, de televisión)
el enfermero, la enfermera
el médico, la médica
el / la policía
el profesor, la profesora

Estudiante A   Estudiante B

a.   b.   c.
d.   e.   f.   g.

*Note that whenever we make a general statement about a profession we use a masculine singular noun.

366   Capítulo 11

Options

Strategies for Reaching All Students

Spanish-Speaking Students
Exs. 1–4: Pair bilingual with non-bilingual students, if possible.

Students Needing Extra Help
Ex. 1: Give additional examples of the footnote. Remind students that the asterisk is not part of the spelling. Review *ninguno* and the *a personal*.
Ex. 2: Give students time to pair the appropriate responses and fill in the *jugar* blank. Remind them to use the appropriate form, depending on the gender of the person with whom they are speaking, when they see the male and the female writer.

Enrichment
Ex. 1: You may want students to expand on this exercise by giving a person's name: *¿Conoces a algún dentista? Sí, conozco a uno, el doctor Fernández; trabaja en... Sí, conozco a una, la doctora Gómez; trabaja en....*

2

A —¡Ah! ¿Entonces eres *escritor(a)*?
B —Sí, me dedico a *escribir novelas*.

Estudiante A

a.

b.

c.

d.

e.

f.

g.

Estudiante B

dar las noticias en el canal 7

enseñar física en la universidad

escribir novelas

hacer negocios en un banco

investigar crímenes

jugar ___

reparar coches

Vocabulario para conversar   367

2 **ESTUDIANTE A**
a. ¡Ah! ¿Entonces eres deportista?
b. ...detective?
c. ...mujer / hombre de negocios?
d. ...mecánico(a)?
e. ...científico(a)?
f. ...locutor(a)?
g. Questions will vary.
ESTUDIANTE B
a. Sí, me dedico a jugar ___.
b. ...investigar crímenes.
c. ...hacer negocios en un banco.
d. ...reparar coches.
e. ...enseñar física en la universidad.
f. ...dar las noticias en el canal 7.
g. Answers will vary.

Ex. 3: As a follow-up to this exercise, write the following sentences on the chalkboard, calling on students to complete them: *Para ser científico(a) es necesario ser muy ___. También hay que sacar buenas notas, especialmente en estas materias: ___.*
Point out that students should name personality traits for the first sentence.

Extended Written Practice/Homework
1. Write two pairs of sentences of advice concerning what subjects one should study for different professions: *Si quieres ser . . . es importante estudiar . . . También debes dedicarte a . . .*
2. Choose a profession or occupation that interests you for the future. Write three sentences telling what you would like to be and what you would like to do in this profession or occupation.

Multiple Intelligences
Verbal/Linguistic
1) Have students write brief descriptions of their possible future professions and read them to the class. Have them make up new professions for the twenty-first century.
2) See Exs. 1–2.

Practice & Apply

Re-enter / Recycle
Ex. 4: TV and movie character types from Chap. 10
Ex. 5: school subjects from Chap. 2

Answers: Empecemos a conversar

3 ESTUDIANTE A
a. ¿Te interesan los negocios?
b. . . . interesa la música?
c. . . . interesa la tecnología?
d. . . . interesa la medicina?
e. . . . interesa la educación?
f. Questions will vary.

ESTUDIANTE B
a. Sí, quisiera ser hombre / mujer de negocios / trabajar en una oficina; *or* no me interesan los negocios.
b. . . . ser músico(a) / bailarín (bailarina) / cantante *or* no me interesa la música.
c. . . . ser técnico(a) *or* no me interesa la tecnología.
d. . . . ser médico(a) / enfermero(a) / trabajar en un hospital; *or* no me interesa la medicina.
e. . . . ser profesor(a) / trabajar en una escuela / universidad; *or* no me interesa la educación.
f. Answers will vary.

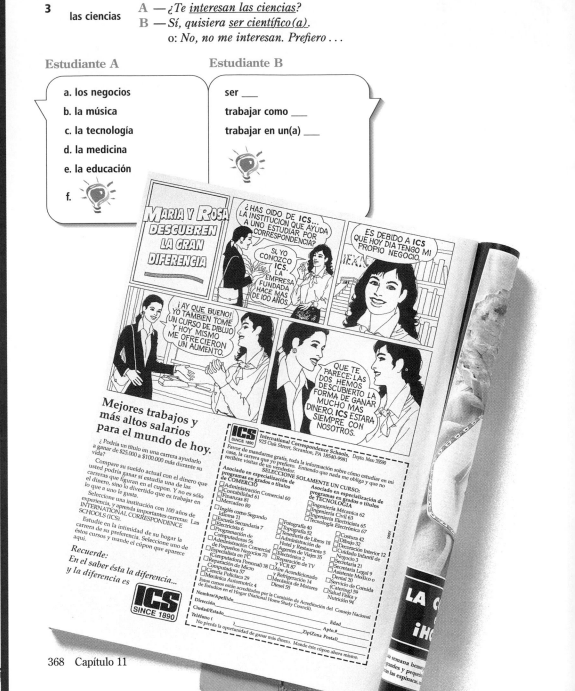

3 las ciencias
A — ¿Te *interesan las ciencias*?
B — Sí, quisiera *ser científico(a)*.
o: *No, no me interesan. Prefiero . . .*

Estudiante A
a. los negocios
b. la música
c. la tecnología
d. la medicina
e. la educación
f.

Estudiante B
ser ___
trabajar como ___
trabajar en un(a) ___

368 Capítulo 11

Options

Strategies for Reaching All Students

Spanish-Speaking Students
Ex. 7: *¿Qué profesiones crees que no se necesitarán en el futuro? ¿Por qué?*

 Un paso más Ex. 11-C

Students Needing Extra Help
Ex. 3: Model using a singular subject. Complete the blanks in the *Estudiante B* response. Do the exercise once using the affirmative response, then again using the negative response after modeling a completed *Prefiero* statement.
Ex. 4: Brainstorm the vocabulary for the *Estudiante B* responses and why people choose the careers they do.
Ex. 5: Review *escolares* and *mejores*.

If available, use the vocabulary section of the Book 2, Chap. 1 Organizer.
Ex. 6: Point out the connections between students' interests and a career. Brainstorm possible answers to the *¿Por qué?* question.
Ex. 7: Use the vocabulary section of the Organizer. Brainstorm with students which professions will be important in the future, and the advantages and disadvantages of each. Model possible answers for the *¿Por qué?* question.

4 detective / bombero(a)

A —¿Te gustaría ser *detective* o *bombero(a)*?

B —*Bombero(a)* porque quiero dedicarme a *ayudar a la gente.*

o: *Ni detective ni bombero(a). Quisiera ser...*

Estudiante A

a. mecánico(a) / técnico(a) de computadoras

b. astronauta / científico(a)

c. hombre (mujer) de negocios / abogado(a)

d. enfermero(a) / médico(a)

e. político(a) / juez

f. actor (actriz) / locutor(a)

g. cantante / bailarín (bailarina)

h.

Estudiante B

Empecemos a escribir

Escribe tus respuestas en español.

5 ¿Cuáles son tus actividades favoritas? ¿Qué materias escolares te gustan más? ¿En qué materias sacas las mejores notas?

6 ¿En qué profesiones podrías hacer lo que más te interesa? ¿Qué es más importante para ti, una profesión que te gusta mucho o una en que ganas mucho dinero? ¿Por qué? ¿Te gustaría ir a la universidad o a una escuela técnica? ¿Qué quisieras estudiar? ¿Cómo te gustaría ganarte la vida?

7 En tú opinión, ¿qué profesiones son mejores para el futuro? ¿Por qué? ¿Cuáles son las ventajas y desventajas de esas profesiones?

¿A ti te gustaría diseñar juguetes para niños?

La Nave, centro de diseño en Valencia, España

MORE PRACTICE

- Más práctica y tarea, p. 558
- Practice Workbook 11–1, 11–2

También se dice

el trabajador, la trabajadora

el bailador, la bailadora
el / la danzante

el cantador, la cantadora

Vocabulario para conversar   369

Present

Chapter Theme
Changes in the future

Communicative Objectives
- To describe homes of the future
- To describe the world of the future
- To discuss the environment

 Overheads 54–55

 Vocabulary Art BLMs/CD-ROM

 Vocabulary Tape 11-2

Grammar Preview
Habrá, tendrán, and *será* are presented here lexically. The paradigm of future-tense verbs is on p. 379.

Teaching Suggestions
Preparing students to speak: Use one or two options from each of the categories of Comprehensible Input, Physical Response, and Limited Verbal Response. For a complete explanation of these categories and some sample activities, see pp. T20–T21.

Class Starter Review
On the day following the presentation of vocabulary, you might begin the class with this activity: Ask students to list five features

Vocabulario para conversar

¿Qué cambios habrá en el futuro?
Aquí tienes el resto del vocabulario que necesitas en este capítulo para hablar sobre el futuro.

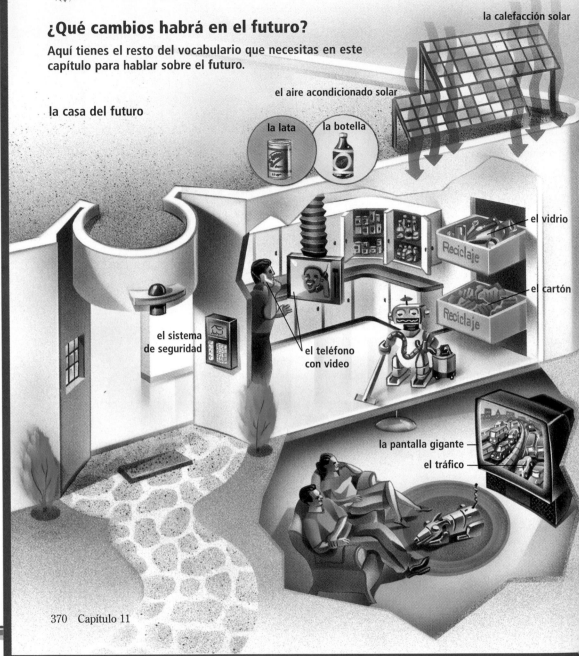

370   Capítulo 11

Options

Strategies for Reaching All Students

Spanish-Speaking Students
Añade otras palabras relacionadas a este tema a tu vocabulario personal. Mira la casa del futuro. ¿Qué te gustaría tener en tu propia casa? ¿Por qué? ¿En cuál de las actividades para proteger el medio ambiente crees que debemos todos participar? ¿Por qué?

 Un paso más Ex. 11-D

Students Needing Extra Help
Remind students who used Book 1 that they have seen some of these words before. *También necesitas . . . :* Review the present, preterite, and imperfect forms of *haber.*

Learning Spanish Through Action
STAGING VOCABULARY: *Levanten*
MATERIALS: Vocabulary Art BLMs/CD-ROM
DIRECTIONS: After copying and cutting the appropriate Vocabulary Art BLMs, distribute to students. Give a message to transmit to outer space describing life on Earth. Have students hold up pictures of the items as you mention them in the message.

el espacio

el planeta

la Luna

la paz

la guerra

el océano

la Tierra

el río

el bosque

También necesitas . . .

el medio ambiente	*environment*	
por supuesto	*of course*	
echar	*to throw out; to dump*	
gastar	*here: to waste*	
haber: habrá	*there will be*	
ser: (él / ella) será	*he / she / it will be*	
tener: (Uds. / ellos / ellas) tendrán	*you / they will have*	

¿Y qué quiere decir . . . ?

automático, -a	el ser humano
económico, -a	contaminar
eficiente	explorar
gigante	reciclar
solar	reducir *(c →zc)*
el cambio	separar

Vocabulario para conversar   371

that will make the house of the future better than present-day houses.

Multicultural Perspectives

The rain forests of Costa Rica are an invaluable resource, as evidenced by the findings of U.S. botanist Monie S. Hudson. Of the more than 1,500 rain forest plants examined by Hudson, 15 percent were found to be possible anti-cancer agents. To save these plants, and the many others that may have medicinal value, the Costa Rican government has instituted two unique programs. "Debt for nature" is an agreement between Costa Rica and its lender nations forgiving the country's foreign debt in exchange for the promise that rain forests will be set aside as protected national parks. Another program teaches farmers how to re-use land instead of clearing rain forest. This is accomplished through controlled watering, and the planting of indigenous trees to prevent soil erosion and loss of nutrients. Ask students how we can help conserve the rain forests, and what they think rain forests may provide for us in the twenty-first century.

www Internet Activities

Juegos

Extended Written Practice/Homework
1. Choose three vocabulary items from pp. 370–371 and tell about your family's practices or if you have these items already in your home: *Mi familia y yo ya reciclamos botellas de vidrio.*
2. Refer to pp. 230–231 and 370–371 and write three sentences naming features that your house in the future will have: *En el futuro, mi casa tendrá . . .*

3. Write four sentences saying what we should or should not do to protect the environment. Consider using: *deber, es importante, es necesario, hay que, tener que.*

Multiple Intelligences
Bodily/Kinesthetic
See Learning Spanish Through Action.

Logical/Mathematical
Have students make a list of ways that technology makes household chores easier. Then have them add to their lists possible future technological innovations for the home.
Verbal/Linguistic
See Vocabulary Tape 11-2.
Visual/Spatial
See Overheads 54–55, the Vocabulary Art BLMs/CD-ROM, and Class Starter Review.

Practice & Apply

Answers: Empecemos a conversar

8 ESTUDIANTE A

a. ¿Te parece que en todas las casas del futuro habrá teléfonos con video?
b. ... habrá sistemas de seguridad?
c. ... habrá robots?
d. ... habrá aire acondicionado solar?
e. ... habrá pantallas gigantes?
f. ... habrá microondas?
g. Questions will vary.

ESTUDIANTE B

a.–g. Answers will vary.

9 ESTUDIANTE A

a. ¿Crees que es importante explorar los planetas?
b. ... el espacio?
c. ... el océano?
d. ... las ruinas?
e. ... la selva?

ESTUDIANTE B

a.–e. Answers will vary.

Empecemos a conversar

8

A — ¿Te parece que en todas las casas del futuro habrá *calefacción solar*?
B — ¡Por supuesto, *es mucho más económico*!
  o: *Creo que no, pero . . .*

Estudiante A

a. b. c.
d. e. f. g.

Estudiante B

es mucho más económico

es mucho más eficiente

será mejor para el medio ambiente

será más divertido

es necesario protegerse de los ladrones

9

A — ¿Crees que es importante explorar *la Luna*?
B — *Sí, por supuesto.*
  o: *No. Pienso que hay cosas más importantes. Por ejemplo, debemos . . .*

Estudiante A

a. b. c.
d. e.

Estudiante B

Options

Strategies for Reaching All Students

Spanish-Speaking Students
Exs. 8–9: Pair Spanish-speaking students if possible.
Ex. 10: Have students write out this exercise using declarative statements instead of questions and answers: *Para reducir la basura, podemos reciclar las botellas.*
Ex. 13: *¿Te gustaría explorar el espacio? ¿Por qué? ¿Adónde te gustaría ir?*

 Un paso más Ex. 11-E

Students Needing Extra Help
Ex. 8: Help students recall *calefacción central* from Chap. 7 with the given artwork. Encourage them to use a response from the *Estudiante B* list rather than *Creo que no.*
Ex. 9: Brainstorm possible responses. Discourage use of the *por supuesto* response.
Ex. 10: Explain why the participle is not paired with a form of *estar.*
Ex. 12: Brainstorm possible vocabulary.

Ex. 13: Emphasize that *humano* is a part of *el ser humano.* Point out the meaning of *enviar* in this context. Brainstorm possible responses to the *¿Por qué?* question.
Ex. 14: Do this exercise as a whole class, emphasizing the vocabulary used.
Ex. 15: If available, use the vocabulary section of the Book 1, Chap. 13 Organizer, as well as the Organizer from this chapter. Refer to Ex. 10.

10 reducir la basura

A — ¿Cómo podemos _reducir la basura_?
B — _Reciclando las botellas._

Estudiante A

a. reducir el tráfico
b. no gastar agua
c. conservar energía
d. no contaminar el aire
e. proteger el océano
f. no dañar la selva
g.

Estudiante B

¡NO OLVIDES!

Do you remember these words for talking about the environment?
el agua
la energía
la luz, _pl._ las luces
ahorrar
conservar
la electricidad
eléctrico, -a

Empecemos a escribir y a leer

Escribe tus respuestas en español.

11 ¿Qué profesión te gustaría tener? ¿Una profesión tradicional o una más moderna? ¿Cuál?

12 ¿Es más importante resolver los problemas de la Tierra o explorar el espacio? ¿Por qué piensas así?

13 ¿Debemos enviar a seres humanos o a robots a explorar los planetas? ¿Por qué?

14 ¿Crees que siempre habrá guerra en la Tierra? ¿Es posible tener paz en el futuro? En grupos pequeños, hagan una lista de lo que podemos hacer para tener paz. Después, todos juntos, hablen de las listas que hicieron.

15 Aquí tienes unas reglas _(rules)_ para proteger el medio ambiente. Con un(a) compañero(a), léelas y escribe otras dos en cada categoría.

Para proteger el medio ambiente en la Tierra, debemos:
• hacer más bosques
• ir a pie o usar bicicletas

No debemos:
• usar tanto papel
• echar basura en los ríos, lagos y océanos

Después, todos juntos, hagan un cartel para la sala de clases. Pueden ponerle fotos y dibujos.

También se dice

el tránsito

www.pasoapaso.com

MORE PRACTICE

Más práctica y tarea, p. 558
Practice Workbook 11–3, 11–4

Vocabulario para conversar 373

10 ESTUDIANTE A
a. ¿Cómo podemos reducir el tráfico?
b. . . . no gastar agua?
c. . . . conservar energía?
d. . . . no contaminar el aire?
e. . . . proteger el océano?
f. . . . no dañar la selva?
g. Questions will vary.
ESTUDIANTE B
a.–g. Answers will vary.

Answers: Empecemos a escribir y a leer
11–14 Answers will vary.

15 Answers will vary, but may include:
Debemos reducir la basura y reciclar el vidrio.
No debemos usar tanta electricidad ni contaminar el aire.

 Practice Wkbk. 11-3, 11-4

 Audio Activity 11.2

 Writing Activities 11-B, 11-C

 Pruebas 11-3, 11-4

Enrichment
Ex. 8: In groups of three, have students discuss the following question and report their findings to the class. _¿Te parece que el ser humano será muy diferente en el futuro? ¿Cómo cambiará?_ Guide students to consider changes that medical or technological advances may bring.
Ex. 10: As a homework assignment, have students write about their community's effort to protect the environment. Suggest the following questions to help them get started: _¿Hay camiones en tu comunidad que recojan cosas que se pueden reciclar? ¿Qué hace tu comunidad para reducir el tráfico? ¿Qué hace para proteger el medio ambiente? ¿Qué problemas están causando las fábricas de los Estados Unidos y de otros países en el norte de México?_
Ex. 13: Additional questions: _¿Para qué trabajos crees que un robot sirve mejor que un ser humano? ¿Por qué piensas así? ¿Qué trabajos crees que un robot nunca podrá hacer? ¿Por qué piensas así?_

Multiple Intelligences
Verbal/Linguistic
See Enrichment and Audio Activity 11.2.
Verbal/Linguistic and Interpersonal/Social
See Exs. 8–10.
Visual/Spatial
See Practice Wkbk. 11-3 and 11-4 and Writing Activities 11-B and 11-C.

Practice

¡Comuniquemos!

Aquí tienes otra oportunidad para usar el vocabulario de este capítulo.

1 Dile a un(a) compañero(a) qué profesión crees que debe tener él o ella en el futuro. Dile también por qué piensas así.

A — *Yo creo que debes ser . . .*
B — *¿ ___ ? ¿Yo? ¡Nunca! ¿Por qué lo dices?*
A — *Pues, porque . . .*
B — *. . .*

2 Con un(a) compañero(a), hablen de las ventajas y desventajas de varias profesiones. Hablen de:

- cuánto tiempo hay que estudiar
- en qué y cuánto hay que trabajar
- cuánto dinero se puede ganar
- si es interesante o no y por qué
- si sirve para el futuro y por qué

Options

Strategies for Reaching All Students

Spanish-Speaking Students
Ex. 3: Have students write out this exercise. Afterwards, have them conduct a survey. *Haz una encuesta. Pregúntales a tus compañeros sobre la profesión que quieren seguir despúes de terminar sus estudios. Luego, en un cartel, indica qué profesiones escogen y cuántos las escogen. Presenta tu información a la clase.*

Students Needing Extra Help
Ex. 1: As a class, generate a list of careers and the qualities, interests, and talents needed to succeed in them. Model an example.
Ex. 2: Limit the number of professions to five. You might divide the class into five groups and have each discuss one profession. Have materials available that will help students complete this activity. Or you might just choose one profession and do as a whole class.

Ex. 3: Brainstorm in order to develop two ideas about each topic. Do a complete model. Students may need help articulating their ideas.
¿Qué sabes ahora?: Have students write this so they can record their progress.

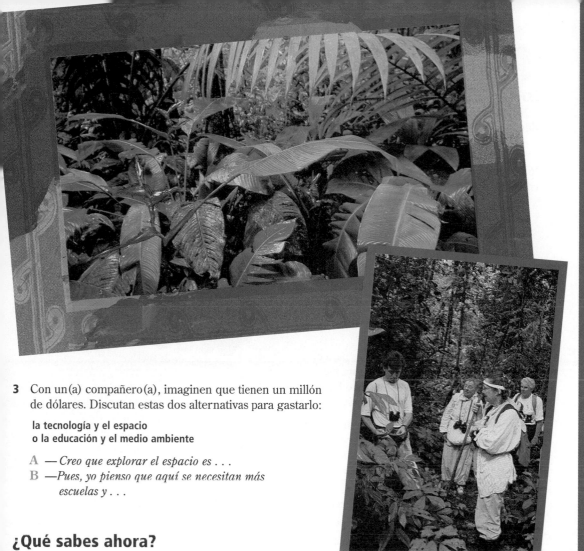

3 Con un(a) compañero(a), imaginen que tienen un millón de dólares. Discutan estas dos alternativas para gastarlo:

**la tecnología y el espacio
o la educación y el medio ambiente**

A — *Creo que explorar el espacio es . . .*
B — *Pues, yo pienso que aquí se necesitan más escuelas y . . .*

¿Qué sabes ahora?

Can you:

■ **discuss professions?**
  —Me gustaría ser ___ y trabajar en ___.

■ **say what you think the world will be like in the future?**
  —Creo que en las casas del futuro habrá ___ y ___.

■ **talk about protecting the environment?**
  —Creo que debemos ___ todos los (todas las) ___.

En la selva del Río Napo, Ecuador

Vocabulario para conversar   375

Answers: ¿Qué sabes ahora?
Answers will vary, but may include:
• hombre (mujer) de negocios / un banco
• teléfonos con video / sistemas de seguridad
• reciclar / periódicos (latas)

 Audio Activity 11.3

 Comm. Act. BLM 11-1

 Pasos vivos 2 CD-ROM
Boom Box, Clip Art Album, Notas culturales, Slide Projector, Laboratorio de grabar

Strategies for Reaching All Students
MULTIPLE INTELLIGENCES
Interpersonal/Social and Bodily/Kinesthetic
See Cooperative Learning.
Interpersonal/Social and Verbal/Linguistic
See Exs. 1–3.
Verbal/Linguistic
See Audio Activity 11.3.
Visual/Spatial
See Comm. Act. BLM 11-1.

Cultural Notes ☀

Cooperative Learning
In groups of four, have students create a brochure for a recycling center. Each student is responsible for a paragraph about one recyclable: *el papel, el cartón, las latas,* or *el vidrio.* Students should include the following information: advantages of recycling that item, how much money the recycled item is worth, and how the recycled material will be used afterwards. Display the finished brochures.

(p. 374, realia)
Banco Santander, Spain's largest banking group, has branches throughout Europe. The bank offers the *Cuenta ahorro infantil* for children from birth to 18 years of age. These accounts feature high interest, a monthly gift of age-appropriate books, and donations to the Spanish affiliate of the World Wildlife Fund. After age 18 until age 26, the account may be converted to a *Cuenta ahorro joven* for continued special savings.

(p. 375, photos)
The greatest diversity of plant and animal life exists in rain forests, found in tropic and subtropic regions. Over 2,000 species of trees, including hardwoods such as rosewood, mahogany, ebony, and teak, are found in the rain forests of Latin America. Some of these trees may reach heights of 150 feet or more. Some plants common to rain forests are bromeliads, orchids, and ferns.

Present & Apply

Cultural Objective

- To compare Latin American and U.S. attitudes toward the future

Answers

Answers to inductive questions will vary, but students may say that it is important to make plans for the future to ensure that it turns out well. Students may say that the young people in the photos may choose to continue studying in the respective fields pictured, and that the parade queen may do community work.

Answers: La cultura desde tu perspectiva

1 Answers will vary, but students may say that, in general, Americans view the future as nearby and controllable, while Latin Americans view it as further away and often beyond their control.

Perspectiva cultural

¿Crees que es importante hacer planes para el futuro? ¿Qué crees que los jóvenes en estas fotos piensan hacer después de terminar la escuela secundaria?

Aprendiendo a tocar la trompeta en una escuela en España

Rubén, un joven norteamericano, está hablando con Ricardo, un costarricense.

RUBÉN   Estudiar en la universidad es muy caro. Por eso, cuando nací, mis padres abrieron una cuenta de ahorros para mis gastos universitarios.

RICARDO   Los míos tienen algunos ahorros, pero no tienen ninguna cuenta bancaria especial para mis estudios. Yo no sé si estudiaré en los Estados Unidos o en Costa Rica.

(Los latinoamericanos hacen planes para el futuro, pero generalmente no para un futuro lejano. Por ejemplo, normalmente no hacen planes especiales para los gastos universitarios.)

RUBÉN   Además, mis padres no me permiten gastar todo lo que gano cortando céspedes cada verano. Una gran parte de ese dinero es para pagar mis estudios.

RICARDO   ¿Ahorras dinero para tus estudios?

RUBÉN   Sí. ¿En Costa Rica no lo hacen?

RICARDO   No es muy común. No cuesta mucho ir a la universidad allá. ¿Sabes ya lo que vas a estudiar?

RUBÉN   Sí, química. Pienso ser ingeniero químico. ¿Y tú?

RICARDO   Quizás estudiaré derecho.

RUBÉN   ¿Quieres ser abogado?

RICARDO   Realmente no, pero en Costa Rica es más fácil ser ejecutivo en una gran compañía si eres abogado.

376 Capítulo 11

Una estudiante de arquitectura en Guadalajara

Las universidades latinoamericanas dan mucha importancia a los estudios humanísticos, como la filosofía, la literatura y el arte. También dan importancia a las profesiones tradicionales, como el derecho y la medicina. Por eso, muchas veces un graduado no practica la profesión que estudió.

La cultura desde tu perspectiva

1 ¿Cómo crees que muchos norteamericanos ven el futuro?

2 ¿Qué ventajas y desventajas ves en la manera que tienen los latinoamericanos de ver el futuro?

Cultural Activity   www.pasoapaso.com

En Nueva York, una locutora entrevista a la reina del desfile dominicano.
(inset) Este joven de Málaga, España, quizás será locutor.

Options

Strategies for Reaching All Students

Spanish-Speaking Students

Ask: *¿Cómo piensas prepararte para el futuro? ¿Vas a seguir estudiando? ¿Cómo pagarás los gastos? ¿Crees que es importante hacer planes para el futuro? ¿Por qué?*

 Un paso más Ex. 11-F

Students Needing Extra Help

Have students take notes for use in the *¿Lo sabes bien?* section.
Ex. 1: Discuss in depth the cultural differences in terms of saving money for college, knowing what you want to study, and actually working in that field.
Ex. 2: Brainstorm the advantages and disadvantages with the whole class. Write two lists on the chalkboard.

Enrichment

Ex. 1: Additional questions: *¿Por qué crees que los norteamericanos ven el futuro de esa manera? ¿Qué ideas hay en la cultura norteamericana que influyen ese punto de vista?*

Multiple Intelligences

Visual/Spatial and Verbal/Linguistic
See Using Photos.

2 Answers will vary, but may include: Advantages: Latin Americans can enjoy living in the present and accept whatever the future brings. Disadvantages: They are not as prepared for changes in fortune and they could miss opportunities.

Encourage students to discuss what there might be in U.S. history that encourages long-range planning, and what in Latin American history might cause someone to live from day to day. Possible answers: The U.S. has a history of stable government, while Latin American history shows frequent changes in government that were usually beyond the control of the average citizen. In addition, students may mention a U.S. sense that one's destiny is within one's own control, while many Latin Americans hold a deeply religious acceptance of life as it is.

Using Photos
Give the following assignment:
Escribe un diálogo corto entre la locutora y la reina del desfile.

 Pasos vivos 2 CD-ROM

Maps

 Internet Activities

Perspectiva cultural

Cultural Notes ☀

(p. 376, top photo)
Originally from the U.S., jazz music is becoming increasingly popular in Spain. Two major jazz festivals, both held in July, are in Vitoria and San Sebastián. Artists from all over the world perform for thousands of fans in concert halls and on the streets. The festivals are supported by the government and the private sector, and there are radio and television transmissions of the concerts.

(p. 376, bottom photo)
Increasingly, women are entering such previously male-dominated fields as architecture. At the Universidad de Guadalajara, for example, 30 percent of the students in *la facultad de arquitectura* are women.

(p. 377, photo)
Every summer, floats and marchers stream along Madison from 38th St. to 55nd St. in the annual Dominican parade. Many of New York's 350,000 Dominicans live in the Washington Heights neighborhood between 168th St. and 190th St. Dominican immigration to New York began in the early 1960s and increased during the 1970s and 1980s. Dominicans are the second-largest Hispanic group in New York City after Puerto Ricans.

Preview

Overhead 56

Teaching Suggestions
B: You may want to point out the verb forms *será, harán,* and *habrán*. Help students figure out that they come from the infinitives *ser, hacer,* and *haber.*

Answers
A The Spanish infinitives are *vivir(emos), vivir(án), estudiar(á), dormir(án), trabajar(án). /* The endings *-emos, -án, -á* have been added to the infinitives. The future is being talked about. / *Comerán.*

B The infinitive is *tener que.* The word that follows it is *dirigir.* The infinitive is *poder.*

Gramática en contexto

Una estación espacial en el año 2002

¿Viviremos en el espacio algún día? ¿Podremos viajar a las estrellas fácilmente? Algunos científicos norteamericanos dicen que el espacio será nuestro.

Diseño de una estación espacial (1994)

El primer paso será la construcción de una estación espacial en el año 2002. Se harán experimentos de biología y se estudiará el medio ambiente. Al principio, los científicos tendrán que dirigir la estación desde la Tierra.

Pero luego, seis astronautas vivirán allí. Dormirán en la nave y trabajarán en la estación. El proyecto costará mucho dinero, pero si tiene éxito, habrá bases en la Luna y, más tarde, se harán viajes a Marte.

A Some of the verb forms in this article contain an infinitive. Can you find the Spanish infinitives for *live, study, sleep,* and *work?* Now look at the complete forms. What has been added to the infinitive? What period of time is being talked about? What verb form do you think you would use to tell what the astronauts will eat?

B Now look for the expression *tendrán que.* What do you think the infinitive is? What word follows it? Look for the verb *podremos.* What do you think the infinitive is?

378   Capítulo 11

Options

Strategies for Reaching All Students

Students Needing Extra Help
Begin the grammar section of the Organizer.
A: Emphasize that the infinitive is contained within another verb form. Review subject pronouns.
B: Tell students that *tendrán* and *podremos* are irregular, and to look at the first three letters of the words to find a clue to the infinitive.

El futuro: Point out to students that this is the first time they are adding something to the infinitive, rather than taking something away. Give further examples of the two ways students already know to express future tense. Stress the written accents. Write some regular infinitives on the chalkboard and have students conjugate them in the future tense.

Extended Written Practice/Homework
1. Choose three of the following verbs and write sentences saying whether or not we will do positive things to protect our environment in the future: *echar, ahorrar, reciclar, reducir, proteger, separar. En el futuro reciclaremos todas las cajas de cartón.*
2. Choose a friend or family member and predict his or her future using three or more of these verbs: *vivir, ser, dedicarse, ganar, estudiar, ir.*

378   Standards 1.2; 3.1; 4.1

El futuro

You have learned two ways to talk about future events. One way is by using the present tense with a time expression.

El tren **sale** a las dos.

The other way is by using *ir a* + infinitive.

Este sábado **voy a reciclar** todas las botellas.

A third way is to use the future tense. For most verbs, the stem for the future tense is the infinitive, so learning this tense is easy.

En el futuro, la gente **vivirá** en la Luna.

Here are all the forms of *hablar*, *aprender*, and *vivir* in the future tense. Note that all three kinds of verbs have the same endings.

hablar

hablar**é**	hablar**emos**
hablar**ás**	hablar**éis**
hablar**á**	hablar**án**

aprender

aprender**é**	aprender**emos**
aprender**ás**	aprender**éis**
aprender**á**	aprender**án**

vivir

vivir**é**	vivir**emos**
vivir**ás**	vivir**éis**
vivir**á**	vivir**án**

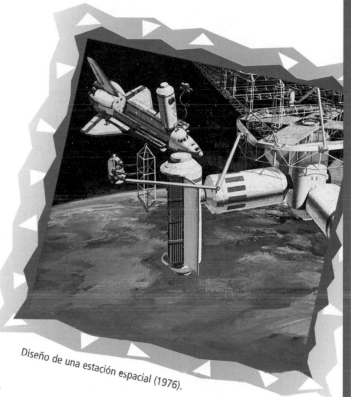

Diseño de una estación espacial (1976).

• Note that all the forms need a written accent except the *nosotros / nosotras* form.

Gramática en contexto   379

Present

Class Starter Review
On the day following presentation of the future tense, you might begin the class with this activity: In pairs, students take turns saying what they will do next summer. Have them continue until they find three things they both plan to do, and three they both plan not to do. Have students write their sentences out and share them with the class.

Present & Practice

Answers

1 ESTUDIANTE A

a. ¿Vivirás solo(a) después de la escuela secundaria?

b. ¿Irás a la universidad . . .

c. ¿Te dedicarás a . . .

d. ¿Serás . . .

e. ¿Aprenderás a . . .

f. ¿Ganarás . . .

g. ¿Te casarás . . .

h. ¿Echarás . . .

i. Questions will vary.

ESTUDIANTE B

a.–i. Answers will vary, but should include the correct *yo* form in the future tense.

2 ESTUDIANTE A

a. ¿Qué será Andrés en el futuro?

b. . . . seremos Miguel y yo . . .

c. . . . serán tus hermanas . . .

d. . . . serás (tú) . . .

e. . . . serán Uds. . . .

f. . . . será Claudia . . .

g. . . . será tu hermano . . .

h. . . . seré (yo) . . .

ESTUDIANTE B

a. Creo que será veterinario. Trabajará en una clínica de animales.

b. Creo que seremos escritores. Escribiremos una novela.

c. Creo que serán deportistas. Correrán en los Juegos Olímpicos.

d. Creo que seré astronauta. Exploraré nuevos planetas.

---

1 ¿Qué vas a hacer después de la escuela secundaria? Pregunta y contesta según lo que piensas hacer.

trabajar

A — *¿Trabajarás después de la escuela secundaria?*
B — *Sí, trabajaré en un banco.*
   o: *No. Pienso . . .*

a. vivir solo(a)

b. ir a la universidad

c. dedicarse a . . .

d. ser . . .

e. aprender (a) . . .

f. ganar tu propio dinero

g. casarse

h. echar en la basura todos los cuadernos escolares

i.

2 Di qué serán estas personas en el futuro. Después, escoge elementos de la lista y di lo que harán. Pregunta y contesta según el modelo.

Sonia

A — *¿Qué será Sonia en el futuro?*
B — *Creo que será música. Tocará en una orquesta.*

proteger a las víctimas de crímenes
trabajar en una clínica de animales
dirigir un banco
correr en los Juegos Olímpicos

explorar nuevos planetas
reparar calefacciones solares
escribir una novela
servir al país

a. Andrés   **b. Miguel y yo**   **c. tus hermanas**   **d. (tú)**

e. Uds.   **f. Claudia**   **g. tu hermano**   **h. (yo)**

380   Capítulo 11

Options

Strategies for Reaching All Students

Students Needing Extra Help

Ex. 1: Give another model using a reflexive verb. Remind students to change the verb form when answering questions. Brainstorm possibilities for the blanks in *c, d,* and *e.* Have students vary their answers, and discourage use of the negative response.

Ex. 2: You may want to write the paradigm of *ser* in the future tense. Point out that in the future it is completely regular. Review future endings. Use the vocabulary section of the Organizer. Allow time for students to

match the columns before they start the exercise.

Ex. 3: Brainstorm possible resolutions. Point out that each statement is in the *yo* form and should reflect their own thinking.

El futuro: continuación: Students may need to see the complete paradigms of these irregular verbs. Give additional examples of *si* + a regular verb in the present tense.

Ex. 4: Model using a non-reflexive verb. Have students do all except *g,* which you can do as a whole-class activity.

Enrichment

Ex. 1: In groups of four, have students interview one another on aspects of their daily routine tomorrow. Tell students to ask the following questions and write down the answers to report to the rest of the class: *¿A qué hora te levantarás mañana? ¿A qué hora te ducharás o bañarás? ¿A qué hora te acostarás?* Call on representatives to report each group's responses.

3 Es el fin de año. Dile a un(a) compañero(a) cinco resoluciones que vas a hacer para el año nuevo. Por ejemplo:

Estudiaré por lo menos una hora y media todos los días.

El futuro: continuación

The verbs *tener, poder, saber,* and *hacer* have irregular stems in the future tense: *tendr-, podr-, sabr-, har-.* The endings, however, are the same as for regular verbs.

Si viajas al espacio, **¿tendrás que** llevar un traje especial?
Claro, **tendré que** llevar un traje de astronauta.

¿Podrás ver la Tierra desde la Luna?
Sí, creo que **podré** verla.

¿Sabrás qué hacer en caso de emergencia?
Sí, me parece que **sabré**.

¿Harás informes todos los días?
Pienso que **haré** muchos informes.

- *Habrá* is the future of *haber*. The future stem is *habr-*.

  ¿Crees que en el futuro **habrá** una comunidad de seres humanos en el espacio?

- The future is often used with *si* + a verb in the present tense.

  Si viajas al espacio, **¿tendrás que** comer comida especial?

4 ¿Cómo será el futuro? Forma frases con los siguientes elementos.

**(nosotros) /
poder verse en los
teléfonos con video**

*En el futuro, podremos vernos
en los teléfonos con video.*

a. (tú y yo) / poder vivir debajo del océano
b. las familias / hacer viajes en coches solares
c. los científicos / saber más sobre los otros planetas
d. un robot / hacer todos nuestros quehaceres
e. nuestro planeta / no tener bastante comida para todos
f. nuestros océanos / tener menos contaminación
g. haber ciudades en el espacio

Gramática en contexto 381

¡NO OLVIDES!

Like *hay, había,* and *hubo, habrá* is used only in the singular.

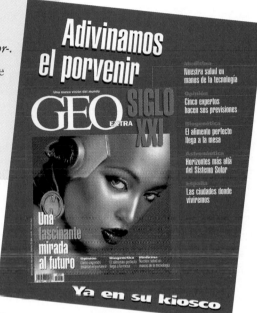

---

e. Creo que seremos mécanicos. Repararemos calefacciones solares.
f. Creo que será mujer de negocios. Dirigirá un banco.
g. Creo que será político. Servirá al país.
h. Creo que serás abogado(a). Protegerás a las víctimas de crímenes.

3 Answers will vary, but should include the future tense.

4 a. En el futuro, (tú y yo) podremos vivir debajo del océano.
b. ...las familias harán viajes en coches solares.
c. ...los científicos sabrán más sobre los otros planetas.
d. ...un robot hará todos nuestros quehaceres.
e. ...nuestro planeta no tendrá bastante comida para todos.
f. ...nuestros océanos tendrán menos contaminación.
g. ...habrá ciudades en el espacio.

 **Practice Wkbk.
11-5, 11-6**

 **Writing Activities
11-D, 11-E**

 Pruebas 11-5, 11-6

Ex. 4: As a homework assignment, have students write five other ways in which the future will be different, using the verbs *tener, poder, saber,* and *hacer.* Encourage students to be creative and to use as much of their vocabulary as possible.

Extended Written Practice/Homework
1. Write three sentences telling what you believe will happen next year at your school. Refer to pp. 89 and 157 for ideas: *Mis amigos escribirán para la revista literaria.*

2. Write three sentences comparing what an athlete, movie star, and musician do now vs. what they will do in the future: *Ahora Shaquille O'Neal juega básquetbol. En el futuro será abogado y sabrá ayudar a los jugadores de básquetbol.*

**Multiple Intelligences
Interpersonal/Social and Verbal/Linguistic**
See Exs. 1 and 3.
Visual/Spatial
See Practice Wkbk. 11-5 and 11-6 and Writing Activities 11-D and 11-E.

Cultural Notes

(p. 381, realia)
This ad for the popular science magazine *Geo* is alluring to readers on various levels. First, on the level of the articles it contains, which deal with the promising future of health, food, travel, and cities. Second, on the level of beauty–the physical appeal of the robot model in the ad, and the artistic design of the ad itself. Discuss with students the choice of words, type, color, and other elements in this ad.

Practice

Answers

5 Questions will vary, but should include the future tense and an interrogative word.

6 Answers will vary, but should include the present tense in the first part and the future tense in the second part of the sentence.

Multicultural Perspectives

According to data from the U.S. Census Bureau, the Hispanic population grew by 53 percent between 1980 and 1990, to a total of over 22 million. At its current rate of growth, it will double by the year 2020—making it the single largest minority group in the U.S. Because it is increasing faster than any other ethnic group, it affects the educational programs in such large states as California, Texas, and Florida, as well as in such cities as New York and Chicago. Bilingual and bicultural programs are in great demand. Teachers who study how LEP (Limited English Proficient) students learn in a second-language classroom, in addition to their chosen field of education, often earn significantly higher salaries and have an easier time finding work after graduation. Ask students how they think knowing Spanish will help them in their chosen career.

5 Con un(a) compañero(a), hagan los papeles de un escritor y un científico en una entrevista sobre el futuro. Escojan un elemento de cada columna para hacer por lo menos siete preguntas. Por ejemplo:

ESCRITOR — *¿Dónde podremos echar la basura?*
CIENTÍFICO — *No tendremos basura, por supuesto.*
  La reciclaremos.

¿Quién?	hacer
¿Qué?	tener
¿Cómo?	haber
¿Cuándo?	poder
¿Dónde?	saber

En el parque de Chapultepec piden a la gente que recicle.

También piden que la gente proteja el parque.

6 Combina elementos de las dos columnas para hacer frases como la siguiente.

si mi papá me presta el coche   *Si mi papá me presta el coche, tú y yo iremos (o: podremos ir) a la playa mañana.*

a. si te interesa la tecnología
b. si compro un sistema de seguridad
c. si hay seres extraterrestres
d. si trabajo todo el verano
e. si viajas al espacio
f. si hay paz en la Tierra
g. si se puede vivir en la Luna
h. si pensamos en el medio ambiente
i. si reducimos la contaminación
j. 💡

tú
tú y yo
yo
nosotros / nosotras
(nombre)
(dos nombres)

382   Capítulo 11

Options

Strategies for Reaching All Students

Students Needing Extra Help
Ex. 5: Brainstorm possible phrases to link with the infinitives. Do as a whole class activity.
Ex. 6: Brainstorm possible responses to the *si* clauses. Do as a whole class activity.
Ahora lo sabes: Have students write this so that they can record their progress.

Extended Written Practice/Homework
1. Write three sentences about your privileges and responsibilities after high school. Use: *tener que, poder, hacer. Después de graduarme, podré salir con mis amigos todas las noches.*
2. Write three sentences telling what you think your community will be like in the future: *En el futuro, mi comunidad tendrá más negocios de tecnología.*

Multiple Intelligences
Naturalist
Have students make a list of possible future environmental changes in their area: *Habrá menos árboles y más casas en el futuro.*
Verbal/Linguistic
See Ex. 5 and Audio Activities 11.4 and 11.5.
Visual/Spatial
See Practice Wkbk. 11-7, 11-8, and 11-9; Writing Activities 11-F and 11-G; and Comm. Act. BLMs 11-2 and 11-3.

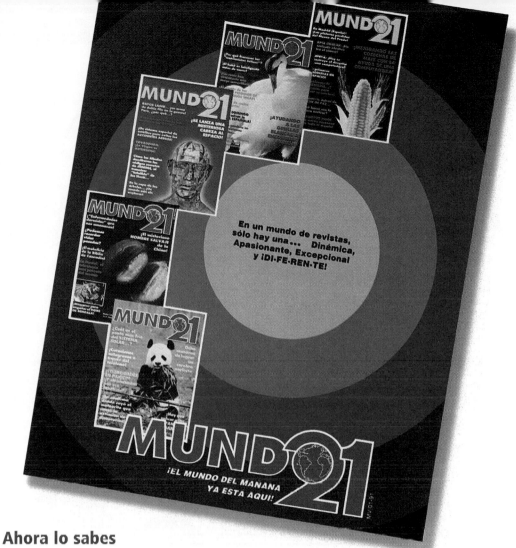

En un mundo de revistas, sólo hay una... Dinámica, Apasionante, Excepcional y ¡DI-FE-REN-TE!

MUNDO 21
¡EL MUNDO DEL MAÑANA YA ESTÁ AQUÍ!

Using Realia

Ask: *¿Por qué se llama "Mundo 21" esta revista? ¿De qué se trata?*

Answers: Ahora lo sabes
- estudiaré
- seré / seremos
- iré

 Practice Wkbk.
11-7, 11-8, 11-9

 Audio Activities
11.4, 11.5

 Writing Activities
11-F, 11-G

 Pruebas 11-7, 11-8

 Comm. Act. BLMs
11-2, 11-3

 Pasos vivos 2
CD-ROM

Bulletin Board, Slide Presentation Maker, Spindle, Treadmill

Ahora lo sabes

Can you:

- say what will happen in the future?
  —El próximo año (yo) ___ química.
- say what you and your friends will be in the future?
  —Yo ___ médico(a) y dos de nosotros(as) ___ abogados(as).
- talk about possibilities in the future?
  —Si tengo tiempo mañana, ___ al centro comercial.

> ### MORE PRACTICE
>
> Más práctica y tarea, p. 559
> Practice Workbook 11–5, 11–9

Gramática en contexto   383

Cultural Notes

(p. 383, realia)
The magazine *Mundo 21* presents contemporary science-related news with an eye to possible future changes in such social institutions as food production, health care, family life, education, transportation, ecology, and communications.

Apply

 Video Activity A

Using the Video

Episode 11 begins in Silvestre Aguilar's office at La Jacaranda. His lawyer, who has read La Catrina's will, tells him that Jamie probably has legal rights to the inheritance. Silvestre responds angrily and sends his bodyguards to Jamie's house to look for the will. Santana can be seen outside Silvestre's office, listening.

In the next scene, Felipe and María choose a movie and watch it at María's house. After the movie, they talk about their future.

Later, as María and Jamie are getting ready for bed, one of Silvestre's bodyguards enters the house and rummages through the drawers of a desk. María and Jamie drive him out of the house and Santana helps chase him away. The will is still safe because Jamie had hidden it.

 La Catrina: Capítulo 11

Play

Actividades

1 Formen grupos. Díganle a su grupo lo que quisieran ser en el futuro. Cada miembro les dará un consejo *(advice)*.

    A —*Quisiera ser . . .*
    B —*Si quieres ser . . . tendrás que . . .*
    C —*Para ser . . . , habrá que estudiar . . .*
    D —*Podrás . . .*

2 ¿Cómo será el futuro de tus compañeros(as) de clase? Dividan la clase en cuatro grupos. Cada grupo va a predecir el futuro de los miembros de otro grupo.

Juan escribirá una novela.
Julia será veterinaria, por supuesto.

3 ¿Qué cambios crees que son necesarios para tener un futuro mejor? En grupo, escriban frases como la siguiente:

Si el sistema escolar tiene más dinero, tendremos mejor educación.
Si hay paz en la Tierra, . . .
Si vamos a la Luna, . . .
Si . . .

384   Capítulo 11

Options

Strategies for Reaching All Students

Spanish-Speaking Students
Exs. 1–2: If possible, have one Spanish-speaking student in each group.
Ex. 3: If possible, group Spanish-speaking students together.

 Un paso más Ex. 11-G

Students Needing Extra Help
Ex. 1: Give a complete model. As a class, generate a list of careers and the qualities, interests, and talents needed to succeed in them.
Ex. 2: Brainstorm phrases and write them on the chalkboard. Let students match them up with their classmates. Encourage creativity.
Ex. 3: Brainstorm some *si* clauses. Students may need help articulating their thoughts about the future.

Enrichment
As a homework assignment, have students write about one of the following topics: *Para eliminar el racismo (las armas, la delincuencia, el desempleo, las drogas, la pobreza), tendremos que . . .*

Candombe, cuadro del pintor uruguayo Pedro Figari (1861–1938)

Conexiones

¿Qué pasará aquí?

En este cuadro se ve una escena de fines del siglo diecinueve en Montevideo, Uruguay. Míralo con un(a) compañero(a).

1 Describe qué están haciendo los personajes del cuadro. Puedes hacer una tabla como la siguiente.

Personajes	¿Qué están haciendo?
Los bailarines	están bailando
El músico	está . . .
El hombre detrás de la ventana	
Las mujeres delante de la puerta	

2 Imagina qué va a pasar después del baile. Agrega *(Add)* una tercera columna a la tabla: *¿Qué harán los personajes después?* Usa tu imaginación para llenar *(fill in)* esa columna para cada uno de los personajes.

3 En grupos de cinco o seis, túrnense para leer sus descripciones del futuro de la escena.

4 Cada grupo escogerá las dos descripciones más imaginativas y las leerá a la clase.

Todo junto   385

 Video Activity B

 Para entender mejor

Play

 Video Activity C

Answers: Actividades
1–3 Answers will vary, but should include a wide variety of chapter vocabulary and correct use of the present and future tenses where appropriate.

Answers: Conexiones
1. El músico está tocando percusión.
El hombre detrás de la ventana está mirando la fiesta.
Las mujeres delante de la puerta están charlando.
2. Answers will vary, but look for logical predictions and use of the future tense.
3–4. Descriptions will vary.

 Writing Activity 11-H

 Comm. Act. BLMs 11-4, 11-5

 Pasos vivos 2 CD-ROM
A Jugar, Laboratorio de grabar, Maps, Video Monitor, Video Presentation Maker

Cooperative Learning
In groups of five, have students envision their community in the year 2200. Each student gives three predictions about one of the following areas: housing, schools, transportation, environment, and energy. Have them make a captioned poster illustrating how they predict their community will look.

Multiple Intelligences
Interpersonal/Social and Bodily/Kinesthetic
See Cooperative Learning.
Interpersonal/Social and Verbal/Linguistic
See Ex. 1.
Visual/Spatial
See Using the Video, Enrichment, *Conexiones,* Writing Activity 11-H, and Comm. Act. BLMs 11-4 and 11-5.

Cultural Notes

(p. 385, photo)
This painting is part of a series by Uruguayan artist Pedro Figari (1861–1938) on the ritual dances of Candombe, an African religion. Figari is known for his paintings of rural and social themes and for his brilliant use of color. He had no formal artistic training and did not begin displaying his work until he was sixty. Ask students: Name other artists you know who have painted on the same themes and used color in a similar way.

Apply

Process Reading
For a description of process
reading, see p. 52.

Answers
Antes de leer
Answers will vary, but may
include: the use of lightweight
materials, an aerodynamic front, a
solar panel that can be adjusted to
best capture the sun's rays, rear-
wheel drive, and a weight of 180
kilograms.

Mira la lectura
Answers will vary, but may include
the following cognates: *materiales,
aerodinámica, panel solar orientable, tracción, kilogramos*

¡Vamos a leer!

Antes de leer

STRATEGY ➤ Using prior knowledge

Look at the photo of this energy-efficient solar-
powered car. List in English four or five features
relating to energy sources and body design that
it might have.

Mira la lectura

STRATEGY ➤ Scanning

Now scan the selection to see if you can find
Spanish cognates of the features you listed.
Write them next to the corresponding English
terms on your list.

Tonatiuh, el hijo del Sol para los aztecas, dio
su nombre al primer automóvil solar
mexicano. El coche Tonatiuh fue diseñado
por un grupo de jóvenes universitarios que
querían ayudar a controlar el alto nivel de
contaminación de muchos lugares en México.
El proyecto está basado en la alta eficiencia y
en el uso de fuentes renovables de energía.
Por eso se usaron materiales ligeros y se
diseñó un área frontal aerodinámica que
ofrece muy poca resistencia al viento.

El chasis está hecho de fibras compuestas
que pueden soportar un conjunto pesado de
baterías y toda la electrónica. Tiene un panel
solar orientable, es decir, que se puede
mover para recibir los rayos del Sol. Tiene
tres ruedas y tracción en la de atrás. Pesa
alrededor de 180 kilogramos. El proyecto
costó aproximadamente 150 mil dólares.

Tonatiuh:
Automóvil Solar

386   Capítulo 11

Options

Strategies for Reaching All Students

Spanish-Speaking Students
*Aplicación: ¿Crees que un coche solar será
práctico? ¿Por qué? ¿Qué te gustaría cambiar en el coche que se describe aquí para
hacerlo más práctico? Explica.*

Students Needing Extra Help
Discuss car model names (Bronco, Pinto,
Mustang, etc.). Brainstorm why manufactur-
ers name their cars this way. Background
knowledge will be very limited for some students. Discuss some basic background
material before the actual reading.
Infórmate: Students may be unfamiliar with
the English word "to orient." Model its use
and give synonyms.

Infórmate

STRATEGIES Using cognates
Understanding suffixes

1 There are many cognates in this selection that will help you understand it. Among them are the words *renovables* and *orientable*. *Renovable* is formed from the verb *renovar*. It has the same Latin root as the adjective *nuevo*. Given what you know of prefixes (*re-*) and suffixes (*-able*), what do you think *renovable* means?

In the same way, *orientable* is formed from the verb *orientar*. What do you think it means?

2 Now list in Spanish the three most important features of the solar car. Compare your list with that of a partner. Discuss any differences in your lists and agree on one set of the most important features.

PASO CULTURAL

El tren eléctrico AVE (alta velocidad española) puede llegar a más de 350 kilómetros por hora. Hay 28 trenes AVE que salen todos los días de la Estación de Atocha en Madrid y llegan en dos horas y quince minutos a la Estación de Santa Justa en Sevilla. Hay trenes de alta velocidad en varios otros países, por ejemplo, Francia y Japón. ¿Te gustaría tener acceso a un tren como el AVE donde tú vives? ¿Por qué crees que no hay más trenes en los Estados Unidos?

Tren de alta velocidad española

Aplicación

Think about the features of the car described in this selection and, with a partner, compare them to corresponding features of cars you are familiar with.

¡Vamos a leer! 387

Infórmate

1. renewable, movable (can be positioned to capture the sun's rays)
2. Answers will vary, but may include the following:
Usa materiales ligeros.
El chasis está hecho de fibras compuestas.
El coche tiene un panel solar orientable.

Aplicación
Answers will vary.

 Internet Activities

Cultural Notes ☀

Paso cultural
Answers will vary, but students may mention the fact that transportation in the U.S. is dominated by the automobile: *En los Estados Unidos casi todos tienen coche.*

(p. 387, photo)
The inauguration of *el tren de alta velocidad española* (AVE) coincided with the opening of the Expo 92 in Sevilla. The state-of-the-art AVE is similar to Japan's Shinkansen Supertrains and France's TGV.

Apply

Teaching Suggestions
Ex. 1: Be sure to display all the descriptions on a bulletin board so that students who are doing the second writing task can choose one.

Process Writing
For information regarding developing a writing portfolio, see p. 54.

Todo junto

¡Vamos a escribir!

Los aparatos electrónicos de hoy están cambiando. ¿Cómo será el televisor del futuro? ¿La radio? ¿El teléfono? Vamos a describirlos.

1 Primero, escoge un aparato y piensa en cómo será en el futuro. Dibuja el aparato. Luego, escribe una breve descripción según este modelo. Pídele comentarios a un(a) compañero(a) y sigue los otros pasos del proceso de escribir. Por ejemplo:

APARATO:	teléfono con video de bolsillo
DESCRIPCIÓN:	un teléfono celular con una pantalla pequeña
VENTAJAS:	las personas que hablan se pueden ver; tamaño de bolsillo; no daña el medio ambiente
COSTO:	30 dólares

388   Capítulo 11

Options

Strategies for Reaching All Students

Students Needing Extra Help
Have students use the vocabulary section of the Organizer from Chap. 7. Brainstorm ways that some of these appliances could be modified in the future. Do the exercise in pairs or small groups. Try to group an artistic student, a mechanically inclined student, and a strong language student together.

Ex. 2: Students may need help with the vocabulary. Present a paragraph based on the information given in the model. Discourage students from keeping their ideas in list form, rather than a paragraph.

Enrichment
Have students list *aparatos electrónicos* that are common in homes today, but that were rare or nonexistant twenty years ago *(video-caseteras, hornos microondas, teléfonos celulares,* etc.).

2 Ahora lee todas las descripciones y escoge uno de los aparatos del futuro. Piensa en los cambios sociales que traerá. Por ejemplo, el videoteléfono traerá los siguientes cambios:

- Las personas que se conocen no necesitarán identificarse.
- Será necesario peinarse y maquillarse antes de hablar con alguien que no conoces.
- Las familias se sentirán más unidas.

Escribe un párrafo breve sobre los cambios que traerá el aparato.

3 Para distribuir su trabajo, pueden:

- enviar las descripciones y los ensayos al periódico o a la revista escolar
- coleccionarlos en un libro titulado *Nuestro futuro electrónico*
- exhibirlos en la sala de clases
- incluirlos en sus portafolios

**Multiple Intelligences
Visual/Spatial**
See Enrichment.

Assess & Summarize

Test Preparation
You may want to assign parts of this section as written homework or as an in-class writing activity prior to administering the *Examen de habilidades*.

Answers
Listening: *No sé a qué profesión me dedicaré. Me gusta escribir, pero los escritores no ganan mucho. También me gusta cantar y bailar, pero la vida de una cantante o bailarina no será fácil. Mi hermana prefiere las ciencias. Le gustan los animales. Ella será médica o veterinaria.*
High-school courses recommended for the speaker: creative writing, English, literature, chorus, dancing; courses recommended for the speaker's sister: science courses, especially biology.

Reading: The ad is for a large-screen TV; *combinar, adaptar;* to combine, to adapt

Writing: Interviews will vary.

Culture: Answers will vary, but should include the information that a Latin American is less likely than a North American to make long-range plans.

Speaking: Dialogues will vary.

Esta sección te ayudará a prepararte para el examen de habilidades, donde tendrás que hacer tareas semejantes.

Listening
Can you understand when people talk about professions? Listen as your teacher reads a sample similar to what you will hear on the test. What high-school courses would you recommend to the speaker? And to her sister?

Reading
Óscar is reading an ad in his favorite magazine. What is the ad for? What verbs do *combinable* and *adaptable* come from? What do the verbs mean?

El futuro ya llegó.

Tiene una pantalla gigante de 41 pulgadas.

Tiene control remoto.

Tiene ajuste automático de color y de sonido.

Combinable con sus videojuegos y adaptable al cable.

La pantalla se puede colgar de la pared o montarse en el aparato.

¡Llévese el futuro a casa por sólo 725 dólares!

Writing
Can you interview a scientist about the planet Earth in the year 3000? Write three more questions like the following one. Then write a logical answer to each.

1. ¿En qué tipo de casa vivirá la gente en el año 3000?

Culture
Can you compare how a North American and a Latin American might plan for the future?

Speaking
Create a dialogue in which you talk to your partner about a possible future career.

A — *¿A qué piensas dedicarte?*
B — *Pienso estudiar para ser abogado.*
A — *Necesitarás estudiar por muchos años, ¿no?*
B — *Sí, pero trabajaré mientras estudio. Y tú, ¿cómo te ganarás la vida?*
A — . . .

Self Test www.pasoapaso.com

390 Capítulo 11

Options

Strategies for Reaching All Students

Students Needing Extra Help
Have students write out this exercise so that they can check off what they have mastered. *Lo sabes bien:* Remind students that this is only a sample of the actual test.
Listening: Read more than once. Remind students that they did something similar to this in *Todo junto,* Ex. 1. Brainstorm for what words students should be listening.

Reading: Review cognates. Remind students that they did something similar in *Infórmate* in the *¡Vamos a leer!* section.
Writing: Have students use the Organizer to write a sample interview before the test. Point out that they have to answer the questions they create. Remind them that they did something similar in Exs. 4–5, pp. 381–382.

Culture: Have students review the notes they took during the first reading of the *Perspectiva cultural.* Give them time to gather their ideas.
Speaking: Use the vocabulary section of the Organizer. Limit the number of lines of dialogue. Give a complete model. Remind students to think about which tenses they need to use.

Resumen del vocabulario

Usa el vocabulario de este capítulo para:

■ discuss various professions
■ say what you think the world will be like in the future
■ discuss how to protect the environment

to discuss professions
la profesión, *pl.* las profesiones
el abogado, la abogada
el /la juez, *pl.* los /las jueces
el político, la política
la política
el /la astronauta
el bailarín, la bailarina
el /la cantante
el músico, la música
el escritor, la escritora
la novela
el pintor, la pintora
el /la deportista
el mecánico, la mecánica
el obrero, la obrera
el técnico, la técnica
  (de computadoras)
la tecnología
el hombre de negocios,
  la mujer de negocios
los negocios
el secretario, la secretaria
el veterinario, la veterinaria

to talk about career education
la educación
la universidad
la ventaja
la desventaja
dedicarse (a)
ganarse la vida

to describe homes of the future
la pantalla gigante
el sistema de seguridad
el teléfono con video
automático, -a
económico, -a
eficiente
gigante
solar

to describe the world of the future
el cambio
el futuro
la guerra
la paz
el espacio
la Luna
el planeta

el ser humano
la Tierra
explorar

to discuss the environment
el medio ambiente
el bosque
el océano
el río
la botella
el cartón
la lata
el tráfico
el vidrio
contaminar
echar
gastar
reciclar
reducir *(c → zc)*
separar

other useful words and expressions
querer: (yo) quisiera,
  (tú) quisieras
por supuesto

Resumen 391

Assessment

 Prueba cumulativa

 Examen de habilidades

 Test Generator

Additional Assessment Options

 Comm. Act. BLMs

Small Group Activities
Situation Cards

 Pasos vivos 2 CD-ROM
Slide Presentation Maker, Video
Presentation Maker, Word
Processor, Spindle

 ¿Lo sabes bien? Video Quiz

Internet Activities
Self-Test

CAPÍTULO 12

THEME: TRAVEL

COMMUNICATION

Topics

Tourism

Customs

Air travel

Places in an airport

Objectives

To compare accommodations in Spain with those in the U.S.

To discuss travel arrangements

To describe a plane trip

To discuss tourist accommodations

To discuss tourist activities

CULTURE

Accommodations in Spain

GRAMMAR

Repaso: Los mandatos afirmativos con tú

Los mandatos negativos con tú

Los mandatos negativos: continuación

Ancillaries available for use with Chapter 12

Multisensory/Technology	Print	Assessment

Multisensory/Technology

 Overheads, 57–61

 Audio Tapes and CDs

 Vocabulary Art Blackline Masters for Hands-On Learning, pp. 63–67/CD-ROM

Classroom Crossword

La Catrina

 Pasos vivos 2 CD-ROM

 Internet Activities www.pasoapaso.com

Print

 Practice Workbook, pp. 115–124

 Writing, Audio & Video Activities, pp. 71–76, 126–128, 173–174

 Communicative Activity Blackline Masters

  Pair and Small Group Activities, pp. 78–83

  Situation Cards, p. 84

 Un paso más: Actividades para ampliar tu español, pp. 67–72

 RESOURCE PRO

Planning Express, Teaching Resources Library, and Clip Art Library

Assessment

 Assessment Program

  Pruebas, pp. 174–183

  Examen de habilidades, pp. 184–187

 Test Generator

 ¿Lo sabes bien? Video Quiz

Video still from Chap. 12

International Travel

When planning a trip to a foreign country, it is important to know what documentation is needed. Most countries require travelers to present their passports in order to obtain a tourist visa, which authorizes visits lasting from a few weeks to several months. Some span a period of several years, and allow multiple entries with the same visa. Some countries require the visa to be secured before departure, while others allow tourists to obtain one at the port of entry. It is always best to check with a travel consultant, airline representative, or consulate agent to verify entrance requirements to a particular country.

Once the destination has been decided and the entrance requirements fulfilled, the next step is to determine how to actually travel to that country. Many Spanish-speaking countries have their own international airlines which provide direct service from major U.S. cities like New York, Chicago, Los Angeles, Houston, or Miami. More flights to Latin America leave from Miami than any other U.S. city. The only major difference between airports in the U.S. and those in Latin America is that when the plane lands, passengers usually disembark on the runway and walk or take a shuttle bus to the customs area.

Spain and Latin America offer an impressive variety of places to visit. Spain presents historical sites and artifacts dating back to before the Roman Empire. Some of the most notable buldings are the *alcázares,* palaces built by the Arabs who occupied Spain for nearly 800 years. Aside from these historical treasures, some of the most popular beaches in Europe are found along Spain's Costa del Sol, as well as fine ski resorts in the Sierra Nevada and Pyrenees. Locations to visit in Latin America include complex pre-Columbian archeological sites such as Chichén Itzá in Mexico, Tikal in Guatemala, and Machu Picchu in Peru. Many of the objects originally found at these sites are now displayed in museums in Mexico City, San José, Costa Rica, Bogotá, and Lima. Colorful marketplaces, particularly Chichicastenango in Guatemala and Otavalo in Ecuador, are popular with tourists looking for authentic native crafts. Beautiful colonial architecture, blending the seventeenth and eighteenth century Spanish styles with that of the indigenous people, appears throughout Central and South America. Two of the best examples are found in Guadalajara, Mexico: the Palacio de Gobierno and the Templo de Aranzazú. For the sports enthusiast, ski resorts in the southern Andes are open from June through August, and scuba-diving off the coast of Mexico's Yucatán peninsula and Honduras' Roatán Island is available year-round.

Tourism is a major industry in Spain and Latin America. Both government and private agencies can provide information and tours to accommodate anyone's travel interests.

Introduce

Re-entry of Concepts

The following list represents words, expressions, and grammar topics re-entered from Book 1 and Book 2 (Chaps. 8 and 11):

Book 1
time-telling, leisure-time activities, nature items, recyclables

Chapter 8
places in a community

Chapter 11
nature
recyclables

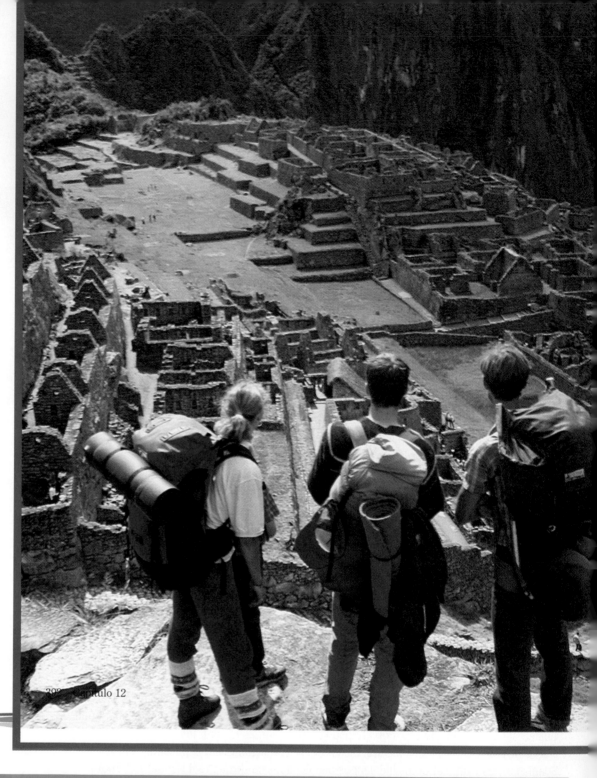

392 Capítulo 12

Planning

Cross-Curricular Connections

Mathematics and Geography Connection *(pp. 406-407)*
In pairs, have students choose one Latin American country. They are to make a train or plane schedule listing trips between the capital and five major cities. The schedule should include the cities, their distances from the capital in kilometers, arrival and departure times using the 24-hour clock, and the fare amount in the currency of that country. These can be passed to other groups or photocopied for the whole class

to use in question-and-answer sessions or to practice travel vocabulary.

Geography Connection *(pp. 410–411)*
In pairs, have students choose a favorite monument, either in the U.S. or in another country. They will prepare a travel guide, either in poster or brochure form. This should include a short tour, which takes the tourists through the monument's different rooms or points out its features and tells of its historical or cultural significance.

Students should use command forms and preterite and imperfect tenses as needed.

Spanish in Your Community
In small groups, have students create a poster to attract Spanish-speaking tourists to their community. Posters should include a "town motto" and written descriptions of four places in the community that tourists would want to visit. Display posters around the class or have volunteers ask Spanish-speaking store owners if they would like to display them.

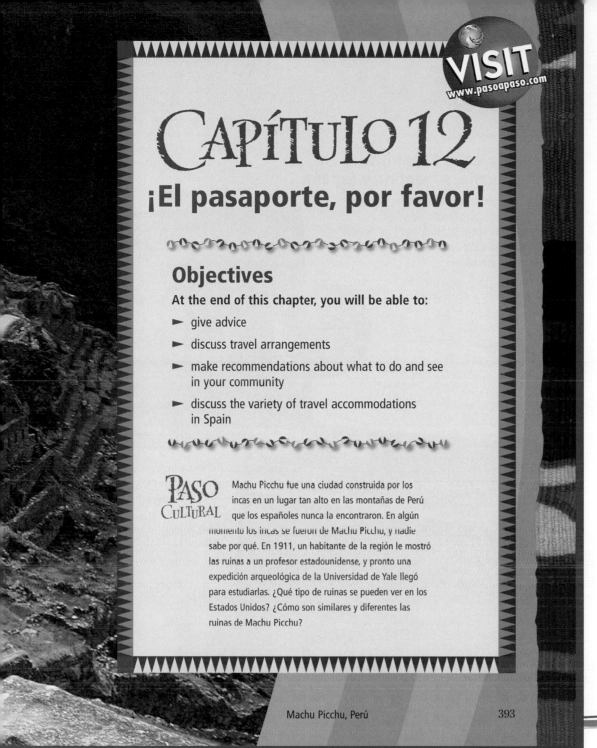

CAPÍTULO 12
¡El pasaporte, por favor!

Objectives

At the end of this chapter, you will be able to:

► give advice

► discuss travel arrangements

► make recommendations about what to do and see in your community

► discuss the variety of travel accommodations in Spain

PASO CULTURAL

Machu Picchu fue una ciudad construida por los incas en un lugar tan alto en las montañas de Perú que los españoles nunca la encontraron. En algún momento los incas se fueron de Machu Picchu, y nadie sabe por qué. En 1911, un habitante de la región le mostró las ruinas a un profesor estadounidense, y pronto una expedición arqueológica de la Universidad de Yale llegó para estudiarlas. ¿Qué tipo de ruinas se pueden ver en los Estados Unidos? ¿Cómo son similares y diferentes las ruinas de Machu Picchu?

Machu Picchu, Perú   393

Strategies for Reaching All Students
MULTIPLE INTELLIGENCES
Naturalist
Have groups of students make a travel brochure for Machu Picchu. Have them include information such as the location and setting, the "discovery" in 1911, and the various theories about the functions of the site for the Incas.

Cultural Notes ☀

Paso cultural
En los Estados Unidos se ven los túmulos *(burial mounds)* en muchas partes del este del país y los pueblos de escalamiento *(cliff dwellings)* del suroeste. Machu Picchu está en un lugar escondido *(hidden)* como los pueblos de escalamiento, pero en los Estados Unidos no se puede ver ruinas tan grandes como las de Machu Picchu.

(pp. 392–393, photo)
These three hikers are looking northwest across the main ruins of Machu Picchu to the peak of Huayna Picchu. They may have arrived by train from Cuzco, as do many tourists visiting Peru's most famous Incan ruins, or they may have hiked. More adventurous visitors elect to take the four-day walk, passing through or near other Incan ruins. Visitors to Machu Picchu (8,000 feet) and Cuzco (11,500 feet) must let their bodies adjust to the high altitudes before exerting themselves. Altitude sickness *(soroche)* can cause dizziness, headaches, nausea, body pains, and troubled breathing.

Preview

- To discuss travel in Spanish-speaking countries

Multicultural Perspectives

By A.D. 718, the Moors had conquered nearly all of the Iberian Peninsula, and would occupy it for 700 years. As a result, Moorish culture greatly affected that of Spain. For example, Arabic-language influences are present in place names, such as the Andalusian (Al-Andaluz) towns of Almería, Alicante, and Algeciras. Many Spanish agricultural, architectural, administrative, and commercial terms also come from Arabic because of their heavy involvement in these areas during the occupation. Examples include *café* (coffee), *algarroba* (carob), *tamarindo* (tamarind), *alcázar* (palace), *alcantarilla* (sewer or underground aqueduct), *jabega* (fishing net), *álgebra* (algebra), *azumbre* ("azumbre" or a liquid measurement approximately equal to two liters). If available, have students research the different languages that influence Spanish by looking up five words in a standard dictionary and finding their origins. If no standard Spanish dictionary is available, have students research word origins in English using standard English dictionaries.

¡Piensa en la CULTURA!

De viaje en la República Dominicana, Argentina y España

Mira las fotos. Los estudiantes que vemos están hablando de viajes. ¿Hiciste un viaje alguna vez? ¿Adónde fuiste? ¿Crees que hiciste lo mismo que estos jóvenes?

> **Santo Domingo, República Dominicana**

"Es agradable hacer una excursión en bote."
Cada día, muchas personas en la región del delta del río Paraná, al norte de Buenos Aires, van a su trabajo en bote.

PASO CULTURAL

El Parc Güell en Barcelona es una de las creaciones más famosas del arquitecto Antonio Gaudí (1852-1926). Miles de azulejos *(tiles)* de muchos colores decoran las estructuras fantásticas del parque. El banco *(bench)* en esta foto es un ejemplo del estilo ondeante *(curving)* de Gaudí. Imagina que eres arquitecto(a) y vas a construir un parque fantástico. ¿Cómo va a ser tu parque, y cuáles son los materiales naturales de tu área que puedes usar para construirlo?

"¿Sabías que ésta es la iglesia más antigua del Caribe? ¡Tiene más de 450 años!"
Jóvenes turistas francohablantes de Martinique visitan la catedral en Santo Domingo.

> **Tigre, Argentina**

394 Capítulo 12

Options

Strategies for Reaching All Students

Spanish-Speaking Students
Ask: *¿Has viajado en avión? ¿Adónde ibas? ¿Te gustaría viajar a otro país? ¿Qué necesitas para viajar de un país a otro?*

 Un paso más Ex. 12-A

Cultural Notes

(p. 394, top photo)
The Santo Domingo cathedral is famous as the first cathedral in the Americas and—until 1992, when his remains were transferred to a specially built lighthouse—the final resting place of Christopher Columbus. Despite all this attention, Dominicans consider it bad luck to pronounce Columbus's name, referring to him in daily speech as *el almirante*. Ask students: Why do you think Dominicans feel this way?

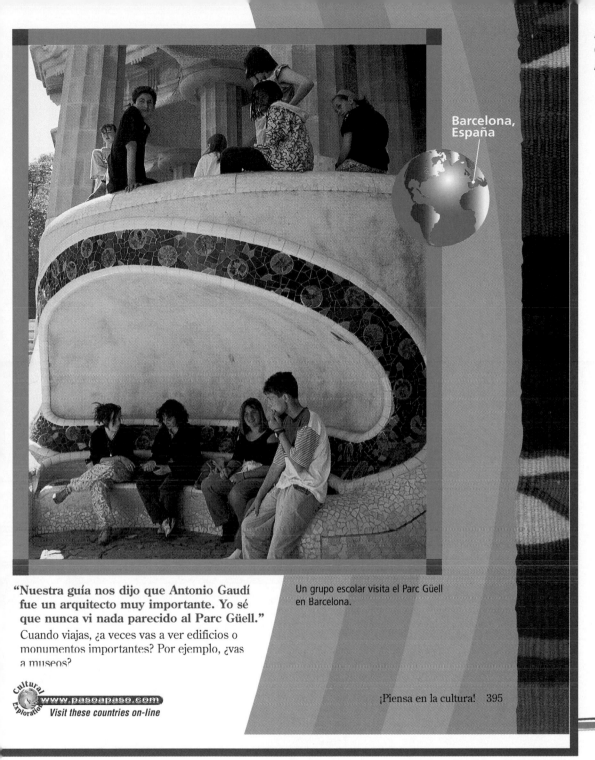

Barcelona,
España

**"Nuestra guía nos dijo que Antonio Gaudí
fue un arquitecto muy importante. Yo sé
que nunca vi nada parecido al Parc Güell."**

Cuando viajas, ¿a veces vas a ver edificios o
monumentos importantes? Por ejemplo, ¿vas
a museos?

Un grupo escolar visita el Parc Güell
en Barcelona.

*Cultural
Exploration*
www.pasoapaso.com
Visit these countries on-line

¡Piensa en la cultura! 395

(p. 394, bottom photo)
Located just outside of Buenos Aires, the
town of Tigre is a popular weekend
destination for *porteños* (inhabitants of
Buenos Aires). Many come for Tigre's
famous fruit market, but the suburb's
greatest draws are the rivers, canals, and
lush marshlands of the Río Paraná delta.
These boys are touring the delta on one of
Tigre's many taxi launches. Other visitors
come for such water sports as yachting,
rowing, and fishing.

Paso cultural
Answers will vary.

(p. 395, photo)
Antonio Gaudí's Parc Güell, with its organic,
asymmetrical forms and brilliantly patterned
surfaces, is representative of the architect's
eclectic style combining elements of
mudéjar (Spain's characteristic Christian-
Muslim amalgam), Gothic, and baroque
architecture. Gaudí declared that his buildings should "stand as trees stand" and
designed them without any internal bracing
or external buttressing. He often used tilted
piers and columns to transmit the construction's diagonal thrusts. Gaudí was a major
figure in the Catalan *Renaixensa,* or artistic
and political revival.

Present

Chapter Theme
At the airport

Communicative Objectives
• To discuss travel arrangements
• To describe a plane trip

 Overheads 57–58

 Vocabulary Art BLMs/CD-ROM

 Vocabulary Tape 12-1

Teaching Suggestions
Preparing students to speak: Use one or two options from each of the categories of Comprehensible Input, Physical Response, or Limited Verbal Response. For a complete explanation of these categories and some sample activities, see pp. T20–T21.

If there are any students who have been through customs, ask them to describe the experience.

¡El pasaporte, por favor!

Vocabulario para conversar

¿Compraste un boleto de ida y vuelta?

Vas a necesitar estas palabras y expresiones para hablar sobre viajes. Después de leerlas varias veces, practícalas con un(a) compañero(a).

Options

Strategies for Reaching All Students

Spanish-Speaking Students
Ask: *¿Sabes otras palabras relacionadas al tema? Escríbelas en tu vocabulario personal.*

 Un paso más Exs. 12-B, 12-C

Students Needing Extra Help
Begin the vocabulary section of the Organizer. Point out that *piloto* is spelled the same, for both men and women. Point out that *avión* loses its accent in the plural. Show the word family of *ventanilla*. *También necesitas . . . :* Explain the "going and returning" concept of *de ida y vuelta.* Show the complete paradigm of *conseguir* for those students who need to see it. Explain the steps involved in going through customs in the U.S. and abroad.

Enrichment
As homework, have students rank the travel-related professions according to how much they would like to be in them. Ask them to explain their choices for the top and bottom of the list.

Learning Spanish Through Action
STAGING VOCABULARY: *Levanten* MATERIALS: envelope containing copies of items from the Vocabulary Art BLMs/CD-ROM to remember before leaving for the airport

la auxiliar de vuelo

el pasillo

abrocharse

desabrocharse*

el piloto   la piloto

el cinturón
(de seguridad)

el pasajero   la pasajera

el auxiliar de vuelo

la agencia de viajes

hacer
la maleta

CASTILLOS
en España

¡No te aburras! Disfruta
de la vida venezolana.

el /la agente
(de viajes)

deshacer*
la maleta

Class Starter Review
On the day following the presentation of vocabulary, you might begin the class with this activity: Prepare a list of three travel destinations, including information about the season in which the travel would occur. In groups of three, have students list three items they would take with them to those destinations. Poll the class to see what the most popular item was for each destination.

www Internet Activities
Juegos

También necesitas . . .

el boleto (de ida y vuelta)	*(round-trip) ticket*	con destino a	*going to*
la escala	*stopover*	procedente de	*arriving from*
el retraso	*delay*		
la tarjeta de embarque	*boarding pass*		
el vuelo	*flight*		
facturar	*to check (baggage)*		
conseguir *(e → i)*	*to get, to obtain*		
pasar por	*to pass / go through*		
registrar	*to inspect, to search*		
viajar	*to travel*		
a mano	*by hand*		

¿Y qué quiere decir . . . ?
el cheque de viajero
el viajero, la viajera
la línea aérea
la reservación,
   pl. las reservaciones
sin escala
sólo de ida

* Notice that *des-* is the equivalent of *un-* in English.

Vocabulario para conversar   397

DIRECTIONS: Play the part of a parent checking to see if a child has everything ready for the departure. Give each student one picture, then direct them to hold up the appropriate picture as you ask who has that item.

Extended Written Practice/Homework
1. Refer to the illustrations on p. 396. Write three sentences telling what will happen at the airport: *Los pasajeros pasarán por la puerta C-3.*
2. Using the illustrations on p. 397, write three sentences saying what is happening now: *Un señor está haciendo su maleta.*
3. Write three sentences saying what must or should happen while traveling. Use *es importante, es necesario, deber,* and *hay que.*

Multiple Intelligences
Bodily/Kinesthetic
See Learning Spanish Through Action.
Interpersonal/Social
See Class Starter Review.
Logical/Mathematical
See Enrichment.
Verbal/Linguistic
See Vocabulary Tape 12-1.
Visual/Spatial
See Overheads 57–58 and the Vocabulary Art BLMs/CD-ROM.

Standards 1.1; 1.2; 4.1; 5.1   **397**

Practice

Answers: Empecemos a conversar

1 ESTUDIANTE A

a. ¿Quiénes sirven la comida en el avión?

b. ...les facturan el equipaje a los pasajeros?

c. ...se abrochan el cinturón?

d. ...muestran la tarjeta de embarque?

e. ...registran las maletas?

f. ...pasan por la aduana?

g. ...dicen que hay que abrocharse los cinturones?

h. ...venden boletos?

ESTUDIANTE B

a. Los auxiliares de vuelo.

b. Los empleados de la línea aérea.

c. Los pasajeros.

d. Los pasajeros.

e. Los aduaneros.

f. Los pasajeros.

g. Los auxiliares de vuelo.

h. Los agentes de viajes / los empleados de la línea aérea.

2 ESTUDIANTE A

a. Perdone, ...¿a qué hora llega el vuelo número 115 procedente de Medellín?

b. ...aterriza el vuelo 093 de Bogotá?

c. ...sale el vuelo con destino a Cali?

d. ...llega el vuelo de Cartagena?

e. ...aterriza el avión procedente de Barranquilla?

f. ...despega el vuelo con destino a Santa Marta?

Empecemos a conversar

Túrnate con un(a) compañero(a) para ser *Estudiante A* y *Estudiante B*. Reemplacen las palabras subrayadas en el modelo con palabras representadas o escritas en los recuadros. Si ven 💡 pueden dar su propia respuesta.

1 necesitar tarjetas de embarque

A — *¿Quiénes necesitan tarjetas de embarque?*
B — *Los pasajeros.*

Estudiante A

a. servir la comida en el avión

b. facturarles el equipaje a los pasajeros

c. abrocharse el cinturón

d. mostrar la tarjeta de embarque

e. registrar las maletas

f. pasar por la aduana

g. decir que hay que abrocharse los cinturones

h. vender boletos

Estudiante B

398   Capítulo 12

Options

Strategies for Reaching All Students

Spanish-Speaking Students
Exs. 1–2: Pair bilingual with non-bilingual students, if possible.
Ex. 3: Pair Spanish-speaking students if possible.

Students Needing Extra Help
Ex. 1: Review stem-changing and reflexive verbs, and the present-tense forms of *decir*. Point out that the *Estudiante B* responses can be used more than once if appropriate.
Ex. 2: Read through the schedule as a class. Model a response without using the *retraso* phrase. You may want to review time-telling before beginning this exercise. Point out that all of these cities are in Colombia.
Ex. 3: Point out that this is not a linear match for answers.

Enrichment
Ex. 3: To extend this exercise, call on the entire class to suggest things the people named usually say. You may want to make a chart with the following headings: *Lo que dice un(a) piloto, Lo que dice un(a) auxiliar de vuelo, Lo que dice un(a) agente de viajes,* etc.

398   Standards 1.1; 3.2

2 salir / el avión
para Pasto

A —*Perdone, señor (señora / señorita), ¿a qué hora*
sale el avión para Pasto?
B —*A las 9:25. Tiene un retraso de 25 minutos.*

Estudiante A

a. llegar / el vuelo número 115 procedente
de Medellín

b. aterrizar / el vuelo 093 de Bogotá

c. salir / el vuelo con destino a Cali

d. llegar / el vuelo de Cartagena

e. aterrizar / el avión procedente de Barranquilla

f. despegar / el vuelo con destino a Santa Marta

Estudiante B

Vuelo	Ciudad	Llegada	Salida
353	Cali		8:30 (retraso de 30 min.)
297	Cartagena	9:20	
116	Pasto		9:25 (retraso de 25 min.)
093	Bogotá	10:50	
115	Medellín	11:10	
193	Santa Marta		3:00 (retraso de 15 min.)
245	Barranquilla	5:45	

3 el piloto

A —*¿Qué dijo el piloto?*
B —*Dijo que íbamos a aterrizar en 20 minutos.*

Estudiante A

a. el empleado de la línea aérea

b. la auxiliar de vuelo

c. ese mecánico

d. el agente de viajes

e. esa pasajera

f. el aduanero

g.

Estudiante B

íbamos a aterrizar en (20) minutos

íbamos a salir por la puerta número 3

quería un asiento cerca de la ventanilla

había que registrar todas las maletas

había que comprar los boletos en seguida

tenía que reparar algo en el avión

debíamos abrocharnos el cinturón

Vocabulario para conversar   399

ESTUDIANTE B
a. A las 11:10.
b. . . . 10:50.
c. . . . 8:30. Tiene un retraso de 30 minutos.
d. . . . 9:20.
e. . . . 5:45.
f. . . . 3:00. Tiene un retraso de 15 minutos.

3 ESTUDIANTE A
a. ¿Qué dijo el empleado de la línea aérea?
b. . . . la auxiliar de vuelo?
c. . . . ese mecánico?
d. . . . el agente de viajes?
e. . . . esa pasajera?
f. . . . el aduanero?
g. Questions will vary.

ESTUDIANTE B
a. Dijo que íbamos a salir por la puerta número tres.
b. . . . debíamos abrocharnos el cinturón.
c. . . . tenía que reparar algo en el avión.
d. . . . había que comprar los boletos en seguida.
e. . . . quería un asiento cerca de la ventanilla.
f. . . . había que registrar todas las maletas.
g. Answers will vary.

Extended Written Practice/Homework
1. Write a sequence of four sentences telling what you or another person did as a part of a trip: *Primero fui a . . . Conseguí . . . Luego hice . . . Tuve que . . .*
2. Choose three of these people and write statements that you might hear them say: *empleado(a) de la línea aérea, aduanero(a), piloto, auxiliar de vuelo, agente de viajes.*

Multiple Intelligences
Bodily/Kinesthetic and Verbal/Linguistic
In small groups, have students write brief dialogues between passengers and airline personnel on a plane. Have each group present their dialogue to the class in the form of a skit.
Verbal/Linguistic
See Exs. 1–3 and Enrichment.

Practice & Apply

Answers: Empecemos a conversar

4 ESTUDIANTE A

a. ¿Conseguiste un vuelo sin escala?

b. ¿Conseguiste un asiento cerca de la ventanilla?

c. ¿Compraste un boleto sólo de ida?

d. ¿Cambiaste la reservación?

e. ¿Conseguiste un vuelo por la mañana?

f. ¿Hiciste reservaciones en el hotel en Montevideo?

g. ¿Compraste un boleto barato?

h. Questions will vary.

ESTUDIANTE B

a. No, todos hacen escala en Panamá.

b. . . . prefiero estar cerca del pasillo.

c. . . . de ida y vuelta.

d. . . . había que pagar $100 más.

e. . . . conseguí uno a las 3:00.

f. . . . allí nunca hay mucha gente.

g. Por suerte no fue demasiado caro.

h. Answers will vary.

4 comprar un boleto de ida y vuelta a Santiago

A — *¿Compraste un boleto de ida y vuelta a Santiago?*

B — *No, sólo de ida.*

Estudiante A

a. conseguir un vuelo sin escala

b. conseguir un asiento cerca de la ventanilla

c. comprar un boleto sólo de ida

d. cambiar la reservación

e. conseguir un vuelo por la mañana

f. hacer reservaciones en el hotel en Montevideo

g. comprar un boleto barato

h.

Estudiante B

No, sólo de ida.

No, prefiero estar cerca del pasillo.

Por suerte no fue demasiado caro.

No, allí nunca hay mucha gente.

No, conseguí uno a las 3:00.

No, había que pagar $100 más.

No, todos hacen escala en Panamá.

No, de ida y vuelta.

Options

Strategies for Reaching All Students

Spanish-Speaking Students

Ex. 4: Pair Spanish-speaking students if possible.

Ex. 9: Add: *¿Has pasado por la aduana? ¿Qué tuviste que mostrarles a los aduaneros?*

 Un paso más Exs. 12-D, 12-E

Students Needing Extra Help

Ex. 4: Review preterite verb forms. Pair students who haven't flown before with those who have.

Empecemos a escribir: Answer these questions as a class, to include those who have never traveled.

Ex. 5: Point out that more than one tense will be used.

Ex. 6: Remind students that *te* in the question becomes *me* in the answer. Point out that more than one tense is used.

Cooperative Learning

In pairs, have students choose one of the situations presented in Ex. 4. Have them create a ten-line dialogue acting out that situation. Scenes can be amusing or serious: encourage creativity and wide use of vocabulary. After students have practiced their scene, have each pair present their dialogue to the class. The class should try to guess which situation is being presented.

Pasajeros después de aterrizar en Santo Domingo

Empecemos a escribir

Escribe tus respuestas en español.

5 ¿Tienes pasaporte? ¿Cuánto tiempo hace que lo tienes? ¿Para qué lo necesitaste? Si no tienes uno, ¿a quién conoces que tiene pasaporte? ¿A qué país viajaba cuando lo consiguió?

6 ¿Viajaste en avión alguna vez? ¿Adónde fuiste? ¿Por qué prefiere la gente los vuelos sin escala? ¿Te gusta (o te gustaría) viajar en avión o te da miedo?

7 Cuando viajas, ¿llevas mucho o poco equipaje? Cuando haces la maleta, ¿es difícil decidir qué llevar? ¿Cuál es mejor, facturar el equipaje o llevarlo en la mano? ¿Por qué?

8 En tú opinión, ¿cuáles son las ventajas y desventajas de ser piloto o auxiliar de vuelo? ¿Y las ventajas de ser agente de viajes o empleado(a) de una línea aérea?

9 ¿Sabes cuándo y por qué hay que pasar por la aduana? ¿Crees que los aduaneros deben registrar todas las maletas o no? ¿Por qué?

También se dice

la aeromoza, el aeromozo
la azafata

In addition to saying *facturar*, we also say *chequear*.

MORE PRACTICE

- Más práctica y tarea, p. 560
- Practice Workbook 12–1, 12–2

Vocabulario para conversar 401

Cultural Notes

(p. 400, left realia)
Portugal lies in the southwestern corner of Europe on the Iberian Plateau facing the Atlantic Ocean. Its Mediterranean climate offers mild winters and hot, dry summers. This ad invites the Spanish tourist to "hurry" or "come flying" to Portugal.

(p. 400, right realia)
Venezuela attracts visitors with such sites as its Amazon jungle, the world's highest waterfall (Cataratas Ángel), and the beaches of las Islas Margarita. Venezuela's population is 67 percent mestizo, 21 percent white, 10 percent black, and 2 percent Indian, including the Warao of the eastern Orinoco Delta and the Yanomami of the Amazonas territory.

(p. 401, photo)
International visitors to the Dominican Republic, which shares the island of Hispaniola with Haiti, land at Las Américas airport in Santo Domingo, the country's capital city. Bartholomew Columbus, brother of Christopher, founded Santo Domingo in 1496, making it the oldest city established by Europeans in the Americas. Many areas in the city have been restored to their colonial style.

Present

Chapter Theme
Tourism

Communicative Objectives
- To discuss tourist accommodations
- To discuss tourist activities

 Overheads 59–60

 Vocabulary Art BLMs/CD-ROM

 Vocabulary Tape 12-2

Grammar Preview
Affirmative and negative *tú* commands are presented here lexically. They are explained on pp. 411–414.

Teaching Suggestions
Preparing students to speak: Use one or two options from each of the categories of Comprehensible Input, Physical Response, or Limited Verbal Response. For a complete explanation of these categories and some sample activities, see pp. T20–T21.

Vocabulario para conversar

¿Dónde puedo cambiar cheques de viajero?

la oficina telefónica

la oficina de turismo

la artesanía

la guía

el /la turista

el mercado

la guía

la casa de cambio

DÓLARES-PESOS

402   Capítulo 12

Options

Strategies for Reaching All Students

Spanish-Speaking Students
Ask: *¿Puedes añadir palabras a esta lista? Escríbelas en tu vocabulario personal.*
Exs. 10–11: Pair bilingual with non-bilingual students, if possible.

 Un paso más Ex. 12-F

Students Needing Extra Help
Point out that *turista* is masculine and feminine. Explain that *habitación* loses its accent in the plural. Explain the concept of the long-distance telephone office.
También necesitas . . . : Define "indigenous." Show students that the verb forms of *regatear* and *planear* will look similar. Remind them of *bucear.*

¿Y qué quiere decir . . . ?: Explain the difference between *un viaje* and *una excursión.* Write out the *recomendar* paradigm for students who need to see it.
Ex. 10: Accept any logical answer.

Enrichment
Ex. 10: To extend this dialogue, *Estudiante A* can ask *Estudiante B* to elaborate by asking, *¿Por qué dices eso?*

402 **Standards** 1.1; 1.2; 1.3; 3.1; 3.2

la habitación, *pl.* las habitaciones

la habitación individual

el guía

la habitación doble

También necesitas . . .

el pueblo	*town*
la pensión, *pl.* las pensiones	*inexpensive lodging*
la naturaleza	*nature*
cambiar	*here: to cash*
disfrutar de	*to enjoy*
incluir: incluye	*to include: it includes*
planear	*to plan*
regatear	*to bargain*
ir: ve; no vayas	*go!; don't go!*
tener cuidado (con): ten cuidado	*to be careful (of / with): be careful!*
indígena	*indigenous, native*
pintoresco, -a	*picturesque*

¿Y qué quiere decir . . . ?
el palacio
el viaje
hacer una excursión
recomendar (*e* → *ie*)

Practice

Class Starter Review
On the day following the presentation of vocabulary, you might begin the class with this activity: Describe a situation in which a tourist may find himself or herself in a Spanish-speaking country. Have students write down a solution to the problem. For example: *Tomás necesita información sobre el Museo Nacional. ¿Adónde debe ir? (a la oficina de turismo)*

www Internet Activities
Juegos

Answers: Empecemos a conversar *(p. 404)*
10 ESTUDIANTE A
a.–f. ¿Me recomiendas . . . ?
g. Questions will vary.
ESTUDIANTE B
Answers will vary, but may include:
a. Sí, si te gustan los edificios viejos.
b. . . . gusta la naturaleza.
c. . . . gusta la naturaleza.
d. . . . gustan los lugares pintorescos.
e. . . . gusta pasear en bote.
f. . . . gusta esquiar.
g. Answers will vary.

Learning Spanish Through Action
STAGING VOCABULARY: *Señalen*
MATERIALS: signs for *el hotel, la casa de cambio, la oficina de turismo, la oficina telefónica, el mercado, la agencia de viajes* placed in different areas of the classroom
DIRECTIONS: Have students imagine they are vacationing in Venezuela. Direct them to point to the place they would go to do the activities you mention.

Extended Written Practice/Homework
1. Imagine that you visited the town on pp. 402–403. Write four sentences describing what you saw: *Había un mercado donde vendían artesanía.*
2. Write four sentences describing a trip you would like to take: *Quisiera ir a . . . Me gustaría viajar en . . . Prefiero quedarme en . . . Pienso hacer una excursión . . .*

Multiple Intelligences
Bodily/Kinesthetic
See Learning Spanish Through Action.
Verbal/Linguistic
See Vocabulary Tape 12-2.
Visual/Spatial
See Overheads 59–60 and the Vocabulary Art BLMs/CD-ROM.
Visual/Spatial and Verbal/Linguistic
See Class Starter Review.

Standards 1.1; 1.2; 4.1; 5.1   **403**

Practice & Apply

Re-enter / Recycle

Exs. 11 and 14: places in a community from Chap. 8

Answers: Empecemos a conversar

11 ESTUDIANTE A

a. ¿Dónde puedo encontrar un(a) guía?

b. ...comprar artesanías?

c. ...conseguir un boleto de avión?

d. ...buscar un mapa?

e. ...llamar a los Estados Unidos?

f. ...comprar tarjetas postales?

g. ...encontrar una habitación barata?

h. Questions will vary.

ESTUDIANTE B

a. Ve a una oficina de turismo.

b. ...un mercado.

c. ...una agencia de viajes.

d. ...una oficina de turismo / una agencia de viajes / un quiosco.

e. ...la oficina telefónica.

f. ...un quiosco.

g. ...una pensión.

h. Answers will vary.

12 ESTUDIANTE A

a. ¿Prefiere pagar con tarjeta de crédito o con cheques de viajero?

b. ...un hotel o una pensión?

c. ...hacer una excursión al mercado o al Palacio Nacional?

d. ...ir con guía o solo(a)?

¡El pasaporte, por favor!

Empecemos a conversar

10 ir a los mercados
A —¿Me recomiendas *ir a los mercados*?
B —Sí, si te gusta *regatear*.

Estudiante A

a. ver los palacios
b. visitar una selva tropical
c. hacer una excursión a las cataratas
d. hacer un viaje a los pueblos
e. ir a los lagos y los ríos
f. hacer una excursión a las montañas
g. 💡

Estudiante B

esquiar	los lugares pintorescos
pasear en bote	los edificios viejos
regatear	la naturaleza
la artesanía indígena	💡

11 cambiar cheques de viajero
A —¿Dónde puedo *cambiar cheques de viajero*?
B —Ve a *una casa de cambio*.

Estudiante A

a. encontrar un(a) guía	e. llamar a los Estados Unidos
b. comprar artesanías	f. comprar tarjetas postales
c. conseguir un boleto de avión	g. encontrar una habitación barata
d. buscar un mapa	h. 💡

Estudiante B

la oficina telefónica	una pensión
una casa de cambio	un quiosco
una agencia de viajes	💡
un mercado	
una oficina de turismo	

12 una habitación doble /individual
A —¿Prefiere *una habitación doble o una individual*?
B —*Una individual. Viajo solo*.

Estudiante A

a. pagar con tarjeta de crédito / con cheques de viajero	e. quedarse en un lugar pintoresco / moderno
b. un hotel /una pensión	f. una habitación al fondo /con ventanas a la calle
c. hacer una excursión al mercado / al Palacio Nacional	g. 💡
d. ir con guía /solo(a)	

Estudiante B

404   Capítulo 12

Options

Strategies for Reaching All Students

Spanish-Speaking Students
Exs. 12–13: Pair bilingual with non-bilingual students, if possible.
Ex. 16: *Haz un folleto o pequeño cartel que anuncie algunos de los lugares de interés turístico en nuestra comunidad.*

Students Needing Extra Help
Ex. 12: Brainstorm possible second sentences in the *Estudiante B* response. *Empecemos a escribir y a leer:* Answer these questions as a class, to include those who have not traveled before.
Ex. 13: Discuss different types of excursions.
Ex. 14: As a class, review the concept of bargaining.

Ex. 15: Answer questions one at a time as a class to help students stay focused. Write the list of things to be careful of on the chalkboard.
Ex. 16: Generate a list of positive and negative features of your community, then have students use the list to create statements they could make to tourists.

Empecemos a escribir y a leer

Escribe tus respuestas en español.

13 ¿Qué tipo de excursión te gustaría hacer? ¿Disfrutas más de la naturaleza o de las ciudades? ¿Por qué?

14 ¿En qué lugares crees que se puede regatear? ¿Regateaste alguna vez? ¿Dónde? ¿Hay lugares en tu pueblo o ciudad donde se puede regatear?

15 ¿Alguna vez hiciste un viaje a un pueblo, ciudad o país que no conocías? ¿Adónde fuiste? ¿Cómo planeaste el viaje? ¿Fuiste a una agencia de viajes? ¿Con quién(es) viajaste? ¿Qué tuviste que hacer como turista? ¿Con qué debe tener cuidado un(a) turista? Haz una lista para un(a) compañero(a).

Ten cuidado con el dinero.
Ten cuidado con . . .
No vayas al parque por la noche.
No vayas a . . .

16 Imagina que eres guía en tu comunidad. ¿Qué le recomiendas a un(a) turista?

17 Con un(a) compañero(a), lee los tres anuncios de excursiones. Escoge cuál te gustaría hacer y di por qué.

www.pasoapaso.com

MORE PRACTICE
- Más práctica y tarea, p. 561
- Practice Workbook 12–3, 12–4

Ciudad de México • Oaxaca • Mérida
8 días por *sólo*

$440 por persona / hab. doble

Incluye:
- Boleto de ida y vuelta
- 7 noches en hoteles de turista superior
- Transporte diario en autobús con guía en español
- Visita a todas las ruinas, pirámides y lugares pintorescos de la región
- Transporte:
  aeropuerto → hotel → aeropuerto

Santo Domingo
8 días por *sólo*

$520 por persona / hab. individual

Incluye:
- 7 noches en el Hotel Boca Chica (frente al océano)
- Programa completo de deportes acuáticos
- Alimentación completa
- Una camiseta por persona con el logo del hotel
- Transporte:
  aeropuerto → hotel → aeropuerto

Ciudad de Panamá
3 días por *sólo*

$127 por persona / hab. triple

Incluye:
- 2 noches en un hotel turista superior
- Transporte:
  aeropuerto → hotel → aeropuerto
- Transporte todos los días de ida y vuelta a los almacenes en la zona libre*
- Visita al Canal con guía en español

*Zona libre = tax-free

---

e. . . . quedarse en un lugar pintoresco o moderno?
f. . . . una habitación al fondo o con ventanas a la calle?
g. Questions will vary.
ESTUDIANTE B
a.–g. Answers will vary.

Answers: Empecemos a escribir y a leer
13–16 Answers will vary, but look for correct use of the present, preterite, and the impersonal *se* where appropriate.

17 Answers will vary, but may include the following:
Escogimos el viaje a México porque nos interesan los pirámides / necesitamos un(a) guía / incluye un boleto de ida y vuelta.
Escogimos el viaje a Santo Domingo porque queremos nadar, y además es muy barato porque tiene alimentación completa.
Escogimos el viaje a Panamá porque nos gusta ir de compras y queremos mucho ver el Canal.

 Practice Wkbk. 12-3, 12-4

 Audio Activity 12.2

 Writing Activity 12-C

 Pruebas 12-3, 12-4

 Comm. Act. BLM 12-1

Enrichment
Ex. 14: Additional questions: *¿Te gusta regatear? ¿Por qué sí o no? ¿Conoces a alguien que sepa regatear bien? ¿Cómo es esa persona?*
Ex. 17: To expand this exercise, have students who chose the same trip form groups and plan it.

Extended Written Practice/Homework
1. Write four sentences telling where to go to accomplish different travel-related tasks: *Para comprar artesanía, ve al mercado.*
2. Write four sentences giving recommendations to classmates concerning a place you have visited: *Recomiendo . . . Es un pueblo . . . Debes . . . Ten cuidado . . . Ve a . . . pero no vayas a . . .*

Multiple Intelligences
Intrapersonal/Introspective
Ask students to write a paragraph describing their ideal vacation spot, including a physical description and possible activities.
Verbal/Linguistic
See Exs. 10–12 and Audio Activity 12.2.
Visual/Spatial
See Practice Wkbk. 12-3 and 12-4, Writing Activity 12-C, and Comm. Act. BLM 12-1.

Practice

Teaching Suggestions

Ex. 1: To prepare for this exercise you may want to ask students to pick up brochures from different Latin American countries at a local travel agency.

Answers:
¡Comuniquemos!

1–3 Answers will vary, but look for a wide variety of chapter vocabulary and correct use of the future tense where appropriate.

Multicultural Perspectives

In rural areas of Colombia, the most practical form of travel is the *chiva* (goat), so called because this converted school bus provides transportation to places only a mountain goat would go. A typical multi-colored, double-decker *chiva* has the destinations it serves written on the bus, along with the name of the company running the service. When people need to travel from one small town to another, they wait at the side of the road and flag down a passing *chiva*. The *chiva* not only carries people from place to place, but doubles as a freight carrier, bringing livestock and agricultural products along with their owners to a given destination. Discuss with students modes of transportation which are unique to a particular region or country.

¡Comuniquemos!

Aquí tienes otra oportunidad para usar el vocabulario de este capítulo.

1 Con un(a) compañero(a), planea un viaje o una excursión a algún país o lugar específico. Hablen de:

- adónde irán
- en qué irán
- qué necesitarán hacer primero
- cuánto tiempo se quedarán
- qué llevarán
- qué harán allá

2 Con un(a) compañero(a), hagan los papeles de un(a) agente de viajes y un(a) cliente.

A —*Quisiera un . . . para ir a . . .*
B — *. . .*
A —*¿Dónde puedo . . . ?*
B —*En . . .*
A —*¿Sabe Ud. si hay que . . . ?*
B — *. . .*

3 Con un(a) compañero(a), hagan los papeles de un(a) auxiliar de vuelo y un(a) pasajero(a). Escojan por lo menos tres de las situaciones que siguen.

A —*Señor (Señorita), por favor, ¿(me) podría . . . ?*
B —*Claro que sí, señor(ita) . . .*
  o: *Lo siento, señor(ita), pero . . .*

1. Tienes sed. El/La auxiliar te ofrece varias bebidas.
2. Quieres leer un periódico y sólo hay revistas.
3. No puedes abrocharte el cinturón de seguridad. Crees que está roto.
4. Quieres cambiar de asiento.
5. Tu maleta es demasiado grande y no puedes ponerla debajo del asiento.
6. Pediste pollo para la cena, pero no hay más.

406   Capítulo 12

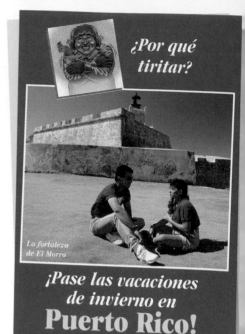

¿Por qué tiritar?

La fortaleza de El Morro

¡Pase las vacaciones de invierno en **Puerto Rico!**

Córdoba

La mezquita (hoy la catedral)

donde Ud. encontrará el cruce de las culturas musulmana, judía y cristiana

Options

Strategies for Reaching All Students

Spanish-Speaking Students
Ex. 3: Pair Spanish-speaking students if possible, to prepare this activity and present it to the class. It can be used as a listening comprehension exercise for others, especially if it is recorded.

Students Needing Extra Help
Ex 2: Present a complete model. Provide specific criteria for completing the dialogue.
Ex. 3: Remind students to change the suggestions from the *tú* form to the *yo* form. For the dialogues they develop, point out the necessity for both people to use the *Ud.* form.
¿Qué sabes ahora?: Have students write out this list so they can record their progress.

Cooperative Learning
Have students list three types of excursions they would enjoy on vacation, then circulate through the class to find three others with similar responses. As a group, each must generate one reason why theirs is the ideal vacation. Students will create a poster using words, photos, drawings, etc. Within the group, one pair will be responsible for creating the poster and one pair will generate the reasons why it is ideal.

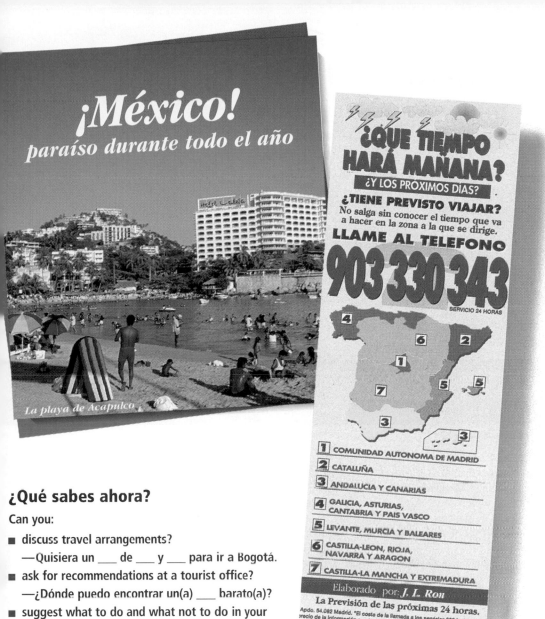

¡México!
paraíso durante todo el año

La playa de Acapulco

¿QUE TIEMPO HARÁ MAÑANA?
¿Y LOS PRÓXIMOS DÍAS?

¿TIENE PREVISTO VIAJAR?
No salga sin conocer el tiempo que va a hacer en la zona a la que se dirige.

LLAME AL TELEFONO

903 330 343
SERVICIO 24 HORAS

1. COMUNIDAD AUTONOMA DE MADRID
2. CATALUÑA
3. ANDALUCIA Y CANARIAS
4. GALICIA, ASTURIAS, CANTABRIA Y PAIS VASCO
5. LEVANTE, MURCIA Y BALEARES
6. CASTILLA-LEON, RIOJA, NAVARRA Y ARAGON
7. CASTILLA-LA MANCHA Y EXTREMADURA

Elaborado por: **J. L. Ron**
La Previsión de las próximas 24 horas.

Apdo. 54.082 Madrid. *El costo de la llamada a los servicios 903 incluye el precio de la información o entretenimiento que usted recibe. Beneficiese de las tarifas nocturnas y de días festivos*. Precio llamada e información 60 ptas. minuto. noches y festivos 42 ptas. Sin IVA.

¿Qué sabes ahora?

Can you:

- discuss travel arrangements?
  —Quisiera un ___ de ___ y ___ para ir a Bogotá.
- ask for recommendations at a tourist office?
  —¿Dónde puedo encontrar un(a) ___ barato(a)?
- suggest what to do and what not to do in your hometown?
  —Ve a ___. No ___ a ___.

Vocabulario para conversar 407

Using Realia
Have students compare the two images presented in the top photo on p. 406. Then ask: *¿Qué quiere decir "tiritar?"* (to shiver)

Answers: ¿Qué sabes ahora?
- boleto / ida / vuelta
- Answers will vary, but may include *habitación* or *pensión*.
- Locations will vary; verb should be *vayas*.

Strategies for Reaching All Students
MULTIPLE INTELLIGENCES
Interpersonal/Social, Bodily/Kinesthetic, and Visual/Spatial
See Cooperative Learning.
Interpersonal/Social and Verbal/Linguistic
See Exs. 1–3.
Musical/Rhythmic
Using a familiar melody, have students write a jingle to use with the brochures/ads on pp. 406–407.
Verbal/Linguistic
See Audio Activity 12.3.

 Audio Activity 12.3

Pasos vivos 2 CD-ROM
Boom Box, Clip Art Album, Slide Projector, Laboratorio de grabar

---

Cultural Notes ☀

(p. 406, top photo)
San Juan, Puerto Rico, is one of the oldest cities in the Americas. It was originally settled in 1508, and by 1533 the Spanish settlers and military had begun to build fortifications to protect the island. El Morro castle and the fort of San Cristóbal lie at either end of the viejo San Juan historic section. They are part of the San Juan National Historic Site run by the U.S. National Park Service.

(p. 406, bottom photo)
Córdoba's *mezquita* (mosque) contains vast interior space divided by rows of columns supporting stone piers that carry a second tier of arches, creating a light, airy effect. Construction began in 786 and was finished in 987. Since 1236, it has been used as a cathedral. It remains a breathtaking example of the *mudéjar* style of architecture.

(p. 407, photo)
Acapulco is a popular beach resort with Mexican families and international tourists. Some of the city's most famous beaches are Condesa, Playa Larga, and Revolcadero. The city also has a renowned night life, good restaurants, and many luxury hotels as well as economical *pensiones*.

Perspectiva cultural

¿Qué son estos edificios? ¿Castillos o palacios? ¿Museos? ¿Casas privadas? ¿Hoteles o edificios de apartamentos? ¿Por qué crees eso?

El parador de Sigüenza

¿Te gustaría pasar una noche en el Hospital Real fundado por Isabel de Castilla y Fernando de Aragón en 1499? ¿Quisieras quedarte en un castillo construido hace mil años? ¿Qué tal un convento franciscano del siglo dieciséis? ¿O quizás prefieres un edificio que fue primero un templo romano, luego una basílica visigoda y después un convento de la Orden de Santiago? Es posible quedarte en todos estos lugares si vas a España.

En España estos hoteles especiales se llaman *paradores*. En 1926 el gobierno español decidió establecer una cadena de paradores para atraer a los turistas a los lugares donde no había hoteles.

Los primeros paradores estaban a una distancia de un día de viaje uno de otro. Claro que ahora, con las carreteras modernas, el mismo viaje toma mucho menos tiempo. En total, hay 85 paradores en toda España.

Además de paradores, también hay varios tipos de hoteles y albergues (pensiones) para jóvenes en España. Desde la Expo 92 en Sevilla y los Juegos Olímpicos en Barcelona en el mismo año, también es posible pasar la noche en muchas casas privadas. Por lo general, le ofrecen al viajero la habitación y una comida al día. Es una manera muy buena de conocer a la gente y la vida de España.

Cultural Activity www.pasoapaso.com

408 Capítulo 12

Options

Strategies for Reaching All Students

Spanish-Speaking Students
Ask: *Además de hoteles y moteles, ¿qué otros tipos de lugares en los Estados Unidos serían buenos para atraer a los turistas de otros países? Piensa en nuestra área y en diferentes partes del país. Un ejemplo puede ser un rancho de ganado en Texas.*

 Un paso más Ex. 12-G

Students Needing Extra Help
Have students take notes they can use to review in the *¿Lo sabes bien?* culture section. Discuss the types of places in which tourists can stay in the U.S., then compare them to what students see in the photos. Ex. 2: Model a response to the *¿por qué?* question.

Enrichment
Additional questions: *¿Te gustaría tener turistas en tu casa? ¿Por qué sí o no?*

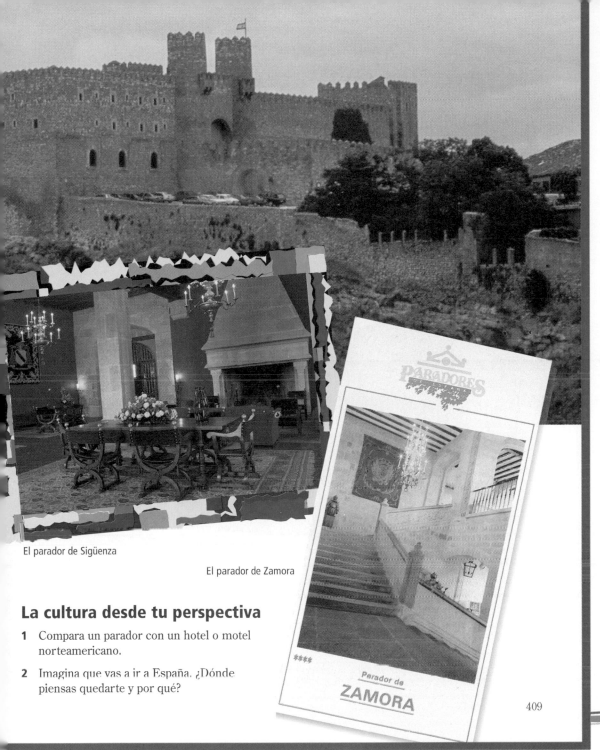

El parador de Sigüenza

El parador de Zamora

Parador de
ZAMORA

409

La cultura desde tu perspectiva

1 Compara un parador con un hotel o motel norteamericano.

2 Imagina que vas a ir a España. ¿Dónde piensas quedarte y por qué?

Answers: La cultura desde tu perspectiva

1 Answers will vary, but should include the following: The Spanish government established the *paradores,* whereas American hotels are privately owned. Many *paradores* are located in a historically significant place: a castle, a palace, or an old convent.

2 Answers will vary, but students may say that they will stay in a *parador* because a palace or a castle would be interesting, but if they want to save money, they would stay in a *pensión* because it is less expensive and usually includes a meal.

Pasos vivos 2 CD-ROM
Maps, Notas culturales

www Internet Activities
Perspectiva cultural

Cultural Notes ☼

(pp. 408–409, photos)
Parador de Sigüenza, near Guadalajara, was originally a Visigoth castle occupied for a time by the Moors. Famous guests of the castle have included King Ferdinand and Queen Isabela, Cardinal Mendoza, and Juana la Loca.

(p. 409, right photo)
Paradores were historically the lodging of distinguished or respectable travelers. Parador de Zamora, in the medieval city of Zamora, is a Renaissance palace built on the ruins of a Romanesque building.

Preview

Overhead 61

Teaching Suggestions

A: Point out that if a pronoun is added to a command form of two or more syllables, a written accent is needed, as in *búscalas* (paragraph 1). Provide writing and pronunciation practice.

Answers

A The command forms are *busca, consigue, usa, aprende, habla.* They are the same as the *Ud. / él / ella* forms of the present tense. The *tú* command forms of *viajar, vender,* and *escribir* would be *viaja, vende,* and *escribe.*

B If the command form of *ir* were regular, it would be *va.* It is *ve.* (It is irregular in its ending.)

C The verb forms are *no olvides* and *no seas.* They come from *olvidar* and *ser.* You would tell a friend, *"No factures tu equipaje."*

Gramática en contexto

América Latina: Destino de jóvenes

¿Tienes poco dinero y quieres viajar?

¡Ve a América Latina en cualquier época del año!

Busca una de nuestras pensiones para jóvenes. Están en todas las ciudades grandes y operan todo el año. Búscalas en las oficinas de turismo.

Consigue un carnet estudiantil. Así podrás conseguir descuento en muchos lugares.

Usa el transporte público. Es fácil de usar y siempre barato.

¡Y no olvides! Aprende algunas palabras del idioma—¡y no seas tímido! Habla con la gente. ¡Es amable, alegre . . . vital!

A These tips for student travelers address the reader as *tú.* What are the command forms meaning "look for," "get," "use," "learn," and "talk"? What forms of the present tense are the same? What do you think the *tú* command forms of *viajar, vender,* and *escribir* might be?

B Find the command form of *ir.* What would you expect it to be if it were regular?

C The reader is also urged *not* to do two things. What verbs do you think they come from? How do you think you might tell a friend, "Don't check your baggage"?

410   Capítulo 12

Options

Strategies for Reaching All Students

Students Needing Extra Help
Begin the grammar section of the Organizer. If available, use the grammar section of the Book 1, Chap. 13 Organizer.
Repaso: Mandatos afirmativos con tú: Give additional examples of *tú* commands, isolated and in sentences. Give additional examples of *pon, haz,* and *di* in sentences.

Ex. 1: Remind students that all *Estudiante A* statements will be in the *yo* form, and all the *Estudiante B* responses will be in the *tú* command form. Review the ¡No olvides! and give further examples before doing the exercise.

Extended Written Practice/Homework
1. Write four sentences telling classmates what to do to have a successful school experience: *Participa en una actividad extracurricular.*
2. Write four sentences telling friends and family members what to do to be in good physical shape: *Corre por lo menos tres veces a la semana.*

Repaso: Mandatos afirmativos con *tú*

You already know how to give affirmative commands to someone you address as *tú*.

> **Pasa** por la aduana.
> **Aprende** a regatear.
> **Escribe** tarjetas postales.

- You also know the irregular command forms *pon (poner)*, *haz (hacer)*, and *di (decir)*. Here are some other verbs that have irregular command forms.

> **salir**
> **Sal** por las escaleras en caso de emergencia.
>
> **ir**
> **Ve** al aeropuerto por lo menos dos horas antes del vuelo.
>
> **ser**
> **Sé** amable con los otros pasajeros.
>
> **tener**
> **¡Ten** cuidado!

¡NO OLVIDES!

Remember that pronouns can be attached to commands. When a pronoun is added to a command form of two or more syllables, a written accent mark is needed.
—¿Dónde facturo el equipaje?
—Factúralo en el mostrador de la línea aérea.

1 Imagina que estás haciendo un viaje con tu compañero(a).

necesitar una
tarjeta de
embarque

A —*Necesito una tarjeta de embarque.*
B —*Pues, habla con el empleado de la línea aérea.*

a. **querer planear un viaje**

b. **necesitar conseguir cheques de viajero**

c. **querer saber qué tiempo hace**

d. **no querer hacer escala**

e. **preferir otro asiento**

f. **tener que enviar mi dirección a casa**

hablar con el empleado de la línea aérea

escribir una tarjeta postal

preguntarle al auxiliar de vuelo

leer el pronóstico de tiempo

cambiar la reservación

visitar una agencia de viajes

comprarlos en una casa de cambio

Gramática en contexto   411

Present & Practice

Answers

1 ESTUDIANTE A
a. Quiero planear un viaje.
b. Necesito conseguir cheques de viajero.
c. Quiero saber qué tiempo hace.
d. No quiero hacer escala.
e. Prefiero otro asiento.
f. Tengo que enviar mi dirección a casa.

ESTUDIANTE B
a. Pues, visita una agencia de viajes.
b. ...cómpralos en una casa de cambio.
c. ...lee el pronóstico de tiempo.
d. ...cambia la reservación.
e. ...pregúntale al auxiliar de vuelo.
f. ...escribe una tarjeta postal.

---

3. Write three sentences telling others what positive things to do to help the environment: *Apaga las luces cuando sales de un cuarto para conservar energía.*

Multiple Intelligences
Logical/Mathematical
Have students create a graphic organizer for planning a vacation, including information about weather, necessary clothing, and itinerary.
Verbal/Linguistic
See Ex. 1.
Visual/Spatial
See Overhead 61.

Present & Practice

Re-enter / Recycle

Ex. 3: environment and recyclables from Chap. 11

Answers

2 ESTUDIANTE A

a. ¿Dónde pongo la maleta?

b. ¿Qué hago si el avión aterriza de emergencia?

c. ¿Dónde encuentro las maletas?

d. ¿Qué hago en la aduana?

e. ¿Cómo regateo bien?

f. ¿Dónde puedo poner mi pasaporte?

g. ¿Cuándo debo hacer reservaciones?

h. Questions will vary.

ESTUDIANTE B

a. Ponla debajo del asiento.

b. Sal rápido del avión.

c. Ve a la terminal de equipaje.

d. Di lo que tienes en tu maleta.

e. Sé amable con los vendedores.

f. Ten cuidado y guárdalo en un bolsillo.

g. Hazlas en seguida.

h. Answers will vary.

 Practice Wkbk.
12-5, 12-6

 Writing Activity
12-D

---

2 Vas a viajar a otro país por primera vez y le pides consejos *(advice)* a un(a) amigo(a). Por ejemplo:

dónde / cambiar   A — *¿Dónde cambio cheques de viajero?*
cheques de viajero   B — *Ve a la casa de cambio.*

a. dónde / poner la maleta

b. qué / hacer si el avión aterriza de emergencia

c. dónde / encontrar las maletas

d. qué / hacer en la aduana

e. cómo / regatear bien

f. dónde / poder poner mi pasaporte

g. cuándo / deber hacer reservaciones

h.

---

ir a la casa de cambio

ir a la terminal de equipaje

hacerlas en seguida

tener cuidado y guardarlo en un bolsillo

ser amable con los vendedores

ponerla debajo del asiento

salir rápido del avión

decir lo que tienes en tu maleta

Los mandatos negativos con *tú*

To form negative *tú* commands with regular verbs, we drop the *o* of the present-tense *yo* form and add the following endings:

hablar
hablo → habl- + **es**   **No hables** ahora.

comer
como → com- + **as**   **No comas** eso.

abrir
abro → abr- + **as**   **No abras** esa puerta.

Notice that *-ar* verbs take the ending *-es* and that *-er* and *-ir* verbs take the ending *-as*.

• In stem-changing verbs the stem change remains.

   No devuelvas el boleto todavía.
   No recomiendes esa pensión a nadie.
   No sigas a esa guía.

412   Capítulo 12

Options

Strategies for Reaching All Students

Students Needing Extra Help

Los mandatos negativos con tú: Give further examples of regular and stem-changing negative commands. Emphasize that forming the negative command requires changes besides just adding *no*.

Ex. 3: Brainstorm possibilities for two additional rules. Have students refer to Book 2, Chap. 11 for ideas.

Ex. 4: Review stem-changing verbs and the rule for forming negative *tú* commands.

Enrichment

Ex. 2: As an in-class written assignment, have students change this exercise by making up entirely new commands or attaching pronouns to commands based on the verb in the original question. For example:
¿Dónde cambio cheques de viajero? / Cámbialos en la casa de cambio.

Ex. 4: Have students work in pairs to generate three additional rules for being a good roommate. You might also have them work

in pairs to create rules for riding on a tour bus, going on a field trip *(excursión)*, etc.

Multiple Intelligences

Interpersonal/Social and Visual/Spatial
See Class Starter Review.

Verbal/Linguistic
See Exs. 2–4.

Visual/Spatial
See Practice Wkbk. 12-5, 12-6, and 12-7 and Writing Activities 12-D and 12-E.

3 ¿Qué se debe hacer para proteger el medio ambiente? Con un(a) compañero(a), haz estas reglas y por lo menos dos reglas más.

echar las pilas viejas en la basura   *No eches las pilas viejas en la basura.*

a. depender sólo de la energía eléctrica
b. contaminar el agua
c. echar las botellas de vidrio ni de plástico en la basura
d. escribir en las paredes de los edificios
e. cortar las flores
f. usar lo que no puedes reciclar
g.

4 Tú y tu compañero(a) tienen una habitación doble en una pensión. Uds. se pelean desde la mañana hasta la noche. Túrnense para ser la persona mandona *(bossy)*.

encender el televisor
A —*No enciendas el televisor.*
B —*¿Por qué?*
A —*Porque no quiero verlo.*

a. cerrar la ventana
b. encender la luz
c. perder las llaves
d. mostrar mis fotos a nadie
e. pedir comida ahora
f. devolver el secador de pelo todavía
g.

Texas. De Todo Un Poco. Y Más.

La iglesia de la misión San José (1720) en San Antonio, Texas

Gramática en contexto   413

Class Starter Review
On the day following the presentation of negative *tú* commands, you might begin the class with this activity:
In small groups, have students prepare a list of five rules for the incoming class. The list should include both positive and negative commands. As a class, decide on the five most useful rules.

3 a. No dependas sólo de la energía eléctrica.
b. No contamines el agua.
c. No eches las botellas de vidrio ni de plástico en la basura.
d. No escribas en las paredes de los edificios.
e. No cortes las flores.
f. No uses lo que no puedes reciclar.
g. Answers will vary.

4 Second part will vary.
a. No cierres la ventana. / Porque tengo calor.
b. No enciendas la luz. / . . . quiero dormir.
c. No pierdas las llaves. / . . . no estaré aquí cuando regreses.
d. No muestres mis fotos a nadie. / . . . son malas.
e. No pidas comida ahora. / . . . comeremos muy pronto.
f. No devuelvas el secador de pelo todavía. / . . . necesito usarlo.
g. Answers will vary.

 Practice Wkbk. 12-7

 Writing Activity 12-E

Cultural Notes

(pp. 412–413, photo)
Catholic missions throughout the Americas functioned as churches, residences, trade schools, and granaries, and were instrumental in Spanish colonization efforts. Of the five missions built near San Antonio, Texas, the most famous is misión San José, known for its beautiful stonework that includes a stone *acequia* (aqueduct) used to bring irrigation water from the San Antonio River to the mission's fields.

(p. 413, realia)
Texas and Mexico have shared much of their histories and key elements of their cultures since 1536, when Cabeza de Vaca led an expedition from Galveston on the Gulf Coast through Texas and down to Mexico City. Spain lost Texas when Mexico declared its independence in 1821. Texas declared itself an independent republic in 1836, and became a state on February 19, 1846. Twenty-five percent of its population is Hispanic, and the majority of those are Mexican American. Commerce and tourism remain important links between Texas and Mexico.

Present & Practice

Re-enter / Recycle
Ex. 5: places in a community from Chap. 8

Answers

5 ESTUDIANTE A
a. No salgas solo(a).
b. No hagas reservaciones en un hotel.
c. No pongas el pasaporte en la maleta.
d. No llegues tarde al aeropuerto.
e. No vayas al centro solo(a) por la noche.
f. No seas maleducado(a).
g. No traigas muchos regalos.
h. No cruces la calle cuando el semáforo está en rojo.
i. Statements will vary.

ESTUDIANTE B
Answers will vary, but could include the following:
a. Sal (con otros miembros de tu grupo).
b. Haz (reservaciones en una pensión).
c. Pon (el pasaporte en el bolsillo de tu chaqueta).
d. Llega (tan temprano como posible).
e. Ve (con un[a] amigo[a]).
f. Sé educado(a).
g. Trae (sólo lo que necesitas).
h. Cruza (sólo cuando está en verde).
i. Advice will vary.

¡El pasaporte, por favor!

Los mandatos negativos: continuación

Verbs ending in -car, -gar, and -zar have the following spelling changes in negative *tú* commands in order to maintain the original sound.

-car *(c → qu)*
tocar
toco → to**qu**- + **es**   **No toques** el piano.

-gar *(g → gu)*
llegar
llego → lle**gu**- + **es**   **No llegues** tarde.

-zar *(z → c)*
cruzar
cruzo → cru**c**- + **es**   **No cruces** aquí.

• Verbs whose present-tense *yo* form ends in *-go (caerse, decir, hacer, poner, salir, tener, traer)* form their negative *tú* commands according to the regular rule.

  No pongas la maleta sobre el asiento.
  No hagas ruido en el avión.
  No le **digas** eso a la auxiliar de vuelo.
  No salgas de tu asiento.

• Some verbs, such as *ir* and *ser*, have irregular negative *tú* command forms.

  No vayas al bosque por la noche.
  No seas tímido. Pide lo que necesitas.

5 Imagina que alguien viaja solo(a) por primera vez. Tú y tu compañero(a) le dan consejos. ¿Qué le dicen?

poner la artesanía   A —*No pongas la artesanía en el equipaje.*
en el equipaje   B —*De acuerdo. Ponla en un bolso.*

a. salir solo(a)
b. hacer reservaciones en un hotel
c. poner el pasaporte en la maleta
d. llegar tarde al aeropuerto
e. ir al centro solo(a) por la noche
f. ser maleducado(a)
g. traer muchos regalos
h. cruzar la calle cuando el semáforo está en rojo
i. 🔦

414   Capítulo 12

Options

Strategies for Reaching All Students

Students Needing Extra Help
Los mandatos negativos: continuación: On the chalkboard, copy this list of -car, -gar, and -zar verbs that students know:

buscar	apagar	aterrizar
explicar	colgar	empezar
indicar	despegar	cruzar
picar	entregar	
practicar	jugar	
sacar	llegar	
secar	pagar	
tocar		

Then form their affirmative and negative commands. Repeat with the -go verbs, *ir*, and *ser*.
Ex. 5: Brainstorm additional advice to complete the *Estudiante B* response. Point out that the command for *Estudiante A* is negative, but that for *Estudiante B* it is affirmative.
Ex. 6: Have students generate a list of possible activities.
Ahora lo sabes: Have students write out this list so they can record their progress.

Enrichment
As a homework assignment, have students think of a well-known fairy tale, legend, or story and give the main character advice on things not to do or say, places not to go, etc.

Extended Written Practice/Homework
1. Write four commands telling a person who lives in an apartment building what *not* to do: *No toques la música por la noche.*

414   **Standards** 1.1; 3.1

6 Un estudiante nuevo llega a tu escuela. Con un(a) compañero(a), dile lo que debe hacer y lo que no. Recomiéndale por lo menos ocho cosas. Por ejemplo:

Ve a todos los partidos de fútbol.
Visita . . .
No vayas . . .

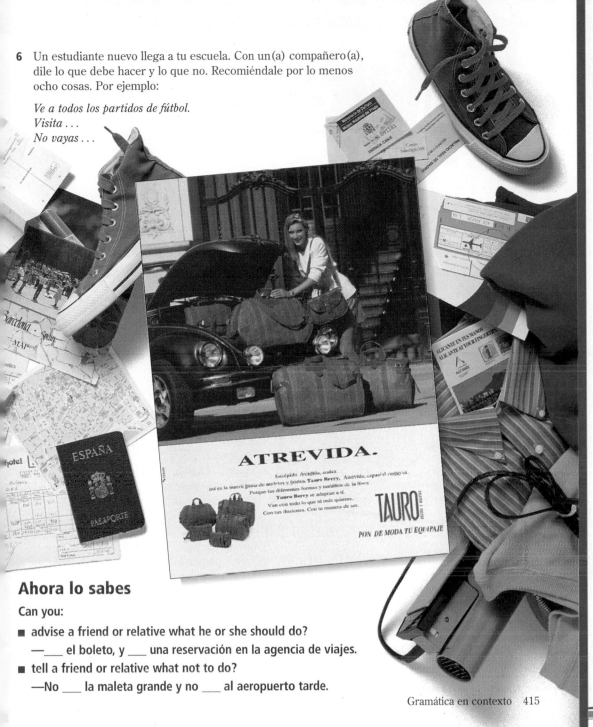

ATREVIDA.

TAURO
PON DE MODA TU EQUIPAJE

Ahora lo sabes

Can you:

■ advise a friend or relative what he or she should do?

—___ el boleto, y ___ una reservación en la agencia de viajes.

■ tell a friend or relative what not to do?

—No ___ la maleta grande y no ___ al aeropuerto tarde.

Gramática en contexto 415

---

2. Choose an activity that interests you (playing a sport, going shopping, watching movies, etc.) and write four sentences containing advice for this activity: *No vayas de compras en el centro porque allí la ropa es muy cara. Ve a un centro comercial con dos o más almacenes.*
3. Write three sentences of advice to children concerning good behavior: *No mientas nunca a tus padres.*

Multiple Intelligences
Verbal/Linguistic
See Audio Activities 12.4 and 12.5.
Visual/Spatial
See Enrichment, Practice Wkbk. 12-8 and 12-9, Writing Activity 12-F, and Comm. Act. BLMs 12-2 and 12-3.

Cultural Notes

(p. 415, realia)
This ad brings to mind the flair and daring of the Spanish *taurino* culture, suggesting that the owner of Tauro luggage can be as daring as a bullfighter.

Apply

¿Recuerdas?

Play

Video Activity A

Using the Video

Jamie and Carlos visit various Mexico City sites. They also go to el Museo Diego Rivera and see the mural *Sueño de una tarde dominical en la Alameda Central*. Later, they visit Carolina Beltrán, a lawyer who is reviewing La Catrina's will for them. In Licenciada Beltrán's opinion, the will is valid. She advises Jamie to begin legal proceedings to claim La Catrina's property.

La Catrina: Capítulo 12

Play

Madrid
Metro a Metro.

PRECIADOS
Preciados, 3.
GOYA
Goya, 76—Felipe II, 7.
CASTELLANA
Raimundo Fdez. Villaverde, 79
PRINCESA
Princesa, 42 – Alberto Aguilera, 39

Horario: 6 de la mañana a 130 de la madrugada.
• Estación con horario restringido.

416   Capítulo 12

Actividades

1 Imagina que llega a la escuela un estudiante de un país hispanohablante. En grupo, preparen una lista de direcciones para ir de la escuela a varios lugares importantes o populares. Incluyan un mapa y varios mandatos. Pueden decirle:

- ir a . . .
- seguir por . . .
- no tomar la calle/la carretera . . .
- doblar en la calle . . .
- no doblar en la calle . . .
- buscar . . .
- no ir a . . .

Si hay transporte público, pueden decirle:

- comprar el boleto en . . .
- tomar el autobús/el metro en . . .
- no tomar el número . . .
- bajar en la calle . . .

2 ¿Qué se debe hacer si ocurre una emergencia durante un viaje? En grupo, hablen de eso. Luego, hagan recomendaciones a la clase usando mandatos. ¿Qué debe hacer alguien si . . . ?

- se enferma
- tiene un accidente
- pierde los anteojos o los lentes de contacto
- pierde el pasaporte o el boleto de avión
- alguien le roba

Options

Strategies for Reaching All Students

Spanish-Speaking Students
Ex. 2: Have students write out this exercise.

 Un paso más Ex. 12-H

Students Needing Extra Help
If there are time constraints, have students do Ex. 2 only.
Ex. 1: Do the map first as a class so that students have a visual to help them. Present a complete model. Point out all the components in giving directions: street names, buildings, directions, etc. Use the vocabulary section of the Book 2, Chap. 10 Organizer.
Ex. 2: Brainstorm possibilities for what to do in an emergency. Review commands.

Cooperative Learning
As a class, discuss situations in which there may be unwritten rules: traveling, being a tourist in another culture, dating, friendship, talking to an authority figure, etc. Tell pairs of students to select a topic and develop a set of ten rules. One partner will write five

Conexiones

La geografía

¿Se necesita pasaporte o no?

Tú y un(a) amigo(a) están haciendo planes para viajar. Con un(a) compañero(a), mira estos itinerarios para decidir adónde irán.

- Con tu compañero(a), escoge dos de estos itinerarios. Uno de los viajes debe ser desde los Estados Unidos.

- Hagan una tabla similar a ésta para cada itinerario y complétenla.

Itinerario: De _____ a _____

Modos de viaje posibles:

   Por avión   Por mar   Por tren   En auto

   Otro: _____

Si por avión: Línea aérea: _____

   Vuelo directo   Sí   No

   Si no, con escala en _____

Se necesita pasaporte   Sí   No

Hay que pasar por la aduana   Sí   No

Es necesario cambiar dinero   Sí   No

   Unidad monetaria oficial: _____

- Comparen su tabla con las de otros grupos de la clase.

- Presenten sus resultados a la clase.

Todo junto 417

 Video Activity B

 Para entender mejor

Play

 Video Activity C

Answers: Conexiones
Charts will vary. Assuming students have U.S. passports, they would be needed for Spain, England, France, Australia, and New Zealand, but not for Puerto Rico. In Mexico, passports are highly recommended but not obligatory. It's necessary to pass through customs and change money for all of these countries with the exception of Puerto Rico.
Currencies:
México: nuevos pesos mexicanos
Puerto Rico: dólares (EE.UU.)
España: pesetas (euros)
Inglaterra: libras
Francia: francos (euros)
Australia: dólares australianos
Nueva Zelanda: dólares neozelandeses

 Writing Activities 12-G, 12-H

 Comm. Act. BLMs 12-4, 12-5

 Pasos vivos 2 CD-ROM
A Jugar, Laboratorio de grabar, Maps, Video Monitor, Video Presentation Maker

---

affirmative commands, and the other five negative commands. Each command should employ a different verb. Partners should exchange lists to assure appropriateness to the situation. Have students present their lists and discuss them with the class.

Multiple Intelligences
Interpersonal/Social
See *Actividades* 1–2.
Interpersonal/Social and Verbal/Linguistic
See Cooperative Learning.
Visual/Spatial
See Using the Video, *Conexiones,* Writing Activities 12-G and 12-H, and Comm. Act. BLMs 12-4 and 12-5.

Cultural Notes

(p. 416, realia)
With a total of eleven lines, the *metro* system of Madrid is quite extensive, reaching most areas of the city. Due to government subsidies, it is also inexpensive. In 1998, one ride cost only 130 *pesetas* (less than a dollar) and a ten-ride pass cost 670 *pesetas* (about five dollars). Ask students: Why do you think that the government subsidizes the Madrid *metro?* Do you think subsidizing public transportation is a good idea? Why or why not?

Apply

Process Reading
For a description of process reading, see p. 52.

Answers
Antes de leer
Answers will vary, but students may mention:
Check doors and windows to make sure they're locked.
Ask neighbors to pick up the mail.
Put house lights on a timer.
Tell only a few people that you will be away.

Mira la lectura
Answers will vary.

¡Vamos a leer!

Antes de leer

STRATEGY > Using prior knowledge

This is a public service ad about protecting your house before you go on vacation. Make a list in English of six things you think you should do.

Mira la lectura

STRATEGY > Skimming

Now skim the reading selection to get a general idea of what it's about.

Acostumbre a su casa a quedarse sola

Este verano, usted va a disfrutar de unas merecidas vacaciones, pero su vivienda se quedará sola, sin su protección. No se preocupe, unas sencillas medidas de seguridad, ayudarán a que su hogar no quede tan vulnerable como usted imagina. Además, las Fuerzas y Cuerpos de Seguridad del Estado, van a dedicar todo su esfuerzo para que a su regreso, encuentre todo tal y como usted lo dejó.

1 Recuerde que la puerta de su casa debe reunir unas condiciones mínimas de seguridad.

2 Haga un inventario de sus efectos personales, indicando marca, tipo y número de fabricación, y procure marcar sus objetos de valor.

3 Compruebe que todas las posibles entradas de la casa quedan perfectamente cerradas, incluyendo las ventanas que dan a patios.

4 No conviene dejar señales visibles de que su vivienda está desocupada: encargue a algún vecino la recogida de la correspondencia de su buzón.

5 No comente su ausencia con personas desconocidas ni deje notas indicando cuando piensa volver.

6 Existen diferentes entidades de crédito que durante sus vacaciones pueden hacerse cargo de sus objetos de valor: no los deje nunca en casa, ni tampoco dinero.

Para más información llame al: 900 150 000

Ministerio del Interior
Secretaría de Estado para la Seguridad

OPERACIÓN VERANO 91

418 Capítulo 12

Options

Strategies for Reaching All Students

Students Needing Extra Help
Ex. 1: Review vocabulary from Book 2, Chap. 8, and from Book 1, Chap. 10.

Infórmate

STRATEGY ➤ Coping with unknown words

1 Check your list against the ad. Which of your suggestions were included in the selection?

Remember, you already know several ways to figure out unknown words:

- recognizing a cognate
- recognizing a stem that appears in another Spanish word you know
- using the meaning of the phrases before and after the unknown word

2 What do you think these words mean? Explain to a partner how you figured them out.

merecidas	valor
vivienda	encargue
regreso	recogida
marca	ausencia
fabricación	hacerse cargo de

3 Now read the selection again and try out your meanings. If you prefer, try out these choices and identify the correct meanings.

1. merecidas
   a. merciful
   b. deserved
   c. safe
2. vivienda
   a. living
   b. life
   c. house
3. regreso
   a. return
   b. regret
   c. leaving
4. marca
   a. mark
   b. brand
   c. stain
5. número de fabricación
   a. serial number
   b. how many you own
   c. manufacturer's phone number
6. valor
   a. bravery
   b. value
   c. validity
7. encargue
   a. drive
   b. put in charge of
   c. send
8. recogida
   a. collecting
   b. recognizing
   c. knowing
9. ausencia
   a. absence
   b. audience
   c. plan
10. hacerse cargo de
   a. to park
   b. to send
   c. to take charge of

Aplicación

Can you understand the meaning of these sentences? Confirm your understanding with a partner.

1. El viaje que le regalaron sus padres era muy merecido.
2. Para su viaje compró una cámara de marca japonesa.
3. En el avión dieron la película *El regreso de Godzilla.*
4. Va a hacer muchas compras; el valor del dólar es alto.

¡Vamos a leer! 419

Infórmate

1–2 Answers will vary.

3 1. b
   2. c
   3. a
   4. b
   5. a
   6. b
   7. b
   8. a
   9. a
   10. c

Aplicación

Answers will vary, but should be similar to the following:
1. The trip his parents gave him was well deserved.
2. For his trip, he bought a Japanese camera.
3. On the plane, they showed the movie *The Return of Godzilla.*
4. He is going to buy many things; the value of the dollar is high.

www **Internet Activities**

Cultural Notes

(p. 418, realia)
Summer vacations and holidays, when homes and apartments may be unoccupied for extended periods, are when burglaries are most frequent. For that reason, the *Ministerio del interior* sponsored this program in 1991 to help homeowners increase their home security. Telephone 900 numbers, similar to 800 numbers in the U.S., are reserved for public service and toll-free calls.

Apply

Process Writing
For information regarding developing a writing portfolio, see p. 54.

see p. 54.

Todo junto

¡amos a escribir!

¿Prefieres viajar solo(a) o con un grupo? Vamos a comparar un viaje independiente a uno de excursión.

1 Primero, piensa en las ventajas y desventajas de las dos maneras de viajar. Piensa en estas cosas, entre otras:

- el costo
- los compañeros
- la necesidad de planear el transporte y los hoteles
- la oportunidad de conocer un lugar nuevo
- la oportunidad de practicar otro idioma

Escribe un párrafo breve empezando con la frase *Prefiero viajar solo(a) / con un grupo porque ...*

Disfruta.

Pásalo bien. Estés donde estés.
Porque Europ Assistance está siempre cerca.
Para que nunca te sientas demasiado lejos.

No te preocupes por nada.
Tienes un equipo humano a tu disposición
las 24 horas del día. Cuando te lo necesites.
Incluso aunque no seas usuario.

Asegúrate de que tu próximo viaje sea
de placer. Hazte socio de Europ Assistance.
Y disfruta.

europ assistance
(91) 597 21 25

En su Banco, Agencia de Viajes o Agente de Seguros y en Cajeros Automáticos de la red Telebanco 4B.

Un policía en Barcelona ayudando a una turista

420   Capítulo 12

Options

2 Ahora piensa en la gente que viaja: jóvenes, familias, ancianos *(senior citizens)*. Escoge un tipo de viajero y recomienda la mejor manera de viajar para esta persona. Empieza con la frase *Para (un anciano) es mejor viajar solo/con un grupo porque* ...

3 Para distribuir tu trabajo, puedes:

- hacer un debate sobre el tema *Para un(a) jóven es mejor viajar solo(a)*
- enviarlo a la revista o al periódico escolar
- exhibirlo en la escuela o en la sala de clases
- incluirlo en tu portafolio

Una chilena lee su revista en la playa.

Un grupo escolar visita el Jardín Botánico en Madrid.

421

(p. 420, bottom photo)
During the 1990s, the Spanish tourism industry has grown to well over 50 million visitors annually. The greatest number of visitors come from Europe (86 percent), followed by Africa (4 percent), and the Americas (3 percent). The majority of tourists say they visit Spain for fun, to visit historic sites, or to increase their understanding of Spanish culture.

(p. 421, top photo)
Just north of the historic Chilean port city of Valparaíso is the famous beach resort of Viña del Mar, whose beaches are filled during the summer months of December, January, and February with vacationers from all over Latin America and Europe. Viña del Mar is noted for its sunshine, good seafood, and beautiful scenery. The city is surrounded by wooded areas, and many scenic gardens explain its nickname, *Ciudad Jardín.*

(pp. 420–421, photo)
Botanical gardens were originally associated with medical schools to train students and to raise medicinal plants. Today they display ornamental plants, drawing visitors to view regional and more exotic plants of special interest. While ethnobotanists continue to study the traditional uses of plants for medicinal purposes, most such gardens today stress cultivation.

Assess & Summarize

Test Preparation

You may want to assign parts of this section as written homework or as an in-class writing activity prior to administering the *Examen de habilidades.*

Teaching Suggestions

The customs form used in the writing section is found on p. 78 of the Vocabulary Art BLMs/CD-ROM and on Overhead 88. Photocopy the BLM for your students.

Answers

Listening: —*Perdón, ¿por dónde queda la terminal de equipaje?*
—*Por este pasillo.*
—*¿Y la aduana?*
—*Está en la salida de la terminal de equipaje, al lado de la casa de cambio.*
—*Muchas gracias.*
The passenger is arriving (he or she is asking for the baggage claim area). It is an international flight (the passenger is asking where the customs area is).

Reading
1. d
2. e
3. b
4. c
5. a

Repaso ¿Lo sabes bien?

Esta sección te ayudará a prepararte para el examen de habilidades, donde tendrás que hacer tareas semejantes.

Listening

Can you understand when people talk about places at an airport? Is this passenger leaving or arriving? Is it an international flight or not? How do you know?

Reading

This is a notice given to hotel guests. Match the Spanish words with their English meanings.

> **En caso de robo, el primer paso es denunciarlo en la estación de policía más cercana; en caso de emergencias solamente, llamar al 911. Si pierde o le roban el pasaporte, hay que acudir al consulado de su país para su reemplazo temporal.**

1. denunciar	a. *temporary*
2. cercana	b. *go to*
3. acudir	c. *replacement*
4. reemplazo	d. *report*
5. temporal	e. *near*

Writing

Can you fill out a customs form for Spanish-speaking travelers arriving in the United States? Your teacher will give you a copy to fill out. Imagine that you have purchased *at least* one item that has to be declared.

Culture

Can you name three kinds of places to stay in Spain and describe at least one of them?

Speaking

Create a dialogue in which you buy an airline ticket at a travel agency.

A — *¿Cuánto cuesta un boleto de ida y vuelta a Cancún?*
B — *Esta semana la línea aérea Aeroméxico tiene una excursión de seis días a Cancún por sólo $569.*
A — *¿Incluye el hotel?*
B — *Sí, incluye un boleto de ida y vuelta, el hotel y el almuerzo.*
A — *¡Fantástico!*

www.pasoapaso.com

Options

Strategies for Reaching All Students

Students Needing Extra Help
¿Lo sabes bien?: Have students write out this section so that they can check off what they have mastered. Remind them that this is only a sample of what the real test will be like.
Listening: Remind students that they are listening for only two pieces of information. Brainstorm with students for what words they should be listening.
Reading: Review cognates and recognizing verb stems. Remind students that they prac-

ticed something similar in *Infórmate* in the *¡Vamos a leer!* section.
Writing: Most students will not be familiar with the concept of declaring purchases or the terminology related to it. Explain the idea of declaring and of monetary limits. For items 8, 9, and 10, draw a distinction between the three categories. Have students highlight the main words or phrases. They need not fully understand the fine print on the back of the form; you may, however, want to paraphrase it for them.

Culture: Have students review the notes they took during their first reading of the *Perspectiva cultural.*
Speaking: Remind students not to copy the model directly. Bring in some travel ads that state ticket prices, accommodations, etc. Use the vocabulary section of the Organizer. Limit the number of lines of dialogue. Remind students to use the present tense.

Resumen del vocabulario

Usa el vocabulario de este capítulo para:

- give advice
- discuss travel arrangements
- make recommendations about what to do and see in your community

to discuss travel arrangements
el viaje
el viajero, la viajera
la agencia de viajes
el /la agente (de viajes)
planear
viajar
la reservación, *pl.* las reservaciones
el boleto (de ida y vuelta)
sólo de ida
el cheque de viajero
el equipaje
la terminal de equipaje
facturar
hacer la maleta
deshacer la maleta
recomendar *(e → ie)*

to describe a plane trip
el aeropuerto
el avión, *pl.* los aviones
la línea aérea
el pasillo
el /la piloto
la puerta
la tarjeta de embarque
la ventanilla
el vuelo
aterrizar
despegar

la escala
sin escala
con destino a
procedente de
el /la auxiliar de vuelo
el empleado, la empleada (de la línea aérea)
abrocharse
desabrocharse
pasar por
registrar
la aduana
el aduanero, la aduanera
el cinturón (de seguridad)
el pasajero, la pasajera

to discuss tourist accommodations
la habitación, *pl.* las habitaciones
una (habitación) doble
una (habitación) individual
la pensión, *pl.* las pensiones

to discuss tourist activities
el /la guía
la guía

la oficina telefónica
el /la turista
la oficina de turismo
hacer una excursión
la casa de cambio
cambiar
la artesanía
el mercado
la naturaleza
el palacio
el pueblo
regatear
indígena
pintoresco, -a

other useful words and expressions
el retraso
conseguir *(e → i)*
disfrutar de
incluir: incluye
tener cuidado (con): ten cuidado
ir: ve; no vayas
a mano

Resumen   423

Writing: Tell students to fill out the forms completely in order to avoid delays in customs.

Culture
1. *paradores:* government-run inns often located in old and historic palaces, castles, or convents
2. hotels
3. youth hostels
4. private homes (which usually provide a room and one meal a day)

Speaking: Dialogues will vary.

Assessment

 Prueba cumulativa

 Examen de habilidades

 Test Generator

Additional Assessment Options

 Comm. Act. BLMs
Small Group Activities
Situation Cards

 Pasos vivos 2 CD-ROM
Slide Presentation Maker, Video Presentation Maker, Word Processor, Spindle

¿Lo sabes bien? Video Quiz

www Internet Activities
Self-Test

CAPÍTULO 13

THEME: MEALS

COMMUNICATION

Topics

Food preparation

Nutrition

Fruit

Objectives

To discuss food preparation customs in Spanish-speaking cultures

To name foods

To describe dishes and their ingredients

To discuss cooking

To discuss nutrition

To name snacks and beverages

To make suggestions

CULTURE

Meals and food preparation in Latin America

GRAMMAR

Repaso: Mandatos negativos

El subjuntivo

Ancillaries available for use with Chapter 13

Multisensory/Technology

 Overheads, 62–66

 Audio Tapes and CDs

 Vocabulary Art Blackline Masters for Hands-On Learning, pp. 68–72/CD-ROM

 Classroom Crossword

 La Catrina

 Pasos vivos 2 CD-ROM

 Internet Activities www.pasoapaso.com

Print

 Practice Workbook, pp. 125–135

 Writing, Audio & Video Activities, pp. 77–82, 129–131, 175–177

 Communicative Activity Blackline Masters

  Pair and Small Group Activities, pp. 85–90

  Situation Cards, p. 91

 Un paso más: Actividades para ampliar tu español, pp. 74–79

 RESOURCE PRO®

Planning Express, Teaching Resources Library, and Clip Art Library

Assessment

 Assessment Program

  Pruebas, pp. 188–198

  Examen de habilidades, pp. 199–202

 Test Generator

 ¿Lo sabes bien? Video Quiz

Video still from Chap. 13

423A

Regional Cuisine

Many basic foods eaten in Spain and Latin America today have been a part of diets there since pre-Columbian times. Indigenous Latin American staples include potatoes, squash, peppers, and chocolate, but corn is perhaps the most common. The Mexican corn *tortilla* is used rather than bread during meals, and also in the preparation of typical dishes such as *enchiladas* and *tacos*. The *tortilla* is popular in Central America as well, but it is smaller and thicker than its Mexican counterpart. Another popular corn dish in Mexico and Central America is *tamales.* Also known as *nacatamales* in Nicaragua, these can be sweet or spicy, wrapped in corn husks or banana leaves, and will vary in shape and size depending on the region in which they are made. Although *tortillas* and *tamales* are not native to South America, numerous corn dishes are found throughout the continent. In Ecuador, *mote* is a typical part of family meals. It is simply a platter of cooked, large, white corn kernels that is placed in the center of the table: spoonfuls are taken directly rather than placed on individual plates.

Another food staple which dates back to pre-Columbian times is beans. By far, the most common entree in Central America and parts of the Caribbean is black beans and rice. This combination has acquired two colorful names. In Nicaragua, it is known as *gallo pinto* (speckled rooster), and in Costa Rica and Cuba it is referred to as *moros y cristianos* (Moors and Christians, in reference to the Arab invasion of Spain). It is often served with a dry, white cheese on top and accompanied by fried or boiled plantains.

Seafood is also a basic ingredient for those who live along the coasts of Spain and Latin America. Some of the most prized shellfish come from Chile's coastal waters, and are used in many delicious combinations, including the traditional *curanto* (a steaming hot seasoned serving of various shellfish) in southern Chile.

In Spain, the region best known for seafood is Galicia along the northwest coast. One of the most popular dishes there is boiled octopus sliced into medallions and covered with hot olive oil and garlic. The most universally recognized Spanish entree—*paella*—also contains seafood. Originally from Valencia on Spain's east coast, it consists of saffron-seasoned rice, abundant amounts of shellfish in its shell, pork and chicken, and other regional delicacies.

Introduce

Re-entry of Concepts

The following list represents words, expressions, and grammar topics re-entered from Book 1 and Book 2 (Chaps. 4 and 6):

Book 1

numbers 0–31, food, drink, expressing preferences, numbers 32–100

Chapter 4

sports, leisure-time activities

Chapter 6

holidays

Planning

Cross-Curricular Connections

Mathematics Connection *(pp. 446–447)*
Have each student choose a favorite recipe and write it out in Spanish. All directions must be in the command form, with use of the subjunctive encouraged. All the ingredient amounts must be metric. You may want to orchestrate a potluck day so that students can demonstrate these recipes and bring the foods to class.

Health Connection *(pp. 448–449)*
In pairs, have students role play dieticians. They will prepare menus for clients with varying needs: people who must lower their cholesterol or gain weight, vegetarians, people who need low sugar or high protein, etc. Have each pair create two menus and share them with the class.

Spanish in Your Community
Have students determine which restaurants in their community serve foods and dishes from Spain. Have students visit this (these) restaurant(s) for a meal or to talk with the chef. Students may wish to invite a chef or a parent who specializes in Spanish food to visit the class, discuss Spanish food, and perhaps prepare a dish. Students might also want to visit the local grocery store to find out which Spanish foods are available.

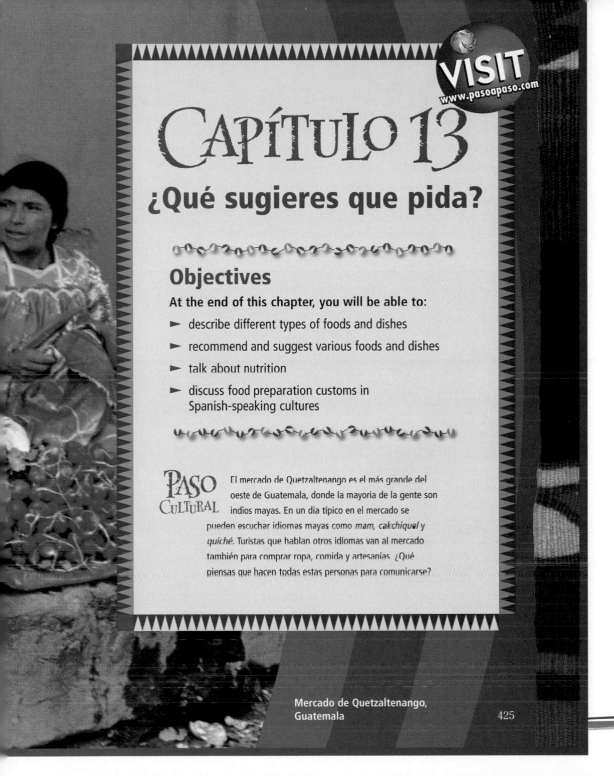

CAPÍTULO 13
¿Qué sugieres que pida?

Objectives

At the end of this chapter, you will be able to:

► describe different types of foods and dishes

► recommend and suggest various foods and dishes

► talk about nutrition

► discuss food preparation customs in Spanish-speaking cultures

PASO CULTURAL
El mercado de Quetzaltenango es el más grande del oeste de Guatemala, donde la mayoría de la gente son indios mayas. En un día típico en el mercado se pueden escuchar idiomas mayas como *mam, cakchiquel* y *quiché*. Turistas que hablan otros idiomas van al mercado también para comprar ropa, comida y artesanías. ¿Qué piensas que hacen todas estas personas para comunicarse?

Mercado de Quetzaltenango, Guatemala

425

Paso cultural
Se comunican con gestos *(gestures)* y con algunas palabras del español y, a veces, del inglés u otro idioma. Muchas veces la gente del mercado aprende palabras importantes para poder vender.

(pp. 424–425, photo)
Quetzaltenango, also called Xela, is an industrial city and a major trading center for villages in Guatemala's western highlands. Avenida 15 is home to a large market where produce as well as woven and ceramic *artesanía* from the surrounding villages are sold. These two women selling *rábanos* (radishes), *zanahorias,* and *maravillas* (mari-

golds) in the market are wearing *huipiles* typical of their home village. Each village has a distinctive *huipil* with a characteristic woven or embroidered design. Often these ornate designs form a cross when the blouse is laid open and flat. The cross shape is emblematic of eternal life and also represents the four cardinal points, the four winds, and the four phases of the moon.

Preview

Cultural Objective
• To discuss meals and food preparation in Latin America

Critical Thinking: Classifying Information
Have students make a two-column list with the headings *Bueno(a) para la salud* and *Malo(a) para la salud*. Have them categorize the foods shown in the photos. Using this information, have them make a second list with the headings *Lo que como frecuentemente, Lo que como a veces,* and *Lo que no como nunca.*

Answers: ¡Piénsalo bien!
Answers to inductive questions will vary.

¡Piensa en la CULTURA!

Restaurantes en México, Colombia y España

Mira las fotos. Las personas que vemos están hablando de la alimentación. ¿Hay comida en estas fotos que reconoces?

"A toda la familia le gustan las barbacoas y los picnics."

A ti, ¿qué te gusta comer en una barbacoa?

PASO CULTURAL Cada región de España tiene sus platos especiales, como el gazpacho de Andalucía y la paella de Valencia. Pero como España tiene costas extensas con el Atlántico y el Mediterráneo, los españoles comen mucho pescado. Y como España produce muchas frutas y verduras, éstas también forman gran parte de la dieta allí. Mira lo que esta familia española está comiendo en su picnic. ¿Qué diferencias ves entre este picnic y un picnic americano?

Granada, España

Una familia española disfrutando de un picnic

426   Capítulo 13

Options

Strategies for Reaching All Students

Spanish-Speaking Students
Ask: *¿Cuáles de estas comidas te gustan? ¿Cuáles te gustaría probar? ¿Has probado paella? ¿Te gustó? ¿Cómo se prepara?*

 Un paso más Ex. 13-A

Multiple Intelligences
Logical/Mathematical
See Critical Thinking.

Cultural Notes

Paso cultural
Possible answer: No hay muchas diferencias entre este picnic y un picnic americano. Están comiendo carne y ensalada. También hay jugos y otras bebidas en la mesa.

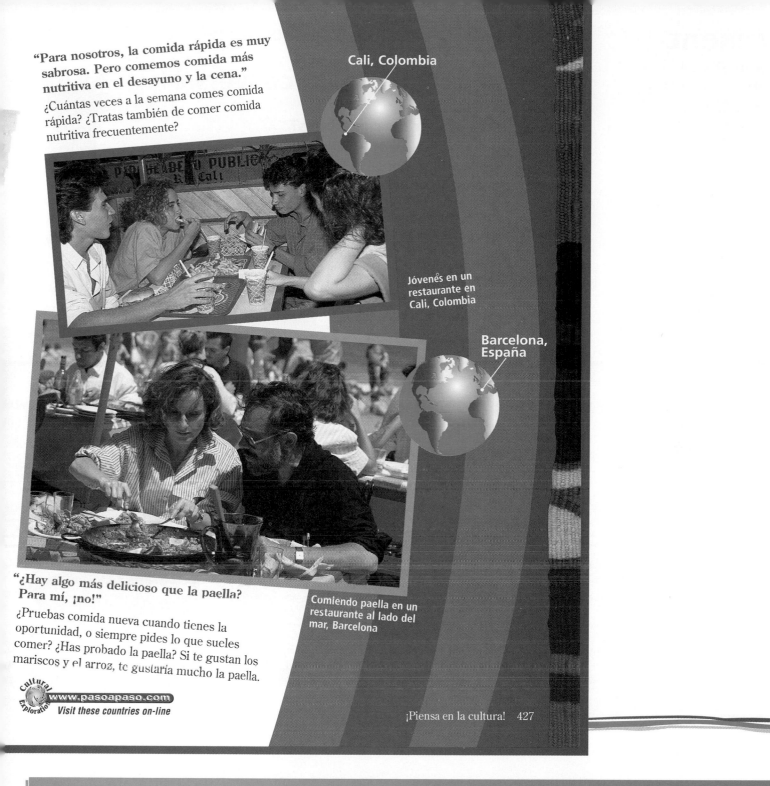

"Para nosotros, la comida rápida es muy sabrosa. Pero comemos comida más nutritiva en el desayuno y la cena."

¿Cuántas veces a la semana comes comida rápida? ¿Tratas también de comer comida nutritiva frecuentemente?

Cali, Colombia

Jóvenes en un restaurante en Cali, Colombia

Barcelona, España

"¿Hay algo más delicioso que la paella? Para mí, ¡no!"

¿Pruebas comida nueva cuando tienes la oportunidad, o siempre pides lo que sueles comer? ¿Has probado la paella? Si te gustan los mariscos y el arroz, te gustaría mucho la paella.

Comiendo paella en un restaurante al lado del mar, Barcelona

Cultural Exploration
www.pasoapaso.com
Visit these countries on-line

(p. 427, top photo)
Colombia has many fast-food chains offering the familiar burger and fries combination. For regional variety, though, Colombian street vendors offer many eat-while-you-walk foods, such as *pan de queso* (a ring of cheese bread), *chuzos* (skewers of beef), *tostones* (plantain chips), *buñuelos* (fritters made with corn flour and grated cheese), and a medley of tropical fruit drinks such as *guanábana* (soursop: a large, acid, succulent fruit with short, fleshy spines) and *mora* (mulberry).

(p. 427, bottom photo)
Seafood is abundant in Barcelona, a major Mediterranean seaport. Popular regional dishes include *bullabesa* (fish stew similar to the French *bouillabaisse), zarzuela de mariscos* (an "operetta" of shellfish), *bacalao* (cod), *lenguado* (sole) and *lubina* (sea bass). Catalan cooking combines elements of Spanish and French cuisine, and features spicy sauces including *all i oli,* garlic-flavored olive oil used for poultry.

Present

Chapter Theme
Cooking

Communicative Objectives
- To name foods
- To describe dishes and their ingredients
- To discuss cooking
- To discuss nutrition
- To name snacks and beverages

 Overheads 62–63

 Vocabulary Art BLMs/CD-ROM

 Vocabulary Tape 13-1

Teaching Suggestions
Preparing students to speak: Use one or two options from each of the categories of Comprehensible Input, Physical Response, or Limited Verbal Response. For a complete explanation of these categories and some sample activities, see pp. T20–T21.

Vocabulario para conversar

¿Quieres probar los camarones?

Vas a necesitar estas palabras y expresiones para hablar sobre la alimentación. Después de leerlas varias veces, practícalas con un(a) compañero(a).

la piña

guisado, -a

el champiñón, *pl.* los champiñones

el espárrago

el durazno

el limón, *pl.* los limones

el camarón, *pl.* los camarones

al horno

a la parrilla

asado, -a

hacer una barbacoa

428   Capítulo 13

Options

Strategies for Reaching All Students

Spanish-Speaking Students
Ask: *¿Puedes añadir algunas palabras a esta lista? Escríbelas en tu vocabulario personal.*

 Un paso más Ex. 13-B

Students Needing Extra Help
Begin the vocabulary section of the Organizer. Separate the foods into categories: fruits, vegetables, condiments, etc. Point out that *champiñón* and *camarón* lose their accents in the plural. Point out that *enlatada* contains the Spanish word *lata*, which they already know. Point out the differences between the cooking terms for students unfamiliar with them.

También necesitas . . . : Remind students that they have seen *dañar* before with a similar meaning. Give examples for *hacer daño a* and *mantenerse sano.* Point out the difference between *el dulce* as a noun and *dulce* as an adjective. Point out that *salado* contains the Spanish word *sal.*

frito, -a

el aceite

el vinagre

la salsa

el dulce

la mostaza

la mayonesa

las espinacas

fresco, -a

congelado, -a

enlatado, -a

el cerdo

También necesitas . . .

la alimentación	*nourishment, food*	dulce	*sweet*
hacer daño a	*to make ill; not to agree with (food)*	grasoso, -a	*greasy*
		soso, -a	*tasteless*
mantenerse* sano, -a	*to stay healthy*		
amargo, -a	*bitter*		
agrio, -a	*sour*		
salado, -a	*salty*		

> **¿Y qué quiere decir . . . ?**
> la caloría   la proteína
> el carbohidrato   la vitamina

*Mantenerse follows the pattern of tener.

Vocabulario para conversar   429

Class Starter Review

On the day following the presenta-tion of vocabulary, you might begin the class with this activity: In groups of three, have students list three foods in each of these categories: roasted, fried, and grilled. Within a given time limit, they should try to make their lists as unique as possible. Have volun-teers from each group read the lists to determine the most unusu-al foods mentioned.

Multicultural Perspectives

Names for many common foods vary from region to region in Latin America. This is at least partly due to the different native dialects spo-ken in these regions before the Spanish conquest. Sometimes the variation is so extreme that a request for a certain food using the incorrect name for that region will not be understood. Following is a list of some of these common foods and their regional names.

United States	Mexico / Ctrl America	South America
avocado	aguacate	palta
beans	frijoles	porotos
cake	pastel	torta
corn	elote	choclo
hot peppers	chile	ají
squash	calabaza	zapallo
strawberry	fresa	frutilla

 Internet Activities
Juegos

Learning Spanish Through Action

STAGING VOCABULARY: *Levántense*
MATERIALS: 2ʺ x 2ʺ cutouts of vocabulary items, cards for *frutas, salsas, verduras, preparación de carne*
DIRECTIONS: Place cards in different loca-tions around the room. Distribute vocabu-lary pictures. Direct students to stand, hold-ing up the picture, under the sign for the proper category.

Extended Written Practice/Homework

1. Refer to pp. 428–429 and write four sen-tences telling what kinds of foods you eat and how often: *En casa, comemos pescado al horno de vez en cuando.*
2. Write four sentences naming foods you like or dislike and telling why: *No me gustan nada los guisantes enlatados porque son sosos.*
3. Write three sentences comparing different kinds of foods: *Las espinacas frescas son más sabrosas que las espinacas enlatadas.*

Multiple Intelligences

Bodily/Kinesthetic
See Learning Spanish Through Action.
Verbal/Linguistic
See Vocabulary Tape 13-1.
Visual/Spatial
See Overheads 62–63, the Vocabulary Art BLMs/CD-ROM, and Class Starter Review.

Standards 1.1; 1.2; 1.3; 2.1; 5.1   **429**

Practice

Reteach / Review: Vocabulary

Before beginning these exercises, you may want to review Chaps. 4 and 12 of Book 1, in which food vocabulary is introduced.
Ex. 2: To extend this exercise, when *Estudiante B* replies that the food is too bitter, salty, etc., *Estudiante A* can offer to add or do something to the food to make it taste better.

Teaching Suggestions

Ex. 1: Point out that *al horno* and *a la parrilla* are expressions whose forms never change. However, *asado, guisado,* and *frito* are adjectives that agree in gender and number with the nouns they follow.

Answers: Empecemos a conversar

1 **ESTUDIANTE A**
(The adjective chosen may vary.)
a. ¿Quieres probar los camarones fritos?
b. ...el cerdo frito?
c. ...la carne (de res) frita?
d. ...el pollo frito?
e. ...el pescado frito?
f. Questions will vary.
ESTUDIANTE B
a.–f. Answers will vary, but may begin with *Me encanta(n)* and show correct adjective agreement.

Empecemos a conversar

Túrnate con un(a) compañero(a) para ser *Estudiante A* y *Estudiante B*. Reemplacen las palabras subrayadas en el modelo con las palabras representadas o escritas en los recuadros. Si ven 💡 pueden dar su propia respuesta.

1
A — ¿Quieres probar *las papas fritas*?
B — Sí. *Me encantan las papas fritas*.
o: No. Prefiero *las papas asadas*.

¡NO OLVIDES!

Do you remember these words for common foods?
la carne de res
el pollo
el pescado
las frutas
la leche
el pan
el arroz
las verduras
las papas

Estudiante A   Estudiante B

a.   b.

c.   d.

e.   f.

430   Capítulo 13

Options

Strategies for Reaching All Students

Spanish-Speaking Students
Exs. 1–2: Pair bilingual with non-bilingual students, if possible.

Students Needing Extra Help
¡No olvides!: If available, have students review the vocabulary sections of Book 1, Chaps. 4 and 12.
Ex. 1: Review cooking terms. Point out that *Estudiante A* has to combine the pictured food with a cooking term.
Ex. 2: Brainstorm other possibilities for the *prefiero* blank. Do the exercise twice, first using the *Estudiante B* response to practice the adjectives, then using the *prefiero* response.

Enrichment
Ex. 1: As homework, have students list three entrées that would appear on a menu in a family restaurant and write brief but detailed descriptions of each one. Tell students that the description should make the food as appealing as possible to the customer. For example, *Carne asada con arroz mexicano sabroso, y verduras frescas y una ensalada de espinacas, lechuga y tomates, servida con nuestra salsa fantástica.*

2

A —¿Prefieres _café_ o _té_?
B —_Té, por favor. El café es demasiado amargo._
   o: _Ninguno, gracias. Prefiero ____._

Estudiante A

a.
b.
c.
d.
e.
f.

Estudiante B

amargo, -a	grasoso, -a
agrio, -a	dulce
soso, -a	salado, -a

Letrero de
una frutería en
San Francisco

431

2 ESTUDIANTE A
a. ¿Prefieres papas al horno o papas fritas?
b. ... limones o naranjas?
c. ... duraznos o manzanas?
d. ... pollo frito o pollo a la parrilla?
e. ... jamón o pescado?
f. Questions will vary.
ESTUDIANTE B
a.–f. Answers will vary, but should show correct adjective agreement.

Using Photos
Ask: _Si una yucateca es alguien de Yucatán, ¿de dónde es una mazatleca?_

Cultural Notes

Extended Written Practice/Homework
1. Write three sentences telling what kinds of food you order in different restaurants: _En el restaurante La Venezolana, siempre pido pollo al horno con papas._
2. Write three sentences describing foods that different people serve on different occasions: _Cuando mi familia celebra un cumpleaños, mi mamá sirve pollo o cerdo asado._

3. Write four sentences telling how different kinds of food affect a person's health: _Los camarones fritos son sabrosos pero tienen muchas calorías._

Multiple Intelligences
Verbal/Linguistic
See Exs. 1–2.
Visual/Spatial
See Enrichment.

(p. 431, photo)
The nostalgic name of this fruit store in San Francisco's Mission District suggests that the owner may be from Mazatlán, Mexico. The Mission District includes a sizable Hispanic population and is famous for its many murals reflecting the rich cultural influence of Latin America.

Practice & Apply

Teaching Suggestions

Ex. 4: Tell students to pretend they are planning a meal for this exercise.

Answers: Empecemos a conversar

3 ESTUDIANTE A

a. ¿Quieres camarones?

b. ... piña?

c. ... pastel?

d. ... dulce?

e. ... vinagre?

f. ... espinacas?

g. Questions will vary.

ESTUDIANTE B

a.–g. Answers will vary.

4 ESTUDIANTE A

a. ¿Qué servimos, espinacas frescas o enlatadas?

b. ... piña fresca o enlatada?

c. ... espárragos frescos o enlatados?

d. ... pescado fresco o enlatado?

e. ... duraznos frescos o enlatados?

f. ... champiñones frescos o enlatados?

g. Questions will vary.

ESTUDIANTE B

a.–g. Answers will vary.

¿Qué sugieres que pida?

3

A — ¿Quieres *refresco*?

B — No, gracias. *Los refrescos me hacen daño.*

o: *Sí, un poco, por favor.*

Estudiante A — Estudiante B

___ me hace(n) daño.

No me gusta(n) ___.

Nunca como ___.

Tiene(n) muchas calorías.

a. b. c. d. e. f. g.

4

A — ¿Qué servimos, *jamón fresco o enlatado*?

B — *Enlatado. Es más práctico.*

o: *¿Por qué no servimos ___?*

Estudiante A — Estudiante B

Tiene(n) más vitaminas.

Es más práctico.

Se consigue(n) durante todo el año.

Es (Son) mejor(es).

Es (Son) muy bueno(a)(s) para la salud.

También podemos servir ___ congelado(a).

a. b. c. d. e. f. g.

432   Capítulo 13

Options

Strategies for Reaching All Students

Spanish-Speaking Students

Exs. 3–4: Pair bilingual with non-bilingual students, if possible.

Ex. 8: *Haz una lista de un menú ideal para un(a) joven. Incluye algo de cada grupo nutritivo. ¿Sigues tú una dieta nutritiva? ¿De qué debes comer más? ¿De qué debes comer menos?*

 Un paso más Ex. 13-C

Students Needing Extra Help

Ex. 3: Give examples of how to fill in the blanks in the *Estudiante B* responses.

Ex. 4: Point out that if *Estudiante B* chooses the *¿por qué?* response, he or she must fill in the blank with an appropriate choice.

Ex. 8: Explain carbohydrates, calories, etc. for students who are unfamiliar with these terms.

Enrichment

Ex. 4: Point out that if students suggest that another food be served, they should give reasons for the suggestion.

Ex. 6: Additional question: *¿Quién prepara la comida cuando hacen barbacoas en tu casa?*

Empecemos a escribir

Escribe tus respuestas en español.

5　¿Qué frutas y verduras comen en tu casa? Generalmente, ¿son frescas, congeladas o enlatadas? ¿Qué otras cosas enlatadas o congeladas comen? ¿Crees que es mejor comer comidas frescas? ¿Por qué?

6　¿Cuándo hacen barbacoas en tu casa? Generalmente, ¿qué comidas sirven en una barbacoa? ¿Cuál es tu comida favorita en una barbacoa? ¿Cómo prefieres las carnes—asadas, fritas, al horno o a la parrilla?

7　¿Le pones aceite y vinagre o alguna otra salsa a la ensalada? ¿A qué le pones mayonesa? ¿Y mostaza?

8　¿Sabes qué tipos de alimentación tienen muchas calorías? ¿Y pocas? ¿En qué comidas hay muchos carbohidratos? ¿Y proteínas? ¿Qué alimentación debe tener una persona para mantenerse sana?

También se dice

el caramelo
el confite

el ananá

el hongo
la seta

el aderezo
el aliño

el melocotón

el chancho
el cochino
el gorrino
el guarro
el marrano
el puerco

al carbón
a la plancha

rostizado, -a

In addition to *hacer una barbacoa*, we also say *hacer un asado*.

MORE PRACTICE

- Más práctica y tarea, p. 563
- Practice Workbook 13–1, 13–2

Vocabulario para conversar　433

Answers: Empecemos a escribir

5–8 Answers will vary, but should include correct use of the present tense. In Ex. 7, look for correct use of the indirect object pronoun.

Using Realia
Ask: *¿Cuál de estos dos platillos prefieres? ¿Por qué?*

Practice Wkbk. 13-1, 13-2

Audio Activity 13.1

Pruebas 13-1, 13-2

Multiple Intelligences
Interpersonal/Social and Bodily/Kinesthetic
Have students place the names or pictures of food items on index cards. With a piece of tape, affix a card to the back of each student. In pairs, have them guess the food item taped to their backs by asking questions: *¿Es una fruta? ¿Es carne? ¿Es de color verde?*

Verbal/Linguistic
See Exs. 3–8 and Audio Activity 13.1.
Visual/Spatial
See Practice Wkbk. 13-1 and 13-2.

Present

Chapter Theme
Recipes

Communicative Objectives
• To name foods
• To describe dishes and their ingredients
• To discuss cooking
• To discuss nutrition
• To name snacks and beverages
• To make suggestions

 Overheads 64–65

 Vocabulary Art BLMs/CD-ROM

 Vocabulary Tape 13-2

Grammar Preview
The subjunctive is presented here lexically. The explanation is on pp. 443–444.

Teaching Suggestions
Preparing students to speak: Use one or two options from each of the categories of Comprehensible Input, Physical Response, or Limited Verbal Response. For a complete explanation of these categories and some sample activities, see pp. T20–T21.

Vocabulario para conversar

¿De qué está hecha una empanada?

Aquí tienes el resto del vocabulario que necesitas en este capítulo para hablar sobre la alimentación.

hervir (e → ie)

revolver (o → ue)

el gazpacho

el pepino

la receta

el ajo

el pimiento verde

el chorizo

la masa

el relleno

la empanada

la fresa

la tarta

Options

Strategies for Reaching All Students

Spanish-Speaking Students
Ask: *¿Qué otros ingredientes sabes que se necesitan para completar estas recetas? Escríbelos en tu vocabulario personal.*

 Un paso más Ex. 13-D

Students Needing Extra Help
Point out that *el melón* loses its accent in the plural. Stress that this is canteloupe and not watermelon. Write out the full paradigms for *hervir* and *revolver,* including

command forms, for those students who need to see them. If available, use the vocabulary sections of the Organizers from Book 1, Chaps. 4 and 12. Emphasize that a *tortilla española* is an omelet, not a Mexican tortilla.
También necesitas . . . : Explain the concept of *las tapas.* Write out the complete *sugerir* paradigm, emphasizing its similarity to *hervir.* Refer to Exs. 10 and 12, where *que pidas* and *que haga* are used in context. Give additional examples.

Learning Spanish Through Action
STAGING VOCABULARY: *Levántense, Pongan*
MATERIALS: 2″ x 2″ pictures of ingredients for *paella, gazpacho, empanada, ensalada de frutas,* six mixing bowls
DIRECTIONS: Distribute pictures of vocabulary items. Play the role of a chef in a Spanish restaurant. Direct students to help

434 Standards 1.1; 1.2; 1.3; 3.1

la calabaza

picar

el huevo duro

la paella

el perro caliente

la tortilla española

la cereza

el melón, *pl.* los melones

la sandía

la ensalada de frutas

También necesitas . . .

el bocadillo	*Spanish sandwich made with French-type roll*
las tapas	*appetizer-size dishes served in restaurants in Spain*
mezclar	*to mix*
sugerir *(e → ie)*	*to suggest*
cocido, -a	*cooked*
(estar) hecho, -a (de)	*(to be) made (of)*
que pidas *(from: pedir)*	*that you ask for / order*
que haga *(from:* hacer)	*that I do*

¿Y qué quiere decir . . . ?
el cocinero, la cocinera
el ingrediente
cortar

Multicultural Perspectives
Latin American recipes contain some ingredients not commonly found in the U.S. *Plátanos* (green bananas or plantains) are used as vegetables that can be boiled, fried, or baked. This type of banana must be cooked before it can be eaten. In Puerto Rico and Cuba, it is fried and sliced to make *tostones*. Yucca (cassava, or manioc) is a root with a thick, barklike covering and a white starchy interior. It can be prepared in a variety of ways, from boiled with a garlic sauce to ground into flour that is then baked. *Jícama* is a Mexican root that is becoming popular in the Southwestern U.S. A member of the potato family, it can be peeled and eaten raw, or used in salads. Ask students from Spanish-speaking countries to share recipes from home.

www Internet Activities
Juegos

you create the items on the menu. As you read the recipes, ask students holding the picture of the ingredient mentioned to put the item in the mixing bowl.

Extended Written Practice/Homework
1. Write four sentences describing foods on pp. 434–435: *Algunas cerezas son dulces pero otras son muy agrias.*

2. Choose three items from pp. 434–435 and write sentences saying if you have tried them before. Tell if you liked them or would like to try them: *He probado gazpacho una vez. No me gustó mucho.*
3. Write three sentences saying in which dishes or kinds of foods different ingredients are used: *El ajo es un ingrediente importante en la comida mexicana y española.*

Multiple Intelligences
Bodily/Kinesthetic
See Learning Spanish Through Action.
Verbal/Linguistic
See Vocabulary Tape 13-2 and Class Starter Review.
Visual/Spatial
See Overheads 64–65 and the Vocabulary Art BLMs/CD-ROM.

Practice

Reteach / Review: Vocabulary

Ex. 10: To extend this exercise, *Estudiante B* can ask why *Estudiante A* suggests that particular food with the latter giving his or her reason.

Re-enter / Recycle

Ex. 11: holidays from Chap. 6

Answers: Empecemos a conversar

9 ESTUDIANTE A

a. ¿De qué está hecho el gazpacho?

b. ...hecha la paella?

c. ...hecha una tortilla española?

d. ...hecha una ensalada de frutas?

e. ...hecha una empanada?

f. ...hecho un bocadillo?

g. Questions will vary.

ESTUDIANTE B

a.–g. Answers will vary.

10 ESTUDIANTE A

a. Te sugiero que pidas un bocadillo de ___.

b. ...una empanada de ___.

c. ...unas tapas.

d. ...una tortilla española.

e. ...una sopa de ___.

f. ...un perro caliente.

g. Statements will vary.

ESTUDIANTE B

a.–g. Answers will vary.

Empecemos a conversar

9

A —¿De qué está *hecho un pastel*?

B —Está *hecho de harina, huevos, leche, mantequilla y azúcar*.

Estudiante A

Estudiante B

a.

b.

c.

d.

e.

f.

g.

10

un pastel de ___

A — *Te sugiero que pidas un pastel de chocolate*.

B — *Sí, buena idea, y además, quiero un café*.

o: *No, prefiero una ensalada de frutas*.

Estudiante A

Estudiante B

a. un bocadillo de ___

b. una empanada de ___

c. unas tapas

d. una tortilla española

e. una sopa de ___

f. un perro caliente

g.

436   Capítulo 13

Options

Strategies for Reaching All Students

Spanish-Speaking Students

Exs. 9–10: Pair Spanish-speaking students, if possible.

Exs. 11–12: Pair bilingual with non-bilingual students, if possible.

Students Needing Extra Help

Exs. 10 and 12: Explain the subjunctive expressions for meaning only. Avoid discussion of grammar.

Ex. 10: Explain the context of this exercise, (a waiter making suggestions for dinner). Break the expression *Te sugiero que pidas* into parts for students. Brainstorm possibilities for the blanks and for the *Estudiante B* responses.

Ex. 12: Help students match the *Estudiante A* and *Estudiante B* responses before beginning the exercise. Review commands.

11

A —¿Hacemos _pavo_ para _el Día de Gracias_?

B —_Sí, y tarta de calabaza también._

   o: ¿Por qué no hacemos ___?

el Día de Gracias

Estudiante A

Estudiante B

a. tu cumpleaños   b. el picnic   c. el Día de la Independencia

d. la fiesta de sorpresa   e. la fiesta de graduación   f. la barbacoa   g.

12   el café

A —¿Qué quieres que haga para _el café_?

B —_Primero, hierve el agua._

Estudiante A

a. la barbacoa   f. las empanadas

b. el pastel

c. los camarones fritos   g.

d. el gazpacho

e. la paella

Estudiante B

picar la cebolla   mezclar la harina y el azúcar

cortar los chorizos

conseguir los perros calientes   preparar el aceite

revolver el relleno   hervir el agua

Vocabulario para conversar   437

Practice & Apply

 Practice Wkbk. 13-3, 13-4

 Audio Activity 13.2

 Pruebas 13-3, 13-4

 Comm. Act. BLM 13-1

Empecemos a escribir y a leer

Escribe tus respuestas en español.

13 ¿Has probado alguna vez la comida española? ¿Qué probaste? ¿Dónde? Imagina que estás en un restaurante español. ¿Qué piensas pedir?

14 ¿Qué comida española te gustaría hacer tú mismo(a)? ¿Te gusta la comida con ajo? ¿Y con cebolla?

15 ¿Cómo se prepara el pavo en los Estados Unidos? ¿De qué es el relleno? ¿Cómo ayudarás a preparar el pavo la próxima vez? ¿En qué otras cosas ayudarás? ¿Crees que ser cocinero(a) es una buena profesión? ¿Por qué?

16 Aquí tienes unas recetas para hacer diferentes cosas. Adivina *(guess)* para qué son y completa los nombres de las recetas.

a. ____ **de papas**

4 papas cocidas	mayonesa
2 huevos duros	sal y pimienta
1 cebolla	

Corta las papas y los huevos. Pica la cebolla. Mezcla todos los ingredientes.

b. ____ **vinagreta**

2 cucharadas de vinagre
$\frac{1}{2}$ taza de aceite de oliva
sal y pimienta

Con un tenedor, mezcla los ingredientes.

c. ____ **de manzanas**

5–6 manzanas	$\frac{1}{2}$ taza de azúcar
2 tazas de harina	sal
4 onzas de mantequilla	agua

Antes de comenzar, enciende el horno a 450 grados. Para preparar la masa, mezcla primero la harina y la mantequilla con un tenedor. Después, ponle un poco de sal y agua. Extiende la masa y ponla en un molde. Corta las manzanas y ponlas sobre la masa. Por último, espolvorea el azúcar sobre las manzanas. Ponlo en el horno por 10 minutos. Después, reduce la temperatura a 350 grados y cocina por 30 minutos más.

i ME encanta cocinar!

EL LIBRO DE LA COCINA LATINOAMERICANA

www.pasoapaso.com

MORE PRACTICE

- Más práctica y tarea, p. 563
- Practice Workbook 13–3, 13–4

Options

Strategies for Reaching All Students

Spanish-Speaking Students
Ex. 15: Additional questions: *¿Se hacen comidas especiales en tu casa? ¿Cuándo se sirven esas comidas?*
Ex. 2: Instead of this exercise, tell students: *Escribe un párrafo sobre el (la) mejor cocinero(a) que conoces. Di por qué crees que es tan bueno(a) y describe una o dos de sus especialidades.*

 Un paso más Ex. 13-E

Students Needing Extra Help
Encourage students to finish all questions.
Ex. 13: Remind students that Spanish, Mexican, and Carribean foods are different from each other. Help them see how regional dishes are based on the ingredients which were originally readily available.
Ex. 14: Use the vocabulary section of the Organizer and the corresponding artwork. Point out that Exs. 15–16 can be completed by students unfamiliar with foreign foods.

Ex. 15: Assign this a few days in advance so that students can ask about it at home or contact the home economics teacher. Model responses to *¿En qué otras cosas ayudarás?* Give details of what a *cocinero(a)* does on a daily basis.
¡Comuniquemos! Ex. 1: Emphasize the health-related phrases suggested here. Model an entire dialogue to encourage students to create responses.
Ex. 2: Present a complete model. Use the vocabulary section of the Organizer. If avail-

¡Comuniquemos!

Aquí tienes otra oportunidad para usar el vocabulario de este capítulo.

1 Compara tu almuerzo con el de un(a) compañero(a).

A —*Para el almuerzo como . . . ¿Qué comes tú?*
B —*Yo como . . .*
A —*Me parece que comes mucho(a) / poco(a) . . . No debes comer tanto(a) / Debes comer más . . .*

Puedes usar las siguientes frases:

muchas / pocas proteínas	dulce
suficiente carbohidratos	fresco
algunas vitaminas	es mejor

2 Túrnate con un(a) compañero(a) para hablar del mejor cocinero o cocinera que tú conoces.

A — *(Mi abuelita) es la mejor cocinera que conozco.*
B —*¿Por qué?*
A —*Porque hace / Siempre cocina / Sabe preparar . . .*

3 Consigue una receta de alguna comida que te gusta mucho. Prepara una lista de los ingredientes. Explícale a tu compañero(a) cómo hacerla.

A —*Aquí tienes una receta para hacer un(a) . . .*
B —*¿De qué está hecho(a)?*
A — *. . .*
B —*¿Cómo se hace?*
A — *. . .*

¿Qué sabes ahora?

Can you:

■ discuss food preferences and explain why?
 —No me gusta el (la) ___ frito(a) porque es muy ___.
■ describe dishes and ingredients?
 —La tortilla española está ___ de ___, ___ y ___.
■ suggest to a friend or relative which dishes to order?
 —Te sugiero que ___ un(a) ___.

También se dice

el huevo cocido

el ayote
el zapallo

el chile dulce
el chiltoma
el ají

la salchicha

el melón de agua

Vocabulario para conversar   439

Answers:
¡Comuniquemos!
1–2 Answers will vary.

3 Answers will vary, but should include appropriate *tú* commands, use of the reflexive, or present-tense *tú* forms.

Answers: ¿Qué sabes ahora?
• Answers will vary. / Answers will vary, but may include *amargo(a), agrio(a), dulce, grasoso(a), salado(a),* or *soso(a).*
• hecha / cebolla / papas / huevos
• pidas / *Answers will vary.*

Strategies for Reaching All Students
MULTIPLE INTELLIGENCES
Interpersonal/Social and Verbal/Linguistic
See Cooperative Learning and Exs. 1–3.
Verbal/Linguistic
See Exs. 13–16 and Audio Activity 13.3.
Visual/Spatial
See Practice Wkbk. 13-3 and 13-4, Comm. Act. BLM 13-1, and Writing Activities 13-A, 13-B, and 13-C.

 Audio Activity 13.3

 Writing Activities 13-A, 13-B, 13-C

 Pasos vivos 2 CD-ROM
Boom Box, Clip Art Album, Slide Projector, Laboratorio de grabar

able, use the Organizers from Book 1, Chaps. 4 and 12.
Ex. 3: Assign in advance so that students can bring in recipes, or have recipes available. Remind students that they did something similar in Ex. 16c. Review commands needed for cooking.
¿Qué sabes ahora?: Have students write out this exercise so that they can record their progress.

Cooperative Learning
On index cards, list the ingredients of *la paella, el gazpacho, la tortilla española, la ensalada de frutas,* and *la empanada* according to the art on p. 434. Divide the class into five groups, but do not tell them which dish they will represent. Tape one index card to each student's back, keeping

all the ingredients for each dish in the same group. Students then ask *sí / no* questions within their respective groups to figure out which ingredient is written on his or her back. When everyone has discovered his or her ingredient, students should verify which dish the group represents.

Present & Apply

Cultural Objective
• To discuss the traditional importance of meals and food preparation in Latin America

Multicultural Perspectives
Kitchens, especially during holidays or special events, are the center of most households. In many Latin American countries, the preparation of special dishes involves the entire family. In Puerto Rico, everyone is needed to make *pasteles* for Christmas. These are made from mashed green bananas and seasonings that are then wrapped in banana leaves and steamed. A similar dish is popular in Mexico, where *tamales* are made from meat rolled in cornmeal and wrapped in corn husks that are then steamed. *Nacatamales* are a special holiday treat in some Central American countries. They contain not just corn, but meat, potato, and rice as well. Ask students to share a special event that involves the entire family in food or other preparations.

Perspectiva cultural

¿En qué se parece lo que ves en estas fotos a lo que hacen tú y tu familia? ¿En qué se diferencia?

Mercado al lado de la catedral, Granada

Muchas familias latinoamericanas viven en casas o apartamentos pequeños. Los padres trabajan, y padres e hijos comen un almuerzo ligero y cenan platos que se compran ya hechos.

Pero otras familias todavía viven de una manera tradicional. En estas casas, la cocina es un cuarto muy importante. Tiene que ser grande porque se usa todos los días y es un lugar de reunión. La preparación de los platos dura mucho tiempo. Por eso, mientras la madre o la abuela cocina, los miembros de la familia entran y salen, se sientan a charlar y ayudan a cocinar.

En la familia tradicional, la abuela vive con su hijo o hija y sus nietos. Tiene un papel muy importante. Puede encargarse de la casa o cuidar a los niños. Pero sobre todo, se encarga de la comida. Hace las compras por la mañana. Después pasa muchas horas lavando, cortando y preparando los ingredientes de sopas y guisados deliciosos para la cena familiar.

Las familias que viven de una manera tradicional siempre compran por la mañana los ingredientes

para las comidas de ese día. Así la familia puede disfrutar de una cena fresca y sabrosa todos los días.

www.pasoapaso.com

La cultura desde tu perspectiva

1 Compara la cocina tradicional latinoamericana con la norteamericana. ¿Quiénes pasan mucho tiempo en la cocina? ¿Qué hacen?

2 Muchas familias que compran comida fresca todos los días tienen refrigerador y no tienen que hacer las compras tan a menudo. ¿Qué valor cultural tienen estas familias?

440 Capítulo 13

Options

Strategies for Reaching All Students

Spanish-Speaking Students
Ask: *Piensa en la cocina de tu mamá o la de tu abuela. ¿Qué crees que recordarás de esa cocina en el futuro? ¿Los olores, los sabores, el calor . . . ? Explica por qué.*

 Un paso más Ex. 13-F

Students Needing Extra Help
Have students take notes to use in the *¿Lo sabes bien?* section.

Enrichment
Additional questions: *¿Cuáles son las ventajas y desventajas de hacer compras todos los días? ¿Cómo es diferente el papel de la abuela en una familia norteamericana de su papel en una familia hispana?*

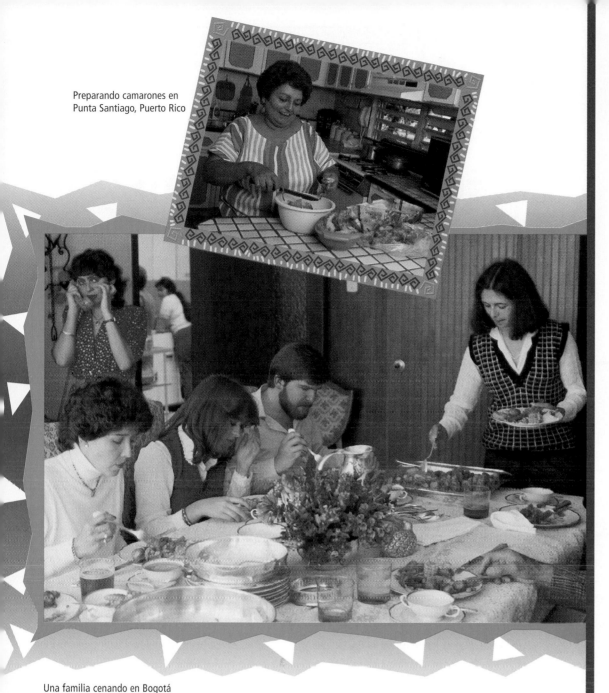

Preparando camarones en Punta Santiago, Puerto Rico

Una familia cenando en Bogotá

Perspectiva cultural   441

Answers: La cultura desde tu perspectiva

1 Answers will vary, but may include the following:
Kitchens in the U.S. are not as large as the traditional Latin American kitchen. There is less activity in the U.S. kitchen. In the traditional Latin American home, family members spend a lot of time in the kitchen. They come and go, chat, and help with the cooking. In U.S. households, family members don't spend as much time in the kitchen. Usually only one or two people use the kitchen to cook.

2 For families who buy fresh food every day, it is important to prepare healthful meals with the freshest possible ingredients. Going to the market is part of their daily routine. Other people prefer not to go shopping so often, and stock enough food for one or more weeks.

 Pasos vivos 2 CD-ROM
Maps, Notas culturales

 Internet Activities
Perspectiva cultural

Cultural Notes

(p. 440, photo)
The city of Granada in southeastern Spain was founded by the Moors in about A.D. 750, and was the center of Moorish wealth and culture in the thirteenth century. In 1492, when the armies of Fernando and Isabel took possession of the city, it was the last Moorish stronghold in Europe. The tombs of the king and queen are in the Royal Chapel of Granada's cathedral.

(p. 441, top photo)
Shrimp is a key ingredient in certain Puerto Rican dishes. One such dish is *caldo santo,* eaten during holy week. Ingredients include coconut milk, *recaíto* (a mixture of spices and vegetables), *alcaparrado* (a combination of olives, capers, and pimento), *yuca* (cassava), *yautía* (taro root), *batata* (sweet potato), *ñame* (yam), plantains, shrimp, *bacalao* (salt codfish), blue crab, and red snapper.

Preview

Overhead 66

Answers

A *Encienda* is from an *-er* verb. The present-tense *tú* form is *enciendes*. The negative *tú* command form is *no enciendas*. It means "we recommend that you light."

B The form of *usar* is *use*. The related form, *use*, is used in negative commands: *No la use nunca . . . .* It is different because it ends in *e* rather than *a*. The verb form *lave* is also different because it ends in *e* rather than *a*.

Multicultural Perspectives

In Argentina, beef is an important part of the economy and of the cuisine. *Gauchos* began the tradition of the *asado criollo,* an outdoor feast featuring meats as the main course. All types of meats—sausages, ribs, steaks, and delicacies such as liver—are cooked *a la parrilla.* Sometimes an entire animal is split open and put on an iron spit to cook slowly as it turns. Different sauces are prepared to accompany the meats. Have students investigate the Pampas region of Argentina and the culture of the *gauchos.*

Gramática en contexto

¡Lo felicitamos!

Compró Ud. la mejor barbacoa que se fabrica hoy, la Barbacoa Barcelona.

Le recomendamos que encienda su Barbacoa Barcelona en un lugar seguro. Si la enciende dentro de la casa o cerca de un árbol puede provocar un incendio.

Le sugerimos que use su Barbacoa Barcelona sólo para asar. Nunca la use para hornear o guisar.

Le sugerimos que lave su barbacoa con agua, detergente y un cepillo de metal. ¡Y ahora, que la disfrute! Estamos seguros que estará Ud. satisfecho con su Barbacoa Barcelona.

A A recommendation is made in the first caption. Look at the verb form *encienda*. Is it an *-ar, -er,* or *-ir* verb? What is the present-tense *tú* form? What is the negative *tú* command form? What do you think *Le recomendamos que encienda* means?

B A suggestion is made in the second caption. What form of *usar* is used? What is the related form that you know? How is this different from what you might expect? Find another suggestion in the third caption. How does the verb form that comes after *que* differ from what you might expect?

442   Capítulo 13

Options

Strategies for Reaching All Students

Students Needing Extra Help
Begin the grammar section of the Organizer. Review commands before beginning this section. Emphasize the vowel changes in the command form. Refer to the grammar section of the Chap. 12 Organizer.
Ex. 1: Review negative commands. Brainstorm possible reasons why the child shouldn't do these things. Emphasize the vowel change as a bridge to the subjunctive.

El subjuntivo: Make sure students take careful notes, or have a handout available with this information. Read the explanation and models aloud twice. The second time, when you come to the sentence "We use it to say . . . ," have students tell you the Spanish word for "want," "tell," "suggest," and "recommend." Then give the students the following formula: subject + *querer,* etc. + *que* + other subject + subjunctive.

Emphasize that each sentence will have two subjects and two different verbs, connected by *que.* The subjunctive verb will appear after *que.* Refer to the models to point out the different parts of the formula.

Repaso: Mandatos negativos

You already know how to give negative commands to someone you address as *tú*.

1 Imagina que cuidas a un(a) niño(a) que siempre quiere hacer lo que no debe. Tú le dices que no y él (ella) siempre pregunta por qué. Turnándote con un compañero(a), hagan los dos papeles. Por ejemplo:

beber otro refresco

A —*No bebas otro refresco.*
B —*¿Por qué no?*
A —*Porque te puede hacer daño.*

a. patinar en el pasillo
b. comer más dulces
c. cortar las flores
d. mezclar la sal con el azúcar
e. abrir ese guardarropa
f. saltar a la cuerda en la casa
g. echar los espárragos en la basura

El subjuntivo

Up to now you have been using verbs in the *indicative mood,* which is used to talk about facts or actual events. For example:

Tomás no **come** camarones.
Javier y yo **mezclamos** los ingredientes.
Tú **escribes** toda la receta.

Spanish has another way of using verbs called the *subjunctive mood.* We use it to say what one person does or doesn't want, tell, suggest, or recommend someone else to do. A sentence that includes the subjunctive form has two parts connected by the word *que.* For example:

Sus padres **no quieren que** Tomás **coma** camarones.
La profesora **sugiere que** Javier y yo **mezclemos** los ingredientes.
El cocinero **recomienda que escribas** toda la receta.

Gramática en contexto   443

Vitaminas de refresco.

Ahora que aprieta el calor, lo mejor es refrescarse con vitaminas. Mucho hielo, agua y zumo de limón. El refresco más natural, más barato y con más vitaminas. Este verano sácale todo su jugo al limón.

Alimentos de España
DISFRÚTALOS.

Extended Written Practice/Homework
1. Write four negative commands telling another person what *not* to do in order to stay healthy: *Para mantenerte sano, no uses demasiada mayonesa en los sándwiches.*
2. Choose four of these verbs and write negative commands telling another person what *not* to do while cooking: *quemar, usar, poner, hervir, cortar, revolver, mezclar. No hiervas el chocolate cuando haces dulces.*

Multiple Intelligences
Visual/Spatial
See Overhead 66, Practice Wkbk. 13-5, and Writing Activity 13-D.

Cultural Notes

(p. 443, realia)
This ad suggests that *limonada* is the ideal drink for cooling down during warm weather. Although *refresco* most commonly refers to a soft drink, it literally means "refresher" and can be used to describe any drink that fulfills that meaning.

Present & Practice

Class Starter Review
On the day folllowing the presentation of the subjunctive mood, you might begin the class with this activity:

Have each student imagine being a waiter or waitress in a Spanish restaurant. They should prepare to share with the class what they would recommend to someone trying Spanish food for the first time.

• We form the present subjunctive of most verbs the same way we form negative *tú* commands. We drop the *-o* of the present-tense indicative *yo* form and add the subjunctive endings.

infinitive *-ar*

que (yo)	hable	que (nosotros) que (nosotras)	hable**mos**
que (tú)	hable**s**	que (vosotros) que (vosotras)	hablé**is**
que Ud. que (él) que (ella)	hable	que Uds. que (ellos) que (ellas)	hable**n**

infinitive *-er/-ir*

que (yo)	com**a** /viv**a**	que (nosotros) que (nosotras)	com**amos** /viv**amos**
que (tú)	com**as** /viv**as**	que (vosotros) que (vosotras)	com**áis** /viv**áis**
que Ud. que (él) que (ella)	com**a** /viv**a**	que Uds. que (ellos) que (ellas)	com**an** /viv**an**

• We form the *yo*, *tú*, and *Ud./él/ella* forms of the subjunctive of stem-changing verbs the same way as regular verbs. We drop the *-o* of the present-tense *yo* form and add the subjunctive endings.

> El camarero quiere que **pruebes** la tarta de limón.
> El cocinero no quiere que **hierva** el agua.
> Te recomiendo que **pidas** una tarta de cerezas.

PIÑA FRESCA DE THAILANDIA

Options

Strategies for Reaching All Students

Students Needing Extra Help
Rewrite the three subjunctive charts on the chalkboard. Write out separate charts for *comer* and *vivir*. Have students copy the charts. Make sure they include the *que*. Remind them that stem-changing *-ar* and *-er* verbs have the stem change in all except the *nosotros* and *vosotros* forms. There are "boot" verbs in the subjunctive also. Write out some complete paradigms of *-ar*, *-er*, and *-ir* "boot" verbs *(probar, encender, servir)*.

Before presenting the *-car*, *-gar*, and *-zar* verbs, remind students that those verbs had a spelling change in the *yo* form of the preterite. In the subjunctive, the change will appear in all forms. Write out the complete paradigms of these verbs on the chalkboard. Have lists available of the verbs students already know that fall into these categories. Practice all irregular verb forms daily.
Ex. 2: Review subjunctive endings. Point out that none of the verbs used here are stem-changing or spelling-change verbs.

Enrichment
As homework, have students list the recommendations the following people would make in the given situation: a teacher advising students on how to prepare for a test, a parent instructing a babysitter on his or her toddler's evening routine, a guidance counselor telling a student how to prepare for a job interview. If they prefer, students can think of people in other situations giving recommendations.

- Verbs whose infinitives end in *-car*, *-gar*, and *-zar* have a spelling change in all the forms of the present subjunctive in order to retain the original sound.

-car *(c → qu)*
buscar
  Buscamos ajo y cebolla para el gazpacho.
  Mamá quiere que **busquemos** ajo y cebolla para el gazpacho.

-gar *(g → gu)*
apagar
  Juan apaga la barbacoa con un poco de agua.
  Recomendamos que Juan **apague** la barbacoa con un poco de agua.

-zar *(z → c)*
cruzar
  Cruzamos la calle para ir a la pescadería.
  Sugiero que **crucemos** la calle para ir a la pescadería.

2 ¿Qué les recomienda el médico a sus pacientes que quieren mantenerse sanos?

Gloria /
desayunar cereal,
melón y leche
El médico recomienda que Gloria desayune cereal, melón y leche.

a. Tomás / no comer tanta comida salada
b. Sra. González / tomar más vitaminas
c. los estudiantes / escribir una lista de lo que comen
d. (nosotros) / beber ocho vasos de agua al día
e. (tú) / cambiar tu alimentación
f. (yo) / preparar platos de verduras y frutas frescas
g. nadie / comer comida grasosa
h. Graciela y Ricardo / cocinar la carne a la parrilla
i. María Elena y yo / tomar una clase de ejercicio

Una frutería en la Ciudad de México

445

Answers
2 a. El médico recomienda que Tomás no coma tanta comida salada.
b. ...la Sra. González tome más vitaminas.
c. ...los estudiantes escriban una lista de lo que comen.
d. ...bebamos ocho vasos de agua al día.
e. ...cambies tu alimentación.
f. ...prepare platos de verduras y frutas frescas.
g. ...nadie coma comida grasosa.
h. ...Graciela y Ricardo cocinen la carne a la parrilla.
i. ...María Elena y yo tomemos una clase de ejercicio.

**Practice Wkbk.
13-6, 13-7**

Extended Written Practice/Homework
1. Choose five of these verbs and write sentences telling a student who is studying Spanish what you recommend that he or she do to be successful: *hablar, estudiar, repasar, aprender, escribir, leer, practicar, entregar. Recomiendo que hables español con muchas personas.*
2. Write five sentences telling what your parents want you to do at home. Use: *arreglar, sacudir, cortar, limpiar, lavar, quitar,* *sacar. Mis padres quieren que mi hermano y yo limpiemos el baño.*

Multiple Intelligences
Logical/Mathematical and Visual/Spatial
See Students Needing Extra Help.
Verbal/Linguistic
See Class Starter Review.
Visual/Spatial
See Enrichment and Practice Wkbk. 13-6 and 13-7.

Cultural Notes

(p. 445, photo)
Most open-air *mercados* in Mexico feature a *frutería*. This one is in the colonial suburb of San Ángel, which lies in the southern section of Mexico City along Avenida Insurgentes, not far from the Universidad Autónoma de México.

Practice

Re-enter / Recycle
Ex. 4: sports and leisure-time activities from Chap. 4

Answers
3 *Estudiante A* asks throughout, *¿Qué quieres que haga?*

ESTUDIANTE B
a. Quiero que piques . . .
b. . . . mezcles . . ./c. . . . abras . . .
d. . . . saques . . ./e. . . . busques . . .
f. . . . apagues . . ./g. . . . cortes . . .
h. Statements will vary.

4 ESTUDIANTE A
a. Mi mamá me dice que monte en bicicleta o a caballo.
b. . . . me dice que corra . . .
c. . . . me dicen que nade . . .
d. . . . me dice que camine . . .
e. . . . me dice que patine . . .
f. Statements will vary.

ESTUDIANTE B
a.–f. Answers will vary.

5 Order may vary, but should include:
Mis padres no quieren que yo escuche cintas cuando cenamos.
. . . use ropa tan sucia.
. . . suba montañas.
. . . me maquille demasiado.
. . . toque mi trompeta a medianoche.

6 ESTUDIANTE A
a. ¿Qué hago con la tortilla española?
b. . . . el gazpacho?
c. . . . el horno?
d. . . . los camarones?

---

3 Túrnate con un(a) compañero(a). Imagina que estás preparando una cena y un(a) amigo(a) está ayudándote. Dile lo que tiene que hacer. Por ejemplo:

lavar los camarones
A —¿Qué quieres que haga?
B —Quiero que laves los camarones.

a. picar la cebolla
b. mezclar los huevos y la leche
c. abrir la lata de champiñones
d. sacar el pollo congelado
e. buscar chorizos en la carnicería
f. apagar el horno
g. cortar la sandía
h. 💡

4 ¡No sé qué tipo de ejercicio hacer! Todo el mundo me dice algo diferente. Túrnate con un(a) compañero(a). Por ejemplo:

mis hermanas / levantar pesas
A —Mis hermanas me dicen que levante pesas. ¿Qué me sugieres tú?
B —Te sugiero que juegues básquetbol.

a. mi mamá / montar en bicicleta o a caballo
b. mi entrenador(a) / correr dos kilómetros tres veces a la semana
c. mis amigos / nadar por la mañana
d. mi papá / caminar en el parque
e. mi abuela / patinar por una hora
f. 💡

5 Hay muchas cosas que nuestros padres no quieren que hagamos. Di lo que no te permiten a ti tus padres. Usa los dibujos u otras ideas. Por ejemplo:

Mis padres no quieren que lleve arete.

446   Capítulo 13

Options

Strategies for Reaching All Students

Students Needing Extra Help
Ex. 3: Point out that some of the verbs used here have spelling changes. Remind students that the verb forms will change in the answer. Show them how *quieres* becomes *quiero,* followed by the *que,* and *haga* is replaced by a verb from the list.
Ex. 4: Review the *decir* paradigm. Brainstorm possible suggestions for *Estudiante B.*
Ex. 5: Brainstorm expressions students will need. Make sure students realize that *tocar* is a spelling-change verb.

Ex. 6: Have students match the art with the expressions. Have them tell the correct *tú* form of the subjunctive for the *Estudiante B* verbs. Remind students where to place the object pronouns.
Ex. 7: Present a model. Remind students that they did something similar in Ex. 2, p. 445. Point out that *pedir* and *encontrar* are stem-changing verbs.
Ahora lo sabes: Have students write out this list so that they can record their progress.

Enrichment
Ex. 5: You might extend this exercise by asking students about parentally approved activities. For example: *Mis padres quieren que lleve ropa más o menos como la suya.*

446   Standards 1.1

6 Imagina que es tu primer día de trabajo en un restaurante. Pregúntale al (a la) cocinero(a) qué hacer.

A —¿Qué hago con la leche?
B —Te sugiero que no la hiervas.

a.   b.   c.

d.   e.   f.   g.

no hervirla

recomendarla

servirla en seguida

revolverlos con el tomate
y la cebolla

encenderlo a 345 grados

probarlo antes de servirlo

devolverlo a la cocina

7 Imagina que quieres organizar una barbacoa con tus compañeros de clase. Diles, a por lo menos siete de ellos, lo que recomiendas que hagan. Usa estos verbos u otros:

cambiar	encontrar	llevar	preparar
cocinar	gastar	pedir	querer
comprar	invitar	pedir prestado(a)	sugerir

Ahora lo sabes

Can you:

■ say that you want someone to do something?

—Quiero que ___ tres cebollas, por favor.

■ say that you are telling someone to do something?

—Le digo a Carlos que ___ unas empanadas para la cena.

■ make suggestions and recommendations?

—Señor, le recomiendo que ___ un café con esa tarta de piña.

—Le sugiero que no ___ tantos carbohidratos.

Gramática en contexto   447

e. . . . el relleno?
f. . . . la tarta de fresa?
g. Questions will vary.

ESTUDIANTE B
a. Te sugiero que la sirvas . . .
b. . . . lo pruebes . . .
c. . . . lo enciendas . . .
d. . . . los revuelvas . . .
e. . . . lo devuelvas . . .
f. . . . la recomiendas.
g. Answers will vary.

7 Answers will vary.

Answers: Ahora lo sabes

• Answers will vary, but may include *piques, cortes,* or another verb in the subjunctive.
• Answers will vary, but may include *compre, cocine,* or another verb in the subjunctive.
• *tome* or *pida / coma*

Practice Wkbk.
13-8, 13-9, 13-10

Audio Activities
13.4, 13.5

Writing Activities
13-E, 13-F

Pruebas 13-6, 13-7,
13-8

Comm. Act. BLM
13-2

Pasos vivos 2
CD-ROM
Phone Task, Slide Presentation
Maker, Spindle, Treadmill

Apply

 ¿Recuerdas?

Play

 Video Activity A

Using the Video
Carlos and Jamie talk about the approaching court case against Silvestre Aguilar.

Later, in court, the lawyers of Jamie and Silvestre present their cases about who should be the rightful owner of La Catrina's property. The judge rules that all of it belongs to Jamie.

After the court case, at a big party to celebrate the decision, Demetrio finally introduces Jamie and Carlos to Santana, whose mission is now complete.

Jamie tells Carlos that she feels uncomfortable in her new situation and needs to talk to her family.

 La Catrina: Capítulo 13

Play

En Madrid

Actividades

1 En grupo, preparen algunas sugerencias para unos visitantes hispanohablantes que quieren probar comida típica de los Estados Unidos. Recomiéndenles restaurantes, a qué hora comer y qué deben pedir. Usen estas frases u otras:

* Yo sugiero que ...
* Yo recomiendo que ...

beber	empezar
buscar	pedir
cenar	planear
comer	probar
desayunar	visitar

2 En grupos de cinco, hagan los papeles de cuatro clientes en un restaurante y un(a) camarero(a). Primero, preparen un menú con sus precios, y después, pregúntenle y pídanle al (a la) camarero(a) la comida que quieren. Usen estos verbos u otros:

beber	costar	pedir
cambiar	devolver	preparar
cocinar	encontrar	recomendar
comer	gastar	servir
cortar	llevar	sugerir

448   Capítulo 13

Options

Strategies for Reaching All Students

Spanish-Speaking Students
Ex. 1: *Escribe la primera actividad. Puedes escribir de la comida de los Estados Unidos, o de cualquier otro país cuya comida típica conozcas.*

 Un paso más Ex. 13-G

Students Needing Extra Help
Have some menus on hand. Use the vocabulary section of the Organizer. If available, use the Organizers from Book 1, Chaps. 4 and 12.
Ex. 1: Present a complete model. Remind students that *empezar, pedir,* and *probar,* are stem-changing verbs.

Ex. 2: Present a complete model. Remind them that *costar, devolver, encontrar, pedir, recomendar, servir,* and *sugerir* are stem-changing verbs. Remind students that *costar* is usually only used in the third-person singular and plural.

Conexiones

La pirámide de la alimentación

Mira la Pirámide Nutritiva del Departamento de Agricultura de los Estados Unidos. De los alimentos que se muestran, ¿cuáles son tus favoritos? ¿Cuáles comes menos?

Los estudiantes se van a dividir en seis grupos para preparar informes sobre la alimentación. Cada grupo escogerá uno de los seis grupos de alimentos.

1 Investiguen:

• las sustancias nutritivas (proteínas, vitaminas, carbohidratos) que tienen los alimentos de este grupo

• la cantidad que se debe comer diariamente

• en qué consiste una porción

2 Hagan recomendaciones o sugerencias sobre esos alimentos. Por ejemplo:

Se recomienda . . . / Se sugiere . . .

El Departamento de Agricultura sugiere / recomienda que . . .

Los médicos /científicos dicen que . . .

3 Presenten su informe a la clase oralmente o por escrito

los azúcares y las grasas

la leche y sus productos

las carnes, los pescados, los huevos y los frijoles

las verduras

las frutas

el pan, los cereales, el arroz y la pasta

Todo junto   449

 Video Activity B

 Para entender mejor

Play

 Video Activity C

Teaching Suggestions
Ex. 2: You may want to elicit some ideas before the groups separate. Students who choose to be waiters (waitresses) may want to use a folded napkin on their arm and a small notebook to take orders.

Answers: Actividades
1–2 Answers will vary, but should include correct use of subjunctive.

Answers: Conexiones
Answers and presentations will vary, but look for logical information and the use of chapter vocabulary.

 Writing Activities 13-G, 13-H

 Comm. Act. BLMs 13-3, 13-4, 13-5

 Pasos vivos 2 CD-ROM
A Jugar, Laboratorio de grabar, Maps, Video Monitor, Video Presentation Maker

Cooperative Learning
In groups of four, tell students to imagine they are members of a charity that has decided to purchase $100 worth of food for a family of one adult and three children. Within the group, one pair should make the shopping list, including amounts spent, using foods from the food pyramid on p. 449. When each group is finished they should present the list to the class, letting the class vote on whether or not the food was worth the money.

Multiple Intelligences
Interpersonal/Social
See Ex. 1.
Interpersonal/Social and Logical/Mathematical
See Cooperative Learning.
Visual/Spatial
See Using the Video, *Conexiones,* Writing Activities 13-G and 13-H, and Comm. Act. BLMs 13-3, 13-4, and 13-5.

Cultural Notes

(p. 448, photo)
There are more than three thousand restaurants in Madrid, accommodating virtually every taste and budget. In general, foreign restaurants open for dinner earlier than Spanish restaurants, in which dinnertime tends to run from nine to late in the night.

Apply

Process Reading

For a description of process reading, see p. 52.

Answers
Antes de leer

Answers will vary, but students may say the olive tree originated in Asia Minor. Olive trees grow in the Mediterranean, and the Spaniards introduced the olive tree to Peru, Mexico, Chile, and California.

¡Vamos a leer!

www.pasoapaso.com

Antes de leer

STRATEGY Using prior knowledge

Do you know where the olive tree originated? Where do olive trees grow nowadays? How did they get there?

Mira la lectura

STRATEGY Skimming

Skim the article "El aceite de oliva" to get the gist of it.

El aceite de oliva

El aceite de oliva se extrae de la aceituna, que es el fruto de un árbol llamado olivo. La palabra española se deriva del árabe "azzait."

Su historia

El olivo se considera originario de Asia Menor, y desde allí su cultivo se extendió a todos los países del Mediterráneo y a sus islas. En el sur de Europa — Grecia, Italia y España — se cultivaba ya el olivo antes de la era cristiana. Se cree que los fenicios introdujeron el olivo en España. Los romanos y más tarde los árabes intensificaron su cultivo en Andalucía, y desde entonces el olivo es el árbol más representativo de la región andaluza. Los españoles llevaron el olivo a Perú, México, Chile y, más tarde, a California.

El aceite de oliva en la dieta mediterránea

Las propiedades beneficiosas del aceite de oliva residen en su alto contenido en ácido oléico (el ácido mejor absorbido por el organismo humano) y vitamina E.

Este aceite siempre ha constituido uno de los elementos claves de la dieta mediterránea, reconocida en la actualidad como una de las más saludables. La cocina española, tanto tradicional como moderna, utiliza el aceite de oliva en la mayoría de sus platos: ensaladas, salsas, vinagretas, paellas, etc.

Options

Strategies for Reaching All Students

Students Needing Extra Help

Point out that *oliva* and *aceituna* both mean "olive."

Infórmate

By now you have learned many strategies for helping you to understand a reading selection. Read this article carefully. Use what you know about articles and essays, the subject of olive oil, and reading strategies to help you. Which of the following strategies do you think will help you the most?

- Using prior knowledge
- Recognizing word families
- Using cognates

To check your comprehension, read these statements. Some are true, and some are false. Change the false ones to true ones.

1. Los árabes introdujeron el olivo en España.
2. El olivo se cultiva en California.
3. El olivo se cultiva en los países del Mediterráneo.
4. La palabra "olivo" es el nombre del árbol, no de la fruta.
5. El aceite de oliva no es ni bueno ni malo para la salud.

Aplicación

1. The olive was brought to the Americas by Europeans. Name three foods that were taken to Europe from the Americas.

2. What do some people use in place of olive oil? Where do those foods come from?

¡Vamos a leer!   451

Infórmate

Answers to inductive question will vary.
1. false *(Los fenicios introdujeron el olivo a España.)*
2.–4. true
5. false *(El aceite de oliva es bueno para la salud: contiene ácido oléico y vitamina E. Forma parte de la dieta mediterránea, que es muy saludable.)*

Aplicación

1. Answers will vary, but students may mention chocolate, tomatoes, corn, and potatoes.
2. Answers will vary, but students may say that some people use corn oil (which comes from corn), vegetable oil (from vegetables), or safflower oil (from safflower seeds).

www **Internet Activities**

Cultural Notes

(p. 450, photo)
Spain is one of the world's leading commercial producers of olives. Fresh olives are too bitter to eat, so they must be treated. In Spain, they are harvested before ripening, and then are soaked in lye to neutralize the oleuropein, the substance causing the bitter taste. The washed olives are then soaked in brine and packaged. The olive may be pitted and stuffed with a hand-rolled pimento. Olive trees may live as long as 1,500 years.

Apply

Teaching Suggestions

Ex. 1: Be sure to exhibit all student work on a bulletin board so that those doing the second exercise can base their work on it.

Process Writing

For information regarding developing a writing portfolio, see p. 54.

¡Vamos a escribir!

¿Comes mucha comida rápida? ¿Debes comer más comida nutritiva y saludable? Vamos a escribir algunas sugerencias.

1 Primero, piensa en las siguientes cosas:

- ¿Qué tipo de comida rápida es saludable?
- ¿Qué comida saludable puede sustituir a la comida rápida?
- ¿Qué meriendas saludables conoces?

Escribe una lista de sugerencias. Luego, ponlas en grupos lógicos. Pídele comentarios a un(a) compañero(a), y sigue los otros pasos del proceso de escribir.

2 Ahora, basándote en las sugerencias de todos los estudiantes, prepara un cartel sobre meriendas saludables. Usa mandatos afirmativos y negativos. Por ejemplo:

No comas dulces.

¡Come uvas!

La uva es la merienda de la naturaleza. Tamaño perfecto para poner en la boca.

Fácil de servir — si quieres sólo una o si quieres muchas.

¡Y el jugo de uvas es delicioso!

452 Capítulo 13

Options

Strategies for Reaching All Students

Students Needing Extra Help

Ex. 1: Divide the class into groups of three. Explain the term "logical groups." Review commands.

Ex. 2: Give students the option of using magazine cutouts. Explain that they should choose one snack and elaborate on its healthful aspects.

Multiple Intelligences

Naturalist

Have students list advantages and disadvantages of organic farming techniques: *La comida orgánica es más cara. Las verduras y frutas orgánicas son más sanas.*

3 Para distribuir su trabajo, pueden:

- enviar las sugerencias al periódico o a la revista escolar
- exhibirlas en la sala de clases o en la escuela
- usarlas para preparar un folleto
- enviar los carteles a una escuela primaria donde hay alumnos hispanohablantes
- enviarlos a una clínica que tenga clientes hispanohablantes
- incluir las sugerencias y los carteles en su portafolio

453

Cultural Notes ☀

(p. 453, realia)
Zumo is the most commonly used word for "juice" in Spain, but in some parts of Mexico and Central America, *zumo* refers to the zest: the thin, fragrant, oily outer skin of an orange or lemon. The oil from the zest is combined with alcohol to make flavorings or extracts. The zest itself is bitter, and the vapor it emits when the fruit is peeled or abrased is an eye irritant.

Test Preparation

You may want to assign parts of this section as written homework or as an in-class writing activity prior to administering the *Examen de habilidades*.

Answers

Listening: —*¿Qué pasó?*
—(crying) *Un desastre. Los perros calientes se quemaron. ¡Y el perro comió las hamburguesas!*
—*No llores. Sugiero que sirvas los perros calientes quemados y que prepares más hamburguesas.*
—*No. No vale la pena. Tampoco tenemos mostaza. ¿Por qué no vamos a un restaurante?*
The food is being barbecued or grilled.

Reading: The recipe is for an appetizer (guacamole).

Writing: Reasons will vary, but should include subjunctive phrases where appropriate.

Culture: In traditional Latin American homes, the kitchen is central to the home and serves as a gathering place for the family.

Speaking: Dialogues will vary.

CAPÍTULO 13
Repaso ¿Lo sabes bien?

Esta sección te ayudará a prepararte para el examen de habilidades, donde tendrás que hacer tareas semejantes.

Listening

Can you understand when people talk about food? Listen as your teacher reads a sample similar to what you will hear on the test. How is this food being cooked?

Reading

Luisa is reading a recipe. Is it for a soup, a main dish, or an appetizer?

Ingredientes
½ cebolla
1 tomate
2 aguacates
½ taza de cilantro
jugo de ½ limón
sal, pimienta, chile jalapeño al gusto

Preparación
1. Pique la cebolla.
2. Pele los tomates y los aguacates.
3. Aplástelos con un tenedor en una fuente.
4. Añada el jugo de limón, el cilantro picado y el chile jalapeño.
5. Agregue sal y pimienta y está listo para servir.

Culture

Can you describe the role of the kitchen in a traditional Latin American home?

Speaking

Create a dialogue with your partner in which you are deciding what to order in a Spanish restaurant.

A —*¿Qué vas a probar primero?*
B —*Pues, me encantan las tapas, pero si como muchas, no podré comer otra cosa.*
A —*Entonces sugiero que pidas sólo unos camarones y unos espárragos frescos.*
B —*Bueno. ¿Y cómo es la paella en este restaurante?*
A —*Sabrosa. Va bien con una ensalada de lechuga y tomate.*
B — ...

Self Test www.pasoapaso.com

Writing

The Spanish Club has asked you to help them write a letter suggesting that Spanish and Latin American food be served in the cafeteria. Here is one reason:

Sugerimos que preparen comida que nos ayudará a aprender sobre las culturas de otros países.

Write two more reasons.

454   Capítulo 13

Options

Strategies for Reaching All Students

Students Needing Extra Help

Have students write this out so that they can check off what they have mastered.
¿Lo sabes bien?: Remind students that this is just a sample of what the real test will be like.
Listening: Read more than once. Brainstorm for which words students should be listening. Point out the cooking terms *(al horno, a la parrilla,* etc.) if students do not realize these on their own.

Reading: Brainstorm what ingredients would be found in a main dish or soup recipe. Guide students through the preparation section. Encourage them to use context clues.
Writing: Have students use the Organizer and write two sample suggestions before the test as practice. Brainstorm reasons for serving Spanish and Latin American foods.

Culture: Have students review the notes they took during their first reading of the *Perspectiva cultural.* Give them guidelines for the type and amount of information needed.
Speaking: Use the vocabulary section of the Organizer. Limit the number of lines of dialogue. Present a complete model. Remind students to think about which tenses they need to use.

Resumen del vocabulario

Usa el vocabulario de este capítulo para:

- describe different types of foods and dishes
- recommend and suggest various foods and dishes
- talk about nutrition

to name foods
el camarón, *pl.* los camarones
el cerdo
el perro caliente
el huevo duro
la calabaza
el champiñón, *pl.* los
   champiñones
la cereza
el durazno
la fresa
el limón, *pl.* los limones
el melón, *pl.* los melones
la piña
la sandía
el espárrago
las espinacas

to describe dishes and their ingredients
la paella
el ajo
el chorizo
el gazpacho
el aceite
el vinagre
la salsa
la mayonesa
la mostaza
el pepino
el pimiento verde
la empanada

la masa
el relleno
la ensalada de frutas
la tortilla española
la tarta
agrio, -a
amargo, -a
dulce
grasoso, -a
salado, -a
soso, -a

to discuss cooking
el cocinero, la cocinera
el ingrediente
la receta
estar hecho, -a de
cortar
hervir *(e → ie)*
mezclar
picar
revolver *(o → ue)*
congelado, -a
enlatado, -a
fresco, a
al horno
a la parrilla
asado, -a
cocido, -a
frito, -a
guisado, -a
hacer una barbacoa

to discuss nutrition
la alimentación
la caloría
el carbohidrato
la proteína
la vitamina
hacer daño a
mantenerse sano, -a

to name snacks and beverages
el bocadillo
el dulce
las tapas

to make suggestions
que haga *(from:* hacer)
que pidas *(from:* pedir)
sugerir *(e → ie)*

Resumen 455

Assessment

 Prueba cumulativa

 Examen de habilidades

 Test Generator

Additional Assessment Options

 Comm. Act. BLMs

Small Group Activities
Situation Cards

 Pasos vivos 2 CD-ROM

Slide Presentation Maker, Video Presentation Maker, Word Processor, Spindle

¿Lo sabes bien? Video Quiz

Internet Activities
Self-Test

CAPÍTULO 14

THEME: THE OUTDOORS

COMMUNICATION

Topics

Camping

Hiking

Outdoor sports

Wild animals

Objectives

To discuss health problems tourists may encounter

To discuss camping

To describe nature

To discuss outdoor activities

To discuss plants and animals

CULTURE

Health problems tourists may encounter

GRAMMAR

El subjuntivo de ciertos verbos irregulares

El subjuntivo de los verbos ir y ser

El subjuntivo con expresiones impersonales

Ancillaries available for use with Chapter 14

Multisensory/Technology

 Overheads, 67–71

 Audio Tapes and CDs

 Vocabulary Art Blackline Masters for Hands-On Learning, pp. 73–77/CD-ROM

 Classroom Crossword

 La Catrina

 Pasos vivos 2 CD-ROM

 Internet Activities www.pasoapaso.com

Print

 Practice Workbook, pp. 136–146

 Writing, Audio & Video Activities, pp. 83–88, 132–134, 177–180

 Communicative Activity Blackline Masters

   Pair and Small Group Activities, pp. 92–97

   Situation Cards, p. 98

 Un paso más: Actividades para ampliar tu español, pp. 79–84

Assessment

 Assessment Program

   Pruebas, pp. 203–213

   Examen de habilidades, pp. 214–217

 Test Generator

 ¿Lo sabes bien? Video Quiz

Video still from Chap. 14

Parques y reservas nacionales

Latin America has many undeveloped regions providing travelers the opportunity to experience many unusual animal and plant species. National parks and biological reserves have been established to preserve a region's ecology and, in some instances, promote ecotourism, a concept started in the mid-1980s. Three such parks are worth special mention.

The lush and pristine Monte Verde Cloud Forest Reserve, in subtropical mountains along Costa Rica's continental divide, consists of some 48,000 acres that are home to a proliferation of plant and mammal species, including almost 500 emerald green and pink *quetzal* birds, held sacred among the pre-Columbian peoples of Mesoamerica. Another of its more unusual animal species is the delicate golden toad, which despite bold efforts to maintain ecological balance in the reserve, is on the verge of extinction. Entrance fees to Monte Verde, as well as to other national parks, have fostered the creation of more scientific institutes and educational programs dedicated to protecting the environment.

In stark physical contrast to Monte Verde is Chile's Torres del Paine National Park and Biosphere Reserve, offering one of the most dramatic landscapes in our hemisphere, with glaciers and ice fields, steep-rising jagged peaks, gentle plateaus, lakes, rivers, and waterfalls. Animal species include the South American condor, ducks, geese, flamingos, swans, small herds of guanaco (cousin of the llama), and Patagonian pumas. Despite its harsh, windy climate, tourism to the region has increased dramatically in recent years. Many come merely to relish the park's distinctive arctic beauty, while others engage in such activities as hiking, mountain climbing, and kayaking. The 450,000-acre park is considered one of Latin America's most well-managed and successful parks.

Perhaps the most well known of all the national parks and biological reserves in the world are the Galápagos Islands, approximately 600 miles from Ecuador's Pacific coast. Consisting of some 70 volcanic islands, they were discovered in 1835 by Charles Darwin who arrived at his theory of evolution based on environmental adaptation by observing that many of the islands contained their own unique animal species. Among the species inhabiting the Galápagos today are sea lions, giant tortoises, the flightless cormorant, and the albatross. To preserve this important natural habitat, the surrounding waters have been declared a marine reserve. Visitors are allowed to visit only a handful of the islands and must be accompanied by guides who educate them about the area's ecology and help enforce the islands' strict rules.

Introduce

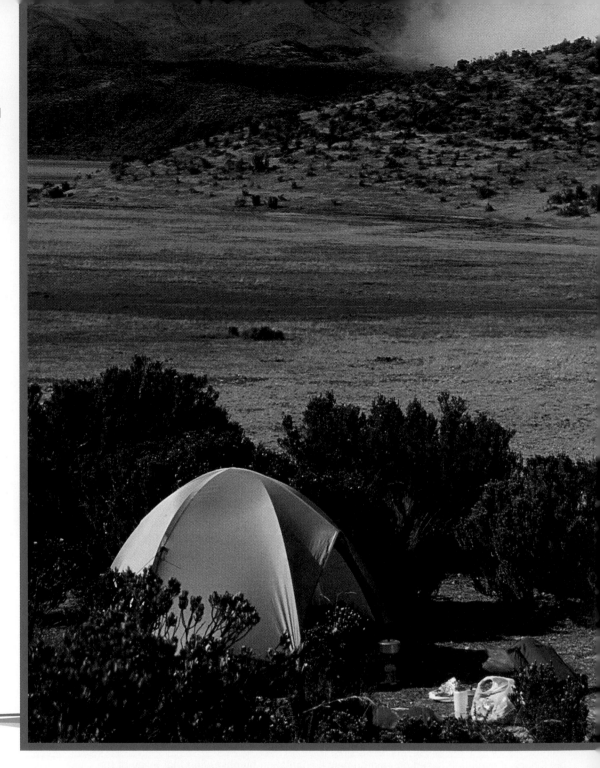

Planning

Cross-Curricular Connections

Geography Connection *(pp. 460–461)*
In groups of four, have students plan a camping trip to a site in a Spanish-speaking country. Within each group, they should choose a specific location and locate it on a map. Then they should describe the topographical and / or climatic features that influenced their choice, and which outdoor activities are available in the summer months.

Science Connection *(pp. 476–477)*
Have students choose one of the animals, plants, or natural features from this chapter and write a brief article for a science magazine. Without revealing their chosen subject, students should write three paragraphs: one describing its physical characteristics and special attributes, one telling its importance to the Earth or to our civilization, and one making recommendations as to how we can help conserve or protect it. Tell students to use as much chapter vocabulary and as many subjunctive phrases as possible. The following day, have students read their paragraphs aloud to the class, who must then guess the identity of the subject.

CAPÍTULO 14

¡Me encanta la naturaleza!

Objectives

At the end of this chapter, you will be able to:

► discuss popular outdoor activities

► describe the natural environment

► express attitudes and opinions about the environment

► explain why it may be unwise to drink the water in unfamiliar places

PASO CULTURAL El volcán Cotopaxi tiene una historia muy larga. Los indígenas de la región lo veneraban y consideraban la actividad volcánica como un mensaje divino. En 1534, los conquistadores llegaron a Ecuador y escribieron sus impresiones de esta extraña montaña con humo. Después, durante una batalla entre los conquistadores y los indígenas, el Cotopaxi entró en erupción. ¿Qué diferencias crees que hubo entre la reacción de los conquistadores y la de los indígenas?

Campamento en un valle cerca de El Cotopaxi, Ecuador, el volcán activo más alto (5.896 m.) del mundo

457

Answers: Paso cultural
Los conquistadores no tenían experiencia con volcanes y sentían terror. Los indígenas veneraban el volcán y sentían inspiración con la erupción. Lo tomaron como mensaje divino que les daba fuerzas en la batalla.

Cultural Notes

Spanish in Your Community
Have students go to a national park or park district office and interview the park director concerning the information available to the local Hispanic community. Have them present this to the class. If none is available, have students collect information in English to use as a model to create a Spanish brochure to present to the national park or park district office.

(pp. 456–457, photo)
INEFAN *(Instituto Ecuatoriano Forestal y de Áreas Naturales y Vida Silvestre)* administers Cotopaxi National Park, which lies along the Pan American Highway, south of Quito. The park is a destination for people interested in hiking up to the snowline of Mt. Cotopaxi (19,346 ft.) or for those wishing to view some of the wildflowers, lichens, birds, and majestic scenery of the mountain's lower slopes and protected gorges. Among the other parks administered by INEFAN are the Galápagos Islands.

Preview

Cultural Objective
• To discuss health problems tourists may encounter

Critical Thinking: Summarizing Information
Have students describe the three photos. Write responses on the chalkboard, and then have students summarize what the photos have in common.

Answers: ¡Piensa en la cultura!
Answers will vary.

¡Piensa en la CULTURA!

Preservando la naturaleza en España, Perú y Ecuador

Mira las fotos. Los estudiantes que vemos están hablando de la naturaleza. ¿Te gustaría viajar a estos lugares? ¿Por qué sí o por qué no?

PASO CULTURAL

Muchas agencias de viajes internacionales dicen que ir de camping en los Andes, como lo están haciendo aquí en la Cordillera Vilcanota en Perú, es muy diferente de ir de camping en otros lugares. ¿Qué diferencias puede haber entre la experiencia de escalar montañas en los Andes y en los Estados Unidos? ¿Cómo puedes disfrutar más de un viaje a los Andes sabiendo algo de la cultura de la región?

"Me gustaría ir de camping a las montañas: poca gente, aire puro, agua limpia de la nieve . . ."

¿Fuiste de camping alguna vez? ¿Adónde fuiste? ¿Cuándo lo hiciste? ¿Con quiénes? ¿Por cuánto tiempo?

Campamento en la Cordillera Vilcanota, Perú

Perú

"Cuando hace buen tiempo, nos gusta mucho dar caminatas por el bosque."

¿Disfrutas mucho de la naturaleza? ¿Dan caminatas tú y tus amigos? ¿Dónde? ¿Hay bosques donde vives? Si hay bosques, ¿cómo son?

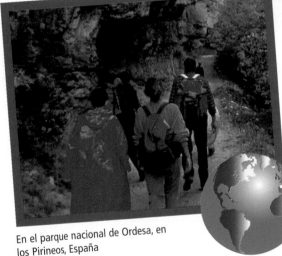

En el parque nacional de Ordesa, en los Pirineos, España

los Pirineos, España

458   Capítulo 14

Options

Strategies for Reaching All Students

Spanish-Speaking Students
¿En cuáles de estas actividades te gustaría participar? ¿En cuáles ya has participado?

 Un paso más Ex. 14-A

Multiple Intelligences
Verbal/Linguistic
See Critical Thinking.
Visual/Spatial and Verbal/Linguistic
For extra credit, have students prepare a presentation/report about Hurricane Mitch of 1998 and its devastating effects in Central America.

Cultural Notes ☀

(p. 458, left photo)
The Parque Nacional de Ordesa y Monte Perdido was founded in 1918 to protect the natural environment of the central Pyrenees. The park includes many varieties of pine, fir, larch, beech, and poplars. Several species of protected wildlife live there, including boar, chamois (a small type of antelope), and the *Capra Pyrenaica* mountain goat.

Las Islas Galápagos de Ecuador son picos *(peaks)* de volcanes sumergidos en el Océano Pacífico que tienen más de tres millones de años. Los habitantes de las islas son pingüinos, tortugas gigantes, iguanas y otras especies, muchas de las cuales están en peligro de extinción. Se limita el número de turistas que puede visitar las islas cada año. ¿Por qué crees que se puso ese límite? ¿Cuáles pueden ser las ventajas y desventajas del turismo para las islas?

"Sólo una foto más . . . ¡No te muevas, iguana!"

¿Tienes una cámara? ¿De qué sacas fotos? ¿De la gente? ¿De tu familia y tus amigos? ¿De los edificios? ¿De los animales y la naturaleza?

Cultural Exploration
www.pasoapaso.com
Visit these countries on-line

las Islas Galápagos, Ecuador

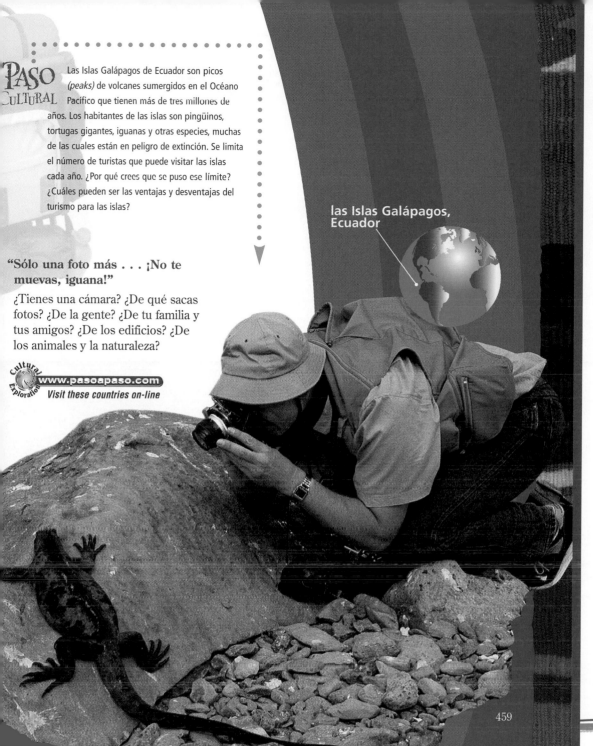

459

Answers: Paso cultural

(p. 458) En Perú, la gente vive en las montañas altas hasta 4,500 metros *(almost 15,000 feet)*. Saber algo de la cultura de la región es importante porque escalar montañas en Perú no es solamente disfrutar de la naturaleza, sino que se puede también conocer una cultura antigua *(ancient)* y una vida muy diferente de la vida de los Estados Unidos y de muchos otros países. En los Andes también se encuentran muchas ruinas de los incas y de otros grupos indígenas.

(p. 459) Se puso el límite para proteger el medio ambiente y los animales en peligro de extinción. El turismo puede cambiar el equilibrio del ecosistema, pero también puede servir para dar más atención y protección a los animales de las Islas Galápagos.

(p. 458, right photo)
This campground is set up in the Cordillera Vilcanota near Cuzco, Peru. While other Latin American countries have single *cordilleras* (mountain ranges) running through them, Peru's Andes are characterized by a number of separate but converging ranges. The Peruvian Andes are much wider than ranges to the north or south and have several sharp, snow-covered peaks that are favored by experienced mountain climbers.

(p. 459, photo)
The six Galápagos Islands, called *las islas encantadas* by Spanish explorers, lie 600 miles off the coast of Ecuador. It is believed that the Incas may have journeyed to the islands in large ocean-going rafts. Charles Darwin's observations of life on the islands

led to his theory of evolution described in *The Origin of Species*. Each island carries an English name as well as a Spanish one. Located at the southeastern extreme of the group is Hood Island *(Isla Española)*. The Galápagos are an Ecuadorian national park and wildlife sanctuary.

Present

Chapter Theme
Camping

Communicative Objectives
- To discuss camping
- To describe nature
- To discuss plants and animals

 Overheads 67–68

 Vocabulary Art BLMs/CD-ROM

 Vocabulary Tape 14-1

Grammar Preview
Several subjunctive phrases are presented here lexically. The explanation of the subjunctive of certain irregular verbs is on p. 475.

Teaching Suggestions
Preparing students to speak: Use one or two options from each of the categories of Comprehensible Input, Physical Response, or Limited Verbal Response. For a complete explanation of these categories and some sample activities, see pp. T20–T21.

Reteach / Review: Vocabulary
También necesitas . . . : Remind students of the other meaning of the word *roto* (broken).

Vocabulario para conversar

¿Das caminatas a menudo?

Vas a necesitar estas palabras y expresiones para hablar sobre la naturaleza. Después de leerlas varias veces, practícalas con un(a) compañero(a).

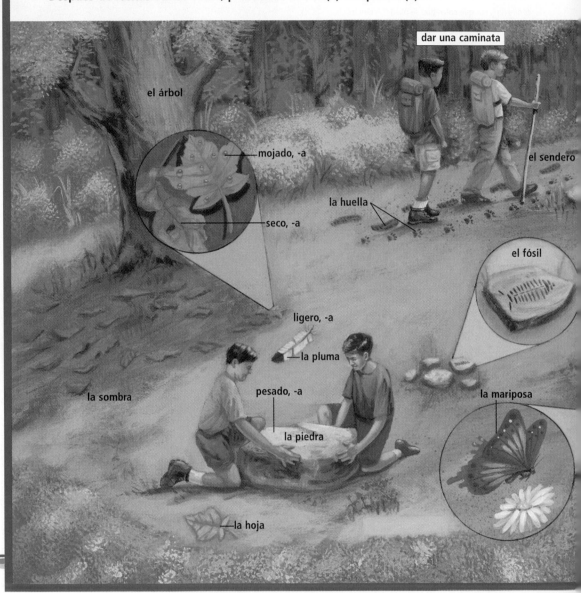

Options

Strategies for Reaching All Students

Spanish-Speaking Students
Ask: *¿Sabes otras palabras que se relacionen a este tema? Escríbelas en tu vocabulario personal.*

 Un paso más Ex. 14-B

Students Needing Extra Help
Begin the vocabulary section of the Organizer. Point out the word families of *el abrelatas, seco, caminata,* and *pesado. También necesitas . . . :* Give examples of how *que lo hagamos, pongamos,* and *recojamos* are used in sentences.

Enrichment
Have students make two lists: one headed *Lo que es necesario llevar,* the other headed *Lo que está en la naturaleza.* Tell students to place the new vocabulary under the appropriate heading.

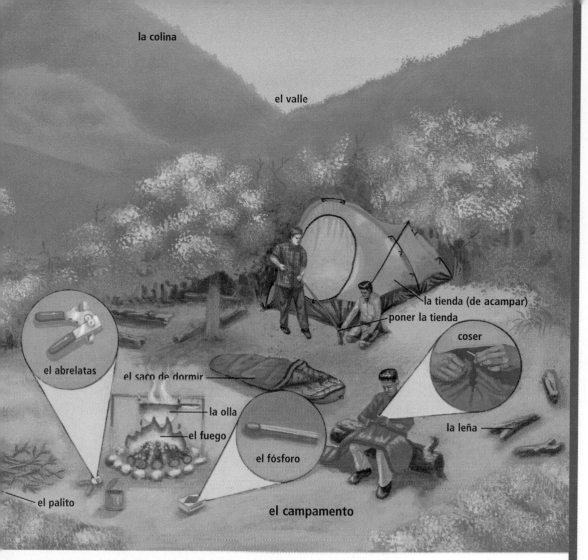

la colina

el valle

la tienda (de acampar)

poner la tienda

coser

el abrelatas

el saco de dormir

la olla

el fuego

la leña

el fósforo

el palito

el campamento

También necesitas . . .

recoger $(g \rightarrow j)$ *to pick up, to gather*
roto, -a   here: *torn*
al aire libre   *outdoors*

¿Y qué quiere decir . . . ?

contaminado, -a
ir de camping
secar $(c \rightarrow qu)$

que lo (la) hagamos
que lo (la) pongamos
que lo (la) recojamos

Vocabulario para conversar   461

Class Starter Review
On the day following the initial presentation of vocabulary, you might begin the class with this activity:
Have students name items they would carry in their backpack to go on a camping trip.

www Internet Activities
Juegos

Learning Spanish Through Action
STAGING VOCABULARY: *Levanten, Señalen*
MATERIALS: reproductions of vocabulary transparency or Vocabulary Art BLMs/CD-ROM
DIRECTIONS: Tell students to listen to the story of a recent camping trip. Have students raise or point to items as you mention them. For example: *Llegamos al campa-mento temprano. Pusimos la tienda (de acampar) y luego sacamos el abrelatas y la olla de la mochila pesada. Hicimos un fuego con palitos secos debajo de un árbol en la sombra y cocinamos la comida. ¡Qué bonito es comer al aire libre, lejos de la ciudad contaminada!*

Multiple Intelligences
Bodily/Kinesthetic
See Learning Spanish Through Action.
Logical/Mathematical and Visual/Spatial
See Enrichment.
Verbal/Linguistic
See Vocabulary Tape 14-1 and Class Starter Review.
Visual/Spatial
See Overheads 67–68 and the Vocabulary Art BLMs/CD-ROM.

Standards 1.1; 1.2; 4.1; 5.1   **461**

Practice

Reteach / Review: Commands

Ex. 1: As a variation of this exercise, have students redo it with *Estudiante B* using a negative command first, and then an affirmative command to tell *Estudiante A* what to do. For example: *¿Qué hago? El plato está roto. / Pues, no lo uses. Usa otra cosa.*

Answers: Empecemos a conversar

1 ESTUDIANTE A

a. ¿Qué hago? La leña está mojada.
b. ...El agua está contaminada.
c. ...La olla está sucia.
d. ...La tienda (de acampar) está rota.
e. ...El abrelatas está roto.
f. ...La mochila está demasiado pesada.
g. Statements will vary.

ESTUDIANTE B

Answers will vary, but may include the following:
a. Pues, tendrás que secarla.
b. ...hervirla.
c. ...lavarla.
d. ...coserla.
e. ...buscar otro.
f. ...sacarle algo.
g. Answers will vary.

Empecemos a conversar

Túrnate con un(a) compañero(a) para ser *Estudiante A* y *Estudiante B*. Reemplacen las palabras subrayadas en el modelo con palabras representadas o escritas en los recuadros. Si ven 💡 pueden dar su propia respuesta.

1
A — *¿Qué hago? El plato está roto.*
B — *Pues, tendrás que usar otra cosa.*

roto

Estudiante A

a. mojado(a)
b. contaminado(a)
c. sucio(a)
d. roto(a)
e. roto(a)
f. demasiado pesado(a)
g.

Estudiante B

usar otra cosa
lavarlo(la)
hervirlo(la)
coserlo(la)
secarlo(la)
sacarle algo
buscar otro(a)

La etiqueta en esta mariposa sirve para que los científicos estudien su migración. Millones de mariposas monarcas pasan el invierno en México.

Options

Strategies for Reaching All Students

Spanish-Speaking Students
Exs. 1–2: Pair bilingual with non-bilingual students, if possible.
Ex. 3: Pair Spanish-speaking students, if possible.

Students Needing Extra Help
Ex. 2: Review location words. Discuss the details of the picture. Remind students of the change in the object pronoun at the beginning of the *Estudiante B* response.

Enrichment
Ex. 2: To extend this exercise, have *Estudiante A* respond affirmatively to *Estudiante B*'s question. Either student can continue by suggesting another place to look for the item in question.

2

A — *No encontré <u>los champiñones</u>.*
B — *¿<u>Los</u> buscaste <u>en la sombra, debajo de los árboles</u>?*

Estudiante A

a.   b.   c.

Estudiante B

d.   e.   f.

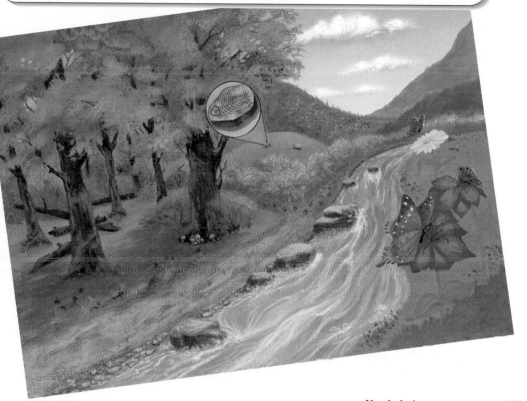

Vocabulario para conversar   463

2 ESTUDIANTE A
a. No encontré las huellas.
b. ...los fósiles.
c. ...las flores.
d. ...las piedras.
e. ...las mariposas.
f. ...la leña.
ESTUDIANTE B
Answers will vary, but may include the following:
a. ¿Las buscaste en el sendero?
b. ¿Los ...en la colina?
c. ¿Las ...en el valle?
d. ¿Las ...en el río?
e. ¿Las ...sobre las flores?
f. ¿La ...en el bosque?

Extended Written Practice/Homework
1. Use the vocabulary on pp. 460–461 and write three sentences describing a spot in nature that you are familiar with.
2. Write three sentences saying what you or others do during a camping trip: *Mis hermanos y yo ponemos las tiendas de acampar.*
3. Write a series of four commands saying what to do when you arrive at a campsite: *Primero recoge leña.*

Multiple Intelligences
Naturalist and Bodily/Kinesthetic
Have students make a poster that provides information about rain forests, including the animals, plants, and trees that live there.
Verbal/Linguistic
See Exs. 1–2.

Cultural Notes

(p. 462, photo)
The butterfly reserve at El Rosario, Michoacán, lies in the mountains between Morelia, Michoacán, and Toluca, Mexico. From November through February every year, millions of monarch butterflies migrate to this area from the north, covering the branches of the area's tall pine trees.

Standards 1.1; 3.1   **463**

Practice & Apply

Re-enter / Recycle
Ex. 7: leisure-time activities and sports from Chap. 4

3 ESTUDIANTE A

a. ¿Qué se debe hacer con los fósforos?

b. ...el fuego?

c. ...la basura?

d. ...la tienda (de acampar)?

e. ...los palitos?

f. ...la leña?

g. ...la sopa?

h. Questions will vary.

ESTUDIANTE B

Answers will vary, but may include the following:

a. Es necesario que los busques.

b. ...lo apagues.

c. ...la recojas.

d. ...la pongas.

e. ...los enciendas.

f. ...la consigas.

g. ...la hagas.

h. Answers will vary.

3   A — ¿Qué se debe hacer con <u>el agua</u>?
        B — Es necesario que <u>la hiervas</u>.

Estudiante A   Estudiante B

a.   b.   c.

d.   e.

f.   g.   h.

apagues

busques

consigas

enciendas

hagas

hiervas

pongas

recojas

seques

464   Capítulo 14

Options

Strategies for Reaching All Students

Spanish-Speaking Students
Ex. 7: *¿Qué se puede hacer cerca de donde vives? ¿En qué estación del año te gusta más estar al aire libre?*

Un paso más Ex. 14-C

Students Needing Extra Help
Ex. 3: Put this exercise in context. Have students decide on the object pronouns and match them to the verbs before beginning this activity.

Ex. 4: Decide on which area the students should base the activity before beginning this exercise. Have information available if a specific place is chosen. Brainstorm camping activities and important related information.
Ex. 5: Brainstorm things to be careful of. Explain the expressions that begin with *¿con qué . . . .*
Ex. 6: Brainstorm possible answers.

Ex. 8: Give students a specific number of things to be included on the lists. Use the vocabulary section of the Chap. 11 Organizer.

Enrichment
Additional questions: *Hay personas que nunca van de camping porque no les gusta nada la idea de pasar sus vacaciones en un campamento. ¿Por qué crees que piensan así? ¿Crees que tienen razón?*

Empecemos a escribir

Escribe tus respuestas en español.

4 ¿Fuiste a un campamento alguna vez o te gustaría ir a alguno? ¿Adónde? ¿Qué actividades hay en un campamento que te gustan mucho? ¿Crees que es importante saber cocinar si vas de camping? ¿Qué más es importante saber?

5 Si das una caminata en el campo, ¿con qué hay que tener cuidado? ¿Con qué hay que tener cuidado en el bosque? ¿Qué te gusta hacer cuando das una caminata?

6 ¿Qué se necesita para hacer un fuego? ¿Cómo se enciende? ¿Cómo se apaga? ¿Cómo se puede proteger el bosque de un incendio?

7 ¿Qué te gusta hacer al aire libre?

8 ¿Crees que es importante llevar cosas ligeras cuando vas de camping? Haz una lista de lo que hay que llevar y una de lo que no se debe llevar. Haz una lista de lo que te gustaría recomendarle a alguien para que no contamine ni haga ningún daño a la naturaleza.

También se dice

la fogata

la cerilla
el cerillo

el abridor de latas

la loma

la roca

MORE PRACTICE

- Más práctica y tarea, p. 565
- Practice Workbook 14–1, 14–2

Este joven argentino va de camping a los Andes.

Vocabulario para conversar   465

Answers: Empecemos a escribir

4–8 Answers will vary, but should include correct use of present and preterite tenses where appropriate.

 Practice Wkbk. 14-1, 14-2

Audio Activity 14.1

Writing Activity 14-A

Pruebas 14-1, 14-2

Cooperative Learning
Using the question in Ex. 7, have students interview three classmates. They should then form a pair with someone they did not interview and share the responses they received. Have pairs prepare a graph illustrating their combined results and present it to the class.

Multiple Intelligences
Logical/Mathematical, Interpersonal/Social, and Verbal/Linguistic
See Cooperative Learning.
Verbal/Linguistic
See Ex. 3 and Audio Activity 14.1.
Visual/Spatial
See Practice Wkbk. 14-1 and 14-2 and Writing Activity 14-A.

Cultural Notes

(p. 465, photo)
Aconcagua, in Argentina, rises 22,834 feet. Although the Andes reach their highest elevations around Aconcagua, the relatively short distance across the mountains between Santiago de Chile and Mendoza, Argentina, makes this crossing well traveled. These mountains are rocky and dry with low, scrubby vegetation. On the Argentine side, orange, pink, red, crimson, and black rock formations color the landscape.

Standards 1.1; 1.2; 1.3; 3.1   **465**

Present

Chapter Theme
Nature

Communicative Objectives
- To describe nature
- To discuss outdoor activities
- To discuss plants and animals

 Overheads 69–70

 Vocabulary Art BLMs/CD-ROM

 Vocabulary Tape 14-2

Teaching Suggestions
Preparing students to speak: Use one or two options from each of the categories of Comprehensible Input, Physical Response, or Limited Verbal Response. For a complete explanation of these categories and some sample activities, see pp. T20–T21.

Vocabulario para conversar

¿Qué ves en el desierto?

Aquí tienes el resto del vocabulario que necesitas en este capítulo para hablar sobre la naturaleza.

la ardilla

el amanecer

el búho

el venado

la venada

la rana

la serpiente

el lobo, la loba

el parque nacional

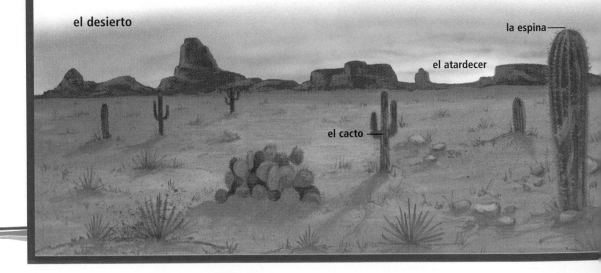

el desierto

la espina

el atardecer

el cacto

Options

Strategies for Reaching All Students

Spanish-Speaking Students
¿Puedes añadir otras palabras relacionadas al tema? Escríbelas en tu vocabulario personal.

Un paso más Ex. 14-D

Students Needing Extra Help
Point out the feminine form of *el lobo.* Remind students of the word family for *atardecer (tarde).* Divide the vocabulary into three sections: animals, activities, and equipment.
También necesitas . . . : Remind students that *salvaje* and *silvestre* both mean "wild."

Learning Spanish Through Action
STAGING VOCABULARY: *Señalen*
MATERIALS: Photos or posters of vacation spots
DIRECTIONS: Place the various photos or posters around the room and describe them, having students indicate which one is being described.

el elefante

el gorila

el coyote

el gorila

la ballena

la balsa

navegar en balsa

la canoa

navegar en canoa

la tabla
(de surf)

hacer surf

la vela

hacer surf de vela

la moto acuática

hacer moto acuática

hacer esquí acuático

el trampolín, pl.
los trampolines

dar saltos

escalar montañas

También necesitas . . .

el animal salvaje	*wild animal*	
la planta silvestre	*wild plant*	
venenoso, -a	*poisonous*	

¿Y qué quiere decir . . . ?
el oxígeno
doméstico, -a
peligroso, -a
los animales en peligro de extinción

Vocabulario para conversar 467

Practice

Re-enter / Recycle
Ex. 9: leisure-time activities and sports from Chap. 4
Ex. 11: environment from Chap. 11

Reteach / Review: Vocabulary
Ex. 10: Have students choose three settings for which they have already learned vocabulary, and list the objects, animals, or people they would see if they went there.
For example: *En la fiesta habrá pastel y una piñata. En el parque habrá árboles, flores y ardillas.*

Answers: Empecemos a conversar

9 ESTUDIANTE A
a. ¿Qué te gustaría hacer este verano, hacer moto acuática o bucear?
b. . . . hacer surf o navegar en balsa?
c. . . . escalar montañas o hacer esquí acuático?
d. . . . navegar en canoa o hacer surf de vela?
e. . . . montar en bicicleta o patinar?
f. . . . jugar béisbol o dar saltos?
g. Questions will vary.

ESTUDIANTE B
a.–g. Answers will vary.

10 ESTUDIANTE A
a. Si voy a un océano, ¿qué puedo hacer?
b. . . . una selva tropical, ¿qué puedo ver?

Empecemos a conversar

9

A — ¿Qué te gustaría hacer este verano, *dar caminatas o montar a caballo*?
B — *Montar a caballo. Es más divertido.*
   o: *Ni una cosa ni la otra. Prefiero ___.*

¡NO OLVIDES!
Do you remember these words associated with sports?
bucear
correr
esquiar
los esquíes
el campeón, la campeona
el entrenador, la entrenadora
la piscina

Estudiante A   Estudiante B

468   Capítulo 14

Options

Strategies for Reaching All Students

Spanish-Speaking Students
Exs. 9 and 11: Pair bilingual with non-bilingual students, if possible.
Ex. 10: Pair Spanish-speaking students, if possible.

Students Needing Extra Help
Ex. 9: Brainstorm possible adjectives that describe the preferred activity. Point out that if students choose the second response, they need to fill in the blank following *Prefiero* with another activity.
Ex. 10: Brainstorm what students might do or see in these particular places.

Ex. 11: Avoid discussing the subjunctive. Match *Estudiante A* and *B* responses as a class. Encourage students to incorporate their own ideas into the answers. Accept all logical answers.

10 ver

A —*Si voy a un río, ¿qué puedo ver?*
B —*Ranas, peces, serpientes y plantas silvestres.*

Estudiante A

a. hacer
b. ver
c. ver
d. hacer
e. hacer
f. ver
g.

Estudiante B

11 los bosques

A —*¿Por qué es necesario que protejamos los bosques?*
B —*Porque allí viven los animales salvajes.*

Estudiante A

a. los desiertos
b. los océanos
c. los parques nacionales
d. los elefantes
e. las selvas tropicales
f. el medio ambiente
g. los búhos
h.

Estudiante B

allí viven los animales salvajes
están en peligro de extinción
los seres humanos los están matando
sus plantas y árboles nos dan oxígeno
necesitamos aire y agua limpios
allí viven los lobos y los coyotes
allí viven las ballenas y los peces
allí protegen la naturaleza

Vocabulario para conversar   469

c. ...un parque nacional, ¿qué puedo ver?
d. ...un lago, ¿qué puedo hacer?
e. ...un bosque, ¿qué puedo hacer?
f. ...un desierto, ¿qué puedo ver?
g. Questions will vary.

ESTUDIANTE B
a.–g. Answers will vary.

11 ESTUDIANTE A
a. ¿Por qué es necesario que protejamos los desiertos?
b. ...los océanos?
c. ...los parques nacionales?
d. ...los elefantes?
e. ...las selvas tropicales?
f. ...el medio ambiente?
g. ...los búhos?
h. Questions will vary.

ESTUDIANTE B
Answers will vary, but may include:
a. Porque allí viven los lobos y los coyotes.
b. ...allí viven las ballenas y los peces.
c. ...allí protegen la naturaleza.
d. ...los seres humanos los están matando.
e. ...sus plantas y árboles nos dan oxígeno.
f. ...necesitamos aire y agua limpios.
g. ...están en peligro de extinción.
h. Answers will vary.

Comm. Act. BLM 14-1

Enrichment
Ex. 9: To extend this exercise, have *Estudiante A* ask *Estudiante B* to elaborate on the answer. For example, *¿Por qué crees que es más divertido?* or *¿Por qué prefieres ése?*

Cooperative Learning
Make signs for each of the sports listed on pp. 466–467 and post them around the room. Tell students they have received a scholarship to a summer camp that specializes in one of these sports. Give students time to decide which they would choose, and ask them to move to that location in the room. When all groups are formed, have each student tell the members of his or her

group one reason why he or she chose that sport. Groups should combine the reasons and present a list to the class.

Multiple Intelligences
Interpersonal/Social
See Cooperative Learning.
Visual/Spatial
See Comm. Act. BLM 14-1.

Practice & Apply

Re-enter / Recycle
Ex. 16: clothing from Chap. 3

Answers: Empecemos a escribir y a leer

12–15 Answers will vary.

16 a. Para protegerte del zumaque te recomiendo que nunca camines sin zapatos.
b. ...que uses ...
c. ...que lleves ...
d. ...que te abroches ...
e. ...que lleves ...
f. Answers will vary.

Practice Wkbk. 14-3, 14-4

Audio Activity 14.2

Writing Activities 14-B, 14-C

Pruebas 14-3, 14-4

Empecemos a escribir y a leer

Escribe tus respuestas en español.

12 ¿Cómo es el desierto? ¿Qué animales hay? ¿Qué no hay en un desierto?

13 ¿Cómo es el campo donde vives? ¿Qué animales hay? ¿Qué se puede hacer? ¿Se pueden hacer deportes acuáticos? ¿Cuáles? ¿Cuáles haces tú? ¿Cuál prefieres? ¿Cuál te parece el deporte acuático más peligroso? ¿Y el más divertido? ¿Por qué?

14 ¿Te gusta ver los amaneceres o los atardeceres? Describe uno de los dos. ¿Por qué no es prudente quedarse en el bosque después del atardecer?

15 ¿Qué animales salvajes te dan miedo? ¿Por qué? ¿Por qué se debe tener cuidado con algunos animales? ¿Con cuáles? ¿Y con qué plantas? ¿Por qué?

16 Lee el texto sobre el zumaque venenoso. Luego, dale recomendaciones de la lista a un(a) compañero(a). Agrega *(add)* otra recomendación tuya.

El zumaque venenoso abunda en los Estados Unidos. Causa una alergia muy dolorosa y en algunos casos muy peligrosa, sobre todo para los niños pequeños. Para protegerte del zumaque te recomiendo que:

a. nunca caminar sin zapatos
b. usar guantes si quieres recoger flores o plantas silvestres
c. llevar camisas de manga larga y pantalones largos
d. abrocharse todos los botones de la camisa
e. llevar siempre la camisa dentro de los pantalones y los pantalones dentro de las botas
f. 💡

www.pasoapaso.com

470   Capítulo 14

Mono araña en la selva panameña

Una foca con su recién nacid en las islas Galápagos

MORE PRACTICE
- Más práctica y tarea, p. 566
- Practice Workbook 14–3, 14–4

Options

Strategies for Reaching All Students

Spanish-Speaking Students
Ex. 15: *¿Crees que debemos proteger estos animales? ¿Por qué?*
Ex. 2: *Escoge una actividad. Escribe un párrafo que dice cómo se puede evitar hacerle daño a la naturaleza y a la vez, disfrutar de la actividad.*

 Un paso más Exs. 14-E, 14-F

Students Needing Extra Help
Ex. 12: Use the vocabulary section of the Organizer. Have information available about desert activities.
Ex. 14: Brainstorm adjectives to describe the sunrise and sunset.
Ex. 15: If available, use the vocabulary section of the Book 1, Chap. 13 Organizer. Use the vocabulary section of the Chap. 9 Organizer.
Ex. 16: Do *a.* as a class. Point out that *b.–e.* are affirmative suggestions.

¡Comuniquemos!
Ex. 1: Present a complete model. Have students set up columns for each category and brainstorm possible answers. Use the vocabulary section of the Organizer.
Ex. 2: Present a complete model. Brainstorm positive and negative aspects of each activity.
¿Qué sabes ahora?: Have students write out this exercise to record their progress.

¡Comuniquemos!

Aquí tienes otra oportunidad para usar el vocabulario de este capítulo.

1 En grupo, hablen de adónde quisieran ir durante las vacaciones y por qué.

A —*¿Te gustaría ir a un desierto?*
B —*A un desierto, no. Allí no hay . . . Hay que llevar . . . Prefiero . . .*
C —*A mí me gustaría ir a un desierto porque . . .*

2 Habla con un(a) compañero(a) sobre algunas actividades o deportes que le pueden hacer daño a la naturaleza. Por ejemplo:

coleccionar plantas silvestres hacer moto acuática
esquiar ir de camping
hacer esquí acuático ir de pesca

A —*¿Qué piensas de hacer moto acuática?*
B —*Creo que es un . . .*
A —*Estoy de acuerdo, pero . . .*

3 Habla con un(a) compañero(a) sobre el campamento ideal. Hablen sobre:

- dónde está el campamento
- cómo es el campo por allí
- qué animales se pueden ver allí
- si es necesario hacer una reservación
- qué hay que llevar
- si hay agua, electricidad, servicios, duchas, etc.
- qué se puede hacer y qué no se puede hacer

¿Qué sabes ahora?

Can you:

■ talk about water sports?
—Me encanta ___. Es un deporte ___, pero muy divertido.

■ discuss our natural environment?
—En el estado donde vivo hay ___, ___ y ___.

■ talk about protecting animals and the environment?
—Es necesario que protejamos los ___ porque ___.

También se dice

el tecolote
la lechuza

la culebra

surfear

hacer saltos de trampolín
hacer clavados

la piragua

hacer alpinismo

Vocabulario para conversar 471

Practice

Answers:
¡Comuniquemos!
1–3 Answers will vary.

Answers: ¿Qué sabes ahora?
Answers will vary, but may include the following:
- la moto acuática / peligroso
- coyotes / lobos / ardillas
- búhos / están en peligro de extinción

Strategies for Reaching All Students
MULTIPLE INTELLIGENCES
Verbal/Linguistic
See Exs. 1–3 and Audio Activities 14.2 and 14.3.
Visual/Spatial
See Practice Wkbk. 14-3 and 14-4 and Writing Activities 14-B and 14-C.

 Audio Activity 14.3

 Pasos vivos 2 CD-ROM
Boom Box, Clip Art Album, Notas culturales, Slide Projector, Laboratorio de grabar

Cultural Notes

Enrichment
Ex. 12: *¿Qué cosas debes llevar si vas a visitar el desierto por algunas horas?*
Ex. 16: *¿En qué lugar te gusta más la naturaleza: los desiertos, los océanos, los bosques, los ríos o las selvas tropicales? ¿Por qué?*

(p. 470, top photo)
The spider monkey, small with a notably long tail, is a genus found only in the Americas. It is characterized by long, slender limbs, a rudimentary thumb, and a prehensile tail. Chocó Indians, who inhabit the province of Darién, in eastern Panama, have traditionally hunted spider monkeys using blow guns and bows and arrows.

(p. 470, bottom photo)
Although many of the species of animals found on the Galápagos are unique, others, such as the California sea lion, may be found elsewhere. This animal is known for its intelligence and memory and is popular in zoos and marine shows since it is easily trained. The California sea lion's coat is brown, but appears black when wet. Galápagos park regulations protect the sea lion.

Present & Apply

Cultural Objective
• To discuss health problems tourists may encounter

Multicultural Perspectives

Major cities in Latin America use water filtration systems much like those in the U.S. In rural areas, however, the quality of water can be dramatically lower. Many people do not have potable water: they have to obtain their drinking water from rivers contaminated by animals and farm runoff.

Untreated water carries many diseases and is one of the leading causes of infant mortality in Latin America. Intestinal bacteria can affect infants through prolonged diarrhea, which causes dehydration and sometimes death. Rural areas also experience outbreaks of other water-born diseases such as cholera, typhoid, and hepatitis. Have students research the efforts of Latin American governments and world health organizations to provide clean water throughout the region. Ask students to share their findings with the class.

Perspectiva cultural

¿Hay comida y bebidas que puedes identificar en las fotos? Imagina que vas a ir a estos lugares. ¿Qué comida comerás? ¿Qué bebidas beberás? ¿Cuáles no? ¿Por qué?

Imagina que estás visitando la ciudad de Guadalajara en México con unos compañeros. Hace mucho calor y tienen sed. En un quiosco ven a un vendedor de aguas frescas. Tiene botellas grandes de vidrio que contienen pedazos de hielo y de naranjas, piñas o sandía flotando en el líquido refrescante. Algunos de tus compañeros quieren comprar un vaso de agua fresca. Otros no. ¿Qué harás tú?

¿Es verdad que los turistas no deben beber el agua en ciertos países? Toda agua contiene microbios. Diversos países usan diversos sistemas para purificarla. Y, por lo general, la gente está acostumbrada al agua de su país. En otras palabras, el agua no le hace daño porque suele beberla. Por eso, los viajeros deben tomar precauciones para no tener problemas.

¿Qué precauciones debes tomar? Primero, bebe sólo agua hervida o agua mineral que se venda en botella. Cepíllate los dientes con esa misma agua. No bebas bebidas hechas con agua regular. No comas verduras o frutas lavadas con agua regular. Pela la fruta. Si quieres, antes de viajar, puedes pedirle a tu médico que te recete un antibiótico para protegerte.

Además del agua, hay otras causas de problemas del estómago. En la mayoría de los casos, se deben a la deshidratación o al cansancio (*fatigue*), no al agua.

La cultura desde tu perspectiva

1 ¿Por qué los microbios les hacen daño a algunas personas y a otras no?

2 ¿Qué le puedes decir a un(a) turista que está en los Estados Unidos por primera vez que te pregunta si debe beber el agua?

Vendedor de aguas frescas en el mercado de San Miguel de Allende, México

472 Capítulo 14

Options

Strategies for Reaching All Students

Spanish-Speaking Students
Ex. 2: After this exercise, have students answer in writing: *Como dice el artículo, hay otras causas de problemas del estómago, además del agua, para los turistas. ¿Qué consejos les darías a los turistas para no sentirse mal cuando viajen? Haz una lista.*

 Un paso más Ex. 14-G

Students Needing Extra Help
Have students take notes to be used later in the culture section of *¿Lo sabes bien?*
Ex. 1: You might want to change *los microbios les hacen* to *el agua les hace.*

Enrichment
As an additional assignment, have students research advice given in guidebooks regarding food, drink, and general health questions for people traveling to foreign countries. Have them prepare a brief report to share with the class, naming the guidebook and the recommendations given.

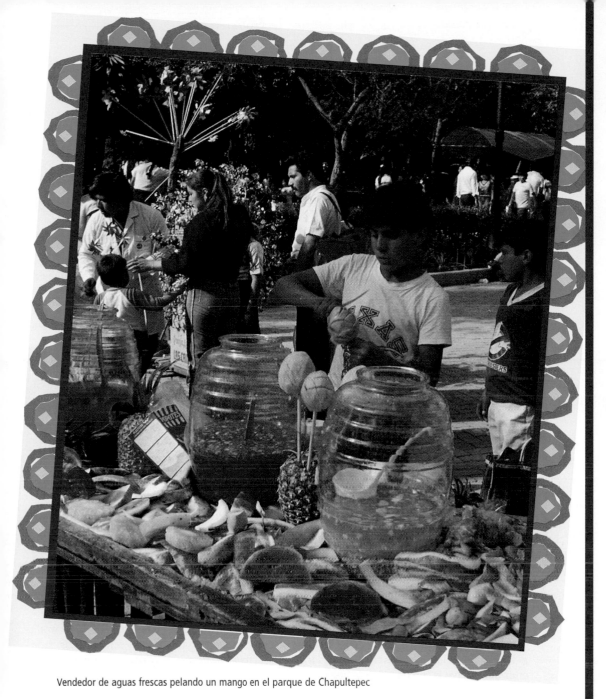

Vendedor de aguas frescas pelando un mango en el parque de Chapultepec

Perspectiva cultural   473

Cultural Notes

Multiple Intelligences

Verbal/Linguistic
Have students write a paragraph about the people in the photo on p. 473.

Visual/Spatial
See Enrichment.

(pp. 472–473, photos)
Glass jars filled with *aguas frescas* are a familiar sight in any Mexican market or *zócalo*. Three common *aguas* are *horchata*, *agua de jamaica,* and *agua de tamarindo*. *Horchata* is made with rice, blanched almonds, cinnamon, sugar, and water. *Agua de jamaica* is made from calyxes of the hibiscus blossom, sugar, and water. Tamarind pods are shelled and then boiled with sugar and water to prepare *agua de tamarindo.*

Standards 2.2; 5.1   **473**

Preview

 Overhead 71

Reteach / Review: Subjunctive

B: As a review, ask students to compare the subjunctive forms *cruces* and *apagues* with the corresponding *yo* forms of the present tense, and ask how the stem changes in the subjunctive.

Answers

A The two examples are *es importante limpiar* and *es necesario quitar*. The word *que* follows *es necesario*. It changes (from *haces* to *hagas*). The infinitive of *hagas* is *hacer*. The negative *tú* command form is *no hagas*.

B The verbs are *uses*, from *usar*; *cruces*, from *cruzar*; and *apagues*, from *apagar*. You would use the subjunctive form *lleves*.

Gramática en contexto

Para hacer un fuego

Primero, es importante limpiar bien el área. Es necesario quitar las piedras, los palos y las hojas del lugar.

El fuego debe quedar limitado al área que escogiste. Para eso es necesario que hagas un círculo con piedras en el centro del área.

Pon palitos y papeles dentro del círculo. Es importante que uses palitos secos. Si están mojados, será difícil encenderlos.

Luego, pon la leña sobre los palitos y los papeles. Es importante que cruces los palitos y la leña para permitir la entrada del aire.

Al final, enciende los palitos de abajo con un fósforo. Pronto se encenderá la leña. Recuerda: Es muy importante que apagues el fuego antes de acostarte o de salir del área.

A You have seen *es importante* and *es necesario* followed by infinitives. Find two examples in the first caption. In the second caption, the writer is saying that it is necessary for someone to do something. What word follows *es necesario*? What happens to the verb form after *que*? What is the infinitive of *hagas*? What is the negative *tú* command form?

B Each of the other captions contains a suggestion using *es importante*. Look at the verbs that follow *que* and identify the infinitive of each. What form of *llevar* would you use to complete this sentence: *Es importante que tú (llevar) fósforos secos?*

474   Capítulo 14

Options

Strategies for Reaching All Students

Students Needing Extra Help
Have students begin the grammar section of the Organizer. Tell them to take careful notes.
A: Write the expressions on the chalkboard as students find them.
B: Write the three *Es importante . . .* sentences on the chalkboard. Underline *uses*, *cruces*, and *apagues*. Have students identify

the infinitive of each verb form. Point out that all are *-ar* verbs if they do not see this on their own. Write the new sentence on the chalkboard, leaving room for students to supply the correct form of *llevar*.
El subjuntivo de ciertos verbos irregulares: Write out the complete paradigm of the listed verbs.

Ex. 1: Match the responses as a class. Write the model on the chalkboard, underlining the parts that change. Review the placement of object pronouns. Brainstorm possible *Estudiante B* responses.

El subjuntivo de ciertos verbos irregulares

As in negative commands, irregular verbs that add a *g* to the stem in the present-tense *yo* form (including *caerse, decir, hacer, poner, salir, tener,* and *traer*) also have a *g* in the present subjunctive.

hacer → ha**g-o** → **haga**
tener → ten**g-o** → **tenga**

Mi papá quiere que yo **haga** esquí acuático.
Mi mamá quiere que **tengamos** mucho cuidado.

¡NO OLVIDES!
We form the present subjunctive of most verbs in the same way we form negative *tú* commands. Add the subjunctive endings to the stem of the present-tense *yo* form.

1 La directora del campamento les da recomendaciones a un grupo de excursionistas.

los mosquitos

A —*¿Qué debemos hacer con tantos mosquitos?*
B —*Les recomiendo que traigan repelente.*

a. con las tiendas de acampar
b. con los fuegos
c. con los fósforos
d. en las caminatas
e. con los animales salvajes
f. con las latas
g. con lo que hay que llevar

ponerlos en un lugar seco
hacer una mochila con sólo cosas necesarias
no salir muy lejos del campamento
traer un abrelatas
no hacerlos cerca de las tiendas
no ponerlas donde hay piedras
tener mucho cuidado con ellos

Ahora tú, dales otras tres recomendaciones a los excursionistas.

h. con las flores y las plantas silvestres
i. con la comida
j. con la leña y los palitos

Gramática en contexto   475

Present & Practice

Answers
1 ESTUDIANTE A
a. ¿Qué debemos hacer con las tiendas de acampar?
b. ...con los fuegos?
c. ...con los fósforos?
d. ...en las caminatas?
e. ...con los animales salvajes?
f. ...con las latas?
g. ...con lo que hay que llevar?
h. ...con las flores y las plantas silvestres?
i. ...con la comida?
j. ...con la leña y los palitos?
ESTUDIANTE B
Answers may include:
a. Les recomiendo que no las pongan donde hay piedras.
b. ...que no los hagan cerca de las tiendas.
c. ...que los pongan en un lugar seco.
d. ...que no salgan muy lejos del campamento.
e. ...que tengan mucho cuidado con ellos.
f. ...que traigan un abrelatas.
g. ...que hagan una mochila con sólo cosas necesarias.
h. ...que no las corten.
i. ...que la conserven.
j. ...que no los mojen.

 Practice Wkbk. 14-5, 14-6

 Writing Activity 14-D

Extended Written Practice/Homework
1. Refer to the expressions on p. 467 that use *hacer.* Write a sentence for each saying whether your parents want you and your brothers, sisters, or friends to do these things: *Mis padres quieren que hagamos esquí acuático.*
2. Write four sentences stating what you want to have happen in your school. Use *caerse, decir, hacer, poner, salir, tener,* and *traer: Quiero que salgamos de la escuela a la una de la tarde.*

Multiple Intelligences
Visual/Spatial
See Overhead 71, Practice Wkbk. 14-5 and 14-6, and Writing Activity 14-D.

Standards 1.1   475

Present & Practice

Answers

2 ESTUDIANTE A

a. ¿Me recomiendas que vaya a un desierto?

b. ¿Le . . . que vaya a un parque nacional?

c. ¿Nos . . . que vayamos a un lago?

d. ¿Les . . . que vayan a un campamento?

e. ¿Me . . . que vaya a una selva?

f. ¿Nos . . . que vayamos a una ciudad?

g. Questions will vary.

ESTUDIANTE B

Answers may include:

a. Sí. Y te recomiendo también que seas prudente con el agua.

b. . . . le . . . sea obediente a las reglas.

c. . . . les . . . no sean tímidos(as) de nadar.

d. . . . les . . . sean limpios(as) con la comida.

e. . . . te . . . seas paciente para ver los animales.

f. . . . les . . . sean sociables con la gente.

g. Answers will vary.

El subjuntivo de los verbos *ir* y *ser*

Ir and *ser* have irregular subjunctive forms. They are just like the negative *tú* command forms.

(yo)	**vaya / sea**	(nosotros) (nosotras)	**vayamos / seamos**
(tú)	**vayas / seas**	(vosotros) (vosotras)	**vayáis / seáis**
Ud. (él) (ella)	**vaya / sea**	Uds. (ellos) (ellas)	**vayan / sean**

2 Pregúntale a un(a) compañero(a) qué recomienda.

A — *¿Me recomiendas que vaya a una playa?*

B — *Sí. Y te recomiendo también que seas prudente con la tabla de surf.*

me

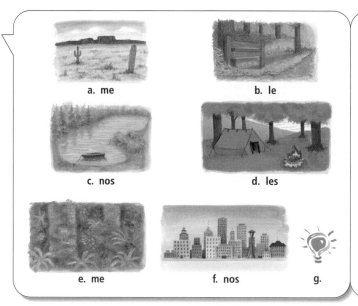

a. me
b. le
c. nos
d. les
e. me
f. nos
g.

paciente
(no) desobediente
ordenado, -a
(no) desordenado, -a
limpio, -a
sociable
(no) tímido, -a
(no) perezoso, -a

476 Capítulo 14

Options

Strategies for Reaching All Students

Students Needing Extra Help
Review the negative *tú* command forms of *ir* and *ser*. Refer students to the grammar section of the Chap. 12 Organizer. Point out that there is a written accent mark on *vayáis*.
Ex. 2: Do this exercise as a class, separating it into two parts. First, do the exercise eliminating the *ser* + adjective phrase. Repeat the exercise, including the *ser* + adjective phrase, choosing one adjective to repeat throughout.

El subjuntivo con expresiones impersonales: Refer to the captions in the art in the *Gramática en contexto* section. Give additional examples of using infinitives as opposed to the subjunctive. Have students keep a running list of subjunctive expressions. Review regular subjunctive using the Chap. 12 Organizer. Write the *yo* forms of those verbs on the chalkboard.

Enrichment
El subjuntivo de los verbos ir *y* ser: As homework, have students think of a place (restaurant, school, theater, hospital, etc.) to which they would never recommend that anyone go, and give three reasons why.
El subjuntivo con expresiones impersonales: Ask pairs of students to create sayings about life in general using the expressions presented. Encourage students to be humorous and creative. Let them share their sayings with the class.

El subjuntivo con expresiones impersonales

You know how to make suggestions and recommendations using certain impersonal expressions with the infinitive. For example:

Es mejor dar una caminata por la mañana.

When we want to specify *who* should do something, we use the subjunctive.

Es mejor que Samuel y sus amigos vayan de camping a un parque nacional.

Some of the expressions that we use this way are *es mejor, es necesario,* and *es importante.*

¿**Es necesario que yo vaya** con ellos?
Es importante que regresen antes del atardecer.

Navegando en canoa en el Río Napa, Ecuador

Dando una caminata en las montañas de California

477

Class Starter Review
On the day following the presentation of the subjunctive with impersonal expressions, you might begin the class with this activity: In pairs, have students take turns telling each other precautions that must be taken when going camping. For example: *Es importante que traigas agua pura.*

Multicultural Perspectives
Tortuguero National Park in Costa Rica is the most important breeding area in the world for the green sea turtle. From July to October, up to 3,000 female turtles come to Tortuguero to nest. A female may come ashore two or three times to nest, each time laying over 100 eggs. Because this is one of the most scientifically studied areas, tourists can sometimes participate in the tagging of female turtles to see if they return to the same nesting place. This type of eco-tourism is a new way to experience exotic places. Ask students if they know of other areas which promote ecotourism.

 Practice Wkbk.
14-7, 14-8

 Writing Activities
14-E, 14-F

 Pruebas 14-5, 14-6

Cultural Notes

Cooperative Learning
In pairs, have students use the adjectives in Ex. 2 on p. 476 to create six recommendations for a classmate who is running for class president. Each student is responsible for three recommendations and the rationale behind them. As a pair, students should prioritize their recommendations and present them to the class.

Extended Written Practice/Homework
1. Write recommendations for protecting our environment. Use *es mejor, es necesario,* and *es importante: Es importante que protejamos los animales que están en peligro de extinción.*
2. Choose a place that you would recommend as a good vacation spot. Write three sentences telling other people what you recommend that they do: *Recomiendo que vayas a… Es mejor que … Es importante que …*

(p. 477, right photo)
The Oriente region of Ecuador drops from the eastern side of the Andes to the headwaters of the Amazon River. The Napo River is the major tributary of the Amazon. Those traveling alone, who don't mind rustic accommodations, can begin a trip at Puerto Napo in a motorized canoe, stopping for the night in guest houses, army posts, and settlers' homes.

Practice & Apply

Teaching Suggestions
Ex. 3: To further practice the subjunctive, you may want to repeat this exercise using *todos, alguien,* and *algunos* as subjects.

Answers

3 ESTUDIANTE A
a. ¿Qué debemos hacer para ver los animales salvajes?
b. ...dar una caminata larga?
c. ...cocinar al aire libre?
d. ...poner la tienda de acampar?
e. ...escalar una montaña?
f. ...proteger el bosque?
g. ...proteger la comida de las hormigas?
h. Questions will vary.

ESTUDIANTE B
a. Es necesario que seamos pacientes y que estemos callados.
b. ...que llevemos agua pura para beber.
c. ...que recojamos palitos y leña para el fuego.
d. ...que quitemos las piedras.
e. ...que llevemos una cuerda.
f. ...que apaguemos bien el fuego.
g. ...que la guardemos en el coche.
h. Answers will vary.

3 Túrnate con un(a) compañero(a) para decir qué es mejor, qué es necesario o qué es importante hacer en un campamento.

proteger el
parque nacional

A —*¿Qué debemos hacer para proteger el parque nacional?*
B —*Es necesario que recojamos toda la basura.*

a. ver los animales salvajes
b. dar una caminata larga
c. cocinar al aire libre
d. poner la tienda de acampar
e. escalar una montaña
f. proteger el bosque
g. proteger la comida de las hormigas

recoger toda la basura
quitar las piedras
guardarla en el coche
llevar agua pura para beber
ser paciente y estar callado(a)
recoger palitos y leña para el fuego
llevar una cuerda
apagar bien el fuego

4 Dile a un(a) compañero(a) lo que quisieras hacer este verano. Tu compañero(a) te dará algunas ideas.

escalar una
montaña

A —*Este verano quisiera escalar una montaña.*
B —*Es importante que consigas unas botas buenas.*

a. hacer ...
b. ir a ...
c. ir de camping ...
d. navegar en ...
e. practicar ...

f. recoger ...
g. ver ...
h. viajar ...

es necesario que ...
es importante que ...
es mejor que ...

478   Capítulo 14

Options

Strategies for Reaching All Students

Students Needing Extra Help
Ex. 3: If possible, divide the class into groups with at least one experienced camper in each. Review verbs from Chap. 13. Remind students to use only the *nosotros* form.

Ex. 4: Brainstorm possible completions for the *Estudiante A* statement and the *Estudiante B* response.
Ahora lo sabes: Have students write out this list so they can record their progress.

Multiple Intelligences
Verbal/Linguistic
See Exs. 3–4 and Audio Activities 14.4 and 14.5.
Visual/Spatial
See Practice Wkbk. 14-9 and 14-10 and Comm. Act. BLM 14-2.

Subiendo un árbol en la selva de San Blas, Panamá

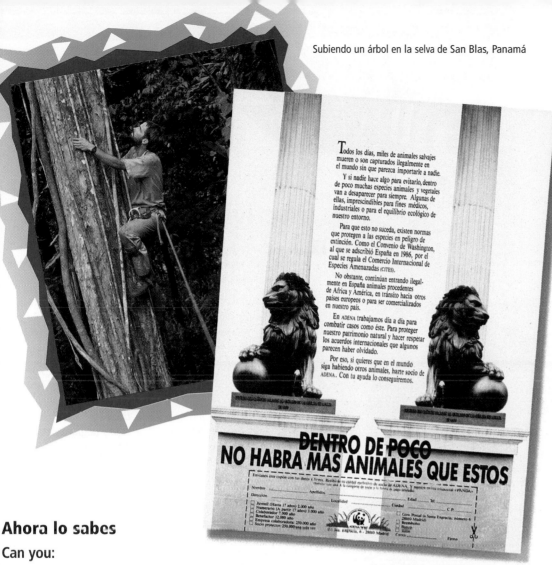

Todos los días, miles de animales salvajes mueren o son capturados ilegalmente en el mundo sin que parezca importarle a nadie.

Y si nadie hace algo para evitarlo, dentro de poco muchas especies animales y vegetales van a desaparecer para siempre. Algunas de ellas, imprescindibles para fines médicos, industriales o para el equilibrio ecológico de nuestro entorno.

Para que esto no suceda, existen normas que protegen a las especies en peligro de extinción. Como el Convenio de Washington, al que se adscribió España en 1986, por el cual se regula el Comercio Internacional de Especies Amenazadas (CITES).

No obstante, continúan entrando ilegalmente en España animales procedentes de África y América, en tránsito hacia otros países europeos o para ser comercializados en nuestro país.

En ADENA trabajamos día a día para combatir casos como éste. Para proteger nuestro patrimonio natural y hacer respetar los acuerdos internacionales que algunos parecen haber olvidado.

Por eso, si quieres que en el mundo siga habiendo otros animales, hazte socio de ADENA. Con tu ayuda lo conseguiremos.

DENTRO DE POCO
NO HABRÁ MÁS ANIMALES QUE ESTOS

Answers: Ahora lo sabes
- pongamos
- vayas
- sean

 Practice Wkbk. 14-9, 14-10

 Audio Activities 14.4, 14.5

 Pruebas 14-7, 14-8

 Comm. Act. BLM 14-2

 Pasos vivos 2 CD-ROM
Bulletin Board, Slide Presentation Maker, Spindle, Treadmill

Ahora lo sabes

Can you:

- tell someone what it is necessary, important, or advisable to do?
  —Es mejor que (nosotros) ___ la tienda antes de comer.
- recommend that someone not go somewhere?
  —Te recomiendo que no ___ al desierto en el verano.
- say that it is important for someone not to be a certain way?
  —Es importante que los niños no ___ maleducados.

MORE PRACTICE

Más práctica y tarea, pp. 566–567
Practice Workbook 14–5, 14–10

Gramática en contexto   479

Cultural Notes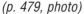

(p. 479, photo)
The archipelago of 365 San Blas Islands lies just off the Caribbean coast of Panama. Rain forests, such as the one in San Blas, have a characteristic structure generally consisting of several layers: the ground surface, the undergrowth, and the upper canopy, or treetops. Many animals live out their entire lifespan in only one of these layers. This forest reserve is significant because wild areas in other parts of Panama are being encroached upon by developers.

(p. 479, realia)
Spain's unique geographic location makes it an important European port of entry. Unfortunately, illegal smuggling of wildlife has been known to follow this same route. By combatting this activity in its own territory, the Spanish government helps to stem the mistreatment of wildlife internationally. These two stone lions are at the entrance of the Spanish Parliament.

Apply

 Video Activity A

Using the Video
In Episode 14, Jamie calls her parents in Los Angeles and tells them about the inheritance. They advise her not to give up her opportunity to go to college by staying in Mexico to see to the property. Later, Jamie explains to Carlos her decision to return to Los Angeles and donate the Hacienda La Jacaranda to Operación Aztlán. In a declaration before a judge, she adds that the Hotel will still belong to her family.

The final scene takes place at the train station, where Jamie and Felipe are saying good-bye to everyone they have met. Felipe and María agree to stay in touch and see each other again. Carlos promises Jamie he will visit Los Angeles and wait for her to return to Querétaro.

Actividades

1 Escoge por lo menos cuatro lugares que te gustaría visitar. Un(a) compañero(a) te hará sugerencias. Pueden usar frases como las siguientes. Por ejemplo:

A — *¿Qué recomiendas que haga si voy al océano?*
B — *Te sugiero que traigas mucho bronceador. Te recomiendo que hagas surf de vela y que seas muy prudente.*

- aprender a ...
- ir a ...
- divertirse
- ser prudente
- no ser desordenado(a) / demasiado atrevido(a)
- escalar la montaña
- ponerse / quitarse

- hacer una excursión en coche / autobús / tren
- navegar en ...
- traer ...
- salir / llegar antes del amanecer / atardecer
-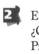

2 En grupo, piensen en el año escolar que termina. ¿Qué hicieron para tener éxito en la clase de español? Preparen algunas sugerencias para los estudiantes nuevos. ¿Qué les recomiendan que hagan y que no hagan? Usen frases como éstas:

- Es necesario / importante (que) ...
- Les sugerimos / les recomendamos que ...
- El (la) profesor(a) quiere que ...

Pueden escribir sus sugerencias en un cartel y ponerlo en la pared de la sala de clases para los estudiantes del año próximo.

Parque Nacional

480   Capítulo 14

Options

Strategies for Reaching All Students

Spanish-Speaking Students
Ex. 1: Give students this alternative assignment: *Escribe un párrafo acerca de lo que se puede hacer en dos de los lugares. Incluye también unas advertencias o alguna precaución que debe tomar el turista.*

 Un paso más Ex. 14-H

Students Needing Extra Help
If time is a factor, do only one activity.
Ex. 1: Brainstorm possibilities to complete the verb phrase used in the *Estudiante B* response. Review the rule for forming the subjunctive of reflexive verbs. Remind students that *ponerse* is also irregular.
Ex. 2: Brainstorm suggestions for success. Have students sign their names, or take a picture of the class and put it on the list.

Multiple Intelligences
Interpersonal/Social and Verbal/Linguistic
See Exs. 1–2.
Intrapersonal/Introspective and Naturalist
Have students write a paragraph about a nearby wilderness area. Have them tell whether or not they are interested in spending time there and give reasons for their preference.

Conexiones

La biología

La contaminación del agua

Mira este diagrama.

La contaminación térmica Las fábricas usan agua como refrigerante y después la echan a los ríos.

El petróleo Cae al mar desde los petroleros, flota en la superficie y mata los peces, pájaros y mamíferos acuáticos.

El plomo (lead) Los conductos del agua se hacían antes de plomo, el cual se disuelve y produce efectos tóxicos.

Los pesticidas Cuando se usan en exceso para proteger las plantas o matar los insectos, hacen daño al ecosistema.

La contaminación radioactiva Generalmente procede de las centrales nucleares. Su efecto sobre los seres vivos puede ser mortal.

¿CÓMO SE CONTAMINA EL AGUA?

1 Trabajando en grupo, comenten:

- las diferentes clases de contaminación y los efectos que tiene en el agua cada una de ellas
- cuál(es) de esas clases existe(n) en la región donde Uds. viven
- otras clases de contaminación del agua que Uds. conozcan

2 Digan qué se debe hacer para mejorar la calidad del agua. Por ejemplo:

> Es importante que las fábricas . . .
>
> Es necesario que tengamos cuidado . . .
>
> Es mejor que las personas no echen . . .

3 Compartan (share) dos o tres de las recomendaciones de su grupo con la clase.

Todo junto   481

La Catrina: Capítulo 14

Play

Video Activity B

Para entender mejor

Play

Video Activity C

Answers: Actividades
1–2 Answers will vary, but should include correct use of subjunctive where appropriate.

Answers: Conexiones
Recommendations will vary, but look for logical suggestions and the use of chapter vocabulary.

Writing Activities 14-G, 14-H

Comm. Act. BLMs 14-3, 14-4, 14-5

Pasos vivos 2 CD-ROM
A Jugar, Laboratorio de grabar, Maps, Video Monitor, Video Presentation Maker

Visual/Spatial
See Using the Video, *Conexiones,* Writing Activities 14-G and 14-H, and Comm. Act. BLMs 14-3, 14-4, and 14-5.

Apply

Process Reading
For a description of process reading, see p. 52.

Answers
Antes de leer
Answers will vary, but students may mention that they would expect to find pictures of the endangered plants or animals, and a description of what the area will be like.

Mira la lectura
Answers will vary, but students may say that Ecuador has more than twice the species of animals and plants than all of North America. Just one river of the Equatorial Amazon contains 473 species of fish; compared to only 70 in the European continent. Ecuador also is home to over 20 percent of the world's population of birds.

¡Vamos a leer!

Antes de leer
STRATEGY ➤ Using prior knowledge

Ecotourism is travel to areas that need protection because they have endangered species of plants and/or animals. What would you expect to find in an ad for ecotours?

Mira la lectura
STRATEGY ➤ Scanning

Scan the ad to find three attractions in Ecuador for travelers who are interested in protecting the environment.

Entre las miles de especies que viven en las islas Galápagos, hay piqueros (pájaros de patas azules), muchos tipos de iguanas terrestres y marinas y tortugas gigantes que tienen cientos de años.

Infórmate
STRATEGY ➤ Coping with unknown words

1 Read the ad carefully and make a list of words you don't know. Underline the ones that you think are important to know. Work with a partner to figure them out. Then use a dictionary to verify the meanings.

2 Now read the ad again. Then read the following sentences based on it. Some are true and some are false. Change the false sentences to true ones.

   a. Hay más especies de peces en Ecuador que en Europa.

   b. No hay montañas en Ecuador.
   c. Hay sólo dos tipos de bosques en Ecuador.
   d. Samoa Turismo tiene un catamarán y un yate a motor.
   e. Los Estados Unidos tiene un número mayor de especies animales y vegetales que Ecuador.

Aplicación

What would be an attractive destination in the United States for an ecotourist? Write three sentences in Spanish telling why.

482   Capítulo 14

Options

Strategies for Reaching All Students

Spanish-Speaking Students
Investiga algún lugar en otro país que se presta al ecoturismo. Di dónde está, qué tipo de lugar es (una selva tropical, un río, un cañón, etc.) y qué se puede ver allí.

Students Needing Extra Help
Mira la lectura: Emphasize scanning and the fact that students are looking for three pieces of information.
Infórmate: Emphasize the strategy for coping with unknown words. Limit the number of words on the list. Do the activity as a class, one paragraph at a time, until students learn the technique. On the chalkboard, write a list of words students don't understand.
Aplicación: Brainstorm possible locations.

Cultural Notes

(p. 482, left photo)
Blue-footed boobies are a type of gannet, or fish-eating off-shore sea bird. During courtship, male boobies fly toward their future mates, exposing the brilliant blue soles of their feet as they land. Since there are few natural predators on the islands, boobies show little fear when observed close-up by humans.

ECUADOR:
¡Bienvenido a la experiencia!

La primera consideración de Samoa Turismo al ofrecerle visitar Ecuador es naturaleza, mezclada con comodidad, seguridad y mucha simpatía.

Visitar nuestro país de apenas 283.561 kilómetros cuadrados, realmente es una hermosa experiencia; es uno de los países de mayor biodiversidad de la Tierra, tomando en cuenta su pequeña superficie, y con una riqueza florística excepcional que corresponde al 50% de la flora de Brasil y al 10% de la flora mundial.

Posee más del doble de especies animales y vegetales que toda Norteamérica y podemos citar que en un solo río de la Amazonía ecuatoriana habitan 473 especies de peces mientras que todo el continente europeo tiene 70.

En Sudamérica existen 3.500 especies de aves y en todo el mundo 8.600, en Ecuador viven 1.800 especies que representarían más del 20% de la avifauna mundial.

Posee tres de los puntos excepcionales

para la conservación de las especies: las estribaciones orientales de los Andes, el bosque lluvioso noroccidental y los bosques secos, semihúmedos y húmedos tropicales.

Samoa Turismo también le brinda la oportunidad de visitar las Islas Galápagos, una de las maravillas naturales del mundo, Patrimonio de la Humanidad y la selva Amazónica, considerada el pulmón de la tierra.

Al ofrecerle nuestros servicios, Samoa Turismo garantiza una operación segura, en nuestros propios yates: **"American Enterprise"**, lujoso catamarán para 16 pasajeros y 8 tripulantes; y **"Samoa I"**, yate a motor, clase turista superior para 12 pasajeros y 6 tripulantes, además de su **"Amazon Jungle Resort Village"** en la selva Amazónica ecuatoriana y sus demás servicios en el resto del país, Andes y Costa que harán de su visita algo realmente inolvidable.

SAMOA TURISMO
Bienvenido a la experiencia ...

Infórmate
a. true
b. false; *Los Andes están en Ecuador.*
c. false; *Hay el bosque lluvioso noroccidental y los bosques secos, semihúmedos y húmedos tropicales.*
d. true
e. false; *Ecuador posee más del doble de especies animales y vegetales que toda Norteamérica.*

Aplicación
Answers will vary, but students may mention the Grand Canyon, Yosemite, Yellowstone, the Rocky Mountains, or Alaska.

www **Internet Activities**

(p. 482, center photo)
Although the name "iguana" is generally applied to any herbivacious lizard with a dorsal crest, the Galápagos iguanas are a unique genus of lizard. The Galápagos marine iguana, which grows to as much as five feet, uses its tail to swim and dive. It grazes on underwater seaweed, and the Galápagos land iguana feeds on berries and cactus.

(p. 482, right photo)
The Galápagos tortoise is an ancient animal that existed in Texas and other parts of the southwestern U.S. some 25,000 years ago. The majority of them live today near the Alcedo volcano on the island of Isabela. Behaving in a manner typical of many Galápagos animals, the tortoise demonstrates little fear of humans. The giant tortoises weigh as much as 600 pounds and have a natural life span of 100 years or more.

Galápagos is Spanish for "tortoise" and the animal has come to symbolize the uniqueness of the islands' reptiles, birds, and plants. About 10,000 of these animals remain in the wild.

Apply

Teaching Suggestions
Ex. 1: Display all student work so that students doing the second task can choose a poet about whom to write.

Process Writing
For information regarding developing a writing portfolio, see p. 54.

¡Vamos a escribir!

Vamos a escribir unos poemas haiku. Los poemas haiku tienen tres líneas. La primera tiene 5 sílabas, la segunda tiene 7 y la tercera tiene 5. Por lo general, tratan de la naturaleza y de los sentimientos que inspira.

1 Para empezar, piensa en los lugares al aire libre que te gustan más, por ejemplo, un parque, un bosque o una playa. ¿Qué sientes cuando estás en uno de esos lugares? Trata de expresar tus sentimientos de una manera muy concreta y sencilla. Aquí hay unos ejemplos.

En el desierto,
la serpiente descansa.
Comió ardilla.

Al aire libre,
las hojas, el sendero,
tú y yo, tristes.

Montañas altas,
dar una caminata,
estoy cansado.

Cuenta las sílabas. No olvides que necesitas 5, 7 y 5 sílabas. Pídele sus comentarios a un(a) compañero(a) y revisa tu haiku si quieres.

484   Capítulo 14

Options

Strategies for Reaching All Students

Students Needing Extra Help
Explain haiku format. Have English-language haiku available. Use the vocabulary section of the Organizer.
Ex. 2: Give examples of the type of short biography found on book jackets. Pair students who like the same poem.

2 Un libro de poesía generalmente tiene datos sobre los poetas y las poetisas. Escoge un haiku que te gusta mucho y entrevista al (a la) compañero(a) que lo escribió. Luego, haz una nota biográfica sobre él o ella. Incluye estos datos:

- cómo se llama
- cuándo y dónde nació
- qué actividades le gustan más
- cuánto tiempo hace que escribe poesía
- qué piensa ser en el futuro

3 Para distribuir su trabajo, pueden:

- hacer un libro que se llama *La naturaleza en haiku*
- enviar su trabajo al periódico o revista escolar
- enviarlo a un periódico o revista local
- exhibirlo en la sala de clases o en otro lugar de la escuela
- incluirlo en su portafolio

¡Vamos a escribir!   485

Assess & Summarize

Test Preparation

You may want to assign parts of this section as written homework or as an in-class writing activity prior to administering the *Examen de habilidades*.

Answers

Listening: —*¡Qué aventura! Estábamos dando una caminata cuando Julio decidió escalar una montaña. Pero, ¿qué le pasó? De repente, ¡se cayó en un cacto! No se lastimó mucho, pero todavía tiene unas espinas que le duelen mucho. Ahora siempre les dice a sus amigos, "Es mejor que lleven zapatos especiales para escalar montañas."*
While mountain climbing, Julio fell on a cactus and hurt himself on the thorns.

Reading: You might see this sign in a national park.

Writing: Statements will vary; look for the subjunctive following each of the phrases.

Culture: A foreigner traveling in the U.S. might have an upset stomach because he or she is unaccustomed to the water, or because of dehydration or fatigue.

Speaking: Dialogues will vary.

Repaso ¿Lo sabes bien?

Esta sección te ayudará a prepararte para el examen de habilidades, donde tendrás que hacer tareas semejantes.

Listening

Can you understand when people talk about outdoor activities? Listen as your teacher reads a sample similar to what you will hear on the test. What happened to Julio?

Reading

How well can you understand signs that deal with wildlife? Where might you see this sign?

En este lugar hay lobos, venados, coyotes y serpientes de muchas especies. Algunos de estos animales están en peligro de extinción. Por lo tanto les pedimos que sigan por el sendero, que tengan cuidado con los animales que encuentren y que tomen precauciones contra las plantas venenosas.

Se prohíbe encender fuegos.

Self Test
www.pasoapaso.com

486   Capítulo 14

Writing

This is an excerpt from a brochure that gives advice on camping. Finish statements 2 to 4.

1. Es importante que lleven fósforos secos.
2. Se recomienda que . . .
3. Es mejor que . . .
4. Es necesario que . . .

Culture

Can you explain why a foreigner traveling in the United States might have stomach upsets?

Speaking

You and your partner have gone camping. Create a dialogue in which you solve a problem. Here is an example:

A —*¡Vaya! ¡Los fósforos están mojados!*
B —*Yo sé encender palitos con un lente de mis anteojos.*
A —*¡No me digas! ¿De verdad?*
B —*Créeme. Pero necesito que me ayudes.*
A —*Bueno. ¿Qué hago?*
B —*Primero, busca palitos y hojas secas. Luego, . . .*

MORE PRACTICE

Más práctica y tarea, pp. 568–571

Options

Strategies for Reaching All Students

Students Needing Extra Help
¿Lo sabes bien?: Remind students that this is just a sample of what the test will be like.
Listening: Read the sample more than once. Remind students they only need to listen for one piece of information. Brainstorm words students should be listening for.
Reading: Remind students to use context clues.
Writing: Have students use the Organizer to write sample suggestions as practice.

Culture: Have students review the notes they took during their first reading of the *Perspectiva cultural.* Encourage them to give an explanation rather than a short answer.
Speaking: Use the vocabulary section of the Organizer. Limit the number of lines of dialogue. Encourage students to use the subjunctive. Brainstorm problems that might arise on a camping trip and their possible solutions.
Have students write out this exercise so that they can check off what they have mastered.

Resumen del vocabulario

Usa el vocabulario de este capítulo para:
- discuss popular outdoor activities
- describe the natural environment
- express attitudes and opinions about the environment

to discuss camping
ir de camping
al aire libre
el campamento
la tienda (de acampar)
poner la tienda
el saco de dormir
el fósforo
el fuego
la leña
el palito
el abrelatas
la olla
ligero, -a
pesado, -a
mojado, -a
seco, -a
contaminado, -a
roto, -a

to describe nature
el amanecer
el atardecer
el desierto
el parque nacional
la colina
el valle
el fósil
la huella
la piedra
el sendero
la sombra

to discuss outdoor activities
dar una caminata
dar saltos
el trampolín, *pl.* los
    trampolines
escalar montañas
hacer esquí acuático
hacer moto acuática
la moto acuática
hacer surf
hacer surf de vela
la tabla (de surf)
la vela
navegar en balsa
la balsa
navegar en canoa
la canoa

to discuss plants and animals
el animal salvaje
la ardilla
la ballena
el búho
el coyote
el elefante
el gorila
el lobo, la loba
la mariposa
la pluma
la rana
la serpiente
el venado, la venada
los animales en peligro de
    extinción
doméstico, -a
peligroso, -a
venenoso, -a
el árbol
la hoja
el cacto
la espina
la planta silvestre

**other useful words
and expressions**
el oxígeno
coser
recoger
secar

Assessment

 Prueba cumulativa

 **Examen de
habilidades**

 Test Generator

**Additional Assessment
Options**

 Comm. Act. BLMs

Small Group Activities
Situation Cards

 **Pasos vivos 2
CD-ROM**

Slide Presentation Maker, Video
Presentation Maker, Word
Processor, Spindle

 **¿Lo sabes bien?
Video Quiz**

 Internet Activities

Self-Test

Verbos

Regular Verbs

estudiar		
	PRESENT INDICATIVE	estudio, estudias, estudia; estudiamos, estudiáis, estudian
	PRESENT SUBJUNCTIVE	estudie, estudies, estudie; estudiemos, estudiéis, estudien
	PRETERITE	estudié, estudiaste, estudió; estudiamos, estudiasteis, estudiaron
	IMPERFECT	estudiaba, estudiabas, estudiaba; estudiábamos, estudiabais, estudiaban
	FUTURE	estudiaré, estudiarás, estudiará; estudiaremos, estudiaréis, estudiarán
	TÚ COMMANDS	estudia, no estudies
	PRESENT PARTICIPLE	estudiando

comer		
	PRESENT INDICATIVE	como, comes, come; comemos, coméis, comen
	PRESENT SUBJUNCTIVE	coma, comas, coma; comamos, comáis, coman
	PRETERITE	comí, comiste, comió; comimos, comisteis, comieron
	IMPERFECT	comía, comías, comía; comíamos, comíais, comían
	FUTURE	comeré, comerás, comerá; comeremos, comeréis, comerán
	TÚ COMMANDS	come, no comas
	PRESENT PARTICIPLE	comiendo

vivir		
	PRESENT INDICATIVE	vivo, vives, vive; vivimos, vivís, viven
	PRESENT SUBJUNCTIVE	viva, vivas, viva; vivamos, viváis, vivan
	PRETERITE	viví, viviste, vivió; vivimos, vivisteis, vivieron
	IMPERFECT	vivía, vivías, vivía; vivíamos, vivíais, vivían
	FUTURE	viviré, vivirás, vivirá; viviremos, viviréis, vivirán
	TÚ COMMANDS	vive, no vivas
	PRESENT PARTICIPLE	viviendo

Reflexive Verbs

lavarse		
	PRESENT INDICATIVE	me lavo, te lavas, se lava; nos lavamos, os laváis, se lavan
	PRESENT SUBJUNCTIVE	me lave, te laves, se lave; nos lavemos, os lavéis, se laven
	PRETERITE	me lavé, te lavaste, se lavó; nos lavamos, os lavasteis, se lavaron
	IMPERFECT	me lavaba, te lavabas, se lavaba; nos lavábamos, os lavabais, se lavaban
	FUTURE	me lavaré, te lavarás, se lavará; nos lavaremos, os lavaréis, se lavarán
	TÚ COMMANDS	lávate, no te laves
	PRESENT PARTICIPLE	lavándose

Stem-Changing Verbs *(You will learn the forms that are in italics next year.)*

cerrar (e → ie)
PRESENT INDICATIVE cierro, cierras, cierra; cerramos, cerráis, cierran
PRESENT SUBJUNCTIVE cierre, cierres, cierre; *cerremos, cerréis, cierren*
PRETERITE cerré, cerraste, cerró; cerramos, cerrasteis, cerraron
IMPERFECT cerraba, cerrabas, cerraba; cerrábamos, cerrabais, cerraban
FUTURE cerraré, cerrarás, cerrará; cerraremos, cerraréis, cerrarán
TÚ COMMANDS cierra, no cierres
PRESENT PARTICIPLE cerrando

Other verbs that follow the pattern of **cerrar: despertarse, pensar,** *and* **recomendar.**

dormir (o → ue)
PRESENT INDICATIVE duermo, duermes, duerme; dormimos, dormís, duermen
PRESENT SUBJUNCTIVE duerma, duermas, duerma; *durmamos, durmáis, duerman*
PRETERITE dormí, dormiste, durmió; dormimos, dormisteis, durmieron
IMPERFECT dormía, dormías, dormía; dormíamos, dormíais, dormían
FUTURE dormiré, dormirás, dormirá; dormiremos, dormiréis, dormirán
TÚ COMMANDS duerme, no duermas
PRESENT PARTICIPLE durmiendo

empezar (e → ie)
PRESENT INDICATIVE See *cerrar.*
PRESENT SUBJUNCTIVE empiece, empieces, empiece; *empecemos, empecéis, empiecen*
PRETERITE empecé, empezaste, empezó; empezamos, empezasteis, empezaron
IMPERFECT See *cerrar.*
FUTURE See *cerrar.*
TÚ COMMANDS See *cerrar.*
PRESENT PARTICIPLE See *cerrar.*

jugar (u → ue)
PRESENT INDICATIVE juego, juegas, juega; jugamos, jugáis, juegan
PRESENT SUBJUNCTIVE juegue, juegues, juegue; *juguemos, juguéis, jueguen*
PRETERITE jugué, jugaste, jugó; jugamos, jugasteis, jugaron
IMPERFECT jugaba, jugabas, jugaba; jugábamos, jugabais, jugaban
FUTURE jugaré, jugarás, jugará; jugaremos, jugaréis, jugarán
TÚ COMMANDS juega, no juegues
PRESENT PARTICIPLE jugando

llover (o → ue)
PRESENT INDICATIVE llueve
PRESENT SUBJUNCTIVE llueva
PRETERITE llovió
IMPERFECT llovía
FUTURE lloverá
PRESENT PARTICIPLE lloviendo

nevar (e → ie)
PRESENT INDICATIVE nieva
PRESENT SUBJUNCTIVE nieve
PRETERITE nevó
IMPERFECT nevaba
FUTURE nevará
PRESENT PARTICIPLE nevando

Verbos 489

pedir (e → i)	PRESENT INDICATIVE	pido, pides, pide; pedimos, pedís, piden
	PRESENT SUBJUNCTIVE	pida, pidas, pida; *pidamos, pidáis, pidan*
	PRETERITE	pedí, pediste, pidió; pedimos, pedisteis, pidieron
	IMPERFECT	pedía, pedías, pedía; pedíamos, pedíais, pedían
	FUTURE	pediré, pedirás, pedirá; pediremos, pediréis, pedirán
	TÚ COMMANDS	pide, no pidas
	PRESENT PARTICIPLE	pidiendo

Other verbs that follow the pattern of pedir: **conseguir, despedirse, seguir, servir,** *and* **vestirse.**

perder (e → ie)	PRESENT INDICATIVE	pierdo, pierdes, pierde; perdemos, perdéis, pierden
	PRESENT SUBJUNCTIVE	pierda, pierdas, pierda; *perdamos, perdáis, pierdan*
	PRETERITE	perdí, perdiste, perdió; perdimos, perdisteis, perdieron
	IMPERFECT	perdía, perdías, perdía; perdíamos, perdíais, perdían
	FUTURE	perderé, perderás, perderá; perderemos, perderéis, perderán
	TÚ COMMANDS	pierde, no pierdas
	PRESENT PARTICIPLE	perdiendo

| poder (o → ue) | See Irregular Verbs. |

preferir (e → ie)	PRESENT INDICATIVE	prefiero, prefieres, prefiere; preferimos, preferís, prefieren
	PRESENT SUBJUNCTIVE	prefiera, prefieras, prefiera; *prefiramos, prefiráis, prefieran*
	PRETERITE	preferí, preferiste, prefirió; preferimos, preferisteis, prefirieron
	IMPERFECT	prefería, preferías, prefería; preferíamos, preferíais, preferían
	FUTURE	preferiré, preferirás, preferirá; preferiremos, preferiréis, preferirán
	TÚ COMMANDS	prefiere, no prefieras
	PRESENT PARTICIPLE	prefiriendo

Other verbs that follow the pattern of **preferir: divertirse, encender, hervir, mentir, sentirse,** *and* **sugerir.**

probar (o → ue)	PRESENT INDICATIVE	pruebo, pruebas, prueba; probamos, probáis, prueban
	PRESENT SUBJUNCTIVE	pruebe, pruebes, pruebe; *probemos, probéis, prueben*
	PRETERITE	probé, probaste, probó; probamos, probasteis, probaron
	IMPERFECT	probaba, probabas, probaba; probábamos, probabais, probaban
	FUTURE	probaré, probarás, probará; probaremos, probaréis, probarán
	TÚ COMMANDS	prueba, no pruebes
	PRESENT PARTICIPLE	probando

Other verbs that follow the pattern of **probar: acostarse, colgar, encontrar, mostrar, probarse,** *and* **recordar.**

| querer (e → ie) | See Irregular Verbs. |

soler (o → ue)	PRESENT INDICATIVE	suelo, sueles, suele; solemos, soléis, suelen
	PRESENT SUBJUNCTIVE	suela, suelas, suela; *solamos, soláis, suelan*
	PRETERITE	solí, soliste, solió; solimos, solisteis, solieron
	IMPERFECT	solía, solías, solía; solíamos, solíais, solían
	FUTURE	soleré, solerás, solerá; soleremos, soleréis, solerán
	TÚ COMMANDS	suele, no suelas
	PRESENT PARTICIPLE	soliendo

Other verbs that follow the pattern of **soler: devolver** *and* **revolver.**

490   Verbos

Verbs with Spelling Changes

actuar (u → ú)

PRESENT INDICATIVE	actúo, actúas, actúa; actuamos, actuáis, actúan
PRESENT SUBJUNCTIVE	actúe, actúes, actúe; actuemos, actuéis, actúen
PRETERITE	actué, actuaste, actuó; actuamos, actuasteis, actuaron
IMPERFECT	actuaba, actuabas, actuaba; actuábamos, actuabais, actuaban
FUTURE	actuaré, actuarás, actuará; actuaremos, actuaréis, actuarán
TÚ COMMANDS	actúa, no actúes
PRESENT PARTICIPLE	actuando

Other verbs that follow the pattern of **actuar: graduarse.**

apagar (g → gu)

PRESENT INDICATIVE	apago, apagas, apaga; apagamos, apagáis, apagan
PRESENT SUBJUNCTIVE	apague, apagues, apague; apaguemos, apaguéis, apaguen
PRETERITE	apagué, apagaste, apagó; apagamos, apagasteis, apagaron
IMPERFECT	apagaba, apagabas, apagaba; apagábamos, apagabais, apagaban
FUTURE	apagaré, apagarás, apagará; apagaremos, apagaréis, apagarán
TÚ COMMANDS	apaga, no apagues
PRESENT PARTICIPLE	apagando

Other verbs that follow the pattern of **apagar: despegar, entregar, investigar, llegar, navegar,** *and* **pagar.**

buscar (c → qu)

PRESENT INDICATIVE	busco, buscas, busca; buscamos, buscáis, buscan
PRESENT SUBJUNCTIVE	busque, busques, busque; busquemos, busquéis, busquen
PRETERITE	busqué, buscaste, buscó; buscamos, buscasteis, buscaron
IMPERFECT	buscaba, buscabas, buscaba; buscábamos, buscabais, buscaban
FUTURE	buscaré, buscarás, buscará; buscaremos, buscaréis, buscarán
TÚ COMMANDS	busca, no busques
PRESENT PARTICIPLE	buscando

Other verbs that follow the pattern of **buscar: explicar, indicar, picar, practicar, sacar, secar(se),** *and* **tocar.**

conocer (c → zc)

PRESENT INDICATIVE	conozco, conoces, conoce; conocemos, conocéis, conocen
PRESENT SUBJUNCTIVE	conozca, conozcas, conozca; conozcamos, conozcáis, conozcan
PRETERITE	conocí, conociste, conoció; conocimos, conocisteis, conocieron
IMPERFECT	conocía, conocías, conocía; conocíamos, conocíais, conocían
FUTURE	conoceré, conocerás, conocerá; conoceremos, conoceréis, conocerán
TÚ COMMANDS	conoce, no conozcas
PRESENT PARTICIPLE	conociendo

Other verbs that follow the pattern of **conocer: desobedecer, obedecer,** *and* **parecer.**

creer (e → y)

PRESENT INDICATIVE	creo, crees, cree; creemos, creéis, creen
PRESENT SUBJUNCTIVE	crea, creas, crea; creamos, creáis, crean
PRETERITE	creí, creíste, creyó; creímos, creísteis, creyeron
IMPERFECT	creía, creías, creía; creíamos, creíais, creían
FUTURE	creeré, creerás, creerá; creeremos, creeréis, creerán
TÚ COMMANDS	cree, no creas
PRESENT PARTICIPLE	creyendo

Other verbs that follow the pattern of **creer: leer.**

Verbos   491

cruzar (z → c)	PRESENT INDICATIVE	cruzo, cruzas, cruza; cruzamos, cruzáis, cruzan
	PRESENT SUBJUNCTIVE	cruce, cruces, cruce; crucemos, crucéis, crucen
	PRETERITE	crucé, cruzaste, cruza; cruzamos, cruzasteis, cruzaron
	IMPERFECT	cruzaba, cruzabas, cruzaba; cruzábamos, cruzabais, cruzaban
	FUTURE	cruzaré, cruzarás, cruzará; cruzaremos, cruzaréis, cruzarán
	TÚ COMMANDS	cruza, no cruces
	PRESENT PARTICIPLE	cruzando

Other verbs that follow the pattern of **cruzar: lanzar.**

dirigir (g → j)	PRESENT INDICATIVE	dirijo, diriges, dirige; dirigimos, dirigís, dirigen
	PRESENT SUBJUNCTIVE	See *escoger.*
	PRETERITE	See *escoger.*
	IMPERFECT	See *escoger.*
	FUTURE	See *escoger.*
	TÚ COMMANDS	See *escoger.*
	PRESENT PARTICIPLE	See *escoger.*

empezar (z → c)   See Stem-Changing Verbs.

escoger (g → j)	PRESENT INDICATIVE	escojo, escoges, escoge; escogemos, escogéis, escogen
	PRESENT SUBJUNCTIVE	escoja, escojas, escoja; escojamos, escojáis, escojan
	PRETERITE	escogí, escogiste, escogió; escogimos, escogisteis, escogieron
	IMPERFECT	escogía, escogías, escogía; escogíamos, escogíais, escogían
	FUTURE	escogeré, escogerás, escogerá; escogeremos, escogeréis, escogerán
	TÚ COMMANDS	escoge, no escojas
	PRESENT PARTICIPLE	escogiendo

Other verbs that follow the pattern of **escoger: proteger(se)** *and* **recoger.**

incluir (i → y)	PRESENT INDICATIVE	incluyo, incluyes, incluye; incluimos, incluís, incluyen
	PRESENT SUBJUNCTIVE	incluya, incluyas, incluya; incluyamos, incluyáis, incluyan
	PRETERITE	incluí, incluiste, incluyó; incluimos, incluisteis, incluyeron
	IMPERFECT	incluía, incluías, incluía; incluíamos, incluíais, incluían
	FUTURE	incluiré, incluirás, incluirá; incluiremos, incluiréis, incluirán
	TÚ COMMANDS	incluye, no incluyas
	PRESENT PARTICIPLE	incluyendo

Other verbs that follow the pattern of **incluir: destruir.**

jugar (g → gu)   See Stem-Changing Verbs.

Irregular Verbs *(You will learn the forms that are in italics next year.)*

| **caerse** | PRETERITE | me caí, te caíste, se cayó; nos caímos, os caísteis, se cayeron |
| | | *For all other forms, see* **traer** *and Reflexive Verbs.* |

dar	PRESENT INDICATIVE	doy, das, da; damos, dais, dan
	PRESENT SUBJUNCTIVE	*dé, des, dé; demos, deis, den*
	PRETERITE	di, diste, dio; dimos, disteis, dieron
	IMPERFECT	daba, dabas, daba; dábamos, dabais, daban
	FUTURE	daré, darás, dará; daremos, daréis, darán
	TÚ COMMANDS	da, *no des*
	PRESENT PARTICIPLE	dando

decir		
	PRESENT INDICATIVE	digo, dices, dice; decimos, decís, dicen
	PRESENT SUBJUNCTIVE	diga, digas, diga; digamos, digáis, digan
	PRETERITE	dije, dijiste, dijo; dijimos, dijisteis, dijeron
	IMPERFECT	decía, decías, decía; decíamos, decíais, decían
	FUTURE	diré, dirás, dirá; diremos, diréis, dirán
	TÚ COMMANDS	di, no digas
	PRESENT PARTICIPLE	diciendo

estar		
	PRESENT INDICATIVE	estoy, estás, está; estamos, estáis, están
	PRESENT SUBJUNCTIVE	*esté, estés, esté; estemos, estéis, estén*
	PRETERITE	estuve, estuviste, estuvo; estuvimos, estuvisteis, estuvieron
	IMPERFECT	estaba, estabas, estaba; estábamos, estabais, estaban
	FUTURE	estaré, estarás, estará; estaremos, estaréis, estarán
	TÚ COMMANDS	está, *no estés*
	PRESENT PARTICIPLE	estando

haber		
	PRESENT INDICATIVE	hay
	PRESENT SUBJUNCTIVE	*haya*
	PRETERITE	hubo
	IMPERFECT	había
	FUTURE	habrá

hacer		
	PRESENT INDICATIVE	hago, haces, hace; hacemos, hacéis, hacen
	PRESENT SUBJUNCTIVE	haga, hagas, haga; hagamos, hagáis, hagan
	PRETERITE	hice, hiciste, hizo; hicimos, hicisteis, hicieron
	IMPERFECT	hacía, hacías, hacía; hacíamos, hacíais, hacían
	FUTURE	haré, harás, hará; haremos, haréis, harán
	TÚ COMMANDS	haz, no hagas
	PRESENT PARTICIPLE	haciendo

ir		
	PRESENT INDICATIVE	voy, vas, va; vamos, vais, van
	PRESENT SUBJUNCTIVE	vaya, vayas, vaya; vayamos, vayáis, vayan
	PRETERITE	fui, fuiste, fue; fuimos, fuisteis, fueron
	IMPERFECT	iba, ibas, iba; íbamos, ibais, iban
	FUTURE	iré, irás, irá; iremos, iréis, irán
	TÚ COMMANDS	ve, no vayas
	PRESENT PARTICIPLE	*yendo*

mantenerse	See *tener* and Reflexive Verbs.

nacer		
	PRETERITE	nací, naciste, nació; nacimos, nacisteis, nacieron

poder		
	PRESENT INDICATIVE	puedo, puedes, puede; podemos, podéis, pueden
	PRESENT SUBJUNCTIVE	pueda, puedas, pueda; *podamos, podáis, puedan*
	PRETERITE	pude, pudiste, pudo; pudimos, pudisteis, pudieron
	IMPERFECT	podía, podías, podía; podíamos, podíais, podían
	FUTURE	podré, podrás, podrá; podremos, podréis, podrán
	TÚ COMMANDS	puede, no puedas
	PRESENT PARTICIPLE	*pudiendo*

poner		
	PRESENT INDICATIVE	pongo, pones, pone; ponemos, ponéis, ponen
	PRESENT SUBJUNCTIVE	ponga, pongas, ponga; pongamos, pongáis, pongan
	PRETERITE	puse, pusiste, puso; pusimos, pusisteis, pusieron
	IMPERFECT	ponía, ponías, ponía; poníamos, poníais, ponían
	FUTURE	pondré, pondrás, pondrá; pondremos, pondréis, pondrán
	TÚ COMMANDS	pon, no pongas
	PRESENT PARTICIPLE	poniendo

Verbos   493

querer	PRESENT INDICATIVE	quiero, quieres, quiere; queremos, queréis, quieren
	PRESENT SUBJUNCTIVE	quiera, quieras, quiera; *queramos, queráis, quieran*
	PRETERITE	quise, quisiste, quiso; quisimos, quisisteis, quisieron
	IMPERFECT	quería, querías, quería; queríamos, queríais, querían
	FUTURE	querré, querrás, querrá; querremos, querréis, querrán
	TÚ COMMANDS	quiere, no quieras
	PRESENT PARTICIPLE	queriendo
saber	PRESENT INDICATIVE	sé, sabes, sabe; sabemos, sabéis, saben
	PRESENT SUBJUNCTIVE	*sepa, sepas, sepa; sepamos, sepáis, sepan*
	PRETERITE	*supe, supiste, supo; supimos, supisteis, supieron*
	IMPERFECT	sabía, sabías, sabía; sabíamos, sabíais, sabían
	FUTURE	sabré, sabrás, sabrá; sabremos, sabréis, sabrán
	TÚ COMMANDS	sabe, *no* sepas
	PRESENT PARTICIPLE	sabiendo
salir	PRESENT INDICATIVE	salgo, sales, sale; salimos, salís, salen
	PRESENT SUBJUNCTIVE	salga, salgas, salga; salgamos, salgáis, salgan
	PRETERITE	salí, saliste, salió; salimos, salisteis, salieron
	IMPERFECT	salía, salías, salía; salíamos, salíais, salían
	FUTURE	saldré, saldrás, saldrá; saldremos, saldréis, saldrán
	TÚ COMMANDS	sal, no salgas
	PRESENT PARTICIPLE	saliendo
ser	PRESENT INDICATIVE	soy, eres, es; somos, sois, son
	PRESENT SUBJUNCTIVE	sea, seas, sea; seamos, seáis, sean
	PRETERITE	fui, fuiste, fue; fuimos, fuisteis, fueron
	IMPERFECT	era, eras, era; éramos, erais, eran
	FUTURE	seré, serás, será; seremos, seréis, serán
	TÚ COMMANDS	sé, no seas
	PRESENT PARTICIPLE	*siendo*
tener	PRESENT INDICATIVE	tengo, tienes, tiene; tenemos, tenéis, tienen
	PRESENT SUBJUNCTIVE	tenga, tengas, tenga; tengamos, tengáis, tengan
	PRETERITE	tuve, tuviste, tuvo; tuvimos, tuvisteis, tuvieron
	IMPERFECT	tenía, tenías, tenía; teníamos, teníais, tenían
	FUTURE	tendré, tendrás, tendrá; tendremos, tendréis, tendrán
	TÚ COMMANDS	ten, no tengas
	PRESENT PARTICIPLE	teniendo
traer	PRESENT INDICATIVE	traigo, traes, trae; traemos, traéis, traen
	PRESENT SUBJUNCTIVE	traiga, traigas, traiga; traigamos, traigáis, traigan
	PRETERITE	traje, trajiste, trajo; trajimos, trajisteis, trajeron
	IMPERFECT	traía, traías, traía; traíamos, traíais, traían
	FUTURE	traeré, traerás, traerá; traeremos, traeréis, traerán
	TÚ COMMANDS	trae, no traigas
	PRESENT PARTICIPLE	trayendo
ver	PRESENT INDICATIVE	veo, veas, ve; vemos, veis, ven
	PRESENT SUBJUNCTIVE	vea, veas, vea; veamos, veáis, vean
	PRETERITE	vi, viste, vio; vimos, visteis, vieron
	IMPERFECT	veía, veías, veía; veíamos, veíais, veían
	FUTURE	veré, verás, verá; veremos, veréis, verán
	TÚ COMMANDS	ve, no veas
	PRESENT PARTICIPLE	viendo

VOCABULARIO ESPAÑOL-INGLÉS

This *Vocabulario* contains all active vocabulary from PASO A PASO 1 and 2.

A dash (—) represents the main entry word. For example, **al** — after **el horno** means **al horno**.

The number following each entry indicates the chapter in which the word or expression is presented. A Roman numeral (I) indicates that the word was presented in PASO A PASO 1.

The following abbreviations are used: *adj.* (adjective), *dir. obj.* (direct object), *f.* (feminine), *fam.* (familiar), *ind. obj.* (indirect object), *inf.* (infinitive), *m.* (masculine), *pl.* (plural), *prep.* (preposition), *pron.* (pronoun), *sing.* (singular).

a, al *(a + el)* at; to (I)
la **abeja** bee (9)
el **abogado, la abogada** lawyer (11)
abrazarse to hug, to embrace (6)
el **abrelatas** can opener (14)
el **abrigo** coat (I)
abril April (I)
abrir to open (I)
abrocharse to fasten (12)
el **abuelo, la abuela** grandfather, grandmother (I)
los **abuelos** grandparents (I)
aburrido, -a boring (I)
aburrir to bore (I)
—**se** to be bored (4)
acampar: la tienda de — tent (14)
el **accidente** accident (9)
acción: la película de — action film (10)
Acción *see* **Día**
el **aceite** oil (13)
acondicionado *see* **aire**
acostarse *(o → ue)* to go to bed (2)
la **actividad** activity (2)
el **actor, la actriz** actor, actress (I)
la **actuación** acting (10)
actuar to act (10)
acuático, -a *see* **esquí, moto**
acuerdo: estar de — to agree (I)
además in addition, besides (9)
adiós good-by (I)
¿adónde? (to) where? (I)
la **aduana** customs (12)
el **aduanero, la aduanera** customs agent (12)
aérea: la línea — airline (12)
el **aeropuerto** airport (12)
afeitar:
—**se** to shave (8)
la crema de — shaving cream (8)
la máquina de — razor (8)
la **agencia de viajes** travel agency (12)
el/la **agente (de viajes)** (travel) agent (12)
agosto August (I)

agrio, -a sour (13)
el **agua** *f.* water (I)
el **aguacate** avocado (I)
ahora now (I)
ahorrar to save (7)
el **aire** air (I)
al — **libre** outdoors (14)
el — **acondicionado** air conditioning (7)
el **ajedrez** chess (4)
el **ajo** garlic (13)
alegre happy, festive (4)
el **alemán** German *(language)* (1)
la **alergia** allergy (9)
alérgico, -a (a) allergic (to) (9)
el **álgebra** *f.* algebra (1)
algo something (I)
— **más** something else (I)
el **algodón** cotton (3)
alguien someone, somebody (I, 3)
alguno (algún), -a some (I, 1)
—**a vez** ever (I)
la **alimentación** nourishment, food (13)
allí there (I)
— **está** there it is (I)
el **almacén** department store (I)
el **almuerzo** lunch (I)
en el — for lunch (I)
alto, -a tall (I)
el **alto: la señal de** — stop sign (8)
el **aluminio** aluminum (I)
amable kind, nice (I)
el **amanecer** dawn, sunrise (14)
amargo, -a bitter (13)
amarillo, -a yellow (I)
el **ambiente** atmosphere (I)
el **medio** —environment (I, 11)
la **ambulancia** ambulance (9)
la **amenaza** threat (I)
el **amigo, la amiga** friend (I)
el **análisis** medical test (9)
anaranjado, -a orange *(color)* (I)
el **anillo** ring (7)
el **animal** animal (I, 5)
el — **de peluche** stuffed animal (5)

el **aniversario (de boda)** (wedding) anniversary (6)
anoche last night (I)
los **anteojos (de sol)** (sun)glasses (I, 7)
antes de + *verb* before + *verb* + -ing (2)
antialérgico, -a non-allergenic (9)
el **antibiótico** antibiotic (9)
antiguo, -a old, traditional (I)
antipático, -a unfriendly, unpleasant (I)
el **anuario** yearbook (2)
el **anuncio** ad, commercial (I)
el **año** year (I)
a los . . . —s at the age of . . . (6)
el — **Nuevo** New Year's Day (6)
¿cuántos — tienes? how old are you? (I)
cumplir —s to have a birthday (6)
la fiesta de fin de — New Year's Eve party (I)
el fin de — New Year's Eve (6)
tener . . . —s to be . . . years old (I)
apagar to turn off (I, 7); to blow out *(candles)* (6)
el **aparato** appliance, device (7)
el **apartamento** apartment (I)
aprender to learn (I)
apretado, -a tight *(clothing)* (3)
aquel, aquella; aquellos, -as that (over there); those (over there) (3)
aquél, aquélla; aquéllos, -as *pron.* that one (over there); those (over there) (3)
aquí here (I)
— **está** here it is (I)
por — around here (I)
la **araña** spider (9)
el **árbol** tree (I, 14)
la **ardilla** squirrel (14)
el **arete** earring (I, 7)
el **argumento** plot (10)
el **armario** locker (1)
arreglar to clean up (I)
arrestar to arrest (10)

el **arroz** rice (I)
el **arte** art (I, 4)
  las—**s marciales** martial arts (2)
la **artesanía** handcrafts (12)
artístico, -a artistic (I)
asado, -a roasted (13)
el **ascensor** elevator (8)
asco: ¡qué —! yuck! that's disgusting! (I)
así, así so-so, fair (I)
el **asiento** seat (1)
la **aspiradora** vacuum cleaner (I)
  pasar la — to vacuum (I)
el/la **astronauta** astronaut (11)
el **atardecer** sunset (14)
aterrizar to land (12)
atractivo, -a attractive (I)
atrevido, -a bold, daring (I)
el **auditorio** auditorium (1)
el **autobús** bus (I)
  la parada del — bus stop (I)
automático, -a automatic (11)
el/la **auxiliar de vuelo** flight attendant (12)
la **avenida** avenue (I)
aventura: la película de —s adventure film (I)
el **avión** airplane (12)
¡ay! ouch! (I)
ayer yesterday (I)
la **ayuda** help, assistance (10)
ayudar to help (I)
el **azúcar** sugar (I)
azul, *pl.* **azules** blue (I)

bailar to dance (I, 6)
el **bailarín, la bailarina** dancer (11)
el **baile** dance (I, 6)
baja: el sube y — seesaw (5)
bajo, -a short *(height)* (I)
la **ballena** whale (I, 14)
el **balón** *(inflated)* ball (4)
la **balsa** raft (14)
  navegar en — to go river rafting (14)
bañarse to take a bath (2)
el **banco** bank (I)
la **banda** band (2)
la **bandera** flag (1)
el **baño** bathroom (I)
  el traje de — bathing suit (I)
barato, -a cheap, inexpensive (I)
la **barbacoa** barbecue (13)
  hacer una — to have a barbecue (13)
basado, -a (en) based (on) (10)

básquetbol: jugar — to play basketball (I)
bastante rather, quite (I, 4)
la **basura** garbage (I)
el **bate** (baseball) bat (4)
beber to drink (I)
la **bebida** beverage (I)
el **béisbol** baseball (I)
besarse to kiss (6)
la **biblioteca** library (I)
la **bicicleta** bicycle (I, 4)
  montar en — to ride a bike (4)
bien well (I)
la **biología** biology (1)
el **bisabuelo, la bisabuela** great-grandfather, great-grandmother (6)
el **bistec** steak (I)
blanco, -a white (I)
el **bloque** block *(toy)* (5)
la **blusa** blouse (I)
la **boca** mouth (I)
el **bocadillo** Spanish-style sandwich (13)
la **boda** wedding (6)
el **boleto (de ida y vuelta)** (round-trip) ticket (12)
el **bolígrafo** pen (I)
los **bolos** bowling (4)
el **bolsillo** pocket (3)
el **bolso** gym bag, book bag (1); purse (3)
el **bombero, la bombera** firefighter (8)
  la estación de —s fire station (8)
el **bombillo** light bulb (7)
bonito, -a pretty (I)
el **bosque** woods (11)
la **bota** boot (I)
el **bote** rowboat (I)
  pasear en — to row (I)
la **botella** bottle (I, 11)
el **botín** half boots (3)
el **botón** button (3)
el **brazo** arm (I)
el **bronceador** suntan lotion (I)
bucear to skin-dive (I)
bueno (buen), -a good (I)
  bueno OK, fine, all right (I)
la **bufanda** muffler, scarf (I)
el **bufet de ensaladas** salad bar (1)
el **búho** owl (14)
el **burrito** burrito (I)
buscar to look for (I)
el **buzón** mailbox (8)

el **caballero: la ropa para —s** men's wear (8)
el **caballo** horse (10)
  montar a — to ride a horse (10)
la **cabeza** head (I)
  tener dolor de — to have a headache (I)
el **cacto** cactus (14)
la **cadena** chain (7)
caerse to fall down (9)
el **café** coffee (I)
la **cafetería** cafeteria (1)
la **caja** cashier's station (8)
el **cajero, la cajera** cashier (3)
el **cajón de arena** sandbox (5)
la **calabaza** pumpkin (13)
la **calamina** calamine lotion (9)
el **calcetín** sock (I)
la **calculadora** calculator (I)
la **calefacción** heating (7)
el **calentador** heater (7)
caliente: el perro — hot dog (13)
callado, -a quiet (I)
la **calle** street (I)
calor:
  hace — it's hot (out) (I)
  tener — to be hot *(person)* (I)
la **caloría** calorie (13)
la **cama** bed (I)
la **cámara** camera (I)
el **camarero, la camarera** waiter, waitress (I)
el **camarón** shrimp (13)
cambiar to change (10); to cash (12)
el **cambio** change (11)
  la casa de — currency exchange (12)
caminar to walk (5)
caminata: dar una — to go hiking (14)
el **camión** truck (5)
la **camisa** shirt (I)
la **camiseta** T-shirt (I)
el **campamento** campground (14)
el **campeón, la campeona** champion (4)
el **campeonato** championship (4)
camping: ir de — to go camping (14)
el **campo** countryside (I)
el **canal** (TV) channel (I)
la **canción** song (2)
la **canoa** canoe (14)
  navegar en — to go canoeing (14)
canoso: pelo — gray hair (I)
cansado, -a tired (I)

el/la **cantante** singer (11)
    cantar to sing (I, 2)
el **capítulo** chapter (1)
la **cara** face (2)
el **carbohidrato** carbohydrate (13)
    cariñoso, -a affectionate, loving (I)
la **carne (de res)** beef (I)
el **carnet de identidad** ID card (7)
la **carnicería** butcher shop (8)
    caro, -a expensive (I)
la **carpeta** pocket folder (I)
    la **— de argollas** three-ring binder (I)
la **carretera** highway (8)
el **carrusel** merry-go-round (5)
la **carta** letter (I)
    a la — a la carte (I)
el **cartel** poster (I)
la **cartera** wallet (3)
el **cartón** cardboard (I, 11)
la **casa** house (I)
    la **— de cambio** currency exchange (12)
    en — at home (I)
    la **especialidad de la —** house specialty (I)
    casado, -a (con) married (to) (6)
    casarse (con) to marry, to get married to (6)
el **casco** helmet (4)
el **casete** cassette (4)
    casi almost (I)
    caso: en — de in case of (7)
    castaño: pelo — brown (chestnut) hair (I)
el **catálogo** catalog (3)
las **cataratas** waterfall (I)
la **catedral** cathedral (I)
    catorce fourteen (I)
la **cebolla** onion (I)
la **celebración** celebration (6)
    celebrar to celebrate (6)
la **cena** dinner (I)
    central central (7)
el **centro** center (I); downtown (8)
    el **— comercial** mall (I)
    cepillarse (los dientes) to brush (one's teeth) (2)
el **cepillo** brush (8)
    el **— de dientes** toothbrush (8)
    cerca (de) near (I)
el **cerdo** pork (13)
el **cereal** cereal (I)
la **cereza** cherry (13)
    cero zero (I)
    cerrar *(e → ie)* to close (I)
el **césped** lawn (I)

el **cesto de la ropa sucia** laundry hamper (3)
el **chaleco** vest (3)
el **champiñón** mushroom (13)
el **champú** shampoo (I)
el **chandal** sweatsuit (3)
la **chaqueta** jacket (I)
el **chaquetón** car coat (3)
    charlar to chat (6)
el **cheque** check (3)
    el **— de viajero** traveler's check (12)
el **chile** chili pepper (I)
    el **— con carne** beef with beans (I)
    el **— relleno** stuffed pepper (I)
el **chocolate** hot chocolate (I)
el **chorizo** sausage (13)
el **churro** churro (I)
    cien one hundred (I)
la **ciencia ficción** science fiction (I)
las **ciencias** science (I)
    — de la salud health (science) (I)
    — sociales social studies (I)
el **científico, la científica** scientist (10)
    ciento uno, -a; ciento dos; etc. 101, 102, etc. (I)
    cinco five (I)
    cincuenta fifty (I)
el **cine** movies, movie theater (I)
el **cinturón** belt (3)
    el **— de seguridad** seatbelt (12)
la **ciudad** city (I)
el **clarinete** clarinet (2)
    claro: ¡— que sí/no! of course (not) (I)
    claro, -a light *(color)* (3)
la **clase (de)** class; kind, type (I)
    después de las —s after school (I)
    la **sala de —s** classroom (I)
    clásico, -a classical (4)
la **clínica** clinic (I)
el **club** club (2)
el **coche** car (I)
    cocido, -a cooked (13)
la **cocina** kitchen (I)
    cocinar to cook (I)
el **cocinero, la cocinera** cook (13)
el **codo** elbow (9)
la **colección** collection (5)
    coleccionar to collect (5)
    colgar *(o → ue)* to hang (3)
la **colina** hill (14)
el **collar** necklace (I, 7)

el **color** color (I)
    ¿de qué —? what color? (I)
    en —es in color (I)
el **columpio** swing (5)
la **comedia** comedy, sitcom (I)
el **comedor** dining room (I)
el **comentario (sobre)** review (of) (10)
    comer to eat (I)
los **comestibles** groceries (I)
    cómico, -a comical (I)
la **comida** meal, food (I)
    como like, as (I)
    tan + *adj.* + **—** as + *adj.* + as (1)
    tanto(s), -a(s) + noun + **—** as much (many) + *noun* + as (3)
    ¿cómo? how? (I)
    ¿— eres? what are you like? (I)
    ¿— estás/está Ud.? how are you? (I)
    ¡— no! certainly! (I)
    ¿— se dice . . . ? how do you say . . . ? (I)
    ¿— se llama(n)? what is his/her/their name? (I)
    ¿— te llamas? what's your name? (I)
la **cómoda** dresser (I)
    cómodo, -a comfortable (I)
el **compañero, la compañera** classmate (I)
la **composición** composition (1)
    comprar to buy (I)
    compras:
    hacer las — to shop (8)
    ir de — to go shopping (I)
    el **programa de —** home shopping show (10)
la **computadora** computer (1)
la **comunidad** community (I)
    con with (I)
el **concierto** concert (I)
    concursos: el programa de — game show (10)
    congelado, -a frozen (13)
    conmigo with me (I)
    conocer *(c → zc)* to know, to be aquainted with (I, 1)
    conseguir *(e → i)* to get, to obtain (12)
el **consejero, la consejera** counselor (1)
el **consejo estudiantil** student council (2)
    consentido, -a spoiled *(child)* (5)
    conservar to conserve, to save (I, 7)
    contaminado, -a contaminated, polluted (I, 14)

contaminar to pollute (11)
contestar to answer (1)
contigo with you (I)
el **contrabajo** bass (2)
el **control remoto** remote control (7)
la **corbata** necktie (I, 3)
el **coro** chorus, choir (2)
el **correo** post office (I)
correr to run, to jog (4)
cortar to cut (I, 13)
   —se to cut oneself (9)
corto, -a short *(length)* (I)
la **cosa** thing (I)
coser to sew (14)
costar *(o → ue)* to cost (I)
el **coyote** coyote (14)
crédito: la tarjeta de — credit
   card (3)
creer to think, to believe (I)
   creo que sí (no) I (don't) think
   so (I)
la **cremallera** zipper (3)
el **crimen** crime (10)
el/la **criminal** criminal (10)
el **cruce** intersection (8)
el **crucigrama** crossword puzzle (4)
cruzar to cross (8)
el **cuaderno** spiral notebook (I)
la **cuadra** block (I)
cuadrado, -a square (I)
el **cuadro** picture (I)
cuadros: a — plaid, checked (3)
¿cuál(es)? what? which? which
   one(s)? (I)
cuando, ¿cuándo? when (I)
   de vez en — sometimes (7)
¿cuánto? how much? (I)
   ¿— (tiempo) hace que . . . ?
     how long has it been since . . . ?
     (I)
   ¿cuántos, -as? how many? (I)
   ¿— años tiene . . . ? how old is .
     . .? (I)
cuarenta forty (I)
cuarto, -a quarter; fourth (I)
   y — *(time)* quarter after, quarter
     past (I)
el **cuarto** room (I)
cuatro four (I)
cuatrocientos four hundred (I)
la **cucaracha** cockroach (9)
la **cuchara** spoon (I)
el **cuchillo** knife (I)
el **cuello** neck (I)
   el suéter de — alto turtleneck
     (3)
la **cuenta** bill *(restaurant)* (I)

la **cuerda** rope (5)
   saltar a la — to jump rope (5)
el **cuero** leather (I)
   de — (made of) leather (I)
el **cuerpo** body (I)
cuidado: tener — (con) to be
   careful (with / of) (12)
cuidar niños to baby-sit (2)
el **cumpleaños** birthday (I, 6)
   ¡feliz —! happy birthday! (I)
   la fiesta de — birthday party (I)
   la tarjeta de — birthday card (I)
cumplir años to have a birthday
   (6)
el **cuñado, la cuñada** brother-in-law,
   sister-in-law (6)

damas: la ropa para — ladies'
   wear (8)
las **damas** checkers (4)
dañar to damage (10)
daño: hacer — a to make ill, not
   to agree with *(food)* (13)
dar to give (I)
   — + *movie or TV program* to
     show (I)
   — una caminata to go hiking
     (14)
   — miedo a to scare (I)
   — saltos to dive (14)
   —se la mano to shake hands (6)
   (me) da igual it's all the same
     (to me) (3)
de, del *(de + el)* from; of; **—** 's,
   — s' (I)
   — + *material* made of (I)
   — nada you're welcome (I)
   — postre for dessert (I)
   ¿— veras? really? (I)
debajo de under(neath) (I)
deber ought to, should (I)
decir to say, to tell (I)
   ¿cómo se dice . . . ? how do you
     say . . . ? (I)
   —se "¡Hola!" to say hello (6)
   ¡no me digas! really?, you don't
     say! (I)
   ¿qué quiere — . . . ? what does
     . . . mean? (I)
   se dice . . . it is said (I)
la **decoración** decoration (I)
dedicarse (a) to be involved in; to
   devote oneself (to) (11)
el **dedo** finger (I)
   el — del pie toe (I)
delante de in front of (I)
demasiado too (I)
dental: la seda — dental floss (8)

el/la **dentista** dentist (I)
depender (de) to depend (on) (I, 2)
los **deportes** sports (I)
deportista athletic (I)
el/la **deportista** athlete (11)
deportivo, -a *adj.* sports (I)
depositar to deposit (I)
derecha: a la — (de) to the right
   (of) (I)
derecho, -a right (I)
el **derrumbe** landslide (10)
desabrocharse to unfasten (12)
el **desastre** disaster (4)
desayunar to have breakfast (2)
el **desayuno** breakfast (I)
descansar to rest (I)
el **descuento: la tienda de —s**
   discount store (I)
desde (que + *verb*) since, from (6)
desear: ¿qué desea Ud? may I
   help you? (I)
el **desfile** parade (4)
el **desierto** desert (14)
desobedecer *(c → zc)* to disobey
   (5)
desobediente disobedient (5)
el **desodorante** deodorant (8)
desordenado, -a messy (I)
despedirse *(e → i)* **(de)** to say
   goodby (to) (6)
despegar *(plane)* to take off (12)
el **despertador** alarm clock (2)
despertarse *(e → ie)* to wake up (2)
después de + *inf.* after + *verb*
   + -ing (I, 2)
destino: con — a going to (12)
destruir to destroy (10)
la **desventaja** disadvantage (11)
el/la **detective** detective (10)
   el programa de —s detective
     show (I)
el **detector de humo** smoke detector
   (7)
detrás (de) behind (I)
devolver *(o → ue)* to return
   (something) (I)
el **día** day (I)
   buenos —s good morning (I)
   el — de fiesta holiday (6)
   el plato del — daily special (I)
   ¿qué — es hoy? what day is it?
     (I)
   todos los —s every day (I)
el **Día de (Acción de) Gracias**
   Thanksgiving (6)
el **Día de los Enamorados** Valentine's Day (6)
el **Día de la Independencia** Independence Day (6)

el **Día de la Madre** Mother's Day (6)
el **Día del Padre** Father's Day (6)
el **Día de la Raza** Columbus Day (6)
la **diapositiva** slide (1)
dibujar to draw (I)
el **dibujo** drawing (I)
    los **—s animados** cartoons (I)
el **diccionario** dictionary (I)
diciembre December (I)
diecinueve nineteen (I)
dieciocho eighteen (I)
dieciséis sixteen (I)
diecisiete seventeen (I)
los **dientes** teeth (2)
    el **cepillo de —** toothbrush (8)
diez ten (I)
difícil difficult, hard (I)
digas *see* **decir**
el **dinero** money (I)
el **dinosaurio** dinosaur (5)
la **dirección** address (8); direction (10)
el **director, la directora** *(school)* principal (1); *(film)* director (10)
dirigir *(g → j)* to direct (10)
el **disco** disk (4)
    el **— compacto** compact disk (4)
    el **— (de hockey)** (hockey) puck (4)
disfraces: la fiesta de — costume party (I, 4)
disfrutar de to enjoy (12)
la **distancia** distance (8)
la **diversión** fun, entertainment (4)
    el **parque de —es** amusement park (I)
divertido, -a amusing, funny (I)
divertirse *(e → ie)* to have fun (4)
divorciado, -a (de) divorced (from) (6)
doblar to turn (8)
doble double (12)
doce twelve (I)
el **documental** documentary (I)
el **dólar** dollar (I)
doler *(o → ue)* to hurt, to ache (I)
dolor: tener — de . . . to have a . . . ache (I)
doméstico, -a domestic (14)
domingo Sunday (I)
    el **—** on Sunday (I)
donde, ¿dónde? where (I)
dormir *(o → ue)* to sleep (I)
    el **saco de —** sleeping bag (14)
el **dormitorio** bedroom (I)
dos two (I)
doscientos two hundred (I)
ducharse to take a shower (2)

dulce sweet (13)
el **dulce** candy (13)
durar to last (I)
el **durazno** peach (13)
duro: el huevo — hard-boiled egg (13)

echar to throw out, to dump (11)
económico, -a economical (11)
la **edad: ¿a qué —?** at what age? (6)
el **edificio** building (1)
la **educación** education (11)
educado, -a polite, well-mannered (5)
educativo, -a educational (I)
efectivo: (el dinero) en — cash (3)
los **efectos especiales** special effects (10)
eficiente efficient (11)
el **ejercicio** exercise (I, 1)
    hacer — to exercise (I)
el the *m. sing.* (I)
él he; him *after prep.* (I)
la **electricidad** electricity (7)
eléctrico, -a electric (7)
el **elefante** elephant (I, 14)
elegante elegant (I, 3)
ella she; her *after prep.* (I)
ellos, ellas they; them *after prep.* (I)
el **embarque: la tarjeta de —** boarding pass (12)
la **emergencia** emergency (7)
    en caso de — in case of emergency (7)
    la sala de — emergency room (9)
emocionante exciting, funny (I)
la **empanada** turnover (13)
empatar to tie *(in scoring)* (4)
empezar *(e → ie)* to begin, to start (I)
el **empleado, la empleada** employee (12)
en in, at, on (I)
    — + *vehicle* by (I)
Enamorados *see* **Día**
enamorarse (de) to fall in love (with) (10)
encantado, -a delighted (I)
encantar to love (I)
encender *(e → ie)* to light (6); to turn on (7)
la **enchilada** enchilada (I)
encima (de) on (top of) (I)
encontrar *(o → ue)* to find (3)
    —se *(o → ue)* to meet (6)
la **energía** energy (I, 7)

enero January (I)
la **enfermedad** illness (9)
la **enfermería** nurse's office (I)
el **enfermero, la enfermera** nurse (9)
enfermo, -a ill, sick (I)
enfrente (de) facing, opposite, in front of (I)
enlatado, -a canned (13)
la **ensalada** salad (I)
    el **bufet de —s** salad bar (1)
    la **— de frutas** fruit salad (13)
enseñar to teach (I)
la **entrada** entrance (8)
entre between, among (I)
entregar to deliver (I); to hand in (1)
el **entrenador, la entrenadora** coach (4)
la **entrevista** interview (10)
    el **programa de —s** talk show (I)
enviar to send, to mail (I)
el **equipaje** baggage (12)
    la **terminal de —** baggage claim (12)
el **equipo** team (2)
    el **— de sonido** stereo (I)
la **erupción** eruption (10)
la **escala** stopover (12)
    sin — nonstop (12)
escalar montañas to go mountain climbing (14)
la **escalera** stairs (8)
    la **— mecánica** escalator (8)
la **escena** scene (10)
el **escenario** stage (1)
escoger *(g → j)* to choose (I, 3)
escolar *adj.* school (1)
esconder to hide *(something)* (10)
    —se to hide (10)
escribir to write (I, 1)
    ¿cómo se escribe . . . ? how do you spell . . . ? (I)
    —se to write each other (6)
el **escritor, la escritora** writer (11)
el **escritorio** desk (I)
escuchar to listen (to) (I)
la **escuela** school (I)
ese, -a; -os, -as that; those (I, 3)
ése, -a; -os, -as *pron.* that one; those (3)
el **esmalte de uñas** nail polish (8)
eso: por — that's why (I)
el **espacio** space (11)
la **espalda** back (I)
el **español** Spanish *(language)* (I)
el **espárrago** asparagus (13)
especial special (6)

la **especialidad de la casa** house specialty (I)
el **espejo** mirror (I)
la **espina** thorn, spine (14)
las **espinacas** spinach (13)
el **esposo, la esposa** husband, wife (6)
el **esquí** ski (4)
    el **— acuático** water skiing (14)
    hacer — acuático to water ski (14)
    esquiar to ski (I)
la **esquina** corner (I)
la **estación** season; station (I)
el **estadio** stadium (I)
el **estante** shelf (7)
    estar to be (I)
    ¿cómo estás/está Ud.? how are you? (I)
    la sala de — family room (I)
    este, -a; -os, -as this; these (I, 3)
    éste, -a; -os, -as *pron.* this one; these (3)
el **estómago** stomach (I)
    tener dolor de — to have a stomachache (I)
    estornudar to sneeze (9)
el/la **estudiante** student (I)
    estudiantil *adj.* student (2)
    estudiar to study (I)
la **estufa** stove (I)
    exagerado, -a exaggerated (10)
el **examen** exam, test (1)
    excelente excellent (10)
la **excursión** excursion, short trip (12)
    hacer una — to take an excursion (12)
    éxito: tener — to be successful (10)
    explicar to explain (1)
    explorar to explore (I, 11)
la **exposición (de arte)** (art) exhibit (4)
la **extinción: en peligro de —** endangered (I, 14)
    extracurricular extracurricular (2)
el/la **extraterrestre** alien (10)

la **fábrica** factory (I)
    fácil easy (I)
    fácilmente easily (2)
    facturar to check *(baggage)* (12)
la **falda** skirt (I)
    faltar to be lacking, to be missing (I)
la **familia** family (I)
    familiar *adj.* family (6)
    fantástico, -a fantastic (I)

la **farmacia** drugstore (I)
    fascinante fascinating (I)
    fascinar to fascinate (I)
    febrero February (I)
la **fecha** date (I)
    ¡felicidades! congratulations! (6)
    felicitar to congratulate (6)
    ¡feliz cumpleaños! happy birthday! (I)
    feo, -a ugly (I)
la **fiebre** fever (I)
    tener — to have a fever (I)
la **fiesta** party (I, 3)
    el día de — holiday (6)
    la — de cumpleaños birthday party (I, 6)
    la— de disfraces costume party (I, 4)
    la — de fin de año New Year's Eve party (I, 6)
    la — de sorpresa surprise party (I, 6)
    fila: hacer — to line up, to stand in line (1)
el **fin:**
    el— de año New Year's Eve (6)
    el — de semana on the weekend (I)
    la fiesta de — de año New Year's Eve party (I)
    físico, -a: la educación —a physical education (I)
el **flan** flan (I)
la **flauta** flute (2)
    flojo, -a loose *(clothing)* (3)
la **flor** flower (I, 6)
    floreado, -a flowered (3)
la **floristería** flower shop (8)
    fondo: al — in the back (8)
    formar parte de to be a part of (I)
el **fósforo** match (14)
el **fósil** fossil (14)
la **foto** photo (I)
    sacar —s to take pictures (I)
la **fotografía** photography (10)
el **fracaso** failure (10)
el **francés** French *(language)* (1)
el **fregadero** sink (7)
los **frenillos** braces (9)
la **fresa** strawberry (13)
    fresco, -a fresh (13)
    fresco: hace — it's cool outside (I)
el **frijol** bean (I)
    los —es refritos refried beans (I)

    frío:
    hace — it's cold outside (I)
    tener — to be cold *(person)* (I)
    frito, -a fried (13)
la **fruta** fruit (I)
la **frutería** fruit store (8)
el **fuego** fire (14)
    los —s artificiales fireworks (6)
    fuerte strong (9)
    fui, fuiste *see* **ir, ser**
    funcionar to work, to function (7)
el **fútbol** soccer (I)
    el — americano football (I)
el **futuro** future (11)

el **galán** *(film)* hero (10)
    ganar to earn money (2); to win (4)
    —se la vida to earn a living (11)
la **ganga** bargain (I)
el **garaje** garage (I)
la **garganta** throat (I)
    las pastillas para la — throat lozenges (I)
    tener dolor de — to have a sore throat (I)
    gastar to spend (8); to waste (11)
el **gato** cat (I)
el **gazpacho** gazpacho (I, 13)
el **gemelo, la gemela** twin (I)
    generalmente usually, generally (I)
    generoso, -a generous (I)
    ¡genial! great! wonderful! (I)
la **gente** people (I)
la **geografía** geography (1)
la **geometría** geometry (1)
    gigante: la pantalla — big screen TV (11)
el **gimnasio** gymnasium (I)
el **gol** goal (4)
el **golf** golf (4)
el **gorila** gorilla (I, 14)
la **gorra** cap (3)
el **gorro** ski cap (I)
las **gotas (para los ojos)** (eye)drops (9)
la **grabadora** tape recorder (I)
    gracias thank you (I)
las **Gracias** *see* **Día**
    gracioso, -a funny (I)
la **graduación** graduation (6)
    graduarse to graduate (6)
    grande big, large (I, 3)
la **grapadora** stapler (1)
    grasoso, -a greasy (13)
la **gripe** flu (I)
    tener — to have the flu (I)
    gris gray (I)

el **guacamole** avocado dip (I)
el **guante** glove (I)
guapo, -a handsome, good-looking (I)
guardar to put away, to keep (3)
el **guardarropa** closet (I)
la **guardería infantil** day-care center (5)
la **guerra** war (11)
el/la **guía** guide (12)
la **—** guidebook (12)
la **— telefónica** phone book (I)
el **guión** script (10)
guisado, -a stewed (13)
el **guisante** pea (I)
la **guitarra** guitar (I)
gustar to like (I)
me (te) gustaría I'd (you'd) like … (I)

haber:
hay there is / are (I)
hubo there was / were (10)
la **habitación** hotel room (12)
hablar to talk, to speak (I)
—se to talk to each other (6)
se habla is spoken (8)
hacer to do, to make (I)
hace + *(time)* … **ago** (I)
hace + *(time)* + **que** it's been *(time)* since (I)
— ejercicio to exercise (I)
se hace(n) con … it's (they're) made with … (I)
hambre: tener — to be hungry (I)
la **hamburguesa** hamburger (I)
la **harina** flour (I)
hasta until (I)
— luego see you later (I)
hay there is / are (I)
— que + *inf.* it's necessary to (I, 2)
hecho, -a (de) made (of) (I, 13)
el **hecho** fact (I, 10)
la **heladería** ice cream shop (8)
helado: el té — iced tea (I)
el **helado** ice cream (I)
el **hermano, la hermana** brother, sister (I)
los **hermanos** brothers; brother(s) and sister(s) (I)
la **heroína** heroine (10)
hervir *(e → ie)* to boil (13)
hice, hiciste see **hacer**
el **hielo** ice (4)
el **hijo, la hija** son, daughter (I)
los **hijos** sons; children (I)
la **historia** history (1)

histórico, -a historic(al) (8)
el **hockey** hockey (4)
la **hoja** leaf (14)
la **— de papel** sheet of paper (I)
¡hola! hi!, hello! (I)
el **hombre** man (I)
el **— de negocios** businessman (11)
la **hora** period ; time (I)
¿a qué —? at what time? (I)
¿qué — es? what time is it? (I)
el **horario** schedule (I)
la **hormiga** ant (9)
el **horno** oven (7)
al — baked (13)
horrible horrible (I)
el **horror** horror (4)
el **hospital** hospital (I)
el **hotel** hotel (I)
hoy today (I)
— no not today (I)
hubo see **haber**
la **huella** footprint (14)
el **hueso** bone (9)
el **huevo** egg (I)
el **— duro** hard-boiled egg (13)
humano, -a human (11)
humo: el detector de — smoke detector (7)
humor: de buen / mal — in a good / bad mood (2)
el **huracán** hurricane (10)

ida see **boleto**
sólo de — one way (12)
la **identidad: el carnet de —** ID card (7)
la **identificación** identification (7)
el **idioma** language (1)
la **iglesia** church (I)
igual: (me) da — it's all the same (to me) (3)
igualmente likewise (I)
impaciente impatient (I)
el **impermeable** raincoat (I)
el **incendio** fire (7)
el **extinguidor de —s** fire extinguisher (7)
incluir to include (12)
incómodo, -a uncomfortable (I)
indicar to indicate, to show, to point out (8)
indígena indigenous, native (12)
individual: la habitación — single room (12)
infantil see **guardería**
la **infección** infection (9)
la **información** information (10)

el **informe** report (1)
el **inglés** English *(language)* (I)
el **ingrediente** ingredient (I, 13)
el **insecticida** insecticide (9)
el **instrumento** instrument (2)
inteligente intelligent (I)
el **interés** interest (I)
interesante interesting (I)
interesar to interest (I)
internacional international (10)
la **inundación** flood (10)
investigar to investigate (10)
el **invierno** winter (I)
la **invitación** invitation (I, 6)
el **invitado, la invitada** guest (I)
invitar to invite (I, 6)
la **inyección** injection, shot (9)
poner una — to give an injection (9)
ir to go (I)
— a + *inf.* to be going to + *verb* (I)
izquierda: a la — (de) to the left (of) (I)
izquierdo, -a left (I)

el **jabón** soap (I)
el **jaguar** jaguar (I)
el **jamón** ham (I)
el **jarabe (para la tos)** cough syrup (9)
los **jeans** jeans (I)
joven *adj.* young (I)
el/la **joven** young man, young woman (I)
los **jóvenes** young people (I)
las **joyas** jewelry (I)
las **judías verdes** green beans (I)
jueves Thursday (I)
el — on Thursday (I)
el/la **juez** judge (11)
el **jugador, la jugadora** player (4)
jugar *(u → ue)* to play (I)
el **juguete** toy (5)
de — *adj.* toy (5)
el **jugo** juice (I)
julio July (I)
junio June (I)

el **kilómetro** kilometer (8)
el **kindergarten** kindergarten (5)

la the *f.sing.;* her, it *dir. obj. pron.* (I)
los **labios** lips (8)
el lápiz de— lipstick (8)
el **laboratorio** laboratory (1)

lado: al — de next to, beside (I)

el **ladrón, la ladrona** thief (10)

el **lago** lake (I)

la **lámpara** lamp (I)

la **lana** wool (3)

lanzar to shoot (6)

el **lápiz** pencil (I)

  el — de labios lipstick (8)

largo, -a long (I)

las the *f.pl.;* them *dir. obj. pron.* (I)

lástima: ¡qué —! that's too bad! what a shame! (I)

lastimar to hurt (I)

la **lata** can (I, 11)

el **lavadero** laundry room (I)

la **lavadora** (clothes) washer (7)

el **lavaplatos** dishwasher (7)

lavar to wash (I)

  —se (la cara, etc.) to wash (one's face, etc.) (2)

le *ind. obj. pron.* (to) him, her, it, you (I)

la **lección** lesson (1)

la **leche** milk (I)

la **lechuga** lettuce (I)

leer to read (I)

lejos (de) far (from) (I)

la **leña** firewood (14)

los **lentes de contacto** contact lenses (7)

les *ind. obj. pron.* (to) them (I)

levantar to lift (4)

  —se to get up (2)

leve light, minor (9)

libre: al aire — outdoors (14)

la **librería** bookstore (I)

el **libro** book (I)

la **liga** league (4)

ligero, -a light *(weight)* (14)

el **limón** lemon, lime (13)

la **limonada** lemonade (I)

limpiar to clean (I)

limpio, -a clean (I)

la **línea aérea** airline (12)

la **linterna** flashlight (7)

la **liquidación** sale (3)

  estar en — to be on sale (3)

liso, -a plain (3)

literario, -a literary (2)

la **literatura** literature (1)

llamar to call (I)

  —se to be named (I)

la **llave** key (7)

el **llavero** keychain (7)

llegar to arrive (I)

llevar to wear; to take, to carry along (I)

llorar to cry (5)

llover *(o → ue)* to rain (I)

llueve it rains, it's raining (I)

la **lluvia** rain (I)

lo *dir. obj. pron.* him, it (I)

  — que what (3)

  — siento I'm sorry (I)

el **lobo, la loba** wolf (I, 14)

local local (10)

el **locutor, la locutora** announcer (10)

la **lona** canvas (3)

los the *m.pl.; dir. obj. pron.* them (I)

  — + *day of week* on (I)

luego then, if (I)

el **lugar** place (I)

el **lujo** luxury (7)

la **Luna** moon (11)

lunes Monday (I)

  el — on Monday (I)

la **luz** light (I)

la **madera** wood (I)

  de — (made of) wood (I)

la **madre** mother (I)

el **maíz** corn (I)

mal badly (I)

  menos — que . . . it's a good thing that . . . (I)

  me siento — I feel ill (I)

maleducado, -a rude, impolite (5)

la **maleta** suitcase (I, 12)

  (des)hacer la — to (un)pack (12)

malo, -a bad (I)

manera: de ninguna — not at all (I)

la **manga** sleeve (3)

la **mano** hand (I)

  a — by hand (12)

  darse la — to shake hands (6)

  hecho, -a a — handmade (I)

el **mantel** tablecloth (I)

mantenerse sano, -a to stay healthy (13)

la **mantequilla** butter (I)

la **manzana** apple (I)

mañana tomorrow (I)

la **mañana** morning (I)

  de/por la — in the morning (I)

el **mapa** map (1)

el **maquillaje** make-up (8)

maquillarse to put on makeup (8)

el **mar** sea (I)

el **marcador** marker (I)

la **mariposa** butterfly (14)

los **mariscos** seafood (9)

marrón brown (I)

martes Tuesday (I)

  el — on Tuesday (I)

marzo March (I)

más more, *adj.* + -er (I)

  el/la/los/las — + *adj.* the most + *adj.*, the *adj.* + -est (I, 1)

la **masa** dough (13)

matar to kill (10)

las **matemáticas** mathematics (I)

la **materia** school subject (1)

mayo May (I)

la **mayonesa** mayonnaise (13)

mayor older (I)

  el — the oldest, biggest (I)

me *obj. pron.* me (I)

mecánico, -a: la escalera —a escalator (8)

el **mecánico, la mecánica** mechanic (11)

media:

  una hora y — an hour and a half (I)

  — hora *f.* half an hour (I)

  y — half-past (I)

mediano, -a medium *(in sizes)* (3)

la **medianoche** midnight (I)

la **medicina** medicine (9)

el **médico, la médica** doctor (I)

medio: *(número)* **y —** and a half *(in sizes)* (3)

el **medio ambiente** environment (I, 11)

el **mediodía** noon (I)

mejor better (I)

  el/la — the best (I)

el **melón** cantaloupe (13)

menor younger (I)

menos:

  el/la/los/las — + *adj.* the least + *adj.* (I, 1)

  — mal que . . . it's a good thing that . . . (I)

  por lo — at least (2)

mentir *(e → ie)* to lie (5)

el **menú** menu (I)

menudo: a — often (I)

el **mercado** market (12)

la **merienda** afternoon snack (I)

  de — for a snack (I)

el **mes** month (I)

la **mesa** table (I)

  la — de noche night table (7)

metal: de — (made of) metal (I)

meter un gol to score a goal (4)

el **metro** subway (I); meter *(measurement)* (8)

mezclar to mix (13)

mi, mis my (I)

mí me *after prep.* (I)

el **microondas** microwave (oven) (7)

el **miembro** member (2)

   ser — de to be a member of (2)

mientras while (8)

miércoles Wednesday (I)

   el — on Wednesday (I)

mil one thousand (I)

la **milla** mile (8)

el **minuto** minute (I)

mío, -a my, (of) mine (7)

el **mío, la mía** mine (7)

mismo, -a same (2)

   lo — the same thing (I)

   (yo) — myself (7)

el **mocasín** loafer (3)

la **mochila** backpack (I)

la **moda** fashion (3)

   estar de — to be fashionable (3)

moderno, -a modern (I)

mojado, -a wet (14)

molestar to bother, to annoy (5)

la **moneda** coin (7)

el **monstruo** monster (10)

la **montaña** mountain (I)

montar:

   — a caballo to ride horseback (10)

   — en bicicleta to ride a bike (I, 4)

el **monumento** monument (I)

morado, -a purple (I)

la **mosca** fly (9)

el **mosquito** mosquito (9)

la **mostaza** mustard (13)

el **mostrador** counter (8)

mostrar *(o → ue)* to show (7)

la **moto acuática** jet skiing (14)

   hacer — to jet ski (14)

el **muchacho, la muchacha** boy, girl (I)

mucho, -a a lot of, much (I)

   —as veces many times (I)

   —gusto pleased / nice to meet you (I)

los **muebles** furniture (I)

las **muelas: tener dolor de —** to have a toothache (I)

muerto, -a dead (6)

la **mujer** woman (I)

   la — de negocios businesswoman (11)

las **muletas** crutches (9)

la **muñeca** doll (5); wrist (9)

el **muñeco** action figure (5)

el **músculo** muscle (9)

el **museo** museum (I)

la **música** music (I)

musical *adj.* musical (I, 2)

   el video — music video (4)

el **músico, la música** musician (11)

muy very (I)

nacer to be born (6)

nacional national (14)

nada nothing, not at all (I)

   de — you're welcome (I)

nadar to swim (I)

nadie no one (I)

la **naranja** orange (I)

la **nariz** nose (I)

la **naturaleza** nature (12)

navegar *see* **balsa, canoa**

la **Navidad** Christmas (6)

necesario, -a necessary (2)

la **necesidad** necessity (7)

necesitar to need (I)

los **negocios** business (11)

   el hombre / la mujer de — businessman, businesswoman (11)

negro, -a black (I)

   en blanco y — in black and white (I)

nevar: nieva it snows, it's snowing (I)

ni . . . ni neither . . . nor, not . . . or (I)

el **nieto, la nieta** grandson, granddaughter (6)

la **nieve** snow (I)

el **nilón** nylon (3)

ninguno (ningún), -a no, not any (I, 8)

   —a parte nowhere, not anywhere (I)

el **niño, la niña** boy, girl (5)

   cuidar niños to baby-sit (2)

   los niños children (5)

no no, not (I)

   ¿no? don't you?, aren't I?, etc. (I)

la **noche** evening (I)

   buenas —s good evening, good night (I)

   de la — at night (I)

   por la — in the evening (I)

la **Nochebuena** Christmas Eve (6)

el **nombre** name (I)

nos *obj. pron.* us (I)

nosotros, -as we (I); us *after prep.* (I)

la **nota** grade (1)

las **noticias** news (I)

novecientos nine hundred (I)

la **novela** novel (11)

noventa ninety (I)

noviembre November (I)

el **novio, la novia** boyfriend, girlfriend (I)

nuestro, -a our (I); (of) ours (7)

el **nuestro, la nuestra** ours (7)

nueve nine (I)

nuevo, -a new (I)

   de — again (6)

el **número** number (I); (shoe) size (3)

nunca never (I)

o or (I)

obedecer *(c → zc)* to obey (5)

obediente obedient (5)

la **obra de teatro** play (4)

el **obrero, la obrera** laborer (11)

el **océano** ocean (I, 11)

ochenta eighty (I)

ocho eight (I)

ochocientos eight hundred (I)

octavo, -a eighth (I)

octubre October (I)

ocupado, -a busy (I)

ocurrir to occur, to happen (10)

el **oeste: la película del —** western (I)

la **oficina** office (1)

el **oído** ear (I)

   tener dolor de — to have an earache (I)

el **ojo** eye (I)

la **olla** pot (14)

once eleven (I)

la **operación** operation (9)

ordenado, -a neat, tidy (I)

el **oro** gold (7)

   de — (made of) gold (7)

la **orquesta** orchestra (2)

oscuro, -a dark *(color)* (3)

el **oso** bear (I, 5)

el **otoño** fall, autumn (I)

otro, -a another, other (I)

el **oxígeno** oxygen (14)

paciente *adj.* patient (I)

el **padre** father (I)

   los —s parents (I)

la **paella** paella (13)

pagar to pay (I)

la **página** page (1)

el **país** country (I)

el **pájaro** bird (I, 5)

el **palacio** palace (12)

el **palito** twig; *pl.* kindling (14)

el **palo (de golf, de hockey)** golf club, hockey stick (4)
el **pan** bread (I)
    el **— tostado** toast (I)
la **panadería** bakery (8)
la **pantalla** screen (11)
los **pantalones** pants (I)
las **pantimedias** pantyhose (I)
el **pañuelo** scarf (3)
la **papa** potato (I)
    la **— frita** French fry (I)
el **papel** paper (I); part, role (10)
    hacer el — (de) to play the part (of) (10)
    la hoja de — sheet of paper (I)
para for, in order to (I)
la **parada del autobús** bus stop (I)
el **paraguas** umbrella (I)
parecer to appear, to seem (7)
la **pared** wall (1)
el **pariente, la parienta** relative (I, 6)
el **parque** park (I)
    el — de diversiones amusement park (I)
la **parrilla: a la —** grilled (13)
partes: por todas — all over, everywhere (3)
participar (en) to participate (in) (2)
el **partido** match, game (I, 4)
pasado, -a last, past (I)
el **pasajero, la pasajera** passenger (12)
el **pasaporte** passport (I)
pasar to pass; to happen (I)
    — la aspiradora to vacuum (I)
    —lo bien / mal to have a good / bad time (I, 4)
    ¿qué pasa? what's the matter? (I)
el **pasatiempo** pastime, hobby (I)
pasear:
    ir a — to take a walk (I)
    — en bote to row (I)
el **pasillo** aisle (12)
la **pasta dentífrica** toothpaste (I)
el **pastel** cake (I, 6)
la **pastilla** pill (I, 9)
el **patín** skate (4)
patinar to skate (I)
    — sobre hielo to ice skate (4)
el **patio de recreo** playground (5)
el **pavo** turkey (6)
la **paz** peace (11)
pedir *(e → i)* to ask for, to order (I)
    — prestado, -a (a) to borrow (from) (4)
peinarse to comb one's hair (2)

el **peine** comb (7)
pelearse to fight (5)
la **película** film, movie (I)
el **peligro** danger (I, 14)
    en — de extinción endangered (I, 14)
peligroso, -a dangerous (14)
pelirrojo, -a red-haired (I)
el **pelo** hair (I, 2)
    el secador de — hair dryer (7)
la **pelota** ball (4)
peluche:
    el animal de — stuffed animal (5)
    el oso de — teddy bear (5)
pensar *(e → ie)* to think (I)
    — + *inf.* to plan (I)
la **pensión** inexpensive lodging (12)
peor worse (I)
    el/la — the worst (I)
el **pepino** cucumber (13)
pequeño, -a small (I, 3)
    de — as a child (5)
perder *(e → ie)* to lose (4)
perdón excuse me (I)
perdonar to excuse, to pardon (8)
    perdone (Ud.) excuse me, pardon me (8)
perezoso, -a lazy (I)
el **perfume** perfume (8)
el **periódico** newspaper (I, 2)
permitir to permit, to allow (1)
    se permite it's allowed (1)
pero but (I)
el **perro** dog (I)
    el — caliente hot dog (13)
la **persona** person (I)
el **personaje** character (10)
personal personal (I)
pesado, -a heavy (14)
las **pesas** weights (4)
pesca: ir de — to go fishing (I)
la **pescadería** fish store (8)
el **pescado** fish *(cooked)* (I)
el **pez,** *pl.* **los peces** fish *(live)* (5)
el **piano** piano (2)
la **picadura (de insecto)** insect bite, sting (9)
picante spicy, peppery, hot *(flavor)* (I)
    no — mild *(flavor)* (I)
picar to sting (9); to chop (13)
el **picnic** picnic (4)
    hacer un — to have a picnic (4)
el **pie** foot (I)
    a — walking, on foot (I)
    el dedo del — toe (I)
la **piedra** rock, stone (14)

la **piel** fur (I)
la **pierna** leg (I)
la **pila** battery (7)
el/la **piloto** pilot (12)
la **pimienta** pepper *(seasoning)* (I)
el **pimiento verde** green pepper (13)
la **piña** pineapple (13)
el **pintor, la pintora** painter (11)
pintoresco, -a picturesque (12)
la **pirámide** pyramid (I)
la **piscina** pool (I)
el **piso** story, floor (I)
la **pistola (de agua)** (water) pistol (5)
la **pizarra** chalkboard (I)
planear to plan (12)
el **planeta** planet (11)
la **planta** plant (I, 14)
el **plástico** plastic (I, 3)
    de — (made of) plastic (I)
la **plata** silver (7)
    de — (made of) silver (7)
el **plátano** banana (I)
el **platillo** saucer (I)
el **plato** dish, plate (I)
    el — del día daily special (I)
la **playa** beach (I)
la **plaza** town square (I)
la **pluma** feather (14)
poco: un — (de) a little (I)
poder *(o → ue)* can, to be able (I)
    ¿podría(s)? could you? (8)
el **polen** pollen (9)
el/la **policía** police officer (10)
    la — the police (I)
la **política** politics (11)
el **político, la política** politician (11)
el **pollo** chicken (I)
el **polvo** dust (9)
poner to put, to place (I)
    —la mesa to set the table (I)
    —se to put on *(clothing, make-up, etc.)* (8)
    —una tienda to pitch a tent (14)
por for (I, 9); *(+ place)* by, through, at (8)
    — aquí around here (I)
    — eso that's why, therefore (I)
    — la mañana / la tarde / la noche in the morning / afternoon / evening (I)
    — lo menos at least (2)
    ¿— qué? why? (I)
    — supuesto of course (I, 11)
    — todas partes all over, everywhere (3)
porque because (I)
portarse (bien / mal) to behave (well / badly) (5)

la **posesión** possession (7)

el **postre** dessert (I)

    de — for dessert (I)

practicar to practice (I)

práctico, -a practical (I)

preferir *(e → ie)* to prefer (I)

la **pregunta** question (1)

    hacer una — to ask a question (1)

preguntar to ask (1)

preparar to prepare (I)

presentar to introduce (I)

    te presento a . . . I'd like you to meet . . . (I)

prestado, -a: pedir — (a) to borrow (from) (4)

prestar to lend (4)

primaria: la escuela — elementary school (5)

la **primavera** spring (I)

primero (primer), -a first (I)

el **primo, la prima** cousin (I)

principal *adj.* main, principal (10)

probar *(o → ue)* to try, to taste (I)

    —se to try on (3)

el **problema** problem (1)

procedente de arriving from (12)

la **profesión** profession (11)

el **profesor, la profesora** teacher (I)

el **programa** program (I)

prohibir to prohibit (1)

    se prohíbe it's prohibited (1)

el **pronóstico del tiempo** weather forecast (I)

propio, -a own (7)

proteger(se) *(g → j)* to protect (oneself) (I, 9)

la **proteína** protein (13)

próximo, -a next (1)

el **proyector** projector (1)

prudente cautious (I)

la **prueba** quiz (1)

público, -a public (8)

pude, pudiste *see* **poder**

el **pueblo** town (12)

la **puerta** door (I); gate (12)

pues well *(to indicate pause)* (I)

la **pulsera** bracelet (I, 7)

    el reloj — wristwatch (I, 7)

las **puntadas** stitches (9)

    hacer — to stitch *(surgically)* (9)

punto: en — sharp, on the dot (I)

puntualmente on time (I)

el **pupitre** student desk (I)

puro, -a pure, clean (I)

puse, pusiste *see* **poner**

que that, who (I)

    lo — what (3)

¿qué? what? (I)

    ¿de — es...? what's it made of? (3)

    ¡— + *adj.*! how + *adj.!* (I)

    ¿— tal? how's it going? (I)

    ¿— tal es . . . ? how is . . .? (10)

quedar to fit; to be located (I)

    —se (en la cama) to stay (in bed) (I)

el **quehacer (de la casa)** (household) chore (I)

quemar(se) to burn (oneself) (9)

querer *(e → ie)* to want (I)

    ¿qué quiere decir...? what does . . . mean? (I)

    quisiera(s) I'd / you'd like (I, 11)

la **quesadilla** quesadilla (I)

el **queso** cheese (I)

¿quién(es)? who? whom? (I)

la **química** chemistry (1)

quince fifteen (I)

quinientos five hundred (I)

quinto, -a fifth (I)

el **quiosco (de periódicos)** newsstand (8)

quisiera *see* **querer**

quitar la mesa to clear the table (I)

quitarse to take off *(clothing, makeup, etc.)* (8)

el **radio** radio (set) (7)

la **radiografía** X-ray (9)

    sacar una — to take an X-ray (9)

la **rana** frog (14)

la **raqueta (de tenis)** (tennis) racket (4)

rayas: a — striped (3)

la **Raza** *see* **Día**

razón: (no) tener — to be right (wrong) (I)

la **reacción** reaction (9)

real real (I)

realista realistic (I)

la **receta** prescription (9); recipe (13)

recetar to prescribe (9)

recibir to receive (I)

el **reciclaje: el centro de —** recycling center (I)

reciclar to recycle (I, 11)

recoger *(g → j)* to gather, to pick up (I, 14)

recomendar *(e → ie)* to recommend (12)

recordar *(o → ue)* to remember (5)

recreo: el patio de — playground (5)

el **recuerdo** souvenir (I)

redondo, -a round (I)

reducir *(c → zc)* to reduce (I, 11)

el **refresco** soft drink (I)

el **refrigerador** refrigerator (I)

regalar to give a gift (I, 6)

el **regalo** gift (I)

    la tienda de —s gift shop (I)

regatear to bargain (12)

registrar to inspect, to search (12)

la **regla** ruler (I)

regresar to come back, to return (I)

regular so-so, fair (I)

el **relleno** filling (13)

el **reloj** clock (1)

    el — (pulsera) wristwatch (I, 7)

reparar to repair, to fix (7)

repartir to deliver (2)

repasar review (1)

el **repelente** insect repellent (9)

la **reservación** reservation (12)

el **resfriado** cold (I)

la **respuesta** answer (1)

el **restaurante** restaurant (I)

el **retraso** delay (12)

la **reunión** gathering, get-together (I, 6)

la **revista** magazine (I, 2)

revolver *(o → ue)* to stir (13)

el **río** river (11)

robar to rob (10)

el **robot** robot (5)

rock: la música — rock music (4)

la **rodilla** knee (9)

rojo, -a red (I)

romántico, -a romantic (I)

el **rompecabezas** jigsaw puzzle (4)

romperse to break *(a bone)* (9)

la **ropa** clothes (I)

    la — para caballeros men's wear (8)

    la — para damas ladies' wear (8)

    la — para niños children's wear (8)

rosado, -a pink (I)

roto, -a broken (9); torn (14)

rubio, -a blonde (I)

la **rueda: la silla de —s** wheelchair (9)

las **ruinas** ruins (I)

sábado Saturday (I)
  el — on Saturday (I)
saber to know (how) (I, 4)
sabroso, -a delicious, tasty (I)
el **sacapuntas** pencil sharpener (1)
sacar to take; to take out (I)
  — dinero to withdraw money (I)
  — fotos to take pictures (I)
  — una buena / mala nota to get a good / bad grade (1)
  — un libro to check out a book (I)
el **saco de dormir** sleeping bag (14)
sacudir to dust (I)
la **sal** salt (I)
la **sala** living room (I)
  la — de clases classroom (I)
  la — de emergencia emergency room (9)
  la — de estar family room (I)
salado, -a salty (13)
la **salida** exit (8)
salir to go out, to leave (I)
la **salsa** sauce, dressing (I, 13)
saltar a la cuerda to jump rope (5)
saltos: dar — to dive (14)
la **salud** health (I)
saludar to greet (6)
salvaje wild (*animals*) (14)
la **sandía** watermelon (13)
el **sandwich** sandwich (I)
la **sangre** blood (9)
sano, -a healthy (13)
el **saxofón** saxophone (2)
el **secador de pelo** hair dryer (7)
la **secadora** (clothes) dryer (7)
secar to dry (14)
  —se (el pelo) to dry (one's hair) (2)
la **sección** section (8)
seco, -a dry (14)
el **secretario, la secretaria** secretary (11)
sed: tener — to be thirsty (I)
la **seda dental** dental floss (8)
seguida: en — right away (I)
seguir *(e → i)* to follow; to continue (8)
según according to (2)
segundo, -a second (I)
la **seguridad:**
  el cinturón de — seatbelt (12)
  el sistema de — security system (11)
seis six (I)
seiscientos six hundred (I)

el **sello** stamp (I)
la **selva** forest (I)
  la — tropical rain forest (I)
el **semáforo** traffic light (8)
la **semana** week (I)
  el fin de — on the weekend (I)
el **semestre** semester (I)
sencillo, -a simple (3)
el **sendero** path (14)
sensacionalista sensationalistic (10)
sentir:
  lo siento I'm sorry (I)
  —se *(e → ie)* to feel (9)
la **señal de alto** stop sign (8)
señor Mr.; sir (I)
señora Mrs.; ma'am (I)
señorita Miss; miss (I)
separado, -a (de) separated (from) (6)
separar to separate; to sort (I, 11)
septiembre September (I)
séptimo, -a seventh (I)
ser to be (I)
el **ser humano** human being (11)
serio, -a serious (I)
la **serpiente** snake (I, 14)
el **servicio: la estación de —** gas station (I)
los **servicios** restroom (8)
la **servilleta** napkin (I)
servir *(e → i)* to serve (I)
sesenta sixty (I)
setecientos seven hundred (I)
setenta seventy (I)
sexto, -a sixth (I)
si if, whether (I)
sí yes; do + *verb (emphatic)* (I)
siempre always (I)
siete seven (I)
la **silla** chair (I)
  la — de ruedas wheelchair (9)
el **sillón** armchair (I)
silvestre wild (*plants*) (14)
simpático, -a nice, friendly (I)
sin without (2)
sintético, -a synthetic (3)
el **síntoma** symptom (9)
el **sistema de seguridad** security system (11)
sobre about; on (I)
  patinar — hielo to ice skate (4)
el **sobrino, la sobrina** nephew, niece (6)
sociable outgoing (I)
el **sofá** sofa (I)

el **sol** sun (I)
  los anteojos de — sunglasses (I)
  hace — it's sunny (I)
  tomar el — to sunbathe (I)
solar solar (11)
soler *(o → ue) + inf.* to be in the habit of (I, 2)
solo, -a alone (I)
sólo only (I)
soltero, -a single, unmarried (6)
la **sombra** shade (14)
sonido: el equipo de — stereo (I)
la **sopa** soup (I)
soportar to tolerate, to stand (4)
la **sorpresa: la fiesta de —** surprise party (I, 6)
soso, -a tasteless (13)
el **sótano** basement (I)
su, sus his, her; your *formal;* their (I)
el **sube y baja** seesaw (5)
subir to climb (I)
sucio, -a dirty (I)
la **sudadera** sweatshirt (I)
el **suelo** floor (3)
sueño: tener — to be sleepy (I)
suerte: por — luckily (1)
el **suéter** sweater (I)
  el — de cuello alto turtleneck (3)
suficiente sufficient, enough (7)
sugerir *(e → ie)* to suggest (13)
el **sujetapapeles** paper clip (1)
el **supermercado** supermarket (I)
supuesto: por — of course (I, 11)
surf:
  hacer — to surf (14)
  hacer — de vela to windsurf (14)
  la tabla de — surfboard (14)
suyo, -a (of) his, her (of hers), your (of yours), their (of theirs) (7)
el **suyo, la suya** yours, his, hers, theirs (7)

la **tabla (de surf)** surfboard (14)
tacaño, -a stingy (I)
el **taco** taco (I)
el **tacón** heel (I, 3)
tal:
  ¿qué —? how's it going? (I)
  ¿qué — es . . . ? how is? (10)
la **talla** clothing size (3)
el **tamaño** size (3)
también also, too (I)
el **tambor** drum (2)

tampoco neither, not either (I)
tan + *adj.* + **como** as + *adj.* + as (1)
tanto, -a + *noun* + **como** as much / many + *noun* + as (3)
las **tapas** Spanish-style appetizers (13)
tarde late (I)
la **tarde** afternoon (I)
　　buenas —s good afternoon, good evening (I)
　　de/por la — in the afternoon (I)
la **tarea** homework (I)
la **tarjeta** card (I)
　　la — de crédito credit card (3)
　　la — de embarque boarding pass (12)
　　la — postal post card (I)
la **tarta** pie (13)
el **taxi** taxi (I)
la **taza** cup (I)
el **tazón** bowl (I)
te *fam. obj. pron.* you (I)
el **té** tea (I)
　　el — helado iced tea (I)
el **teatro** theater (I)
　　la obra de — play (4)
el **técnico, la técnica (de computadoras)** (computer) technician (11)
la **tecnología** technology (11)
la **tela** fabric, cloth (3)
telefónico, -a: la oficina —a telephone office (12)
el **teléfono** telephone (I)
　　el número de — phone number (I)
　　por — on the telephone (I)
　　el — con video video telephone (11)
　　el — público public (pay) phone (8)
la **telenovela** soap opera (I)
la **tele(visión)** television (I)
el **televisor** TV set (7)
el **templo** temple (I)
temprano early (I)
el **tenedor** fork (I)
tener to have (I)
　　¿qué tienes? what's wrong? (I)
　　— que + *inf.* to have to (I)
el **tenis** tennis (I)
los **tenis** sneakers (I)
tercer, -a third (I)
la **terminal de equipaje** baggage claim (12)
terminar to end (I)
el **terremoto** earthquake (10)

terrible terrible (I)
terror: la película de — horror film (I)
ti you *fam. after prep.* (I)
el **tiempo** time; weather (I)
　　hace buen/mal — the weather is nice/bad (I)
　　el pronóstico del — weather forecast (I)
　　¿qué — hace? what's the weather like? (I)
　　tener — de + *inf.* to have time + *inf.* (4)
la **tienda** store (I)
　　poner una — to pitch a tent (14)
　　la — (de acampar) tent (14)
la **Tierra** Earth (I, 11)
el **tigre** tiger (I)
tímido, -a shy (5)
el **tío, la tía** uncle, aunt (I)
　　los tíos uncles; aunts and uncles (I)
típico, -a typical (I, 10)
el **tobillo** ankle (9)
el **tobogán** slide (5)
el **tocacintas** tape player (7)
tocar to play (I)
todavía still (I)
　　— no not yet (I)
todos, -as all; everyone (I)
　　— los días every day (I)
tomar to take (I)
　　— el sol to sunbathe (I)
el **tomate** tomato (I)
tonto, -a silly, dumb (I)
la **tormenta** storm (10)
la **tortilla** tortilla (I)
　　la — española potato and onion omelet (13)
la **tortuga** turtle (5)
la **tos** cough (9)
　　el jarabe (para la —) cough syrup (9)
toser to cough (9)
tostado: el pan — toast (I)
el **tostador** toaster (7)
trabajador, -a hardworking (I)
trabajar to work (I)
traer to bring (I)
el **tráfico** traffic (11)
el **traje** suit (I, 3)
　　el — de baño bathing suit (I)
el **trampolín** diving board (14)
el **transporte** transportation (8)
tratarse de to be about (10)
travieso, -a mischievous, naughty (5)
trece thirteen (I)

treinta thirty (I)
el **tren** train (I)
　　el — de juguete train *(toy)* (5)
tres three (I)
trescientos three hundred (I)
el **triciclo** tricycle (5)
　　montar en — to ride a tricycle (5)
triste sad (I)
la **trompeta** trumpet (2)
tu, tus your *fam.* (I)
tú you *fam.* (I)
turismo: la oficina de — tourist office (12)
el/la **turista** tourist (12)
el **tutor, la tutora** tutor (2)
tuve, tuviste *see* **tener**
tuyo, -a your, (of) yours (7)
el **tuyo, la tuya** yours (7)

último, -a last (4)
la **uña** fingernail (8)
　　el esmalte de —s nail polish (8)
único, -a only (I)
la **universidad** university (11)
uno (un), una a, an, one (I)
　　es la una it's one o'clock (I)
　　— one, a person (2)
unos, -as a few, some (I)
usar to use (I, 1); to wear (3)
usted (Ud.) you *formal sing.* (I)
ustedes (Uds.) you *formal pl.* (I)
la **uva** grape (I)

la **vaca** cow (I)
las **vacaciones** vacation (I)
　　ir de to go on vacation (I)
　　valer: (no) vale la pena it's (not) worthwhile (I)
el **valle** valley (14)
el **vaquero, la vaquera** cowboy, cowgirl (10)
el **vaso** glass (I)
¡vaya! my goodness! gee! wow! (I)
el **vecino, la vecina** neighbor (5)
veinte twenty (I)
veintiuno (veintiún) twenty-one (I)
la **vela** candle (6); sail (14)
el **venado, la venada** deer (14)
la **venda** bandage (8)
el **vendedor, la vendedora** salesperson (3)
vender to sell (I)
　　— se to be sold (8)
venenoso, -a poisonous (14)
la **ventaja** advantage (11)
la **ventana** window (I)
la **ventanilla** *(plane)* window (12)

el **ventilador** electric fan (7)
ver to see, to watch (I)
    a — let's see (I)
    —se to see each other (6)
el **verano** summer (I)
    veras: ¿de — ? really? (I)
la **verdad** truth (5)
    ¿—? isn't that so?, right? (I)
verde green (I)
la **verdulería** greengrocer (8)
las **verduras** vegetables (I)
el **vestido** dress (I)
vestirse *(e → i)* to get dressed (2)
el **veterinario, la veterinaria**
    veterinarian (11)
la **vez,** *pl.* **las veces** time (I)
    a la — at the same time (I)
    alguna — ever (I)
    a veces at times, sometimes (I)
    de — en cuando sometimes (7)
    dos veces twice (I)
    muchas veces many times (I)
    una — one time, once (I)
viajar to travel (12)
el **viaje** trip, voyage (12)
    la agencia de —s travel agency (12)
    el / la agente de —s travel agent (12)

el **viajero, la viajera** traveler (12)
    el cheque de — traveler's check (12)
la **víctima** victim (10)
la **vida** life (I)
    ganarse la — to earn a living (11)
    el programa de hechos de la — real fact-based program (I)
el **video** video (4)
la **videocasetera** VCR (I)
el **videojuego** video game (I)
el **vidrio** glass (I, 11)
    de — (made of) glass (I)
viejo, -a old (I)
el **viento** wind (I)
    hace — it's windy (I)
viernes Friday (I)
    el — on Friday (I)
el **vinagre** vinegar (13)
la **violencia** violence (10)
violento, -a (10)
el **violín** violin (2)
el **virus** virus (9)
visitar to visit (I)
la **vitamina** vitamin (13)
vivir to live (I)
el **vóleibol** volleyball (I)

voluntario(a): trabajar como —
    to volunteer (2)
vomitar to vomit (9)
vosotros(as) you *pl.* (I)
el **vuelo** flight (12)
    el/la auxiliar de — flight attendant (12)
vuelta *see* **boleto**

y and (I)
ya already (I)
    — no no longer, not anymore (I)
el **yeso** cast (9)
yo I (I)

la **zanahoria** carrot (I)
la **zapatería** shoe store (I)
el **zapato** shoe (I)
    los —s de tacón alto high-heeled shoes (I, 3)
el **zoológico** zoo (I)

ENGLISH-SPANISH VOCABULARY

This *Vocabulary* contains all active vocabulary from PASO A PASO 1 and 2.

A dash (—) represents the main entry word. For example, **to — for** following **to ask** means **to ask for.**

The number following each entry indicates the chapter in PASO A PASO 2 in which the word or expression is first introduced. Two numbers indicate that it is introduced in one chapter and elaborated upon in a later chapter. A Roman numeral (I) indicates that the word was presented in PASO A PASO 1.

The following abbreviations are used: *adj.* (adjective), *dir. obj.* (direct object). *f.* (feminine), *fam.* (familiar), *ind. obj.* (indirect object), *inf.* (infinitive), *m.* (masculine), *pl.* (plural), *prep.* (preposition), *pron.* (pronoun), *sing.* (singular).

a, an un, una (I)
able: to be — poder *(o → ue)* (I)
about sobre (I)
   to be — tratarse de (10)
accident el accidente (9)
according to según (2)
ache el dolor (I)
acquainted: to be — with conocer (I, 1)
to **act** actuar (10)
acting la actuación (10)
action:
   — figure el muñeco (5)
   — film la película de acción (10)
activity la actividad (2)
actor, actress el actor, la actriz (I)
ad el anuncio (I)
addition: in — además (9)
address la dirección, *pl.* las direcciones (8)
advantage la ventaja (11)
adventure film la película de aventuras (I)
affectionate cariñoso, -a (I)
after después (de) (I)
   — + *verb* **+ -ing** después de + *inf.* (2)
   — school después de las clases (I)
afternoon la tarde (I)
   — snack la merienda (I)
   good — buenas tardes (I)
   in the — por la tarde (I)
again de nuevo (6)
age:
   at the age of... a los... años (6)
   at what — ? ¿a qué edad? (6)
ago hace + *(time)* ... (I)
to **agree** estar de acuerdo (I)
   not to — with *(food)* hacer daño a (13)
air el aire (I)
   — conditioning el aire acondicionado (7)
airline la línea aérea (12)

airplane el avión, *pl.* los aviones (12)
airport el aeropuerto (12)
aisle el pasillo (12)
alarm clock el despertador (2)
algebra el álgebra *f.* (1)
alien el / la extraterrestre (10)
all todo, -a (I)
   — over por todas partes (3)
   — right bueno (I)
   — the same (to me) (me) da igual (3)
allergic (to) alérgico, -a (a) (9)
allergy la alergia (9)
to **allow** permitir (1)
   it's —ed se permite (1)
almost casi (I)
alone solo, -a (I)
already ya (I)
also también (I)
aluminum el aluminio (I)
always siempre (I)
ambulance la ambulancia (9)
among entre (I)
amusement park el parque de diversiones (I)
amusing divertido, -a (I)
and y (I)
animal el animal, *pl.* los animales (I, 5)
   stuffed — el animal de peluche (5)
   wild — el animal salvaje (14)
ankle el tobillo (9)
anniversary el aniversario (6)
announcer el locutor, la locutora (10)
to **annoy** molestar (5)
another otro, -a (I)
answer la respuesta (1)
to **answer** contestar (1)
ant la hormiga (9)
antibiotic el antibiótico (9)
any: not — ningúno (ningún), -a (I, 8)

anywhere: not — ninguna parte (I)
apartment el apartamento (I)
appetizers *(Spanish-style)* las tapas (13)
apple la manzana (I)
appliance el aparato (7)
April abril (I)
arm el brazo (I)
armchair el sillón, *pl.* los sillones (I)
around here por aquí (I)
to **arrest** arrestar (10)
to **arrive** llegar (I)
arriving from procedente de (12)
art el arte (I, 4)
   — exhibit la exposición, *pl.* las exposiciones de arte (4)
artistic artístico, -a (I)
as:
   — + *adj.* **—** tan + *adj.* + como (1)
   — much (many) + *noun* + **—** tanto, -a (tantos, -as) + *noun* + como (3)
to **ask** preguntar (1)
   to — a question hacer una pregunta (1)
   to — for pedir (I)
asparagus el espárrago (13)
assistance la ayuda (10)
astronaut el / la astronauta (11)
at en; a (I); por (8)
athlete el / la deportista (11)
athletic deportista (I)
atmosphere el ambiente (I)
attractive atractivo, -a (I)
auditorium el auditorio (1)
August agosto (I)
aunt la tía (I)
   —s and uncles los tíos (I)
automatic automático, -a (11)
autumn el otoño (I)
avenue la avenida (I)
avocado el aguacate (I)
   — dip el guacamole (I)

English-Spanish Vocabulary   509

to **baby-sit** cuidar niños (2)
back la espalda (I)
   in the — al fondo (8)
backpack la mochila (I)
bad mal, -a (I)
   to have a — time pasarlo mal (I, 4)
baggage el equipaje (12)
   — claim la terminal de equipaje (12)
baked *adj.* al horno (13)
bakery la panadería (8)
ball la pelota (4); *(inflated)* el balón, *pl.* los balones (4)
banana el plátano (I)
band la banda (2)
bandage la venda (8)
bank el banco (I)
barbecue la barbacoa (13)
   to have a — hacer una barbacoa (13)
bargain la ganga (I)
to **bargain** regatear (12)
baseball el béisbol (I)
based (on) basado, -a (en) (10)
basement el sótano (I)
basketball el básquetbol (I)
bass el contrabajo (2)
bat *(baseball)* el bate (de béisbol) (4)
bath: to take a — bañarse (2)
bathing suit el traje de baño (I)
bathroom el baño (I)
battery la pila (7)
to **be** estar; ser (I)
   to — about tratarse de (10)
beach la playa (I)
beans los frijoles (I)
   green — las judías verdes (I)
   refried — los frijoles refritos (I)
bear el oso (I)
because porque (I)
bed la cama (I)
   to go to — acostarse *(o → ue)* (2)
bedroom el dormitorio (I)
bee la abeja (9)
beef la carne (de res) (I)
before + *verb* + *-ing* antes de + *inf.* (2)
to **begin** empezar *(e → ie)* (I)
to **behave (well / badly)** portarse (bien / mal) (5)
behind detrás (de) (I)
to **believe** creer (I)
belt el cinturón, *pl.* los cinturones (3)
beside al lado de (I)
besides además (9)

best el / la mejor (I)
better mejor (I)
between entre (I)
beverage la bebida (I)
bicycle la bicicleta (I, 4)
   to ride a — montar en bicicleta (I, 4)
big grande (I)
   — screen TV la pantalla gigante (11)
bike *see* **bicycle**
bill *(restaurant)* la cuenta (I)
binder (3-ring) la carpeta de argollas (I)
biology la biología (1)
bird el pájaro (I, 5)
birthday el cumpleaños (I)
   — card la tarjeta de cumpleaños (I)
   — party la fiesta de cumpleaños (I, 6)
   happy —! ¡feliz cumpleaños! (I)
   to have a — cumplir años (6)
bite *(insect)* la picadura (9)
to **bite** *(insect)* picar (9)
bitter amargo, -a (13)
black negro, -a (I)
   in — and white en blanco y negro (I)
block la cuadra (I); *(toy)* el bloque (5)
   how many —s (from . . .)? ¿a cuántas cuadras (de . . .)? (I)
blond rubio, -a (I)
blood la sangre (9)
blouse la blusa (I)
to **blow out** *(candles)* apagar (6)
blue azul (I)
boarding pass la tarjeta de embarque (12)
body el cuerpo (I)
to **boil** hervir *(e → ie)* (13)
bold atrevido, -a (I)
bone el hueso (9)
   to break a — romperse (9)
book el libro (I)
   — bag el bolso (1)
bookstore la librería (I)
boot la bota (I)
   half — el botín, *pl.* los botines (3)
to **bore** aburrir (I)
bored: to be — aburrirse (4)
boring aburrido, -a (I)
born: to be — nacer (6)
to **borrow (from)** pedir prestado, -a (a) (4)
to **bother** molestar (5)

bottle la botella (I, 11)
bowl el tazón, *pl.* los tazones (I)
bowling los bolos (4)
boy el muchacho (I); el niño (5)
boyfriend el novio (I)
bracelet la pulsera (I, 7)
braces los frenillos (9)
bread el pan (I)
to **break** *(a bone)* romperse (9)
breakfast el desayuno (I)
   for — en el desayuno (I)
   to have — desayunar (2)
to **bring** traer (I)
broken roto, -a (9)
brother el hermano (I)
   —s and sisters los hermanos (I)
   —-in-law el cuñado (6)
brown marrón, *pl.* marrones; *(hair)* castaño (I)
to **brush** *(one's teeth, hair, etc.)* cepillarse (los dientes, el pelo, etc.) (2)
building el edificio (1)
to **burn** quemar (9)
   to — oneself quemarse (9)
burrito el burrito (I)
bus el autobús, *pl.* los autobuses (I)
   — stop la parada del autobús (I)
business los negocios (11)
   —man, —woman el hombre / la mujer de negocios (11)
busy ocupado, -a (I)
but pero (I)
butcher shop la carnicería (8)
butter la mantequilla (I)
butterfly la mariposa (14)
button el botón, *pl.* los botones (3)
to **buy** comprar (I)
by por; + *vehicle* en (I)

cactus el cacto (14)
cafeteria la cafetería (1)
cake el pastel (6)
calamine lotion la calamina (9)
calculator la calculadora (I)
to **call** llamar (I)
calorie la caloría (13)
camera la cámara (I)
campground el campamento (14)
camping: to go — ir de camping (14)
can poder *(o → ue)* (I); la lata (I, 11)
   — opener el abrelatas (14)
candle la vela (6)

candy el dulce (13)
canned enlatado, -a (13)
canoe la canoa (14)
   to go —ing navegar en canoa (14)
cantaloupe el melón, *pl.* los melones (13)
canvas la lona (3)
cap la gorra (3)
   ski — el gorro (I)
car el coche (I)
   — coat el chaquetón, *pl.* los chaquetones (3)
carbohydrate el carbohidrato (13)
card la tarjeta (I)
   ID — el carnet de identidad (7)
cardboard el cartón (I, 11)
careful: to be — (of / with) tener cuidado (con) (12)
carousel el carrusel (5)
carrot la zanahoria (I)
carte: a la — a la carta (I)
cartoons los dibujos animados (I)
case: in — of en caso de (7)
cash (el dinero) en efectivo (3)
to cash cambiar (12)
cashier el cajero, la cajera (3)
   —'s station la caja (8)
cassette el casete (4)
cast el yeso (9)
cat el gato (I)
catalog el catálogo (3)
cathedral la catedral (I)
cautious prudente (I)
CD el disco compacto (4)
to celebrate celebrar (6)
celebration la celebración, *pl.* las celebraciones (6)
center el centro (I)
   recycling — el centro de reciclaje (I)
   shopping — el centro comercial (I)
central central (7)
cereal el cereal (I)
chain la cadena (7)
   key— el llavero (7)
chair la silla (I)
chalkboard la pizarra (I)
champion el campeón, *pl.* los campeones; la campeona (4)
championship el campeonato (4)
change el cambio (11)
to change cambiar (10)
channel el canal (I)
chapter el capítulo (1)
character el personaje (10)
to chat charlar (6)

cheap barato, -a (I)
check el cheque (3)
to check *(baggage)* facturar (12)
   to — out a book sacar un libro (I)
checked *(design)* a cuadros (3)
checkers las damas (4)
cheese el queso (I)
chemistry la química (1)
cherry la cereza (13)
chess el ajedrez (4)
chestnut(-colored) castaño, -a (I)
chicken el pollo (I)
   — soup la sopa de pollo (I)
child el niño, la niña (5)
   as a — de pequeño, -a (5)
   only — el hijo único, la hija única (I)
children los niños (5)
   —'s wear la ropa para niños (8)
chili pepper el chile (I)
chocolate: hot — el chocolate (I)
choir el coro (2)
to choose escoger *(g → j)* (I, 3)
to chop picar (13)
chore el quehacer(I)
   household — el quehacer de la casa (I)
chorus el coro (2)
Christmas la Navidad (6)
   — Eve la Nochebuena (6)
church la iglesia (I)
churro el churro (I)
city la ciudad (I)
clarinet el clarinete (2)
class la clase (de) (I)
classical clásico, -a (4)
classmate el compañero, la compañera (I)
classroom la sala de clases (I)
clean limpio, -a; puro, -a (I)
to clean limpiar (I)
   to — up arreglar (I)
to clear the table quitar la mesa (I)
to climb subir (I)
clinic la clínica (I)
clock el reloj (1)
   alarm — el despertador (2)
to close cerrar *(e → ie)* (I)
closet el guardarropa (I)
cloth la tela (3)
clothes la ropa (I)
club el club, *pl.* los clubes (2)
coach el entrenador, la entrenadora (4)
coat el abrigo (I)
   car — el chaquetón, *pl.* los chaquetones (3)

cockroach la cucaracha (9)
coffee el café (I)
coin la moneda (7)
cold frío, -a (I)
   to be (very) — tener (mucho) frío (I)
   to have a — tener (un) resfriado (I)
   it's — out hace frío (I)
to collect coleccionar (5)
collection la colección, *pl.* las colecciones (5)
color el color (I)
   in — en colores (I)
   what —? ¿de qué color? (I)
Columbus Day el Día de la Raza (6)
comb el peine (2)
to comb one's hair peinarse (2)
comedy la comedia (I)
comfortable cómodo, -a (I)
comical cómico -a (I)
commercial el anuncio (de televisión) (I)
community la comunidad (I)
compact disc el disco compacto (4)
composition la composición (1)
computer la computadora (1)
   — technician el técnico, la técnica de computadoras (11)
concert el concierto (I)
congratulations! ¡felicidades! (6)
to congratulate felicitar (6)
to conserve conservar (I, 7)
contact lenses los lentes de contacto (7)
to contaminate contaminar (11)
contaminated contaminado, -a (I, 11)
cook el cocinero, la cocinera (13)
to cook cocinar (13)
cooked cocido, -a (13)
cool: it's — out hace fresco (I)
corn el maíz (I)
   — tortilla la tortilla de maíz (I)
corner la esquina (I)
to cost costar *(o → ue)* (I)
costume party la fiesta de disfraces (I, 4)
cotton el algodón (3)
cough la tos (9)
   — syrup el jarabe (para la tos) (9)
to cough toser (9)
could you...? ¿podría (Ud.) / podrías (tú) + *inf.?* (8)

English-Spanish Vocabulary   511

counselor el consejero, la consejera (1)

counter el mostrador (8)

country el país (I)

countryside el campo (I)

course: of — claro que sí (I); por supuesto (I, 11)

cousin el primo, la prima (I)

cow la vaca (I)

cowboy, cowgirl el vaquero, la vaquera (10)

coyote el coyote (14)

credit card la tarjeta de crédito (3)

crime el crimen (10)

criminal el / la criminal (10)

to **cross** cruzar (8)

crossword puzzle el crucigrama (4)

crutches las muletas (9)

to **cry** llorar (5)

cucumber el pepino (13)

cup la taza (I)

currency exchange la casa de cambio (12)

customs la aduana (12)

   — agent el aduanero, la aduanera (12)

to **cut** cortar (I)

   to — oneself cortarse (9)

daily special el plato del día (I)

to **damage** dañar (10)

dance el baile (I, 6)

to **dance** bailar (I, 6)

dancer el bailarín, la bailarina (11)

danger el peligro (I, 14)

dangerous peligroso, -a (14)

daring atrevido, -a (I)

dark *(color)* oscuro, -a (3)

date la fecha (I)

   what's today's —? ¿cuál es la fecha de hoy? (I)

daughter la hija (I)

dawn el amanecer (14)

day el día (I)

   every — todos los días (I)

day-care center la guardería infantil (5)

dead muerto, -a (6)

December diciembre (I)

decoration la decoración, *pl.* las decoraciones (I)

deer el venado, la venada (14)

delay el retraso (12)

delicious sabroso, -a (I)

delighted encantado, -a (I)

to **deliver** repartir (2)

dental floss la seda dental (8)

dentist el / la dentista (I)

deodorant el desodorante (8)

department store el almacén, *pl.* los almacenes (I)

to **depend (on)** depender (de) (I, 2)

to **deposit** depositar (I)

desk el escritorio; *(student)* el pupitre (I)

desert el desierto (14)

dessert el postre

   for — de postre (I)

to **destroy** destruir (10)

detective el / la detective (10)

   — show el programa de detectives (I)

device el aparato (7)

to **devote oneself (to)** dedicarse (a) (11)

dictionary el diccionario (I)

difficult difícil (I)

dining room el comedor (I)

dinner la cena (I)

   for — en la cena (I)

dinosaur el dinosaurio (5)

to **direct** dirigir *(g → j)* (10)

direction la dirección, *pl.* las direcciones (10)

director *(film)* el director, la directora (10)

dirty sucio, -a (I)

disadvantage la desventaja (11)

to **disagree** no estar de acuerdo (I)

disaster el desastre (4)

discount store la tienda de descuentos (I)

disgusting: that's — ! ¡qué asco! (I)

dish el plato (I)

dishwasher el lavaplatos (7)

disk el disco (4)

disobedient desobediente (5)

to **disobey** desobedecer *(c → zc)* (5)

distance la distancia (8)

to **dive** dar saltos (14)

diversion la diversión, *pl.* las diversiones (4)

diving board el trampolín, *pl.* los trampolines (14)

divorced (from) divorciado, -a (de) (6)

to **do** hacer (I)

documentary el documental (I)

dog el perro (I)

doll la muñeca (5)

dollar el dólar (I)

domestic doméstico, -a (14)

door la puerta (I)

dot: on the — en punto (I)

double doble (12)

dough la masa (13)

downtown el centro (8)

to **draw** dibujar (I)

drawing el dibujo (I)

dress el vestido (I)

   party — el vestido de fiesta (I)

dressed: to get — vestirse *(e → i)* (2)

dresser la cómoda (I)

to **drink** beber (I)

drops las gotas (9)

drugstore la farmacia (I)

drum el tambor (2)

dry seco, -a (14)

to **dry** secar (14)

   to — one's hair secarse el pelo (2)

dryer:

   clothes — la secadora (7)

   hair — el secador de pelo (7)

dumb tonto, -a (I)

to **dump** echar (11)

dust el polvo (9)

to **dust** sacudir (I)

ear el oído (I)

   —ache el dolor de oído (I)

early temprano (I)

to **earn** ganar (2)

   to — a living ganarse la vida (11)

earring el arete (I, 7)

Earth la Tierra (I, 11)

earthquake el terrremoto (10)

easily fácilmente (2)

easy fácil (I)

to **eat** comer (I)

economical económico, -a (11)

education la educación (11)

educational educativo, -a (I)

efficient eficiente (11)

egg el huevo (I)

   hard-boiled — el huevo duro (13)

eight ocho (I)

   — hundred ochocientos (I)

eighteen dieciocho (I)

eighth octavo, -a (I)

eighty ochenta (I)

either: not — no ... tampoco (I)

elbow el codo (9)

electric eléctrico, -a (7)

   — fan el ventilador (7)

electricity la electricidad (7)

elegant elegante (I, 3)

elementary school la escuela primaria (5)
elephant el elefante (I, 14)
elevator el ascensor (8)
eleven once (I)
else: anything — algo más (I)
to **embrace** abrazarse (6)
emergency la emergencia (7)
  — room la sala de emergencia (9)
  in case of — en caso de emergencia (7)
employee el empleado, la empleada (12)
enchilada la enchilada (I)
to **end** terminar (I)
endangered en peligro de extinción (I, 14)
energy la energía (I, 7)
English (*language*) el inglés (I)
to **enjoy** disfrutar de (12)
enough suficiente (7)
entertainment la diversión, *pl.* las diversiones (4)
entrance la entrada (8)
environment el medio ambiente (I, 11)
eruption la erupción, *pl.* las erupciones (10)
escalator la escalera mecánica (8)
evening la noche (I)
  good — buenas noches / tardes (I)
  in the — por la noche / tarde (I)
ever alguna vez (I)
every day todos los días (I)
everyone todos, -as (I)
everywhere por todas partes (3)
exaggerated exagerado, -a (10)
exam el examen, *pl.* los exámenes (1)
excellent excelente (10)
exciting emocionante (I)
excursion la excursión, *pl.* las excursiones (12)
  to take an — hacer una excursión (12)
to **excuse** perdonar (8)
  — me perdón (I); perdone (Ud.) (8)
exercise el ejercicio (I, 1)
to **exercise** hacer ejercicio (I)
exhibit (*art*) la exposición, *pl.* las exposiciones (de arte) (4)
exit la salida (8)
expensive caro, -a (I)
to **explain** explicar (1)

to **explore** explorar (I)
extracurricular extracurricular (2)
eye el ojo (I)
  — drops las gotas para los ojos (9)

fabric la tela (3)
face la cara (2)
facing enfrente (de) (I)
fact el hecho (I, 10)
  —-based program el programa de hechos de la vida real (I)
factory la fábrica (I)
failure el fracaso (10)
fair regular; así, así (I)
fall el otoño (I)
to **fall (down)** caerse (9)
  to — in love (with) enamorarse (de) (10)
family la familia (I); *adj.* familiar (6)
  — room la sala de estar (I)
fan (*electric*) el ventilador (7)
fantastic fantástico, -a (I)
far (from) lejos (de) (I)
to **fascinate** fascinar (I)
fascinating fascinante (I)
fashion la moda (3)
fashionable: to be — estar de moda (3)
to **fasten** abrocharse (12)
father el padre (I)
  —'s Day el Día del Padre (6)
feather la pluma (14)
February febrero (I)
to **feel** sentirse (*e → ie*) (9)
  how do you —? ¿cómo te sientes? (I)
festive alegre (4)
fever la fiebre (I)
  to have a — tener fiebre (I)
few: a — unos, unas (I)
fifteen quince (I)
fifth quinto, -a (I)
fifty cincuenta (I)
to **fight** pelearse (5)
filling el relleno (13)
film la película (I)
to **find** encontrar (*o → ue*) (3)
finger el dedo (I)
fingernail la uña (8)
  — polish el esmalte de uñas (8)
fire el incendio (7); el fuego (14)
  — extinguisher el extinguidor de incendios (7)
  — station la estación de bomberos (8)

firefighter el bombero, la bombera (8)
firewood la leña (14)
fireworks los fuegos artificiales (6)
  to shoot — lanzar fuegos artificiales (6)
first primero (primer), -a (I)
fish (*cooked*) el pescado (I); (*live*) el pez, *pl.* los peces (5)
  — store la pescadería (8)
  to go —ing ir de pesca (I)
to **fit** quedar (I)
five cinco (I)
  — hundred quinientos (I)
to **fix** reparar (7)
flag la bandera (1)
flan el flan (I)
flashlight la linterna (7)
flight el vuelo (12)
  — attendant el / la auxiliar de vuelo (12)
flood la inundación, *pl.* las inundaciones (10)
floor (*story*) el piso (I); el suelo (3)
floss: dental — la seda dental (8)
flour la harina (I)
  — tortilla la tortilla de harina (I)
flower la flor (I, 6)
  — shop la floristería (8)
flowered floreado, -a (3)
flu la gripe (I)
  to have the — tener gripe (I)
flute la flauta (2)
fly la mosca (9)
folder la carpeta (I)
to **follow** seguir (*e → i*) (8)
food la comida (I); la alimentación (3)
foot el pie (I)
  on — a pie (I)
football el fútbol americano (I)
footprint la huella (14)
for para; por (I)
  — + *time expression* por (9)
forest la selva (I)
  rain — la selva tropical (I)
fork el tenedor (I)
forty cuarenta (I)
fossil el fósil (14)
four cuatro (I)
  — hundred cuatrocientos (I)
fourteen catorce (I)
French (*language*) el francés (1)
  — fries las papas fritas (I)
fresh fresco, -a (13)
Friday viernes (I)
  on — el viernes (I)

English-Spanish Vocabulary 513

fried frito, -a (13)
friend el amigo, la amiga (I)
friendly simpático, -a (I)
frog la rana (14)
from de (I); desde (6)
front: in — of enfrente de; delante de (I)
frozen congelado, -a (13)
fruit la fruta (I)
— **salad** la ensalada de frutas (13)
— **shop** la frutería (8)
fun: to have — divertirse *(e → ie)* (4)
to **function** funcionar (7)
funny gracioso, -a; emocionante; divertido, -a (I)
fur la piel (I)
furniture los muebles (I)
future el futuro (11)

game el partido (I, 4)
— **show** el programa de concursos (10)
garage el garaje (I)
garbage la basura (I)
garlic el ajo (13)
gas station la estación de servicio (I)
gate la puerta (12)
to **gather** recoger (14)
gathering la reunión, *pl.* las reuniones (I, 6)
gazpacho el gazpacho (13)
gee! ¡vaya! (I)
generally generalmente (I)
generous generoso, -a (I)
geography la geografía (1)
geometry la geometría (1)
German *(language)* el alemán (1)
to **get** conseguir *(e → i)* (12)
to — up levantarse (2)
get-together la reunión, *pl.* las reuniones (I, 6)
gift el regalo (I)
— **shop** la tienda de regalos (I)
to give a — regalar (I, 6)
girl la muchacha (I); la niña (5)
girlfriend la novia (I)
to **give** dar (I)
to — a gift regalar (I, 6)
to — an injection poner una inyección (9)
glass el vaso (I); *(material)* el vidrio (I, 11)
(made of) — de vidrio (I)
glasses los anteojos (I, 7)

glove el guante (I)
baseball — el guante de béisbol (4)
to **go** ir (I)
to be —ing to + *verb* ir a + *inf.* (I)
to — fishing ir de pesca (I)
— **on!** ¡vaya! (I)
to — on a trip hacer una excursión (12)
to — on vacation ir de vacaciones (I)
to — shopping ir de compras (I)
to — to bed acostarse *(o → ue)* (2)
to — to school ir a la escuela (I)
to — through pasar por (12)
goal el gol (4)
going to con destino a (12)
gold el oro (7)
(made of) — de oro (7)
good bueno (buen), -a (I)
— **afternoon** buenas tardes (I)
— **evening** buenas noches (I)
— **morning** buenos días (I)
— **night** buenas noches (I)
it's a — thing that . . . menos mal que . . . (I)
golf el golf (4)
— **club** el palo (de golf) (4)
good buen(o), -a (I)
to have a — time pasarlo bien (I, 4)
good-by adiós (I)
to say — (to) despedirse *(e → i)* (de) (6)
good-looking guapo, -a (I)
goodness: my —! ¡vaya! (I)
gorilla el gorila (I, 14)
grade la nota (1)
to get a good / bad — sacar una buena / mala nota (1)
to **graduate** graduarse (6)
graduation la graduación, *pl.* las graduaciones (6)
granddaughter la nieta (6)
grandfather el abuelo (I)
grandmother la abuela (I)
grandparents los abuelos (I)
grandson el nieto (6)
grape la uva (I)
gray gris, *pl.* grises (I)
— **hair** pelo canoso (I)
greasy grasoso, -a (13)
great! ¡genial! (I)
great-grandfather / grandmother el bisabuelo, la bisabuela (6)

green verde (I)
— **beans** las judías verdes (I)
— **pepper** el pimiento verde (13)
greengrocer la verdulería (8)
to **greet** saludar (6)
grilled a la parrilla (13)
groceries los comestibles (I)
guest el invitado, la invitada (I)
guide el / la guía (12)
guidebook la guía (12)
guitar la guitarra (I)
gym el gimnasio (I)
— **bag** el bolso (1)

habit: to be in the — of soler *(o → ue)* + *inf.* (I, 2)
hair el pelo (I)
to comb one's — peinarse (2)
— **dryer** el secador de pelo (7)
half:
and a — *(in sizes)* y medio (3)
— **an hour** media hora (I)
— **boots** el botín, *pl.* los botines (3)
—-**past** y media (I)
ham el jamón (I)
hamburger la hamburguesa (I)
hamper: laundry — el cesto de la ropa sucia (3)
hand la mano (I)
by — a mano (12)
—**made** hecho, -a a mano (I)
to shake —s darse la mano (6)
to **hand in** entregar (1)
handcrafts la artesanía (12)
handsome guapo, -a (I)
to **hang** colgar *(o → ue)* (3)
to **happen** pasar (I); ocurrir (10)
what —ed to you? ¿qué te pasó? (9)
happy alegre (4)
hard difícil (I)
hard-boiled egg el huevo duro (13)
hard-working trabajador, -a (I)
to **have** tener (I)
to — fun divertirse *(e → ie)* (4)
to — a good / bad time pasarlo bien / mal (I, 4)
to — time + *inf.* tener tiempo de + *inf.* (4)
to — to tener que + *inf.* (I)
he él (I)
head la cabeza (I)
—**ache** el dolor de cabeza (I)

health la salud (I); *(class)* las ciencias de la salud (I)
healthy sano, -a (13)
  to stay — mantenerse sano, -a (13)
heater el calentador (7)
heating la calefacción (7)
heavy pesado, -a (14)
hello! ¡hola! (I)
helmet el casco (4)
help la ayuda (10)
to **help** ayudar (I)
  may I — you? ¿qué desea (Ud.)? (I)
her *adj.* su, sus (I); suyo, -a (7); *dir. obj. pron.* la; *ind. obj. pron.* le (I)
here aquí (I)
  around — por aquí (I)
  — it is aquí está (I)
hero *(film)* el galán, *pl.* los galanes (10)
heroine la heroína (10)
hers el suyo, la suya, los suyos, las suyas (7)
hi! ¡hola! (I)
to **hide** esconder(se) (10)
high-heeled shoes los zapatos de tacón alto (I, 3)
highway la carretera (8)
hiking: to go — dar una caminata (14)
hill la colina (14)
him *dir. obj. pron.* lo; *ind. obj. pron.* le (I)
his *adj.* su, sus (I), suyo, -a (7), *pron.* el suyo, la suya, los suyos, las suyas (7)
historic(al) histórico, -a (8)
history la historia (1)
hobby el pasatiempo (I)
hockey el hockey (4)
  — puck el disco (de hockey) (4)
  — stick el palo (de hockey) (4)
holiday el día de fiesta (6)
home la casa (I)
  — shopping show el programa de compras (10)
homework la tarea (I)
horrible horrible (I)
horror el horror (4)
  — movie la película de terror (I)
horse el caballo (I, 10)
  to ride —back montar a caballo (10)
hospital el hospital (I)
hot *(flavor)* picante (I)
  to be — *(person)* tener calor (I)
  it's — out hace calor (I)

hot dog el perro caliente (13)
hotel el hotel (I)
  — room la habitación, *pl.* las habitaciones (12)
house la casa (I)
  — special la especialidad de la casa (I)
household chore el quehacer de la casa (I)
¡how! qué + *adj.* (I)
how? ¿cómo? (I)
  — are you? ¿cómo estás /está (Ud.)? (I)
  — long has it been since … ¿cuánto (tiempo) hace que …? (I)
  — many? ¿cuántos, -as? (I)
  — much? ¿cuánto? (I)
  — old is … ? cuántos años tiene … ? (I)
  —'s it going? ¿qué tal? (I)
  — is…? ¿qué tal es…? (10)
to **hug** abrazarse (6)
human being el ser humano (11)
hundred cien; ciento (I)
hungry: to be — tener hambre (I)
hurricane el huracán, *pl.* los huracanes (10)
to **hurt** doler *(o → ue);* lastimarse + *part of body* (I)
husband el esposo (6)

I yo (I)
ice el hielo (4)
  to — skate patinar sobre hielo (4)
ice cream el helado (I)
  — shop la heladería (8)
iced tea el té helado (I)
identification la identificación (7)
  — card la carnet de identidad (7)
if si (I)
ill enfermo, -a (I)
  to feel — sentirse *(e → ie)* mal (I)
  to make — hacer daño a (13)
illness la enfermedad (9)
impatient impaciente (I)
impolite maleducado, -a (5)
in en (I)
  — order to para + *inf.* (I)
to **include** incluir (12)
Independence Day el Día de la Independencia (6)
to **indicate** indicar (8)
indigenous indígena (12)
inexpensive barato, -a (I)
  — lodging la pensión, *pl.* las pensiones (12)

infection la infección, *pl.* las infecciones (9)
information la información (10)
ingredient el ingrediente (I, 13)
injection la inyección, *pl.* las inyecciones (9)
  to give an — poner una inyección (9)
insect el insecto (9)
  — bite la picadura (de insecto) (9)
  — repellent el repelente (9)
insecticide el insecticida (9)
to **inspect** registrar (12)
instrument el instrumento (2)
intelligent inteligente (I)
interest: place of — el lugar de interés (I)
to **interest** interesar (I)
interesting interesante (I)
international internacional (10)
intersection el cruce (8)
interview la entrevista (10)
to **introduce** presentar (I)
to **investigate** investigar (10)
invitation la invitación, *pl.* las invitaciones (I, 6)
to **invite** invitar (I, 6)
involved: to be — in dedicarse (a) (11)
it *dir. obj.* lo (I)

jacket la chaqueta (I)
jaguar el jaguar (I)
January enero (I)
jeans los jeans (I)
to **jet ski** hacer moto acuática (14)
jet skiing la moto acuática (14)
jewelry las joyas (I)
jigsaw puzzle el rompecabezas (4)
to **jog** correr (4)
judge el / la juez, *pl.* los / las jueces (11)
juice el jugo (I)
  orange — el jugo de naranja (I)
July julio (I)
to **jump (rope)** saltar (a la cuerda) (5)
  — rope la cuerda (5)
June junio (I)

to **keep** guardar (3)
key la llave (7)
  —chain el llavero (7)
to **kill** matar (10)
kilometer el kilómetro (8)
kind *adj.* amable; la clase (I)

English-Spanish Vocabulary   515

kindergarten el kindergarten (5)
kindling los palitos (14)
to **kiss** besarse (6)
kitchen la cocina (I)
knee la rodilla (9)
knife el cuchillo (I)
to **know** conocer (c → zc) (I, 1); saber (I, 4)
    to — how saber (I, 4)

lab(oratory) el laboratorio (1)
laborer el obrero, la obrera (11)
lacking: to be — faltar a (I)
ladies' wear la ropa para damas (8)
lake el lago (I)
lamp la lámpara (I)
to **land** aterrizar (12)
landslide el derrumbe (10)
language el idioma (1)
large grande (I, 3)
last pasado, -a (I); último, -a (4)
    — night anoche (I)
to **last** durar (I)
late tarde (I)
    see you —r hasta luego (I)
laundry hamper el cesto de la ropa sucia (3)
laundry room el lavadero (I)
lawn el césped (I)
    to mow the — cortar el césped (I)
lawyer el abogado, la abogada (11)
lazy perezoso, -a (I)
leaf hoja (14)
league la liga (4)
to **learn** aprender (I)
least el / la / los / las menos + *adj.* (I)
    at — por lo menos (2)
leather el cuero (I)
    (made of) — de cuero (I)
to **leave** salir (I)
left izquierdo, -a (I)
    to the — (of) a la izquierda (de) (I)
leg la pierna (I)
lemon el limón, *pl.* los limones (13)
lemonade la limonada (I)
to **lend** prestar (4)
lenses: contact — los lentes de contacto (7)
less menos (I)
    more or — más o menos (I)
lesson la lección, *pl.* las lecciones (1)
letter la carta (I)

lettuce la lechuga (I)
library la biblioteca (I)
to **lie** mentir *(e → ie)* (5)
life la vida (I)
to **lift** levantar (4)
light *(color)* claro, -a (3); *(minor)* leve (9); *(weight)* ligero, -a (14)
light la luz, *pl.* las luces (I)
    — bulb el bombillo (7)
    traffic — el semáforo (8)
to **light** encender *(e → ie)* (6)
to **like** gustar a (I)
    I'd (you'd) — quisiera(s); me (te) gustaría (I)
likewise igualmente (I)
lime el limón, *pl.* los limones (13)
line: to — up hacer fila (1)
lips los labios (8)
lipstick el lápiz *(pl.* los lápices) de labios (8)
to **listen (to)** escuchar (I)
literary literario, -a (2)
lit(erature) la literatura (1)
little pequeño, -a (I)
    a — un poco (de) (I)
to **live** vivir (I)
    living: to earn a — ganarse la vida (11)
living room la sala (I)
loafer el mocasín, *pl.* los mocasines (3)
local local (10)
located: to be — quedar (I)
locker el armario (1)
lodging: inexpensive — la pensión, *pl.* las pensiones (12)
long largo, -a (I)
to **look (at)** mirar (I)
    to — for buscar (I)
loose *(clothing)* flojo, -a (3)
to **lose** perder *(e → ie)* (4)
lot: a — of mucho, -a (I)
love: to fall in — (with) enamorarse (de) (10)
to **love** encantar (I)
loving cariñoso, -a (I)
luckily por suerte (1)
lunch el almuerzo (I)
    for — en el almuerzo (I)
luxury el lujo (7)

ma'am señora (I)
made hecho, -a (I, 13)
    it's — of... es de... (3)
    — of de + *material* (I)
    what's (it) — of ? de qué es...? (3)

magazine la revista (I)
to **mail** enviar (I)
mailbox el buzón, *pl.* los buzones (8)
main principal (10)
to **make** hacer (I)
make-up el maquillaje (8)
    to put on — maquillarse (8)
mall el centro comercial (I)
man el hombre (I)
many muchos, -as (I)
    as — as tantos, -as + *noun* + como (3)
map el mapa (1)
March marzo (I)
market el mercado (12)
marker el marcador (I)
married (to) casado, -a (con) (6)
    to get — (to) casarse (con) (6)
martial arts las artes marciales (2)
match *(game)* el partido (I); el fósforo (14)
mathematics las matemáticas (I)
matter: what's the —? ¿qué pasa? (I)
May mayo (I)
mayonnaise la mayonesa (13)
me *obj. pron.* me; *after prep.* mí (I)
meal la comida (I)
mechanic el mecánico, la mecánica (11)
medical test el análisis, *pl.* los análisis (9)
medicine la medicina (9)
medium *(in sizes)* mediano, -a (3)
to **meet** encontrarse *(o → ue)* (6)
    I'd like you to — te presento a... (I)
    pleased to — you mucho gusto; encantado, -a (I)
member el miembro (2)
    to be a — of ser miembro de (2)
men's wear la ropa para caballeros (8)
menu el menú (I)
merry-go-round el carrusel (5)
messy desordenado, -a (I)
metal el metal (I)
    (made of) — de metal (I)
meter *(measurement)* el metro (8)
microwave oven el microondas (7)
midnight la medianoche (I)
mild *(flavor)* no picante (I)
mile la milla (8)
milk la leche (I)

mine el mío, la mía, los míos, las mías (7)
minor leve (9)
minute el minuto (I)
mirror el espejo (I)
mischievous travieso, -a (5)
miss (la) señorita (I)
miss: to be —ing faltar a (I)
to **mix** mezclar (13)
modern moderno, -a (I)
Monday lunes (I)
  on — el lunes (I)
money el dinero (I)
monster el monstruo (10)
month el mes (I)
monument el monumento (I)
mood: in a good / bad — de buen / mal humor (2)
moon la Luna (11)
more más (I)
  — or less más o menos (I)
morning la mañana (I)
  good — buenos días (I)
  in the — por la mañana (I)
mosquito el mosquito (9)
most: the — el / la / los / las más + *adj.* (I)
mother la madre (I)
  —'s Day el Día de la Madre (6)
mountain la montaña (I)
  to go — climbing escalar montañas (14)
mouth la boca (I)
movie la película (I)
  —s el cine (I)
  — theater el cine (I)
  to show a — dar una película (I)
to **mow the lawn** cortar el césped (I)
Mr. (el) señor (I)
Mrs. (la) señora (I)
much mucho, -a (I)
  as — as tanto, -a + *noun* + como (3)
  how —? ¿cuánto? (I)
muffler la bufanda (I)
muscle el músculo (9)
museum el museo (I)
mushroom el champiñón, *pl.* los champiñones (13)
music la música (I)
  — program el programa musical (I)
  — video el video musical (4)
musical musical (I)
musician el músico, la música (11)

mustard la mostaza (13)
my mi, mis (I); mío, -a (7)
myself (yo) mismo, -a (7)

nail *see* **fingernail**
name el nombre (I)
  my — is me llamo (I)
  what's your —? ¿cómo te llamas? (I)
named: to be — llamarse (I)
napkin la servilleta (I)
national nacional (14)
native *adj.* indígena (12)
nature la naturaleza (12)
naughty travieso, -a (5)
near cerca (de) (I)
neat ordenado, -a (I)
necessary: it's — to hay que + *inf.* (I, 2); es necesario (2)
necessity la necesidad (7)
neck el cuello (I)
necklace el collar (I, 7)
necktie la corbata (I, 3)
to **need** necesitar (I)
neighbor el vecino, la vecina (5)
neither . . . nor ni . . . ni (I)
nephew el sobrino (6)
never nunca (I)
new nuevo, -a (I)
  — Year's Day el Año Nuevo (6)
  — Year's Eve el fin de año (6)
news las noticias (I)
newspaper el periódico (I, 2)
newsstand el quiosco (de periódicos) (8)
next próximo, -a (I)
  — to al lado (de) (I)
nice amable; simpático, -a (I)
niece la sobrina (6)
night la noche (I)
  at — de la noche (I)
  good — buenas noches (I)
  last — anoche (I)
  — table la mesa de noche (7)
nine nueve (I)
  — hundred novecientos (I)
nineteen diecinueve (I)
ninety noventa (I)
no no (I)
  — longer ya no (I)
nobody, no one nadie (I)
nonallergenic antialérgico, -a (9)
nonstop sin escala (12)
noon el mediodía (I)
nor: neither . . . — ni . . . ni (I)
nose la nariz (I)

not no (I)
  — anymore ya no (I)
  — at all de ninguna manera (I)
  — yet todavía no (I)
notebook el cuaderno (I)
nothing nada (I)
nourishment la alimentación (13)
novel la novela (11)
November noviembre (I)
now ahora (I)
nowhere ninguna parte (I)
number el número (I)
  phone — el número de teléfono (I)
nurse el enfermero, la enfermera (9)
  —'s office la enfermería (I)
nylon el nilón (3)

obedient obediente (5)
to **obey** obedecer *(c → zc)* (5)
to **obtain** conseguir *(e → i)* (12)
to **occur** ocurrir (10)
ocean el océano (I, 11)
October octubre (I)
of de (I)
— course claro que sí (I); por supuesto (I, 11)
office la oficina (1)
  telephone — la oficina telefónica (12)
  tourist — la oficina de turismo (12)
often a menudo (I)
oil el aceite (13)
ok bueno (I)
old viejo -a; antiguo, -a (I)
  how — is . . . ? ¿cuántos años tiene . . . ? (I)
older mayor (I)
omelet *(Spain)* la tortilla española (13)
on en; sobre (I)
  — the dot en punto (I)
  — time puntualmente (I)
  — top (of) encima (de) (I)
once una vez (I)
one uno (un), una (I); *(a person)* uno (2)
  it's — o'clock es la una (I)
  —-way sólo de ida (12)
onion la cebolla (I)
only sólo (I)
  — child el hijo único, la hija única (I)
to **open** abrir (I)
operation la operación, *pl.* las operaciones (9)

English-Spanish Vocabulary 517

opposite enfrente (de) (I)
or o (I)
   not . . . — ni . . . ni (I)
orange anaranjado, -a; la naranja (I)
   — juice el jugo de naranja (I)
orchestra la orquesta (2)
order: in — to para + *inf.* (I)
to **order** pedir *(e → i)* (I)
other otro, -a (I)
ouch! ¡ay! (I)
ought to deber (I)
our nuestro, -a (I)
ours el nuestro, la nuestra, los
   nuestros, las nuestras (7)
outdoors al aire libre (14)
outgoing sociable (I)
oven el horno (7)
over: all — por todas partes (3)
owl el búho (14)
own propio, -a (7)
oxygen el oxígeno (14)

to **pack** hacer la maleta (12)
paella la paella (13)
page la página (1)
painter el pintor, la pintora (11)
palace el palacio (12)
pants los pantalones (I)
pantyhose las pantimedias (I)
paper el papel (I)
   — clip el sujetapapeles, *pl.* los
      sujetapapeles (1)
   sheet of — la hoja de papel (I)
parade el desfile (4)
to **pardon** perdonar (8)
   — me perdone (Ud.) (8)
parents los padres (I)
park el parque (I)
   amusement — el parque de
      diversiones (I)
part: to be a — of formar parte de
   (I)
part *(film, play)* el papel (10)
   to play the — (of) hacer el
      papel (de) (10)
to **participate (in)** participar (en) (2)
party la fiesta (I)
   birthday — la fiesta de cumple-
      años (I, 6)
   costume — la fiesta de disfraces
      (I, 4)
   New Year's Eve — la fiesta de
      fin de año (I, 6)
   surprise — la fiesta de sorpresa
      (I, 6)
to **pass** pasar (I)
passenger el pasajero, la pasajera
   (12)

passport el pasaporte (I)
past:
   half- — y media (I)
   quarter — y cuarto (I)
pastime el pasatiempo (I)
pastry el pastel (I)
path el sendero (14)
patient *adj.* paciente (I)
to **pay** pagar (I)
pea el guisante (I)
peace la paz (11)
peach el durazno (13)
pen el bolígrafo (I)
pencil el lápiz, *pl.* los lápices (I)
   — sharpener el sacapuntas, *pl.*
      los sacapuntas (1)
people la gente (I)
pepper la pimienta (I)
   green — el pimiento verde (13)
   stuffed — el chile relleno (I)
peppery picante (I)
perfume el perfume (8)
period la hora (I)
to **permit** permitir (1)
   it's —ted se permite (8)
person la persona (I)
   a — uno (2)
personal personal (I)
phone el teléfono (I)
   on the — por teléfono (I)
   pay — el teléfono público (8)
   — book la guía telefónica (I)
   — number el número de teléfono
      (I)
photo la foto (I)
photography la fotografía (10)
physical education la educación
   física (I)
physician el médico, la médica (I)
piano el piano (2)
to **pick up** recoger (I, 14)
picnic el picnic (4)
   to have a — hacer un picnic (4)
picture el cuadro (I)
picturesque pintoresco, -a (12)
pie la tarta (13)
pill la pastilla (9)
pilot el/la piloto (12)
pineapple la piña (13)
pink rosado, -a (I)
pistol la pistola (5)
to **pitch a tent** poner una tienda (14)
place el lugar (I)
   — of interest el lugar de interés
      (I)
to **place** poner (I)
plaid a cuadros (3)
plain liso, -a (3)
to **plan** pensar + *inf.* (I); planear (12)

plane el avión, *pl.* los aviones (12)
planet el planeta (11)
plant la planta (I, 14)
plastic el plástico (I, 3)
   (made of) — de plástico (I)
plate el plato (I)
play la obra de teatro (4)
to **play** jugar *(u → ue)* (I)
   to — the part (of) hacer el
      papel (de) (10)
player el jugador, la jugadora (4)
playground el patio de recreo (5)
pleased to meet you mucho gusto;
   encantado, -a (I)
plot el argumento (10)
pocket el bolsillo (3)
   — folder la carpeta (I)
to **point out** indicar (8)
poisonous venenoso, -a (14)
police la policía (I)
   — officer el / la policía (10)
   — station la estación de policía
      (I)
polish: nail — el esmalte de uñas
   (8)
polite (bien) educado, -a (5)
politician el político, la política (11)
politics la política (11)
pollen el polen (9)
to **pollute** contaminar (11)
polluted contaminado, -a (I, 14)
pool la piscina (I)
pork el cerdo (13)
possession la posesión, *pl.* las
   posesiones (7)
post card la tarjeta postal (I)
poster el cartel (I)
post office el correo (I)
pot la olla (14)
potato la papa (I)
   baked — la papa al horno (I)
   French-fried — la papa frita (I)
practical práctico, -a (I)
to **practice** practicar (I)
to **prefer** preferir *(e → ie);* gustar más
   (I)
to **prescribe** recetar (9)
prescription la receta (9)
to **prepare** preparar (I)
pretty bonito, -a (I)
principal *(school)* el director, la directora (1); *adj.* principal (10)
problem el problema (1)
profession la profesión, *pl.* las
   profesiones (11)
program el programa (I)

to **prohibit** prohibir (1)
 it's —ed se prohíbe (1)
projector el proyector (1)
to **protect (oneself)** proteger(se)
 (g →j) (I, 9)
protein la proteína (13)
public público, -a (8)
puck el disco (de hockey) (4)
pumpkin la calabaza (13)
pure puro, -a (I)
purple morado, -a (I)
purse el bolso (3)
to **put** poner (I)
 to — away guardar (3)
 to — on *(clothes)* ponerse (8);
 (make-up) maquillarse (8)
pyramid la pirámide (I)

quarter cuarto, -a (I)
 — past y cuarto (I)
quesadilla la quesadilla (I)
question la pregunta (1)
 to ask a — hacer una pregunta
 (1)
quiet callado, -a (I)
quite bastante (4)
quiz la prueba (1)

racket: tennis — la raqueta de
 tenis (4)
radio *(set)* el radio (7)
raft la balsa (14)
 to go —ing navegar en balsa
 (14)
rain la lluvia (I)
to **rain** llover *(o → ue)* (I)
 it's —ing llueve (I)
raincoat el impermeable (I)
rain forest la selva tropical (I)
rather bastante (I)
razor la máquina de afeitar (8)
reaction la reacción, *pl.* las
 reacciones (9)
to **read** leer (I)
real real (I)
realistic realista (I)
really? ¿de veras?; ¡no me digas! (I)
to **receive** recibir (I)
recipe la receta (13)
to **recommend** recomendar *(e → ie)*
 (12)
to **recycle** reciclar (I, 11)
recycling center el centro de
 reciclaje (I)
red rojo, -a (I)
 —-haired pelirrojo, -a (I)
to **reduce** reducir *(c → zc)* (I, 11)

refrigerator el refrigerador (I)
relative el pariente, la parienta (I, 6)
to **remember** recordar *(o → ue)* (5)
remote control el control remoto
 (7)
to **repair** reparar (7)
repellent el repelente (9)
report el informe (1)
reservation la reservación, *pl.* las
 reservaciones (12)
to **rest** descansar (I)
restaurant el restaurante (I)
restroom los servicios (8)
to **return** regresar; devolver *(o → ue)*
 (I)
review (of) el comentario (sobre)
 (10)
to **review** repasar (1)
rice el arroz (I)
to **ride:**
 to — a bike montar en bicicleta
 (4)
 to — horseback montar a caballo
 (10)
right derecho, -a (I)
 to be — tener razón (I)
 —? ¿verdad? (I)
 — away en seguida (I)
 to the — (of) a la derecha (de)
 (I)
ring el anillo (7)
river el río (11)
roasted asado, -a (13)
to **rob** robar (10)
robot el robot, *pl.* los robots (5)
rock la piedra (14); *(music)* la
 música rock (4)
role el papel (10)
 to play the — (of) hacer el
 papel (de) (10)
romantic movie la película
 romántica (I)
room el cuarto (I); *(hotel)* la
 habitación, las habitaciones
 (12)
rope la cuerda (5)
 to jump — saltar a la cuerda (5)
round redondo, -a (I)
 —-trip ticket el boleto de ida y
 vuelta (12)
to **row** pasear en bote (I)
rowboat el bote (I)
rude maleducado, -a (5)
ruins las ruinas (I)
ruler la regla (I)
to **run** correr (4)

sad triste (I)
sail la vela (14)
salad la ensalada (I)
 fruit — la ensalada de frutas
 (13)
 — bar el bufet de ensaladas (1)
 — dressing la salsa (13)
sale la liquidación, *pl.* las liquidaciones (3)
 to be for — se vende (8)
 to be on — estar en liquidación
 (3)
salesperson el vendedor, la vendedora (3)
salt la sal (I)
salty salado, -a (13)
same mismo, -a (2)
 it's all the — (to me) (me) da
 igual (3)
 the — thing lo mismo (I)
sandbox el cajón, *pl.* los cajones de
 arena (5)
sandwich el sandwich (I); *(Spanish-
style)* el bocadillo (13)
Saturday sábado (I)
 on — el sábado (I)
sauce la salsa (I)
saucer el platillo (I)
sausage el chorizo (13)
to **save** conservar (I, 7); ahorrar (7)
sax(ophone) el saxofón, *pl.* los
 saxofones (2)
to **say** decir (I)
 how do you — ...? ¿cómo se
 dice ...? (I)
 it is said ... se dice (I)
 to — good-by (to) despedirse
 (e → i) (de) (6)
 to — hello decirse "¡Hola!" (6)
 you don't — ! ¡no me digas! (I)
to **scare** dar miedo a (I)
scarf la bufanda (I); el pañuelo (3)
scene la escena (10)
schedule el horario (I)
school la escuela (I); *adj.* escolar
 (1)
 after — después de las clases (I)
 elementary — la escuela
 primaria (5)
science las ciencias (I)
 — fiction la ciencia ficción (I)
scientist el científico, la científica
 (10)
to **score (a goal)** meter (un gol) (4)
screen la pantalla (11)
 big — TV la pantalla gigante (11)

script el guión, *pl.* los guiones (10)
sea el mar (I)
seafood los mariscos (9)
to **search** *(baggage)* registrar (12)
season la estación, *pl.* las estaciones (I)
seat el asiento (1)
seatbelt el cinturón, *pl.* los cinturones de seguridad (12)
second segundo, -a (I)
secretary el secretario, la secretaria (11)
section la sección, *pl.* las secciones (8)
security system el sistema de seguridad (11)
to **see** ver (I)
    let's — a ver (I)
    to — each other verse (6)
seesaw el sube y baja (5)
to **sell** vender (I)
semester el semestre (I)
to **send** enviar (I)
sensationalistic sensacionalista (10)
to **separate** separar (I, 11)
    separated (from) separado, -a (de) (6)
September septiembre (I)
serious serio, -a (I)
to **serve** servir *(e → i)* (I)
to **set** poner (I)
    — the table poner la mesa (I)
seven siete (I)
    — hundred setecientos (I)
seventeen diecisiete (I)
seventh séptimo, -a (I)
seventy setenta (I)
to **sew** coser (14)
    shade la sombra (14)
to **shake hands** darse la mano (6)
shampoo el champú (I)
sharp en punto (I)
sharpener: pencil — el sacapuntas (1)
to **shave** afeitarse (8)
    shaving cream la crema de afeitar (8)
she ella (I)
shelf el estante (7)
shirt la camisa (I)
    T-— la camiseta (I)
shoe el zapato (I)
    high-heeled —s los zapatos de tacón alto (I)
    — store la zapatería (I)
to **shoot fireworks** lanzar fuegos artificiales (6)

to **shop** hacer las compras (8)
shopping:
    to go — ir de compras (I)
    — center el centro comercial (I)
short *(height)* bajo, -a; *(length)* corto, -a (I)
shorts los pantalones cortos (I)
shot la inyección, *pl.* las inyecciones (9)
    to give a — poner una inyección (9)
should deber + *inf.* (I)
show el programa (I)
    game — el programa de concursos (10)
    home shopping — el programa de compras (10)
to **show** *movie or TV program* dar (I); mostrar *(o → ue)* (7); indicar (8)
shower: to take a — ducharse (2)
shrimp el camarón, *pl.* los camarones (13)
shy tímido, -a (5)
sick enfermo, -a (I)
    to feel — sentirse *(e → ie)* mal (I)
silly tonto, -a (I)
silver la plata (7)
    (made of) — de plata (7)
simple sencillo, -a (3)
since desde (que + *verb*) (6)
    it's been *(time)* **—** hace + *(time)* + que (I)
to **sing** cantar (I, 2)
singer el / la cantante (11)
single *(unmarried)* soltero, -a (6); *(room)* individual (12)
sink el fregadero (7)
sir señor (I)
sister la hermana (I)
sister-in-law la cuñada (6)
sitcom la comedia (I)
six seis (I)
    — hundred seiscientos (I)
sixteen dieciséis (I)
sixth sexto, -a (I)
sixty sesenta (I)
size el tamaño (3); *(clothing)* la talla (3); *(shoe)* el número (de zapatos) (3)
skate el patín, *pl.* los patines (4)
to **skate** patinar (I)
    to ice — patinar sobre hielo (4)
ski el esquí, *pl.* los esquíes (4)
    — cap el gorro (I)
to **ski** esquiar (I)

to **skin-dive** bucear (I)
skirt la falda (I)
to **sleep** dormir *(o → ue)* (I)
sleeping bag el saco de dormir (14)
sleepy: to be — tener sueño (I)
sleeve la manga (3)
slide *(photograph)* la diapositiva (1); *(playground)* el tobogán, *pl.* los toboganes (5)
small pequeño, -a (I)
smoke detector el detector de humo (7)
snack *(afternoon)* la merienda (I)
    for a — de merienda (I)
snake la serpiente (I, 14)
sneakers los tenis (I)
to **sneeze** estornudar (9)
snow la nieve (I)
to **snow** nevar *(e → ie)* (I)
    it's —ing nieva (I)
soap el jabón (I)
    — opera la telenovela (I)
soccer el fútbol (I)
social studies las ciencias sociales (I)
sock el calcetín, *pl.* los calcetines (I)
sofa el sofá (I)
soft drink el refresco (I)
solar solar (11)
sold: to be — venderse (8)
some unos, unas (I); alguno (algún), -a (1)
someone, somebody alguien (I, 3)
something algo (I)
    — else algo más (I)
sometimes a veces (I); de vez en cuando (7)
son el hijo (I)
    —s; —s and daughters los hijos (I)
song la canción, *pl.* las canciones (2)
sorry: I'm — lo siento (I)
to **sort** separar (I)
so-so así, así; regular (I)
soup la sopa (I)
sour agrio, -a (13)
souvenir el recuerdo (I)
space el espacio (11)
    — heater el calentador (7)
Spanish español, -a; *(language)* el español (I)

special especial (6)
    daily — el plato del día (I)
    — effects los efectos especiales (10)
spell: how do you — . . . ? ¿cómo se escribe . . . ? (I)
to **spend** gastar (8)
spicy picante (I)
spider la araña (9)
spinach las espinacas (13)
spine *(on plant)* la espina (14)
spoiled *(child)* consentido, -a (5)
spoken: is — se habla (8)
spoon la cuchara (I)
sports los deportes (I)
    — program el programa deportivo (I)
spring la primavera (I)
square cuadrado, -a (I)
squirrel la ardilla (14)
stadium el estadio (I)
stage el escenario (1)
stairs la escalera (8)
stamp el sello (I)
to **stand** soportar (4)
    to — in line hacer fila (1)
stapler la grapadora (1)
to **start** empezar *(e → ie)* (I)
station la estación, *pl.* las estaciones (I)
to **stay** quedarse (I)
    to — in bed quedarse en la cama (I)
    to — healthy mantenerse sano, -a (13)
steak el bistec (I)
stereo el equipo de sonido (I)
steward, stewardess el / la auxiliar de vuelo (12)
stewed guisado, -a (13)
still todavía (I)
sting *(insect)* la picadura (9)
to **sting** *(insect)* picar (9)
stingy tacaño, -a (I)
to **stir** revolver *(o → ue)* (13)
to **stitch** *(surgically)* hacer puntadas (9)
stitches las puntadas (9)
stomach el estómago (I)
    —ache el dolor de estómago (I)
stone la piedra (14)
stopover la escala (12)
stop sign la señal de alto (8)
store la tienda (I)
    clothing — la tienda de ropa (I)
    department — el almacén, *pl.* los almacenes (I)
    discount — la tienda de descuentos (I)

storm la tormenta (10)
story *(of a building)* el piso (I)
stove la estufa (I)
strawberry la fresa (13)
street la calle (I)
striped a rayas (3)
strong fuerte (9)
student el / la estudiante (I)
    — council el consejo estudiantil (2)
to **study** estudiar (I)
stuffed animal el animal de peluche (5)
subject *(in school)* la materia (1)
subway el metro (I)
    — station la estación del metro (I)
successful: to be — tener éxito (10)
sufficient suficiente (7)
sugar el azúcar (I)
to **suggest** sugerir *(e → ie)* (13)
suit el traje (I, 3)
    bathing — el traje de baño (I)
suitcase la maleta (I, 12)
summer el verano (I)
sun el sol (I)
to **sunbathe** tomar el sol (I)
Sunday domingo (I)
    on — el domingo (I)
sunglasses los anteojos de sol (I, 7)
sunny: it's — hace sol (I)
sunrise el amanecer (14)
sunset el atardecer (14)
suntan lotion el bronceador (I)
supermarket el supermercado (I)
to **surf** hacer surf (14)
surfboard la tabla (de surf) (14)
surprise party la fiesta de sorpresa (I, 6)
sweater el suéter (I)
    turtleneck — el suéter de cuello alto (3)
sweatshirt la sudadera (I)
sweatsuit el chandal (3)
sweet dulce (13)
to **swim** nadar (I)
swimming pool la piscina (I)
swing el columpio (5)
symptom el síntoma (9)
synthetic sintético, -a (3)
system el sistema (11)

table la mesa (I)
    to clear the — quitar la mesa (I)
    night — la mesa de noche (7)
    to set the — poner la mesa (I)
tablecloth el mantel (I)

taco el taco (I)
to **take** llevar; sacar; tomar (I)
    to — a bath bañarse (2)
    to — off *(clothes, make-up, etc.)* quitarse (2); *(aircraft)* despegar (12)
    to — out sacar (I)
    to — pictures sacar fotos (I)
    to — a shower ducharse (2)
    to — a walk ir a pasear (I)
to **talk** hablar (I)
    to — to each other hablarse (6)
talk show el programa de entrevistas (I)
tall alto, -a (I)
tape player el tocacintas, *pl.* los tocacintas (7)
tape recorder la grabadora (I)
to **taste** probar *(o → ue)* (I)
tasteless soso, -a (13)
tasty sabroso, -a (I)
taxi el taxi (I)
tea el té (I)
    iced — el té helado (I)
to **teach** enseñar (I)
teacher el profesor, la profesora (I)
team el equipo (2)
technican el técnico, la técnica (11)
technology la tecnología (11)
teddy bear el oso de peluche (5)
teeth las muelas (I); los dientes (2)
telephone el teléfono (I); *see also* **phone**
    — office la oficina telefónica (12)
    video — el teléfono con video (11)
television la tele(visión) (I)
    — set el televisor (7)
    to watch — ver la tele(visión) (I)
to **tell** decir (5)
temple el templo (I)
ten diez (I)
tennis el tenis (I)
    — racket la raqueta de tenis (4)
tent la tienda (de acampar) (14)
    to pitch a — poner una tienda (14)
terrible terrible (I)
test el examen, *pl.* los exámenes (1)
    medical — el análisis, *pl.* los análisis (9)
Thanksgiving el Día de (Acción de) Gracias (6)
thank you gracias (I)

English-Spanish Vocabulary   521

that que (I); ese, esa; (I, 3); aquel, aquella (3)
   isn't — so? ¿verdad?(I)
   — one ése, ésa, (I, 3); aquél, aquélla (3)
   —'s too bad! ¡qué lástima! (I)
   —'s why por eso (I)
the el, la, los, las (I)
theater *(movie)* el cine; el teatro (I)
their su, sus (I); suyo, -a (7)
theirs el suyo, la suya, los suyos, las suyas (7)
them *dir. obj. pron.* los, las; *after prep.* ellos, ellas; *ind. obj. pron.* les (I)
then luego (I)
there allí (I)
   — is / are hay (I)
   — it is allí está (I)
   — used to be había (5)
   — was / were había (5); hubo (10)
   — will be habrá (11)
therefore por eso (I)
these estos, -as (I, 3); *pron.* éstos, -as (3)
they ellos, ellas (I)
thief el ladrón, *pl.* los ladrones; la ladrona (10)
thing la cosa (I)
to **think** creer; pensar *(e → ie)* (I); parecer (que) (7)
   I (don't) — so creo que sí (no) (I)
   to — about pensar en (I)
third tercer, -a (I)
thirsty: to be — tener sed (I)
thirteen trece (I)
thirty treinta (I)
this este, esta (I, 3)
   — one éste, ésta (3)
thorn la espina (14)
those esos, -as (I, 3); aquellos, -as (3); *pron.* ésos, -as; aquéllos, -as (3)
thousand mil (I)
threat la amenaza (I)
three tres (I)
   — hundred trescientos (I)
   —-ring binder la carpeta de argollas (I)
throat la garganta (I)
   sore — el dolor de garganta (I)
   — lozenges las pastillas para la garganta (I)
through por (8)
to **throw out** echar (11)
Thursday jueves (I)
   on — el jueves (I)

ticket el boleto (12)
tidy ordenado, -a (I)
tie la corbata (I, 3)
to **tie** *(in scoring)* empatar (4)
tiger el tigre (I)
tight *(clothing)* apretado, -a (3)
time la hora; el tiempo; la vez (I)
   at the same — a la vez (I)
   at —s a veces (I)
   at what — ¿a qué hora ? (I)
   to have a good / bad — pasarlo bien / mal (I, 4)
   many —s muchas veces (I)
   on — puntualmente (I)
   what — is it? ¿qué hora es? (I)
tired cansado, -a (I)
to a (I)
   in order — para + *inf.* (I)
toast el pan tostado (I)
toaster el tostador (7)
today hoy (I)
   not — hoy no (I)
toe el dedo del pie (I)
to **tolerate** soportar (4)
tomato el tomate (I)
   — soup la sopa de tomate (I)
tomorrow mañana (I)
too también (I); demasiado (I)
toothache el dolor de muelas (I)
toothbrush el cepillo de dientes (8)
toothpaste la pasta dentífrica (I)
top: on — of encima de (I)
torn roto, -a (14)
tortilla la tortilla (I)
tourist el / la turista (12)
   — office la oficina de turismo (12)
town el pueblo (12)
   — square la plaza (I)
toy el juguete (5); *adj.* de juguete (5)
traffic el tráfico (11)
   — light el semáforo (8)
train el tren (I)
   — station la estación del tren (I)
transportation el transporte (8)
to **travel** viajar (12)
travel agency la agencia de viajes (12)
   — agent el/la agente de viajes (12)
traveler el viajero, la viajera (12)
   —'s check el cheque de viajero (12)
tree el árbol (I, 14)
tricycle el triciclo (5)
   to ride a — montar en triciclo (5)

trip el viaje (12)
   short — la excursión, *pl.* las excursiones (12)
truck el camión, *pl.* los camiones (5)
trumpet la trompeta (2)
truth la verdad (5)
to **try** probar *(o → ue)* (I)
   to — on probarse *(o→ ue)* (3)
T-shirt la camiseta (I)
Tuesday martes (I)
   on — el martes (I)
turkey el pavo (6)
to **turn** doblar (8)
   to — off apagar (I, 7)
   to — on encender *(e → ie)* (7)
turnover la empanada (13)
turtle la tortuga (5)
   —neck (sweater) el suéter de cuello alto (3)
tutor el tutor, la tutora (2)
twelve doce (I)
twenty veinte (I)
twice dos veces (I)
twig el palito (14)
twin el gemelo, la gemela (I)
two dos (I)
   — hundred doscientos (I)
type la clase (I)
typical típico, -a (I, 10)

ugly feo, -a (I)
umbrella el paraguas (I)
uncle el tío (I)
uncomfortable incómodo, -a (I)
under(neath) debajo de (I)
to **unfasten** desabrocharse (12)
unfriendly antipático, -a (I)
university la universidad (11)
unmarried soltero, -a (6)
to **unpack** deshacer la maleta (12)
unpleasant antipático, -a (I)
until hasta (I)
to **upset** *(one's stomach)* hacer daño a (13)
us *obj. pron.* nos; *after prep.* nosotros, -as (I)
to **use** usar (I)
usually generalmente (I)

vacation las vacaciones (I)
   to go on — ir de vacaciones (I)
to **vacuum** pasar la aspiradora (I)
vacuum cleaner la aspiradora (I)
Valentine's Day el Día de los Enamorados (6)
valley el valle (14)

VCR la videocasetera (I)
vegetable la verdura (I)
    — **soup** la sopa de verduras (I)
very muy (I)
vest el chaleco (3)
veterinarian el veterinario, la veterinaria (11)
victim la víctima (10)
video el video (4)
    — **game** el videojuego (I)
vinegar el vinagre (13)
violence la violencia (10)
violent violento, -a (10)
violin el violín, *pl.* los violines (2)
virus el virus (9)
to **visit** visitar (I)
vitamin la vitamina (13)
volleyball el vóleibol (I)
to **volunteer** trabajar como voluntario (2)
to **vomit** vomitar (9)
voyage el viaje (12)

waiter, waitress el camarero, la camarera (I)
to **wake up** despertarse *(e → ie)* (2)
to **walk** caminar (5)
walking a pie (I)
wall la pared (1)
wallet la cartera (3)
to **want** querer *(e → ie)* (I)
war la guerra (11)
to **wash** lavar (I)
    — **one's face, hair, etc.** lavarse la cara, el pelo, etc. (2)
washer:
    clothes — la lavadora (7)
    dish— el lavaplatos (7)
to **waste** gastar (11)
watch el reloj (pulsera) (I, 7)
to **watch** ver (I)
water el agua *f.* (I)
    — **pistol** la pistola de agua (5)
    to — **ski** hacer esquí acuático (14)
    — **skiing** el esquí acuático (14)
waterfall las cataratas (I)
watermelon la sandía (13)
we nosotros, -as (I)
to **wear** llevar (I); usar (3)
weather el tiempo (I)
    the — **is nice (bad)** hace buen (mal) tiempo (I)
    — **forecast** el pronóstico del tiempo (I)
    what's the — **like?** ¿qué tiempo hace? (I)

wedding la boda (6)
    — **anniversary** el aniversario (de boda) (6)
Wednesday miércoles (I)
    on — el miércoles (I)
week la semana (I)
weekend el fin de semana (I)
weights las pesas (4)
    to lift — levantar pesas (4)
welcome: you're — de nada (I)
well bien (I); *(to indicate pause)* pues (I)
well-mannered (bien) educado, -a (5)
western la película del oeste (I)
wet mojado, -a (14)
whale la ballena (I, 14)
what ¿qué? (I); lo que (3)
wheelchair la silla de ruedas (9)
when ¿cuándo?; cuando (I)
where? ¿dónde?; donde (I)
    from —? ¿de dónde? (I)
    (to) —? ¿adónde? (I)
whether si (I)
while mientras (8)
white blanco, -a (I)
    in black and — en blanco y negro (I)
who? whom? ¿quién(es)? (I)
why ¿por qué? (I)
    that's — por eso (I)
wife la esposa (6)
wild *(animal)* salvaje (14); *(plant)* silvestre (14)
to **win** ganar (4)
wind el viento (I)
window la ventana (I); *(plane)* la ventanilla (12)
to **windsurf** hacer surf de vela (14)
winter el invierno (I)
with con (I)
    — **me** conmigo (I)
    — **you** contigo (I)
to **withdraw** *(money)* sacar (I)
without sin (2)
wolf el lobo, la loba (I, 14)
woman la mujer (I)
    young — la joven (I)
wonderful fantástico; ¡genial! (I)
wood la madera (I)
    (made of) — de madera (I)
woods el bosque (11)
wool la lana (3)
to **work** trabajar (I); *(machines)* funcionar (7)
worse peor (I)
worst el / la (los / las) peor(es) (I)

worthwhile: it's (not) — (no) vale la pena (I)
wow! ¡vaya! (I)
wrist la muñeca (9)
    —**watch** el reloj pulsera (I, 7)
to **write** escribir (I, 1)
    to — **to each other** escribirse (6)
writer el escritor, la escritora (11)
wrong:
    to be — no tener razón (I)
    what's —? ¿qué tienes? (I)

X-ray la radiografía (9)
    to take an — sacar una radiografía (9)

year el año (I)
    to be . . . —**s old** tener . . . años (I)
    New —**'s Day** el Año Nuevo (6)
    New —**'s Eve** el fin de año (6)
    New —**'s Eve party** la fiesta de fin de año (I)
yearbook el anuario (2)
yellow amarillo, -a (I)
yes sí (I)
yesterday ayer (I)
you *fam.* tú *; formal* usted (Ud.); *pl.* ustedes (Uds.); *dir. obj. pron.* lo, la, los, las; *fam. dir. obj. pron.* te; *ind. obj. pron.* le, les; *fam. after prep.* ti (I)
young *adj.* joven (I)
    —**er** menor, *pl.* menores (I)
    — **lady** la joven (I)
    — **man** el joven (I)
    — **people** los jóvenes (I)
your tu, tus *fam.;* su, sus *formal & pl.* (I); tuyo, -a; suyo, -a (7)
yours *fam.* el tuyo, la tuya, los tuyos, las tuyas; *formal & pl.* el suyo, la suya, los suyos, las suyas (7)
yuck! ¡qué asco! (I)

zero cero (I)
zipper la cremallera (3)
zoo el zoológico (I)

Más práctica y tarea

Aquí tienes una oportunidad adicional de practicar el vocabulario y la gramática de *PASO A PASO 2*. Escribe todas tus respuestas en una hoja aparte.

PASODOBLE

¿Qué tiempo hace? y El mundo hispano (páginas 2–4)

1 **El clima y los meses** Escoge la letra de la respuesta apropiada.

1. Septiembre, octubre y noviembre son los meses de ___.
   a. invierno   **b.** otoño   **c.** verano

2. En Puerto Rico, generalmente ___.
   a. hace frío   **b.** nieva   **c.** hace sol

3. Cuando la temperatura es de 76°F debes llevar ___.
   a. los anteojos de sol   **b.** una bufanda   **c.** un abrigo

4. En invierno en las montañas ___.
   a. hace calor   **b.** llueve mucho   **c.** nieva

5. Marzo, abril y mayo son los meses de ___.
   a. otoño   **b.** Colombia   **c.** primavera

6. ¿Cuál de estos países es una isla?
   a. Cuba   **b.** México   **c.** Nicaragua

(Do Practice Workbook PD-1 and PD-2.)

Características, actividades y el verbo *gustar* (páginas 5–16)

1 **Los fines de semana** ¿Qué les gusta hacer a estas personas los fines de semana? Completa cada frase con la forma apropiada del verbo en el presente.

Ud. ___ música. (escuchar)   *escucha*

1. Elena y Marta ___ ropa. (comprar)
2. Yo ___ en el parque. (patinar)
3. Tú ___ fotos. (sacar)
4. Clara, Pepe y yo ___ vóleibol. (jugar)
5. Uds. ___ la tarea. (hacer)
6. Los hermanos ___ la casa. (arreglar)
7. La señora Guzmán ___ de compras. (ir)
8. Alejandro ___ hamburguesas. (comer)
9. Yo ___ al parque. (ir)

¿Qué tiempo hace? y El mundo hispano (páginas 2–4)

Exercise 1
1. b
2. c
3. a
4. c
5. c
6. a

Características, actividades y el verbo *gustar* (páginas 5–16)

Exercise 1
1. compran
2. patino
3. sacas
4. jugamos
5. hacen
6. arreglan
7. va
8. come
9. voy
10. sacuden
11. vemos
12. pasea
13. lees
14. vivimos

¿Qué tiempo hace? y El mundo hispano (páginas 2–4)

Exercise 2

1. Es deportista.
2. Es trabajadora.
3. Son artísticos.
4. Es perezosa.
5. Es generoso.
6. Son calladas.
7. Es simpática.

Exercise 3

1. A ellos les gusta hacer ejercicio.
2. A ella le gusta comer.
3. A él le gusta escribir cartas.
4. A ti te gusta leer.
5. A mí me gusta hablar.
6. A nosotros nos gusta nadar.
7. A mí me gusta cocinar.
8. A ustedes les gusta comprar ropa.

10. Eduardo y María ___ los muebles. (sacudir)
11. Nosotros ___ videos. (ver)
12. El señor Lugones ___ en bote. (pasear)
13. Tú ___ libros. (leer)
14. Mi familia y yo ___ en el campo. (vivir)

2 **¿Cómo son?** Escoge la palabra apropiada del recuadro *(box)* para cada frase. Sigue el ejemplo.

A Juana le gusta esquiar y hacer cosas nuevas.
Es atrevida.

artísticos	deportista	simpática
atrevida	generoso	trabajadora
calladas	perezosa	

1. A Ramón le gusta jugar béisbol y fútbol americano.
2. Los sábados Julia limpia la casa y hace toda su tarea.
3. A Samuel y a Teresa les gusta dibujar e ir a los museos de arte.
4. A Esperanza sólo le gusta ver la tele.
5. Pedro siempre ayuda a las personas viejas.
6. Gloria y Rebeca prefieren no decir nada en clase.
7. Susi es la persona más popular de la clase.

3 **¿Qué les gusta hacer?** Escoge la frase apropiada del recuadro para describir a estas personas. Sigue el ejemplo.

Josefina va al centro comercial.
A ella le gusta ir de compras.

A ella le gusta comer.	A ustedes les gusta comprar ropa.
A nosotros nos gusta nadar.	A ti te gusta leer.
A ellos les gusta hacer ejercicio.	A mí me gusta cocinar.
A mí me gusta hablar.	A él le gusta escribir cartas.

1. Luis y Toño van al gimnasio.
2. Ceci compra fruta, pan y queso.
3. El señor Castillo va al correo.
4. Tú sacas libros de la biblioteca.
5. Yo hablo mucho por teléfono con mis amigos.
6. Mi amigo y yo vamos a la piscina.
7. Yo preparo postres deliciosos.
8. ¡Tú y Elisa tienen 30 camisetas!

4 **¿Qué hicieron** *(What did they do)* **anoche?** Escribe lo que hicieron anoche tus amigos. Escoge el verbo apropiado en el pretérito. Sigue el ejemplo.

—Benjamín, *¿lavaste* tú los platos? (lavé/lavaste)
—No, *estudié* matemáticas. (estudié/estudio)

1. —¿___ tú y David el bistec? (Cocinamos/Cocinaron)
   —No, nosotros ___ por teléfono. (hablaron/hablamos)

2. —¿___ Anita al zoológico? (Fue/Fui)
   —No, ella ___ en la piscina. (nadó/nadé)

3. —¿___ Esteban y Miguel con sus amigos? (Salen/Salieron)
   —No, los ___ por teléfono. (llamó/llamaron)

4. —¿___ tú el fútbol? (Practicaron/Practicaste)
   —No. Yo ___ fútbol americano. (jugué/jugó)

5. —¿___ Uds. paella? (Comimos/Comieron)
   —No. Nosotros ___ limonada. (bebimos/bebieron)

(Do Practice Workbook PD-3, PD-4, PD-5, PD-6, PD-7, and PD-8.)

Las vacaciones y la casa (páginas 17–25)

1 **Las vacaciones** Estas personas preguntan y hablan sobre sus vacaciones. Escribe lo que hacen. Sigue el ejemplo.

¿Qué prefiere ver Fernando? (la selva)
Prefiere ver la selva.

1. ¿Qué prefiere hacer Beatriz? (tomar el sol)
2. ¿Adónde puedes ir tú? (a Ecuador)
3. ¿Qué podemos hacer nosotros? (esquiar)
4. ¿Qué piensan hacer ustedes? (visitar las ruinas aztecas)
5. ¿Qué quieren hacer los turistas? (comprar recuerdos)

2 **¿Cómo es tu casa?** Escoge la letra de la respuesta apropiada.

1. En nuestro patio hay ___ y plantas.
   a. cuartos   **b.** flores   **c.** teles
2. Veo la tele con mis amigos en ___ .
   a. la sala de estar   **b.** el patio   **c.** la ventana
3. Nuestra ___ está cerca del centro comercial.
   a. puerta   **b.** casa   **c.** mesa
4. Sus vestidos nuevos están en el ___.
   a. guardarropa   **b.** videocasetera   **c.** escritorio

(Do Practice Workbook PD-9 and PD-10.)

Exercise 4
1. Cocinaron, hablamos
2. Fue, nadó
3. Salieron, llamaron
4. Practicaste, jugué
5. Comieron, bebimos

Las vacaciones y la casa (páginas 17–25)
Exercise 1
1. Prefiere tomar el sol.
2. Puedo ir a Ecuador.
3. Pueden esquiar.
4. Pensamos visitar las ruinas aztecas.
5. Quieren comprar recuerdos.

Exercise 2
1. b
2. a
3. b
4. a

Vocabulario para conversar (páginas 30–33)

Exercise 1

1. el reloj
2. el laboratorio
3. el armario
4. la computadora
5. buenas notas
6. el bolso
7. páginas
8. geometría

Exercise 2

1. biología
2. geografía
3. historia
4. francés
5. páginas/lecciones
6. bandera

Exercise 3

1. Luis hace su informe de química todos los jueves.
2. Yo leo mi composición de francés.
3. Nosotros repasamos las lecciones todas las tardes.
4. Mi amiga Julia estudia para el examen de geometría.

Aquí tienes una oportunidad adicional de practicar el vocabulario y la gramática. Escribe todas tus respuestas en una hoja aparte.

Capítulo 1

Vocabulario para conversar (páginas 30–33)

1 **En la escuela** Las clases terminan y algunos estudiantes conversan sobre la escuela. Completa cada frase con la palabra apropiada del recuadro *(box)*.

el armario	buenas notas	geometría	páginas
el bolso	la computadora	el laboratorio	el reloj

1. Son las 14:00 P.M., pero en ___ de la escuela son las 13:45 P.M.
2. En ___ practicamos la química.
3. María no lleva todos sus libros a casa. Los pone en ___.
4. Necesito ___ para escribir mi tarea.
5. Ellos sacaron ___ en todas las materias.
6. Tú llevas los libros a casa en ____.
7. No puedo leer este libro en un día. ¡Hay 200 ___!
8. ¿Ya estudiaron para el examen de ___?

2 **Las clases** Julio y sus amigos conversan sobre sus clases. Completa cada frase con la palabra apropiada.

1. Estudiamos los animales en la clase de ___.
2. Repasamos las ciudades de los países en la clase de ___.
3. Aprendemos sobre el pasado en la clase de ___.
4. Mi profesora de ___ es de París.
5. Hay muchas ___ en tu libro.
6. La ___ de México es de tres colores: verde, blanco y rojo.

3 **¿Qué haces en tus clases?** Luis y Juan le dicen a su prima lo que hacen en su escuela. Escribe frases en el presente con la información de abajo *(below)*.

1. Luis/hacer/su informe de química todos los jueves
2. yo/leer/mi composición de francés
3. nosotros/repasar/las lecciones todas las tardes
4. mi amiga Julia/estudiar/para el examen de geometría

(Do Practice Workbook 1-1 and 1-2.)

Vocabulario para conversar (páginas 34–37)

1 **¿En dónde?** Completa cada frase con la expresión apropiada.

1. Los estudiantes pueden comer en la ___ de la escuela.
2. En el ___ hay muchas verduras.
3. Cuando el director quiere hablar con los estudiantes, todos van al ___.
4. El ___ de todos los países está en la sala de clases.

2 **Mis clases** Escoge la palabra apropiada para cada frase.

1. Los padres de Pedro conocen al ___ de la escuela. (libro/consejero)
2. La oficina del ___ está al lado de mi sala de clases. (director/asiento)
3. Las clases de alemán son más interesantes cuando hay___. (sacapuntas/diapositivas)
4. Los estudiantes hacen ___ en la cafetería escolar. (fila/materia)

(Do Practice Workbook 1-3 and 1-4.)

Gramática en contexto (páginas 42–49)

El verbo *salir* (páginas 43–44)

1 **¿Cuándo?** Ricardo y su familia van a visitar mañana a la abuela. Su mamá y él conversan sobre el horario de cada persona. Completa el siguiente diálogo con la forma apropiada del presente del verbo *salir*.

—Ricardo, ¿a qué hora __1__ mañana de la escuela?
—__2__ a las dos de la tarde, porque tengo examen de geometría.
—Y tu hermana, ¿a qué hora __3__?
—No sé. Creo que ella y sus compañeros __4__ de la clase de álgebra a las 2:30 de la tarde.
—Mmm…
—Papá __5__ de la oficina a las 3:30 mañana.
—Si nosotros __6__ de casa a las tres, podemos llegar a su oficina a las 3:30.
—Entonces vamos a llegar a casa de la abuela a las 4:00 de la tarde.

(Do Practice Workbook 1-5.)

La forma comparativa: *tan...como* (páginas 44–45)

2 **¿Cómo son?** Unos estudiantes comparan las cosas y las personas de su escuela. Completa las frases con *tan* + adjetivo + *como*.

1. La literatura es ___ la historia. (interesante)
2. La geografía es ___ el álgebra. (fácil)
3. La oficina del director es ___ la sala de clases. (grande)
4. El profesor de alemán es ___ la profesora de francés. (simpático)

(Do Practice Workbook 1-6.)

Vocabulario para conversar (páginas 34–37)
Exercise 1
1. cafetería
2. bufet de ensaladas
3. auditorio
4. mapa

Exercise 2
1. consejero
2. director
3. diapositivas
4. fila

Gramática en contexto (páginas 42–49)
Exercise 1
1. sales
2. Salgo
3. sale
4. salen
5. sale
6. salimos

Exercise 2
1. tan interesante como
2. tan fácil como
3. tan grande como
4. tan simpático como

Exercise 3

1. la más aburrida
2. el más difícil
3. la/más interesante
4. la mejor

Exercise 4

1. la
2. los
3. las
4. lo
5. la
6. los

Exercise 5

1. Tienes
2. traen
3. conocemos
4. tienen
5. traigo
6. conoce
7. tienen
8. trae

Repaso: La forma superlativa (página 45)

3 **La mejor** Unos estudiantes comparan las materias que les gustan. Completa las frases con la forma superlativa del adjetivo.

1. La historia es ___ de todas las materias. (aburrida)
2. El examen de álgebra va a ser ___ de todos los exámenes. (difícil)
3. La química es ____ materia ___ de todas. (interesante)
4. La clase de biología es ___ de todas. (mejor)

(Do Practice Workbook 1-7.)

Repaso: El complemento directo: los pronombres *lo, la, los, las* (página 46)

4 **La escuela empieza.** Los padres de Roberto y María quieren ayudarlos. Completa las frases con los pronombres de complemento directo.

1. —¿Escribiste la composición de literatura?
   —Sí, ___ escribí ayer.
2. —¿Ya hizo tu hermano los ejercicios de geometría?
   —No, todavía no ___ hizo.
3. —¿Estudiaron las cuatro páginas de historia?
   —Sí, ___ estudiamos hoy por la mañana.
4. —¿Traes sacapuntas?
   —No, no ___ traigo.
5. —¿Repasó tu hermano la lección de francés?
   —Sí, ___ repasó con su amigo.
6. —¿Tienes los sujetapapeles en tu mochila?
   —No, no ___ tengo.

(Do Practice Workbook 1-8.)

Repaso: Los verbos *tener* y *traer* / El verbo *conocer* (páginas 47–49)

5 **Nuestras materias** Completa cada frase con el presente del verbo.

1. ¿___ tú clases de francés? (tener)
2. Ustedes ___ muchos libros en la mochila. (traer)
3. Nosotros ___ al profesor de historia. (conocer)
4. Ustedes ___ tarea de álgebra. (tener)
5. Yo ___ mi composición de literatura. (traer)
6. Ella ___ Barcelona. (conocer)
7. Ustedes ___ el examen de geometría mañana. (tener)
8. Él ___ el libro sobre la historia del reloj. (traer)

(Do Practice Workbook 1-9 and 1-10.)

CAPÍTULO 2

Vocabulario para conversar (páginas 62–65)

1 **Pati y sus amigos van a una fiesta.** Completa cada frase con la expresión apropiada del recuadro.

a la misma hora	antes de	después de	se cepilla
acostarse	de mal humor	por lo menos	se viste

1. Luis quiere bañarse ___ ir a la fiesta.
2. Pati ___ el pelo.
3. Luis ___ antes de peinarse.
4. Pati y Melisa llegan ___ a la fiesta. Llegan temprano.
5. Luis llega ___ una hora.
6. Pati está ___.
7. Luis baila con Pati. ___ él sabe bailar muy bien.
8. Melisa está cansada y quiere ___ temprano.

2 **Después de la fiesta** Completa cada frase con la expresión apropiada del recuadro. Puedes usar cada una más de una vez.

antes de	hay que	según
después de	mismo	sin

—Ya es tarde. _1_ salir, _2_ llamar a un taxi. ¿Dónde está Luis?
—No lo sé. Podemos llamar al _3_ taxi que tomamos antes.
—_4_ el señor del taxi, él está muy ocupado esta noche.
—Voy a llamar a otro _5_ ponerme el suéter.
—¡Un momento! ¡No podemos irnos _6_ Luis!

(Do Practice Workbook 2-1 and 2-2.)

MÁS PRÁCTICA Y TAREA

Vocabulario para conversar (páginas 62–65)

Exercise 1
1. antes de
2. se cepilla
3. se viste
4. a la misma hora
5. después de
6. de mal humor
7. Por lo menos
8. acostarse

Exercise 2
1. Antes de
2. hay que
3. mismo
4. Según
5. después de/antes de
6. sin

Vocabulario para conversar (páginas 66–69)

Exercise 1

1. cuidar niños
2. repartir
3. ser miembro
4. participar
5. trabajar como voluntario
6. ganar

Exercise 2

1. el coro
2. el saxofón
3. el violín
4. las artes marciales
5. el periódico
6. el anuario

Gramática en contexto (páginas 74–81)

Exercise 1

1. te levantas
2. me levanto
3. se levanta
4. se lava
5. bañarse
6. ducharnos
7. lavarme
8. me cepillo

Vocabulario para conversar (páginas 66–69)

1 **Después de las clases** Completa cada frase con la expresión más apropiada del recuadro.

cuidar niños	participar	ser miembro
ganar	repartir	trabajar como voluntario

1. A mí me gusta ayudar a los niños. Por eso voy a ___ por las tardes.
2. Para ___ los periódicos, prefiero montar en bicicleta.
3. Me gusta hablar con otros estudiantes. Voy a ___ del club de estudiantes.
4. Canto muy bien. Me gustaría ___ en el coro de la escuela.
5. Yo quiero ___ en mi comunidad.
6. Me interesan las computadoras. Voy a ___ mucho dinero.

2 **Actividades extracurriculares** Completa cada frase con las palabras más apropiadas.

1. Los estudiantes cantan en ___. (el coro/la orquesta)
2. Lin prefiere tocar ___, un instrumento de metal grande. (el saxofón/el piano)
3. Consuelo aprende a tocar ___, un instrumento pequeño de madera. (el tambor/el violín)
4. A Vera y a Carlos les gustan los deportes y por eso practican ___. (las canciones/las artes marciales)
5. Nos gusta escribir para ___ de la escuela. (el contrabajo/el periódico)
6. Antes de terminar el año escolar, algunos estudiantes preparan ___. (las clases/el anuario)

(Do Practice Workbook 2-3 and 2-4.)

Gramática en contexto (páginas 74–81)

Los verbos reflexivos (páginas 75–77)

1 **Por la mañana** Pilar y sus amigos hablan sobre lo que hacen antes de ir a la escuela. Completa cada frase con el presente del verbo apropiado.

—Pilar, por la mañana, ¿a qué hora _1_ (dormirse/levantarse) tú?

—A las 6:45. Si duermo bien, _2_ (tocar/levantarse) de buen humor.

—Yo también, pero mi hermano no. Él _3_ (levantarse/correr) de mal humor. Luego, _4_ (depender/lavarse) la cara porque no le gusta _5_ (subir/bañarse) por la mañana.

—A todos en mi familia, nos gusta _6_ (ducharse/abrir) por las mañanas. Tengo el pelo corto, y me gusta _7_ (vestirse/lavarse) el pelo casi todos los días.

—Después de desayunar, yo _8_ (peinarse/cepillarse) los dientes. Llego a la escuela a las 7:45.

2 **¿Cuándo lo haces?** Completa las frases con el presente del verbo.

1. —Julio, ¿cuándo ___? (cepillarse los dientes)
   —Yo ___ después de comer.
2. —Ustedes, ¿cómo ___ para ir a la escuela? (vestirse)
   —Nosotros ___ de pantalones y camiseta.
3. —¿A qué hora ___ ustedes? (levantarse)
   —Nosotros ___ todos los días a la misma hora.

(Do Practice Workbook 2-5 and 2-6.)

Repaso: Verbos con los cambios *o* → *ue, e* → *ie* y *e* → *i* (páginas 78–79)

3 **¿Qué suelen hacer?** Escribe frases en el presente con la información de abajo.

1. ¿a qué hora/acostarse/tus hermanos?
2. ellos/acostarse temprano
3. ¿a qué hora/despertarse/Elisa?
4. ella/despertarse/a las 6:30 de la mañana
5. nosotros/vestirse/antes de desayunar

(Do Practice Workbook 2-7 and 2-8.)

Antes *de* / *después de* + infinitivo (páginas 80–81)

4 **¿Cuándo lo haces?** Escribe frases en el presente con la expresión *antes de* o *después de*.

1. Se cepilla los dientes ___ la cena.
2. Él se ducha ___ peinarse.
3. Tú vas a la piscina ___ salir de clases.
4. Ella hace la cama ___ levantarse.
5. Yo hago la tarea ___ acostarme.

5 **Vacaciones en Puerto Rico** Elena escribe una carta a Juan. Completa cada frase con la expresión apropiada del recuadro.

antes de	después de	me baño	se acuestan
antes de regresar	después de pasear	me despierto	se levantan

Querido Juan:

Estoy en Puerto Rico. Todos los días __1__ temprano sin despertador. Me gusta practicar las artes marciales __2__ desayunar. Luego yo __3__. Mis hermanos __4__ muy tarde, porque todas las noches __5__ muy tarde. __6__ desayunar, vamos a pasear en bote. __7__ vamos a escuchar una banda. ¡Me gusta mucho la música de Puerto Rico! Vamos a ir a San Juan __8__ a casa.

Hasta luego,
Elena

(Do Practice Workbook 2-9 and 2-10.)

Exercise 2
1. te cepillas los dientes, me cepillo los dientes
2. se visten, nos vestimos
3. se levantan, nos levantamos

Exercise 3
1. ¿A qué hora se acuestan tus hermanos?
2. Ellos se acuestan temprano.
3. ¿A qué hora se despierta Elisa?
4. Ella se despierta a las 6:30 de la mañana.
5. Nosotros nos vestimos antes de desayunar.

Exercise 4
1. después de
2. antes de
3. después de
4. después de
5. antes de

Exercise 5
1. me despierto
2. antes de
3. me baño
4. se levantan
5. se acuestan
6. Después de
7. Después de pasear
8. antes de regresar

Más práctica y tarea   533

Vocabulario para conversar (páginas 94–97)

Exercise 1

1. a
2. c
3. b
4. a
5. b
6. c
7. a
8. a

Vocabulario para conversar (páginas 98–103)

Exercise 1

1. los botones
2. la cremallera
3. el cheque
4. el número
5. el catálogo
6. la liquidación
7. la talla
8. el cajero
9. la tarjeta de crédito

Capítulo 3

Vocabulario para conversar (páginas 94–97)

1 **¿Qué ropa te gusta?** Escoge la letra de la respuesta apropiada.

1. Me gusta ponerme ___ en el cuello.
   a. un pañuelo   b. un zapato   c. un chandal
2. Quiero comprar ___ para este invierno.
   a. una zanahoria   b. unos anteojos   c. unos botines
3. Pon el dinero en ___.
   a. la moda   b. la cartera   c. los zapatos
4. Si tienes frío, lleva ___.
   a. el chaquetón   b. el nilón   c. el plástico
5. Alejandro, los pantalones te quedan grandes. Usa ___.
   a. un zapato   b. un cinturón   c. una tela
6. Prefiero la ropa de ___ porque es más cómoda.
   a. traje   b. tacón alto   c. algodón
7. Los pantalones ___ están de moda.
   a. a cuadros   b. de bolso   c. de manga corta
8. Me duelen los pies, por eso prefiero usar ___.
   a. mocasines   b. zapatos de tacón alto c. un suéter de cuello alto

(Do Practice Workbook 3-1 and 3-2.)

Vocabulario para conversar (páginas 98–103)

1 **En la tienda de ropa** ¿Qué necesita Pepe? ¿A quién busca? Escribe las palabras apropiadas para cada frase.

La mujer que vende la ropa.   *la vendedora*

1. Son redondos y pequeños. Los usamos para cerrar una camisa.
2. La usamos para cerrar una falda. Puede ser de plástico o de metal.
3. Quiere pagar con esto. Es de papel y tiene que escribir su nombre.
4. Va a comprar zapatos. Necesita saber esto para ver si le quedan bien.
5. Prefiere estar en casa y mirar esto para escoger la ropa.
6. Cuando la ropa cuesta menos.
7. Para comprar la ropa que le queda necesita saber esto.
8. El hombre que recibe el dinero que paga Pepe.
9. No es ni dinero ni cheque, pero la puedes usar para comprar cosas.

2 **De compras** Ana y Raúl quieren comprar ropa y zapatos. Completa cada frase con la palabra más apropiada.

1. Los pantalones son grandes para Raúl. Le quedan ___. (pequeños/flojos)
2. El traje es muy pequeño para Ana. Le queda ___. (apretado/de moda)
3. Por eso, Ana necesita una ___ más grande. (lana/talla)
4. Raúl prefiere las camisas de ___ larga. (oscura/manga)
5. A Raúl le gustan las camisas de ___. (algodón/tacón alto)
6. También le gusta llevar ___ con los trajes. (corbata/chandal)
7. A Ana no le gustan los colores oscuros; ella prefiere los colores ___. (claros/aprctados)
8. Ellos quieren suéteres de ___ porque hace frío. (lona/lana)
9. Ana prefiere el suéter ___. (de cuello alto/de tacón alto)
10. Raúl va a comprar una corbata ___. (a rayas/en efectivo)

(Do Practice Workbook 3-3 and 3-4.)

Gramática en contexto (páginas 108–115)

Repaso: El pretérito de los verbos regulares (páginas 109–111)

1 **¿Qué compraron?** Ana y Raúl conversan con sus amigos sobre las cosas que compraron. Completa cada frase con el pretérito del verbo.

1. Raúl ___ pantalones. (buscar)
2. Nosotros ___ suéteres de lana. (escoger)
3. Y ustedes, ¿qué ___? (comprar)
4. Ellos ___ con tarjeta de crédito. (pagar)
5. Ella ___ la cartera en el bolso. (guardar)
6. Tú ___ los zapatos. (buscar)
7. Yo ___ una talla más grande. (pedir)
8. ¿Cuánto ___ el traje? (costar)
9. ¿___ ustedes los mocasines? (encontrar)
10. Yo ___ un chandal de algodón. (buscar)
11. Y tú, ¿ ___ el chaquetón? (devolver)
12. Ellos ___ la ropa en su guardarropa. (colgar)

2 **¿Qué hicieron?** Escribe frases en el pretérito con la información de abajo.

1. ellos/acostarse/temprano
2. nosotros/subir/la montana
3. tú/montar/en bicicleta
4. ella/ver/la tele
5. tú/vivir/con tus abuelos

(Do Practice Workbook 3-5, 3-6, and 3-7.)

Exercise 2
1. flojos
2. apretado
3. talla
4. manga
5. algodón
6. corbata
7. claros
8. lana
9. de cuello alto
10. a rayas

Gramática en contexto (páginas 108–115)

Exercise 1
1. buscó
2. escogimos
3. compraron
4. pagaron
5. guardó
6. buscaste
7. pedí
8. costó
9. encontraron
10. busqué
11. devolviste
12. colgaron

Exercise 2
1. Ellos se acostaron temprano.
2. Nosotros subimos la montaña.
3. Tú montaste en bicicleta.
4. Ella vio la tele.
5. Tú viviste con tus abuelos.

Exercise 3

1. este, aquél
2. aquellos, éstos
3. este, aquél
4. aquel, éste
5. esa, aquélla
6. este, aquél
7. aquellos, éstos

Exercise 4

1. tan, como
2. tantos, como
3. tan, como
4. tantas, como
5. tan, como
6. tan, como
7. tantas, como
8. tan, como
9. tan, como
10. tan, como
11. tantos, como
12. tantos, como

Adjetivos y pronombres demostrativos (páginas 112–114)

3 **Leo y sus hermanos van a ir a una fiesta.** Completa cada frase con las formas apropiadas de los adjetivos y pronombres demostrativos. Por ejemplo:

—¿Te gustan ___ botines? (este) —¿Te gustan _estos_ botines?
—No, prefiero ___. (ese) —No, prefiero _ésos_.

1. —¿Te gusta ___ pañuelo? (este)
   —No, prefiero ___. (aquel)
2. —¿Te gustan ___ mocasines? (aquel)
   — No, prefiero ___. (este)
3. —¿Te gusta ___ chaleco? (este)
   —No, prefiero ___. (aquel)
4. —¿Te gusta ___ bolso? (aquel)
   —No, prefiero ___. (este)
5. —¿Te gusta ___ corbata? (ese)
   —No, prefiero ___. (aquel)
6. —¿Te gusta ___ cinturón? (este)
   —No, prefiero ___. (aquel)
7. —¿Te gustan ___ mocasines? (aquel)
   —No, prefiero ___. (este)

(Do Practice Workbook 3-8 and 3-9.)

Los comparativos: *tanto(a)...como* (páginas 114–115)

4 **En la fiesta** Unos amigos conversan. Completa cada frase con la expresión *tan...como* o *tanto(a)/tantos(as)...como*.

Julia reparte ___ periódicos ___ Clara.
Julia reparte tantos periódicos como Clara.

1. María es ___ elegante ___ Susi.
2. Pedro tiene ___ amigos ___ Luisa.
3. La otra orquesta es ___ grande ___ ésta.
4. Isabel tiene ___ tarjetas de crédito ___ Raquel.
5. Esa música es ___ fascinante ___ aquélla.
6. Estos zapatos son ___ cómodos ___ ésos.
7. Lalo tiene ___ gorras ___ Carlos.
8. Meche canta ___ bien ___ Gloria Estefan.
9. Ese chaquetón es ___ caro ___ aquél.
10. Este estudiante es ___ inteligente ___ ése.
11. José toca ___ instrumentos musicales ___ Benjamín.
12. Felipe comió ___ tacos ___ Mariana.

(Do Practice Workbook 3-10.)

Vocabulario para conversar (páginas 128–133)

1 **El campeonato** En la escuela los estudiantes se preparan para participar en un campeonato. Completa las frases con las palabras apropiadas.

1. —Vamos al parque a jugar fútbol.
   —Sí, ahora traigo ___. (el balón/el patín)
2. —El sábado tenemos ___ de fútbol. (el sacapuntas/el partido)
   —Tenemos que ___. (lavar/ganar)
3. —Paco ___ en el partido de ayer. (metió un gol/compró una camisa)
   —Y su equipo ___. (prestó/ganó)
4. —Yo prefiero ___ sobre hielo. (levantar/patinar)
   —Y, ¿tienes ___? (bolos/patines)
5. —Sí, tengo patines porque juego ___ en la escuela. (fútbol/hockey)
   —¡Vaya! ¿Juegas con el equipo de la escuela?
6. —¿Me prestas el bate?
   —Ah, ¿juegas ___? (hockey/béisbol)
7. —Me duelen los brazos.
   —Porque ___ por mucho tiempo. (levantaste pesas/corriste)
8. —Vamos a jugar tenis.
   —Lo siento. No tengo ___. (bate/raqueta)

2 **¿Qué hacen?** Los estudiantes que no participan en el campeonato hacen otras cosas. Escribe frases con la información de abajo.

1. María/montar en bicicleta
2. los estudiantes/correr/en el parque
3. la jugadora de golf/jugar/en el campo de golf
4. nosotros/jugar/bolos
5. tú/usar/el casco en el partido de hockey
6. ustedes/patinar sobre hielo
7. yo/pedir prestado/un guante
8. usted/prestar/sus esquíes a un amigo

(Do Practice Workbook 4-1 and 4-2.)

Vocabulario para conversar (páginas 128–133)

Exercise 1
1. el balón
2. el partido, ganar
3. metió un gol, ganó
4. patinar, patines
5. hockey
6. béisbol
7. levantaste pesas
8. raqueta

Exercise 2
1. María monta en bicicleta.
2. Los estudiantes corren en el parque.
3. La jugadora de golf juega en el campo de golf.
4. Nosotros jugamos bolos.
5. Tú usas el casco en el partido de hockey.
6. Ustedes patinan sobre hielo.
7. Yo pido prestado un guante.
8. Usted prestó sus esquíes a un amigo.

Vocabulario para conversar (páginas 134–139)

Exercise 1

1. disfraces
2. hacer un picnic
3. un desfile
4. una obra de teatro
5. lo pasan bien
6. música rock
7. una exposición
8. videos musicales

Gramática en contexto (páginas 144–149)

Exercise 1

1. fue
2. fuiste
3. fuimos
4. fueron
5. fueron
6. fui

Exercise 2

1. hice
2. pudimos
3. hicieron
4. pudiste
5. hicieron
6. pudo
7. hicimos
8. pudieron

Vocabulario para conversar (páginas 134–139)

1 **Después del campeonato** Los estudiantes preparan una fiesta. Completa cada frase con la expresión apropiada del recuadro.

un desfile	una exposición	lo pasan bien	una obra de teatro
disfraces	hacer un picnic	música rock	videos musicales

1. Casi todos dicen que en una fiesta de ___ se divierten bastante.
2. Susana prefiere ___ en el campo.
3. Hay ___ para los campeones de béisbol en el centro.
4. Martín piensa hacer ___ con algunos actores.
5. Algunos ___ en un concierto.
6. Otros prefieren un grupo de ___.
7. Pilar y Pedro quieren hacer ___ con fotos del campeonato.
8. Julio quiere traer ___ para la fiesta.

(Do Practice Workbook 4-3 and 4-4.)

Gramática en contexto (páginas 144–149)

El pretérito del verbo *ser* (páginas 145–146)

1 **¿Cómo fue?** Completa cada frase con el pretérito del verbo *ser*.

1. El campeonato de vóleibol del año pasado ___ el mejor.
2. Tú ___ miembro de la liga de béisbol.
3. Nosotros ___ los mejores jugadores el año pasado.
4. Ustedes ___ campeones hace dos años.
5. Ustedes ___ voluntarios para dar la fiesta escolar.
6. Yo ___ estudiante de la profesora Mendoza.

(Do Practice Workbook 4-5 and 4-6.)

El pretérito de los verbos *hacer* y *poder* (páginas 146–147)

2 **¿Qué hicieron?** Completa cada frase con el pretérito del verbo *hacer* o *poder*.

1. Yo ___ la tarea.
2. Nosotros no ___ ver el campeonato.
3. Ellos ___ la cena.
4. Tú ___ ver el campeonato en la televisión.
5. Ustedes ___ un rompecabezas.
6. Ella ___ ir al concierto de música rock.
7. Nosotros ___ un cartel para la exposición.
8. Mis primos ___ jugar damas.

3 **En el periódico** Pilar escribió sobre el campeonato para el periódico de la escuela. Completa cada frase con el verbo apropiado del pretérito del recuadro.

fueron	hice	hizo	pudieron	pudiste
fui	hicieron	pude	pudimos	tuvieron

LOS DEPORTES

El sábado pasado yo __1__ al campeonato de deportes de la escuela. No todos __2__ tiempo de ir a los partidos. Algunos compañeros no __3__ ir, porque tenían exámenes. Pero, ¡todos fueron a la fiesta de disfraces! Nadie se aburrió.

Los partidos __4__ muy interesantes. __5__ muy buen tiempo.

Yo __6__ sacar muchas fotos bastante divertidas. Luego yo __7__ una exposición de las fotos. Si tú no __8__ verla durante la fiesta, la puedes ver el viernes en la cafetería de la escuela.

A los miembros del equipo de béisbol les __9__ un desfile. Todos nosotros __10__ ver el desfile antes de ir a la fiesta.

¡Todos lo pasamos bien!

(Do Practice Workbook 4-7 and 4-8.)

Repaso: El verbo *saber* (páginas 148–149)

4 *¿Saber o conocer?* Completa cada frase con el verbo apropiado. Usa el presente del verbo.

1. José no ___ dónde está el rompecabezas. (saber/conocer)
2. Yo no ___ jugar golf. (saber/conocer)
3. Nosotros ___ a los actores de esa obra de teatro. (saber/conocer)
4. Tú no ___ al entrenador. (saber/conocer)
5. Uds. ___ jugar tenis. (saber/conocer)

(Do Practice Workbook 4-9.)

El pretérito de los verbos reflexivos (página 149)

5 *¿Qué hicieron ayer?* Escribe frases completas con la información de abajo. Usa el pretérito de los verbo reflexivos.

1. nosotros/levantarse/ayer a las siete de la mañana
2. el jugador de hockey/probarse/el casco nuevo
3. tú/aburrirse/en el entrenamiento
4. yo/quedarse/en casa a ver el partido
5. ellos/lastimarse/en el partido de fútbol americano
6. nosotros/ducharse/después del entrenamiento

(Do Practice Workbook 4-10.)

Exercise 3
1. fui
2. tuvieron
3. pudieron
4. fueron
5. Hizo
6. pude
7. hice
8. pudiste
9. hicieron
10. pudimos

Exercise 4
1. sabe
2. sé
3. conocemos
4. conoces
5. saben

Exercise 5
1. Nosotros nos levantamos ayer a las siete de la mañana.
2. El jugador de hockey se probó el casco nuevo.
3. Tú te aburriste en el entrenamiento.
4. Yo me quedé en casa a ver el partido.
5. Ellos se lastimaron en el partido de fútbol americano.
6. Nosotros nos duchamos después del entrenamiento.

CAPÍTULO 5

Vocabulario para conversar (páginas 162–165)

1 **Cuando era niña** La abuela de Lupita escribe una carta sobre lo que ella hacía cuando era niña. Completa cada frase con la expresión apropiada del recuadro.

a la cuerda	los bloques	niña	de peluche	tren
bien educada	las muñecas	los peces	tortuga	triciclo

Querida Lupita:

Cuando yo era __1__ , me gustaba jugar con __2__ , y saltar __3__ . Tenía muchos animales __4__ . Creo que era obediente. Mi mamá me decía que tenía que ser __5__ . En la casa también teníamos animales. Me gustaba mirar __6__ y jugar con la __7__ . Me gustaba montar en bicicleta y a mi hermano le gustaba montar en __8__ . A veces él jugaba con su __9__ . También nos gustaba hacer casas con __10__ . Tú y tu hermano, ¿son obedientes?

(Do Practice Workbook 5-1 and 5-2.)

Vocabulario para conversar (páginas 166–169)

1 **Yo también** Lupita también le escribe a su abuela una carta sobre lo que ella hacía cuando era niña. Completa cada frase con la expresión apropiada del recuadro.

cajón de arena	dinosaurio	osos
camiones	juguetes	patio de recreo

Querida abuelita:

Cuando yo era niña, me gustaba jugar con toda clase de __1__ . Mi animal favorito era un __2__ de juguete. Yo también coleccionaba __3__ de peluche. A mí me gusta jugar con mi hermano pequeño. A él le gustaría tener un coche como Papá. Por eso, él juega con sus __4__ . Es divertido ir con él al __5__ . A él le gusta jugar en el __6__ . ¡Claro que sí somos muy obedientes!

2 En el patio de recreo Después de las clases, algunos estudiantes cuidan niños. Escribe la letra de la respuesta apropiada.

1. En ___ sólo pueden jugar dos niños.
   a. el robot   **b.** el sube y baja   **c.** el triciclo
2. En el patio de recreo de la escuela tenemos ___.
   a. un carrusel   **b.** un bloque   **c.** un oso de peluche
3. Nos gustaba poner agua en ___.
   a. la cuerda   **b.** las pistolas de agua   **c.** el columpio
4. De pequeña, mi hermana no obedecía a mis padres. Ella era ___.
   a. desobediente   **b.** grande   **c.** alta
5. A mi abuelo le gustaba ___ tarjetas de animales.
   a. montar en triciclo   **b.** saltar a la cuerda   **c.** coleccionar
6. En la guardería infantil me ___. Era travieso.
   a. portaba mal   **b.** bañaba   **c.** lloraba

(Do Practice Workbook 5-3 and 5-4.)

Gramática en contexto (páginas 174–181)

El imperfecto de los verbos que terminan en *-ar* (páginas 175–176)

1 ¿Cómo te portabas? Escribe frases en el imperfecto con la información de abajo.

1. tú/cantar/en el coro de la escuela
2. yo/portarse bien/los fines de semana
3. mi padre/tocar/un instrumento musical cuando era niño
4. nosotros/usar/pantalones de tela sintética
5. mis hermanos/tomar/el autobús para ir a la escuela
6. ustedes/tocar/en la orquesta

(Do Practice Workbook 5-5.)

El imperfecto de los verbos que terminan en *-er* e *-ir* (páginas 177–178)

2 ¿Qué hacían? Completa las frases con el imperfecto del verbo.

1. Él ___ hacer los crucigramas. (saber)
2. Nosotros ___ con los abuelos en el campo. (vivir)
3. Ellos ___ en las fiestas escolares. (divertirse)
4. Tú ___ muchos dulces. (comer)
5. Yo ___ a mi abuela su muñeca. (pedir)
6. Ellos ___ leer muy bien. (poder)
7. Ustedes ___ al árbol. (subir)
8. Ella ___ muñecas de papel. (hacer)

(Do Practice Workbook 5-6 and 5-7.)

Exercise 2
1. b
2. a
3. b
4. a
5. c
6. a

Gramática en contexto (páginas 174–181)
Exercise 1
1. Tú cantabas en el coro de la escuela.
2. Yo me portaba bien los fines de semana.
3. Mi padre tocaba un instrumento musical cuando era niño.
4. Nosotros usábamos pantalones de tela sintética.
5. Mis hermanos tomaban el autobús para ir a la escuela.
6. Ustedes tocaban en la orquesta.

Exercise 2
1. sabía
2. vivíamos
3. se divertían
4. comías
5. pedía
6. podían
7. subían
0. hacía

Exercise 3

1. iba
2. eran
3. ibas
4. era, era
5. eran, iban
6. iba
7. era
8. iban
9. éramos
10. iban
11. iba
12. era

Exercise 4

1. caminaba
2. ponía
3. teníamos
4. gustaba
5. hacían
6. tocaban
7. jugaban
8. quería
9. tomaba
10. saltabas

Exercise 5

1. montábamos
2. mentía
3. obedecíamos
4. tenían
5. se peleaban
6. hacías

El imperfecto de los verbos *ir* y *ser* (páginas 179–180)

3 *¿Ir o ser?* Completa cada frase con el imperfecto del verbo *ir* o del verbo *ser.*

1. A veces Margarita ___ al centro comercial.
2. Ustedes ___ muy pequeños, cuando llegó el tío Mario de Perú.
3. Tú ___ a la escuela a las siete todas las mañanas.
4. Mi hermana ___ muy obediente cuando ___ pequeña.
5. Cuando mis abuelos ___ niños, ___ a la escuela a pie.
6. Él ___ al parque todos los días para jugar fútbol americano.
7. Un niño en mi clase ___ muy maleducado.
8. Mis primos ___ al gimnasio cerca de casa.
9. Nosotros ___ muy traviesos.
10. Ellas ___ al cine todos los sábados.
11. Usted ___ a menudo al restaurante mexicano.
12. Yo ___ impaciente, pero ahora soy muy paciente.

4 **Cuando éramos niños...** Completa cada frase con el imperfecto del verbo.

1. Muchas veces, la gente ___ largas distancias para ir a la escuela. (caminar)
2. Generalmente, yo ___ la mesa antes de comer. (poner)
3. A menudo nosotros ___ que lavar los platos. (tener)
4. A mi hermana siempre le ___ hacer picnics en el campo. (gustar)
5. Y tus amigos, ¿qué ___? (hacer)
6. Ustedes ___ en la orquesta escolar. (tocar)
7. Todos los días, ellos ___ con los vecinos. (jugar)
8. Nicolás nunca ___ patinar solo. (querer)
9. ¿Ud. ___ limonada cuando era niño? (tomar)
10. Tú ___ a la cuerda con tus amigos. (saltar)

5 **Lo que hacíamos** Completa cada frase con el imperfecto del verbo que mejor corresponda.

hacer	montar	pelearse
mentir	obedecer	tener

1. Nosotros ___ en triciclo cuando éramos pequeños.
2. Algunas veces mi prima ___ cuando era niña. Era muy traviesa.
3. Nosotros siempre ___ a nuestros padres.
4. Ellos ___ que hacer la tarea antes de jugar.
5. A veces mis hermanos ___, pero ahora son amigos.
6. ¿Qué ___ tú de pequeño?

(Do Practice Workbook 5-8 and 5-9.)

CAPÍTULO 6

Vocabulario para conversar (páginas 194–197)

1 **El cumpleaños** Hay una reunión familiar para celebrar el cumpleaños del abuelo. Completa cada frase con la expresión apropiada del recuadro.

especial	invitó	regalan	separados
está soltero	un pastel	se abrazan	velas

1. La abuela ___ a toda la familia a la fiesta de cumpleaños.
2. Es una celebración ___ para el abuelo.
3. Todos ___ cuando llegan.
4. Mamá trajo ___ a la reunión.
5. Mi hermano puso en el pastel 85 ___.
6. El tío Alex todavía ___. Llega solo.
7. Mis primos le ___ al abuelo una videocasetera.
8. Mis tíos están ___; ya no viven en la misma casa.

2 **En las celebraciones** Escoge la(s) palabra(s) apropiada(s) del recuadro para cada definición.

bisabuelo	cuñado	despedirse	familiar	invitar
boda	darse la mano	estar muerto	graduación	sobrina

1. Celebramos esto después de terminar la escuela secundaria.
2. Cuando dos personas quieren casarse, celebran esto.
3. Cuando te presentan a alguien, generalmente hay que hacer esto.
4. Cuando dices "Adiós."
5. El esposo de tu hermana.
6. La hija de tu hermano.
7. El papá de tu abuelo.
8. Que es de la familia.
9. Lo que haces cuando quieres dar una fiesta.
10. Cuando una persona ya no vive.

(Do Practice Workbook 6-1 and 6-2.)

Vocabulario para conversar (páginas 194–197)

Exercise 1
1. invitó
2. especial
3. se abrazan
4. un pastel
5. velas
6. está soltero
7. regalan
8. separados

Exercise 2
1. graduación
2. boda
3. darse la mano
4. despedirse
5. cuñado
6. sobrina
7. bisabuelo
8. familiar
9. invitar
10. estar muerto

Vocabulario para conversar (páginas 198–203)

Exercise 1

1. Día de la Madre
2. Día de la Independencia
3. la invitación
4. bailes
5. fuegos artificiales

Gramática en contexto (páginas 208–213)

Exercise 1

1. pedimos
2. pediste
3. pidieron
4. pedí
5. pidió
6. pidieron

Exercise 2

1. dieron
2. dio
3. dieron
4. dimos
5. dieron
6. di

Vocabulario para conversar (páginas 198–203)

1 **¿Cómo lo celebras?** Escribe la palabra apropiada para completar la frase.

1. El ___ se celebra el segundo domingo de mayo. (Día de la Madre/cumpleaños)
2. El 4 de julio se celebra el ___. (Año Nuevo/Día de la Independencia)
3. Quiero saber a qué hora empieza la fiesta. ¿Dónde está ___? (la vela/la invitación)
4. Los ___ siempre son divertidos si hay música buena. (bailes/muñecos)
5. El 4 de julio lanzan muchos ___. (animales de peluche/fuegos artificiales)

(Do Practice Workbook 6-3 and 6-4.)

Gramática en contexto (páginas 208–213)

El pretérito de los verbos con el cambio *e →i* (páginas 209–211)

1 **Una fiesta de sorpresa** Completa cada frase con la forma apropiada del pretérito del verbo *pedir.*

1. Nosotros les ___ música para bailar.
2. Tú ___ comida para tu fiesta.
3. Ellos ___ unos carteles.
4. Yo ___ pasteles.
5. Ella ___ un regalo de Luis.
6. Ustedes ___ limonadas.

(Do Practice Workbook 6-5, 6-6, and 6-7.)

El pretérito del verbo *dar* (páginas 211–212)

2 **¿Qué le diste?** Completa cada frase con la forma apropiada del pretérito del verbo *dar.*

1. Mis padres me ___ una bicicleta para mi cumpleaños.
2. Pilar le ___ una invitación a Ramón.
3. Ellos nos ___ pastel y sandwiches en su fiesta.
4. Nosotros ___ una fiesta de sorpresa. ¡Qué divertido!
5. Ustedes ___ una fiesta para celebrar su aniversario.
6. Yo le ___ un regalo a mi amiga.

(Do Practice Workbook 6-8.)

Otros usos del imperfecto (página 212)

3 **Antes...** Completa cada frase con el imperfecto del verbo que mejor corresponda.

celebrar	haber	ser	tener
charlar	llegar	servir	vivir

Cuando ellos _tenían_ la fiesta, _había_ mucha gente.

1. La casa de campo ___ muy grande.
2. Mis abuelos ___ el aniversario de su boda cada año.
3. Mi tía ___ una espléndida cena.
4. Los parientes ___ a felicitar a los abuelos.
5. Todos nosotros ___ hasta muy tarde en la fiesta.
6. Todavía ___ gente en la fiesta a las dos de la mañana.
7. Yo ___ tres años cuando me regalaron un perrito.
8. Mi amigo y yo ___ en la misma calle cuando éramos pequeños.

(Do Practice Workbook 6-9.)

Los verbos reflexivos recíprocos (página 213)

4 **¿Qué se hacen?** Juanita charla con Luis sobre lo que hacen en su país en las fiestas. Completa cada frase con el presente del verbo reflexivo recíproco.

1. Cuando llegamos a una fiesta, nosotros ___. (abrazarse)
2. Todos los parientes ___. (saludarse)
3. Si no podemos ir a una fiesta, ___ por teléfono. (hablarse)
4. Los primos y los cuñados ___ para dar las fiestas. (ayudarse)
5. Nosotros casi nunca ___. (pelearse)
6. Algunas veces ___ cuando no nos podemos ver. (escribirse)

5 **¡Más práctica!** Escribe frases en el pretérito o en el imperfecto, según corresponda, con la siguiente información.

yo/lastimarse/una pierna en un partido de básquetbol (ayer)
Yo me lastimé una pierna en un partido de básquetbol.

1. nosotros/encontrarse/con nuestros primos en la fiesta de sorpresa (ayer)
2. ustedes/charlar/sobre la celebración del Día de los Enamorados (antes)
3. yo/felicitar/a mis abuelos en su aniversario de boda (ayer)
4. mi primo/graduarse (ayer)
5. tú/enviar/ una invitación a tu amiga cada año (antes)
6. su mamá siempre/encender/las velas del pastel (antes)

(Do Practice Workbook 6-10.)

Exercise 3
1. era
2. celebraban
3. servía
4. llegaban
5. charlábamos
6. había
7. tenía
8. vivíamos

Exercise 4
1. nos abrazamos
2. se saludan
3. nos hablamos
4. se ayudan
5. nos peleamos
6. nos escribimos

Exercise 5
1. Nosotros nos encontramos con nuestros primos en la fiesta de sorpresa.
2. Ustedes charlaban sobre la celebración del Día de los Enamorados.
3. Yo felicité a mis abuelos en su aniversario de boda.
4. Mi primo se graduó.
5. Tú enviabas una invitación a tu amiga cada año.
6. Su mamá siempre encendía las velas del pastel.

Vocabulario para conversar (páginas 226–229)

Exercise 1

1. el collar
2. el anillo
3. el televisor
4. el secador de pelo
5. las llaves
6. el tocacintas
7. los lentes de contacto
8. el peine
9. el carnet de identidad
10. el oro

Exercise 2

1. plata
2. televisor
3. radio
4. collar
5. anteojos
6. llave

CAPÍTULO 7

Vocabulario para conversar (páginas 226–229)

1 **¿Sabes qué cosa es?** Escoge la expresión apropiada del recuadro para cada frase.

el anillo	las llaves	el secador de pelo
el carnet de identidad	el oro	el televisor
el collar	el peine	el tocacintas
los lentes de contacto		

1. Lo pones en el cuello.
2. Lo pones en el dedo.
3. Puedes ver tus programas favoritos en esto.
4. Lo usas para secarte el pelo.
5. Con ellas, abres las puertas de tu casa.
6. Puedes usar esto para escuchar música.
7. Los usas para ver mejor.
8. Te peinas con esto todos los días.
9. Es una tarjeta que dice quién eres.
10. Un metal muy caro y de color amarillo.

2 **¿Qué cosa es?** Completa cada frase con la palabra que mejor corresponda.

1. —¿De qué es tu anillo?
   —Mi anillo es de ___. (plata/cuero)
2. —¿Tienes ___ en tu cuarto? (televisor/arroz)
   —Sí. Hace muchos años que lo tengo.
3. —¿Puedes escuchar música en tu cuarto?
   —¡Claro! Tengo un ___ que me regaló mi hermano. (llavero/radio)
4. —¿Qué llevas en el cuello?
   —Es mi ___ de plata. (pulsera/collar)
5. —¿No puedes ver bien?
   —No, necesito ___. (anillos/anteojos)
6. —No puedo abrir la puerta.
   —¿Dónde dejaste tu ___? (llave/moneda)

(Do Practice Workbook 7-1 and 7-2.)

Vocabulario para conversar (páginas 230–235)

❶ **¿Para qué los usamos?** Pedro le explica a su hermana pequeña para qué usamos las cosas de la casa. Escoge la letra de la respuesta apropiada.

1. Necesitamos ___ en caso de incendio.
a. despertador
b. reloj
c. extinguidor de incendios

2. Lavamos los platos en el ___.
a. control remoto
b. cuarto
c. fregadero

3. En invierno usamos la ___.
a. calefacción central
b. moneda
c. cadena

4. Puedes poner tus cosas en el ___.
a. estante
b. calentador
c. tocacintas

5. Cuando hace calor, puedes usar el ___.
a. detector de incendios
b. ventilador
c. fregadero

6. Por la noche enciendes el ___ para ver mejor.
a. microondas
b. incendio
c. bombillo

7. Si la ropa está sucia, la lavas en la ___.
a. lavadora
b. mesa de noche
c. pila

8. Usamos el ___ en el verano.
a. calentador
b. aire acondicionado
c. llavero

(Do Practice Workbook 7-3 and 7-4.)

Gramática en contexto (páginas 240–247)

Los adjetivos posesivos (páginas 241–242)

❶ **Anuncios por la radio** Pedro escucha algunos anuncios por la radio. Completa cada frase con el adjetivo posesivo apropiado. Sigue el ejemplo.

"<u>Nosotros</u> pensamos que *nuestro* programa de radio ¡es el mejor! <u>Usted</u> no puede escuchar tan buenas noticias como las nuestras por _1_ tele."

"De noche, <u>tú</u> puedes usar _2_ linterna. Compra las linternas Luz."

"¡Qué <u>voy</u> a hacer! _3_ lavadora ya no funciona."

"<u>Luis</u> compró zapatos muy buenos. _4_ zapatos son de nuestra tienda El Calzado Elegante."

❷ Ahora usa el adjetivo posesivo apropiado después del objeto.

"<u>Nosotros</u> pensamos que el programa de radio _1_ ¡es el mejor! <u>Usted</u> no puede escuchar tan buenas noticias como las nuestras en la tele _2_."

"De noche, <u>tú</u> puedes usar la linterna _3_. Compra las linternas Luz."

"¡Qué <u>voy</u> a hacer! La lavadora _4_ ya no funciona."

"<u>Luis</u> compró zapatos muy buenos. Los zapatos _5_ son de nuestra tienda El Calzado Elegante."

(Do Practice Workbook 7-5.)

Vocabulario para conversar (páginas 230–235)
Exercise 1
1. c
2. c
3. a
4. a
5. b
6. c
7. a
8. b

Gramática en contexto (páginas 240–247)
Exercise 1
1. su
2. tu
3. Mi
4. Sus

Exercise 2
1. nuestro
2. suya
3. tuya
4. mía
5. suyos

Exercise 3

1. suyas
2. tuyo
3. suyo
4. nuestra
5. suyas

Exercise 4

1. suyas
2. tuyo
3. suya
4. tuyas

Exercise 5

1. es
2. son
3. es
4. soy
5. somos
6. eres

Los pronombres posesivos (páginas 243–245)

3 **¡Es mío!** Completa cada frase con el pronombre posesivo apropiado. Sigue el ejemplo.

—¿De quién es este tocacintas?
—Es _mío_. (de mí)

—¿De quién son estas monedas?
—Son __1__. (de ellos)
—¿De quién es este tostador?
—Es __2__. (de ti)
—¿De quién es este reloj pulsera?
—Es __3__. (de ella)
—¿De quién es esta lavadora?
—Es __4__. (de nosotros)
—¿De quién son estas llaves?
—Son __5__. (de usted)

4 **Tienes las tuyas.** Completa cada frase con el pronombre posesivo apropiado. Sigue el ejemplo.

—¿Dónde está el secador de pelo de Luis?
—El _suyo_ está en su cuarto.

—No encuentro nuestras monedas.
—Aquí están las __1__.
—Éste es mi llavero, ¿verdad?
—Sí, el __2__ es negro. El mío es marrón.
—Ésta es la pulsera de mamá, ¿verdad?
—No, la __3__ es de oro.
—Estas cadenas de oro son mías, ¿verdad?
—¡No, las __4__ son pequeñas!

(Do Practice Workbook 7-6 and 7-7.)

Repaso: Los usos del verbo *ser* (páginas 246–247)

5 **Mi amigo es de Buenos Aires.** Luis escribe una carta a su amigo en Buenos Aires. Completa las frases con el presente del verbo *ser*.

Querido Juan:

Mi escuela __1__ muy grande. Mis amigos __2__ muy divertidos y jugamos hockey todos los sábados. El próximo partido __3__ el sábado. Yo __4__ tan atrevido como ellos. Nosotros __5__ buenos amigos. Pero tú, ¡__6__ mi mejor amigo!

Un abrazo,
Luis

(Do Practice Workbook 7-8.)

CAPÍTULO 8

Vocabulario para conversar (páginas 260–265)

1 **¿Dónde queda?** Elena y su prima van en coche al centro. Completa cada frase con la palabra apropiada del recuadro.

buzón	hacer las compras	la pescadería
el cruce	una heladería	semáforo
la dirección	la panadería	la verdulería

—Hace calor. ¿Por qué no compramos un helado?

—Mmm… ¡Buena idea! ¿Dónde hay _1_ ?

—Tenemos que pasar _2_ de las calles Cinco y Sol.

—¡Ah! Queda cerca del _3_ donde enviamos las cartas.

—Podemos enviar la carta que escribiste ayer. ¿Ya escribiste _4_ en la carta?

—Sí, ya lo hice. ¡Cuidado! La luz del _5_ está roja.

—Mira, allí podemos comprar pan.

—Sí, en _6_ . Ahora la luz está verde.

—No hay nada en el refrigerador. Tenemos que _7_ .

—Vamos a comprar algunas verduras en _8_ .

—Yo quiero comer pescado. Vamos también a _9_ .

—¡Lo vamos a pasar bien! Ya llegamos a la heladería…

2 **¡Vamos al cine en el centro!** Más tarde, Elena y su prima quieren ir al cine. Completa cada frase con la palabra que mejor corresponda.

—Hay una película muy buena. Vamos al _1_ . (centro/semáforo)

—¿Vamos al cine que está cerca de _2_ ? (la estación de bomberos/la dirección)

—No, el que está al lado de donde venden flores.

—¡Ah! _3_ de la amiga de tu mamá, ¿verdad? (La carretera/La floristería)

—Sí, ésa es. Pero creo que mi papá va a necesitar el coche.

—Entonces vamos a usar _4_ . (el transporte público/el teléfono público)

—Sí, está bien. ¿Sabes? No sé a qué hora empieza la película.

—Vamos a comprar un periódico en _5_ . (el quiosco/el buzón)

—¿Dónde hay uno cerca?

—Hay uno a 300 _6_ de aquí. (kilómetros/metros)

(Do Practice Workbook 8-1 and 8-2.)

Vocabulario para conversar (páginas 260–265)

Exercise 1
1. una heladería
2. el cruce
3. buzón
4. la dirección
5. semáforo
6. la panadería
7. hacer las compras
8. la verdulería
9. la pescadería

Exercise 2
1. centro
2. la estación de bomberos
3. La floristería
4. el transporte público
5. el quiosco
6. metros

Vocabulario para conversar (páginas 266–271)

Exercise 1

1. al fondo
2. te pones
3. mientras
4. crema de afeitar
5. pasta dentífrica
6. seda dental
7. la escalera mecánica
8. la caja
9. una venda

Gramática en contexto (páginas 276–283)

Exercise 1

1. La ropa está limpia.
2. Nosotros estamos al fondo, en la sección de ropa para niños.
3. Yo estoy comprando desodorante y crema de afeitar.
4. Tú estás al lado del ascensor.
5. Las joyas están en ese mostrador.
6. Ustedes están en la sección de ropa para caballeros.

Exercise 2

1. Usted está comprándolos.
2. Yo estoy colgándolas.
3. Mamá está bañándolo.
4. Ustedes están buscándola.

Vocabulario para conversar (páginas 266–271)

 En el almacén Leo y Lola van de compras. Completa cada frase con la palabra apropiada del recuadro.

al fondo	crema de afeitar	seda dental
la caja	la escalera mecánica	te pones
pasta dentífrica	mientras	una venda

1. Los servicios no están aquí, están ___.
2. ¿Por qué no ___ ese chaquetón para ver si te gusta?
3. Yo voy a ver las faldas ___ tú ves los chandales.
4. Si te vas a afeitar, ¿por qué no compras ___?
5. No me cepillé los dientes porque no tengo ___.
6. ¿Por qué no compras un cepillo de dientes y también ___?
7. Estoy cansada. Vamos a subir al tercer piso por ___.
8. Vamos a pagar las compras. ¿Dónde está ___?
9. ¡Ay! Me lastimé el pie. ¿Por qué no compras ___?

(Do Practice Workbook 8-3 and 8-4.)

Gramática en contexto (páginas 276–283)

Repaso: Los usos de *estar* (página 277)

 ¿Dónde está? Escribe frases con la información de abajo. Usa el presente del verbo *estar.*

el mostrador/estar/en el primer piso
El mostrador está en el primer piso.

1. la ropa/estar/limpia
2. nosotros/estar/al fondo, en la sección de ropa para niños
3. yo/estar/comprando desodorante y crema de afeitar
4. tú/estar/al lado del ascensor
5. las joyas/estar/en ese mostrador
6. ustedes/estar/en la sección de ropa para caballeros

(Do Practice Workbook 8-5.)

Repaso: El presente progresivo (páginas 278–280)

2 **¿Quién está haciéndolo?** Escribe frases en el presente progresivo y usa *lo, la, los* o *las* después del verbo. Sigue el ejemplo.

nosotros/cruzar la calle
Nosotros estamos cruzándola.

1. usted/comprar los sombreros
2. yo/colgar las corbatas
3. Mamá/bañar al niño
4. ustedes/buscar la seda dental

(Do Practice Workbook 8-6 and 8-7.)

Construcciones negativas (páginas 280–281)

 3 **Alguien compró esmalte de uñas.** Completa cada frase con la palabra apropiada del recuadro.

algo	alguna	ningún	nunca
alguien	nada	ninguna	siempre
algún	nadie	ninguno	tampoco

—¿ 1 te afeitas por la noche?
—No, 2 me afeito por la noche.
—¿Tiene 3 una venda?
—No, 4 tiene una.
—¿Te gusta 5 de esas pulseras?
—No, no me gusta 6 .
—Quiero regalarte 7 para tu cumpleaños.
—No, no necesitas regalarme 8 . Gracias.
—A Luisa no le gusta usar esmalte de uñas.
—A María 9 le gusta usar esmalte de uñas.
—¿Encontraste 10 perfume?
—No, no encontré 11 perfume. No me gusta 12 .

(Do Practice Workbook 8-8.)

El *se* impersonal (páginas 282–283)

4 **Se venden perfumes.** Escribe frases usando el *se* impersonal con la información de abajo. Sigue el ejemplo.

vender regalos de toda clase
Aquí se venden regalos de toda clase.

1. permitir tocar el piano hasta las 10:00 de la noche
2. celebrar muchas fiestas
3. tocar sólo música rock
4. hacer llaves

(Do Practice Workbook 8-9.)

Más práctica y tarea 551

Exercise 3
1. Siempre
2. nunca
3. alguien
4. nadie
5. alguna
6. ninguna
7. algo
8. nada
9. tampoco
10. algún
11. ningún
12. ninguno

Exercise 4
1. Aquí se permite tocar el piano hasta las 10:00 de la noche.
2. Aquí se celebran muchas fiestas.
3. Aquí se toca sólo música rock.
4. Aquí se hacen llaves.

Vocabulario para conversar (páginas 296–299)

Exercise 1

1. me rompí
2. una silla de ruedas
3. sangre
4. codo
5. Me corté

Exercise 2

1. medicinas
2. ambulancia
3. enfermero
4. yeso
5. frenillos

Vocabulario para conversar (páginas 300–305)

Exercise 1

1. f
2. a
3. d
4. e
5. b
6. c

Capítulo 9

Vocabulario para conversar (páginas 296–299)

1 **La opción correcta** Escoge la(s) palabra(s) que mejor complete(n) cada frase.

1. Creo que (me rompí/tuve) la muñeca.
2. No puedo caminar y por eso necesito (puntadas/una silla de ruedas).
3. Él tuvo un accidente y le tienen que poner (sangre/músculo).
4. Me rompí el (tobillo/codo) y tengo que llevar un yeso en el brazo.
5. (Me corté/Me quemé) la mano y por eso necesito puntadas.

2 **La respuesta correcta** Completa cada frase con la palabra más apropiada del recuadro.

ambulancia	frenillos	radiografía
enfermero	medicinas	yeso

1. A los niños no les gusta tomar las ___.
2. La ___ me llevó al hospital.
3. El ___ me puso la inyección.
4. Me rompí la muñeca, y fue necesario ponerme un ___.
5. De niña, tenía que llevar ___ en los dientes.

(Do Practice Workbook 9-1 and 9-2.)

Vocabulario para conversar (páginas 300–305)

1 **Definiciones** Aquí hay una lista de palabras y una lista de definiciones. Empareja *(Match)* cada palabra con su definición.

1. pastilla   a. Medicina en forma líquida.
2. jarabe   b. La necesitas cuando quieres comprar medicina.
3. estornudar   c. Usas esto si no te gustan los insectos.
4. picar   d. Cuando tienes un resfriado y dices "¡Achís!"
5. receta   e. Los mosquitos hacen esto.
6. insecticida   f. Medicina en forma de tableta.

(Do Practice Workbook 9-3 and 9-4.)

Gramática en contexto (páginas 310–317)

El imperfecto progresivo (páginas 311–312)

1 **¿Qué estaba pasando?** Completa cada frase usando el imperfecto progresivo del verbo.

1. Cuando entré en la sala de clases, mis compañeros ya (prepararse) para salir.
2. Cuando mi madre entró en el hospital, la enfermera (ponerme) una inyección.
3. Cuando llegó a su casa, el niño ya (sentirse) mal.
4. Cuando te caíste ayer, nosotros (mirar) el partido.
5. Cuando fuimos a ver al médico, tú ya (toser) mucho.
6. Cuando el abuelo llamó, mi padre (descansar) en su dormitorio.

(Do Practice Workbook 9-5.)

El uso del pretérito y del imperfecto progresivo (página 313)

2 **Cuando . . .** Escribe cada frase usando las formas correctas del pretérito o del imperfecto progresivo de los verbos.

1. Cuando Mario (entrar), el señor López (hablar) por teléfono.
2. Cuando la enfermera (salir), el médico (hablar) con los pacientes.
3. Cuando Susana (comprar) la medicina, su mamá ya (sentirse) mejor.
4. Cuando mi hermano (caerse), yo (dormir).

(Do Practice Workbook 9-6.)

El pretérito de *caerse, creer* y *leer* (páginas 314–315)

3 **¿Cómo . . . ?** Aquí hay grupos de palabras que no están en orden. Escribe frases completas al ordenar las palabras correctamente y cambiar los verbos al pretérito.

1. caerse / en / Mateo / la ducha
2. libros / dos / anoche / yo / leer
3. amigos / mis / creerme / no
4. del / caerse / yo / árbol
5. leer / la / nosotros / receta

(Do Practice Workbook 9-7.)

Gramática en contexto (páginas 310-317)

Exercise 1
1. se estaban preparando/estaban preparándose
2. me estaba poniendo/estaba poniéndome
3. se estaba sintiendo/estaba sintiéndose
4. estábamos mirando
5. estabas tosiendo
6. estaba descansando

Exercise 2
1. entró; estaba hablando
2. salió; estaba hablando
3. compró; se estaba sintiendo/estaba sintiéndose
4. se cayó; estaba durmiendo

Exercise 3
1. Mateo se cayó en la ducha.
2. Yo leí dos libros anoche.
3. Mis amigos no me creyeron.
4. Yo me caí del árbol.
5. Nosotros leímos la receta.

Exercise 4

1. puso
2. pusiste
3. puse
4. pusimos
5. pusieron

El pretérito del verbo *poner* (páginas 316–317)

 Se pone . . . Completa las frases usando el pretérito del verbo *poner.*

1. El médico me ___ una inyección.
2. ¿Dónde ___ tú el repelente?
3. A ver, ¿dónde ___ yo la receta?
4. Nosotros ___ las muletas en la ambulancia.
5. Los jugadores se ___ los uniformes y los cascos.

(Do Practice Workbook 9-8 and 9-9.)

CAPÍTULO 10

Vocabulario para conversar (páginas 330–335)

1 **La sopa de letras** Pon los siguientes grupos de letras en orden correcto para formar palabras del vocabulario.

1. r m n c i e
2. n e c a s e
3. s n o g u i e
4. u a c r a t
5. o t n e m u g r a
6. s o e j r e p a n

2 **La respuesta correcta** Completa cada frase con la palabra apropiada.

1. No puedo entender el ___ de esa película. (argumento/papel)
2. Los ___ especiales de esa película son muy buenos. (ladrones/efectos)
3. El ___ está investigando quién es el ladrón. (criminal/detective)
4. Una actriz muy famosa hace el ___ de la científica. (papel/guión)

3 **¿Qué hacen?** Completa cada frase con una palabra relacionada con la segunda parte de cada grupo. Sigue el ejemplo.

El policía arresta. El criminal _mata_.

1. El detective investiga. El ladrón ___.
2. La directora dirige. La actriz ___.
3. Él hace el papel del galán. Ella hace el papel de ___.

(Do Practice Workbook 10-1 and 10-2.)

Vocabulario para conversar (páginas 336–339)

1 **Definiciones** Aquí hay una lista de palabras y una lista de definiciones. Empareja cada palabra con su definición.

1. entrevista
2. locutora
3. fracaso
4. tormenta
5. huracán

a. Viento muy violento.
b. Un programa que no tiene éxito es esto.
c. Cuando llueve muchísimo.
d. Cuando el locutor le hace preguntas a alguien.
e. La persona que habla en un programa de televisión.

Vocabulario para conversar (páginas 330–335)
Exercise 1
1. crimen
2. escena
3. guiones
4. actuar
5. argumento
6. personaje

Exercise 2
1. argumento
2. efectos
3. detective
4. papel

Exercise 3
1. roba
2. actúa
3. la heroína

Vocabulario para conversar (páginas 336–339)
Exercise 1
1. d
2. e
3. b
4. c
5. a

Exercise 2
1. destruyó
2. comentarios
3. terremotos
4. locutor
5. tormenta

Gramática en contexto (páginas 344–351)

Exercise 1
1. Eran, llegó
2. Era, mató
3. era, entró
4. Era, arrestó

Exercise 2
1. Lloré porque estaba triste.
2. Fuimos a la cafetería porque teníamos hambre.
3. Él durmió porque estaba cansado.
4. Me llamaste porque querías verme.

---

2 **La mejor opción** Completa cada frase con la palabra más apropiada.

comentarios	destruyó	locutor	terremotos	tormenta

1. La erupción del volcán ___ todo.
2. Vinieron expertos para hacer ___ sobre la situación.
3. En lugares donde hay muchos ___, no se debe tener edificios muy altos.
4. El ___ leyó las noticias sobre el derrumbe.
5. La ___ causó muchos problemas en mi ciudad.

(Do Practice Workbook 10-3 and 10-4.)

Gramática en contexto (páginas 344–351)

El pretérito y el imperfecto 1 (páginas 345–346)

1 **¿Qué hora...?** Para cada frase escribe el imperfecto del primer verbo en paréntesis y el pretérito del segundo. Usa las formas correctas de los verbos.

1. ___ (ser) las ocho cuando Antonio ___ (llegar).
2. ___ (ser) la una cuando el criminal ___ (matar) a la víctima.
3. ¿Qué hora ___ (ser) cuando el ladrón ___ (entrar) en la casa?
4. ___ (ser) la medianoche cuando el policía ___ (arrestar) a la ladrona.

(Do Practice Workbook 10-5.)

El pretérito y el imperfecto 2 (páginas 346–347)

2 **¿Por qué?** Cambia los verbos en cada frase al pretérito o al imperfecto, según corresponda.

1. Lloro porque estoy triste.
2. Vamos a la cafetería porque tenemos hambre.
3. Él duerme porque está cansado.
4. Me llamas porque quieres verme.

(Do Practice Workbook 10-6 and 10-7.)

El pretérito y el imperfecto 3 (páginas 348–349)

3 **¿Qué estabas haciendo?** Cambia las frases al tiempo pasado. Sigue el ejemplo.

Jorge almuerza. Suena el timbre.
Jorge estaba almorzando cuando sonó el timbre.

1. La niña camina. Se cae.
2. El criminal se esconde. El policía lo encuentra.
3. Me baño. Hay un terremoto.
4. Vemos el programa de concursos. Alguien grita.

(Do Practice Workbook 10-8.)

El pretérito del verbo *decir* (página 350)

4 **¿Qué dijiste?** Cambia el verbo *decir* en estas frases al pretérito.

1. Yo no digo eso.
2. Decimos nuestros nombres.
3. ¿Qué dice el criminal?
4. Y ustedes, ¿por qué dicen que no?

(Do Practice Workbook 10-9.)

Exercise 3
1. La niña estaba caminando cuando se cayó.
2. El criminal se estaba escondiendo cuando el policía lo encontró.
3. Me estaba bañando cuando hubo un terremoto.
4. Estábamos viendo el programa de concursos cuando alguien gritó.

Exercise 4
1. Yo no dije eso.
2. Dijimos nuestros nombres.
3. ¿Qué dijo el criminal?
4. Y ustedes, ¿por qué dijeron que no?

Vocabulario para conversar (páginas 364–369)

Exercise 1
1. mecánico
2. cantante
3. veterinario
4. escritora
5. deportista

Exercise 2
1. escritor(a)
2. secretario(a)
3. bailarín/ bailarina
4. juez
5. mecánico(a)

Vocabulario para conversar (páginas 370–373)

Exercise 1
1. e
2. a
3. d
4. c
5. b

Exercise 2
1. un sistema de seguridad
2. el vidrio
3. la paz
4. La Tierra
5. el medio ambiente

CAPÍTULO 11

Vocabulario para conversar (páginas 364–369)

1 **¿A qué me dedico?** Completa cada frase con la palabra apropiada del recuadro.

cantante	deportista	escritora	mecánico	veterinario

1. Me dedico a reparar coches. Soy ___.
2. Doy conciertos y mis discos compactos son populares. Soy ___.
3. Cuido la salud de los animales. Soy ___.
4. Mis libros se leen por todas partes. Soy ___.
5. Soy entrenadora y me gustan los deportes. Soy ___.

2 **¿Qué sabes hacer?** Lee cada frase y decide a qué profesión se refiere *(is referred to).*

1. Generalmente esta persona trabaja sola. Necesita silencio para escribir.
2. Esta persona contesta teléfonos y ayuda a otros en la oficina.
3. Esta persona sabe bailar bien.
4. Esta persona escucha a los abogados antes de tomar una decisión.
5. Esta persona sabe mucho sobre los coches.

(Do Practice Workbook 11-1 and 11-2.)

Vocabulario para conversar (páginas 370–373)

1 **Definiciones** Empareja cada palabra con su definición.

1. botella	a. conflicto entre dos grupos
2. guerra	b. donde hay muchos árboles
3. océano	c. la vemos de noche
4. la Luna	d. donde viven los peces
5. bosque	e. generalmente es de vidrio o de plástico

2 **La opción correcta** Completa cada frase con la expresión apropiada.

1. Para proteger una casa, se necesita (una pantalla gigante/un sistema de seguridad).
2. Es necesario reciclar (el espacio/el vidrio).
3. Algo que todos los países deben buscar es (la paz/la guerra).
4. (La Luna/La Tierra) es un planeta.
5. Tenemos que proteger (el medio ambiente/el tráfico).

(Do Practice Workbook 11-3 and 11-4.)

Gramática en contexto (páginas 378–383)

El futuro (páginas 379–381)

1 **¿Qué pasará?** Cambia las palabras subrayadas *(underlined)* al tiempo futuro del verbo en infinitivo.

1. En el año 2050, voy a trabajar en una oficina en la Luna.
2. Voy a vivir en una casa con calefacción solar.
3. Mi familia va a ver la tele en una pantalla gigante.
4. Mis amigos y yo vamos a hablar usando el teléfono con video.
5. Todos vamos a reducir la basura.

(Do Practice Workbook 11-5 and 11-6.)

El futuro: continuación (páginas 381–382)

2 **¿Qué harán?** Cambia cada verbo subrayado al tiempo futuro.

1. ¿Hay mucha gente allí?
2. Tenemos que reciclar los periódicos.
3. El ser humano puede ir a muchos planetas.
4. No hay más guerras.
5. Todos pueden ver la televisión en una pantalla gigante.
6. Tú eres astronauta.
7. Nosotros sabemos qué hacer.
8. Ustedes hacen informes.

3 **En el futuro** Usa el futuro del verbo entre paréntesis para completar cada frase.

1. Si es posible, yo (ir) contigo.
2. Ella (tener) un secretario.
3. Nosotros (explorar) nuevos planetas.
4. Los astronautas (visitar) otras galaxias.
5. Tú (seguir) con la protección del medio ambiente.
6. Los mecánicos (reparar) mi coche.
7. Ustedes (poder) visitarme mañana.
8. Él (participar) en el consejo estudiantil.

(Do Practice Workbook 11-7, 11-8, and 11-9.)

Gramática en contexto (páginas 378–383)

Exercise 1
1. trabajaré
2. Viviré
3. verá
4. hablaremos
5. reduciremos

Exercise 2
1. Habrá
2. Tendremos
3. podrá
4. habrá
5. podrán
6. serás
7. sabremos
8. harán

Exercise 3
1. iré
2. tendrá
3. exploraremos
4. visitarán
5. seguirás
6. repararán
7. podrán
8. participará

Vocabulario para conversar (páginas 396–401)

Exercise 1
1. aterrizar
2. desabrocharse
3. hacer la maleta
4. ida y vuelta
5. procedente de

Exercise 2
1. con destino a
2. hacer la maleta
3. abróchense los cinturones
4. aterrizar
5. facturar
6. la terminal de equipaje

Exercise 3
1. a
2. e
3. b
4. c
5. d

CAPÍTULO 12

Vocabulario para conversar (páginas 396–401)

1 **Antónimos** Escribe la palabra o frase que sea lo contrario de las siguientes expresiones.

1. despegar
2. abrocharse
3. deshacer la maleta
4. sólo de ida
5. con destino a

2 **La respuesta correcta** Completa cada frase con la(s) palabra(s) apropiada(s) del recuadro.

abróchense los cinturones	facturar
aterrizar	hacer la maleta
con destino a	la terminal de equipaje

1. El avión ___ Montevideo sale en una hora.
2. Mañana voy a viajar. Esta noche tengo que ___.
3. Atención pasajeros, vamos a despegar ahora. Por favor, ___.
4. El avión no pudo ___ porque hacía mal tiempo.
5. Tienes que ___ la maleta. Es muy grande.
6. ¿Puede decirme dónde está ___? Necesito buscar mi maleta.

3 **Definiciones** Empareja cada palabra con su definición.

1. aduana
2. puerta
3. maleta
4. auxiliar de vuelo
5. boleto

a. Donde te registran las maletas cuando llegas de otro país.
b. Pones tus cosas en esto cuando viajas.
c. Ayuda a los pasajeros en el avión.
d. Lo compras si quieres viajar.
e. Pasas por aquí para entrar en el avión.

(Do Practice Workbook 12-1 and 12-2.)

Vocabulario para conversar (páginas 402–405)

1 **La opción correcta** Completa cada frase con la expresión apropiada.

1. Si necesitas dinero de otro país, puedes ir a una (casa de cambio/oficina de turismo).
2. En (una habitación doble/una guía) pueden dormir dos personas.
3. (La pensión/La habitación individual) es un lugar donde se puede dormir por poco dinero.
4. Cuando viajo, me gusta comprar (artesanías/pueblos).
5. El mercado de ese pueblo es muy (a mano/pintoresco).

(Do Practice Workbook 12-3 and 12-4.)

Gramática en contexto (páginas 410–415)

Repaso: Mandatos afirmativos con *tú* (páginas 411–412)

1 **Haz esto.** Completa cada frase usando el mandato afirmativo del verbo.

1. Cristóbal, ___ (facturar) tu maleta.
2. ___ (escribir) tarjetas postales.
3. ___ (ir) con Nicolás a la terminal.
4. ___ (tener) cuidado con tus maletas.
5. ___ (decir) siempre la verdad.

(Do Practice Workbook 12-5 and 12-6.)

Los mandatos negativos con *tú* (páginas 412–413)

2 **No lo hagas.** Cambia las palabras subrayadas a mandatos negativos con *tú*.

1. <u>Enciende</u> la radio.
2. <u>Habla</u> por teléfono ahora.
3. <u>Cierra</u> la puerta.
4. <u>Sigue</u> a la guía.
5. <u>Pide</u> ayuda para hacer tu tarea.
6. <u>Echa</u> los periódicos viejos en la basura.
7. <u>Usa</u> las manos para comer.
8. <u>Come</u> chocolate antes del almuerzo.
9. <u>Pierde</u> tu cuaderno.
10. <u>Sube</u> al árbol.

(Do Practice Workbook 12-7.)

Vocabulario para conversar (páginas 402–405)
Exercise 1
1. casa de cambio
2. una habitación doble
3. La pensión
4. artesanías
5. pintoresco

Gramática en contexto (páginas 410–415)
Exercise 1
1. factura
2. Escribe
3. Ve
4. Ten
5. Di

Exercise 2
1. No enciendas la radio.
2. No hables por teléfono ahora.
3. No cierres la puerta.
4. No sigas a la guía.
5. No pidas ayuda para hacer tu tarea.
6. No eches los periódicos viejos en la basura.
7. No uses las manos para comer.
8. No comas chocolate antes del almuerzo.
9. No pierdas tu cuaderno.
10. No subas al árbol.

Exercise 3

1. Juan, no pongas tu boleto en el asiento.
2. Felipe, no hagas tu maleta ahora.
3. Mariel, no vayas al mercado.
4. Luisa, no cruces la plaza.
5. Patricio, no llegues tarde a la reunión.
6. Cecilia, no juegues en el parque.
7. Silvia, no vayas sola al mercado.
8. Andrés, no seas atrevido.
9. Armando, no digas lo que piensas.
10. Soledad, no traigas al perro.

Los mandatos negativos: continuación (páginas 414–415)

 No lo hagan. Cambia estas frases usando mandatos negativos con *tú*. Sigue el ejemplo.

Antonio quiere tocar la guitarra.
Antonio, no toques la guitarra.

1. Juan quiere poner su boleto en el asiento.
2. Felipe quiere hacer su maleta ahora.
3. Mariel quiere ir al mercado.
4. Luisa quiere cruzar la plaza.
5. Patricio quiere llegar tarde a la reunión.
6. Cecilia quiere jugar en el parque.
7. Silvia quiere ir sola al mercado.
8. Andrés quiere ser atrevido.
9. Armando quiere decir lo que piensa.
10. Soledad quiere traer al perro.

(Do Practice Workbook 12-8 and 12-9.)

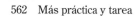

CAPÍTULO 13

Vocabulario para conversar (páginas 428–433)

1 **Definiciones** Completa cada frase con la palabra apropiada.

1. El ___ es una fruta amarilla que se usa en las comidas y en las bebidas.
2. A mucha gente le gustan las hamburguesas a la ___.
3. Me gusta poner vinagre y ___ a la ensalada.
4. Hay demasiada sal en esta sopa. Está muy ___.
5. Su madre hace sus pasteles al ___.

2 **La diferencia** Escoge la palabra en cada grupo que no vaya con las otras.

1. espárrago / espinacas / salsa
2. champiñón / piña / durazno
3. a la parrilla / dulce / al horno
4. agrio / amargo / cerdo
5. aceite / salado / soso
6. mostaza / mayonesa / barbacoa

(Do Practice Workbook 13-1 and 13-2.)

Vocabulario para conversar (páginas 434–438)

1 **De un color diferente** Escoge la comida que sea de un color diferente en cada grupo.

1. ajo, camarón, azúcar
2. fresa, mostaza, limón
3. cereza, tomate, huevo
4. pepino, espinaca, mayonesa
5. calabaza, melón, sandía

2 **Vamos a comer.** Completa cada frase con la expresión apropiada del recuadro. Van a sobrar dos palabras *(two words will be left over)*.

amargo	paella
calabaza	relleno
hierve	tortilla española

1. En los Estados Unidos, esta fruta se usa para hacer muchas cosas en octubre y noviembre. Es la ___.
2. La parte interior de la empanada se llama el ___.
3. Para hacer una ___ hay que usar muchos huevos.
4. Para preparar sopa, primero ___ el agua.

(Do Practice Workbook 13-3 and 13-4.)

Vocabulario para conversar (páginas 428–433)

Exercise 1
1. limón
2. parrilla
3. aceite
4. salada
5. horno

Exercise 2
1. salsa
2. champiñón
3. dulce
4. cerdo
5. aceite
6. barbacoa

Vocabulario para conversar (páginas 434–438)

Exercise 1
1. camarón
2. fresa
3. huevo
4. mayonesa
5. sandía

Exercise 2
1. calabaza
2. relleno
3. tortilla española
4. hierve

Gramática en contexto
(páginas 442–447)

Exercise 1

1. No te portes mal.
2. No te levantes tarde.
3. No salgas a la calle por la noche.
4. No bebas otra limonada.

Exercise 2

1. traiga
2. muestre
3. recomiende
4. sirva
5. preparemos
6. cocinen

Exercise 3

1. bebas
2. prueben
3. hierva
4. vivas
5. cruce
6. coma
7. hablen
8. pidamos

Gramática en contexto (páginas 442–447)

Repaso: Mandatos negativos (página 443)

1 **No lo hagas.** Escribe mandatos negativos con *tú* con las siguientes frases. Sigue el ejemplo.

comer muchas papas fritas
No comas muchas papas fritas.

1. portarse mal
2. levantarse tarde
3. salir a la calle por la noche
4. beber otra limonada

(Do Practice Workbook 13-5.)

El subjuntivo (páginas 443–447)

2 **En un restaurante** Completa el siguiente diálogo entre un camarero y un cliente, cambiando los infinitivos en paréntesis al subjuntivo.

CAMARERO: Buenas tardes. ¿Qué desea?
CLIENTE: Necesito que me __1__ (traer) agua, por favor.
CAMARERO: Bien. ¿Quiere que le __2__ (mostrar) el menú?
CLIENTE: No, prefiero que me __3__ (recomendar) algo.
CAMARERO: El cerdo es nuestra especialidad. ¿Quiere que le __4__ (servir) eso?
CLIENTE: Sí, por favor.
CAMARERO: ¿Y cómo quiere que nosotros lo __5__ (preparar)?
CLIENTE: Prefiero que lo __6__ (cocinar) al horno.

3 **Recomiendo que . . .** Escoge el verbo más apropiado del recuadro para cada frase y cámbialo al subjuntivo.

beber	cruzar	hervir	probar
comer	hablar	pedir	vivir

1. Sugiero que tú ___ más jugo de naranja.
2. Recomiendo que ustedes ___ la comida de ese restaurante.
3. Es necesario que Matilde ___ el agua para hacer huevos duros.
4. Sugiero que tú ___ más cerca de la escuela.
5. No quiero que ella ___ la calle sola.
6. Es necesario que usted ___ más frutas y verduras.
7. Recomiendo que ustedes ___ con un médico sobre una dieta práctica.
8. Sugiero que nosotros les ___ ayuda a nuestros amigos para organizar la fiesta.

(Do Practice Workbook 13-6, 13-7, 13-8, 13-9, and 13-10.)

CAPÍTULO 14

Vocabulario para conversar (páginas 460–465)

1 **Lo contrario** Escoge la expresión más apropiada del recuadro para cada frase.

colina	caminata	ligera	mojada	sombra

1. Esta hoja está seca, pero ésa está ___.
2. Esa piedra es pesada, pero la otra es ___.
3. Podemos poner la tienda de acampar en el valle o en la ___.
4. En el sol hace calor, en la ___ hace frío.
5. Ustedes pueden descansar mientras nosotros vamos a dar una ___.

2 **Sopa de letras** Pon los siguientes grupos de letras en orden correcto para formar palabras.

1. l i o a t p
2. m o r s a b
3. a s a p i r o m
4. d e e n o r s
5. l a s t a r a b c
6. n e m o t a p c m a
7. ó f s l i
8. ó f s f o o r

3 **Definiciones** Escribe la palabra que corresponda a cada definición.

1. Es por donde vas si quieres hacer una caminata.
2. Lo necesitas para abrir comida enlatada.
3. Un insecto bonito y de colores.
4. Madera que se usa para hacer fuegos.
5. Se usa para encender el fuego.

(Do Practice Workbook 14-1 and 14-2.)

Vocabulario para conversar (páginas 460–465)

Exercise 1
1. mojada
2. ligera
3. colina
4. sombra
5. caminata

Exercise 2
1. palito
2. sombra
3. mariposa
4. sendero
5. abrelatas
6. campamento
7. fósil
8. fósforo

Exercise 3
1. sendero
2. abrelatas
3. mariposa
4. leña
5. fósforo

Vocabulario para conversar (páginas 466–470)

Exercise 1

1. elefante
2. gorila
3. Navegar en balsa
4. el atardecer
5. hacer esquí acuático
6. animales salvajes

Exercise 2

1. parque nacional
2. mar
3. desierto
4. parque nacional
5. mar
6. desierto
7. parque nacional

Gramática en contexto (páginas 474–479)

Exercise 1

1. Quiero que Wilfredo y Dolores busquen leña.
2. Quiero que Cándida ponga la tienda.
3. Quiero que José escale montañas.
4. Quiero que Sergio navegue en balsa hoy.
5. Quiero que Laura y yo demos una caminata.

Vocabulario para conversar (páginas 466–470)

1 **La mejor opción** Escoge la(s) palabra(s) apropiada(s) para completar cada frase.

1. El animal más grande de la selva es el (elefante/gorila).
2. El (gorila/coyote) tiene muchas características similares al ser humano.
3. (Dar caminatas/Navegar en balsa) es una actividad bastante peligrosa.
4. Entre el día y la noche, está (el atardecer/la espina).
5. Ese lago es perfecto para (escalar montañas/hacer esquí acuático).
6. Los (animales salvajes/fósiles) viven en el parque nacional.

2 **¿Dónde?** Decide si las siguientes frases se refieren a un desierto, a un parque nacional o al mar.

1. ¡Mira, una ardilla!
2. Esa ballena es enorme.
3. Aquí sólo hay piedras y hace muchísimo calor.
4. Pongamos la tienda al lado de esos árboles.
5. Ya me aburrí de hacer surf.
6. No toques ese cacto. Tiene muchas espinas.
7. Allí hay unos venados.

(Do Practice Workbook 14-3 and 14-4.)

Gramática en contexto (páginas 474–479)

El subjuntivo de ciertos verbos irregulares (página 475)

1 **Quiero que . . .** Usa la expresión *Quiero que* para cambiar las siguientes frases a la forma subjuntiva. Sigue el ejemplo.

Antonio tiene cuidado de los animales.
Quiero que Antonio tenga cuidado de los animales.

1. Wilfredo y Dolores buscan leña.
2. Cándida pone la tienda.
3. José escala montañas.
4. Sergio navega en balsa hoy.
5. Laura y yo damos una caminata.

(Do Practice Workbook 14-5 and 14-6.)

El subjuntivo de los verbos *ir* y *ser* (página 476)

 Quiere que . . . Completa cada frase con el subjuntivo del verbo *ir* o *ser.*

1. Ellos quieren que yo ___ al desierto contigo.
2. ¿Por qué no quiere usted que nosotros ___ a San Antonio?
3. Tino le sugiere a Julia que ella ___ más prudente cuando hace esquí acuático.
4. Javier quiere que Micaela y Carmen ___ menos traviesas.

(Do Practice Workbook 14-7 and 14-8.)

El subjuntivo con expresiones impersonales (páginas 477–478)

3 **Es necesario que . . .** Escribe frases completas usando la forma subjuntiva con expresiones impersonales.

1. es mejor que / Josefina y Eugenio / no escalar esa montaña
2. es necesario que / Francisco / recoger la leña
3. es importante que / Patricia y yo / aprender a navegar en canoa
4. es mejor que / Beatriz / llevar un saco de dormir al campamento
5. es necesario que / todos / divertirse en la fiesta

(Do Practice Workbook 14-9 and 14-10.)

Exercise 2
1. vaya
2. vayamos
3. sea
4. sean

Exercise 3
1. Es mejor que Josefina y Eugenio no escalen esa montaña.
2. Es necesario que Francisco recoja la leña.
3. Es importante que Patricia y yo aprendamos a navegar en canoa.
4. Es mejor que Beatriz lleve un saco de dormir al campamento.
5. Es necesario que todos se diviertan en la fiesta.

A.

1. a
2. c
3. c
4. c
5. a
6. b
7. c
8. b
9. a
10. b

Examen cumulativo

A. Below you will find a series of sentences, each with four possible choices selected from the vocabulary of *PASO A PASO 2*. On a separate sheet of paper, write the letter of the item that best completes the statement or answers the question.

1. Una materia que me gusta es ___ .
   a. la química
   b. la grapadora
   c. la prueba
   d. la bandera

2. Me gusta cantar. Voy a participar en ___ .
   a. la orquesta
   b. la banda
   c. el coro
   d. el anuario

3. Quisiera tener una camisa blanca de ___ corta.
   a. bufanda
   b. gorra
   c. manga
   d. lana

4. Para montar en bicicleta necesito mi ___ .
   a. guante
   b. pelota
   c. casco
   d. palo

5. ___ es un juguete que les gusta a los niños.
   a. El camión
   b. La canoa
   c. El pájaro
   d. La tortuga

6. El esposo de mi hermana es mi ___ .
   a. bisabuelo
   b. cuñado
   c. nieto
   d. sobrino

7. Si no tienes tu ____, no puedes entrar en tu casa.
   a. llavero
   b. peine
   c. llave
   d. pulsera

8. Estoy buscando ____ para comprar una revista.
   a. el semáforo
   b. el quiosco
   c. el buzón
   d. la carretera

9. Me rompí la pierna y necesito ____ para ayudarme a caminar.
   a. muletas
   b. jarabe
   c. calamina
   d. frenillos

10. En el campo hay animales como ___ .
    a. los directores
    b. los caballos
    c. los monstruos
    d. las víctimas

11. Me gusta mucho la ____ porque quiero ser presidente.
 a. política
 b. juez
 c. novela
 d. pantalla

12. Vamos a hacer ____ en Buenos Aires.
 a. aduana
 b. escala
 c. habitación
 d. maleta

13. El ____ es una comida buena en el invierno.
 a. grasoso
 b. ingrediente
 c. relleno
 d. guisado

14. En los árboles se ven ___ .
 a. las balsas
 b. las ranas
 c. los búhos
 d. las velas

15. Necesito un sacapuntas. ¿Tienes uno?
 a. Sí. ¿Vas al bufet de ensaladas?
 b. Por suerte tengo sujetapapeles.
 c. Sí. ¿Vas a escribir un informe?
 d. No, no me gusta la química.

16. Soy miembro de muchos clubes. Me gustan ___ .
 a. estar de moda
 b. las actividades extracurriculares
 c. los animales de peluche
 d. los fuegos artificiales

17. ¿De qué son los pantalones?
 a. Son de lona.
 b. Son de algodón.
 c. Uso el tamaño mediano.
 d. Están en liquidación.

18. Necesitamos una diversión nueva.
 a. ¡Juguemos ajedrez!
 b. Voy a meter un gol esta noche.
 c. Lo pasamos muy bien anoche.
 d. ¿Dónde están los palos?

19. Los niños quieren jugar hoy. ¿Qué pueden hacer?
 a. Te gustaban las materias.
 b. Son maleducados.
 c. Pueden ir a la escuela primaria.
 d. Pueden ir al patio de recreo.

20. No tenemos nada que hacer en octubre.
 a. ¡Pero hay el Día de la Raza!
 b. ¡Pero hay el Día de los Enamorados!
 c. ¡Pero hay el Día de Gracias!
 d. ¡Pero hay el Día del Padre!

21. Tenemos una emergencia. ¿Dónde está ___?
 a. el estante
 b. el extinguidor de incendios
 c. la secadora
 d. los aretes

22. ¿Dónde está la sección de ropa para niños?
 a. Tiene que subir por la escalera.
 b. En la estación de bomberos.
 c. No hay mostradores por aquí.
 d. No haces las compras hoy.

11. a
12. b
13. d
14. c
15. c
16. b
17. b
18. a
19. d
20. a
21. b
22. a

23. a
24. d
25. a
26. d
27. c
28. d

B.
1. b
2. a
3. a
4. b
5. b
6. d
7. b
8. b
9. b

23. En el verano tengo muchos resfriados y yo ___ .
    a. estornudo mucho
    c. saco una radiografía
    b. necesito más polvo
    d. necesito muletas

24. Hay mucha información sensacionalista, ¿no?
    a. Sí. Fue un fracaso total.
    c. Es porque el actor no tiene éxito.
    b. Sí, me gustan las entrevistas.
    d. Sí. Todo es exagerado a veces.

25. ¿Es importante tener una buena educación?
    a. Sí. Es una ventaja.
    c. Debes echar basura.
    b. Es bueno explorar el planeta.
    d. Sí. Me dedico a no contaminar.

26. Voy a hacer una excursión a México.
    a. ¿Te gusta regatear?
    c. Hablas con los aduaneros.
    b. Ah, quieres ser guía.
    d. ¿Necesitas un pasaporte?

27. Sirven postres buenos en este restaurante. Debes probarlos.
    a. Me gustan los bocadillos.
    c. ¿Qué sugieres que yo pida?
    b. Los champiñones son buenos.
    d. Quiero hacer una barbacoa.

28. ¿Quieres ir de camping conmigo?
    a. Sí, me gustan las artes marciales.
    c. Hay que sacar una radiografía.
    b. No me gusta ir de compras.
    d. Sí, me gusta dar caminatas.

B. In the following paragraph, the family of twins Emilia and Estefanía talk about the girls. Below the paragraph are four possible answers for each blank. Select the most appropriate choice and mark its letter on a separate sheet of paper.

Emilia leía __1__ su gemela Estefanía. Las dos __2__ muy inteligentes. Ellas se leían frecuentemente y __3__ a comprender las novelas. También en nuestra casa había muchas discusiones sobre la literatura. El mes pasado, cuando ellas __4__ 15 años, la familia __5__ una celebración para __6__. Esa noche, todos nosotros __7__ a la librería. Allí les __8__ novelas de tres de sus escritores favoritos. Creo que un día en el futuro todos __9__ sobre las tres novelas.

1. a. tan como
   b. tanto como
   c. tanta como
   d. tantos como

2. a. eran
   b. fueron
   c. estuvieron
   d. estaban

6. a. sus
   b. suyas
   c. su
   d. ellas

7. a. tuvimos
   b. fuimos
   c. pudimos
   d. hicimos

3. a. se ayudaban
   b. se ayudaron
   c. se estaban ayudando
   d. se ayudarán

4. a. tuvieron
   b. tenían
   c. estaban
   d. estuvieron

5. a. tuvieron
   b. tuvo
   c. tenían
   d. ellas

8. a. dijimos
   b. dimos
   c. dijeron
   d. dieron

9. a. hablamos
   b. hablaremos
   c. hablaron
   d. hablaban

C. Below are two passages. In the first passage, Pablo writes about his memories of childhood. In the second passage, a father writes to his son about the responsibilities of adulthood. On a separate sheet of paper, write the correct form of the word in parentheses to complete each sentence.

Yo __1__ (ser) un niño contento. También yo __2__ (tener) muchos amigos diferentes. Es decir, nosotros __3__ (hacer) muchas actividades en grupo y __4__ (divertirse) mucho. Tengo unos recuerdos espléndidos de un día de octubre cuando __5__ (llegar) a jugar unos amigos __6__ (mío). Yo los consideraba los muchachos __7__ (más popular) del pueblo. Ese día yo __8__ (levantarse) temprano y todos nosotros __9__ (salir) a jugar y a subir colinas. Lo __10__ (pasar) muy bien. ¡Qué recuerdos __11__ (magnífico) tengo de mis amigos y de nuestras actividades!

Hijo, para ser un adulto responsable, recomiendo que tú __1__ (tener) un buen trabajo que te guste. Además, recuerda lo que siempre te digo: "__2__ (salir) con personas buenas, __3__ (ser) bien educado con todos y no __4__ (hablar) mal de otros." También sugiero que tú y tus hermanos __5__ (ayudarse) y que no __6__ (pelearse). Y si tienes un amigo bueno, tú __7__ (estar) contento.

C.
1. era
2. tenía
3. hacíamos
4. nos divertíamos
5. llegaron
6. míos
7. más populares
8. me levanté
9. salimos
10. pasamos
11. magníficos

1. tengas
2. Sal
3. sé
4. hables
5. se ayuden
6. se peleen
7. estarás

Índice

In almost all cases, structures are first presented in the *Vocabulario para conversar*, where they are practiced lexically in conversational contexts. They are explained later, usually in the *Gramática en contexto* section of that chapter. Light-face numbers refer to pages where structures are initially presented or, after explanation, where student reminders occur. Bold-face numbers refer to pages where structures are explained or otherwise highlighted.

ACKNOWLEDGMENTS

Illustrations   Mapping Specialists Limited: pp. **XII-XV**; Iskra Johnson: pp. **8-9**; Elizabeth Wolf: pp. **10-11**; Scott Snow: p. **17**; Susan Aiello: pp. **75, 86, 210-211, 438, 484**; Kevin Bapp: pp. **42-43**; Andrea Barrett: pp. **162-166, 169-171, 176, 189, 216-217**; Robert Burger: pp. **337, 345-346**; John Ceballos: pp. **418-419**; Rick Clubb pp. **194-201, 203, 208, 210, 212, 221, 276, 364-367, 369, 380, 384, 391**; Guy Crittenden: pp. **480-481**; Lane Dupont: pp. **62-63, 65-69, 71, 76-77, 80, 89, 245**; John Edens: p. **174**; George Eisner: pp. **344, 354, 356, 406**; Susan Greenstein: pp. **448, 454**; Doug Henry: p. **310**; Robin Hotchkiss: pp. **348-349**; Andy Lendway: pp. **215, 296-302, 304-306, 312, 315-316, 318, 325, 446**; Jude Maceren: pp. **451-452**; Peg Magovern: pp. **282, 311, 410, 417**; James Mellett: pp. **128-141, 145, 147, 157, 281, 390, 442**; Steve Musgrave pp. **351, 355, 387, 444, 484**; Andy Myer: pp. **52-53, 152-153, 320-321**; Ortelius Design: p. **286**; Julie Pace: pp. **94-105, 112, 114-115, 122-123**; Leif Peng: pp. **396-398, 401-403, 423, 474**; Donna Perrone: pp. **222-223**; Bob Shein: p. **485**; Ken Smith: pp. **64, 68**; Scott Snow: pp. **322-323, 449**; Jim Starr: pp. **30-37, 44-46, 48-49, 51, 56-57, 116, 357, 370-373, 388, 391, 428-437, 439, 446-447, 455**; Richard Stergulz: pp. **460-469, 470, 476, 484, 487**; Joe Scrofani: pp. **260-269, 271, 272-273, 278-279, 281, 283, 291**; Rod Vass: pp. **226-235, 237, 242-244, 255, 330-333, 335-336, 338-339, 350**; Gary Yealdhall: pp. **50, 182-183, 240**; John Zielinsky: p. **108**

Photography   **Front Cover:** Haroldo Castro/FPG International; **Back Cover, II:** F. Catala-Roca, Barcelona; **V, VIII** (t), **7, 20** (b), **29** (b), **38** (inset), **80, 181, 225** (t), **238** (b), **313, 392-393, 440, 450, 472-473**: Robert Frerck/Odyssey/Chicago; **IV, 47, 72, 120** (br), **121** (t), **124-125, 126** (b), **137** (l), **179, 202** (l), **284** (b), **394** (b), **412-413, 431**: Robert Fried; **2** (l), **87** (tl), **93** (t), **106-107, 113** (t), **120** (t), **309** (t), **363, 406** (t), **407, 421** (t), **426**: David R. Frazier Photolibrary; **38, 41** (b), **50, 55, 60** (b), **72, 120** (br), **121** (t), **126** (b), **137** (l), **167, 187** (b), **204, 294** (r), **295, 308, 465**: Chip & Rosa Maria de la Cueva Peterson; **8** (b), **23** (tr), **160** (t), **259** (b), **284** (t), **329** (t), **441** (b): Stuart Cohen/The Image Works; **206-207, 401**: Martha Cooper/Viesti Collection; **239, 264** (t): Ric Ergenbright Photography; **158-159, 207** (t), **218-219, 236, 288** (b), **314-315, 458** (b): Joe Viesti/Viesti Collection; **87** (bl), **113** (b), **173, 222-223, 270, 347** (t), **377, 394** (t), **395, 406** (b), **420-421**: Beryl Goldberg; **154** (b), **202** (r), **445**: Mary Altier; **XVI, 61** (b), **79, 93** (b), **116** (t), **118, 127, 259** (t), **341** (t), **420**: Owen Franken; **2** (c), **3, 160** (b), **168, 180, 318** (b): Tony Arruza; **2** (r), **23** (tl): Glenn Randall; **5** (l): Cynthia Lum/Sports Light; **5** (r): Focus on Sports; **6**: Arthur Tilley/FPG International; **16** (t): Yoram Kahana/Shooting Star; **16** (b): Joel Holzman/Shooting Star; **18**: José Luis Martín Mena, courtesy Semana; **19**: Hoviv, courtesy ¡Hola!; **20** (t), **29** (t): Chris Sharp/DDB Stock Photo; **20** (c): DDB Stock Photo; **22-23, 23** (b): Gary Braasch; **24-25**: Jack Parsons; **26-27**: Ken Laffal; **28** (r): Scala/Art Resource, NY, ©ARS, NY; **28** (l), **82** (t): Robert Fried/DDB Stock Photo; **40, 82** (b), **427** (t): Victor Englebert; **41** (t), **73** (b), **120** (bl), **304-305**: Nancy D'Antonio; **51, 60, 126-127, 151, 160** (l, r), **182** (t, c, b), **192, 214** (l, r), **224** (l, t), **258, 259, 294, 318** (t), **362** (br), **426** (t), **459** (t): PhotoDisc; **58-59, 133**: Bob Daemmrich Photography; **60** (t), **130, 208** (r): Tony Freeman/PhotoEdit; **61** (t): The Museum of Modern Art, New York. Mrs. Simon Guggenheim Fund. Photograph ©1995 The Museum of Modern Art; **75, 87** (tr), **378-379**: NASA; **84, 225** (b): Bob Daemmrich/Stock Boston; **86, 87** (br), **217, 362** (b): Richard Lord; **90-91**: Will & Deni McIntyre/Tony Stone Images; **103**: V.O. Press/PhotoEdit; **110**: Suzanne L. Murphy/DDB Stock Photo; **121** (b), **233**: M. Antman/The Image Works; **126** (t), **186**: Cameramann International, Ltd.; **131**: Jacques Halber; **137** (r), **369, 376** (b), **427** (b): Peter Menzel; **139**: Susan Watts/Retna, Ltd.; **142-143**: Bob Schalkwijk/Art Resource, NY; **144**: Courtesy Foreign Imported Productions & Publishing, Inc.; **148**: Art Gingert/Comstock; **154** (t): Krasner/Trebitz-E.R.S.; **161**: The Metropolitan Museum of Art, The Jules Bache Collection, 1949 (49.7.41); **172, 185** (t): UPI/Corbis-Bettmann; **175**: David J. Sams/Stock Boston; **184**: Courtesy of the Pittsburgh Pirates Baseball Club/Photo by Dave Arrigo; **187** (t): D. Boroughs/The Image Works; **190-191**: Peter Menzel/Material World; **192** (t): ©1994 Fernando Botero/VAGA,NY, courtesy the Marlborough Gallery; **192** (b): Scala/Art Resource, NY; **193**: Chester Dale Collection, ©1995, National Gallery of Art, Washington DC; **207** (b): Ann Trulove/Unicorn Stock Photos; **208** (l): Karen Huntt Mason/Corbis; **209**: Diego Goldberg/Material World; **213**: Allan Landau for ScottForesman, courtesy Mexican Fine Arts Center, Chicago; **218**: Peter Millen/The Image Bank; **219** (inset): Steve Vidler/Leo de Wys; **224** (inset): Steve Vidler/Leo de Wys; **224** (l): B. Barbey/Magnum Photos; **238** (t), **252** (artifacts): Lee Boltin Picture Library; **247, 387**: Daniel Aubry/Odyssey/Chicago; **253**: Dana White/PhotoEdit; **256-257**: B. W. Hoffmann/envision; **258, 317**: Owen Franken/Stock Boston; **264** (b): Collection of the Art Museum of the Americas, OAS, Washington, DC; **264-265**: Tom Gibson/envision; **274-275, 424-425**: Miriam Lefkowitz/envision; **285**: Bibliothèque Nationale, Paris; **288** (t): The Metropolitan Museum of Art, H. O. Havemeyer Collection, Bequest of Mrs. H. O. Havemeyer, 1929; **289**: Courtesy Michael Realty Company, Toledo,OH; **292-293, 376** (t): David Simson/Stock Boston; **294** (l): Alyx Kellington/DDB Stock Photo; **309** (b): M. Rangell/The Image Works; **326-327**: R. Crandall/The Image Works; **328**: Jeffrey J. Foxx; **329** (b), **362** (t): Larry Mangino/The Image Works; **334**: Photofest; **335**: The Kobal Collection; **341** (b): Jack Demuth for ScottForesman; **342-343**: Courtesy Coral Picture Corporation/Radio Caracas Televisión, Venezuela; **347** (b): Stuart Cohen; **360-361**: Monique Salaber/The Image Works; **375** (t): Michael Fogden/Bruce Coleman, Inc.; **377** (inset): Robert Frerck/Tony Stone Images; **382**: William Dyckes; **385**: Courtesy Oscar Bonilla; **386**: Courtesy Universidad Nacional Autónoma de México, Instituto de Ingeniería, Sunrayce '95, Proyecto Tonatiuh; **408-409, 409** (bl): Courtesy Parador de Sigüenza; **409** (br): Courtesy Parador de Zamora; **441** (t): K. Mcglynn/The Image Works; **448**: Lionel Delevingne/Stock Boston; **456-457**: Eric A. Wessman/Viesti Collection; **458** (t): J. Buchardi/Leo de Wys; **375** (b), **459, 470** (b), **477** (r), **482** (l, c): Walt Anderson; **462**: Patti Murray/Animals Animals; **470** (t): Michael Fogden/DRK Photo; **477** (l): José Carrillo/PhotoEdit; **479**: D. Cavagnaro/DRK Photo; **482** (r): Leonard Lee Rue III.